UNDERSTANDING STRUCTURED COBOL
SECOND EDITION

UNDERSTANDING STRUCTURED COBOL
SECOND EDITION

Michel Boillot
Pensacola Junior College

West Publishing Company
St. Paul   New York   Los Angeles   San Francisco

Copyediting Pamela McMurry
Design Judith Getman
Art Carlisle Graphics
Composition Carlisle Graphics
Cover design Delor Erickson
Smorgasbord Studio

COPYRIGHT © 1982 BY WEST PUBLISHING CO.
COPYRIGHT © 1986 by WEST PUBLISHING CO.
50 West Kellogg Boulevard
P.O. Box 64526
St. Paul, MN 55164-1003

All rights reserved

Printed in the United States of America

Library of Congress Cataloging in Publication Data

Boillot, Michel H.
    Understanding structured COBOL, second edition.

    Includes index.
    1. COBOL (Computer program language) 2. Structured programming. I. Title.
QA76.73.C25B63   1986   005.13'3   85-22719
Softcover ISBN: 0-314-93155-4
Hardcover ISBN: 0-314-99083-6

CONTENTS

Preface ix
Acknowledgment xiii

CHAPTER 1 Introduction to Programming 1
    1-1 Computers—What Are They? 2
    1-2 Computer Languages and Pseudo Code 8
    1-3 Programming Tools and Program Design and Structure 9
    1-4 File Processing—An Application 24
    1-5 You Might Want to Know 24
    1-6 Exercises 27

CHAPTER 2 Getting Started: The First COBOL Program 33
    2-1 Problem Specification 34
    2-2 How and Where to Start 35
    2-3 COBOL Code Interpretation 42
    2-4 Exercises 51

CHAPTER 3 Structure and Syntax 57
    3-1 Elements of the COBOL Language 58
    3-2 The Identification Division 73
    3-3 The Environment Division 73
    3-4 The Data Division 75
    3-5 The Procedure Division 89
    3-6 Writing Programs 98
    3-7 Exercises 104

CHAPTER 4 The Editing Process and Arithmetic Statements 115
    4-1 Processing Numbers with Decimal Points 116
    4-2 The Editing Process 122
    4-3 Data Transfer through Arithmetic Operations 141
    4-4 You Might Want to Know 153
    4-5 Writing Programs 156
    4-6 Exercises 164

CHAPTER 5 Screen Processing 177

- 5-1 Alternate Forms of Input and Output 178
- 5-2 The Accept and Display Statements 179
- 5-3 Formatted Screens 194
- 5-4 Exercises 201

CHAPTER 6 The Decision and Iteration Structures, Program Design, and Data Validation 207

- 6-1 The Decision Structure 208
- 6-2 The Perform Statement and the Accumulation Process 227
- 6-3 Putting It Together: The Program Development Process 238
- 6-4 Writing Programs and the Input Validation Process 249
- 6-5 You Might Want to Know 266
- 6-6 Exercises 269

CHAPTER 7 Additional Features and Reports 299

- 7-1 The Redefines Statement 300
- 7-2 Condition Names 309
- 7-3 Character Manipulating Statements 312
- 7-4 Reports 329
- 7-5 You Might Want to Know 347
- 7-6 Exercises 354

CHAPTER 8 One- and Two-Dimensional Tables 371

- 8-1 One-Dimensional Tables 372
- 8-2 Elements of the COBOL Language 379
- 8-3 Table Manipulation 387
- 8-4 Two-Dimensional Tables 407
- 8-5 Writing Programs 424
- 8-6 Three-Dimensional Tables 440
- 8-7 You Might Want to Know 448
- 8-8 Exercises 449

CHAPTER 9 Searching and Sorting 489

- 9-1 Indexing 490
- 9-2 The Search Feature 493
- 9-3 Sorting 501
- 9-4 Sorting without the Sort Statement 517
- 9-5 Programming Exercises 520

CHAPTER 10 Sequential File Processing 531

- 10-1 Problem Example: Creation of a Tape/Disk Data File Through COBOL 532
- 10-2 Files and Physical Devices 533
- 10-3 Sequential File Processing 542
- 10-4 Common File-Processing Tasks 546
- 10-5 A Multiple-File Programming Problem: Grade Report 566
- 10-6 You Might Want to Know 571
- 10-7 Programming Exercises 573

CHAPTER 11 Indexed Sequential Files 583
    11-1 Indexed Files 584
    11-2 Processing an Indexed File Sequentially (Access Mode Is Sequential) 590
    11-3 Processing Records Randomly 604
    11-4 Processing an Indexed File Dynamically 612
    11-5 Exercises 620

APPENDIX A USAGE Clause and RENAMES A-1
APPENDIX B American National Standard COBOL Format Summary and Reserved Words B-1
APPENDIX C General Form of Cobol Statements C-1
INDEX I-1

PREFACE

One of the main objectives in writing this book was to produce a textbook that would be enjoyable, easy to read and to understand, yet not lacking in substance or completeness. Since a great deal of learning takes place by watching others and since pictures, diagrams and program listings are worth a thousand written words, the emphasis has been put on a visual presentation of concepts through varied illustrations, reinforced by numerous displays of complete COBOL programs. However, therein lay the obstacle: the sheer size of a typical COBOL program requires that its display be spread over several pages of a regular-size textbook, and this physical segmentation of program code on two or more consecutive pages generally creates an awkward, if not adverse, learning environment for the reader. The reader is forced constantly to thumb back and forth between pages to recall various data item entries, and to follow the logic of the program. Thus the reader loses his or her train of thought and concentration. In order to eliminate this visual Ping-Pong of information across pages, the decision was made to lay out the complete COBOL on facing pages. Thus at one glance, in a panoramic view of sorts, the reader can visually embrace all the components of the COBOL program including the layout of the input data, the layout of the output report, occasional structured diagrams and the line-by-line interpretation of the COBOL code. Altogether this text presents 30 such pages displaying complete COBOL programs.

The major differences between this edition and the first edition can be summarized as follows:

1. This new edition represents a seventy percent rewrite effort.
2. Fold out pages have been eliminated.
3. Color is used to highlight areas of importance.
4. Illustrations, diagrams and other visual aids have been added.
5. Chapter 5 is a new chapter on screen processing.
6. Chapter 11 on indexed files has been significantly expanded.
7. The INSPECT, STRING and UNSTRING instructions are fully detailed in chapter 7.
8. Many of the flowcharts have been replaced by pseudo code.
9. All COBOL programs display both input and output files.
10. Many programming assignments specify the input/output data layout.
11. DO IT NOW sections provide short questions and answers allowing students to test their comprehension on material they have just covered (syntax and programming applications).
12. "My System Is Different" sections gives extra writing space to students to make notations for their specific system(s).

Most chapters conclude with a section containing a self test, programming exercises and answers to the self test. The "Test Yourself" enables the reader to test his or her understanding of the material covered in the chapter as well as the ability to write short COBOL coding segments covering important programming techniques. Answers to the self test are provided at the end of each chapter for immediate feedback. The programming exercise subsection contains an extensive collection of problems ranging over a wide variety of subject areas and levels of difficulty. Problems are generally presented in graduated order of difficulty. Many of these problems are traditional-type problems; some are more advanced, i.e., "total problems" requiring the student to design a complete system. Some instructors and students alike may feel intimidated by the sheer number of programming exercises at the conclusion of each chapter. The rationale for this plethora of problems is the result of my belief that considerable knowledge, experience, learning and language proficiency can be gained by a student when that student is given the opportunity to read, analyze and criticize programs written by classroom peers. In the course of a semester or quarter, students are generally concerned with writing only eight or nine programs. They rarely get a chance to look at others' programs. To provide greater exposure to a variety of programming situations, the instructor may wish to handle programming assignments as follows.

Given a typical class size of 30 to 40 students, the instructor may want to break the class into groups of five or ten students and assign to each group a different programming exercise which each student in that group solves independently. When the program assignments are turned in, the instructor selects from each group an "outstanding" program which he or she can then run on a computer to obtain 30 or so copies for distribution to the whole class. In this manner each student builds his or her own portfolio or minilibrary of programs that he or she can refer to at any given time for ideas, style, technique, syntax purposes, and so on. Even a casual glance at any of these programs can benefit the student in the sense that he or she becomes aware of the variety of ways in which a program can be written, ways that the student (or the instructor!) would never have imagined or thought possible!

Such a learning process can only add to the student's understanding of the COBOL language and of the problem-solving process in general. Additionally, such diversity of programming experiences should enhance the student's imagination and stimulate creativity and objectivity.

The author would appreciate any correspondence with users regarding errors or suggestions dealing with the improvement of this book.

I would like to thank Bennett Kramer, Massasoit Community College, Rob Dependahl, Santa Barbara City College, Marylyn Puchalski, Bucks County Community College, William Carlborg, Prairie State College, Linda Love, Thornton Community College, Carol Clark, Saint Louis Community College at Florissant Valley, Patricia Bartos Foutz, Virginia Polytechnic Institute and State University, and Marilyn Moore, Indiana University Northwest for their helpful comments and criticisms during the review stages of the manuscript. I am greatly indebted to Sheila Castañeda, Clarke College, for reviewing and proofreading the galleys of this text and to Pamela McMurry for her superb copyediting of the manuscript.

Such a text could not have been produced without the tremendous effort put forth by Carlisle Graphics. In particular I would like to thank John Carlisle and Beth Segilia.

Not to be forgotten in this adventure is my good friend Gary Woodruff, my friend and editor Peter Marshall, and Developmental Editor Phyllis Mueller, all of whom provided guidance and support and never tired of showing encouragement. I would also like to thank Kim Bornhoft, Beth Kennedy and all the other silent support personnel at West who have made this project a reality.

PREFACE xi

I would like to dedicate this book to this great team of people, named or unnamed, that I have mentioned above—I must not forget my wife Mona (the miracle typist) without whose help the manuscript would have never seen daylight. Thank you Mona.

It is difficult to remain of sane mind during such a two year adventure. Many of my little friends (Rabs and Orgs) some of which are shown below, accompanied me during this journey. Their unceasing humor and zest for life made it possible for me to complete this trip. Thank you guys.

ACKNOWLEDGMENT

The following extract is reproduced from COBOL Edition 1965, which was published by the Conference on Data Systems Languages (CODASYL) and printed by the U.S. Government Printing Office under Form Number 1965-0795689, and is presented for the information and guidance of the user:

Any organization interested in reproducing the COBOL report and specifications in whole or in part, using ideas taken from this report as the basis for an instruction manual or for any other purpose is free to do so. However, all such organizations are requested to reproduce this section as a part of the introduction to the document. Those using a short passage, as in a book review, are requested to mention "COBOL" in acknowledgment of the source, but need not quote this entire section.

COBOL is an industry language and is not the property of any company or group of companies, or of any organization or group of organizations.

No warranty, expressed or implied, is made by any contributor or by the COBOL Committee as to the accuracy and functioning of the programming system and language. Moreover, no responsibility is assumed by any contributor, or by the committee, in connection therewith.

Procedures have been established for the maintenance of COBOL. Inquiries concerning the procedures for proposing changes should be directed to the Executive Committee of the Conference on Data Systems Languages.

The authors and copyright holders of the copyrighted material used herein

FLOW–MATIC (Trademark of Sperry Rand Corporation), Programming for the Univac I and II, Data Automation Systems copyrighted 1958, 1959, by Sperry Rand Corporation; IBM Commercial Translator Form No. F28-8013, copyrighted 1959 by IBM; FACT, DSI 27A5260-2760; copyrighted 1960 by Minneapolis-Honeywell

have specifically authorized the use of this material in whole or in part, in the COBOL specifications. Such authorization extends to the reproduction and use of COBOL specifications in programming manuals of similar publications.

UNDERSTANDING STRUCTURED COBOL
SECOND EDITION

CHAPTER 1

INTRODUCTION TO PROGRAMMING

1–1 COMPUTERS—WHAT ARE THEY?

1–2 COMPUTER LANGUAGES AND PSEUDO CODE

1–3 PROGRAMMING TOOLS AND PROGRAM DESIGN AND STRUCTURE

1–4 FILE PROCESSING—AN APPLICATION

1–5 YOU MIGHT WANT TO KNOW

1–6 EXERCISES

INTRODUCTION This chapter gives a brief introduction to computers, hardware and software, and programming languages. It then focuses on the fundamental principles of program design—the use of pseudo code, the concept of structured programming, program control structures, documentation, and structured diagrams. An example of file processing (one of COBOL's most important uses) is also discussed.

1-1 COMPUTERS—WHAT ARE THEY?

Computers are automatic electronic machines that can:

1. Accept (read) data.
2. Store the accepted data in memory.
3. Manipulate the stored data according to directions given by the user.
4. Produce intelligible reports (results) from the manipulated data.

1-1-1 DATA, INSTRUCTIONS, AND INFORMATION

The objective of computer data processing is to convert raw data into information that can be used for decision making. *Data* refers to raw facts that have been collected from various sources. Consider, for example, the number 2909. Is that number someone's street address, or is it the balance in his/her checking account? The number 2909 is data, but once it has meaning it becomes information. *Data* can be defined as unprocessed facts, while *information* is the result of organizing unprocessed facts into a meaningful arrangement.

Data is generally fed to a computer to produce information, i.e., data is input to the computer, and information is output from the computer (see Figure 1-1). *Instructions* tell the computer how to process the data. A *program* is a set of instructions written to solve a particular problem.

The computer can accept:

1. The set of instructions (program) that tell it what to do, i.e., how to solve the particular problem.
2. The specific data to be processed by the program to produce the desired information.

Thus, the program and the data are clearly independent entities. For example, a program might consist of the set of instructions telling the computer how to sort a list of names in alphabetical order, while the data could be any list of

INTRODUCTION TO PROGRAMMING 3

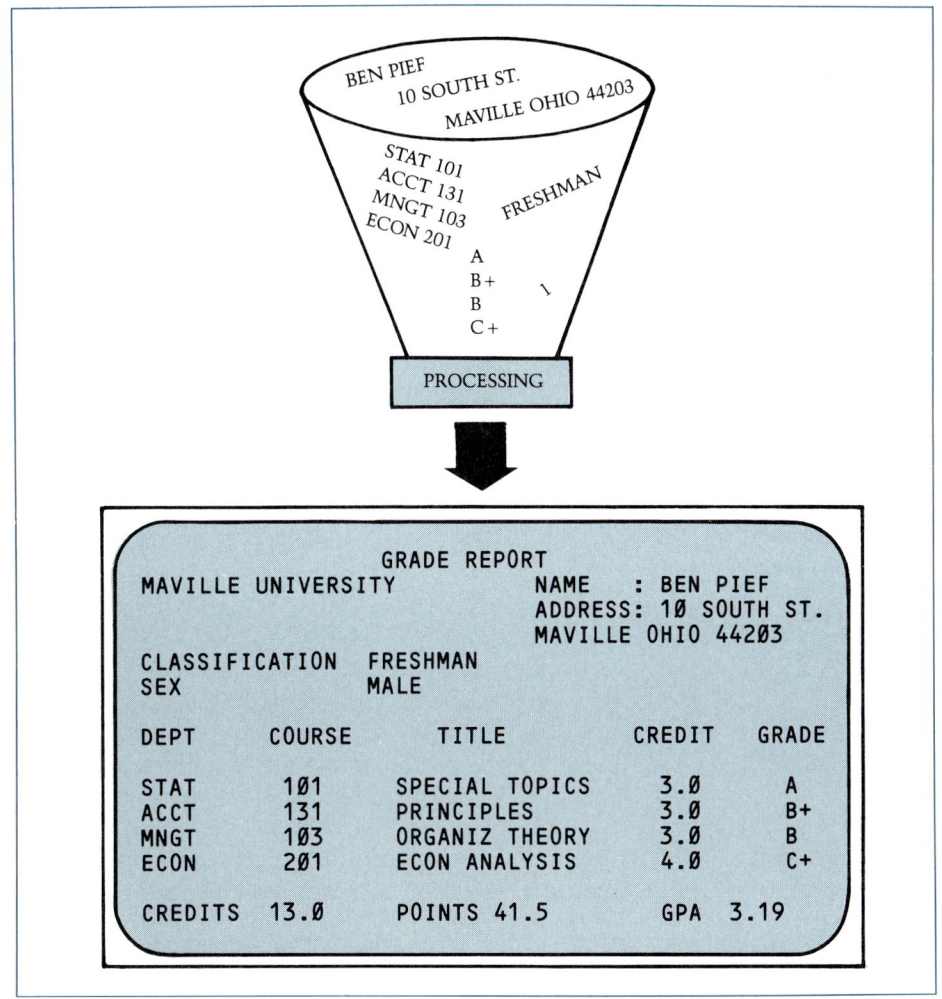

FIGURE 1-1
DATA VERSUS INFORMATION

names. The program would be general enough to process different lists containing various numbers of names.

1-1-2 COMPUTER HARDWARE

The term *hardware* refers to the physical components of the computer (the term *software* refers to programs or systems of programs written to accomplish specific tasks).

Computers accept (read) programs and data from a variety of input devices. Punched cards used to be a common way to feed data to a computer, but the punched card has now given way to other forms of data entry. Terminals allow the user to enter programs and data directly on the computer using either a visual screen (cathode ray tube, CRT) or a hard copy terminal (paper display typewriters). Flexible magnetic disks, called *diskettes* or *floppy disks*, have also replaced punched cards as a medium for data entry. The user typically inserts a diskette into a slot (disk drive) on the terminal and uses the keyboard to write the input data and programs onto the diskette (see Figure 1-2). These programs

FIGURE 1-2
MICROCOMPUTER HARDWARE AND STORAGE DEVICES

and data can then be read and processed by the computer at a time convenient to the user. Such systems are widely used in schools to provide economical and easy computer access for students. In industry and in any large data processing center, data and programs are usually stored on mass storage devices such as magnetic tape and magnetic disks (see Figure 1-3).

Before a program can be executed by a computer, it must first be loaded into the computer's memory, which consists of many cells (locations) into which data and program instructions can be stored. This memory is often referred to as *primary storage.*

Once the program is stored in memory, the central processing unit (CPU) of the computer carries out (executes) the instructions one by one. Executing an instruction may mean adding or multiplying numbers or comparing two numbers to determine the larger of the two. It can also involve input/output operations such as reading data into storage or printing results onto a terminal, a printer, or some other type of storage device such as a magnetic disk. Storage media such as magnetic disk drives, which are not part of memory, are referred to as *secondary storage* devices.

From this discussion, we can see that a typical computer system consists of input and output devices and a processing unit (see Figure 1-4); the processing unit is generally composed of the following units:

1. *Memory* Programs and data are stored in memory locations.

2. *Arithmetic/Logic* This unit can add, subtract, multiply, divide, and raise to a power. It can also compare numbers algebraically and compare words (one character at a time).

3. *Control* The control unit fetches program instructions or data in memory and executes each instruction in conjunction with the arithmetic/logic unit.

In Figure 1-5 the problem of alphabetizing a list of names is illustrated in terms of program instructions, input of data, output of information, and hardware requirements. Notice the relationship between program execution and input/output and the role of the hardware in each step.

INTRODUCTION TO PROGRAMMING

FIGURE 1–3
THE MAINFRAME SYSTEM WITH MASS STORAGE DEVICES

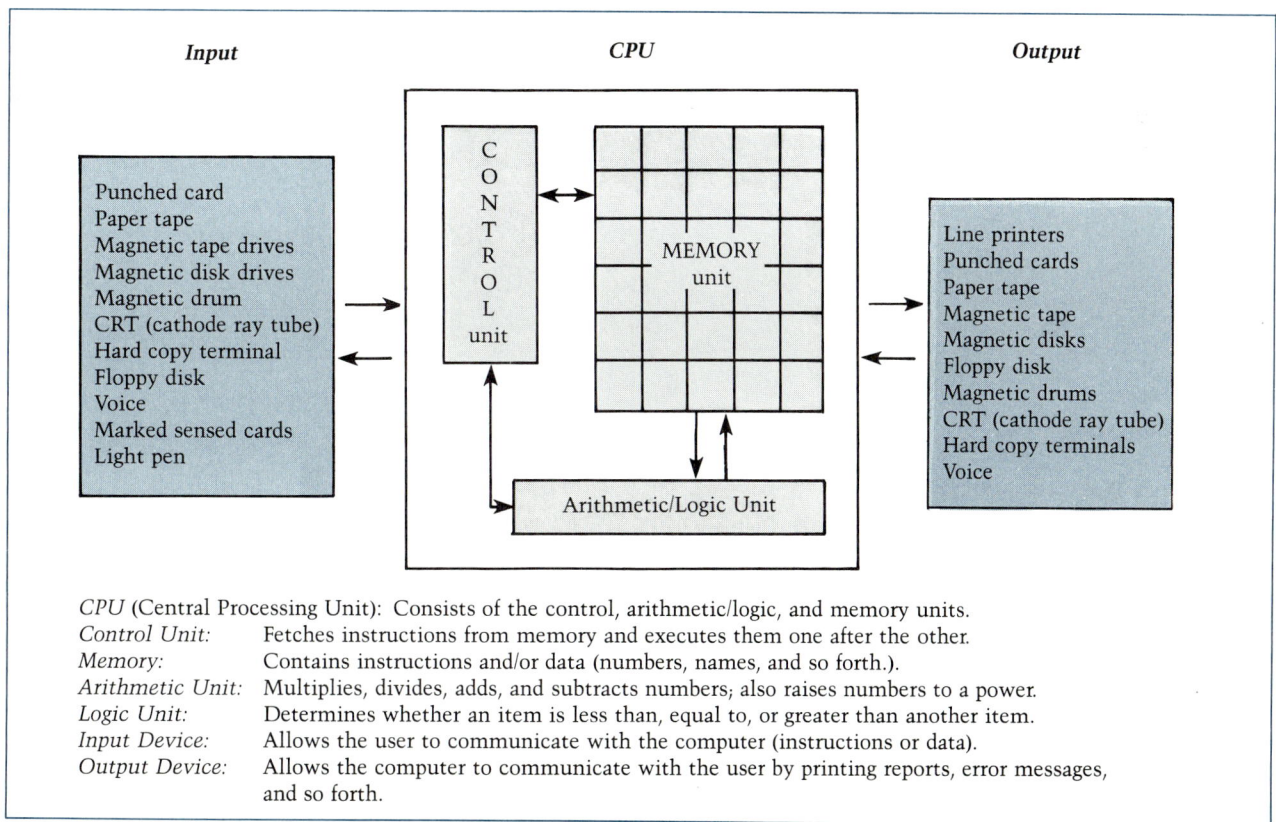

FIGURE 1–4
FUNCTIONAL UNITS OF A COMPUTER

6 UNDERSTANDING STRUCTURED COBOL

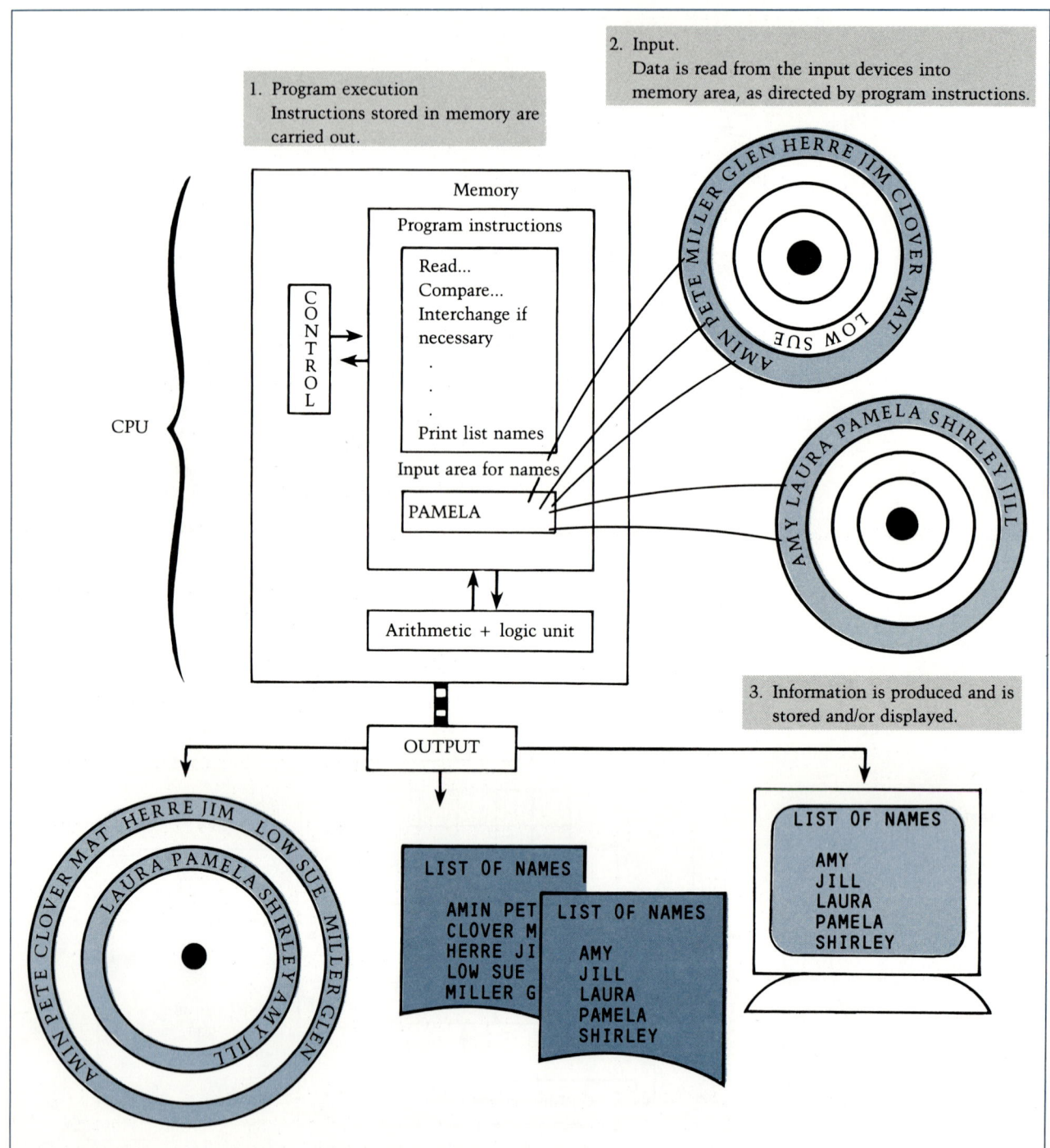

FIGURE 1-5
INPUT, PROCESSING, AND OUTPUT

1-1-3 SOFTWARE

The term *software* is generally used to describe the set of programs, written by programmers, that causes the computer hardware to function. There are three basic software categories:

1. Translation programs.
2. Operating system programs.
3. User processing programs.

Translation programs (*compilers*) are programs used by the computer system to translate high-level languages or problem-oriented languages into machine language. (High-level languages and machine language will be discussed in more detail in the next section.)

Operating system program are usually supplied by the computer manufacturer to assist in the overall operation of the computer system. They are used to regulate and supervise the sequence of activities going on at any time in the system. These programs minimize operator intervention in the actual operation of the computer and ensure a smooth, fast, and efficient transition among the varied tasks performed by the system. Other operating system programs, such as utility and library programs, aid the programmer in his/her work. The following functions are performed by some operating system programs:

1. Load programs into memory from mass storage.
2. Print messages for the operator and the programmer regarding the status of the program.
3. Perform job accounting by keeping track of who uses the computer and for how long.
4. Handle requests for input/output from executing programs.
5. Handle the collection of data from telecommunication lines (in a time-sharing system).
6. Schedule the slice of time to be allocated to each user's program (in a time-sharing or multiprogramming system).
7. Perform some routine processing of data, such as sorting and copying the contents of one data set onto a specified device.
8. Maintain the store of programs on the mass storage device—adding programs to the store, deleting those no longer needed, and so forth.
9. Attempt to recover from and/or correct errors that may occur in any segment of the computing system.
10. Interpret the job set-up and job control instructions specified by the programmer.

At the heart of most operating systems is a program variously called the *supervisor*, the *executive*, or the *monitor*. This program is usually resident in memory at all times and performs many essential tasks such as program loading and error checking. This resident portion of the operating system loads other less frequently used routines as they are required.

User processing programs, sometimes called *applications programs*, are those programs written by individual users to solve particular problems. They may be written in a generalized fashion and modified as needed to fit the peculiar requirements of a particular system, or they may be constructed exactly to satisfy specific needs. For example, a company may construct its own payroll system or it may purchase (or rent) a general set of payroll programs and modify them if necessary. Companies guard their processing programs as a very important company asset. Extensive security measures are taken to avoid the loss or theft of programs. A considerable store of programs is usually available to a computer user; in fact, the usefulness of a computer may well depend more on the variety and efficiency of the available software than on any single aspect of the hardware.

1-2 COMPUTER LANGUAGES AND PSEUDO CODE

1-2-1 HIGH-LEVEL LANGUAGES

An electronic computer may be called an electronic brain, but its function and problem-solving ability depend on the intelligence of the human beings who direct and control the machine. These people (*programmers* and *operators*) give the computer a set of instructions consisting of the steps required to solve a given problem and see that those instructions (i.e., the program) are carried out by the computer.

A program can be executed (processed) by the computer only when it is stored in the computer's memory and is in binary form represented by 1's and 0's (machine language code). Machine language is the only language the central processing unit can understand. It is a language in which all operations are represented by machine-recognizable numeric codes and in which memory locations containing data and program instructions are represented by numeric addresses. Machine language programs are very detailed, time-consuming, and difficult to write. Machine languages vary from one computer manufacturer to another; they are machine-specific, reflecting the design of each computer. Other types of languages (called *high-level languages*) have been developed to allow the user to formulate problems in a much more convenient and efficient manner.

COBOL (Common Business Oriented Language) is an example of a high-level language—high-level in the sense that it can tell the computer how to solve business-type problems yet it still approximates the English language. Because the central processing unit cannot carry out COBOL instructions directly, they must first be translated into machine code. A special program referred to as a *language translator* and called the COBOL *compiler* is made available to the central processing unit to perform this translation task. Typically the compiler reads the COBOL instructions (often referred to as *source* code) and translates these English-looking instructions into machine code (often referred to as *object* code).

The process of creating, translating, and executing a COBOL program is illustrated in the three time frames of Figure 1–6 (the same computer is shown in each time frame). On some systems the compiler, the source code, the object code, and the input data all reside on the same disk. On other systems the compiler is stored on a separate disk while the source code, object code, and input data are on some other disk(s).

1-2-2 PSEUDO CODE

Computers are problem-solving tools, but they are useful only when we can provide them with the step-by-step description of the method to solve a given problem. This account of how we proceed from one step to the next in order to arrive at the solution of the problem is called the *logic* of a problem.

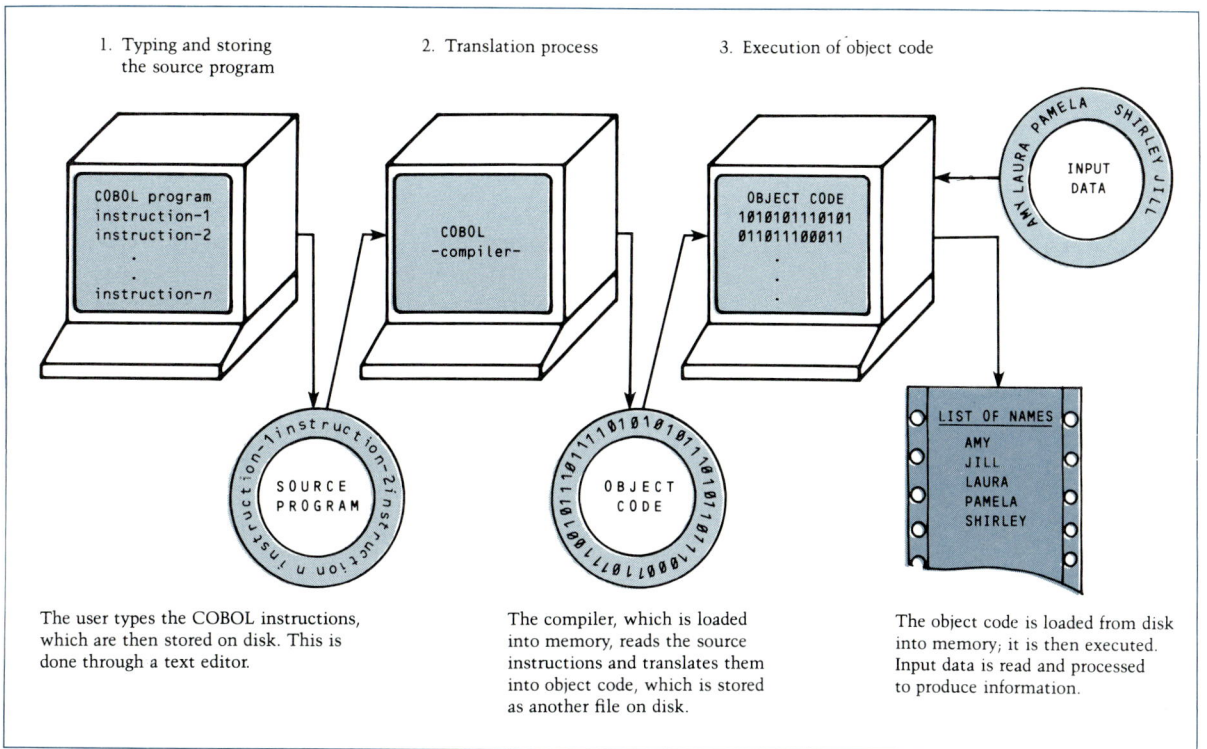

FIGURE 1-6
SOURCE PROGRAM/COMPILATION/EXECUTION

Pseudo code is a very practical tool for expressing the logic of a given problem. It is an abbreviated form of expression that uses the English language and certain key words that have special meaning. Pseudo code sentences are typically written one per line; occasionally they are indented for readability and clarity. Pseudo code is not subject to the strict grammatical rules of the COBOL language, thus the writer can concentrate on developing the proper structure of the logic without worrying about the details of a programming language. Pseudo code captures the essence of structured program design and is also semantically close to the COBOL language. Thus, converting pseudo code into COBOL is a simple process. Pseudo code has an inherent structure that allows the reader to start reading at the top and proceed sequentially downwards, just as one would when reading a paragraph in a novel.

We will begin to use pseudo code for program development in the next section.

1-3 PROGRAMMING TOOLS AND PROGRAM DESIGN AND STRUCTURE

1-3-1 A FIRST ATTEMPT AT PROGRAM DEVELOPMENT

Consider the following problem:

You, your two brothers, and your sister own a small company. As executive officers of the company, you are paid at the fixed rate of $20 per hour, while your part-time employees (who may vary in number from week to week) are paid $4 or $5 per hour, depending on their position in the company ($5 per hour for pay code 1, and $4 dollars per hour for pay code 2). You keep daily records of the hours worked by everyone. At the end of the week, you summarize the work activities of the four company officers and the part-timers as follows:

```
NAME     HOURS  CODE

JONES M    2           ⎫
JONES L    5           ⎬  The summary always starts with the four records of the
JONES S    0           ⎬  officers of the company.
JONES T    4           ⎭  Each record consists of two entries: name and hours.
                          Officers are paid at a fixed rate of $20 per hour.

HUNT  L   30     1     ⎫  Part-time work force. Assume at least 1 part-time record.
LARD  S   35     2     ⎬  Each record consists of 3 entries: name, hours, and pay code.
■                      ⎭  The special symbol ■ identifies the end of the summary.
```

Such a collection of records is called a *file*. To physically identify the end of the file, you place a marker or symbol ■. In this way, when the computer reads the symbol ■, it knows that the end of the file has been encountered.

Note that officers' records consist of two entries, while part-time workers' records consist of three entries (name, hours, and position-code). Such entries within records are generally referred to as *fields* or *data items*.

We will now to write the logic to read and process the above file as input to produce the following pay report:

```
NAME     HOURS    PAY

JONES M    2      40.00    ⎫
JONES L    5     100.00    ⎬  This report consists of 6 records (output lines).
JONES S    0       0.00    ⎬  Each record contains three fields: the name, the
JONES T    4      80.00    ⎬  hours, and the pay.
HUNT  L   30     150.00    ⎬
LARD  S   35     140.00    ⎭
```

1-3-2 TASKS, MODULES, AND TOP-DOWN DESIGN

The main objective in the program development process is to produce code that will obviously solve the intended problem, but that will also be easy to read, easy to understand, and easy to correct or change if the need arises. One way to achieve this goal is to decompose the logic into separate tasks (sometimes called modules), each defining and carrying out certain functions (clearly defined tasks) that are independent of one another.

Breaking down a problem into smaller pieces or subtasks allows the programmer to focus more easily on a particular part of the problem without having to worry about the overall problem. These subtasks are easier to program and are much more manageable since each performs a specific function. Of course, some of these subtasks may need to be further broken down into other subtasks, each reflecting decreased levels of responsibility.

Thus a hierarchy of tasks is created where each task can be respecified into a sequence of subtasks describing what is to be performed at an increasing level of detail. At the very top level, a main-logic task or module is written to coordinate all sublevel modules. This coordinating module initiates the channel of command. This technique of expanding a program plan into several levels of detail (subplans) is sometimes referred to as a *top-down* design.

1-3-3 PSEUDO CODE SOLUTION TO PROBLEM

The modularization process discussed in the above section (decomposition of a problem into a task structure) is made possible through the sequence structure, the decision structure (*if then/else*), and the looping structure (*perform*). These structures are illustrated in Figure 1-7, which displays the pseudo code solution of our pay report problem, and they will be discussed further in section 1-3-4.

Figure 1-8 displays the step-by-step execution of the pseudo code in Figure 1-7. The pseudo code is broken down into three tasks (or *paragraphs*, as they are called in COBOL): coordinating-module, compute-executive-pay, and compute-part-timer-pay. Each of these represents distinct activities. The coordinating-module coordinates the other two modules (tasks) and also gives an overview of the logic, i.e., the general plan of action.

The *perform* statement at line 2 passes control to the compute-executive-pay module (line 6), which reads the first employee name and corresponding hours (JONES M, 2), computes the pay ($40), and prints out the name, the hours worked, and the pay (see Figure 1-8). At this point, the end of the compute-executive-pay module is reached and control automatically passes back to the *perform* statement at line 2. Since this *perform* statement specifies that the compute-executive-pay module must be carried out four times, that module is carried out three more times to produce the payroll report for the four company executives.

The *read* statement at line 3 then reads the fifth record, which is actually the first part-timer record. The employee-name is HUNT L, the hours-worked is 30, and the position code is 1.

```
 1:  Coordinating-module.
 2:      Perform compute-executive-pay 4 times
 3:      Read employee-name, hours-worked, and position-code
 4:      Perform compute-part-timer-pay until end-of-file is encountered
 5:      Stop

 6:  Compute-executive-pay.
 7:      Read employee-name and hours-worked
 8:      Compute pay = hours-worked × 20
 9:      Write employee-name, hours-worked, and pay

10:  Compute-part-timer-pay.
11:      If position-code = 1
12:      Then
13:          Compute pay = hours-worked × 5
14:      Else
15:          compute pay = hours-worked × 4
16:      Endif
17:      Write employee-name, hours-worked, and pay
18:      Read employee-name, hours-worked, and position-code
```

input file:

name	hours-worked	position code
JONES M	2	
JONES L	5	
JONES S	0	
JONES T	4	
HUNT L	30	1
LARD S	35	2

FIGURE 1-7
A FIRST ATTEMPT AT STRUCTURED CODE

	Employee-name	Hours-worked	Position-code	Pay	
Coordinating-module.					input file ↓
┌─ Perform compute-executive-pay 4 times					JONES M 2
│ Read employee-name, hours-worked, and position-code	HUNT L	30	1		JONES L 5
│ Perform compute-part-timer-pay					JONES S 0
│ until end-of-file is encountered					JONES T 4
↓ Stop					HUNT L 30 1
Compute-executive-pay.					LARD S 35 2
Read employee-name and hours-worked	JONES M	2			■
Compute pay = hours-worked × 20				40.00	output
↓ Write employee-name, hours-worked, and pay					JONES M 2 40.00
Compute-executive-pay.					
Read employee-name and hours-worked	JONES L	5			
Compute pay = hours-worked × 20				100.00	
↓ Write employee-name, hours-worked, and pay					JONES L 5 100.00
Compute-executive-pay.					
Read employee-name and hours-worked	JONES S	0			
Compute pay = hours-worked × 20				0.00	
↓ Write employee-name, hours-worked, and pay					JONES S 0 0.00
Compute-executive-pay.					
Read employee-name and hours-worked	JONES T	4			
Compute pay = hours-worked × 20				80.00	
Write employee-name, hours-worked, and pay					JONES T 4 80.00
Compute-part-timer-pay.					
If position-code = 1					
Then					
Compute pay = hours-worked × 5				150.00	
Else					
compute pay = hours-worked × 4					
Endif					
Write employee-name, hours-worked, and pay					HUNT L 30 150.00
Read employee-name, hours-worked, and position-code	LARD S	35	2		
Compute-part-timer-pay.					
If position-code = 1					
Then					
Compute pay = hours-worked × 5					
Else					
compute pay = hours-worked × 4				140.00	
Endif					
Write employee-name, hours-worked and pay					LARD S 35 140.00
Read employee-name, hours-worked, and position-code	■end file				

FIGURE 1–8
STEP-BY-STEP EXECUTION OF FIGURE 1–7 Note that the data read, computed, and written by the program is aligned with the corresponding pseudo code *read*, *compute*, and *write* statements.

The *perform* statement at line 4 is a variation of the *perform* statement at line 2. It carries out a module until a specific condition is satisfied. In this case, the compute-part-timer-pay module (line 10) is to be carried out until the end-of-file record is read. Note that the *perform until* statement first determines whether or not the condition is satisfied. If the condition is satisfied at the outset, then the specified module is *not* carried out at all. In our case, the end-of-file condition is not satisfied (the end-of-file record has not been read yet), so the compute-part-timer-pay module is carried out for employee HUNT L.

The *if* sentence that terminates with the *endif* statement at line 16 asks whether the position code is 1. If it is, the statement specified by the *then* phrase is carried out (line 13); otherwise (position-code not equal to 1) the statements(s) between the *else* and *endif* is (are) carried out (line 15). In our case, position code is 1 so we compute pay = 30 × 5 = 150. Control is then passed to line 17 where the pay data for HUNT is printed. Line 18 is then executed and the three items LARD S, 35, and 2 are read. At this point, the end of the module is reached and control is passed back to the *perform until* statement at line 4. Since the end-of-file condition is not satisfied, the compute-part-timer-pay module (line 10) is carried out one more time. This time, position code = 2 and LARD's pay is computed at line 15. The output line for LARD is then printed out and the next record is read, which turns out to be the end-of-file marker ∎. Control is then passed again to the *perform until* statement at line 4 where, this time, the end-of-file condition is satisfied. Control is passed to the next instruction (line 5) and the program stops.

Note that if there were no part-timer records in the input file, the *read* statement at line 3 would read the end-of file symbol ∎ and, since the end-of-file condition would be satisfied at line 4, the program would stop!

1-3-4 TOOLS FOR STRUCTURE

As illustrated in the pseudo code of Figure 1-7, the decomposition of a problem into a well-designed task structure is made possible by the sequence, decision, and looping structures.

The Loop Structure

To *loop* means to do something over and over again. In the context of structured design, *looping* means repeating a task one or more times. The loop structure (sometimes referred to in the literature as the *iteration* or the *repetition* structure) is made possible through different forms of the *perform* statements.

Case 1: perform compute-executive-pay 4 times   (line 2)

The *perform* statement tells us to carry out the sentences in the compute-executive-pay paragraph four times. After this task has been carried out four times, control is automatically passed to the sentence following the *perform*.

Case 2: perform compute-part-timer-pay until end-of-file is encountered
(line 4)

This form of the *perform* statement tells us to carry out the sentences in the compute-part-timer-pay paragraph until the end of file is encountered, at which time control is passed to the sentence following the *perform* statement. Because of the *until* clause, the question, Is the end of file encountered? must be answered first before the paragraph in question is carried out. If the answer to the question is yes, then the paragraph is *not* carried out and control is passed to the sentence following the *perform* statement. If the answer is no, then the paragraph is carried out.

Notice, also, that the very first time the compute-part-timer-pay paragraph is executed, the *if* sentence (line 11) asks a question about position-code, and the computation sentences (lines 13 and 15) refer to hours-worked. In order for both of these items to be defined, the first record must already be known before this paragraph is executed; otherwise the value of these items (position-code and hours-worked) will be unknown. This is accomplished by including a separate *read* statement (line 3) just before the *perform until* statement.

The Decision Structure

Decisions are based on whether certain condition(s) are met. The decision structure is illustrated in the compute-part-timer-pay paragraph, as follows:

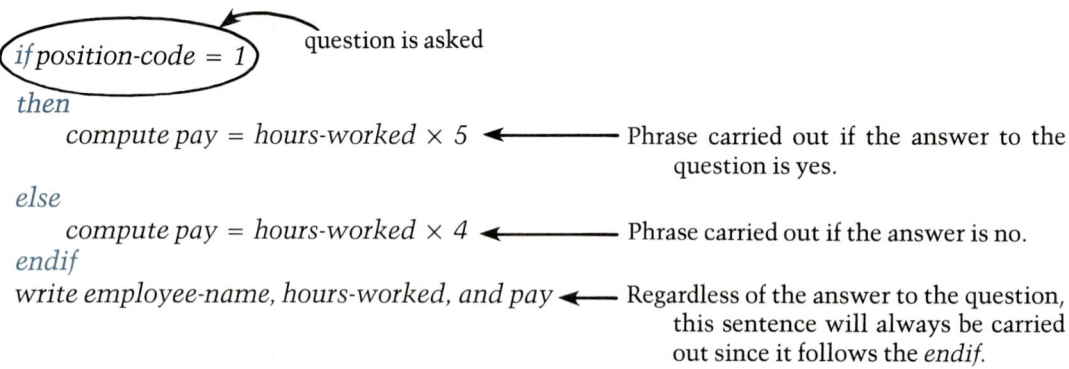

The *endif* is a visual marker that defines the "reach" of the *if* statement.

The Sequence Structure

The sequence structure is illustrated in each paragraph; sentences are executed sequentially one after the other. Since *if* sentences are often quite lengthy, they are generally typed on several lines to improve readability. In the case of Figure 1-7, the decision sentence starts with the *if* word and spreads out over six lines, ending with the *endif* phrase.

1-3-5 DATA DESCRIPTION

The idea of structure goes beyond the area of program logic and into the area of data definition and description. Input and output data and logic are inseparable entities—logic needs input data to produce output (information).

One characteristic of the COBOL language is that data is always read one entire record at a time and data is always written one entire record at a time. For example, a WRITE instruction will print a complete line of output that generally consists of many entries. This suggests that the user must prepare the output record, i.e., all the various entries to be printed must be moved into the output record, before the WRITE instruction is executed. Therefore the layout or configuration of such records must be made known to the program. In Figure 1-9 this is accomplished informally by naming the input and output records and by listing the various items that make up each record. In addition, the length and the type of each item are specified. The length of a data item refers to the number of characters it occupies in the record, and the type specifies whether the item is numeric or alphanumeric. (Numeric items can be processed algebraically, i.e., they can be compared to one another as signed numbers, and added, subtracted, and so forth. Alphanumeric items, on the other hand, cannot be processed numerically; they can, however, be compared to one another, just like alphabetical data.)

Notice that Figure 1-9 contains a slight change in the pseudo code in terms of the input/output statements (see lines 13, 17, 19, 27 and 28). The *read* and *write* statements specify record names, not individual data items. This is common practice when writing pseudo code, especially when there are many items in an input or output record. The reader can always look up the individual items in the data definition and description section.

```
1:      Data Definition and Description.
2:      Input-record.
3:          · Employee-name  [10 alphanumeric characters]
4:          · Hours-worked   [ 2 digit numeric field]
5:          · Position-code  [ 1 numeric digit]

6:      Output-record.
7:          · Employee-name  [10 alphanumeric characters]
8:          · Hours-worked   [ 2 digit numeric field]
9:          · Pay            [ 6 digit decimal number]

10:     Program Development.
11:     Coordinating-module.
12:         Perform compute-executive-pay 4 times
13:         Read input-record
14:         Perform compute-part-timer-pay until end-of-file is encountered
15:         Stop

16:     Compute-executive-pay.
17:         Read input-record
18:         Compute pay = hours-worked × 20
19:         Write output-record

20:     Compute-part-timer-pay.
21:         If position-code = 1
22:         Then
23:             Compute pay = hours-worked × 5
24:         Else
25:             compute pay = hours-worked × 4
26:         Endif
27:         Write output-record
28:         Read input-record
```

FIGURE 1-9
AN ALTERNATIVE VERSION OF PSEUDO CODE

Figure 1-9 contains both the pseudo code and the data definition and description. It is actually not necessary to include the data definition and description when writing the pseudo code for the logic, but its presence documents the data used by the logic and thus ties the data and the logic into a complete structure. Such a data dictionary, which identifies all the records and data items referred to in the logic, can be quite useful for illustrating the infrastructure of the various records and the interrelationships between data items and records. Its inclusion in Figure 1-9 is a forewarning to the student that a COBOL program is divided into parts called *divisions*, of which one will be the logic or procedure division and another will be the data division, which corresponds to the data definition and description in Figure 1-9.

1-3-6 READABILITY AND DOCUMENTATION

In the pseudo code of Figure 1-7 we could have written the *if* sentence or, for that matter, the entire compute-part-timer-pay paragraph as follows:

compute-part-timer-pay.
if position-code = 1 then compute pay = hours-worked × 5 else compute pay = hours-worked × 4 endif write employee-name, hours-worked and pay read employee-name, hours-worked and position-code

But this linear arrangement is difficult to read and therefore to understand. For that reason we usually write one instruction per line, and in the case of the *if* statement, we use indentation to emphasize visually what actions are to be carried out if the answer to the question asked is yes or no.

Note that each module or paragraph is given a name that is self-documenting in the sense that it summarizes the function of the paragraph. The names of data items should also be meaningful, i.e., they should describe accurately the nature of the item in question. Hyphens can be used to connect a multi-word name to make a name reference even more self-explanatory. In this way pseudo code sentences becomes much more like English sentences that can be understood by all. Beginning COBOL students sometimes have a tendency to use short, secretive names for data items because it takes less time and effort to write them. Sentences such as "compute P = H × R + B" are often written to compute a pay. However a more documented and meaningful sentence might be "compute pay = hours-worked × rate + bonus." Think of looking at these two formulas two months later; which version would be easier to understand? The additional time required now to write this sentence will be much less trouble than the headaches and hours of lost time that might result later from the more telegraphic form of expression.

The physical layout of the pseudo code is also very important to its readability. Note that the text (sentences) making up each paragraph is offset to the right, and that indentation is used in the *if* sentence, as we have discussed. If a sentence is too long to fit on one line, it can be continued on the next line in indented fashion (see the *perform until* in Figure 1-8).

Although pseudo code is very descriptive, there may still be a need to explain or summarize the function of groups of statements and describe how they relate to the entire logic. Lines that begin with an asterisk (*) are *comments*; comments can be interspersed at any point in the pseudo code. These comments serve as internal documentation and are an important part of the program development phase.

In a real-life environment, a programmer seldom writes a program just for himself/herself; it is usually for a friend, a customer, or the company for which he/she works. Thus, the program needs to be understood by others, and it may even need to be revised, updated, or expanded by others. It is, therefore, very important that the program be self-documenting and that it contain explanations and comments to help the reader understand its nature and purpose. Comment statements can also help the programmer recapture the essence of some of his/her original thoughts. Once again comments are **not** instructions—they are not executed by the computer, they are merely observations or explanations to help the reader better understand the program or logic (see Figure 1–10 for example).

1-3-7 A MODIFIED VERSION OF A STRUCTURED DESIGN

Figure 1–10 shows another version of the logic in Figure 1–7. Look at it carefully to see what changes have been made. The size of the coordinating module has been reduced. The two *perform* sentences in the coordinating module of Figure 1–10 are the essence of the program; the pay is first computed for the company officers and then for the part-time employees. The specific *read* sentence that was present in the coordinating module of Figure 1–7 has now been relegated to the part-time-employee module, where it really belongs. The part-time pay computations have now been assigned to a separate module, since these computations and the *read* and *write* operations that followed were really separate functions.

In the process of breaking down the code into more modules, each module becomes a little more specific. In the real world of program design and development, a sizable and complex software project can be decomposed into many independent modules that can be subcontracted to different programmers or software teams for individual or group development. These modules can then be run and tested independently of one another and subsequently "sewed" together by coordinating modules for the final testing phases. With this kind of structure, making one change in a particular module is a very local intervention that does not require an understanding of all other modules.

There are more modules in Figure 1–10 than there are in Figure 1–7—this leads to the questions: How long should each module be? and How many modules should there be for a given problem? There are no specific or quick answers to such questions—general guidelines will be discussed throughout this text. In general, the code should be broken down into manageable tasks that are independent of one another. Other technical considerations, such as screen size, can also affect the size of modules. In any event, guidelines on modularization will still leave the programmer ample room for flexible designs.

As noted earlier, pseudo code is simply a tool that can be used by a programmer to sketch or "rough out" his/her ideas about the logic of a program; in very informal language, the programmer explores and expresses the way in which a problem can be solved. The degree of precision of the individual pseudo code sentences is really a matter of personal judgment. For example, in the part-time-pay computation of figure 1–10 the programmer might initially write "compute $5 pay," instead of "compute pay = hours-worked × 5"; this form of abbreviation especially makes sense in programs that include typing long and complex

Program development
* *Purpose of program is to compute company personnel pay*

Coordinating-module.
    Perform executive-pay 4 times
    Perform part-time-employees
    Stop

* *This module computes the pay for the 4 company officers*
Executive-pay.
    Read input-record
    Compute pay = hours-worked × 20
    Write output-record

* *This module takes care of all part-time employees*
Part-time-employees.
    Read input-record
    Perform part-time-process until end-of-file is encountered

Part-time-process.
    Perform part-time-pay-computation
    Write output-record
    Read input-record

Part-time-pay computation.
* *A code of 1 implies a rate of 5 dollars an hour*
    If position-code = 1
    Then
        compute pay = hours-worked × 5
* *A code of 2 implies a rate of 4 dollars an hour*
    Else
        compute pay = hours-worked × 4
    Endif

FIGURE 1–10
A SECOND VERSION OF A STRUCTURED DESIGN

sets of operations or formulas, the specifics of which will have to be eventually coded into COBOL anyhow! The important point to keep in mind is that pseudo code is on the user's side; it is an ally and not a hindrance or a barrier to one's own style of thinking. If the programmer feels more comfortable with the statement "compute overtime pay" instead of spelling out the many individual sentences to compute an overtime pay, this is certainly his/her prerogative.

1-3-8 DO IT NOW

1. Could the logic outlined in Figure 1–7 have taken care of not just two part-timers but an unknown number of part-timers?

INTRODUCTION TO PROGRAMMING 19

2. Suppose the *read* sentence at line 3 of Figure 1–7 had been omitted. What consequences would this omission have on the results and the logic? Explain specifically what happens.

3. Suppose that the very last *read* sentence in Figure 1–7 had been omitted. What consequences would this omission have on the logic of the program? Explain what happens.

4. Consider the following code, which is almost identical to the one shown in Figure 1–7. The *read* sentences in the coordinating module and in the part-time module have been replaced with a single *read* sentence at the beginning of the part-time module. What effect does this have on the logic of the program?

   Coordinating-module.
       Perform compute-executive-pay 4 times
       Perform compute-part-timer-pay until end-of-file is encountered
       Stop

   Compute executive-pay.
       Read input-record
       Compute pay = hours-worked × 20
       Write output-record

   Compute-part-timer-pay.
       Read input-record
       If position-code = 1
       Then
           compute pay = hours-worked × 5
       Else
           compute pay = hours-worked × 4
       Endif
       Write output-record

5. Change the logic of Figure 1–10 so that the sentence *read* input-record is actually coded only once in the pseudo code.

ANSWERS TO SELECTED EXERCISES

2. The pay for T. JONES is processed twice. The last record read before the *perform until* sentence is carried out at line 4 is that of T. JONES, who worked 4 hours. Hence the first time the module compute-part-timer-pay is performed, the position code is undefined (no position code is stated for company officer T. JONES). Since the position code is not equal to 1, the *else* clause is executed, yielding $16.00. The records of the part-time employees would then be read by line 18 in the compute-part-time pay module, and their pays would be computed correctly.

3. The compute-part-timer pay module would be carried out indefinitely using the first part-time employee record, since the end-of-file record would never be encountered.

4. The output line LARD S 35 140.00 will be printed out twice since, after the end-of-file record is read, the *if* sentence and the *write output-record* are carried out again.

5. Replace every occurrence of the sentence "read input-record" with the sentence "perform read-operation" and create a new module called read-operation that has "read input-record" as its only sentence.

1-3-9 STRUCTURED DIAGRAMS

Pseudo code can be useful for describing the logical activities within particular modules. However, it is less useful for showing the relationships between all modules and their hierarchy. A *structured diagram*, is a pictorial representation of a program's network of modules. This network consists of rows or levels of boxes (modules) that project the structural design of the program. A structured diagram illustrates the chain of command (up-down) among the various levels of modules (up-down). The box at the top (the first level) is the coordinating module. The boxes along the second row are those modules that are performed (carried out) by the coordinating module. Each new level shows what has to be done to accomplish the functions specified at the preceding level. Control modules are those giving rise to one or more modules at a lower level. Each module can be entered only from the module above it. The function name or phrase appearing in a box should reflect the overall function of the particular module and can be the same as the module identifier used in the pseudo code.

For example, the pseudo code in Figure 1–7 can be represented by the following structured diagram.

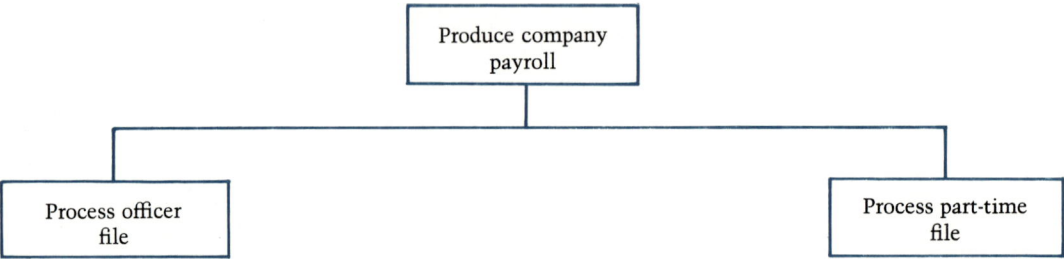

The following structured diagram captures the structure of the pseudo code in Figure 1–10:

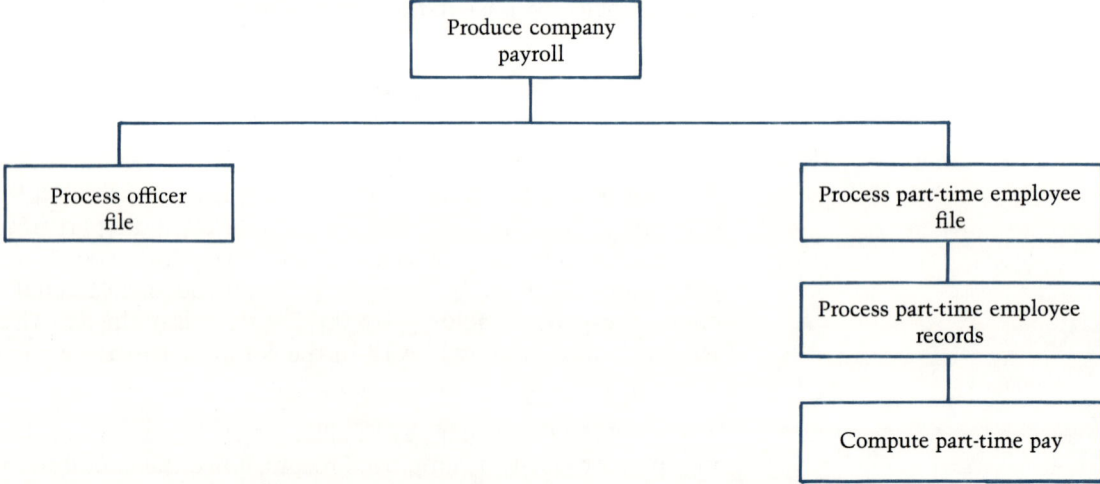

Structured diagrams are an excellent form of documentation and can be very helpful in organizing, constructing, and testing a design for proper structure. Many people find it very difficult to draw a structured diagrams first and then write the corresponding code—this is the proper sequence of events. In fact, in too many beginners' minds, structured diagrams are just not worth the bother—the logic and structure, they say, comes naturally to them. However, in the majority of cases, code that is not based on a structured diagram is terrifyingly involved and unnecessarily complicated. The ability to first draw structured diagrams and then write the corresponding code requires a great deal of experience and maturity of logic that many beginners do not possess. Yet writing pseudo code or COBOL code without a structured diagram leaves the programmer little idea as to whether his/her program is properly structured—the program can be run on the computer, of course, but that does not in itself provide any indication of valid structure.

The important questions are: How do you know your code is properly structured? What do you compare it to in order to ensure "good" design? Is the number of modules too few or too many? Is this module too short or too long? Does this control module have too few or too many subordinate modules? Are the modules really independent of one another?

The following discussion attempts to provide very general guidelines on what to look for and what to avoid and give a sense of "structured direction" to the novice coder. The most important rule is: **draw a structured diagram,** even if you have already written the pseudo code or the COBOL code. Drawing a diagram will force you to better understand, assess, and criticize your program logic, structure, and code readability. The diagram will also immediately reveal any structural flaws, and chances are you will want to make changes to your code. In addition, as you draw more structured diagrams, you will gain better insight into the process of thinking about and writing structured code.

What to Look For. It is interesting to note that there are certain parallels between structured diagrams, sometimes called *hierarchy charts* for programs and hierarchy charts in human organizations, such as management organizational structures. In the context of an institution's organizational structure, consider the following two charts.

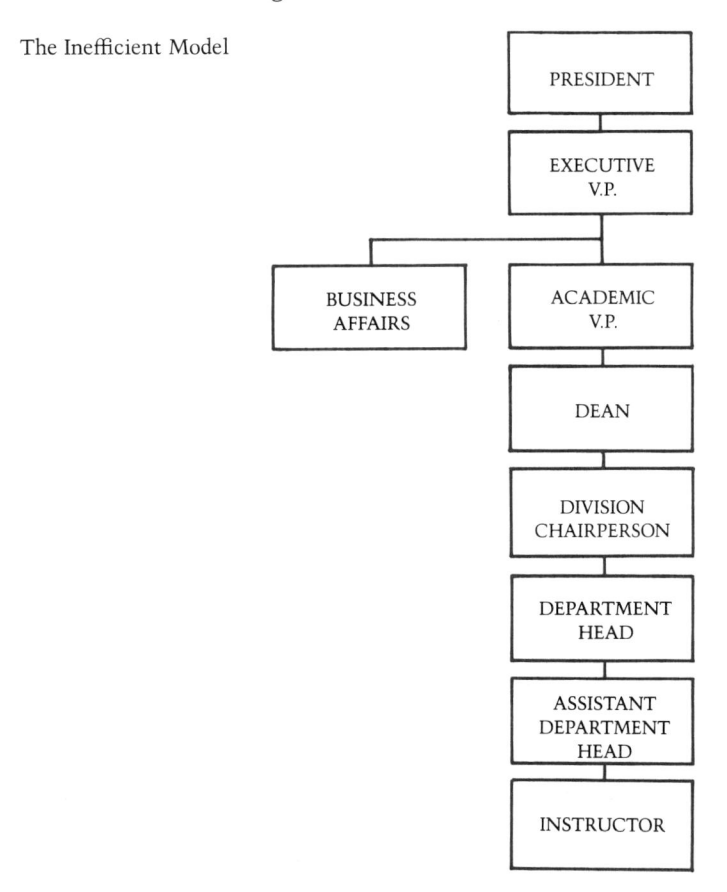

The Inefficient Model

This structure leads one to suspect an overstaffed administration. A few positions could easily be eliminated without affecting the quality of management. In this example the manager manages the manager who manages the manager.... In a structured program environment, a high level control module should do more than call a subordinate module that perpetuates what is done to it! Such a structure is clearly inefficient. Certain modules should either be taken out, be absorbed by higher level modules, or be rearranged horizontally.

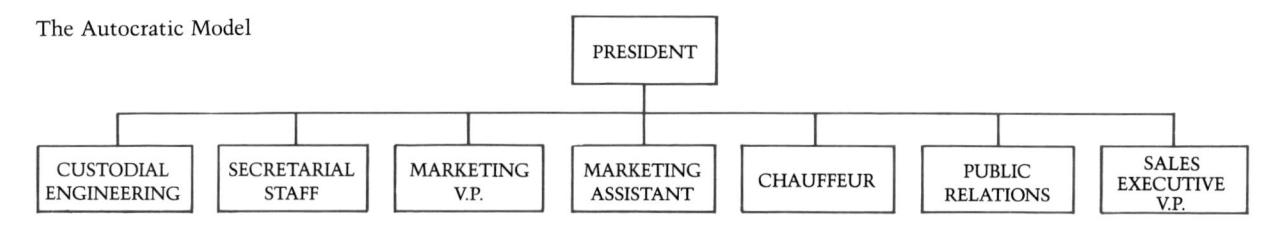

The Autocratic Model

```
                              PRESIDENT
    ┌───────────┬──────────┬─────────┼─────────┬──────────┬───────────┐
 CUSTODIAL  SECRETARIAL  MARKETING MARKETING  CHAUFFEUR  PUBLIC     SALES
ENGINEERING    STAFF       V.P.    ASSISTANT            RELATIONS  EXECUTIVE
                                                                     V.P.
```

In this example, the company president has become so caught up in the day-to-day minutiae that his/her ability to devote time to central issues and to the decision-making process is severely impaired. His/her effectiveness is compromised by the multitude of responsibilities. Likewise, in a structured design such a wide control span of responsibilities should be avoided or should be delegated to subordinate levels. In general, one should not coordinate more than seven or eight subordinate paragraphs at any given level.

Each module in a structured design should be functional, i.e., each should have a clearly defined responsibility, a very specific objective that can be described very succinctly. In the pseudo code of Figure 1–7, modules such as compute-executive-pay and compute-part-time-pay are examples of specific tasks that are self-contained and independent of one another. One way to ensure that a module is functional is to give it a module name that expresses its function in a three-word sentence:

verb-adjective-noun   such as   compute-overtime-pay

For example, modules with such names as
assign-bonus-to-officers-and-compute-part-time-pay or
check-position-code-and-write-output-record
could be broken down into more elementary functions.

1-3-10 DO IT NOW

1. Rewrite the pseudo code for the part-time-employees and part-time-process modules of Figure 1–10, based on the following structured chart:

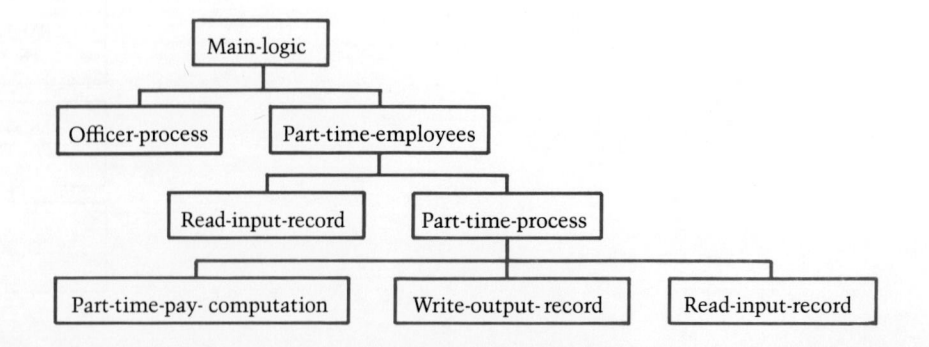

```
                        Main-logic
                    ┌───────┴────────┐
            Officer-process    Part-time-employees
                            ┌───────┴────────┐
                    Read-input-record    Part-time-process
                                    ┌────────┼─────────┐
                        Part-time-pay-   Write-output-  Read-input-
                         computation       record         record
```

2. Write the pseudo code to solve the payroll problem in Figure 1–7, with the added stipulations:
   (a) Officers pay a state tax of 6% of gross and a federal tax off 25% of gross amount over $500. The output record should include the gross and net pay and the state and federal tax. Note that the federal tax paid could equal 0.
   (b) Part-timers get a bonus of $50 if their base pay exceeds $250.

ANSWERS

1. *Part-time-employees.*
       perform read-input-record
       perform part-time-process until end of file is encountered
   Part-time-process.
       perform part-time-pay-computation
       perform write-output-record
       perform read-input-record

2. *Program Development.*
       *Purpose of program is to compute company personnel pay
   Main-logic.
       perform officer-process 4 times
       perform part-time-employees
       stop
   Officer-process.
       read input-record
       compute pay = hours-worked × 20
       perform tax-computations
       compute net-pay = pay − state-tax − fed-tax
       write output-record (pay, net-pay, fed-tax, state-tax)
   Tax-computations.
       compute state-tax = 0.06 × pay
       if pay is greater than 500
           compute fed-tax = 0.25 × (pay − 500)
       else
           compute fed-tax = 0
       endif
   Part-time-employees.
       read input-record
       perform part-time-process until end of file is encountered
   Part-time-process.
       perform part-time-pay-computation
       write output-record
       read input-record
   Part-time-pay-computation.
       if position-code = 1
           compute pay = hours-worked × 5
       else
           compute pay = hours-worked × 4
       endif
       if pay is greater than 250
           compute pay = pay + 50
       else
           compute pay = pay
       endif

24 UNDERSTANDING STRUCTURED COBOL

1-4 FILE PROCESSING—AN APPLICATION

1-4-1 COBOL: A FILE-PROCESSING LANGUAGE

As we have noted earlier, COBOL is a language designed to process large volumes of information. This generally implies recording, reading, and processing vast amounts of data to produce detailed reports such as inventories, mailing lists, payrolls, personnel information, et cetera. COBOL is, then, essentially a transaction type or file-oriented language that feeds on vast quantities of data. Defining and understanding the nature of a file is thus of primary importance.

1-4-2 FILES, RECORDS, AND DATA ITEMS

Study Figure 1–11 carefully. It involves a transaction between a parts manufacturing company located in New York state and a customer plant in Texas. Note the data typed in the small windows on the screen; this is an example of a *record*. This record consists of numerous *fields* or *data items*—the customer company name, the commodity number ordered, the item amount, et cetera. Thus a *record* is defined as a collection of related data items. Some of these data items (such as the date) are broken down into *subitems* (month/day). Each data item (field) is a collection of related and contiguous column/storage positions (screen/printer/diskette/memory). For example, the data typed on the screen in columns 3–12 identifies the customer name.

The screen record in figure 1–11 is an order record for 40 sq. shank swivels from the General Manufacturing Company. A similar record would also be typed for 75 flat top rigid items, et cetera. The typewritten invoice lists altogether six separate items, implying that the input order file for the New Mexico Company must have consisted of six order records.

Quite obviously, the General Manufacturing Company also supplies other firms throughout the country with the same or other equipment. At the conclusion of a business day, the General Manufacturing plant typically collects all the order files (one for each company). All these separate files, stored on magnetic disk, are then combined into one large file to represent all transactions for the day. This daily file can be processed accordingly by the company's data processing center to produce general/detailed sales reports and to obtain a new master list for an updated inventory from which reorder decisions can be made.

Note that to generate the invoice of Figure 1–11, the billing program must search General Manufacturing's master client file to look up the address of the client firm (the New Mexico Company), the various item descriptions and corresponding costs, the company's standard method of shipment, its customary payment terms, et cetera.

Other output items such as the total bill, the customer's order number, and invoice number are either computed or assigned values by the invoice/billing program.

1-5 YOU MIGHT WANT TO KNOW

1. How long has COBOL been around?

   Answer: CODASYL (Conference on Data Language Systems)—a commit-

INTRODUCTION TO PROGRAMMING

Order typed in by GENERAL MANUFACTURING COMPANY employee

Order Screen Forms

customer name	customer number	date mo day	commodity number	quantity	salesman number
NEW MEX CO	59751	12 31	11202	00040	67

Data item → (pointing to NEW MEX CO)

input-record
(collection of related data items)

GENERAL MANUFACTURING COMPANY
ENDICOTT, N.Y.

CUSTOMER'S ORDER NO. 331   INVOICE DATE 12-31   INVOICE NO. 12349

SOLD TO   New Mexico Company
           216 Wysor Building   CUSTOMER NO. 59751
           Houston, Texas

SHIP TO   Above   SALESMAN Macy-67

Make all checks payable to
GENERAL MANUFACTURING COMPANY
Endicott, N.Y.

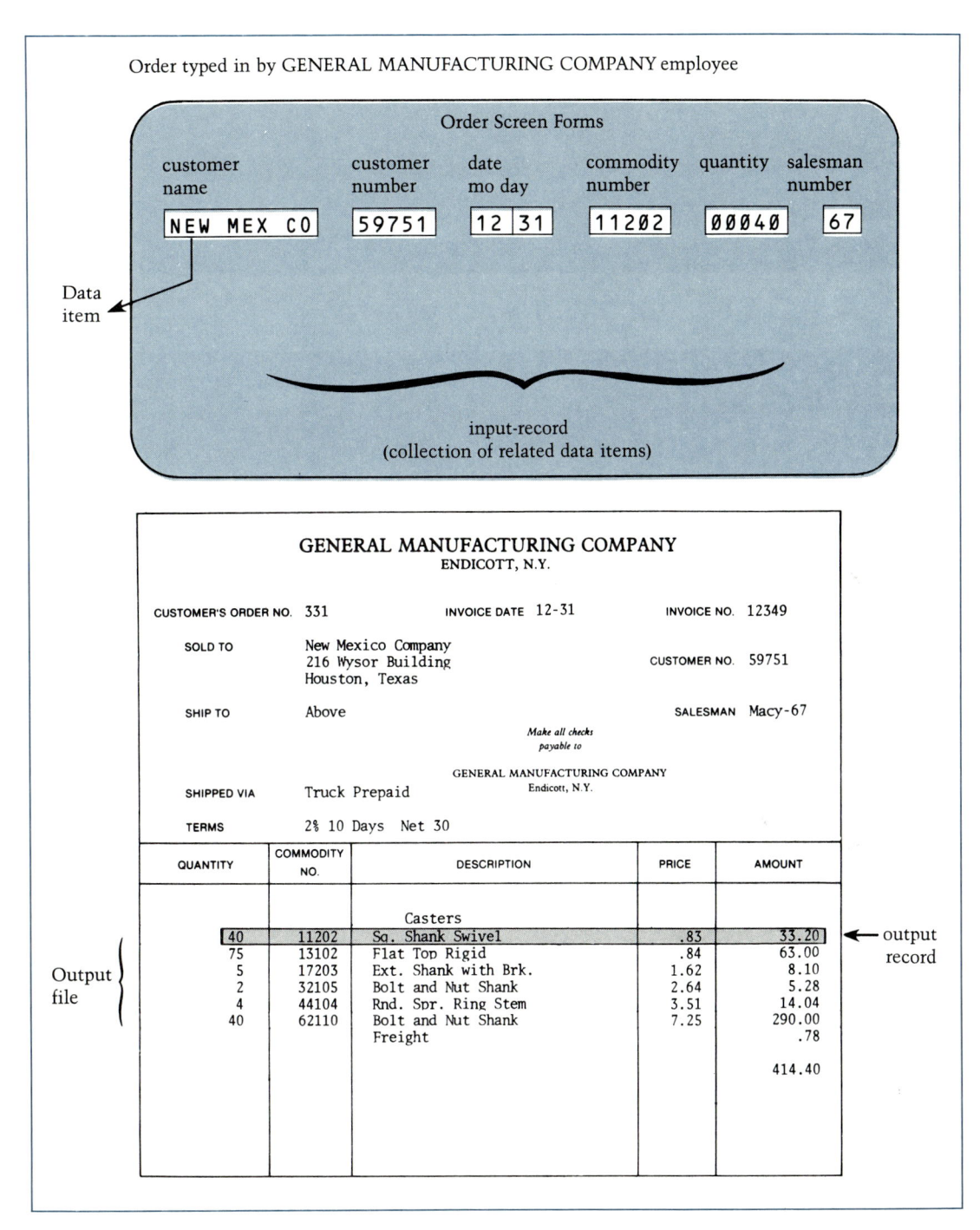

SHIPPED VIA   Truck Prepaid

TERMS   2% 10 Days Net 30

QUANTITY	COMMODITY NO.	DESCRIPTION	PRICE	AMOUNT
		Casters		
40	11202	Sq. Shank Swivel	.83	33.20
75	13102	Flat Top Rigid	.84	63.00
5	17203	Ext. Shank with Brk.	1.62	8.10
2	32105	Bolt and Nut Shank	2.64	5.28
4	44104	Rnd. Spr. Ring Stem	3.51	14.04
40	62110	Bolt and Nut Shank	7.25	290.00
		Freight		.78
				414.40

Output file ← (bracketing the table)
output record → (pointing to the 40/11202/Sq. Shank Swivel row)

FIGURE 1-11
FILES, RECORDS, AND DATA ITEMS

tee of government, business, computer manufacturers, academics and users—supervised the development of COBOL in 1959.

2. Does COBOL vary from one computer to another?

   Answer: In 1968 the American National Standards Institute (ANS, ANSI) adopted a standard COBOL language. This initial standard of 1968 was revised in 1974. Some computer companies, such as IBM, still adhere to 1968 standards, with special features of their own, but many of IBM's features are also present in 1974 standards. This textbook uses 1974 ANS COBOL. The manufacturer's technical COBOL manual, probably available at the reader's computer laboratory, is a worthwhile investment and may save hours of frustration and inconvenience because it will show the particular provisions and/or restrictions of the compiler used by the reader's computer.

3. When are new standards projected for COBOL?

   Answer: Possibly in 1986!

4. Is COBOL available on microcomputers?

   Answer: Yes. 1974 ANS COBOL is available on most micros with at least 64 K of memory. In most cases, however, it is a "low-intermediate" COBOL, meaning that it does not support certain functional processing modules, such as Report Writer, Sort/Merge, and Communication. However, the capabilities of the microcomputer are sufficient for many educational institutions and businesses.

5. What is the story behind structured programming?

   Answer: In 1966 the *Communications of the ACM* (a publication of the Association for Computing Machinery) published a paper by Messrs. Boehm and Jacopini, which had been presented two years earlier during an international colloquium on algebraic linguistics. The essence of the paper was that a program with one entry and one exit could be written using only three control patterns: the sequence, the selection (*if then else*) and the *do while* patterns.

   In 1968 Mr. Dijkstra of the Netherlands proposed that program code could be written without the use of the *go to* statement. Mr. Dijkstra considered the *go to* statement harmful and stated, "I discovered why the use of the *go to* statement has such disastrous effects, and I became convinced that the *go to* statement should be abolished from all higher level programming languages..."

   Subsequently, Dr. Mills of the IBM Corporation wrote an article on the mathematical foundation of structured programming. With Terry Baker of IBM, the New York Times Project was developed using structured program concepts.

   From 1971 on, structured programming has been an alternative to the traditional program development methods that are progressively disappearing from the programming scene.

6. What other types of languages are there besides COBOL?

   Answer: One survey reported 600 computer languages in more or less widespread use. Among the more common are FORTRAN (scientific processing), RPG (Report Program Generator—for small shops), ALGOL (scientific and system language), BASIC (Beginners All Symbolic Instruction Code), PL/1 (a sister language to COBOL, well suited for business and for scientific problems), and PASCAL.

7. In terms of coding productivity, how does structured programming compare to traditional COBOL programming?

   Answer: Studies in the mid-1960s revealed that professional programmers coded approximately 12 lines of tested code per day. Some studies show that this figure jumps to 100 lines of tested code per day when structured designs are used.

8. What is a flowchart?

   Answer: A flowchart is a pictorial representation (a graphic outline) of the logic used to solve a particular problem. Each step in the flowchart is represented either by a rectangle (computations), a parallelogram (input-output or a diamond (decisions). An oval is used to identify the beginning and the end of the flowchart. These geometric blocks are linked to one another by means of flow lines which specify the order in which these steps (blocks) are to be carried out. Thus the reader can easily visualize the entire logic of the problem through its network of action routes.

9. What are the different symbols for flowcharting?

    Answer:

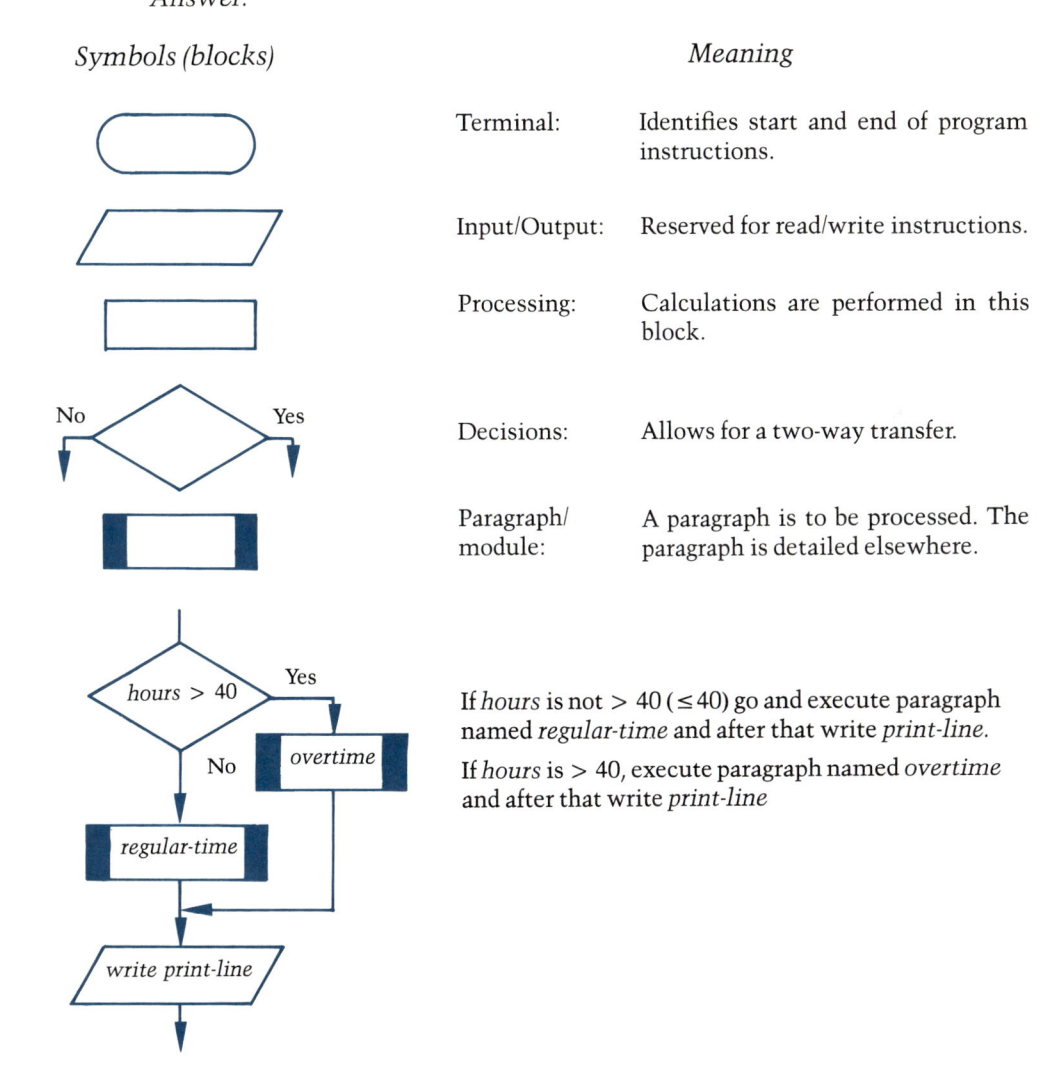

Symbols (blocks)		Meaning
(oval)	Terminal:	Identifies start and end of program instructions.
(parallelogram)	Input/Output:	Reserved for read/write instructions.
(rectangle)	Processing:	Calculations are performed in this block.
(diamond, No/Yes)	Decisions:	Allows for a two-way transfer.
(module symbol)	Paragraph/module:	A paragraph is to be processed. The paragraph is detailed elsewhere.

Flowchart: *hours > 40* decision — Yes branch to *overtime*, No branch to *regular-time*, both leading to *write print-line*.

If *hours* is not > 40 (≤ 40) go and execute paragraph named *regular-time* and after that write *print-line*.

If *hours* is > 40, execute paragraph named *overtime* and after that write *print-line*

1–6 EXERCISES

1–6–1 TEST YOURSELF

1. Define the following words:
    a. Computer
    b. Data
    c. Instruction
    d. Information
    e. Memory
    f. Central processing unit
    g. Input/output devices
    h. Hardware/software
    i. High-level language

2. List the five components of a computer system. Explain the function of each.

3. Determine which of the following is true or false:

   a. A compiler is a program that translates machine code into a high-level language.
   b. Computer hardware consists of all the physical components that make up a computer system.
   c. High-level languages are machine-independent.
   d. The term *software* refers to such material as diskettes, paper/magnetic tapes, et cetera.
   e. ANS recognized COBOL in 1959.
   f. Pseudo code is a language that can be processed by a computer.
   g. In top-down design, the lowest level modules contain the greatest level of detail.

In Questions 4–10 select the most appropriate answer.

4. Operating systems

   a. are considered hardware.
   b. assist and, in part, control the operations of the computer.
   c. are designed to allow several programs to share the same computer resources.
   d. perform all problem solving.
   e. Both b and c.

5. A language translator program transforms source program statements into

   a. high-level language
   b. job control language
   c. a compiler
   d. an object program

6. Modules of a program solution and their relationships can be depicted graphically using a

   a. structured diagram
   b. flowchart
   c. pseudo code
   d. graph

7. Pseudo code is

   a. a simple version of COBOL.
   b. a debugging technique.
   c. an English-like description of the processing steps in a program.
   d. difficult to understand.

8. Structured programming

   a. increases testing time.
   b. tries to do away with the loop pattern.
   c. has the objective of reducing the complexity of a program.
   d. Both b and c.

9. In each case, which statements (other than the PERFORM statement) is executed after the sentence SING? Draw the corresponding structured diagram for each case.

a. A.
      PERFORM B.
      GET DRY.
    B.
      PERFORM C.
      EAT.
    C.
      WASH UP.
      SING.

b. A.
      PERFORM B.
      GET DRY.
    B.
      PERFORM C.
    C.
      WASH UP.
      SING.

c. A.
      PERFORM B.
      EAT.
    B.
      PERFORM D.
      PERFORM C.
    C.
      PERFORM E.
    D.
      SING.
    E.
      PERFORM F.
    F.
      GRUNT.
      PERFORM D.

10. How many processing levels do you count in the following structured diagram?

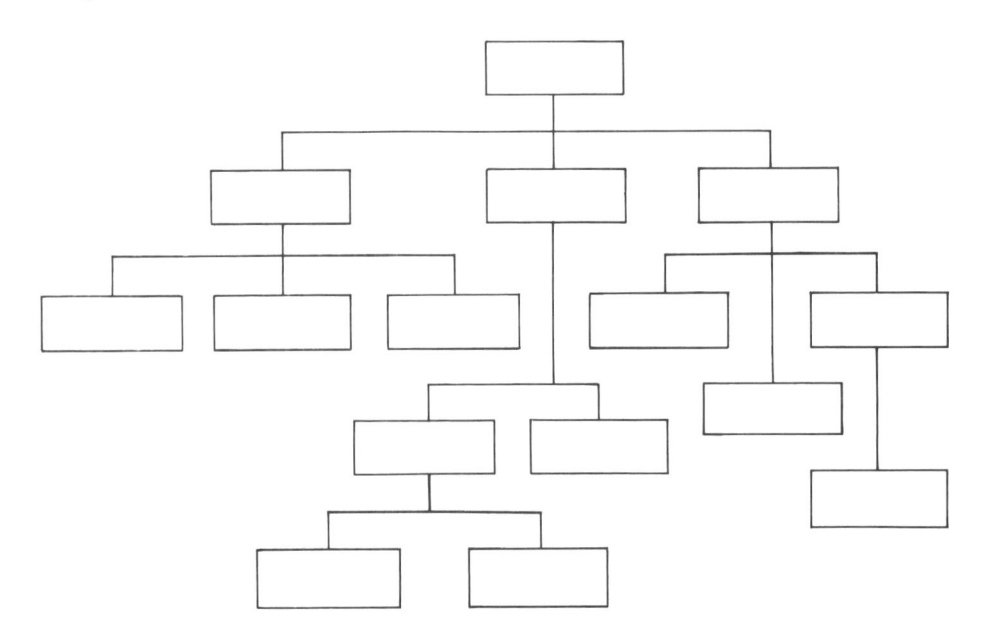

11. An input file consists of exactly five records, each containing an employee-name and a number of hours worked. Write the pseudo code to read these five records and compute each employee's pay as follows: If the employee has worked more than 40 hours, the hourly rate of pay is $5.00 per hour (over 40); otherwise it is $3.76 per hour. Print each output record.

12. Change the pseudo code solution for exercise 11 so that it will process correctly a file containing an unknown number of records.

13. Translate the following flowchart into pseudo code, using Figures 1–7 and 1–9 for guidance. Generate two modularized versions, and draw the corresponding structured diagrams.

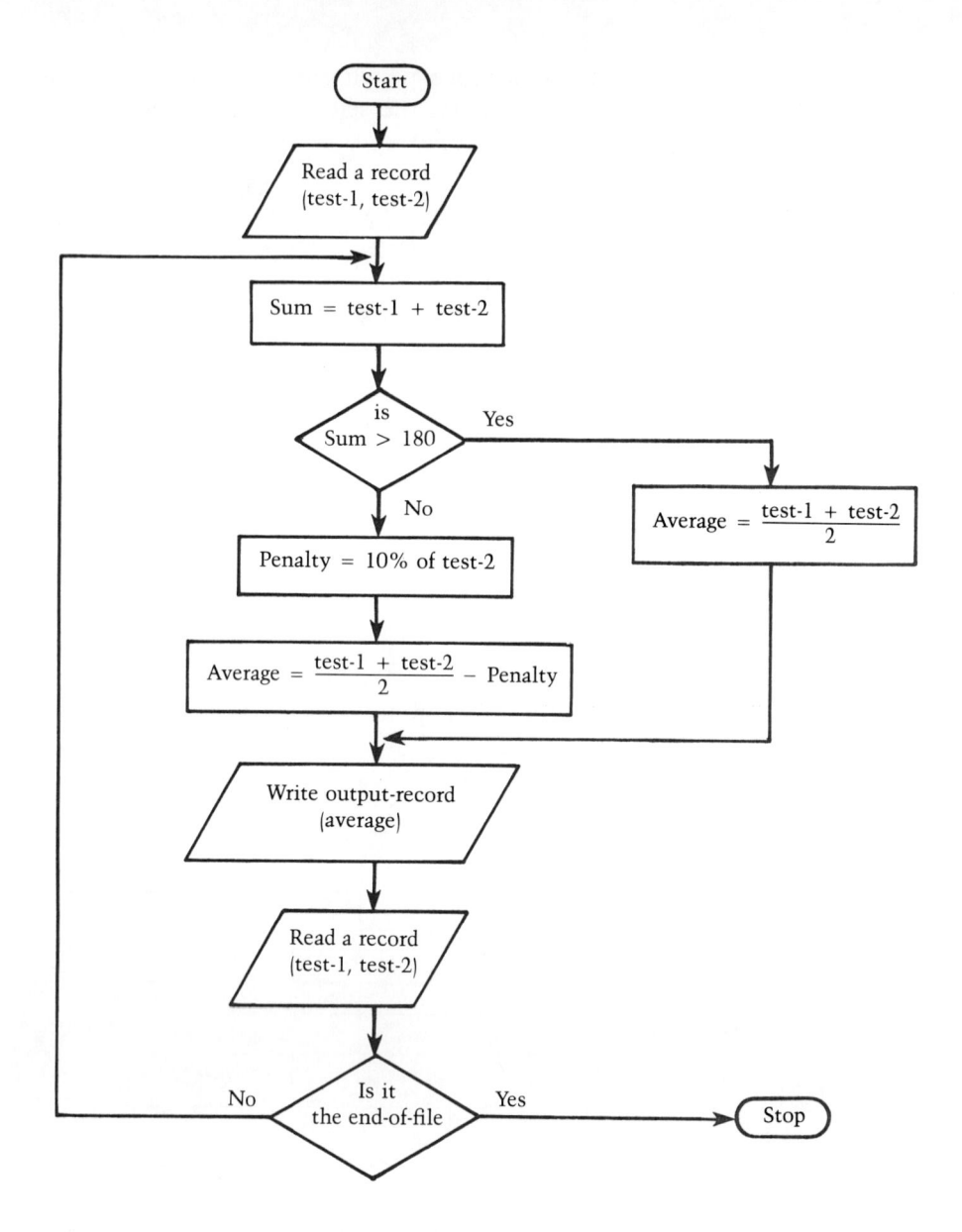

```
                          ┌─────────┐
                          │  Start  │
                          └────┬────┘
                               ▼
                       ╱─────────────╲
                      ╱ Read a record  ╲
                      ╲ (test-1, test-2)╱
                       ╲─────────────╱
                               │
       ┌──────────────────────▶│
       │                       ▼
       │           ┌───────────────────────┐
       │           │ Sum = test-1 + test-2 │
       │           └───────────┬───────────┘
       │                       ▼
       │                   ╱───────╲        Yes
       │                  ╱   is    ╲──────────────────┐
       │                  ╲ Sum > 180╱                  │
       │                   ╲───┬───╱                    │
       │                     No│                        ▼
       │                       ▼              ┌──────────────────────┐
       │           ┌───────────────────────┐  │          test-1+test-2│
       │           │ Penalty = 10% of test-2│ │ Average = ─────────── │
       │           └───────────┬───────────┘  │               2       │
       │                       ▼              └──────────┬───────────┘
       │    ┌────────────────────────────┐               │
       │    │          test-1 + test-2   │               │
       │    │Average = ─────────────── - Penalty         │
       │    │                2            │              │
       │    └──────────────┬─────────────┘               │
       │                   ▼◀──────────────────────────── 
       │           ╱─────────────────╲
       │          ╱  Write output-record╲
       │          ╲     (average)       ╱
       │           ╲─────────────────╱
       │                   │
       │                   ▼
       │           ╱─────────────╲
       │          ╱ Read a record  ╲
       │          ╲ (test-1, test-2)╱
       │           ╲─────────────╱
       │                   │
       │                   ▼
       │               ╱───────╲
       │      No      ╱  Is it  ╲    Yes     ┌──────┐
       └─────────────╲the end-of-file╱──────▶│ Stop │
                      ╲─────────╱            └──────┘
```

1-6-2 SELECTED ANSWERS TO TEST YOURSELF

1. a. **Computer** A machine that can perform arithmetic operations and make decisions based on comparisons by following a set of instructions stored in its memory.
   b. **Data** Raw facts; raw material for information.
   c. **Instruction** A statement specifying one or more operations to be performed.
   d. **Information** Data that has been organized and processed so that it is meaningful.
   e. **Memory** Physical component of a computer that stores instructions and data.
   f. **Central Processing Unit** Brain headquarters of a computer, consisting of memory, arithmetic and logic unit, and control unit.
   g. **Input/Output Devices** Devices from which the computer can accept data and information and onto which it can write or store data/information.

      h. **Hardware** Physical components of a computing system.
         Software Computer programs.
      i. **High-Level Language** A language that can be used to communicate with computers in a semi-English written language.

2. Input, output, memory, arithmetic/logic and control.

3. a. F   b. T   c. T   d. F   e. F   f. F   g. T

4. (e) Operating systems permit a computer system to manage its own operations and provide a control system. Operating systems also handle the allocation of computer resources to several programs.

5. (d) The language translator program transforms the source program statements into a machine-executable program known as an object program.

6. (a) A structured diagram graphically depicts the hierarchical relationship of the modules.

7. (c) Pseudo code is used to express program logic by describing the processing steps in an English-like manner. Pseudo code is easily understood, even to those unfamiliar with the program logic.

8. (c) Structured programming emphasizes dividing a program into logical sections in order to reduce testing time, increase programming productivity, and bring clarity to programming by reducing complexity.

9. a. Eat   b. Get dry   c. Grunt, eat

10. Four levels

CHAPTER 2

GETTING STARTED: THE FIRST COBOL PROGRAM

2–1 PROBLEM SPECIFICATION

2–2 HOW AND WHERE TO START

2–3 COBOL CODE INTERPRETATION

2–4 EXERCISES

INTRODUCTION

This chapter presents the first complete COBOL program and data file and gives instructions for typing them and running the program. The COBOL program code is explained. The four divisions of a COBOL program—IDENTIFICATION, ENVIRONMENT, DATA, AND PROCEDURE—are introduced, and the requirements of each are specified. Detailed instructions for describing records and data items in the DATA division are also given.

2-1 PROBLEM SPECIFICATION

Using your text editor:

1. Create an input file consisting of three student records, where each record contains a student name and two test scores. The physical layout of the record is as follows:

```
ARDEN LIZ   050060
JONES MIKE  060050   } to be typed
ABBOTT BRIAN040090
```

Name: positions 1–12
Test1: positions 13–15
Test2: positions 16–18

2. Write the COBOL program to read the input file created in step 1 and print out the student records according to the following design. Assume each printer line is 80 characters long.

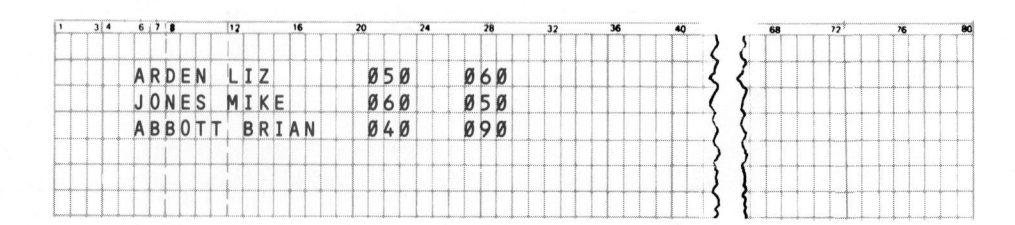

```
      ARDEN LIZ     050  060
      JONES MIKE    060  050
      ABBOTT BRIAN  040  090
```

2-2 HOW AND WHERE TO START

2-2-1 PRACTICAL CONSIDERATIONS: COMMUNICATING WITH YOUR SYSTEM

Because of the many types of operating systems and the wide variety of computers, ranging from the microcomputers to large mainframe computers, the ways in which input data files and COBOL programs are typed, stored on disk, and then submitted for processing vary considerably from one system or installation to another. Specific information regarding access to your particular system is not discussed in this chapter; it is available from your instructor, computer lab assistants, or appropriate technical reference manuals. Section 2-2-5 is left open for you to record this information.

2-2-2 TEXT EDITORS

Both the input file and the source file (COBOL program) consist of lines of text that must be typed and recorded on some device (usually a disk) before they can be processed by the computer. Text editors are used for this purpose. Text editors are essentially unsophisticated word processors that allow you to type lines of text and display the text on screens or hard copy terminals. Such lines can then be *edited* at will, i.e., lines can be deleted or added, and text within a line can be changed. The resulting lines of text can then be stored (saved) on disk under a particular file name (catalogued).

Text editors have their own commands or instructions for the various editing functions. Keep in mind that these text editing commands have *nothing* to do with the COBOL language! The text editor is used solely to create and edit files (you could even use a text editor to write letters or essays!).

Typically, each line of text is automatically numbered by the editor; this makes it possible for you to refer to the particular line number that you wish to edit. Even though the line numbers appear on the screen or on your hard copy terminal, these line numbers are ignored by COBOL when it reads your COBOL source file or the data file, i.e., as far as COBOL is concerned, position 1 starts after the numeric label provided by the text editor (on screens, at the beginning cursor position).

Figure 2-1 shows text processed by two different types of text editors.

Once the input or source file has been typed, a text editor command is used to save that file on disk. The user gives the file a name so that it can be catalogued on disk for subsequent retrieval. The user-chosen file name is added to the directory of the disk, which contains the names of all the files currently on the disk.

Use the open space provided in section 2-2-5 to record the following:

1. How to load (call) your text editor.
2. The text editor commands that you are likely to use, i.e., those to insert, delete, and change lines of text.
3. How to save a file and give it a name.

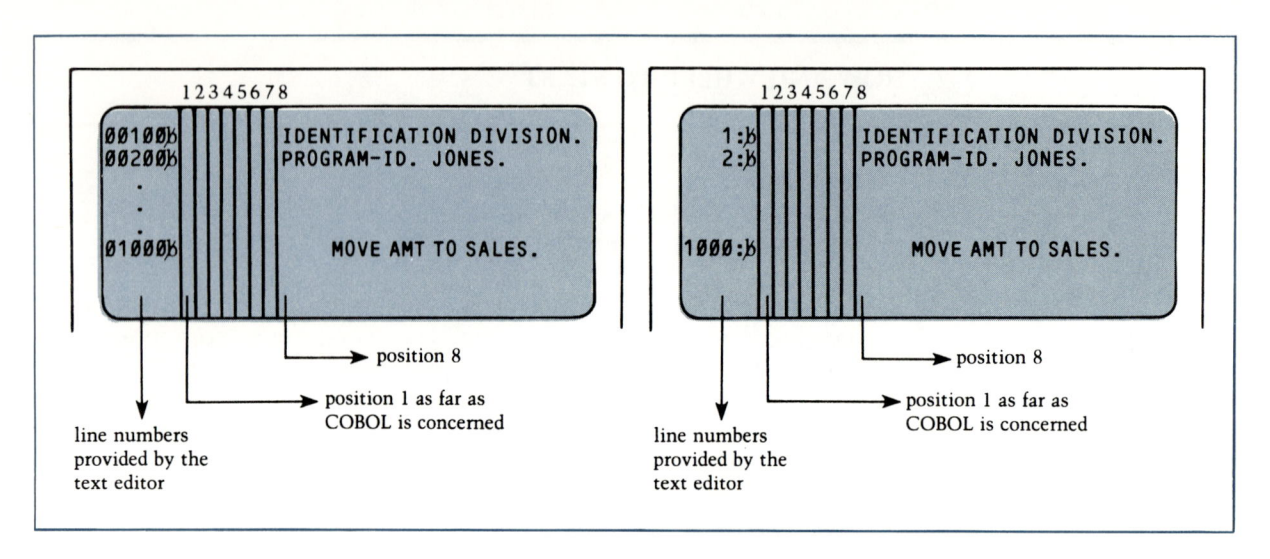

FIGURE 2-1
TYPICAL TEXT EDITOR SCREENS

4. How to print the text file and how to access the disk directory in case you forget the names of your files.

Depending on the system you use to run your COBOL program, you may need to create two separate files using your text editor—one for the input data file and the other for the COBOL program. These files will then be stored independently of one another on disk. On some other systems the data file and the COBOL program consist of just one file—the data file is typed immediately after the various COBOL statements, and special control statements separate the source program from the data file. The following discussion pertains to a typical system where two distinct files must be created.

2-2-3 CREATING THE DATA FILE

Using your text editor, type the input file as specified in section 2-1. Note that the name field goes into columns 1-12 and that the first and second test scores start in columns 13 and 16, respectively. (Don't forget to type the leading 0's for the scores.) After you have typed the second test score for each record, press the RETURN or ENTER key to start a new record. When you have entered the last record, store the data file on disk. The system will automatically insert an end-of-file record following the last record you typed; it is represented in Figure 2-2 by the symbol ■. You will need to give your data file a name so that it will appear on the disk directory. Let's name the data file ROSTER; this will allow us to retrieve and edit it later on. Figure 2-2 shows the data file on the screen and on the disk.

2-2-4 TYPING YOUR COBOL PROGRAM: PRACTICAL CONSIDERATIONS

Now, using your text editor, type the COBOL program shown in Figure 2-3.

GETTING STARTED: THE FIRST COBOL PROGRAM 37

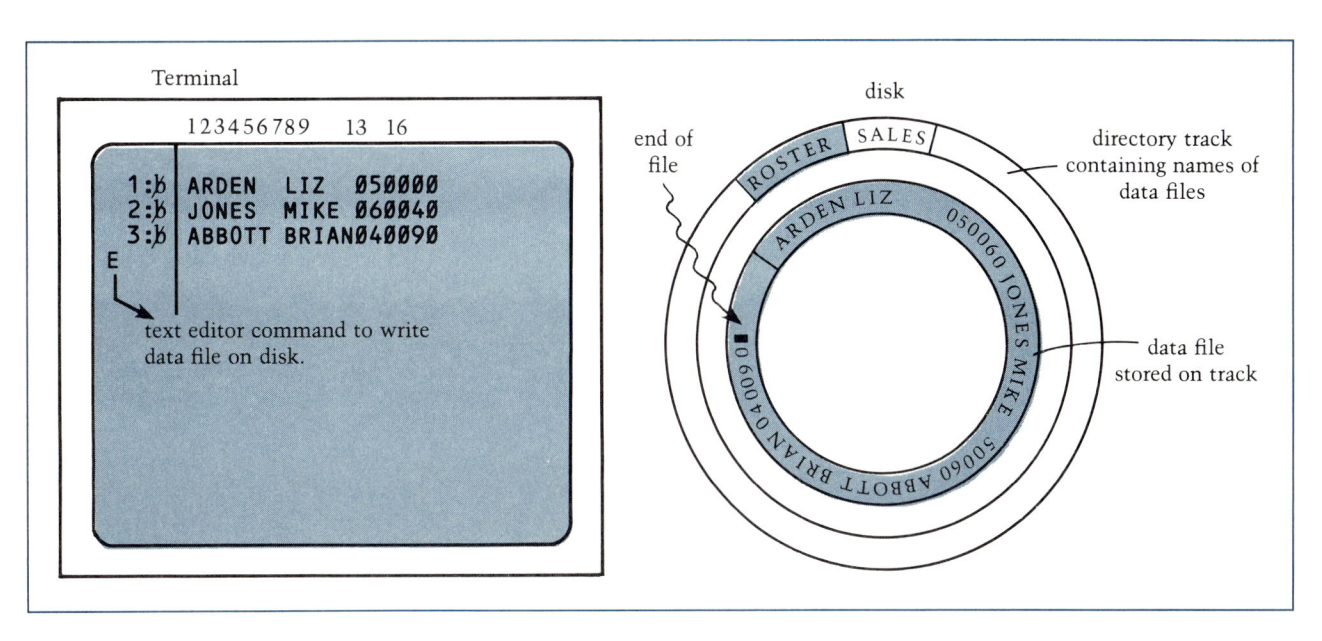

```
        Terminal
         123456789   13  16

       1:b  ARDEN   LIZ   050000
       2:b  JONES   MIKE  060040
       3:b  ABBOTT  BRIAN040090
        E

       text editor command to write
       data file on disk.
```

disk — directory track containing names of data files
end of file
ROSTER SALES
ARDEN LIZ 050060 JONES MIKE 060040 ABBOTT BRIAN 040090
data file stored on track

FIGURE 2–2
INPUT FILE DISPLAYED ON SCREEN AND STORED ON DISK

1. Note that the COBOL statements start in either position 7 (asterisk lines), position 8, or position 12. Remember that position 1 actually starts after the line numbers provided by the text editor.

2. Make sure that you type each line exactly as shown. The lines starting with an asterisk in column 7 may actually be typed in free form, because they are comment lines.

3. Do not forget the periods, the hyphens, and the blank spaces following the periods, as in lines 2, 3, 13, and 14, for example. Note that some lines do *not* terminate with a period, such as lines 24, 32, 50, and 69.

4. Note that apostrophes (single quotation marks) are used at lines 37, 51, 53, and 70. Some COBOL versions may allow double quotation marks.

5. The system input/output device names PRINTER and DISK at lines 17 and 18 may have to be changed to work with your system. Ask your instructor or the computer lab assistant for the appropriate entries, and record this information in section 2–2–5.

6. When you have entered the last line of text, carefully check what you have typed against the text shown in Figure 2–3 and correct any errors.

7. Store the COBOL program on disk. You will need to give your program file a name so that it can be catalogued on disk; let's give it the name PROG1.

At this point your data file and program file should both be stored on disk with the disk directory showing two separate entries, ROSTER and PROG1 (see Figure 2–4).

```cobol
       IDENTIFICATION DIVISION.
       PROGRAM-ID. STUDENT-LISTING.
       AUTHOR. JONES.
      ****************************************************************
      *                                                              *
      *       THIS PROGRAM READS STUDENT RECORDS FROM A DISK FILE    *
      *       AND PRINTS OUT EACH STUDENT NAME AS WELL AS HIS/HER    *
      *       TWO TEST SCORES.                                       *
      *                                                              *
      ****************************************************************
       ENVIRONMENT DIVISION.
       CONFIGURATION SECTION.
       SOURCE-COMPUTER. IBM.
       OBJECT-COMPUTER. IBM.
       INPUT-OUTPUT SECTION.
       FILE-CONTROL.
           SELECT REPORT-FILE  ASSIGN TO PRINTER.
           SELECT STUDENT-FILE ASSIGN TO DISK.
      *
       DATA DIVISION.
       FILE SECTION.
      *
       FD  STUDENT-FILE
           LABEL RECORDS ARE STANDARD
           DATA RECORD IS STUDENT-RECORD.
       01  STUDENT-RECORD.
           05 SR-NAME  PIC X(12).
           05 SR-TEST1 PIC 999.
           05 SR-TEST2 PIC 999.
      *
       FD  REPORT-FILE
           LABEL RECORDS ARE OMITTED
           DATA RECORD IS PRINT-LINE.
       01  PRINT-LINE  PIC X(80).
      *
       WORKING-STORAGE SECTION.
       01  END-FILE    PIC XXX    VALUE 'NO'.
       01  DETAIL-LINE.
           05 FILLER   PIC X(5)   VALUE SPACES.
           05 DL-NAME  PIC X(12).
           05 FILLER   PIC XXX    VALUE SPACES.
           05 DL-TEST1 PIC 999.
           05 FILLER   PIC XXX    VALUE SPACES.
           05 DL-TEST2 PIC 999.
           05 FILLER   PIC X(51)  VALUE SPACES.
      *
       PROCEDURE DIVISION.
       100-COORDINATING-MODULE.
           OPEN INPUT STUDENT-FILE, OUTPUT REPORT-FILE.
           READ STUDENT-FILE
               AT END MOVE 'YES' TO END-FILE.
           PERFORM 200-PROCESS-RECORD
               UNTIL END-FILE = 'YES'.
           CLOSE STUDENT-FILE, REPORT-FILE.
           STOP RUN.
      ****************************************************************
      *                                                              *
      *       THIS MODULE MOVES THE VARIOUS INPUT FIELDS INTO THE    *
      *       SPECIFIED POSITIONS THAT THEY ARE TO OCCUPY ON THE     *
      *       OUTPUT-LINE.                                           *
      *                                                              *
      ****************************************************************
       200-PROCESS-RECORD.
           MOVE SR-NAME  TO DL-NAME.
           MOVE SR-TEST1 TO DL-TEST1.
           MOVE SR-TEST2 TO DL-TEST2.
           MOVE DETAIL-LINE TO PRINT-LINE.
           WRITE PRINT-LINE.
           READ STUDENT-FILE
               AT END MOVE 'YES' TO END-FILE.
```

FIGURE 2-3
FIRST COBOL PROGRAM

Line numbers
↓

1 Always start with the IDENTIFICATION DIVISION. Don't forget the period. Start in Column 8.
2 User chooses a name for the program. STUDENT-LISTING. Don't forget the hyphen.
3 The AUTHOR entry is optional.
4–10 are comment lines. To create a comment line you must type an asterisk in column 7; thereafter you can type any comment you want. In this case, a box of asterisks was drawn to highlight the comments. Lines 6 through 8 describe the purpose of the program. Comments are optional but their inclusion in the program makes the program more self-documenting. The practice of inserting comments at key points in a program is strongly recommended.
11–14 These lines identify the computer facility. Ask your instructor or the lab assistant. Don't forget the hyphen in both lines 13 and 14 and a blank space after the first period.
15–18 The user gives symbolic names to his/her input and output file and assigns a device for each file.
16 Don't forget the hyphen in FILE-CONTROL.
17 COBOL requires the user to choose names for both the input and output file. REPORT-FILE is the name chosen to identify the output file (results). PRINTER is the system name that designates which device will be used to process (write) the output file. The designation PRINTER will need to be changed for your system.
18 Let us give the name STUDENT-FILE to the input file. DISK is the system name of the device on which the input file resides. You need to determine the system name for the input device on your system.
19 This blank comment separates the divisions of the program and makes it more readable.
20 The DATA division allocates memory space for the various records and data items used in the program.
21 Only the input and output records are described in this section.
23 Lines 23–25 actually represent one long statement spread over three lines. Note the absence of periods at lines 23 and 24. FD stands for file description.
25 Optional entry. The user explicitly states the name of the input record whose structure will represent all input records.
26 The name of the input file record is STUDENT-RECORD. The level number 01 is required to designate a complete record, which in this case is 18 positions long.
27–29 The three 05 level numbers indicate that the record is broken down into three distinct fields. Each field is given a name. The length of the item and its type (numeric (9), alphanumeric (X)) are specified through the picture clause PIC.
31 Lines 31 through 33 represent one long statement spread over 3 lines. Note the absence of periods at lines 31 and 32. FD stands for file description.
33 Optional. PRINT-LINE is the name chosen for the output record.
34 The output line consists of 80 alphanumeric positions.
36 This section describes all records and data items used in the logic of the program.
37 END-FILE is a data item used by the program to let it know when there are no more records to read.
38–45 DETAIL-LINE is a temporary storage area used to create the image of the output line that is to be printed. This 80-character record is broken down into 7 fields, some of which contain blank spaces (FILLER) and others that contain the student name and his/her two test scores.
47 This entry identifies the start of the logic, which is broken down into two modules.
48 This is the coordinating module.
49 Both input and output files must be OPENed before they can be processed.
50–51 The READ sentence carries over two lines. The first record is read.
51 If the end of the file is detected, the value 'YES' is placed in END-FILE (not likely for the first READ).
52–53 As long as the value of END-FILE is not 'YES', lines 64–70 are repeated over and over again.
54 Both files must be closed before the program is terminated (line 55).
64–66 The student name and two test scores are transferred to the image of the output line.
67–68 The image of the output line is moved into the output area and then printed.
69–70 A new input record is read; if the end of file is read, 'YES' is stored in END-FILE. In any event, control is returned to line 52 where END-FILE is tested. If it contains 'YES', control is passed to line 54, otherwise the paragraph at line 63 is carried out to process the record just read at line 69.

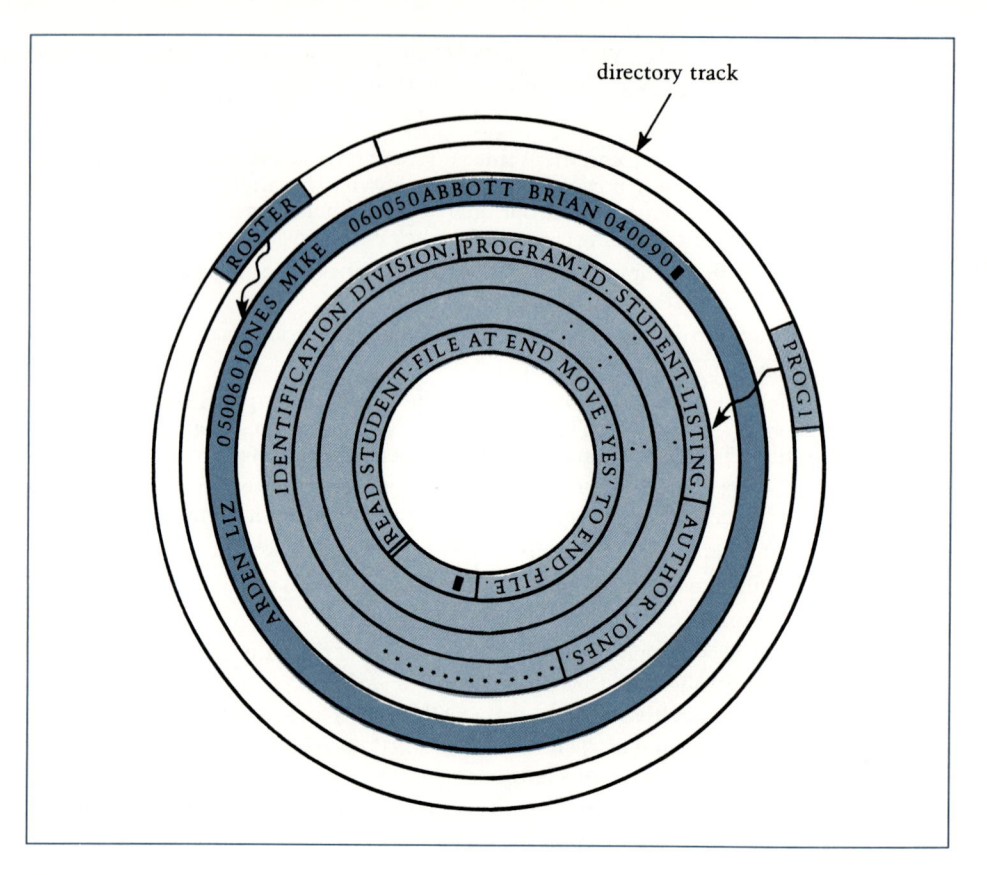

FIGURE 2-4
DISK CONTAINING COBOL PROGRAM AND DATA FILE

2-2-5 MY SYSTEM IS DIFFERENT

In this section record the various text editor commands that you will use, as well as any system or COBOL statements that need to be changed or added so that your program will run on your system.

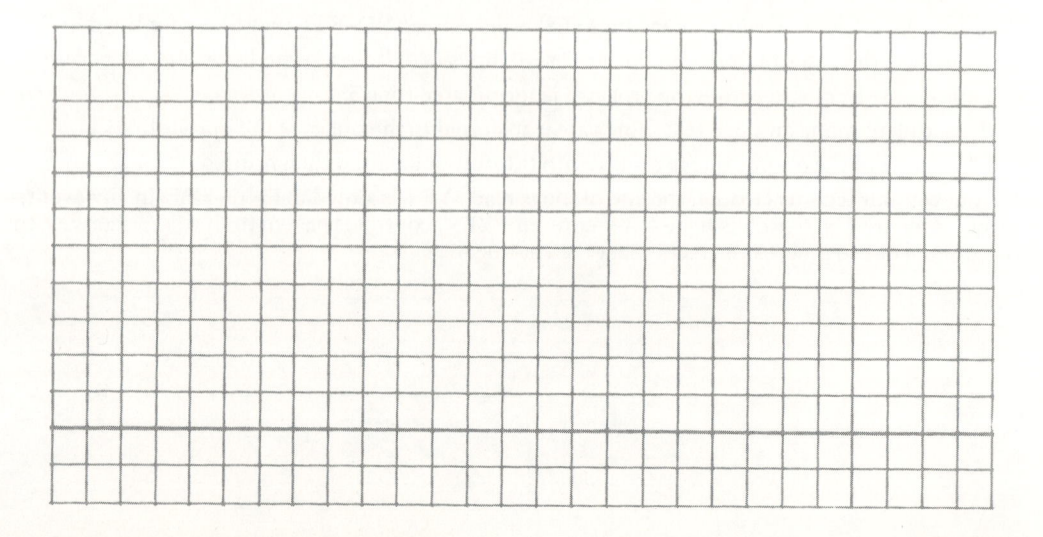

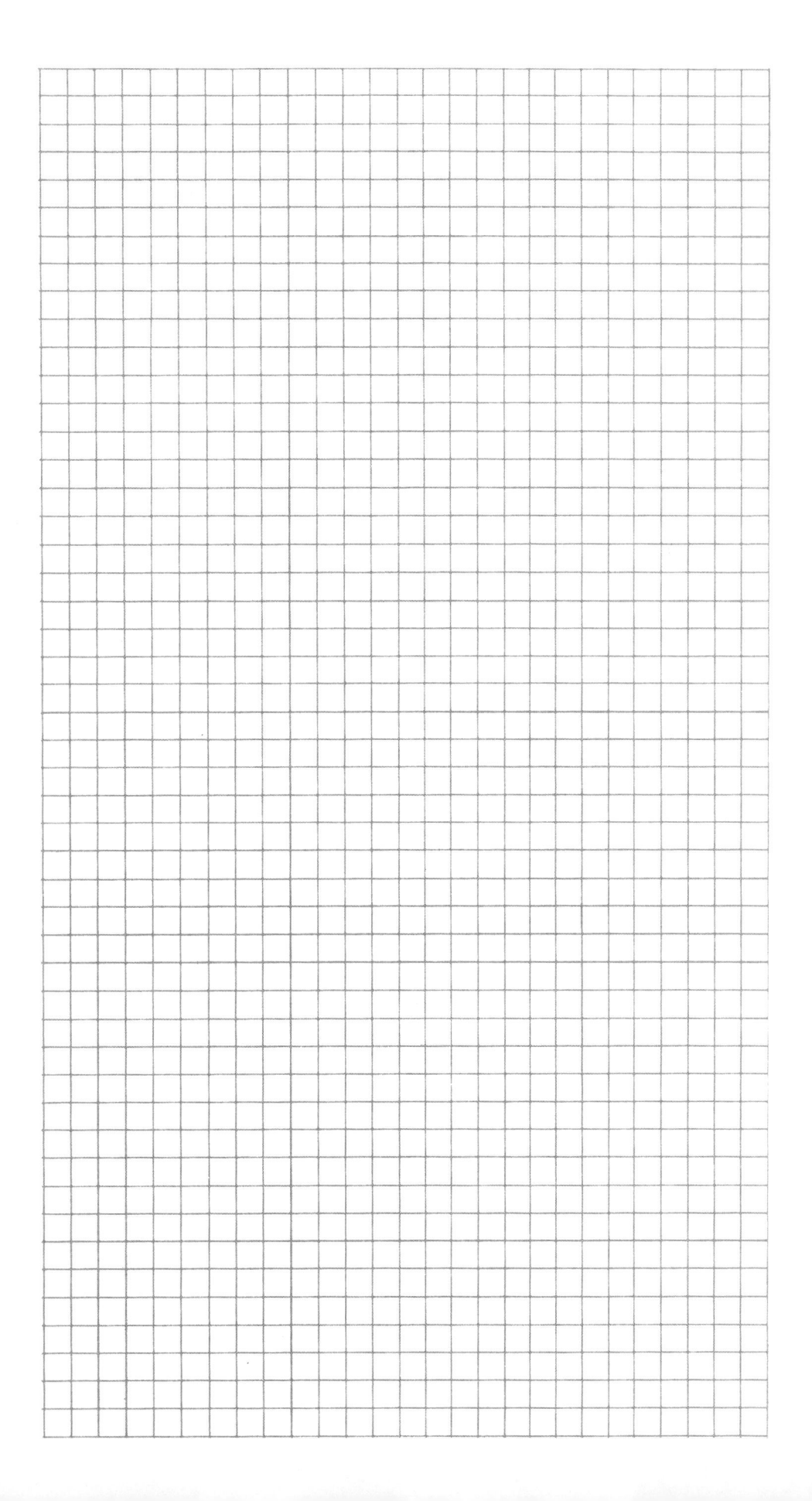

2-2-6 COMPILING YOUR PROGRAM

Now that the COBOL program is stored on disk under the name PROG1, it must be translated into machine language (object code) before it can be executed by the central processing unit. Special system commands such as COMPILE *program-name* (COMPILE PROG1) or other types of job control instructions are used to initiate this compilation process. Record the instructions for your system in section 2–2–5.

If you have introduced errors while typing your program (forgotten period or hyphen, incorrect spelling, et cetera), the compiler will not be able to translate the corresponding COBOL entries. The compiler will list errors by line numbers, and if errors are present, you must correct them by loading the text editor and going through the editing process described in section 2–2–2.

2-2-7 RUNNING YOUR PROGRAM

If no errors occurred during the compilation process, the program (actually the corresponding object code) is now ready to be executed. Special system instructions such as RUN *program-name* (RUN PROG1) or some other job control instructions are used to initiate this process. The program should then produce the desired results. If these results are incorrect (for example, if there is only one line of output, or if the various entries are not in their proper column positions) you must look carefully at your logic and correct those COBOL instructions that spawned the errors. The entire process of text editing, compiling, and running your COBOL program is illustrated in Figure 2–5.

2-3 COBOL CODE INTERPRETATION

2-3-1 GENERAL CONSIDERATIONS: AN OVERVIEW

The words in color in the COBOL program of Figure 2–3 identify those reserved words that have special meaning to COBOL. These words must be spelled exactly as shown. The other words are user-chosen names for files, records, and data item names.

Comment lines can be interspersed throughout the program. Comment lines must start with an asterisk in column 7. Comments are directed at the user or reader and are strictly for documentation purposes. These explanatory comments help the reader understand the program better. Comments are optional.

A COBOL program is always broken down into four parts called *divisions*, which must appear in the following order: the IDENTIFICATION, the ENVIRONMENT, the DATA, and the PROCEDURE divisions.

Recall that COBOL is a file-processing language. Files consist of records, while records consist of items (data items). The structure of the COBOL language requires that the user describe these files, records, and items very carefully. Describing a file means giving the file a user-chosen name and letting COBOL know what particular device will process that file, i.e., will it be a magnetic tape, a diskette, or a hard disk? This description is given in the ENVIRONMENT division.

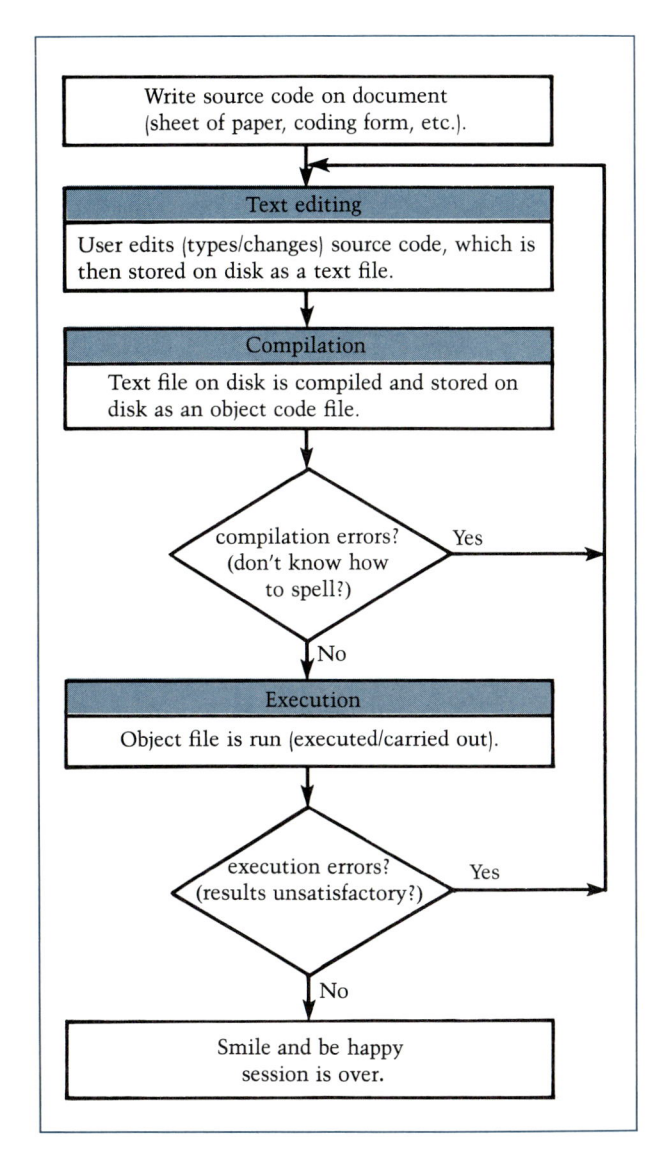

FIGURE 2–5
PROGRAM SUBMISSION PROCESS

Since a file generally consists of one or more records, it is also necessary to describe each different type of record in the file. (In our case all records have identical formats, i.e., a name and two test scores.) Describing a record means giving it a name and letting COBOL know the structure of the particular record, i.e., the number of items making up the record. Describing an item means giving it a name, stating its length (number of characters or positions it occupies), and letting COBOL know whether that item is to be processed arithmetically (added, multiplied, et cetera) or alphabetically, like characters in a word, for example. These descriptions are given in the DATA division.

Finally, the PROCEDURE division contains the logic of the program.

2-3-2 THE IDENTIFICATION DIVISION

The COBOL program always starts with the IDENTIFICATION division. In the PROGRAM-ID entry, the user specifies a name for the COBOL program. This name is generally different from the name given to the source program when it is typed and catalogued on disk using the text editor. The AUTHOR entry is optional.

2-3-3 THE ENVIRONMENT DIVISION

The ENVIRONMENT division follows the IDENTIFICATION division. It specifies the type of computer used and the particular devices that will be used for input and output.

In the INPUT-OUTPUT section of the ENVIRONMENT division, the user gives a name to both the input and the output files by means of the SELECT verb at lines 17 and 18. The user then specifies the particular devices that will process the input file and the output file by means of the ASSIGN verb. In our program, the results (REPORT-FILE) will be written on the printer (system device name PRINTER) and the input file (STUDENT-FILE) will be read from disk (system device name DISK). As mentioned earlier, both PRINTER and DISK references will need to be changed to run the program on your system.

On some systems the ASSIGN verb must designate not only the name of the system input device where the input file resides, but also the name of the data file itself, i.e., the name you gave it when you created the data file through the text editor. On some other systems the name of the data file must be specified in the file description entries at lines 23–25, and on still other systems the name of the data file is specified outside the COBOL program in job control statements. Figure 2–6 shows examples of such configurations. Note that the name given to the input file in the COBOL program (the file name used by the logic of the COBOL program) is different from the name under which the data file was catalogued on disk. Any reference to the input file in the COBOL program must use STUDENT-FILE and *not* ROSTER.

2-3-4 THE DATA DIVISION

In the third division of a COBOL program, the DATA division, the user provides a detailed description of all records and data items that are used in the logic of the program. By creating this dictionary of records and data items, the user instructs COBOL to allocate the appropriate memory storage for each record and each item, as specified in the description of the data.

File Section:

In the FILE section of the DATA division, the user specifies file characteristics for all input and output files. The key word FD (File Description) is used to identify the input or output file whose characteristics are to be described. The name of that particular file must have already been declared in the SELECT clause of the INPUT-OUTPUT section (lines 17 and 18). Labels are another important file characteristic that must be specified in the FD entry; in our case, labels are standard, i.e., on a disk, a label record is written at the beginning of the file. With punched cards, the statement LABEL RECORDS ARE OMITTED should be used instead.

In the FD entry, the user also names the storage area (memory locations) into which an input record will be moved as a result of a READ operation or from which a record is sent to the output device (printer) as a result of a WRITE operation. These user-named areas are referred to as the input and output areas, respectively, (STUDENT-RECORD and PRINT-LINE—lines 26 and 34 in Fig-

GETTING STARTED: THE FIRST COBOL PROGRAM   **45**

```
1.   SELECT STUDENT-FILE ASSIGN TO DISK.
     .
     .
     .
     FD  STUDENT-FILE
         LABEL RECORDS ARE STANDARD
         VALUE OF { FILE-ID / TITLE } IS 'ROSTER'.
         DATA RECORD IS STUDENT-RECORD.

2.   SELECT STUDENT-FILE ASSIGN TO INPUT 'ROSTER'.   } Tandy computers
3.   SELECT STUDENT-FILE ASSIGN UT-S-ROSTER         } IBM 4331
                                                      Needs JCL DD entry
```

Callouts:
- In the logic of the COBOL program, the user uses the name STUDENT-FILE to refer to the input file
- system device name of device containing the input file (IBM PC, Burroughs 7900)
- name under which the data file was catalogued on disk by text editor

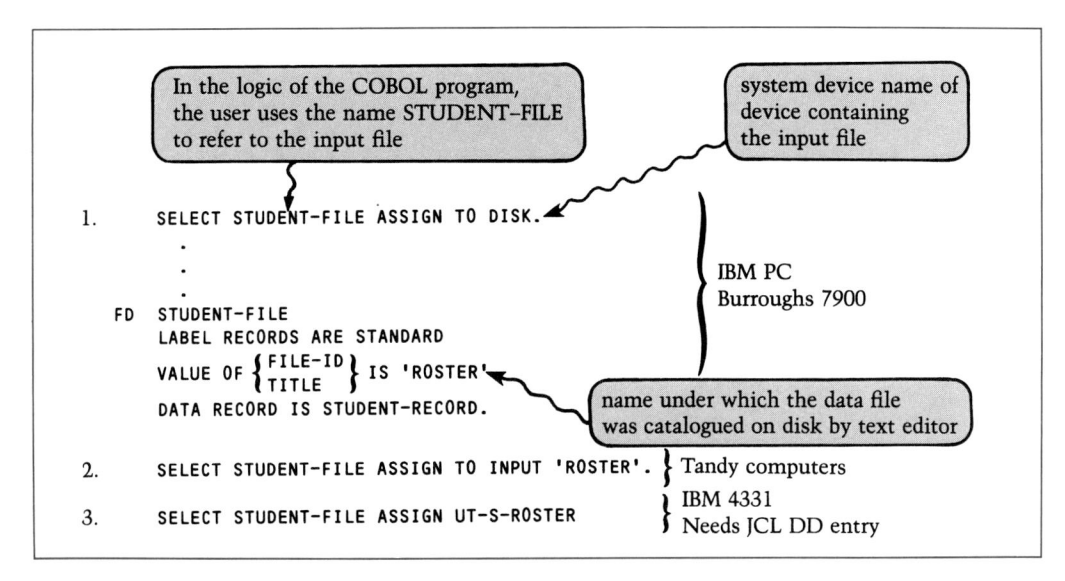

FIGURE 2–6
EXAMPLES OF SELECT/ASSIGN ENTRIES FOR VARIOUS COMPUTERS

ure 2–3); they are optionally identified as such through the DATA RECORD IS entry in the file description (lines 25 and 33).

In general, the input area has the same physical size as the input record, while the output area reflects the length of the output record (the length of a printed line, for example). If an 80-character-wide printer is designated as the output device, the output area would be 80 memory positions long; for an 18-character-long input record, the input area would be 18 memory positions long. Note that *only one* physical record (area) is assigned to each file.

From now on we will refer to the input area as the input record, realizing of course that this is technically somewhat incorrect, since the real input records are in fact physically stored on disk! In a COBOL program, a reference to the input record simply implies a reference to the data that has been moved (read) into the input area as a result of a READ operation. Likewise, we will refer henceforth to the output area as the output record; the image of the line to be printed is formed in the output area and then sent to the output device by means of the WRITE instruction (see Figure 2–7).

The structure, design, or format of the input record is then described following the input file FD entry (line 26). The description of an entire record always starts with the number 01 (called the level number), followed by the user-chosen name for that record.

The organization of the data on the input record reflects a structure or hierarchy among the various data items:

First comes the name of the   (level 1)   STUDENT–RECORD
entire record   ┌──────┼──────┐

and then the name of the   (level 2)   SR–NAME SR–TEST1 SR–TEST 2
various data items, three
in this particular case.

This hierarchical structure is expressed in terms of levels. STUDENT–RECORD is at the top (first level) while the three data items are at the second level. Level numbers are used in COBOL to indicate level relationships between data items

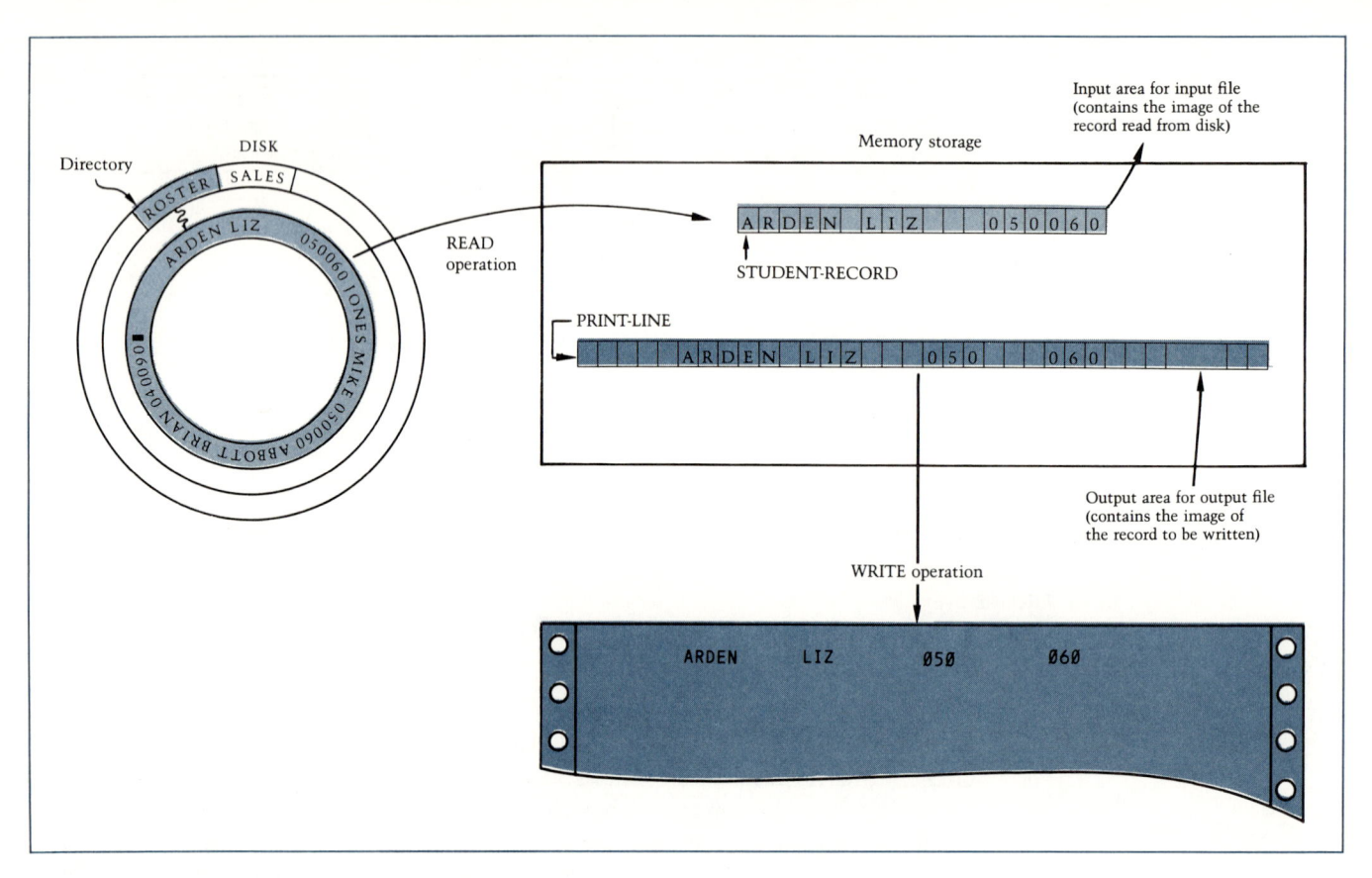

FIGURE 2-7
INPUT AREA AND OUTPUT AREA

(a genealogical tree of sorts). The level 01 is always used to designate a physical record, i.e., an entire record, while other level numbers such as 02, 03, ..., 49 are used to indicate *subordinate* levels. For example, the above input record STUDENT-RECORD could have been described with level numbers as follows:

```
01 STUDENT-RECORD.        01 STUDENT-RECORD.        01 STUDENT-RECORD.
   02 SR-NAME ...            05 SR-NAME...             31 SR-NAME...
   02 SR-TEST1...   or       05 SR-TEST1...   or       31 SR-TEST1...
   02 SR-TEST2...            05 SR-TEST2...            31 SR-TEST2...
```

Since SR-NAME, SR-TEST1, and SR-TEST2 are all at the same level, their corresponding level numbers are the same. Successively lower levels must be described by successively higher level numbers.

The prefix SR in SR-NAME, SR-TEST1, and SR-TEST2 is optional. Its presence alerts the reader to the fact that such data items are part of *S*TUDENT-*R*ECORD, i.e., the subordinate items of that record have the SR prefix. Such a convention for naming records contributes to the consistency of programs and makes them easier to debug and modify, as we will see later on.

In addition to describing the levels of the various data items within a particular record, it is also necessary to identify the length (number of characters/positions) of each data item and the nature or type of each data item, i.e., whether it is to be processed numerically (added, multiplied, etc.) or processed like letters of the alphabet (alphanumeric information). These two characteristics, field length and data type, are expressed in COBOL through the keyword PICTURE, which can be abbreviated to PIC. For example:

05 SR-NAME PIC XXXXXXXXXXXX. SR–NAME identifies a string of 12 characters (positions), and these characters serve as place holder positions for alphanumeric data. Each X symbol denotes an alphanumeric character.

05 SR-TEST1 PICTURE 999. SR–TEST1 is the name given to 3 memory positions which at one time or another will be filled with 3 digits. This entire 3-digit number can then be processed arithmetically by the arithmetic unit of the computer.

The complete record entry description for the input record in Figure 2–3 can be typed as:

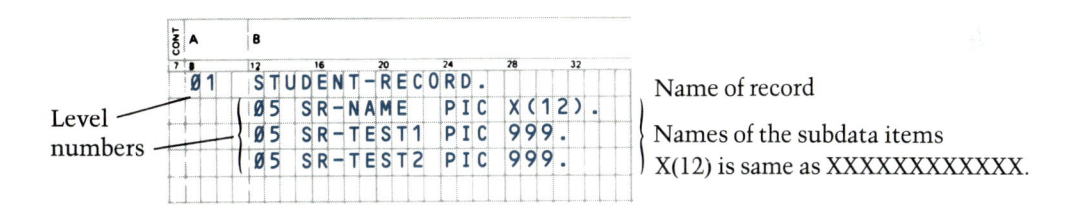

```
01  STUDENT-RECORD.
    05  SR-NAME   PIC  X(12).
    05  SR-TEST1  PIC  999.
    05  SR-TEST2  PIC  999.
```

Level numbers

Name of record
Names of the subdata items
X(12) is same as XXXXXXXXXXXX.

This entry describes the physical characteristics of the input record. When the computer is told to READ the input record, the data on the record will thus find its way into memory as:

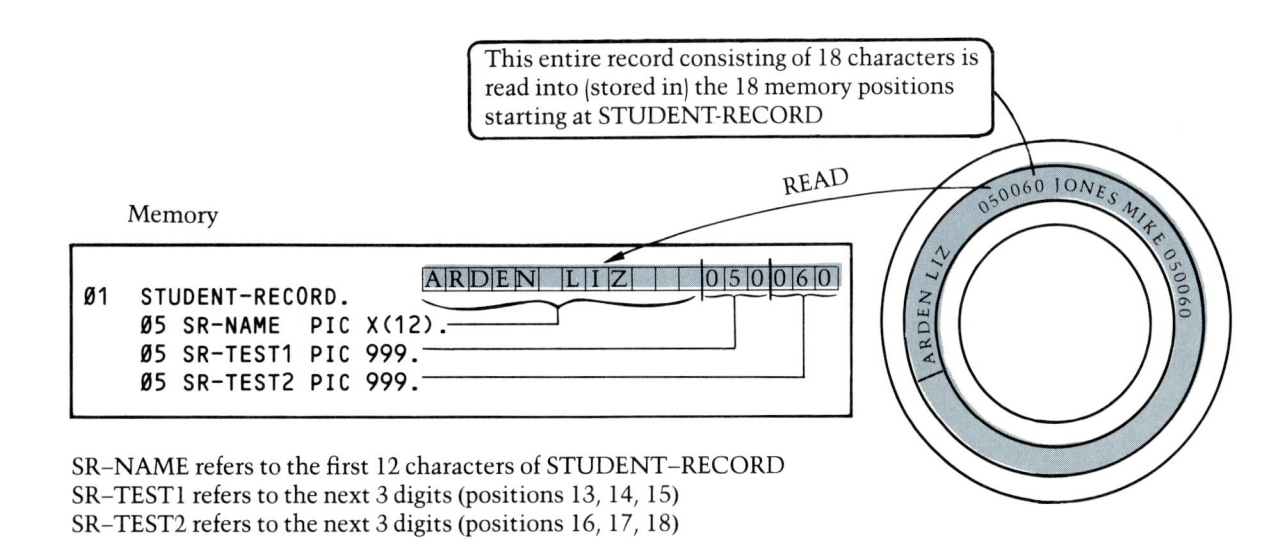

This entire record consisting of 18 characters is read into (stored in) the 18 memory positions starting at STUDENT-RECORD

Memory

```
01  STUDENT-RECORD.         ARDEN LIZ   050060
    05  SR-NAME   PIC X(12).
    05  SR-TEST1  PIC 999.
    05  SR-TEST2  PIC 999.
```

SR–NAME refers to the first 12 characters of STUDENT-RECORD
SR–TEST1 refers to the next 3 digits (positions 13, 14, 15)
SR–TEST2 refers to the next 3 digits (positions 16, 17, 18)

Just as in the case of the input record, the description of the output record (line 34) follows the FD entry for the output file. The output record in Figure 2–3 is named PRINT–LINE; 80 memory positions (the size of an output line for an 80-character-wide printer) are reserved for it.

Working Storage

It is important to realize that whenever a WRITE instruction is specified in the logic of the program, COBOL writes out whatever happens to be in the output record at that time. Hence if something meaningful is to be written, the programmer must first assemble all the elements that make up a particular line (i.e., all the different result fields on a single line) and position these elements in the desired slots for that line. This image of the final line is generally prepared not in the output record but in another record that is located in an area of memory called WORKING–STORAGE (an area that can have numerous blueprint records under preparation). In Figure 2–3 this record is DETAIL–LINE (line 38). The programmer then moves the preassembled line from WORKING–STORAGE to the output record so that when the WRITE instruction is carried out, the desired output line is printed.

Before any record or any data item can be processed by a COBOL program, it must first be declared either in the FILE section (for input/output records only) or in the WORKING–STORAGE section of the DATA division. Declaring a record or a data item in WORKING–STORAGE is done in the same manner as declaring an input or output record in the FILE section. A user-chosen name is given to the record, the structure of the record is conveyed by means of level numbers, and appropriate pictures are specified for the various data items. In the process, COBOL reserves the storage space required for each of these records. In Figure 2–3 DETAIL–LINE is the blueprint record for the typical output line. It is the replica of the line that will eventually be printed. Before it can be printed, however, certain areas of the line have to be filled in with the appropriate information (name and test scores). The process of moving information into DETAIL–LINE takes place in the logic of the program (PROCEDURE DIVISION). Declaring entries in the WORKING–STORAGE section simply reserves memory locations.

The FILLER fields are used for left and right margins on the output line and as blank areas between the various data fields. The key words VALUE SPACES initialize the corresponding PICTURE fields to blank spaces. The DETAIL–LINE entries (lines 38 through 45) specify the following memory arrangement:

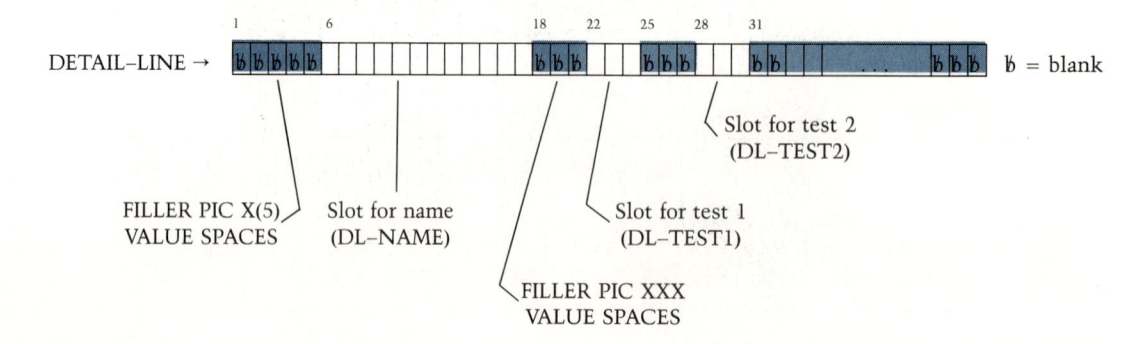

DETAIL-LINE diagram showing positions 1, 6, 18, 22, 25, 28, 31 with:
- FILLER PIC X(5) VALUE SPACES
- Slot for name (DL-NAME)
- FILLER PIC XXX VALUE SPACES
- Slot for test 1 (DL-TEST1)
- Slot for test 2 (DL-TEST2)
- ♭ = blank

Note that the name (DL–NAME) and test score fields (DL–TEST1, DL–TEST2) at the time of their declaration do *not* contain blank spaces. If the contents of DETAIL–LINE were printed at that time, the name and test score fields would be unintelligible since whatever characters were in those fields would be printed.

The entry END–FILE is a three-character-long record that is initialized to the characters NO . This data item is used in the logic of the program to let the program know when to stop processing input records (i.e., when to stop reading the input file). As long as there are still records to be read, the value of

END–FILE remains unchanged (its value remains "NO"); when the end-of-file record is read, the value "YES" is placed in END–FILE. The program, meanwhile, constantly monitors the value of END–FILE. When END–FILE has value "YES", no further attempt should be made to read the input file.

2-2-5 THE PROCEDURE DIVISION

Conceptual Overview:

The last division in a COBOL program is the PROCEDURE division. It is the part of the program where, after all of our files, records and data items have been described, we specify the way in which this data is to be processed (logic).

Our programming problem at first appears very simple in terms of what actions are to be taken. We are to instruct the computer to read three data fields from a record—a student name and two test scores—and then have the computer write out these three items in such a way that they are nicely spread out (edited) on the output form (printed page). That same task is to be repeated as many times as there are input records, of course. This leads to the following approach:

Plan of attack

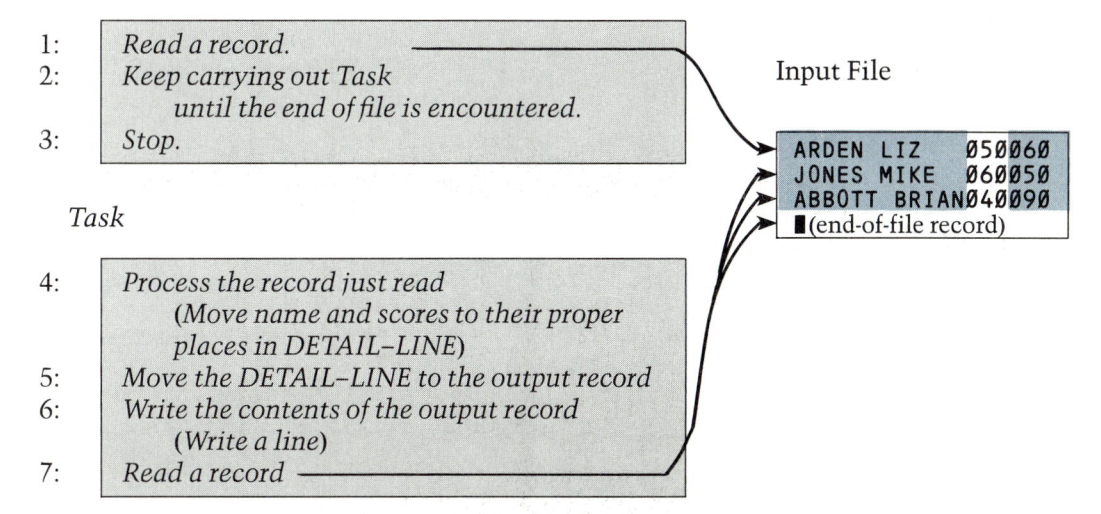

1: Read a record.
2: Keep carrying out Task
     until the end of file is encountered.
3: Stop.

Input File

```
ARDEN LIZ    050060
JONES MIKE   060050
ABBOTT BRIAN040090
■(end-of-file record)
```

Task

4: Process the record just read
     (Move name and scores to their proper
     places in DETAIL–LINE)
5: Move the DETAIL–LINE to the output record
6: Write the contents of the output record
     (Write a line)
7: Read a record

The problem has now been broken down into two parts: lines 1–3 and lines 4–7. The first time line 4 is carried out, we will be processing the record read at line 1 (ARDEN LIZ . . .). The data in that record (name and test scores) is then moved into the appropriate slots in DETAIL–LINE, which is then moved into the output record and written. The next record is then read at line 7 (JONES MIKE . . .). Since there are no more instructions in the Task module, control is automatically returned to line 2. Since the record read was not the end-of-file record, the Task module is processed again. The process of carrying out Task over and over again, goes on until the record read at line 7 is the end-of-file record. At that point control returns to line 2, and since the condition stated at that line is no longer true, the program stops.

This approach is conceptually valid and lends itself quite well to a structured COBOL design except for line 2, for which there is no COBOL equivalent. We therefore reformulate line 2 as:

2: Keep carrying out TASK
     until such time as END–FILE = "YES".

where END–FILE is a data item that initially has the value "NO". We also rewrite line 7 in more COBOL-like fashion as:

> 7: Read a record
>   and if it is the end of file, move the value "YES" to END–FILE.

Thus every time a record is read, either the value YES is stored in END–FILE (when the end-of-file record is read) or END–FILE remains unchanged (when the record read is not the end of file).

With these two modifications the logic is rewritten as follows (assume END–FILE = "NO" initially):

> 1: Coordinating Module
> 2:   Read a record
>   and if it is the end of file, move the value "YES" to END–FILE.
> 3:   Keep carrying out Task
>   until END–FILE = "YES".
> 4:   Stop.
> 5: Task
> 6:   Process record just read.
> 7:   Move detail-line to output record.
> 8:   Write the output record.
> 9:   Read a record
>   and if it is the end of file, move the value "YES" to END–FILE.

Let us "walk through" the code and carry out each step one at a time, starting with line 2. The lines executed are as follows:

line 2: Record read is: `ARDEN LIZ 050060` and END–FILE = `NO`
line 3: Since END–FILE is not "YES", Task is carried out.
line 6: Move name and scores in DETAIL-LINE   `ARDEN LIZ 050 060 ...`
line 7: Move DETAIL-LINE to output record STUDENT-RECORD   `ARDEN LIZ 050 060 ...`
line 8: Line is printed.
line 9: Record read is: `JONES MIKE 060050` and END–FILE = `NO`

line 3: Since END–FILE is not 'YES', Task is carried out.
line 6: Move name and scores in DETAIL-LINE   `JONES MIKE 060 050 ...`
line 7: Move DETAIL-LINE to output record STUDENT-RECORD   `JONES MIKE 060 050 ...`
line 8: Line is printed.
line 9: Record read is: `ABBOTT BRIAN040090` and END–FILE = `NO`

line 3: Since END–FILE is not 'YES', Task is carried out.
line 6: Move name and scores in DETAIL-LINE   `ABBOTT BRIAN 040 090 ...`
line 7: Move DETAIL-LINE to output record STUDENT-RECORD   `ABBOTT BRIAN 040 090 ...`
line 8: Line is printed.
line 9: Record read is the end of file ■   and END–FILE = `YES`

line 3: Since END–FILE = 'YES', next instruction (line 4) is carried out.
line 4: Stop.

Note that the instruction at line 3 first checks the value of END–FILE before it decides whether or not to carry out Task. If END–FILE is equal to "YES", the Task module is *not* carried out and control passes to line 4; otherwise, Task is carried out.

COBOL Code

Lines 47–70 of Figure 2–3 show the COBOL coded version of the preceding pseudo code. The program is broken down into two paragraphs that begin at lines 48 and 63. Each paragraph consists of sentences that are indented to column 12.

GETTING STARTED: THE FIRST COBOL PROGRAM

The OPEN sentence tells the system to make the input file, STUDENT-FILE, available for processing (disk is mounted and readied). Likewise the system output device is readied for action to print REPORT-FILE.

Lines 50 and 51 represent one sentence that has been spread over two lines for improved readability. The key word READ must *always* specify the name of the input file; the AT END clause (required) tells the system what action to take in the event the end-of-file record is read (in this case MOVE 'YES' TO END-FILE). Even though the name of the file is specified for the READ operation, each READ operation will only read one input record—the entire input file is not read at one time.

The PERFORM sentence at lines 52 and 53 causes paragraph 200-PROCESS-RECORD to be carried out over and over again UNTIL END-FILE changes from 'NO' to 'YES'. This will happen when the end of file is read at line 69.

All files that have been opened *must* be CLOSEd before the program is terminated at line 55.

Paragraph 200-PROCESS-RECORD moves the name and test scores from the input record to their respective slots in DETAIL-LINE. The 80 characters of DETAIL-LINE are then moved to the output record, which is then written out by line 68. Note that to write the output record, the word WRITE is used, followed by the name of the *output record, not* the name of the output file, i.e., WRITE PRINT-LINE (not WRITE STUDENT-FILE).

Figure 2-8 illustrates the sequence of activities required by COBOL to read, process, and print records from an input file. Analyze this figure very carefully.

2-4 EXERCISES

2-4-1 TEST YOURSELF

1. Answer True or False.

   a. The compiler translates the object code into a machine-recognizable code.
   b. Text editing commands are part of the COBOL language.
   c. Punctuation errors in COBOL sentences are flagged at RUN time.
   d. A COBOL program consists of the IDENTIFICATION, the ENVIRONMENT, the CONFIGURATION, and the PROCEDURE divisions.
   e. The SELECT verb specifies the name of the input or output record.
   f. Every record description entry must have a level number.
   g. The WORKING-STORAGE section describes all COBOL records.
   h. Record names are always user-chosen.
   i. PIC 999 identifies alphanumeric data.
   j. PIC X(5) and PIC 9(5) reserve the same number of memory positions.
   k. READ *name-of-input-record* is the correct way to read a record.
   l. WRITE *name-of-output-record* is the correct way to write a record.
   m. The STOP instruction causes the COBOL program to stop execution of instructions.
   n. Moving one item of record-1 to a slot in record-2 implies that the item moved is no longer part of record-1.
   o. The sentence CLOSE INPUT *name-of-input file* is valid.
   p. An error message will be written by the text editor as a result of typing IDENTICATION DIVISION.

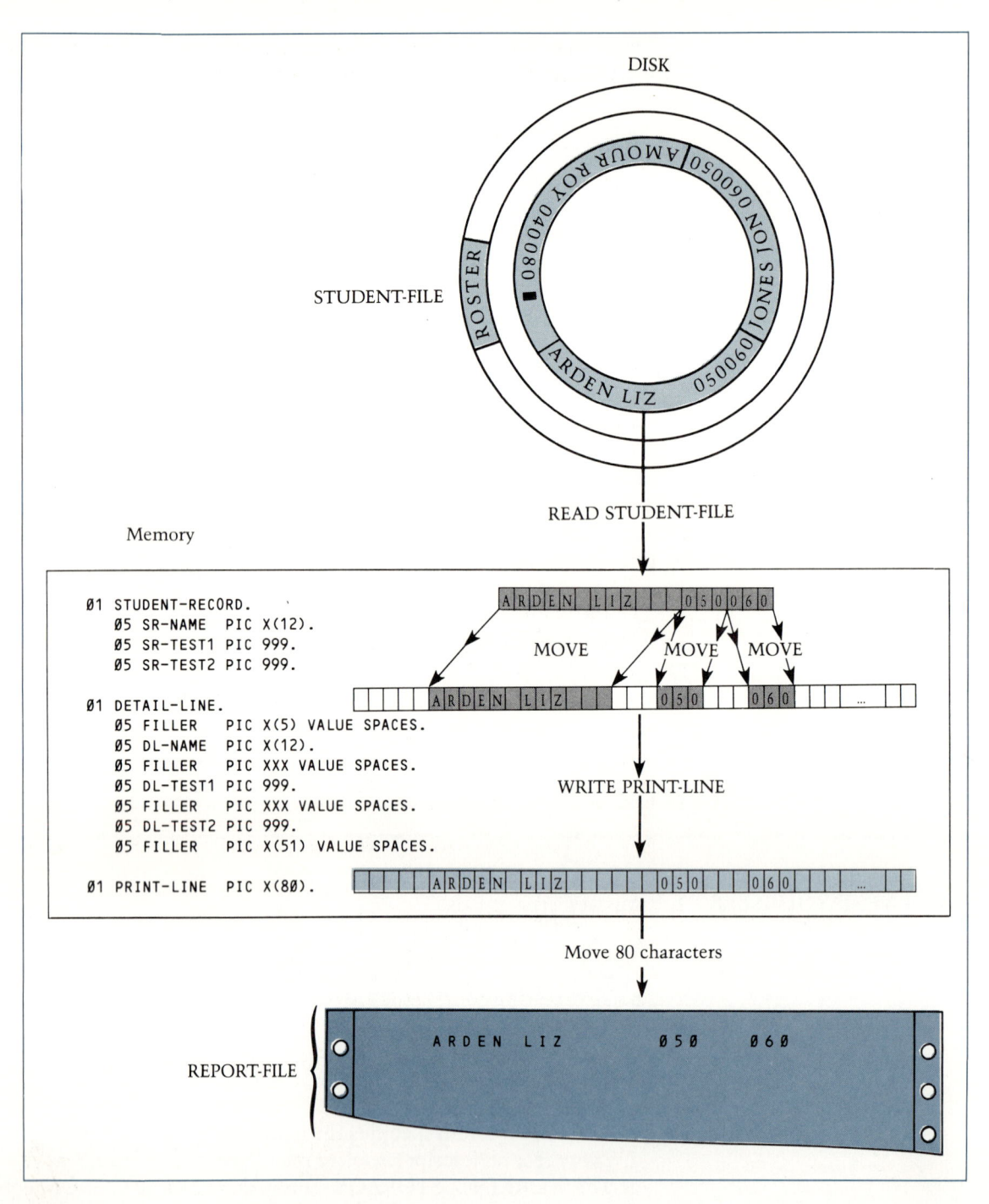

FIGURE 2-8
INPUT, PROCESSING, AND OUTPUT OF RECORDS

2. The following questions deal with the COBOL program in Figure 2-3.
   a. Assume STUDENT-FILE contains no student records. What action will be taken by the program? Specify the lines that will be executed.
   b. Specify what happens if lines 69 and 70 are left out.
   c. Specify what happens if lines 50 and 51 are left out.
   d. Specify what happens if lines 64–68 are left out.
   e. Specify what happens if line 53 is left out.
   f. Specify what happens if lines 56–62 are left out.

3. In the program of Figure 2–3 would you be more likely to get a compilation error or execution error if for some reason you:

   a. left out line 13?
   b. forgot to include line 33?
   c. typed line 40 as DL–NAME PIC X(30) instead of PIC X(12)?

4. Would the program in Figure 2–9 accomplish the same objectives as the program in Figure 2–3? [Look at difference in WORKING–STORAGE].

```
 1:     IDENTIFICATION DIVISION.
 2:     PROGRAM-ID. STUDENT-LISTING.
 3:     AUTHOR. JONES.

 4.     ENVIRONMENT DIVISION.
 5:     CONFIGURATION SECTION.
 6:     SOURCE-COMPUTER. IBM.
 7:     OBJECT-COMPUTER. IBM.
 8:     INPUT-OUTPUT SECTION.
 9:     FILE-CONTROL.
10:         SELECT REPORT-FILE ASSIGN TO PRINTER.
11:         SELECT STUDENT-FILE ASSIGN TO DISK.

12:     DATA DIVISION.
13:     FILE SECTION.
14:     FD  STUDENT-FILE
15:         LABEL RECORDS ARE STANDARD
16:         DATA RECORD IS STUDENT-RECORD.
17:     01  STUDENT-RECORD.
18:         05 SR-NAME  PIC X(12).
19:         05 SR-TEST1 PIC 999.
20:         05 SR-TEST2 PIC 999.
21:     FD  REPORT-FILE
22:         LABEL RECORDS ARE OMITTED
23:         DATA RECORD IS PRINT-LINE.
24:     01  PRINT-LINE.
25:         05 FILLER   PIC X(5).
26:         05 PL-NAME  PIC X(12).
27:         05 FILLER   PIC XXX.
28:         05 PL-TEST1 PIC 999.
29:         05 FILLER   PIC XXX.
30:         05 PL-TEST2 PIC 999.
31:         05 FILLER   PIC X(51).
32:     WORKING-STORAGE SECTION.
33:     01  END-FILE    PIC XXX.

34:     PROCEDURE DIVISION.
35:     100-COORDINATING-MODULE.
36:         OPEN INPUT STUDENT-FILE, OUTPUT REPORT-FILE.
37:         READ STUDENT-FILE
38:             AT END MOVE 'YES' TO END-FILE.
39:         PERFORM 200-PROCESS-RECORDS
40:             UNTIL END-FILE = 'YES'.
41:         CLOSE STUDENT-FILE, REPORT-FILE.
42:         STOP RUN.
43:     200-PROCESS-RECORDS.
44:         MOVE SPACES  TO PRINT-LINE.   (clear out PRINT-LINE).
45:         MOVE SR-NAME  TO PL-NAME.
46:         MOVE SR-TEST1 TO PL-TEST1.
47:         MOVE SR-TEST2 TO PL-TEST2.
48:         WRITE PRINT-LINE.
49:         READ STUDENT-FILE
50:             AT END MOVE 'YES' TO END-FILE.
```

FIGURE 2–9

5. Identify possible errors in the following COBOL program; make the necessary corrections.

```
01  IDENTIFICATION DIVISION.
02  AUTHOR.MJONES.
03  ENVIRONMENT DIVISION
04  INPUT-OUTPUT SECTION.
05  FILE CONTROL.
06  SELECT CARD ASSIGN TO PRINTER.
07  SELECT JOE ASSIGN TO DISK.
08  DATA DIVISION.
09  FD CARD.
10      LABEL RECORDS ARE OMITTED
11      DATA RECORD IS CARD-RECORD.
12  01 CARD-RECORD PIC X(132).
13  FD JOE
14      DATA RECORD IS JOE-CARD
15      LABEL RECORDS ARE OMITTED.
16  01 JOE-CARD PIC X(80)
17
18  PROCEDURE DIVISION.
19      OPEN INPUT CARD.
20      OPEN OUTPUT JOE-CARD.
21      PERFORM WRITE 4 TIMES.
22      STOP RUN.
23  WRITE.
24      READ JOE-CARD.
25      MOVE JOE-CARD TO CARD-RECORD.
26      WRITE CARD-RECORD.
27      END.
```

6. Add two more input records to the input file of Figure 2–3 (ROSTER) and run the COBOL program. Do you need to recompile the COBOL program?

7. Write a program to print your initials in expanded notation as shown here.

```
MMM        MMM   BBBBBBBBBB
MMMM      MMMM   BBB       B
MMMMM    MMMMM   BBBBBBBBBB
MMM MM MM MMM    BBB       B
MMM  MMM  MMM    BBBBBBBBBB
```

Produce this report by: (a) reading input records, each record containing the equivalent of an output line.
(b) modifying the original solution to create each line in the DATA division (no records should be read).

8. Create an input file consisting of the following records:

Customer (1–12)	Commodity (14–18)	Quantity (19–22)	City (23–32)
NEW MEXICO CO.	11202	0040	TUCSON
TRI X STAR	12201	0100	PHOENIX
SOUTHERN GAS	10231	8000	PENSACOLA

and write the program to produce the following report:

GETTING STARTED: THE FIRST COBOL PROGRAM   55

```
TUCSON      0040   11202   NEW MEXICO CO.
PHOENIX     0100   12201   TRI X STAR
PENSACOLA   8000   10231   SOUTHERN GAS
```

2-4-2 ANSWERS

1. a. F. The compiler translates source code into object code.
   b. F. They are part of a totally different language.
   c. F. Punctuation errors are flagged at compilation time.
   d. F. There is a DATA division but no CONFIGURATION division.
   e. F. It specifies the name of the input/output file.
   f. T.
   g. F. The FILE section describes input/output records.
   h. T.
   i. F. It identifies numeric data.
   j. T.
   k. F. Read *name-of-input-file* reads a record from the input file.
   l. T.
   m. F. STOP RUN.
   n. F. The data is simply copied.
   o. F. CLOSE *name-of-input-file* is valid.
   p. F. The compiler writes the error message.

2. a. Lines 49, 50, 51, 52, 53, 54, and 55 are executed in sequence.
   b. Since no additional records will be read, END–FILE will never contain 'YES', paragraph 200-PROCESS-RECORD will be carried out over and over again, causing the first line to be printed repeatedly.
   c. When instructions 64–66 are carried out for the first time, the first line printed will contain unpredictable characters, since SR–NAME, SR–TEST1, and SR–TEST2 will not contain the data of the first record.
   d. The input file is read but nothing is printed.
   e. Only the first record will be printed, since paragraph 200-PROCESS-RECORD will be carried out only once.
   f. Comments do not affect execution of programs. The output remains the same.

3. a. Compilation error.
   b. No error—statement is optional.
   c. No error—output would just look different.

4. Yes.

5. Missing PROGRAM–ID paragraph.
   Line 02 A U T H O R . ␣ M J O N E S .   (Blank space after the first period)
   Line 03 Missing period.
       COBOL requires the CONFIGURATION and SOURCE/OBJECT–COMPUTER entries.
   Line 05 FILE–CONTROL.
   Line 09 No period after CARD.
   Line 16 Missing period after X(80).
   Line 17 Some compilers may not accept a blank line (place a * in position 7).

Line 18   Need a paragraph name after PROCEDURE DIVISION, i.e., MAIN-LOGIC.
Line 19–20   OPEN OUTPUT CARD, INPUT JOE.
Line 21   WRITE is a reserved word; use WRITE-OUTPUT-LINE.
Line 22   Forgot to close files before ending execution.
Line 24   READ JOE AT END . . . The AT END clause is required.
Line 27   No such statement as END; use STOP RUN.

CHAPTER 3

STRUCTURE AND SYNTAX

3–1 ELEMENTS OF THE COBOL LANGUAGE

3–2 THE IDENTIFICATION DIVISION

3–3 THE ENVIRONMENT DIVISION

3–4 THE DATA DIVISION

3–5 THE PROCEDURE DIVISION

3–6 WRITING PROGRAMS

3–7 EXERCISES

INTRODUCTION This chapter discusses the elements and the structure of the COBOL language, including the COBOL characters, COBOL names for paragraphs and data items, and rules for COBOL constants. Details on the use of the COBOL coding form are also given. General structural forms for many types of COBOL statements and clauses are presented, and the requirements of the four COBOL program divisions are given in greater detail. Elementary and group data items are defined in relation to the data record hierarchy; rules for data record descriptions are given, along with detailed examples. Independent data items are also discussed. Examples show how to generate headings and data lines for reports. The WRITE FROM and READ INTO statements are introduced, and COBOL arithmetic operations are introduced. Suggestions for organizing programs and designing report layouts are given, and syntax and logical errors are discussed.

3-1 ELEMENTS OF THE COBOL LANGUAGE

3-1-1 STRUCTURE OF THE COBOL LANGUAGE

In the study of any language, whether human or computer, it is convenient, if not necessary, to define precisely all the components of the written language, starting with a list of the symbols or characters (alphabet) that make up words. Words are then grouped into classes such as verbs and nouns and can be combined to form phrases, clauses, or sentences.

The syntax of a language deals with the physical structure of sentences or clauses, i.e., the way in which words are ordered to form a correct sentence. The grammar, in turn, deals with such aspects of the language as spelling, punctuation, and syntactical relationships. In these senses, COBOL is very much a language. It is a structured language that, like a human language, is composed of a hierarchy of elements (see Figure 3-1).

Divisions, Sections, Paragraphs.

Taking a top-down approach, the first of COBOL's structural elements are the four divisions. With the exception of the IDENTIFICATION DIVISION, divisions are divided into sections. The next hierarchical elements are paragraphs. In the PROCEDURE DIVISION, paragraphs are composed of sentences, in the IDENTIFICATION, ENVIRONMENT, and DATA divisions, paragraphs are composed of entries. (There are no paragraphs in the DATA DIVISION, only entries.)

```
                          DIVISION
                             |
                          SECTION
                             |
                          PARAGRAPH
(PROCEDURE DIVISION)         |          (Other DIVISIONS)
        ┌────────────────────┴────────────────────┐
     Sentences                                 Entries
    ┌────┴────┐                           ┌───────┼───────┐
Statement 1 ... Statement n            Clause 1  Clause 2  ... Clause n
```

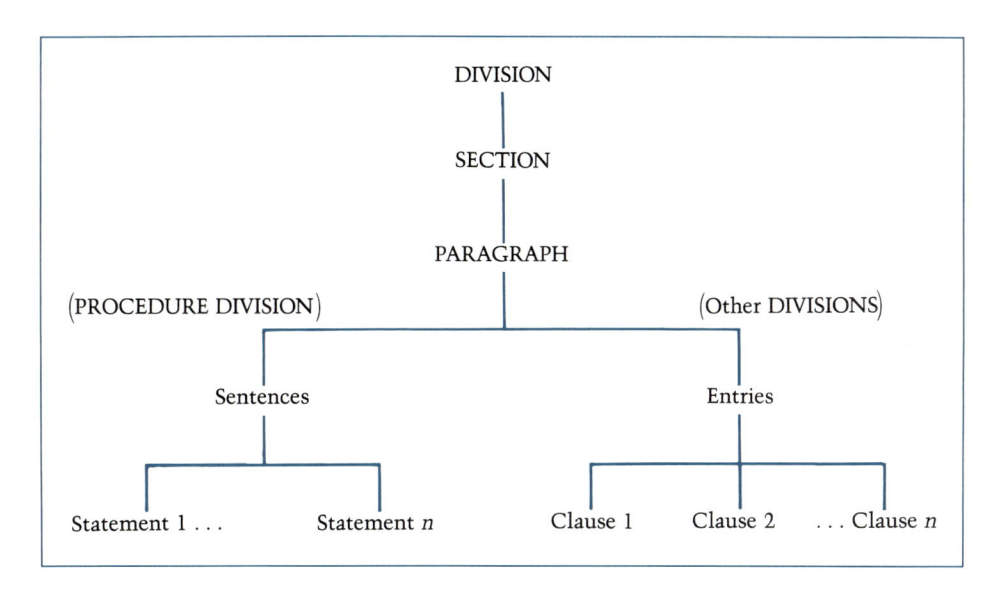

FIGURE 3-1
HIERARCHY OF COBOL ELEMENTS

Entries are composed of one or more clauses, such as the SELECT, ASSIGN clauses in the ENVIRONMENT DIVISION and the PICTURE and VALUE clauses in the record description entries.

In the PROCEDURE DIVISION, paragraphs are broken down into sentences.

Paragraph Names.

The paragraph (task) is the basic unit of organization in the PROCEDURE DIVISION; it is a module containing a set of related instructions. Paragraph names are user-chosen names that must conform to the following rules:

1. Composition: 1 to 30 characters
   - letters of the alphabet   A–Z
   - numerical digits   0–9
   - the hyphen   –

2. Restrictions
   - May not be a reserved word (see appendix A).
   - No imbedded blanks within the name, since a blank denotes the end of a word.
   - First or last character of name may not be a hyphen.

VALID PARAGRAPH NAMES		INVALID	REASON	CORRECTIONS
A	TAX-10	33.24	No special characters	3324
TAX	100-200			
10-TAX	TAX-10-3	LINES	Reserved word	LINES-NEEDED
98	SEARCH-FILE		(check list regularly)	

COBOL programs should be self-documenting and be composed of sentences that are self-explanatory, so that a reader unfamiliar with the COBOL language should be able to read a COBOL program and get a general idea of what the program does. For the same reason, paragraph names must be descriptive. One method to ensure such a trait is to choose names with a verb-modifier-object structure. Consider, for example, the following readable and self-documenting paragraph names:

```
100-PRINT-INVALID-RECORDS.
500-VALIDATE-TAX-REFUNDS.
300-READ-ALL-TRANSACTIONS.
```

Sentences.

Sentences, in turn, are broken down into one or more statements. Broadly speaking, a statement expresses an action to be taken during execution of the program. This action is described by such COBOL reserved words as MOVE, ADD, IF, and ELSE. A combination of these actions, terminated by a period, makes up a sentence. Such actions indicate the way in which data items are to be processed.

Data Item Names.

Recall that data items are symbolic names given to memory storage areas in which data is stored. The rules for forming data item names are as follows:

1. Composition: 1 to 30 characters
   - letters of the alphabet   A–Z
   - numerical digits   0–9
   - the hyphen   –

2. Restrictions
   - May not be a reserved word.
   - No imbedded blanks within the name, since a blank denotes the end of a word.
   - First or last character of name may not be a hyphen.
   - Name must contain at least one alphabetic character.

Like paragraph names, data item names should be meaningful. Obscure or secretive names, such as X or AMT, are to be avoided. The little extra effort required to think of and to type a descriptive name is well worth it in terms of readability (clarity) and documentation.

VALID NAME	INVALID	REASON	CORRECTIONS
A	HOURS.	Period not allowed	HOURS-WORKED
PAY-123	OVER 30	Blank space not allowed	OVER-30
123--PAY	TAX-	No trailing hyphen	TAX-DUE
HOURS-WORKED	$AMOUNT	Invalid character $	AMOUNT-PAID
AMOUNT-EARNED	TABLE	Reserved word	TAX-TABLE
COUNT-OF-MEN-OVER-30-N-MARRIED	100	All numeric	100-PROCESS

Figure 3–2 shows examples of how the various hierarchical COBOL elements are combined in the four divisions of a program.

STRUCTURE AND SYNTAX 61

Language Structure	COBOL Program Example	Examples of the Language

Division
    Paragraph
    Paragraph
	IDENTIFICATION DIVISION.
	PROGRAM-ID. PAYROLL.
	AUTHOR. BOILLOT.
	.
	.
	.
		} Entries
		  (external name,
		  comments)

Division
    Section
 	
    Paragraph
	ENVIRONMENT DIVISION.
	CONFIGURATION SECTION.
	.
	.
	.
	FILE-CONTROL.
	    SELECT SALES-FILE
	    ASSIGN TO READER.
		
		Clause } Entry
		Clause } (file)

Division
    Section
 	
    Section
	DATA DIVISION.
	FILE SECTION.
	FD INPUT-FILE
	    LABEL REORD IS OMITTED
	    DATA RECORD IS IN-SALES.
	.
	.
	.
	WORKING-STORAGE SECTION.
	01 DETAIL-LINE.
	    05 FILLER PIC X(12)
	            VALUE SPACES.
	    05 NAME PIC X(20).
		
		Clause } Entry
		Clause } (file description)
		
		Clause
		Clause } Entry
		Clause } (record description)

Division
    Paragraph
 	
    Paragraph
	PROCEDURE DIVISION.
	MAIN-LOGIC.
	    PERFORM COMPUTATION.
	    MOVE NET TO NET-OUT.
	    IF HOURS > 40
	        PERFORM OVER-TIME
	    ELSE
	        PERFORM REG-TIME.
	COMPUTATION.
	.
	.
		
		Statement (sentence)
		
		statement
		statement } Sentence
		statement
		statement

FIGURE 3–2
STRUCTURE OF COBOL PROGRAM

NOTATION	MEANING	EXAMPLE
Capitalized words underlined	COBOL keyword required if feature is used.	<u>VALUE</u>
Capitalized words not underlined	Noise word—optional. Improves readability.	IS
Lowercase words	Programmer-supplied entries, e.g., data names.	<u>PROGRAM-ID</u>. Program-name.
Square brackets [ ]	Indicates elements that are optional.	<u>WRITE</u> record-name [<u>FROM</u> data-name]
Braces { }	One of the enclosed must be chosen.	<u>LABEL</u> { RECORD IS / RECORDS ARE }
Ellipsis . . .	Any number of the preceding type may be repeated.	<u>ADD</u> {data-name-1 / literal-1} {data-name-2 / literal-2} [{data-name-3 / literal-3}] ...

FIGURE 3–3
CONVENTIONAL NOTATION FOR GENERAL FORM OF COBOL ELEMENTS

3-1-2 COBOL ELEMENTS AND THEIR GENERAL FORM

The layout of a division refers to the nature, structure, and number of entries in a particular division. Since some of the division entries may vary somewhat from one computer manufacturer's COBOL to another, the reader is encouraged to check his/her installation's COBOL reference manual or COBOL reference card to determine the specifics of the various COBOL divisions and statements.

Figure 3–3 shows the notation commonly used to describe the general forms of COBOL elements. Appendix C contains the general forms for each COBOL element. To see how these general forms are used, let us illustrate the way in which particular COBOL elements can be derived from their general forms given in Figure 3–3. Consider the following three examples:

Examples:

1. **The general form of a data item entry in a record description is**

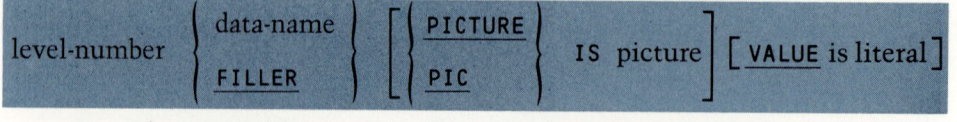

   level-number { data-name / FILLER } [{ PICTURE / PIC } IS picture] [<u>VALUE</u> is literal]

   From this general form we can derive the following entries:

   1. `01 STUDENT-RECORD.`   Record name, no PICTURE clause.
   2. `10 FLDA PIC X(17).`
      `10 FLDA PIC IS X(17).`
      `10 FLDA PICTURE X(17).`
      `10 FLDA PICTURE IS X(17).`   } All these forms are equivalent.
   3. `05 FLAG PIC 999 VALUE IS 123.`
   4. `49 FILLER PIC X(20) VALUE 'DIVISION BY ZERO'.`

STRUCTURE AND SYNTAX 63

2. **The general form of the MOVE instruction is**

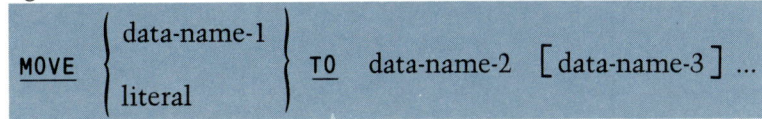

$$\underline{\text{MOVE}} \left\{ \begin{array}{l} \text{data-name-1} \\ \text{literal} \end{array} \right\} \underline{\text{TO}} \text{ data-name-2 } [\text{data-name-3}] \ldots$$

We can use this general form to generate the following entries:

```
                          ┌─────────────────── literal
                          ▼
1.  MOVE 'IN SEQUENCE' TO DL-MESSAGE. ◄── data-name
2.  MOVE 0 TO COST1  COST2  COST3.
3.  MOVE ZEROS TO FIELD.
4.  MOVE 0 TO FIELD.
5.  MOVE ALL '*' TO STAR-LINE.
6.  MOVE LAST-NAME TO PRINT-LAST-NAME.
```

3. **The general form of the ENVIRONMENT division is**

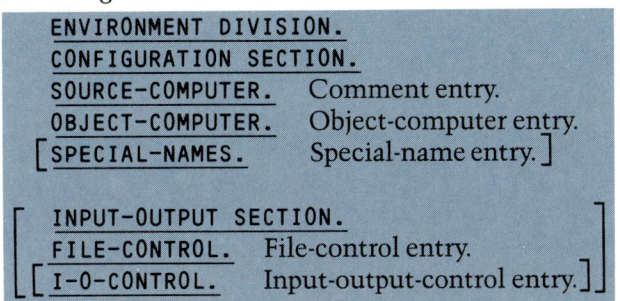

```
ENVIRONMENT DIVISION.
CONFIGURATION SECTION.
SOURCE-COMPUTER.    Comment entry.
OBJECT-COMPUTER.    Object-computer entry.
[SPECIAL-NAMES.     Special-name entry.]

[INPUT-OUTPUT SECTION.
 FILE-CONTROL.      File-control entry.
 [I-O-CONTROL.      Input-output-control entry.]]
```

From this we can generate the following entries:

```
1.  ENVIRONMENT DIVISION.              2.  ENVIRONMENT DIVISION.
    CONFIGURATION SECTION.                 CONFIGURATION SECTION.
    SOURCE-COMPUTER. IBM.                  SOURCE-COMPUTER. IBM.
    OBJECT-COMPUTER. BURROUGHS.            OBJECT-COMPUTER. IBM.
                                           INPUT-OUTPUT SECTION.
                                           FILE-CONTROL.
```

3-1-3 THE COBOL CHARACTER SET

The COBOL character set is composed of three classes of characters: alphabetic characters (A–Z), the numeric characters (0–9), and alphanumeric characters (any combination of alphabetic, numeric, or special characters). The standard character set consists of the following 52 characters:

0–9	Digits	;	Semicolon
A–Z	Alphabetic characters	)	Right parenthesis
"	Quotation mark	*	Asterisk
'	Apostrophe (alternate for quotation mark)	$	Currency sign
		+	Plus sign
>	Greater than symbol	(	Left parenthesis
,	Comma	<	Less than symbol
/	Slash	.	Period or decimal point
–	Hyphen (minus sign)		Blank (space bar)
=	Equal sign		

3-1-4 CONSTANTS

Unlike a data name whose value varies depending on what is stored (moved) into the data name, a constant remains fixed in value. There are two types of constants, and there are restrictions on their length and composition:

1. Literal constants
   - Numeric
     - Composition: digits 0–9 + – . (period)
     - Length: 1–18 digits
     - Remark: may not end with decimal point
     - Examples: −1.34   +1000   .00067
   - Nonnumeric
     - Composition: Any alphanumeric character
     - Length: 1–120 characters
     - Remark: must be enclosed in quotation marks
     - Examples: '12 NORTH ST.'   'XYZ COMPANY'

2. Figurative constants: Reserved words expressing both commonly used numeric and nonnumeric constants
   - Examples: SPACES meaning " " (alphanumeric)
   - ZERO meaning 0 (numeric)

Numeric Literals.

A numeric literal is a quantity whose value is fixed and explicitly stated. It must contain at least one but no more than 18 digits. The allowed characters are the digits 0 through 9, the plus (optional) and minus symbols (+, −) and the decimal point (period .). No numeric constant may end with a decimal point.

VALID NUMERIC LITERALS	INVALID	REASON	CORRECTIONS
1.0	10.	Ends with a period	10 or 10.0 or 10.00
−200003	3,442.00	Has a comma	3442.00
+123456789012345678	111-22-4444	Has a hyphen	
−.06	− 403.50	Leading blank	−403.50
0.78	3 0 4	Has blank spaces	304

Numeric literals can be used in COBOL sentences or entries as follows:

Examples:

NUMERIC LITERAL	COBOL USE	
123.4	MOVE 123.4 TO AMOUNT	→ Numeric literal / → Data name
+33, −31.4	ADD +33 −31.4 TO WS-SUM	→ Numeric literals / → Data name
−0.0056	IF J-HRS > −0.0056	→ Data name / → Numeric literal
1	05 END-FILE PIC 9 VALUE 1.	→ Data name / → Numeric literal

Nonnumeric Literals.

Nonnumeric literals, sometimes called alphanumeric constants, are used to create titles, headers, identification labels, captions, messages, et cetera. Nonnumeric literals consist of alphanumeric data. Such literals can be compared to one another but cannot be processed arithmetically.

Nonnumeric literal constants are strings of no more than 120 characters enclosed in double (") or single (apostrophe ') quotation marks. Any available character is permitted within the quotation marks. Blanks, special characters, and reserved words can be used in nonnumeric literals.

Examples:	**COBOL use**
"XYZ COMPANY"	`05 FILLER PIC X(11) VALUE "XYZ COMPANY".`
'TUESDAY 7TH 1986'	`MOVE 'TUESDAY 7TH 1986' TO DATE-FLD.`
'DIVISION BY ZERO'	`DISPLAY 'DIVISION BY ZERO'.` (The message DIVISION BY 0 is displayed on screen/terminal)
"YES"	`IF FLAG = "YES" MOVE 1 TO X.`

Figurative Constants.

Figurative constants (one guesses, "figures," what they represent) are reserved COBOL words that represent commonly used values. These constants should not be enclosed in quotation marks.

Examples:

FIGURATIVE CONSTANTS	VALUE	EXAMPLE OF USE	MEANING
ZEROES ZEROS ZERO	0 0 0	`MOVE ZERO TO WS-COUNT.`	Initialize WS–COUNT to 0. Equivalent to the numeric value 0 or character "0".
SPACES SPACE	blank(s)	`MOVE SPACES TO LINE-1.`	Initialize field LINE–1 to blanks. Equivalent to " ".
ALL [literal]	literal	The literal must be a nonnumeric literal or a figurative constant. ALL allows one to form a literal in which the characters specified by ALL are repeated. `MOVE ALL '7' TO FLD-1.`	FLD–1 = 7 7 7 7 (if FLD–1 has picture XXXX.)
	alphanumeric	`IF FLDB = ALL '*' ...`	If FLDB consists of only asterisks, then ...
HIGH-VALUES HIGH-VALUE			Represents one or more occurrences of the character (PIC X) that has the highest value in the computer's collating sequence (hexadecimal value 'FF').
LOW-VALUES LOW-VALUE			One or more of the characters (PIC X) that have the lowest value (hexadecimal '00').
QUOTE QUOTES		`QUOTE HELLO QUOTE ("HELLO")` `MOVE QUOTE TO FLDA.`	Represents one or more of the quotation mark characters; cannot be used to enclose a nonnumeric literal; i.e., is invalid. Moves a quotation mark to the field FLDA.

3–1–5 THE COBOL CODING SHEET

Rules governing the positioning of the various program statements are very important. COBOL is a very "picky" language and much frustration can be avoided by being aware of all the rules. The novice programmer will find it advantageous to invest in COBOL coding forms similar to the one shown in Figure 3–4.

The coding form is essentially broken down into four areas: columns 1–6, column 7, columns 8–72 and columns 73–80 (see Figure 3–5).

Columns 1–6: Sequencing (optional)

These columns are used for sequencing purposes. Columns 1–3 are used for page numbers, while columns 4–6 are used for individual line numbers.

If sequencing is used, the six-digit numbers should be in sequence. Since a COBOL program will generally require many COBOL coding sheets, each new sheet (new page) should start with a new page number in columns 1–3. Note that the coding form shows 20 preprinted lines per page. This does not mean that you must use all 20 lines; for example, you may need to use only 16 lines to write a short paragraph on page three—the last line on that page would then be 003160 and you would start the next coding form at line number 004010.

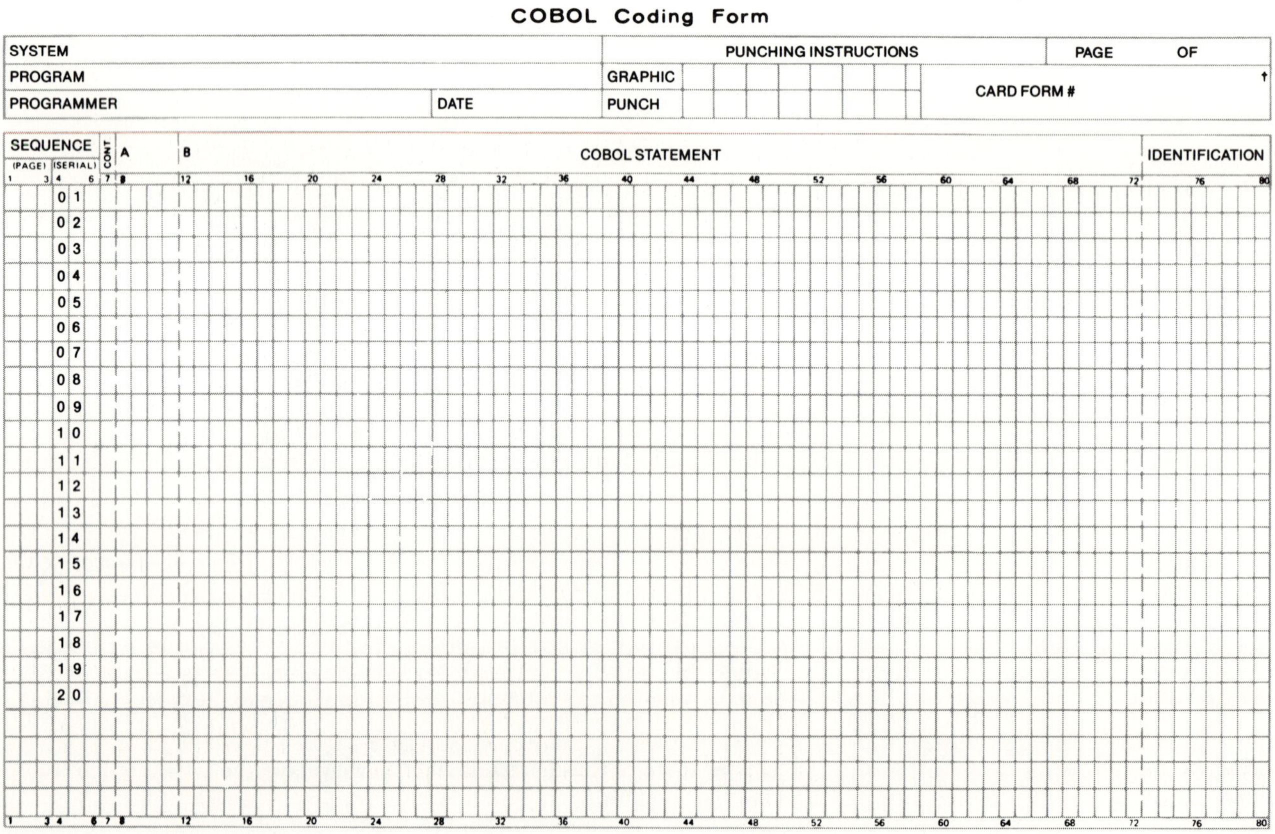
COBOL Coding Form

SYSTEM | PUNCHING INSTRUCTIONS | PAGE OF

PROGRAM | GRAPHIC | CARD FORM #

PROGRAMMER | DATE | PUNCH

SEQUENCE (PAGE) (SERIAL) | CONT. | A | B | COBOL STATEMENT | IDENTIFICATION

1 3 4 6 7 8 12 16 20 24 28 32 36 40 44 48 52 56 60 64 68 72 76 80

01
02
03
04
05
06
07
08
09
10
11
12
13
14
15
16
17
18
19
20

FIGURE 3–4
A COBOL CODING FORM

STRUCTURE AND SYNTAX

To avoid a waste of your time and possible typing errors, you may leave columns 1–6 unnumbered. Sequencing is generally used by professional COBOL programmers in data processing installations where the actual keying in of the program is done by data entry personnel.

Column 7

The Asterisk for Program Documentation. As we discussed in chapter 2, it is very important that a COBOL program be self-documenting and that it contain explanations and comments to help the reader understand its nature and purpose. For this reason, COBOL allows the programmer to intersperse comments throughout the COBOL code. Comment lines can be inserted anywhere in a program by entering an asterisk in position 7 (see Figure 3–6). When the compiler reads the * in position 7, it realizes that the information in that statement is just for the programmer; it does not view the statement as a COBOL instruction and does not translate it into machine language. The * in position 7 also causes the comment statement to be listed as part of the COBOL program.

It is good practice to start a program with comments identifying the purpose of the program. It is also an excellent idea to preface most paragraphs (modules) with explanatory text describing the objective(s) of the paragraph in question.

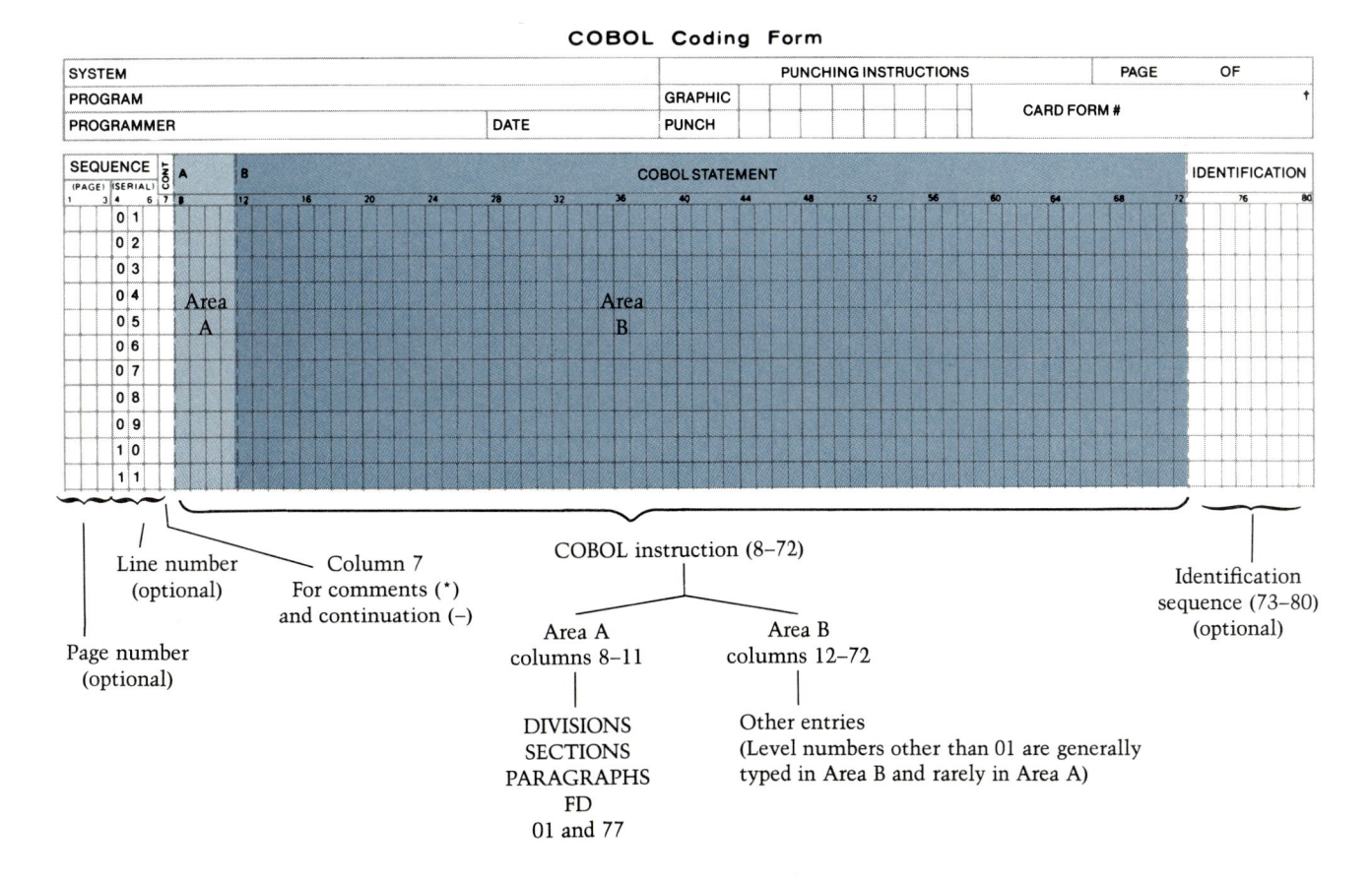

FIGURE 3–5
FUNCTIONAL AREAS OF THE CODING SHEET

```
SEQUENCE   |C|A   B                          COBOL STATEMENT
(PAGE)(SERIAL)|O|
 1  3 4  6 7 8   12    16   20   24   28   32   36   40   44   48   52   56   60   64   68   72
     01  *THIS PARAGRAPH SEARCHES FOR THE LOWEST SCORE IN THE TABLE
     02  *
     03   100-SEARCH-TABLE.
     04  *
     05  *IF THE ITEM NUMBER IS FOUND THEN UPDATE
     06  *ITS CORRESPONDING STOCK-LEVEL QUANTITY
     07           IF IR-ITEM-NO = MF-ITEM-NO (INDX)
     08
     09  ***********************
     10  * CODE MEANING              *
     11  *                           *
     12  *    1: SINGLE              *
     13  *    2: MARRIED             *
     14  *    3: CONSIDERING DIVORCE *
     15  *    4: WIDOWED             *
     16  ***********************
     17
     18
     19   IF WS-ERROR-FLAG = 1
     20       DISPLAY ' CHECK IMMEDIATLY WITH THE HEAD SECURITY OFFICER AND
      -              'TELL HIM OF POSSIBLE BREACH OF SECURITY ON TAPE 007-
      -              'GSA-42. IN THE MEAN-TIME TURN SYS-302 OFF.'.
```

FIGURE 3-6
USING THE ASTERISK AND HYPHEN IN COLUMN 7

The Hyphen for Continuation. A hyphen (-) in column 7 indicates continuation of literals, words, entries, or sentences. Check your technical reference manual for details. This feature should only be used in the very rare instance where a nonnumeric literal is too long to fit in columns 12-72. In that case the literal should extend all the way to column 72 and continue on the next line, where the hyphen is placed in column 7 and where the literal resumes in area B; quotation marks must precede the continued text (see Figure 3-6 last two lines).

Columns 8-72: Margin and Areas A and B

Record positions 8-72 contain the COBOL program statements. Margin A is defined to be record column 8, while area A refers to record columns 8-11 inclusive. Margin B identifies column 12, while area B refers to columns 12-72 inclusive (see Figure 3-5).

The following types of COBOL statements can appear in areas A and B:

Area A	DIVISION header: must be all by itself on line.
(8-11)	SECTION header: must be all by itself on line.
	Paragraph names.
	File Description FD.
	01 and 77 level entries.
Area B	Paragraph sentences.
Area A or B	02-49 level entries.

Figure 3-7 illustrates the way in which areas are used in a COBOL program.

STRUCTURE AND SYNTAX 69

```
000010 IDENTIFICATION DIVISION.              Division header: Area A
000020 PROGRAM-ID. BOILLOT.
000030 ENVIRONMENT DIVISION.                 Paragraph entries.
000040 CONFIGURATION SECTION.                Area A
000050 SOURCE-COMPUTER. IBM.
000060 OBJECT-COMPUTER. IBM.
000070 INPUT-OUTPUT SECTION.                 Section header: Area A
000080 FILE-CONTROL.                         Paragraph entry Area A
000090*
000100     SELECT INPUT-FILE ASSIGN TO READER.   } Clause entries: Area B
000110     SELECT PRINT-FILE ASSIGN TO PRINTER.
000120*
000130 DATA DIVISION.                        Division header: Area A
000140 FILE SECTION.                         Section header: Area A
000150 FD PRINT-FILE                         FD entries: Area A
000160    LABEL RECORDS ARE OMITTED          } FD entries: Area B
000170    DATA RECORD IS PRINT-LINE.
000180 01 PRINT-LINE        PIC X(133).      01 record entry Area A
000190 FD INPUT-FILE                         Area A
000200    LABEL RECORDS ARE STANDARD
000210    DATA RECORD IS INPUT-RECORD.
000220 01 INPUT-RECORD.
000230    05 IR-ITEM-NO     PIC X(06).       Generally Area B.
000240    05 IR-ITEM-DESCR  PIC X(10).       Level numbers 05 may
000250    05 IR-UNIT-COST   PIC 9999V99.     start in area A.
000260    05 IR-SELLING-PRICE PIC 9999V99.
000270    05 FILLER         PIC X(52).
000280*
000290 WORKING-STORAGE SECTION.              Section header: Area A
000300 77 WS-GROSS-MARGIN   PIC S999V99.     77 level numbers: Area A
000310 01 STAR-LINE.                         Area B
000320    05 FILLER PIC X(01) VALUE SPACES.  (may start in Area A)
000330    05 FILLER PIC X(75) VALUE ALL '*'.
           .
           .
           .
000730 PROCEDURE DIVISION.                   Area A
000740 05-MAIN-LOGIC.                        Paragraph entry: Area A
000750    OPEN INPUT INPUT-FILE, OUTPUT PRINT-FILE.   Paragraph sentences
000760    PERFORM 10-HEADER-ROUTINE.         Area B
000770    PERFORM 20-READ-PRINT 6 TIMES.
000780    WRITE PRINT-LINE FROM STAR-LINE AFTER 1.
000790    CLOSE INPUT-FILE, PRINT-FILE.
000800    STOP RUN.
000810*
000820 10-HEADER-ROUTINE.
000830    WRITE PRINT-LINE FROM HEADER-1 AFTER 3.
000840    WRITE PRINT-LINE FROM HEADER-2 AFTER 3.
```

FIGURE 3–7
AREAS A AND B

Since areas A and B are actually groups of columns, area A entries can start in columns 8, 9, 10, or 11. Similarly, area B elements can start in 12, 13, 14, ..., 72. For the sake of readability and consistency, it is recommended that area A entries start at column 8 and area B entries start at column 12.

Because of COBOL's flexibility in positioning COBOL sentences and entries, the coding style in Figure 3–8 is eccentric but still legal; in contrast, Figure 3–9 shows the recommended coding of the same program segment. The code shown in Figure 3–8 is sloppily arranged only to show the reader what he/she can and cannot do. Being off by 1 column is not a major crime and may not

```
    SEQUENCE    A   B                          COBOL STATEMENT
  (PAGE)(SERIAL)
01      INPUT-OUTPUT SECTION.
02      FILE-CONTROL. SELECT REPORT-FILE ASSIGN      More than 1 entry per line.
03          PRINTER. SELECT    STUDENT-FILE          Intervening blanks don't count.
04          ASSIGN TO DISK.
05      DATA DIVISION.
06          FILE SECTION.                            Area A but not starting in 8.
07      FD  STUDENT-FILE LABEL RECORDS STANDARD.     FD and clauses on one line.
08      01  STUDENT-RECORD.
09          05  SR-NAME PIC X(12).                   05 level in area B
10      05  SR-TEST1 PIC 999.                        05 level in area A
11
12      PROCEDURE DIVISION.
13      100-COORDINATING-MODULE.  OPEN               More than one sentence per line
14          INPUT STUDENT-FILE OPEN
15          OUTPUT REPORT-FILE.
16
```

FIGURE 3-8
USE OF AREAS A AND B (NOT RECOMMENDED)

```
01      INPUT-OUTPUT SECTION.
02      FILE-CONTROL.
03          SELECT REPORT-FILE ASSIGN TO PRINTER.
04          SELECT STUDENT-FILE ASSIGN TO DISK.
05  *
06      DATA DIVISION.
07      FILE SECTION.
08  *
09      FD  STUDENT-FILE
10          LABEL RECORDS ARE STANDARD.
11      01  STUDENT-RECORD.
12          05  SR-NAME  PIC X(12).
13          05  SR-TEST1 PIC 999.
14
15      PROCEDURE DIVISION.
16      100-COORDINATING-MODULE.
17          OPEN INPUT   STUDENT-FILE.
18          OPEN OUTPUT  REPORT-FILE.
19
```

FIGURE 3-9
USE OF AREAS A AND B (RECOMMENDED)

warrant retyping an entire line(s), but note the striking difference in terms of appearance (readability) between the program segments. Model your design on Figure 3-9, where the code is easy to work with; notice how easy it would be to look up entries and correct errors.

Use of Commas, Semicolons, and Periods in COBOL Statements.

Commas, semicolons, and periods are used as follows:

- All entries or sentences must terminate with a period.
- Semicolons and commas may be used for punctuation at the discretion of the programmer, for example, to separate two statements or two data names from each another in a sentence.
- Commas, semicolons, and periods must be typed immediately to the right of the last character of the COBOL word and should be followed by at least one blank space.

Consider the following examples:

VALID PUNCTUATION:

```
    OPEN INPUT TAX-FILE, OUTPUT PRINT-FILE.
    SELECT INVEN-1; ASSIGN TO READER.
    MOVE 10.6 TO LINE-OUT. MOVE C TO D.
```

INVALID PUNCTUATION:

```
    OPEN INPUT TAX-FILE,OUTPUT PRINT-FILE.        Commas must be followed by blank.
    SELECT INVEN-1 ; ASSIGN TO READER.            Semicolon must follow word immediately.
    MOVE 10.6 TO LINE-OUT.MOVE C TO D.            Period should be followed by blank.
```

COBOL statements may extend over several lines (records) as long as words or literals are not split from one line to another and as long as the continued text starts in area B; the continuation character (hyphen in column 7) is not used in this case. Consider the following examples:

VALID

```
    COMPUTE TOTAL-HOURS =
        RATE * HOURS.
    READ TAX-FILE
        AT END MOVE
        1324 TO CODE-OUT.
    READ TAX-FILE
        AT END MOVE
        "CHECK INPUT FILE"
        TO ERR-MSSG.
05 LAS PIC X(9) VALUE
        "LAST NAME".
```

INVALID

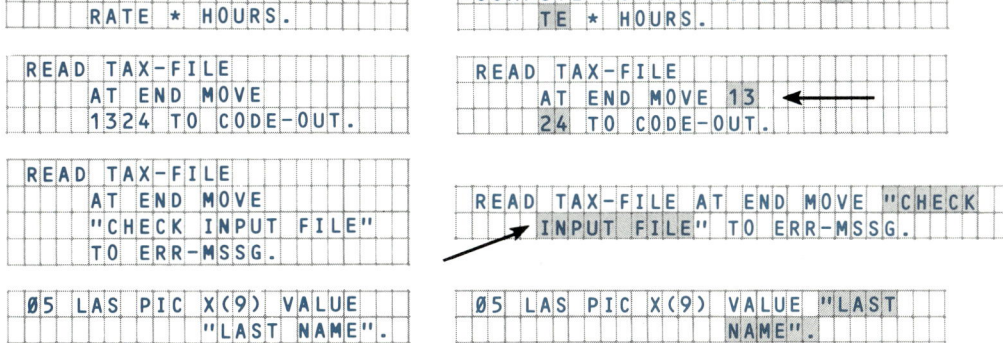

```
    COMPUTE TOTAL-HOURS = RA  ←
        TE * HOURS.
    READ TAX-FILE
        AT END MOVE 13  ←
        24 TO CODE-OUT.
    READ TAX-FILE AT END MOVE "CHECK
        INPUT FILE" TO ERR-MSSG.
05 LAS PIC X(9) VALUE "LAST
        NAME".
```

Columns 73–80: Identification Field (optional)

This field is seldom used today. When using punched cards, the program name entered in the PROGRAM-ID paragraph would be punched in columns 73–80 of the punched card.

3-1-6 DO IT NOW

True or false (if false, explain why):

1. A COBOL sentence may contain only one reserved word; for example, MOVE A TO B MOVE A TO C. is invalid since it has two reserved words and only one period.
2. The sentence MOVE A TO B can be written on two lines as: MOVE A TO B
3. The DATA division is made up of paragraphs.
4. $25 is a valid paragraph name.
5. PARAGRAPH NAME is an invalid paragraph name.
6. 1--- is a valid paragraph name.
7. 123 is a valid data item name.
8. COBOL is an invalid data item name.
9. A paragraph name reserves an area of storage for all sentences in it.
10. The following ENVIRONMENT division structure is valid:
    ENVIRONMENT DIVISION.
    CONFIGURATION SECTION.
    SOURCE-COMPUTER. IBM.
    OBJECT-COMPUTER. IBM.
    I-O-CONTROL. Input-output-control entry.
11. The entry 08 DATA ITEM.   is a valid data item description.
12. '.12.4' is a valid nonnumeric literal.
13. 123- is not a numeric literal, hence it is a valid nonnumeric literal.
14. MOVE ALL 'SPACES'   is a valid beginning of a COBOL sentence.
15. All level numbers can be typed in area B.
16. Only 01 level numbers can be typed in area A.
17. Only one sentence may be typed on one line.
18. Commas, colons, and periods are used for punctuation purposes.

ANSWERS:

1. F
2. T
3. F
4. F (special characters)
5. T (blank space)
6. F (cannot end with hyphen)
7. F (missing alphabetic character)
8. T
9. F
10. F (needs INPUT–OUTPUT section)
11. F (invalid item name)
12. T
13. F (needs quotes)
14. T
15. F (not 01)
16. F
17. F
18. F (colon invalid)

3-2 THE IDENTIFICATION DIVISION

As we noted in chapter 2, a COBOL program consists of four divisions that must appear in the following order: the IDENTIFICATION, the ENVIRONMENT, the DATA, and the PROCEDURE divisions.

The purpose of the IDENTIFICATION division is to provide background information about the particular program, i.e., the name of the program, its author, the particular installation where it is used or maintained, the date it was written and subsequently compiled, and any specific instructions related to operational security procedures (access by authorized personnel, classified files, et cetera). The IDENTIFICATION division is important in that it serves to document the program's origin and history, its place of application, and time references (dates). In any company's data processing center, where scores of programmers work on a multitude of projects, program documentation and accountability play a very important role. Data processing managers, project team leaders, and individual programmers need or may need to have access to such information. The general format of the IDENTIFICATION division is shown in Figure 3-10.

The PROGRAM-ID entry gives a user-chosen name to the entire COBOL program. In many systems the program-name is limited to eight characters (the first letter must be alphabetic, the remaining optional characters can be letters of the alphabet and/or digits; hyphens may be used, but not as the last character.) In some systems, COBOL communicates the user-chosen names to the operating system, which flashes the name of the program currently being run on the operations console.

All entries in the IDENTIFICATION division are called paragraphs. All paragraph entries must be followed by a period and a space; then the user comments follow. Examples of IDENTIFICATION divisions are shown in Figure 3-11.

3-3 THE ENVIRONMENT DIVISION

The ENVIRONMENT division is the part of the COBOL program that allows you to interface your COBOL program's input/output software with your system's input/output hardware. The fact that different computing systems have different hardware characteristics does not mean that your COBOL program cannot be run on other systems. You write hardware-independent programs by creating (SELECTing) your own symbolic names for your various input/output files and then by using those user-created file references throughout the logic of your program. In so doing, you never need to worry about the actual physical devices that will be used to process these files.

At some point of course (when the program is ready to be run), the computing system must be told which of its system devices will be needed to carry out the various input/output operations (what is the system name of the device, where the data file is stored, what is the name of the particular output device that is to be used, et cetera—these system names vary considerably from one computer or system to another). Such an ASSIGNment of user-named files to corresponding physical devices takes place in the ENVIRONMENT division.

```
IDENTIFICATION DIVISION.
PROGRAM-ID.     Program-name.
[ AUTHOR.       [Comment-entry]... ]
[ INSTALLATION. [Comment-entry]... ]
[ DATE-WRITTEN. [Comment entry]... ]
[ DATE-COMPILED.[Comment-entry]... ]
[ SECURITY.     [Comment-entry]... ]
```

FIGURE 3–10
GENERAL FORMAT OF THE IDENTIFICATION DIVISION

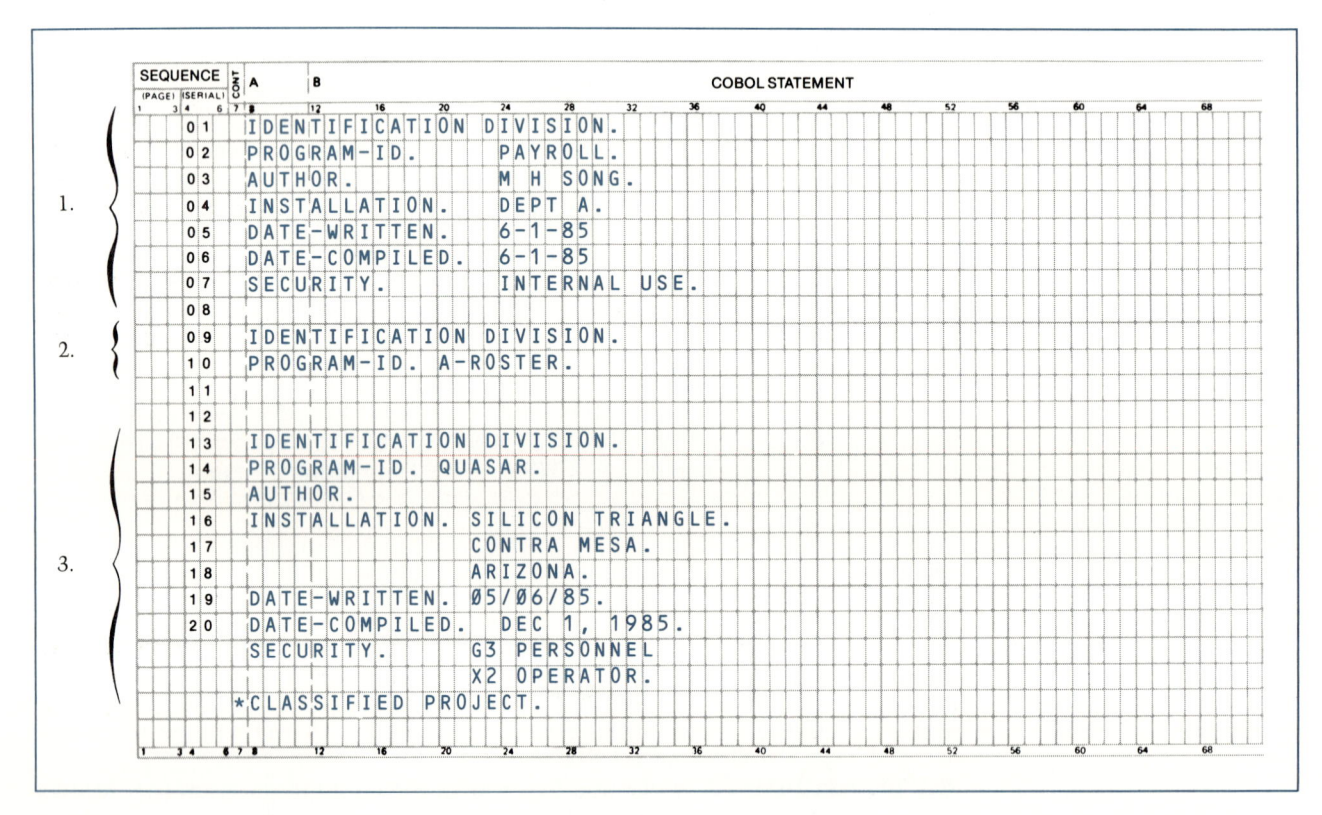

```
01  IDENTIFICATION DIVISION.
02  PROGRAM-ID.     PAYROLL.
03  AUTHOR.         M H SONG.
04  INSTALLATION.   DEPT A.
05  DATE-WRITTEN.   6-1-85
06  DATE-COMPILED.  6-1-85
07  SECURITY.       INTERNAL USE.
08
09  IDENTIFICATION DIVISION.
10  PROGRAM-ID. A-ROSTER.
11
12
13  IDENTIFICATION DIVISION.
14  PROGRAM-ID. QUASAR.
15  AUTHOR.
16  INSTALLATION. SILICON TRIANGLE.
17                CONTRA MESA.
18                ARIZONA.
19  DATE-WRITTEN. 05/06/85.
20  DATE-COMPILED. DEC 1, 1985.
    SECURITY.     G3 PERSONNEL
                  X2 OPERATOR.
   *CLASSIFIED PROJECT.
```

FIGURE 3–11
EXAMPLES OF IDENTIFICATION DIVISIONS

Thus you can tailor or adjust your input/output needs to the specific requirements of any particular computer and in the process never have to change one line of code in the IDENTIFICATION, the DATA, or the PROCEDURE division.

The skeletal format of the ENVIRONMENT division is shown in Figure 3–12. The complete format is shown in appendix C.

The ENVIRONMENT division is broken down into two parts (called sections) that identify:

1. The hardware (particular computer) used to process the program. The hardware description is provided in the CONFIGURATION section.

2. The system input/output devices that process the programmer's file. This information is provided in the INPUT-OUTPUT section.

In Figure 3-13, the SOURCE-COMPUTER paragraph (line 13) designates an IBM computer to compile the source code into object code. This object code will be executed also by an IBM computer as specified in the OBJECT-COMPUTER paragraph.

Since a particular input or output file can be processed on different types of input/output devices (magnetic tape, printer, magnetic disks, et cetera), the programmer must identify the particular device needed to process his/her files. Unfortunately, different computers have different system names for their various input/output devices. To make the COBOL program as hardware-independent as possible, the programmer selects a symbolic name (any name that is not a reserved word) for the input/output files so that he/she can work with them in the logic of the program and then assigns (links) those file names to the particular input/output hardware units of his/her system.

This linkage between the user-chosen file name and the physical device that processes that file is specified in the FILE-CONTROL paragraph of the INPUT-OUTPUT section through the sentence SELECT...ASSIGN (see lines 16-22 of Figure 3-13). Hence, if a user wishes to execute a program on a different computer, he/she needs only to reassign the files to the host computer device designations by changing the name of the system devices specified in the ASSIGN clause.

In Figure 3-13, lines 21 and 17 show the SELECT...ASSIGN sentences that associate the programmer's input file (STUDENT-FILE) to the physical device DISK (a particular IBM disk) and the output file (REPORT-FILE) to the device PRINTER (an IBM printer).

3-4 THE DATA DIVISION

The purpose of the DATA division is twofold: (1) to document the use of *all* data items in the logic of the program and (2) to reserve appropriate memory space for all data items. It is in the DATA division that you describe the nature and organization of all the data used by the program.

```
ENVIRONMENT DIVISION.
CONFIGURATION SECTION.
SOURCE-COMPUTER.   Computer-name-entry.
OBJECT-COMPUTER.   Computer-name-entry.
INPUT-OUTPUT SECTION.
FILE-CONTROL.
     SELECT   file-name   ASSIGN   to device-name ...
   *[ORGANIZATION IS [LINE] SEQUENTIAL].
```
*This entry may be required for diskette files.

```
01  ENVIRONMENT DIVISION.
02  CONFIGURATION SECTION.
03  SOURCE-COMPUTER.  IBM.
04  OBJECT-COMPUTER.  IBM.
05  INPUT-OUTPUT SECTION.
06      SELECT STUDENT-FILE
07          ASSIGN TO DISK.
08      SELECT REPORT-FILE
09          ASSIGN TO PRINTER.
10
```

FIGURE 3-12
SKELETAL FORMAT OF THE ENVIRONMENT DIVISION

```
 1:      IDENTIFICATION DIVISION.
 2:      PROGRAM-ID. STUDENT-LISTING.
 3:      AUTHOR. JONES.
 4:      ************************************************************
 5:      *                                                          *
 6:      *   THIS PROGRAM READS STUDENT RECORDS FROM A DISK FILE    *
 7:      *   AND PRINTS OUT EACH STUDENT NAME AS WELL AS HIS/HER    *
 8:      *   TWO TEST SCORES.                                       *
 9:      *                                                          *
10:      ************************************************************
11:      ENVIRONMENT DIVISION.
12:      CONFIGURATION SECTION.
13:      SOURCE-COMPUTER. IBM.
14:      OBJECT-COMPUTER. IBM.
15:      INPUT-OUTPUT SECTION.
16:      FILE-CONTROL.
17:          SELECT REPORT-FILE ASSIGN TO PRINTER.
18:      *
19:      *
20:      *
21:          SELECT STUDENT-FILE ASSIGN TO DISK
22:          ORGANIZATION IS LINE SEQUENTIAL.
23:      *
24:      DATA DIVISION.
25:      FILE SECTION.
26:      *
27:      FD  STUDENT-FILE
28:          LABEL RECORDS ARE STANDARD
29:          VALUE OF FILE-ID IS 'ROSTER'
30:          DATA RECORD IS STUDENT-RECORD.
31:      01  STUDENT-RECORD.
32:          05  SR-NAME  PIC X(12).
33:          05  SR-TEST1 PIC 999.
34:          05  SR-TEST2 PIC 999.
35:      *
36:      FD  REPORT-FILE
37:          LABEL RECORDS ARE OMITTED
38:          DATA RECORD IS PRINT-LINE.
39:      01  PRINT-LINE  PIC X(80).
40:      *
41:      WORKING-STORAGE SECTION.
42:      01  END-FILE   PIC XXX    VALUE 'NO'.
43:      01  DETAIL-LINE.
44:          05  FILLER   PIC X(5)   VALUE SPACES.
45:          05  DL-NAME  PIC X(12).
46:          05  FILLER   PIC XXX    VALUE SPACES.
47:          05  DL-TEST1 PIC 999.
48:          05  FILLER   PIC XXX    VALUE SPACES.
49:          05  DL-TEST2 PIC 999.
50:          05  FILLER   PIC X(51)  VALUE SPACES.
51:      *
52:      PROCEDURE DIVISION.
53:      100-COORDINATING-MODULE.
54:          OPEN INPUT STUDENT-FILE, OUTPUT REPORT-FILE.
55:          READ STUDENT-FILE
56:              AT END MOVE 'YES' TO END-FILE.
57:          PERFORM 200-PROCESS-RECORDS
58:              UNTIL END-FILE = 'YES'.
59:          CLOSE STUDENT-FILE, REPORT-FILE.
60:          STOP RUN.
61:      ************************************************************
62:      *                                                          *
63:      *   THIS MODULE MOVES THE VARIOUS INPUT FIELDS INTO THE    *
64:      *   SPECIFIED POSITIONS THAT THEY ARE TO OCCUPY ON THE     *
65:      *   OUTPUT-LINE.                                           *
66:      *                                                          *
67:      ************************************************************
68:      200-PROCESS-RECORDS.
69:          MOVE SR-NAME  TO DL-NAME.
70:          MOVE SR-TEST1 TO DL-TEST1.
71:          MOVE SR-TEST2 TO DL-TEST2.
72:          MOVE DETAIL-LINE TO PRINT-LINE.
73:          WRITE PRINT-LINE.
74:          READ STUDENT-FILE
75:              AT END MOVE 'YES' TO END-FILE.
```

1. User gives names to files and works with these names in the logic of the program without worrying about the actual physical devices.
2. Through the SELECT/ASSIGN clauses, the user specifies which files will be processed by which system device.

FIGURE 3–13
FILE NAMES AND INPUT/OUTPUT DEVICES

3-4-1 DATA ITEMS

In COBOL, data items occur either as one or more entries within a record or as independent entities (not related or part of any record) or as entries in tables (discussed in chapter 9). Recall from chapters 1 and 2 that a data item is actually a memory area, a disk area, or a screen area into or on which one or more characters (an entity) have been stored or displayed and to which we have given a symbolic name (data item name). For example, we talk about a record being divided into different fields (data items)—a name field, an address field, an age field, et cetera; these fields (or collections or related character positions) are called data items. Note that a data item can just as well be one character of information (a one-digit gender code) as 80 characters of information (a typical print-line).

Sometimes, a data item can be broken down into smaller data items called *subitems*. A data item such as an address might be broken down into four subitems: a street number, a city, a state, and a zip code. In turn, a subitem may be further subdivided; for example, a zip code number might be broken down into a region center and a locality code. Figure 3–14 shows the data items and sub-

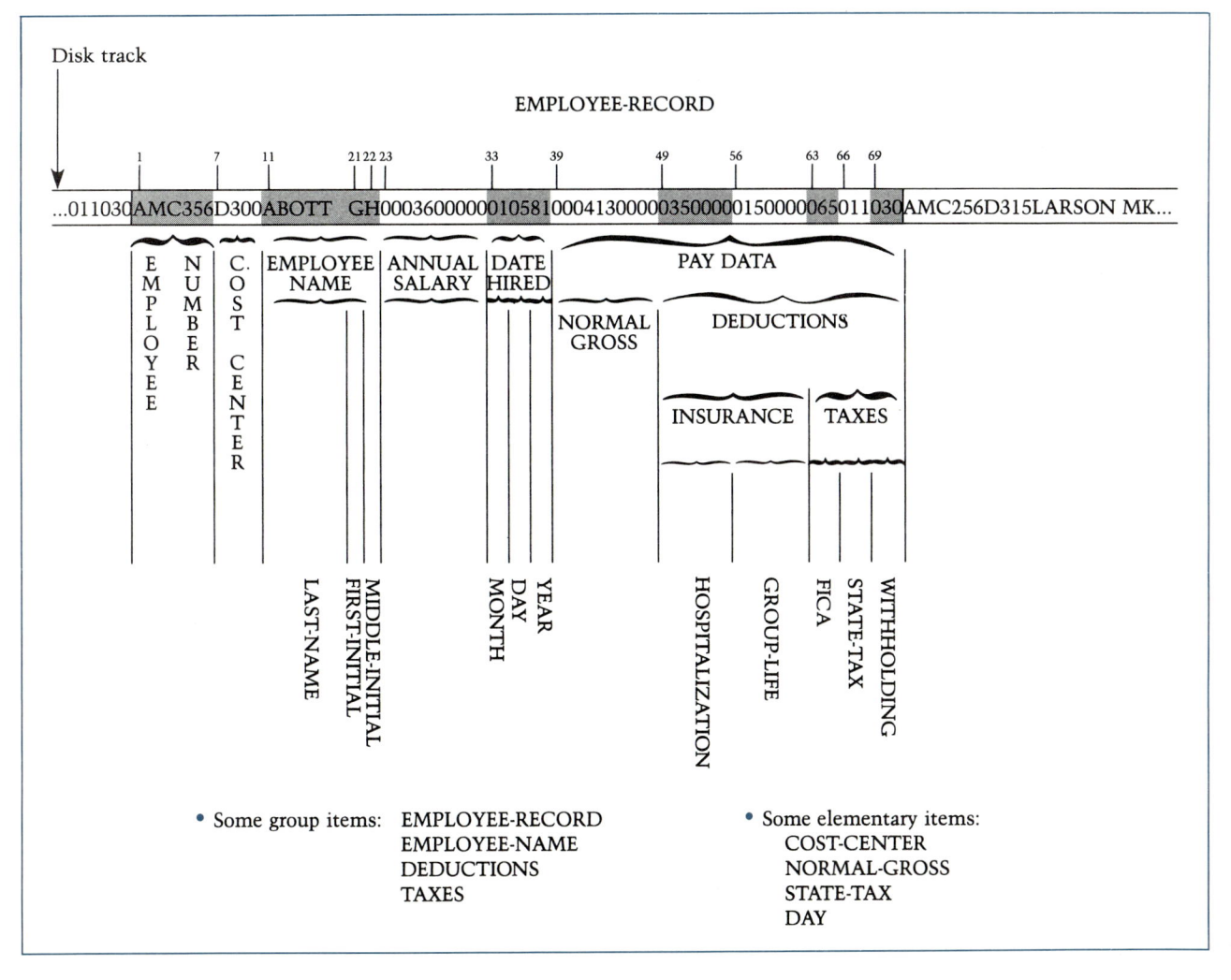

FIGURE 3–14
RECORDS AND DATA ITEMS

items of an employee record stored on disk. We distinguish between those data items that are subdivided and those that are not:

Definition: A *group item* is a data item that is further subdivided.

Definition: An *elementary* data item is a data item that is not further subdivided.

3-4-2 DATA ITEM TYPE AND THE PICTURE CLAUSE

There are basically two types of data items: alphanumeric data items (sometimes referred to as character strings) and numeric data items.

Alphanumeric data items consist of characters such as digits, letters of the alphabet, and special characters. Such items can be moved (copied) from one area of memory to another and can also be compared to one another (the character A, for example, is less than the character Z, and the character 3 is less than the character 9). Alphanumeric items can thus be arranged in character sequence (sorting out a list of names in alphabetical order, for example). Digits, of course, can be part of an alphanumeric item, as in the string of characters "1304 NORTH 12TH AVE." The reader at first thought might think there is no difference between the alphanumeric item 1304 and the numeric item 1304—but there is! COBOL cannot add character strings together; it cannot add the string 1304 to the string 24 just as it cannot add the character strings PAUL and SUE. It can compare these strings, however—in fact, the character string 24 is greater than the character string 1304 since the first character '2' is larger than the character '1'. How does COBOL know, then, whether to treat the digits 1304 as alphanumeric or numeric data? (*Answer:* through the PICTURE field, which we will discuss shortly.)

Numeric items (see section 3-1-4), on the other hand, can be processed algebraically as signed numbers. They can be added, subtracted, multiplied, divided, raised to a power, and compared to one another.

All data items must be declared in the DATA division. A data declaration must indicate the type of the data item (alphanumeric or numeric) and the length of the item, i.e., the number of characters or digits. This information is conveyed by the PICTURE clause, where the symbol 9 is used to represent numeric digit positions and the symbol X is used to represent character positions for alphanumeric items. The general form of a data item description entry is shown in Figure 3-15.
Thus

`TOTAL-DAYS PICTURE 9999`	reserves four memory positions for a numeric item.
`NAME PICTURE XXXXXXXX`	reserves eight memory positions for an alphanumeric item.

Note that the digit 9 and the character X serve as place holder positions for numeric and alphanumeric data respectively. The number of occurrences of those characters (9 or X) in the PICTURE field determines the length of the item. For example, TOTAL-DAYS will never exceed four digits. If an attempt is made to move the number 12345 into TOTAL-DAYS, only the digits 2345 will actually be stored in TOTAL-DAYS! Also note that the PICTURE clause does not initialize the data item to any value; the PICTURE clause simply reserves memory storage for the item and tells COBOL whether to treat the data within that memory area as numeric data or alphanumeric data.

STRUCTURE AND SYNTAX 79

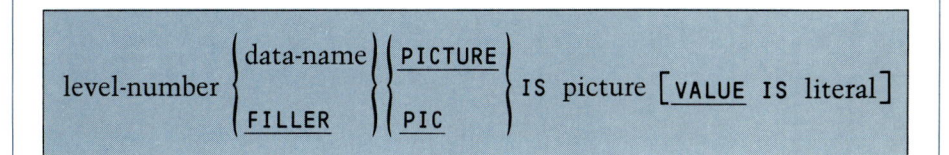

$$\text{level-number} \begin{Bmatrix} \text{data-name} \\ \underline{\text{FILLER}} \end{Bmatrix} \begin{Bmatrix} \underline{\text{PICTURE}} \\ \underline{\text{PIC}} \end{Bmatrix} \text{IS picture} \begin{bmatrix} \underline{\text{VALUE}} \text{ IS literal} \end{bmatrix}$$

where:

- level-number can be 01, 02, ..., 49, or 77.

- picture identifies the type of data (A = alphabetic, X = alphanumeric, 9 = numeric) and the size of the field in terms of storage positions.

- VALUE is used to initialize the data item to numeric or alphanumeric values. On some compilers VALUE can be abbreviated to VA.

- the VALUE clause may not be used to describe input/out records in the FILE section.

- a PICTURE clause is required for elementary items. It must not be used with a group item entry.

- literal can be any one of the following:

    a nonnumeric literal, i.e., a string of characters enclosed in quotes.

    a numeric literal, i.e., a sequence of digits 0 through 9 with or without a decimal point. The plus (+) sign or minus (−) sign may be used but should immediately precede the first digit.

    a figurative constant such as SPACE, ZERO, ALL...

FIGURE 3–15
A DATA ITEM DESCRIPTION ENTRY

The word PICTURE may be abbreviated to PIC, and multiple occurrences of the character 9 or X can be shortened to a form of expression such as X(k) or 9(k) where k is the field length for the item. Thus PICTURE XXXXXXXX can be rewritten as PIC X(8).

Consider the following examples of data item entries:

05 SR-NUM1	PIC 9	VALUE 0.	a 1-digit field set to 0 initially.
05 SR-NUM2	PIC 9(4)	VALUE 3451.	a 4-digit number equal to 3451.
05 SR-NUM3	PIC 99	VALUE ZEROES.	a 2-digit number equal to 0.
10 DL-NAME	PIC A(10)	VALUE 'ELIZABETHE'.	a data item name consisting of 10 characters (alphabetic).
10 DL-ADRESS	PIC X(12)	VALUE '7 N. 8TH ST.'.	consists of 12 alphanumeric characters.
10 DL-PHONE	PIC X(7)	VALUE IS '1234567'.	a string of 7 alphanumeric characters (cannot be processed arithmetically).
25 ER-LINE2	PIC IS X(132)	VALUE ALL '-'.	a string of 132 underline characters.
49 FILLER	PIC IS X(10)	VALUE IS SPACES.	Record entry initialized to 10 blanks.

It is also possible to initialize data items to decimal/fractional values such as VALUE IS −33.256. or VALUE IS +0.0056.; however, corresponding PICTURES must be appropriately described to include a reference to the internal position of the decimal point and the sign of the number. This will be discussed in chapter 4.

It is very important that the literal specified by the VALUE clause agree with the PICTURE definition of the particular data item. If the PICTURE clause specifies a numeric field, then the corresponding literal value should be numeric. If the PICTURE clause specifies a nonnumeric field, the corresponding literal value should be nonnumeric.

Avoid the errors in the following invalid data item descriptions:

INVALID DATA ITEMS	REASON
05 CODEX PIC 999 VALUE '123'.	Value is nonnumeric. PICTURE is numeric. Should be VALUE 123 or PIC XXX.
05 LARG PIC X(3) VALUE 345.	Value is numeric; requires PIC 999.

01 STUDENT-RECORD PIC X(24).
  05 SR-NAME   PIC X(18).
  05 SR-TEST1   PIC 999.
  05 SR-TEST2   PIC 999.
	Group items do not have picture clauses. The length of STUDENT-RECORD is the sum of the lengths of its subitems. (24 in this case).

3-4-3 RECORD DESCRIPTION

To describe the physical layout of a record, the programmer must:

- Identify by name the various data items making up the record.
- Identify the nature (type) of the data items (numeric or alphanumeric), since these are treated differently by the computer.
- Specify the length of each data item, i.e., is the item 8 digits long or is it 92 characters long?

Consider the following employee record:

```
STEVENS JOEL    4018 SPRING ST.       CLEVELAND  OHIO  4216548
```

Name: 1–15
Address: 16–57
Age: 58–59

One can describe this employee record in many different ways, each reflecting different access to the various fields.

1. If all that is needed is to process the record as one block of 59 characters, the hierarchy of the record can consist of just one element that can be described in COBOL as

    HIERARCHY   RECORD DESCRIPTION

    1st level   EMPLOYEE-RECORD   01 EMPLOYEE-RECORD PIC X(59).

    In this case there is only one level of elements and the level number 01 must always be used to refer to this first level.

STRUCTURE AND SYNTAX

2. The first record description permitted only a reference to all 59 characters, with no option of referring to items within the record. If we needed to refer to the name, address, and age fields, we would set up a hierarchy of elements consisting of the entire record at the first level and these three items at the next lower level.

```
HIERARCHY                                    RECORD DESCRIPTION

1st level         EMPLOYEE-RECORD            01  01  EMPLOYEE-RECORD.
                         |                   02      05  ER-NAME     PIC X(15).
2nd level       NAME  ADDRESS  AGE           03      05  ER-ADDRESS  PIC X(42).
                                             04      05  ER-AGE      PIC 99.
```

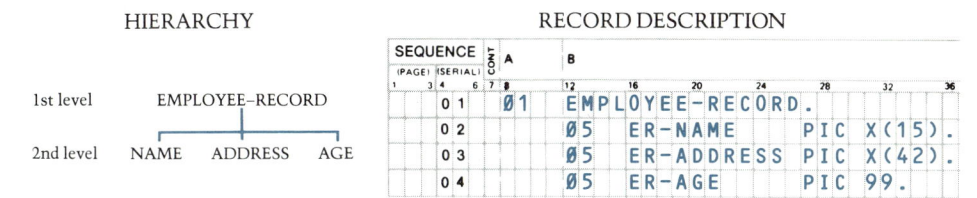

The different levels in the hierarchy of a record are indicated by different level numbers, with the level number 01 used exclusively to identify the physical record at the highest level. Subordinate levels in the hierarchy of the record are represented by successively higher level numbers in the record description entry. The numbers 02–49 can be used. A common practice is to use the level numbers 05, 10, 15, 20, ..., where 05 identifies 2nd level items, 10 identifies 3rd level items, et cetera.

Recall that a data item that is further subdivided is called a *group* item. A group item may not be described with a picture field; such an item is always treated as an alphanumeric item regardless of the picture type of its various subordinate items. An elementary item is an item that is not further subdivided—such an item *must* be described with a picture field. The length of a group item is the sum of the lengths of all its elementary items. In the above example, EMPLOYEE-RECORD is a group item consisting of 59 alphanumeric positions. ER-NAME and ER-ADDRESS are alphanumeric elementary items, and ER-AGE is a two-digit numeric elementary item.

3. The second record description allows no reference to the first and last name of the employee, but the following hierarchy would permit such references:

```
HIERARCHY                                              RECORD DESCRIPTION

1st level              EMPLOYEE-RECORD                 01  01  EMPLOYEE-RECORD.
                              |                        02      05  ER-LAST-NAME   PIC X(8).
2nd level  LAST-NAME  FIRST-NAME  ADDRESS  AGE         03      05  ER-FIRST-NAME  PIC X(7).
                                                       04      05  ER-ADDRESS     PIC X(42).
                                                       05      05  ER-AGE         PIC 99.
```

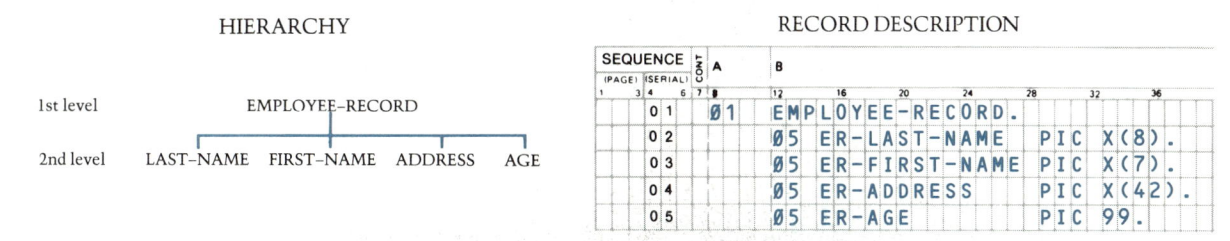

The third record description, however, does not make it possible to refer to the name as a whole unit. The following record description does:

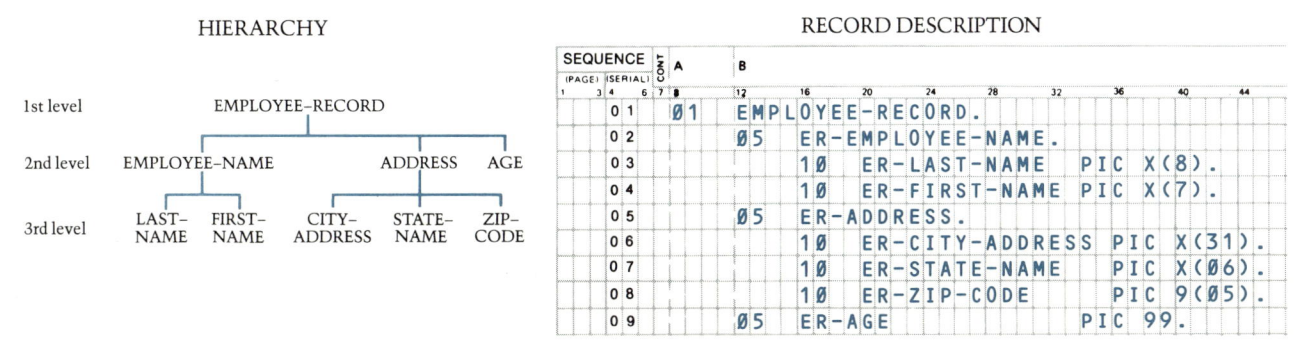

```
HIERARCHY                                                    RECORD DESCRIPTION

1st level                 EMPLOYEE-RECORD                    01  01  EMPLOYEE-RECORD.
                                 |                           02      05  ER-EMPLOYEE-NAME.
2nd level       EMPLOYEE-NAME         ADDRESS      AGE       03          10  ER-LAST-NAME     PIC X(8).
                    |                    |                   04          10  ER-FIRST-NAME    PIC X(7).
3rd level     LAST-  FIRST-      CITY-   STATE-  ZIP-        05      05  ER-ADDRESS.
              NAME   NAME        ADDRESS NAME    CODE        06          10  ER-CITY-ADDRESS  PIC X(31).
                                                             07          10  ER-STATE-NAME    PIC X(06).
                                                             08          10  ER-ZIP-CODE      PIC 9(05).
                                                             09      05  ER-AGE               PIC 99.
```

ER-EMPLOYEE-NAME is now a group item and LAST-NAME and FIRST-NAME are elementary items.

> **REMEMBER**
>
> - The level number 01 or 1 is used exclusively to describe a record entry.
> - Levels 02, 03, ..., 49 are used to describe data item levels of subdivision.
> - Group data items must never be described with a PICTURE clause.
> - Elementary data items must always be described with a PICTURE clause specifying the data type and the field length of the data item.
> - Successive levels of subdivision should be indicated by successively higher level numbers (ascending level number order). However, these level numbers need not be consecutive.

3-4-4 THE FILE SECTION

The FILE section describes the characteristics of all the input/output files; it specifies the layout or structure of the various records of the input/output files and reserves one input area for each input file and one output area for each output file. The skeletal form of the FILE section is shown in Figure 3–16. The general form is shown in appendix C.

The characteristics of all input/output files are described under the COBOL entry FD. The keyword FD stands for File Description. One FD entry is required for each input/output file. This entry, among other things, identifies the name of the file to be processed by the program and the names of the records associated with this file (generally there is only one record name, since all the records in the file will usually be identical in terms of data structure). Note that the name of the file specified by the FD entry must have been previously declared in a SELECT entry in the INPUT–OUTPUT SECTION, so that the computer knows which physical input/output device to use to process that file.

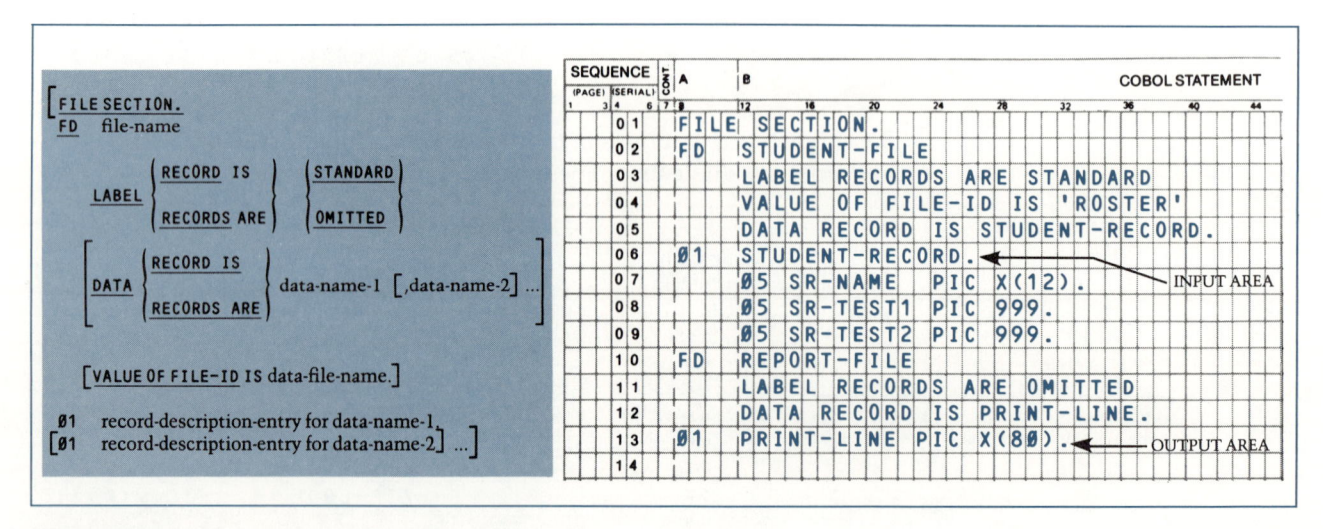

```
[FILE SECTION.
 FD  file-name

       LABEL  {RECORD IS   } {STANDARD}
              {RECORDS ARE }  {OMITTED }

     [DATA   {RECORD IS   } data-name-1 [,data-name-2] ...]
             {RECORDS ARE }

     [VALUE OF FILE-ID IS data-file-name.]

 01  record-description-entry for data-name-1
[01  record-description-entry for data-name-2] ...
```

```
01  FILE SECTION.
02  FD  STUDENT-FILE
03      LABEL RECORDS ARE STANDARD
04      VALUE OF FILE-ID IS 'ROSTER'
05      DATA RECORD IS STUDENT-RECORD.
06  01  STUDENT-RECORD.          ← INPUT AREA
07      05  SR-NAME   PIC X(12).
08      05  SR-TEST1  PIC 999.
09      05  SR-TEST2  PIC 999.
10  FD  REPORT-FILE
11      LABEL RECORDS ARE OMITTED
12      DATA RECORD IS PRINT-LINE.
13  01  PRINT-LINE  PIC X(80).   ← OUTPUT AREA
```

FIGURE 3–16
SKELETAL FORM OF THE FILE SECTION

STRUCTURE AND SYNTAX

The FD entry also specifies the presence or absence of labels that are often used in connection with magnetic tape or disk files. These labels identify device numbers and provide summary information about the data on the device. For disk files the entry LABEL RECORDS ARE STANDARD should be specified. Labels are not used in conjunction with card readers or printer files; however, the label entries are required in the file description, so use LABEL RECORDS ARE OMITTED.

On many systems it may also be necessary to use the VALUE OF FILE-ID entry to specify the catalogued name of the input data file(s) that is (are) to be accessed on disk.

The DATA RECORD IS entry is optional, but it is a good idea to include this entry for documentation. **In any event, the input/output record description entry or entries should immediately follow the last entry of the FD paragraph.** Even though a file may contain different types of records requiring different record entry descriptions, only one input/output area is reserved for each file. (Multiple input/output records are discussed in chapter 7).

3-4-5 THE WORKING-STORAGE SECTION

Record Description

The FILE section describes and allocates memory storage for the input and output records. The WORKING-STORAGE section similarly describes and allocates memory storage for all other records, all data items, and all tables used in the logic of the program.

In WORKING-STORAGE, the user designs all the various skeletal (as yet unfilled) records that the computer will work with to produce the different types of output lines that will make up the report (final results). Then, during execution of the program, WORKING-STORAGE becomes a busy construction site where each skeletal record is filled in with the appropriate information before it is dispatched to output. A report typically consists of output records (lines) of different formats, as shown in Figure 3-17, where the report consists of four different types of output lines.

Each of those records (output lines) is described as a group item in WORKING-STORAGE. Some of these records contain solely caption-type data that never changes, such as the major and minor heading in Figure 3-17. These records are formatted in WORKING-STORAGE as shown on the following page (assume an 80-character-wide output line):

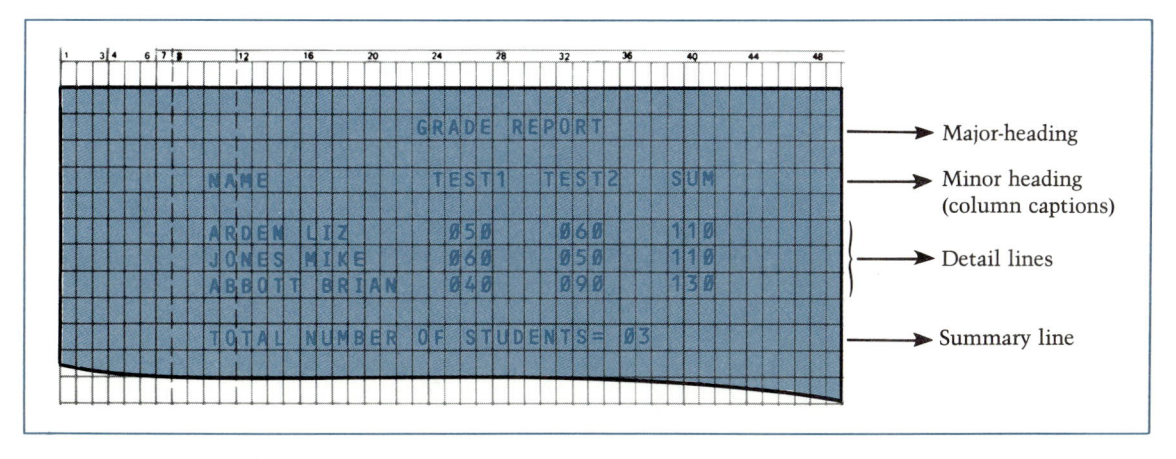

FIGURE 3-17
REPORTS AND OUTPUT LINES

RECORD DESCRIPTION

```
01  WORKING-STORAGE.
02  01  MAJOR-HEADING.
03      05  FILLER    PIC X(21) VALUE SPACES.
04      05  FILLER    PIC X(12) VALUE 'GRADE REPORT'.
05      05  FILLER    PIC X(47) VALUE SPACES.
06
07  01  MINOR-HEADING.
08      05  FILLER    PIC X(09) VALUE SPACES.
09      05  FILLER    PIC X(04) VALUE 'NAME'.
10      05  FILLER    PIC X(09) VALUE SPACES.
11      05  FILLER    PIC X(05) VALUE 'TEST1'.
12      05  FILLER    PIC X(02) VALUE SPACES.
13      05  FILLER    PIC X(05) VALUE 'TEST2'.
14      05  FILLER    PIC X(03) VALUE SPACES.
15      05  FILLER    PIC X(03) VALUE 'SUM'.
16      05  FILLER    PIC X(40) VALUE SPACES.
```

MEMORY ALLOCATION IN WORKING–STORAGE

MAJOR–HEADING — GRADE REPORT

MINOR–HEADING — NAME | TEST1 | TEST2 | SUM

← 80 characters →

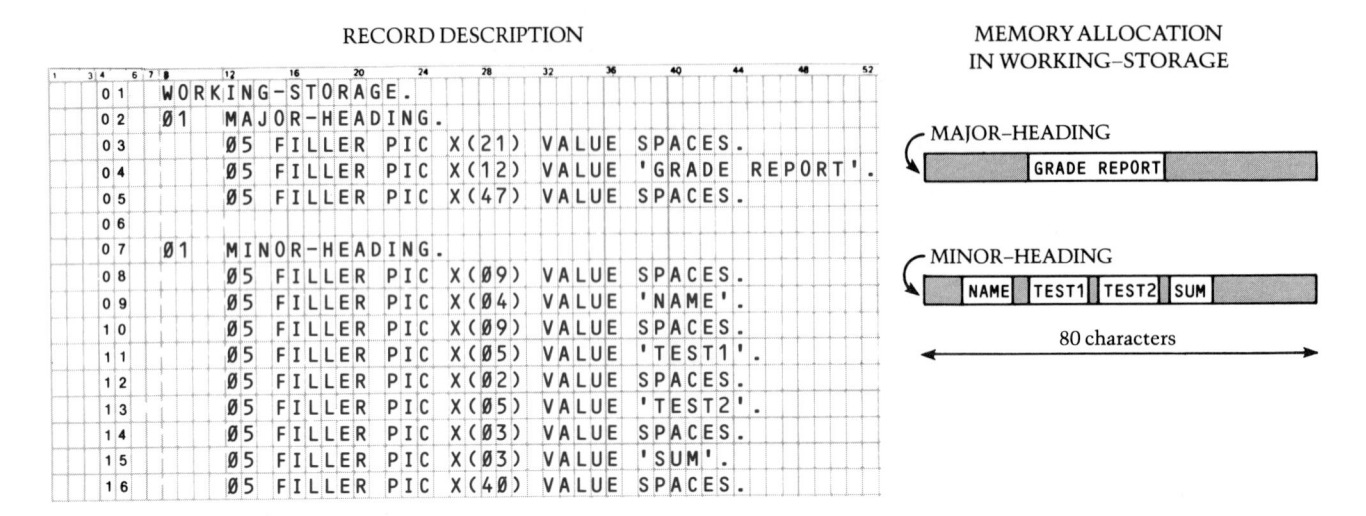

The other records, DETAIL-LINE and SUMMARY-LINE, are designed with pre-positioned open areas into which information is to be moved during execution of the program. These two records could be formatted as follows:

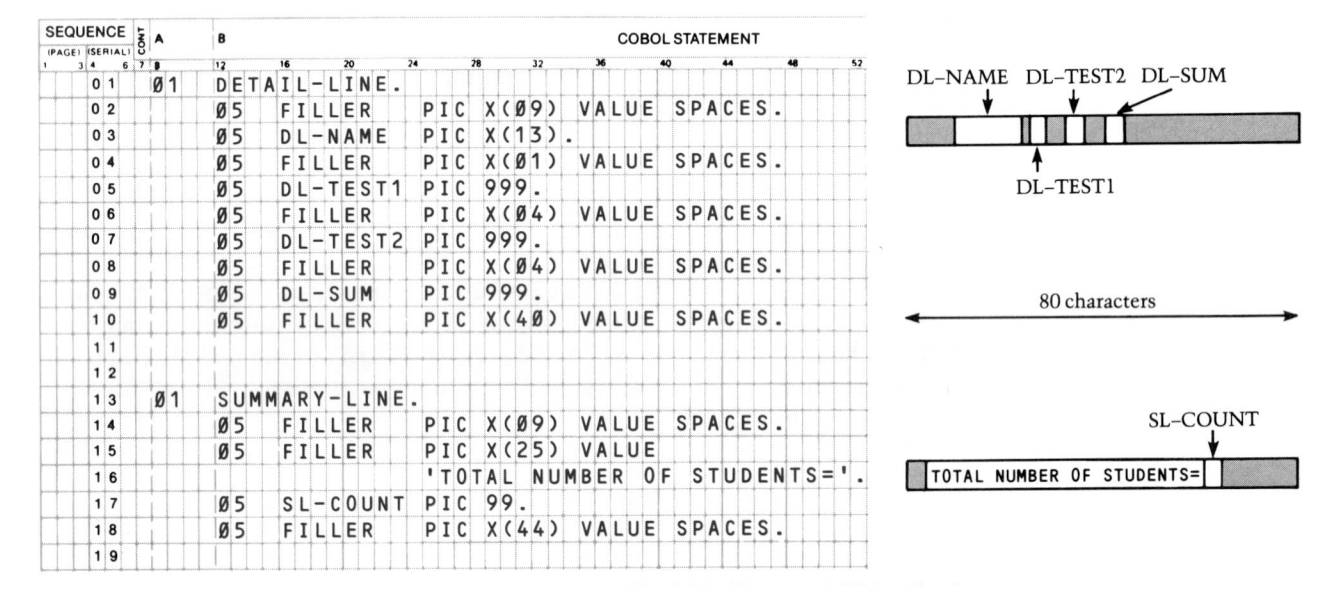

```
01  01  DETAIL-LINE.
02      05  FILLER    PIC X(09) VALUE SPACES.
03      05  DL-NAME   PIC X(13).
04      05  FILLER    PIC X(01) VALUE SPACES.
05      05  DL-TEST1  PIC 999.
06      05  FILLER    PIC X(04) VALUE SPACES.
07      05  DL-TEST2  PIC 999.
08      05  FILLER    PIC X(04) VALUE SPACES.
09      05  DL-SUM    PIC 999.
10      05  FILLER    PIC X(40) VALUE SPACES.
11
12
13  01  SUMMARY-LINE.
14      05  FILLER    PIC X(09) VALUE SPACES.
15      05  FILLER    PIC X(25) VALUE
16              'TOTAL NUMBER OF STUDENTS='.
17      05  SL-COUNT  PIC 99.
18      05  FILLER    PIC X(44) VALUE SPACES.
19
```

DL–NAME   DL–TEST2   DL–SUM
DL–TEST1

← 80 characters →

SL–COUNT
TOTAL NUMBER OF STUDENTS=

In the logic of the program, a lot of shuffling takes place between WORKING-STORAGE and the output record. Records are constantly prepared and completed in WORKING-STORAGE and then moved out to the output record for printing. The following outline could be used to produce a report similar to the one shown in Figure 3–17. Study this outline carefully, along with Figure 3–18, and use the latter to trace visually the data movement from the input records to WORKING-STORAGE to the output record.

1. Initialize a counter to 0 to count the number of records.
2. MOVE the MAJOR-HEADING from WORKING-STORAGE to the output record and print it.
3. MOVE the MINOR-HEADING from WORKING-STORAGE to the output record and print it.
4. READ the first record into the input area.
5. Carry out steps 9 through 14 until the end of file is encountered.

STRUCTURE AND SYNTAX 85

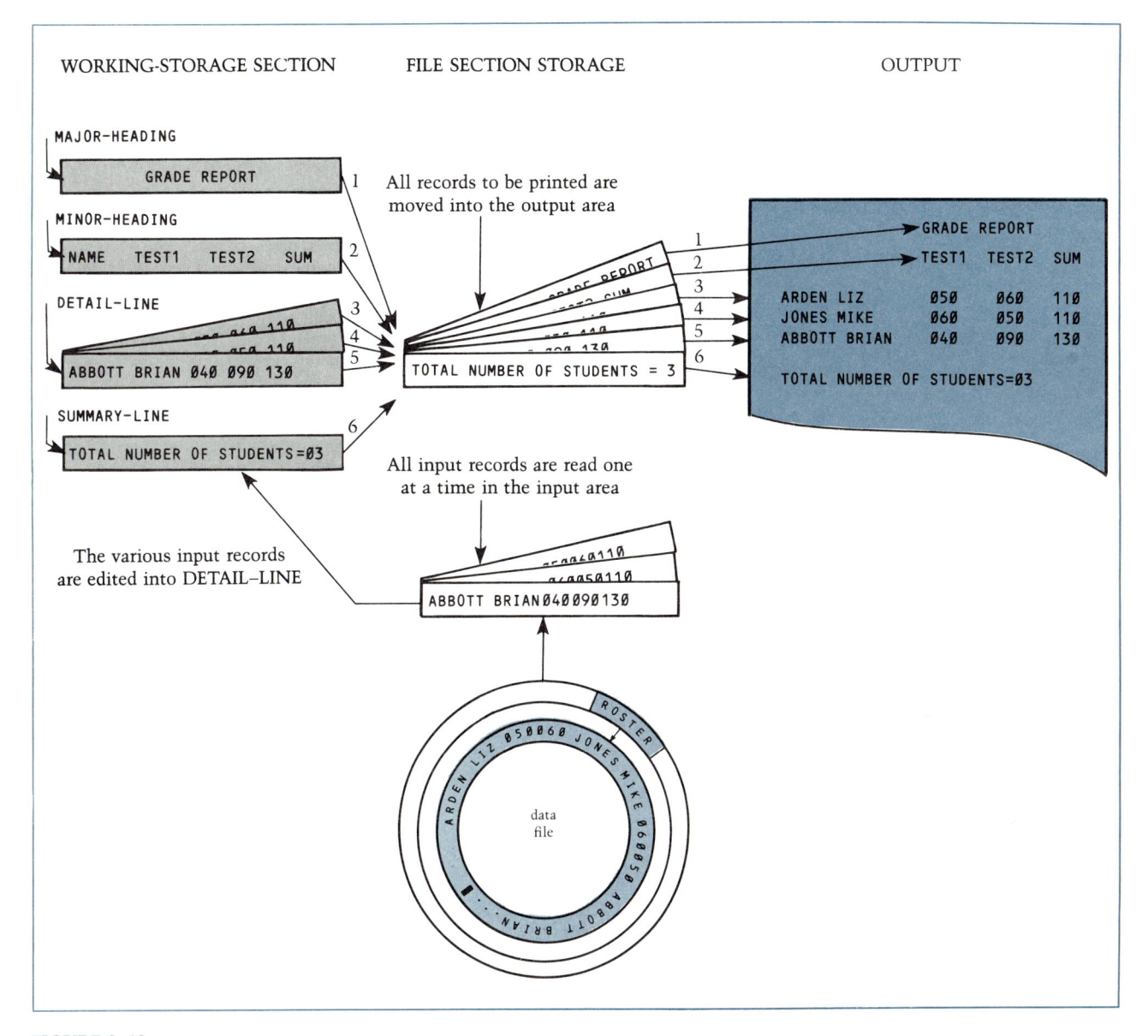

FIGURE 3–18
DATA MOVEMENT BETWEEN INPUT/WORKING-STORAGE/AND OUTPUT

6. Move counter to appropriate slot into SUMMARY–LINE (SL–COUNT).

7. Move SUMMARY–LINE to the output record and print it.

8. STOP.

9. Move the data from the input record to WORKING–STORAGE (appropriate slots in DETAIL–LINE).

10. Add 1 to the counter.

11. Compute the sum of the two scores.

12. Move the sum of the two scores to its appropriate place in the DETAIL–LINE (DL–SUM).

13. Move the DETAIL–LINE to the output area and print it.

14. Read the next record into the input area.

Independent Data Items

Most data items declared in WORKING–STORAGE are generally part of a record that is eventually printed out. In some cases, however, a data item does not belong to any record—such an item is called an *independent* item. It is an elementary item, yet it is not part of a record. In chapter 2 we encountered an independent item, END–FILE, which was used to stop reading an input file. This item was never printed! Independent items are also used to hold intermediate results (temporary storage areas). For example, if we want to print the average of a set of scores, we must first compute the sum of the scores. This sum is just an intermediate result and is of no value once the average has been computed. To distinguish this "orphan" type of item from data items belonging to records, COBOL lets you create a unique class of items that are identified by the special level number 77. These independent items can be initialized to certain values through the VALUE clause, and they can be interspersed throughout WORKING–STORAGE. A commonly observed practice, however, is to declare them before all other 01 record entry descriptions, i.e., right after the line specifying WORKING–STORAGE.

In the logic of the program to produce Figure 3–17, three items could be declared as 77-level items: one to take care of the end-of-file processing (WS–END–FILE), another to compute the sum of the two scores (WS–SUM–TESTS) and, finally, a counter (WS–RECORD–COUNTER) to count the number of records. These three independent items would appear in WORKING–STORAGE as:

```
01  WORKING-STORAGE.
02  77  WS-END-FILE            PIC XXX VALUE 'NO'.
03  77  WS-SUM-TESTS           PIC 999 VALUE 0.
04  77  WS-RECORD-COUNTER      PIC 99  VALUE 0.
```

Since none of these items belong to a record, the optional prefix WS (*WORKING–S*TORAGE) is used to identify them as 77-level items. 77-level items should be listed in alphabetical order to facilitate a visual search when the list is lengthy.

It should be noted that the current trend is to discourage the use of 77 levels. To provide better documentation and structure, independent data items are grouped by category (class) into records of similar type items, for example:

```
01  WORKING-STORAGE SECTION.
02  01  COUNTERS.
03      05  WS-RECORD-COUNTER   PIC 99 VALUE 0.
04      05  WS-PAGE-COUNTER     PIC 99 VALUE 0.
05      05  WS-LINE-COUNT       PIC 99 VALUE 0.
06  01  ACCUMULATORS.
07      05  WS-TOTAL-PAY        PIC ...
08      05  WS-SUBTOTAL         PIC ...
09  01  FLAGS-N-SWITCHES.
10      05  WS-EOF              PIC XXX VALUE 'NO'.
11      05  WS-ERROR-SWITCH     PIC 9   VALUE 0.
```

3-4-6 DO IT NOW

1. Answer true or false, or fill in blanks when necessary.
   a. The ENVIRONMENT division describes the particular input/output records that are to be processed by the hardware.
   b. The SELECT clause identifies the hardware device to process the input or output file.
   c. The SELECT/ASSIGN entries allow the user to specify the input/output devices that will be used to process the files that are referred to in the logic of the program.
   d. System device names are standard, just like COBOL reserved words.
   e. Subordinate data items must always be described with a PICTURE clause.
   f. Group items are always treated by COBOL as alphanumeric data.
   g. If a program works with 3 input files, _____ SELECT clauses will be required in the _____ division.
   h. The nonnumeric literal ' – 123' is less than '123' since negative numbers are less than positive numbers.
   i. The VALUE clause may not be used in the definition of an output record.
   j. Assume the record description

   ```
   01 FLDA.
       05 FLDB PIC 9 VALUE 2.
       05 FLDC PIC 9 VALUE 3.
   ```

   The value of FLDA will be 24 if 1 is added to FLDA.
   k. The FD entry must specify the _____ that is also declared in the _____ entry of the INPUT/OUTPUT section.
   l. The input/output records are defined in WORKING–STORAGE.
   m. Independent data items must be declared with 77-level numbers.

2. Define the record structure to capture the following data. Preserve the column positions and assume the entire record is 80 positions long.

1 2 3 4 5 6	7 8 9 10 11 12 13 14 15 16 17 18 19 20	21 22 23 24 25 26 27 28 29	30 31 32 33 34 35 36 37 38 39 40 41 42 43 44 45 46 47 48
DATE	EMPLOYEE NAME	S. SECURITY	ADDRESS
MONTH / DAY / YEAR	LAST FIRST M		NO. / STREET / CITY / ZIP (R / C)

3. Given the following record description outlines, determine which data item names should be described with a PICTURE clause.

   ```
   a. 01  A      b. 01  A      c. 01  A      d. 01  A
      02  B         01  B         05  B         02  B
      02  C         05  C         05  C         01  C
      03  D         06  D         06  D         03  D
      04  E         07  E         06  E         04  E
                                  05  F         04  F
   ```

4. Determine whether the following record descriptions are valid or invalid. If invalid, specify errors.

   ```
   a. 01 SALES-SLIP PIC 99999.    b. 01 NAME PIC X(80).
         05 SALESMAN PIC 9.             01 FIRST PIC X(80).
         05 DEPT PIC 9999.
   ```

```
    c. 05 TEST-SCORE.                  d. 10 SALES-RECORD.
          08 DATE-TEST PIC A(8).             15 SALES PIC 999.
          09 GRADE PIC 999.                  20 CODE-ITEM.
                                             20 DEPT-NO.

    e. 01 F1 PIC X(4).                  f. 01 FILLER PIC X(80).
       01 F2.
          05 F3 PIC 99.
          05 F4.
             10 FILLER PIC 9(9).
             10 F5    PIC 9(X).
```

5. Using the following partial record description, decide whether statements a. through l. are true or false.

   ```
   01  A.              a. B is a group item.
       05  B.          b. G is a group item.
           10 C ____   c. H is a group item.
       05  D.          d. C is an elementary item.
           12 E ____   e. H is an elementary item.
           12 F ____   f. A is an elementary item.
           12 G ____   g. A is a record.
       05  H    ____   h. B is a record.
                       i. B is a subitem.
                       j. F is a subitem.
                       k. A is a data item.
                       l. G is a data item.
   ```

ANSWERS:

1. a. F
    b. F
    c. T
    d. F
    e. F
    f. T
    g. 3, ENVIRONMENT
    h. F (the character − is compared to the character 1)
    i. T
    j. F (group item FLDA is alphanumeric and cannot be processed arithmetically)
    k. filename, SELECT
    l. F
    m. F

2.  ```
    01 EMPLOYEE-RECORD.
       05 ER-DATE.
          10 ER-MONTH       PIC 99.
          10 ER-DAY         PIC 99.
          10 ER-YEAR        PIC 99.
       05 EMP-NAME.
          10 ER-LAST        PIC X(7).
          10 ER-FIRST       PIC X(6).
          10 ER-MIDDLE      PIC X.
       05 SOCIAL-SECURITY   PIC 9(9).
       05 EMP-ADDRESS.
          10 ER-NUMBER      PIC X(3).
          10 ER-STREET      PIC X(6).
          10 ER-CITY        PIC X(5).
          10 ER-CODE.
             15 ER-REGION   PIC 99.
             15 ER-CODE     PIC 999.
    ```

3. a. B, E   b. A, E   c. B, D, E, F   d. B, E, F

4. a. Invalid. SALES–SLIP is a group item, no PICTURE clause.
   b. Invalid. FIRST is a reserved word.
   c. Invalid. DATE–TEST is a group item, no PICTURE clause.
   d. Invalid. SALES is a group item, no PICTURE clause. CODE and DEPT should have PICTURE clauses.
   e. Valid. Numeric field for FILLER is not invalid.
   f. Syntactically correct.

5. a. T b. F c. F d. T e. T f. F g. T h. F i. T j. T k. T l. T
    ```

3-5 THE PROCEDURE DIVISION

3-5-1 AN OVERVIEW

The PROCEDURE division contains the COBOL instructions that tell the computer in detail what operations to carry out and the order in which to perform them. The logic (instructions) to solve the problem is spelled out in the PROCEDURE division, but note that if data is to be read and results are to be printed, all input/output files and related records must have been specified and described in the ENVIRONMENT and DATA divisions.

During the execution of the code in the PROCEDURE division, the input data is read (one record at a time) into memory, where it is moved around, operated upon (using arithmetic operations), compared, et cetera, to finally yield results that are printed one line at a time (one output record at a time) on some output medium. This process is illustrated in Figure 3-19.

On the technical level, the PROCEDURE division, whose hierarchical elements are illustrated in Figure 3-1, can be broken down into sections. From a beginner's standpoint, the PROCEDURE division is typically broken down into many paragraphs in which four or fewer types of statements are used.

1. Input/output statements
2. Arithmetic statements
3. Sequence control statements
4. Miscellaneous statements

On a conceptual level, the PROCEDURE division can be thought of as a sequence of modules that each carry out specific objectives, such as initialization, file processing, data manipulation, et cetera.

The skeletal forms of the COBOL statements used in the PROCEDURE division are shown in Figure 3-20.

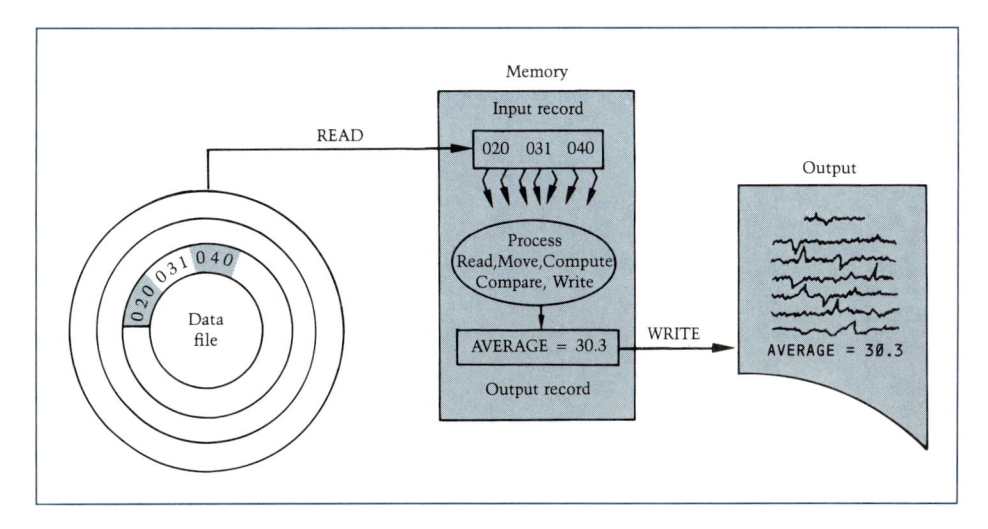

FIGURE 3-19
EXECUTING A PROGRAM

```
PROCEDURE DIVISION.
       OPEN    ⎧ INPUT  filename-1 [,filename-2 ...]  ⎫
               ⎩ OUTPUT filename-3 [,filename-4 ...]  ⎭
       CLOSE   filename-1 [,filename-2 ...]
       READ    filename [INTO data-record] [AT END statement-1 [,statement-2 ...]]
                                                           ⎧ data-name ⎫
       WRITE   record-name [FROM data-record] AFTER [ADVANCING] ⎨           ⎬ [LINES]
                                                           ⎩ integer   ⎭
       COMPUTE data-name = arithmetic-expression
               ⎧ data-name-1 ⎫
       MOVE    ⎨             ⎬ TO data-name-2 [,data-name-3 ...]
               ⎩ literal-1   ⎭
                         ⎧ true-statement-1 [,true-statement-2 ...] ⎫
       IF condition      ⎨                                          ⎬
                         ⎩ NEXT SENTENCE                            ⎭
                         ⎧ false-statement-1 [,false-statement-2 ...] ⎫
       [ELSE             ⎨                                            ⎬
                         ⎩ NEXT SENTENCE                              ⎭
       PERFORM paragraph-name [UNTIL condition]
```

FIGURE 3–20
TYPICAL COBOL STATEMENTS USED IN A PROCEDURE DIVISION

3–5–2 THE WRITE FROM STATEMENT

The general form of the WRITE FROM statement is:

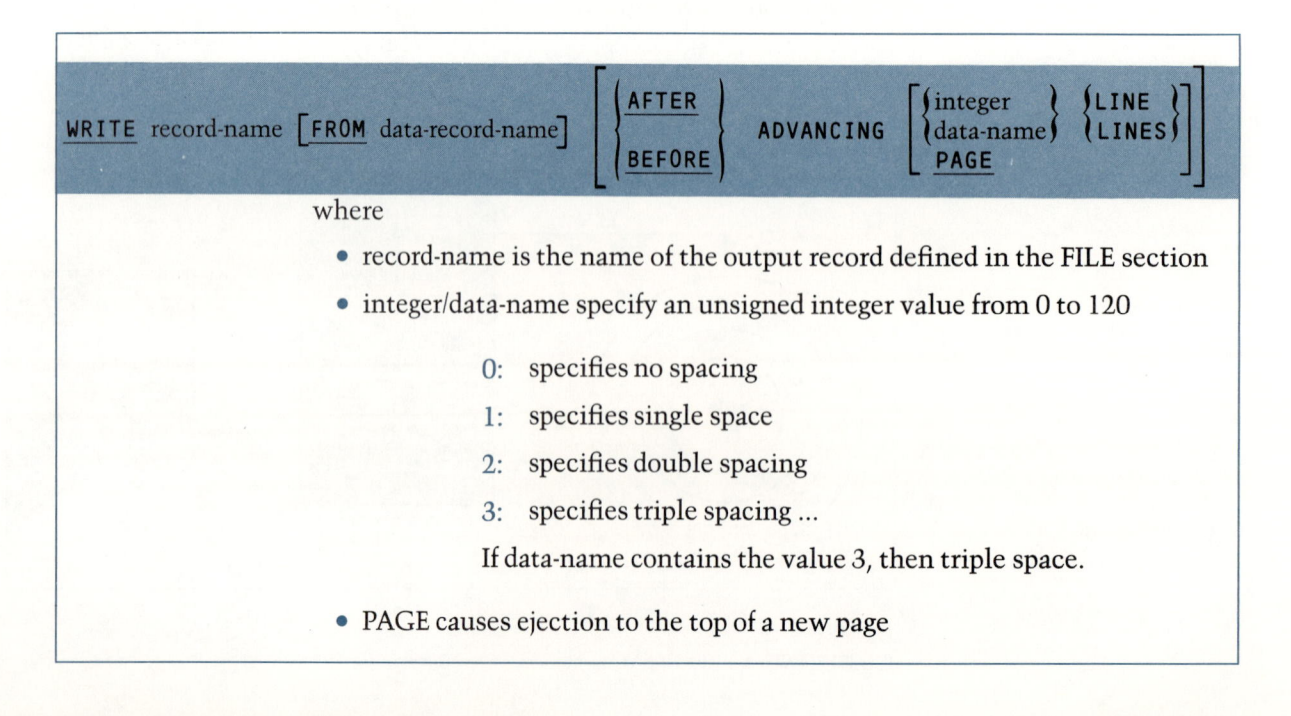

```
                                        ⎧ AFTER  ⎫           ⎧ integer   ⎫ ⎧ LINE  ⎫
WRITE record-name [FROM data-record-name] ⎨        ⎬ ADVANCING ⎨ data-name ⎬ ⎨       ⎬
                                        ⎩ BEFORE ⎭           ⎩ PAGE      ⎭ ⎩ LINES ⎭
```

where
- record-name is the name of the output record defined in the FILE section
- integer/data-name specify an unsigned integer value from 0 to 120

    0: specifies no spacing
    1: specifies single space
    2: specifies double spacing
    3: specifies triple spacing ...

    If data-name contains the value 3, then triple space.

- PAGE causes ejection to the top of a new page

STRUCTURE AND SYNTAX

The WRITE FROM option is very convenient as it allows the user to write records directly from WORKING-STORAGE. The user specifies the record in WORKING-STORAGE that is to be printed and the system automatically moves that record to the output record that is then printed.

Example:
```
         WRITE PRINT-LINE FROM MAJOR-HEADING
FD REPORT-FILE ...
01 PRINT-LINE PIC X(80).
   .
   .
   .
WORKING-STORAGE SECTION.
01 MAJOR-HEADING.
   05 FILLER PIC X(05) VALUE SPACES.
   05 FILLER PIC X(12) VALUE 'GRADE REPORT'.
   05 FILLER PIC X(63) VALUE SPACES.
```

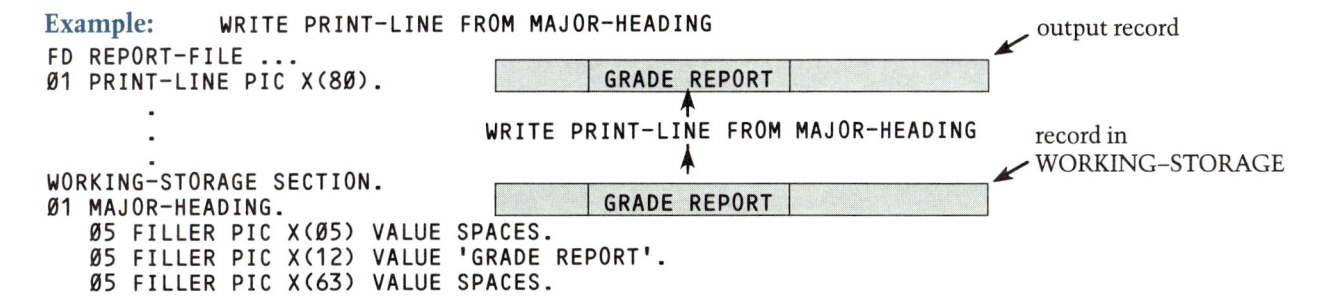

output record — GRADE REPORT

WRITE PRINT-LINE FROM MAJOR-HEADING

record in WORKING-STORAGE — GRADE REPORT

The WRITE FROM statement automatically moves the 80 characters of MAJOR-HEADING into PRINT-LINE (output record) and then writes the record. Thus the statement WRITE PRINT-LINE FROM MAJOR-HEADING is equivalent to the following two lines:

```
MOVE MAJOR-HEADING TO PRINT-LINE.
WRITE PRINT-LINE.
```

It is extremely important to remember that, unlike most other computer languages, COBOL does not write out individual data items. Such sentences as:

`WRITE TOTAL`	Where TOTAL is a data item,
or	
`WRITE HOURS, RATE, PAY`	where HOURS, RATE, PAY are record description entries,

simply don't work in the COBOL environment.

COBOL does not write a list of data items directly. It does, however, write out a complete record, and this record generally consists of many items that have been moved or edited into it. COBOL writes the "whole" and not the "part." Thus it is the programmer's responsibility to move or edit the required data items into predefined slots in the output record. This process obviously requires some forethought since all individual items must be sewed up into one record before printing can take place. We can visualize this process in the following example, which shows the valid process for printing the values for HOURS, RATE, and PAY.

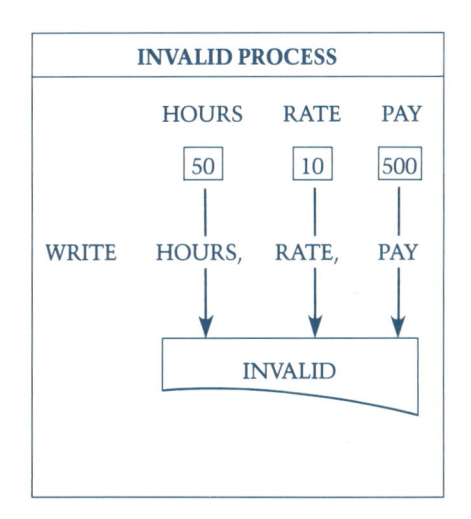

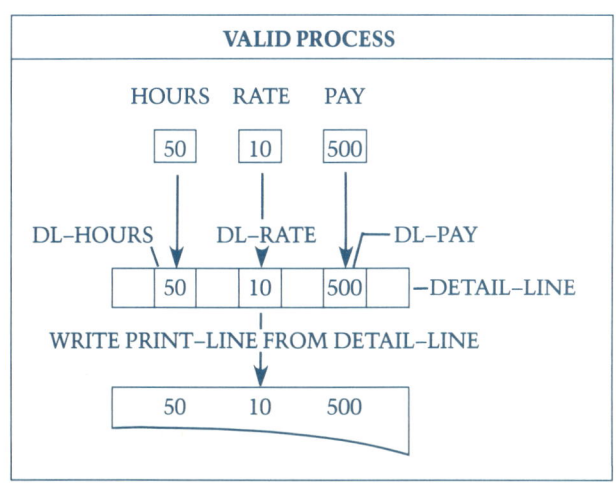

INVALID PROCESS

```
         HOURS  RATE  PAY
          50    10   500
          |     |    |
WRITE  HOURS, RATE,  PAY
          ↓     ↓    ↓
         INVALID
```

VALID PROCESS

```
         HOURS  RATE  PAY
          50    10   500
          ↓     ↓    ↓
DL-HOURS    DL-RATE    DL-PAY
          50    10   500   —DETAIL-LINE

WRITE PRINT-LINE FROM DETAIL-LINE
          ↓
          50    10   500
```

The AFTER/BEFORE ADVANCING clause

Many times the user needs to be able to control vertical spacing on the output form. Spacing between lines can be accomplished through the AFTER/BEFORE option, as illustrated in the following examples.

Examples:

1. To single space:

    ```
    WRITE PRINT-LINE
        AFTER ADVANCING 1 LINE.
    ```

    Action: Start printing on 1st line after the last one that was printed.

2. To double space:

    ```
    WRITE PRINT-LINE FROM DETAIL-LINE
        AFTER 2.
    ```

    Action: Start printing on 2nd line after the last one that was printed.

3. To underline a heading:

    ```
    01 MAJOR-HEADING.
        05 FILLER     PIC X(15) VALUE SPACES.
        05 MH-CAPTION PIC X(12) VALUE 'GRADE REPORT'.
        05 FILLER     PIC X(53) VALUE SPACES.

    WRITE PRINT-LINE FROM MAJOR-HEADING
        AFTER ADVANCING 2 LINES.
    MOVE ALL '_' TO MH-CAPTION.
    WRITE PRINT-LINE FROM MAJOR-HEADING
        AFTER ADVANCING 0 LINES.
    ```

4. To print MAJOR–HEADING, then skip 2 lines, then PRINT SUB–HEADING, then skip 3 lines:

    ```
    WRITE PRINT-LINE FROM MAJOR-HEADING
        BEFORE ADVANCING 2 LINES.
    WRITE PRINT-LINE FROM SUB-HEADING
        BEFORE ADVANCING 3 LINES.
    ```

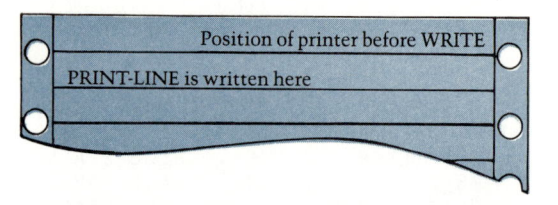

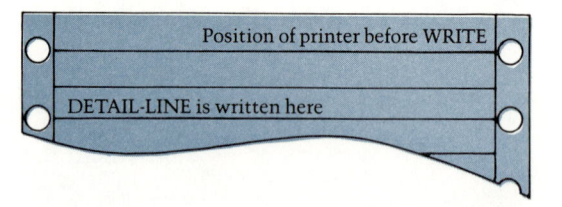

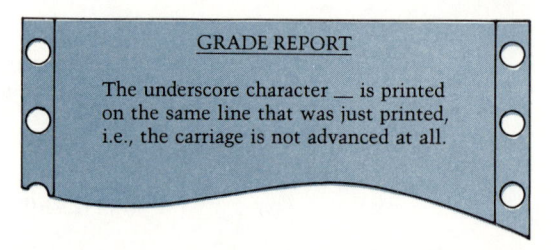

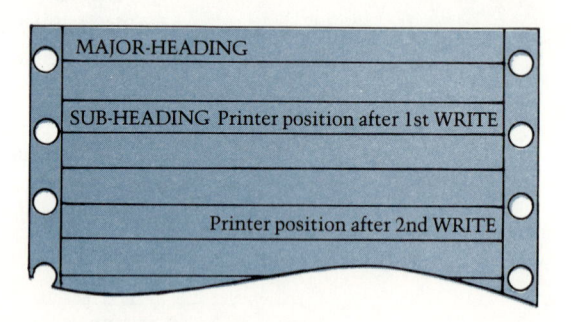

In example 4 note that the MAJOR–HEADING line might be written over (on top of) a line that was previously written by the computer, since the WRITE occurs before the carriage is moved. This would indeed happen if the statement WRITE PRINT–LINE AFTER 1 occurred just before the WRITE PRINT–LINE FROM MAJOR–HEADING.

If you decide to use the ADVANCING feature in a program, you should then use this feature for all WRITE statements for the sake of consistency. In that case single-spacing should always be coded as:

```
WRITE PRINT-LINE FROM DETAIL-LINE AFTER ADVANCING 1 LINE.
```

To avoid ambiguous interpretations and possible overwrites, try to use either the AFTER or the BEFORE feature throughout your program but not both.

3-5-3 THE READ INTO STATEMENT

The general form of the READ INTO statement is

> <u>READ</u> file-name <u>INTO</u> data-record-name [<u>AT</u> <u>END</u> statement ...]
>
> where data-record-name is the name of a record in WORKING–STORAGE or the name of the output record area in the FILE section.

The input record is read into the input area defined in the FD entry. That same record is then automatically MOVEd into data-record-name by the system. (See Figure 3–21, line 86.) The data-record-name can be an entry defined in WORKING–STORAGE or an output record area in the FILE section. As a result, two images of the input record are available in memory: one in the FILE section and the other one in the WORKING–STORAGE section.

The READ INTO statement is conceptually akin to the WRITE FROM statement. Whereas we can write a "print-line" from various types of heading-lines, detail-lines, summary-lines, et cetera, we can now read different types of input records into different areas in WORKING–STORAGE. So far, of course, the input records that we have processed have had the same physical layout. This is not always the case and, in fact, in many applications different types of records will generally be encountered in the input file. This requires that we specify separate record description entries for each type of input record. One way to do this is to provide these record descriptions in WORKING–STORAGE and then use the READ INTO feature to read these records into the appropriate entry in WORKING–STORAGE.

In addition, it is good management from a documentation standpoint to use the READ INTO statement. It allows us to structure our WORKING–STORAGE section into clearly defined sets of distinct record types (see figure 3–21, lines 36, 43, and 50). In one visual scoop, the reader can identify all the various types of records used in the PROCEDURE division, simply by looking at the WORKING–STORAGE section.

3-5-4 ARITHMETIC OPERATIONS: THE COMPUTE, ADD, AND SUBTRACT STATEMENTS

COBOL allows the user to express arithmetic operations in two different ways:

1. **Simple arithmetic** uses the COBOL verbs ADD, SUBTRACT, MULTIPLY, and DIVIDE. Only one arithmetic verb may be specified in one operation. Simple uses of the ADD and SUBTRACT statements are discussed in this section. A complete discussion of simple arithmetic will be given in chapter 4.

2. **Compound arithmetic** uses the COMPUTE statement, which allows the user to compound or combine the various arithmetic operators +, −, /, *, and ** (exponentiation) in one expression.

Skeletal forms of the COMPUTE, ADD, and SUBTRACT statements are shown in Figure 3–22.

When the COMPUTE statement is encountered, the associated expression is evaluated and the result is stored in the data name specified by the COMPUTE verb.

```
17:    FILE-CONTROL.
18:        SELECT REPORT-FILE  ASSIGN TO PRINTER.
19:        SELECT STUDENT-FILE ASSIGN TO DISK
20:        ORGANIZATION IS LINE SEQUENTIAL.
21: *
22:    DATA DIVISION.
23:    FILE SECTION.
24: *
25:    FD  STUDENT-FILE
26:        LABEL RECORDS ARE STANDARD
27:        VALUE OF FILE-ID IS 'ROSTER'
28:        DATA RECORD IS INPUT-AREA.
29:    01  INPUT-AREA PIC X(18).
30:    FD  REPORT-FILE
31:        LABEL RECORDS ARE OMITTED
32:        DATA RECORD IS PRINT-LINE.
33:    01  PRINT-LINE  PIC X(80).
34:    WORKING-STORAGE SECTION.
35: *
36: * INDEPENDENT ITEMS
37: *
38:    01  FLAGS-AND-COUNTERS.
39:        05  WS-END-FILE        PIC XXX VALUE 'NO'.
40:        05  WS-RECORD-COUNTER  PIC 99  VALUE 0.
41:        05  WS-SUM-TESTS       PIC 999 VALUE 0.
42: *
43: * INPUT RECORDS
44: *
45:    01  STUDENT-RECORD.
46:        05 SR-NAME  PIC X(12).
47:        05 SR-TEST1 PIC 999.
48:        05 SR-TEST2 PIC 999.
49: *
50: * OUTPUT RECORDS
51: *
52:    01  MAJOR-HEADING.
53:        05 FILLER   PIC X(21) VALUE SPACES.
54:        05 FILLER   PIC X(12) VALUE 'GRADE REPORT'.
55:        05 FILLER   PIC X(47) VALUE SPACES.
56:    01  MINOR-HEADING.
57:        05 FILLER   PIC X(09) VALUE SPACES.
58:        05 FILLER   PIC X(04) VALUE 'NAME'.
59:        05 FILLER   PIC X(09) VALUE SPACES.
60:        05 FILLER   PIC X(05) VALUE 'TEST1'.
61:        05 FILLER   PIC X(02) VALUE SPACES.
62:        05 FILLER   PIC X(05) VALUE 'TEST2'.
63:        05 FILLER   PIC X(03) VALUE SPACES.
64:        05 FILLER   PIC X(03) VALUE 'SUM'.
65:        05 FILLER   PIC X(39) VALUE SPACES.
66:    01  DETAIL-LINE.
67:        05 FILLER   PIC X(09) VALUE SPACES.
68:        05 DL-NAME  PIC X(13).
69:        05 FILLER   PIC X(01) VALUE SPACES.
70:        05 DL-TEST1 PIC 999.
71:        05 FILLER   PIC X(04) VALUE SPACES.
72:        05 DL-TEST2 PIC 999.
73:        05 FILLER   PIC X(04) VALUE SPACES.
74:        05 DL-SUM   PIC 999.
75:        05 FILLER   PIC X(40) VALUE SPACES.
76:    01  SUMMARY-LINE.
77:        05 FILLER   PIC X(09) VALUE SPACES.
78:        05 FILLER   PIC X(25) VALUE
79:                    'TOTAL NUMBER OF STUDENTS='.
80:        05 SL-COUNT PIC 99.
81:        05 FILLER   PIC X(42) VALUE SPACES.
82: *
83:    PROCEDURE DIVISION.
84:    100-COORDINATING-MODULE.
85:        OPEN INPUT STUDENT-FILE, OUTPUT REPORT-FILE
86:        READ STUDENT-FILE INTO STUDENT-RECORD
87:            AT END MOVE 'YES' TO WS-END-FILE.
```

READ STUDENT-FILE INTO STUDENT-RECORD AT END MOVE 'YES' TO WS-END-FILE.

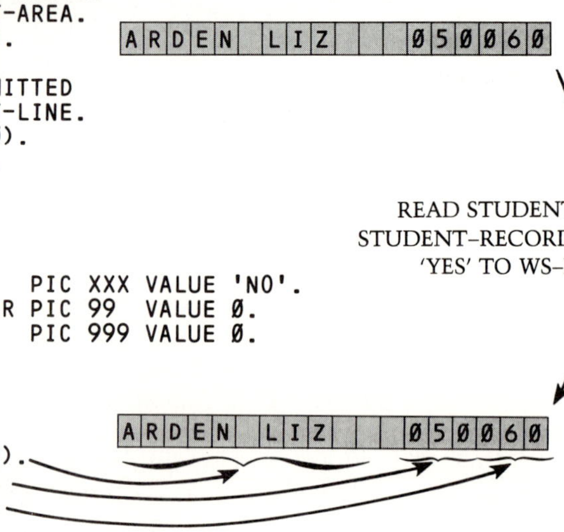

Note how the WORKING-STORAGE section is well structured and documented in terms of independent items, input records and output records.

In the PROCEDURE division we use the READ INTO feature.

FIGURE 3-21
THE READ INTO FEATURE

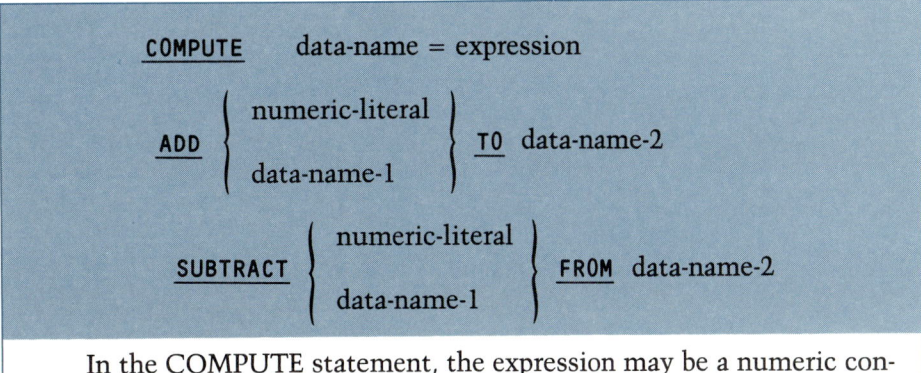

STRUCTURE AND SYNTAX

> COMPUTE data-name = expression
>
> ADD { numeric-literal / data-name-1 } TO data-name-2
>
> SUBTRACT { numeric-literal / data-name-1 } FROM data-name-2
>
> In the COMPUTE statement, the expression may be a numeric constant or a data name or any combination of data names or numeric literals linked by the arithmetic operators:
>
> - `+` Addition `*` Multiplication `**` Exponentiation
> - `-` Subtraction `/` Division (raising to a power)
>
> Parentheses may be included to denote the order of computations.
>
> Examples:
>
> ```
> ADD 1 TO WS-COUNT.            WS-COUNT is now equal to WS-COUNT + 1
> SUBTRACT 3.6 FROM SR-PER.     SR-PER is now equal to SR-PER - 3.6
> COMPUTE DL-PAY = IR-HOURS * IR-RATE * .20.
> ```

FIGURE 3-22
A SIMPLE FORM OF COMPUTE/ADD/SUBTRACT

The following rules must be strictly observed when using the COMPUTE statement (some compilers may be less restrictive—check your reference manual):

1. Arithmetic operators and the equal sign (=) must be immediately preceded and followed by at least one space.

2. There should be at least one space before each open parenthesis "(" and one space following each close parenthesis ")".

   ```
   COMPUTE PAY = REG-PAY + (HRS - 40) * 1.5 * RATE.
   ```

3. No space should follow the open parenthesis and no space should precede the close parenthesis.

4. No two arithmetic operators may follow one another.

5. A period may immediately follow a close parenthesis if it is the end of the sentence.

Examples of COMPUTE statements:

```
COMPUTE INTEREST = PRINCIPAL * RATE * DURATION.
COMPUTE CELSIUS = 5 / 9 * (FAHRENHEIT - 32).
COMPUTE AMOUNT = PRINCIPAL * (1 + INTEREST) ** YEARS.

COMPUTE PAYMENT = (INTEREST * PRINCIPAL / COMPOUND) /
    (1 - (INTEREST / COMPOUND + 1)
    ** (COMPOUND * YEARS) ).
```

The COBOL language is not designed to solve problems of a scientific nature. However, the COMPUTE verb does allow one to express any type of algebraic expression. The following examples of COBOL and equivalent algebraic expressions might benefit readers who feel unsure about interpreting algebraic expressions correctly.

COBOL EXPRESSION	ALGEBRAIC EXPRESSION
A	A
14	14
(A / B) * C	$\frac{A}{B} \cdot C$
A * B - 30.	$A \cdot B - 30$
-C	$-C$
(A * B) ** 2	$(AB)^2$
(-C + B) * D	$(-C + B)D$
A ** B	A^B
-3.7	-3.7
A ** .5	$\sqrt{A}$

INVALID COMPUTE STATEMENTS:

1. PAY = HOURS * RATE — COMPUTE verb missing.
2. COMPUTE HOURS * RATE = PAY — A data name, not an expression, should be to the left of the equal sign.
3. COMPUTE HOURS * RATE — No equal sign and no data name into which to store the result.
4. COMPUTE T = 3 (A + JB) — Operator missing after the 3.
5. COMPUTE T = A - (B + C * (K) — Unpaired parentheses. Should be A - (B + C * (K)).
6. COMPUTE T = X * - 3 — Two operators side by side. Should be X * (-3).
7. COMPUTE T = 3+4 — Spaces should precede and follow the + sign.
8. COMPUTE T = (3 + (2 * 4)) — Space should be provided between the last two parentheses.

In the case of examples 7 and 8, the user should check with his/her COBOL reference manual. Some COBOL compilers may accept 7 and 8 as written above.

Rules of Precedence for Arithmetic Operations

When there are parentheses in an expression, the operation within the parentheses is performed first.

Examples:

1.   *Expression*   *Evaluation*

            3 * (4 + 5)   3 * (4 + 5) = 3 * 9 = 27

    If parentheses are nested in an expression, then the operation in the innermost set of parentheses is performed first.

2.   *Expression*   *Evaluation*

            3 * (4 + (8/2))   3 * (4 + (8/2)) = 3 * (4 + 4) = 3 * 8 = 24

Operations within an expression are performed according to the following rules of precedence:

OPERATION	SYMBOL	PRECEDENCE
grouping	( )	highest precedence
exponentiation	**	↓
multiplication/division	* /	
addition/subtraction	+ −	lowest precedence

Operations with higher precedence are performed before operations with lower precedence, thus

$$4 * 3 ** 2 = 4 * 9 = 36$$

Additions/subtractions and multiplications/divisions are performed in order from left to right according to the rules of precedence, for examples

$$2 + 3/4 * 2 = 2 + .75 * 2 = 2 + 1.5 = 3.5$$

Exponentiations are performed in order from left to right, for example

$$2 ** 2 ** 3 = 2 ** 8 = 4 ** 3 = 64$$

Note that raising a number to the one half power is equivalent to calculating the square root of that number, for example, 4 ** 0.5 = 2.

The following example illustrates the rules of precedence.

3 ** 2 + (2 * 2 ** 3 / 4 + 1) − 2 / 3	Grouping then exponentiation
3 ** 2 + (2 * 8 / 4 + 1) − 2 / 3	Multiplication (left to right)
3 ** 2 + (16 / 4 + 1) − 2 / 3	Division
3 ** 2 + (4 + 1) − 2 / 3	Add (because of the parentheses)
3 ** 2 + 5 − 2 / 3	Exponentiation
9 + 5 − 2 / 3	Division
9 + 5 − .67	Addition
14 − .67	Subtraction
13.33	

Examples:

1. `A - B + C` — B is subtracted from A and the result is increased by C.
   `3 - 2 + 5` — (3 − 2) + 5 = 1 + 5 = 6

2. `A + B * C` — Since multiplication has priority, B * C is computed; the result is then added to A giving (B * C) + A.
   `3 + 2 * 3` — 3 + (2 * 3) = 3 + 6 = 9

3. `A / B * C` — Since multiplication and division have same priority, B is first divided into A, i.e., A/B, and the result of the division is multiplied by C. This is quite different from A / (B * C).
   `9 / 4 * 2` — (9/4) * 2 = 2.25 * 2 = 4.50

4. `A / B / C` — First A / B is performed and the result is divided by C. The answer would have been the same if A / (B * C) had been computed.
   `8 / 4 / 2` — (8 / 4) / 2 = (2) / 2 = 1

5. `A * B + C / D` — First A * B is performed. Then C is divided by D. The sum of the two results is then performed.
   `3 * 4 + 8 / 2` — 3 * 4 + 8 / 2 = 12 + 4 = 16

6. `(A + B) / C * D` — The parentheses indicate that the sum of A + B is to be performed first. The sum is then divided by C and the result is multiplied by D giving

   $$\frac{A+B}{C} * D \quad \text{and not} \quad \frac{A+B}{C * D}$$

   `(3 + 6) / 3 * 6` — 9 / 3 * 6 = 3 * 6 = 18

7. `A + B * C ** 2` — Since exponentiation has highest priority, C^2 is computed. This result is then multiplied by B since multiplication has the next highest priority. Finally this result is added to A giving ((C ** 2) * B) + A.
   `3 + 3 * 2 ** 2` — $3 + 3 * (2)^2 = 3 + 3 * 4 = 3 + 12 = 15$

8. `A ** B ** C` — Exponentiation is evaluated from left to right. Therefore A is raised to the power B. This result is raised to the power of C giving: ((A ** B) ** C), i.e., $(A)^B$ ** C.
   `3 ** 2 ** 3` — (3 ** 2) ** 3 = 9 ** 3 = 729

3–6 WRITING PROGRAMS

3–6–1 PROBLEM SPECIFICATION

An input file consists of an unknown number of records, each containing a name and two test scores. The physical layout of each record is as follows:

```
ARDEN LIZ    050060
JONES MIKE   060050
ABBOTT BRIAN 040090
```

Name: positions 1–12
Test1: positions 13–15
Test2: positions 16–18

STRUCTURE AND SYNTAX 99

Write a program to read this input file and produce the following report. Assume each printer line is 80 characters wide.

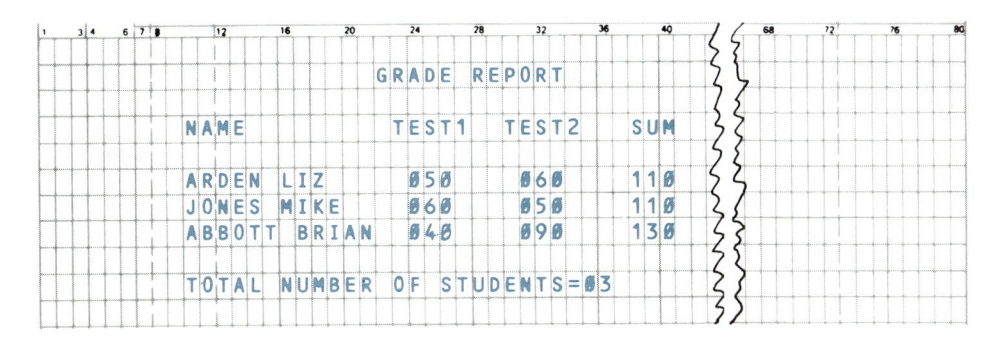

```
                   GRADE REPORT

        NAME           TEST1   TEST2   SUM

        ARDEN LIZ      050     060     110
        JONES MIKE     060     050     110
        ABBOTT BRIAN   040     090     130

        TOTAL NUMBER OF STUDENTS=03
```

3-6-2 PROGRAM ANALYSIS

The program to solve this problem is shown in Figure 3–23. Note the four different types of output lines in the final report. These lines are constructed in WORKING-STORAGE at lines 52, 57, 68, and 79. During execution of the program these records are successively moved into the output record for printing.

To ensure readability and structure, the coordinating module calls on four paragraphs to coordinate all program tasks. Note that paragraph 300-READ-RECORD is called from two different paragraphs (lines 93 and 122). Paragraph 400-PROCESS-RECORD terminates with a PERFORM statement at line 122; thus, after that PERFORM statement is carried out, control resumes at line 94.

To count the total number of records we initialize a counter WS-RECORD-COUNTER to 0 at line 40. Then we add 1 to that counter every time a record is read and processed (line 121). Note that the end-of-file record is not reflected in the count for WS-RECORD-COUNTER since the counting operation precedes the READ instruction.

3-6-3 TIPS AND HINTS

- To give your program breathing room and to improve its physical appearance, use blank lines (with asterisk in position 7 if necessary) to separate record descriptions and paragraphs from one another.

- Break down sentences consisting of two or more clauses over a number of lines, and use indentation for each successive line. For example, in Figure 3–23

  OPEN statement (lines 90, 91)

  PERFORM/UNTIL (lines 94, 95)

  WRITE/AFTER ADVANCING (lines 119, 126)

- Align PICTURE clauses within a record description; also align the VALUE clause. If the VALUE clause is too long for one line, type the literal separately on the next line, as shown at line 83.

Layout Design

The user is often responsible for designing the layout of the final report, i.e., he/she must decide where all the various headers, column titles, captions, et cetera must be positioned. This is a major task that can become quite frustrating un-

```
 1:      IDENTIFICATION DIVISION.
 2:      PROGRAM-ID. STUDENT-REPORT.
 3:      AUTHOR. JONES.
 4:      ***************************************************************
 5:      *                                                             *
 6:      *     THIS PROGRAM READS AN INPUT FILE WHERE EACH RECORD      *
 7:      *     CONSISTS OF A NAME AND TWO TEST SCORES. THE PROGRAM     *
 8:      *     PRINTS THE SUM OF THE TWO TEST SCORES AS WELL AS THE    *
 9:      *     NUMBER OF RECORDS READ.                                 *
10:      *                                                             *
11:      ***************************************************************
12:      ENVIRONMENT DIVISION.
13:      CONFIGURATION SECTION.
14:      SOURCE-COMPUTER. IBM.
15:      OBJECT-COMPUTER. IBM.
16:      INPUT-OUTPUT SECTION.
17:      FILE-CONTROL.
18:          SELECT REPORT-FILE  ASSIGN TO PRINTER.
19:          SELECT STUDENT-FILE ASSIGN TO DISK
20:          ORGANIZATION IS LINE SEQUENTIAL.
21:      *
22:      DATA DIVISION.
23:      FILE SECTION.
24:      *
25:      FD  STUDENT-FILE
26:          LABEL RECORDS ARE STANDARD
27:          VALUE OF FILE-ID IS 'ROSTER'
28:          DATA RECORD IS INPUT-AREA.
29:      01  INPUT-AREA PIC X(18).
30:      FD  REPORT-FILE
31:          LABEL RECORDS ARE OMITTED
32:          DATA RECORD IS PRINT-LINE.
33:      01  PRINT-LINE  PIC X(80).
34:      WORKING-STORAGE SECTION.
35:      *
36:      * INDEPENDENT ITEMS
37:      *
38:      01  FLAGS-AND-COUNTERS.
39:          05  WS-END-FILE         PIC XXX VALUE 'NO'.
40:          05  WS-RECORD-COUNTER PIC 99   VALUE 0.
41:          05  WS-SUM-TESTS        PIC 999.
42:      *
43:      * INPUT RECORDS
44:      *
45:      01  STUDENT-RECORD.
46:          05  SR-NAME  PIC X(12).
47:          05  SR-TEST1 PIC 999.
48:          05  SR-TEST2 PIC 999.
49:      *
50:      * OUTPUT RECORDS
51:      *
52:      01  MAJOR-HEADING.
53:          05 FILLER    PIC X(21) VALUE SPACES.
54:          05 FILLER    PIC X(12) VALUE 'GRADE REPORT'.
55:          05 FILLER    PIC X(47) VALUE SPACES.
56:      *
57:      01  MINOR-HEADING.
58:          05 FILLER    PIC X(09) VALUE SPACES.
59:          05 FILLER    PIC X(04) VALUE 'NAME'.
60:          05 FILLER    PIC X(09) VALUE SPACES.
61:          05 FILLER    PIC X(05) VALUE 'TEST1'.
62:          05 FILLER    PIC X(02) VALUE SPACES.
63:          05 FILLER    PIC X(05) VALUE 'TEST2'.
```

Input file:
```
ARDEN LIZ   050060
JONES MIKE  060050
ABBOTT BRIAN040090
```

Output file:
```
            GRADE REPORT

   NAME         TEST1   TEST2   SUM

   ARDEN LIZ     050     060    110
   JONES MIKE    060     050    110
   ABBOTT BRIAN  040     090    130

   TOTAL NUMBER OF STUDENTS=03
```

FIGURE 3–23
A GRADE REPORT

```
64:          05 FILLER     PIC X(03) VALUE SPACES.
65:          05 FILLER     PIC X(03) VALUE 'SUM'.
66:          05 FILLER     PIC X(39) VALUE SPACES.
67:     *
68:     01  DETAIL-LINE.
69:          05 FILLER     PIC X(09) VALUE SPACES.
70:          05 DL-NAME    PIC X(13).
71:          05 FILLER     PIC X(01) VALUE SPACES.
72:          05 DL-TEST1   PIC 999.
73:          05 FILLER     PIC X(04) VALUE SPACES.
74:          05 DL-TEST2   PIC 999.
75:          05 FILLER     PIC X(04) VALUE SPACES.
76:          05 DL-SUM     PIC 999.
77:          05 FILLER     PIC X(40) VALUE SPACES.
78:     *
79:     01  SUMMARY-LINE.
81:          05 FILLER     PIC X(09) VALUE SPACES.
82:          05 FILLER     PIC X(25) VALUE
83:                'TOTAL NUMBER OF STUDENTS='.
84:          05 SL-COUNT   PIC 99.
85:          05 FILLER     PIC X(42) VALUE SPACES.
86:     *
87:     PROCEDURE DIVISION.
88:     *
89:     100-COORDINATING-MODULE.
90:         OPEN INPUT STUDENT-FILE
91:              OUTPUT REPORT-FILE.
92:         PERFORM 200-WRITE-HEADINGS.
93:         PERFORM 300-READ-RECORD.
94:         PERFORM 400-PROCESS-RECORD
95:             UNTIL WS-END-FILE = 'YES'.
96:         PERFORM 500-TERMINATION.
97:         CLOSE STUDENT-FILE, REPORT-FILE.
98:         STOP RUN.
99:     *
100:    200-WRITE-HEADINGS.
101:        WRITE PRINT-LINE FROM MAJOR-HEADING
102:            AFTER ADVANCING 1 LINE.
103:        WRITE PRINT-LINE FROM MINOR-HEADING
104:            AFTER ADVANCING 2 LINES.
105:        MOVE SPACES TO PRINT-LINE.
106:        WRITE PRINT-LINE
107:            AFTER ADVANCING 1 LINE.
108:    *
109:    300-READ-RECORD.
110:        READ STUDENT-FILE INTO STUDENT-RECORD
111:            AT END MOVE 'YES' TO WS-END-FILE.
112:    *
113:    400-PROCESS-RECORD.
114:        MOVE SR-NAME   TO DL-NAME.
115:        MOVE SR-TEST1  TO DL-TEST1.
116:        MOVE SR-TEST2  TO DL-TEST2.
117:        COMPUTE WS-SUM-TESTS = SR-TEST1 + SR-TEST2.
118:        MOVE WS-SUM-TESTS TO DL-SUM.
119:        WRITE PRINT-LINE FROM DETAIL-LINE
120:            AFTER ADVANCING 1 LINE.
121:        ADD 1 TO WS-RECORD-COUNTER.
122:        PERFORM 300-READ-RECORD.
123:    *
124:    500-TERMINATION.
125:        MOVE WS-RECORD-COUNTER TO SL-COUNT.
126:        WRITE PRINT-LINE FROM SUMMARY-LINE
127:            AFTER ADVANCING 2 LINES.
```

FIGURE 3-23
(*continued*)

less a systematic approach is taken to solve such a problem. Many programs have been rerun just to readjust a caption here or a column there, only to cause further havoc or distortion to the report. The **solution** is as follows:

Method: First, purchase a printer layout worksheet. It is more than worth it! Then identify all different lines (in terms of format) that your program is expected to generate. For example, 2 header lines, 1 detail line, 1 summary line, et cetera, as in:

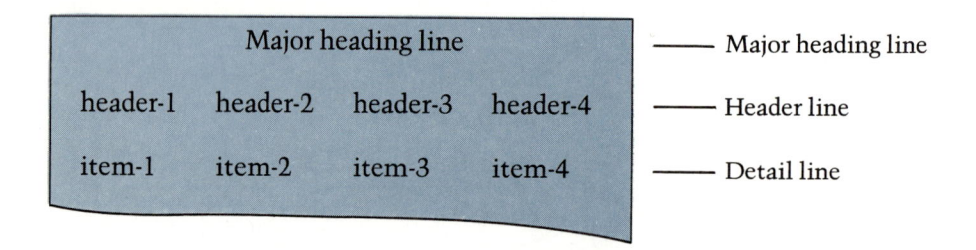

```
                  Major heading line              ——— Major heading line

   header-1   header-2   header-3   header-4      ——— Header line

   item-1     item-2     item-3     item-4        ——— Detail line
```

Then, before you describe the major heading and the header line records, start with header-1 and item-1 and decide which of the two is the widest (remember to choose an example data item that represents the maximum length of a field). Assume it is item-1. Enter on your printer layout worksheet a dummy field for item-1, and then position header-1 above item-1. Then go to header-2 and item-2. If header-2 is wider than item-2, write down header-2 and position item-2 below header-2. Repeat the same procedure until you run out of items.

Once this is completed, position your major and summary entries on the design form. Finally, code your record-description entries. The following diagram illustrates the sequence in which entries on the output form are assembled. In any event, do use a systematic approach.

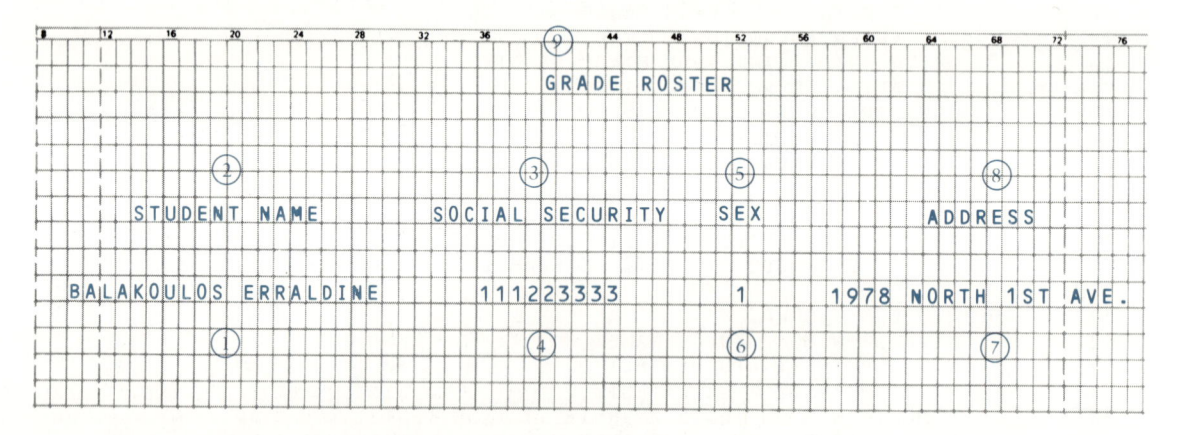

```
                                    GRADE ROSTER

        (2)                 (3)                 (5)              (8)
     STUDENT NAME        SOCIAL SECURITY        SEX           ADDRESS

     BALAKOULOS ERRALDINE   111223333            1         1978 NORTH 1ST AVE.
        (1)                 (4)                 (6)              (7)
```

3–6–4 ERRORS: COMPILE–TIME AND EXECUTION–TIME

Errors, unfortunately, go hand in hand with programming. To the novice programmer, however, errors should be viewed in a positive context, as lessons are quickly learned. (The programmer soon learns to be humble!) In fact, many lessons are learned, as COBOL does not scrimp in handing out a fascinating variety of error messages. Each COBOL compiler seems to affirm its own personality through its seemingly ever-expanding reservoir of warnings, diagnostics, and error messages.

The treatment of error messages is somewhat difficult due to the nonstandard manner in which COBOL compilers confront human errors. The best tool in error inquiry is the COBOL reference manual at the student's installation.

The most frequent errors occur as a result of forgetting a period or by improperly positioning a COBOL statement in margin A or margin B. COBOL prints its interpretation of the error in the source listing. It may or may not make sense. However, its very presence indicates something "fishy" in the neighborhood. This neighborhood may be the line immediately preceding the error message or the line(s) before it! One small error may cause the compiler to spew out literally hundreds of warnings or error messages.

Errors are not uncommon when writing programs. There can be keypunching/typing errors, grammatical errors, logical errors (the program does not solve the intended problem), execution errors, job control errors, or workflow errors. Errors (or *bugs* as they are commonly called) confront the beginner on all fronts. How good a programmer really is depends, to a certain extent, on his/her ability to *debug* (locate errors in) programs!

There are two distinct classes of errors that are likely to occur in a predefined time sequence during the processing of a program on a computer.

Compile-time Errors (Syntax Errors) and Warnings

These errors are caught by the compiler during the machine language translation process. They result from incorrectly structured statements or from not following grammatical rules. A list of these errors is generally provided on the printout form with the program listing.

Examples:

```
PEFORM WEEK-TOTALS.              The word PERFORM is misspelled.
WORKING STORAGE.                 Should be WORKING-STORAGE.
COMPUTE PAY = (HOURS - 40 * R.   Close parenthesis is missing.
```

In some systems, depending on the gravity of the syntactical errors and the number of errors, the job will be aborted at the conclusion of the compilation. (Why execute a set of unsound instructions?)

Always remember that the compiler merely translates COBOL statements into machine instructions; it does not execute the machine instructions and hence cannot determine whether the instructions (commands) are feasible or not.

Execution Time Errors (Logical Errors)

Logical errors are the traditional enemies of beginning and professional programmers alike. Logical errors are present in a program whenever the program does not solve the intended problem, i.e., the results produced by the computer are incorrect. Such incorrect results may occur because of one silly but critical typographical error or because of incorrect reasoning or an incorrect sequence of instructions. In between these extremes lie hundreds of other possible sources of errors.

Logical errors are the hardest ones to find in a program because the computer generally prints no error message during the execution of the program, i.e., as far as COBOL is concerned, the instructions are all syntactically sound and therefore the results must be correct.

A program will not solve the intended problem if logical errors are present. Logical errors are often very well camouflaged and can look perfectly innocent to the programmer as well as to the computer; for example the instruction COMPUTE PAY = HOURS + RATE is a perfectly valid instruction syntactically speaking but the result is clearly incorrect.

Thus, it is important that the programmer not put blind faith in whatever the computer prints out. The fact that the computer prints out numbers does not necessarily mean that those numbers are correct! The programmer should always check and analyze computer-produced results most carefully.

A logical error may also be picked up by the operating system. For example an instruction causing an infinite loop in the program may cause the message "time exceeded" to be printed. Similarly, a logic error causing 1000 pages of results to be printed may force the system to print "print limit exceeded."

Certain execution errors can cause immediate cancellation of the job. A list of execution-time errors, their codes, and meaning are provided by the system on the printout form. It is recommended that the reader consult the manufacturer's COBOL technical reference manual for a complete description and explanation of each of the different types of execution-time errors.

3-7 EXERCISES

3-7-1 TEST YOURSELF

1. Identify the four COBOL divisions and describe succinctly the purpose of each division.

2. What information can/should be present in the following columns (COBOL coding sheet):

   a. Columns 1–3   c. Column 7   e. Columns 73–80
   b. Columns 4–6   d. Columns 8–72

3. Which of the following are valid data item names? If invalid, write a corrected version.

   a. NET PAY   d. $COST   g. GROSS–PAY   j. ADD–SUBTRACT
   b. 111–AB   e. ZERO   h. PRODUCT.
   c. 123   f. A - B   i. ITEM–NAME

4. Which of the following are numeric literals? Nonnumeric literals? Figurative constants? If invalid, state the reasons.

   a. ZEROS   e. ALL "0"   i. SPACE   m. "50,000.25"
   b. –00056.3   f. $5.75   j. " "   n. –.5
   c. +3.   g. "SUBTRACT"   k. 10**2   o. 3*5
   d. 30,000   h. ALL   l. 3^2

5. Define the record structure to capture the following data. Assume the entire record is 80 positions long and preserve the approximate column positions. Use realistic data-item names.

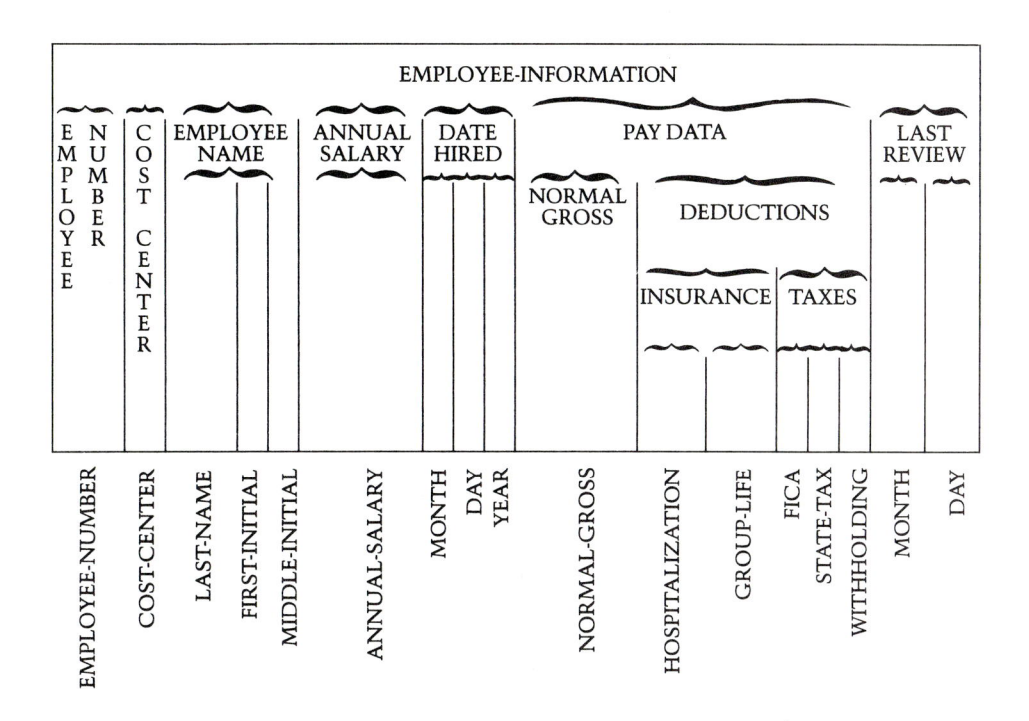

```
                                    EMPLOYEE-INFORMATION
                                              ⌒
┌─┬─┬────────┬───────┬──────┬─────────────────────────────┬──────┐
│E│C│EMPLOYEE│ANNUAL │ DATE │           PAY DATA          │ LAST │
│M│O│  NAME  │SALARY │HIRED │                             │REVIEW│
│P│S│        │       │      │ NORMAL  │   DEDUCTIONS      │      │
│L│T│        │       │      │  GROSS  │                   │      │
│O│ │        │       │      │         │                   │      │
│Y│C│        │       │      │         │ INSURANCE │TAXES  │      │
│E│E│        │       │      │         │           │       │      │
│E│N│        │       │      │         │           │       │      │
│ │T│        │       │      │         │           │       │      │
│ │E│        │       │      │         │           │       │      │
│ │R│        │       │      │         │           │       │      │
└─┴─┴────────┴───────┴──────┴─────────┴───────────┴───────┴──────┘
```

(labels, reading each column: EMPLOYEE-NUMBER, COST-CENTER, LAST-NAME, FIRST-INITIAL, MIDDLE-INITIAL, ANNUAL-SALARY, MONTH, DAY, YEAR, NORMAL-GROSS, HOSPITALIZATION, GROUP-LIFE, FICA, STATE-TAX, WITHHOLDING, MONTH, DAY)

6. In the following computer-produced reports, define a record description common to each of the output lines. Assume each line is 80 positions long.

   a.

   ```
                          GRADE REPORT

        DEPT         COURSE      TITLE         CREDIT      GRADE

        MATH         101         ALGEBRA         3           A
        MATH         103         GEOMETRY        3           B
        ENGLISH      100         COMPOSITION     4           C
   ```

   b.

   ```
        EMPLOYEE NO.                NAME                       NO.
        CODE     DEPT      FIRST    LAST      SEX           CHILDREN

        103      AMH       JOE      STARK      1              13
        200      MOC       LISA     TRAP       2              00
   ```

7. Design input record description entries to capture the following data:

   a. Name, courses (4 possible courses), student classification, sex, age, and address (number, street, city, zip (region, location)).
   b. Employee number, birth date (month, day, year), hours worked (regular, overtime), telephone (area code, number).

8. True or False.
   a. A data item can be a group item.
   b. An elementary data item can be a record name.
   c. A record is an example of a data item.
   d. An alphabetic data item can be specified using the X picture.
   e. Alphabetic data items cannot be processed arithmetically.
   f. Digit fields specified by the X picture can be processed arithmetically.
   g. Subordinate data items can be declared in a record description entry with an 01 level.
   h. FILLER fields are data items.
   i. Periods or semicolons can be used interchangeably for punctuation purposes.
   j. An asterisk in record position 8 means that the particular line of code is a comment statement.
   k. An 05 level number can be used to describe a record name.
   l. Level numbers may start in area A.
   m. An 01 level number can be used to describe an elementary data item.
   n. A record name must be described with an 01 level number.
   o. A COBOL statement must start in either column 8 or column 12.
   p. It is possible to write a PROCEDURE division without using reserved words.
   q. The letter X is a reserved word since it is used to describe alphanumeric picture clauses.
   r. The IDENTIFICATION division serves to identify the computing system.
   s. Records are described in the ENVIRONMENT division.
   t. The FD entry may be used to identify the name of the record associated with a particular input/output file.
   u. If PAYROLL is the name of an input file consisting of three records, the statement READ PAYROLL AT END STOP RUN. will cause the computer to read all three records into memory at one time.
   v. If A and B are alphanumeric data items containing 3 and 13, respectively, the sum A + B is equal to 16.
   w. Given the following: 01 A.
                               05 B PIC X(3).
                               05 C PIC 9(7).
   A reference to A implies a reference to the three characters at B.
   x. A Group item can consist of only one elementary item.
   y. The AT END phrase in the READ statement is optional.
   z. Record oriented input/output means that if 3 data items D1, D2 and D3 are to be read or printed, these 3 data items must be specified in the READ/WRITE instruction.
   aa. The WRITE statement must always specify the name of the record to be printed.
   bb. The READ statement must always specify the name of the record to be read.
   cc. In the instruction MOVE A TO B, the data in memory storage A is moved to storage B, leaving the contents of storage A unknown.
   dd. Columns 1 through 6 of a COBOL program may be left blank.
   ee. Margin A refers to columns 8–11 of the COBOL coding sheet.
   ff. MOVE A TO B MOVE A TO C. is correctly punctuated.
   gg. The IDENTIFICATION division identifies the author and the computer used to process the program.

STRUCTURE AND SYNTAX 107

hh. The ENVIRONMENT division, among other purposes, specifies the physical devices to be used by the program as well as the names selected by the programmer to represent his/her input/output records.
ii. The name given by the programmer to the input file is independent of the particular computer used.
jj. The FD entry identifies the physical devices used for input and output.
kk. A data item may not represent more than 30 characters of information.
ll. In a record description, subitems at successively lower levels of subdivision are defined by successively higher level numbers.
mm. In some cases, in a record description, elementary items need no PICTURE clauses.
nn. Entries with different level numbers must be indented in a record description.
oo. A group data item must not be described with the VALUE clause.
pp. The grammatical rules related to the naming of a paragraph are the same as those for naming data items.
qq. Numeric literals are composed of 1 to 30 digits with the plus (+) and minus (−) signs allowed as well as the decimal point.
rr. MOVE 1. TO X. is a valid COBOL sentence.
ss. Nonnumeric literal constants may not consist of more than 120 digits.
tt. MOVE "SPACES" TO SPACE–OUT is valid.
uu. MOVE SPACES TO "SPACES" is invalid.
vv. MOVE SPACES TO SPACES is valid.
ww. The sentence CLOSE INPUT CARD–FILE, OUTPUT PRINT–FILE is valid.

9. Are the following record descriptions valid or invalid? If a record description is invalid, explain why.

a.
```
01  CARD  PIC   X(80).
```

b.
```
40  A.
    05  B  PIC  X.
    05  C  PIC  X.
```

c.
```
01  X.
    02  Y  PIC  A.
    03  Z  PIC  X.
```

d.
```
01  PAY.
    49  NAME  PIC  A.
    49  EMP.
        55  KODE  PIC  X.
        55  DEPT  PIC  9.
    48  SCHOOL  PIC  XX.
```

e.
```
01  T.
    05  S.
        08  X.
            10  Z  PIC  9.
            10  T  PIC  X.
```

f.
```
01  T.
    05  S.
        08  X.
            10  Z  PIC  X.
            10  L.
                11  A  PIC  9.
```

g.
```
01  A.
    05  B.
        10  P  PIC  9.
        10  Y  PIC  99.
            20  Z  PIC  9.
```

h.
```
01  A.
    05  B.
        10  C  PIC  9.
        10  K  PIC  X.
    05  D.
        15  E  PIC  X.
        15  F  PIC  9.
```

i.
```
01  A
    05  B.
        10  X  PIC  9.
        10  Y  PIC  99.
    05  C.
        15  D.
            25  F  PIC  X.
```

```
j. 01 A.                          k. 01 ABC.
      05 B.                               10 FILLER    PIC  XX.
         10  C  PIC  9.                   10 ITEM-NAME XXX.
         10  K  PIC  XX.
      05 D.
         10  L  PIC  X.            l. 01 Z
         10  E  PIC  99.                  05 X  PIC  99.
      05 F.                                05 Z  PIC  XX.
```

10. Answer the following questions in one or two sentences:

    a. Why is it important that all input records have the same format or layout?
    b. Define what is meant by the COBOL source and object code.
    c. Why is it important to make a distinction between alphanumeric and numeric data items?
    d. Must the PROCEDURE division always read an input file?
    e. Differentiate between a statement and a clause.
    f. Derive four possible COBOL sentences from the following form of the SUBTRACT verb.

$$\text{SUBTRACT} \begin{Bmatrix} \text{name-1} \\ \text{literal-1} \end{Bmatrix} \begin{bmatrix} \text{,name-2} \\ \text{,literal-2} \end{bmatrix} \ldots \text{FROM} \ \ \text{name-3} \ \ \text{GIVING} \ \ \text{name-4} \ \ [\text{ROUNDED}]$$

    g. What are the largest positive and negative numeric literals?
    h. Specify the number of characters permitted in the longest nonnumeric literal.
    i. Are the OPEN and CLOSE verbs always required in the PROCEDURE division?
    j. Could you write a COBOL program without the ENVIRONMENT division? without the CONFIGURATION section?

11. Answer the following:

    a. Differentiate between a compilation error and an execution-time error; give examples of each.
    b. Write the code to perform the following:
        i. Skip a line and then print MAJOR–HEADING.
        ii. Print REPORT–TITLE, then skip two lines.
        iii. Print COLUMN–HEADING; on the next line print SUMMARY–LINE and then skip 3 lines.
        iv. Print MALE–REPORT, then on the same line print REPORT–NUMBER; on the next line print FEMALE–REPORT and then skip one line.
        v. Skip two lines, then print ROW–LINE, then skip 2 lines before printing DETAIL–LINE.
        vi. Separate HEADER–1 from HEADER–2 by one blank line.
    c. The sentence COMPUTE AVERAGE = WS–SUM / TOTAL–COUNT where TOTAL–COUNT is 0 is more likely to cause what type of error?

3-7-2 PROGRAMMING EXERCISES

1. Each input record consists of a person's name and address. Write a program to produce a mailing list similar to the following one. Note the two sets of addresses for each individual.

```
     ---------------------------          ---------------------------
     ADAMS JOEL                           ADAMS JOEL
     3241 N 12TH ST.                      3241 N 12TH ST.
     SIOUX CITY N.D. 21560                SIOUX CITY N.D. 21560
     ---------------------------          ---------------------------



     ---------------------------          ---------------------------
     GLEASON GARY                         GLEASON GARY
     1345 LINETREE DR.                    1345 LINETREE DR.
     PENSACOLA FL. 32504                  PENSACOLA FL. 32504
     ---------------------------          ---------------------------
```

2. Write a program to produce personalized form letters like the following one. Only the underlined words may be read from an input file.

```
THE SMITHS
123 NORTH ST
MOBILE    ALABAMA

DEAR MR AND MRS SMITH

ONLY YOU HAVE BEEN SELECTED IN THE MOBILE    AREA TO APPLY FOR OUR ONCE-
IN-A-LIFETIME SPECIAL ALUMINUM SIDING BARGAIN OF THE YEAR. THE SMITH
FAMILY SHOULD REJOICE IN HAVING THEIR DELIGHTFUL HOME AT 123 NORTH ST
BE RESTYLED WITH THE FINEST MATERIAL FROM ALABAMA.
                                        MANAGEMENT


THE DURKINS
212 SHADY AVE
PARIS     MAINE

DEAR MR AND MRS DURKIN

ONLY YOU HAVE BEEN SELECTED IN THE PARIS     AREA TO APPLY FOR OUR ONCE-
IN-A-LIFETIME SPECIAL ALUMINUM SIDING BARGAIN OF THE YEAR. THE DURKIN
FAMILY SHOULD REJOICE IN HAVING THEIR DELIGHTFUL HOME AT 212 SHADY AVE
BE RESTYLED WITH THE FINEST MATERIAL FROM MAINE.
                                        MANAGEMENT
```

Example of Input data

1-10	11-26	27-35	36-49
SMITH	123 NORTH ST	MOBILE	ALABAMA
DURKIN	212 SHADY AVE	PARIS	MAINE

3. Alpha College has very inflexible course schedules. All students must meet on Monday, Wednesday and Friday mornings from 8–9, 9–10 and 10–11 for

three distinct courses and on Tuesday and Thursday mornings from 9–10 for another course. Each record in an input file contains a student's schedule:

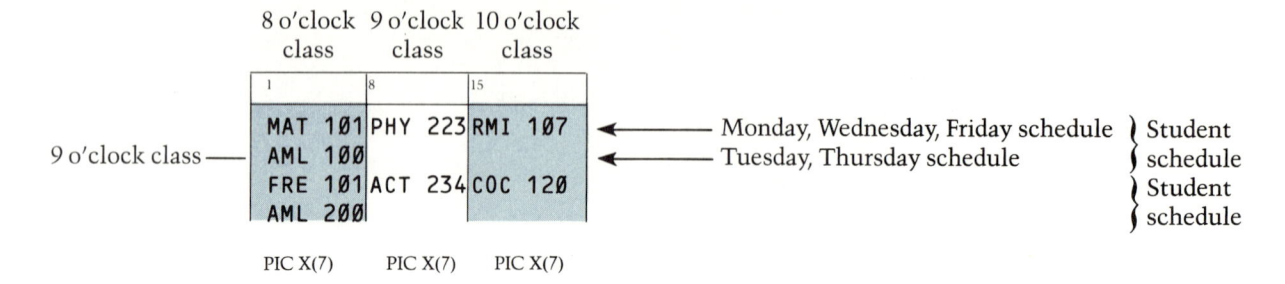

```
           8 o'clock  9 o'clock  10 o'clock
            class      class       class
           ┌─────────┬─────────┬─────────┐
           │1        │8        │15       │
           │MAT 101  │PHY 223  │RMI 107  │  ←── Monday, Wednesday, Friday schedule  ⎫ Student
9 o'clock──│AML 100  │         │         │  ←── Tuesday, Thursday schedule          ⎬ schedule
  class    │FRE 101  │ACT 234  │COC 120  │                                          ⎫ Student
           │AML 200  │         │         │                                          ⎬ schedule
           └─────────┴─────────┴─────────┘
            PIC X(7)  PIC X(7)  PIC X(7)
```

Write a program to provide each student with his/her weekly class schedule, as follows:

```
           MONDAY    TUESDAY   WEDNESDAY  THURSDAY   FRIDAY

  8- 9    MAT 101              MAT 101               MAT 101
  9-10    PHY 223   AML 100    PHY 223    AML 100    PHY 223
 10-11    RMI 107              RMI 107               RMI 107
```

4. Write a program to approximate the Julian date (introduced by Julius Caesar in 46 B.C.) equivalent to a calendar date given in the form: month, day. The Julian date is the day of the year. January 1 has Julian date 1, February 2 has Julian date 33, December 31 has Julian date 365, et cetera. A formula for approximating the Julian date is (month − 1) * 30 + day. Compute the Julian dates for November 7, May 25, and March 21 by reading an input file with the dates written in numeric form such as 1107, 0525, et cetera.

5. You work for a federal prison as a social worker and are asked to provide certain information about the prisoners. Data concerning prisoners is recorded as follows:

  1–10 Prisoner's last name.
  11–13 Sentence length in months.
  16–18 Month entered prison.
  20–23 Year entered prison.
  25–27 Age of prisoner when incarcerated.

A typical input file might be as follows:

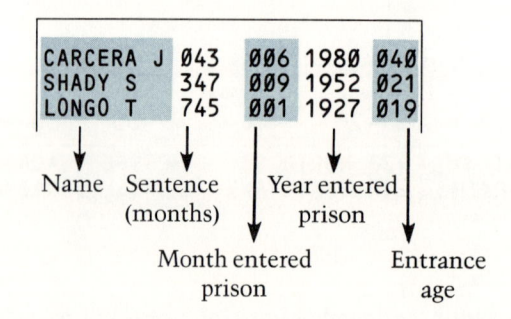

```
CARCERA J  043  006 1980 040
SHADY   S  347  009 1952 021
LONGO   T  745  001 1927 019
   │       │     │    │    │
   ▼       ▼     ▼    ▼    ▼
  Name  Sentence  Year entered  Entrance
        (months)    prison        age
                Month entered
                   prison
```

Write a program to indicate release time information about each prisoner (age at release time, year, and month of release) and produce a report similar to the following:

NAME	SENTENCE MONTHS	ENTERED PRISON AGE	YEAR	MONTH	RELEASE TIME AGE	YEAR	MONTH
CARCERA J	043	040	1980	006	044	1984	001
SHADY S	347	021	1952	009	050	1981	008
LONGO T	745	019	1927	001	081	1989	002

6. An input file consists of records showing the grades obtained in the various courses taken by a particular student. Each record identifies the subject area, the course title, the number of credits and the grade. Write a program to compute the grade point totals for each course. A sample input and output file are shown below:

Input file

```
MATH     1014A
MATH     1023B
FRENCH   1003D
LYCEUM   1501A
CHEM LAB 1172C
```

Output file

GRADE POINT REPORT

SUBJECT AREA	COURSE NUMBER	NUMBER CREDITS	GRADE	GRADE POINT TOTALS
MATH	101	4	A	12
MATH	102	3	B	09
FRENCH	100	3	D	03
LYCEUM	150	1	A	04
CHEM LAB	117	2	C	04

3-7-3 ANSWERS TO SELECTED EXERCISES

2. b. Individual labeling of lines
   d. Body of COBOL instruction
   e. Any information; identification sequence

3. a. Invalid (NET–PAY)
   c. Invalid (A123)
   e. Invalid (reserved word)
   g. Valid
   i. Valid

4. b. Numeric literal
   c. Invalid; must not end with decimal point
   e. Nonnumeric
   g. Nonnumeric
   h. Invalid
   i. Figurative
   j. Nonnumeric
   k. invalid (operation)
   m. Nonnumeric
   o. Invalid; (operation)

5.  ```
    01 EMPLOYEE-REC.
        05 EMP-NO              PIC 9(5).
        05 COST-CENTER         PIC 9(4).
        05 EMP-NAME.
            10 LAS             PIC X(13).
            10 FIRS            PIC X.
            10 MIDDLE          PIC X.
        05 SALARY              PIC 9(8).
        05 DATE-HIRED.
            10 MONTH           PIC 99.
            10 DAYS            PIC 99.
            10 YEAR            PIC 99.
        05 PAY-DATA.
            10 GROSS           PIC 9(8).
            10 DEDUCTIONS.
                15 INSURANCE.
                    20 HOSPITAL PIC 9(6).
                    20 GR-LIFE  PIC 9(6).
                15 TAXES.
                    20 FICA     PIC 9(6).
                    20 STATE    PIC 9(6).
                    20 WITHOLD  PIC 9(6).
        05 LAST-REVIEW.
            10 LR-MONTH        PIC 99.
            10 LR-DAY          PIC 99.
    ```

6. b.
    ```
    01 MAJOR-HEADING.
        05 FILLER PIC X(5)    VALUE SPACES.
        05 FILLER PIC X(12)   VALUE 'EMPLOYEE NO.'.
        05 FILLER PIC X(6)    VALUE SPACES.
        05 FILLER PIC X(4)    VALUE 'NAME'.
        05 FILLER PIC X(9)    VALUE SPACES.
        05 FILLER PIC XXX     VALUE 'SEX'.
        05 FILLER PIC XXX     VALUE SPACES.
        05 FILLER PIC XXX     VALUE 'NO.'.
        05 FILLER PIC X(35)   VALUE SPACES.
    01 MINOR-HEADING.
        05 FILLER PIC X(5)    VALUE SPACES.
        05 FILLER PIC X(12)   VALUE 'CODE    DEPT'.
        05 FILLER PIC XX      VALUE SPACES.
        05 FILLER PIC X(12)   VALUE 'FIRST    LAST'.
        05 FILLER PIC X(11)   VALUE SPACES.
        05 FILLER PIC X(8)    VALUE 'CHILDREN'.
        05 FILLER PIC X(30)   VALUE SPACES.
    01 OUTPUT-REC.
        05 FILLER PIC X(5).
        05 EMP-NO.
            10 CODE-NO PIC 999.
            10 FILLER  PIC X(5).
            10 DEPT-NO PIC XXX.
        05 FILLER PIC X(3).
        05 NAME.
            10 FIRST-N PIC X(7).
            10 FILLER  PIC X.
            10 LAST-N  PIC X(9).
        05 FILLER PIC X
        05 SEX    PIC X(6).
        05 FILLER PIC X(6).
        05 KIDS   PIC 99.
        05 FILLER PIC X(34).
    ```

8.
b. T	l. T	v. F	ff. T	pp. F
d. T	n. T	x. T	hh. F	rr. F
f. F	p. F	z. F	jj. F	tt. T
h. T	r. F	bb. F	ll. T	vv. F
i. F	s. F	cc. F	mm. F	ww. F
j. F	t. T	dd. T	nn. F	
    ```

STRUCTURE AND SYNTAX

9. c. Invalid. There should be no PICTURE clause for Y.
   f. Valid
   g. Invalid. Y is a group item.
   h. Valid
   j. Invalid. F needs PICTURE clause.
   l. Invalid. No period after Z.

10. a. Because only one record description is provided in the FILE SECTION.
    c. Because numeric items must be converted internally into an acceptable form before the arithmetic unit can process these operands.
    d. No, but generally the program will need input data in order to produce a report.
    e. A statement is used in the PROCEDURE DIVISION. A clause is generally used with entries in the other three divisions.
    f. ```
SUBTRACT X FROM Y GIVING Z.
SUBTRACT X, Y FROM Z GIVING T.
SUBTRACT 3, 4, T, -1.2 FROM AMT GIVING L ROUNDED.
```
    g. Largest numeric literal: $10^{19} - 1$ and $-10^{19} + 1$.
    h. 120 characters.
    i. Yes, if input and output files are to be processed, otherwise not.

11. a. A compilation error occurs during the translation phase (COBOL to object code), while an execution error occurs while the machine instruction(s) code corresponding to a COBOL instruction is actually being carried out by the arithmetic or logical unit.

    Examples: SUBTACT 3 FROM AMT. Compilation error (SUBTRACT)
    COMPUTE RESULT = TOTAL / NBER   Execution error if NBER = 0

    b. ii. ```
WRITE PRINT-LINE FROM REPORT-TITLE BEFORE ADVANCING 3.
```
       iii. ```
WRITE PRINT-LINE FROM COLUMN-HEADING BEFORE 1.
WRITE PRINT-LINE FROM SUMMARY-LINE BEFORE 4.
```
       iv. ```
WRITE PRINT-LINE FROM MALE-REPORT AFTER 1.
WRITE PRINT-LINE FROM REPORT-NUMBER AFTER 0.
WRITE PRINT-LINE FROM FEMALE-REPORT AFTER 1.
MOVE SPACES TO PRINT-LINE. WRITE PRINT-LINE AFTER 1.
```
       vi. ```
WRITE PRINT-LINE FROM HEADER-1 AFTER 1.
WRITE PRINT-LINE FROM HEADER-2 AFTER 2.
```
```

CHAPTER 4

THE EDITING PROCESS AND ARITHMETIC STATEMENTS

4.1 PROCESSING NUMBERS WITH DECIMAL POINTS

4.2 THE EDITING PROCESS

4.3 DATA TRANSFER THROUGH ARITHMETIC OPERATIONS

4.4 YOU MIGHT WANT TO KNOW

4.5 WRITING PROGRAMS

4.6 EXERCISES

INTRODUCTION Two important topics are the subject of this chapter. The first is the editing process, by which numeric output can be displayed with desirable features such as commas, decimal points, dollar signs, and other symbols. The second major topic is arithmetic operations; detailed instructions are given for using the ADD, SUBTRACT, MULTIPLY, and DIVIDE commands and several related options. Examples of COBOL programs and exercises are also included.

4–1 PROCESSING NUMBERS WITH DECIMAL POINTS

4–1–1 OVERVIEW

As we noted earlier, COBOL can carry out arithmetic operations (additions, subtractions, et cetera) *only* with numeric items, i.e., items that have a picture field of 9's. Internally, numeric items consist only of the digits 0 through 9; *no* other characters are allowed in the internal representation of a numeric item— no decimal points (.), no commas (,), no plus signs (+), and no minus signs (−). There is an exception in the case of the plus or minus sign, however, if a special form of the PICTURE clause is used to declare a numeric field. In that case the plus or minus sign occupies a separate position in the internal form of the number (see section 4–1–4).

Other than this exception, any data item that contains any character other than 0 through 9 is no longer considered numeric and therefore cannot participate in any numeric operation. For example, if A internally consists of the three characters ⟨3⟩⟨.⟩⟨1⟩ and B consists of the three characters ⟨0⟩⟨3⟩⟨.⟩ then it is not possible to add A and B together since neither is a numeric item (because of the decimal point). Similarly, it is not possible to add ⟨−⟩⟨3⟩⟨1⟩ to ⟨3⟩⟨2⟩ because of the minus symbol (−). Such fields are not numeric; they are alphanumeric. This discussion raises the following questions:

1. How can we process numbers with fractional parts, i.e., how can we add 32.4 to 4.6?

2. How can we process negative numbers, since the minus sign is not allowed as a character in the internal form of a number?

3. How can we read negative numbers?

4. How can we print numbers with decimal points, since no decimal point is actually present in the number, and similarly, how can we print the negative sign if the number is negative?

4-1-2 THE V SYMBOL: IMPLIED DECIMAL POINT

Consider the numeric internal representations for the numbers A, B, and C:

A: |1|2|3| B: |1|2|3| C: |1|2|3|

All three numbers seem to have the value 123! Yet, as far as COBOL is concerned, A could be used as 0.123, B could be 12.3, and C could be 1.23! Since the decimal point is not physically present in the number, how does COBOL know where the decimal point is? The answer is simple: by looking at the PICTURE corresponding to the particular item. The programmer notifies the computer of the assumed position of the decimal point by placing the symbol V at the desired position in the numeric string of 9's in the PICTURE clause. The computer then uses this marker for alignment purposes. Consider the following examples:

DATA ITEM DEFINITION	ASSUMED MEMORY CONTENT	VALUE TAKEN ON WHEN PROCESSED BY PROGRAM
77 A PIC 999V9	|1|2|3|4|	123.4
05 B PIC V9999.	|0|0|1|2|	.0012
10 C PIC 9V999.	|3|0|0|5|	3.005
05 D PIC 999V.	|0|1|6|	16.
77 E PIC 99V99 VALUE 2.34.	|0|2|3|4|	2.34
77 F PIC 9V999 VALUE .5.	|0|5|0|0|	.5

Note that the number of memory positions reserved for a numeric literal is equal to the number of 9's in the PICTURE clause. Thus item A above occupies four memory positions because its PICTURE clause has four nines. The symbol V is simply a position marker and does not occupy a memory location. It exists solely to inform the computer of the assumed position of the decimal point when that number is to be processed.

To understand how the computer processes numeric literals, consider the following numeric literals A, B and C.

```
A PIC 99V99.     |1|2|3|4|
B PIC 9999V9.    |2|1|9|8|2|
C PIC 9999V999.  |?|?|?|?|?|?|?|
```

and let us see how the computer adds A to B and stores the result in C. The computer, simply by looking at the four and five memory positions for A and B, does not know where the decimal point is (remember there is no decimal point physically present in the numbers), so it looks for the decimal marker V in each picture (for A and B) and aligns the digits of both numbers according to the assumed decimal point. This process can be visualized as follows:

PROGRAM LOGIC	DATA ITEM DEFINITION	MEMORY STORAGE BEFORE OPERATION	ALIGNMENT AND ARITHMETIC PROCESSING	MEMORY STORAGE AFTER OPERATION; RESULT IS STORED IN C
COMPUTE C = A + B	A PIC 99V99.	|1|2|3|4|	A |1|2|3|4|	A |1|2|3|4|
	B PIC 9999V9.	|2|1|9|8|2|	B |2|1|9|8|2| +	B |2|1|9|8|2|
	C PIC 9999V999.	|?|?|?|?|?|?|?|	C |2|2|1|0|5|4|0|	C |2|2|1|0|5|4|0|

4-1-3 NEGATIVE NUMBERS AND THE S SYMBOL

As we have seen, the internal representation of a numeric data item consists solely of the digits 0, 1, 2, ..., 8, 9. The sign of a numeric item is included in, or is a part of, the right-most digit. (An exception to this rule is discussed in section 4-1-4.)

The sign is a built-in code that is always present in the right-most digit of the numeric field. It is represented internally in the following symbolic form:

VALUE	INTERNAL REPRESENTATION	
+ 120		1	2	0⁺	
− 3		3⁻	
28		2	8		No internal sign symbol since 28 is assumed positive
− 0.0076		0	0	0	7	6⁻	

Note that the sign and the right-most digit together occupy only one memory position.

How does the user insert the sign in the right-most digit of the number? How does the programmer inform COBOL that a number may or may not take on a negative value? Is it sufficient, for example, to define A as PIC 999 VALUE −123 and hope that COBOL will sign A properly? The answer is no. The programmer must explicitly inform COBOL whether the number is to be signed. This is accomplished by prefixing the PICTURE field of the numeric literal with the symbol S. The S symbol informs COBOL that the number can either take on a positive or a negative value; the absence of the S symbol, however, implies that the number can never take on a negative value.

Examples:

DATA ITEM DEFINITION	INTERNAL REPRESENTATION	COMMENTS
1. AMT1 PIC ⓢ999 VALUE −132.	1 3 2̄	Because of the symbol S in AMT1, the number is negatively signed in the right-most digit.
2. AMT2 PIC ⓢ999 VALUE 132.	1 3 2	The symbol S does not affect the sign of the number, but AMT2 can now handle both positive and negative numbers.
3. AMT3 PIC ⑨⑨⑨ VALUE −132.	1 3 2	AMT3 is stored as a positive number since the symbol S is absent from the PICTURE clause.

The symbol S, like the symbol V, does not occupy a memory position. Thus PIC S999 and PIC S9V99 each occupy three memory positions. Also note that PIC 99V is identical to PIC 99.

The absence of the S symbol in the picture field of a numeric item implies that the item will always be treated as a positive number without regard to whether that number is initialized to a negative value (as in example 3 above) or whether a negative number is moved into the field, as in the following example:

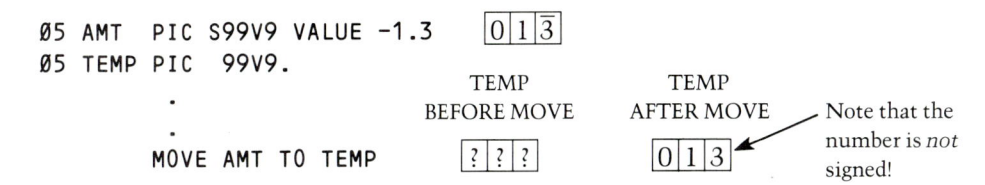

```
05 AMT  PIC S99V9 VALUE -1.3    |0|1̄|3|
05 TEMP PIC  99V9.
                                TEMP            TEMP
       .                        BEFORE MOVE     AFTER MOVE      Note that the
       .                                                        number is not
       MOVE AMT TO TEMP         |?|?|?|         |0|1|3|         signed!
```

Since TEMP is not signed (the symbol S is missing from its PICTURE field), the value stored in TEMP will be positive. To avoid errors of this kind, many programmers make it a habit always to include the S symbol in PICTUREs defining numeric items, as in the following PICTUREs for A, C, D, and E:

	PICTURE	FIELD LENGTH	MEMORY	VALUE	
A	PIC S9V.	1	|3̄|	−3.	
B	PIC V999.	3	|0|0|3|	.003	always positive
C	PIC S99V9.	3	|2|2|2̄|	−22.2	
D	PIC SV9999.	4	|0|0|3|2̟|	.0032	
E	PIC S99.	2	|1|0|	10.	
F	PIC 999V9	4	|1|2|3|4|	123.4	always positive

4-1-4 INPUT OF SIGNED NUMBERS WITH DECIMAL POINTS

Suppose you are to create an input file where each record consists of one signed number that is to be read under a S999V99 picture, and suppose the numbers are

$$111.55, \quad 20.6, \quad 0.05, \quad -3.02, \quad -21.3, \quad -2, \quad 3$$

The question arises: How are the numbers to be typed on the data records so that they will be read correctly? Two methods are presented. The first one is applicable to all IBM mainframes and IBM microcomputers, as well as to the majority of other systems. If, however, this method does not "work" on your system, consult your technical reference manual for appropriate information or switch to method 2.

Method 1

1. Each typed item on the data record should consist of exactly 5 positions (PIC S999V99). Leading and/or trailing zeros should be provided if necessary. The first three positions are those for the "whole" part of the number, while the last two are for the fractional positions.

2. If the number is negative, the right-most digit in the data field should be replaced by the corresponding character in the list below:

If the number is negative and the last digit is 1, type J instead of 1.

If the number is negative and the last digit is 2, type K instead of 2.

If the number is negative and the last digit is 3, type L instead of 3.

If the number is negative and the last digit is 4, type M instead of 4.

If the number is negative and the last digit is 5, type O instead of 5.

If the number is negative and the last digit is 6, type P instead of 6.

If the number is negative and the last digit is 7, type Q instead of 7.

If the number is negative and the last digit is 8, type R instead of 8.

If the number is negative and the last digit is 9, type S instead of 9.

If the number is negative and the last digit is 0, type } instead of 0.

(Depending on the system used, the symbol for negative 0 may be different than the right brace symbol }.)

3. Neither the decimal point nor the + or − symbols should be typed. As a result, the data file would take on the following appearance:

LIST OF NUMBERS		DATA FILE (1-9)	read in memory as
111.55	record #1	1 1 1 5 5	1 1 1 5 5 +
20.6	record #2	0 2 0 6 0	0 2 0 6 0 +
0.05	record #3	0 0 0 0 5	0 0 0 0 5 +
− 3.02	record #4	0 0 3 0 K	0 0 3 0 2 −
− 21.3	record #5	0 2 1 3 }	0 2 1 3 0 −
− 2	record #6	0 0 2 0 }	0 0 2 0 0 −
3	record #7	0 0 3 0 0	0 0 3 0 0 +

Method 2: Use of the SIGN clause with SEPARATE CHARACTER

Each typed number on the data record occupies six positions, with the leading or the trailing position reserved for the + or − character, depending on the SIGN clause of the PICTURE entry. In memory, the number is also read into six positions with the + or − sign occupying one memory position. To ensure that the + and − signs are treated as valid characters in numeric operations, the SEPARATE CHARACTER option of the SIGN clause must be used. The general form of the SIGN clause is:

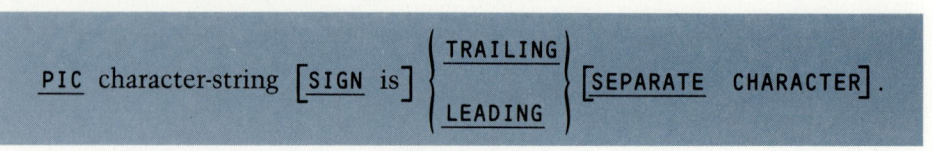

PIC character-string [SIGN is] { TRAILING / LEADING } [SEPARATE CHARACTER].

THE EDITING PROCESS AND ARITHMETIC STATEMENTS 121

If SEPARATE is not used, the sign of the number is either embedded in the trailing or leading digit of the number field, depending on the TRAILING or LEADING option used.

For our example, we will use the following PICTURE form:

```
PIC S999V99 SIGN IS { TRAILING / LEADING } SEPARATE CHARACTER.
```

Note that in this case the appropriate sign is stored as a separate character in memory i.e., the S symbol represents a memory position. With this option, our data file can be typed in either of the two following ways:

PIC S999V99 SIGN IS TRAILING SEPARATE.   PIC S999V99 SIGN IS LEADING SEPARATE.

	DATA FILE	MEMORY STORAGE	DATA FILE	MEMORY STORAGE
record #1	11155+	11155+	+11155	+11155
record #2	02060+	02060+	+02060	+02060
record #3	00005+	00005+	+00005	+00005
record #4	00302−	00302−	−00302	−00302
record #5	02130−	02130−	−02130	−02130
record #6	00200−	00200−	−00200	−00200
record #7	00300+	00300+	+00300	+00300

Many signed numbers can be read from one record, as illustrated by the following example:

```
01 SIGNED-NUMBERS.
   05 A PIC S99V99.
   05 B PIC SV999 TRAILING SEPARATE.
   05 C PIC S999   LEADING SEPARATE.
```

Stored in memory as

After READ operation:
A: 0134
B: 032−
C: +123

data record → 0134 032− +123   A = 1.34, B = −0.032, C = 123
              A   B   C

With these definitions for A, B, and C, it is now possible, for example, to add A to B, or add B to C, even though B and C internally contain the + or − character.

Once again arithmetic operations can be performed only on numeric data items. In the memory of the computer, a numeric data item is expressed only in terms of the digits 0 through 9 and a special code for the sign, which is always included in (part of) the right-most digit (except when the SIGN SEPARATE option is used). The presence of any other character in a numeric field (except for the + and − characters in the SIGN SEPARATE option) will cause an error to take place if an arithmetic operation is to be carried out on the data item. Consider the following values and their internal numeric representation:

VALID NUMERIC FIELDS

NUMERIC VALUE	PICTURE	INTERNAL REPRESENTATION
+120	S9V99	|1|2|0⁺|
−3	S9	|3⁻|
28	99		2	8	

Internal representation for numeric values consists solely of the digits 0–9 and the sign code.

Numbers of this form can be processed numerically.

The following memory character fields do not define values that can be processed numerically:

INVALID NUMERIC FIELDS

CHARACTER FIELD	PICTURE	INTERNAL REPRESENTATION	
12.35	PIC 999V99.	|1|2|.|3|5|	. is an illegal character.
−123	PIC XXXX.	|−|1|2|3|	invalid picture field for numeric processing.
1,558	PIC 9999.	|1|,|5|5|8|	, is an illegal character.

Fields to be processed numerically must contain only digits 0–9 and an internal sign code.

In the first of the three invalid examples, the reader may wonder how it is possible to initialize a numeric picture field 999V99 so that its resulting internal field consists of the characters |1|2|.|3|5| . We know that PIC 999V99 VALUE 12.35 yields an internal field |0|1|2|3|5| . The only way these five characters (12.35) can be stored in a picture field 999V99 is if they are read from a data record. This can be done, and *no* READ error will occur, since COBOL does not check the field type into which the data is to be read. An error will occur, however, as soon as any arithmetic operations are to be carried out on that field (12.35), since the arithmetic unit does not recognize the period as a digit!

4-2 THE EDITING PROCESS

Since no decimal point is recorded internally for a number that is to be processed numerically, the question may be asked, How is the decimal point printed on the output form? For that matter, how can dollar signs, negative signs, and commas be edited into numerical results? How can leading 0's be suppressed and changed into blanks to produce realistic report entries such as one sees in invoices, bank statements, and accounting reports? The answer to all these questions is that the programmer tells the computer where to physically place the decimal point, the commas, the dollar signs, et cetera by means of a preformatted PICTURE field.

COBOL allows the user to construct preformatted PICTURE fields (sometimes referred to as *numeric edited* or *report items*) where the decimal point

THE EDITING PROCESS AND ARITHMETIC STATEMENTS 123

and other characters such as the dollar sign or the comma are physically present in the report field. The programmer then MOVEs the numeric result to be printed into the numeric edited field. Under the MOVE instruction, the computer inserts the digits of the numeric field into the report field (to the left and to the right of the already present decimal point) in such a way that alignment of the decimal point is observed. This final edited field is no longer a numeric field but an alphanumeric field, and thus it can no longer be processed arithmetically.

As an example, suppose we want to print the sum of AMT1 (PIC 99V99) and AMT2 (PIC 99V99) in such a way that the resulting field displays 2 fractional digits, the decimal point, and no leading 0's. A special field called a *numeric edited field* is created for that purpose as follows:

```
05 RL-TOTAL PIC ZZZ.99.
```

This field occupies 6 memory positions—3 positions are reserved for the whole part of the number, 2 for the fractional part, and 1 for the decimal point. The character Z is a *replacement character*, just like the 9 character, except that it replaces leading 0's with blank spaces. The period is called an *insertion character*, and it physically occupies one position in the numeric edited field. When the sum of the two numbers is moved into the numeric edited field, the three whole digits are placed to the left of the decimal point and the two fractional digits are positioned to the right of the decimal point. Leading 0's, if any, are replaced by blank spaces. For example, if AMT1 = 17.35 and AMT2 = 14.22, then the sum 31.57 is edited as follows:

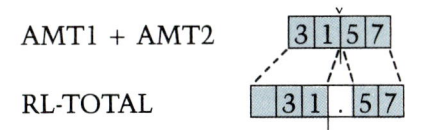

AMT1 + AMT2   3157

RL-TOTAL   31 . 57

The entire process is illustrated in Figure 4–1

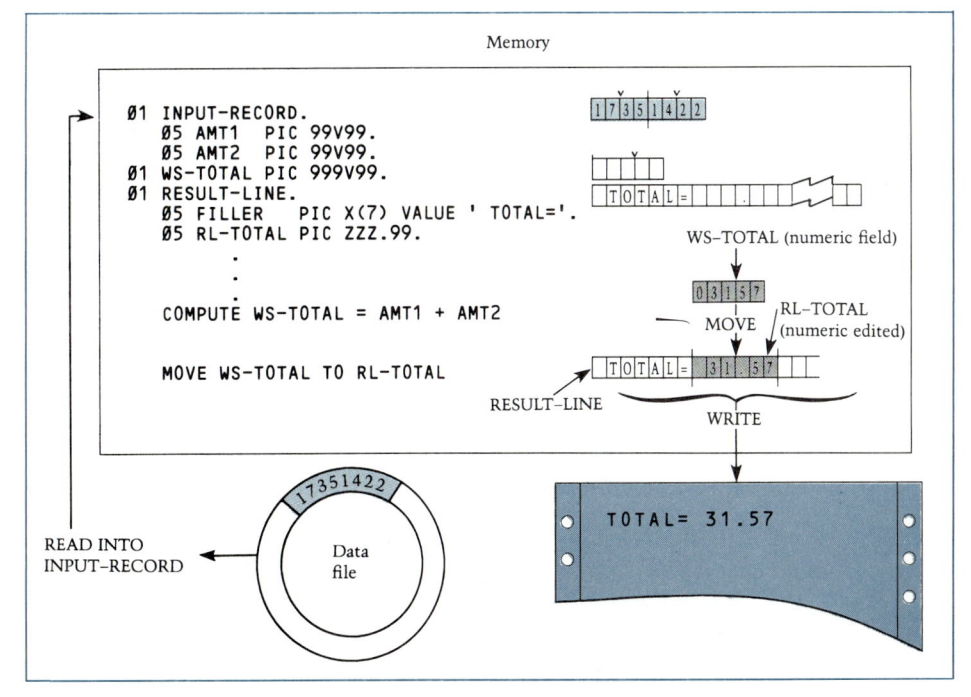

FIGURE 4–1

READING, ADDING, EDITING, AND WRITING

124 UNDERSTANDING STRUCTURED COBOL

Note the difference between the following report fields used for output purposes and the numeric fields used for input or computational purposes:

NUMERIC EDITED DATA ITEMS (FOR OUTPUT)	MEMORY STORAGE	NUMERIC DATA ITEMS (FOR INPUT OR COMPUTATION)	MEMORY STORAGE
05 N1 PIC 99.99.	☐☐.☐☐	05 N1 PIC S99V99.	☐☐ᵥ☐☐
05 N2 PIC 9.999.	☐.☐☐☐	05 N2 PIC 9V999.	☐ᵥ☐☐☐
05 N3 PIC 999.	☐☐☐	05 N3 PIC S999V.	☐☐☐ᵥ
05 N4 PIC .9999.	.☐☐☐☐	05 N4 PIC V9999.	ᵥ☐☐☐☐

From input to output, the evolution of numeric data generally goes through the following phases:

INPUT   Read the numeric data into memory.
↓
PROCESS   Calculate, compare, add, multiply, et cetera.
↓
EDIT   Prepare for output by dressing up results.
↓
OUTPUT   Write out the results.

The editing process is illustrated in Figure 4–2.

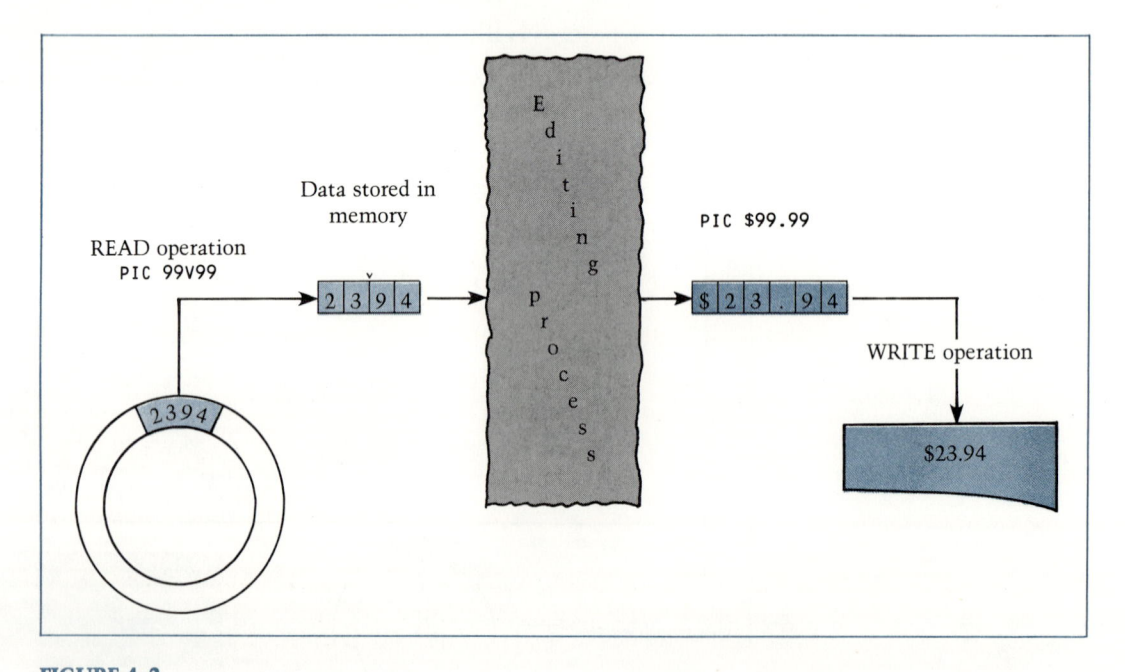

FIGURE 4–2
THE EDITING PROCESS The editing process is carried out by certain arithmetic instructions and the MOVE instruction.

4-2-1 DATA TRANSFER

Other than the READ and WRITE instructions, which transfer data externally in and out of the computer, the only COBOL instructions that transfer data internally are:

- The MOVE instruction, whose general form is shown in Figure 4-3.
- The arithmetic instructions: ADD, SUBTRACT, MULTIPLY, and DIVIDE with the GIVING clause and the COMPUTE verb.

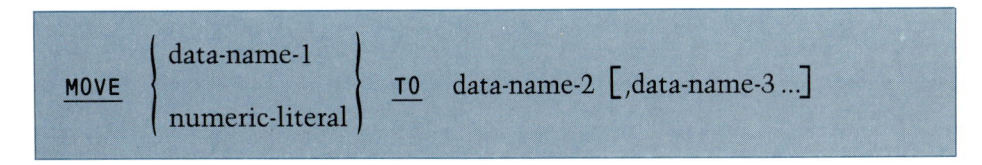

$$\underline{\text{MOVE}} \left\{ \begin{array}{c} \text{data-name-1} \\ \text{numeric-literal} \end{array} \right\} \underline{\text{TO}} \text{ data-name-2 } [\text{,data-name-3} \ldots]$$

FIGURE 4-3
GENERAL FORM OF THE MOVE STATEMENT

When data is transferred from one memory area to another using the MOVE instruction, it usually goes through an editing process that may or may not involve numeric edited fields. It is important to realize that these transfers can affect the value of the data. For example, what happens if a 5-digit data item is moved into a 3-digit numeric field?

Case 1: MOVE between numeric fields.

If the receiving field is larger than the sending field, the implied decimal point position of the sending item is aligned with the implied decimal point position of the receiving field. Any unfilled positions on either end of the receiving field are filled with 0's.

If the receiving field is smaller than the sending field, the implied decimal point position of the sending item is aligned with the implied decimal point position of the receiving field; the excess digits of the sending item are truncated on either or both ends of the decimal point in the receiving field.

In the examples in this section, we will illustrate data transfer using the following graphic notation:

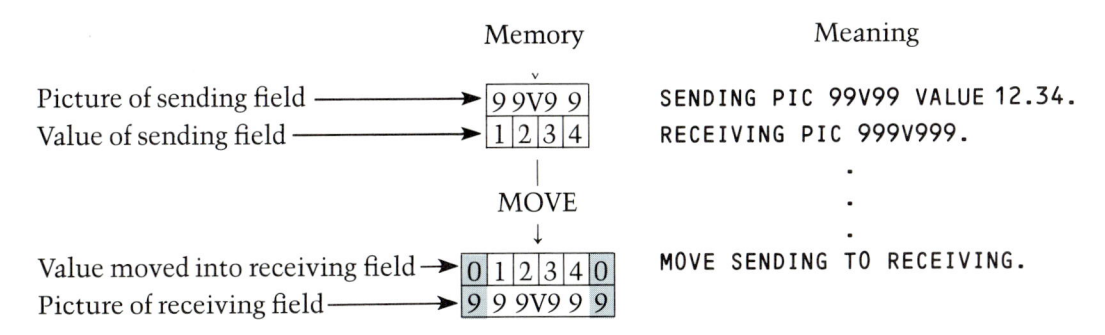

```
                              Memory                    Meaning

Picture of sending field ──▶  9 9V9 9      SENDING PIC 99V99 VALUE 12.34.
Value of sending field  ──▶  1 2 3 4       RECEIVING PIC 999V999.
                                |                      .
                              MOVE                     .
                                ↓                      .
Value moved into receiving field ──▶ 0 1 2 3 4 0    MOVE SENDING TO RECEIVING.
Picture of receiving field ──▶ 9 9 9V9 9 9
```

In this case, the receiving field is wider on both ends than the sending field, hence leading and trailing 0's are provided.

Examples: In all the following examples the shaded areas display the results.

DATA TRANSFER | EXPLANATION

1. `MOVE 123.45 TO` | 9 9V9 | → 9 9 9V9 9 / 1 2 3 4 5 — MOVE → 2 3 4 / 9 9V9 | Receiving field is smaller on both sides of the decimal point; truncation of leading and trailing digits.

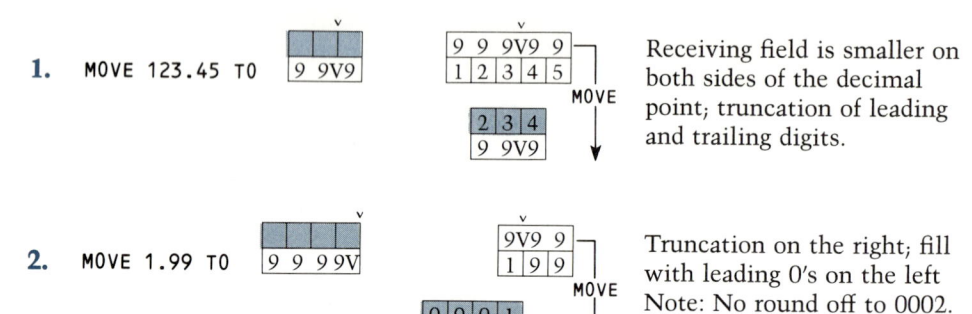

2. `MOVE 1.99 TO` | 9 9 9 9V | → 9V9 9 / 1 9 9 — MOVE → 0 0 0 1 / 9 9 9 9V | Truncation on the right; fill with leading 0's on the left. Note: No round off to 0002.

Note that COBOL does not inform the programmer directly when the truncation process occurs. But when truncation does occur, the sign of the number is not lost, i.e., if the number is negative, it remains negative, as in example 3.

`MOVE -1.234 TO` | 9 9V9 9 | → 9V9 9 9 / S 1 2 3 4 — MOVE → 0 1 2 3 / S 9 9V9 9 | Fill with leading 0's. Truncate on the right. The sign is not lost, however.

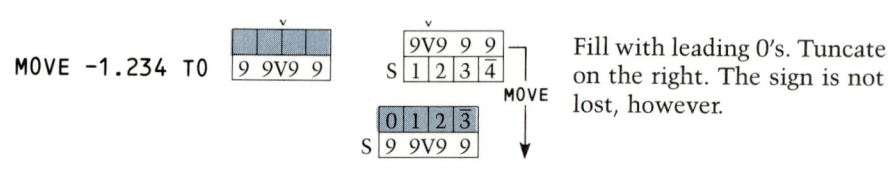

Consider the following cases where negative numbers are transferred:

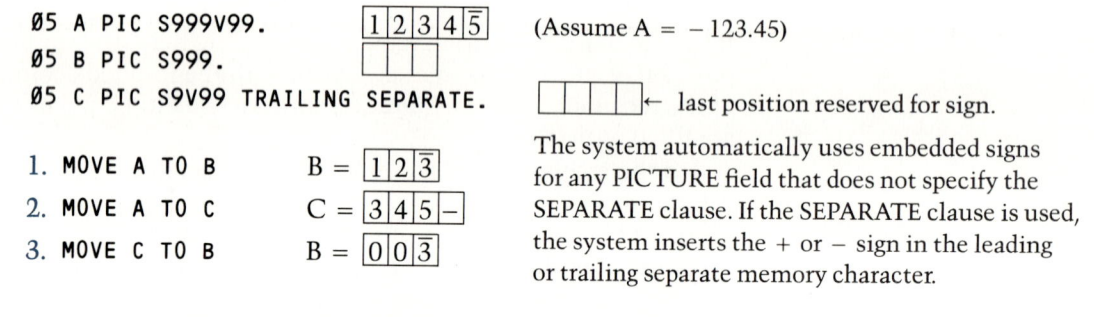

```
05 A PIC S999V99.        1 2 3 4 5̄      (Assume A = -123.45)
05 B PIC S999.
05 C PIC S9V99 TRAILING SEPARATE.    ☐☐☐☐ ← last position reserved for sign.
```

1. `MOVE A TO B`   B = 1 2 3̄
2. `MOVE A TO C`   C = 3 4 5 –
3. `MOVE C TO B`   B = 0 0 3̄

The system automatically uses embedded signs for any PICTURE field that does not specify the SEPARATE clause. If the SEPARATE clause is used, the system inserts the + or − sign in the leading or trailing separate memory character.

Case 2: MOVE between alphanumeric fields.

In the case of alphanumeric MOVEs:

- If the receiving field is smaller than the sending field, truncation of excess characters occurs to the right.
- If the receiving field is wider than the sending field, blanks pad the receiving field to the right.

Examples:

DATA TRANSFER | EXPLANATION

1. `MOVE 'HELLO' TO` | A A | → A A A A A / H E L L O — MOVE → H E | Receiving field too small; truncation occurs on the right.

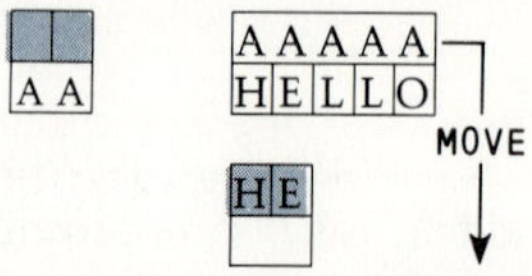

2. MOVE '32 NORTH' TO ⬚⬚⬚   Receiving field too small; truncation on the right.

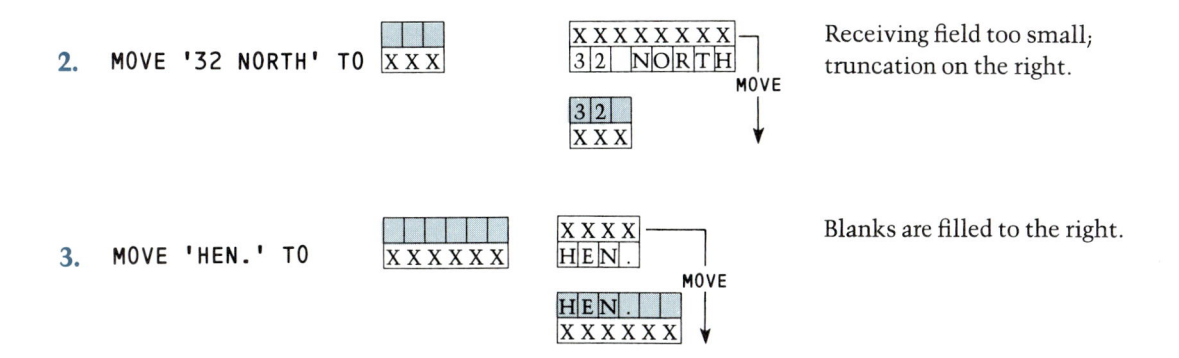

3. MOVE 'HEN.' TO ⬚⬚⬚⬚⬚⬚   Blanks are filled to the right.

Initialization of data names through the VALUE clause in a PICTURE field is subject to the same rules as specified above in cases 1 and 2. Consider the following examples:

1.	SALES-AMOUNT	PIC 9999V99	VALUE 23.4.	`002340`	Leading and trailing 0's.
2.	NEGATIVE-NO	PIC S999	VALUE -3.9.	`003`	Truncation on the right.
3.	AMOUNT	PIC 99	VALUE 789.	`89`	Truncation on the left
4.	FILLER	PIC X(5)	VALUE 'THE EARTH'.	`THE E`	Truncation on the right.
5.	FILLER	PIC X(5)	VALUE 'A'.	`A`	Fill to the right with blanks.

Case 3: MOVE from numeric to numeric edited fields.

Writing a business or scientific report generally involves writing out numerical information that should be readable and self-explanatory. In a business report a host of special characters are generally used to refine computed numerical results: Numbers may be prefixed with a currency symbol such as a dollar sign and will generally include a decimal point with two trailing digits. Numbers with large magnitudes might sport commas. A string of asterisks often prefaces a dollar amount in computer-printed checks. In some accounting reports, the credit symbol (CR) and debit symbol (DB) are appended to the right-most digit in the number field. In other reports the symbols + or − might prefix the result. Leading zeros are generally suppressed.

COBOL allows the programmer to prepare a numeric edited field (report field) containing insertion characters (see Figure 4-4) such as the dollar symbol ($), the comma (,) and the decimal point (.). For example, it is possible to dress up raw data into refined data as follows:

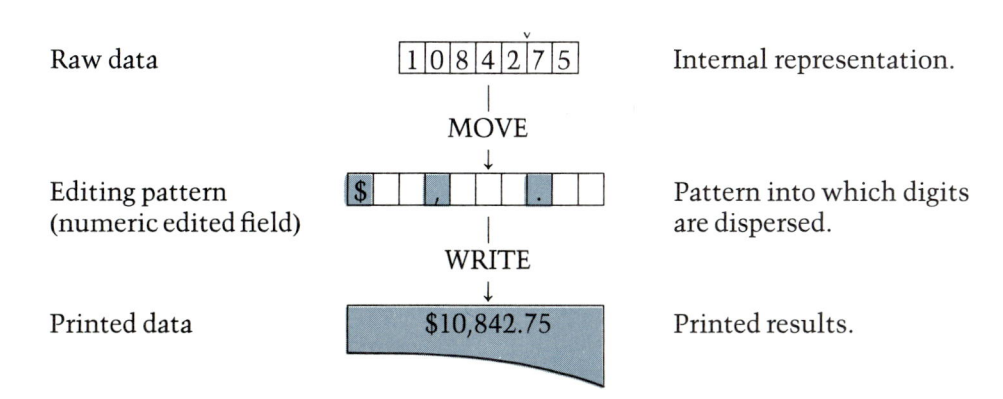

Raw data	`1084275`	Internal representation.
	↓ MOVE	
Editing pattern (numeric edited field)	`$ , .`	Pattern into which digits are dispersed.
	↓ WRITE	
Printed data	$10,842.75	Printed results.

Insertion Characters

.	Insert a decimal point.
,	Insert a comma. Comma is suppressed if all digits to left of the comma are 0's; it is replaced by a blank space, an asterisk or a $ sign depending on the replacement character used in the picture field.
$ or £	Currency symbol is inserted to the left of the left-most digit or decimal point.
B	Insert a blank.
/	Insert a slash where present (check your system for this character).
+, −	Can be used as first or last character of edited field. Will insert a + or − character as first or last character in output field.
CR, DB	Occupies two characters in report field. If the number is negative, either DB or CR will be printed as the two right-most characters of the output field. Otherwise (if the number is positive) the two right-most characters will be blank.

Replacement Characters

Z	Replace leading 0's and suppressed commas with blanks. One or more consecutive Z's can be used.
*	Replace leading 0's and suppressed commas by asterisks. One or more consecutive *'s may be used.
$, −, +	A leading string of identical symbols will cause the particular symbol used to be placed to the immediate left of the first non-zero digit. Any leading zeros or suppressed commas will be replaced by blanks, asterisk, or a $ sign depending on the replacement character used.

FIGURE 4–4
EDITING CHARACTERS

COBOL also allows the programmer to use replacement characters (Figure 4–4) such as Z or asterisk (*) that will cause leading 0's to be replaced with leading blanks or asterisks. For example:

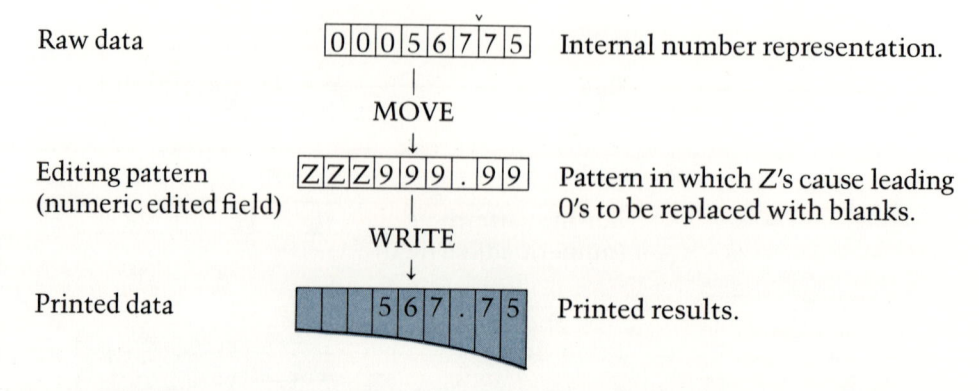

Raw data   `0 0 0 5 6 7 5`   Internal number representation.

MOVE

Editing pattern   `Z Z Z 9 9 9 . 9 9`   Pattern in which Z's cause leading
(numeric edited field)   0's to be replaced with blanks.

WRITE

Printed data   `    5 6 7 . 7 5`   Printed results.

The use of replacement and insertion characters in preparing numeric edited fields will be the subject of sections 4–2–3 through 4–2–10.

4-2-2 DO IT NOW

1. Answer true or false:
   a. The memory string $\boxed{1|2|.|3}$ cannot be processed numerically.
   b. The memory string $\boxed{+|1|2|3}$ can be processed numerically if the PICTURE field specifies the SEPARATE CHARACTER option.
   c. The number of memory positions reserved for PIC SV99 is two.
   d. PIC VS999 is a valid picture clause.
   e. A PIC S99V9 VALUE − 1.299 will give rise to A: $\boxed{0|1|\overline{3}}$ internally.

2. Display the memory positions of the receiving field as a result of successively carrying out the operations a–f.

   ```
   A PIC S999V9   LEADING SEPARATE VALUE -10.3.
   B PIC S999     TRAILING SEPARATE.
   C PIC S99V9.
   D PIC S99V9    VALUE -123.4.
   E PIC 99V999   VALUE -0.06.
   ```
   a. MOVE A TO B.
   b. MOVE A TO C
   c. MOVE C TO B
   d. MOVE D TO C
   e. COMPUTE B = A**2 + .89
   f. MOVE E TO A

ANSWERS

1. a. True
   b. True
   c. True
   d. False (The symbol S must come first)
   e. False $\boxed{0|1|\overline{2}}$

2. a. $\boxed{0|1|0|-}$ b. $\boxed{1|0|3|-}$ c. $\boxed{0|1|0|-}$
   d. $\boxed{2|3|\overline{4}}$ e. $\boxed{1|0|6|+}$ f. $\boxed{+|0|0|0|0}$

4-2-3 EDITING WITH THE DECIMAL POINT (.)

The implied decimal position of the incoming numeric item is aligned with the explicit decimal point position in the edited numeric field. Any unfilled positions on either end of the edited numeric field are filled with 0's. If the incoming numeric data item contains more digits than positions available in the receiving field on either side of the decimal point, the excess digits of the incoming data item are truncated.

Examples:

DATA TRANSFER

1. MOVE 12.83 TO `| | |.| | |` / `|9|9|.|9|9|`

`|9|9V9|9|` / `|1|2|8|3|` MOVE `|1|2|.|8|3|` / `|9|9|.|9|9|`

EXPLANATION

If the numerical value 1283 with PICTURE 99V99 is moved into report field with PICTURE 99.99, the edited result will be 12.83.

DATA TRANSFER

EXPLANATION

2. MOVE 10.83 TO `9999.999`

```
 9 9V9 9
 1 0 8 3    MOVE
 0 0 1 0 . 8 3 0
 9 9 9 9 . 9 9 9
```

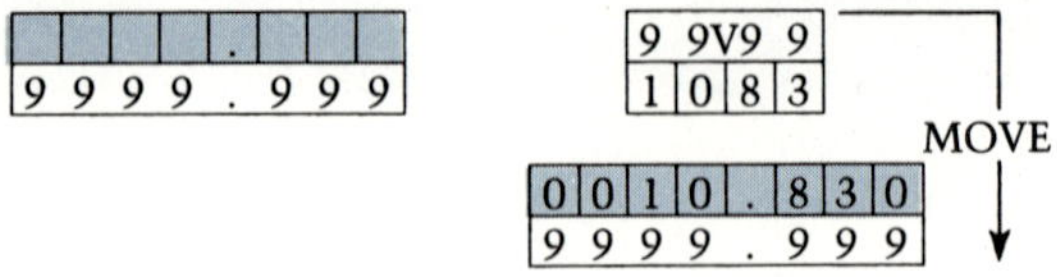

Leading and trailing 0's are provided. Result field occupies 8 characters.

3. MOVE 10.83 TO `99`

```
 9 9V9 9
 1 0 8 3    MOVE
 1 0
 9 9
```

Digits are truncated to the right of the decimal point.

4. MOVE 10.83 TO `9.9`

```
 9 9V9 9
 1 0 8 3    MOVE
 0 . 8
 9 . 9
```

Leading and trailing digits are truncated. Result field is 3 characters.

5. MOVE 10.83 TO `999.9`

```
 9 9V9 9
 1 0 8 3    MOVE
 0 1 0 . 8
 9 9 9 . 9
```

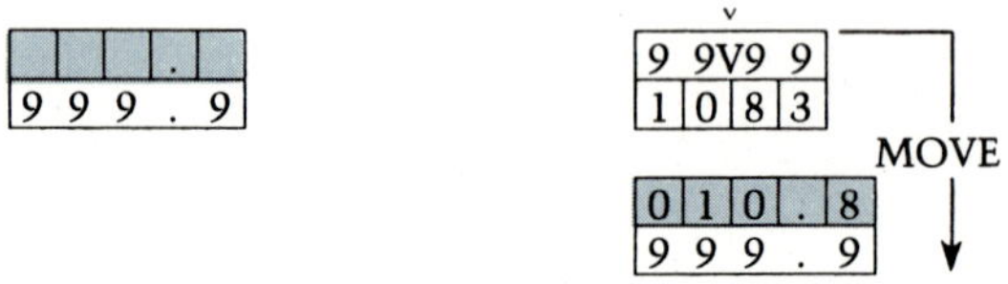

Leading 0's are provided; trailing digit truncated.

6. MOVE 12.96 TO `9.`

```
 9 9V9 9
 1 2 9 6    MOVE
 2 .
 9 .
```

Truncation on both sides; result field is two characters.

When truncation occurs, no error message is given and the edited result is *not* rounded off.

4-2-4 EDITING WITH THE ZERO SUPPRESSION CHARACTER Z

The Zero suppression character Z suppresses leading zeros and replaces them with blanks. Zero suppression terminates when the first nonzero digit is encountered (examples 1 and 3) or when the decimal point is encountered (example 4), whichever comes first. If the sending value is 0 and the edited field is all Z's, the entire edited field will be blank (example 6).

DATA TRANSFER

EXPLANATION

1. MOVE 200 TO `ZZZZ`

```
 9 9 9 9
 0 0 2 0 0   MOVE
     2 0 0
 Z Z Z Z
```

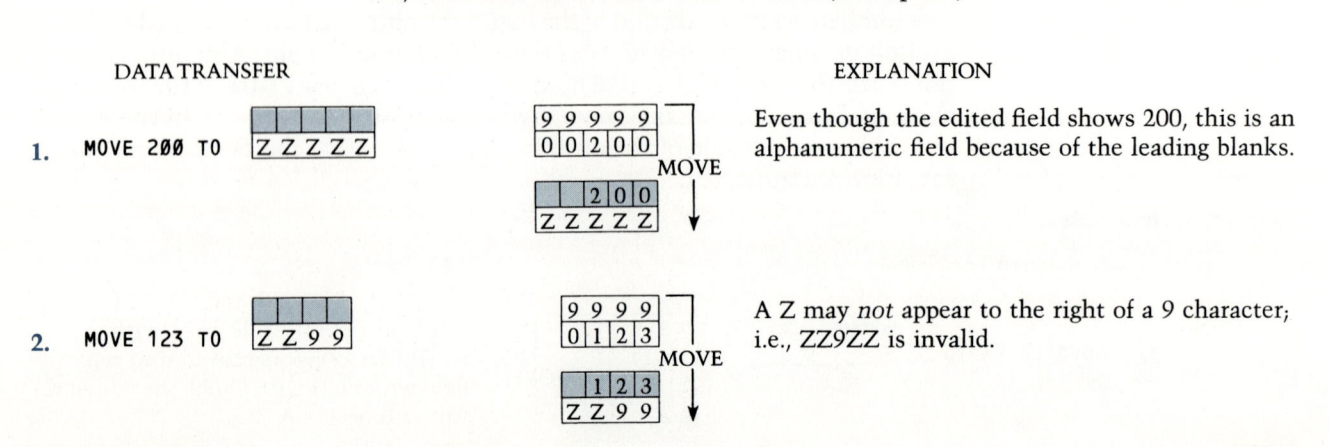

Even though the edited field shows 200, this is an alphanumeric field because of the leading blanks.

2. MOVE 123 TO `ZZ99`

```
 9 9 9 9
 0 1 2 3    MOVE
   1 2 3
 Z Z 9 9
```

A Z may *not* appear to the right of a 9 character; i.e., ZZ9ZZ is invalid.

3. MOVE 10 TO `ZZZZ.ZZ`

```
9 9 9 9V9 9
0 0 1 0 0 0
```
MOVE →
```
      1 0 . 0 0
Z Z Z Z . Z Z
```

A Z may appear to the right of the decimal point as long as all positions to the right of the decimal point are Z's.

4. MOVE .08 TO `ZZZZ.ZZ`

```
9 9 9 9V9 9
0 0 0 0 0 8
```
MOVE →
```
          . 0 8
Z Z Z Z . Z Z
```

Zero suppression stops at the decimal point.

5. MOVE .08 TO `ZZZZ.99`

```
9 9 9 9V9 9
0 0 0 0 0 8
```
MOVE →
```
          . 0 8
Z Z Z Z . 9 9
```

To avoid confusion, make it a habit to use 9's to the right of the decimal point.

6. MOVE 0 TO `ZZZZ.ZZ`

```
9 9
0 0
```
MOVE →
```
Z Z Z Z . Z Z
```

The resulting field is all blank.

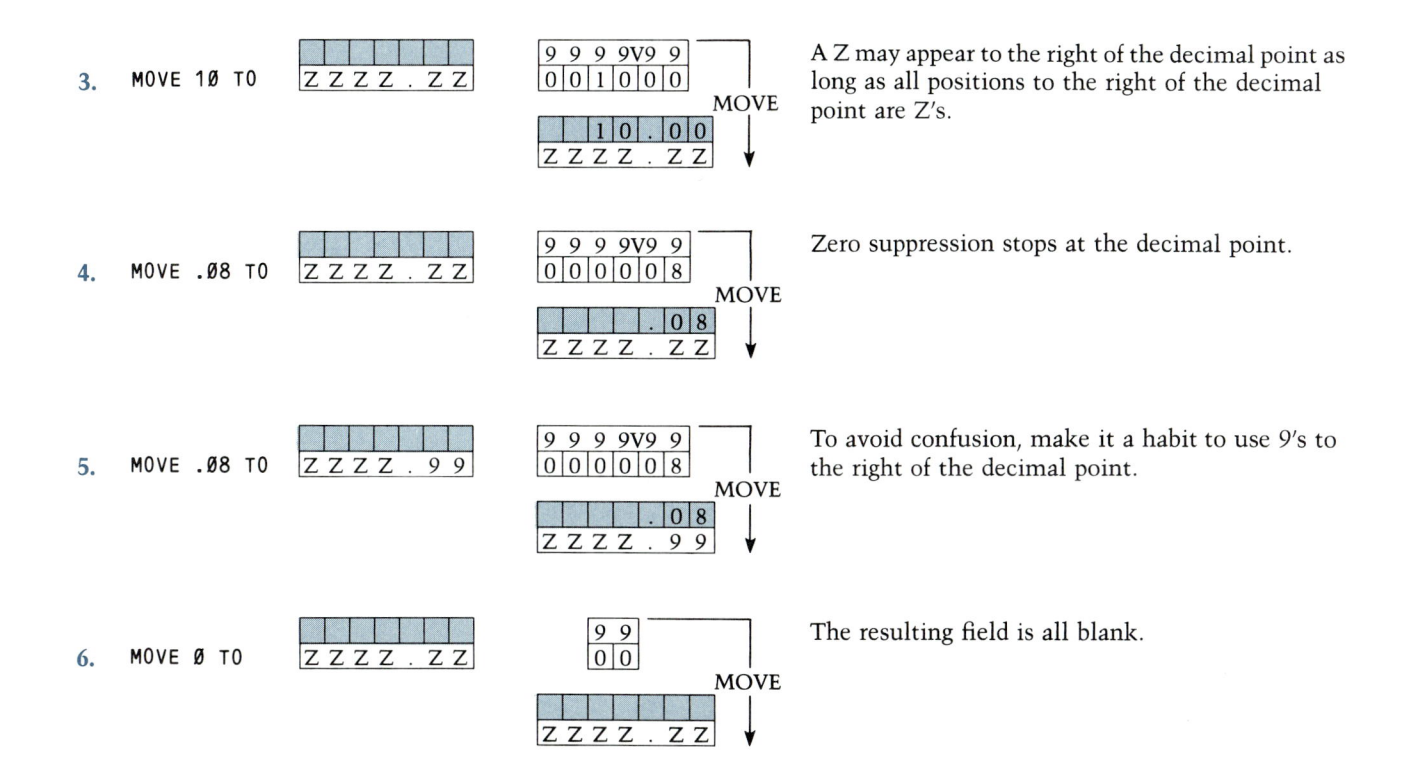

4-2-5 EDITING WITH THE CURRENCY SYMBOL ($) or (£)

Case 1: The first character of the receiving picture is a $ sign and no other $ signs follow; in that case the $ symbol does not represent a digit position.

Result: A dollar sign is printed as the first character in the result field. The dollar sign counts as 1 character in the size of the result field. No $ sign is printed if the sending field is all 0's.

Case 2: The first characters of the receiving picture are a string of $ signs.

Result: The dollar signs act as zero suppression characters. A $ sign is printed to the immediate left of the first nonzero digit or to the left of the decimal point, whichever comes first. In determining the size of the result field, all $ signs count for 1 position each. No $ sign is printed if the sending field is all 0's, i.e., the receiving field is blanked out.

Examples:

DATA TRANSFER   EXPLANATION

1. MOVE 123.45 TO `$999.99`

```
9 9 9V9 9
1 2 3 4 5
```
MOVE →
```
$ 1 2 3 . 4 5
$ 9 9 9 . 9 9
```

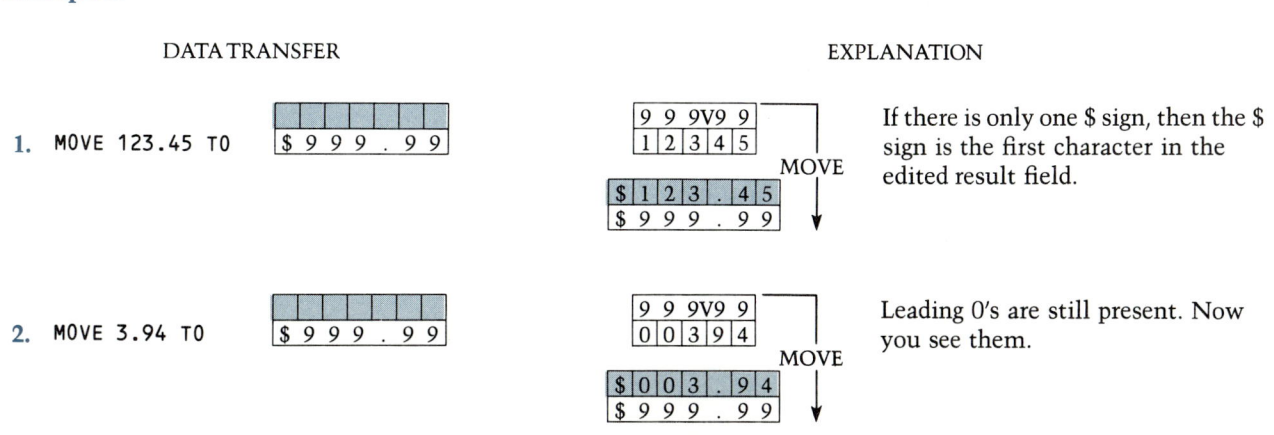

If there is only one $ sign, then the $ sign is the first character in the edited result field.

2. MOVE 3.94 TO `$999.99`

```
9 9 9V9 9
0 0 3 9 4
```
MOVE →
```
$ 0 0 3 . 9 4
$ 9 9 9 . 9 9
```

Leading 0's are still present. Now you see them.

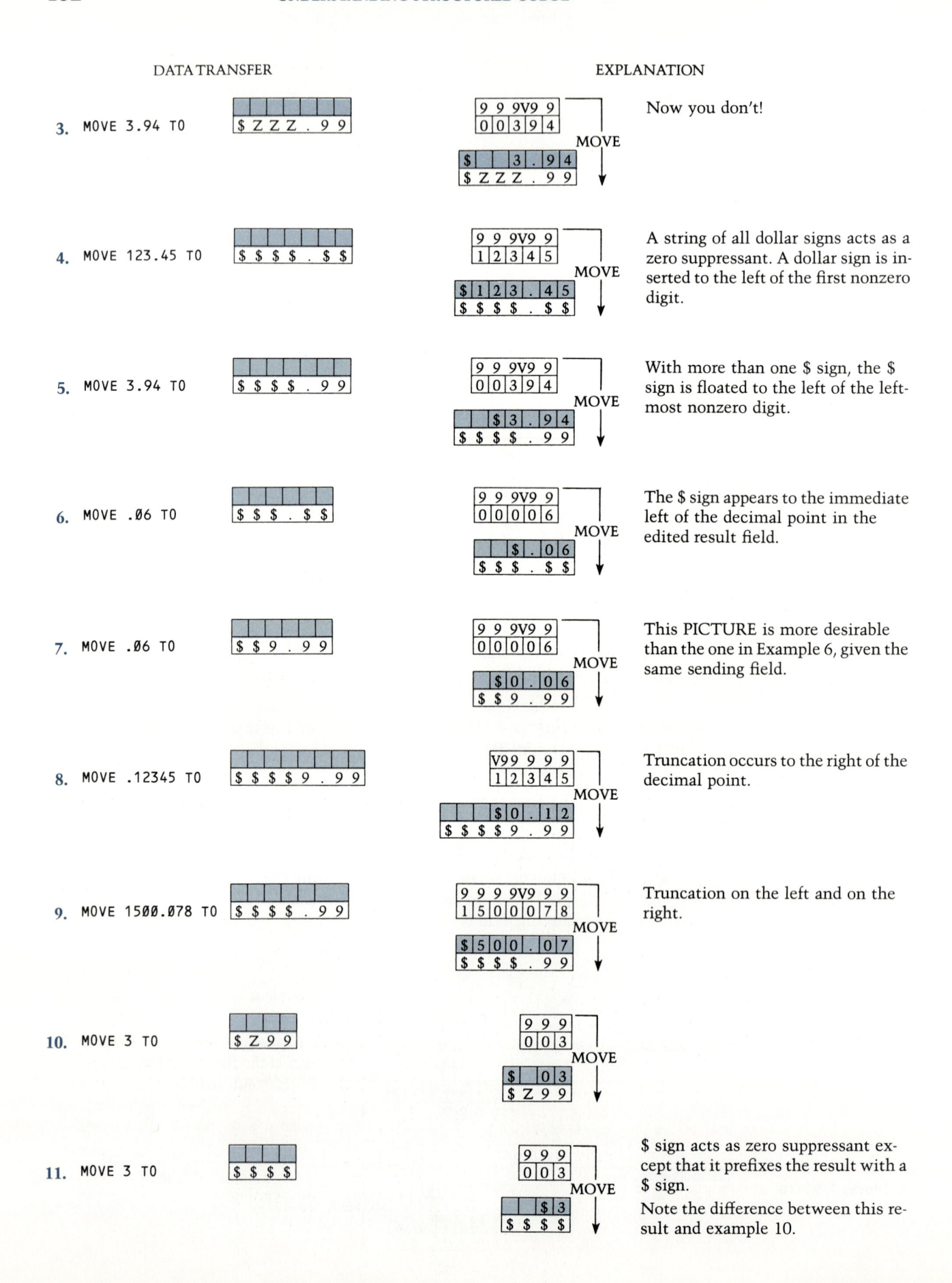

DATA TRANSFER | | EXPLANATION

3. MOVE 3.94 TO `$ZZZ.99`

```
9 9 9V9 9
0 0 3 9 4
          MOVE
$      3.9 4
$ Z Z Z . 9 9
```

Now you don't!

4. MOVE 123.45 TO `$$$$.$$`

```
9 9 9V9 9
1 2 3 4 5
          MOVE
$ 1 2 3 . 4 5
$ $ $ $ . $ $
```

A string of all dollar signs acts as a zero suppressant. A dollar sign is inserted to the left of the first nonzero digit.

5. MOVE 3.94 TO `$$$$.99`

```
9 9 9V9 9
0 0 3 9 4
          MOVE
      $ 3 . 9 4
$ $ $ $ . 9 9
```

With more than one $ sign, the $ sign is floated to the left of the leftmost nonzero digit.

6. MOVE .06 TO `$$$.$$`

```
9 9 9V9 9
0 0 0 0 6
          MOVE
        $ . 0 6
$ $ $ . $ $
```

The $ sign appears to the immediate left of the decimal point in the edited result field.

7. MOVE .06 TO `$$9.99`

```
9 9 9V9 9
0 0 0 0 6
          MOVE
      $ 0 . 0 6
$ $ 9 . 9 9
```

This PICTURE is more desirable than the one in Example 6, given the same sending field.

8. MOVE .12345 TO `$$$$9.99`

```
V99 9 9 9
 1 2 3 4 5
          MOVE
      $ 0 . 1 2
$ $ $ $ 9 . 9 9
```

Truncation occurs to the right of the decimal point.

9. MOVE 1500.078 TO `$$$$.99`

```
9 9 9 9V9 9 9
1 5 0 0 0 7 8
              MOVE
$ 5 0 0 . 0 7
$ $ $ $ . 9 9
```

Truncation on the left and on the right.

10. MOVE 3 TO `$Z99`

```
9 9 9
0 0 3
      MOVE
$     0 3
$ Z 9 9
```

11. MOVE 3 TO `$$$$`

```
9 9 9
0 0 3
      MOVE
      $ 3
$ $ $ $
```

$ sign acts as zero suppressant except that it prefixes the result with a $ sign.

Note the difference between this result and example 10.

THE EDITING PROCESS AND ARITHMETIC STATEMENTS 133

12. MOVE 0 TO $ZZ.Z

    999 → 000
    MOVE → $ZZ.Z

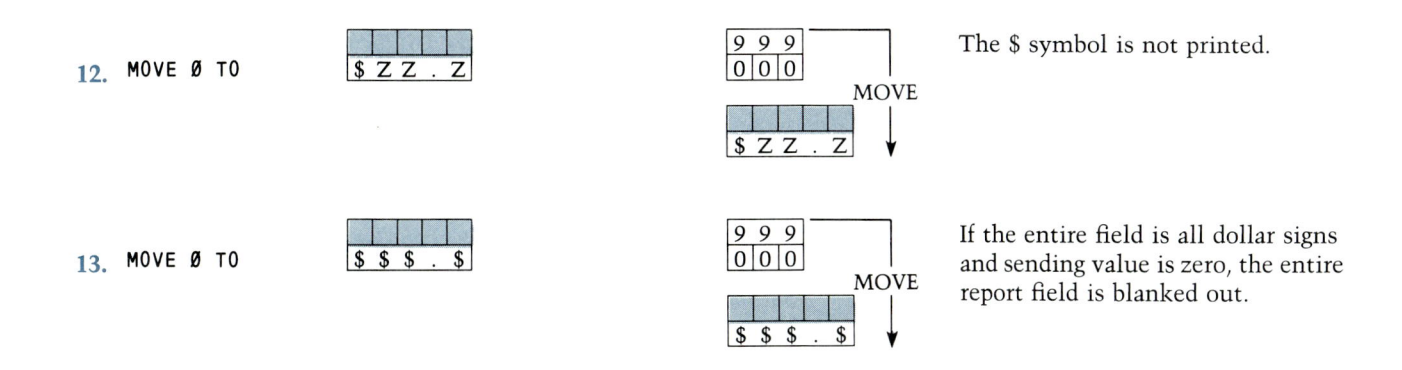

    The $ symbol is not printed.

13. MOVE 0 TO $$$.$

    999 → 000
    MOVE → $$$.$

    If the entire field is all dollar signs and sending value is zero, the entire report field is blanked out.

4-2-6 EDITING WITH THE COMMA (,)

A comma will be inserted at the designated comma position in the edited result field. If the character immediately to the left of the comma is a suppressed 0, the comma is not printed; it can also become a blank character, a dollar sign, an asterisk, or a − or + symbol depending on the replacement character used. In any event it accounts for one position in the result field.

Examples:

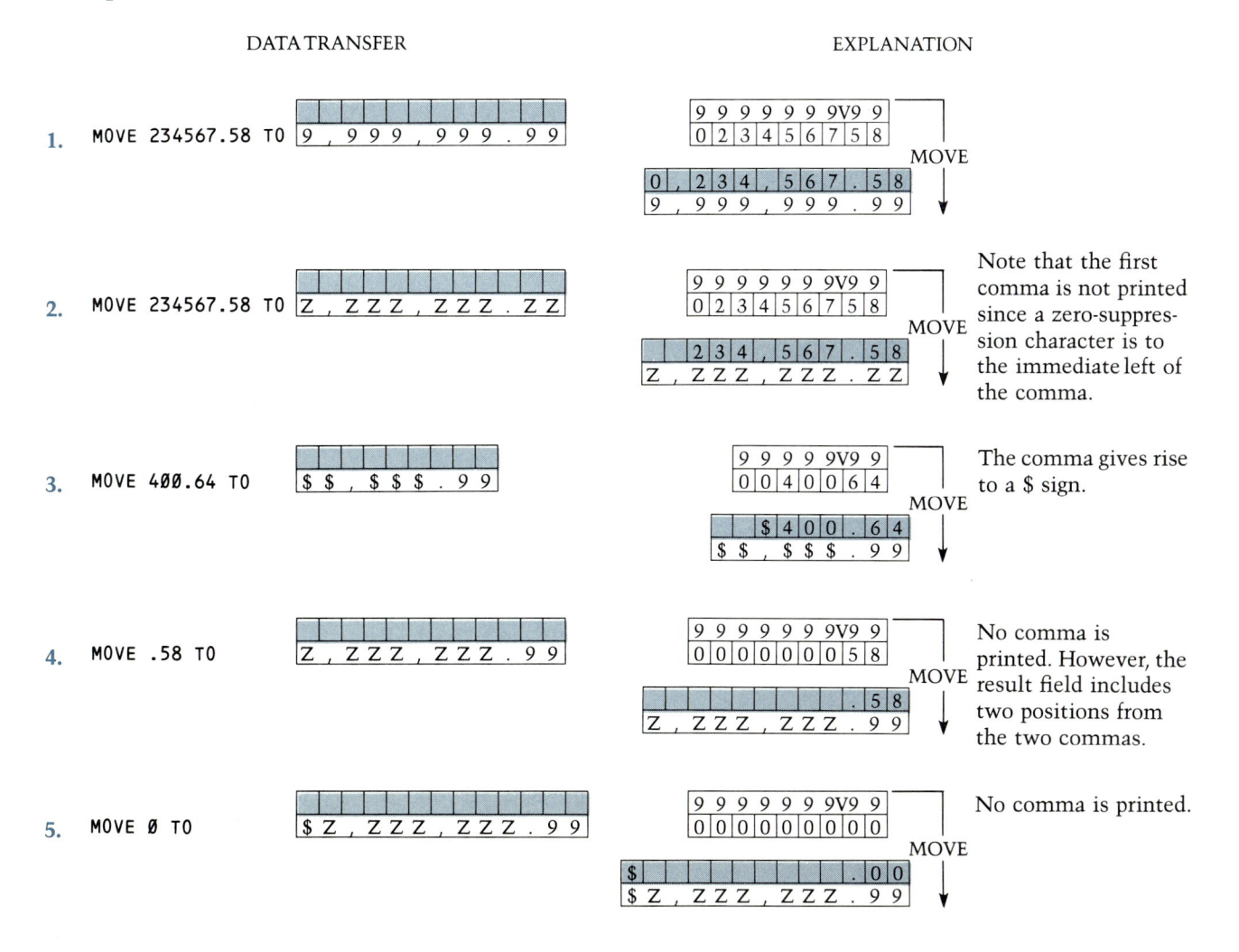

DATA TRANSFER | EXPLANATION

1. MOVE 234567.58 TO 9,999,999.99

    999999V99 → 02345758
    MOVE → 0,234,567.58 / 9,999,999.99

2. MOVE 234567.58 TO Z,ZZZ,ZZZ.ZZ

    999999V99 → 02345758
    MOVE → 234,567.58 / Z,ZZZ,ZZZ.ZZ

    Note that the first comma is not printed since a zero-suppression character is to the immediate left of the comma.

3. MOVE 400.64 TO $$,$$$.99

    9999V99 → 040064
    MOVE → $400.64 / $$,$$$.99

    The comma gives rise to a $ sign.

4. MOVE .58 TO Z,ZZZ,ZZZ.99

    999999V99 → 00000058
    MOVE → .58 / Z,ZZZ,ZZZ.99

    No comma is printed. However, the result field includes two positions from the two commas.

5. MOVE 0 TO $Z,ZZZ,ZZZ.99

    999999V99 → 00000000
    MOVE → $ .00 / $Z,ZZZ,ZZZ.99

    No comma is printed.

134 UNDERSTANDING STRUCTURED COBOL

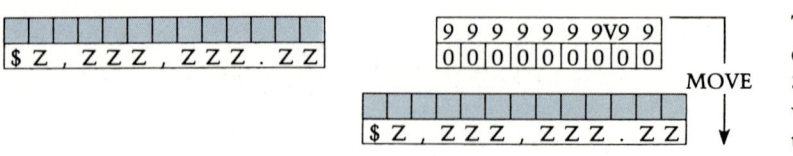

	DATA TRANSFER		EXPLANATION
6.	MOVE 0 TO $Z,ZZZ,ZZZ.ZZ	9 9 9 9 9 9 9V9 9 / 0 0 0 0 0 0 0 0 → MOVE → $Z,ZZZ,ZZZ.ZZ	The same result would occur if all Z's had been $ signs. No nonzero digit was encountered, hence the result field is all blanks.

4-2-7 EDITING WITH THE CHECK PROTECTION CHARACTER (*)

The check protection character is mainly used to ensure that the figure amount of a check cannot be changed. For example, instead of printing a check as $ 347.55, editing with the check protection feature will give $***347.55.

Leading 0's and any suppressed commas will be replaced by an asterisk. The asterisk insertion process stops upon encountering the first nonzero digit or the decimal point, whichever comes first. The decimal point is *always* printed.

Examples:

	DATA TRANSFER		EXPLANATION
1.	MOVE 3.45 TO ***.**	9 9 9V9 9 / 0 0 3 4 5 → MOVE → **3.45	An asterisk may be used to the right of the decimal point, but then all digit positions to the right of the decimal point must be asterisks.
2.	MOVE 1305.56 TO $*,***.**	9 9 9 9V9 9 / 1 3 0 5 5 6 → MOVE → $1,305.56	Insertion characters come to life.
3.	MOVE .08 TO $*,***.**	9 9 9 9V9 9 / 0 0 0 0 0 8 → MOVE → $****.08	The asterisk insertion stops at the decimal point (except when sending value is zero—see example 5).
4.	MOVE 305.56 TO $*,***.99	9 9 9 9V9 9 / 0 3 0 5 5 6 → MOVE → $**305.56	The comma is replaced by an asterisk.
5.	MOVE 0 TO $*,***.**	9 9 9 9V9 9 / 0 0 0 0 0 0 → MOVE → $****.**	No nonzero digits were found: The entire result field is filled with asterisks except for the decimal point.
6.	MOVE 0 TO $**,*99	9 9 9 9 9 / 0 0 0 0 0 → MOVE → $***00	The 9's forced the insert character $ to appear.

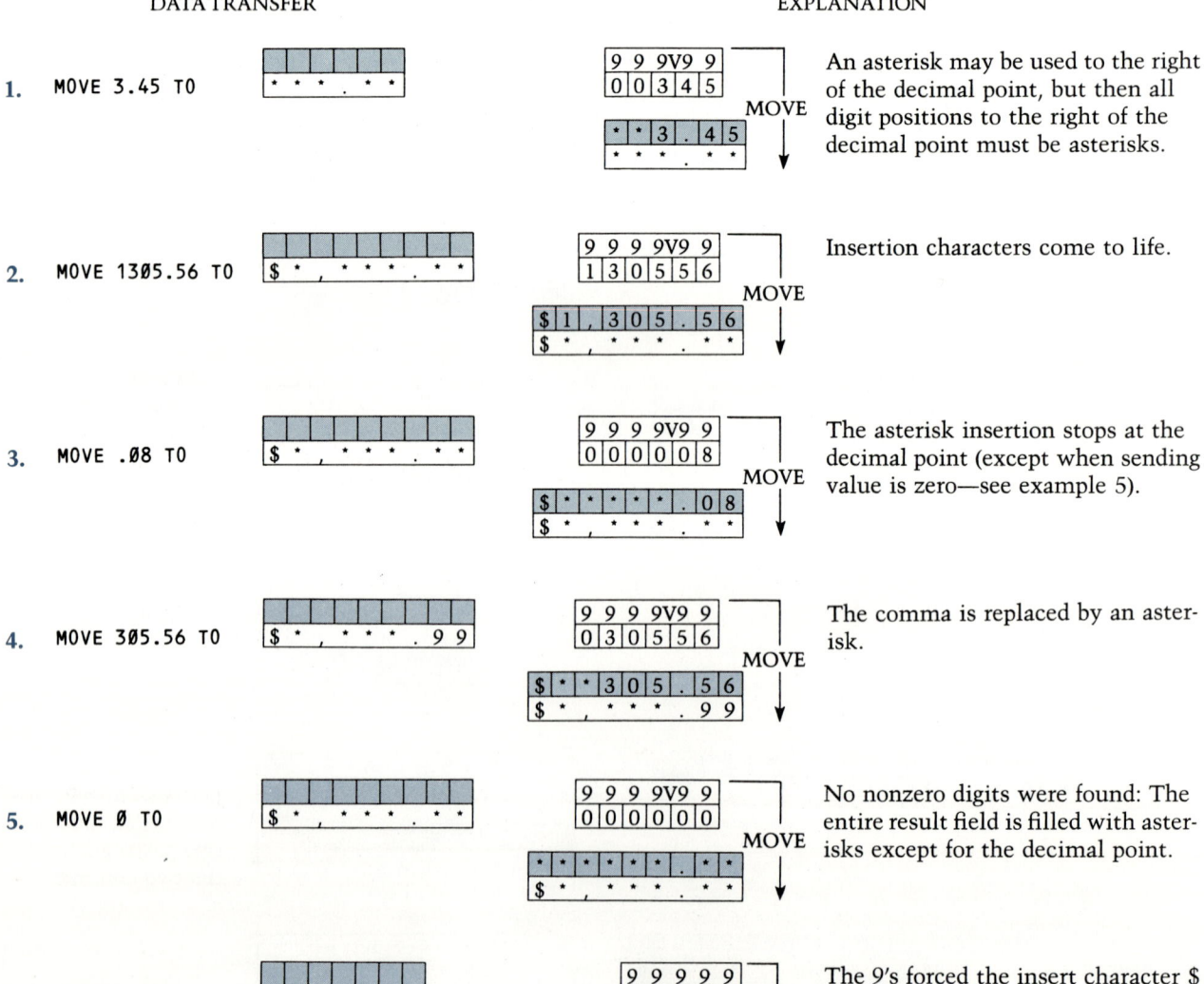

4-2-8 EDITING WITH THE SIGN INSERTION SYMBOLS (+) AND (−)

The + and − symbols are used on output to indicate the sign of a particular item; they may either precede or follow the result. These symbols may be used either as insert characters (one symbol) or as zero-suppression characters (string).

Case 1: The sign symbol as an insert character.

The symbol or character + can be used as either the first or last character in the PICTURE clause. If the sending field is positive, the + symbol will then be inserted at the beginning or at the end of the result field, depending on the + sign's position in the field. If the number is negative, the minus sign − will be inserted as the first or last character in the result field. In any event, the resulting sign + or − counts as one character in the result field.

The minus editing symbol − behaves like the + symbol, except that the + sign is not printed if the result field is positive. (See Figure 4–5.)

Examples:

	DATA TRANSFER		EXPLANATION
1.	MOVE -1.23 TO +9.999	S 9 9V9 9 / 0 1 2 3 →MOVE -1.230 / +9.999	Since the sending field is negative, the insert character − is printed in the first position of the report field.
2.	MOVE -1.26 TO +ZZZ.9	S 9 9V9 9 / 0 1 2 6̄ →MOVE - / 1 . 2 / +ZZZ.9	The negative sign could have been floated (see case 2). Note truncation to the right.
3.	MOVE 1.23 TO +99.99	9 9V9 9 / 0 1 2 3 →MOVE +01.23 / +99.99	Note the absence of the S symbol in the sending field. This does not matter; the number is considered positive.
4.	MOVE 1.23 TO ZZ.ZZ+	9 9V9 9 / 0 1 2 3 →MOVE 1.23+ / ZZ.ZZ+	The sign symbol is positioned as the right-most character in the PICTURE. Note its position in the result field.
5.	MOVE -1.23 TO ZZ.ZZ+	S 9 9V9 9 / 0 1 2 3̄ →MOVE 1.23- / ZZ.ZZ+	The negative sign occupies the right-most position in the result field.
6.	MOVE 1.23 TO ZZ.ZZ-	9 9V9 9 / 0 1 2 3 →MOVE 1.23 / ZZ.ZZ-	A blank instead of a + sign is inserted in the right-most position of the result field.

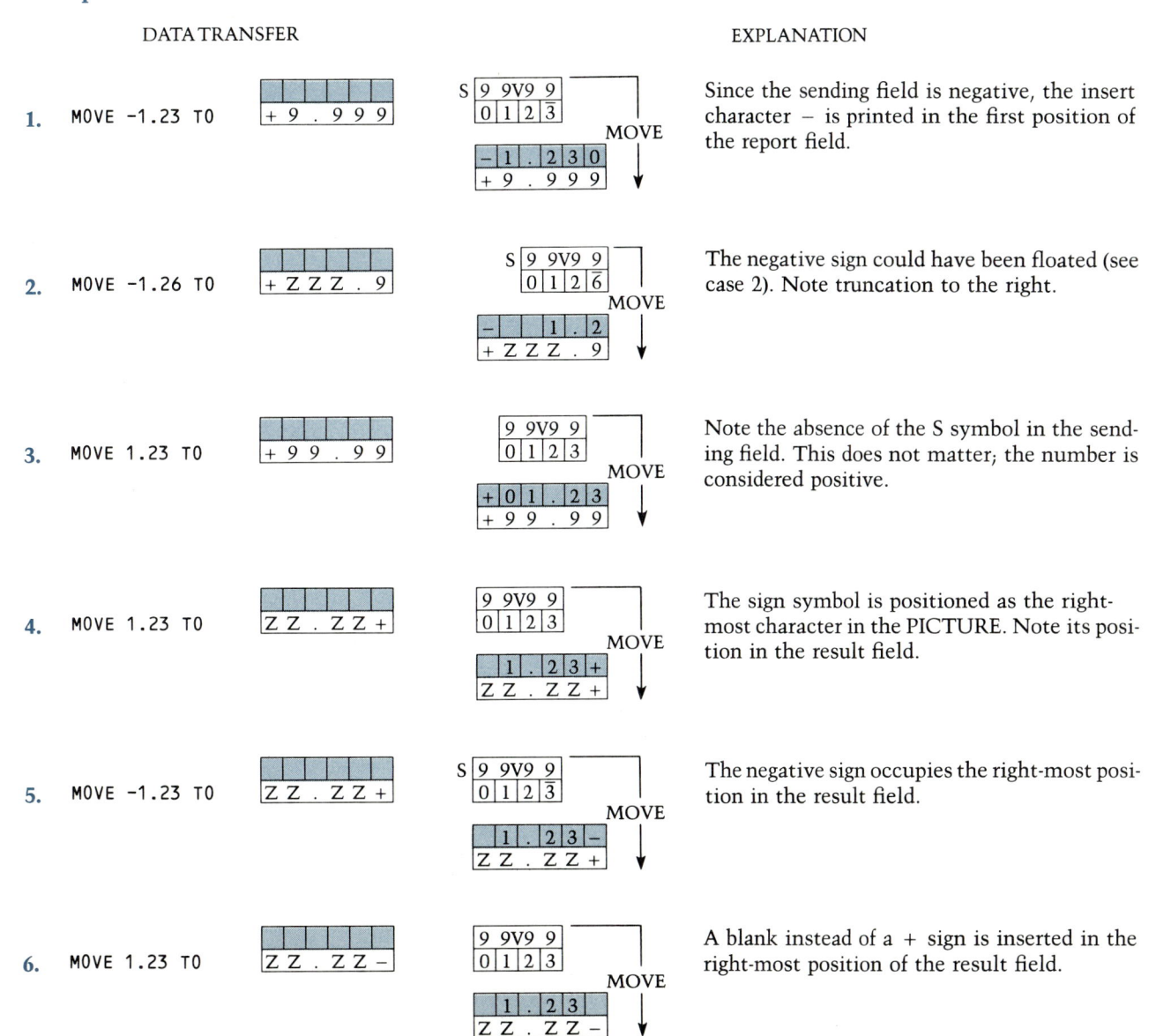

	DATA TRANSFER		EXPLANATION
7.	MOVE 84.34 TO `-Z.999`	`99 9V9 9` / `0 8 4 3 4` → `4 . 3 4 0` / `-Z . 9 9 9`	Same as example 7, with truncation on the left.
8.	MOVE -1.23 TO `-Z99.9`	`S 9 9V9 9` / `0 1 2 3` → `- 0 1 . 2` / `-Z 9 9 . 9`	Minus sign is printed.
9.	MOVE -0 TO `-ZZ.ZZ`	`S 9 9V9 9` / `0 0 0 0` → (blank) / `-Z Z . Z Z`	No nonzero digits were found: insertion characters do not get printed.

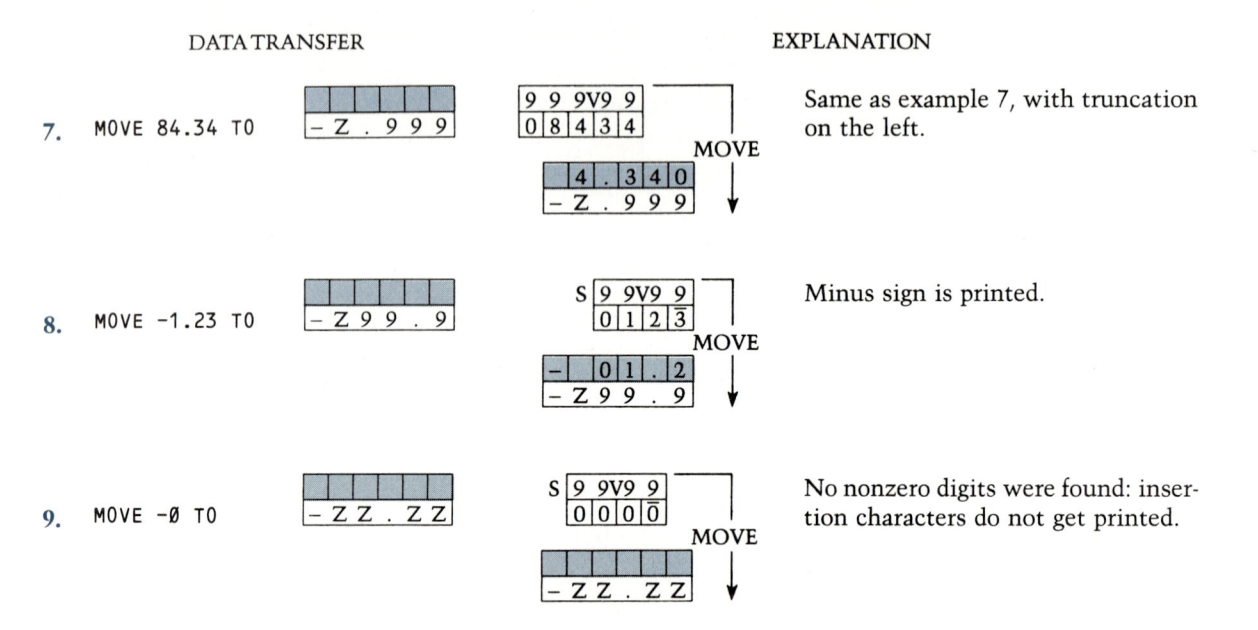

Case 2: The sign symbol as a string.

The + or − sign can be floated throughout the PICTURE clause. In that capacity it acts as a zero-suppression character and behaves like the floating $ sign. The appropriate sign will precede the first nonsuppressed 0.

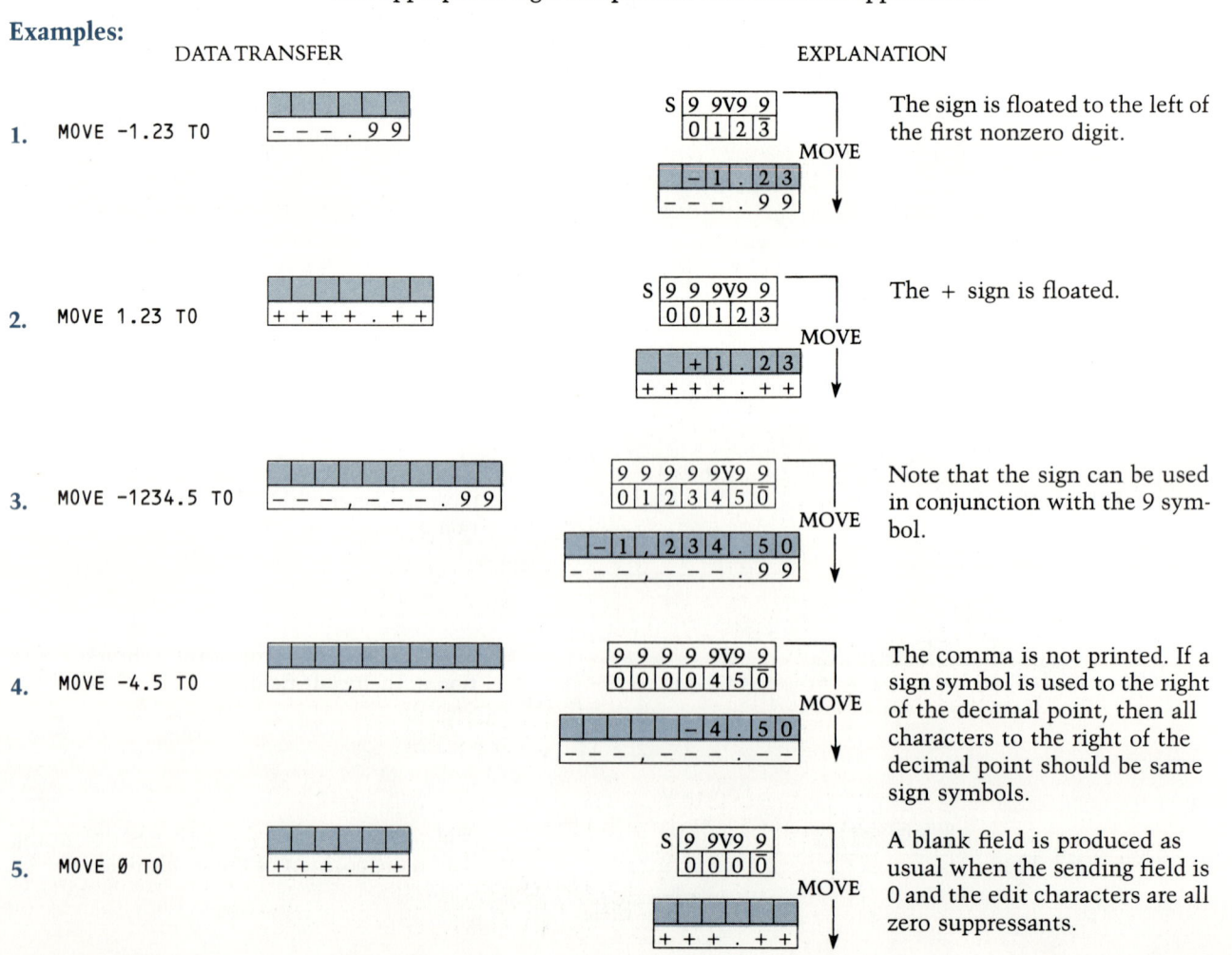

Examples:

	DATA TRANSFER		EXPLANATION
1.	MOVE -1.23 TO `---.99`	`S 9 9V9 9` / `0 1 2 3` → `- 1 . 2 3` / `- - - . 9 9`	The sign is floated to the left of the first nonzero digit.
2.	MOVE 1.23 TO `+++.++`	`S 9 9 9V9 9` / `0 0 1 2 3` → `+ 1 . 2 3` / `+ + + + . + +`	The + sign is floated.
3.	MOVE -1234.5 TO `---,---.99`	`9 9 9 9 9V9 9` / `0 1 2 3 4 5 0` → `- 1 , 2 3 4 . 5 0` / `- - - , - - - . 9 9`	Note that the sign can be used in conjunction with the 9 symbol.
4.	MOVE -4.5 TO `---,---.--`	`9 9 9 9 9V9 9` / `0 0 0 0 4 5 0` → `- 4 . 5 0` / `- - - , - - - . - -`	The comma is not printed. If a sign symbol is used to the right of the decimal point, then all characters to the right of the decimal point should be same sign symbols.
5.	MOVE 0 TO `+++.++`	`S 9 9V9 9` / `0 0 0 0` → (blank) / `+ + + . + +`	A blank field is produced as usual when the sending field is 0 and the edit characters are all zero suppressants.

Editing symbol in edited field	Result field	
	Sending field is positive or zero	Sending field is negative
+	+ sign	− sign
−	1 space	− sign
CR	2 spaces	CR
DB	2 spaces	DB

FIGURE 4–5
THE SIGN AND DB/CR CHARACTERS

4-2-9 EDITING WITH THE CREDIT AND DEBIT SYMBOLS (CR) AND (DB)

If the symbols CR or DB are to be used, they must be specified as the last two characters in the PICTURE clause.

- If the two characters DB are specified in the edited field, the two letters D and B will appear in the two right-most positions of the result field *if* the sending field is negative. If the sending number is positive, two blanks will occupy the two right-most positions of the result field.

- If the two characters CR are specified in the edited field, the two letters C and R will appear in the two right-most positions of the result field *if* the sending field is negative. If the sending number is positive, two blanks will occupy the two right-most positions of the result field. (See Figure 4–5.)

If the result is positive and the user wants either DB or CR to be displayed up in the edited field, then he/she must multiply the sending field's value by −1.

Examples:

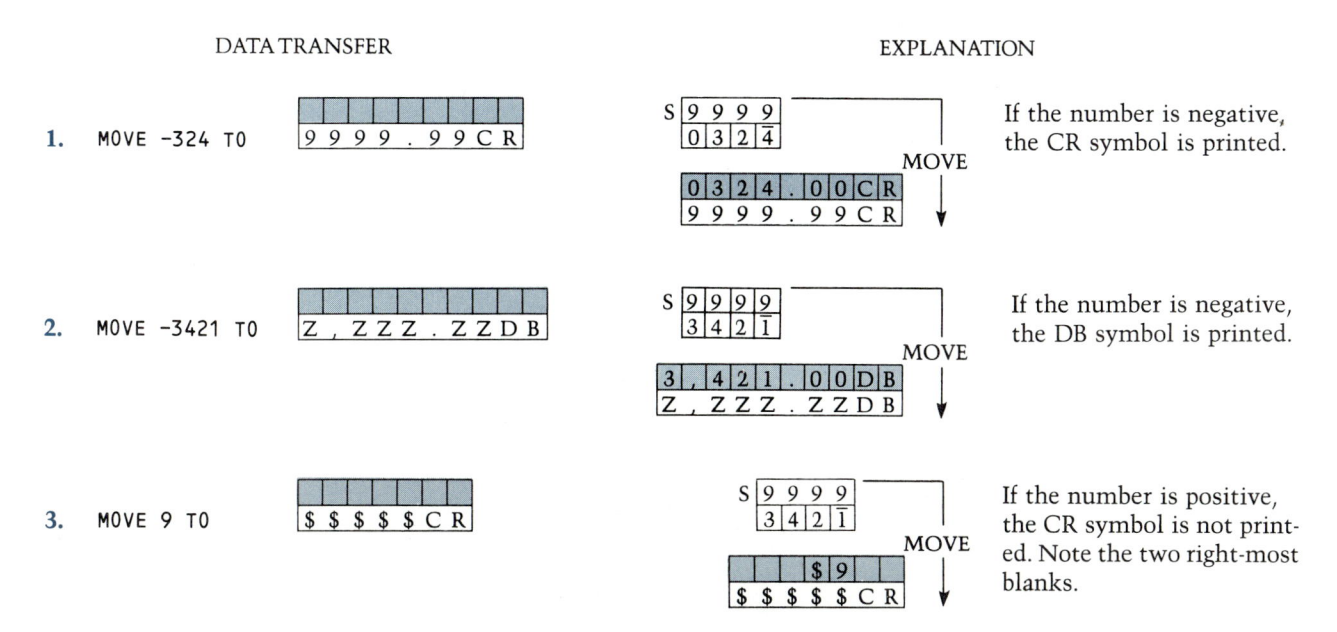

DATA TRANSFER / EXPLANATION

1. MOVE -324 TO 9 9 9 9 . 9 9 C R
   S 9 9 9 9 / 0 3 2 4̄ → MOVE → 0 3 2 4 . 0 0 C R / 9 9 9 9 . 9 9 C R
   If the number is negative, the CR symbol is printed.

2. MOVE -3421 TO Z , Z Z Z . Z Z D B
   S 9 9 9 9 / 3 4 2 1̄ → MOVE → 3 , 4 2 1 . 0 0 D B / Z , Z Z Z . Z Z D B
   If the number is negative, the DB symbol is printed.

3. MOVE 9 TO $ $ $ $ $ C R
   S 9 9 9 9 / 3 4 2 1̄ → MOVE → $ 9 / $ $ $ $ $ C R
   If the number is positive, the CR symbol is not printed. Note the two right-most blanks.

138   UNDERSTANDING STRUCTURED COBOL

DATA TRANSFER   EXPLANATION

4. MOVE -.75 TO   `$*,***.99CR`

S|9 9V9 9|
|0 0 7 5|
MOVE
|$ * * * . 7 5 C R|
|$ * , * * * . 9 9 C R|

This is similar to example 1, except with an asterisk as an insert.

5. MOVE .476 TO   `9.99DB`

|9 9V9 9 9|
|0 0 4 7 6|
MOVE
|0 . 4 7|
|9 . 9 9 D B|

If the number is positive, the DB symbol is not printed; note the 2 blanks.

4-2-10 EDITING WITH THE BLANK INSERTION SYMBOL (B) AND THE SLASH SYMBOL (/)

The character B is used to insert a space in a result field. Wherever the character B is positioned in the PICTURE clause, a blank character will be inserted in the corresponding position in the result field. The character B can be used in conjunction with any other editing character. This editing symbol doesn't require the sending field to be numeric. Most versions of COBOL also use the slash (/) as an insert character.

Examples:

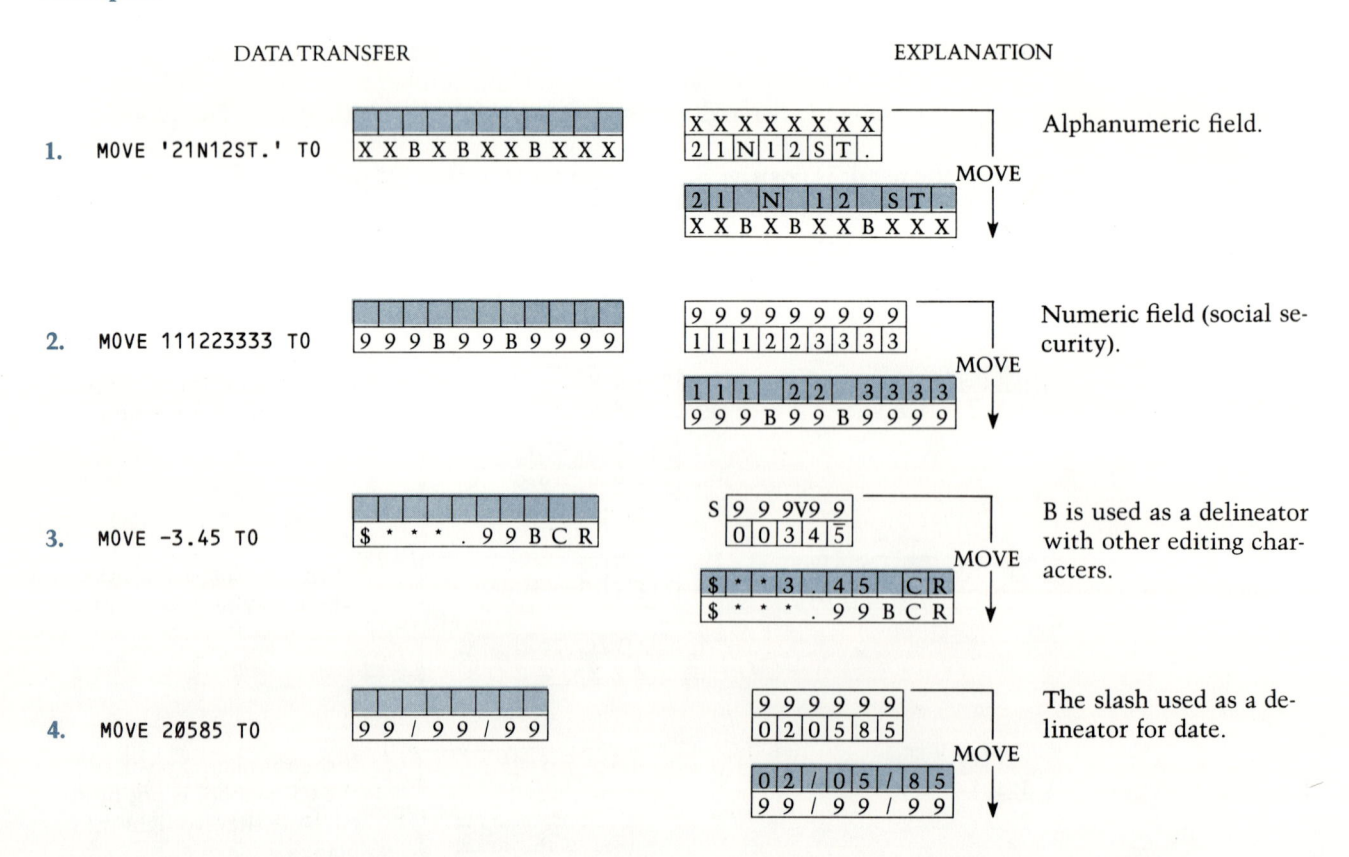

DATA TRANSFER   EXPLANATION

1. MOVE '21N12ST.' TO   `X X B X B X X B X X X`

|X X X X X X X|
|2 1 N 1 2 S T .|
MOVE
|2 1   N   1 2   S T .|
|X X B X B X X B X X X|

Alphanumeric field.

2. MOVE 111223333 TO   `999B99B9999`

|9 9 9 9 9 9 9 9 9|
|1 1 1 2 2 3 3 3 3|
MOVE
|1 1 1   2 2   3 3 3 3|
|9 9 9 B 9 9 B 9 9 9 9|

Numeric field (social security).

3. MOVE -3.45 TO   `$***.99BCR`

S|9 9 9V9 9|
|0 0 3 4 5|
MOVE
|$ * * 3 . 4 5   C R|
|$ * * * . 9 9 B C R|

B is used as a delineator with other editing characters.

4. MOVE 20585 TO   `99/99/99`

|9 9 9 9 9 9|
|0 2 0 5 8 5|
MOVE
|0 2 / 0 5 / 8 5|
|9 9 / 9 9 / 9 9|

The slash used as a delineator for date.

THE EDITING PROCESS AND ARITHMETIC STATEMENTS 139

> **ATTENTION   ATTENTION   ATTENTION**
>
> - A Z may not follow a 9, an asterisk (*) or any   PIC 99ZZ.
>   floating string.   (OK ZZ99)
>
> - An * may not follow a 9, a Z or any floating   PIC 99**.99.
>   string.   (OK **99.99.)
>
> - If any of the replacement characters +, −, $, *   PIC ZZZ.++.
>   or Z appear to the right of the decimal point,   (OK +++.++.)
>   then all numeric characters in the PICTURE
>   must be the same.

4-2-11 DO IT NOW

1. Which of the following PICTUREs are valid or invalid? Specify error if any.

   a. PIC .9999.
   b. PIC S9.99.
   c. PIC 9..
   d. PIC V9.
   e. PIC S9V9.
   f. PIC -V9.99.
   g. PIC +++,++.99 LEADING SEPARATE.

2. Display the memory positions of the receiving fields. Identify blanks by the symbol ƀ.

SENDING FIELD	RECEIVING FIELD	SENDING FIELD	RECEIVING FIELD
a. 3V0$\overline{8}$	PIC 9	m. 48	$****
b. 3V0$\overline{8}$	PIC S99V9	n. 10000V45	$*,***.9
c. 140	PIC S99 LEADING SEPARATE	o. 0	$**,***.**
d. V0078	PIC 9(6)	p. 1V3	−ZZ.Z
e. 0	PIC 99.99	q. V07$\overline{3}$	$99.9+
f. 0V8	PIC ZZ	r. 131V$\overline{2}$	ZZ.Z+
g. 31V$\overline{6}$	PIC ZZZ.99	s. 10V3	$ZZ.ZZ−
h. 0	PIC Z.Z	t. 123	+ZZ99
i. V0076	PIC ZZ.ZZ	u. 12$\overline{3}$	99ZZ−
j. 1V3	PIC Z9Z9.Z	v. 33V1	−***.**
k. 9V	PIC $ZZZ.Z	w. 0	+++,+(3).++
l. 31V31	PIC $999.9	x. 13V$\overline{1}$	−(3).−(3)

ANSWERS

1.
   a. Valid
   b. Invalid: Not both S and .
   c. Invalid: only one period
   d. Valid
   e. Valid
   f. Invalid: V is for numeric fields
   g. Invalid: Cannot be numeric edited with LEADING SEPARATE.

2.
   a. 3̄
   b. 03̄0
   c. +40
   d. 000000
   e. 00.00
   f. ᵬᵬ
   g. ᵬ31.60
   h. ᵬᵬᵬ
   i. ᵬᵬ.00
   j. Invalid picture; should not alternate Z and 9.
   k. $ᵬᵬ9.0
   l. $031.3
   m. $**48
   n. $*****.4
   o. *******.**
   p. ᵬᵬ1.3
   q. $00.0+
   r. 31.2−
   s. $10.30ᵬ
   t. +ᵬ12.3
   u. Invalid picture
   v. ᵬ*33.10
   w. 10 blanks
   x. −13.100

4-2-11 PERMISSIBLE MOVES

In the following discussion, we will classify data into three groups:

1. Alphanumeric data—represented by the X data descriptor code.
2. Numeric data—containing only the S, V, and 9 data descriptor codes.
3. Numeric edited—containing the descriptor codes $, *, ., +, −, CR, DB, B, et cetera.

In sections 4-2-1 through 4-2-10 various types of moves within particular data groups have been discussed: numeric to numeric, alphanumeric to alphanumeric, and numeric to numeric edited. Other types of moves between one data group and another are shown in Figure 4-6.

It should be noted that group items can also be moved. In fact, all output lines, including the various types of detail lines, are group items that are constantly moved from WORKING–STORAGE to the output area for printing. Remember that a group item is treated as one long alphanumeric record.

	RECEIVING		
SENDING	NUMERIC	ALPHANUMERIC	NUMERIC EDITED
NUMERIC	Yes	Yes: sign is dropped	Yes
ALPHANUMERIC	No	Yes	No
NUMERIC EDITED	No	Yes	No

FIGURE 4-6
PERMISSIBLE MOVES

4–3 DATA TRANSFER THROUGH ARITHMETIC OPERATIONS

4–3–1 THE ADD INSTRUCTION

The two general forms of the ADD statement are shown in Figure 4–7.

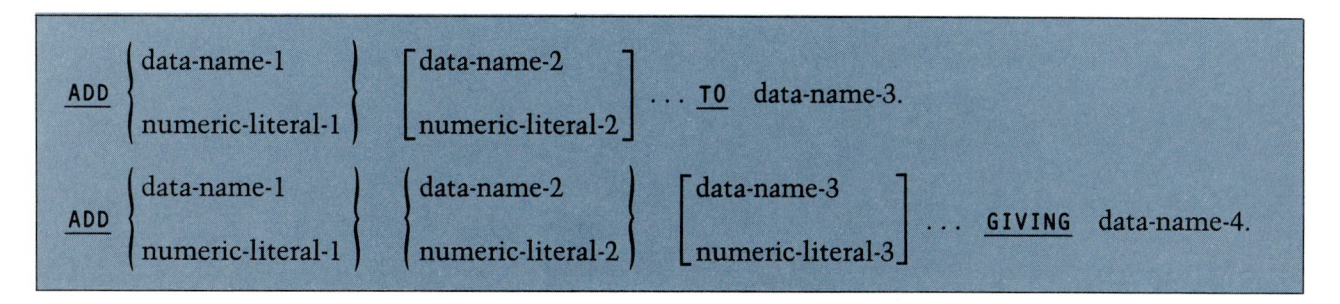

$$\underline{\text{ADD}} \begin{Bmatrix} \text{data-name-1} \\ \text{numeric-literal-1} \end{Bmatrix} \begin{bmatrix} \text{data-name-2} \\ \text{numeric-literal-2} \end{bmatrix} \ldots \underline{\text{TO}} \text{ data-name-3}.$$

$$\underline{\text{ADD}} \begin{Bmatrix} \text{data-name-1} \\ \text{numeric-literal-1} \end{Bmatrix} \begin{Bmatrix} \text{data-name-2} \\ \text{numeric-literal-2} \end{Bmatrix} \begin{bmatrix} \text{data-name-3} \\ \text{numeric-literal-3} \end{bmatrix} \ldots \underline{\text{GIVING}} \text{ data-name-4}.$$

FIGURE 4–7
THE ADD STATEMENT

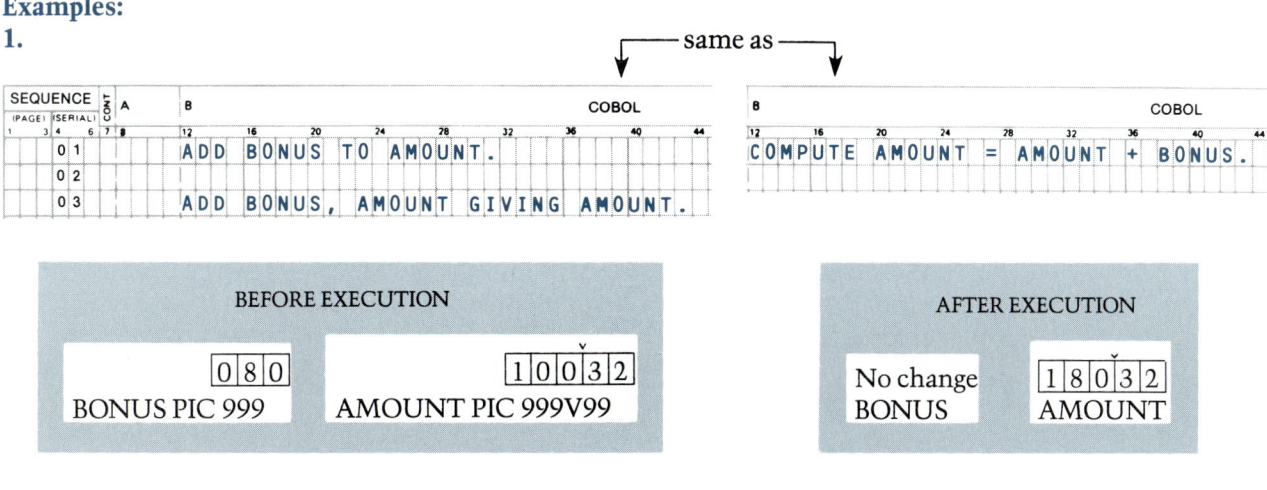

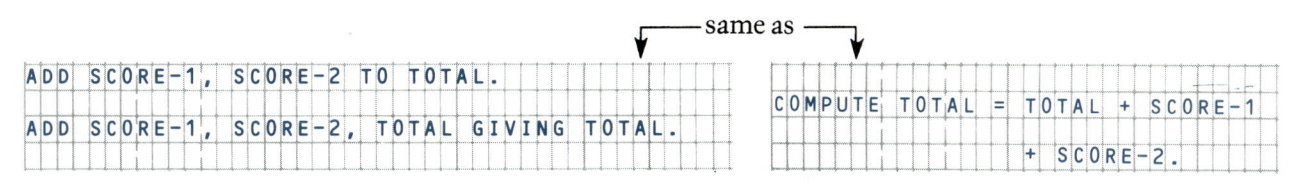

Examples:

1.

— same as —

```
ADD BONUS TO AMOUNT.
                                    COMPUTE AMOUNT = AMOUNT + BONUS.
ADD BONUS, AMOUNT GIVING AMOUNT.
```

BEFORE EXECUTION

BONUS PIC 999 = 080
AMOUNT PIC 999V99 = 100ˇ32

AFTER EXECUTION

No change BONUS
AMOUNT = 180ˇ32

2.

— same as —

```
ADD SCORE-1, SCORE-2 TO TOTAL.
                                    COMPUTE TOTAL = TOTAL + SCORE-1
ADD SCORE-1, SCORE-2, TOTAL GIVING TOTAL.                + SCORE-2.
```

BEFORE EXECUTION

SCORE-1 PIC 999 = 080
SCORE-2 PIC 999 = 100
TOTAL PIC 9999 = 0400

AFTER EXECUTION

No change SCORE-1
No change SCORE-2
TOTAL = 0580

3.

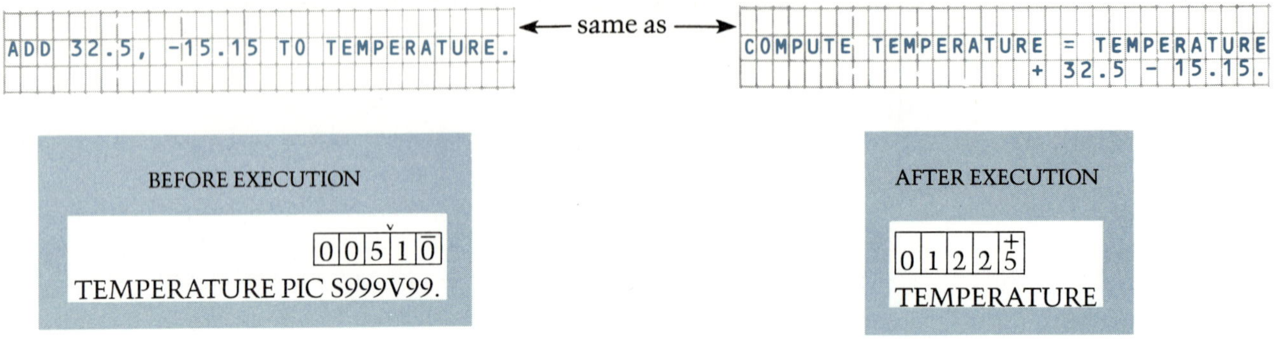

`ADD 32.5, -15.15 TO TEMPERATURE.` ←— same as —→ `COMPUTE TEMPERATURE = TEMPERATURE + 32.5 - 15.15.`

BEFORE EXECUTION

`0 0 5 1 0`
TEMPERATURE PIC S999V99.

AFTER EXECUTION

`0 1 2 2 5` (+)
TEMPERATURE

4.

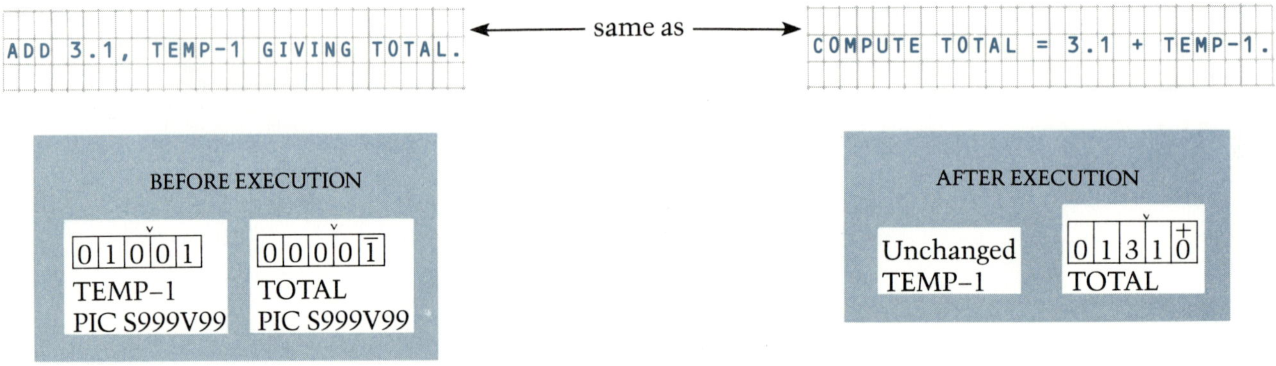

`ADD 3.1, TEMP-1 GIVING TOTAL.` ←— same as —→ `COMPUTE TOTAL = 3.1 + TEMP-1.`

BEFORE EXECUTION

`0 1 0 0 1` `0 0 0 0 1`
TEMP-1   TOTAL
PIC S999V99 PIC S999V99

AFTER EXECUTION

Unchanged   `0 1 3 1 0` (+)
TEMP-1   TOTAL

All arithmetic operations with the COMPUTE verb or the GIVING clause allow results to be edited directly into the field specified by the COMPUTE or the GIVING clause, if the resultant field does not take part in the arithmetic operation itself, as in ADD X,Y GIVING X. However, if the resultant field of the COMPUTE or GIVING clause is a numeric edited field, it can no longer be processed arithmetically.

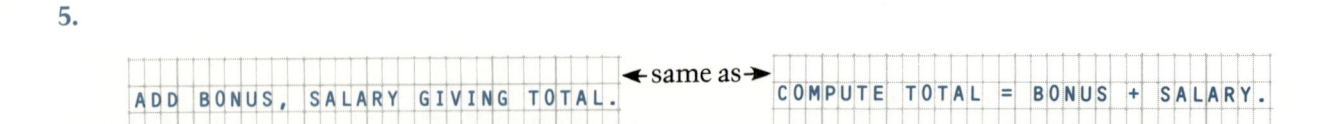

5.

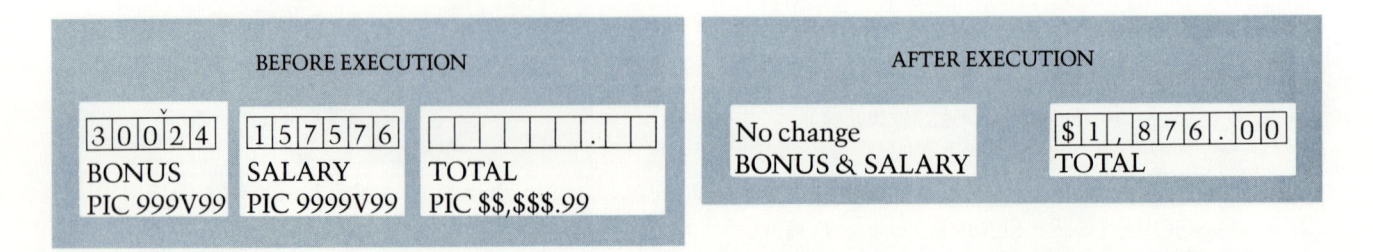

`ADD BONUS, SALARY GIVING TOTAL.` ←same as→ `COMPUTE TOTAL = BONUS + SALARY.`

BEFORE EXECUTION

`3 0 0 2 4` `1 5 7 5 7 6` `| | | | | . | |`
BONUS   SALARY   TOTAL
PIC 999V99   PIC 9999V99   PIC $$,$$$.99

AFTER EXECUTION

No change   `$ 1 , 8 7 6 . 0 0`
BONUS & SALARY   TOTAL

> **CAUTION** In COBOL, you can get results like 150 + 50 = 50 and 50 − 100 = 50! Yes, this is true!! Suppose PAY is defined as PIC 99 VALUE 50; consider the instruction
>
> ADD 100 TO PAY.
>
> Since the result field consists of only two digit positions, the left-most digit 1 of 150 is left out (truncated). Unlike other computer languages, where arithmetic operations are always carried out to the maximum number of significant digits allowed by the particular system, COBOL depends on the user to tell it how many digit positions are needed for the result. Hence forethought is needed to determine the size of the result field; otherwise, if the field is insufficiently large, truncation will occur on the left of the "whole" part of the number and on the right of the fractional digits. For example, to add 50.75 and 80.40 we must reserve an area field of 999V99 to accommodate all digits—PIC 999 would result in 131, while 9V99 would result in 1.15.
>
> Similarly, result fields should be signed when performing arithmetic with negative numbers or when carrying out subtractions. For that reason, many professional programmers always make it a practice to sign all numeric fields.
>
> These comments apply to all arithmetic operations and not just to additions and subtractions.

INVALID ADD STATEMENTS—COMMON MISTAKES	EXPLANATIONS AND CORRECTIONS
1. 01 PAY PIC 99.99. . . ADD BONUS, PAY GIVING PAY.	Since PAY is a numeric edited field, it *cannot* participate in an arithmetic operation; an execution error would occur. To correct, change PAY to PIC 99V99 and use ADD BONUS, PAY GIVING GROSS where GROSS is a numeric edited field.
2. ADD TEST1 TO TEST2 GIVING TOTAL.	Cannot use TO and GIVING at the same time. To correct, use: ADD TEST1,TEST2 GIVING TOTAL.
3. ADD TOTAL TO 30. ADD 30. TO TOTAL.	The item specified by the TO clause must be a data name. 30. is an invalid numeric literal. To correct, use: ADD 30 TO TOTAL.
4. ADD HOURS * RATE TO TOTAL.	HOURS * RATE is not a data name. To correct, use: COMPUTE TOTAL = TOTAL + HOURS * RATE.

4-3-2 THE SUBTRACT INSTRUCTION

The general form of the SUBTRACT statement is shown in Figure 4–8.

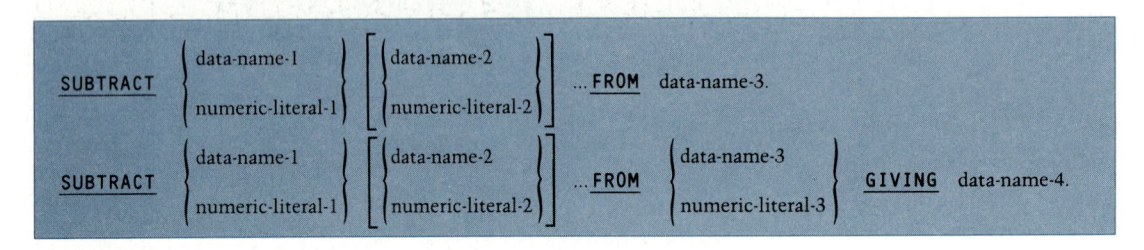

$$\underline{\text{SUBTRACT}} \left\{ \begin{array}{l} \text{data-name-1} \\ \text{numeric-literal-1} \end{array} \right\} \left[\left\{ \begin{array}{l} \text{data-name-2} \\ \text{numeric-literal-2} \end{array} \right\} \right] \ldots \underline{\text{FROM}} \text{ data-name-3}.$$

$$\underline{\text{SUBTRACT}} \left\{ \begin{array}{l} \text{data-name-1} \\ \text{numeric-literal-1} \end{array} \right\} \left[\left\{ \begin{array}{l} \text{data-name-2} \\ \text{numeric-literal-2} \end{array} \right\} \right] \ldots \underline{\text{FROM}} \left\{ \begin{array}{l} \text{data-name-3} \\ \text{numeric-literal-3} \end{array} \right\} \underline{\text{GIVING}} \text{ data-name-4}.$$

FIGURE 4–8
THE SUBTRACT VERB

Examples:

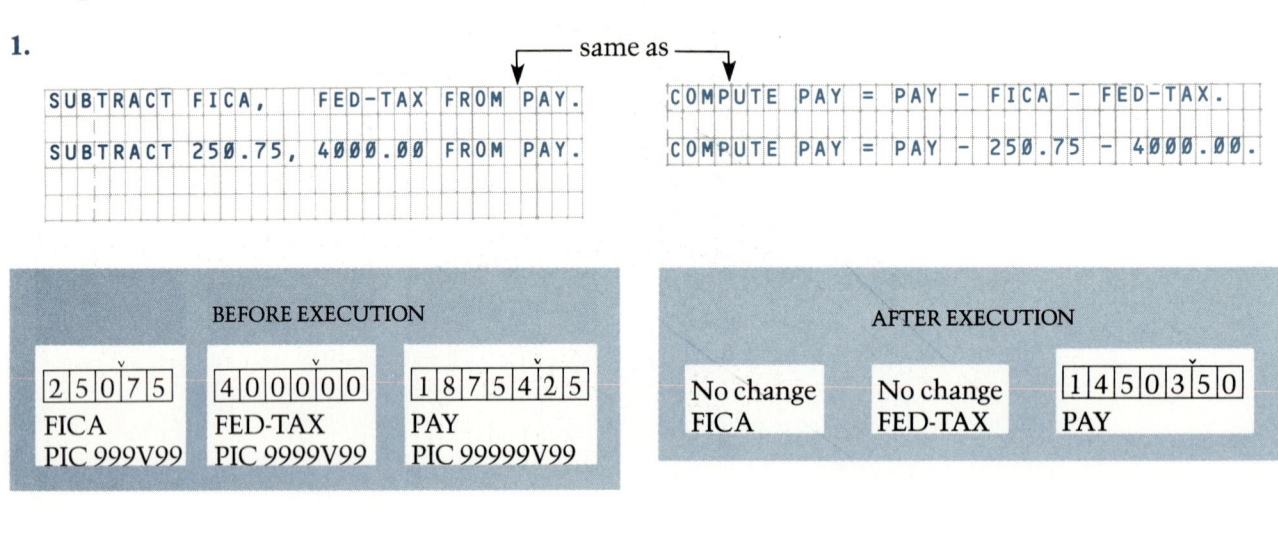

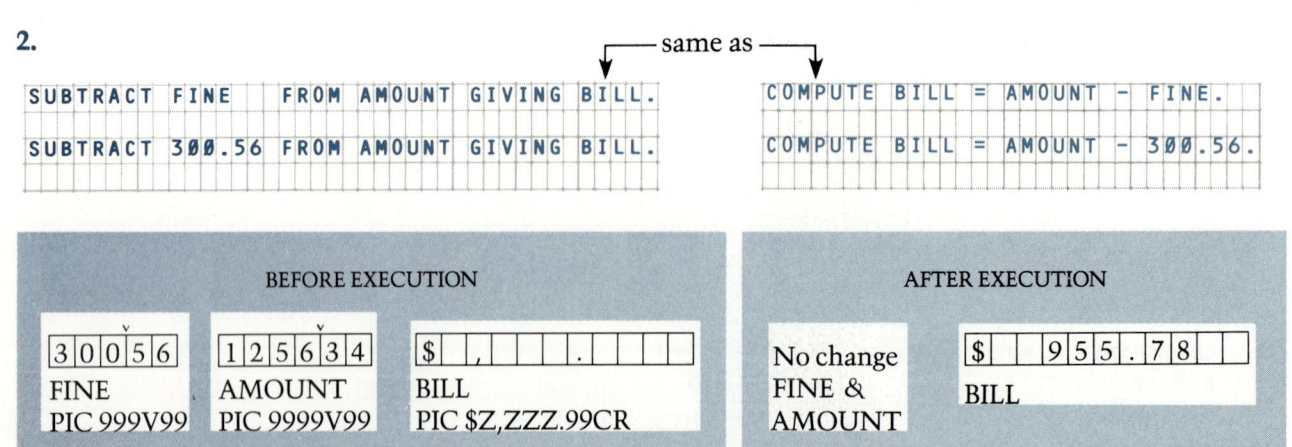

1.

— same as —

```
SUBTRACT FICA, FED-TAX FROM PAY.        COMPUTE PAY = PAY - FICA - FED-TAX.
SUBTRACT 250.75, 4000.00 FROM PAY.      COMPUTE PAY = PAY - 250.75 - 4000.00.
```

BEFORE EXECUTION

250ˇ75	4000ˇ00	1875ˇ425
FICA	FED-TAX	PAY
PIC 999V99	PIC 9999V99	PIC 99999V99

AFTER EXECUTION

No change FICA   No change FED-TAX   1450ˇ350 PAY

2.

— same as —

```
SUBTRACT FINE FROM AMOUNT GIVING BILL.     COMPUTE BILL = AMOUNT - FINE.
SUBTRACT 300.56 FROM AMOUNT GIVING BILL.   COMPUTE BILL = AMOUNT - 300.56.
```

BEFORE EXECUTION

300ˇ56	1256ˇ34	$, .
FINE	AMOUNT	BILL
PIC 999V99	PIC 9999V99	PIC $Z,ZZZ.99CR

AFTER EXECUTION

No change FINE & AMOUNT $ 955.78   BILL

4-3-3 THE MULTIPLY INSTRUCTION

The general form of the MULTIPLY verb is shown in Figure 4–9.

THE EDITING PROCESS AND ARITHMETIC STATEMENTS 145

1. MULTIPLY $\begin{Bmatrix} \text{data-name-1} \\ \text{numeric-literal-1} \end{Bmatrix}$ <u>BY</u> data-name-2.

(Meaning: data-name-2 = data-name-2 · data-name-1)

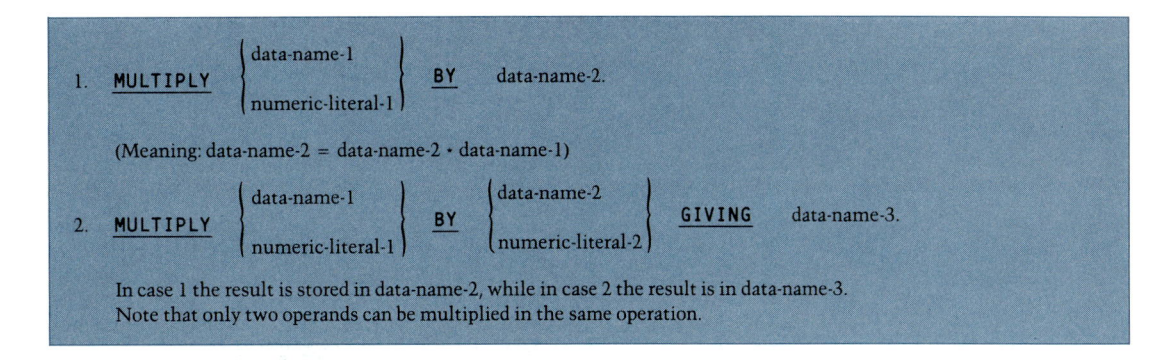

2. MULTIPLY $\begin{Bmatrix} \text{data-name-1} \\ \text{numeric-literal-1} \end{Bmatrix}$ <u>BY</u> $\begin{Bmatrix} \text{data-name-2} \\ \text{numeric-literal-2} \end{Bmatrix}$ <u>GIVING</u> data-name-3.

In case 1 the result is stored in data-name-2, while in case 2 the result is in data-name-3.
Note that only two operands can be multiplied in the same operation.

FIGURE 4–9
THE MULTIPLY VERB

Examples:

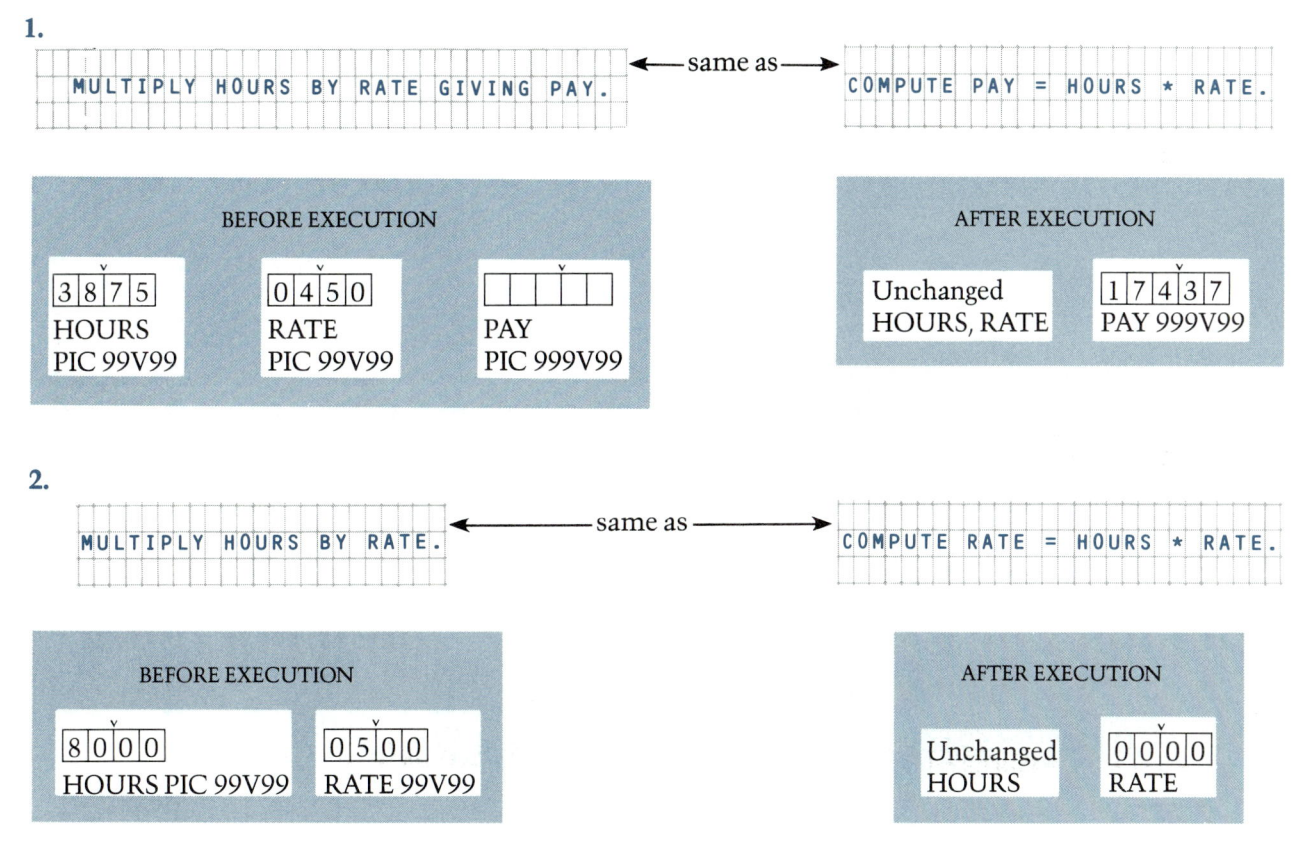

1.

MULTIPLY HOURS BY RATE GIVING PAY.   ←— same as —→   COMPUTE PAY = HOURS * RATE.

BEFORE EXECUTION

3 8 7 5		0 4 5 0		
HOURS		RATE		PAY
PIC 99V99		PIC 99V99		PIC 999V99

AFTER EXECUTION

Unchanged | 1 7 4 3 7 |
HOURS, RATE | PAY 999V99 |

2.

MULTIPLY HOURS BY RATE.   ←— same as —→   COMPUTE RATE = HOURS * RATE.

BEFORE EXECUTION

| 8 0 0 0 | | 0 5 0 0 |
| HOURS PIC 99V99 | | RATE 99V99 |

AFTER EXECUTION

Unchanged | 0 0 0 0 |
HOURS | RATE |

Note that the result is stored in RATE. Also note that the result in RATE is 0! That is because the picture field is not large enough to accomodate the left-most digit 4. (Solution: Use RATE PIC 999V99.)

Just as in the preceding arithmetic operations, care must be taken to specify the size of the result field as well as the number of positions to the left and right of the decimal point. If two operands, operand-1 and operand-2, are to be multiplied, and if operand-1 contains m digits in all with m_1 digits to the left of the decimal point, and operand-2 contains n digits in all with n_1 digits to the left of the decimal point, then:

- The result field cannot exceed $m + n$ digits.
- The number of digits to the left of the decimal point cannot exceed $m_1 + n_1$.

Example: A = −12.6 and B = 10.34 and we wish to MULTIPLY A BY B. The number of digits to the left of the decimal point for the result field B cannot exceed 4; hence the PICTURE for B should be S9999V999.

	Before execution	After execution
MULTIPLY A BY	B	B
1 2 6̄ / S 9 9V9	0 0 1 0 3 4 0 / S 9 9 9 9V9 9 9	0 1 3 0 2 8 4̄ / S 9 9 9 9V9 9 9

4-3-4 THE DIVIDE INSTRUCTION

The various forms of the DIVIDE statements are shown in Figure 4–10.

Division requires a little more attention than the other arithmetic operations since the programmer must decide ahead of time how many digits to the right of the decimal point should be reatined.

Example: Suppose we wish to divide B into A (A/B) where A = 22 and B = 7, using the statement

```
DIVIDE B INTO A
```

or the equivalent statement

```
COMPUTE A = A / B.
```

1. <u>DIVIDE</u> {data-name-1 / numeric-literal-1} <u>INTO</u> data-name-2.

$$\left(\text{meaning: data-name-2} = \frac{\text{data-name-2}}{\text{data-name-1}}\right)$$

2. <u>DIVIDE</u> {data-name-1 / numeric-literal-1} <u>INTO</u> {data-name-2 / numeric-literal-2} <u>GIVING</u> data-name-3.

$$\left(\text{meaning: data-name-3} = \frac{\text{data-name-2}}{\text{data-name-1}}\right)$$

3. <u>DIVIDE</u> {data-name-1 / numeric literal-1} <u>BY</u> {data-name-2 / numeric-literal-2} <u>GIVING</u> data-name-3.

$$\left(\text{meaning: data-name-3} = \frac{\text{data-name-1}}{\text{data-name-2}}\right)$$

FIGURE 4–10
THE DIVIDE VERB

We know the value of 22/7 = 3.1428571.... How many of the digits to the right of the decimal point do we want? If we want two digits to the right of the decimal point, then A should be defined with a PICTURE of 99V99 (remember that the result is going to be stored in A), as is done below:

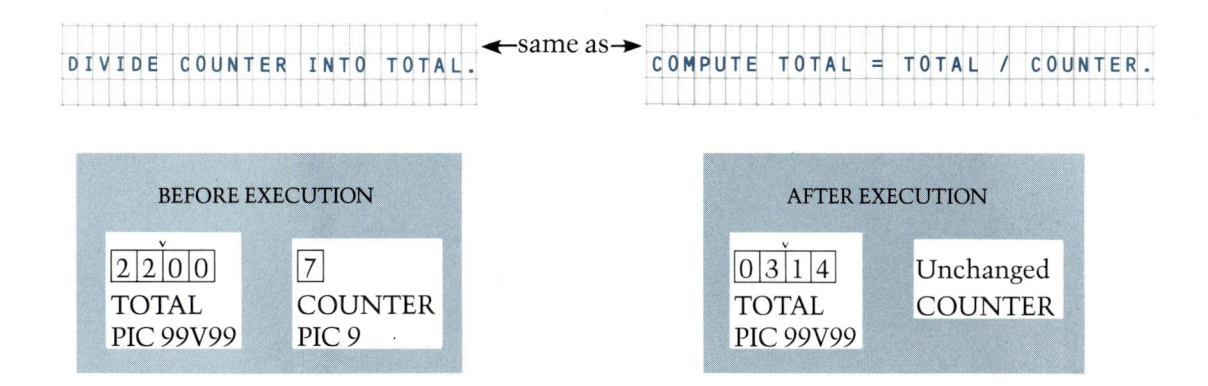

```
DIVIDE COUNTER INTO TOTAL.      ←same as→      COMPUTE TOTAL = TOTAL / COUNTER.
```

BEFORE EXECUTION

2200	7
TOTAL	COUNTER
PIC 99V99	PIC 9

AFTER EXECUTION

0314	Unchanged
TOTAL	COUNTER
PIC 99V99	

As we have noted for other arithmetic operations, data names specified by the GIVING verb can be report-type fields (except when the data name itself is to participate in the operation).

Example: Suppose we write DIVIDE A BY B GIVING C (A/B→C) where A = −1500 and B = 3:

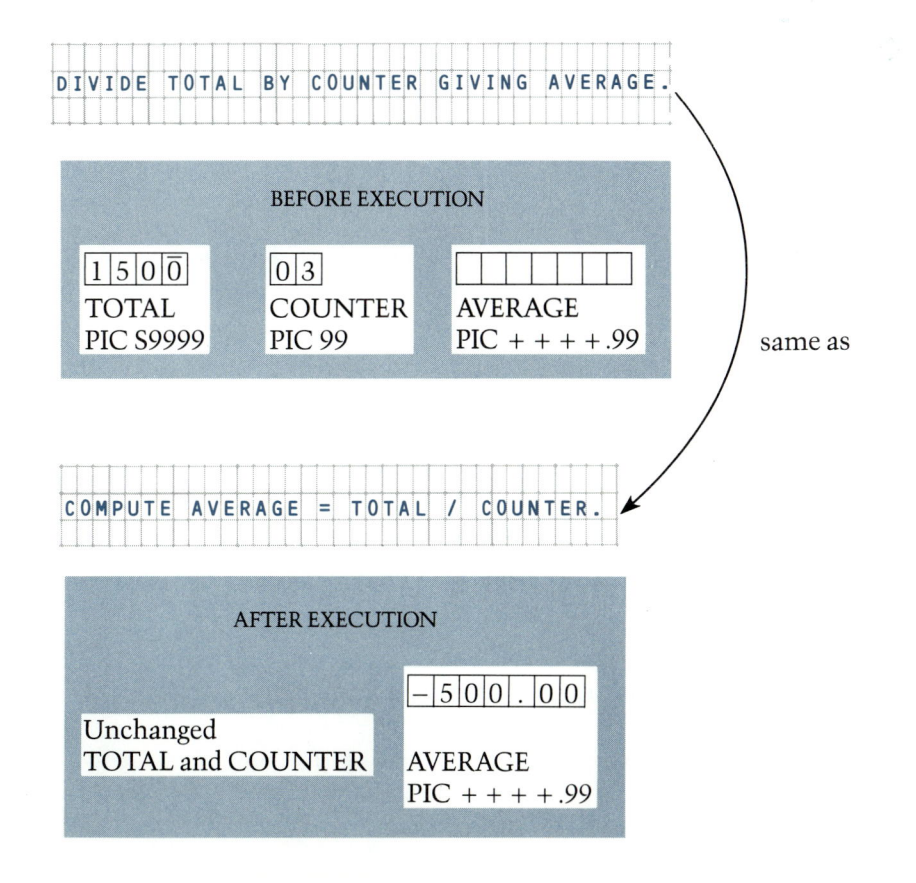

```
DIVIDE TOTAL BY COUNTER GIVING AVERAGE.
```

BEFORE EXECUTION

1500	03	[ ]
TOTAL	COUNTER	AVERAGE
PIC S9999	PIC 99	PIC + + + + .99

same as

```
COMPUTE AVERAGE = TOTAL / COUNTER.
```

AFTER EXECUTION

Unchanged TOTAL and COUNTER

| −500.00 |
| AVERAGE |
| PIC + + + + .99 |

The REMAINDER Option

Sometimes it may be important to know the remainder of a division operation. The remainder is given by the formula:

$$\text{Remainder} = \text{Dividend} - (\text{Quotient} * \text{Divisor})$$

Examples:

1. dividend → $\dfrac{17}{3}$ = 5 + $\dfrac{2}{3}$ ← remainder   (2 = 17 − 5 * 3)
   divisor →

   ↑ quotient

2. $\dfrac{4.37}{16.33}$ = .26 + $\dfrac{.1242}{16.33}$ ← remainder   The quotient (.26) accounts for 2 digits to the right of the decimal point.

3. $\dfrac{4.37}{16.33}$ = .2 + $\dfrac{1.104}{16.33}$ ← remainder   The quotient (.2) accounts for only 1 digit to the right of the decimal point. Notice the difference in the remainder.

Note that the maximum number of digits for the remainder will never exceed the number of digits in the divisor, i.e., 4 (16.33) examples 2 and 3.

The REMAINDER clause can only be used in conjunction with the GIVING option. To code item 2 above, we would use the following sentence:

```
DIVIDE 4.37 BY 16.33 GIVING X REMAINDER Z.
```

In this case the PICTURE for X might be 99V99 and the PICTURE for Z might be V9999.

One of many applications of the REMAINDER option is to break a dollar amount into the least number of coins possible—half dollars, quarters, dimes, nickels, and pennies. The REMAINDER function could be used as follows:

To break $1.98, convert to cents and divide by 50 for number of half dollars.

1. $\dfrac{198}{50}$ = 3 half dollars.   Remainder = 48. Next, divide remainder by 25.

2. $\dfrac{48}{25}$ = 1 quarter.   Remainder = 23. Next, divide remainder by 10.

3. $\dfrac{23}{10}$ = 2 dimes.   Remainder = 3. Next, divide remainder by 5.

4. $\dfrac{3}{5}$ = 0 nickels.   Remainder = 3.

Thus $1.98 = 3 half dollars + 1 quarter + 2 dimes + 0 nickels + 3 pennies.

4-3-5 ARITHMETIC OPERATION OPTIONS

Figure 4–11 displays the general forms of the various arithmetic statements that use the ROUNDED, ON SIZE ERROR, and REMAINDER options.

The ROUNDED Option

If the result of an arithmetic operation contains more decimal positions than are reserved in the result field, the excess right-most digits are truncated. The ROUNDED option can be used to round off the right-most digit in the receiving field.

Rounding off a number to n significant digits means leaving the nth digit unchanged if the $(n + 1)$th digit is either a 0, 1, 2, 3 or 4, or adding 1 to the nth digit if the $(n + 1)$th digit is 5 or above.

Examples:

1. A = 1.349, B = 3.268 both with PICTURE 9V999.

    ```
    ADD    A         B      GIVING   C   ROUNDED.
           ↓         ↓               ↓
        ┌─┬─┬─┬─┐ ┌─┬─┬─┬─┐       ┌─┬─┬─┐
        │1│3│4│9│ │3│2│6│8│       │4│6│2│
        ├─┼─┼─┼─┤+├─┼─┼─┼─┤   =   ├─┼─┼─┤
        │9V9 9 9│ │9V9 9 9│       │9V9 9│
        └─┴─┴─┴─┘ └─┴─┴─┴─┘       └─┴─┴─┘
    ```

    1.349 + 3.268 = 4.617 real answer.
    1.349 + 3.268 = 4.61 truncated to 2 fractional positions.
    1.349 + 3.268 = 4.62 rounded to 2 fractional positions.

2. Assume

    ```
    A PICTURE 99V9 VALUE 46.8.
    B PICTURE S99V99 VALUE 31.05.

    SUBTRACT   A    FROM    B    GIVING   C    ROUNDED.
               ↓            ↓             ↓
            ┌─┬─┬─┐     ┌─┬─┬─┬─┐      ┌─┬─┬─┐
            │4│6│8│     │3│1│0│5│      │ │-│1│6│
            ├─┼─┼─┤     ├─┼─┼─┼─┤  =   ├─┼─┼─┤
            │S 9 9V9│   │S 9 9V9 9│    │- - 9 9│
            └─┴─┴─┘     └─┴─┴─┴─┘      └─┴─┴─┘
    ```

    31.05 − 46.8 = − 15.75 real answer.
    31.05 − 46.8 = − 15. truncated to 0 fractional position.
    31.05 − 46.8 = − 16. rounded to 0 fractional position.

3. Assume

    ```
    A PIC 9V9 VALUE 6.4.
    B PIC 9V9 VALUE .5.
    C PICTURE 9.

    COMPUTE C ROUNDED  =  A  +  B.
            ↓             ↓     ↓
          ┌─┐           ┌─┬─┐ ┌─┬─┐
          │7│           │6│4│ │0│5│
          ├─┤           ├─┼─┤ ├─┼─┤
          │9│           │9V9│ │9V9│
          └─┘           └─┴─┘ └─┴─┘
    ```
    Note where the ROUNDED option is placed.

    6.4 + 0.5 = 6.9 real result.
    6.4 + 0.5 = 6. truncated to 0 fractional positions.
    6.4 + 0.5 = 7. rounded to 0 fractional positions.

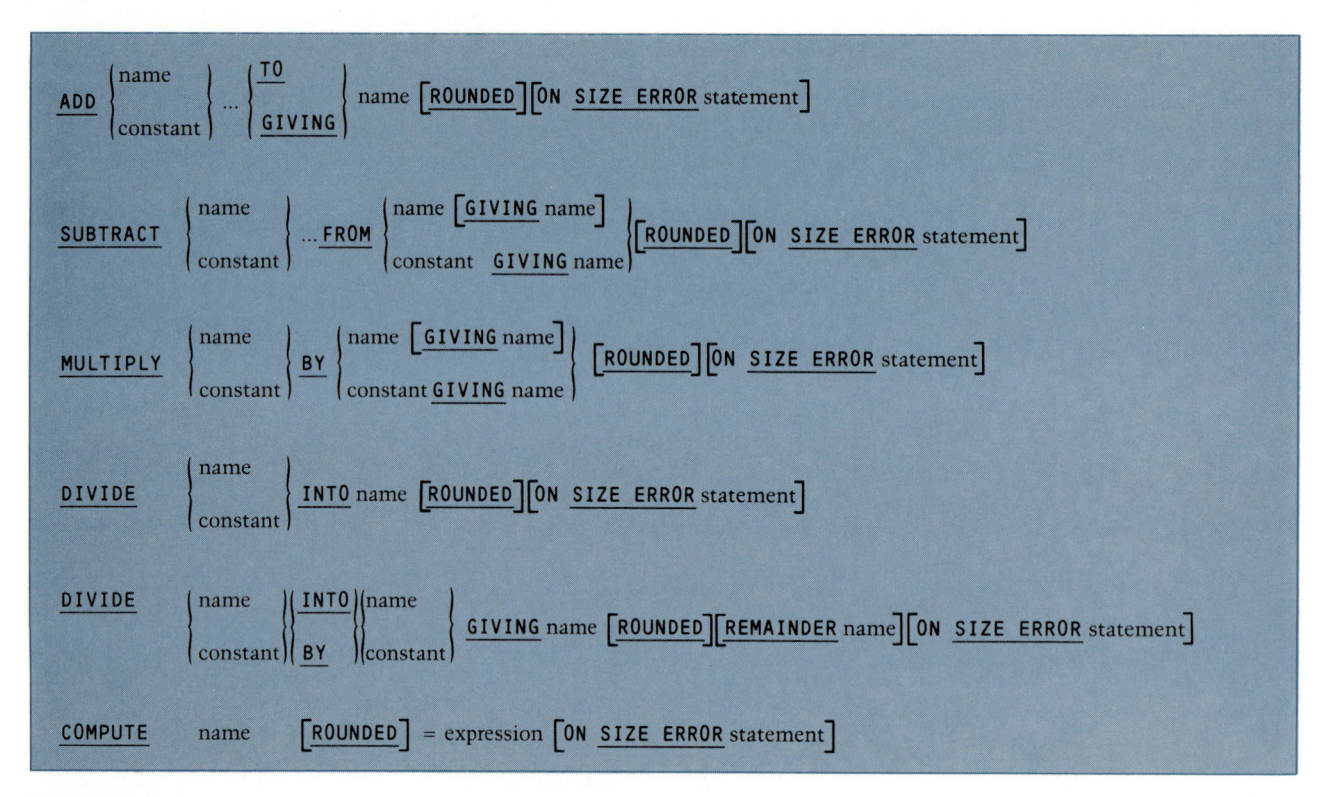

```
ADD      {name    } ... {TO    } name [ROUNDED][ON SIZE ERROR statement]
         {constant}     {GIVING}

SUBTRACT {name    } ...FROM {name    [GIVING name]} [ROUNDED][ON SIZE ERROR statement]
         {constant}          {constant GIVING name}

MULTIPLY {name    } BY {name    [GIVING name]} [ROUNDED][ON SIZE ERROR statement]
         {constant}     {constant GIVING name}

DIVIDE   {name    } INTO name [ROUNDED][ON SIZE ERROR statement]
         {constant}

DIVIDE   {name    }{INTO}{name    } GIVING name [ROUNDED][REMAINDER name][ON SIZE ERROR statement]
         {constant}{BY  }{constant}

COMPUTE  name [ROUNDED] = expression [ON SIZE ERROR statement]
```

FIGURE 4–11

ARITHMETIC OPERATION FORMATS *Constant* refers to a numeric literal and *name* refers to a data item (numeric).

4. Assume

   C PICTURE 9V9.
   D PICTURE 99V99.

   DIVIDE 4.36 BY 16.3 GIVING C REMAINDER D ROUNDED.

   without ROUNDED OPTION → | 0 | 2 | | 0 | 3 | ← with ROUNDED option
                            | 9V9 | | 9V9 |

   Note the quotient is rounded, not the remainder.

The ON SIZE ERROR Option

While the ROUNDED option applies to the loss of digits on the right, the ON SIZE ERROR applies to the loss of digits (significant) on the left. The ON SIZE ERROR option allows the programmer to specify what action or actions the computer is to take in either of the following events:

1. A division by 0 occurs during execution time.
2. Digits to the left of the decimal point are truncated as a result of a receiving field being too small to accommodate results of a numeric calculation.

THE EDITING PROCESS AND ARITHMETIC STATEMENTS   151

Example:

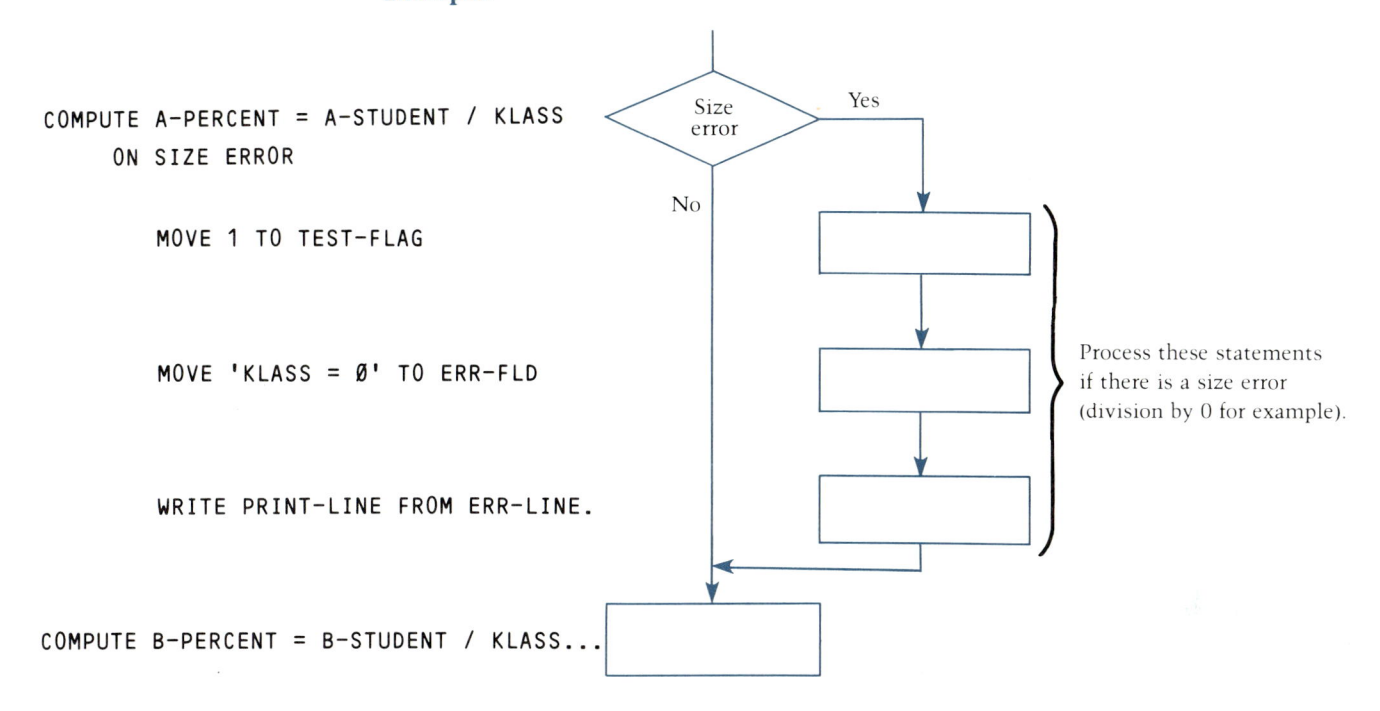

```
COMPUTE A-PERCENT = A-STUDENT / KLASS
    ON SIZE ERROR

       MOVE 1 TO TEST-FLAG


       MOVE 'KLASS = 0' TO ERR-FLD


       WRITE PRINT-LINE FROM ERR-LINE.


COMPUTE B-PERCENT = B-STUDENT / KLASS...
```

Process these statements if there is a size error (division by 0 for example).

If KLASS is 0, a division by 0 will occur. At this point the sequence of statements specified by the ON SIZE ERROR is carried out (all statements up to the first period encountered). After these statements have been carried out, the program resumes execution at the next statement (COMPUTE B-PERCENT...).

If KLASS is not 0, then there is no division by 0 and all statements specified by the ON SIZE ERROR are skipped. Control resumes at the next sentence (COMPUTE B-PERCENT...).

Moving a 1 into TEST-FLAG allows the programmer to test TEST-FLAG at various points in the program and take appropriate action.

If the ERROR option had not been included in the DIVIDE instruction, the system would have terminated the program right at the DIVIDE instruction with a division by 0 error message.

> **CAUTION** If the period after the sentence WRITE PRINT-LINE FROM ERR-LINE had been omitted, then the statement COMPUTE B-PERCENT... would become part of the ON SIZE ERROR routine and that statement would never be executed if the division were "all right"!

Example: Assume

```
77 A PIC 99 VALUE 21.
77 B PIC 99 VALUE 85.
```

Consider now the sentences

```
ADD A TO B ON SIZE ERROR PERFORM OVFLOW-WRITE.
MOVE B TO FLDA.
```

Since B is too small to accommodate 106 (85 + 21) in a two-digit field, the paragraph specified by the ON SIZE ERROR is carried out, after which the next sentence (MOVE B TO FLDA) is executed.

If the size of B accommodates the result, the statements specified by the ERROR clause are bypassed and execution resumes at the next sentence (MOVE B TO FLDA).

Whether or not the ON SIZE ERROR is specified, the truncated result (06 in this case) is stored in the receiving field. If the ERROR option is not specified, no error message will be given by the computer.

Data validation techniques (chapter 6) are often used to reduce or eliminate the need for the ON SIZE ERROR option. It is important to understand both.

4-3-6 DO IT NOW

1. True or false (if false, explain why):
   a. `PIC S999.9 VALUE -123.5.` is a valid PICTURE field.
   b. `ADD BONUS, PAY TO TOTAL` is equivalent to
      `ADD BONUS, PAY GIVING TOTAL.`
   c. `COMPUTE TEMP = 32.5 + -15.3` is a valid statement.
   d. `SUBTRACT FINE FROM 56.75.` is an invalid statement.
   e. `SUBTRACT FINE FROM -2.5 GIVING AMT` is a valid statement.
   f. `MULTIPLY 3.2, X, 4.5 BY BILL GIVING TOTAL` is a valid statement.
   g. `MULTIPLY A BY 40` is a valid statement.
   h. `MULTIPLY HOURS BY RATE` where `RATE` has `PICTURE 99.9` is a valid statement.
   i. `DIVIDE A BY B` is a valid statement.

2. Specify the value of PAY after execution of the statement ADD BONUS TO PAY, where initially BONUS = 50.75, PAY = 80.40 and both fields have PICTURE 99V99.

3. If T has PICTURE ----.9, specify value of T as a result of
   MULTIPLY 3 BY − 10.5 GIVING T.

4. Assume

   ```
   N1 PIC XXX VALUE'123'.
   N2 PIC XXX VALUE'-123'.
   ```

   What value will be stored in N2 as a result of ADD N1 to N2?

5. Display the memory contents of D after the following operations. Assume D has PICTURE S999V9.

	A PIC	A VALUE	B PIC	B VALUE	C PIC	C VALUE	D PIC
a. ADD A B C GIVING D.	S99V99	0200	S999	03$\bar{2}$	V999	300	S999V9
b. SUBTRACT B C FROM A GIVING D.							
c. MULTIPLY A BY B GIVING D ROUNDED.							
d. DIVIDE A BY B GIVING D.							
e. COMPUTE D = (A + B) ** A - 2.							

THE EDITING PROCESS AND ARITHMETIC STATEMENTS

6. Display the contents of D after the following operations. Assume W has PICTURE 9.

	A		B		C		D
	PIC	VAL	PIC	VAL	PIC	VAL	PIC
	S99V99	0200	S999	03$\bar{2}$	V999	300	S999V9

```
a. COMPUTE D = C ON SIZE ERROR
      MOVE 1 TO D.
b. COMPUTE D = B + 1032
      ON SIZE ERROR MOVE 1 TO D.
c. DIVIDE B BY 5 GIVING W
      REMAINDER D.
d. COMPUTE D = A - C * 12
      ON SIZE ERROR MOVE 3 TO D.
```

ANSWERS

1.
   a. False. The symbol S may only be used in a numeric PICTURE field.
   b. False. It is equivalent to ADD BONUS, PAY, TOTAL GIVING TOTAL.
   c. False. No two arithmetic operators may be side by side.
   d. True. (SUBTRACT 56.75 FROM FINE.)
   e. True.
   f. False. Only one data field may follow the MULTIPLY verb.
   g. True. 4O (and not 40) is a valid data name!
   h. False. RATE is a numeric edited field and cannot be processed arithmetically.
   i. False. The BY option requires GIVING.

2. 31.15

3. | |−|3|1|.|5|

4. Error. Arithmetic operations cannot be performed on alphanumeric data.

5. a. 029V$\bar{7}$ b. 033V7   c. 064V$\bar{0}$ d. 000V0   e. 898V0

6. a. 000V3   b. 001V0   c. 002V$\bar{0}$ d. 001V$\bar{6}$

4-4 YOU MIGHT WANT TO KNOW

1. When writing an arithmetic statement without the COMPUTE verb, I forget which operand stores the result. Is there any easy way to remember?

   Answer: Yes. The result is always stored in the right-most operand.

Examples:

```
ADD        A    TO      B  ⎫
MULTIPLY   A    BY      B  ⎬ → The result is always stored
SUBTRACT   A    FROM    B  ⎪   in the right-most operand, B.
DIVIDE     A    INTO    B  ⎭
```

2. Sometimes I wish I could use the same name to refer to a particular field defined in two different records. For example, my input record might consist of data items such as NAME, ADDRESS, and OCCUPATION. Do I have to think of brand new names to identify these data items in my output record, such as NAME-OUT, ADDRESS-OUT, and OCCUPATION-OUT et cetera?

   Answer: No. You can use the same data-item names in both record descriptions. However, any reference to these data names must be qualified, i.e., you must indicate the records pertaining to these items. This is accomplished as follows:

```
01  INPT-RECORD.                    01  DETAIL-LINE.
    05  NAME        PIC X(20).          05  FILLER      PIC X(5).
    05  ADDRESS.                        05  NAME        PIC X(20).
        10  STREET  PIC X(6).           05  ADDRESS.
        10  ZIP     PIC 9(5).               10  FILLER  PIC X(5).
    05  SEX         PIC 9.                  10  STREET  PIC X(6).
                                            10  FILLER  PIC X(5).
                                            10  ZIP     PIC 9(5).
                                        05  FILLER      PIC X(40).
```

   In the PROCEDURE division you can then write the following:

$$\text{MOVE NAME} \begin{Bmatrix} \text{IN} \\ \text{OF} \end{Bmatrix} \text{INPT-RECORD TO ...}$$

$$\text{MOVE ADDRESS} \begin{Bmatrix} \text{IN} \\ \text{OF} \end{Bmatrix} \text{DETAIL-LINE TO ...}$$

   choose either IN or OF

   For elementary items at two levels of subdivision, two levels of qualification are required, as in:

            level 2   level 1   level 2   level 1

   `MOVE ZIP OF ADDRESS OF INPT-RECORD TO ZIP IN ADDRESS OF DETAIL-LINE.`

3. Question 2 has given me some ideas. Could I just move INPT-RECORD to DETAIL-LINE (defined in question 2) and hope that each elementary item of the sending group item will be moved into its corresponding named location in the receiving field? After all, the names are the same. For instance, will NAME of the input record find its way to NAME of the output record?

   Answer: In essence, yes, you can! But you must use the MOVE CORRESPONDING option, which will move all data item names common to both records but not those that are different. For example, using the record descriptions in question 2, we can write the following:

$$\text{MOVE} \begin{Bmatrix} \text{CORRESPONDING} \\ \text{CORR} \end{Bmatrix} \text{INPT-RECORD TO DETAIL-LINE.}$$

   This instruction will move NAME, STREET, and ZIP of INPT-RECORD to their corresponding named locations in DETAIL-LINE. SEX, however, will not be moved (there is no recipient by the same name in DETAIL-LINE). It should be noted that the CORRESPONDING move will move the common names (NAME, STREET, and ZIP) regardless of whether the common names are listed in the same order in both records. In addition, the common name PICTUREs can be of different lengths and/or types. Numeric elementary items of the sending field can be edited into same-named report fields in the receiving group item.

4. Sometimes I wish I could include in my report the date and/or time at which my program was run. Is there an easy way to do this without reading the date or time from a data record?

   Answer: In many COBOL compilers there is a way to extract the date or time from the computing system through certain reserved words. (Check your own technical reference manual.) In many systems CURRENT–DATE will return the date in the format MMDDYY (MM = month, DD = day, YY = year). Thus,

   ```
   MOVE CURRENT-DATE TO HEADER-OUT
   ```

   is permissible. The reserved word TIME (N), where N is an integer, will also return the time in different formats, depending on the value of N. On some compilers, the ACCEPT verb can also be used to capture the date and time. (See chapter 5).

5. I am writing a report with dollar amounts spread out over many columns that have PICTURE $Z,ZZ9.99. I don't want zero dollar fields such as $0.00 on my report; instead I prefer blank fields. How can I force the system to print blanks for these fields?

   Answer: Use the BLANK WHEN ZERO option. This option will print blanks for any numeric or numeric edited elementary data items that specify the BLANK WHEN ZERO clause in the record description entry. Obviously blanks will be printed out only if the receiving field contains a zero result.

   Examples:

   ```
   77 X        PIC 999       BLANK WHEN ZERO.
   05 DATE-IN  PIC 99B99B99  BLANK WHEN ZERO.
   05 AMT      PIC $$,$$$.99 BLANK WHEN ZERO.
   ```

   If zeros are moved into any of these three fields, blanks will be printed if the field is printed.

6. Is there any easy way to tell the computer to print a blank line?

   Answer: Depending on the objective sought, lines can be skipped by using the AFTER ADVANCING option used with the WRITE statement. In all other cases you can move SPACES to your output record and then print the output record. For example, assume PRINT–LINE is the output record:

   ```
   MOVE SPACES TO PRINT-LINE.
   WRITE PRINT-LINE AFTER ADVANCING 1 LINE.
   ```

7. My program did more than I expected it to do! I forgot to include the STOP RUN in the PROCEDURE division. What did the computer do?

   Answer: Since no STOP RUN was present, the computer continued on to the next paragraph to get its next instruction.

8. I have this lengthy PICTURE $ – – – – 9999.99999. Can I use repetition factors, as in PICTURE $ – (5)9(4).9(5).?

   Answer: Yes, but it is not very readable!

9. Can the minus sign also be printed with the DB and CR symbols?

   Answer: Yes. For example, if FLD has PICTURE – – –.99DB then MOVE – 3.4 TO FLD will result in FLD = | |–|3|.|4|0|D|B|
   The only time DB or CR will be printed, however, is if the value is negative.

10. When writing COBOL programs, I seem to be spending most of my time writing out record entries for my headers! Can I reduce the size of these header records?

    Answer: Yes. Consider the following headers:

Long Way	Short Way
`01 HEADING-1.`	`01 HEADING-11.`
`   05 FILLER PIC X(10) VALUE SPACES.`	`   05 FILLER PIC X(10) VALUE SPACES.`
`   05 FILLER PIC X(04) VALUE "NAME".`	`   05 FILLER PIC X(20) VALUE "NAME".`
`   05 FILLER PIC X(16) VALUE SPACES.`	`   05 FILLER PIC X(11) VALUE "ADDRESS".`
`   05 FILLER PIC X(06) VALUE "ADDRESS".`	`   05 FILLER PIC X(07) VALUE "SEX".`
`   05 FILLER PIC X(05) VALUE SPACES.`	`   05 FILLER PIC X(07) VALUE "EARNING".`
`   05 FILLER PIC X(03) VALUE "SEX".`	
`   05 FILLER PIC X(04) VALUE SPACES.`	
`   05 FILLER PIC X(07) VALUE "EARNING".`	
`   05 FILLER PIC X(78) VALUE SPACES.`	

Both records are identical. In the record on the right, the spaces are included in the various header fields. Note, also, that there is no need for trailing spaces in record HEADING-11, i.e., PIC X(78) has been left out; when the record is moved to the output record, spaces will automatically be provided to the right of the EARNING field to match up the record length of the output record. (See the rules for the MOVE statement when the receiving field is larger than the sending field.)

This shortcut is fine for getting you quickly to the PROCEDURE DIVISION. However, your instructor may disapprove of this technique. In that event, when your program has been debugged, you can reconstruct the headings appropriately (they will need to be changed anyway!).

4-5 WRITING PROGRAMS

4-5-1 PROBLEM SPECIFICATION: A FULLY EDITED REPORT

An input file consists of an unknown number of records each containing the following seven fields:

Positions 1-10: Author name PIC X(10).

Positions 11-20: Book title PIC X(10).

Positions 21-25: Number of copies sold PIC 99999.

Positions 26–30: Number of copies returned PIC 99999.

Positions 31–34: Cost of book PIC 99V99.

Positions 35–36: Contract percentage, for example,
15% of net sales PIC V99.

Positions 37–39: Percentage of royalties in case
book is coauthored PIC 9V99.
(For example if there are three authors, each gets 33.3% of royalties.)

An example of an input file is shown below:

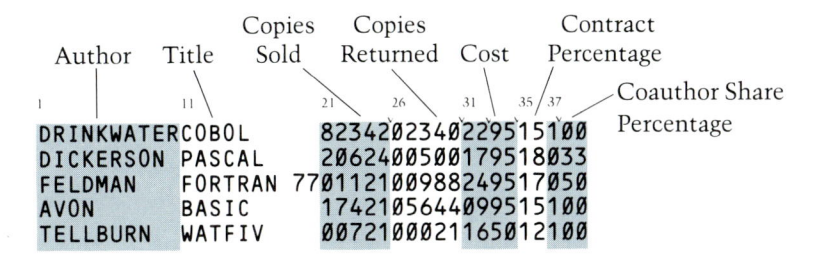

```
                 Copies  Copies         Contract
        Author   Title   Sold  Returned  Cost  Percentage
        1        11      21    26        31    35 37   Coauthor Share
        DRINKWATERCOBOL       8234202340229515100   Percentage
        DICKERSON PASCAL      2062400500179518033
        FELDMAN   FORTRAN 7701121009882249517050
        AVON      BASIC       1742105644099515100
        TELLBURN  WATFIV      0072100021165012100
```

Write a program to compute net sales, total royalty amount, and author royalty due. The report should also specify the author's name, the book title, the number of copies sold, the number of copies returned, the author percentage expressed in a nonfractional form, and the royalty rate contract. The output should be similar to the following:

```
                              PUBLICATION REPORT
                    COPIES                     NET      ROYALTY    COAUTHOR     ROYALTY   ROYALTY
AUTHOR      TITLE   SOLD    RETURNS   COST     SALES    AMOUNT     PERCENTAGE   RATE      DUE

DRINKWATER  COBOL       82,342  2,340  $22.95  1,836,045.90  275,406.88  100.00%   15%   $275,406.88
DICKERSON   PASCAL      20,624    500  $17.95    361,225.80   65,020.64   33.00%   18%   $ 21,456.81
FELDMAN     FORTRAN 77   1,121    988  $24.95      3,318.35      564.11   50.00%   17%   $    282.05
AVON        BASIC       17,421  5,644   $9.95    117,181.15   17,577.17  100.00%   15%   $ 17,577.17
TELLBURN    WATFIV         721     21  $16.50     11,550.00    1,386.00  100.00%   12%   $  1,386.00
                        -------  -----          ------------                              -----------
                        122,229  9493          2,329,321.20                              $316,108.91
```

Understanding the Program

The program to solve this problem is shown in Figure 4–12.

To compute the net sales, we must subtract the number of books returned from the total number of copies sold and multiply that number by the cost of the book (see line 190).

The royalty amount for a particular book is a percentage of the net sales, as specified by the royalty rate (see line 191).

The royalty due to the author is 100 percent of the royalty amount if there is only one author or a percentage of that amount if there are coauthors (see line 194).

To keep track of the total number of copies sold, returns, net sales, and royalties due, we set four data item names (called accumulators) to 0, as shown in lines 47 through 50. For example each time we read a record, we add the number

```
 1:    IDENTIFICATION DIVISION.
 2:    PROGRAM-ID. ROYALTIES.
 3:    AUTHOR. JONES.
 4:   **************************************************************
 5:   *  OBJECTIVE:  PRODUCE A REPORT FOR A PUBLISHING COMPANY TO   *
 6:   *              COMPUTE ROYALTY DUE TO AUTHORS BASED ON NUMBER *
 7:   *              BOOKS SOLD AND CONTRACT RATES.                 *
 8:   *                                                             *
 9:   *  INPUT:  AUTHOR; BOOK TITLE; COPIES SOLD; BOOK RETURNS; COST; *
10:   *          CONTRACT RATE: TYPICAL CONTRACT IS 15% OF NET SALES; *
11:   *          AUTHOR SHARE OF ROYALTIES IN CASE OF COAUTHORS (50%) *
12:   *                                                             *
13:   *  OUTPUT: PRINT ALL INPUT DATA AND COMPUTE NET SALES, TOTAL  *
14:   *          ROYALTY AMOUNT AND ROYALTY DUE FOR EACH AUTHOR.    *
15:   *          ACCUMULATE TOTAL COPIES SOLD, TOTAL RETURNS, TOTAL *
16:   *          ROYALTY AMOUNTS AND TOTAL ROYALTIES DUE TO AUTHORS *
17:   **************************************************************
18:    ENVIRONMENT DIVISION.
19:    CONFIGURATION SECTION.
20:    SOURCE-COMPUTER. IBM.
21:    OBJECT-COMPUTER. IBM.
22:    INPUT-OUTPUT SECTION.
23:    FILE-CONTROL.
24:        SELECT REPORT-FILE  ASSIGN TO PRINTER.
25:        SELECT AUTHOR-PUBLICATIONS ASSIGN TO DISK
26:        ORGANIZATION IS LINE SEQUENTIAL.
27:   *
28:    DATA DIVISION.
29:    FILE SECTION.
30:   *
31:    FD  AUTHOR-PUBLICATIONS
32:        LABEL RECORDS ARE STANDARD
33:        VALUE OF FILE-ID IS 'ROSTER'
34:        DATA RECORD IS INPUT-RECORD.
35:    01  INPUT-RECORD PIC X(39).
36:    FD  REPORT-FILE
37:        LABEL RECORDS ARE OMITTED
38:        DATA RECORD IS PRINT-LINE.
39:    01  PRINT-LINE PIC X(132).
40:   *
41:    WORKING-STORAGE SECTION.
42:   *
43:   *    INDEPENDENT ITEMS
44:   *
45:    01  ACCUMULATORS-AND-FLAGS.
46:        05  WS-END-FILE        PIC XXX    VALUE 'NO'.
47:        05  WS-TOTAL-COPIES    PIC 999999    VALUE 0.
48:        05  WS-TOTAL-NET-SALES PIC 99999999V99 VALUE 0.
49:        05  WS-TOTAL-RETURNS   PIC 999999    VALUE 0.
50:        05  WS-TOTAL-ROYALTIES PIC 9999999V99 VALUE 0.
51:   *
52:    01  COMPUTATIONAL-ITEMS.
53:        05  WS-COAUTHOR-PERCENTAGE PIC 999V99.
54:        05  WS-ROYALTY-RATE        PIC 99.
55:        05  WS-NET-SALES           PIC 9999999V99.
56:        05  WS-ROYALTY-AMOUNT      PIC 999999V99.
57:        05  WS-ROYALTY-DUE         PIC 999999V99.
58:   *
59:   *    INPUT RECORD DESCRIPTION
60:   *
61:    01  AUTHOR-RECORD.
62:        05  AR-AUTHOR              PIC X(10).
63:        05  AR-TITLE               PIC X(10).
64:        05  AR-COPIES-SOLD         PIC 9(05).
65:        05  AR-RETURNS             PIC 9(05).
66:        05  AR-TITLE-COST          PIC 99V99.
67:        05  AR-ROYALTY-RATE        PIC V99.
68:        05  AR-COAUTHOR-PERCENTAGE PIC 9V99.
69:   *
70:   *    OUTPUT LINE DESCRIPTIONS
71:   *
72:    01  MAJOR-HEADING.
73:        05  FILLER PIC X(53) VALUE SPACES.
74:        05  FILLER PIC X(18) VALUE
75:                   'PUBLICATION REPORT'.
76:        05  FILLER PIC X(61) VALUE SPACES.
77:   *
78:    01  MINOR-HEADING-2.
79:        05  FILLER PIC X(06) VALUE 'AUTHOR'.
80:        05  FILLER PIC X(07) VALUE SPACES.
81:        05  FILLER PIC X(05) VALUE 'TITLE'.
82:        05  FILLER PIC X(09) VALUE SPACES.
83:        05  FILLER PIC X(04) VALUE 'SOLD'.
84:        05  FILLER PIC X(05) VALUE SPACES.
85:        05  FILLER PIC X(07) VALUE 'RETURNS'.
86:        05  FILLER PIC X(05) VALUE SPACES.
87:        05  FILLER PIC X(04) VALUE 'COST'.
88:        05  FILLER PIC X(09) VALUE SPACES.
89:        05  FILLER PIC X(05) VALUE 'SALES'.
90:        05  FILLER PIC X(10) VALUE SPACES.
91:        05  FILLER PIC X(06) VALUE 'AMOUNT'.
92:        05  FILLER PIC X(05) VALUE SPACES.
93:        05  FILLER PIC X(10) VALUE 'PERCENTAGE'.
94:        05  FILLER PIC X(03) VALUE SPACES.
95:        05  FILLER PIC X(04) VALUE 'RATE'.
96:        05  FILLER PIC X(07) VALUE SPACES.
97:        05  FILLER PIC X(03) VALUE 'DUE'.
98:        05  FILLER PIC X(18) VALUE SPACES.
```

Input file — Copies Sold, Copies Returned, Cost, Contract Percentage, Coauthor Split

```
DRINKWATER COBOL    82342 02340 2295 15 100
DICKERSON  PASCAL   20624 00500 1795 18 033
FELDMAN    FORTRAN  77011 21009 88 2495 17 050
AVON       BASIC    17421 05644 0995 15 100
TELLBURN   WATFIV   00721 00021 1650 12 100
```

FIGURE 4–12
AUTHOR ROYALTY PROGRAM

```cobol
 99:  *
100:  01  MINOR-HEADING-1.
101:      05  FILLER  PIC X(26) VALUE SPACES.
102:      05  FILLER  PIC X(06) VALUE 'COPIES'.
103:      05  FILLER  PIC X(30) VALUE SPACES.
104:      05  FILLER  PIC X(03) VALUE 'NET'.
105:      05  FILLER  PIC X(10) VALUE SPACES.
106:      05  FILLER  PIC X(07) VALUE 'ROYALTY'.
107:      05  FILLER  PIC X(05) VALUE SPACES.
108:      05  FILLER  PIC X(08) VALUE 'COAUTHOR'.
109:      05  FILLER  PIC X(04) VALUE SPACES.
110:      05  FILLER  PIC X(07) VALUE 'ROYALTY'.
111:      05  FILLER  PIC X(03) VALUE SPACES.
112:      05  FILLER  PIC X(07) VALUE 'ROYALTY'.
113:      05  FILLER  PIC X(16) VALUE SPACES.
114:  *
115:  01  DETAIL-LINE.
116:      05  DL-AUTHOR              PIC X(10).
117:      05  FILLER                 PIC X(03) VALUE SPACES.
118:      05  DL-TITLE               PIC X(10).
119:      05  FILLER                 PIC X(03) VALUE SPACES.
120:      05  DL-COPIES-SOLD         PIC ZZ,ZZ9.
121:      05  FILLER                 PIC X(04) VALUE SPACES.
122:      05  DL-RETURNS             PIC ZZ,ZZ9.
123:      05  FILLER                 PIC X(05) VALUE SPACES.
124:      05  DL-TITLE-COST          PIC $$9.99.
125:      05  FILLER                 PIC X(05) VALUE SPACES.
126:      05  DL-NET-SALES           PIC Z,ZZZ,ZZ9.99.
127:      05  FILLER                 PIC X(04) VALUE SPACES.
128:      05  DL-ROYALTY-AMOUNT      PIC ZZZ,ZZ9.99.
129:      05  FILLER                 PIC X(04) VALUE SPACES.
130:      05  DL-COAUTHOR-PERCENTAGE PIC ZZ9.99.
131:      05  FILLER                 PIC X(06) VALUE '%'.
132:      05  DL-ROYALTY-RATE        PIC Z9.
133:      05  FILLER                 PIC X(06) VALUE '%'.
134:      05  DL-ROYALTY-DUE         PIC $ZZZ,ZZ9.99.
135:      05  FILLER                 PIC X(13) VALUE SPACES.
136:  *
137:  01  SUMMARY-LINE.
138:  *
139:      05  FILLER                 PIC X(25) VALUE SPACES.
140:      05  SL-COPIES-SOLD         PIC ZZZ,ZZ9.
141:      05  FILLER                 PIC X(03) VALUE SPACES.
142:      05  SL-RETURNS             PIC ZZ,ZZ9.
143:      05  FILLER                 PIC X(15) VALUE SPACES.
144:      05  SL-NET-SALES           PIC ZZ,ZZZ,ZZ9.99
145:      05  FILLER                 PIC X(38) VALUE SPACES.
146:      05  SL-ROYALTY-DUE         PIC $ZZZ,ZZ9.99.
147:      05  FILLER                 PIC X(13) VALUE SPACES.
148:  *
149:  01  UNDER-LINE.
150:      05  FILLER                 PIC X(25) VALUE SPACES.
151:      05  FILLER                 PIC X(07) VALUE ALL '_'.
152:      05  FILLER                 PIC X(03) VALUE SPACES.
153:      05  FILLER                 PIC X(07) VALUE ALL '_'.
154:      05  FILLER                 PIC X(15) VALUE SPACES.
155:      05  FILLER                 PIC X(13) VALUE ALL '_'.
156:      05  FILLER                 PIC X(38) VALUE SPACES.
157:      05  FILLER                 PIC X(11) VALUE ALL '_'.
158:      05  FILLER                 PIC X(13) VALUE SPACES.
159:      05  FILLER                 PIC X(07) VALUE ALL '_'.
160:  *
161:  PROCEDURE DIVISION.
162:  100-COORDINATING-MODULE.
163:      OPEN INPUT  AUTHOR-PUBLICATIONS
164:           OUTPUT REPORT-FILE.
165:      PERFORM 200-WRITE-HEADINGS.
166:      PERFORM 300-READ-RECORD.
167:      PERFORM 400-PROCESS-RECORD
168:          UNTIL WS-END-FILE = 'YES'.
169:      PERFORM 500-SUMMARY-RESULTS.
170:      CLOSE AUTHOR-PUBLICATIONS, REPORT-FILE.
171:      STOP RUN.
172:  *
173:  200-WRITE-HEADINGS.
174:      WRITE PRINT-LINE FROM MAJOR-HEADING
175:          AFTER ADVANCING 1 LINE.
176:      WRITE PRINT-LINE FROM MINOR-HEADING-1
177:          AFTER ADVANCING 2 LINES.
178:      WRITE PRINT-LINE FROM MINOR-HEADING-2
179:          AFTER ADVANCING 1 LINE.
180:      MOVE SPACES TO PRINT-LINE.
181:      WRITE PRINT-LINE
182:          AFTER ADVANCING 1 LINE.
183:  *
184:  300-READ-RECORD.
185:      READ AUTHOR-PUBLICATIONS INTO AUTHOR-RECORD
186:          AT END MOVE 'YES' TO WS-END-FILE.
187:  *
188:  400-PROCESS-RECORD.
189:      COMPUTE WS-NET-SALES =
190:          (AR-COPIES-SOLD - AR-RETURNS) * AR-TITLE-COST.
191:      COMPUTE WS-ROYALTY-AMOUNT =
192:          WS-NET-SALES * AR-ROYALTY-RATE.
193:      COMPUTE WS-ROYALTY-DUE =
194:          WS-ROYALTY-AMOUNT * AR-COAUTHOR-PERCENTAGE.
195:      COMPUTE WS-ROYALTY-RATE = AR-ROYALTY-RATE * 100.
196:      COMPUTE WS-COAUTHOR-PERCENTAGE =
197:          AR-COAUTHOR-PERCENTAGE * 100.
198:  *
199:  *    ACCUMULATE ALL TOTALS
200:  *
201:      ADD WS-NET-SALES    TO WS-TOTAL-NET-SALES.
202:      ADD WS-ROYALTY-DUE  TO WS-TOTAL-ROYALTIES.
203:      ADD AR-COPIES-SOLD  TO WS-TOTAL-COPIES.
204:      ADD AR-RETURNS      TO WS-TOTAL-RETURNS.
205:      PERFORM 600-FILL-IN-DETAIL-LINE.
206:      WRITE PRINT-LINE FROM DETAIL-LINE
207:          AFTER ADVANCING 1 LINE.
208:      PERFORM 300-READ-RECORD.
209:  *
210:  500-SUMMARY-RESULTS.
211:      MOVE WS-TOTAL-COPIES     TO SL-COPIES-SOLD.
212:      MOVE WS-TOTAL-RETURNS    TO SL-RETURNS.
213:      MOVE WS-TOTAL-NET-SALES  TO SL-NET-SALES.
214:      MOVE WS-TOTAL-ROYALTIES  TO SL-ROYALTY-DUE.
215:      WRITE PRINT-LINE FROM UNDER-LINE
216:          AFTER ADVANCING 1 LINE.
217:      WRITE PRINT-LINE FROM SUMMARY-LINE
218:          AFTER ADVANCING 1 LINE.
219:  *
220:  600-FILL-IN-DETAIL-LINE.
221:      MOVE AR-AUTHOR               TO DL-AUTHOR.
222:      MOVE AR-TITLE                TO DL-TITLE.
223:      MOVE AR-COPIES-SOLD          TO DL-COPIES-SOLD.
224:      MOVE AR-RETURNS              TO DL-RETURNS.
225:      MOVE AR-TITLE-COST           TO DL-TITLE-COST.
226:      MOVE WS-NET-SALES            TO DL-NET-SALES.
227:      MOVE WS-ROYALTY-AMOUNT       TO DL-ROYALTY-AMOUNT.
228:      MOVE WS-COAUTHOR-PERCENTAGE  TO DL-COAUTHOR-PERCENTAGE.
229:      MOVE WS-ROYALTY-RATE         TO DL-ROYALTY-RATE.
230:      MOVE WS-ROYALTY-DUE          TO DL-ROYALTY-DUE.
```

FIGURE 4–12
(*continued*)

of copies sold to the total number of copies sold so far. (line 203) et cetera. (lines 201-204).

To make the detail line attractive, we use numeric edited fields to suppress leading 0's and provide commas and dollar signs wherever needed.

Documentation and Structure. To make the WORKING-STORAGE section readable and self-documenting, we break it down into three classes of items: independent items, input record(s), and output records. Each class is then split into subclasses of items: accumulators/flags and computational items for the independent item class, and various types of output lines for the output line class.

Note that the READ INTO option reads the input record into the input area (line 35) and into WORKING-STORAGE at AUTHOR-RECORD (line 61).

1. Assume line 208 had been omitted. Specify exactly what would happen.

2. Suppose the VALUE clauses at lines 47 through 50 had been left out. What would happen?

3. What would happen if line 50 had been coded as:
   WS-TOTAL-ROYALTIES PIC 9(7).99 VALUE 0?

4. What would happen if line 171 had been forgotten?

5. Suppose the COPIES SOLD entry in the 5th data record had been coded as ƀƀ721 (ƀ = blank)? What would the program do?

6. What would the program do if the first record of the input file were the end-of-file record?

7. Could line 189, for example, have been written as:

   ```
   COMPUTE DL-NET-SALES =
       (AR-COPIES-SOLD - AR-RETURNS) * AR-TITLE-COST
   ```

   For that matter, is it really necessary to use all the computational items in lines 53 through 57, since they already exist in the DETAIL-LINE?

4-5-2 PROBLEM SPECIFICATION: A CHECKBOOK ANALYSIS

An input file consists of one header record containing the name of a customer, the customer's account number, and a balance forward. Following the header record we have an unknown number of check records each containing a check number or the caption "deposit", a date, and an amount (a positive or negative number to represent deposits and withdrawals). The input layout is as follows:

Header Record:
    Positions 1-15 Name   PIC X(15)
    Positions 16-19 Account number PIC 9999.
    Positions 20-27 Balance forward   PIC S99999V99 LEADING SEPARATE.

Check Record (all records following the header record):
    Positions 1-7   Check number PIC X(07).
    Positions 8-13 Date   PIC 999999.
    Positions 14-20 Check amount   PIC S9999V99 LEADING SEPARATE.

THE EDITING PROCESS AND ARITHMETIC STATEMENTS   **161**

For example, an input file might be:

```
                    Account    Balance
          Name      Number     Forward
            ↓         ↓          ↓
     ANDERSON MARIA 1212+0350010
     DEPOSIT010286+010000  ⎫
     DEPOSIT010486+030056  ⎪
     1121311010586-005620  ⎬   Check records:   1st field is the check number
     1121312010686-100005  ⎪                    2nd field is the date
     DEPOSIT010786+100078  ⎪                    3rd field is the check amount
     1121314010786-050000  ⎭
```

Write a program to list each check amount or deposit and compute and print the current remaining balance. Negative amounts should be identified with the debit symbol DB. Also print the total number of transactions written. The output should be similar to the following report:

```
                      CHECKBOOK  ANALYSIS
      ANDERSON MARIA  ACCT#:1212    BALANCE FORWARD: 3,500.10

      TRANSACTIONS    DATE         AMOUNT
      DEPOSIT         01/02/86     100.00          3,600.10
      DEPOSIT         01/04/86     300.56          3,900.66
      1121311         01/05/86      56.20 DB       3,844.46
      1121312         01/06/86   1,000.05 DB       2,844.41
      DEPOSIT         01/07/86   1,000.78          3,845.19
      1121314         01/07/86     500.00 DB       3,345.19

      NUMBER TRANSACTIONS = 6
```

Understanding the Program

Four questions must be answered before proceeding with the solution to this problem, which is shown in Figure 4–13.

1. How do we read and process different types of input records (header and check records)?

2. How do we accumulate a sum of positive and negative values (deposits and withdrawals)?

3. How do we count the number of transactions?

4. How do we type positive and negative numbers in the data file to represent deposits and withdrawals?

We solve the first problem by reading the very first record into HEADER–RECORD and all remaining records into CHECK–RECORD. This is accomplished by means of the READ INTO instruction. In this way the data in the header record is preserved in HEADER–RECORD (line 52) and not overwritten by subsequent transaction records, which are read into CHECK–RECORD (line 57). Thus the balance forward remains intact. Lines 52 through 60, document the two types of input records.

With regard to question 2, the current balance is computed by successively adding the various transaction amounts to the balance forward (read from the header record). On output, the current balance will display the DB symbol if the amount is negative (line 133).

```
 1:*  IDENTIFICATION DIVISION.
 2:   PROGRAM-ID. CHECKBOOK.
 3:   AUTHOR.  JONES.
 4:  ****************************************************************
 5:  * OBJECTIVE:   LIST DATED CHECKS SHOWING DEPOSITS, WITHDRAWALS  *
 6:  *              AND CURRENT BALANCE.                             *
 7:  *                                                               *
 8:  * INPUT:   1. HEADER RECORD: NAME, ACCOUNT NUMBER AND BALANCE.  *
 9:  *          2. CHECK RECORDS: CHECK NUMBER, DATE, AND AMOUNT.    *
10:  *             NEGATIVE AMOUNT REPRESENTS WITHDRAWALS            *
11:  *             POSITIVE AMOUNT REPRESENTS DEPOSITS               *
12:  *                                                               *
13:  * OUTPUT: REPORT IDENTIFYING NAME, ACCOUNT NUMBER AND BALANCE   *
14:  *         FORWARD AND LIST OF CHECKS BY DATE INDICATING         *
15:  *         DEPOSITS AND WITHDRAWALS AS WELL AS CURRENT BALANCES. *
16:  ****************************************************************
17:   ENVIRONMENT DIVISION.
18:   CONFIGURATION SECTION.
19:   SOURCE-COMPUTER. IBM.
20:   OBJECT-COMPUTER. IBM.
21:   INPUT-OUTPUT SECTION.
22:   FILE-CONTROL.
23:       SELECT REPORT-FILE  ASSIGN TO PRINTER.
24:       SELECT CHECK-FILE   ASSIGN TO DISK
25:       ORGANIZATION IS LINE SEQUENTIAL.
26:  *
27:   DATA DIVISION.
28:   FILE SECTION.
29:  *
30:   FD  CHECK-FILE
31:       LABEL RECORDS ARE STANDARD
32:       VALUE OF FILE-ID IS 'CHECKS'
33:       DATA RECORD IS INPUT-RECORD.
34:   01  INPUT-RECORD   PIC X(29).
35:   FD  REPORT-FILE
36:       LABEL RECORDS ARE OMITTED
37:       DATA RECORD IS PRINT-LINE.
38:   01  PRINT-LINE  PIC X(80).
39:  *
40:   WORKING-STORAGE SECTION.
41:  *
42:  *    INDEPENDENT ITEMS
43:  *
44:   01  FLAGS.
45:       05  WS-END-FILE         PIC 9 VALUE 0.
46:  *
47:   01  COMPUTATIONAL-ITEMS.
48:       05  WS-CHECK-COUNT      PIC 999 VALUE 0.
49:  *
50:  *    INPUT RECORD DESCRIPTION
51:  *
52:   01  HEADER-RECORD.
53:       05  HR-NAME             PIC X(15).
54:       05  HR-ACCOUNT-NO       PIC 9999.
55:       05  HR-BALANCE-FORWARD  PIC S99999V99 LEADING SEPARATE.
56:  *
57:   01  CHECK-RECORD.
58:       05  CR-CHECK-NO         PIC X(07).
59:       05  CR-DATE             PIC 999999.
60:       05  CR-AMOUNT           PIC S9999V99 LEADING SEPARATE.
61:  *
62:  *    OUTPUT LINE DESCRIPTIONS
63:  *
64:   01  HEADING-1.
65:       05  FILLER              PIC X(27) VALUE SPACES.
66:       05  FILLER              PIC X(53) VALUE
67:                                    'CHECKBOOK ANALYSIS'.
68:   01  TITLE-LINE.
69:       05  FILLER              PIC X(09) VALUE SPACES.
70:       05  TL-NAME             PIC X(15).
```

Sample output:

```
                         CHECKBOOK ANALYSIS
ANDERSON MARIA     ACCT#:1212    BALANCE FORWARD: 3,600.10

TRANSACTIONS       DATE          AMOUNT
 DEPOSIT          01/02/86        100.00              3,600.10
 DEPOSIT          01/04/86        300.56              3,900.66
 1121311          01/05/86         56.20 DB           3,844.46
 1121312          01/06/86      1,000.05 DB           2,844.41
 DEPOSIT          01/07/86      1,000.78              3,845.19
 1121314          01/07/86        500.00 DB           3,345.19

NUMBER TRANSACTIONS = 6
```

Header Record / Name / Account Number / Balance Forward

```
ANDERSON MARIA 1212+0350010
DEPOSIT010286+010000
DEPOSIT010486+030056
1121311010586-005620   ⎫
1121312010686-005620   ⎬ Check Records
DEPOSIT010786+100078   ⎪
1121314010786-050000   ⎭
```

Check Number / Date / Check Amount

FIGURE 4–13

A CHECKBOOK ANALYSIS

```cobol
71:        05  FILLER               PIC X(08) VALUE '  ACCT#:'.
72:        05  TL-ACCOUNT-NO        PIC 9999.
73:        05  FILLER               PIC X(19) VALUE
74:                                         '  BALANCE FORWARD:'.
75:        05  TL-BALANCE-FORWARD   PIC ZZ,ZZ9.99.
76:   *
77:   01  HEADING-2.
78:        05  FILLER               PIC X(09) VALUE SPACES.
79:        05  FILLER               PIC X(20) VALUE 'TRANSACTIONS'.
80:        05  FILLER               PIC X(13) VALUE 'DATE'.
81:        05  FILLER               PIC X(38) VALUE 'AMOUNT'.
82:   *
83:   01  DETAIL-LINE.
84:        05  FILLER               PIC X(10) VALUE SPACES.
85:        05  DL-CHECK-NUMBER      PIC X(07).
86:        05  FILLER               PIC X(10) VALUE SPACES.
87:        05  DL-DATE              PIC 99/99/99.
88:        05  FILLER               PIC X(05) VALUE SPACES.
89:        05  DL-AMOUNT            PIC Z,ZZ9.99BDB.
90:        05  FILLER               PIC X(04) VALUE SPACES.
91:        05  DL-BALANCE           PIC ZZ,ZZ9.99BDB.
92:   *
93:   01  SUMMARY-LINE.
94:        05  FILLER               PIC X(09) VALUE SPACES.
95:        05  FILLER               PIC X(22) VALUE
96:                                         'NUMBER TRANSACTIONS ='.
97:        05  SL-CHECKS-WRITTEN    PIC Z9.
98:   *
99:   01  BLANK-LINE               PIC X(80) VALUE SPACES.
100:  *
101:  PROCEDURE DIVISION.
102:  100-COORDINATING-MODULE.
103:      OPEN INPUT CHECK-FILE, OUTPUT REPORT-FILE.
104:      PERFORM 200-WRITE-HEADINGS.
105:      PERFORM 300-READ-CHECK-FILE.
106:      PERFORM 400-CHECK-PROCESS UNTIL WS-END-FILE = 1.
107:      PERFORM 500-SUMMARY-LINE.
108:      CLOSE CHECK-FILE, REPORT-FILE.
109:      STOP RUN.
110:  *
111:  200-WRITE-HEADINGS.
112:      WRITE PRINT-LINE FROM HEADING-1 AFTER ADVANCING 1 LINE.
113:      READ CHECK-FILE INTO HEADER-RECORD
114:           AT END MOVE 'NO RECORDS IN CHECK-FILE' TO PRINT-LINE
115:                  WRITE PRINT-LINE AFTER ADVANCING 1 LINE
116:                  STOP RUN.
117:      MOVE HR-NAME             TO TL-NAME.
118:      MOVE HR-ACCOUNT-NO       TO TL-ACCOUNT-NO.
119:      MOVE HR-BALANCE-FORWARD  TO TL-BALANCE-FORWARD.
120:      WRITE PRINT-LINE FROM TITLE-LINE AFTER ADVANCING 1 LINE.
121:      WRITE PRINT-LINE FROM BLANK-LINE AFTER ADVANCING 1 LINE.
122:      WRITE PRINT-LINE FROM HEADING-2  AFTER ADVANCING 1 LINE.
123:  *
124:  300-READ-CHECK-FILE.
125:      READ CHECK-FILE INTO CHECK-RECORD
126:           AT END MOVE 1 TO WS-END-FILE.
127:  *
128:  400-CHECK-PROCESS.
129:      ADD CR-AMOUNT TO HR-BALANCE-FORWARD.
130:      ADD 1 TO WS-CHECK-COUNT.
131:      MOVE CR-CHECK-NO         TO DL-CHECK-NUMBER.
132:      MOVE CR-DATE             TO DL-DATE.
133:      MOVE CR-AMOUNT           TO DL-AMOUNT.
134:      MOVE HR-BALANCE-FORWARD TO DL-BALANCE.
135:      WRITE PRINT-LINE FROM DETAIL-LINE AFTER ADVANCING 1 LINE.
136:      PERFORM 300-READ-CHECK-FILE.
137:  *
138:  500-SUMMARY-LINE.
139:      MOVE WS-CHECK-COUNT TO SL-CHECKS-WRITTEN.
140:      WRITE PRINT-LINE FROM SUMMARY-LINE AFTER ADVANCING 2 LINES.
```

FIGURE 4–13
(continued)

We resolve the last question by typing the check amounts with a leading sign in position 14 followed by six digits in positions 15–20. The LEADING–SEPARATE CHARACTER clause is used to allow for the sign character. In memory the amount item occupies 7 positions.

Test Your Understanding of the Program.

1. What will the program do if there are no input records in the input file?
2. How could you print the successive forward balances with the CR symbol, assuming these balances are positive?
3. How could you print the value of the total withdrawals? of the total deposits?
4. How would you change detail line entries so that the + and /or the − symbols would be printed instead of the DB symbol?
5. What would happen if WS–CHECK–COUNT were defined simply as PIC 999 with no VALUE clause?
6. Specify exactly what the program would do if line 136 were omitted?
7. What would happen exactly if the input record (line 34) were specified as PIC X(20) instead of PIC X(29)?
8. Retype the input file without the + and − signs prefixing the transaction amounts. What changes then need to be made in the input record description entries?

4–6 EXERCISES

4–6–1 TEST YOURSELF

1. Are the following operations valid or invalid? Specify reasons if invalid.

   a. ADD X TO Y GIVING Z.
   b. ADD X, Y GIVING K.
   c. ADD 5.1 5.3 GIVING L.
   d. ADD X TO 4.1.
   e. ADD 1 2 3 TO X.
   f. ADD X + Y TO Z.
   g. ADD 3.1 4.7 TO 6.8.
   h. ADD "915" TO TOTAL.
   i. COMPUTE B = C / D REMAINDER K.
   j. SUBTRACT -8.1 FROM -Z.
   k. SUBTRACT X X X FROM X GIVING X.
   l. SUBTRACT A, B, C, FROM 2.3.
   m. COMPUTE X = (B + C) / -4.
   n. COMPUTE Y = A (B + C).
   o. MULTIPLY 3.1 BY X.
   p. MULTIPLY NUMBER BY ZERO.
   q. MULTIPLY 3 4 L BY C GIVING T.
   r. MULTIPLY 3, 4 GIVING TWELVE.
   s. MULTIPLY 99V9 BY C GIVING C.
   t. MULTIPLY C BY .0001.
   u. DIVIDE A BY B REMAINDER C.
   v. DIVIDE A BY B INTO C.
   w. DIVIDE X BY X.
   x. DIVIDE Z INTO T GIVING $$$.99.
   y. DIVIDE 8 INTO 4 GIVING L.
   z. DIVIDE 8 INTO 4.
   aa. COMPUTE Z + 4 = 3.
   bb. COMPUTE -3 + TERM.
   cc. SUBTRACT 6.1 - 4 FROM Z.
   dd. COMPUTE X = Y / 3 ROUNDED.

THE EDITING PROCESS AND ARITHMETIC STATEMENTS   **165**

2. Write the following expressions in one sentence without using the COMPUTE verb and using the options as indicated.

   a. C = -A -B.
   b. X = X * (-6.1).
   c. F = A + B + C + F.   Use ROUNDED option.
   d. Z = A / B.   Use ON SIZE ERROR option.
   e. F = 1.2 - 3.6 + 40 - C   Use ROUNDED and ON SIZE ERROR options.
   f. G = -C - D + L.
   g. M = (A + B) - (C + D).

3. Are the following PICTUREs valid or invalid? Specify any error.

   a. PIC 5(9)V5(9).   e. PIC $ZZ99.ZZ.
   b. PIC SV999.   f. PIC $Z(4)9(3).9(4).
   c. PIC 9V9.99.   g. PIC -,---.99.
   d. PIC $ZZ99.99.

4. Determine the internal representation for each of the following:

   a. A PIC 999V99 VALUE -123.1.   d. D PIC 9.9   VALUE 1.
   b. B PIC 99V99 VALUE 100.   e. E PIC 9(9) VALUE ALL ZEROS.
   c. C PIC S99V   VALUE -.001.

5. Given the instruction MOVE ITEM-1 TO ITEM-2, fill in the blank entries wherever they occur in the following table. A ƀ represents a blank space. Indicate blank positions in the result field.

	PICTURE-1	←ITEM-1→ CONTENT-1	PICTURE-2	←ITEM-2→ CONTENT-2
a.	999V99	01230	99999	
b.	9V9	12		ᵛ20
c.		1123		$ƀƀ11.230
d.	V9999	0124	9999V	
e.	S9(5)	00100		$ƀƀƀ100.00
f.	V9(5)			$ƀƀƀƀ.12
g.	9(9)	000123456	$ZZZ,ZZZ,ZZZ	
h.	9(6)V99	00123450	$(7).99	
i.	S9(5)	00123		-ƀ123.00
j.	99V9	373	999	
k.	S99	13	+9	
l.		UWFSYS		UWF
m.		9340		-9340
n.	9(5)	12345	999B.B99	
o.	X(6)	$123.6	X(4)	
p.	9(6)V99	00100000	$Z99,999.99	
q.		001234		**12.34
r.	V9(5)	12789	$$$,$$9.99	
s.	9(5)			$12,345.00
t.	S99V9(3)	12345	------.99	
u.	9(5)	00000	$**,***.**	
v.	S9(5)	12345		12345.00+
w.	9(4)V99	001234		2.3400
x.	999	002		$ƀ02
y.	S9999	0988		0988-
z.	S99V9	503	$$,$$$.99CR	
aa.	S9(4)V99	582040	$$,$$$.99DB	
bb.	S9(4)	9910		9910-
cc.	9(3)V99	12345		1ƀ2ƀ3
dd.	9(5)	00123	$**,**9.99	
ee.	999V99	00001		$.01
ff.	99999	00000	$**,*99	
gg.	S99999	20013	----.99	
hh.	99V99	0000	$$$.$$	
ii.	99V99	0008	$$.$$	

6. True or false:
   a. Before a record is printed, the record must first be moved into the output record defined in WORKING–STORAGE.
   b. If a decimal point is present in the internal representation of a number, that number cannot be processed arithmetically.
   c. The number of memory positions allocated by the PICTURE 99V9 is 4.
   d. The VALUE clause can be used to describe an output record in the FILE section.
   e. PICTURE 99V. is the same as PICTURE 99.
   f. The S symbol in a PICTURE does not occupy a memory position.
   g. If A has PICTURE 99, then A can never be a negative number.
   h. The memory field $\boxed{1}\boxed{2}\boxed{.}\boxed{3}$ can be interpreted as an alphanumeric string.
   i. If A has PICTURE – 999V9. this means A can take on a negative value.
   j. The record description entry A PIC 99.9 VALUE 1.3 is valid.
   k. The picture $.99. is a valid numeric edited picture.
   l. The instruction WRITE PRINT–LINE FROM DL–LINE AFTER 3. will result in two blank lines between printed lines.
   m. If B has PICTURE 99V999 and is a subitem of record LIN–1, then, when LIN–1 is written, a decimal point will be inserted between the second and third digits of B.
   n. If A has PICTURE 999.9, the sentence COMPUTE A = A + A will store the equivalent of 2·A in A.
   o. The COMPUTE verb allows the receiving field to be a report-type field.
   p. If the ADVANCING feature is used, then it must be used with *all* WRITE statements.
   q. Before any numeric field can be printed, it must be edited numerically, i.e., the number must be moved into a numeric edited field.
   r. The following record description is valid:

    ```
    01 DETAIL-LINE.
       05 A PIC S99V99.
       05 B PIC 9.9.
       05 C PIC .9(6).
       05 E PIC S9(4)V99.
    ```

   s. The above record is 19 memory positions long.
   t. If LIN has PICTURE Z(13), then a) MOVE SPACES TO LIN is valid.
                                      b) MOVE ZEROS TO LIN is valid.
   u. In order to store the correct result in T as a result of
      MULTIPLY 3 BY – 10.5 GIVING T
      the symbol S should be part of the PICTURE of T.
   v. If A has PICTURE 99.9, the sentence MOVE 99.9 TO A is valid.
   w. If A has PICTURE $$$.9, the sentence MOVE 11V45 TO A is valid.
   x. Given the entry 05 MIN PIC 999V99 VALUE 1000., the value of MIN is 0.
   y. The entry 05 COST–RECORD X(16) VALUE SPACES is valid.
   z. If AMT has PICTURE 9(25), the statement MOVE –1 to AMT is valid.
   aa. A numeric field must be the sending field to a numerically edited receiving field.

7. Determine the values in the receiving fields; show all memory positions of the receiving field by specifying a ƀ for blanks.

THE EDITING PROCESS AND ARITHMETIC STATEMENTS 167

SENDING FIELD	RECEIVING FIELD	SENDING FIELD	RECEIVING FIELD
a. 3V14	PIC $.$	n. 14V25	$$,$$$.99+
b. 22V33	PIC $$.999	o. 100006	+++99
c. 1V009	PIC $ZZ.9	p. 00.03	$$$$
d. 3	PIC $$.$	q. 34$\bar{1}$	ZZZCR
e. 0	PIC $$.$$	r. 3V1	$***.99DB
f. 1000V7	PIC $$,$$$.99	s. 0	$*,***.99CR
g. 100V43	PIC Z,ZZZ.99	t. 3214V476	$$,$$$.99DB
h. 10245V99	PIC $$,$(3).99	u. 31V$\bar{9}$	$999.9DB
i. 0	PIC $$,$$$.$$	v. 0	$.99CR
j. 0	PIC $Z,ZZZ	w. 123	B9B99
k. 98	PIC *ZZ	x. XY.T	XXXBBXX
l. 0	PIC ***,**	y. 444V5$\bar{6}$	$***.99BCR
m. 0	PIC $***9	z. 23V45	+$ZZZ.99

8. Show the contents of the resulting field. Identify any invalid picture fields.

		X		Y		Z
OPERATION		PICTURE	CONTENTS	PICTURE	CONTENTS	PICTURE
a. ADD X Y GIVING Z	i.	999V99	01230	99V999	01230	999V9
	ii.	S99V9	12$\bar{0}$	9V99	120	99V9
	iii.	S99V9	12$\bar{0}$	S99V9	300	S99V9 −
	iv.	99V99	1234	99	12	99999V99
	v.	S99V99	0200	S999	03$\bar{2}$	S999V9
	vi.	S99V9	121	S99V9	139	S99.9
	vii.	S99V9	92$\bar{0}$	S99V9	13$\bar{0}$	− − .9
b. ADD X TO Y	i.	S99V99	1200	S99V99	430$\bar{0}$	
	ii.	S9999	120$\bar{0}$	S9999	030$\bar{0}$	
	iii.	99V9	777	99.9	100	
	iv.	999B	999	999B	999	
c. SUBTRACT X FROM Y	i.	S99V9	120	S99V99	0120	
	ii.	99V9	120	99V9	120	
	iii.	S999	080	99V9	190	
d. SUBTRACT 6.2, −4.23 FROM X GIVING Z	i.	S99V99	123$\bar{4}$			S99V99
	ii.	S999V9	1008			+(4).++
e. MULTIPLY X BY Y GIVING Z	i.	9V99	012	99V9	012	99V9
	ii.	S9V9	1$\bar{2}$	9V99	012	9V9
	iii.	S9V9	1$\bar{2}$	S9V99	012	S99V99
f. MULTIPLY X BY −1.23 GIVING Z ROUNDED	i.	S9V9	1$\bar{2}$			99V9
	ii.	S99V99	0400			$***.**DB
	iii.	S99	10			− − − .−
g. DIVIDE X INTO Y GIVING Z	i.	9V9	48	99	12	99V9
	ii.	V999	009	99	09	$$$.99
h. DIVIDE Y BY X GIVING Z ROUNDED	i.	999V99	20000	99V99	9571	99V99
	ii.	99	99	V99	99	99.999

9. Determine the values in the receiving fields after the following literals are moved.

LITERAL	RECEIVING FIELD	LITERAL	RECEIVING FIELD
a. 32.44	PIC 9V999.	g. "AM"	PIC XXX.
b. −.4732	PIC SV99.	h. "HELLO"	PIC XXX.
c. 111	PIC 9999.	i. 3.246	PIC XXXXX.
d. −98	PIC S9.	j. +324	PIC XXXXX.
e. +.008	PIC S99.	k. "12.3"	PIC ZZ.Z.
f. 38.29	PIC 999V9.	l. SPACES	PIC 9999

10. Given the following input record, specify the contents of A, B, C, D, E, and F as a result of the instruction READ INPUT–FILE... where the input record is INPUT–REC:

INPUT-REC → $0\overline{3}.0059993\ 340188\overline{8}$

a. 01 INPUT-REC.
        05 A   PIC 99.
        05 FILLER PIC X.
        05 B   PIC 999.
        05 C   PIC S9999.
        05 D   PIC 9(8).

b. 01 INPUT-REC.
        05 A PIC S99.
        05 B PIC 9999.
        05 C PIC S999V.
        05 D PIC SV9.
        05 E PIC 999V99.
        05 F PIC XXXX.

11. Answer the following:

    a. Differentiate between a compilation error and an execution-time error; give examples of each.
    b. Write the code to perform the following:
        i. Skip a line and then print MAJOR–HEADING.
        ii. Print REPORT–TITLE, then skip two lines.
        iii. Print COLUMN–HEADING; on the next line print SUMMARY–LINE and then skip 3 lines.
        iv. Print MALE–REPORT, then on the same line print REPORT–NUMBER; on the next line print FEMALE–REPORT and then skip one line.
        v. Skip two lines, then print ROW–LINE, then skip 2 lines before printing DETAIL–LINE.
        vi. Separate HEADER–1 from HEADER–2 by one blank line.
    c. Explain why A and B cannot be added together if both have picture 9.9.
    d. Suppose, under a READ operation, three blank columns are read into HOURS (PICTURE 999.). Will there be a READ error?
    e. How would you be able to detect an overflow when subtracting two numbers? Give an example.
    f. Under what condition can you MOVE A TO B if B is a numeric edited field?
    g. Consider the following output line description:

        01 LINE-OUT.
            05 FILLER PIC X(35).
            05 FILLER PIC X(11) VALUE "ABC COMPANY".
            05 FILLER PIC X(34).

    When LINE-OUT is printed, will the header line be printed the way you would want it printed, i.e., with the caption all by itself on the line?

4-6-2 PROGRAMMING EXERCISES

1. Each record of an input file consists of an item number, a corresponding unit price, and an inventory level for each item. Write a program to read this file and produce the following inventory analysis:

   ```
   INVENTORY ANALYSIS
   ITEM    UNIT    INVENTORY   INVENTORY
   NUMBER  PRICE   LEVEL       AMOUNT

   15202   4.27    544         $ 2,322.88
   15304   16.90   128         $ 2,163.20
   15600   .57     849         $   483.93
   15500   23.99   998         $23,942.02

   TOTAL INVENTORY             $28,912.03
   ```

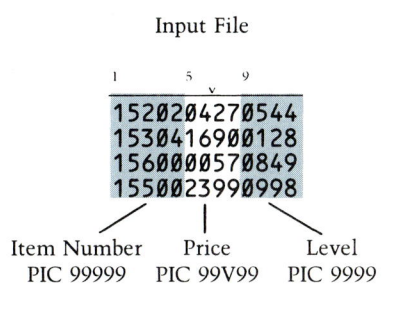

   Input File
   ```
   1    5 v 9
   1520204270544
   1530416900128
   1560000570849
   1550023990998
   ```
   Item Number Price   Level
   PIC 99999   PIC 99V99 PIC 9999

2. Each record of an input file consists of a check amount, the name of the person/store/company to whom the check is made, an item description, and the name of the signer. Write a program to read these data items and position them on a simulated check. The output should be similar to the following:

   ```
   ---------------------------------------
   PAY TO: ALBERTSONS      $*1,234.56

   ITEM: COSMETICS          M DUNKIN
   ---------------------------------------
   PAY TO: PIGGY STORES    $***120.54

   ITEM: GROCERIES          D SANDERS
   ---------------------------------------
   ```

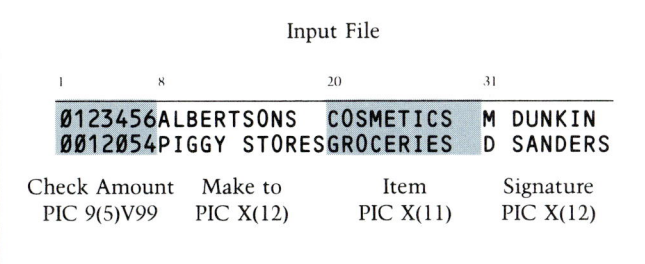

   Input File
   ```
   1      8          20         31
   0123456ALBERTSONS   COSMETICS  M DUNKIN
   0012054PIGGY STORESGROCERIES  D SANDERS
   ```
   Check Amount Make to   Item   Signature
   PIC 9(5)V99   PIC X(12) PIC X(11) PIC X(12)

3. Each record of an input file contains the following information:

RECORD POSITIONS	
1–12	Name
13–21	Social security number
22–23	A monthly deduction X for a health insurance plan, expressed as a percent entry (PIC 9V9). For example, X could be 4.5%. The yearly contribution to this plan is X percent of the first nine months' gross income, with the deductions spread over a 12-month period.
24–25	Number of children N (PIC 99). Child support pays $119.36 per child. This amount is not taxed or subject to social security withholding, and it does not affect payments to life or health insurance plans. It is added to the net monthly income.

26–29   A percent figure T (PIC 99V99) applied to the monthly gross to compute the federal income tax. For example, T might be 15.6%.

30–33   A percent figure Z (PIC 99V99) for a life insurance plan. Monthly payment for life insurance equals Z percent of amount left of monthly gross after social security and federal tax deductions.

38–40   Monthly gross (PIC 99999V99)

Social security withholding is 7.05% of monthly gross.

Write a program to read an input file and produce a report like the following one. Use the debit symbol (DB) to identify any monthly net that is negative. All amounts/results should be rounded off.

NAME	SOCIAL SECURITY	NUMBER CHILDREN	FEDERAL TAX	SOCIAL SS WITHHELD	LIFE INSURANCE	MEDICAL PLAN	GROSS PAY	TOTAL WITHHELD	NET PAY
BARBARA WISE	123 45 6789	10	$.03	$4.23	$.00	$.05	$1,253.60	$3.76	$1,249.84
RAND CHANCE	568 97 4586	2	$139.18	$72.14	$78.86	$34.54	$1,262.08	$315.31	$946.77
BRENDA JOHN	548 72 6533	0	$520.69	$45.85	$85.40	$48.30	$650.45	$694.26	$43.81DB
JACK JEFFERS	114 77 4889	6	$464.44	$165.37	$781.85	$98.52	$3,061.83	$1,488.60	$1,573.23
BETSY JONES	225 85 6335	0	$50,960.27	$6,909.01	$32,826.26	$7,203.04	$98,000.52	$96,997.00	$1,003.52

4. A gross margin analysis is to be performed on six inventory items. The gross profit margin is a measurement used to identify those items that are the most profitable. The gross margin profit is given by the formula:

Gross margin profit = 100 * (selling price − unit cost) / unit cost

Each input record has the following form:

RECORD POSITIONS	DESCRIPTION	ITEM NUMBER	ITEM DESCRIPTION	UNIT COST	SELLING PRICE
1–6	Item number	DRUUCM	INTERFACE	540000	644000
7–16	Item description	KW11LT	TIME CLOCK	000000	000000
17–22	Unit cost	DM11D	BADAPTOR	065000	077785
23–28	Selling price	MR11DB	BOOTSTRAP	057500	050000
		DU11DA	INTERFACE	150000	197500
		DM11AB	MAINFRAME	279000	285000

Write a program to compute the gross margin profit for each of the items in the inventory file. Write an appropriate error message for any item for which the unit cost is zero (this could be the result of an error during the transcription phase and would result in division by 0). Keep in mind that the gross profit margin could be negative if the item is sold at a loss. The output should be similar to the report on the following page.

```
                    GROSS MARGIN ANALYSIS

   ITEM        ITEM         COST PER     SELLING      GROSS MARGIN
   NUMBER      DESCRIPTION  UNIT         PRICE        PROFIT
   ***************************************************************
   DRUU CM     INTERFACE    $5,400.00    $6,440.00    19.26
   KW11 LT     TIME CLOCK      $.00         $.00       .00 CHECK INPUT DATA
   DM11 DB     ADAPTOR       $650.00      $777.85    19.67
   MR11 DB     BOOTSTRAP     $575.00      $500.00    13.04-
   DU11 DA     INTERFACE   $1,500.00    $1,975.00    31.67
   DM11 AB     MAINFRAME   $2,790.00    $2,850.00     2.15
   ***************************************************************
```

5. Each record of an input file contains a students' name, three course descriptions, and the three scores received in these courses. Write a program to compute each student's GPA and produce a report similar to the following one:

```
                          COURSE        COURSE
   STUDENT NAME           DESCRIPTION   NUMBER    GRADE    GPA

   OLDNIX J               MAT           101       1.5
   OLDNIX J               AML           304       2.0
   OLDNIX J               MAN           201       3.5
                                                           2.3

   DEE S                  ECO           100       3.5
   DEE S                  GEA           102       2.5
   DEE S                  AML           103       3.5
                                                           3.2
```

Example of input file:

```
1           13      19 21      27 29      35
OLDNIX J    MAT10115AML30420MAN20135
DEE S       ECO10035GEA10225AML10335

    Name    Subject  Subject  Subject  Grade
   PIC X(12) PIC X(6) PIC X(6) PIC X(6) PIC 9V9

              Grade   Grade
              PIC 9V9 PIC 9V9
```

6. Write a program to break an amount of money read from an input record into half dollars, quarters, nickels, dimes, and pennies. Assume the dollar amount is less than one dollar. See the REMAINDER option in section 4-3-4 for hints. Your program should produce the two following outputs:

a.
```
   AMOUNT        $ .96

   HALF-DOLLARS      1
   QUARTERS          1
   DIMES             2
   NICKELS           0
   PENNIES           1

   AMOUNT        $ .08

   HALF-DOLLARS      0
   QUARTERS          0
   DIMES             0
   NICKELS           1
   PENNIES           3
```

b.

AMOUNT	1/2 DOLLARS	QUARTERS	DIMES	NICKELS	PENNIES
$0.96	1	1	2	0	1
$0.08	0	0	0	1	3

7. Repeat exercise 9 with dollar amounts that do not exceed $10,000. The change should consist of $1,000, $500, $100, $50, $20, $10, $5, and $1 bills, with the remaining change in coins.

8. The date for any Easter Sunday can be computed as follows:

   Let X be the year for which it is desired to compute Easter Sunday.

   Let A be the remainder of the division of X by 19.

   Let B be the remainder of the division of X by 4.

   Let C be the remainder of the division of X by 7.

   Let D be the remainder of the division of (19A + 24) by 30.

   Let E be the remainder of the division of (2B + 4C + 6D + 5) by 7.

   The date for Easter Sunday is then March (22 + D + E). Note that this can give a date in April. Write a program to read values for year X and compute the Easter Sunday date for that year using the formula 22 + D + E.

9. With an interest rate I of 11.5% and a principal P of $1,956.45 deposited for an 11-year period in a savings account,

   Write a program to compute a total principal T given the formula:

   $$T = P(1 + I)^N$$

   where N is the number of years.
   Suppose the interest I is compounded daily for the same time period of 11 years. Add the code to compute:
   a. The total principal given by the formula

   $$T = P\left(1 + \frac{I}{J}\right)^{J \cdot N}$$

   where J is the number of times the interest is compounded per year.
   b. The difference between total amounts when the interest is compounded once and 360 times a year.

10. John Doe must decide whether to buy a house this year at relatively high interest rates or wait until next year when interest rates are anticipated to be lower but when inflation will have increased the cost of the house. This year he can buy a $60,000 house with 10% down and the balance financed at 13.5% for 30 years. Next year he can buy the same house for $63,000 with 10% down and the balance financed at 13% for 30 years. Based on the total cost of the house (principal and interest), should he buy now or wait?

The formula to compute the amount of monthly payment M, given the principal P, interest rate I, and the time in years T, is:

$$M = \frac{P \cdot \dfrac{I}{12}}{1 - \left(\dfrac{1}{1 + \dfrac{I}{12}}\right)^{T \cdot 12}}$$

Write a program to make the decision for John Doe by printing both monthly payments and the difference in cost at the end of 30 years.

11. A wholesaler accepts a $5,000 promissory note at 18% in lieu of cash payment for delivered goods. Write a program to compute the maturity value of the note for a 30-, 60- and 90-day short-term loan. The formula to compute the maturity value S is: S = P(1 + I • N), where P is the principal, I is the interest rate and N is the number of years S(if it is days, expressed as days/360).

4-6-3 ANSWERS TO TEST YOURSELF

1.
   a. Invalid; use either TO or GIVING, not both.
   b. Valid
   c. Valid
   d. Invalid; 4.1 is not a data name.
   e. Valid
   f. Invalid; X + Y is an expression.
   g. Invalid; 6.8 is not a data name.
   h. Invalid; "915" is not numeric.
   i. Invalid; no REMAINDER option with COMPUTE.
   j. Invalid; − Z is not a data name.
   k. Valid
   l. Invalid; 2.3 is not a data name.
   m. Invalid; should be (− 4).
   n. Invalid; missing operator.
   o. Valid
   p. Invalid; ZERO is a reserved word.
   q. Invalid; cannot have R L
   r. Invalid; missing word BY.
   s. Valid (99V9 is a valid data name).
   t. Invalid; .0001 is not a data name.
   u. Invalid; no GIVING.
   v. Invalid; can't have BY & INTO.
   w. Invalid; need GIVING.
   x. Invalid; $$$.99 is not a data name.
   y. Valid
   z. Invalid; 4 is not a data name.
   aa. Invalid; Z + 4 is not a data name.
   bb. Invalid; no receiving field.
   cc. Invalid; 6.1 − 4 is not a literal.
   dd. Invalid; ROUNDED is misplaced.

2.
   a. SUBTRACT A B FROM 0 GIVING C.
   b. MULTIPLY -6.1 BY X.
   c. ADD A, B, C TO F ROUNDED.
   d. DIVIDE A BY B GIVING Z ON SIZE ERROR...
   e. SUBTRACT -1.2, 3.6, -40, C FROM 0 GIVING F ROUNDED, ON SIZE ERROR...
   f. SUBTRACT C, D, FROM L GIVING G.
   g. Cannot do.

3.
   a. Invalid; should be 9(5).
   b. Valid
   c. Invalid; cannot have both V and the decimal point.
   d. Valid
   e. Invalid; no alternating characters in a floating string.
   f. Valid
   g. Invalid; needs 2 starting − symbols to be meaningful.

4. a. |1|2|3|1|0|
   b. |0|0|0|0|
   c. |0|0̄|
   d. |1|.|0|
   e. |0|0|0|0|0|0|0|0|

5. a. 00012
   b. V99
   c. 99V99, $ZZZZ.999
   d. 0000
   e. $ZZZZZZ.99
   f. 12345 or 12000, et cetera; $ZZZZZ.99
   g. $bbbb123, 456
   h. bb$1234.50
   i. −ZZZZ.99
   j. 037
   k. −3
   l. X(6), XXX
   m. S9999, +(5) or −(5)
   n. 345b.b00
   o. $123
   p. $b01,000.00
   q. 9999V99, ****.**
   r. bbbbb$0.12
   s. 12345, $$$,$$$.99
   t. bbb − 12.34
   u. *(7).**
   v. Z(4)9.99+
   w. 9.9999
   x. Z99
   y. 9999+ or 9999−
   z. bbb$50.30CR
   aa. $5,820.40bb
   bb. 9999+ or 9999−
   cc. 9B9B9
   dd. $***123.00
   ee. $.99
   ff. $****00
   gg. −013.00
   hh. bbbbbb
   ii. b$.08

6. a. False; output record defined in FILE section.
   b. True
   c. False; 3 memory positions.
   d. False
   e. True
   f. True except with SEPARATE.
   g. True
   h. True
   i. False; − is an editing symbol.
   j. True
   k. True
   l. True
   m. False; decimal point needed.
   n. False; A is nonnumeric (edited).
   o. True
   p. False
   q. False
   r. True
   s. False; 20
   t. a: false   b: True
   u. False; T could be numeric edited.
   v. Valid
   w. True: Valid data name!
   x. True
   y. False: PIC is missing.
   z. False: PIC 9(18) is maximum.
   aa. True

7. a. $.1
   b. $2.330
   c. $b1.0
   d. $3.0
   e. bbbbb
   f. $1,000.70
   g. bb100.43
   h. $0,245.99
   i. 9 blanks
   j. 6 blanks
   k. *98
   l. ******
   m. $***0
   n. bbb$14.25+
   o. +0006
   p. bbbb
   q. 341CR
   r. $**3.10bb
   s. $*****.00bb
   t. $3,214.47bb
   u. $031.9DB
   v. $.00bb
   w. b1b23
   x. XY.bbTb
   y. $444.56bCR
   z. +$b23.45

8. a. i. 0135 iii. Y invalid (.) iii. 001$\overline{4}$
　　ii. 108 　iv. Y invalid (B) f. i. 015
　　iii. Z invalid c. i. 108$\overline{0}$ ii. $**4.92DB
　　iv. 0002434 　ii. 000 iii. −12.3
　　v. 030$\overline{0}$ 　iii. 610 g. i. 025
　　vi. Z invalid d. i. 143$\overline{1}$ ii. ⌿⌿$.00
　　vii. −5.0 　ii. ⌿+98.83 h. i. 0048
　b. i. 310$\overline{0}$ e. i. 001 ii. 00.010
　　ii. 150$\overline{0}$ 　ii. 01

9. a. 2V440 　　**10.** a. A = 03
　b. V4$\overline{7}$ 　　　　　B = 005
　c. 0111 　　　　　　　　C = 9993
　d. $\overline{8}$ 　　　　　　　　　D = ⌿3401888
　e. 00 　　　　　　　　　b. A = 0$\overline{3}$
　f. 038V2 　　　　　　　B = .005
　g. AM⌿ 　　　　　　　　C = 999
　h. HEL 　　　　　　　　D = 3
　i. 3.246 　　　　　　　E = ⌿3401
　j. 324⌿⌿ 　　　　　　　F = 888R
　k. invalid
　l. invalid

11. a. A compilation error occurs during the translation phase (COBOL to object code), while an execution error occurs while the machine instruction(s) code corresponding to a COBOL instruction is actually being carried out by the arithmetic or logical unit.

　　Examples: SUBTACT 3 FROM AMT. Compilation error (SUBTRACT).
　　　　　　　DIVIDE X INTO Y.　　　If X = 0, execution error.

　b. i. WRITE PRINT-LINE FROM MAJOR-HEADING AFTER 1.
　　ii. WRITE PRINT-LINE FROM REPORT-TITLE BEFORE ADVANCING 3.
　　iii. WRITE PRINT-LINE FROM COLUMN-HEADING BEFORE 1.
　　　　WRITE PRINT-LINE FROM SUMMARY-LINE BEFORE 4.
　　iv. WRITE PRINT-LINE FROM MALE-REPORT AFTER 1.
　　　　WRITE PRINT-LINE FROM REPORT-NUMBER AFTER 0.
　　　　WRITE PRINT-LINE FROM FEMALE-REPORT AFTER 1.
　　　　MOVE SPACES TO PRINT-LINE. WRITE PRINT-LLINE AFTER 2.
　　v. WRITE PRINT-LINE FROM ROW-LINE AFTER 3.
　　　　WRITE PRINT-LINE FROM DETAIL-LINE AFTER 3.
　　vi. WRITE PRINT-LINE FROM HEADER-1 AFTER 1.
　　　　WRITE PRINT-LINE FROM HEADER-2 AFTER 2.

　c. Both fields are report fields (alphanumeric fields) and hence cannot be added.
　d. There is no READ error. Three blanks will be moved into A. If A is processed arithmetically, there will be an execution error for the particular operation since A is an alphanumeric field.
　e. Use the ON SIZE ERROR option:　A PIC S9 VALUE −5.
　　　　　　　　　　　　　　　　　　B PIC S9 VALUE 5.
　　SUBTRACT A FROM B ON SIZE ERROR WRITE PRINT-LINE FROM ERR-MSSG-LINE.
　　The result is 10, which is too large for PIC 9.
　f. If A is a numeric field.
　g. To ensure that the title "ABC COMPANY" prints out all by itself on the output line, the clause VALUE SPACES should be added to both FILLER fields.

CHAPTER 5

SCREEN PROCESSING

5–1 ALTERNATE FORMS OF INPUT AND OUTPUT

5–2 THE ACCEPT AND DISPLAY STATEMENTS

5–3 FORMATTED SCREENS

5–4 EXERCISES

INTRODUCTION The ACCEPT and DISPLAY statements provide another form of input and output. They are used to accept input from a terminal or microcomputer screen and to display results or other output on the screen. This chapter explains how to use the ACCEPT and DISPLAY commands and how to set up formatted screens.

5-1 ALTERNATIVE FORMS OF INPUT AND OUTPUT

5-1-1 OVERVIEW

So far, we have used the READ and WRITE statements for the input of data and the output of results. For input, a data file is created through a text editor and stored on disk; then that data file is read using the READ statement. Similarly, results are printed or written out using the WRITE statement. The record structure of both input and output files is declared in the DATA division, while the specific input/output devices are named in the ENVIRONMENT division through the SELECT/ASSIGN clauses.

Another form of data input and output is available through the ACCEPT and DISPLAY statements. These statements do not require the SELECT/ASSIGN, FD (file description), and associated OPEN and CLOSE clauses.

5-1-2 SCREEN TOOLS: ACCEPT AND DISPLAY

The usefulness and convenience of the ACCEPT and DISPLAY statements are most pronounced with stand-alone terminals or microcomputers where the ACCEPT statement is used to enter data on the screen (terminal) at execution time and the DISPLAY statement is used to print messages or results on the screen. (Those readers familiar with BASIC should equate ACCEPT with INPUT, and DISPLAY with PRINT.) On large mainframe computer systems with terminal networks, the ACCEPT and DISPLAY statements are generally not accessible to students, as this form of communication is used solely by the operator(s) to interact with the various system consoles during the operation of the computing system.

The ACCEPT and DISPLAY statements are most useful (and sometimes necessary) in the following types of situations:

1. Interactive communication. The data is entered spontaneously or in random fashion in response to an on-going process (menus, reservation systems, market quotations queries, games, budgeting and planning, et cetera). Predesigned screens and business forms can be drawn (programmed) on the screen to be completed by the user and processed by the system.

2. As a means of collecting data in interactive or on-line systems. Data is collected through the ACCEPT statement and written on disk in the form of disk files that can then be processed to produce various types of reports. This form of data collection is prevalent in situations where transactions (no matter how small) are continually transmitted to a central computing site for recording purposes (for example, on-line cash registers or election reporting systems with up-to-the-minute voter tabulations and winner/loser projections).

3. As an alternative to text editors for creating data files. The user creates his/her own editor by writing a four- or five-line COBOL program to accept data that is then written onto a disk file. Such a file can be read and processed later by other COBOL programs.

4. Testing and debugging. When logical errors are present in a program and the programmer cannot find the error(s), the DISPLAY statement can be used very constructively to display the contents of particular fields at various locations in the program. In this way the user can visually witness the evolution of "suspect" fields. The DISPLAY statement can also be used to display error messages during program execution.

   Likewise the ACCEPT statement may be used to ACCEPT various experimental input values to test the logic of the program. In this way the input file need not be re-edited for each test run.

5. For time-dependent or date-related functions. The ACCEPT statement enables the user to capture the date and time from the system's clock.

The ACCEPT verb is generally *not* used to manually accept large volumes of data. In such situations, disk files are far more preferable, since they can be processed repeatedly without manually re-entering the data every time the program is run and they can be continuously edited/updated. When the ACCEPT verb is used, the input data *must* be entered each time the program is run; this can become quite a time-consuming and tedious procedure.

There are no truly standardized forms of the ACCEPT or DISPLAY statements. They vary from one COBOL system to another. The ACCEPT and DISPLAY statements discussed in this chapter reflect IBM standards for smaller systems and microcomputers. Because of the increasing number of computer applications involving interactive processing where screen menus, windows, formatted screens, and other business forms are integrated into a total programming system, a fairly complete treatment of the various ACCEPT and DISPLAY statements is presented in the following sections. Even though differences in forms and features may exist between the user's system and the version presented in this chapter, the reader is strongly urged to read this chapter to get a grasp of the dimensions and power of screen processing. In the process, the reader should refer to his/her technical reference manual to convert and execute all the complete screen processing programs illustrated in this chapter.

5-2 THE ACCEPT AND DISPLAY STATEMENTS

The ACCEPT statement is available in four formats, while the DISPLAY statement is available in two formats.

180   UNDERSTANDING STRUCTURED COBOL

The general form of the format 1 ACCEPT statement is:

> **ACCEPT** data-name
>
> where data-name is a record description entry that can be a group item, an elementary item, or an independent item. Data-name can be a numeric edited name.

When the ACCEPT instruction is encountered in the program, the computer stops in scrolling mode to await input of data. The user types the data on the screen (wherever the cursor happens to be at that time) and presses the ENTER key. All characters that were typed before pressing the ENTER key are moved to data-name according to the rules of data transfer discussed in chapter 4. (Exceptions exist for numeric values.) The backspace (or character delete) key can be used to correct or edit the input field **before** the ENTER key is pressed.

Alphanumeric Data Entry

Examples:

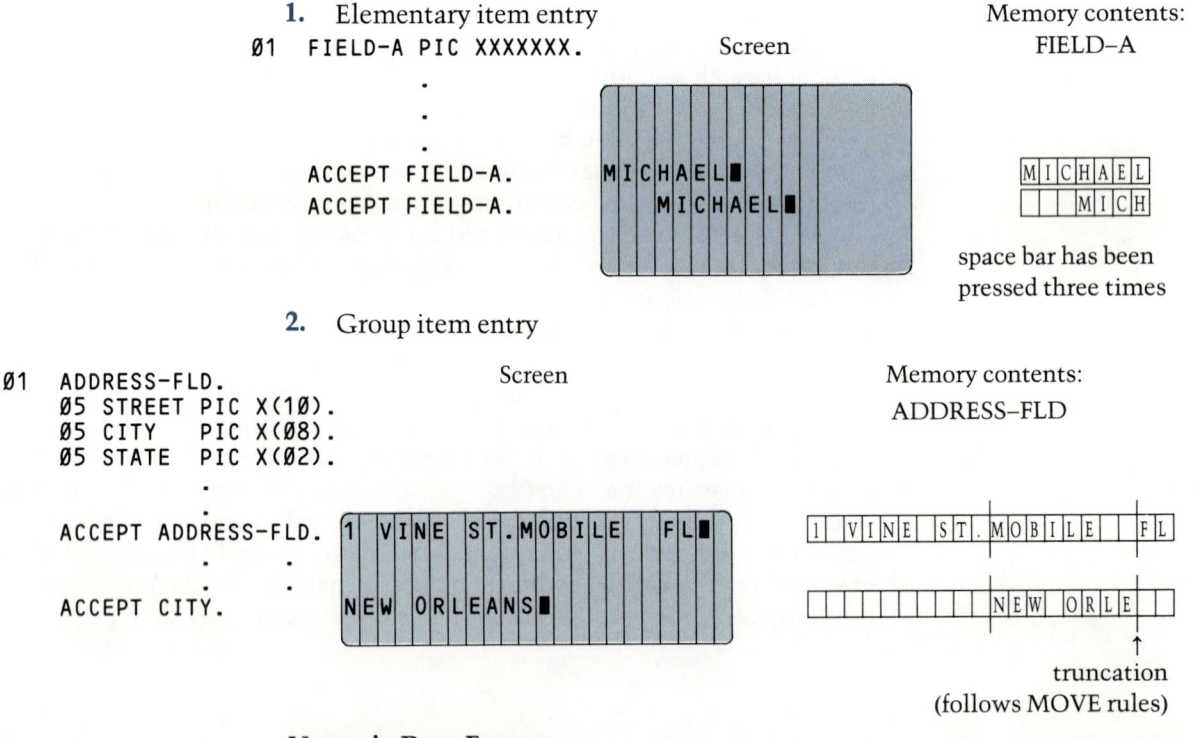

1. Elementary item entry   Memory contents:
   01 FIELD-A PIC XXXXXXX.   Screen   FIELD-A
                .
                .
                .
       ACCEPT FIELD-A.   MICHAEL■   MICHAEL
       ACCEPT FIELD-A.   MICHAEL■   MICH

                                                              space bar has been
                                                              pressed three times

2. Group item entry

   01 ADDRESS-FLD.   Screen   Memory contents:
        05 STREET PIC X(10).   ADDRESS-FLD
        05 CITY   PIC X(08).
        05 STATE PIC X(02).
                .
                .
       ACCEPT ADDRESS-FLD.   1 VINE ST.MOBILE   FL■   1 VINE ST.MOBILE   FL
                .
                .
       ACCEPT CITY.   NEW ORLEANS■   NEW ORLE
                                                                              ↑
                                                                         truncation
                                                                    (follows MOVE rules)

Numeric Data Entry

Transfer of numeric data between input field and receiving field follows the rules governing numeric moves as described in chapter 4, except that the decimal point *must* be typed on the screen if the data entry field specifies fractional digit positions. **For example, if the data entry field has PIC 999V99 and the user enters the digits 12345, the value 34500 will be recorded in memory, *not* 123.45.** Since the user did not type the decimal point, the system assumes it is to the

SCREEN PROCESSING 181

right of the right-most digit typed (5), and since only three whole positions are reserved in the picture field, the two left-most digits—1 and 2—are truncated. The user should have typed 123.45! Such inclusion of the decimal point is necessary for accuracy and readability in the visual environment where screens become actual records for all to behold.

Example: The data entry field is numeric.

Numeric Data Entry Picture Field	Screen Input	Digits Stored in FLDA	Value of FLDA
01 FLDA PIC 999V99.			
ACCEPT FLDA.	1.34■	0 0 1 3 4	1.34
ACCEPT FLDA.	200■	2 0 0 0 0	200.
ACCEPT FLDA.	.7■	0 0 0 7 0	.7
ACCEPT FLDA.	5421.768■	4 2 1 7 6	421.76

The + and − signs can be accepted if the picture for the data entry field specifies the S symbol. Thus, if A has picture S999V99 and the characters −20.4 are typed on the screen, the number stored in memory has value $\boxed{0\,2\,0\,4\,\overline{0}}$.

Example: The data entry field is numeric edited.

Numeric Edited Data Field	Screen Input	Characters Stored in FLDA	Value of FLDA
01 FLDA PIC +999.99.			
ACCEPT FLDA.	1.34■	+0 0 1 . 3 4	No numeric value
ACCEPT FLDA.	1003■	+0 0 3 . 0 0	No numeric value
ACCEPT FLDA.	−21.4■	−0 2 1 . 4 0	No numeric value

Many systems screen the input characters for validity. If the input string contains characters other than the digits 0 through 9, the + or − sign, or the decimal point, the user will be asked to retype the number.

Group items containing numeric fields can also be entered as shown in the following example:

```
01  PAY-DATA
    05  HOURS     PIC 999V99.
    05  RATE-PAY  PIC 99V99.
    05  TAX-RATE  PIC V9999.
    .
    .
    ACCEPT PAY-DATA.
```

Screen Input: `045500500672■`

Memory Contents:
HOURS: 0 4 5 5 0
RATE-PAY: 0 5 0 0
TAX-RATE: 0 6 7 2

Note that in this case **no** decimal points should be typed, since PAY-DATA is a group item and group items are alphanumeric fields. For example, if 045.5005.00.0672 were typed, then the characters 045.5 would be stored in

HOURS, 005. in RATE–PAY, and 00.0 in TAX–RATE—this would cause an execution time error the first time any of these fields participated in an arithmetic operation (computation or condition). The statement ACCEPT HOURS, however, requires the string 45.50 to be entered (with the decimal point), since HOURS is a numeric elementary item.

Figure 5–1 shows more examples of screen data transfers. Note that the operational signs + or – are allowed in the input field only if the editing character S, +, –, CR, or DB is present in the receiving field.

5-2-2 THE DISPLAY STATEMENT

The general form of the DISPLAY statement is:

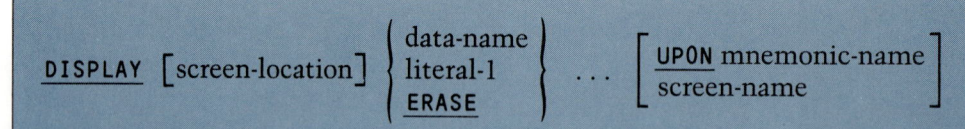

$$\underline{\text{DISPLAY}} \ [\text{screen-location}] \ \left\{ \begin{array}{l} \text{data-name} \\ \text{literal-1} \\ \underline{\text{ERASE}} \end{array} \right\} \ \ldots \ \left[\begin{array}{l} \underline{\text{UPON}} \ \text{mnemonic-name} \\ \text{screen-name} \end{array} \right]$$

where

> screen-location specifies the position (row and column) where the item is to be displayed on the screen.
>
> data-name is a group item, elementary, or independent item.
>
> ERASE can only be used in conjunction with screen-location; it blanks out the screen from screen-location to the bottom of the screen.
>
> screen-name displays predesigned screens (forms/windows). See section 5–3.
>
> UPON is used to identify the system's name for the output device. The mnemonic name may need to be specified in the SPECIAL–NAMES paragraph of the configuration section. If PRINTER is specified, the output is directed to the printer instead of the screen.

Action: the contents of data-name or the literal itself is displayed on the screen at the position designated by screen-location. If screen-location is not specified (or not available on the user's system), the item is displayed in the screen's normal scrolling mode and each DISPLAY verb causes advancement to the next line.

The screen-location has the following general form:

$$\left(\left\{ \begin{array}{l} \underline{\text{LIN}} \ [\pm \text{integer-1}] \\ \text{integer-2} \end{array} \right\} , \left\{ \begin{array}{l} \underline{\text{COL}} \ [\pm \text{integer-3}] \\ \text{integer-4} \end{array} \right\} \right)$$

ROW, COLUMN

Note that a space must follow the comma.

where LIN and COL are COBOL reserved words that are defined internally with numeric picture fields (there is no need to declare them); the user can process LIN and COL numerically. For a standard screen of 24 lines by 80 columns, the value evaluated for the row must be an integer between 1 and 24, while the value

SCREEN INPUT	RECEIVING PICTURE	MEMORY CONTENTS	NUMERIC VALUE
-34	999		Invalid minus character (no S symbol in PICTURE)
1.4	999	001	1
2.4-	S999	00\overline{2}	-2
+46	S99V9	460	46
-20	S99V9	20\overline{0}	-20
+.09	S99V9	000	0
1.21	999.9CR	001.2	No numeric value
15	999.9-	015.0	No numeric value
-1.6	999.9+	001.6-	No numeric value
23	$$$.9	$23.0	No numeric value
3246	$$,$$$.99	$3,246.00	No numeric value
-123.6	$*,***.99DB	$**123.60DB	No numeric value
46-	+999.9	-046.0	No numeric value

FIGURE 5-1
SCREEN EDITING THROUGH THE ACCEPT

evaluated for the column must be a number between 1 and 80. It is the user's responsibility to initialize LIN/COL to the particular values required. If the values of LIN or COL are to be displayed, they must first be moved to WORKING-STORAGE data items that can then be displayed, i.e., DISPLAY LIN is invalid.

Examples of screen locations

(,)	Position of current cursor
(3, 15)	Cursor is positioned at row/line 3 and column 15.
(LIN+1,)	Cursor is positioned at row LIN + 1 and at current column.
(5, COL-2)	Cursor is at row 5 and at column corresponding to COL-2.
(ROW, COLUMN)	Invalid syntax; LIN and COL must be used.
(3,2)	Invalid; a space must follow the comma.

Examples of DISPLAY statements

1.  ```
    01 PAY-DATA.
       05 HOURS PIC 999V99 VALUE 40.5.
       05 RATE  PIC  99V99 VALUE 5.50.

    DISPLAY HOURS RATE.
    DISPLAY HOURS ' ' RATE.
    DISPLAY 'HOURS=' HOURS '  RATE=' RATE.
    DISPLAY PAY-DATA.
    ```

    Screen Output
    ```
    0405００550
    04050 0550
    HOURS=04050    RATE=0550
    0405００550
    ```

2.  ```
    DISPLAY (1, 1) ERASE.    blank out all screen
    DISPLAY ( , ) ERASE.     blank out screen from current cursor position
    ```

3. `DISPLAY EMPLOYEE-RECORD UPON PRINTER.` The data item is printed on the printer.

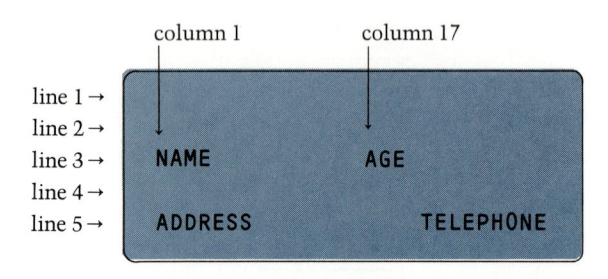

4. ```
   MOVE 3 TO LIN, MOVE 1 TO COL.
   DISPLAY (LIN, COL) ERASE 'NAME', (LIN, COL+16) 'AGE'.
   ADD 2 TO LIN.
   DISPLAY (LIN, COL) 'ADDRESS', (LIN, COL+20) 'TELEPHONE'.
   ```

   This code produces the following screen output:

   ```
              column 1        column 17
                 |                |
   line 1 →
   line 2 →
   line 3 →    NAME             AGE
   line 4 →
   line 5 →    ADDRESS               TELEPHONE
   ```

   Any data above line 3 is **not** erased. The screen is erased from row 3 and column 1 down to row 24 and column 80. The various captions are then displayed as shown.

   The DISPLAY statement can be extremely useful during the debugging phase of a program. Because DISPLAY does not require the SELECT/ASSIGN statement, the FD entry, or the OPEN/CLOSE statements, it is very convenient and easy to DISPLAY one or more item names whose values the user wants to see on the screen. For example, the statement

   ```
   DISPLAY "PAY" DL-PAY, " FLAG= " FLAG
   ```

   could produce the following result on the screen:

   ```
   PAY 001015 FLAG= 2
   ```

   If this statement were part of a loop, the user could then see the different values of these data items at various times and locations in the program.

   Figure 5-2 illustrates the use of the ACCEPT and DISPLAY statements with sample outputs. The program accepts a grocery bill amount and the amount paid by the customer. The program then computes and prints the change, using one dollar bills and the least number of coins. The code displayed could be considerably reduced if the REMAINDER option were used, as shown in comment lines 44, 48, 52, and 60. Since that option may not be available on certain systems, the program uses code that simulate the REMAINDER option.

   Program Questions

   1. Change the logic of the program to include five, ten, twenty, and fifty dollar bills for the change.

   2. What changes would you make in the program to suppress leading 0's on output for the half dollar field. (Be careful!)

   3. How would you change the logic of the program to make it a repetitive loop process? In Figure 5-2 only one change operation is performed, then the program stops.

5-2-3 ACCEPT FORMATS 2 AND 3

Format 2 allows the user to capture the date and the time of day from the system, while format 3 enables the user to accept data from any position on the screen, as opposed to the scrolling position (format 1).
   ```

```cobol
 1:    IDENTIFICATION DIVISION.
 2:    PROGRAM-ID. CHANGE-MAKER.
 3:    ****************************************************************
 4:    * PURPOSE: COMPUTES THE CHANGE OWED TO A CUSTOMER USING THE    *
 5:    *          LEAST NUMBER OF 1 DOLLAR BILLS AND COINS. THE CHANGE*
 6:    *          IS THE DIFFERENCE BETWEEN THE PAYMENT AND THE BILL. *
 7:    *                                                              *
 8:    * INPUT:   PURCHASE BILL & CUSTOMER PAYMENT.                   *
 9:    *                                                              *
10:    * OUTPUT:  DOLLAR BILLS, 50, 25, 10, 5 AND 1 CENT COINS.       *
11:    ****************************************************************
12:    AUTHOR. JONES.
13:    ENVIRONMENT DIVISION.
14:    CONFIGURATION SECTION.
15:    SOURCE-COMPUTER. IBM.
16:    OBJECT-COMPUTER. IBM.
17:    *
18:    DATA DIVISION.
19:    WORKING-STORAGE SECTION.
20:    01  GROCERY-BILL     PIC 999V99.
21:    01  CUSTOMER-PAYMENT PIC 999V99.
22:    01  CHANGE-ITEMS.
23:        05 DOLLAR-BILLS PIC 999.
24:        05 HAF-DOLLAR   PIC 9.
25:        05 QUARTER      PIC 9.
26:        05 DIMES        PIC 9.
27:        05 NICKEL       PIC 9.
28:        05 CENTS        PIC 9.
29:    01  COMPUTATION-ITEMS.
30:        05 CHANGE       PIC 99999.
31:        05 AMOUNT-LEFT  PIC 99999.
32:    *
33:    PROCEDURE DIVISION.
34:    100-COORDINATING-MODULE.
35:        DISPLAY 'ENTER GROCERY BILL'.
36:        ACCEPT GROCERY-BILL.
37:        DISPLAY 'ENTER CUSTOMER PAYMENT'.
38:        ACCEPT CUSTOMER-PAYMENT.
39:    *
40:        COMPUTE CHANGE = (CUSTOMER-PAYMENT - GROCERY-BILL) * 100.
41:    *
42:        COMPUTE DOLLAR-BILLS = CHANGE / 100.
43:        COMPUTE AMOUNT-LEFT  = CHANGE - DOLLAR-BILLS * 100.
44:    *   COMPUTE DOLLAR-BILLS = CHANGE / 100 REMAINDER AMOUNT-LEFT.
45:    *
46:        COMPUTE HAF-DOLLAR   = AMOUNT-LEFT / 50.
47:        COMPUTE AMOUNT-LEFT  = AMOUNT-LEFT - HAF-DOLLAR * 50.
48:    *   COMPUTE HAF-DOLLAR   = AMOUNT-LEFT / 50 REMAINDER AMOUNT-LEFT.
49:    *
50:        COMPUTE QUARTER      = AMOUNT-LEFT / 25.
51:        COMPUTE AMOUNT-LEFT  = AMOUNT-LEFT - QUARTER * 25.
52:    *   COMPUTE QUARTER      = AMOUNT-LEFT / 25 REMAINDER AMOUNT-LEFT.
53:    *
54:        COMPUTE DIMES        = AMOUNT-LEFT / 10.
55:        COMPUTE AMOUNT-LEFT  = AMOUNT-LEFT - DIMES * 10.
56:    *   COMPUTE DIMES        = AMOUNT-LEFT / 10 REMAINDER AMOUNT-LEFT.
57:    *
58:        COMPUTE NICKEL       = AMOUNT-LEFT / 5.
59:        COMPUTE CENTS        = AMOUNT-LEFT - NICKEL * 5.
60:    *   COMPUTE NICKEL       = AMOUNT-LEFT / 5 REMAINDER CENTS.
61:    *
62:        DISPLAY ' '.
63:        DISPLAY 'CHANGE IS:'.
64:        DISPLAY ' '.
65:        DISPLAY DOLLAR-BILLS    ' DOLLAR BILLS'
66:        DISPLAY HAF-DOLLAR      ' HALF DOLLAR'.
67:        DISPLAY QUARTER         ' QUARTER'.
68:        DISPLAY DIMES           ' DIMES'.
69:        DISPLAY NICKEL          ' NICKEL'.
70:        DISPLAY CENTS           ' CENTS'.
71:        STOP RUN.
```

Sample Screen Outputs ↓

```
ENTER GROCERY BILL
5.92
ENTER CUSTOMER PAYMENT
10.00

CHANGE IS:

004 DOLLAR BILLS
0 HALF DOLLAR
0 QUARTER
0 DIMES
1 NICKEL
3 CENTS


ENTER GROCERY BILL
3.7
ENTER CUSTOMER PAYMENT
10.00

CHANGE IS:

006 DOLLAR BILLS
0 HALF DOLLAR
1 QUARTER
0 DIMES
1 NICKEL
0 CENTS


ENTER GROCERY BILL
5.03
ENTER CUSTOMER PAYMENT
10.

CHANGE IS:

004 DOLLAR BILLS
1 HALF DOLLAR
1 QUARTER
2 DIMES
0 NICKEL
2 CENTS


ENTER GROCERY BILL
5.09
ENTER CUSTOMER PAYMENT
10.

CHANGE IS:

004 DOLLAR BILLS
1 HALF DOLLAR
1 QUARTER
1 DIMES
1 NICKEL
1 CENTS
```

FIGURE 5–2
AUTOMATIC CHANGE MAKER

The general form of the format 2 ACCEPT statement is:

```
ACCEPT data-name FROM  { DATE  }
                       { DAY   }
                       { TIME  }
```

DATE, DAY, and TIME are COBOL reserved word that may only be used in the ACCEPT statement; thus DISPLAY DATE is invalid.

DATE returns a 6-digit value of the form YYMMDD (year, month, and day) into data-name.

DAY returns a 5-digit Julian date of the form YYNNN (year, number of days elapsed since the start of the year) into data-name; thus February 1, 1986 is 86032.

TIME returns an 8-digit value of the form HHMMSSFF (hours (00 to 23), minutes (00 to 59), seconds (00 to 59), hundredths of seconds (00 to 99)) into data-name.

The format 3 ACCEPT statement has the general form:

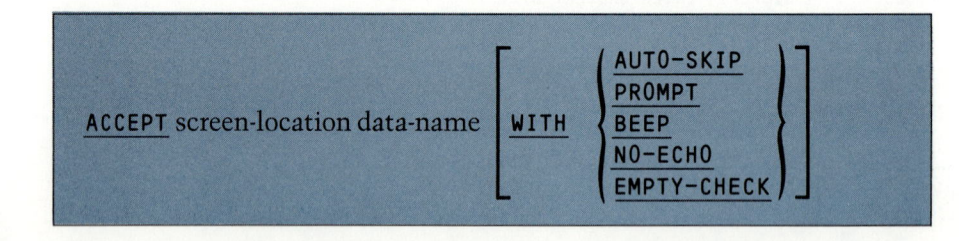

```
ACCEPT screen-location data-name  [ WITH  { AUTO-SKIP    } ]
                                          { PROMPT       }
                                          { BEEP         }
                                          { NO-ECHO      }
                                          { EMPTY-CHECK  }
```

Format 3 enables data to be accepted from any position on the screen by specifying the screen-location parameter, which has the same form as the screen-location parameter used in the DISPLAY statement (see section 5-2-2).

The AUTO–SKIP option causes the ACCEPT to proceed automatically to the next instruction as soon as *all* data input positions have been filled, i.e., the user does not need to press the ENTER key (see also case 1, example 1 below).

The PROMPT clause is an extremely valuable option that should always be specified. Cue or prompt fields (0's for numeric data and periods for alphanumeric data) are displayed on the screen to show the length of the input field.

BEEP causes the speaker to beep at the start of the input operation.

The NO–ECHO option causes an asterisk to be displayed on the screen for each character entered. This option is especially useful when security-sensitive data such as passwords and bank account numbers are to be entered.

The EMPTY–CHECK option requires that at least one character be typed before the ENTER key can be pressed, i.e., blank fields are not accepted.

Case 1: Numeric and Numeric Edited Fields

If the PROMPT option is used, the cue field on the screen shows all digit positions (whole and fractional) as 0's. The decimal point is displayed if there are fractional positions in the PICTURE field. If any of the following editing characters S, +, –, ., CR or DB are present in the picture field, the first position of the cue field is left blank; this position displays the minus sign if the user types in

SCREEN PROCESSING 187

the minus sign. If a character other than a digit, a + sign, or a − sign is typed, it will be rejected. The following diagrams show various screen cues for ACCEPT statements with different receiving field pictures.

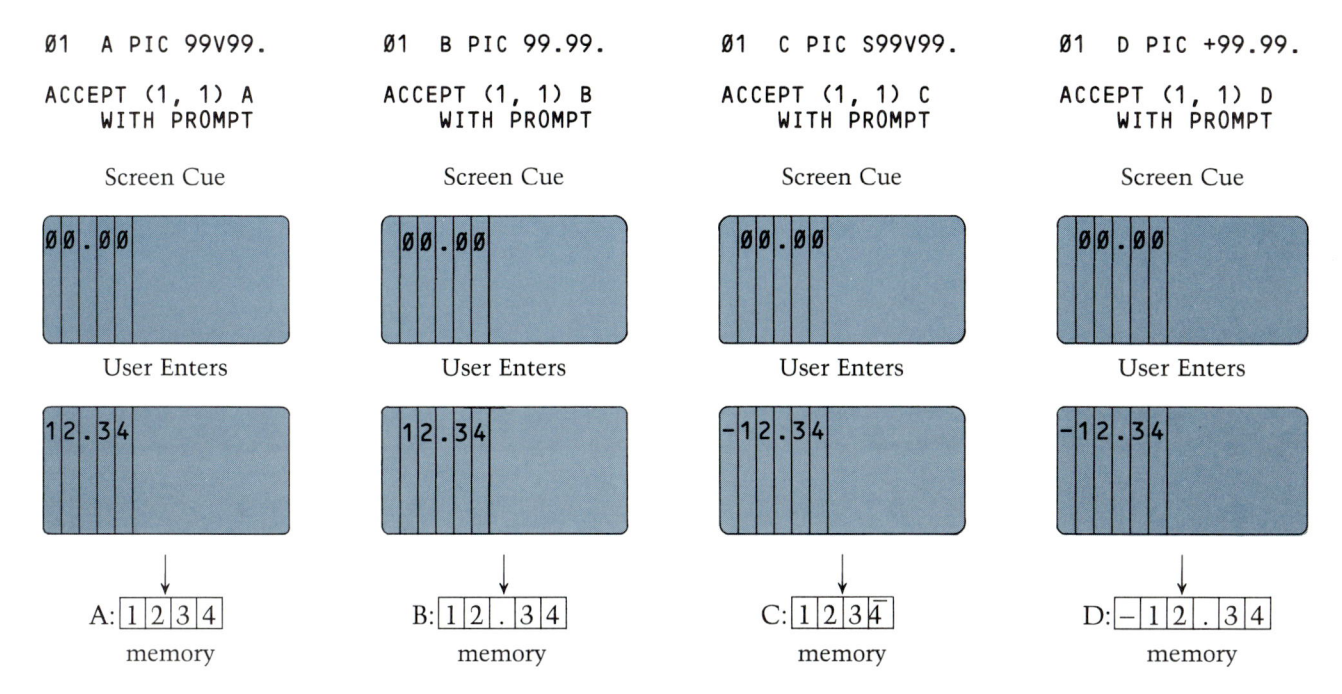

01 A PIC 99V99.	01 B PIC 99.99.	01 C PIC S99V99.	01 D PIC +99.99.
ACCEPT (1, 1) A WITH PROMPT	ACCEPT (1, 1) B WITH PROMPT	ACCEPT (1, 1) C WITH PROMPT	ACCEPT (1, 1) D WITH PROMPT

Screen Cue

| 00.00 | 00.00 | 00.00 | 00.00 |

User Enters

| 12.34 | 12.34 | −12.34 | −12.34 |

| A: 1 2 3 4 | B: 1 2 . 3 4 | C: 1 2 3 4̄ | D: − 1 2 . 3 4 |
| memory | memory | memory | memory |

Note that even though the decimal point appears on the screen in the examples ACCEPT A and ACCEPT C, the value stored in memory is wholly numeric because of the PICTURES of A and C. Furthermore, in the case of ACCEPT C, the minus sign typed on the screen is stored as an internal code in the right-most digit of the receiving field. (The sign position of the cue field stays blank if the user types the + sign.)

The manner in which the system processes the incoming digits as they are typed on the screen may come as a surprise to the user! This process is illustrated in the following examples.

EXAMPLE 1 Suppose A has picture 99V99 and we want to enter the numeric value 12.34 so that the numeric value $\boxed{1|2|3|4}$ is stored in A.

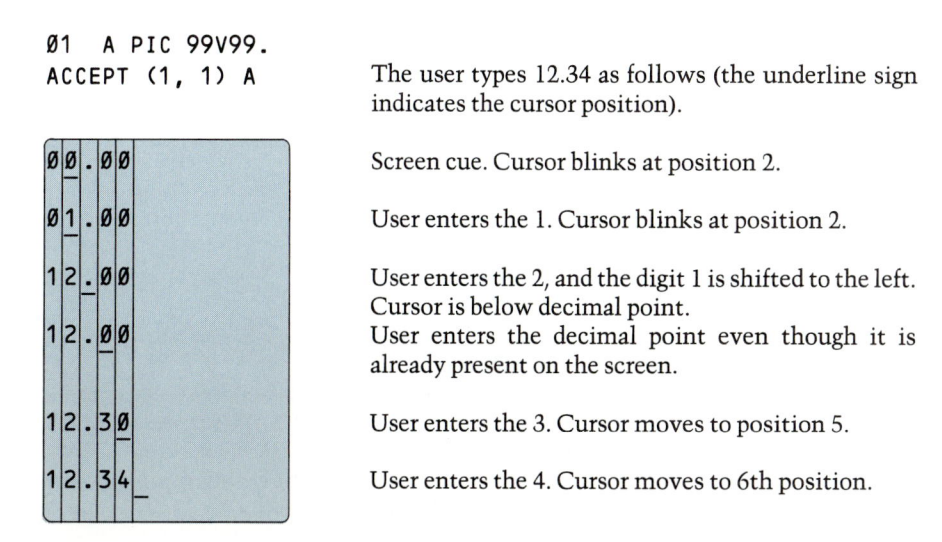

```
01  A PIC 99V99.
    ACCEPT (1, 1) A
```

The user types 12.34 as follows (the underline sign indicates the cursor position).

00.00	Screen cue. Cursor blinks at position 2.
01.00	User enters the 1. Cursor blinks at position 2.
12.00	User enters the 2, and the digit 1 is shifted to the left. Cursor is below decimal point.
12.00	User enters the decimal point even though it is already present on the screen.
12.30	User enters the 3. Cursor moves to position 5.
12.34_	User enters the 4. Cursor moves to 6th position.

As this example shows, each nonfractional (whole) incoming digit is shifted to the left while the cursor remains at the right-most (unit digit) position. When the decimal point is typed, the cursor moves to the first fractional position, then the remaining digits move along with the cursor to the right.

If the AUTO–SKIP option is used and there are fractional digits, the user does not need to type the decimal point; the cursor automatically skips to the fractional positions as soon as all integer positions have been filled. This will happen with numeric as well as with numeric edited fields.

> **CAUTION** If AUTO–SKIP is not specified in the above example and the user types 1, then 2, then 3 (no decimal point), a beep or error message occurs. The system is reminding the user that only two "whole" positions are reserved for the number (PIC 99V99). The user must type the decimal point. If incorrect characters are entered, the backspace key can be used as often as needed (before pressing ENTER) to erase invalid or mistyped characters.

EXAMPLE 2

```
01   A PIC S99V9.
ACCEPT (1, 1) A
```

Assume the value to be stored in A is the numeric value −3. (3)

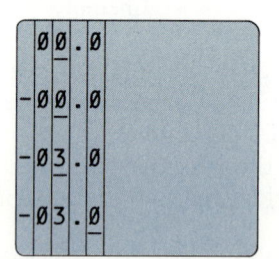

|00.0| Screen cue. Cursor blinks at position 3.

−|00.0| User types the − sign which is automatically displayed in position 1.

−|03.0| The cursor is still in position 3 and the user types 3.

−|03.0| The user types the decimal point and hits ENTER.

In this case, the user could have typed −3 or 3.− and then ENTER; the results would be the same. If the S symbol is not present in the receiving field and the user enters a + sign or − sign, a beep or an error message will be displayed asking the user to retype the character in question.

EXAMPLE 3

```
01   A PIC 99.99+
ACCEPT (1, 1) A
```

Assume the value to be stored in A is the numeric edited value 3 . 4 5 + .

|00.00| Screen cue.

|03.00| User enters 3.

|03.00| User enters the decimal point.

|03.40| User enters 4.

|03.45| User enters the 5. User presses ENTER.

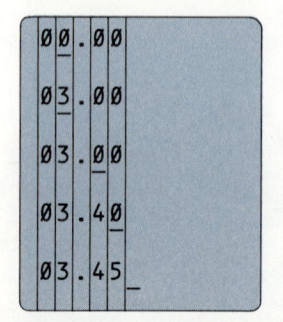

The number could also have been entered in the sequence +3.45, 3.45+, or 03.45 or as 0345 if AUTO–SKIP had been specified.

SCREEN PROCESSING 189

Case 2: Alphanumeric Fields

If the PROMPT option is used, a period is displayed for each alphanumeric position. The cursor is placed on the first period and the input characters are entered on the screen, causing a continuous shift of the cursor to the right. When the ENTER key is pressed, all characters typed are transmitted to the receiving field according to the rules governing alphanumeric data transfer. The following examples contain ACCEPT statements for alphanumeric fields.

EXAMPLE 4   `ACCEPT ( , ) X WITH BEEP AUTO-SKIP.` Beep sound; data is entered at current cursor position.

`ACCEPT (1, 3) PASSWORD WITH NO-ECHO PROMPT.`

`ACCEPT (LIN + 2, COL - 1) IR-NAME WITH PROMPT BEEP EMPTY-CHECK.`

EXAMPLE 5 The following code computes the time interval in minutes between two key strokes:

```
01 START-CLOCK.
   05 SC-HOURS PIC 99.       When the user presses any key, the time will be recorded in START-CLOCK as a result
   05 SC-MIN   PIC 99.       of ACCEPT START-CLOCK FROM TIME.
01 END-CLOCK.
   05 EC-HOURS PIC 99.       When the user presses any key, the time will be recorded in END-CLOCK as a result of
   05 EC-MIN   PIC 99.       ACCEPT END-CLOCK FROM TIME.
01 TIME-DIF    PIC ZZZZ9.    Represents the elapsed time between START and END of clock.
01 X           PIC X.        Represents any key that the user will type during execution of code
   .
   .
   .
   DISPLAY (1, 1) ERASE 'PRESS ANY KEY TO START CLOCK'.    Erase screen and display message.
   ACCEPT ( , ) X WITH AUTO-SKIP.                          Press any key to start counting.
   ACCEPT START-CLOCK FROM TIME.                           Read the hours and the minutes.
   DISPLAY (1, 1) ERASE 'PRESS ANY KEY TO STOP CLOCK'.     Erase screen and display message.
   ACCEPT ( , ) X WITH AUTO-SKIP.                          Press any key to stop the clock.
   ACCEPT END-CLOCK FROM TIME.                             Get the current number of hours and minutes.
   COMPUTE TIME-DIF = (EC-HOURS * 60 + EC-MIN) -           Evaluate the time interval in minutes.
                      (SC-HOURS * 60 + SC-MIN).
   DISPLAY (12, 30) TIME-DIF ' OR SO MINUTES HAVE ELAPSED'. Display approximate results in minutes.
```

5-2-4 PROGRAMMING EXAMPLE

A complete programming example employing various forms of the ACCEPT and DISPLAY statements is shown in Figure 5–3. This program is used by a psychiatrist's receptionist to record the time the physician spends with various patients during the day. A screen prompt asks the receptionist to enter the patient's name, at which time the following data and instructions are displayed on the screen:

```
CLIENT NAME?  BOILLOT          DATE 85/05/05      Lines 105–107
ENTER ANY KEY TO RECORD START OF SESSION          Line 79–80
```

```
 1:    IDENTIFICATION DIVISION.
 2:    PROGRAM-ID. DOCTOR-APPOINTMENT.
 3:    ****************************************************************
 4:    * OBJECTIVE: ALLOWS PSYCHIATRIST'S RECEPTIONIST TO RECORD ON A  *
 5:    *            A DISK FILE THE PATIENTS NAMES & THE TIME SPENT BY *
 6:    *            EACH PATIENT WITH THE DOCTOR.                      *
 7:    *                                                               *
 8:    * INPUT: THE RECEPTIONIST ENTERS PATIENT'S NAME ON THE SCREEN & *
 9:    *        THEN PRESSES ANY KEY TO ACTIVATE THE TIME AT WHICH THE *
10:    *        THE SESSION BETWEEN CLIENT & DOCTOR STARTS. LIKEWISE A *
11:    *        KEY IS PRESSED TO RECORD THE ENDING TIME OF SESSION.   *
12:    *                                                               *
13:    * OUTPUT: SCREEN- CLIENT NAME, DATE, START & END TIME SESSION   *
14:    *         DISK--  CLIENT NAME, DATE, START & END TIME SESSION   *
15:    *                                                               *
16:    * SYSTEM: DATE AND INTERNAL CLOCK ARE READ FROM SYSTEM HARDWARE *
17:    *                                                               *
18:    * VANISHING PROMPTS: CUES TO RECEPTIONIST TO PRESS KEY TO START *
19:    *                    RECORDING CLOCK AT START & END OF SESSION  *
20:    ****************************************************************
21:    AUTHOR. JONES.
22:    ENVIRONMENT DIVISION.
23:    CONFIGURATION SECTION.
24:    SOURCE-COMPUTER. IBM.
25:    OBJECT-COMPUTER. IBM.
26:    INPUT-OUPUT SECTION.
27:    FILE-CONTROL.
28:    *
29:    * NAME, START & END TIME OF SESSION ARE RECORDED ON DISK FILE
30:    *
31:        SELECT AGENDA-FILE ASSIGN TO DISK.
32:    *
33:    DATA DIVISION.
34:    FILE SECTION.
35:    FD AGENDA-FILE
36:        LABEL RECORDS ARE STANDARD
37:        VALUE OF FILE-ID IS 'PATIENT'
38:        DATA RECORD IS AGENDA-RECORD.
39:    01 AGENDA-RECORD.
40:        05 AR-NAME    PIC X(10).
41:        05 AR-DATE    PIC X(08).
42:        05 AR-BEGIN   PIC X(06).
43:        05 AR-END     PIC X(06).
44:    WORKING-STORAGE SECTION.
45:    *
46:    * NAME OF CLIENT THAT IS ENTERED ON SCREEN BY RECEPTIONIST.
47:    01 PATIENT-NAME PIC X(10).
48:
49:    * THE DATE IS READ FROM THE SYSTEM & STORED IN TODAY-DATE.
50:    01 TODAY-DATE PIC Z9/99/99.
51:
52:    * THE SYSTEM CLOCK IS READ INTO BEGIN-SESSION & END-SESSION.
53:    01 BEGIN-SESSION.
54:        05 BS-HOURS     PIC 99.
55:        05 BS-MINUTES   PIC 99.
56:        05 BS-SECONDS   PIC 99.
57:        05 BS-HUNDREDS  PIC 99.
58:    01 END-SESSION.
59:        05 ES-HOURS     PIC 99.
60:        05 ES-MINUTES   PIC 99.
61:        05 ES-SECONDS   PIC 99.
62:        05 ES-HUNDREDS  PIC 99.
63:
64:    * THE USER PRESSES ANY KEY TO RECORD START & END OF SESSION
65:    01 NULL-KEY PIC X.
```

directory name →

Disk Storage

Final Screen Output

```
CLIENT NAME?  BOILLOT     DATE: 85/05/05
TIME IN: 09:06            TIME OUT 09:07

CLIENT NAME?  TENZ        DATE: 85/05/05
TIME IN: 09:08            TIME OUT 09:38

CLIENT NAME?  TROUBLED    DATE: 85/05/05
TIME IN: 09:39            TIME OUT 10:08

CLIENT NAME?  XXX
                              end of file
```

FIGURE 5–3
AN AUTOMATED SESSION-TIME TRACKER

SCREEN PROCESSING

```
 66:   *
 67:   PROCEDURE DIVISION.
 68:   100-COORDINATING-MODULE.
 69:       OPEN OUTPUT AGENDA-FILE.              Disk file to keep track of patient records.
 70:       MOVE 1 TO LIN.
 71:       ACCEPT TODAY-DATE FROM DATE.          Pick up the date and
 72:       PERFORM 200-ENTER-CLIENT-NAME.        determine the name of the patient.
 73:       PERFORM 300-DAY-SCHEDULE UNTIL PATIENT-NAME = 'XXX'.
 74:       CLOSE AGENDA-FILE.
 75:       STOP RUN.
 76:   *
 77:   300-DAY-SCHEDULE.
 78:       DISPLAY (LIN, 30) 'DATE: ', TODAY-DATE.
 79:       DISPLAY (LIN + 1, 1)
 80:           'ENTER ANY KEY TO RECORD START OF SESSION'
 81:       ACCEPT ( , ) NULL-KEY WITH AUTO-SKIP.           Start keeping track of time.
 82:   *
 83:   * THE AUTO-SKIP AUTOMATICALLY PASSES BACK CONTROL TO THE SYSTEM
 84:   * ONCE THE INPUT FIELD IS TYPED ON SCREEN. NO NEED TO PRESS ENTER
 85:   *
 86:       ACCEPT BEGIN-SESSION FROM TIME.                 Pick up time from system.
 87:       DISPLAY (LIN + 1, 1) ERASE.
 88:       DISPLAY (LIN + 1, 1) 'PRESS ANY KEY WHEN SESSION FINISHED'.
 89:       ACCEPT ( , ) NULL-KEY WITH AUTO-SKIP.           Record time at end of session.
 90:       ACCEPT END-SESSION FROM TIME.
 91:       MOVE PATIENT-NAME   TO AR-NAME.
 92:       MOVE TODAY-DATE     TO AR-DATE.
 93:       MOVE BEGIN-SESSION  TO AR-BEGIN.    Record patient record on disk.
 94:       MOVE END-SESSION    TO AR-END.
 95:       WRITE AGENDA-RECORD.
 96:       DISPLAY (LIN + 1, 1) ERASE.
 97:       DISPLAY (LIN + 1, 1)
 98:           'TIME IN: ', BS-HOURS, ':', BS-MINUTES.    Display time in and time out on screen.
 99:       DISPLAY (LIN + 1, 30)
100:           'TIME OUT ', ES-HOURS, ':', ES-MINUTES.
101:       ADD 3 TO LIN.
102:       PERFORM 200-ENTER-CLIENT-NAME.                  Read and process next client.
103:   *
104:   200-ENTER-CLIENT-NAME.
105:       DISPLAY (LIN, 1) ERASE.
106:       DISPLAY (LIN, 1) 'CLIENT NAME?'.
107:       ACCEPT (LIN, 16) PATIENT-NAME WITH PROMPT.
```

FIGURE 5–3
(continued)

Note that the date is automatically displayed by the system (line 78). When the session begins, the receptionist hits any key (line 81); this causes the current time to be saved in memory (line 86). The prompt immediately disappears from the screen (line 87) and is replaced by a new prompt (line 88). At this point the screen has the following display:

```
CLIENT NAME?   BOILLOT        DATE: 85/05/05
PRESS ANY KEY WHEN SESSION FINISHED
```

When the session ends (short session!) the receptionist hits any key (line 89); the time is recorded (line 90), the prompt disappears from the screen (line 96); and the following summary information is then displayed on the screen:

```
CLIENT NAME?    BOILLOT        DATE: 85/05/05
TIME IN: 09:06                 TIME OUT 09:07
```

In the meantime the system builds up a patient file by writing each patient record on disk (line 95); each record consists of the patient's name, the date, and the starting and ending session times (lines 39–43). This data file, catalogued under the name of PATIENT (line 37), is then available for later batch processing, billing, or other reference purposes, for example, the doctor might want to determine the number of visits made by a particular patient or compute the average patient session time. The program terminates when the receptionist enters a name to act as an end-of-file symbol—in this case a name equal to 'XXX' (line 73).

The program in Figure 5–4 reads and lists the data file created by the program in Figure 5–3. The output produced on the printer is as follows:

```
                         Begin    End
Name       Date          Session  Session
BOILLOT    85/05/05      090606   090738
TENZ       85/05/05      090804   093826
TROUBLED   85/05/05      093903   100884
```

The program in Figure 5–4 can be used to list the contents of any disk file created by a COBOL program. The user is prompted to enter the catalogued name of the disk file to be processed (lines 53 and 54). This name, stored in USER–FILE (line 48), is then communicated to the VALUE of the FILE–ID clause (line 28) for disk retrieval purposes. The logical name of the data file retrieved is still DOCTOR–FILE as far as the logic of the COBOL program is concerned (line 26).

Test Your Understanding of the Program in Figure 5–3

1. How would you change the code to write on disk the date field record (LINE 41) as a six-digit numeric field instead of an eight-character field, i.e., the date would be 850505 instead of 85/05/05?

2. What would happen to the display of patient records on the screen after more than 6 or 7 patient records were processed? How would you change the code to take care of this problem?

3. Change the code so that each new patient's two-line summary record is displayed at the top of the screen (all by itself) instead of being scrolled down the screen as the present program does.

4. Make the necessary changes to the program so that it can be run on your system.

5. Using the information in the program of Figure 5–4, what changes would need to be made to the program of Figure 5–3 so that the patient file could be written on disk under a catalogued name specified at execution time?

```cobol
 1:     IDENTIFICATION DIVISION.
 2.     PROGRAM-ID. FILE-LISTER.
 3:     ****************************************************************
 4:     * PURPOSE: READS & LISTS A DATA FILE CREATED BY A COBOL PROGRAM.*
 5:     *          THE USER IS ASKED FOR THE NAME OF THE FILE. IN THIS  *
 6:     *          CASE THE DATA FILE CREATED BY THE PROGRAM OF FIGURE  *
 7:     *          5-3 IS READ, AND LISTED ON PRINTER                   *
 8:     *                                                               *
 9:     * INPUT: THE FILE-NAME IS ENTERED ON THE SCREEN (PATIENT) AND   *
10:     *        THE DATA FILE IS THEN READ                             *
11:     *                                                               *
12:     * OUTPUT: THE CONTENTS OF THE DATA FILE ARE PRINTED             *
13:     ****************************************************************
14:     AUTHOR. JONES.
15:     ENVIRONMENT DIVISION.
16:     CONFIGURATION SECTION.
17:     SOURCE-COMPUTER. IBM.
18:     OBJECT-COMPUTER. IBM.
19:     INPUT-OUTPUT SECTION.
20:     FILE-CONTROL.
21:         SELECT DOCTOR-FILE ASSIGN TO DISK.
22:         SELECT PRINT-FILE  ASSIGN TO PRINTER.
23:     *
24:     DATA DIVISION.
25:     FILE SECTION.
26:     FD DOCTOR-FILE
27:         LABEL RECORDS ARE STANDARD
28:         VALUE OF FILE-ID IS USER-FILE
29:     *
30:     * THE NAME OF THE ACTUAL DISK PATIENT DATA FILE IS ACCEPTED AT
31:     * EXECUTION TIME THROUGH THE DUMMY FIELD "USER-FILE" SPECIFIED IN
32:     * THE FILE-ID CLAUSE AND DEFINED IN WORKING-STORAGE (LINE 48).
33:     *
34:         DATA RECORD IS AGENDA-RECORD.
35:     01  AGENDA-RECORD.
36:         05 DR-NAME  PIC X(10).
37:         05 DR-DATE  PIC X(08).
38:         05 DR-BEGIN PIC 9(06).
39:         05 DR-END   PIC 9(06).
40:     FD  PRINT-FILE
41:         LABEL RECORDS ARE OMITTED
42:         DATA RECORD IS PRINT-LINE.
43:     01  PRINT-LINE PIC X(80).
44:     WORKING-STORAGE SECTION.
45:     *
46:     * USER-FILE IS USED TO ACCEPT THE NAME OF THE DISK FILE TO READ
47:     *
48:     01  USER-FILE       PIC X(08).
49:     01  WS-EOF          PIC 9 VALUE 0.
50:     *
51:     PROCEDURE DIVISION.
52:     100-COORDINATING-MODULE.
53:         DISPLAY 'ENTER NAME OF INPUT FILE'.
54:         ACCEPT USER-FILE.
55:         OPEN INPUT DOCTOR-FILE.
56:         OPEN OUTPUT PRINT-FILE.
57:         READ DOCTOR-FILE
58:             AT END MOVE 1 TO WS-EOF.
59:         PERFORM 200-READ-DOCTOR-FILE
60:             UNTIL WS-EOF = 1.
61:         CLOSE DOCTOR-FILE, PRINT-FILE.
62:         STOP RUN.
63:     *
64:     200-READ-DOCTOR-FILE.
65:         WRITE PRINT-LINE FROM DOCTOR-RECORD AFTER 1 LINE.
66:         READ DOCTOR-FILE
67:             AT END MOVE 1 TO WS-EOF.
```

Line 54: ACCEPT USER-FILE. ←—— User enters PATIENT

Disk Storage — STOCKS, PAYROLL, MORTGAGE, PATIENT

Printer output:
```
BOILLOT    85/05/05090606090738
TENZ       85/05/05090804093826
TROUBLED   85/05/05093903100884
```

FIGURE 5–4
UTILITY PROGRAM TO PRINT A DISK-FILE CREATED BY A COBOL PROGRAM

For example, the program of Figure 5–3 would ask, "What name do you want to give to your disk file?" If the user typed "DOKTOR", the patient file would be catalogued on disk under the name DOKTOR. The program in Figure 5–4 could then be used to retrieve DOKTOR.

Test Your Understanding of the Program in Figure 5–4

1. What problems might occur if the first two lines of the PROCEDURE division started out with the two sentences:

   ```
   OPEN INPUT DOCTOR-FILE.
   OPEN OUTPUT PRINT-FILE.
   ```

2. Make the necessary changes to the program so that it can be run on your system.

3. Write a program to read the patient file created by the program of Figure 5–3 and carry out the following functions:

   a. Compute and print the average duration of all patient sessions.
   b. Print the list of patient names and corresponding session duration (in minutes).
   c. Print the name of the patient with the longest session.
   d. Print the name(s) of any patient(s) who saw the doctor at least two times during the day.

4. Write a billing program for the doctor. Each patient invoice should specify the patient's name, the date, the time in and out of the doctor's office, the duration time in minutes, and the corresponding bill. The doctor charges $80.00 per hour.

5. Produce a summary report showing each patient's name, session duration in minutes, and charge. Compute the total dollar amount. A typical report might have the following form:

   ```
   NAME           DURATION            CHARGE

   AMOS              60                80.00
   HARDY             90               120.00
   LOVE              30                40.00
   SIMS              20                26.67

   TOTAL CHARGES                     $266.67
   ```

6. Can you devise a method to express minutes in terms of hours and minutes (thus 90 mins. = 1:30; 80 mins. = 1:20, et cetera)? Incorporate these changes in your code for exercise 5 above.

5–3 FORMATTED SCREENS

5–3–1 OVERVIEW

Full or partial screen areas can be designed or formatted in the SCREEN SECTION of the DATA division. Formatted screens allow information (literals, data items, and input data to be ACCEPTed) to be displayed in any area of the screen. Thus checks, business forms, menus, and similar displays can be flashed in nonscrolling fashion on the screen and processed as one or more input or output records. In addition, items on a formatted screen can be highlighted (boldface), blinked, displayed in reverse video (with background and foreground colors inverted), underlined (if monitor permits), painted in any available color (if a color monitor is used), et cetera. Screen areas can also be superimposed on top of one another, pasted together, sectioned vertically or horizontally, and of course sent to the printer for printing.

5-3-2 THE SCREEN SECTION

The design of the screen takes place in the SCREEN SECTION of the DATA division. In the PROCEDURE division, the DISPLAY statement causes the screen to be displayed and the ACCEPT statement allows various input items to be captured.

The reader is reminded once again that the screen processing instructions presented in this section may differ somewhat in terms of syntax and hardware function from the user's COBOL system. However, most of the features discussed are available in some form or another on most systems. The reader is therefore strongly encouraged to correlate the various functions described in this section with his/her system's screen processing functions.

Screen items are either group items or elementary items identified by level numbers (01 through 49). Screen items can be used to define

- captions (literals, headings, and so forth)
- screen areas into which data FROM memory (data names) will be moved
- screen areas onto which the user will type data that will be ACCEPTed at execution time and then moved TO memory storage (data names)

Other nondisplay items (that nevertheless have level numbers) are used to specify options relating to sound, color, reverse video state, blank screens, and physical positioning of items on the screen.

The general form of a screen group item is:

---

level-number screen-name [AUTO] [SECURE] [FULL] [REQUIRED]

where screen-name is a group item and the options have the following effects:

AUTO: The system skips to the next data entry field as soon as all current data entry field positions have been typed in by the operator (a data entry field is defined as a screen area that is to be filled by the user/operator as a result of an ACCEPT instruction).

SECURE: An asterisk appears in the data entry field for each character typed by the operator (security function).

FULL: The ENTER key is ignored until all characters have been typed in the data entry field.

REQUIRED: The operator must complete the current data entry field before moving on to the next data entry field (security function).

If any of these options is specified at the group level, it automatically applies to all the group's subordinate items.

The general form of a screen elementary item is:

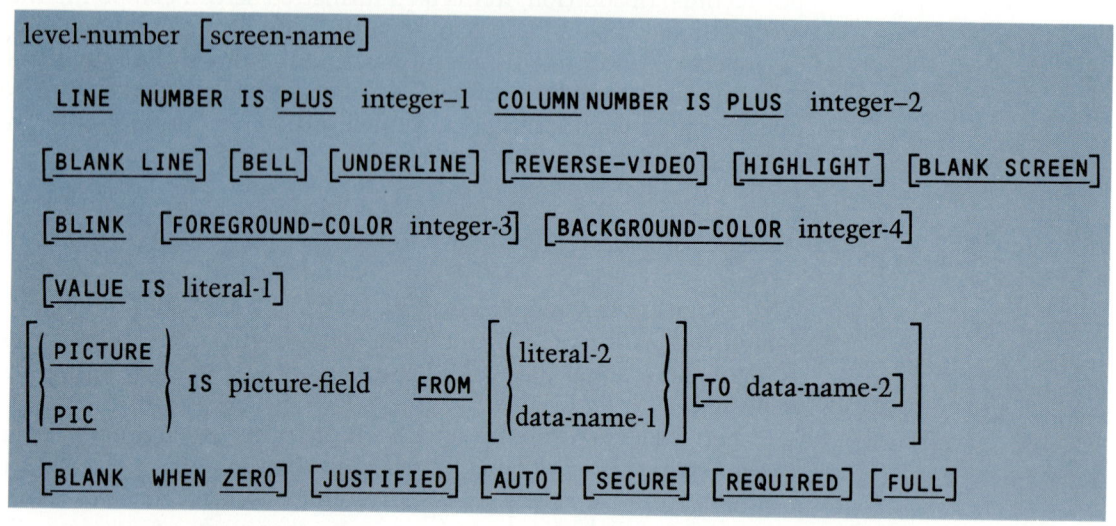

```
level-number [screen-name]

    LINE NUMBER IS PLUS integer-1   COLUMN NUMBER IS PLUS integer-2

    [BLANK LINE] [BELL] [UNDERLINE] [REVERSE-VIDEO] [HIGHLIGHT] [BLANK SCREEN]

    [BLINK] [FOREGROUND-COLOR integer-3] [BACKGROUND-COLOR integer-4]

    [VALUE IS literal-1]

    [ { PICTURE } IS picture-field   FROM  { literal-2    } [TO data-name-2] ]
    [ { PIC     }                           { data-name-1 }                  ]

    [BLANK WHEN ZERO] [JUSTIFIED] [AUTO] [SECURE] [REQUIRED] [FULL]
```

where

LINE and COLUMN specify the screen coordinates of a DISPLAY or ACCEPT item field.

BLANK LINE blanks out the screen from the current cursor position to the end of the line.

BELL emits a beep as a result of an ACCEPT screen instruction.

HIGHLIGHT causes a DISPLAY item to appear in boldface characters (high intensity). This option does not work for ACCEPT data entry fields.

BLINK causes a DISPLAY item to be blinked on the screen. This option does not work for ACCEPT data entry fields.

REVERSE–VIDEO causes a DISPLAY item to appear on the screen with background and foreground colors inverted.

FOREGROUND–COLOR (0–13) and BACKGROUND–COLOR (0–7) can be specified on color monitors to select screen colors using the following numeric code:

0	black	8	gray
1	blue	9	pale blue
2	green	10	pale green
3	cyan	11	pale cyan
4	red	12	pale red
5	magenta	13	pale magenta
6	brown	14	yellow
7	white	15	high intensity blue

(Cyan is a blue-green color. Magenta is reddish purple.)

BLANK SCREEN erases the entire screen and places the cursor at position (1,1). It also returns the screen to its default color. This option may be used with DISPLAY.

UNDERLINE underligns a DISPLAY screen item.

SCREEN PROCESSING

VALUE specifies the literal (quotation marks required) that is to be displayed. (Note the absence of any picture field to describe the literal.)

PICTURE specifies one of the following:

(1) The picture field of an item to be ACCEPTed. The entered item is then automatically moved by the system to the memory location designated by the TO clause.

(2) The picture field of an item to be DISPLAYed. This item is then automatically moved by the system FROM storage to the screen. The FROM clause designates the memory item that is to be displayed.

Both the TO and FROM clauses can be specified in a single screen item.

BLANK WHEN ZERO displays a blank field if the value of the item is 0.

JUSTIFIED causes the item to be right-justified in the screen field.

The remaining options are the same as those described in the screen group item definition.

The following code shows a screen design formatted in four different ways.

Example:

```
IDENTIFICATION DIVISION.
PROGRAM-ID. SCREEN-INPUT.
AUTHOR. JONES.
ENVIRONMENT DIVISION.
CONFIGURATION SECTION.
SOURCE-COMPUTER. IBM.
OBJECT-COMPUTER. IBM.
DATA DIVISION.
WORKING-STORAGE SECTION.
01  DAT PIC 99999 VALUE 85234.
01  EMP PIC X(8).
01  NULL PIC X.
SCREEN SECTION.
```

1.
```
01  TEST1.
    05 VALUE 'DATE'.
    05 PIC 99999 FROM DAT.
    05 VALUE 'NAME'.
    05 PIC X(8) TO EMP.
```

SCREEN OUTPUT

DISPLAY TEST1 → ACCEPT TEST1
DATE85234NAME   DATE85234NAME JONES ← User enters

2.
```
01  TEST2.
    05 BLANK SCREEN.
    05 LINE 1 COLUMN 1 VALUE 'DATE'.
    05 COLUMN 7 PIC 99999 FROM DAT.
    05 LINE 3 COLUMN 1 VALUE 'NAME'.
    05 COLUMN 7 PIC X(8) TO EMP.
```

DISPLAY TEST2 → ACCEPT TEST2
DATE 85234   DATE 85234
NAME   NAME JONES ← User enters

3.
```
01  TEST3.
    05 BLANK SCREEN.
    05 FOREGROUND-COLOR 2.
    05 BACKGROUND-COLOR 9.
    05 LINE 1 VALUE 'DATE'.
    05 HIGHLIGHT COLUMN 7 PIC 9(5) FROM DAT.
    05 REVERSE-VIDEO FOREGROUND-COLOR 6 BLINK
            LINE 3 COLUMN 1 VALUE 'NAME'.
    05 BELL  BACKGROUND-COLOR 10
            COLUMN 7 PIC X(8) TO EMP AUTO SECURE.
```

DISPLAY TEST3 → ACCEPT TEST3
DATE 85234   DATE 85234
NAME   NAME ********

User enters JONES. The screen field is filled with asterisks.

4.
```
01  TEST4.
    05 A.
       10 VALUE 'DATE'.
       10 COLUMN 7 PIC 9(5) FROM DAT.
    05 B.
       10 LINE 3 VALUE 'NAME'.
       10 COLUMN 7 PIC X(8) TO EMP.
```

DISPLAY B
DISPLAY A → ACCEPT B
DATE 85234   DATE 85234
NAME   NAME JONES ← User enters

In example 1, note that the screen is not cleared, the name JONES is stored in memory location EMP.

In example 3, note the background and foreground colors, the highlighted date, the yellow reverse video blinking NAME caption, and the beep emitted as a result of the ACCEPT statement; the characters ACCEPTed are echoed into asterisks as the user types the name. JONES is stored in location EMP.

In example 4, the B screen area is first displayed, then the A screen area is displayed, leaving the B screen area intact on the screen. The resulting screen is identical to the one in example 2.

5-3-3 THE DISPLAY AND ACCEPT SCREEN STATEMENTS

The DISPLAY *screen-name* statement is used to display a screen area. Each item in the screen declaration that has a VALUE or FROM clause, transfers to the screen a literal or a memory storage value, respectively.

The ACCEPT *screen-name* accepts data from an entire formatted screen. A DISPLAY screen operation should always precede an ACCEPT screen instruction so that captions are printed for each data entry field. The data entry fields are accepted in the order the TO clauses appear in the screen definition.

If an error is made while typing a particular data entry field during an ACCEPT operation, the *backspace* key can be used to backtrack to correct the error. If an error has been made in a previously entered data entry field, the *backtab* key can be used to move the cursor to the start of the previous data entry field. For example, pressing the backtab key three times causes the cursor to back over two entry fields and be positioned at the start of the third field back. Backtabbing causes the skipped-over fields to be blanked out on the screen, but it does not affect memory storage. Even though skipped-over data entry fields appear as blank fields on the screen as a result of backtabbing, the original data that was entered on those fields is still intact in memory. Once a particular data entry field has been corrected as a result of a backtab, all records that were skipped-over backwards can be skipped-over forwards by pressing the ENTER key for each record. Once again, this does *not* change their memory contents; thus the operator has the ability to bounce back and forth among the various data entry fields on the screen.

An example of a complete program using screen processing is shown in Figure 5–5. The input screen shown below is to be constructed with the name of the company in boldface, the various captions in reverse video and a blue background and cyan foreground screen. The name, age, sex, address, number of hours worked, and rate of pay are to be accepted from the screen at run time. Whenever a data entry field is filled, the system should automatically move to the next field.

```
              MANPOWER INC
NAME: .........       AGE: ..      SEX: .
ADDRESS
 STREET: .....................  CITY: ..........  ZIP: .....
 HOURS WORKED: ....   RATE OF PAY: .....
```

SCREEN PROCESSING **199**

The program is to compute a gross and net pay, taking into account social security deductions. An output screen is to be displayed below the input screen, with the NET PAY field in red and blinking. The resulting integrated screen is:

```
            MANPOWER INC
NAME: DRINKWATER       AGE: 38      SEX: M
ADDRESS
STREET: 2504 ARIOLA DRIVE    CITY: PENSACOLA    ZIP: 32504
HOURS WORKED: 87.5  RATE OF PAY: 68.85

GROSS PAY: $6,024.37    NET PAY: $5,599.65    FICA: 424.72
```

Note that in the program of Figure 5–5, the SCREEN section follows the WORKING–STORAGE section. The AUTO caption at the group item level (line 44) governs all subordinate items of EMPLOYEE–INPUT–SCREEN. Also note that the various picture items could have been specified right after their corresponding VALUE items, i.e., lines 44–75 could have been coded as:

Picture follows corresponding VALUE field

```
01 EMPLOYEE-INPUT-SCREEN.
   05 BLANK SCREEN FOREGROUND-COLOR 3 BACKGROUND-COLOR 1.
*
*      FOREGROUND IS COLOR OF CHARACTERS, AND BACKGROUND IS
*      COLOR OF THE SCREEN. 3 IS CYAN AND 1 IS BLUE.
*
   05 HIGHLIGHT     LINE 1 COLUMN 12 VALUE 'MANPOWER INC'.
   05 REVERSE-VIDEO LINE 3 COLUMN 01 VALUE 'NAME'.
   05 BELL          LINE 3 COLUMN 07 PIC X(10) TO EMP-NAME.
   05 REVERSE-VIDEO LINE 3 COLUMN 22 VALUE 'AGE'.
   05               LINE 3 COLUMN 27 PIC 99 TO EMP-AGE AUTO.
   05 REVERSE-VIDEO LINE 3 COLUMN 35 VALUE 'SEX'.
   05               LINE 3 COLUMN 40 PIC X  TO EMP-SEX AUTO.
   05               LINE 5 COLUMN 01 VALUE 'ADDRESS'.
   05 REVERSE-VIDEO LINE 7 COLUMN 01 VALUE 'STREET'.
   05               LINE 7 COLUMN 09 PIC X(22) TO EMP-STREET.
   05 REVERSE-VIDEO LINE 7 COLUMN 32 VALUE 'CITY'.
   05               LINE 7 COLUMN 38 PIC X(10) TO EMP-CITY.
   05 REVERSE-VIDEO LINE 7 COLUMN 50 VALUE 'ZIP'.
   05               LINE 7 COLUMN 55 PIC 99999 TO EMP-ZIP AUTO.
   05 REVERSE-VIDEO LINE 8 COLUMN 01 VALUE 'HOURS WORKED'.
   05               LINE 8 COLUMN 15 PIC 99V9 TO EMP-HOURS AUTO.
   05 REVERSE-VIDEO LINE 8 COLUMN 22 VALUE 'RATE OF PAY'.
   05               LINE 8 COLUMN 35 PIC 99V99 TO EMP-RATE AUTO.
```

Figure 5–6 illustrates the mechanics of working with an input screen during the various ACCEPT cycles. The underline symbol shows the position of the cursor on the displayed screen. Whenever the ENTER key is pressed or when the data entry field is filled, the cursor automatically moves to the next field.

```
 1:*     IDENTIFICATION DIVISION.
 2:      PROGRAM-ID. SCREEN-INPUT.
 3:     ****************************************************************
 4:      * PURPOSE: TO ILLUSTRATE SCREEN PROCESSING AS IT RELATES TO    *
 5:      *          SCREEN DESIGN, SCREEN DISPLAY & SCREEN DATA CAPTURE.*
 6:      *                                                              *
 7:      * INPUT: A PREDESIGNED SCREEN LAYOUT IS DISPLAYED AND A WORKERS*
 8:      *        NAME, AGE, SEX, ADDRESS, HOURS WORKED AND RATE OF PAY *
 9:      *        ARE ENTERED ON SCREEN AS PROMPTED BY THE SYSTEM.      *
10:      *                                                              *
11:      * OUTPUT: THE PROGRAM COMPUTES THE GROSS & NET PAY AS WELL AS  *
12:      *         SOCIAL SECURITY TAXES. THE NET PAY IS BLINKED IN RED,*
13:      *         THE INPUT ENTRIES ARE HIGHLIGHTED, THE CAPTIONS ARE  *
14:      *         DISPLAYED IN REVERSE VIDEO & A BEEP SOUNDS AT START. *
15:     ****************************************************************
16:      AUTHOR. JONES.
17:      ENVIRONMENT DIVISION.
18:      CONFIGURATION SECTION.
19:      SOURCE-COMPUTER. IBM.
20:      OBJECT-COMPUTER. IBM.
21:      DATA DIVISION.
22:      WORKING-STORAGE SECTION.
23:      01 EMPLOYEE-INPUT-ITEMS.
24:         05 EMP-NAME    PIC X(10).
25:         05 EMP-AGE     PIC 99.
26:         05 EMP-SEX     PIC X.
27:         05 EMP-STREET  PIC X(22).
28:         05 EMP-CITY    PIC X(10).
29:         05 EMP-ZIP     PIC 99999.
30:         05 EMP-HOURS   PIC 99V9.
31:         05 EMP-RATE    PIC 99V99.
32:      01 COMPUTATIONAL-ITEMS.
33:         05 EMP-GROS    PIC 9999V99.
34:         05 EMP-NET     PIC 9999V99.
35:         05 EMP-FICA    PIC 999V99.
36:      SCREEN SECTION.
37:     *
38:     * THIS SECTION CONSISTS OF TWO SCREENS: ONE TO ACCEPT THE DATA
39:     * (LINES 50-74) AND ANOTHER TO DISPLAY THE RESULTS (LINES 80-87)
40:     * THE 1ST SCREEN IS DISPLAYED (LINE 91). THE ACCEPT VERB IS
41:     * USED AT LINE 92 TO CAPTURE ON THE SCREEN THE NAME, AGE, SEX
42:     * CODE, ADDRESS, HOURS WORKED AND RATE OF PAY OF EMPLOYEE.
43:     *
44:      01 EMPLOYEE-INPUT-SCREEN AUTO.
45:         05 BLANK SCREEN FOREGROUND-COLOR 3 BACKGROUND-COLOR 1.
46:     *
47:     * FOREGROUND IS COLOR OF CHARACTERS, AND BACKGROUND IS COLOR OF
48:     * THE SCREEN. 3 IS CYAN (BLUE/GREEN HUE) AND 1 IS BLUE.
49:     *
50:         05 HIGHLIGHT    LINE 1 COLUMN 12 VALUE 'MANPOWER INC'.
51:         05 REVERSE-VIDEO LINE 3 COLUMN 01 VALUE 'NAME:'.
52:         05 REVERSE-VIDEO LINE 3 COLUMN 22 VALUE 'AGE:'.
53:         05 REVERSE-VIDEO LINE 3 COLUMN 35 VALUE 'SEX:'.
54:         05              LINE 5 COLUMN 01 VALUE 'ADDRESS'.
55:         05 REVERSE-VIDEO LINE 7 COLUMN 01 VALUE 'STREET:'.
56:         05 REVERSE-VIDEO LINE 7 COLUMN 32 VALUE 'CITY:'.
57:         05 REVERSE-VIDEO LINE 7 COLUMN 50 VALUE 'ZIP:'.
58:         05 REVERSE-VIDEO LINE 8 COLUMN 01 VALUE 'HOURS WORKED:'.
59:         05 REVERSE-VIDEO LINE 8 COLUMN 22 VALUE 'RATE OF PAY:'.
60:     *
61:     * LINES 50-59 POSITION THE VARIOUS CAPTIONS ON THE SCREEN WHILE
62:     * LINES 67-74 CAUSE THE USER TO FILL THESE FIELDS BY MEANS OF
63:     * THE ACCEPT SCREEN INSTRUCTION; THE ITEMS ARE ENTERED IN THE
64:     * ORDER DEFINED IN THE SCREEN LAYOUT AND STORED IN THE MEMORY
65:     * LOCATIONS DESIGNATED BY THE VARIOUS "TO" CLAUSES.
66:     *
67:         05 BELL    LINE 3 COLUMN 07 PIC X(10) TO EMP-NAME.
68:         05         LINE 3 COLUMN 27 PIC 99    TO EMP-AGE.
69:         05         LINE 3 COLUMN 40 PIC X     TO EMP-SEX.
```

Final Screen Output

MANPOWER INC

NAME: DRINKWATER   AGE: 38   SEX: M

ADDRESS

STREET: 2504 ARIOLA DRIVE   CITY: PENSACOLA   ZIP: 32504
HOURS WORKED: 87.5   RATE OF PAY: 68.85

GROSS PAY: $6,024.37   NET PAY: $5,599.65   FICA: 424.72

FIGURE 5–5
A SCREEN PROCESSING EXAMPLE

SCREEN PROCESSING   **201**

```
70:        05           LINE 7 COLUMN 09 PIC X(22) TO EMP-STREET.
71:        05           LINE 7 COLUMN 38 PIC X(10) TO EMP-CITY.
72:        05           LINE 7 COLUMN 55 PIC 99999 TO EMP-ZIP.
73:        05           LINE 8 COLUMN 15 PIC 99V9  TO EMP-HOURS.
74:        05           LINE 8 COLUMN 35 PIC 99V99 TO EMP-RATE.
75:   *
76:   * THE INPUT SCREEN OCCUPIES THE 1ST 8 LINES OF THE SCREEN. THE
77:   * OUTPUT SCREEN PICKS UP WHERE THE 1ST SCREEN ENDS AND STARTS AT
78:   * ROW 10. GROSS & NET PAY AND FICA APPEAR ON SCREEN AS OUTPUT.
79:   *
80:   01 EMPLOYEE-OUTPUT-SCREEN.
81:        05 REVERSE-VIDEO LINE 10 COLUMN 01 VALUE 'GROSS PAY:'.
82:        05              LINE 10 COLUMN 12 PIC $Z,ZZ9.99 FROM EMP-GROS.
83:        05 BLINK   FOREGROUND-COLOR 12
84:                        LINE 10 COLUMN 25 VALUE 'NET PAY:'.
85:        05 BLINK        LINE 10 COLUMN 34 PIC $Z,ZZ9.99 FROM EMP-NET.
86:        05 REVERSE-VIDEO LINE 10 COLUMN 47 VALUE 'FICA:'.
87:        05              LINE 10 COLUMN 53 PIC ZZ9.99 FROM EMP-FICA.
88:   *
89:   PROCEDURE DIVISION.
90:   100-COORDINATING-MODULE.
91:        DISPLAY EMPLOYEE-INPUT-SCREEN.
92:        ACCEPT  EMPLOYEE-INPUT-SCREEN.
93:        COMPUTE EMP-GROS = EMP-HOURS * EMP-RATE.
94:        COMPUTE EMP-FICA = EMP-GROS  * 0.0705.
95:        COMPUTE EMP-NET  = EMP-GROS  - EMP-FICA.
96:        DISPLAY EMPLOYEE-OUTPUT-SCREEN.
97:        STOP RUN.
```

FIGURE 5-5
(continued)

5-4 EXERCISES

5-4-1 TEST YOURSELF

1. Assume the PROMPT option in all of the following exercises. In the first blank rectangle, show the cue displayed by the system as a result of the ACCEPT statement; in the second, identify the sequence of characters you would need to type on the screen so that the memory contents would be as indicated in each exercise.

Example:

	MEMORY CONTENTS	SCREEN CUE	USER TYPES
A PIC 999V9 ACCEPT (1, 1) A	0 1 2 3		

Screen cue is 000.0   User types 12.3 or 012.3

	MEMORY CONTENTS	SCREEN CUE	USER TYPES
a. PIC 999V99	0 0 1 3 4		
b. PIC 999999	2 0 0 0 0		
c. PIC 999V99	0 0 0 7 0		
d. PIC S999V99	0 2 0 4 0̄		

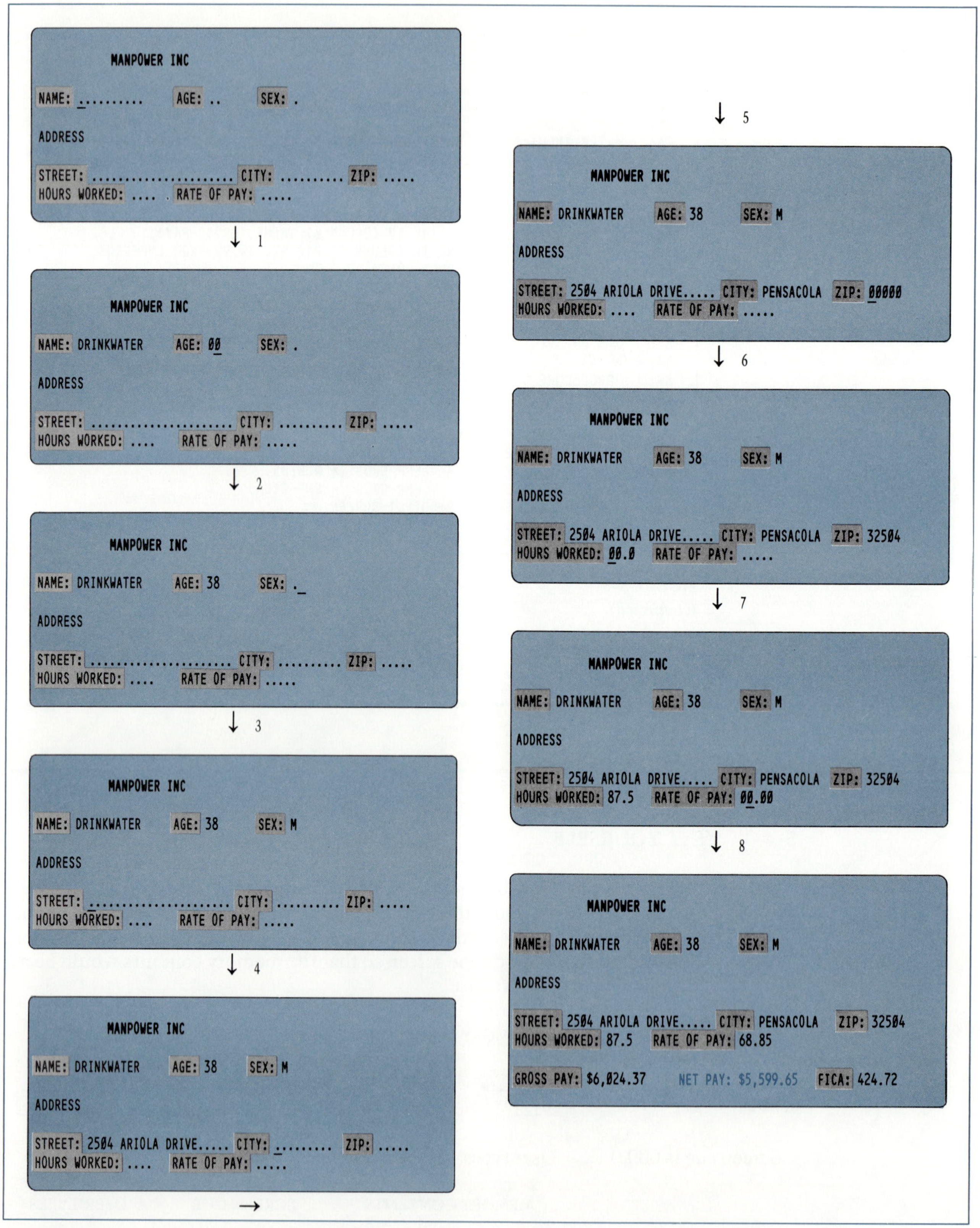

FIGURE 5–6

A STEP BY STEP VIEW OF SCREEN PROCESSING

SCREEN PROCESSING 203

		MEMORY CONTENTS	SCREEN CUE	USER TYPES
e.	PIC S999V99	0 0 0 9 0̄		
f.	PIC +999.99	+ 0 0 1 . 3 4		
g.	PIC +999.99	− 0 2 1 . 4 0		
h.	PIC S99V9	4 6 0̄⁺		
i.	PIC S99V9	2 0 0̄		
j.	PIC 999.9−	0 1 5 . 0		
k.	PIC 999.9+	0 0 1 . 6 −		
l.	PIC $$$.9	$ 2 3 . 0		
m.	PIC $$,$$$.99	$ 3 , 2 4 6 . 0 0		
n.	PIC $*,***.99DB	$ * * 1 2 3 . 6 0 D B		
o.	PIC XXX	A		
p.	PIC −ZZZ.9	− 4 6 . 0		

2. In this exercise you are given the PICTURE of a number to be accepted and you are shown what the user types on the screen. You are to show what number is stored in memory (blank rectangle) as a result. In some cases the system will reject the number typed and you must give the reason for rejection.

Examples:

	USER TYPES	MEMORY STORAGE
PIC 999	1Ø	Ø 1 Ø
PIC 999	ᑯØ	Error: A blank is not permitted.

		USER TYPES	MEMORY STORAGE	
a.	PIC XXXXX	BOILLOT		
b.	PIC XXX	B		
c.	PIC 999V99	5421.768		
d.	PIC +999.99	1ØØ3		
e.	PIC 999	23.		
f.	PIC +999.99	21.4+		
g.	PIC 999	−34		
h.	PIC 999	1.4		
i.	PIC S99V9	+.Ø9		
j.	PIC 999V99	1Ø		
k.	PIC 99V99	1234		with AUTO−SKIP
l.	PIC 999.9CR	−2Ø.		

5-4-2 PROGRAMMING EXERCISES

1. Using three PERFORM and three DISPLAY statements, write the code to display the three columns of numbers shown below. The first column (1–10) should *first* be displayed vertically, followed by the second column and then the third column in that time frame sequence.

```
              ┌─────────────────────────┐
              │  1       11       21    │
              │  2       12       22    │
              │  3       13       23    │
              │  4       14       24    │
              │  .        .        .    │
              │  .        .        .    │
              │  .        .        .    │
              │ 1Ø       2Ø       3Ø    │
              └─────────────────────────┘
```

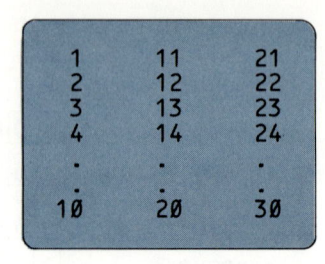

2. Write the code to draw the X figure shown below (made up of asterisks). Use only two DISPLAY statements. Draw one diagonal and then the other diagonal. (Don't draw by rows.)

```
         *           *
           *       *
             *   *
               *
             *   *
           *       *
         *           *
```

3. Write the code to simulate the animation of a falling stone by displaying the character 0 at the top of the screen, then erasing it, then displaying the 0 just below its preceding position, and repeating the process down the length of the screen. This continuous motion should give the impression of a falling object!

4. Write the code to simulate a gas-pumping machine by displaying a gas-volume window and a cost-volume window. As the gas is being pumped, these two windows should display "rolling" digits, i.e., stationary scrolling of numbers within their windows. Volume is in liters and should be displayed in increments of centiliters (1 centiliter = 1/100 liter). Assume the cost of a liter is 30 cents. A photographic image of the pump taken at each centiliter interval would show the following window contents:

LITERS	COST	
0 0 0 . 0 0	$ 0 0 0 . 0 0	Pump at start.
0 0 0 . 0 1	$ 0 0 0 . 0 3	Pump at first centiliter.
0 0 0 . 0 2	$ 0 0 0 . 0 6	Pump at second centiliter.
.	.	
.	.	

Note that only two windows are displayed at any time! Accept a dollar amount and write the code to run the pump until the cost reaches that amount.

5. Write the code to draw a clock on the screen. Start with the number 1 and roll up to the number 12 in circular fashion, as in:

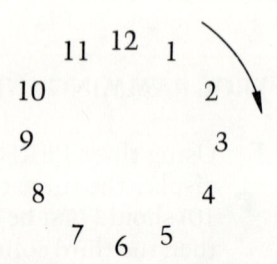

```
              11  12   1
          10              2
          9               3
             8         4
               7  6  5
```

SCREEN PROCESSING   **205**

Can you pick up the time of the system clock and blink the hours position, the minutes (blinking = erasing and displaying)?

6. Write the code to require a user to type in a password before the user is able to execute a particular COBOL program. Make sure that the password is "covered up" on the screen as the user types it.

7. Write a program that will accept the name of a file stored on a disk and make as many copies (listings) of that file as specified. For example, the screen display might be

```
SPECIFY NAME OF FILE
PAYROLL.COB
HOW MANY COPIES
3
```

The program will then make 3 copies of PAYROLL.COB.

5-4-3 ANSWERS TO TEST YOURSELF

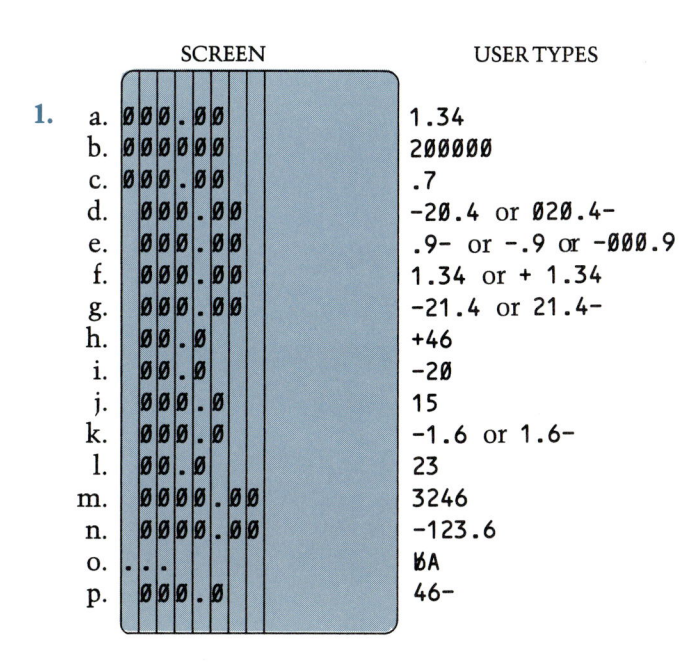

		SCREEN	USER TYPES
1.	a.	000.00	1.34
	b.	000000	200000
	c.	000.00	.7
	d.	000.00	-20.4 or 020.4-
	e.	000.00	.9- or -.9 or -000.9
	f.	000.00	1.34 or + 1.34
	g.	000.00	-21.4 or 21.4-
	h.	00.0	+46
	i.	00.0	-20
	j.	000.0	15
	k.	000.0	-1.6 or 1.6-
	l.	00.0	23
	m.	0000.00	3246
	n.	0000.00	-123.6
	o.	...	ƄA
	p.	000.0	46-

2.   a. BOILL
    b. ƄBƄ
    c. Error occurs when the digit 1 is typed. Too many whole digits.
    d. Error occurs when the digit 3 is typed. Too many whole digits.
    e. 023
    f. +021.40
    g. Error. No sign symbol in picture field.
    h. Error at the digit 4. No fractional positions allowed.
    i. Error at digit 9. Too many fractional digits.
    j. 01000
    k. 1234
    l. 020.0CR

CHAPTER 6

THE DECISION AND ITERATION STRUCTURES, PROGRAM DESIGN, AND DATA VALIDATION

6-1 THE DECISION STRUCTURE

6-2 THE PERFORM STATEMENT AND THE ACCUMULATION PROCESS

6-3 PUTTING IT TOGETHER: THE PROGRAM DEVELOPMENT PROCESS

6-4 WRITING PROGRAMS AND THE INPUT VALIDATION PROCESS

6-5 YOU MIGHT WANT TO KNOW

6-6 EXERCISES

INTRODUCTION   Two of the fundamental concepts of structured programming—the decision and iteration (loop) structures—are discussed in detail in this chapter. The decision structure is implemented through the COBOL IF ELSE sentence; rules are given for forming general and multilevel IF ELSE structures and simple IF statements. The use of simple and compound relational conditions, logical operators, sign and class tests, and numeric and nonnumeric comparisons is also included.

The general PERFORM and the PERFORM UNTIL statements provide COBOL's iterative (loop) structure; general forms and examples are given for both of these statements, along with examples of the counting and accumulation processes.

The program development process and input validation are also important topics of this chapter.

6-1   THE DECISION STRUCTURE

The *sequence*, the *selection* (*decision*), and the *iteration* (loop) structures are those conceptual pillars of structured design. The if-then/else selection structure is implemented in COBOL through the IF ELSE statement.

Recall that the central processing unit (CPU) is capable of carrying out three distinct types of operations:

1. Input/Output: Transferring data into and out of memory.
2. Arithmetic: Adding, multiplying, and so forth (arithmetic unit).
3. Decision making: Deciding which instruction to carry out next based on the outcome of a particular condition (logic unit).

The logic unit enables the computer to compare numeric as well as alphanumeric data and thereby allows the computer to make decisions. For example, by asking a question about the number of hours worked per week (is HOURS–WORKED > 40), a program can determine whether or not to compute overtime pay. Such a question, which has a yes or no answer, is more commonly referred to in COBOL as a *condition*. Conditions are either true or false, i.e., either HOURS–WORKED is greater than 40 or it is not (if it is less than or equal to 40).

The selection or if-then/else structure allows the computer to transfer to nonsequential instructions in a program, depending on whether or not certain conditions are met. In other words, it offers a choice between two program paths based on whether a condition is true or false.

6-1-1 THE IF ELSE SENTENCE

COBOL offers two forms of the selection structure:

1. The simple IF structure, which is a particular case of
2. The general IF ELSE structure.

The General IF ELSE Structure.

The general form of the COBOL IF ELSE is:

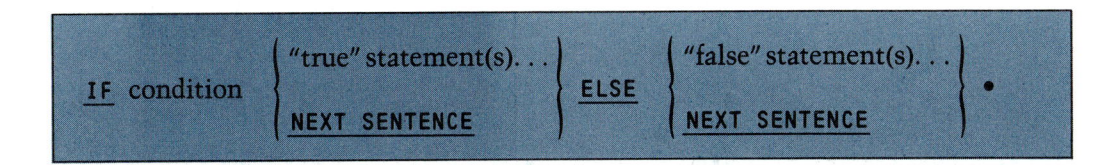

$$\underline{\text{IF}}\ \text{condition} \left\{ \begin{array}{l} \text{"true" statement(s)}\ldots \\ \underline{\text{NEXT SENTENCE}} \end{array} \right\} \underline{\text{ELSE}} \left\{ \begin{array}{l} \text{"false" statement(s)}\ldots \\ \underline{\text{NEXT SENTENCE}} \end{array} \right\} \bullet$$

The IF sentence, which generally consists of many statements telling the computer what action to take if the condition is true or false, *must* terminate with a period. That period determines which statements are part of the IF sentence and which are not. All statements between the key word IF and the first period encountered are governed by (are part of) the IF statement—the statements that follow the period are not! Thus the absence or the misplacement of a period can cause havoc in a COBOL program.

As shown in the general form, the IF sentence can be typed on one or more horizontal lines. However, to improve readability, clarity, and comprehension, the various "true" and "false" statements are each typed on separate lines following the IF and ELSE keywords. A common practice is to indent these statements four positions to the right of the key words, which are themselves aligned. Figure 6–1 illustrates the if-then/else structure and the way it should be

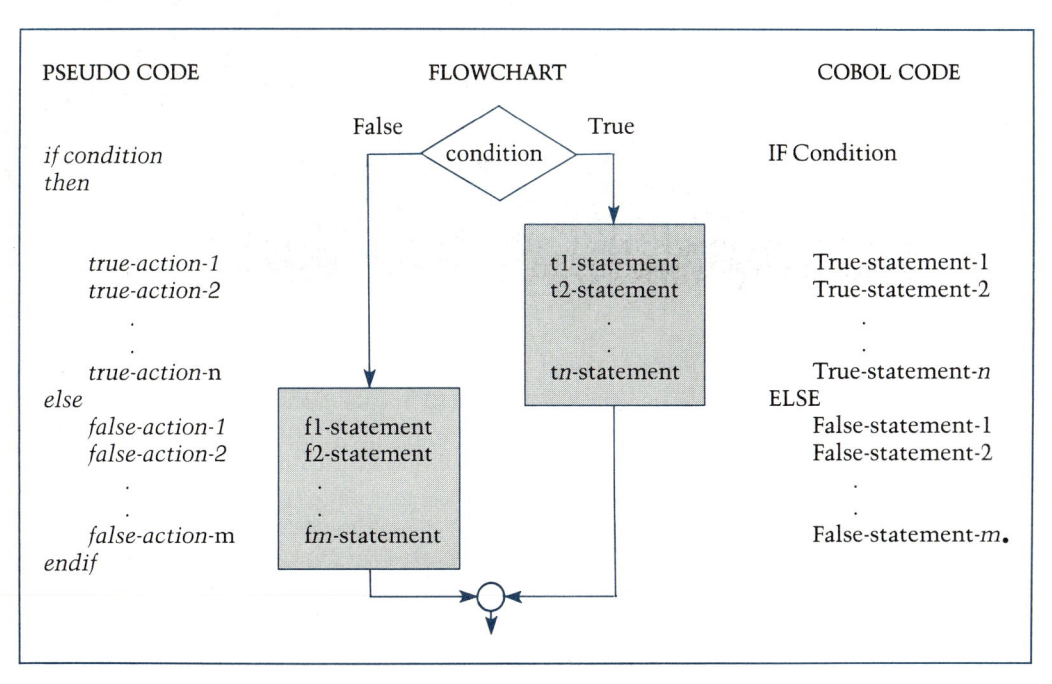

PSEUDO CODE	FLOWCHART	COBOL CODE
if condition then	False ← condition → True	IF Condition

true-action-1
    true-action-2
    .
    .
    true-action-n
	t1-statement
	t2-statement
	.
	.
	tn-statement
		True-statement-1
		True-statement-2
		.
		.
		True-statement-n

else
    false-action-1
    false-action-2
    .
    .
    false-action-m
endif
	f1-statement
	f2-statement
	.
	.
	fm-statement
		ELSE
		False-statement-1
		False-statement-2
		.
		.
		False-statement-m.

FIGURE 6–1
THE IF-THEN/ELSE STRUCTURE

pseudo coded, flowcharted, and coded in COBOL. Note that the end of an if-then/else structure is identified by the word *endif* in pseudo code, a node (circle) in the flowchart, **and a period in the COBOL code.**

If the condition specified by the IF statement in Figure 6–1 is true, true-statements-1,2,3,...n are carried out (all statements up to the ELSE word). Control is then passed to the sentence following the first period encountered. If the condition specified is false, false-statements-1,2,3,...m are carried out (all statements between the ELSE and the first period), then control passes to the next sentence (the sentence starting after the period). Remember that as far as COBOL is concerned, the end of an IF statement is indicated by the period and *not* by the user indentation!

Example: Pay Computation with Overtime Hours

PSEUDO CODE	COBOL CODE
enter hours worked and rate	`ACCEPT HOURS, RATE`
if hours worked > 40	`IF HOURS > 40`
then	
* compute 1st 40 hour pay*	`   COMPUTE REG-PAY  = 40 * RATE`
* compute overtime pay*	`   COMPUTE OVER-PAY = (HOURS - 40) * RATE * 1.5`
* compute total pay*	`   COMPUTE TOT-PAY  = REG-PAY + OVER-PAY`
else	`ELSE`
* compute total pay*	`   COMPUTE TOT-PAY = HOURS * RATE.`
endif	`DISPLAY TOT-PAY.`
display total pay	

Note that the period in the constant 1.5 in the COBOL code does not terminate the IF sentence. To terminate a sentence, a period must be followed by a blank space.

Example: Consider the following coding segments, which are identical except for the position of the period:

CASE 1
```
IF HOURS > 40
    MOVE 100 TO BONUS
ELSE
    MOVE 50 TO BONUS.
DISPLAY BONUS.
```

CASE 2
```
IF HOURS > 40
    MOVE 100 TO BONUS
ELSE
    MOVE 50 TO BONUS
DISPLAY BONUS.
```

CASE 3
```
IF HOURS > 40
    MOVE 100. TO BONUS
ELSE
    MOVE 50 TO BONUS.
DISPLAY BONUS.
```

In case 1 the DISPLAY BONUS sentence is not part of the IF sentence; BONUS is displayed regardless of the value for HOURS. The fact that the DISPLAY sentence is indented and aligned with the MOVE 50 TO BONUS does not mean that it is part of the IF sentence. (Remember that statements can be typed anywhere in columns 8 through 72, or for that matter, continued on another line!).

In case 2 BONUS is displayed only if the condition is false (HOURS is not greater than 40. All statements between the ELSE and the first period encountered are carried out by the IF statement if the condition is false. Once again, the fact that the DISPLAY clause is aligned with the IF and ELSE does not mean that it lies outside the IF sentence!

In case 3 the IF sentence terminates at 100. In terms of syntax, the MOVE statement is invalid, as is the ELSE statement, which has no companion IF!

In some cases the IF statement may be the last sentence executed in a paragraph, in which case the sentence to be processed next will be located in a different paragraph. Consider the following example:

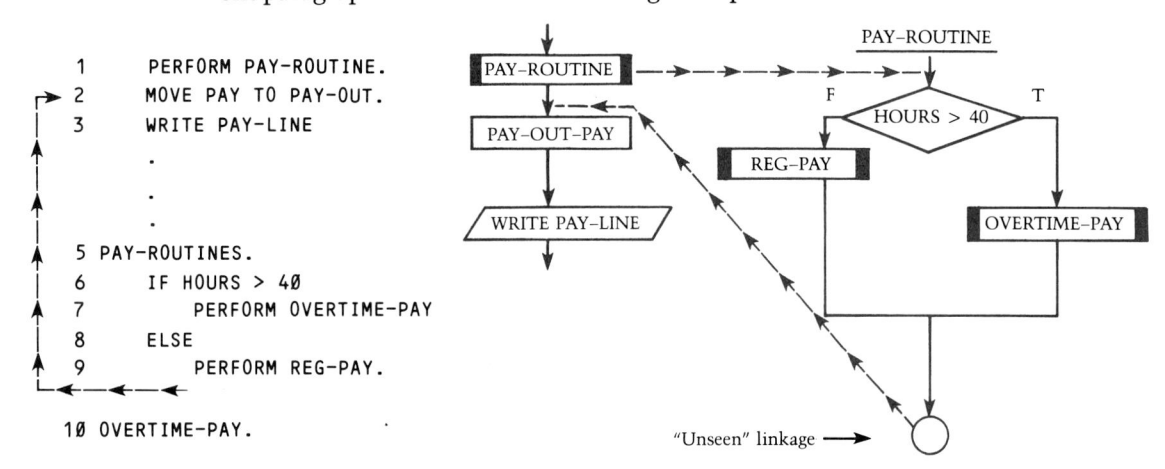

```
 1   PERFORM PAY-ROUTINE.
 2   MOVE PAY TO PAY-OUT.
 3   WRITE PAY-LINE
     .
     .
     .
 5 PAY-ROUTINES.
 6     IF HOURS > 40
 7         PERFORM OVERTIME-PAY
 8     ELSE
 9         PERFORM REG-PAY.
10 OVERTIME-PAY.
```

The statement executed after line 7 is line 2. The statement executed after line 9 is also line 2. The unseen return linkage physically follows the last statement of any paragraph. Any exit from a paragraph must first pass through this linkage.

Sometimes an alternative action is not required if a condition is false. In that case the ELSE key word is omitted, leading to the simpler structure shown in Figure 6–2.

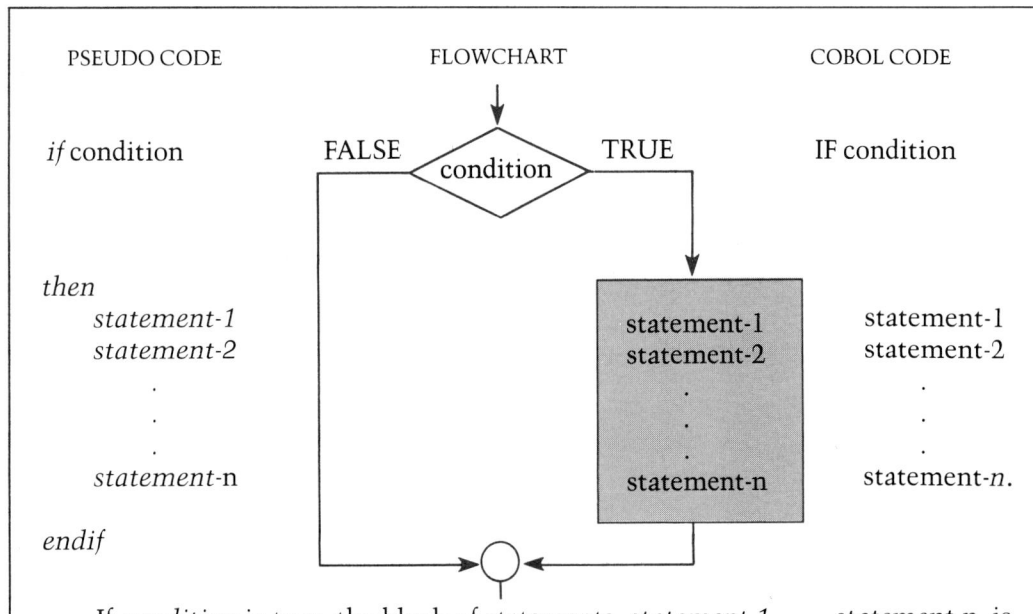

PSEUDO CODE	FLOWCHART	COBOL CODE
if condition	FALSE — condition — TRUE	IF condition

then
  statement-1
  statement-2
  .
  .
  .
  statement-n
endif
	statement-1
	statement-2
	.
	.
	.
	statement-n
		statement-1
		statement-2
		.
		.
		.
		statement-n.

If *condition* is true, the block of statements, *statement 1, . . ., statement n*, is executed and control is passed to the statement following the *endif*.

If *condition* is false, control is passed directly to the statement following the *endif*.

FIGURE 6–2
THE SIMPLE IF STATEMENT

EXAMPLE 1: Assume values for HOURS, RATE, and SALES have been read. Write the code to compute a pay (hours × rate). If SALES exceeds $10,000.00, add 10% of SALES to the pay. In either case, display the pay.

PSEUDO CODE

*compute pay = hours * rate*
if sales > 10,000
then
    add 10% of sales to pay
endif
print pay

COBOL CODE

```
COMPUTE PAY = HOURS * RATE.
IF SALES > 10000
    COMPUTE PAY = .1 * SALES + PAY.
DISPLAY PAY.
```

EXAMPLE 2:
```
10 IF X = 4
20     COMPUTE X = A + B
30     MOVE 1 TO Y
40     PERFORM TAXES
50     WRITE PRINT-LINE.
60 IF X = 5 ...
```
These statements are processed only if X = 4, after which control passes to statement 60. Note that after paragraph TAXES is carried out, return is made to statement 50.

6-1-3 THE NEXT SENTENCE STATEMENT

The statement NEXT SENTENCE transfers control to the statement following the IF sentence, i.e., to the statement following the first period encountered. The purpose of the NEXT SENTENCE statement is to improve readability of multilevel IF sentences (nested IF's). If no actions are to be specified when the condition is true, NEXT SENTENCE can be written after the condition and before the ELSE word. Similarly, if no actions are specified for the ELSE branch, NEXT SENTENCE can be written after the ELSE word. In essence, NEXT SENTENCE specifies explicitly what action is to be taken (nothing!). Consider the following coding segments, which are identical in terms of outcome:

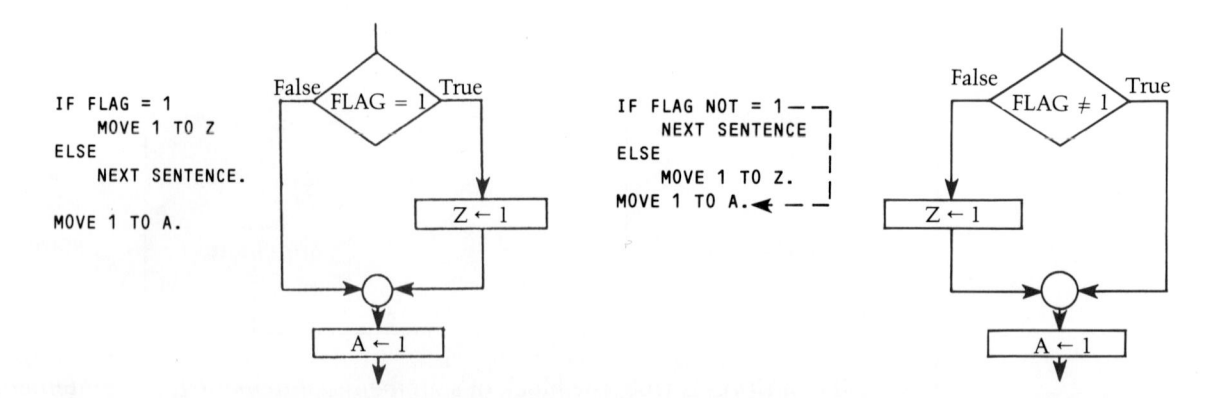

```
IF FLAG = 1
    MOVE 1 TO Z
ELSE
    NEXT SENTENCE.

MOVE 1 TO A.
```

```
IF FLAG NOT = 1
    NEXT SENTENCE
ELSE
    MOVE 1 TO Z.
MOVE 1 TO A.
```

Note that both of these codes could have been written with a simple IF statement, as:

```
IF FLAG = 1
    MOVE 1 TO Z.
MOVE 1 TO A.
```

INVALID CODE	EXPLANATION
10 IF X = 1 20 MOVE A TO B 30 ELSE 40 NEXT SENTENCE 50 MOVE A TO C. 60 MOVE A TO D.	This code is incorrect due to statement 50. The statement NEXT SENTENCE must be all by itself and cannot be carried out in conjunction with other statements.

6-1-4 CONDITIONS

Any of the following types of conditions can be used in an IF statement:

Relational condition: testing for order relationship (<, =, >).

Sign condition: testing for POSITIVE, NEGATIVE, and ZERO value.

Class condition: testing for ALPHABETIC or NUMERIC value.

Condition name: giving conditions a name (discussed in Chapter 7).

A relational condition may be thought of as a proposition, i.e., a statement that is either true or false, for example:

`HOURS IS GREATER THAN 40` is a simple relational condition (only one relational operator in statement).

`EARNING > 40000 OR AGE < 27` is a compound relational condition (2 relational operators, > and <, in one statement).

The outcome of either of these conditions is either true or false.

The general form of a simple relational condition is shown in Figure 6–3. Compound conditions are discussed in the following section.

6-1-5 COMPOUND CONDITIONS

As we have seen, a simple relational condition has the following form:

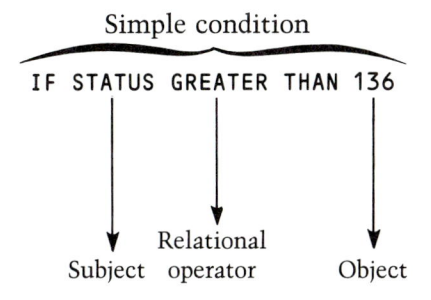

```
           Simple condition
       ⎧―――――――――――――――⎫
       IF STATUS GREATER THAN 136
          ↓        ↓         ↓
       Subject  Relational  Object
                operator
```

Sometimes it may be more practical to combine (conjunct) simple conditions. For example, we might want to know whether "SEX is equal to 1 and STATUS is equal to 4" or "AGE is less than 18 or AGE is greater than 65." Such combinations of simple conditions are called *compound* conditions. To be more precise, a compound condition consists of two or more conditions linked to one another by any of the three *logical operators* AND, NOT, and OR.

214 UNDERSTANDING STRUCTURED COBOL

>   data-name-1   data-name-2
>   literal-1   relational operator literal-2
>   arithmetic expression-1   arithmetic expression-2
>
> where the relational operator can be written either as a symbol or a verbal expression.
>
> ### RELATIONAL OPERATORS
>
> | SYMBOL | VERBAL |
> |--------|--------|
> | = | IS EQUAL TO |
> | < | IS LESS THAN |
> | > | IS GREATER THAN |
> | NOT = | IS NOT EQUAL TO |
> | NOT < | IS NOT LESS THAN (same as greater than or equal to) |
> | NOT > | IS NOT GREATER THAN (same as less than or equal to) |
>
> ### Examples
>
> 1. `EARNING > 40`   identical to   EARNING IS GREATER THAN 40
> 2. `AGE NOT < 65`   identical to   AGE IS NOT LESS THAN 65
> 3. `NAME = 'FONDA'`   identical to   NAME IS EQUAL TO 'FONDA'
>
> A blank space should precede and follow the relational symbol.
> Some systems may disallow arithmetic expression-1 and arithmetic expression-2.

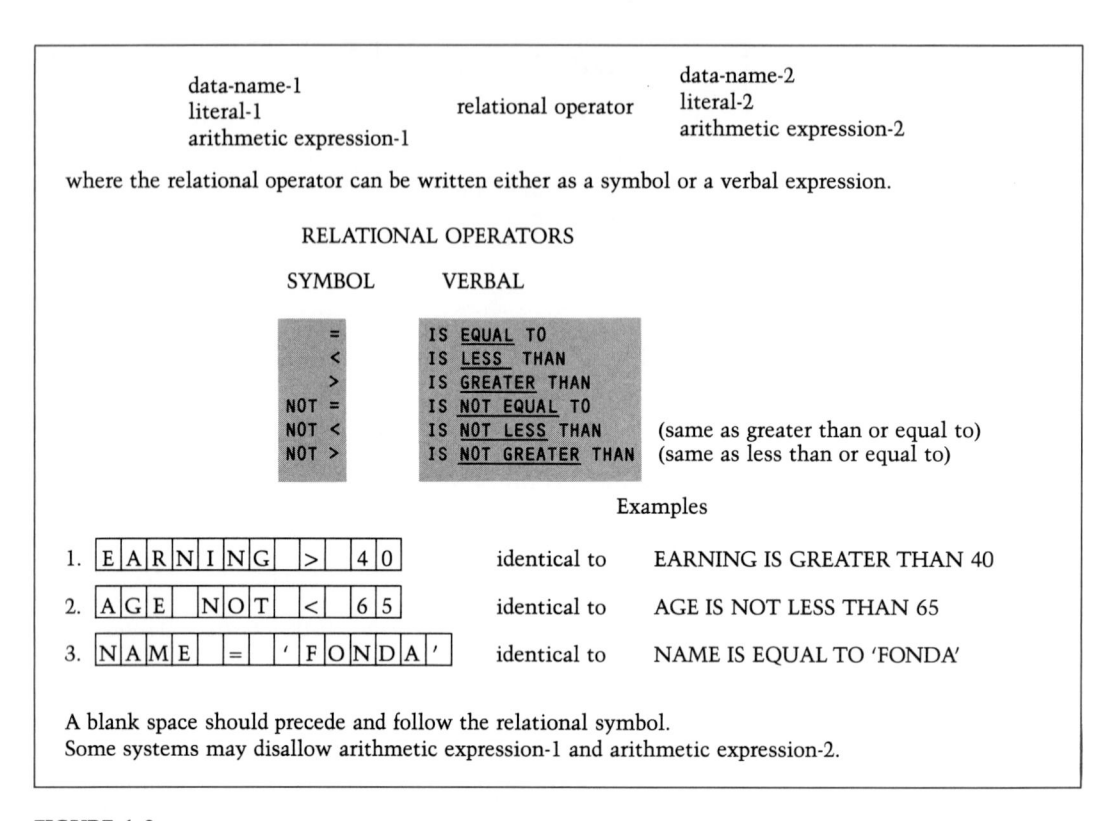

FIGURE 6-3
SIMPLE FORM OF A RELATIONAL CONDITION

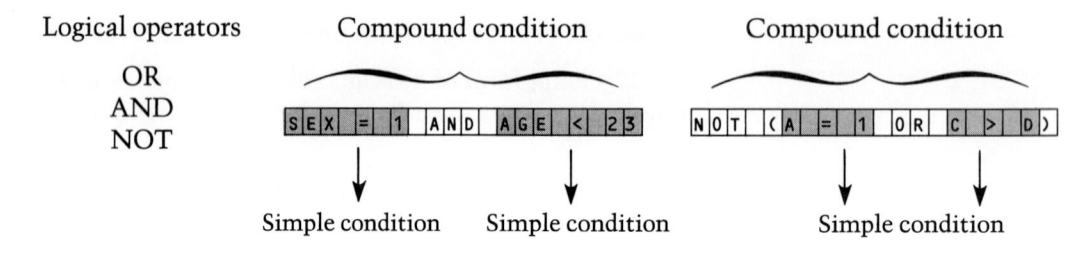

Logical operators
- OR
- AND
- NOT

Compound condition: `SEX = 1 AND AGE < 23`
— Simple condition / Simple condition

Compound condition: `NOT (A = 1 OR C > D)`
— Simple condition / Simple condition

Note that:

- The NOT logical operator can be connected to only one condition (simple or compound).

- No two logical operators may be typed side by side. For example, IF SEX AND OR MARITAL–STATUS = 1 is invalid. (However, see section 6–5 for a discussion of implied logical operators and subjects).

The meaning of the logical operators is illustrated in the following pseudo code examples:

if *condition 1* **and** *condition 2* then ...	Transfer to the *then* statements if both conditions are true; otherwise transfer to the *else* statements, if any.
if *condition 1* **or** *condition 2* then ...	If one condition or both conditions are true, transfer to the *then* statements; otherwise transfer to the *else* statements, if any.

DECISION, ITERATION, PROGRAM DESIGN, DATA VALIDATION

if **not** *condition* then   Transfer to the *then* statements if the condition is NOT true; otherwise transfer to the *else* statements, if any.

The logical operators have the lowest priority in the rules of precedence governing operations:

OPERATIONS	PRECEDENCE
Grouping via parentheses (Arithmetic operators) ** *, / +, − Conditions (Logical operators) NOT AND OR	Highest ↓ Lowest

---

EXAMPLE 1: To determine whether an age is between 18 and 30 (inclusive), the following statement could be used:

```
IF AGE NOT LESS THAN 18 AND AGE NOT GREATER THAN 30 ...
```

EXAMPLE 2: Assume X = 30, Y = 40, and A = 10

```
          IF X + 2  <  Y   OR   Y  NOT =  40   AND   A  >  -3.1
```

Arithmetic expressions are evaluated first: 32., 40., 40., 40., 10., −3.1

Relations are evaluated next: True, False, True

Logical operations are evaluated last according to the precedence rule: True, False → True

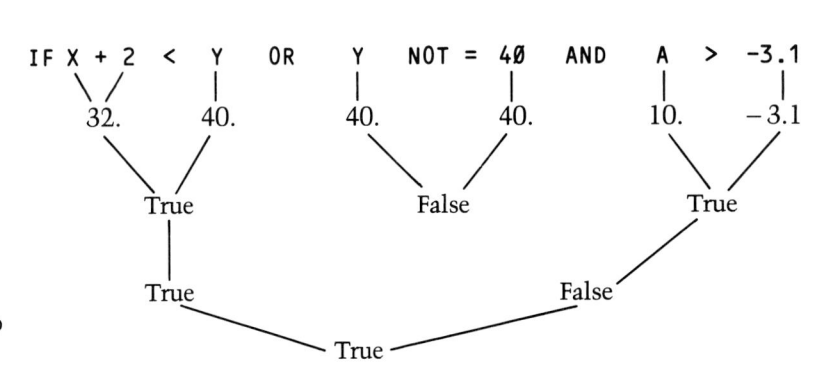

Parentheses can be used to denote the order in which the compound conditions are to be evaluated. Consider, for example, the two following conditions, which have entirely different meanings:

```
IF WEIGHT < 140  OR  AGE < 30   AND  EARNING > 100000
IF (WEIGHT < 140  OR  AGE < 30)  AND  EARNING > 100000
```

In the first case, the condition is true if WEIGHT < 140, regardless of age and earnings, whereas in the second case the condition EARNING > 10000 would always have to be satisfied to make the condition true.

EXAMPLE 3: More examples of compound conditions and their outcomes are shown in the following table:

	X = 4 Y = 2 Z = 2				
CONDITION-1	LOGICAL OPERATOR	CONDITION-2	OUTCOME CONDITION-1	OUTCOME CONDITION-2	OUTCOME COMPOUND
X > Y ** .5	AND	Y EQUAL Z	True	True	True
X < Z	OR	Y NOT EQUAL Z	False	False	False
Y NOT > X	OR	Y + Z < X	True	False	True
X > 5.1	AND	X = 2 * Z	False	True	False
	NOT	X < Y + Z		False	True
	NOT	X NOT < Y		True	False

The NOT logical operator can sometimes befuddle the mind. For example, the clause IF NOT A < B may be somewhat puzzling. One way to look at it is just to read NOT as "it is not true that." The example then reads: IF it is not true that A is less than B (that is, if A is greater than or equal to B). Another way to look at it is to evaluate condition A < B and then take its opposite (negate it), i.e., A ≥ B. Hence the clause IF NOT A < B could have been expressed as IF A GREATER THAN B OR A EQUAL B, which is equivalent to IF A NOT LESS THAN B. We can conclude that NOT A < B is equivalent to A NOT < B.

The logical operator NOT can be joined with a compound expression, in

NOT (A < B OR D = 3.1)

which reads as:

if it is not true that (A < B or D = 3.1).

The reader should remember that the logical operators AND, OR, and NOT can be used only with conditions and not with data names. Try to understand why the following examples are invalid (assume X and Y have numeric PICTURES).

INVALID	EXPLANATION
NOT X	X is not a valid condition; its value is neither true nor false.
X + 1 OR Y + 6	X + 1 and Y + 6 are arithmetic expressions and not conditions.
X < Y + X > 3	Conditions cannot be processed arithmetically. (Logical operator missing.)
X OR Y	Neither X nor Y is a condition.

6-1-6 MULTILEVEL IF STRUCTURES (NESTED IFS)

We often need to include an if then/else structure within another if then/else structure. This usually occurs when more than two alternative actions are associated with the value of a single data item. Three approaches are always possible to solve this type of problem:

1. The nested IF ELSE/IF ELSE/... sentence
2. The nested IF IF IF ... ELSE ELSE ELSE sentence
3. The separate IF ELSE   IF ELSE ... sentences

DECISION, ITERATION, PROGRAM DESIGN, DATA VALIDATION 217

Consider the following problem, where a salesman's commission is based on a graduated sales volume:

SALES	COMMISSION (PERCENTAGE OF SALES)
Under $500	2%
$500 and under $5000	5%
$5000 and over	10%

Let us use the three multilevel IF structures to write the code to compute the salesman's commission based on an amount called SALES.

Method 1 The IF ELSE IF . . . ELSE Approach

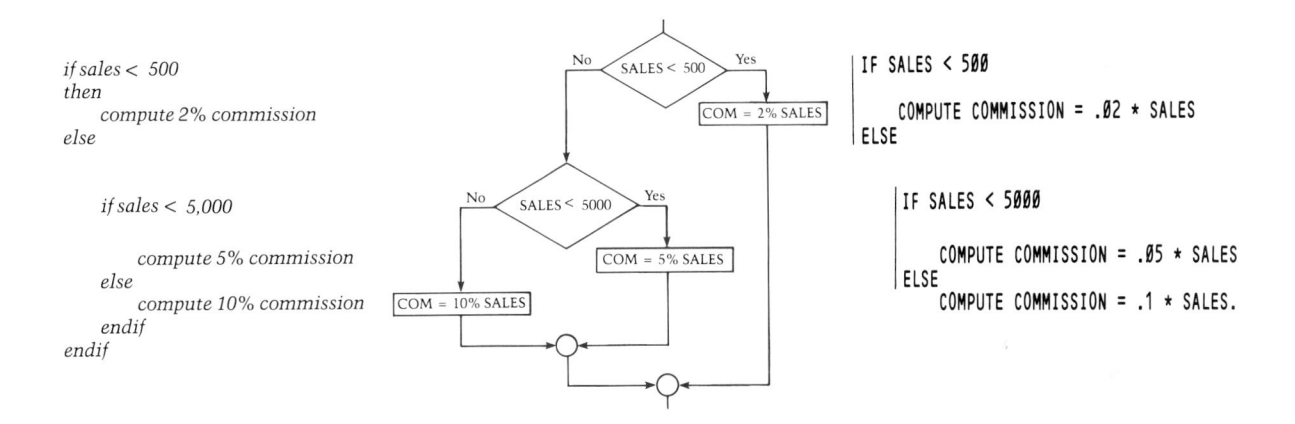

```
if sales < 500
then
    compute 2% commission
else
    if sales < 5,000
    then
        compute 5% commission
    else
        compute 10% commission
    endif
endif
```

```
IF SALES < 500

    COMPUTE COMMISSION = .02 * SALES
ELSE

    IF SALES < 5000

        COMPUTE COMMISSION = .05 * SALES
    ELSE
        COMPUTE COMMISSION = .1 * SALES.
```

Note the indentation of the two pairs of IF/ELSE. Also note that there is only one period in the COBOL code; this code is one long sentence carried over seven lines!

Method 2 The IF IF . . . ELSE ELSE approach

Instead of asking whether SALES is less than 500, we could also solve the problem by asking if SALES is greater than or equal to 500, and if it is, is it greater than or equal to 5,000; we would proceed as follows:

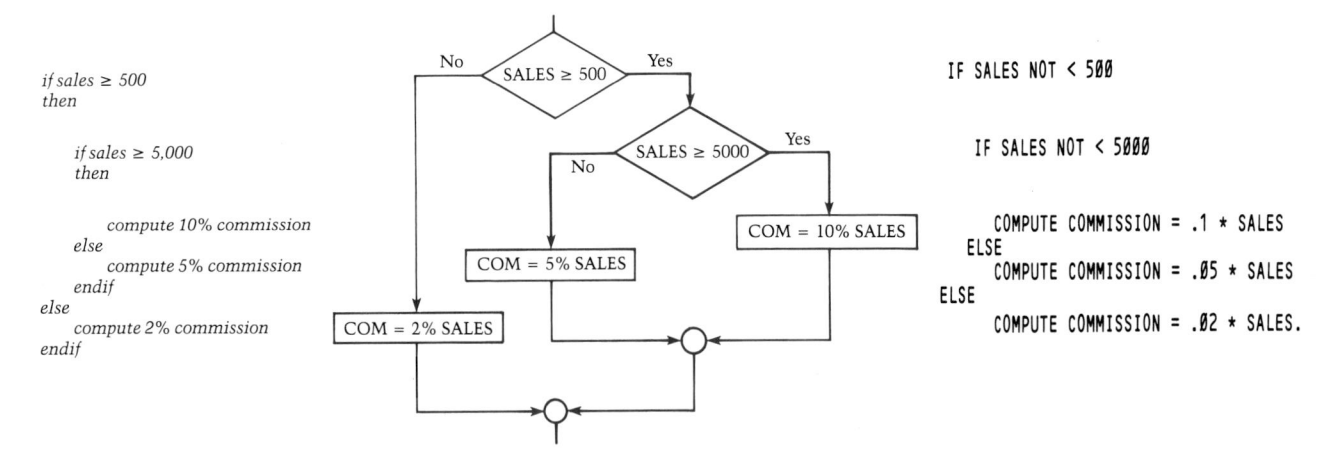

```
if sales ≥ 500
then
    if sales ≥ 5,000
    then
        compute 10% commission
    else
        compute 5% commission
    endif
else
    compute 2% commission
endif
```

```
IF SALES NOT < 500

    IF SALES NOT < 5000

        COMPUTE COMMISSION = .1 * SALES
    ELSE
        COMPUTE COMMISSION = .05 * SALES
ELSE
    COMPUTE COMMISSION = .02 * SALES.
```

At first glance this method may appear a little difficult to follow because of the word NOT in the COBOL code. However, testing sales for not less than $500 is equivalent to testing sales for $500 or above.

Method 3. The separate IF ELSE . . . approach

This approach uses three separate IF ELSE sentences to test for SALES in the three commission ranges.

if sales < 500 　　*then compute 2% commission* *endif*	`IF SALES < 500` 　　`COMPUTE COMMISSION = .02 * SALES.`
if sales ≥ 500 and sales < 5000 　　*then compute 5% commission* *endif*	`IF SALES NOT < 500 AND SALES < 5000` 　　`COMPUTE COMMISSION = .05 * SALES.`
if sales ≥ 5,000 　　*then compute 10% commission* *endif*	`IF SALES NOT < 5000` 　　`COMPUTE COMMISSION = .1 * SALES.`

The selection of one approach over the other depends on the level of efficiency and the level of readability desired. Sometimes the first approach may parallel more closely the formulation of the various conditions stated in the problem, i.e., provide a more direct translation of the phrasing of the problem. Other times, the second approach might be more suitable. In any event, there are two major issues that are conflicting, and they can only be resolved by the user or by policies set forth by the particular COBOL installation in which the programmer works.

In terms of efficiency, structured design, style, and elegance, the first and second approaches tower over the third approach. Indeed, if SALES is less than 500, only one IF statement is executed, whereas three IF statements are executed in the third method. However, in terms of readability and comprehension, the third method, lacking any ELSE statements, is extremely direct, affirmative, and to the point. Deep-nested IF/ELSE statements can be very difficult to read and understand, and trying to unravel the conditions under which an innermost ELSE is carried out can be a harrowing experience.

Many program development managers in industry simply do not tolerate the use of nested IFs in their shops, and parenthetically, many also condemn the use of the NOT logical operator, as it creates a barrier to immediate comprehension. Simplicity, clarity, readability, and ease of comprehension are key issues in program development. This author stays above the mêlée by simply alerting the reader to the varying schools of thought (and heated differences of opinion) among professionals!

Let's look at another problem that requires multilevel IF statements. A special code K is used for different student classifications:

VALUE OF K	VERBAL DESCRIPTION
1	Freshman
2	Sophomore
3	Junior

Write the code to read a numeric value for K and print the verbal description corresponding to the value of K. If K is not 1, 2, or 3, print an error message. Three methods are presented:

Method 1. The IF ELSE IF ELSE . . . approach

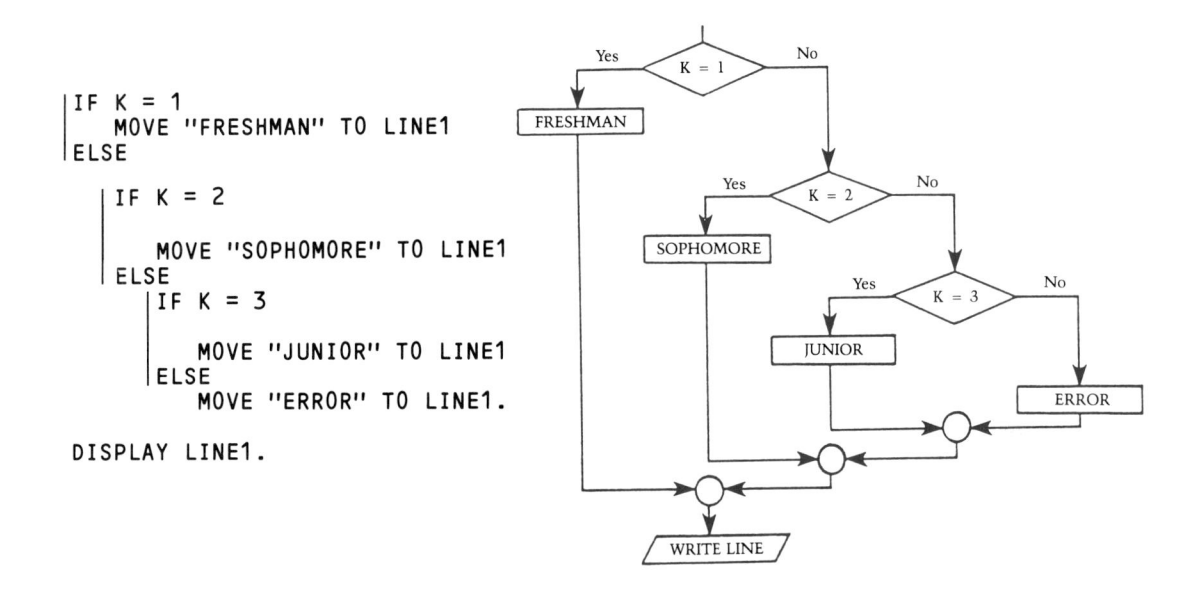

```
IF K = 1
    MOVE "FRESHMAN" TO LINE1
ELSE
    IF K = 2
        MOVE "SOPHOMORE" TO LINE1
    ELSE
        IF K = 3
            MOVE "JUNIOR" TO LINE1
        ELSE
            MOVE "ERROR" TO LINE1.
DISPLAY LINE1.
```

Method 2. The IF IF IF . . . ELSE ELSE ELSE approach

```
IF K NOT = 1
    IF K NOT = 2
        IF K NOT = 3
            MOVE "ERROR" TO LINE1
        ELSE
            MOVE "JUNIOR" TO LINE1
    ELSE
        MOVE "SOPHOMORE" TO LINE1
ELSE
    MOVE "FRESHMAN" TO LINE1.
DISPLAY LINE1.
```

In terms of comprehension, method 1 might be preferable, as the NOT in method 2 somewhat obscures the meaning of the condition.

Method 3. The separate IF ELSE approach

```
*IF K IS NOT 1, 2, OR 3 THEN THERE IS AN ERROR
    MOVE "ERROR" TO LINE1.
    IF K = 1 MOVE 'FRESHMAN' TO LINE1.
    IF K = 2 MOVE 'SOPHOMORE' TO LINE1.
    IF K = 3 MOVE 'JUNIOR' TO LINE1.
    DISPLAY LINE1...
```

In this way if K is not 1, 2, or 3, the message ERROR will already be present in LINE1. If, on the other hand, K is any of the three codes, the message ERROR will be replaced by the appropriate classification.

Although more readable than the two preceding methods, this code is less efficient since regardless of the value of K, three tests will always have to be made before the WRITE statement is executed. However, readability may once again be more important than efficiency, especially for the beginning programmer.

Question: Would the following code be a valid solution to the preceding problem?

```
IF K = 1 MOVE "FRESHMAN"  TO LINE1.
IF K = 2 MOVE "SOPHOMORE" TO LINE1.
IF K = 3 MOVE "JUNIOR"    TO LINE1
ELSE     MOVE "ERROR"     TO LINE1.
```

6-1-7 DO IT NOW

1. Could the sales commission problem in section 6–1–6 have been written as shown in the following coding segments?

   a.
   ```
   IF SALES < 500
      COMPUTE COMMISSION = .02 * SALES.
   IF SALES < 5000
      COMPUTE COMMISSION = .05 * SALES
   ELSE
      COMPUTE COMMISSION = .1 * SALES.
   ```

   b.
   ```
   COMPUTE COMMISSION = .05 * SALES.
   IF SALES < 500 COMPUTE COMMISSION = .02 * SALES.
   IF SALES NOT < 5000 COMPUTE COMMISSION = .1 * SALES.
   ```

   c.
   ```
   COMPUTE COMMISSION = .05 * SALES.
   IF SALES < 500 COMPUTE COMMISSION = .02 * SALES
   ELSE
         IF SALES NOT < 5000 COMPUTE COMMISSION = .1 * SALES.
   ```

2. Under what condition will line 50 be executed?

   ```
   10 IF SALES < 500
   20     IF SALES < 5000
   30         COMPUTE COMMISSION = .05 * SALES
   40     ELSE
   50         COMPUTE COMMISSION = .1 * SALES.
   ```

3. Given the nested sequence IF IF ELSE ELSE, is it possible to place a simple IF in the innermost IF? Discuss and give an example.

4. Which of the following are valid or invalid? Specify reasons if invalid.

   a. IF X = 1.3 PERFORM PAR-1.
   b. IF X = 13. MOVE A TO Z.
   c. IF TEMP IS 0 ADD .5 TO K.
   d. IF HOURS LESS 40
         IF RATE NOT > 13.4
            MOVE X TO A
         ELSE MOVE X TO C.
   e. IF SEX = FEMALE
         ADD 1 TO C-GIRLS.
   f. IF X = 1
         NEXT SENTENCE.
         IF X = 2
            ADD 1 TO Z
            NEXT SENTENCE.
   g. IF A > THAN 3 PERFORM 111.
   h. IF X = NOT 3.1 PERFORM TIDE.
   i. IF Z GREATER OR EQUAL TO L ADD 1 TO X.
   j. IF X = TO 6 PERFORM RIDE.

PUZZLES   PUZZLED   PUZZLES   PUZZLED

5. Does the following COBOL code reflect the logic of the flowchart? If not, propose a solution.

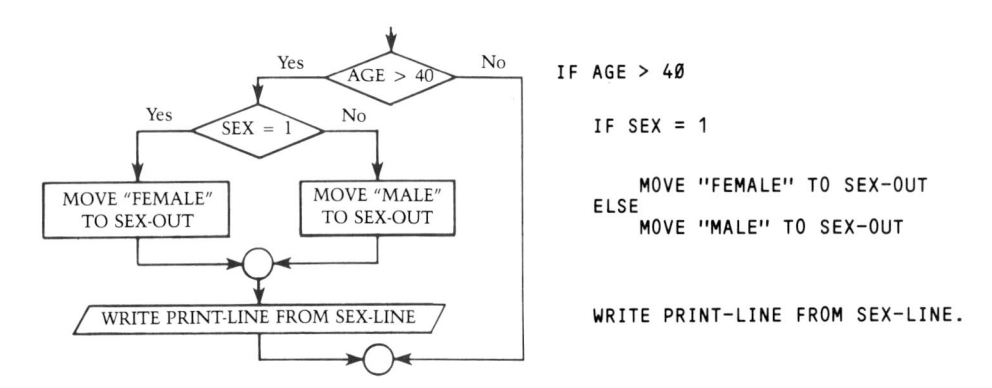

   ```
   IF AGE > 40

       IF SEX = 1

           MOVE "FEMALE" TO SEX-OUT
       ELSE
           MOVE "MALE" TO SEX-OUT

   WRITE PRINT-LINE FROM SEX-LINE.
   ```

6. Which of the following pairs of code are similar?

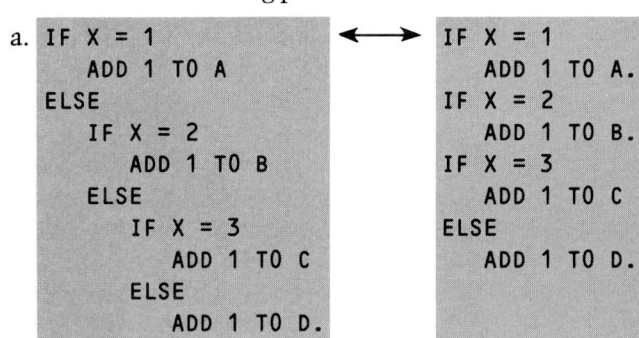

   a.
   ```
   IF X = 1                    IF X = 1
       ADD 1 TO A                  ADD 1 TO A.
   ELSE                        IF X = 2
       IF X = 2                    ADD 1 TO B.
           ADD 1 TO B          IF X = 3
       ELSE                        ADD 1 TO C
           IF X = 3            ELSE
               ADD 1 TO C          ADD 1 TO D.
           ELSE
               ADD 1 TO D.
   ```

b. Check for similarity under the following conditions:
   (i) K is neither 1 nor 2
   (ii) For all values of K.

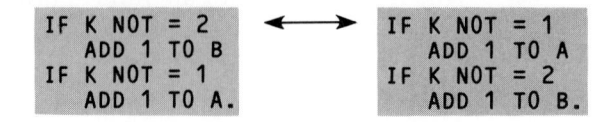

```
IF K NOT = 2                    IF K NOT = 1
    ADD 1 TO B         ⟷           ADD 1 TO A
IF K NOT = 1                    IF K NOT = 2
    ADD 1 TO A.                     ADD 1 TO B.
```

7. In the following three coding segments, assume K takes on integer values between 1 and 6. For which values of K will X be moved to A, B, C, D, E or F? When will line 90 be executed in part c?

```
a. 10 IF K NOT = 1                 b. 10 IF K NOT LESS THAN 3
   20 IF K NOT = 4                    20 IF K LESS THAN 5
   30 IF K > 3                        30     MOVE X TO A
   40     MOVE X TO F                 40 ELSE NEXT SENTENCE.
   50 ELSE MOVE X TO E                50 IF K NOT EQUAL TO 2
   60 ELSE MOVE X TO D                60 NEXT SENTENCE.
   70 ELSE IF K NOT = 2               70 IF K GREATER THAN 3
   80     IF K > 3 MOVE X TO C        80 IF K = 6 MOVE X TO B
   90 ELSE MOVE X TO B                90 ELSE IF K NOT GREATER 6
   95 ELSE MOVE X TO A.               95 MOVE X TO D
                                      97 ELSE NEXT SENTENCE ELSE
                                      99 MOVE X TO C.

c. 10 IF K = 1
   20 MOVE X TO A
   30 IF K = 2
   40     NEXT SENTENCE
   50 ELSE IF K = 3
   60     IF K = 4 NEXT SENTENCE
   70 ELSE MOVE X TO B
   80 ELSE NEXT SENTENCE
   90 MOVE X TO C
   95 ELSE
   97     MOVE X TO D.
```

ANSWERS

1. a. No. Any SALES less than $500 will satisfy not only the first condition but also the second condition; hence the commission on $500 would be computed at 5% instead of 2%.
   b. Yes
   c. Yes

2. Never; the condition at line 20 will always be true!

3. No. If a period terminates the simple IF, then placing it within the innermost IF would create an invalid structure, i.e., one or two ELSE key words would not have an IF companion. On the other hand, if no period is provided for the simple IF, then the simple IF is no longer simple, since the first ELSE statement would be matched with the "simple" IF.

4. a. Valid
    b. Invalid; 13. would terminate the IF.
    c. Invalid; missing operator =
    d. Valid
    e. Valid
    f. Invalid; NEXT SENTENCE should be by itself.
    g. Valid
    h. Invalid; NOT 3.1 is incorrect.
    i. Invalid; cannot have GREATER OR EQUAL
    j. Invalid; = TO is incorrect

Puzzle Answers

5.  ```
    IF AGE > 40
        IF SEX = 1
            MOVE 'FEMALE' TO SEX-OUT
            WRITE PRINT-LINE FROM SEX-LINE
        ELSE
            MOVE 'MALE' TO SEX-OUT
            WRITE PRINT-LINE FROM SEX-LINE.
    ```

6. a. Not similar; see what happens when X = 1.
    b. (i) If K is neither 1 nor 2, the codes are similar.
       (ii) If K takes on all values, codes are dissimilar; see what happens when K = 2.

7. a.

K	
1	B
2,3	E
4	D
5,6	F

    b.

K	
1,2	C
3	A,C
4	A,D
5	D
6	B

    c.

K	
1	A
2,3,4,5,6	D

    line 90 can never be executed

6-1-8 TYPES OF COMPARISONS

In general, comparisons can be made between numeric operands (signed numbers) or between alphanumeric fields.

Numeric Comparisons

Two numeric operands are compared algebraically, i.e., the signs and magnitudes are considered. Consider the following examples:

3 4 5̄	<	2 1̄	−345 is less than −21
2 5	>	3 2 1 5̄	2.5 is greater than −32.15
0 0 0 0 5	<	0 6	0.00005 is less than 0.6
0	=	0̄	0 is equal to −0
    ```

Examples: The following IF statements show comparisons between numeric data items or expressions:

1. IF HOURS IS GREATER THAN 40
        PERFORM OVER-TIME-PAY.

2. IF BONUS + 100.75 > 458
        SUBTRACT 30.75 FROM PAY
        PERFORM BONUS-ADJUST.

3. IF (B ** 2 - 4 * A * C) IS < 0
        WRITE LINE1 FROM NO-ROOTS
    ELSE
        PERFORM REAL-ROOTS.

4. IF EMP-1 + EMP-2 NOT EQUAL TO 2 * EMP-3
        STOP RUN.

5. IF FLDA / 3.14 GREATER THAN ZERO
        MOVE 1 TO ERR-MESSG.

6. IF KODE = FAHRENHEIT
        COMPUTE FAHR = 9 / 5 * CENT + 32
    ELSE
        COMPUTE CENT = 5 / 9 * (FAHR + 32).

Nonnumeric Comparisons

Nonnumeric comparisons can take place between alphanumeric operands. Alphanumeric data are compared character by character from left to right according to the collating sequence shown below. If the two alphanumeric operands to be compared are of unequal length, the shorter operand is filled with blanks to the right until it is as long as the other operand. In COBOL the following collating sequence is always used:

> blank < A < B < C < ... < Y < Z
> and
> 0 < 1 < 2 < ... < 8 < 9

Depending on the code used to represent characters internally (EBCDIC or ASCII, see section 6–5), the digits may all be "less" than the letters of the alphabet (ASCII code) or "larger" than the letters of the alphabet (EBCDIC code).

Examples:

DEAN	<	DEEM	DEAN less than DEEM since A < E.
DAD	>	D	DAD is greater than D since A > blank. (2 trailing blanks are provided).
DAD	=	DAD	1 trailing blank is provided for the first operand. Both operands are equal.
NEW YORK	>	NEW	The first operand is greater than the second since Y > blank.

T̲H̲E	>	␣T̲H̲E	The first operand is greater than the second since T > blank.
A̲3̲B̲	?	3̲B̲4̲	Depends on the internal code used to represent characters.
3̲0	>	2̲9̲3̲	Since 3 is greater than 2!

Examples: Study the following nonnumerical comparisons carefully to see how they can be used in COBOL codes.

`IF CUST-NAME = 'HUGHES'` `    PERFORM IRS-CHECK.`	An alphabetic field is compared to a literal field.
`IF FLDA IS NOT EQUAL TO SPACES` `    MOVE SPACES TO FLDA.`	An alphanumeric field is compared to a figurative constant. If all positions of FLDA are not blanks, FLDA is blanked out.
`IF STAR-LINE = ALL '*'` `    WRITE PRINT-LINE.`	An alphanumeric field is compared to a figurative constant. If all positions of STAR-LINE contain asterisks, PRINT-LINE will be written.
`IF NAME-1 < NAME-2` `    PERFORM INTERCHANGE.`	Two alphabetic fields are compared (assuming alphabetic pictures for names).

6-1-9 CLASS TESTS

It is often necessary to determine whether an alphabetic or an alphanumeric field contains only alphabetic characters and, similarly, whether data in a numeric field is actually numeric. Recall that it is possible to read letters of the alphabet into a numeric picture field and then have an execution time error later on when the CPU tries to process that field! Class tests are generally used to screen invalid data from various sources of input data. The validation process is discussed in detail in section 6-4-2.

The general form of the class test is:

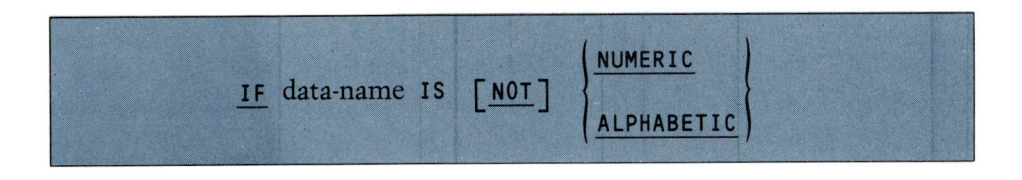

$$\underline{\text{IF}} \text{ data-name IS } [\underline{\text{NOT}}] \left\{ \begin{array}{l} \text{NUMERIC} \\ \text{ALPHABETIC} \end{array} \right\}$$

A data item is considered NUMERIC if the item contains only the characters/digits 0, 1, 2, ..., 9. An internal negative number (3̲2̲5̅) is considered to be numeric.

A data item is considered ALPHABETIC if the field contains only the characters A, B, ..., Z, and the blank character.

Certain restrictions exist as to the types of fields that can be tested. Generally speaking, the user will want to test a numeric field (PICTURE 9's) for NUMERIC and an alphabetic field (PICTURE A'S) for ALPHABETIC, while an alphanumeric field can be tested for both alphabetic and numeric content. Figure 6-4 illustrates the class tests that can be performed on the various data types.

	DATA TYPE	NUMERIC TEST	ALPHABETIC TEST
Numeric	(PIC 9's)	Valid	Invalid
Alphabetic	(PIC A's)	Invalid	Valid
Alphanumeric	(PIC 9's or X)	Valid	Valid

FIGURE 6-4
CLASS TESTS

Examples:

INPUT RECORD OR MEMORY CONTENT	PICTURE	TEST	RESULT	COMMENTS

The test for NUMERIC can be very useful to ensure that no blanks are present in a numeric field (PICTURE 9's).

1 2 3	B PIC S999.	IF B NUMERIC	True	
3 1 4̄	B PIC S9V99.	IF B NUMERIC	True	
␣ 4 2	B PIC 999.	IF B NUMERIC	False	Blank not numeric.
3 . 4	B PIC 999.	IF B NOT NUMERIC	True	Period (.) is not numeric.
1 2 3	B PIC AAA.	IF B NUMERIC	Invalid	Picture is not 9's or X's.

Sometimes it may be necessary to know whether an alphanumeric field contains only digits:

3 2 5	B PIC XXX.	IF B NUMERIC	True	
2 5 ␣	B PIC XXX.	IF B NUMERIC	False	Blank is not numeric.
$ 8 . 9	B PIC $$.9.	IF B NUMERIC	False	$ and . not numeric.

Other times one might want to know whether an alphabetic field contains just alphabetic data:

␣ A T	B PIC AAA.	IF B ALPHABETIC	True	Blank is alphabetic.
B E 3	B PIC AAA.	IF B NOT ALPHABETIC	True	3 is a digit.
A T .	B PIC AAA.	IF B ALPHABETIC	False	Period (.) is not alphabetic.
A B C	B PIC 999.	IF B ALPHABETIC	Invalid	Picture 999.

Alphanumeric fields can also be tested for alphabetic content:

| T H E . | B PIC X(4). | IF B ALPHABETIC | False | Period (.) is not alphabetic. |
| ␣ ␣ ␣ | B PIC $$$. | IF B ALPHABETIC | True | All blanks. |

6-1-10 SIGN TESTS

Sometimes the programmer may wish to determine whether a certain numerical data item or expression is positive, zero, or negative. This can be done, of course, using the relational operators <, = or >. COBOL offers an alternative through the statement:

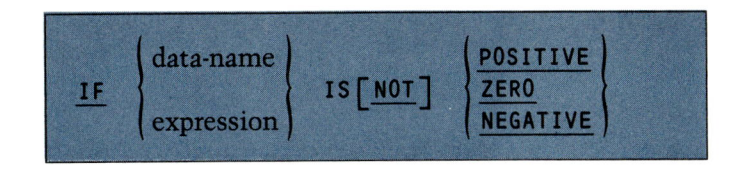

DECISION, ITERATION, PROGRAM DESIGN, DATA VALIDATION 227

$$\underline{IF} \begin{Bmatrix} \text{data-name} \\ \text{expression} \end{Bmatrix} IS [\underline{NOT}] \begin{Bmatrix} \underline{POSITIVE} \\ \underline{ZERO} \\ \underline{NEGATIVE} \end{Bmatrix}$$

For example, the following statements are valid:

1. `IF AMOUNT-REMAINING IS POSITIVE...`
2. `IF B * B - 4 * A * C IS NEGATIVE...`
3. `PERFORM PARA-1 UNTIL MALE-CODE IS ZERO OR FEMALE-CODE IS NOT NEGATIVE.`

Note that testing for NOT NEGATIVE is equivalent to testing for ZERO or POSITIVE. Also, keep in mind that since the sign test is a numerical test (involving algebraic values), it would be invalid to test operands that are alphabetic or alphanumeric.

It is also possible to form compound conditions with class tests, such as

`IF KODE IS POSITIVE OR (NAME IS ALPHABETIC AND KOUNT IS NUMERIC)`

6-2 THE PERFORM STATEMENT AND THE ACCUMULATION PROCESS

As we recall from chapter 1, decomposing a problem into tasks (the modularization process) is made possible through the sequence, the selection (if-then/else), and the iteration structures. The iteration process, implemented through the COBOL statement PERFORM, lies at the heart of structured programming and makes it possible to write programs in top-down fashion. The ability to transfer to a block of code (paragraph), complete that code, and then return to the PERFORM statement or the statement following it is the bedrock of structured programming.

6-2-1 THE SIMPLE PERFORM

The general form of the simple PERFORM is

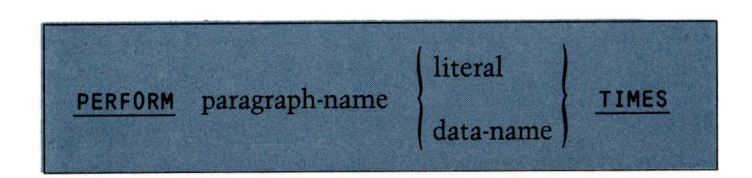

$$\underline{PERFORM} \text{ paragraph-name} \begin{Bmatrix} \text{literal} \\ \text{data-name} \end{Bmatrix} \underline{TIMES}$$

where the literal or data-name (unsigned integer value) specifies the number of times the paragraph in question is to be carried out. Once the paragraph has been carried out the specified number of times, control is passed to the statement or sentence following the PERFORM statement.

The following three examples illustrate the simple iterative process:

Examples:

1.
```
PERFORM PARA-A.
DISPLAY 'THERE'.
    .
    .
PARA-A.
    DISPLAY 'HELLO'.
```

```
HELLO
THERE
```

2.
```
PERFORM PARA-A 3 TIMES.
DISPLAY 'THERE'.
    .
    .
PARA-A.
    DISPLAY 'HELLO'.
```

```
HELLO
HELLO
HELLO
THERE
```

3.
```
ACCEPT N.
PERFORM PARA-A N.
DISPLAY 'THERE'.
    .
    .
PARA-A.
    DISPLAY 'HELLO'.
```

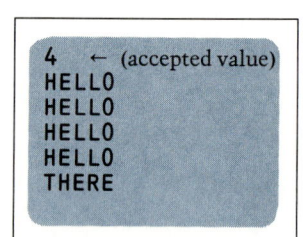

```
4  ← (accepted value)
HELLO
HELLO
HELLO
HELLO
THERE
```

Pseudo Code Representation of the Iterative Process

To preserve a form of expression parallel to the modularized COBOL code, the *perform* verb is used in pseudo code to represent the iterative process. Paragraphs are also used to identify blocks of instructions that are to be processed repeatedly through the PERFORM statement.

6-2-2 THE PERFORM UNTIL STATEMENT

Instead of executing a procedure (paragraph) a fixed number of times, the PERFORM UNTIL statement allows a procedure to be carried out until a particular condition has been satisfied within the procedure. The general form of the PERFORM UNTIL is:

> **PERFORM** paragraph-name **UNTIL** condition

Paragraph-name is carried out repeatedly until the specified condition is met, then control is passed to the sentence following the PERFORM statement. Obviously, the operand(s) specified in the condition must vary or change within paragraph-name; these operands cannot remain constant, or the condition would never change and paragraph-name, theoretically, would be carried on forever (infinite loop).

Every time the paragraph is completed, return is made to the PERFORM statement where the condition is re-tested. The flowchart equivalent of the PERFORM UNTIL is illustrated in Figure 6–5.

It is very important to understand the following points:

1. The condition specified by the UNTIL clause is tested first, before the paragraph is executed. If the condition is already met at the PERFORM state-

ment, paragraph-name is *not* carried out and control passes to the sentence following the PERFORM. If, on the other hand, the condition is not met, paragraph-name is executed. In the pseudo code suntan example in Figure 6–5, the condition is not met initially so "suntan" is carried out. Had the condition stated "until time = 3", then suntan would not have been carried out at all.

2. Even though the condition specified by the PERFORM UNTIL may be met in the very first statements of paragraph-name (e.g., PARA in Figure 6–5), return to the sentence following the PERFORM UNTIL is *not* made at the very moment that the condition is met. Return will be made when the entire paragraph has been completed (the collector or node in the flowchart has been reached).

    At some point, the value of time in the suntan paragraph will be equal to two minutes past three, yet return to the PERFORM statement is not carried out then and there—the entire suntan paragraph must be completed first, i.e., the statement "turn over" must be completed. [How many minutes will the sunbather sunbathe? What will be the position of the sunbather at the time of the "get up" statement—face up or face down?]

    Conditions specified in a PERFORM UNTIL can have varying forms.

Examples:

```
PERFORM 10-XYZ UNTIL X > 10.
PERFORM NAME-SEARCH UNTIL NAME = 'FONDA'.
PERFORM SQUARE-ROOT UNTIL DIFFERENCE IS LESS THAN .0001.
PERFORM HIRE-SEARCH UNTIL AGE NOT < 18 AND YRS-EXP = 3.
PERFORM ART-DISPLAY UNTIL FLDA = ALL '*'.
PERFORM 40-OUT UNTIL FIELDA IS ALPHABETIC.
PERFORM ROOT-10 UNTIL B ** 2 - 4 * A * C NEGATIVE.
```

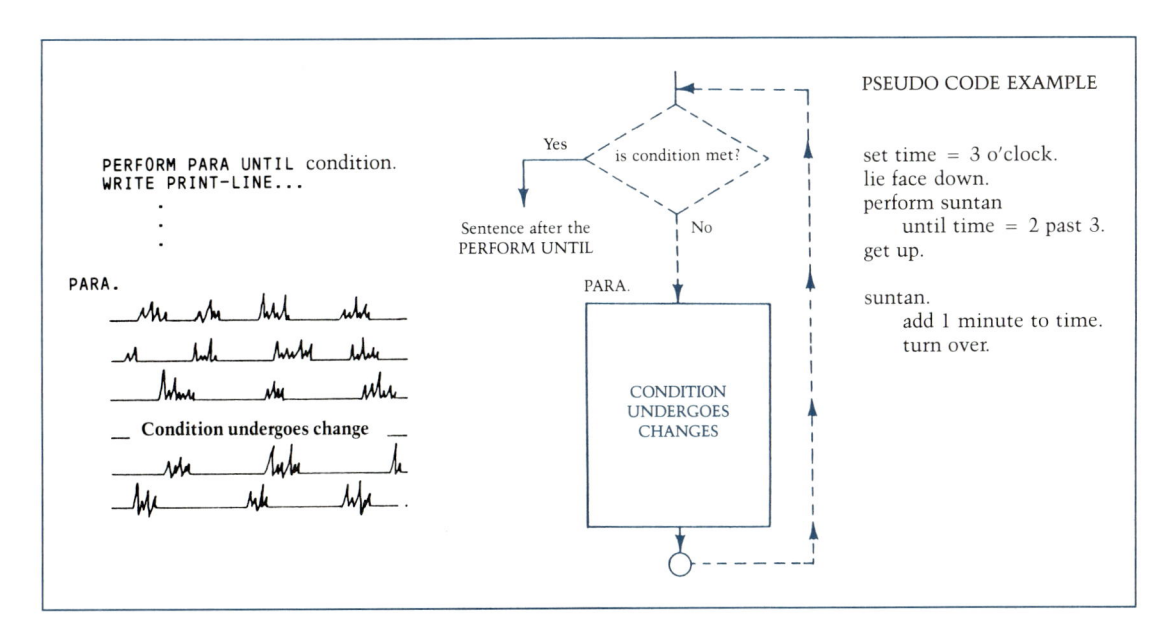

FIGURE 6–5
THE PERFORM UNTIL PROCESS

The following example illustrates the mechanics of the PERFORM statement.

Example:

```
05      MOVE 1 TO X.
10      PERFORM PARA-1 UNTIL X = 2.
         .
         .
15 PARA-1.
20      READ TIME-FILE AT END STOP RUN.
25      MOVE 2 TO X.
30      PERFORM PARA-2.
35      MOVE CUS-NO TO CUS-NO1.
40      ADD 1 TO KOUNT.

45 PARA-2.
50      IF KOUNT = 10
55          NEXT SENTENCE
60      ELSE
65          MOVE 4 TO Z.
```

Line 05–10: X is an operand used in the condition specified in the PERFORM UNTIL. PARA-1 is to be carried out until X = 2.

Line 20: Read a record.

Line 25–40: At this time X is 2. The condition X = 2 is met, however return to the PERFORM statement must await completion of PARA-1. In this case, return is delayed until PARA-2 is completed and the last two statements in PARA-1 are executed.

Line 50–55: NEXT SENTENCE transfers to line 35.

Line 65: After line 65, line 35 is carried out.

6-2-3 DO IT NOW

1. Are the following PERFORM statements valid or invalid? If invalid, state reasons.

   a. PERFORM XYZ EIGHT TIMES.
   b. PERFORM XYZ EIGHT-TIMES.
   c. PERFORM XYZ UNTIL X = "A".
   d. PERFORM PARA MINUS-2 TIMES.
   e. PERFORM T UNTIL X > 10. AND Y < 3.2.
   f. PERFORM T UNTIL YEAR ** 360 / N IS > PAY * Q.

2. Which of the following coding segments will read 10 records?

   a. MOVE 1 TO I.
       PERFORM PARA UNTIL I > 10.
        .
       PARA.
           READ TIME-FILE AT END...
           ADD 1 TO I.

   b. MOVE 10 TO I.
       PERFORM PARA UNTIL I < 0.
        .
       PARA.
           READ TIME-FILE AT END...
           SUBTRACT 1 FROM I.

   c. MOVE 0 TO I.
       PERFORM PARA UNTIL I > 10
           OR I = 10
        .
       PARA.
           ADD 1 TO I.
           READ TIME-FILE AT END...

   d. MOVE 7 TO KOUNT.
       PERFORM PARA UNTIL KOUNT > 17.
        .
       PARA.
           ADD 1 TO KOUNT.
           READ TIME-FILE AT END....

3. How many records will be read by the following coding segments?

a.
```
   77 I PIC 9 VALUE 9.
       .
       PERFORM PARA UNTIL I < 1.
       .
   PARA.
       READ TIME-FILE . . .
       SUBTRACT 1 FROM I.
```
c.
```
   77 I PIC VALUE 0.
       .
       PERFORM PARA UNTIL I > 11.
       .
   PARA.
       READ TIME-FILE . . .
       ADD 1 TO I.
```
b.
```
       MOVE 1 TO I.
       PERFORM PARA UNTIL I > 10.
   PARA.
       ADD 1 TO I.
       READ TIME-FILE . . .
```
d.
```
       MOVE 0 TO X.
       PERFORM PARA-1 UNTIL X > 13.
       .
   PARA-1.
       ADD 1 TO X.
       PERFORM PARA-2 UNTIL X > 12.
   PARA-2.
       ADD 1 TO X.
       READ TIME-FILE . . .
```

ANSWERS

1.
   a. Valid
   b. Valid
   c. Valid
   d. Valid
   e. 10. is invalid.
   f. Some compilers may accept expressions in UNTIL conditions.

2.
   a. Will read 10 records.
   b. Will read 11 records.
   c. Will read 10 records.
   d. Will read 11 records.

3.
   a. 9
   b. 10
   c. Infinite: I will never exceed 9.
   d. 12

6-2-4 PSEUDO CODE: PRACTICAL CONSIDERATIONS

Pseudo code gives us the ability to outline the logic of a problem using a simple form of expression that is syntactically informal but logically rigorous. When we write pseudo code we are not concerned about the specifics or the idiosyncracies of the COBOL language, which only delay our getting to the heart of the solution; we are concerned only with the correctness of the procedural steps. Once the logical infrastructure has been designed, the scene is set for the actual COBOL coding stage.

It is important to understand the implicit meaning of certain verbs or clauses used in pseudo code:

Read input record: means read the list of input items that make up the record. To avoid confusion and to improve documentation and consistency, one common practice is to list in parentheses the names of the various items that are to be referred to in the pseudo code. For example:

Read input record (name, address, sex code)

In this way a later reference to "name" on will cause no surprise as to its origin.

It is also understood that an end-of-file flag is used implicitly with the READ statement.

Write headings: the moves of the various records to the output line are implied.

Initialize: Initialization occurs in either the DATA or PROCEDURE division.

Write output record: The moves of all various items to the output record are implied. Names may also be specified in parentheses.

Open/close files: Open or close all files required in the program.

Stop: means STOP RUN.

Perform paragraph until end file: keep carrying out paragraph until the end of file is encountered.

6-2-5 THE ACCUMULATION PROCESS

Counting

Counting is an essential part of many programs. It may be used to count the number of records read from a file, to repeat a procedure a certain number of times (PERFORM N TIMES), to count the occurrence of specific events, or to generate sequences of numbers for computational use.

EXAMPLE 1: Suppose we want to read and process an input file and we need to know the number of records read. We can use the counting mechanism as follows:

```
01 COUNTERS.
   05 RECORD-COUNT PIC 99 VALUE 0.                Initialize counter to 0.
      .
      .
   READ INPUT-FILE AT END MOVE 1 TO WS-EOF.       Read the first record.
   PERFORM 10-PROCESS-READ UNTIL WS-EOF = 1.      Process the record just read, and read
      .                                           the next record. Repeat these steps
      .                                           until the end of file.
10-PROCESS-READ.
   ADD 1 TO RECORD-COUNT.                         Add 1 to RECORD-COUNT for
   PERFORM 20-PROCESS-RECORD.                     each new record read. Then process
   READ INPUT-FILE AT END MOVE 1 TO WS-EOF.       the record. Read next input record.
```

The data item name RECORD-COUNT, which acts as a counter, is set (initialized) to 0 before the paragraph 10-PROCESS-READ is processed. Every time a record is read, the number 1 is added to RECORD-COUNT to reflect the fact that one more record has been read. Note that when the end of file is encountered, the statement ADD 1 TO RECORD-COUNT is bypassed, i.e., RECORD-COUNT does not count the end-of-file record.

The statement ADD 1 TO RECORD-COUNT is of such importance that we re-emphasize its meaning:

ADD 1 TO RECORD–COUNT means: Add 1 to whatever was in RECORD–COUNT and let this be the new value for RECORD–COUNT; i.e., the newest value of RECORD–COUNT is equal to its old value plus 1.

EXAMPLE 2: Each record of a bank's input file contains, among other information, a savings account number and a current savings amount. The bank wants to determine the number of accounts with savings below $1,000, those between $1,000 and $10,000 inclusive, and those over $10,000.

Figure 6–6 outlines a method to solve this problem. In this case three counters are needed for the three distinct savings categories.

```
*   counting different types of savings accounts
        initialize counters count-below-1000, count-above-10000
            and count-in-between to 0's.
    read a record (savings)
    perform process-savings-file until end of file
    write the three counters
    stop
process-savings-file
    if savings < 1,000
    then
            add 1 to count-below-1000
    else
        if savings ≤ 10,000
        then
            add 1 to count-in-between
        else
            add 1 to count-above-10000
        endif
    endif
    read a record
```

FIGURE 6–6
PSEUDO CODE TO COUNT THREE TYPES OF SAVINGS

Accumulation

We have already seen how counting is made possible by repeated execution of such statements as ADD 1 TO RECORD–COUNT, where RECORD–COUNT is initially set to a beginning value. Each time the statement ADD 1 TO RECORD–COUNT is executed, the value 1 is added to the counter RECORD–COUNT, which takes on successive values 1, 2, 3, 4 and so on (if RECORD–COUNT = 0 initially). Counting can be thought of as accumulating a count.

The main difference between counting and accumulating is that instead of repetitively adding a constant such as 1 to a counter, a data item is added repetitively to an *accumulator* (another data item that is used to keep track of running sums, products, and so forth). For example in the following diagram, the accumulator SUM reflects the sum total of the grades that have been read:

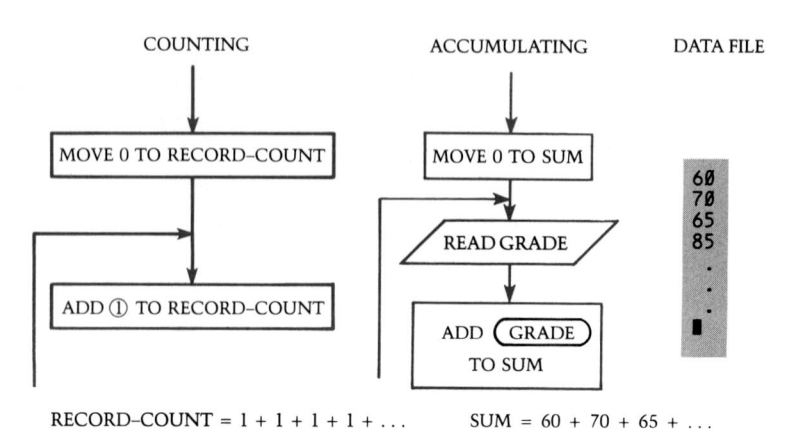

COUNTING   **ACCUMULATING**   **DATA FILE**

```
MOVE 0 TO RECORD-COUNT          MOVE 0 TO SUM             60
                                                          70
                                 READ GRADE               65
ADD ① TO RECORD-COUNT                                     85
                                 ADD GRADE                 .
                                 TO SUM                    .
                                                           ■
```

RECORD-COUNT = 1 + 1 + 1 + 1 + . . .   SUM = 60 + 70 + 65 + . . .

Each time a new grade is entered, it is added to the current SUM.

Let's look at some situations where accumulators are used.

EXAMPLE 1: Computing the sum of the first 100 positive integers.

Let us write the code to compute the sum of the first 100 integers, TOTAL = 1 + 2 + 3 + . . . + 99 + 100.

Before we can compute the sum, we must be able to generate the numbers 1, 2, 3, 4, . . ., 100. This can be done easily by setting RECORD-COUNT to 0 and adding 1 to it repetitively. As each new value for RECORD-COUNT is generated, we add RECORD-COUNT to TOTAL (an accumulator previously set to 0). TOTAL then keeps track of the running or partial sums. There are three very important steps in the code:

1. Counting (ADD 1 TO RECORD-COUNT).

2. Accumulating (ADD RECORD-COUNT TO TOTAL).

3. Testing. Stop the process when RECORD-COUNT = 100.

We can use the following method to solve this problem:

Set counter to 0 initially.
Set accumulator to 0.

Is RECORD-COUNT = 100?
If yes, exit from paragraph SUM-100
If not, add 1 to the counter.
Add RECORD-COUNT to TOTAL.
First 1 will be added to TOTAL
then 2 will be added to TOTAL
then 3, etc. ..., all the way
up to 100.

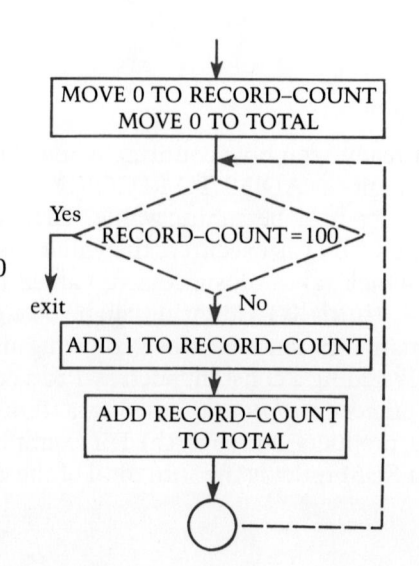

```
MOVE 0 TO RECORD-COUNT
MOVE 0 TO TOTAL

    RECORD-COUNT = 100
Yes               No
exit
    ADD 1 TO RECORD-COUNT

    ADD RECORD-COUNT
         TO TOTAL
```

```
MOVE 0 TO RECORD-COUNT.
MOVE 0 TO TOTAL.

PERFORM SUM-100
    UNTIL RECORD-COUNT = 100.
.
```

```
SUM-100.
    ADD 1 TO RECORD-COUNT.

    ADD RECORD-COUNT TO TOTAL.
```

EXAMPLE 2: Computing an average of grades using the ACCEPT statement

A professor needs to compute the average score for one of her large classes. She has a portable computer and would like to enter the students' scores one at a time and have the computer print out the class average as soon as all the scores have been entered. A negative score is entered to indicate the end of the scores.

The pseudo code to solve this problem is shown in Figure 6–7. Note how the negative score is used in the PERFORM statement to stop the code from reading more scores. Some systems have special keys that act as end-of-file screen markers and that are recognized by the AT END clause of the READ statement. In such a case standard end-of-file flag procedures are observed.

```
*   computing a class average
*   sum is an accumulator to add all scores
*   count counts the number of scores
    initialize count and sum to 0
    accept score
    perform add-scores until score < 0
    compute average = sum/count
    display average
    stop

add-scores
    add 1 to count
    add score to sum
    accept score
*   paragraph add-scores is no longer carried out when a negative score is entered.
```

FIGURE 6–7
COMPUTING A SCORE AVERAGE

EXAMPLE 3: Nesting of paragraphs

A principal P left in a savings account for T years at interest rate R compounded yearly yields a total amount A given by the formula

$$A = P(1 + R)^T$$

Write the pseudo code to compute a total amount A, given a principal of $1,000, for interest rates varying from 9 to 11% in steps of 0.5% for durations of 1, 2, and 3 years. The output should be similar to:

PRINCIPAL	YEARS	INTEREST	AMOUNT
1,000	1	.090	1,090
1,000	1	.095	1,095
1,000	1	.100	1,100
1,000	1	.105	1,105
1,000	1	.110	1,110
1,000	2	.090	1,188
1,000	2	.095	1,199
.	.	.	.
.	.	.	.

Figure 6-8 displays the logic to solve this problem. Note how the process-amount procedure is embedded in the process-years procedure.

```
*   computing principals with varying interest rates
*   years counts the years (1 to 3). interest rates varies from 9 to 11% in steps of .5%
*   principal is $1,000
    initialize years to 1
    initialize principal to 1,000
    open output file
    write headers
    perform process-years until years > 3
    close file
    stop

process-years
    initialize interest rate to 9 percent
    perform process-amount until interest rate > 11 percent
    add 1 to years
    write a blank line

process-amount
    compute amount rounded = principal * (1 + interest rate) ** years
    write output line
    add .5 percent (.005) to interest rate
```

FIGURE 6-8
EFFECTS OF INTEREST RATES AND TIME ON SAVINGS

6-2-6   DO IT NOW

1. Are the following conditions a and b equivalent?

   a. `IF SCORE IS NUMERIC AND SCORE > 100`
   b. `IF SCORE > 100 AND SCORE IS NUMERIC`

2. A marriage proposal letter will be written when the following condition is true. Under how many conditions will the letter be written? Specify the various conditions.

   `IF HAIR = 'BLACK' AND HEIGHT > 5.8 OR EARNING > 100000...`

3. Each record in an input file contains a student's name and the student's test score. Write the partial code to read the student's name and test score and assign a final grade (PASS if score > 90, FAIL otherwise).

4. Records have been typed showing a store's daily sales for the last two weeks. The first entry on each record is the amount of sales for a given day in week 1, and the second entry is the amount of sales for the corresponding day in week 2. Write the code to determine the number of days in week 2 when sales exceeded the corresponding daily sales of week 1 by more than 10% of week 1. Asterisks should identify those "superior" sales days. The input and output have the following form:

INPUT FILE

```
50000 55000
40000 44100
30000 50000
60000 44850
  ↑     ↑
Week1  Week 2
```

SAMPLE OUTPUT

```
FIRST WEEK          SECOND WEEK

   500.00              550.00
   400.00              441.00 **
   300.00              500.00 **
   600.00              448.00

SUPERIOR SALES DAYS NUMBER 2
```

5. Modify the code of Figure 6–7 to allow the professor to calculate averages for all her classes. The output should identify the particular course number, e.g., ENGLISH 101 and the average for that class.

6. Write the COBOL code for Figure 6–6.

7. Write the COBOL code for Figure 6–7.

ANSWERS

1. No. Assume SCORE is not numeric. In that case condition *a* is false since the first simple condition is not met. Condition *b* will give rise to a runtime error message since a nonnumeric value is compared to a signed value (100).

2. A letter will be written under either of the following conditions:

   a. If earning > $100,000
   b. If hair is black and height exceeds 5.8

3.
```
      READ INPUT-FILE AT END MOVE 1 TO EOF.
      PERFORM READ-PROCESS UNTIL EOF = 1.
          .
          .
          .
  READ-PROCESS.
      MOVE CR-NAME TO DL-NAME.
      MOVE CR-GRADE TO DL-GRADE.
      IF CR-GRADE > 90
          MOVE "PASS" TO DL-MESSG
      ELSE
          MOVE "FAIL" TO DL-MESSG.
      WRITE PRINT-LINE FROM DETAIL-LINE.
      READ INPUT-FILE AT END MOVE 1 TO EOF.
```

```
4. WORKING-STORAGE SECTION.
   77  WS-SUP-SALES PIC 9 VALUE 0.
   77  WS-EOF       PIC 9 VALUE 0.
   01  DETAIL-LINE.
        .
   01  SUMMARY-LINE.
        .
       READ INPT-FILE AT END
           MOVE 1 TO WS-EOF.
       PERFORM 10-PROCESS-READ
           UNTIL WS-EOF = 1.
       MOVE WS-SUP-SALES TO SL-COUNT.
       WRITE PRINT-LINE FROM SUMMARY-LINE.
        .
   10-PROCESS-READ.
       MOVE SPACES TO DL-STAR-FLAG.
       IF  CR-SALES-2 > 1.1 * CR-SALES-1
           ADD 1 TO WS-SUP-SALES
           MOVE "**" TO DL-STAR-FLAG.
       MOVE SALES-1 TO DL-SALES-1.
       MOVE SALES-2 TO DL-SALES-2.
       WRITE PRINT-LINE FROM DETAIL-LINE.
       READ INPT-FILE AT END
           MOVE 1 TO WS-EOF.
```

Read the first record to begin processing at paragraph 10-PROCESS-READ.
Keep processing data records until the end of file is encountered.
Write the count of superior sales on output.
Write summary results.

Blank out each line in case the previous line contained the two asterisks.
Keep track of every superior sales day and identify it by two asterisks on the output line.

Print sales for the two corresponding days.
Read the next record.

6-3 PUTTING IT TOGETHER: THE PROGRAM DEVELOPMENT PROCESS

6-3-1 MAJOR PROGRAMMING ACTIVITIES

Computer programming is a complex, creative task that demands a disciplined, organized approach to problem solving. Students often assume that proficiency in one or more computer languages (such as FORTRAN or COBOL) is all that is required to be a good computer programmer. This is equivalent to assuming that proficiency in English ensures the success of a novelist or proficiency in drafting ensures the success of an architect.

The computer programmer must first be able to convert a problem to an *algorithm*, a sequence of well-defined steps that can be carried out by a computer. In some cases, such as computing the area of a rectangular lot, this process is relatively straightforward, since the details of the solution are well understood. In other cases, such as creating economic models or predicting weather patterns, developing the algorithm can be quite complex and time-consuming. Even after an algorithm has been developed and converted into a computer language, the programmer must still make sure that the program is correct and functions as desired in all situations. The actual process of writing statements in COBOL or any other language often represents only a small portion of the time spent on a programming project.

The program development process involves the following five major activities:

- Problem Specification
- Algorithm Design
- Coding
- Data validation and testing
- Documentation

In the following sections we will describe the purpose of each of these activities and techniques of program design.

6-3-2 AN ANALOGY

Before considering the details of the programming process, let us first consider an analogous situation in which an architect is asked to develop plans for a building, as illustrated in Figure 6–9. In the first step, the client must clearly specify the purpose, function, and requirements for the building. If these specifications are not clearly described or if they are incomplete, the architect might design a structure that would not meet the client's needs. This would be a waste of time and money, and the process would have to start again with a more complete set of specifications. The analogous stage in the programming process requires the programmer and problem originator (often the same person) to carefully define the problem to be solved on the computer.

After the client and architect agree on the building specifications, the architect begins a design phase. The architect will probably first develop a general idea of what the structure should look like. Various tools such as sketches and models will be used to help the architect and the client visualize the structure. After many modifications and refinements to the general design, the architect is ready to develop a detailed set of blueprints that describe exactly how the building should be constructed. The programmer also begins by developing a general approach to the problem's solution. The end result of the design stage is an *algorithm* that describes the solution as a sequence of well-defined steps. Various program design tools such as flowcharts and pseudo code are used to describe and develop algorithms.

After the blueprints are completed and carefully checked for errors, the actual construction begins. This stage will probably require the innovative use of building techniques and materials, but for the most part the construction stage is simply a translation of the design into a physical structure. The equivalent stage in programming is called *coding* and involves the translation of the program design into a computer language.

When construction is completed, the architect and client can inspect the building for flaws. Minor construction and design errors can be corrected at some inconvenience and added expense. Major flaws that have progressed beyond the design stage are usually unacceptable and can seriously damage the architect's reputation (e.g., failure to provide access to the fourth floor of a building would impress future clients!). Similarly, the programmer tests a program after it has been translated into a programming language. Like the architect, the good programmer will probably discover and correct a few errors during the design stage. Invariably, however, some errors will exist in the initial program version. Some errors will be obvious minor ones that are easily corrected. Even the best programmers, however, find that it is not uncommon for major flaws to exist in the initial program run, since the programmer does not have the advantage of being able to visualize a physical, static structure. The *testing* stage, during which the programmer tries to develop a reasonable level of confidence in the correctness of a program, often consumes a substantial proportion of the time spent on a program.

A separate, parallel activity that both the architect and programmer must perform is providing *documentation* on the project. The architect will provide the client with blueprints, maintenance procedures, constructions details, and so forth. The programmer also must provide documentation on what the program does, how to use it, and how to keep it up-to-date.

Figure 6–10 illustrates the sequence of programming activities, the time involved in each one, and the typical overlap between the various activities. Many

240 UNDERSTANDING STRUCTURED COBOL

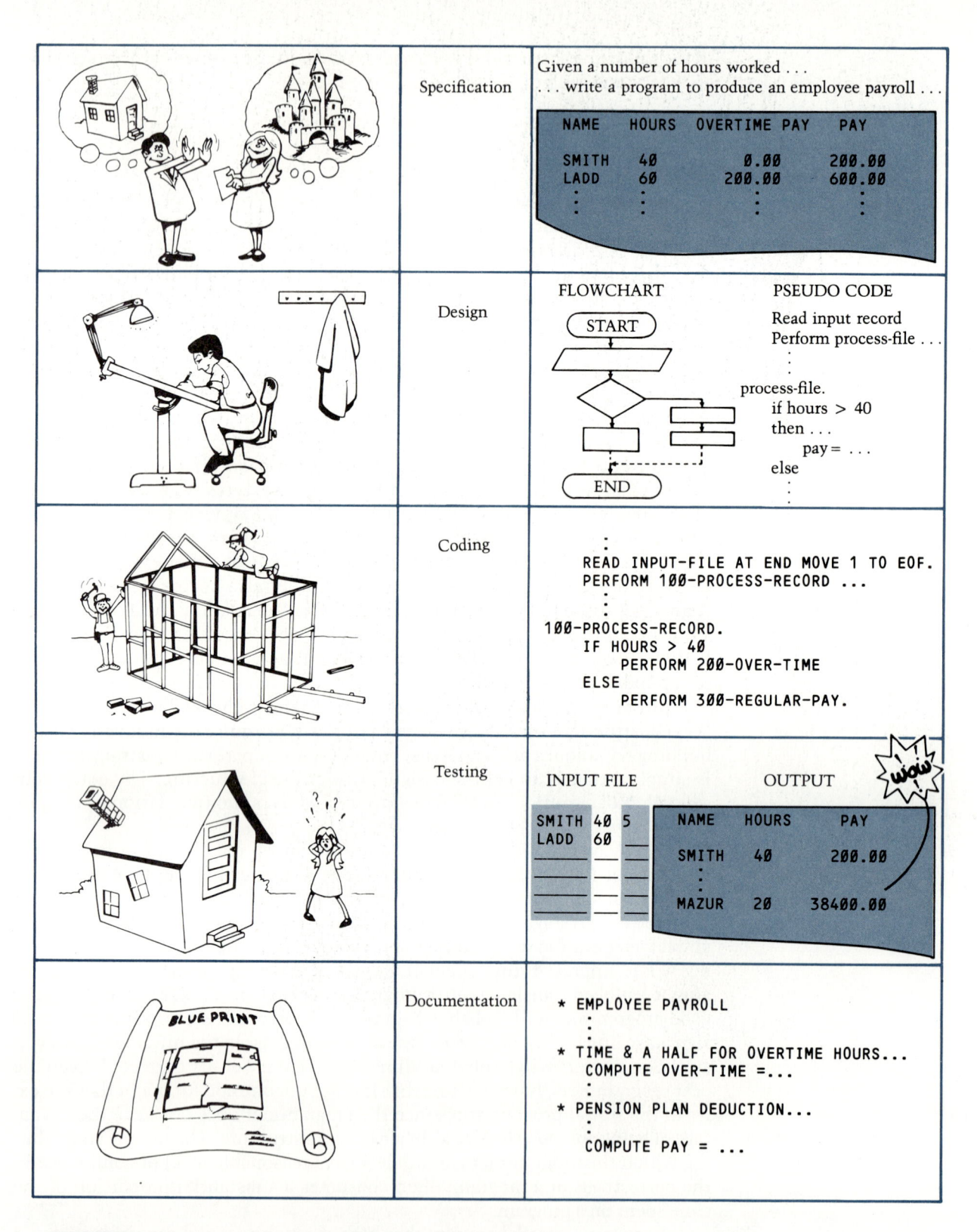

	Specification	Given a number of hours worked... ...write a program to produce an employee payroll... NAME HOURS OVERTIME PAY PAY SMITH 40 0.00 200.00 LADD 60 200.00 600.00

	Design	FLOWCHART PSEUDO CODE
		START
		                           Read input record
		                           Perform process-file...
		
		                           process-file.
		                              if hours > 40
		                              then...
		                                  pay = ...
		END else
| | Coding | ```
       READ INPUT-FILE AT END MOVE 1 TO EOF.
       PERFORM 100-PROCESS-RECORD ...

   100-PROCESS-RECORD.
       IF HOURS > 40
           PERFORM 200-OVER-TIME
       ELSE
           PERFORM 300-REGULAR-PAY.
``` |
| | Testing | INPUT FILE   OUTPUT

SMITH 40 5   NAME   HOURS   PAY
LADD 60
                   SMITH   40   200.00

                   MAZUR   20   38400.00 |
| | Documentation | * EMPLOYEE PAYROLL

* TIME & A HALF FOR OVERTIME HOURS...
   COMPUTE OVER-TIME =...

* PENSION PLAN DEDUCTION...
   COMPUTE PAY = ... |

FIGURE 6–9

PROGRAM DEVELOPMENT ACTIVITIES
```

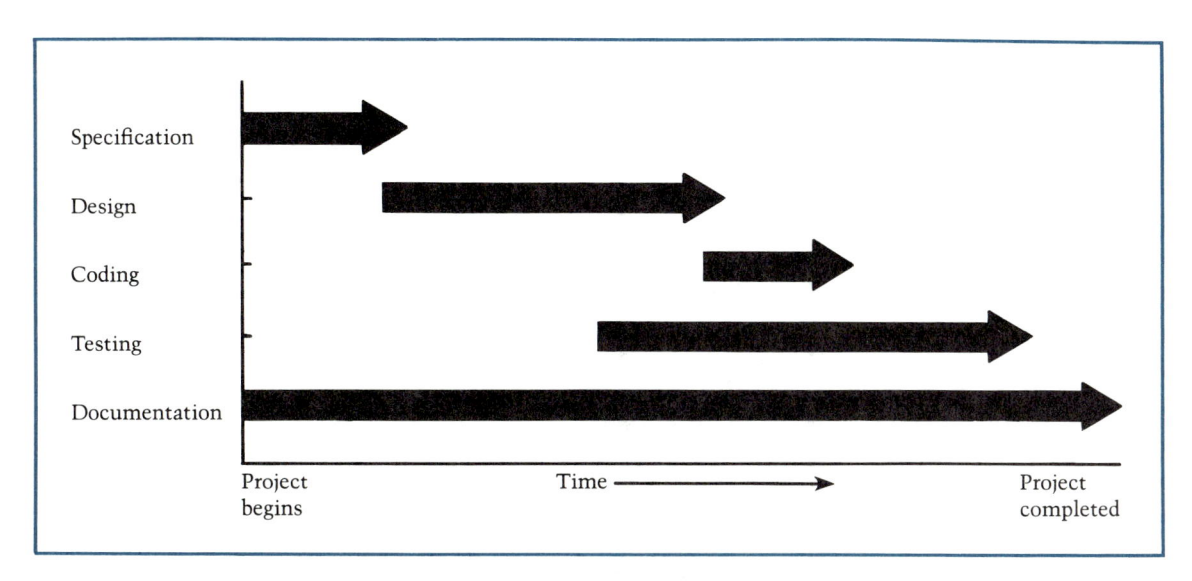

FIGURE 6–10
PROGRAMMING ACTIVITIES—TIME REQUIREMENTS AND TYPICAL OVERLAP

programming projects have failed because one or more of these activities were not given sufficient attention. Students often make the mistake of allowing only enough time to carry out the coding process without regard to the other more time-consuming activities of design and testing. Students who make this mistake usually end up wasting time since they must engage in a long and very frustrating testing phase during which they are continually convinced that their program is *almost* working.

In the following sections we will review the major programming activities and establish techniques for developing algorithms and programs.

6–3–3 PROBLEM SPECIFICATION

A programmer must obviously understand what the problem is before he/she can hope to write a program to solve it. Many programmers, however, have experienced the frustration of writing a program that works perfectly well only to find out that the program does not satisfy the requirements of the problem. For example, suppose that the statement of a problem simply says: *Write a program that will find the area of two rectangular lots*. The programmer would be left with many uncertainties and would have to resolve the questions:

- What type of data will be used by the program?
- How will the data be provided?
- What output should this program produce?
- Should the total area of the two lots be computed?

The programmer's interpretation of these sketchy specifications might result in programs that need to be modified many times. In this simple example, modifications are very straightforward; in a more complex example, however, modifications might easily take as much time as the original solution!

The problem specification stage, therefore, requires that the problem originator clearly state the *function* of the program, what *results* it should produce, and any *special considerations* or methods that should be used in arriving at the results. It is then the programmer's responsibility to study the specifications carefully and to seek clarification on any points that are ambiguous or omitted. Even when the problem originator and the programmer are the same person, the success of the programming project depends on a clear understanding of what is to be achieved.

6-3-4 STRUCTURED PROGRAMMING AND ALGORITHM DESIGN

Once the programmer understands what is to be accomplished, he/she can proceed with the development of an algorithm. This stage requires two skills: a technique for developing a solution and a mechanism for expressing the solution. Both of these areas have received considerable attention in recent years. Until the early seventies there were few formal techniques or guidelines for developing algorithms. Then, in response to the chaotic situation caused by a multitude of individual styles and methods, a new programming discipline called *structured programming* emerged. An exact definition of structured programming is difficult to state since it is usually defined in terms of the alternatives, i.e., the undisciplined approaches of the past. In the most general sense, however, structured programming provides an organized and disciplined approach to design, coding, and testing through the use of the three control structures: sequence, selection, and loop iteration.

Control Structures

In a flowchart, the order in which instructions are to be carried out is specified by the flowlines that connect the flowchart boxes. In pseudo code the order is specified by the use of three well-defined control structures: sequence, selection (if-then/else), and loop iteration (perform until). The exclusive use of these three control structures in writing algorithms is a key principle of structured programming.

One of the more difficult tasks in programming is developing the logic that controls the order in which instructions are performed. A haphazard approach can result in a situation in which following the order of the instructions is like trying to visually pick out the individual strands in a bowl of spaghetti—the logic of the algorithm is so intertwined that the structure is obscured and difficult to comprehend. Structured programming avoids this problem by restricting the ways in which the control logic can be specified. The result is an algorithm that is easier to develop, understand, and modify.

The Sequence Structure

The program in chapter 2 only used the simplest and most basic control structure, the sequence structure. As the name implies, the instructions in a sequence are to be performed one after another. In pseudo code we specify a sequence by simply listing the instructions in the order in which we want them to be performed. A pseudo code sequence and its flowchart equivalent have the following form:

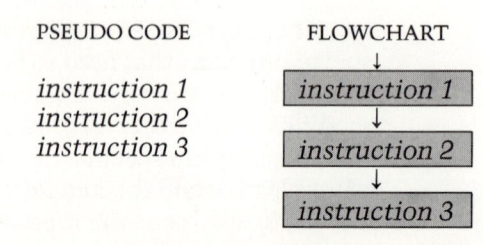

```
         PSEUDO CODE              FLOWCHART
                                      ↓
          instruction 1          [ instruction 1 ]
          instruction 2                ↓
          instruction 3          [ instruction 2 ]
                                      ↓
                                 [ instruction 3 ]
```

The Selection Structure

The selection structure allows alternative actions to be carried out based on the current value of variables in the algorithm. The general form of the selection control structure in pseudo code and in flowchart form is:

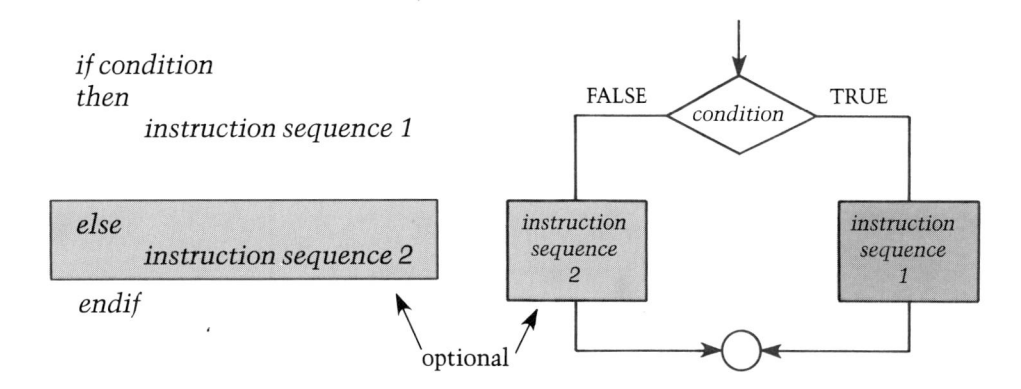

if condition
then
    instruction sequence 1
else
    instruction sequence 2
endif

(optional)

Note that indentation in the pseudo code enhances readability by providing important visual cues that associate actions with conditions.

The Loop (Iteration) Structure:

The loop or iteration control structure allows a set of sequential instructions to be repeated zero or more times. The perform-until has the following general pseudo code and flowchart form:

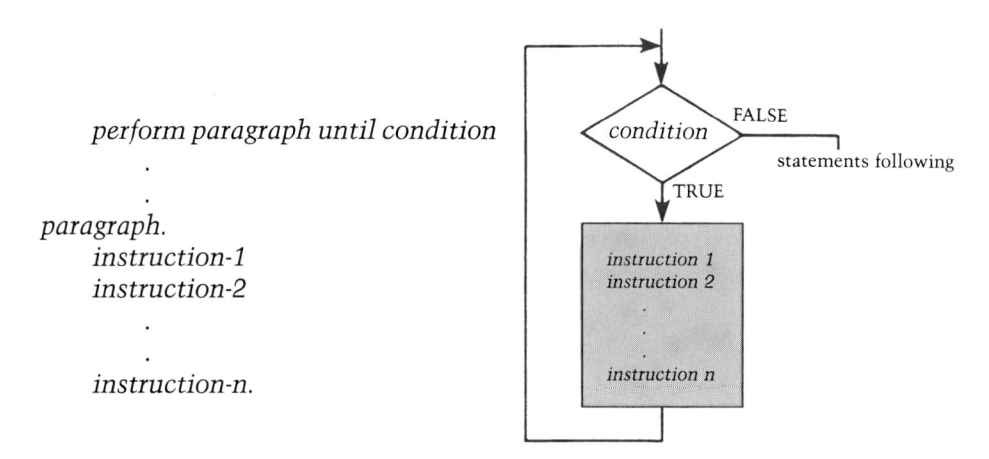

perform paragraph until condition
.
.
.
paragraph.
    instruction-1
    instruction-2
    .
    .
    .
    instruction-n.

As in the if statement, the condition in the perform statement is either true or false. If the condition is true, the paragraph containing the instruction sequence *instruction 1, instruction 2, ..., instruction n* is processed. Completion of the paragraph causes the condition to be tested again. If the condition is still true, the instruction sequence is repeated. This continues until at some point the condition tested is false, at which time control passes to the statement following the perform statement.

If the loop is ever to end, the instructions within the loop must perform an action that will eventually cause the condition to be false. Otherwise the instruction sequence will be repeated forever!

In summary, note that any algorithm can be expressed in pseudo code by using combinations of the loop, selection, and sequence control structures. The selection and the loop control structures incorporate the sequence control structure, and the selection and loop structures themselves can also be combined to form larger sequence structures. Thus an algorithm is initially a sequence of general actions; the algorithm is then refined to incorporate the loop and selection structures necessary to carry out the general actions.

6-3-5 TOP-DOWN DESIGN

The problem of "not being able to see the forest for the trees" can easily occur in the process of developing algorithms. The computer's limited intuitive abilities (compared to those of a human) require that a great deal of detail be incorporated in any problem solution. A programmer can easily become lost in a maze of details if he/she attempts to fully solve each component of a problem before moving on to the next.

A more productive approach is to first formulate the solution in terms of generalized statements. The first version of the algorithm is typically limited to expressing the general logic of the solution, not the details of any particular computation or any specific action. Once the general algorithm has been developed, it can be refined by adding the details that are necessary to perform the general actions. For a complicated problem, this refinement process may be repeated several times with each version containing more detail than the last. The process stops when the translation of the algorithm to a programming language is obvious. This approach, referred to as *stepwise refinement*, is part of a design philosophy called *top-down design*. By using top-down design, we can delay becoming involved in details until the problem has been broken into more manageable segments. This stepwise refinement process is shown in Figure 6–11.

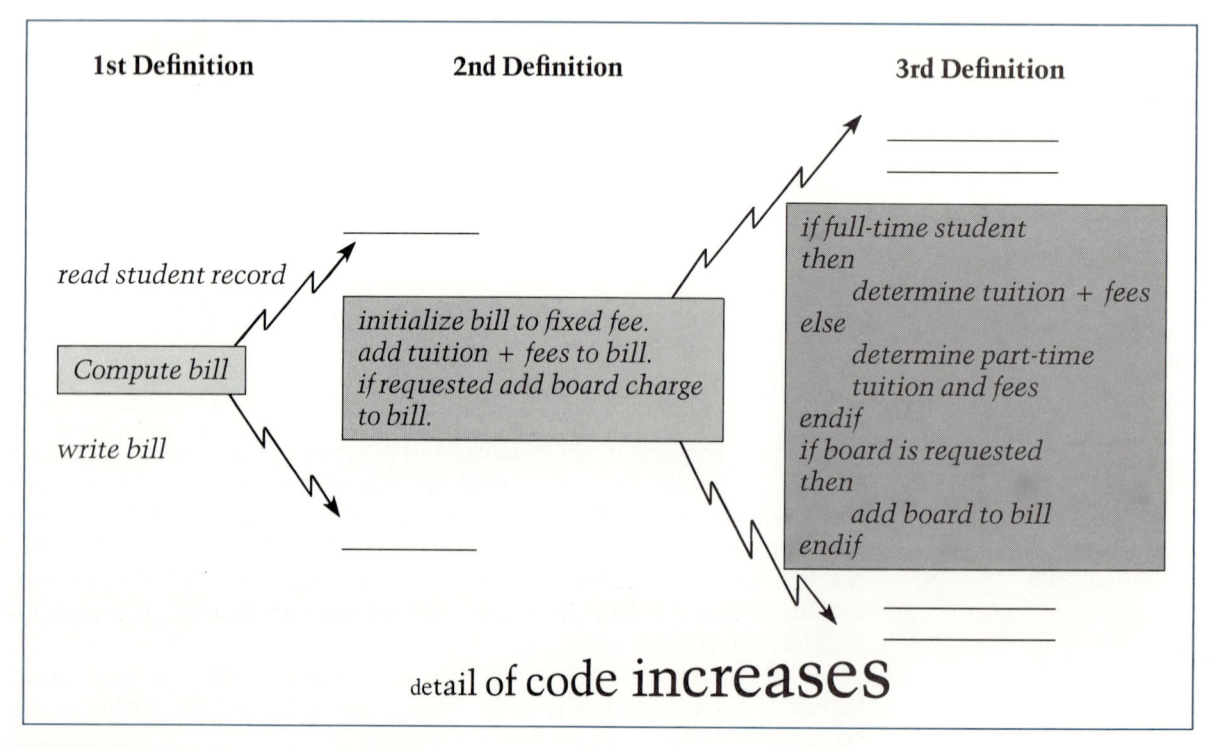

FIGURE 6–11
THE STEPWISE REFINEMENT PROCESS

DECISION, ITERATION, PROGRAM DESIGN, DATA VALIDATION

To illustrate the top-down process, let us consider the following problem:

Problem/Specification: Lurnalot University in Florida has four student classifications for billing purposes: in-state full-time, out-of-state full-time, in-state part-time, and out-of-state part-time. A student who enrolls for less than 12 hours of courses is considered to be a part-time student. The schedule of charges for each classification is summarized in the following table:

SCHEDULE OF CHARGES

	FULL–TIME IN–STATE	FULL–TIME OUT–OF–STATE	PART–TIME IN–STATE	PART–TIME OUT–OF–STATE
TUITION AND FEES	$545	$1,184	$44/hour	$94/hour
FIXED FEE (ALL STUDENTS)	$60			
BOARD	$425			

The university needs a computer program to compute student bills. The input to the program is a file of student records where each record contains a student's

- name
- residence status: the state abbreviation. Florida or 'FL' implies in-state status.
- scheduled hours
- request for board: 'yes' if requested, 'no' otherwise.

The output should list each student's name and total bill. The input and output have the following forms:

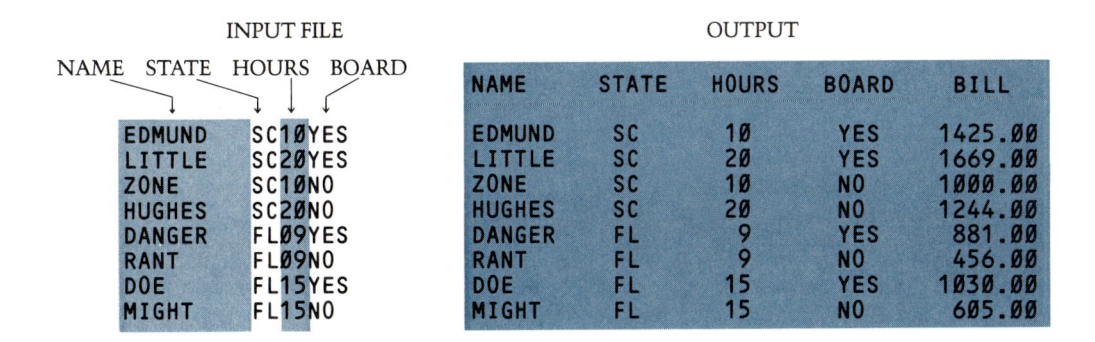

```
          INPUT FILE                           OUTPUT
NAME   STATE  HOURS  BOARD      NAME     STATE   HOURS   BOARD    BILL

EDMUND  SC    10     YES        EDMUND    SC      10      YES     1425.00
LITTLE  SC    20     YES        LITTLE    SC      20      YES     1669.00
ZONE    SC    10     NO         ZONE      SC      10      NO      1000.00
HUGHES  SC    20     NO         HUGHES    SC      20      NO      1244.00
DANGER  FL    09     YES        DANGER    FL       9      YES      881.00
RANT    FL    09     NO         RANT      FL       9      NO       456.00
DOE     FL    15     YES        DOE       FL      15      YES     1030.00
MIGHT   FL    15     NO         MIGHT     FL      15      NO       605.00
```

We begin by considering the actions that are needed to process one student's bill:

- READ the student's record
- Compute the bill
- WRITE the bill.

These very general actions for a single student must obviously be repeated for each student, so our first attempt at an algorithm will include these actions in a loop:

> * student billing problem.
> * version 1—general algorithm
> read a student record.
> perform process-record until end of file.
> stop.
> process-record.
>   compute bill.
>   write student bill.
>   read a student record.

The statement "compute bill" is obviously very general, but at this point in the development process we are simply trying to identify the major components of the problem. Our next version includes somewhat greater detail on how to compute the bill:

> * student billing problem
> * version 2—add some details on bill computation.
> * process individual student bills.
> read student record.
> perform process-record until end of file.
> stop.
> process-record.
>   initialize bill to fixed fee.
>   add tuition and fee charge to bill.
>   if requested, add board charge to bill.
>   write student bill.
>   read student record.

These statements are still very general. We still have not considered the details of how to compute the tuition and fees, for example. A further refinement of the algorithm might expand this by distinguishing between full-time and part-time students:

> * student billing problem
> * version 3—additional details on bill computation
> * process individual student bills
> read student record.
> perform process-record until end of file.
> stop.
> process-record.
>   initialize bill to fixed fee.
>   *determine tuition and fee charge
>   if full-time student
>   then
>   determine full-time tuition and fees charge
>   else
>   determine part-time tuition and fees charge
>   endif
>   add tuition and fees charge to bill.
>   if requested, add board charge to bill.
>   write student bill.
>   read student record.

DECISION, ITERATION, PROGRAM DESIGN, DATA VALIDATION

In this version we continue to delay consideration of the difference between in-state and out-of-state student charges. Incorporating too many details in one refinement step will only obscure the general logic of the algorithm that we are trying to develop.

The final refinement of this algorithm is discussed and shown in section 6–4–2, where the details on how to compute in-state versus out-of-state tuition and fees are included.

6–3–6 TESTING THE DESIGN

Testing is probably the most crucial phase in the program development process, since the fate of the real-life programmer is determined by the correctness of his/her computer-generated results. In an environment where managers and corporate executives increasingly make decisions based on computer-produced reports, a programmer whose program results are faulty has a dismal job outlook. Yet many beginning (and some not-so-beginning) programmers put blind trust in whatever output is produced by their programs, arguing that since no errors showed up during execution, and since captions and numeric values were printed, the results must be correct. Nothing, of course, could be further from the truth. Computer-generated results are often incorrect—the numbers simply do not add up!

The remedy to this problem is to check your results to make sure that they are correct. This, of course, may require a great deal of time. The best way to proceed is to manufacture hypothetical data that will force the program to test each and every path that can be taken during execution of the program. (In a parallel context, if you built a lawn-watering system with numerous cutoff valves, you would want to check that no particular line or pipe was obstructed, i.e., that water would flow through each and every line. Checking just one particular circuit or one component of the pipeline and observing that it worked would not imply that the other lines also worked!) In a programming environment, different types of input values may need to be "invented" so that the action of the program on these dummy values can be observed and checked out. This process is known as *tracing* through a program, (or through a flowchart or pseudo code). You must follow and record what happens to each experimental input item as it travels through the network of instructions until the end of the program is reached. (See Figure 6–12.) You should manufacture as many experimental items as there are paths in the pseudo code or flowchart and you should follow each item through the entire network.

6–3–7 INPUT DATA VALIDATION

Input data validation is another part of design testing. Even though a program may be perfect in the sense that it contains no syntax or logical errors, it may not perform perfectly in the hands of others. Because COBOL is primarily a file-processing language, COBOL programs generally process masses of input data; and where there is a mass of data, there is generally a good potential for masses of errors. In many cases these errors can be traced only indirectly to the COBOL programmer. The programmer comes to grips with the input data during the DATA division phase (identification and description of various data records) and during the program testing phase where he/she manufactures artificial or dummy data to feeds to the program. Once the program logic is found to be sound and the program or system is out of the programmer's hands and into production, the programmer no longer controls the way in which the data finds its

248   UNDERSTANDING STRUCTURED COBOL

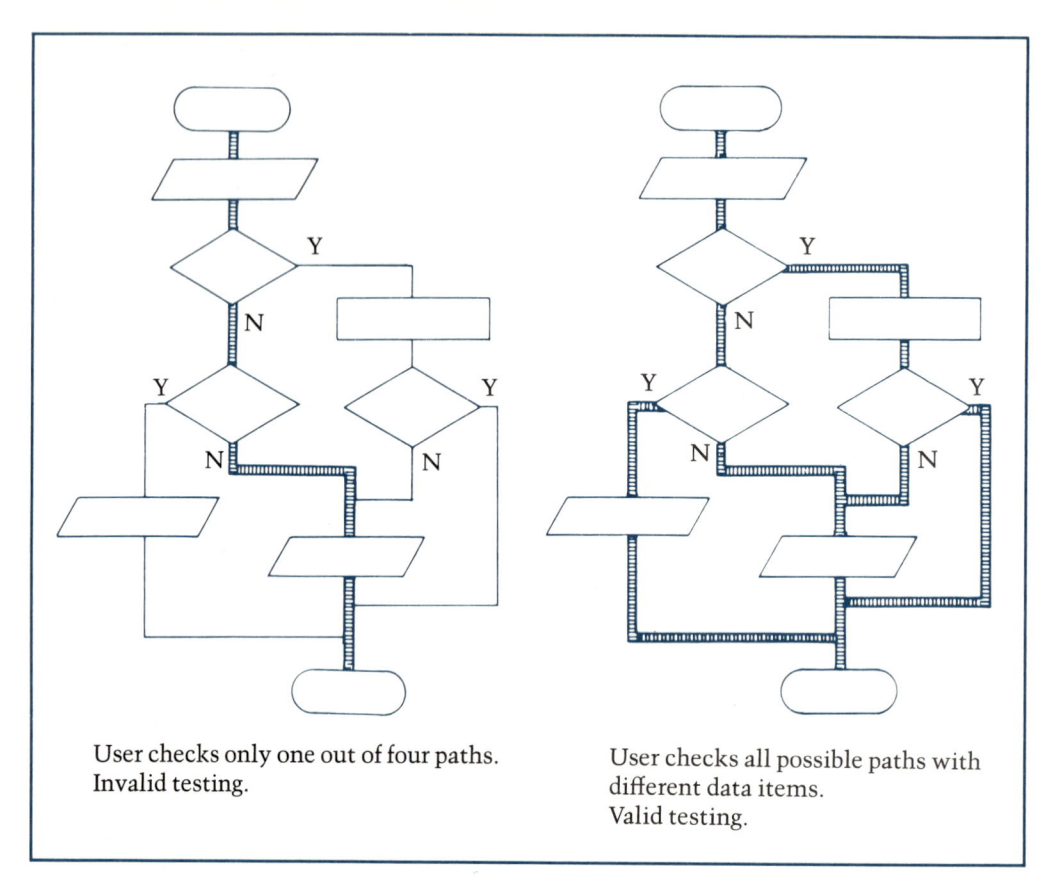

User checks only one out of four paths. Invalid testing.

User checks all possible paths with different data items. Valid testing.

FIGURE 6–12
VALID VERSUS INVALID TESTING

way to the computer. In a typical computerized information processing system many people (data controllers, secretaries, clerks, attendants, and so forth) are responsible for entering data in the computer system.

In a batch-processing environment, I/O controllers (keypunch operators or data entry controllers) capture information from various documents and business forms and transcribe this information onto preformatted/predesigned forms or cards or directly onto magnetic tape/disk (key to tape/disk machines). Such input files are subsequently fed to the computing system. In an on-line inquiry system, data controllers enter information into preformatted records or CRT form images that are directly transmitted to the data base system, which collects, inspects, analyzes, and finally processes the data instantaneously.

In any event, whether in a batch-processing or real-time environment, human errors frequently intervene during the data transcription process: Characters may be mistyped/mispunched, certain fields may be left blank (when they should not be), transposition of characters may occur, or the data itself may be inherently invalid. Many of these errors can be detected during the input (reading) stages of the program before the computer gets into the heart of processing. In a batch-processing environment, an invalid data record should be flagged or listed on output and prevented from being processed. In an on-line system, the system should immediately advise the data controller of the error so that the faulty record/field can be corrected and retransmitted.

Input validation, then, implies checking certain input fields for obvious errors. For example, in a library loan file inquiry system, a typical on-line transaction effected by a library clerk might involve filling in or completing the following delineated fields on a CRT screen:

| LIBRARY CONGRESS NUMBER | BOOK TITLE | CATEGORY | DATE DUE | STATUS |

Upon receiving the CRT record, the system might be set up to ensure that:

1. The first two characters of the Library of Congress number are alphabetic.

2. All fields have been completed (no blank fields).

3. The category field (semester media, monthly media, hold media, and so forth) are valid codes between 1 and 10, for example.

4. The year field in the Date Due should not exceed the current year plus one year. The year could also be checked against the Category code. For example, if the item is monthly media, the borrower should not be allowed to keep the item for more than one month. In general the system should test for simple valid relationships between certain codes or data items.

5. Finally, the Status (faculty, student, etc.) should be checked for valid codes within a certain range.

In an on-line system, the computer can force the input clerk to correct invalid fields/records by flashing certain signals on the screen. Such action screens the program from undesirable (invalid) fields/records that should not be permitted to enter the heart of the processing system.

Certainly the reader can think of numerous applications where input validation should be performed. In a payroll file, social security numbers should be checked for digits only and name fields for alphabetic characters only. In many systems, account numbers already contain a check digit that can be verified to ascertain that no transposition of digits has taken place during the manual input process (see section 6–6–2, exercise 22e). In other cases certain fields should be tested for "reasonable" values or at least questioned if these exceed certain limits, for example, an hourly rate of pay exceeding the company maximum or a $500.00 entry for a breakfast meal in a restaurant's transaction file.

In many file-processing applications, input records may need to be in some sequence, such as ascending name sequence or ascending/descending social security number sequence. In such cases sequence checks should be performed to flag those records that are out of sequence.

COBOL's class test instructions assist the programmer with input validation. Fields can be tested for numeric content or for alphabetic content, and characters can be replaced or inspected for validity through the character manipulation instruction INSPECT (see chapter 7, section 7–3–4).

The input validation process as it relates to the actual COBOL code itself is addressed in detail in different types of programming problems discussed in the following section.

6–4 WRITING PROGRAMS AND THE INPUT VALIDATION PROCESS

6–4–1 A SCREEN-DRIVEN BILLING PROGRAM

Problem/Specification:

Acme Rental charges customers for use of its rental cars based on type of car, insurance purchased, mileage, and number of days. The company rents three types of cars as shown on the following page.

TYPE	DAILY RENTAL	MILEAGE CHARGE
1	$40.00	.06
2	$45.00	.08
3	$50.00	.12

The company offers two insurance plans and selects the plan charging the lesser amount.

PLAN	COST
1	$6 per day of use
2	5% of the total combined daily rental and milage charges, $10 minimum

Write an on-line program to compute a customer's invoice. The agency clerk should enter the data requested by the program through screen prompts: the type of car, the number of miles driven, and the number of days the vehicle was rented. If an invalid entry is typed, the system should inform the clerk about the specific error and allow him/her to retype the entry until it is satisfactory.

When all the data has been entered, the program should display the bill on the screen; the bill should identify the type of car, the number of miles driven, the number of days the vehicle was rented, and the amount due. The insurance amount calculated by the computer is the lesser amount of either insurance plan. A typical session is illustrated as follows:

```
DO YOU WANT TO END THE SESSION?
NO

ENTER TYPE CAR:          1 DIGIT NUMBER
6
ERROR -- TYPE SHOULD BE EITHER 1, 2, OR 3
ENTER TYPE CAR:          1 DIGIT NUMBER
2
ENTER NUMBER OF MILES:  4 DIGIT NUMBER
0010
MILES SHOULD BE NUMERIC -- PLEASE RETYPE
0010
ENTER NUMBER OF DAYS:   3 DIGIT NUMBER
L
DAY SHOULD BE NUMERIC -- PLEASE RETYPE
001

TYPE CAR     :    2
MILES DRIVEN:    10
DAYS RENTED  :    1
AMOUNT DUE  :$   51.80

DO YOU WANT TO END THE SESSION?
YES
```

A program to solve this problem is shown in Figure 6–13.

Program Analysis

1. Note that the daily rental rates, the mileage rates, and the insurance figures could have been specified as constants in the various formulas (lines 165–180) to compute the daily rental, mileage, and insurance costs. However, if

the rental company decided to change these figures, then all these constants would have to be located in the program (be sure to find all of them!) and updated! One way to avoid this dangerous practice would be to initialize all the rates to their respective values in WORKING–STORAGE at lines 47–55, for example, define TYPE1–DAY–RENT PIC 99 VALUE 40 at line 47. A drawback to this approach is that the entire COBOL program must be recompiled for each new respecification of rates. Hence the approach taken by the program in Figure 6–13 is to read these rates from RATE–FILE (lines 36–40).

2. The total combined daily rental and mileage charge is equal to the number of days times the rental charge plus the number of miles driven times the corresponding mileage rate. Insurance plan 2 is simply the number of days times 6 dollars. Insurance plan 1 is either 5% of the total combined cost (rental and mileage) or 10 dollars, whichever figure is the highest. The program then selects the least expensive insurance plan.

3. **Input data validation.** The car type is checked for numeric value. If the value is numeric, the type is then checked for a 1, 2, or 3 value (lines 133–139). Checking first for type values equal to 1, 2, or 3 would cause an execution-time error if the value entered for the type was alphanumeric (invalid comparison between a numeric and nonnumeric value). Hence numeric testing must come first.

   To allow the clerk to correct invalid entries, the program utilizes three error flags (for car type, days, and miles), which are initialized to the value "INCORRECT" (lines 126–128). A PERFORM UNTIL statement is used to force the clerk to type entries until the corresponding error flag for that entry is CORRECT, i.e., PERFORM 500–ENTER–TYPE–CAR UNTIL WS–TYPE–CAR = 'CORRECT'. (lines 117–118). If the data entered is valid, then the value CORRECT is moved to the appropriate flag (line 139) causing the PERFORM UNTIL to terminate.

4. The program concludes when the clerk answers YES to the question "Do you want to end the session?" Notice how lines 92–93 use this response in the PERFORM UNTIL.

6-4-2 A STUDENT BILLING PROBLEM

Problem/Specification:

Lurnalot University in Florida has four student classifications for billing purposes: in-state full-time, out-of-state full-time, in-state part-time, and out-of-state part-time. A student who enrolls for less than 12 hours of courses is considered to be a part-time student. No student may enroll for more than 27 hours. The schedule of charges for each classification is summarized in the following table:

SCHEDULE OF CHARGES

	FULL–TIME		PART–TIME	
	IN–STATE	OUT–OF–STATE	IN–STATE	OUT–OF–STATE
TUITION AND FEES	$545	$1,184	$44/hour	$94/hour
FIXED FEE (ALL STUDENTS)	$60			
BOARD	$425			

```cobol
  1:    IDENTIFICATION DIVISION.
  2:    PROGRAM-ID. STUDENT-REPORT.
  3:    AUTHOR. JONES.
  4: ****************************************************************
  5: * OBJECTIVE: PRODUCE FOR A CAR RENTAL COMPANY AN ON-LINE        *
  6: *            INVOICE PROGRAM TO BILL A CUSTOMER FOR RENTAL OF   *
  7: *            A CAR BASED ON TYPE OF CAR, MILES DRIVEN, NUMBER   *
  8: *            OF DAYS USED AND INSURANCE PLAN.                   *
  9: *                                                               *
 10: * DISK INPUT: RENTAL DAILY CHARGE FOR 3 DIFFERENT TYPES OF CAR, *
 11: *             CORRESPONDING MILEAGE CHARGES, AND INSURANCE COST *
 12: *             (EITHER $6.00 PER DAY OR 5% OF COMBINED DAILY     *
 13: *             AND MILEAGE CHARGE-$10.00 MINIMUM)                *
 14: *                                                               *
 15: * SCREEN OUTPUT :TYPE OF CAR, NUMBER OF MILES DRIVEN, DAYS IN   *
 16: *                POSSESSION OF CAR AND RENTAL BILL.             *
 17: *                                                               *
 18: * SCREEN INPUT  :TYPE OF CAR (1,2, OR 3); MILES DRIVEN (4 DIGIT *
 19: *                NUMBER); NUMBER OF DAYS RENTED (3 DIGIT NUMBER)*
 20: *                                                               *
 21: * VALIDATION    :NUMERIC CAR TYPE NOT GREATER THAN 3; NUMERIC   *
 22: *                ENTRY FOR MILES DRIVEN AND DAYS RENTED.        *
 23: ****************************************************************
```

Lines 24 through 85 are continued in the column to the right

```cobol
 86: *
 87:    PROCEDURE DIVISION.
 88:    100-COORDINATING-MODULE.
 89:        OPEN INPUT RATE-FILE.
 90:        PERFORM 100-INITIALIZE-CAR-RATES.
 91:        PERFORM 300-END-OF-SESSION-DECISION.
 92:        PERFORM 400-ENTER-ON-LINE-DATA
 93:            UNTIL END-SESSION IS EQUAL TO 'YES'.
 94:        CLOSE RATE-FILE.
 95:        STOP RUN.
 96: *
 97: * READ THE DAILY RENTAL RATES, THE MILEAGE CHARGE AND
 98: * THE DATA RELATING TO THE TWO INSURANCE PLANS.
 99: *
100:    100-INITIALIZE-CAR-RATES.
101:        READ RATE-FILE INTO RATE-RECORD
102:            AT END DISPLAY 'NO RECORDS IN RATE-FILE'
103:                   STOP RUN.
104: *
105: * THE USER IS ASKED WHETHER HE/SHE WANTS TO END THE SESSION
106: *
107:    300-END-OF-SESSION-DECISION.
108:        DISPLAY ' '.
109:        DISPLAY 'DO YOU WANT TO END THE SESSION?'
110:        ACCEPT END-SESSION.
111:        DISPLAY ' '.
112: *
113: * TYPE OF CAR, MILES DRIVEN AND DAYS USED ARE ENTERED ON SCREEN
114: *
115:    400-ENTER-ON-LINE-DATA.
116:        PERFORM 450-INITIALIZE-ERROR-FLAGS.
117:        PERFORM 500-ENTER-TYPE-CAR
118:            UNTIL WS-TYPE-CAR = 'CORRECT'.
119:        PERFORM 600-ENTER-MILES-DRIVEN
120:            UNTIL WS-NUMBER-MILES = 'CORRECT'.
121:        PERFORM 700-ENTER-DAYS-DRIVEN
122:            UNTIL WS-NUMBER-DAYS = 'CORRECT'.
123:        PERFORM 800-BILL-COMPUTATION.
124:        PERFORM 300-END-OF-SESSION-DECISION.
125: *
126:    450-INITIALIZE-ERROR-FLAGS.
127:        MOVE 'INCORRECT' TO WS-TYPE-CAR, WS-NUMBER-DAYS,
128:                            WS-NUMBER-MILES.
129: *
130:    500-ENTER-TYPE-CAR.
131:        DISPLAY 'ENTER TYPE CAR: 1 DIGIT NUMBER'.
132:        ACCEPT INPUT-TYPE-CAR.
```

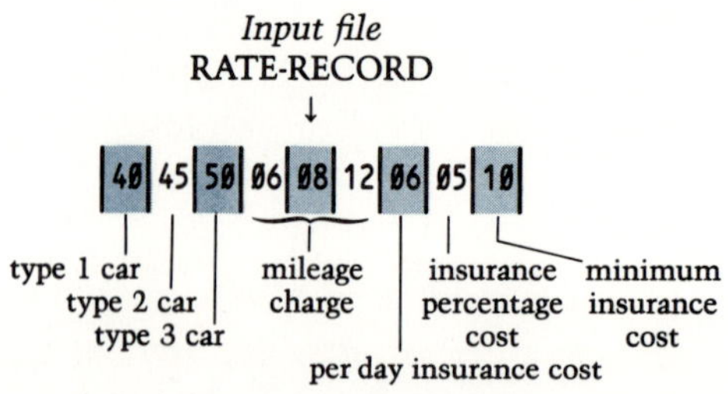

```cobol
 24:    ENVIRONMENT DIVISION.
 25:    CONFIGURATION SECTION.
 26:    SOURCE-COMPUTER. IBM.
 27:    OBJECT-COMPUTER. IBM.
 28:    INPUT-OUTPUT SECTION.
 29:    FILE-CONTROL.
 30:        SELECT RATE-FILE ASSIGN TO DISK
 31:        ORGANIZATION IS LINE SEQUENTIAL.
 32: *
 33:    DATA DIVISION.
 34:    FILE SECTION.
 35: *
 36:    FD  RATE-FILE
 37:        LABEL RECORDS ARE STANDARD
 38:        VALUE OF FILE-ID IS 'RATES'
 39:        DATA RECORD IS INPUT-RECORD.
 40:    01  INPUT-RECORD PIC X(18).
 41: *
 42:    WORKING-STORAGE SECTION.
 43: *
 44: * FILE INPUT RECORD DESCRIPTION
 45: *
 46:    01  RATE-RECORD.
 47:        05  TYPE1-DAY-RENT           PIC 99.
 48:        05  TYPE2-DAY-RENT           PIC 99.
 49:        05  TYPE3-DAY-RENT           PIC 99.
 50:        05  TYPE1-MILEAGE-COST       PIC V99.
 51:        05  TYPE2-MILEAGE-COST       PIC V99.
 52:        05  TYPE3-MILEAGE-COST       PIC V99.
 53:        05  PER-DAY-INSURANCE        PIC 99.
 54:        05  PERCENT-OPTION           PIC V99.
 55:        05  MINIMUM-INSURANCE-COST   PIC 99.
 56: *
 57: * SCREEN DISPLAY OUTPUT ITEMS
 58: *
 59:    01  OUTPUT-TYPE-CAR    PIC ZZZZZ9.
 60:    01  OUTPUT-MILES       PIC ZZZZZ9.
 61:    01  OUTPUT-DAYS        PIC ZZZZZ9.
 62:    01  OUTPUT-BILL        PIC $Z,ZZZ.99.
 63: *
 64: * SCREEN ACCEPT INPUT ITEMS
 65: *
 66:    01  INPUT-TYPE-CAR     PIC 9.
 67:    01  INPUT-MILES        PIC 9999.
 68:    01  INPUT-DAYS         PIC 999.
 69:    01  END-SESSION        PIC XXX VALUE 'NO'.
 70: *
 71: * INDEPENDENT ITEMS
 72: *
 73:    01  FLAGS.
 74:        05  WS-TYPE-CAR              PIC X(09).
 75:        05  WS-NUMBER-DAYS           PIC X(09).
 76:        05  WS-NUMBER-MILES          PIC X(09).
 77: *
 78:    01  COMPUTATIONAL-ITEMS.
 79:        05  WS-MILEAGE-COST          PIC 999V99.
 80:        05  WS-DAY-RENTAL-CHARGE     PIC 9999V99.
 81:        05  WS-INSURANCE-COST-1      PIC 999V99.
 82:        05  WS-INSURANCE-COST-2      PIC 999V99.
 83:        05  WS-INSURANCE-COST        PIC 999V99.
 84:        05  WS-RENTAL-N-MILEAGE-COST PIC 9999V99.
 85:        05  WS-BILL                  PIC 9999V99.
```

Input file
RATE-RECORD
↓

| 40 | 45 | 50 | 06 | 08 | 12 | 06 | 05 | 10 |

type 1 car / type 2 car / type 3 car — mileage charge — per day insurance cost — insurance percentage cost — minimum insurance cost

FIGURE 6–13
A CAR RENTAL PROBLEM

```cobol
133:        IF INPUT-TYPE-CAR IS NOT NUMERIC
134:            DISPLAY 'ERROR -- TYPE SHOULD BE NUMERIC'
135:        ELSE
136:            IF INPUT-TYPE-CAR IS GREATER THAN 3 OR EQUAL TO 0
137:                DISPLAY 'ERROR -- TYPE SHOULD BE EITHER 1, 2, OR 3'
138:            ELSE
139:                MOVE 'CORRECT' TO WS-TYPE-CAR.
140: *
141:    600-ENTER-MILES-DRIVEN.
142:        DISPLAY 'ENTER NUMBER OF MILES: 4 DIGIT NUMBER'.
143:        ACCEPT INPUT-MILES.
144:        IF INPUT-MILES IS NOT NUMERIC
145:            DISPLAY 'MILES SHOULD BE NUMERIC -- PLEASE RETYPE'
146:        ELSE
147:            MOVE 'CORRECT' TO WS-NUMBER-MILES.
148: *
149:    700-ENTER-DAYS-DRIVEN.
150:        DISPLAY 'ENTER NUMBER OF DAYS: 3 DIGIT NUMBER'.
151:        ACCEPT INPUT-DAYS.
152:        IF INPUT-DAYS IS NOT NUMERIC
153:            DISPLAY 'DAY SHOULD BE NUMERIC -- PLEASE RETYPE'
154:        ELSE
155:            MOVE 'CORRECT' TO WS-NUMBER-DAYS.
156: *
157:    800-BILL-COMPUTATION.
158:        PERFORM 850-RENTAL-N-MILEAGE-CHARGES.
159:        PERFORM 900-INSURANCE-PLAN-COMPUTATION.
160:        COMPUTE WS-BILL =
161:            WS-INSURANCE-COST + WS-RENTAL-N-MILEAGE-COST.
162:        PERFORM 950-SCREEN-DISPLAY-REPORT.
163: *
164:    850-RENTAL-N-MILEAGE-CHARGES.
165:        IF INPUT-TYPE-CAR = 1
166:            COMPUTE WS-DAY-RENTAL-CHARGE = TYPE1-DAY-RENT * INPUT-DAYS
167:            COMPUTE WS-MILEAGE-COST = INPUT-MILES * TYPE1-MILEAGE-COST
168:        ELSE
169:            IF INPUT-TYPE-CAR = 2
170:                COMPUTE WS-DAY-RENTAL-CHARGE =
171:                    TYPE2-DAY-RENT * INPUT-DAYS
172:                COMPUTE WS-MILEAGE-COST =
173:                    INPUT-MILES * TYPE2-MILEAGE-COST
174:            ELSE
175:                COMPUTE WS-DAY-RENTAL-CHARGE =
176:                    TYPE3-DAY-RENT * INPUT-DAYS
177:                COMPUTE WS-MILEAGE-COST =
178:                    INPUT-MILES * TYPE3-MILEAGE-COST.
179:        COMPUTE WS-RENTAL-N-MILEAGE-COST =
180:            WS-DAY-RENTAL-CHARGE + WS-MILEAGE-COST.
181: *
182: * THE LEAST COST OF TWO INSURANCE PLANS ARE CALCULATED- EITHER
183: * $6.00 PER DAY OR 5% OF COMBINED RENTAL & MILEAGE CHARGE WITH
184: * A MINIMUM OF $10.00 FOR THE LATTER PLAN.
185: *
186:    900-INSURANCE-PLAN-COMPUTATION.
187:        COMPUTE-WS-INSURANCE-COST-1 = PER-DAY-INSURANCE * INPUT-DAYS.
188:        COMPUTE WS-INSURANCE-COST-2 =
189:            PERCENT-OPTION * WS-RENTAL-N-MILEAGE-COST.
190:        IF WS-INSURANCE-COST-2 IS LESS THAN MINIMUM-INSURANCE-COST
191:            MOVE MINIMUM-INSURANCE-COST TO WS-INSURANCE-COST-2.
192:        IF WS-INSURANCE-COST-1 IS LESS THAN WS-INSURANCE-COST-2
193:            MOVE WS-INSURANCE-COST-1 TO WS-INSURANCE-COST
194:        ELSE
195:            MOVE WS-INSURANCE-COST-2 TO WS-INSURANCE-COST.
196: *
197:    950-SCREEN-DISPLAY-REPORT.
198:        DISPLAY ' '.
199:        MOVE INPUT-TYPE-CAR TO OUTPUT-TYPE CAR.
200:        DISPLAY 'TYPE CAR     :', OUTPUT-TYPE-CAR.
201:        MOVE INPUT-MILES    TO OUTPUT-MILES.
202:        DISPLAY 'MILES DRIVEN:', OUTPUT MILES.
203:        MOVE INPUT-DAYS     TO OUTPUT-DAYS.
204:        DISPLAY 'DAYS RENTED :', OUTPUT-DAYS.
205:        MOVE WS-BILL        TO OUTPUT-BILL.
206:        DISPLAY 'AMOUNT DUE  :', OUTPUT-BILL.
```

```
DO YOU WANT TO END THE SESSION?
NO

ENTER TYPE CAR:       1 DIGIT NUMBER
1
ENTER NUMBER OF MILES: 4 DIGIT NUMBER
0500
ENTER NUMBER OF DAYS: 3 DIGIT NUMBER
001

TYPE CAR     :    1
MILES DRIVEN:   500
DAYS RENTED :    1
AMOUNT DUE  :$   76.00

DO YOU WANT TO END THE SESSION?
NO

ENTER TYPE CAR:       1 DIGIT NUMBER
2
ENTER NUMBER OF MILES: 4 DIGIT NUMBER
0600
ENTER NUMBER OF DAYS: 3 DIGIT NUMBER
010

TYPE CAR     :    2
MILES DRIVEN:   600
DAYS RENTED :   10
AMOUNT DUE  :$  522.90

DO YOU WANT TO END THE SESSION?
NO

ENTER TYPE CAR:       1 DIGIT NUMBER
3
ENTER NUMBER OF MILES: 4 DIGIT NUMBER
10000
ENTER NUMBER OF DAYS: 3 DIGIT NUMBER
001

TYPE CAR     :    3
MILES DRIVEN:    0
DAYS RENTED :    1
AMOUNT DUE  :$   56.00

DO YOU WANT TO END THE SESSION?
NO

ENTER TYPE CAR:       1 DIGIT NUMBER
0
ERROR -- TYPE SHOULD BE EITHER 1, 2 OR 3
ENTER TYPE CAR:       1 DIGIT NUMBER
4
ERROR -- TYPE SHOULD BE EITHER 1, 2 OR 3
ENTER TYPE CAR:       1 DIGIT NUMBER
3
ENTER NUMBER OF MILES: 4 DIGIT NUMBER
1000
MILES SHOULD BE NUMERIC -- PLEASE RETYPE
1000
ENTER NUMBER OF DAYS: 3 DIGIT NUMBER
 20
DAY SHOULD BE NUMERIC -- PLEASE RETYPE
020

TYPE CAR     :    3
MILES DRIVEN: 1000
DAYS RENTED :   20
AMOUNT DUE  :$1,176.00

DO YOU WANT TO END THE SESSION?
YES
```

FIGURE 6–13
(concluded)

The university needs a computer program to compute student bills. The input to the program is a file of student records where each record contains a student's

- name
- residence status: the state abbreviation. Florida or 'FL' implies in-state status.
- scheduled hours
- request for board: YES if requested, NO otherwise.

The output should list each student's name and total bill and perform a thorough input data validation. Examples of the input and output can be seen in Figure 6–14.

INPUT FILE

Name	State	Hours	Board
EDMUND	SC	10	YES
LITTLE	SC	20	YES
ZONE	SC	10	NO
HUGHES	SC	20	NO
DANGER	FL	09	YES
RANT	FL	09	NO
DOE	FL	15	YES
MIGHT	FL	15	NO
WØNG	NY	15	NO
LIU	V3	15	NO
JONES	NY	10	NO
LONG	NY	29	YES
HOPE	NY	09	YEA
LANC1	V3	10	NØ
ABLE	NY	20	NØ
LAMB	V3	15	NØ

Name: positions 1–8
State: positions 9–10
Hours: positions 11–12
Board: positions 13–15

OUTPUT

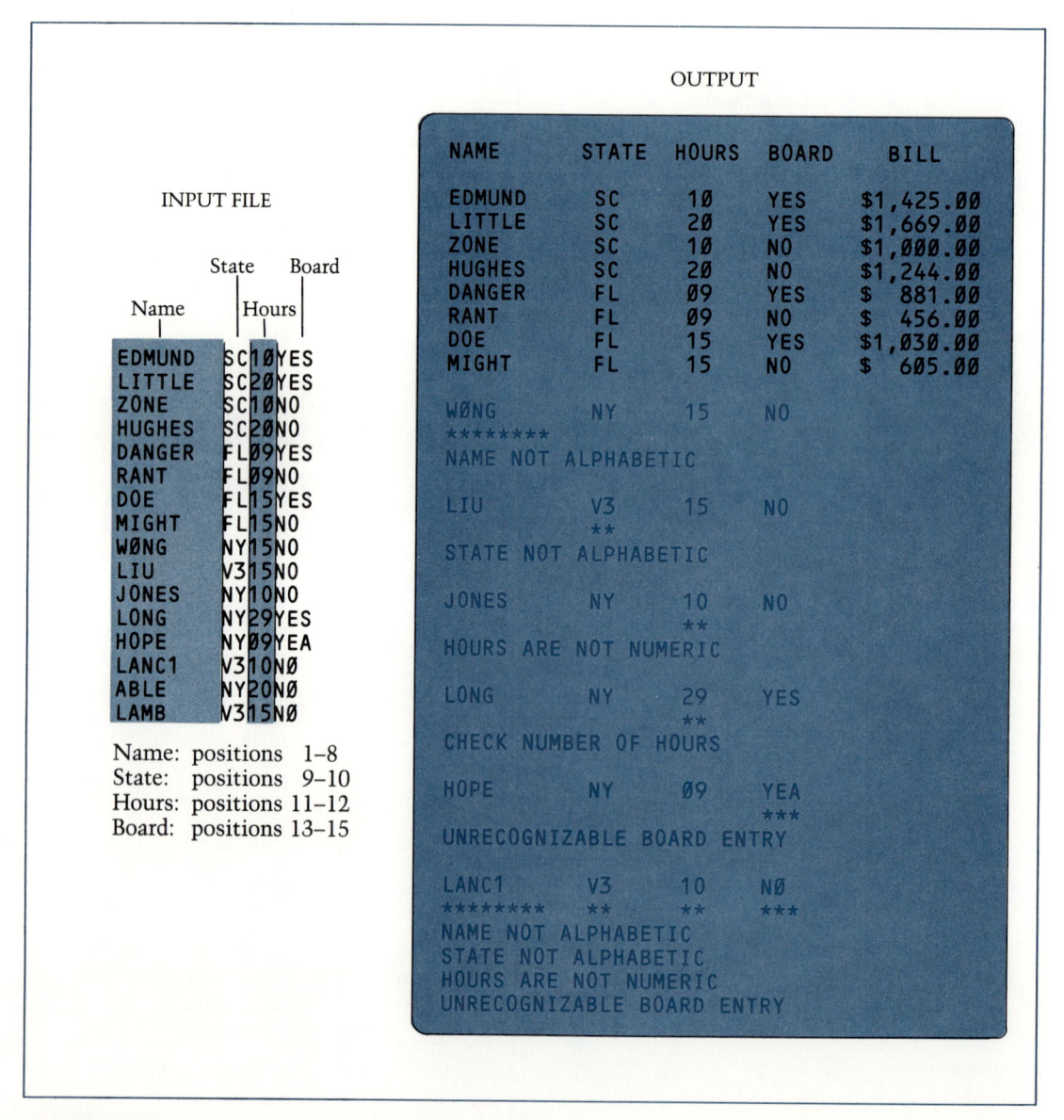

NAME	STATE	HOURS	BOARD	BILL
EDMUND	SC	10	YES	$1,425.00
LITTLE	SC	20	YES	$1,669.00
ZONE	SC	10	NO	$1,000.00
HUGHES	SC	20	NO	$1,244.00
DANGER	FL	09	YES	$ 881.00
RANT	FL	09	NO	$ 456.00
DOE	FL	15	YES	$1,030.00
MIGHT	FL	15	NO	$ 605.00

WØNG   NY   15   NO
****
NAME NOT ALPHABETIC

LIU   V3   15   NO
         **
STATE NOT ALPHABETIC

JONES   NY   10   NO
                **
HOURS ARE NOT NUMERIC

LONG   NY   29   YES
                **
CHECK NUMBER OF HOURS

HOPE   NY   09   YEA
                       ***
UNRECOGNIZABLE BOARD ENTRY

LANC1   V3   10   NØ
******* **   **   ***
NAME NOT ALPHABETIC
STATE NOT ALPHABETIC
HOURS ARE NOT NUMERIC
UNRECOGNIZABLE BOARD ENTRY

FIGURE 6–14
INPUT/OUTPUT FOR STUDENT BILLING PROGRAM

Note the various error messages (typed in blue) on the output whenever a record contains one or more invalid fields; the entire input record is displayed with a string of asterisks placed below the invalid field(s). This provides the reader with a visually compact error view that is complemented by a list of error messages, one per line.

Input Data Validation

The logic of the problem is fairly straightforward, as shown in the pseudo code in Figure 6–15. The corresponding COBOL code in Figure 6–16 is actually very short (lines 197–216). The rest (the major portion) of the code is related to the input data validation process.

The main objective to keep in mind when integrating an input validation component into a COBOL program is to totally separate error handling from the paragraph or paragraphs that actually process the valid input data. Thus, integrity of functions (what to do if data is good, what to do if data is bad) is maintained. No invalid data should ever reach the PROCESS–RECORD paragraph (the code that processes valid records). At this point, invalid records should already have been screened and taken care of. Paragraph PROCESS–RECORD should at no time test input items for validity or generate error messages as a result of invalid input.

To achieve this goal of separation of functions, the structure shown in Figure 6–17 can be used as a model for the input data validation process. This structure can be easily integrated into any COBOL program where input-data validation is required. Within the error-handle module, the programmer can specify what actions (error messages, graphical displays, and so forth) are to be taken in the event of an invalid input field.

Step by Step Analysis In this example the error messages are interspersed within the report itself. These error messages, however, could have been written on disk for subsequent analysis or printed on another printing device, such as an error file.

Since each input record consists of four fields, there is a potential for at least four invalid input fields, and the hours field can give rise to another type of error condition. Let us list the types of possible invalid fields:

- Invalid field name: name must be alphabetic
- Invalid state: state must be alphabetic
- Hours: hours must be numeric and may not exceed 27
- Board: must be equal to either "yes" or "no"

For each type of error, we define a corresponding error flag:

```
01 ERROR-FLAGS.
    05 WS-VALIDATE-NAME      PIC 9.
    05 WS-VALIDATE-STATE     PIC 9.
    05 WS-HOURS-OVER-27      PIC 9.
    05 WS-HOURS-NOT-NUMERIC  PIC 9.
    05 WS-VALIDATE-BOARD     PIC 9.
```

These flags are set to 0 before a record is read (line 144). (Note how each flag is set to 0 by moving zero to the group item ERROR–FLAGS.)

A graph error output line (101–109) is created with a layout identical to the detail line (89–99) that prints the various input fields. This graph line is used to "underline" the invalid field(s) with asterisks. For example, if the hours field is

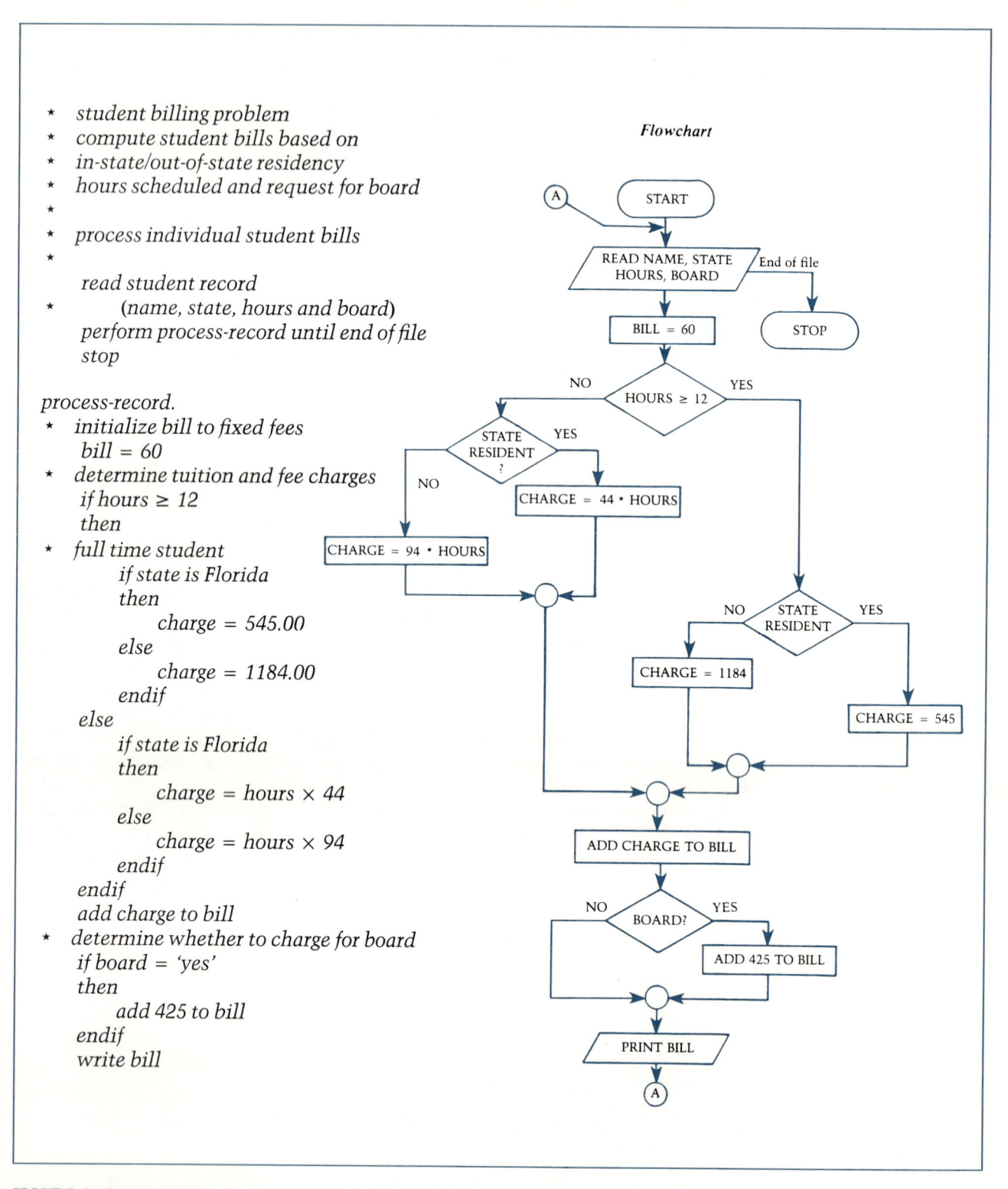

```
*   student billing problem
*   compute student bills based on
*   in-state/out-of-state residency
*   hours scheduled and request for board
*
*   process individual student bills
*
    read student record
*       (name, state, hours and board)
    perform process-record until end of file
    stop

process-record.
*   initialize bill to fixed fees
    bill = 60
*   determine tuition and fee charges
    if hours ≥ 12
    then
*       full time student
        if state is Florida
        then
            charge = 545.00
        else
            charge = 1184.00
        endif
    else
        if state is Florida
        then
            charge = hours × 44
        else
            charge = hours × 94
        endif
    endif
    add charge to bill
*   determine whether to charge for board
    if board = 'yes'
    then
        add 425 to bill
    endif
    write bill
```

Flowchart

FIGURE 6–15
A STUDENT BILLING PROBLEM

invalid, asterisks are moved in those positions of the graph error line that correspond to the positions of the hours field in the detail line. Thus, writing the detail line and followed by the graph error line creates the effect of underlining the invalid field(s) with asterisks. The error line is set to blank before each new record is read, so that previous asterisks are erased (line 145).

Paragraph 500–INPUT–VALIDATION checks the validity of each field. If it finds an invalid field, it sets the corresponding error flag to 1 and moves asterisks to the appropriate area in the graph line (it does not yet print the graph line). It also sets another independent error flag (WS–INVALID–RECORD–FLAG) to 1. The reason for this flag will become apparent shortly.

Upon return from the input validation paragraph (line 134), either the independent flag WS–INVALID–RECORD–FLAG is 1 or 0 (it is always set to 0 prior to reading a record (line 143)). If the flag is 0, then no invalid fields were detected and control passes to 800–COMPUTE–BILL. If the flag is 1, then one or more fields were found to be invalid and control passes to an error-handling routine 700–ERROR–HANDLE. This routine, which begins at line 178, prints the invalid record followed immediately by the graph error line that was prepared in the input validation paragraph (lines 152, 156, 160, 165, 170). It then successively interrogates each error flag to determine which error messages to print (up to a maximum of four error messages per record).

The following discussion is very important in terms of the structure and coding aspects of the validation process. Read it and reread it very carefully, as many times as necessary.

The reader may well question the need for the independent error flag WS–INVALID–RECORD and wonder why it would not be just as simple to insert lines 181–195 right at line 136. Why, upon returning to paragraph 300–PROCESS–RECORD from the input validation routine, don't we print the error graph line and the various error messages right there? The reasons are many. For one, the five IF statements at lines 181–195 would have to be carried out every time a record is processed, even when the record is valid! This is clearly inefficient since, in general, the records are valid! Critically more important, however, are the answers to the questions, What would you do after printing the various error messages? How could you get to line 140 to read the next record without having to compute the bill for the present invalid record? Would you then have to determine one more time whether any of the error flags were on, in order to bypass line 139 (skip the bill computation paragraph) if the record was invalid? Such code would be excessively inefficient. Thus the independent error flag gives rise to an efficient, clear, and well-structured design where paragraphs have very specific responsibilities.

Test Your Understanding of the Program

1. Why is the hours data item defined as it is at lines 72 and 73, and not as 05 SR–HOURS PIC 99?

2. Why is line 145 necessary? line 146?

3. Could the statement at lines 166 and 167 be rewritten as:

    a: IF NOT (SR-BOARD EQUAL TO 'YES' OR SR-BOARD EQUAL TO 'NO')
    b: Same as case *a* without parentheses
    c: IF SR-BOARD NOT = 'YES' OR SR-BOARD NOT = 'NO'

```
 1: IDENTIFICATION DIVISION.
 2: PROGRAM-ID. STUDENT-REPORT.
 3: AUTHOR. JONES.
 4:*****************************************************************
 5:*    OBJECTIVE:  GIVEN A STUDENT ADMISSION FILE, COMPUTE EACH    *
 6:*                STUDENT'S BILL ACCORDING TO THE FOLLOWING:      *
 7:*                                                                *
 8:*...............................................................*
 9:*              .    FULL-TIME    .     PART-TIME                 *
10:*..............................................................*
11:*              . IN-STATE . OUT-OF-STATE . IN-STATE . OUT-OF-STATE *
12:* TUITION      .  $545    .   $1,184     . $44/HOUR .  $94/HOUR  *
13:*..............................................................*
14:* FIXED FEE    .               $60.00                            *
15:* BOARD        .              $425.00                            *
16:*..............................................................*
17:*                                                                *
18:*  INPUT:    NAME, STATE, CREDIT HOURS AND BOARD OPTION.         *
19:*                                                                *
20:*  OUTPUT:   PRINT ALL INPUT DATA AND STUDENT'S BILL.            *
21:*                                                                *
22:*  VALIDATION: NON-ALPHABETICAL NAME, STATE AND BOARD OPTION.    *
23:*              NON-NUMERIC HOURS AND HOURS OVER 27.              *
24:*****************************************************************
25: ENVIRONMENT DIVISION.
26: CONFIGURATION SECTION.
27: SOURCE-COMPUTER. IBM.
28: OBJECT-COMPUTER. IBM.
29: INPUT-OUTPUT SECTION.
30: FILE-CONTROL.
31: SELECT REPORT-FILE  ASSIGN TO PRINTER.
32: SELECT STUDENT-FILE ASSIGN TO DISK
33:     ORGANIZATION IS LINE SEQUENTIAL.
34:*
35: DATA DIVISION.
36: FILE SECTION.
37:*
38: FD  STUDENT-FILE
39:     LABEL RECORDS ARE STANDARD
40:     VALUE OF FILE-ID IS 'ROSTER'
41:     DATA RECORD IS INPUT-RECORD.
42: 01  INPUT-RECORD PIC X(39).
43: FD  REPORT-FILE
44:     LABEL RECORDS ARE OMITTED
45:     DATA RECORD IS PRINT-LINE.
46: 01  PRINT-LINE PIC X(132).
47:*
48: WORKING-STORAGE SECTION.
49:*
50:*   INDEPENDENT ITEMS
51:*
52: 01  FLAGS.
53:     05 WS-END-FILE   PIC XXX VALUE 'NO'.
54:     05 WS-INVALID-RECORD-FLAG PIC 9.
55:*
56: 01  COMPUTATIONAL-ITEMS.
57:     05 WS-BILL     PIC 9999V99.
58:     05 WS-CHARGE   PIC 9999V99.
59:*
60: 01  ERROR-FLAGS.
61:     05 WS-VALIDATE-NAME      PIC 9.
62:     05 WS-VALIDATE-STATE     PIC 9.
63:     05 WS-HOURS-OVER-27      PIC 9.
64:     05 WS-HOURS-NOT-NUMERIC  PIC 9.
65:     05 WS-VALIDATE-BOARD     PIC 9.
66:*
67:*   INPUT RECORD DESCRIPTION
68:*
69: 01  STUDENT-RECORD.
70:     05 SR-NAME           PIC X(08).
71:     05 SR-STATE          PIC X(02).
72:     05 SR-HOURS.
73:         10 SR-HOURS-NUMERIC PIC 99.
74:     05 SR-BOARD          PIC X(03).
75:*
76:*   OUTPUT LINE DESCRIPTIONS
77:*
78: 01  MAJOR-HEADING.
79:     05 FILLER      PIC X(05) VALUE ' NAME'.
80:     05 FILLER      PIC X(06) VALUE SPACES.
81:     05 FILLER      PIC X(05) VALUE 'STATE'.
82:     05 FILLER      PIC X(02) VALUE SPACES.
83:     05 FILLER      PIC X(05) VALUE 'HOURS'.
84:     05 FILLER      PIC X(03) VALUE SPACES.
85:     05 FILLER      PIC X(05) VALUE 'BOARD'.
86:     05 FILLER      PIC X(03) VALUE SPACES.
87:     05 FILLER      PIC X(05) VALUE 'BILL'.
88:*
89: 01  DETAIL-LINE.
90:     05 FILLER      PIC X(01) VALUE SPACES.
91:     05 DL-NAME     PIC X(08).
92:     05 FILLER      PIC X(03) VALUE SPACES.
93:     05 DL-STATE    PIC X(02).
94:     05 FILLER      PIC X(05) VALUE SPACES.
95:     05 DL-HOURS    PIC Z9.
96:     05 FILLER      PIC X(05) VALUE SPACES.
97:     05 DL-BOARD    PIC X(03).
98:     05 FILLER      PIC X(03) VALUE SPACES.
99:     05 DL-BILL     PIC $Z,ZZ9.99.
100:*
101: 01  ERROR-GRAPH-LINE.
102:     05 FILLER     PIC X(01) VALUE SPACES.
103:     05 EG-NAME    PIC X(08).
104:     05 FILLER     PIC X(03) VALUE SPACES.
105:     05 EG-STATE   PIC X(02).
106:     05 FILLER     PIC X(05) VALUE SPACES.
107:     05 EG-HOURS   PIC X(02).
108:     05 FILLER     PIC X(05) VALUE SPACES.
109:     05 EG-BOARD   PIC X(03).
110:*
111: 10  ERROR-MESSAGE-LINE.
112:     05 FILLER     PIC X(01) VALUE SPACES.
113:     05 EM-MESSAGE PIC X(26).
114:*
115: PROCEDURE DIVISION.
116: 100-COORDINATING-MODULE.
117:     OPEN INPUT STUDENT-FILE
118:          OUTPUT REPORT-FILE.
119:     WRITE PRINT-LINE FROM MAJOR-HEADING.
120:     MOVE SPACES TO PRINT-LINE.
121:     WRITE PRINT-LINE AFTER 1 LINE.
122:     PERFORM 200-READ-RECORD.
123:     PERFORM 300-PROCESS-RECORD
124:         UNTIL WS-END-FILE = 1.
125:     CLOSE STUDENT-FILE, REPORT-FILE.
126:     STOP RUN.
127:*
128: 200-READ-RECORD.
129:     READ STUDENT-FILE INTO STUDENT-RECORD
130:         AT END MOVE 1 TO WS-END-FILE.
131:*
132: 300-PROCESS-RECORD.
133:     PERFORM 400-INITIALIZE-ERROR-FLAGS.
134:     PERFORM 500-INPUT-VALIDATION.
135:     PERFORM 600-PREPARE-DETAIL-LINE.
136:     IF WS-INVALID-RECORD-FLAG = 1
137:         PERFORM 700-ERROR-HANDLE
138:     ELSE
139:         PERFORM 800-COMPUTE-BILL.
140:     PERFORM 200-READ-RECORD.
141:*
142: 400-INITIALIZE-ERROR-FLAGS.
143:     MOVE 0 TO WS-INVALID-RECORD-FLAG.
144:     MOVE ALL ZEROES TO ERROR-FLAGS.
```

INPUT FILE

	1	9	13
EDMUND	SC10	YES
LITTLE	SC20	YES
ZONE	SC10	NO
HUGHES	SC20	NO
DANGER	FL09	YES
RANT	FL09	NO
DOE	FL15	YES
MIGHT	FL15	NO
WOONG	NY15	NO
LIU	V315	NO
JONES	NY10	NO
LONG	NY29	YES
HOPE	NY09	YEA
LANC1	V310	NO
ABLE	NY20	N0
LAMB	V315	N,

FIGURE 6–16

AN INPUT VALIDATION EXAMPLE

```
145:        MOVE SPACES TO ERROR-GRAPH-LINE.
146:        MOVE SPACES TO DETAIL-LINE.
147:  *
148:    500-INPUT-VALIDATION.
149:        IF SR-NAME IS NOT ALPHABETIC
150:            MOVE 1 TO WS-INVALID-RECORD-FLAG
151:            MOVE 1 TO WS-VALIDATE-NAME
152:            MOVE ALL '*' TO EG-NAME.
153:        IF SR-STATE IS NOT ALPHABETIC
154:            MOVE 1 TO WS-INVALID-RECORD-FLAG
155:            MOVE 1 TO WS-VALIDATE-STATE
156:            MOVE ALL '*' TO EG-STATE.
157:        IF SR-HOURS IS NOT NUMERIC
158:            MOVE 1 TO WS-INVALID-RECORD-FLAG
159:            MOVE 1 TO WS-HOURS-NOT-NUMERIC
160:            MOVE '**' TO EG-HOURS
161:        ELSE
162:            IF SR-HOURS-NUMERIC IS GREATER THAN 27
163:                MOVE 1 TO WS-INVALID-RECORD-FLAG
164:                MOVE 1 TO WS-HOURS-OVER-27
165:                MOVE '**' TO EG-HOURS.
166:        IF SR-BOARD IS NOT EQUAL TO 'YES'
167:               AND SR-BOARD IS NOT EQUAL TO 'NO'
168:            MOVE 1 TO WS-INVALID-RECORD-FLAG
169:            MOVE 1 TO WS-VALIDATE-BOARD
170:            MOVE '***' TO EG-BOARD.
171:  *
172:    600-PREPARE-DETAIL-LINE.
173:        MOVE SR-NAME  TO DL-NAME.
174:        MOVE SR-STATE TO DL-STATE.
175:        MOVE SR-HOURS TO DL-HOURS.
176:        MOVE SR-BOARD TO DL-BOARD.
177:  *
178:    700-ERROR-HANDLE.
179:        WRITE PRINT-LINE FROM DETAIL-LINE AFTER        2 LINE.
180:        WRITE PRINT-LINE FROM ERROR-GRAPH-LINE AFTER   1 LINE.
181:        IF WS-VALIDATE-NAME = 1
182:            MOVE 'NAME NOT ALPHABETIC' TO EM-MESSAGE
183:            WRITE PRINT-LINE FROM ERROR-MESSAGE-LINE AFTER 1 LINE.
184:        IF WS-VALIDATE-STATE = 1
185:            MOVE 'STATE NOT ALPHABETIC' TO EM-MESSAGE
186:            WRITE PRINT-LINE FROM ERROR-MESSAGE-LINE AFTER 1 LINE.
187:        IF WS-HOURS-OVER-27 = 1
188:            MOVE 'CHECK NUMBER OF HOURS' TO EM-MESSAGE
189:            WRITE PRINT-LINE FROM ERROR-MESSAGE-LINE AFTER 1 LINE.
190:        IF WS-HOURS-NOT-NUMERIC = 1
191:            MOVE 'HOURS ARE NOT NUMERIC' TO EM-MESSAGE
192:            WRITE PRINT-LINE FROM ERROR-MESSAGE-LINE AFTER 1 LINE.
193:        IF WS-VALIDATE-BOARD = 1
194:            MOVE 'UNRECOGNIZABLE BOARD ENTRY' TO EM-MESSAGE
195:            WRITE PRINT-LINE FROM ERROR-MESSAGE-LINE AFTER 1 LINE.
196:  *
197:    800-COMPUTE-BILL.
198:        MOVE 60.00 TO WS-BILL.
199:  *
200:        IF SR-HOURS NOT LESS THAN 12
201:            IF SR-STATE = 'FL'
202:                MOVE 545.00 TO WS-CHARGE
203:            ELSE
204:                MOVE 1184.00 TO WS-CHARGE
205:        ELSE
206:            IF SR-STATE = 'FL'
207:                COMPUTE WS-CHARGE = SR-HOURS-NUMERIC * 44
208:            ELSE
209:                COMPUTE WS-CHARGE = SR-HOURS-NUMERIC * 94.
210:  *
211:        ADD WS-CHARGE TO WS-BILL.
212:        IF SR-BOARD = 'YES'
213:            ADD 425.00 TO WS-BILL.
214:        PERFORM 600-PREPARE-DETAIL-LINE.
215:        MOVE WS-BILL TO DL-BILL.
216:        WRITE PRINT-LINE FROM DETAIL-LINE AFTER 1 LINE.
```

SAMPLE OUTPUT

NAME	STATE	HOURS	BOARD	BILL
EDMUND	SC	10	YES	$1,425.00
LITTLE	SC	20	YES	$1,669.00
ZONE	SC	10	NO	$1,000.00
HUGHES	SC	20	NO	$1,244.00
DANGER	FL	09	YES	$ 881.00
RANT	FL	09	NO	$ 456.00
DOE	FL	15	YES	$1,030.00
MIGHT	FL	15	NO	$ 605.00

```
WONG      NY     15     NO
********
NAME NOT ALPHABETIC

LIU       V3     15     NO
          **
STATE NOT ALPHABETIC

JONES     NY     10     NO
                 **
HOURS ARE NOT NUMERIC

LONG      NY     29     YES
                 **
CHECK NUMBER OF HOURS

HOPE      NY     09     YEA
                        ***
UNRECOGNIZABLE BOARD ENTRY

LANC1     V3     10     NO
********  **     **     ***
NAME NOT ALPHABETIC
STATE NOT ALPHABETIC
HOURS ARE NOT NUMERIC
UNRECOGNIZABLE BOARD ENTRY

ABLE      NY     20     NO
                 **     ***
HOURS ARE NOT NUMERIC
UNRECOGNIZABLE BOARD ENTRY

LAMB      V3     15     NO
          **            ***
STATE NOT ALPHABETIC
UNRECOGNIZABLE BOARD ENTRY
```

FIGURE 6–16
(concluded)

Structured Charts

We can use the structured chart (diagram) shown in Figure 6–18 to better visualize and help clarify the various relationships between the paragraphs of the program in Figure 6–16. So far we have had little use for structured charts, since all our COBOL programs thus far have been relatively simple with fairly straightforward structures. This is not always the case, and structured charts have proved to be an invaluable tool in the overall design of more complex programs.

Recall that a structured chart is a visual description of the interrelationships between modules in a program. In essence, the program has been broken down into a set of small and manageable tasks or modules that are generally independent of one another except for the module coordinating or supervising the particular task in question. A structured diagram shows the hierarchy (channel-lines, lines of authority or command) among the program modules. These modules can then be coded and tested independently. Many people, however, find it difficult if not impossible to design a structured chart first and then write the corresponding code—to these people, the ideas, the logic, and the structure seem to come naturally as they write the code. Many times, however, the resulting code can be terrifyingly involved and unnecessarily complicated.

The ability to first draw structured charts and then write the corresponding code requires a great deal of experience and maturity of logic that many beginners do not possess. The most important rule is: DRAW A STRUCTURED CHART, even if you have already written the COBOL code. Drawing your chart will force you to better understand, assess, and criticize your program's logic, structure, and readability. Your diagram will also immediately reveal any structural flaws, and chances are you will want to make changes to your code. In addition, as you draw more structured diagrams, you will gain better insight into the process of thinking and writing structured code.

Each module in a structured design should be functional, i.e., each should have a clearly defined responsibility, a very specific objective that can be described succinctly. One way to ensure that a paragraph is functional is to express its paragraph name in such a way that its function can be described in a three-word sentence having the form:

VERB – ADJECTIVE – NOUN

for example, PRINT–ERROR–LINE, ASSIGN–WORD–CODES, UPDATE–MASTER–FILE, EDIT–TRANSACTION–FILE. If you cannot describe your paragraph's activities in this telegraphic style but need to say things like: ASSIGN WORD LABELS AND CHECK NUMERIC CODE or READ/VALIDATE/PRINT DATA, then chances are you can break down your procedure into more elementary functions.

In the structured diagram, the lines of communication between paragraphs should always be vertical. A paragraph should be controlled only by the paragraph directly above it. This characteristic implies and ensures paragraph independence. Lateral communications, as well as recursive communications, are not allowed.

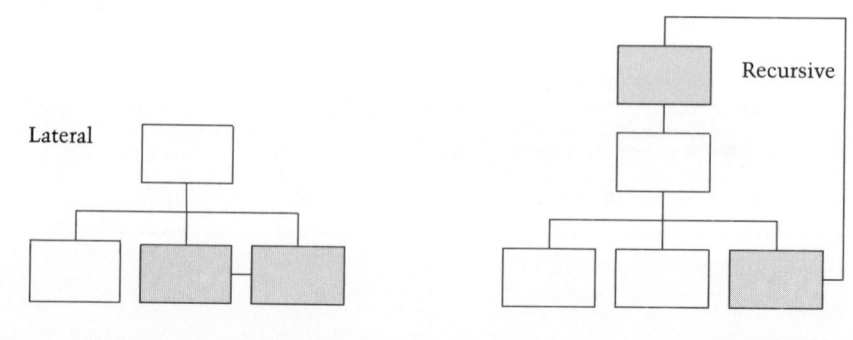

DECISION, ITERATION, PROGRAM DESIGN, DATA VALIDATION

```
*     The input validation process
*     Tasks to carry out when validating input data
*********************************************
*     Invalid-record-flag is turned on if any type of invalid data    *
*     is detected during the input screening phase.                   *
*********************************************
      read a record
      perform job until end of file
               .
               .
job.
      perform error-flag-initialization.
      perform input-data-validation.
      if invalid-record-flag = 1
            perform error-handle
      else
            perform process-record.
      read a record.

error-flag-initialization.
      set invalid-record-flag to 0.
      set all other input-field-error-flags to 0.

input-data-validation.
      test each input field for validity.
      if a field is invalid set the corresponding input-field-error-flag to 1
            and set invalid-record-flag to 1.

error-handle.
      interrogate each input-field-error-flag and
      carry out appropriate action (type error messages/invalid fields, et cetera)

process-record.
      all records treated in this paragraph are valid.
      process them according to statement of problem.
```

FIGURE 6–17
AN INPUT DATA VALIDATION MODEL

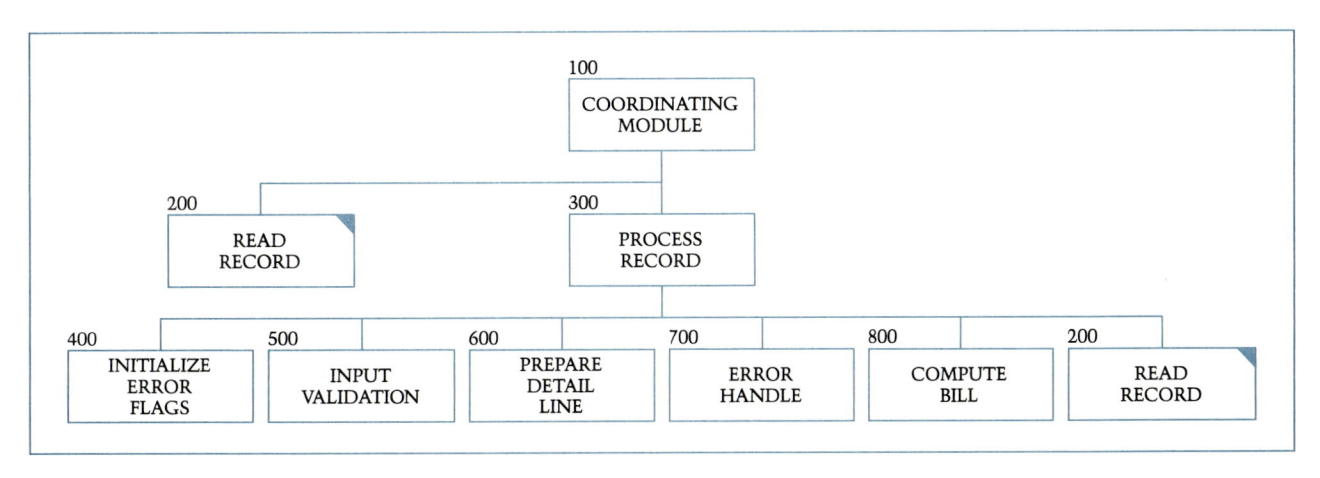

```
                          100
                   COORDINATING
                      MODULE
                   ┌──────┴──────┐
         200                          300
      READ                         PROCESS
     RECORD                         RECORD
                ┌────┬────┬────┬────┬────┐
      400      500     600     700    800     200
  INITIALIZE  INPUT  PREPARE  ERROR  COMPUTE  READ
    ERROR   VALIDATION DETAIL  HANDLE  BILL  RECORD
    FLAGS              LINE
```

FIGURE 6–18
A STRUCTURED CHART

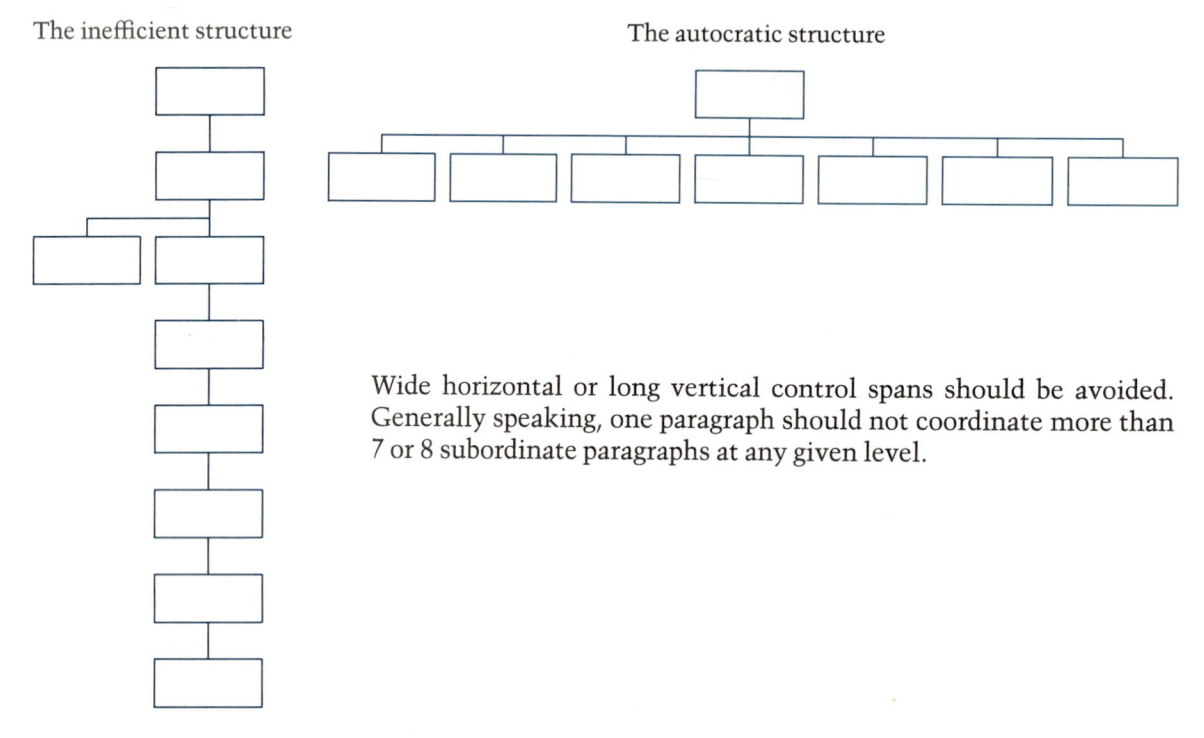

Recall that a well-designed chart should avoid the following types of structure:

The inefficient structure   The autocratic structure

Wide horizontal or long vertical control spans should be avoided. Generally speaking, one paragraph should not coordinate more than 7 or 8 subordinate paragraphs at any given level.

6-4-3 A SEQUENCE CHECK AND SEARCH FOR HIGHEST SCORE

Problem specification

Each record of an input file consists of a student name and a score. The records should already be in alphabetical order by name. Write a program to print the highest score in the input file.

The input data should be validated to identify names that are out of order, names that are not alphabetic, scores that are not numeric, and scores that exceed 100. Invalid scores and scores corresponding to invalid names should not participate in the search for the highest score.

The input and output should have the following forms:

OUTPUT

```
AMOS JOHN                        033
BOILLOT MARC  NOT ALPHABETIC     099
CULVER TIM                       097  ** SCORE NOT NUMERIC**
ARON JIMMY    OUT OF SEQUENCE    089
DILLARD JOE                      076
DOMIN CATHY                      123  *  SCORE IS OVER 100 *
NIELS JON     NOT ALPHABETIC      55  ** SCORE NOT NUMERIC**
NIELS KATE    NOT ALPHABETIC     970  *  SCORE IS OVER 100 *
FARR TED                         077
BAEZ KATE     OUT OF SEQUENCE    068  ** SCORE NOT NUMERIC**
CASSULO JOHN  OUT OF SEQUENCE    143  *  SCORE IS OVER 100 *
SARTRE PAUL                      046

LARGEST SCORE IS 77
```

INPUT FILE

```
1            13
AMOS JOHN    033
BOILLOT MARC 099
CULVER TIM   097
ARON JIMMY   089
DILLARD JOE  076
DOMIN CATHY  123
NIELS JON     55
NIELS KATE   970
FARR TED     077
BAEZ KATE    068
CASSULO JOHN 143
SARTRE PAUL  046
```

Name: positions 1–12
Score: positions 13–15

DECISION, ITERATION, PROGRAM DESIGN, DATA VALIDATION

Notice the various error combinations (eight in all) on the output. Note also that CASSULO is out of sequence even though it follows BAEZ—since BAEZ is out of sequence it cannot serve as a reference point for successive names. Names that are not alphabetic do not participate in the sequence check. The complete program to solve this problem is shown in Figure 6–19.

Program Analysis

Determining the highest score requires successively comparing each new score with the highest score found so far (WS–HIGHEST–SCORE, line 131). If the new score read is larger than WS–HIGHEST–SCORE, we replace WS–HIGHEST–SCORE with the new score. Otherwise we keep on reading scores until we find one that is larger than WS–HIGHEST–SCORE (if there is one). To start the comparison between the very first score and WS–HIGHEST–SCORE, we arbitrarily set WS–HIGHEST–SCORE to 0 (line 49). Then when we compare the first score to WS–HIGHEST–SCORE, the first score is larger than 0 and hence it is moved to WS–HIGHEST–SCORE.

Determining whether the names are in alphabetical order requires checking whether the name just read is larger than the previous name (statement 120 in Figure 6–19). To keep comparing consecutive names, we must remember (save) the name just read in order to compare it with the next name (statement 124). If the next name is less than the previous name, the next name is out of sequence, and an appropriate message is moved to the error line (line 121). Note that we do not want to compare the next name with its immediate predecessor if that predecessor is out of sequence—we want to compare it with the name that was last in sequence. In the input file, for example, we want to compare CASSULO with FARR, and not with BAEZ, since BAEZ is out of sequence. Therefore statement 124 must not be carried out if the next name is less than the previous name.

To start the comparison process between SR–NAME and WS–PREVIOUS–NAME at line 120, we arbitrarily set WS–PREVIOUS–NAME to the value AAA...A (line 50). This way, the first time line 120 is executed, WS–PREVIOUS–NAME will store the name read from the first record.

For input data validation we follow the outline in Figure 6–17, except that we do not need error flags for each field since only one type of error line needs to be printed.

Test Your Understanding of the Program

1. Instead of VALUE ALL 'A' at line 50, could we have used VALUE LOW–VALUES?

2. Could lines 95 and 96 be moved to lines 142 and 143 with the same results?

3. What change(s) would you make to the program to suppress leading 0's in the score field? (Do not suggest DL–SCORE PIC ZZ9 since the MOVE at line 140 would be invalid in the event SR–SCORE is nonnumeric.)

4. The highest score in the sample output is 77. Although 99 is really the highest score, it corresponds to an invalid name and therefore was not considered. Modify the code so that the highest score is printed regardless of the validity of the name.

```
 1:    IDENTIFICATION DIVISION.
 2:    PROGRAM-ID. STUDENT-REPORT.
 3:    AUTHOR. JONES
 4: ****************************************************************
 5:  *   OBJECTIVE:   GIVEN A CLASS ROSTER CONSISTING OF NAMES AND   *
 6:  *               SCORES, IDENTIFY NAMES NOT IN SEQUENCE AND      *
 7:  *               DETERMINE HIGHEST CLASS SCORE                   *
 8:  *                                                               *
 9:  *   INPUT:      STUDENT NAME AND SCORE                          *
10:  *                                                               *
11:  *   OUTPUT:     PRINT CLASS ROSTER AND HIGHEST SCORE. CAPTIONS  *
12:  *               IDENTIFY NAMES OUT OF ORDER & INVALID SCORES    *
13:  *                                                               *
14:  *   VALIDATION: NON-ALPHABETICAL NAMES; NON-NUMERIC SCORES;     *
15:  *               SCORES OVER 100; OUT OF SEQUENCE NAMES          *
16: ****************************************************************
17:    ENVIRONMENT DIVISION.
18:    CONFIGURATION SECTION.
19:    SOURCE-COMPUTER. IBM.
20:    OBJECT-COMPUTER. IBM.
21:    INPUT-OUTPUT SECTION.
22:    FILE-CONTROL.
23:        SELECT REPORT-FILE ASSIGN TO PRINTER.
24:        SELECT STUDENT-FILE ASSIGN TO DISK
25:        ORGANIZATION IS LINE SEQUENTIAL.
26:  *
27:    DATA DIVISION.
28:    FILE SECTION.
29:  *
30:    FD  STUDENT-FILE
31:        LABEL RECORDS ARE STANDARD
32:        VALUE OF FILE-ID IS 'ROSTER'
33:        DATA RECORD IS INPUT-RECORD.
34:    01  INPUT-RECORD PIC X(39).
35:    FD  REPORT-FILE
36:        LABEL RECORDS ARE OMITTED
37:        DATA RECORD IS PRINT-LINE.
38:    01  PRINT-LINE PIC X(132).
39:  *
40:    WORKING-STORAGE SECTION.
41:  *
42:  *    INDEPENDENT ITEMS
43:  *
44:    01  FLAGS.
45:        05  WS-END-FILE PIC XXX VALUE 'NO'.
46:        05  WS-INVALID-RECORD-FLAG PIC 9.
47:  *
48:    01  COMPUTATIONAL-ITEMS.
49:        05  WS-HIGHEST-SCORE PIC 999 VALUE 0.
50:        05  WS-PREVIOUS-NAME PIC X(12) VALUE ALL 'A'.
51:  *
52:  *    INPUT RECORD DESCRIPTION
53:  *
54:    01  STUDENT-RECORD.
55:        05  SR-NAME            PIC X(12).
56:        05  SR-SCORE           PIC 999.
57:  *
58:  *    OUTPUT LINE DESCRIPTIONS
59:  *
60:    01  DETAIL-LINE.
61:        05  FILLER             PIC X(05) VALUE SPACES.
62:        05  DL-NAME            PIC X(12).
63:        05  FILLER             PIC X(03) VALUE SPACES.
64:        05  DL-MESSAGE         PIC X(15).
65:        05  FILLER             PIC X(05) VALUE SPACES.
66:        05  DL-SCORE           PIC X(03)
67:        05  FILLER             PIC X(03) VALUE SPACES.
68:        05  DL-ERROR-MESSG     PIC X(23).
69:        05  FILLER             PIC X(05) VALUE SPACES.
70:  *
```

OUTPUT REPORT

```
AMOS JOHN                        033
BØILLOT MARC   NOT ALPHABETIC    099
CULVER TIM                       097  ** SCORE NOT NUMERIC**
ARON JIMMY     OUT OF SEQUENCE   089
DILLARD JOE                      076
DOMIN CATHY                      123  *  SCORE IS OVER 100 *
N1ELS JON      NOT ALPHABETIC     55  ** SCORE NOT NUMERIC**
N1ELS KATE     NOT ALPHABETIC    970  *  SCORE IS OVER 100 *
FARR TED                         077
BAEZ KATE      OUT OF SEQUENCE   068  ** SCORE NOT NUMERIC**
CASSULO JOHN   OUT OF SEQUENCE   143  *  SCORE IS OVER 100 *
SARTRE PAUL                      046

LARGEST SCORE IS 77
```

INPUT FILE

Name	Score
AMOS JOHN	033
BØILLOT MARC	099
CULVER TIM	097
ARON JIMMY	089
DILLARD JOE	076
DOMIN CATHY	123
NIELS JON	55
NIELS KATE	970
FARR TED	077
BAEZ KATE	068
CASSULO JOHN	143
SARTRE PAUL	046

FIGURE 6–19
A SEQUENCE CHECK AND SEARCH FOR HIGHEST SCORE

```
 72:   01  SUMMARY-LINE.
 73:       05  FILLER            PIC X(05) VALUE SPACES.
 74:       05  FILLER            PIC X(17) VALUE 'LARGEST SCORE IS'.
 76:       05  RL-HIGHEST-SCORE  PIC ZZ9.
 77:       05  FILLER            PIC X(108) VALUE SPACES.
 78:  *
 79:   PROCEDURE DIVISION.
 80:   100-COORDINATING-MODULE.
 81:       OPEN INPUT STUDENT-FILE
 82:            OUTPUT REPORT-FILE.
 83:       PERFORM 200-READ-RECORD.
 84:       PERFORM 300-PROCESS-RECORD
 85:           UNTIL WS-END-FILE = 1.
 86:       PERFORM 600-SUMMARY-TASKS.
 87:       CLOSE STUDENT-FILE, REPORT-FILE.
 88:       STOP RUN.
 89:  *
 90:   200-READ-RECORD.
 91:       READ STUDENT-FILE INTO STUDENT-RECORD
 92:           AT END MOVE 1 TO WS-END-FILE.
 93:  *
 94:   300-PROCESS-RECORD.
 95:       MOVE 0 TO WS-INVALID-RECORD-FLAG.
 96:       MOVE SPACES TO DETAIL-LINE.
 97:       PERFORM 400-INPUT-VALIDATION.
 98:       IF WS-INVALID-RECORD-FLAG = 0
 99:           PERFORM 500-PROCESS-STUDENT
100:       ELSE
101:           PERFORM 700-WRITE-LINE.
102:       PERFORM 200-READ-RECORD.
103:  *
104:   400-INPUT-VALIDATION.
105:       IF SR-SCORE IS NOT NUMERIC
106:           MOVE '** SCORE NOT NUMERIC**' TO DL-ERROR-MESSG
107:           MOVE 1 TO WS-INVALID-RECORD-FLAG
108:       ELSE
109:           IF SR-SCORE IS GREATER THAN 100
110:           MOVE '*  SCORE IS OVER 100 *'   TO DL-ERROR-MESSG
111:           MOVE 1 TO WS-INVALID-RECORD FLAG.
112:  *
113:       IF SR-NAME IS NOT ALPHABETIC
114:           MOVE 'NOT ALPHABETIC '          TO DL-MESSAGE
115:           MOVE 1 TO WS-INVALID-RECORD-FLAG
116:  *
117:  * DETERMINE IF NAME READ IS IN ALPHABETICAL SEQUENCE
118:  *
119:       ELSE
120:           IF SR-NAME IS LESS THAN WS-PREVIOUS-NAME
121:               MOVE 'OUT OF SEQUENCE'      TO DL-MESSAGE
122:               MOVE 1 TO WS-INVALID-RECORD-FLAG
123:           ELSE
124:               MOVE SR-NAME TO WS-PREVIOUS-NAME.
125:  *
126:   500-PROCESS-STUDENT.
127:  *
128:  * DETERMINE IF SCORE READ IS CURRENT HIGHEST SCORE
129:  *
130:       PERFORM 700-WRITE-LINE.
131:       IF SR-SCORE IS GREATER THAN WS-HIGHEST-SCORE
132:           MOVE SR-SCORE TO WS-HIGHEST-SCORE.
133:  *
134:   600-SUMMARY-TASKS.
135:       MOVE WS-HIGHEST-SCORE TO RL-HIGHEST-SCORE.
136:       WRITE PRINT-LINE FROM SUMMARY-LINE AFTER ADVANCING 2 LINES.
137:  *
138:   700-WRITE-LINE.
139:       MOVE SR-NAME  TO DL-NAME.
140:       MOVE SR-SCORE TO DL-SCORE.
141:       WRITE PRINT-LINE FROM DETAIL-LINE AFTER ADVANCING 1 LINE.
```

FIGURE 6–19
(continued)

6-5 YOU MIGHT WANT TO KNOW

1. What is the collation sequence for alphanumeric characters?

   Answer: There are two codes for internal representation of characters. The ASCII (pronounced ask-ee) and EBCDIC (pronounced ebb-si-dic) code.

   The EBCDIC code (Extended Binary Coded Decimal Interchange Code) is a code where each character is represented internally using 8 bits; for example, the character A is C1 in hexadecimal or 11000001 in binary. The EBCDIC code is used by such computers as IBM, Digital PDP–11 series, and Amdahl (large main-frame computers).

   The ASCII code (American Standard Code for Information Interchange) is a 7-bit code used by large computers and by most of the microcomputers including IBM.

   The collating sequence for the two codes is shown as follows:

ASCII CODE			EBCDIC CODE		
CHARACTER	DECIMAL	HEX	CHARACTER	DECIMAL	HEX
space	32	20	space	64	40
!	33	21	.	75	4B
"	34	22	<	76	4C
#	35	23	(	77	4D
$	36	24	+	78	4E
%	37	25	!	79	4F
&	38	26	&	80	50
single quote	39	27	$	91	5B
(	40	28	*	92	5C
)	41	29	)	93	5D
*	42	2A	;	94	5E
+	43	2B	minus −	96	60
comma	44	2C	/	97	61
−	45	2D	comma	107	6B
.	46	2E	%	108	6C
/	47	2F	>	110	6E
0	48	30	?	111	6F
⋮	⋮	⋮	⋮	122	7A
9	57	39	#	123	7B
:	58	3A	@	124	7C
;	59	3B	single quote	125	7D
<	60	3C	=	126	7E
=	61	3D	"	127	7F
>	62	3E	a	129	81
?	63	3F	b	130	82
@	64	40	⋮	⋮	⋮
A	65	41	z	169	A9
⋮	⋮	⋮	A	193	C1
Z	90	5A	⋮	⋮	⋮
a	97	61	Z	233	E9
⋮	⋮	⋮	0	240	F0
z	122	7A	⋮	⋮	⋮
			9	249	F9

Thus in EBCDIC the following is true:
special characters < letter of alphabet < digits 0–9

DECISION, ITERATION, PROGRAM DESIGN, DATA VALIDATION

2. What types of comparisons can be made between data types? For example, can I compare an alphanumeric item with a numeric item?

   Answer: Valid cross-comparisons between data types are shown in the following table. Except when comparing two numeric operands, comparisons are performed one character at a time according to the collating sequences illustrated in the tables of question 1. If a numeric data item is compared to a nonnumeric data item, the nonnumeric operand is treated as an alphanumeric field (some compilers allow such comparisons to take place only if the numeric data item has an integer value).

	Numeric (data names)	Alphabetic (data names)	Alphanumeric (data names)	Literal numeric	Literal nonnumeric
Numeric data names	Valid	Valid	Valid	Valid	Valid
Alphabetic data names	Valid	Valid	Valid	Valid	Valid
Alphanumeric data names	Valid	Valid	Valid	Valid	Valid
Literal numeric	Valid	Valid	Valid	Invalid	Invalid
Literal nonnumeric	Valid	Valid	Valid	Invalid	Invalid

3. Can I write compound conditions as follows?

   ```
   IF A EQUAL TO B OR GREATER THAN C     to mean A = B or A > C (Yes)
   IF A GREATER THAN B AND C             to mean A > B and A > C (Yes)
   ```

   Answer: To discuss the conditions under which these are permissible, recall the terminology for a compound condition:

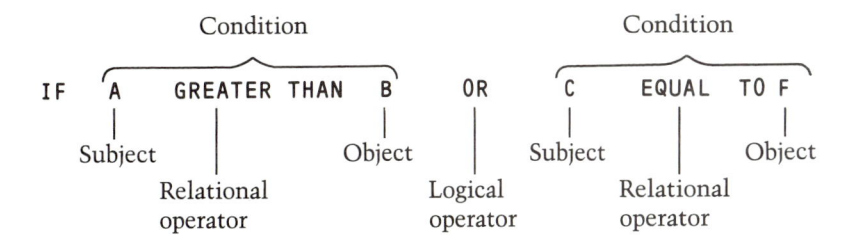

   ```
   IF   A   GREATER THAN   B    OR    C   EQUAL TO   F
        |        |         |    |     |       |      |
     Subject     |       Object  |  Subject    |    Object
             Relational       Logical       Relational
             operator         operator      operator
   ```

   Condition ... Condition

   Omission of The Subject When It Is Implied. The subject may be implied in a simple condition within a compound condition.

   Example:

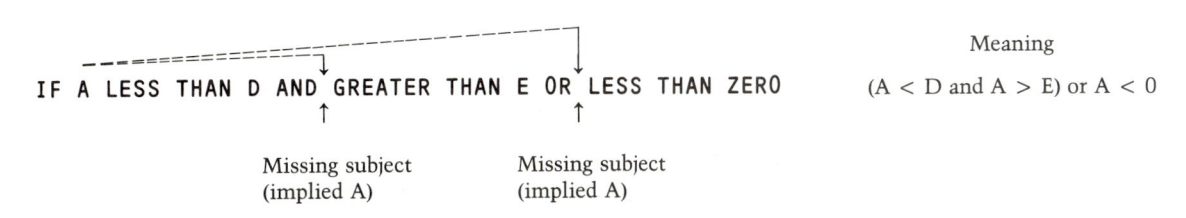

   ```
   IF A LESS THAN D AND GREATER THAN E OR LESS THAN ZERO
                         ↑                 ↑
                    Missing subject    Missing subject
                    (implied A)        (implied A)
   ```

   Meaning: (A < D and A > E) or A < 0

The implied subject is A. Neither D nor E could be subjects since they are themselves objects. Subjects can be implied in a sequence of compound conditions. In that case the implied subject is the closest explicitly stated subject to the left of the implied condition.

Example:

```
IF X = Y AND = Z   OR   W = Z AND = A
```
    Implied subject X   Implied subject W

Closest explicitly stated subject to the left of implied subject

Meaning

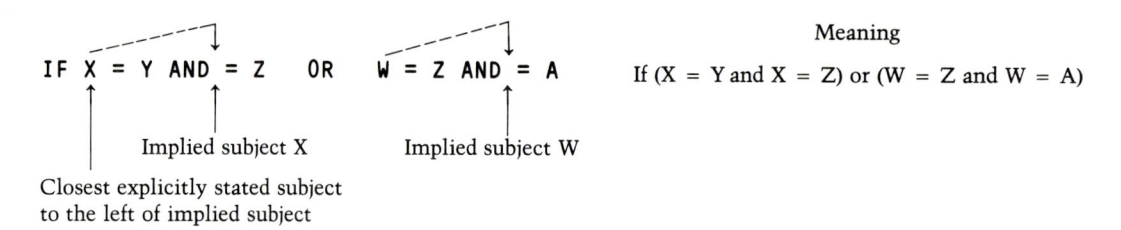

If (X = Y and X = Z) or (W = Z and W = A)

When NOT is used with a relational operator and an implied subject, the NOT is treated as a logical operator.

Example:

```
IF SALES IS LESS THAN 200 OR NOT LESS THAN 5000
```
          Implied subject SALES

Meaning

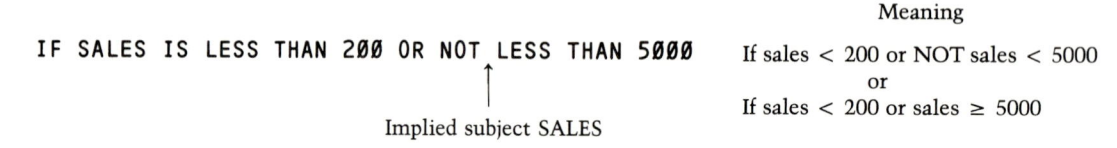

If sales < 200 or NOT sales < 5000
or
If sales < 200 or sales ≥ 5000

In the case of implied subjects, the sequence of operands is as follows:

$$\text{Subject relational-operator object} \begin{Bmatrix} \underline{AND} \\ \underline{OR} \end{Bmatrix} [\underline{NOT}] \text{ relational-operator object...}$$

Implied Subjects and Implied Relational Operators. The subject, as well the relational operator can be implied. The sequence of operands is then:

$$\text{Subject relational-operator object} \begin{Bmatrix} \underline{AND} \\ \underline{OR} \end{Bmatrix} [\underline{NOT}] \text{ object...}$$

Examples

                   Meaning

1. `IF A = B OR C ...`   If A = B or A = C
2. `IF HRS NOT = 40 AND 50 ...` IF HRS ≠ 40 and HRS ≠ 50
3. `IF X NOT = Y AND NOT Z ...` IF X ≠ Y and NOT (X ≠ Z)
4. `IF A LESS THAN B OR C AND D ...` IF A < B or (A < C and A < D)

5. IF COD1 + COD2 EQUAL TO 3 OR 2 * (COD1 + COD2) AND 4

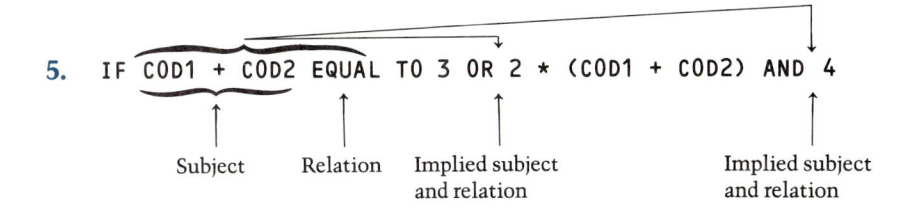

      Subject   Relation   Implied subject   Implied subject
                         and relation   and relation

The implied subject COD1 + COD2 and relation (equal to) are provided appropriately so as to form the sentence:

```
IF (COD1 + COD2) = 3 OR [(COD1 + COD2) = 2 * (COD1 + COD2)
                        AND (COD1 + COD2) = 4]
```

As a general rule, implied subjects and relational operators do not improve program readability and may even confuse a reader not well versed in the rules. It is recommended that subjects and relational operators be specified explicitly. It may take a little longer to code, but it may save time in the long run.

6-6 EXERCISES

6-6-1 TEST YOURSELF

1. Are the following valid or invalid? Specify reasons if invalid.

   a. IF ADR = "17 N. 17 ST"
       MOVE ADR TO 2-ST.
     ELSE SUBTRACT 1 FROM X.
   b. IF H > 40 NEXT SENTENCE.
   c. IF A IS NOT ZERO PERFORM Z.
   d. IF NT IS > THAN L
      ADD 1 TO K.
   e. IF TEMP < 0 NEXT SENTENCE
      ADD 1 TO TEMP-1.
   f. IF X = 4
      IF Y NOT LESS THAN 3
      ELSE MOVE 1 TO X.
   g. IF X NOT 0 ADD 1 TO Z.
   h. IF K = SPACES MOVE A TO B.
   i. IF ALL "1" = ONES MOVE X TO A.
   j. IF X + 1 EQUALS 3 ADD 1 TO Z.
   k. IF L - 1. > 1 - K PERFORM P-1.
   l. IF 13.4 / .005 NOT = TO X ADD 1 TO F.
   m. IF "HUGHES" IS NOT LESS THAN HUGHES...
   n. IF X NOT = 13.4 / .005...
   o. IF P = 3 AND J IS LESS THAN 4 MOVE 3 TO X.
   p. IF L = "HOUSE" OR X NOT EQUAL TO 0 MOVE 1 TO Z.
   q. IF M = 2 OR J + 1 NOT GREATER X + Y - Z
      MOVE 1 TO X.
   r. IF TEMP > "PARTY" OR TEMP IS NOT = 4.5...

2. Which of the following pairs have identical meaning?

   a. IF FLD1 = +123...
      IF FLD1 = 0123...
      IF FLD1 = 123.0...

   b. IF NOT A NOT < ZERO...
      IF A < 0...

   c. IF NOT A LESS THAN B...
      IF A > B...

   d. IF A NOT = B...
      IF NOT (A = B)...

   e. IF HRS > 40 AND RATE NOT < 4.50...
      IF NOT (RATE < 4.50 OR HRS NOT > 40)

3. Are the following valid or invalid? Specify reasons if invalid.

   a. IF A GREATER THAN B OR NOT C...
   b. IF NOT (A NOT < C)...
   c. IF Z GREATER OR = L...
   d. IF X > Y OR C NOT > X...
   e. IF HRS > 30 AND NOT C NOT < B...
   f. IF NOT X = 3 AND NOT Y = 4...
   g. IF NOT 1 OR NOT 2...
   h. IF K IS NOT 1 OR 2...
   i. IF A = B OR C OR D OR E...
   j. IF X OR Y OR Z PERFORM QUERY...
   k. IF A = NOT B OR C...
   l. IF NOT (A + 4.1) > Z-HOUSE...
   m. IF A = B AND NOT C > B...
   n. IF L NOT = 1 OR 2...
   o. IF H NOT < 40 OR NOT 80...

4. Which of the following pairs of coding segments are equivalent?

   a.
   ```
   IF EARNING > 40000                    IF EARNING > 40000
       MOVE "CLASS-1" TO CATALOG-FLD         MOVE "CLASS-1" TO CATALOG-FLD
   IF SEX-CODE = MALE                    IF SEX-CODE = MALE
       MOVE "MALE" TO SEX-FLD                MOVE "MALE" TO SEX-FLD
       WRITE PR-LINE FROM EARN-LINE      ELSE
   ELSE                                      MOVE "FEMALE" TO SEX-FLD.
       MOVE "FEMALE" TO SEX-FLD          WRITE PR-LINE FROM EARN-LINE.
       WRITE PR-LINE FROM EARN-LINE.
   ```

   b.
   ```
   IF X = 1                   IF X = 1
       MOVE X TO A.               MOVE X TO A
   IF X = 2                   ELSE
       MOVE X TO B.               IF X = 2
                                      MOVE X TO B.
   ```

   c.
   ```
   IF X > 1                   IF X > 1
       ADD 1 TO A                 ADD 1 TO 1.
   ELSE                       IF X > 2
       IF X > 2                   ADD 1 TO C.
           ADD 1 TO C.
   ```

   d.
   ```
   IF KODE = 1                IF KODE = 1
       MOVE A TO B                MOVE A TO B
   IF KODE = 2                ELSE IF KODE = 2
       MOVE C TO D.               MOVE C TO D.
   ```

DECISION, ITERATION, PROGRAM DESIGN, DATA VALIDATION   271

In parts e through i assume K may take on values 1, 2, or 3.

e. IF K NOT = 1   IF K = 2
        MOVE K TO A.   IF K = 3
                                                  MOVE K TO A.

f. IF K NOT = 1   IF K = 1   IF K = 2 OR K = 3
        MOVE K TO A   MOVE K TO B   MOVE K TO A
    IF K NOT = 2   ELSE   ELSE
        MOVE K TO B.   MOVE K TO A.   MOVE K TO B.

g. IF K NOT = 1   IF K NOT = 2
        MOVE K TO A.   MOVE K TO B.
    IF K NOT = 2   IF K NOT = 1
        MOVE K TO B.   MOVE K TO A.

h. IF K = 1   IF K NOT = 1
        ADD 1 TO A   IF K NOT = 2
    ELSE   ADD 1 TO C
        IF K = 2   ELSE
            ADD 1 TO B   ADD 1 TO B
        ELSE   ELSE
            ADD 1 TO C.   ADD 1 TO A.

i. IF K > 1   IF K NOT > 1
        ADD 1 TO A   IF K NOT > 2
    ELSE   ADD 1 TO C
        IF K > 2   ELSE
            ADD 1 TO B   ADD 1 TO B
        ELSE   ELSE
            ADD 1 TO C.   ADD 1 TO A.

5. In each of the following cases specify the value(s) for K that will cause A to be moved to any of the locations B, C, D, E, or F. Assume K can take on any integer values between 1 and 6.

a. 10 IF K = 1   b. 10 IF K = 1 MOVE A TO B.
    20   MOVE A TO B   20 IF K = 2 MOVE A TO C.
    30 ELSE   30 IF K = 3 MOVE A TO D.
    40 IF K NOT = 2   40 IF K = 4 MOVE A TO E
    50 IF K = 3   50 ELSE   MOVE A TO F.
    60   MOVE A TO C
    70 ELSE
    80 IF K NOT = 4
    90   MOVE A TO D
    95 ELSE
    97   MOVE A TO E
    98 ELSE
    99   MOVE A TO F.

c. 10 IF K = 1 MOVE A TO B IF K = 2 MOVE A TO C
    20 IF K = 3 MOVE A TO D IF K = 4 MOVE A TO E
    30 ELSE   MOVE A TO F.

d. 10 IF K = 1 MOVE A TO B IF K = 2 MOVE A TO C.
    15 IF K = 3 MOVE A TO D IF K = 4 MOVE A TO E
    20 ELSE MOVE A TO F.

6. Given the code on the right,

   a. What statements are executed after line 25 if X = 2?
   b. What statements are executed starting at line 35 if X = 3?
   c. What statements are executed starting at line 35 if X ≠ 3?

```
10 IF X > 1
20   ADD 1 TO A
25   IF X = 2
30     NEXT SENTENCE
35   ELSE IF X = 3
40     IF X = 4
45       NEXT SENTENCE
50     ELSE ADD 1 TO X
55   ELSE
60     NEXT SENTENCE
65     ADD 1 TO Y
70 ELSE ADD 1 TO Z.
75 ADD 1 TO T.
```

Given the code on the right and assuming that K can take on values 1, 2, 3, 4 or 5:

   d. For what values of K will line 92 be carried out?
   e. For what values of K will line 88 be carried out?

```
80 IF K = 1
81   NEXT SENTENCE
82 ELSE
83   IF K NOT = 2
84     IF K = 3
85       NEXT SENTENCE
86     ELSE
87       IF K NOT EQUAL 4
88         MOVE "ERROR" TO LINE1
89       ELSE
90         NEXT SENTENCE
91   ELSE
92     MOVE "SOPH" TO LINE1.
93 MOVE Z TO D.
```

7. Which of the following coding segments accomplish the same objective as the flowchart?

a.
```
IF SEX = 1
    IF TYPE = 2
        MOVE "N" TO OUT
    ELSE
        MOVE "Y" TO OUT
WRITE OUTPUT-LINE
MOVE Z TO X.
```

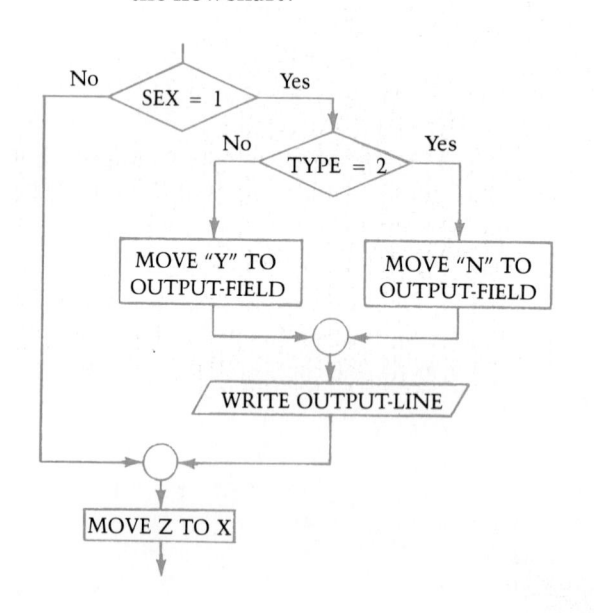

b.
```
IF SEX = 1
    IF TYPE = 2
        MOVE "N" TO OUT
        WRITE OUTPUT-LINE
    ELSE
        MOVE "Y" TO OUT
        WRITE OUTPUT-LINE.
MOVE Z TO X.
```

c.
```
IF SEX = 1
    IF TYPE = 2
        MOVE "N" TO OUT
    ELSE
        MOVE "Y" TO OUT.
    WRITE OUTPUT-LINE.
MOVE Z TO X.
```

d.
```
IF SEX = 1
    MOVE "Y" TO OUT
    IF TYPE = 2
        MOVE "N" TO OUT
WRITE OUTPUT-LINE.
MOVE Z TO X.
```

8. Write the code for the following flowcharts; eliminate any redundancy.

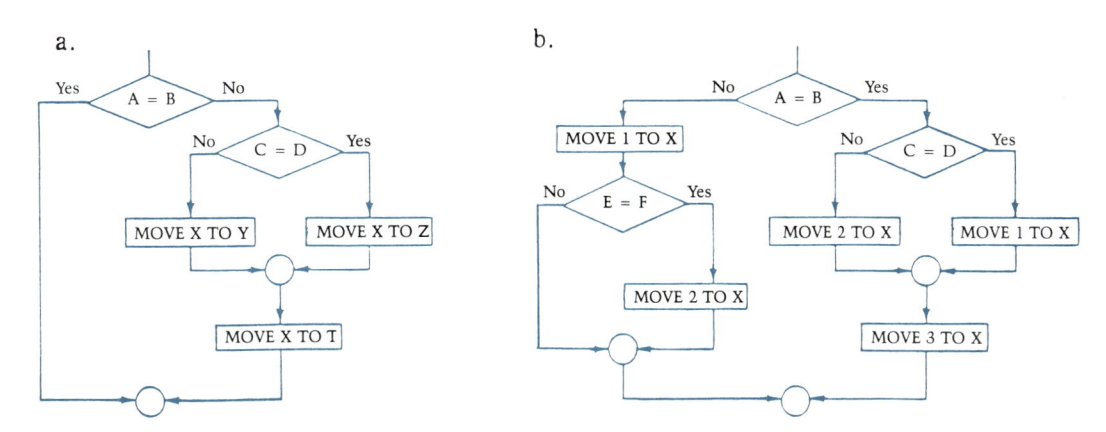

a.

b.

9. Without using compound conditions, translate the following into a sequence of IF statements. If the condition is true, PERFORM TRUE; otherwise PERFORM FALSE:

   a. IF HOURS = 40 OR SEX = 2 OR STAT = 3...
   b. IF HOURS = 40 AND SEX = 2 AND STAT = 3...
   c. IF NAME = "FONDA" OR SEX = 1 AND STAT = 3...
   d. IF NOT (HOURS < 40) AND NOT SEX = 1 OR STAT = 3...
   e. IF NOT (HOURS = 40 OR SEX = 2 OR STAT NOT = 3)...

10. Are the following statements true or false?

    a. The nonnumeric constant "8199" is greater than the constant "10845" when compared together.
    b. The opposite of IF FLAG NOT > 1 is IF NOT FLAG NOT > 1.
    c. The entry 77 EOF PIC 9 can be expressed as 01 EOF PIC 9.
    d. The statement NEXT SENTENCE in a multilevel IF sentence means that control will be transferred to the sentence following the first period encountered.
    e. The following sentence is syntactically correct:
       IF X = 1 ADD 1 TO A, IF Y = 3 ADD 1 TO B.
    f. The following sentence is syntactically incorrect:
       IF X = 1 MOVE A TO B IF Y = 2 MOVE C TO D ELSE STOP RUN.
    g. The following two conditions are identical in terms of outcome:
       1. HRS > 40 AND RATE = 4.6 OR HRS > 40   2. HRS > 40

11. Specify the condition under which the statement at line 50 will be executed.

    ```
    10 READ TIME-FILE AT END
    20                MOVE "ERROR" TO ERR-LIN
    30                WRITE PRINT-LIN FROM ERR-LIN
    40 MOVE AMT-IN TO AMT
    50 WRITE PRINT-LINE FROM DETAIL-LINE.
    ```

12. Rewrite the following without parentheses:

    a. X = 3 OR (A < B AND C = 2)
    b. NOT (A = 0 OR NOT B < 3)
    c. B = 0 AND (A > 3 OR Z = 2)

13. Complete the condition so that exactly 6 data records will be read.
- a. MOVE -1 TO I
        PERFORM PARA UNTIL I _____
        .
     PARA.
        READ TIME-FILE AT END...
        ADD -1 TO I.
- b. MOVE 7 TO I.
        PERFORM PARA UNTIL I _____
        .
     PARA.
        READ TIME-FILE...
        SUBTRACT 1 FROM I.
- c. MOVE 1 TO I.
        PERFORM PARA UNTIL I _____
        .
     PARA.
        READ TIME-FILE...
        ADD .5 TO I.
- d. MOVE 0 TO I.
        PERFORM PARA UNTIL I _____
        .
     PARA.
        ADD 1 TO I.
        READ TIME-FILE...

14. An input file contains an unknown number of records; each record contains a grade. Which of the following coding segments will compute the grade average AVG? Assume AVG-OUT is part of the detail line.

- a. MOVE 0 TO X, SUN, EOF.
        PERFORM AVE UNTIL EOF = 1.
        MOVE AVG TO AVG-OUT...
        .
     AVE.
        READ GRADE-FILE AT END MOVE 1 TO EOF.
        IF EOF = 0
           ADD 1 TO X.
           ADD GRADE TO SUN.
           COMPUTE AVG = SUN / X.

- b. MOVE 0 TO X, SUN, EOF.
        READ GRADE-FILE AT END MOVE 1 TO EOF.
        PERFORM AVE UNTIL EOF = 1.
        COMPUTE AVG = SUN / (X + 1).
        MOVE AVG TO AVG-OUT...

     AVE.
        ADD GRADE TO SUN.
        READ GRADE-FILE AT END MOVE 1 TO EOF.
        ADD 1 TO X.

15. Write out a program to print out multiplication tables from 2 to 12 as follows:

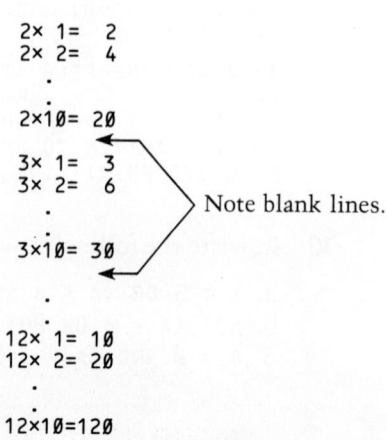

```
2× 1=  2
2× 2=  4
  .
  .
2×10= 20

3× 1=  3
3× 2=  6       ⎫
  .            ⎬ Note blank lines.
  .            ⎭
3×10= 30

  .
  .
12× 1= 10
12× 2= 20
  .
  .
12×10=120
```

16. Each record of an input file contains the following data:

    Employee number

    Employee's yearly base pay

    Employment duration (expressed in years)

    Employee classification: 1 – Hourly 2 – Salaried

    Rating: 1 – Satisfactory 2 – Unsatisfactory

    The policy for determining employee Christmas bonuses at Santa–Claus Inc. is as follows:

    Employees must have been employed with the company at least six months.

    Employees with a satisfactory rating are paid one week's pay for hourly employees, or 20% of monthly pay for salaried employees. If the rating is unsatisfactory, one day's pay will be paid to hourly employees and 5% of monthly pay to salaried employees.

    Employees with more than 10 years of service and a satisfactory rating receive an additional bonus of $400.

    Write the code to compute the bonus.

17. If a year is divisible by 4, it is a leap year, with one exception: years divisible by 100 are not leap years unless they are divisible by 400, in which case they are leap years. Thus 1900 is not a leap year (divisible by 100), but 2000 is a leap year (divisible by 400).
    Write the code to determine whether a year is a leap year.

18. Each record of an input file contains the name of a city and its record high temperature for a year. Cities have been sorted by ascending temperature order. Write the code to print the name of the first city with a temperature of 100 degrees or above. Flush out all remaining input records, if any, i.e., read remaining records, but do not process them.

19. Write the coding segment to generate the following sequences of numbers:

    a. 2, 4, 6, 8, ..., 100
    b. 7.5, 9.5, 11.5, ..., 101.5
    c. 1, 9, 25, 49, ..., 289
    d. 1, 1, 2, 3, 5, 8, 13, 21, ... up to the first 20 terms.
    e. 1, – 1, 1, – 1, ... for the first 20 terms.
    f. – 17, – 15, – 13, ... – 1
    g. 1, 1/2, 1/3, 1/4, ... 1/100

20. Each record of an input file contains a number. Write the code to read the input file and print all the input data up to and including the first number whose sign is different from the preceding ones. For example:

    3, 4, – 3, 2, – 1, . . . would list 3, 4 and – 3.
    – 2, 1, – 3, . . .   would list – 2 and 1.
    1, 2, 3, 4, 5   would list 1, 2, 3, 4 and 5.

21. Each record of an input file contains a dollar amount (PIC 99999). Write the code to read each amount, and print a special message if all dollar amounts read exceed $10,000; otherwise finish reading the input file and *then* perform paragraph COMPUTE–PROCESS.

22. Personpower Inc. needs to find in a hurry the telephone number of the first individual in their personnel file satisfying the following characteristics:

   Male, between 20 and 40, with either 2 years of college or a certificate degree.

   Write the code to print either the telephone number of the individual or a message specifying that no one meets the description. A typical personnel file record is shown below:

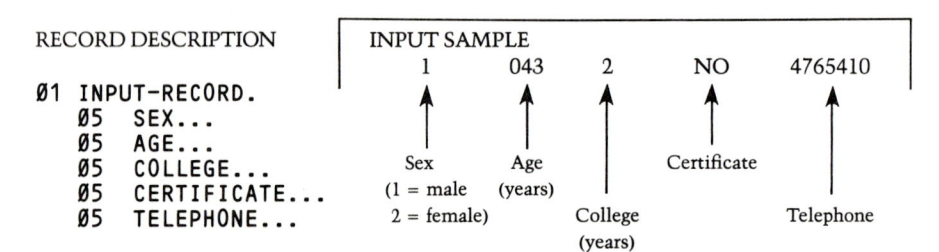

   RECORD DESCRIPTION

   ```
   01 INPUT-RECORD.
       05 SEX...
       05 AGE...
       05 COLLEGE...
       05 CERTIFICATE...
       05 TELEPHONE...
   ```

   INPUT SAMPLE

   ```
   1    043    2    NO    4765410
   ```

   Sex (1 = male, 2 = female), Age (years), College (years), Certificate, Telephone

6-6-2 Programming Exercises

1. Using the screen format discussed in chapter 5, write a screen menu to allow you to select particular colors for the background and foreground of your screen. You can then use your text editor to type your COBOL programs using the colors selected.

2. A student in DP101 has her account number in record positions 1–4 and three tests scores record positions 11–19. The student's average is based on her two best scores. Starting on a new page, print the student's account number and her average on one line and the three test scores on another line (double-space) as follows:

   ```
   ACCT NUMBER: 2136 AVERAGE = 88.5

   TESTS 62 100 77
   ```
   ← Note blank line.

3. In a physical education class, students get either a pass or a fail for the course. If the average of the student's three test scores is below 70, the student fails the course. Examples of the input and output are shown below. Write a program to produce the following output:

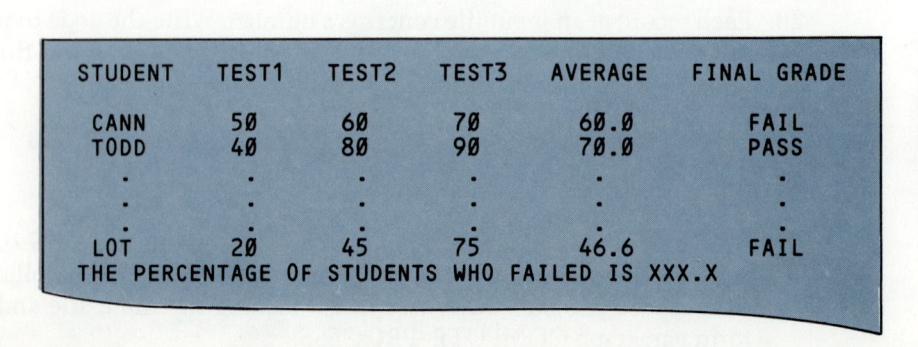

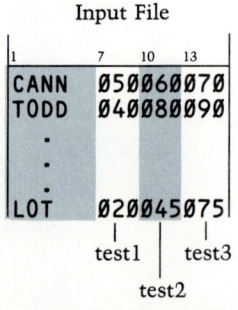

   ```
   STUDENT   TEST1   TEST2   TEST3   AVERAGE   FINAL GRADE

   CANN      50      60      70      60.0      FAIL
   TODD      40      80      90      70.0      PASS
     .        .       .       .        .         .
     .        .       .       .        .         .
     .        .       .       .        .         .
   LOT       20      45      75      46.6      FAIL
   THE PERCENTAGE OF STUDENTS WHO FAILED IS XXX.X
   ```

   Input File
   ```
   1      7  10 13
   CANN   050060070
   TODD   040080090
     .
     .
     .
   LOT    020045075
   ```
   test1, test2, test3

4. The FHA insures home mortgages up to $60,000. The down payment schedule is as follows:

   a. Three precent of the amount up to $25,000.
   b. Ten percent of the next $10,000.
   c. Twenty percent of the remainder.

   Each record in the input file contains a social security number and a mortgage amount. Write a program to calculate the down payment required. The output should contain the applicant's social security number and the down payment. Reject any application over $60,000 and indicate this on the output.

5. Mrs. Spander is spending her money faster than she earns it. She has now decided to keep track of all her expenses. For every purchase or expense, she enters on her home computer the expense description, the amount, and an expense category code (1 = household, 2 = medical, 3 = recreation, 4 = utilities). Then every Sunday night she runs her budget program to obtain the following analysis:

```
                    BUDGET ANALYSIS

              HOUSEHOLD    MEDICAL    RECREATION   UTILITY
              EXPENSES     EXPENSES   EXPENSES     BILLS

   PLANTS       12.33
   MOVIES                              6.50
   MORTGAGE    389.75
   DENTIST                 154.25
   GAS                                              99.66
   VACATION                            1156.56

   SUBTOTALS   402.08      154.25      1163.06      99.66

       TOTAL EXPENSES      $1819.05
```

Write a program to produce this output, given the following input:

RECORD POSITION	MEANING
1–12	Expense description
13–18	Amount (PIC 9999V99)
19	Category code
	1-Household 3-Recreation
	2-Medical 4-Utility

```
INPUT
1            13     19
PLANTS       001233 1
MOVIES       000650 3
MORTGAGE    0389751
DENTIST      0154252
GAS          0099664
VACATION     1156563
```

6. Each data record in a file contains two items: an age and a code for marital status (1 = single, 2 = married, 3 = divorced, and 4 = widowed). Write a program to compute and print:

   a. The percentage of people over 30 years of age.
   b. The number of people who are either widowed or divorced.
   c. The number of people who are over 50 or less than 30 and who are not married.

   Don't forget to print all the input data, and validate the input data.

7. An IRS agent is checking taxpayers' returns in the $20,000 to $30,000 income bracket (gross earnings). Each record of the returns file contains a social security number, gross earnings, and an amount of tax paid. If taxes paid are below 18.5% of gross earnings, compute tax due (assume all taxes in that bracket are 18.5% of gross). If the amount due is above $1,400, add a penalty charge of 1.5% of the amount due. Take care of refunds if necessary. Records of gross earnings outside the interval $20,000 to $30,000 are not to be checked. Print appropriate messages with the results.

8. Drs. Smith and Jones both teach principles of management. Information about students enrolled in the course is recorded as follows:

RECORD POSITIONS	MEANING	SECTION	TEACHER	TIME
1–6	Student ID	1	Smith	Day
10	Course Section (1–4)	2	Smith	Night
15–17	Grade point average 0.0–4.0	3	Jones	Day
20	Type code 1 = part-time, 2 = full-time	4	Jones	Night

Write a program to compute and print:

   a. The percentage of students who are part-time.
   b. The total number of students in Dr. Smith's sections.
   c. A list of the ID numbers of students enrolled in night classes.
   d. The number of day students having a GPA of 2.0 or higher.
   e. The name of the teacher in whose class the highest GPA is found.

9. Employees at Sarah's Style Shop are to receive a year-end bonus. The amount of the bonus depends on the employee's weekly pay, position code, and number of years with the store. Each employee is assigned a bonus based on the following rules:

POSITION CODE	BONUS
1	One week's pay
2	Two weeks' pay; maximum of $700
3	One and a half week's pay

Employees with more than 10 years' experience are to receive $100 in addition to their bonus and employees with less than 2 years' experience are to receive half the bonus derived from the above table.

Write a program to read an employee number, a weekly pay, a position code, and a number of years, then compute and print the employee's bonus. The input and output should be similar to the following:

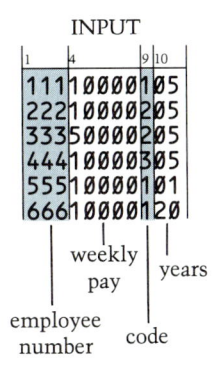

DECISION, ITERATION, PROGRAM DESIGN, DATA VALIDATION   279

```
            INPUT                                OUTPUT
     1    4    9 10
     111 10000 1 05                     EMPLOYEE      BONUS
     222 10000 2 05                     NUMBER
     333 50000 2 05
     444 10000 3 05                        111        100.00
     555 10000 1 01                        222        200.00
     666 10000 1 20                        333        700.00
           |       |                        444        150.00
        weekly   years                      555         50.00
         pay                                666        200.00
     employee   code
      number
```

10. An input file consists of several sets of records, each containing grades obtained by different class sections of an introduction to management course (see illustration below). Each set is identified by a header record specifying the number of scores for a particular section and the section number.

    Write a program to determine the number and percentage of passing scores for each section. Passing scores are those scores above 70. The program should list each section's scores and the output should be similar to the one shown below:

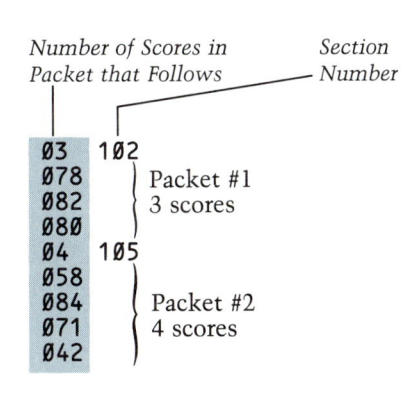

```
Number of Scores in     Section                    SECTION 102
Packet that Follows  ── Number                        SCORES
                                                        78
   03  102                                              82
   078 ⎫                                                80
   082 ⎬ Packet #1
   080 ⎭ 3 scores                          NUMBER OF SCORES IS    3
   04  105                                 NUMBER PASSING SCORES  3
   058 ⎫                                   PASSING PERCENTAGE 100.00
   084 ⎬ Packet #2
   071 ⎭ 4 scores                                    SECTION 105
   042                                                 SCORES
                                                        58
                                                        84
                                                        71
                                                        42

                                          NUMBER OF SCORES IS    4
                                          NUMBER PASSING SCORES  2
                                          PASSING PERCENTAGE    50.0
```

11. The first record of a store's inventory file contains the current date expressed as YYXXX where YY and XXX represent the year and Julian date. For example 86245 represents the 245th day of 1986. Each succeeding record contains (among other items) the date an item was last sold, the number of items on hand, the cost per item, and the regular selling price. A store plans a sale to try to sell slow-moving items. Write a program to produce a report showing recommended sale prices as follows:

    If an item has not been sold in the last 30 days, discount is 10%.

    If an item has not been sold in the last 60 days, discount is 20%.

    If an item has not been sold in the last 90 days, discount is 40%.

However, any item that has sold in the last 30 days is not to be placed on sale. If there is only one of an item left in stock, it is not to be placed on sale no matter when the last sale occurred. In addition, no discount should reduce the sales price below the cost.

Write a program to read the input file and produce a report similar to the following one.

```
CURRENT DATE 86:220

ITEM   LAST SALE   DAYS      NO. IN   COST    REG.    SALE
NO.    DATE        ELAPSED   STOCK            PRICE   PRICE

302    200         20        20       10.00   15.00   15.00
400    189         31         5        6.50   10.00    9.00
101    159         61        15        3.00    5.00    4.00
100    101        119        50        2.00    3.00    2.00
901    100        120         1       12.00   25.00   25.00
999    180         40         2        6.50    7.15    6.50
222    360        225        60       10.00   12.00   10.00
174    100        485         1       30.50   35.50   35.50
```

How would you change your program to handle the case where there is an overlap in years, for example, from 1986 to 1987.

12. Amortization schedule: Suppose you take out a loan of $1,000 at a yearly interest rate of 12% and you intend to repay that loan at $200 (including the interest payment) per month until the loan has been fully repaid. You would like to have an amortization schedule showing the following information: the interest charge, the payment towards the loan, the remaining balance, and the accumulated interest to date. One way to solve this problem is shown here (the monthly interest rate is 1% since the yearly rate is 12%):

The interest for month 1 is	$1000 * .01	= $ 10.00
The payment to capital is	$200 - 10.00	= $190.00
The remaining balance is	$1000 - 190.00	= $810.00
The interest for month 2 is	$810 * .01	= $ 8.10
The payment to capital is	$200 - 8.10	= $191.90
The remaining balance is	$810 - 191.90	= $618.10

The final schedule can then be drawn as follows:

```
                    AMORTIZATION TABLE
            PRINCIPAL  $1000.00   INTEREST 12.00
                 REGULAR PAYMENT  $200.00

       NO.   INTEREST   AMORTIZED   BALANCE   INTEREST TO DATE
        1     10.00       190.00     810.00        10.00
        2      8.10       191.90     618.10        18.10
        3      6.18       193.82     424.28        24.28
        4      4.24       195.76     228.52        28.52
        5      2.29       197.71      30.81        30.81
        6      0.31        30.81       0.00        31.12
       LAST PAYMENT = $31.12
```

Write a program to read a loan amount, a monthly repayment amount, and an interest rate in percentage form (such as 12.75%) and produce a repayment schedule similar to the one above.

13. This is the same as exercise 13, except that the person taking the loan decides to repay the loan for a fixed number of months at a fixed monthly amount. Note that in such a case the last payment may not be the same as the regular monthly payment. Consider the following two examples:

```
                    AMORTIZATION TABLE
PRINCIPAL    $1000.00   INTEREST 12.00  DURATION 3 MONTHS
             REGULAR PAYMENT   $300.00

NO.     INTEREST    AMORTIZED    BALANCE    INTEREST TO DATE
 1       10.00       290.00      710.00          10.00
 2        7.10       292.90      417.10          17.10
 3        4.17       417.10        0.00          21.27
LAST PAYMENT = $421.27
```

```
                    AMORTIZATION TABLE
PRINCIPAL     750.00    INTEREST 12.00  DURATION 3 MONTHS
             REGULAR PAYMENT   $300.00

NO.     INTEREST    AMORTIZED    BALANCE    INTEREST TO DATE
 1        7.50       292.50      457.50           7.50
 2        4.57       295.43      162.07          12.07
 3        1.62       162.07        0.00          13.69
LAST PAYMENT = $163.69
```

Write a program to read a loan amount, a monthly payment, an interest rate, and the term of the loan (such as 5 months, or 1 year and 3 months) and produce a repayment schedule similar to the one above.

14. One method for calculating depreciation is to subtract a fixed percentage of the original value of the item each year. Thus a $100 item depreciated at 10% would be valued at $90 at the end of the first year, $80 at the end of the second, and so forth. Another method for calculating depreciation is to subtract a fixed percentage of the present value of the item. A $100 item depreciated by 10% would be valued at $90 at the end of the first year, $90 − (.1 × 90) = $81 at the end of the second year, and so forth. Write a program to accept as input the original value (V), the depreciation rate (R), and a number of years (N), and produce a table showing the value of the items for the first, second, third, . . . Nth year using both depreciation methods.

15. The Gull Power Electric Company charges supermarkets and small businesses for electricity according to the following scale:

KILOWATT CONSUMPTION	COST
0–300	$5
301–1000	$5 + 6.113 cents for each Kwh over 300 (June thru October)
	$5 + 5.545 cents for each Kwh over 300 (other months)
over 1000	Above rate up to 1000 Kwhs, and 98 percent of either 5.545 or 6.113 cents for each Kwh over 1000 (depending on season)

The input file consists of an unknown number of records that contain the following information:

RECORD POSITION	FIELD DESCRIPTION
10–17	Date
19–23	Meter number
25–30	Account number
32–36	Current reading
38–42	Previous reading

Position 10 ↓

```
04/25/86  12300  SAE558  02335  01998
99XXXXXX  99999  XXXXXX  99999  99999
  Date    Meter  Account Current Previous
          number number  reading reading
```

Write a program to print out a customer's invoice as shown in the following output. Since the month must be processed numerically, declare the first two digits of the date as a numeric picture. Group the day and year together as an alphanumeric item so that the complete date can be printed as is when read from the input record. Note that the line of hyphens are part of the report.

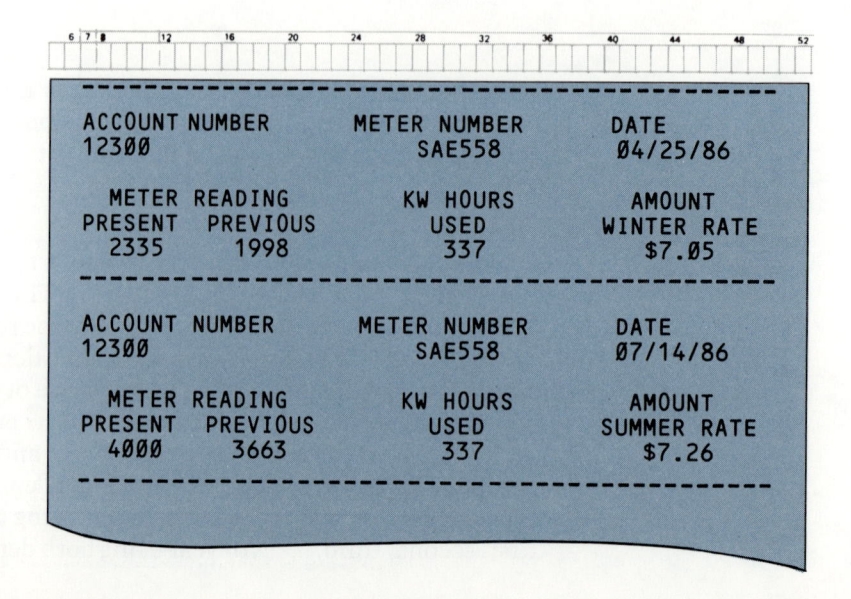

```
------------------------------------------
ACCOUNT NUMBER    METER NUMBER    DATE
12300              SAE558         04/25/86

METER READING     KW HOURS        AMOUNT
PRESENT PREVIOUS  USED            WINTER RATE
 2335    1998      337             $7.05
------------------------------------------
ACCOUNT NUMBER    METER NUMBER    DATE
12300              SAE558         07/14/86

METER READING     KW HOURS        AMOUNT
PRESENT PREVIOUS  USED            SUMMER RATE
 4000    3663      337             $7.26
------------------------------------------
```

16. Read 30 grades already sorted in ascending order and compute the mode. The mode is defined as the score that occurs most frequently. For example, given the grades 10, 15, 15, 17, 17, 17, 20, 21, the mode is 17.

17. Read *N* grades (one per record) already sorted in ascending order (*N* is to be read from the first record) and compute the median. The median is that mark that divides a distribution of scores into two equal parts. For example:

    10, 11, 12, 13, 14, 15, 16   The median is 13.

    10, 11, 12, 13   The median is $\dfrac{11 + 12}{2} = 11.5$.

18. Each record of a data file contains the following information: a name, a sex code (1 = M, 2 = F), and an amount of earnings. Write a program to print the earnings and the names of females earning between ten and twenty thousand dollars; also print the lowest earnings and indicate on the output whether it was earned by a male or a female. For example, either of the following outputs could be produced: (notice the MALE and FEMALE captions).

```
JOMAN                $14300.00
ALLON                $13500.00
LOWEST EARNING = $ 6,736.55 (FEMALE)
```

```
GANDY                $11000.50
LOWEST EARNING = $ 5244.00 (MALE)
```

19. Each record of an input file contains a name and a gross earnings entry. Gross earnings are reduced by federal taxes according to the following schedule:

EARNING	TAX: PERCENT OF GROSS
below $10,000	10%
$10,000 to $18,000	14%
$18,000.01 to $30,000	20%
over $30,000	25%

    and by social security taxes, which are 7.05% of the first $39,600 earned. Write a program to provide a list of names and corresponding gross and net earnings as well as federal and social security taxes.

20. To be eligible for promotion, teachers at Franzia College must have taught there for at least 5 years or somewhere else in the state for at least 7 years. Teachers are not eligible for promotion after 25 years of teaching. To be eligible for promotion to the following ranks, teachers must meet the requirements shown:

RANK	REQUIREMENTS
assistant professor	master's degree in teaching
associate professor	master's degree plus 30 hours in teaching field
full professor	doctorate

In addition, no teacher is eligible for promotion if he/she has not served three full years at his/her rank. The rank below assistant professor is instructor; only four ranks exist at Franzia College. Design a record layout form for personnel to record all faculty data, and write a program to identify the faculty eligible for promotion.

21. Design an employee file where each record specifies the name of an employee, his/her address, a years-experience in field, a department number, an employee number, and salary. Write a program to read the input file and list each employee record subject to the conditions below.

    a. EMP–NAME and CITY must be alphabetic.
    b. EMP–NUM, ZIP, DEPARTMENT–NUM, YEARS–EXPERIENCE, and SALARY must be numeric.
    c. The only valid department numbers are 03, 07, 75, 98, and 99.
    d. All salaries must be in the range of $500 to $1,500.
    e. The 9th digit of the employee number must be equal to the one's digit of the sum of the other eight digits of the employee number. For example, the employee number 123456786 is correct since 1 + 2 + 3 + 4 + 5 + 6 + 7 + 8 = 36 and the one's digit of 36 is 6.

    List each record if valid; if record is invalid, place an asterisk to the right of the record. The programmer who wants to be a little more thorough can identify on the output the invalid field(s) and the cause or reason, instead of placing an asterisk to the right of the invalid record.

22. Write a program to produce the following comparative mortgage tables for principals varying from $50,000 to $100,000 in steps of 10,000, interest rates varying from 9.50% to 12.50% in increments of 0.25% and durations of 20, 25, and 30 years.

```
                    MORTGAGE PAYMENT PLAN
                         JOHN DOE

PRINCIPAL    INTEREST RATE    DURATION    MONTHLY-PAYMENT
  50000          9.50            20           xxxx.xx
                                 25           xxxx.xx
                                 30           xxxx.xx

                 9.75            20           xxxx.xx
                                 25           xxxx.xx
                                 30           xxxx.xx
                  .
                  .
                 12.50           20           xxxx.xx
                                 25           xxxx.xx
                                 30           xxxx.xx

  60000          9.50            20           xxxx.xx
                                 25           xxxx.xx
                                 30           xxxx.xx
                  .
                  .
                 12.50           20           xxxx.xx
                                 25           xxxx.xx
                                 30           xxxx.xx
   .
   .
 100000          9.50            20           xxxx.xx
                                 25           xxxx.xx
                                 30           xxxx.xx
                  .      .         .
                  .      .         .
```

Note the blank lines after every third monthly payment.
The formula to compute the monthly payment is:

$$M = \frac{P \cdot I/12}{1 - \left(\frac{1}{1 + I/12}\right)^{T \cdot 12}} \quad \text{where} \quad \begin{array}{l} P \text{ is the principal} \\ I \text{ is the interest rate} \\ T \text{ is the mortgage duration in years} \end{array}$$

23. Write a program to simulate a bank's handling of a savings account. Each record input into the program will contain a transaction amount, a check number, a transaction date (day of the month), and a transaction code. The records for a particular month should be in ascending date order. The meanings of the codes are as follows:

CODE	MEANING
1	Balance forward
2	Deposit
3	Withdrawal
4	End of transactions (the transaction amount will be ignored while the transaction date will be used for final balance)

    a. Print a report showing all transactions and the account balance after each transaction. The final balance should be clearly labeled. Your report should be similar to the following:

    ```
    DAY    CHECK NO.    WITHDRAWALS    DEPOSITS      BALANCE

     1                                               $3250.00

     4       112          100.00                      3150.00
     6       123          250.00                      2900.00
    19       127                          50.00       2950.00
    25       128                          74.00       3024.00
    31                                 NEW BALANCE   $3024.00
    ```

    b. Modify part a above to compute and credit interest to the account. Assume that interest is based on the average daily balance for the number of days from the beginning of the statement (the date on the balance forward transaction) up to and including the end of the statement (the date of the end of transactions). The interest should be credited to the account on the date of the end of transactions. The average daily balance is computed by adding the daily balances and dividing by the number of days. In the example above, the average daily balance would be

    $$\frac{3 \times 3250 + 2 \times 3150 + 13 \times 2900 + 6 \times 2950 + 6 \times 3024 + 3024}{31} = 2987.67$$

    since the account had a balance of $3,250 for 3 days, $3150 for 2 days, $2,900 for 13 days, ..., and a balance of $3024 on the date ending the period. If the interest rate is 4.75%, the account should then be credited with a monthly interest of $11.82.

24. Write a program to produce a table showing monthly mortgage payments for varying costs of homes at various interest rates. The following information should be accepted from the screen (or data file).

1: home cost range from lowest cost to highest cost.
2: interest range from low interest to high interest.
3: mortgage duration in years.

The output should consist of a table showing monthly mortgage payments starting with lowest range cost at the various interest rates up to highest range cost at same interest rates. The input and output should be similar to the following:

```
ENTER LOWEST COST
085000.0
ENTER HIGHEST COST
105000.0
ENTER LOW INTEREST
.1250
ENTER HIGH INTEREST
.1450
ENTER NUMBER YEARS
20
MORTGAGE   YEARS   INTEREST   MONTHLY     TOTAL
AMOUNT             RATE       PAYMENT     PAYMENT

 85,000.00   20     12.50       965.72   231,772.80
 85,000.00   20     13.50     1,026.27   246,304.80
 85,000.00   20     14.50     1,088.00   261,120.00

 95,000.00   20     12.50     1,079.33   259,039.20
 95,000.00   20     13.50     1,147.01   275,282.40
 95,000.00   20     14.50     1,216.00   291,840.00

105,000.00   20     12.50     1,192.95   286,308.00
105,000.00   20     13.50     1,267.74   304,257.60
105,000.00   20     14.50     1,344.00   322,560.00
```

```
ENTER LOWEST COST
085000.0
ENTER HIGHEST COST
105000.0
ENTER LOW INTEREST
.1250
ENTER HIGH INTEREST
.1450
ENTER NUMBER YEARS
30
MORTGAGE   YEARS   INTEREST   MONTHLY     TOTAL
AMOUNT             RATE       PAYMENT     PAYMENT

 85,000.00   30     12.50       907.17   326,581.20
 85,000.00   30     13.50       973.60   350,496.00
 85,000.00   30     14.50     1,040.87   374,713.20

 95,000.00   30     12.50     1,013.89   365,000.40
 95,000.00   30     13.50     1,088.14   391,730.40
 95,000.00   30     14.50     1,163.33   418,798.80

105,000.00   30     12.50     1,120.62   403,423.20
105,000.00   30     13.50     1,202.68   432,964.80
105,000.00   30     14.50     1,285.78   462,880.80
```

25. The general formula to compute the standard deviation for n grades $x_1, x_2, x_3, \ldots, x_n$ is given by

$$SD = \sqrt{\frac{n(x_1^2 + x_2^2 + x_3^2 + \ldots + x_n^2) - (x_1 + x_2 + x_3 + \ldots + x_n)^2}{n(n-1)}}$$

Write a program to read grades from data records (one grade per record) and compute the average and the standard deviation. Print the grades, the average, and the standard deviation. To compute the standard deviation, it is necessary to:

a. Accumulate the sum of the grades $(x_1 + x_2 + \ldots + x_n)$, where n is the number of grades.
b. Accumulate the sum of the square of each grade $(x_1^2 + x_2^2 + \ldots + x_n^2)$.

26. The Meals on Wheels Company operates a fleet of vans that deliver cold foods at various local plants and construction sites. The management is thinking of purchasing a specially built $18,000 van equipped to deliver hot foods. This new addition to the fleet is expected to generate after-tax earn-

ings $E_1, E_2, \ldots E_6$ (as displayed in the following table) over the next six years, at which time the van's resale value will be zero. Projected repair and maintenance $C_0, C_1, C_2, \ldots, C_6$ over the six years are also shown in the table.

PROJECTED EARNINGS		PROJECTED COSTS	
		C_0	$18,000 (purchase cost of the van)
E_1	$2,500	C_1	610
E_2	2,500	C_2	745
E_3	3,000	C_3	820
E_4	4,500	C_4	900
E_5	6,000	C_5	950
E_6	6,000	C_6	1,000

a. Write a program to determine whether or not the company should acquire the van. The decision depends on the benefit/cost ratio (BCR) (grossly speaking, earnings/expenditures) given by the formula:

$$\text{BCR} = \frac{E_1(1 + i)^6 + E_2(1 + i)^5 + \ldots + E_6(1 + i)^1}{C_0 + C_1(1 + i)^6 + C_2(1 + i)^5 + \ldots + C_6(1 + i)^1}$$

where i is the rate of investment of earnings by the company (use 11% for this problem). If the BCR < 1, then the company should not acquire the van. Use the accumulation process to compute the BCR. The first data record contains E_1 and C_1, the second data record contains E_2 and C_2, and so forth.

b. When shown the projected maintenance costs for the next six years, the repair and maintenance shop foreman argues that these cost figures are unrealistic and proposes instead the following costs for the first through sixth years: 1,000, 1,500, 2,000, 2,000, 2,100, 2,400. Using these figures, determine whether the company should purchase the van.

c. Having found out that the BCR is less than 1 with the projected maintenance costs shown in part b, the management wants to recompute the BCR with the same figures as in part b but setting the resale value of the van at $1,000.00 (the sale of the van represents earnings). Use your program to recompute the BCR.

27. Write a program to perform an analysis of expenses for an automobile trip. Input into the program will be:

number of days

estimated mileage for each day

estimated miles per gallon

estimated cost of gas per gallon

estimated cost of room(s) per day

number of persons

estimated cost of breakfast/lunch/dinner per person

Assume that no more than four persons can occupy a room; if there are more than four persons, additional rooms will be required. Assume that breakfast on the first day and dinner on the last day are not included in trip expenses. Allow 15% of room plus meals per day per person for incidental expenses. (For example, if two persons are sharing a $40 per night room and total meals per day per person is $15, the estimate for incidental expenses per person per day would be .15 × (40/2 + 15) = 5.25.) Allow 15% of total estimated cost of gas for incidental auto expenses.

Write a report showing all input data and a trip expense budget including:

total automotive costs (gas + incidental)

total cost of meals

total cost of rooms

total cost of incidental expenses

total trip estimated expenses.

28. Salaries at the XYZ Corporation are based on job classification, years of service, education, and merit rating. The base pay for all employees is the same; a percentage of the base pay is added to salaries according to the following schedule:

JOB CLASSIFICATION	PERCENTAGE OF BASE PAY	EDUCATION	PERCENTAGE OF BASE PAY
1	0	1(high school)	0
2	5	2(junior college)	10
3	15	3(college)	25
4	25	4(graduate degree)	50
5	50	5(special training)	15

MERIT RATING	PERCENTAGE OF BASE PAY	YEARS OF SERVICE	PERCENTAGE OF BASE PAY PER YEAR
0(poor)	0	0–10 years	5
1(good)	10	each additional year	4
2(excellent)	25		

Write a program to accept numerical codes for each of the four variables and calculate the employee's salary as a percentage of base pay.

29. Each employee working at Slimpower, Inc. is paid at a regular hourly rate of $5.00 for the first 40 hours. The overtime rate is 1.5 times the regular rate. The number of hours worked by each employee is typed into record positions 1–4.

   a. Write a program to compute each employee's pay and produce an output similar to the following:

```
HOURS    RATE    OVERTIME HOURS    PAY
10.00    5.00         0            50.00
50.00    5.00        10           275.00
  .        .           .              .
  .        .           .              .
  .        .           .              .
```

b. Repeat part a, but now the number of hours and the rate of pay are read from data records in positions 1–4 and 7–11, respectively. Also, 6.1% of each employee's pay for the first 30 hours is subtracted from the gross pay for a pension plan. The output should be similar to:

```
HOURS   RATE    PENSION PLAN    PAY
50.00   10.00       18.30      531.70
  .       .           .           .
  .       .           .           .
  .       .           .           .
```

c. Repeat part b, but now a bonus amount for each employee is recorded in positions 15–18 as a three-digit number. If the employee's pay exceeds $500, the bonus is added to the employee's pay; if not, the bonus field is left blank on the output and is not computed into the pay, for example,

```
HOURS   RATE    PENSION PLAN    BONUS    PAY
50.00   10.00       18.30        100    631.70
10.00    5.00        3.05         ___    46.95
  .       .           .                    .
  .       .           .           ↑        .
  .       .           .                    .
                              [Note blank field]
```

30. A rent-a-car company has the following system for computing a customer's rental car bill:

CAR TYPE	RENT/DAY 150 MILES	RENT/WEEK 1050 MILES	EXTRA MILEAGE	EXTRA HOURS
1	$24.95	$140.00	.18	$3.60
2	$32.95	$184.80	.24	$4.80
3	$44.95	$256.95	.26	$7.00

The daily rate includes an allowance of 150 miles, and the weekly rate includes an allowance of 1050 miles.

The extra mileage column in the above table indicates the additional cost for each mile above the mileage allowance for the different car types.

The extra hours column in the above table specifies the additional hourly charge for each hour that the vehicle is used in excess of one day or in excess of one week.

Passenger collision insurance is optional and costs $3.75 per day.

Destination extra charges: There is no extra charge if the vehicle is returned to the renting station; however, if the receiving station is not the renting station, there is an additional charge of 14 cents per mile for the total number of miles driven (including the mileage allowance).

If a car is rented for fewer than 24 hours, the lesser of the following rates is applied: 1. the number of hours of use times the hourly charge (the extra hours charge in the table), or 2. the daily rental charge.

The final invoice should also include a 4% sales tax.

Write a program to compute a customer's bill, based on the charges described above. The following input parameters are used to generate the sample output:

INPUT PARAMETERS	EXAMPLE
Rent code (by the day = 1, by the week = 2)	1
Number of miles driven	1080
Car type	1
Possession of car	
Days	5
Hours	0
Insurance code (1 = yes, 2 = no)	1
Destination extra charge (1 = yes, 2 = no)	1

The output should be similar to:

```
     CAR TYPE            HOURS USED              RENT CODE
        1                   120.                     1


   MILES DRIVEN           1080.
   LESS MILES ALLOWED      750.
   CHARGEABLE MILES        330.  @     .18         $ 59.40
   NUMBER DAYS               5.  @   24.95         $124.75

                          SUBTOTAL                 $184.15
   DESTINATION CHARGES                             $151.20
   COLLISION INSURANCE                             $ 18.75

                          TAXABLE CHARGE           $354.10
                          STATE TAX                $ 14.16

                          NET AMOUNT               $368.26
```

31. The Kiddie Up Company manufactures toys for adults. The company expects fixed costs for the next year to be around $180,000. With the demand for adult toys increasing, the company is looking for sales of $900,000 in the year to come. The variable costs are expected to run at about 74% of sales.

   a. Write a program to determine the breakeven point (BEP) (the dollar amount of sales that must be made to incur neither a profit nor a loss), and compute the expected profit. The formula to compute the BEP is

   $$\text{BEP} = \frac{\text{total fixed costs}}{1 - \frac{\text{variable costs}}{\text{sales}}}$$

DECISION, ITERATION, PROGRAM DESIGN, DATA VALIDATION

b. The Kiddie Up Company management is arguing that with the current rate of inflation, variable costs will run higher for the next year—probably anywhere from 75 to 83% of sales. With sales still projected at $900,000, the management directs its data processing staff to generate the following report to determine the breakeven point and the profits and losses for varying variable costs. Sales and fixed costs remain constant.

```
                    KIDDIE UP COMPANY
                  1986 OPERATIONS FORECAST

PROJECTED SALES: 900,000
FIXED COSTS:     180,000

VARIABLE      VARIABLE COST    BREAK EVEN    PROFIT     DEFICIT
COSTS         PERCENTAGE       POINT
675,000       75               720,000       180,000    ***
   .             .                 .             .         .
   .             .                 .             .         .
   .             .                 .             .         .
747,000       83               1,058,823     ***        158,823
```

Write a program to complete the above report. Place three stars (***) in the profit column if there is no profit. Do the same for deficit.

c. The company employees have just won a new contract. As a result, variable costs are expected to reach 81 or 82% of next year's projected $900,000 sales. A recent internal study carried out by the company on the various aspects of the manufacturing operations disclosed production inefficiencies. Corrective measures could significantly lower fixed costs. Project a range of fixed costs to show a company profit of anywhere from 50 to 100,000 dollars, given that variable costs are expected to reach 81 or 82% of sales next year.

32. XSTAR is a small company supplying major auto parts companies with a single item. The total fixed costs to run the company amount to $40,000 per year. The company has had a steady dollar breakeven point value (BEP) for the last three years, and the president of the company would like to keep the BEP at about the same level ($117,647) for the coming year. The president believes that the selling price per item could range anywhere from $1.10 to $1.30, but that the variable cost per item should not fall below $.75 nor exceed $.83. To help the president consider the options, write a program displaying different combinations of selling prices ($1.10 to $1.30 in increments of one cent) and corresponding variable costs, all yielding a constant BEP of $117,647; that is, generate a table with headings as follows:

```
SELLING     VARIABLE     BREAKEVEN
COSTS       COST/UNIT    POINT        DECISION

$1.10       73           117,647      TOO LOW
 1.11                    117,647         .
   .          .             .            .
   .          .             .            .
   .          .             .            .
 1.30       86           117,647      TOO HIGH
```

If the variable cost per unit falls outside the interval of $.75–$.83, state in the decision column that the variable cost is either too low or too high. The formula to compute the BEP is given by:

$$\text{BEP} = \frac{\text{total fixed costs}}{1 - \dfrac{\text{variable cost/unit}}{\text{selling price/unit}}}$$

33. You have been hired by E. Naddor, Inc., a world-famous firm specializing in inventory control problems, to write a computer program for one of Naddor's largest customers, the Shopping Basket. This firm would like to computerize part of its reordering system to cut down on the cost of replenishing inventories.

    Each Friday at the close of business, the ending inventory of each product is compared to the fixed reorder point for that product. If the ending inventory is equal to or below the reorder point for that product, the Shopping Basket orders enough of the item to bring the amount on hand up to a predetermined order level. Any order placed on Friday is delivered over the weekend so that the company can begin a new week of business with well-stocked shelves. It is possible for the ending inventory to be negative, indicating that demand exceeded supply during the week and some orders were not filled. Shopping Basket policy is to order enough to cover this backordered demand.

    To aid you in your task, you have been given some old records that illustrate how the reorder system works:

ITEM NUMBER DESCRIPTION	15202 TUNA FISH	67180 CHARCOAL LIGHTER FLUID	51435 MOUTHWASH	49415 PIZZA MIX	24361 ASPARAGUS
Unit price (per case)	4.27	8.48	12.29	9.27	15.32
Order level (cases)	30	25	55	75	15
Reorder point (cases)	5	8	10	25	2
Ending inventory (cases)	9	5	7	−10	6

Your task is to write a program to read five data records (using the sample data in the above inventory summary) to determine which items must be ordered and the respective quantities to be ordered for each item. The program should also calculate the cost of such orders and the total cost for all items ordered. The sample input/output layouts are shown below:

INPUT LAYOUT

POSITIONS	FIELD DESCRIPTION
1–5	Item number
31–34	Unit price (dollars and cents)
35–37	Order level (cases)
38–40	Reorder point (cases)
41–44	Ending inventory

SAMPLE RECORD FOR TUNA FISH

15202 427 30 5 9

Item number | Unit price | Order level | Reorder point | Ending inventory

```
              THE SHOPPING BASKET
                  ORDER REPORT

   ITEM    UNIT    ORDER   REORDER   ENDING
  NUMBER   PRICE   LEVEL    POINT   INVENTORY   ORDER     COST

  15202    4.27     30        5         9         0       0.00
  67180    8.48     25        8         5        20     169.60
  51435   12.29     55       10         7        48     589.92
  49415    9.27     75       25       -10        85     787.95
  24361   15.32     15        2         6         0       0.00

                                           TOTAL COST $1547.47
```

Some helpful rules are:

a. Order an item if ending inventory is less than or equal to the reorder point for the item.

b. Amount to order = order-level − ending inventory.

c. Cost of ordering an item = amount ordered * unit price.

6-6-3 ANSWERS TO TEST YOURSELF

1. a. Invalid; sentence may not start with ELSE.
   b. Valid. Serves no purpose.
   c. Invalid; missing relational operator.
   d. Invalid; > THAN is unrecognizable.
   e. Invalid; NEXT SENTENCE should be all by itself.
   f. Invalid; action missing for second IF.
   g. Invalid; missing relational operator.
   h. Valid.
   i. Valid.
   j. EQUALS may not be valid in some systems.
   k. Invalid constant 1.
   l. Invalid; TO not allowed.
   m. Valid.
   n. Valid.
   o. Valid.
   p. Valid.
   q. Valid.
   r. Invalid; TEMP cannot be alphanumeric and numeric.

2. a. Identical
   b. Identical
   c. Not identicals; A ≥ B would be identical.
   d. Identical
   e. Identical

3. a. Valid; same as . . . OR NOT A > C.
   b. Valid; equivalent to if A < C.
   c. Invalid; missing object for Z.
   d. Valid.
   e. Valid.
   f. Valid.
   g. Invalid; no subject.
   h. Invalid; no relational operator.
   i. Valid.
   j. Invalid; missing relational operators and objects.
   k. Invalid object (NOT B).
   l. Invalid; A + 4.1 is not a condition.
   m. Valid.
   n. Valid.
   o. Valid; if H ≥ 40 or H < 80

4. a. Not equivalent. EARN–LINE will always be printed in case 2, whereas in case 1 EARN–LINE will be printed only if EARNING > 40000.
   b. Identical.
   c. Not identical. In case 1, if X = 3, 1 will be added only to A, whereas in case 2, 1 will be added to A and C.
   d. Not identical. C will never be moved to D in the first part of the question.
   e. Not identical. If K = 3, then K is moved to A in case 1, whereas in case 2, K will not be moved to A.
   f. Last two parts are identical.
   g. Identical.
   h. Identical.
   i. Identical.

5.

a.

K	
1	B
2	F
3	C
4	E
5,6	D

b.

K	
1	B
2	C
3	D
4	E
1,2,3,5,6	F

c.

K	
1	B

d.

K	
1	B
3	D
3	F

6. a. 30, 75   b. 40, 50, 65, 75   c. 75   d. If K = 2   e. If K = 5

7. a. No, because the statement WRITE OUTPUT–LINE is not executed if TYPE = 2.
   b. Yes
   c. No, because if SEX ≠ 1, the flowchart does not write OUTPUT–LINE.
   d. No, because OUTPUT–LINE is not printed if TYPE ≠ 2, even though Y will have been moved to OUT.

8. a.
```
   IF A NOT = B
       MOVE X TO T
       IF C = D
           MOVE X TO Z
       ELSE
           MOVE X TO Y.
```
   b.
```
   IF A = B
       MOVE 3 TO X
   ELSE
       IF E = F
           MOVE 2 TO X
       ELSE
           MOVE 1 TO X.
```

9. a.
```
   IF HOURS = 40
       PERFORM TRUE
   ELSE
       IF SEX = 2
           PERFORM TRUE
       ELSE
           IF STAT = 3
               PERFORM TRUE
           ELSE
               PERFORM FALSE.
```
   d.
```
   IF STAT = 3
       PERFORM TRUE
   ELSE
       IF HOURS NOT < 40
           IF SEX NOT = 1
               PERFORM TRUE
           ELSE PERFORM FALSE
       ELSE PERFORM FALSE.
```

10. a. T   b. T   c. T   d. T   e. T   f. F   g. T

11. PRINT–LINE will be written only once, when the end-of-file record is read.

12. a. X = 3 OR A < B AND C = 2
    b. A NOT = 0 AND B < 3
    c. B = 0 AND A > 3 OR B = 0 AND Z = 2

13. a. I = −7   b. I = 1   c. I = 4   d. I = 6

14. a. Code is correct; however, AVG should be computed outside paragraph AVE.
b. No. Should be AVG = SUN/X if same code is to be used.

15.
```
77  I PIC 99 VALUE 2.
77  J PIC 99 VALUE 1.
77  K PIC 999.
    .
    PERFORM TAB1 UNTIL I > 12.
    .
TAB1.
    PERFORM TAB2 UNTIL J > 10.
    ADD 1 TO I.
    WRITE PRINT-LINE FROM BLANK-LINE.
    MOVE 1 TO J.
TAB2.
    COMPUTE K = I * J.
    MOVE I TO DL-I.
    MOVE J TO DL-J.
    MOVE K TO DL-K.
    WRITE PRINT-LINE FROM DL-LINE.
    ADD 1 TO J.
```

16.
```
010 01  INPUT-REC.
020     05 EMP-NO...
030     05 BASE-PAY...
040     05 EMP-TIME...
050     05 KLASS...
060     05 RATING...
          .
          .
          .
075     READ INPUT-FILE AT END MOVE 1 TO EOF.
080     PERFORM READ-PROCESS UNTIL EOF = 1.
090     close files...
100     STOP RUN.
140 READ-PROCESS.
150     IF EMP-TIME < .5
160         PERFORM NO-BONUS-WRITE
170     ELSE
180         PERFORM BONUS-COMPUTE
183         PERFORM BONUS-WRITE.
184     READ INPUT-FILE AT END MOVE 1 TO EOF.
185 BONUS-COMPUTE.
190     IF RATING = 1
192         PERFORM SATISFACTORY-RATING
194     ELSE
196         PERFORM UNSATISFACTORY-RATING.
198 SATISFACTORY-RATING.
200     IF KLASS = 1
210         COMPUTE BONUS = BASE-PAY / 52
220     ELSE
230         COMPUTE BONUS = .2 * BASE-PAY / 12.
240     IF EMP-TIME > 10
250             ADD 400 TO BONUS.
260 UNSATISFACTORY-RATING.
270     IF KLASS = 1
280         COMPUTE BONUS = BASE-PAY / WORKDAYS-PER-YEAR
290     ELSE
300         COMPUTE BONUS = .05 * BASE-PAY / 12.
```

17. 320 DIVIDE YEAR BY 4 GIVING X REMAINDER R.
    325 IF R = 0
    330   DIVIDE YEAR BY 100 GIVING X REMAINDER R
    335   IF R = 0
    340   DIVIDE YEAR BY 400 GIVING X REMAINDER R
    345   IF R = 0
    350   PERFORM LEAP-YEAR
    355   ELSE
    360   PERFORM NOT-LEAP-YEAR
    365   ELSE PERFORM LEAP-YEAR
    370 ELSE PERFORM NOT-LEAP-YEAR.

18.   MOVE 0 TO FLAG, EOF.
        READ INPUT-FILE AT END MOVE 1 TO EOF.
        PERFORM CITY-SEARCH UNTIL EOF = 1.
            .
    CITY-SEARCH.
        IF FLAG = 0
        IF TEMP NOT LESS THAN 100
            MOVE CITY TO CITY-OUT
            WRITE PRINT-LINE FROM CITY-L
            MOVE 1 TO FLAG.
        READ INPUT-FILE AT END MOVE 1 TO EOF.

19. 110 77 X1 PIC 9999.
    120 77 X2 PIC 9999.
    130 77 X3 PIC 9999.
    140 77 I PIC S999V9.
    150 77 K PIC 999 VALUE 0.
    160 77 N PIC 9V999.
    170 PROCEDURE DIVISION.
    180 MAIN-LOGIC.
a   190   MOVE 2 TO I.
    200   PERFORM A UNTIL I > 100.
b   210   MOVE 7.5 TO I.
    220   PERFORM B UNTIL I > 101.5.
c   230   MOVE 1 TO I.
    240   PERFORM C UNTIL K = 289.
d   250   MOVE 1 TO X1, X2.
    260   PERFORM D 18 TIMES.
e   270   MOVE 1 TO I.
    280   PERFORM E 20 TIMES.
f   290   MOVE -17 TO I.
    300   PERFORM F UNTIL I > -1.
g   310   MOVE 1 TO I.
    320   PERFORM G UNTIL I > 100.
    330   STOP RUN.

```
350 A.
370     ADD 2 TO I.
380 B.
400     ADD 2 TO I.
410 C.
420     COMPUTE K = I * I.
440     ADD 2 TO I.
450 D.
460     COMPUTE X3 = X1 + X2.
470     MOVE X2 TO X1.
480     MOVE X3 TO X2.
500 E.
520     MULTIPLY -1 BY I.
530 F.
550     ADD 2 TO I.
560 G.
570     COMPUTE N = 1 / I.
585     ADD 1 TO I.
```

20.
```
090 01 CARD-REC.
100    05 Y PIC S9.
110 77 X PIC S9.
115 77 K PIC S999.
117 77 EOF PIC 9 VALUE 0.
140 PROCEDURE DIVISION.
150 MAINK.
155    OPEN INPUT INPUT-FILE OUTPUT PRINT-FILE.
160    READ INPUT-FILE AT END MOVE 1 TO EOF.
       Write Y onto output form.
180    MOVE Y TO X.
185    READ INPUT-FILE AT END MOVE 1 TO EOF.
190    PERFORM PARA-1 UNTIL K < 0 OR EOF = 1.
200    Close files and stop.
229 PARA-1.
240    COMPUTE K = X * Y.
250    IF K > 0
260        MOVE Y TO X.
270    Write Y onto output form.
275    READ INPUT-FILE AT END MOVE 1 TO EOF.
```

21.
```
    MOVE 1 TO SWITCH.
    READ INPUT-FILE AT END MOVE 1 TO EOF. .
    PERFORM READ-PROCESS UNTIL EOF = 1.
    IF SWITCH = 0
        PERFORM MESSAGE-PRINT
    ELSE
        PERFORM COMPUTE-PROCESS.
               .
READ-PROCESS.
    PERFORM RECORD-PROCESS
    IF DOLLAR-AMT NOT > 10000
        MOVE 0 TO SWITCH.
    READ INPUT-FILE AT END MOVE 1 TO EOF. .
```

22.   PERFORM PROCESS-SEARCH UNTIL
            SEX = 1 AND (AGE > 20 AND AGE < 41)
            AND
            (COLLEGE = 2 OR CERTIFICATE = "YES")
            OR
            EOF = 1.
        IF EOF = 0
            MOVE TELEPHONE TO SL-TELEPHONE
            WRITE PRINT-LINE FROM SL-LINE
        ELSE
            MOVE "NO CANDIDATE" TO DL-MESSG
            WRITE PRINT-LINE FROM DL-LINE.
        STOP RUN.
    PROCESS-SEARCH.
        READ PERSONNEL-FILE AT END MOVE 1 TO EOF.
```
```

CHAPTER 7

ADDITIONAL FEATURES AND REPORTS

7-1 THE REDEFINES STATEMENT

7-2 CONDITION NAMES

7-3 CHARACTER MANIPULATION STATEMENTS

7-4 REPORTS

7-5 YOU MIGHT WANT TO KNOW

7-6 EXERCISES

INTRODUCTION This chapter covers the REDEFINES statement, which is used to give more than one PICTURE field to the same data item, giving names to conditions to make code more readable and easier to write, and character manipulating statements, including the STRING, UNSTRING, EXAMINE, and INSPECT commands and their associated options. The desirable features of reports, including layout, paging, and headings, are also discussed, and reports with single and multiple control breaks are presented and analyzed.

7-1 THE REDEFINES STATEMENT

7-1-1 JUSTIFICATION

Consider the following four coding dilemmas.

Dilemma 1

You are reading an input file consisting of scores (PIC 999) and wish to obtain an edited listing of these scores with leading 0's suppressed. Mistyped scores (nonnumeric digits) must also be listed. For example, the input file shown below should give rise to the following listing:

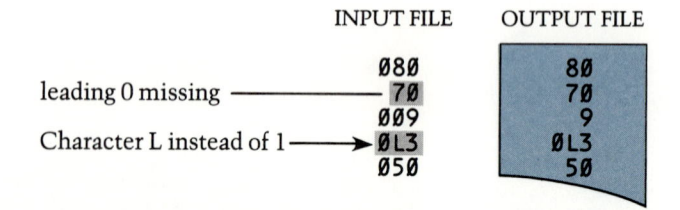

```
                          INPUT FILE    OUTPUT FILE
                             080            80
    leading 0 missing ────── 070            70
                             009             9
  Character L instead of 1 ─► 0L3           0L3
                             050            50
```

Question: How do you define DL-SCORE in the detail line?

If you define DL-SCORE as PIC ZZ9, then you cannot move a nonnumeric score such as 0L3 to DL-SCORE (invalid move). On the other hand, if you define DL-SCORE as PIC XXX then you can not suppress the leading 0's! What you would really like to do in such a situation is to define memory area DL-SCORE both as PIC ZZ9 and PIC XXX and use the first picture for zero suppression and the second picture for nonnumeric entries! This chameleon-like treatment of a data item is made possible in COBOL by the REDEFINES statement, which allows you to redefine the picture of a data item in as many ways as you wish. For example,

```
01  DETAIL-LINE.
    05 FILLER    PIC X(05) VALUE SPACES.
    05 DL-SCORE PIC ZZ9.
    05 DL-ERROR-SCORE REDEFINES DL-SCORE PIC XXX.
```

This "trick" enables you to refer to one memory storage area using different names, where each name is described by a different picture field. Thus DL-SCORE and DL-ERROR-SCORE share the same area of memory, which can be treated in different ways depending on the name used. In our example, you can move the input score (SR-SCORE) to DL-SCORE if the score is numeric, or if it is nonnumeric, you can move SR-SCORE to DL-ERROR-SCORE.

Dilemma 2

An input file consists of different packets of scores (each packet contains the scores of a particular class). A program is to be written to compute the various class averages. Each packet is separated from the others by a record containing the word END. The program should also screen the scores for numeric values.

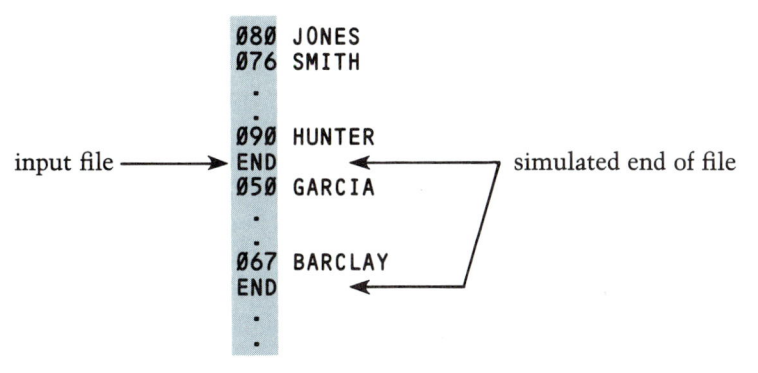

```
                             080 JONES
                             076 SMITH
                              .
                              .
                             090 HUNTER
              input file ──▶ END       ◀──┐
                             050 GARCIA   │ simulated end of file
                              .           │
                              .           │
                             067 BARCLAY  │
                             END       ◀──┘
                              .
                              .
```

Question: How do you define the input record to accomodate both a numeric value (the score) and an alphanumeric value (END)? If the score is defined as PIC 999, then we can test the score for NUMERIC value. But if the score is not numeric, it could either be an invalid score (such as b34) or the characters E, N, and D. To determine whether a nonnumeric score is the END record, we need to compare the score with the literal 'END'—this means comparing a PIC 999 field with a PIC XXX field. To ensure type compatibility and good documentation, we can redefine the score field as an alphanumeric field so that it can be compared to the literal value 'END'.

```
01   INPUT-RECORD
     05 IR-SCORE PIC 999.
     05 IR-END-PACKET REDEFINES IR-SCORE PIC XXX.
     05 IR-NAME   PIC X(10).
      .
      .
     IF  IR-SCORE NUMERIC
         PERFORM 500-PROCESS-SCORE
     ELSE
         IF IR-END-PACKET = 'END'
             PERFORM 600-PROCESS-AVERAGE
         ELSE
             PERFORM 700-PROCESS-INVALID-SCORE.
```

IR-SCORE and IR-END-PACKET share the same storage area while retaining their own identity in terms of data type.

Dilemma 3

A sequence check is to be performed on an input file consisting of seven-digit employee numbers. The meanings of the seven digits are as follows:

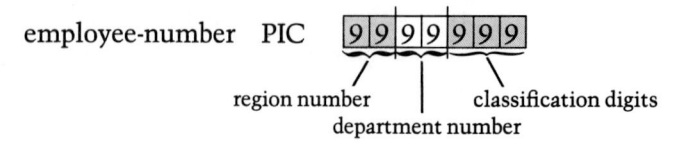

employee-number PIC 9999999

- region number (first 2 digits)
- department number (middle digits)
- classification digits (last digits)

The company also wants to know the number of employees working in department 28.

Question: How can you define the employee number so that you can refer to it as a seven-digit numeric field for sequence checking purposes and at the same time refer to its two middle digits by name in order to count employees in department 28?

Answer: We define the contents of employee-number as follows:

```
01    INPUT-RECORD.
      05   IR-EMPLOYEE-NUMBER PIC 9999999.
      05   IR-RECORD REDEFINES IR-EMPLOYEE-NUMBER.
           10   FILLER   PIC XX.
           10   IR-DEPT  PIC 99.
           10   FILLER   PIC XXX.
```

Note that in this case IR-RECORD is a group item that redefines the employee number. IR-RECORD has three subordinate items, one of which (IR-DEPT) refers to the third and fourth digits of the employee number. In the procedure division we can then write the following IF statements:

```
IF WS-PREVIOUS-NUMBER < IR-EMPLOYEE-NUMBER ...     (for sequence checking)
   .
   .
IF IR-DEPT = 28                                     (for employee count)
   ADD 1 TO WS-DEPT-28.
```

Dilemma 4:

The Medical Center Clinic maintains a patient file where each patient's medical history is recorded on one or more records. Multiple records are used for patients having undergone some form of surgery. The first record identifies the patient's name, address, sex, insurance company, vital statistics, et cetera. Subsequent records for a multirecord patient identify the surgical intervention (such as transplants, fractures, or excisions), the date of the operation, and the name of the physician in charge. A separate record is created for each surgical intervention. A special record identification code is typed in position 1 of every record: a code of 1 identifies a nonsurgical record, while a code of 2 identifies a surgery record (not all patients have such records). The first appearance of a code 2 record follows a code 1 record (only one code 1 record per patient). Thus the input file has the following form:

Record code	Name	Address	Insurance company	Weight	Blood pressure	Age	Blood type	Height
1	GLEASON HAROLD	32 WEST ENG ST	BLUE SHLD/CR	194	130/110	065	O	58
1	SUPPINGER JAN	4206 MAG DR.	EXPLORER'S	135	115/080	033	A+	61
2	CORNEAL TRANSPLANT	THOMPSON JR.	101085					
2	GASTROINTESTINAL	SPENCE M.	101185					

Intervention type — Physician in charge — Operation date

Question: What data structure should be used to permit reference to individual fields within the two different types of records? Remember, there is only one input area into which each record is read. (Each record that is read, whether it is a type 1 or type 2 record, is moved into the *same* memory area—there are *not* two different memory areas.)

The REDEFINES statement can be used as follows:

```
WORKING-STORAGE SECTION.
01  PATIENT-RECORD.
    05  RECORD-CODE    PIC 9.
    05  NAME           PIC X(14).
    05  ADDRESS        PIC X(15).
    05  INSURANCE-CO   PIC X(13).
    05  WEIGHT         PIC 999.
    05  PRESSURE       PIC X(07).
    05  AGE            PIC 999.
    05  BLOOD-TYPE     PIC XX.
    05  HEIGHT         PIC 99.
01  SURGERY-RECORD REDEFINES PATIENT-RECORD
    05  FILLER         PIC 9.
    05  INTERVENTION   PIC X(17).
    05  PHYSICIAN      PIC X(13).
    05  OPERATION-DATE PIC 9(06).
```

Note that in redefining 01 level entries, the length of the redefined item (SURGERY-RECORD) does not have to equal the length of the item that is redefined (PATIENT-RECORD).

7-1-2 THE REDEFINES CLAUSE

In many programming situations it is desirable to allow the same memory area (records or data items in WORKING–STORAGE) to be described by different data description entries. Let's consider another example:

A social security number is a 9-digit field consisting of 3 logical subfields that can be described as follows:

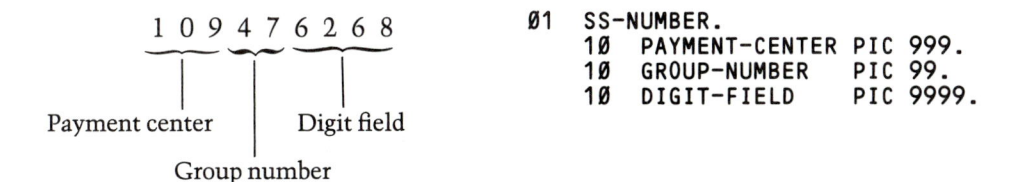

```
    1 0 9  4 7 6  2 6 8        01  SS-NUMBER.
    ‾‾‾‾‾  ‾‾‾‾‾  ‾‾‾‾‾            10  PAYMENT-CENTER PIC 999.
      |      |      |              10  GROUP-NUMBER   PIC 99.
Payment center  Digit field        10  DIGIT-FIELD    PIC 9999.
           Group number
```

This description of a social security number prohibits one from performing any arithmetic operations on the 9-digit field as *one* operand, since any reference to SS–NUMBER (a group item) in the PROCEDURE division implies a nine-character alphanumeric field. Yet in some cases one might want to process the entire social security number arithmetically (add, multiply, et cetera—pseudo random numbers can be generated from arithmetic manipulation of the 9-digit field). The following description would allow numeric processing of a social security number:

```
01  SS-NUMBER    PIC 9(9).
```

but with this definition we would not be able to address or refer to a particular field within the social security number. For example, given a list of social security numbers, we could not determine the number of social security numbers associated with a particular payment center.

We would like to describe the 9-digit field using two different sets of description entries (describing, of course, the same memory area) so that we can refer to SS-NUMBER as a 9-digit numeric field and also refer to PAYMENT-CENTER as a 3-digit numeric item, for example. Thus we need to REDEFINE the original structure of the 9-digit field as follows:

```
05 SS-NUMBER PIC 9(9).
05 SOCIAL  REDEFINES  SS-NUMBER.
   10 PAYMENT-CENTER PIC 999.
   10 GROUP-NUMBER   PIC 99.
   10 DIGIT-FIELD    PIC 9999.
```

SS-NUMBER
(9-digit field)
↓
| 1 | 0 | 9 | 4 | 7 | 6 | 2 | 6 | 8 |

PAYMENT   GROUP   DIGIT
CENTER   NUMBER   FIELD

SOCIAL
(9-character alphanumeric field)

In the PROCEDURE division, references to both structures could be made as follows:

```
IF PAYMENT-CENTER = 109
   MOVE "NEW YORK" TO DL-CENTER
   ADD 1 TO NY-COUNT.
MOVE SOCIAL TO SOCIAL-OUT.
```

or

```
MULTIPLY 287 BY SS-NUMBER.            (287 • 109476268)
SUBTRACT GROUP-NUMBER FROM SS-NUMBER. (109476268−47)
MOVE DIGIT-FIELD TO RANDOM-KEY.       (Move 6268)
```

Many times the question is asked, If I move two different items into the original and into the redefined record, into which of the records are the items moved? The answer is into both, i.e., a redefined record does not reserve a new memory area—it shares the same memory area as the record it redefines. Consider the following example, where data is moved into a redefined memory area.

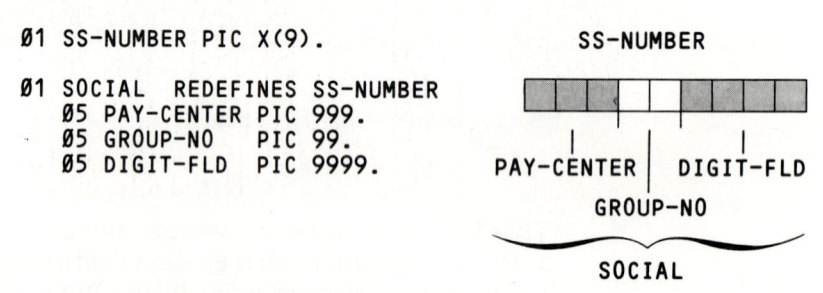

```
01 SS-NUMBER PIC X(9).

01 SOCIAL   REDEFINES SS-NUMBER
   05 PAY-CENTER PIC 999.
   05 GROUP-NO   PIC 99.
   05 DIGIT-FLD  PIC 9999.
```

SS-NUMBER

PAY-CENTER | DIGIT-FLD
GROUP-NO

SOCIAL

INSTRUCTION	OUTCOME	
MOVE 'NEW YORK' TO SS-NUMBER.	`N E W   Y O R K` ↑ Same memory area ↓	A string of nine characters is moved into SS-NUMBER.
MOVE 197 TO DIGIT-FLD.	`N E W Y 0 1 9 7`	The numeric field 0197 is moved into the redefined record, which overwrites the four rightmost positions of SOC-SEC.
ADD 1 TO GROUP-NO.		Execution error, GROUP-NO is an alpha field (` Y `).

The general form of the REDEFINES clause is shown in Figure 7–1.

ADDITIONAL FEATURES AND REPORTS 305

> **level-number   name-1   REDEFINES   name-2**

where:

Level-number can be any level number 01 through 49 or 77.

Name-2 is a record description entry (elementary or group item data-name).

Name-1 is a data item name (elementary or group item) that specifies an alternative layout description for the memory area occupied by name-2.

Name-1 and name-2 must be assigned the same level number.

No entry in a redefined record may contain a VALUE clause, but any entry that has a VALUE clause can be redefined.

The REDEFINES clause must be positioned immediately below the name-2 record entry description if name-2 is an elementary item, or below the last subordinate item of name-2 if name-2 is a group item.

A redefined item must have the same length as the item it redefines except at the 01 level.

Input/output records in the FILE section can be redefined at any level except the 01 level.

Examples:

```
01  RECORD-TYPE.                          01  RECORD-TYPE.
    05  FLD-A PIC 999V9.                      05  RT-NAME PIC X(12).
    05  FLD-B REDEFINES FLD-A PIC XXXX.       05  RT-AGE  PIC 99.
    05  FLD-C PIC 99V99.                  01  INVERSE REDEFINES RECORD-TYPE.
                                              05  IR-AGE  PIC 99.
                                              05  IR-NAME PIC X(12).
```

FIGURE 7–1
THE GENERAL FORM OF THE REDEFINES CLAUSE

EXAMPLE 1:

```
77  A PIC 99999 VALUE 12345.
77  B REDEFINES A PIC 999V99.
```

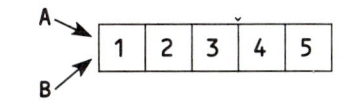

| 1 | 2 | 3 | 4 | 5 |

Even though both A and B share the same five memory positions, the value of A is 12,345 while the value of B is 123.45.

EXAMPLE 2:

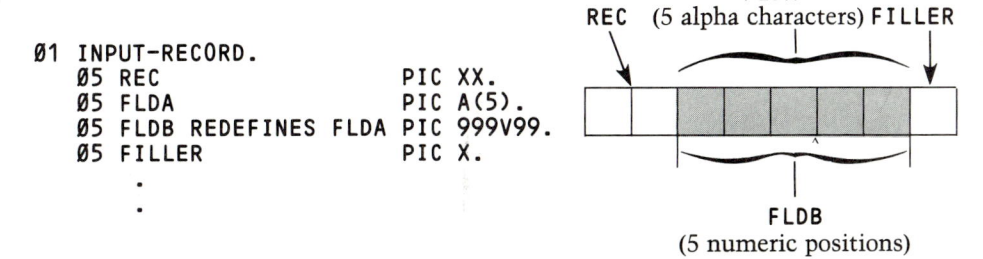

```
01  INPUT-RECORD.
    05  REC                  PIC XX.
    05  FLDA                 PIC A(5).
    05  FLDB REDEFINES FLDA  PIC 999V99.
    05  FILLER               PIC X.
```

REC FLDA (5 alpha characters) FILLER

FLDB (5 numeric positions)

Depending on what is moved or read into INPUT–RECORD, the second data item can be referred to as either an alphabetic data item (FLDA) or a numeric item (FLDB).

EXAMPLE 3:

```
05  FLDA.
    10  CODE-A PIC 999V99 VALUE 33.5.
    10  CODE-B PIC 99.99.

05  FLDB REDEFINES FLDA.
    07  PART-1 PIC XXX.
    07  PART-2 PIC AAA.
    07  PART-3 PIC 9999.
```

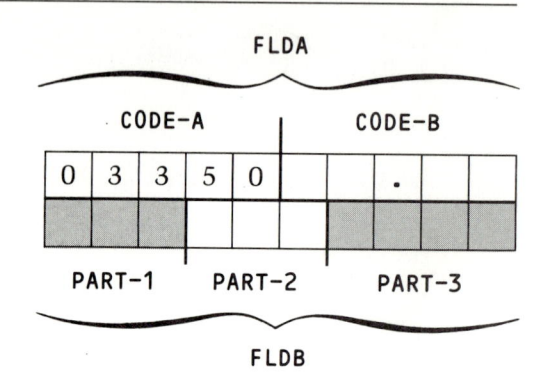

```
          FLDA
 ┌─────────┴─────────┐
  CODE-A        CODE-B
┌─┬─┬─┬─┬─┐   ┌─┬─┬─┬─┐
│0│3│3│5│0│   │ │.│ │ │
├─┼─┼─┼─┼─┤   ├─┼─┼─┼─┤
│▓│ │ │ │▓│   │▓│ │ │▓│
└─┴─┴─┴─┴─┘   └─┴─┴─┴─┘
 PART-1  PART-2  PART-3
 └─────────┬─────────┘
          FLDB
```

In this case PART-1 becomes the alphanumeric string "033". If alphabetic data is moved into PART-2, then CODE-A could not be processed arithmetically since it would contain nonnumeric data in positions 4 and 5.

EXAMPLE 4:

```
01   EMPLOYEE-ID PIC X(18).
01   EMPLOYEE-DESCRIPTION REDEFINES EMPLOYEE-ID.
     05   EMPLOYEE-NUMBER              PIC 9999.
     05   NUMERIC-SEX                  PIC 9.
     05   ALPHA-SEX REDEFINES NUMERIC-SEX PIC X.
     05   EMPLOYEE-ADDRESS             PIC X(13).

01   REGION-FILE-MARKER REDEFINES EMPLOYEE-ID PIC 9(18).
```

As this example illustrates, records can be redefined more than once. Both REGION-FILE-MARKER and EMPLOYEE-DESCRIPTION redefine EMPLOYEE-ID. Note also that in the EMPLOYEE-DESCRIPTION redefinition, ALPHA-SEX redefines NUMERIC-SEX.

To avoid syntax complications in some COBOL systems, do not redefine a record that is itself redefined. For example, do not write:

```
REGION-FILE-MARKER REDEFINES EMPLOYEE-DESCRIPTION.
```

A Program Example with the REDEFINES.

Each record of an input file consists of a salesperson number and various other data items. The salesperson number consists of a seven-digit numeric field subdivided as follows:

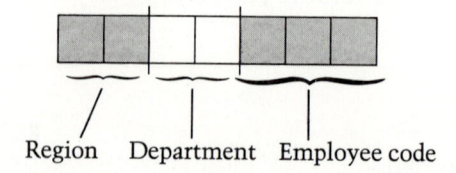

```
┌─┬─┬─┬─┬─┬─┬─┐
│▓│ │ │▓│▓│▓│▓│
└─┴─┴─┴─┴─┴─┴─┘
 └┬┘ └┬┘ └──┬──┘
Region Department Employee code
```

Suppose the input file is arranged in ascending order by salesperson number (seven digits). Let us write the code to:

1. Determine the number of salespeople from department 23.

2. Determine the number of salespeople whose employee codes start with the digit 7.

3. After the input file has been read, print one message at the foot of the report if one or more records are not in ascending order.

ADDITIONAL FEATURES AND REPORTS   307

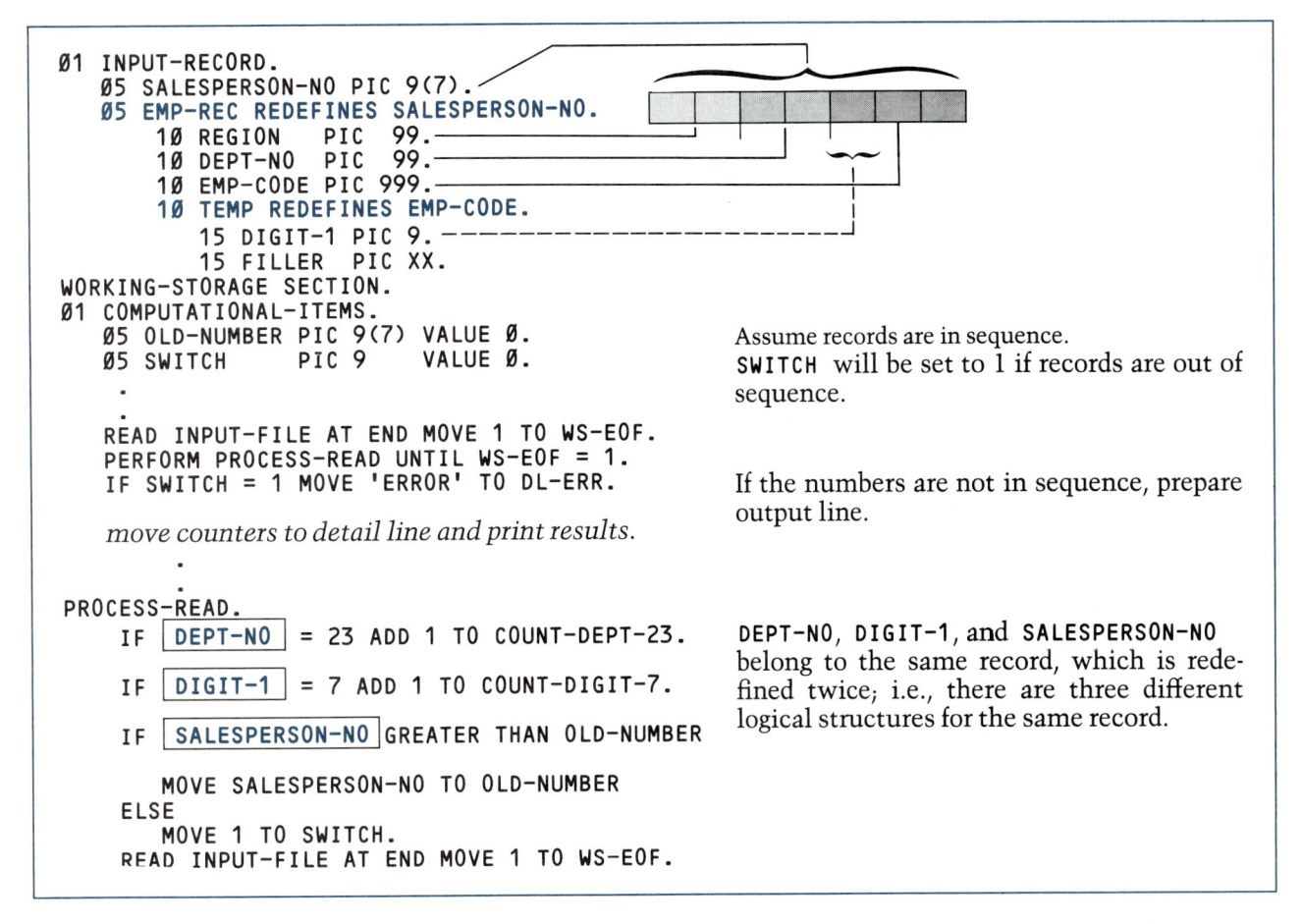

```
01 INPUT-RECORD.
   05 SALESPERSON-NO PIC 9(7).
   05 EMP-REC REDEFINES SALESPERSON-NO.
      10 REGION   PIC 99.
      10 DEPT-NO  PIC 99.
      10 EMP-CODE PIC 999.
      10 TEMP REDEFINES EMP-CODE.
         15 DIGIT-1 PIC 9.
         15 FILLER  PIC XX.
WORKING-STORAGE SECTION.
01 COMPUTATIONAL-ITEMS.
   05 OLD-NUMBER PIC 9(7) VALUE 0.
   05 SWITCH     PIC 9   VALUE 0.
      .
      .
   READ INPUT-FILE AT END MOVE 1 TO WS-EOF.
   PERFORM PROCESS-READ UNTIL WS-EOF = 1.
   IF SWITCH = 1 MOVE 'ERROR' TO DL-ERR.
```
move counters to detail line and print results.
```
      .
      .
PROCESS-READ.
   IF  DEPT-NO  = 23 ADD 1 TO COUNT-DEPT-23.

   IF  DIGIT-1  = 7 ADD 1 TO COUNT-DIGIT-7.

   IF  SALESPERSON-NO  GREATER THAN OLD-NUMBER

      MOVE SALESPERSON-NO TO OLD-NUMBER
   ELSE
      MOVE 1 TO SWITCH.
   READ INPUT-FILE AT END MOVE 1 TO WS-EOF.
```

Assume records are in sequence. SWITCH will be set to 1 if records are out of sequence.

If the numbers are not in sequence, prepare output line.

DEPT-NO, DIGIT-1, and SALESPERSON-NO belong to the same record, which is redefined twice; i.e., there are three different logical structures for the same record.

FIGURE 7–2
REDEFINITION OF A RECORD (REDEFINES).

The program segment to solve this problem is shown in Figure 7–2. Note that the records are not in order if a salesperson record read is less than the preceding salesperson number (OLD–NUMBER). If this is the case, a switch is set to 1 to indicate a sequence error. This switch is interrogated after the input file has been processed. Note that initially OLD–NUMBER is set to 0 so that when the first salesperson number is read, we have two salespersons' numbers to compare. Also note that we need to refer to the salesperson number (the seven-digit number), as well as to two of its subordinate items (DEPT-NO and DIGIT-1).

7-1-3 DO IT NOW

Specify errors, if any, in the following coding segments:

1. ```
   05 FLDA PIC A(15).
   05 FLDB PIC X(15) REDEFINES FLDA.
   ```

2. ```
   05 FLDA PIC X(5).
   04 FLDB REDEFINES FLDA PIC 9(3)V9(2).
   ```

3. 05 FLDA PIC X(10).
   05 FLDB.
      10 FILLER PIC X(5) VALUE SPACES.
      10 FLDC   PIC 999.
   05 FLDD REDEFINES FLDA PIC Z(10).

4. 05 FLDA.
      10 PART-1.
         15 AMT-A PIC X.
         15 AMT-B PIC X.
      10 PART-2 REDEFINES PART-1.
         12 AMT-C PIC 99.

5. 01 FIELDA PIC X(10).
   01 IMAGE REDEFINES FIELDA.
      05 LOC-1 PIC 99 VALUE 0.
      05 LOC-2 PIC XXX VALUE 'YES'.

6. 01 FIELDA PIC X(10) VALUE 'ABCDE'.
   01 IMAGE REDEFINES FIELDA.
      05 LOC-1 PIC 99.
      05 LOC-2 PIC XXX.

7. 05 FLDB PIC X(3).
   05 FLDA REDEFINES FLDB PIC 99.

8. 05 FLDB.
      10 A PIC 99.
      10 B PIC X.
   05 FLDA REDEFINES FLDB.
      10 X PIC XXX.
      10 Y PIC 9.

9. 01 AMT-LINE PIC X(80).
   01 X REDEFINES AMT-LINE PIC 9.

10. 01 RECORD-IN.
       05 FLDB.
          10 FILLER   PIC X(10).
          10 NAME   PIC X(20).
          10 FILLER   PIC X(10).
          10 AMOUNT   PIC 999V99.
       05 FLDA REDEFINES FLDB.
          07 FILLER   PIC X(5).
          07 NAME-IN.
             10 FIRST PIC X(10).
             10 LAST PIC X(10).
          07 FILLER   PIC X(20).
       05 TAX-PIC   PIC X(50).

ANSWERS

1. Invalid. It should be 05 REDEFINES FLDA PIC X(15).
2. Invalid. FLDA and FLDB must have same level number.
3. Invalid. FLDD must be positioned directly below FLDA.
4. Valid.

ADDITIONAL FEATURES AND REPORTS 309

5. Invalid. No VALUE clause is allowed in a REDEFINES clause.
6. Valid.
7. Invalid. Field lengths are unequal (permitted only for 01 levels).
8. Invalid. Field lengths are unequal.
9. Valid (unless it is in the FILE section).
10. Valid.

7-2 CONDITION NAMES

7-2-1 OVERVIEW

Many times, the reader might like to write something like

```
PERFORM 200-READ-PROCESS UNTIL END-OF-FILE.
```

instead of

```
PERFORM 200-READ-PROCESS UNTIL EOF-FLAG = 'YES'.
```

The first sentence flows naturally and is totally self-explanatory; it means: keep processing the READ–PROCESS paragraph until the end-of-file condition is reached.

In another application where a marital status code with the following meanings is read

STATUS	MEANING
1	Single
2	Married
3	Divorced
4	Widowed

it would be nice if the status could be interrogated in English as follows:

```
IF SINGLE                      {IF STAT = 1
    PERFORM SINGLE-PARA.   instead of   PERFORM SINGLE-PARA.

IF DIVORCED OR WIDOWED         {IF STAT = 3 OR 4
    PERFORM DW-PARA.       instead of   PERFORM DW-PARA.
```

To a casual reader, the statement IF STAT = 1 is not too meaningful, since it is not apparent what STAT refers to and what code 1 stands for. The statement IF SINGLE is self-explanatory, however, and of course much more readable.

To improve the readability of COBOL sentences, COBOL allows the user to give names to conditions; then the condition can be referred to by name. In our example,

- The name SINGLE has been given to the condition STAT = 1; hence SINGLE is a condition that is either true or false.
- The name END–OF–FILE has been given to the condition EOF = 'YES'; hence END–OF–FILE is either true or false.

7-2-2 THE VALUE CLAUSE

To give a name to a condition requires, of course, special action. Names generally reserve memory storage—conditions do not reserve memory storage! The way to give a name to a condition is to identify in the DATA division the data item entry that is to be tested in the PROCEDURE division, then specify, directly below the level number of that item, an 88-level entry. This 88-level entry allows you to select a **name** for the condition and the **value** against which the data item is to be tested. For example,

```
05 SEX-CODE PIC 9.
    88 FEMALE VALUE IS 1.
05 AGE      PIC 99.
 .
 .
```

The word FEMALE, as far as COBOL is concerned, does *not* represent a memory storage area. It represents another way to express "SEX–CODE = 1". In your program, when you write IF FEMALE, COBOL interprets this as IF SEX–CODE = 1. Of course you can also write IF NOT FEMALE to express the condition IF NOT SEX–CODE = 1. **But** you *cannot* write IF FEMALE = 2 since COBOL translates this as

$$\text{IF } \underbrace{\text{SEX–CODE} = 1}_{\text{FEMALE}} = 2$$

which is meaningless!

Condition names may appear as 88-level entries in either the FILE section or the WORKING–STORAGE section.

The common form of a condition name clause is:

```
88  Condition-name  VALUE IS  literal
```

Figure 7–3 illustrates the use and declaration of condition names. Note the use of compound condition names such as IF NOT END–OF–FILE or IF JUNIOR OR SENIOR, where END–OF–FILE, JUNIOR and SENIOR are condition names.

Since condition names actually represent conditions, condition names can be used only in connection with statements that make use of conditions, such as the IF statement or the PERFORM UNTIL statement. It would make no sense to move data into a condition name or to process condition names numerically. (How can you move something into SEX = 1?)

The literal defined by the condition name must be consistent with the type of data that it tests. For example, the following condition name is declared incorrectly:

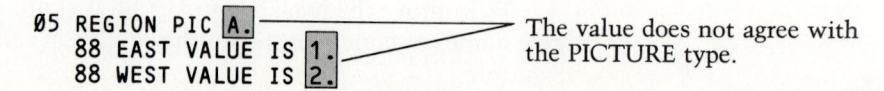

```
05 REGION PIC A.          ──────→  The value does not agree with
   88 EAST VALUE IS 1.               the PICTURE type.
   88 WEST VALUE IS 2.
```

ADDITIONAL FEATURES AND REPORTS

DECLARATION OF CONDITION NAMES	USE OF CONDITION NAMES
| ```
FILE SECTION.
FD  INPUT-FILE
    LABEL RECORDS ARE OMITTED.
01  INPUT-RECORD.
    05 SEX PIC 9.
       88 MALE    VALUE IS 1.
       88 FEMALE  VALUE IS 2.

    05 FILLER PIC X(79).
WORKING-STORAGE SECTION.

77 WS-EOF PIC XXX VALUE 'NO'.
   88 END-OF-FILE VALUE 'YES'.

01 ALTERNATE-RECORD.
   05 NAME           PIC A(20).
   05 CLASSIFICATION PIC 9.
      88 FRESHMAN   VALUE IS 1.
      88 SOPHOMORE  VALUE IS 2.
      88 JUNIOR     VALUE IS 3.
      88 SENIOR     VALUE IS 4.
``` | ```
READ INPUT-FILE
    AT END MOVE 'YES' TO WS-EOF.
    .
    .
    .
    IF MALE PERFORM MALE-PARA
    (meaning IF SEX = 1)
    .
    .
    .
    IF END-OF-FILE  PERFORM LAST-CHORES
    (meaning IF WS-EOF = 'YES')
    .
    .
READ INPUT-FILE INTO ALTERNATE-RECORD
    AT END MOVE 'YES' TO WS-EOF.
IF NOT END-OF-FILE
(meaning IF WS-EOF NOT = 'YES')
    .
    IF JUNIOR OR SENIOR
    (meaning IF CLASSIFICATION = 3
         OR IF CLASSIFICATION = 4)
        PERFORM P-X
    ELSE
        IF FRESHMAN
            PERFORM F-PARA.
``` |

FIGURE 7-3
EXAMPLES OF CONDITION NAMES

Either REGION should be defined with numeric PICTURE, or the value specified in the 88 levels should be alphabetic.

The THRU Option.

The THRU option is a very convenient extension of the VALUE clause in a condition name. The THRU option allows the programmer to specify a range of values for a particular condition name, as illustrated by the following examples.

EXAMPLE 1:
```
05 GRADE PIC 99.
   88 GRADE-SCHOOL  VALUES 1  THRU 6.
   88 JUNIOR-HIGH   VALUES 7, 8, 9.
   88 HIGH-SCHOOL   VALUES 10 THRU 12.
   88 OUTER-ENDS    VALUES 1  THRU 6, 10 THRU 12.
   88 GRADE-ERROR   VALUES 13 THRU 99, 0.
```

USE	MEANING
`IF NOT GRADE-SCHOOL PERFORM TEST1.`	If grade is outside interval 1–6.
`IF JUNIOR-HIGH OR HIGH-SCHOOL` `   PERFORM ADVANCED-LEVEL.`	If grade is in interval 7–12.
`IF GRADE-ERROR` `   PERFORM ERROR-ROUTINE.`	If grade is either 0 or 13–99.

Thus the general form of the VALUE clause for condition names is:

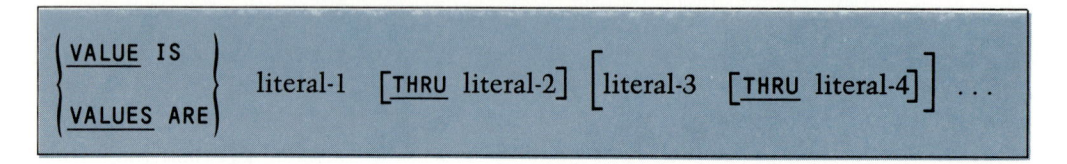

$$\begin{Bmatrix} \underline{\text{VALUE IS}} \\ \underline{\text{VALUES ARE}} \end{Bmatrix} \text{literal-1} \; [\underline{\text{THRU}} \; \text{literal-2}] \; [\text{literal-3} \; [\underline{\text{THRU}} \; \text{literal-4}]] \; \ldots$$

The THRU option can be very useful during the input validation process; with just one condition name the user can screen any invalid code that might have been entered for a particular input data item. In example 1, the condition name GRADE–ERROR tests the input item GRADE for an invalid code.

EXAMPLE 2:
```
05 SALES-AMOUNT PIC 9999V99.
   88 SALES-1 VALUE    0.00 THRU  500.00
   88 SALES-2 VALUE  500.01 THRU 1000.00
   88 SALES-3 VALUE 1000.01 THRU 9999.99.
```

USE	MEANING
IF SALES-1 MOVE .01 TO COMMISSION-RATE.	If sales amount is any value of the form 9999V99 in the interval 0 through 500 ...
IF NOT SALES-2 PERFORM CHECK-OUT.	If sales amount is ≤ 500 or sales amount ≥ 1000.

7–3 CHARACTER MANIPULATING STATEMENTS

COBOL is essentially a file processing language and, as such, it processes huge amounts of data. That data is organized and stored in the form of records that, in many instances, are awkwardly designed in terms of storage allocation. Name fields, for example, may be allocated 25 character positions when most names easily fit in 15 characters. When thousands upon thousands of such records are stored on disk, the resulting space wastage can become mind boggling, as is the time lost in data transmission (for example, from disk/tape to memory or from one computing site to another through telecommunications). An economy of resources can be achieved by compressing or condensing such records, i.e., separating each field by just one blank space. This results in optimal allocation of resources and in cost effectiveness.

Some of these problems can be resolved through the STRING and UNSTRING instructions. The STRING instruction can condense data records while the UNSTRING instruction can restructure them to their original format. In addition, these instructions can be very useful for insertion and deletion of text material in a text processing environment.

In many applications, especially during input data validation, the programmer may also wish to perform such tasks as replacing leading blanks in a numeric field by leading 0's, converting dollar-edited fields to pounds-sterling-edited fields, or replacing single quotes by double quotes. Such search and replace types of functions are available to the COBOL programmer through the EXAMINE and INSPECT verbs.

Other applications of character manipulating statements deal with text analysis and processing. When working with character strings, the programmer will generally want to operate at the character level; i.e., operate on a particular letter or digit within a string. For example, given a paragraph of prose stored in a particular data item, the user might want to count the number of sentences in the paragraph (the number of periods followed by one or more blank spaces), the number of words within a sentence/paragraph (entries sandwiched between blanks), or the number of characters in a particular word.

7-3-1 THE STRING STATEMENT

The STRING statement essentially allows you to take two or more data items (literals or data names) and "glue" them together into one data item consisting of all (or selected parts of) the characters from the original items. For example, we can glue the literal '100' with the literal ' YEARS OLD' to obtain the character string '100 YEARS OLD'. This process is referred to variously as *chaining* or *concatenating* (from the word *concatenation*). The STRING feature is a powerful tool for text manipulation (inserting and deleting characters from character strings). It is also used to condense large records containing many blank spaces into smaller records with fewer spaces.

The general form of the **STRING** statement is shown in Figure 7–4. In the general form, **data-names 1, 2, 4,** and **5** (or **literals 1, 2, 4,** and **5**) are these fields that are to be concatenated and stored **INTO data-name 7**. These fields are referred to as the *sending fields*.

Data names 3 and **6** (or **literals 3** and **6**), specified by the **DELIMITED** clause, are used to indicate what parts of each of the sending fields are to be concatenated. We refer to these fields as the *search pattern field*(s) (*delimited fields*). If **SIZE** is specified, all characters of the sending fields are concatenated. If a search pattern (**literal-3/data-name-3**) is specified instead of **SIZE,** then only those characters *preceding the first occurrence of the search pattern* in the sending field(s) are concatenated. The search pattern may be one or more characters in length. For example, if the search pattern is the letter A (**DELIMITED BY 'A'**) and the data names to be concatenated consist of the characters SAM and LAURA, then S and L are concatenated since they are the only characters preceding the very first occurrence of the letter A in each sending field.

If the search pattern is not found in the sending field(s), then the entire sending field(s) is concatenated into the receiving field. It is possible, of course, to have only one sending field. If the search pattern occurs as the very first character of each sending field, then *no* transfer of data occurs for that field.

The length of the concatenated fields cannot exceed the length of the receiving field. If this is likely to happen, the **ON OVERFLOW** clause can be used to take appropriate action.

Transfer of data into the receiving field is carried out from left to right, just as the sending fields are also processed from left to right. If, for example, the receiving field is 10 characters long and the concatenated data is 4 characters long, then the right-most 6 original characters of the receiving field are not disturbed (the receiving field is *not* padded to the right with blanks, in contrast to alphanumeric moves).

The **POINTER** option specifies a particular position in the receiving field where the concatenated characters are to be moved. **Data-name-8** is a numeric field counter that must be initialized to a value between 1 and the length of the receiving field. That **POINTER** counter is automatically incremented by 1 for each character moved into the receiving field. Note that the concatenation process itself always starts at the first position of the first sending field, the

POINTER does not specify the character position where the concatenation process is to start, but the starting position in the receiving field into which the concatenated data is moved.

The following examples will help clarify the mechanics of the STRING statement.

EXAMPLE 1: For each part, assume the receiving field FLDA has the following picture:

```
    FLDA PIC X(9) VALUE ALL '*'.                              FLDA→  |*|*|*|*|*|*|*|*|*|
a.  STRING 'A', 'B', 'C' DELIMITED BY SIZE INTO FLDA.                |A|B|C|*|*|*|*|*|*|
b.  STRING 'A', 'BA', 'C' DELIMITED BY 'B' INTO FLDA.                |A|C|*|*|*|*|*|*|*|
    The sending field BA is not concatenated since B is the search
    pattern and no characters precede the B of BA.
c.  STRING 'A DOG', 'IN NEW YORK' DELIMITED BY ' ' INTO FLDA.        |A|
 |I|N|*|*|*|*|*|
d.  STRING 'JOHN', 'LAURA' DELIMITED BY 'T' INTO FLDA.               |J|O|H|N|L|A|U|R|A|
e.  STRING 'JIM', 'JOHN' DELIMITED BY 'J' INTO FLDA.                 |*|*|*|*|*|*|*|*|*|
    No characters precede J in either JIM or JOHN.
f.  STRING 'DONNY', ' ', 'MONTY' DELIMITED BY 'ON' INTO FLDA.        |D|
 |M|*|*|*|*|*|*|
g.  STRING 'JIM', 'LAURA' DELIMITED BY 'L' INTO FLDA WITH            |*|*|*|J|I|M|*|*|*|
           POINTER K. (Assume K = 4)                              Value of K is now 7.
h.  STRING 'NEW YORK' DELIMITED BY SPACE INTO FLDA.                  |N|E|W|*|*|*|*|*|*|
i.  STRING 'A', 'BIT' DELIMITED BY 'T
           'OF', 'FUN' DELIMITED BY 'UN' INTO FLDA.                  |A|B|I|O|F|F|*|*|*|
```

EXAMPLE 2: In parts a and b of this example, the data record NAME is condensed into FLDA, an area half its original size.

```
01  NAME.
    05  FOIST PIC X(10) VALUE 'MARC'.     |M|A|R|C| | | | | | |  |J|O|N|E|S| | | | | |
    05  LASTT PIC X(10) VALUE 'JONES'.
01  FLDA  PIC X(10) VALUE ALL '*'.        |*|*|*|*|*|*|*|*|*|*|

 a. STRING FOIST, LASTT DELIMITED BY ' ' INTO FLDA.     |M|A|R|C|J|O|N|E|S|*|
 b. STRING FOIST DELIMITED BY ' '
           SPACE DELIMITED BY SIZE
           LASTT DELIMITED BY SPACE INTO FLDA.          |M|A|R|C| |J|O|N|E|S|
 c. STRING NAME, 'ARC' DELIMITED BY 'RC' INTO FLDA.     |M|A|A|*|*|*|*|*|*|*|
```

In part c, the part of NAME that is to be concatenated consists of all characters preceding RC, i.e., MA. The part of ARC to be concatenated consists of all characters preceding RC, i.e., A. Hence MAA is the result. The trailing asterisks remain in FLDA.

ADDITIONAL FEATURES AND REPORTS 315

$$\underline{\text{STRING}} \left\{ \begin{array}{l} \text{data-name-1} \\ \text{literal-1} \end{array} \right\} \left[\begin{array}{l} \text{,data-name-2} \\ \text{,literal-2} \end{array} \right] \ldots \underline{\text{DELIMITED BY}} \left\{ \begin{array}{l} \text{data-name-3} \\ \text{literal-3} \\ \underline{\text{SIZE}} \end{array} \right\}$$

$$\left[, \left\{ \begin{array}{l} \text{data-name-4} \\ \text{literal-4} \end{array} \right\} \left[\begin{array}{l} \text{,data-name-5} \\ \text{,literal-5} \end{array} \right] \ldots \underline{\text{DELIMITED BY}} \left\{ \begin{array}{l} \text{data-name-6} \\ \text{literal-6} \\ \underline{\text{SIZE}} \end{array} \right\} \right] \ldots$$

$$\underline{\text{INTO}} \text{ data-name-7 } [\text{WITH } \underline{\text{POINTER}} \text{ data-name-8}]$$

$$[\text{ON } \underline{\text{OVERFLOW}} \text{ statement}]$$

sending fields: data-name-1, data-name-2, data-name-4, data-name-5

receiving field: data-name-7

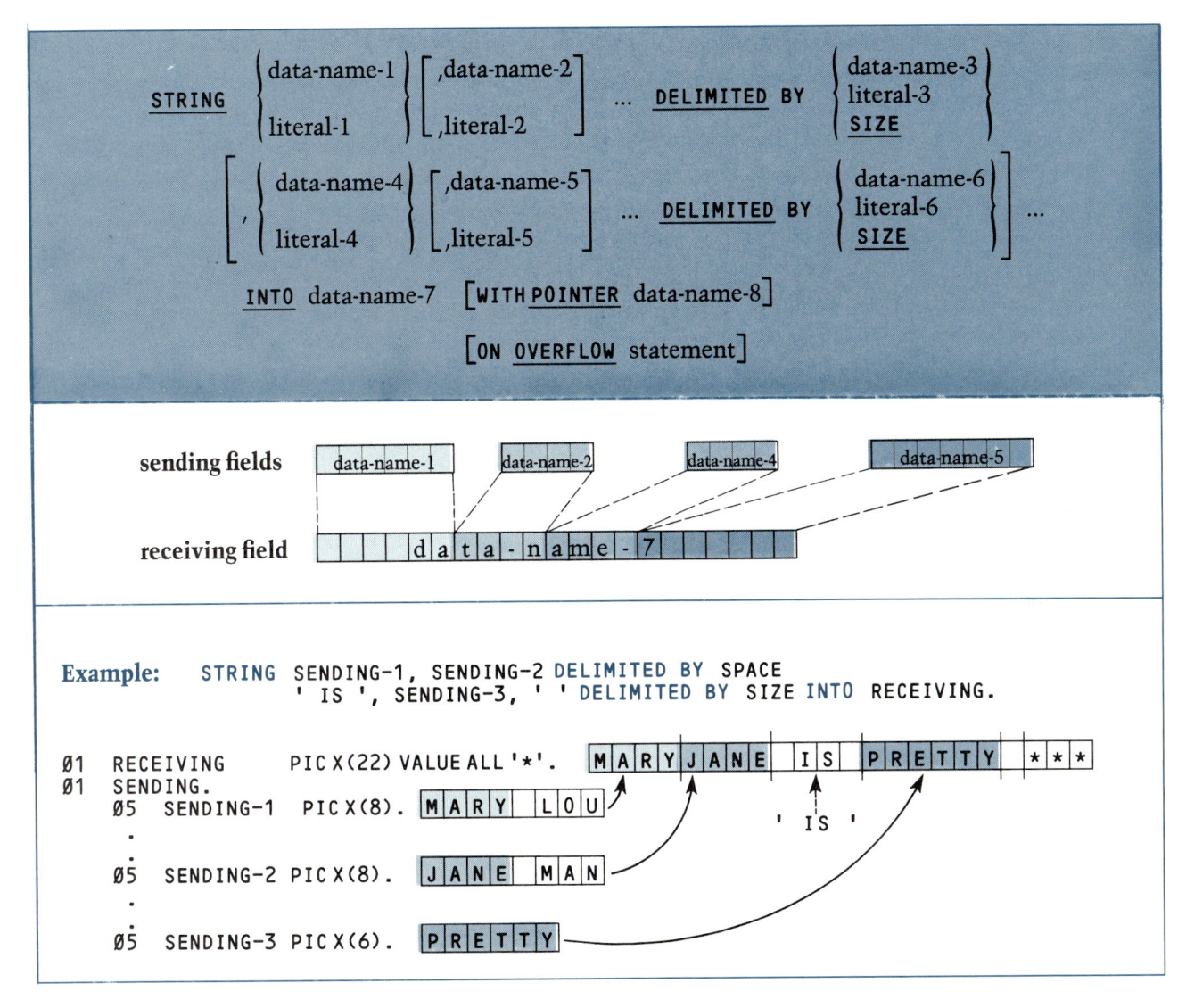

Example: STRING SENDING-1, SENDING-2 DELIMITED BY SPACE
          ' IS ', SENDING-3, ' ' DELIMITED BY SIZE INTO RECEIVING.

```
01  RECEIVING    PIC X(22) VALUE ALL '*'.   MARY JANE IS PRETTY ***
01  SENDING.
    05  SENDING-1  PIC X(8).   MARY LOU
    .
    05  SENDING-2  PIC X(8).   JANE MAN                 ' IS '
    .
    05  SENDING-3  PIC X(6).   PRETTY
```

FIGURE 7–4
THE STRING CLAUSE

EXAMPLE 3: Assume the following numeric data in SS–NUMBER.

```
01  SS-NUMBER.                    1 0 9 3 2 4 1 7 6
    05  PAYMENT-CENTER  PIC 999.
    05  GROUP-NUMBER    PIC 99.
    05  DIGIT-FLD       PIC 9999.
01  SOCIAL-NO           PIC X(11).

    STRING PAYMENT-CENTER, '-', GROUP-NUMBER, '-', DIGIT-FLD
        DELIMITED BY SIZE INTO SOCIAL-NO.
```

1 0 9 - 3 2 - 4 1 7 6

7-3-2 THE UNSTRING STATEMENT

The UNSTRING statement performs the inverse function of the STRING statement. The STRING statement joins separate items together into one field, while the UNSTRING statement disjoins (separates) one field into scattered memory fields. The general form of the UNSTRING statement is shown in Figure 7-5. Data-name-1 must be alphanumeric while data-names 4 and 7 can be alphanumeric or numeric. If the receiving field is wider than the sending field, trailing blanks or leading 0's are provided depending on whether the receiving field is alphanumeric or numeric.

The way in which the UNSTRING statement operates can be better understood by means of several examples:

EXAMPLE 1: MAILING-LIST contains a condensed address record where a slash (/) separates the street, city, state, and zip fields from one another. You are to recreate the address record whose original structure is as follows:

```
01  ADDRESS-RECORD.
    05 STREET PIC X(15).
    05 CITY   PIC X(08).
    05 STATE  PIC X(02).
    05 ZIP    PIC 9(05).
01  MAILING-LIST PIC X(29) VALUE '325 SOUTH ST./VENYCE/FL/37574'.
```

To guide the four substrings of MAILING-LIST into their respective memory areas, we use the instruction:

```
UNSTRING MAILING LIST
         DELIMITED BY '/'
    INTO STREET
         CITY
         STATE
         ZIP.
```

In this case, the substring "325 SOUTH ST." is moved into:

STREET: | 3 | 2 | 5 | | S | O | U | T | H | | S | T | . | | |

and the substring "VENYCE" is moved into:

CITY: | V | E | N | Y | C | E | | | et cetera.

Since STREET is 15 characters long and the substring is only 13 characters long, the STREET field is padded to the right with blank spaces. If the substring had exceeded 15 characters, then only its left-most 15 characters would have been moved to STREET and the extra characters would not be part of the next substring in MAILING-LIST. Only the delimiter (the slash, in this case) can determine the start of a new substring.

If the delimiter had been a blank space (DELIMITED BY ' ') instead of the slash, MAILING-LIST would have been dissected as follows:

STREET | 3 | 2 | 5 | | | | | | | | | | | | |
CITY | S | O | U | T | H | | | |
STATE | S | T |
ZIP | V | E | N | Y | C |

ADDITIONAL FEATURES AND REPORTS 317

$$\begin{bmatrix} \underline{\text{DELIMITED}} \text{ BY } [\underline{\text{ALL}}] \begin{Bmatrix} \text{data-name-2} \\ \text{literal-2} \end{Bmatrix} \begin{bmatrix} , \underline{\text{OR}} [\underline{\text{ALL}}] \begin{Bmatrix} \text{data-name-3} \\ \text{literal-3} \end{Bmatrix} \end{bmatrix} \dots \end{bmatrix}$$

UNSTRING data-name-1

[DELIMITED BY [ALL] {data-name-2 / literal-2} [, OR [ALL] {data-name-3 / literal-3}] ...]

INTO

  data-name-4 [, DELIMITER IN data-name-5] [COUNT IN data-name-6]

  data-name-7 [, DELIMITER IN data-name-8] [COUNT IN data-name-9] ...

  [WITH POINTER data-name-10] [TALLYING IN data-name-11]

  [ON OVERFLOW statement]

sending field: data-name-1

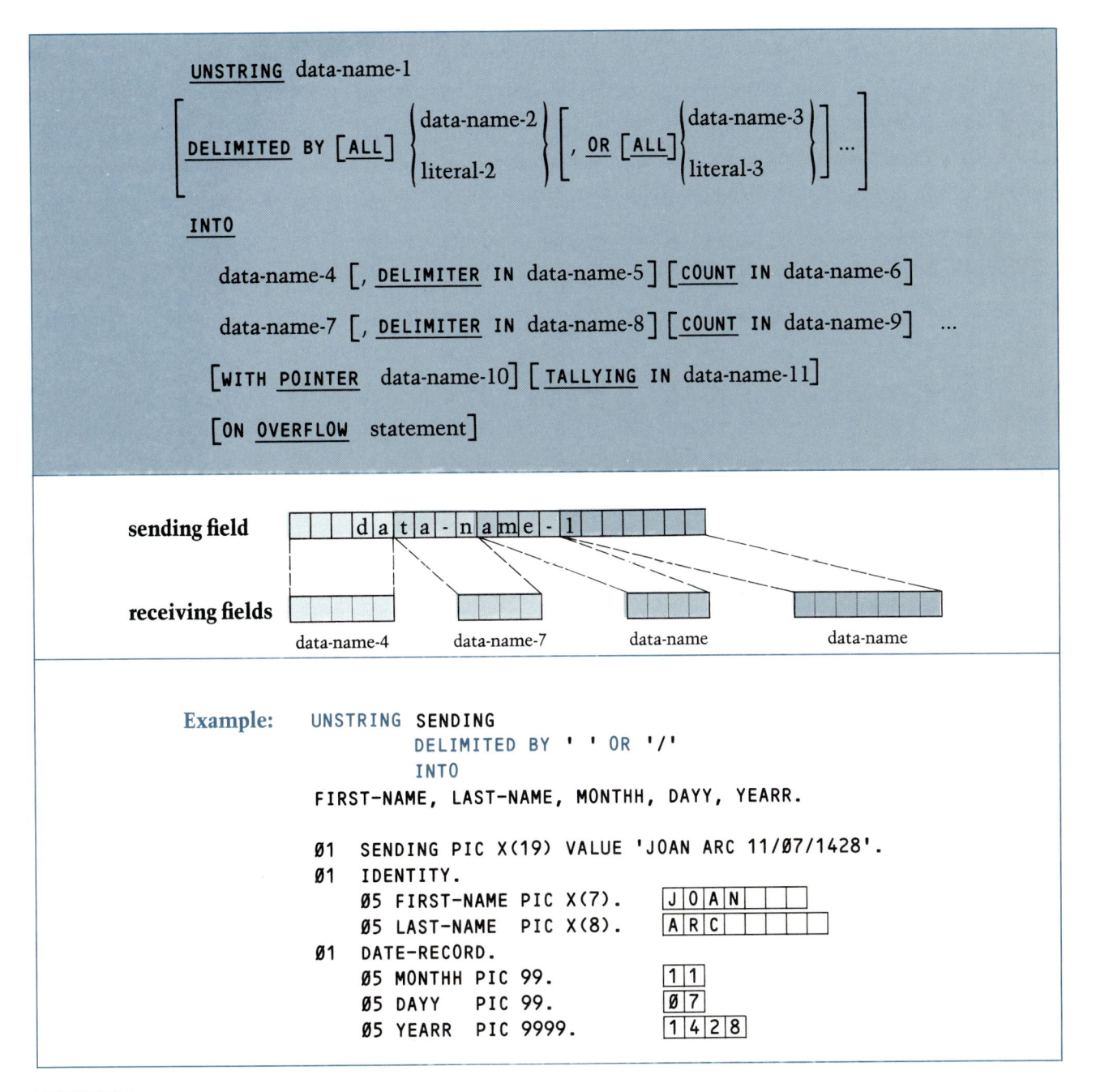

receiving fields: data-name-4, data-name-7, data-name, data-name

Example:
```
          UNSTRING SENDING
                  DELIMITED BY ' ' OR '/'
                  INTO
          FIRST-NAME, LAST-NAME, MONTHH, DAYY, YEARR.

          01  SENDING PIC X(19) VALUE 'JOAN ARC 11/07/1428'.
          01  IDENTITY.
              05  FIRST-NAME PIC X(7).     J O A N
              05  LAST-NAME  PIC X(8).     A R C
          01  DATE-RECORD.
              05  MONTHH PIC 99.           1 1
              05  DAYY   PIC 99.           0 7
              05  YEARR  PIC 9999.         1 4 2 8
```

FIGURE 7–5
THE GENERAL FORM OF THE UNSTRING STATEMENT

If we had unstrung MAILING–LIST into the group item ADDRESS–RECORD with the slash delimiter, i.e., UNSTRING MAILING–LIST ... INTO ADDRESS–RECORD, then the first substring of ADDRESS–RECORD (which is 325 SOUTH ST.) would be moved into the STREET field, while the contents of CITY, STATE and ZIP would not be affected since only one receiving field was specified.

Generally speaking, the number of items specified by the INTO clause corresponds in number to the various substrings present in the sending field. For instance, if we UNSTRING sending-field INTO three items then we expect to have three delimited strings in the sending-field. If, however, there are four delimited strings for three receiving items, then the first three strings are moved to the three memory areas, but the system will give us a message saying that the sending field contains still another substring for which it cannot find a home! This message is in the form of an overflow condition that can be tested by the user through the ON OVERFLOW clause. IF we UNSTRING sending-field INTO four items and there are only two substrings in the sending field, then the two substrings are moved into the first two receiving fields and the last two receiving fields remain unchanged.

If the delimiter is not found in the sending field, then the entire sending field is sent to the first memory area designated by the INTO clause!

EXAMPLE 2 Consecutive occurrences of the delimiter.

```
01  SENDING-FIELD PIC X(15) VALUE 'I AM//13//YEARS'.
01  RECEIVING.
    05 FLD-1  PIC X(4).
    05 FLD-2  PIC 999.
    05 FLD-3  PIC X(4).
    05 FLD-4  PIC X(5).

UNSTRING SENDING-FIELD DELIMITED BY '/'
    INTO FLD-1, FLD-2, FLD-3, FLD-4.
```

The first slash causes $\boxed{\text{I}\ \ \text{AM}}$ to be stored in FLD-1. Since there is no text between the first and second slashes, that substring is considered to be void and numeric 0's are moved to FLD-2 (since FLD-2 is numeric). IF a void substring is moved to an alphanumeric receiving field, the receiving field is filled with blanks. 13 is moved to FLD-3, and blanks are moved into FLD-4.

If the ALL option is used, i.e., DELIMITED BY ALL '/' then any occurrence of consecutive slashes is treated as one delimiter. IF this option were used in the preceding example, FLD-2 would contain 013, FLD-3 would contain YEAR, and FLD-4 would remain unaffected.

The other options that can be used in the UNSTRING statement are discussed here briefly. The reader may wish to refer to the example in Figure 7-6 to understand the various options better.

The OR Option

```
SENDING PIC X(32) VALUE '01/17/84 SOCIAL NO   108-84-6224'.
    .
    .
UNSTRING SENDING DELIMITED BY '/' OR '-' OR ALL SPACES...
```

SENDING now consists of 8 substrings: 01, 17, 84, SOCIAL, NO, 108, 84, 6224

The DELIMITER IN Option

For each substring that is moved to the receiving field, the corresponding delimiter (search pattern character) is stored in the user-designated data item. This feature is used mostly in cases where multiple delimiters are used.

```
                                    FLD-1  FLD-2  FLD-3  FLD-4
SENDING PIC X(21) VALUE 'YES, HIM. THAT'S HIM'.
UNSTRING SENDING DELIMITED BY '.' OR ',' OR ALL ' '
   INTO FLD-1 DELIMITER IN LIM-1     LIM-1 [,]    FLD-1 [Y|E|S]
        FLD-2 DELIMITER IN LIM-2     LIM-2 [b]    FLD-2 0's or spaces
        FLD-3 DELIMITER IN LIM-3     LIM-3 [.]    FLD-3 [H|I|M]
        FLD-4 DELIMITER IN LIM-4.    LIM-4 [b]    FLD-4 0's or spaces
```

Note that in this case the delimiters (comma and blank space) occur side by side (consecutive occurrence as in example 2), causing either spaces or zeroes to be moved into FLD-2 and in FLD-4. Note that an overflow condition would occur since substrings THAT'S and HIM have no receiving fields.

The COUNT IN Option

This option stores the length (number of characters) of each substring processed into the user-designated numeric counter (see Figure 7–6).

The TALLYING IN Option

The TALLYING counter stores in the user-designated numeric item the number of substrings moved to the various receiving fields (see Figure 7–6). This numeric item is initialized to 0 by the system at the start of the instruction.

The POINTER Option

The UNSTRING operation starts at the position in the sending field specified by the value of the pointer. If the value of the pointer is 6, for example, the first five positions of the sending field are ignored. As the UNSTRING instruction is carried out and each character is processed, the value of the pointer field is increased by 1 to reflect the position of the next character to be processed. The value of the pointer may be any number between 1 and the length of the sending field.

7-3-3 DO IT NOW

1. Determine the contents of TEMP as a result of the following STRING instruction:

   a.
   ```
   01 TEMP   PIC X(27) VALUE ALL '*'.
   01 SENT-1 PIC X(9)  VALUE 'I, MICHEL'.
   01 SENT-2 PIC X(9)  VALUE 'HAVE SEEN'.
   01 SENT-3 PIC X(9)  VALUE 'THE LIGHT'.
       STRING SENT-1, SENT-2, SENT-3, '.' DELIMITED BY ','
           INTO TEMP.
   ```

320 UNDERSTANDING STRUCTURED COBOL

```
UNSTRING SENDING DELIMITED BY '/' OR ALL '-'
  INTO
  FLD-1 DELIMITER IN LIM-1 COUNT IN COUNT-1
  FLD-2 DELIMITER IN LIM-2 COUNT IN COUNT-2
  FLD-3 DELIMITER IN LIM-3 COUNT IN COUNT-3
  WITH POINTER POINT
  TALLYING IN TALY
  ON OVERFLOW MOVE 'YES' TO FLAG.
```

Assume value of POINT is initially 1.

SENDING PIC X(10)	FLD-1 PIC XX	FLD-2 PIC 99	FLD-3 PIC XXXX	COUNT-1 PIC 99	COUNT-2 PIC 99	COUNT-3 PIC 99	LIM-1 PIC X	LIM-2 PIC X	LIM-3 PIC X	TALY PIC 99	POINT PIC 99	FLAG PIC XXX
12/34/5678	12	34	5678	02	02	04	/	/	ƀ	03	11	NO
1/2-345678	1ƀ	02	3456	01	01	06	/	-	ƀ	03	11	NO
12345/6789	12	67	ƀƀƀƀ	05	04	00	/	ƀ	ƀ	02	11	NO
1234567890	12	ƀƀ	ƀƀƀƀ	10	00	00	ƀ	ƀ	ƀ	01	11	NO
---2-3--5	ƀƀ		3ƀƀƀ	00	01	01	-	-	-	03	10	YES
12/34/56/7	12	34	56ƀƀ	02	02	02	/	/	/	03	10	YES
12--34--56	12	34	56ƀƀ	02	02	02	-	-	ƀ	03	11	NO
12//34//56	12	00	34ƀƀ	02	00	02	/	/	/	03	08	YES
12/34/-678	12	34	ƀƀƀƀ	02	02	00	/	/	-	03	08	YES
1-/2--3456	1ƀ	00	2ƀƀƀ	01	00	01	-	/	-	03	07	YES
/12--4/567	ƀƀ	12	4ƀƀƀ	00	02	01	/	-	/	03	08	YES
//1/2/3456	ƀƀ	00	1ƀƀƀ	00	00	01	/	/	/	03	05	YES
//123456789	ƀƀ	00	2345	00	00	08	/	/	ƀ	03	11	NO
1/2/3/4/5/	1ƀ	02	3ƀƀƀ	01	01	01	/	/	/	03	07	YES
123456789/	12	ƀƀ	ƀƀƀƀ	09	00	00	/	ƀ	ƀ	01	11	NO
/123456789	ƀƀ	89	ƀƀƀƀ	00	09	00	/	ƀ	ƀ	02	11	NO
123///4567	12	00	ƀƀƀƀ	03	00	00	/	/	/	03	07	YES
////123456	ƀƀ	00	ƀƀƀƀ	00	00	00	/	/	/	03	04	YES
1234567///	12	00	ƀƀƀƀ	07	00	00	/	/	/	03	11	NO
1///2//34	1ƀ	00	ƀƀƀƀ	01	00	00	/	/	/	03	05	YES

FIGURE 7-6
EXAMPLES OF UNSTRING STATEMENTS

```
b. 01  TEMP PIC X(37) VALUE 'I CAME. I SAW. I CONQUERED. I SIGHED.'
   01  K    PIC 99    VALUE 1.

       PERFORM REPLACE-PERIOD UNTIL K > 37.

   REPLACE-PERIOD.
       STRING TEMP, ',' DELIMITED BY '.' INTO TEMP WITH POINTER K.

c. 01  TEMP PIC X(37) VALUE
          'I CAME. I SAW. I CONQUERED. I SIGHED.'.
   01  ALTERNATE REDEFINES TEMP.
       05 FOIST PIC X(7).
       05 SECND PIC X(7).
       05 THIRD PIC X(13).
       05 FORTH PIC X(10).
   01  K PIC 99 VALUE 1.

       STRING FOIST ',' DELIMITED BY '.' INTO TEMP WITH POINTER K.
       STRING SECND ',' DELIMITED BY '.' INTO TEMP WITH POINTER K.
       STRING THIRD ',' DELIMITED BY '.' INTO TEMP WITH POINTER K.
       STRING FORTH ',' DELIMITED BY '.' INTO TEMP WITH POINTER K.
```

ADDITIONAL FEATURES AND REPORTS 321

2. Given the following UNSTRING instruction, determine the contents of memory fields FLD-1, FLD-2, FLD-3, LIM-1, LIM-2, LIM-3, TALY, COUNT-1, COUNT-2, COUNT-3, POINT, and FLAG for the 11 values of SENDING shown below..

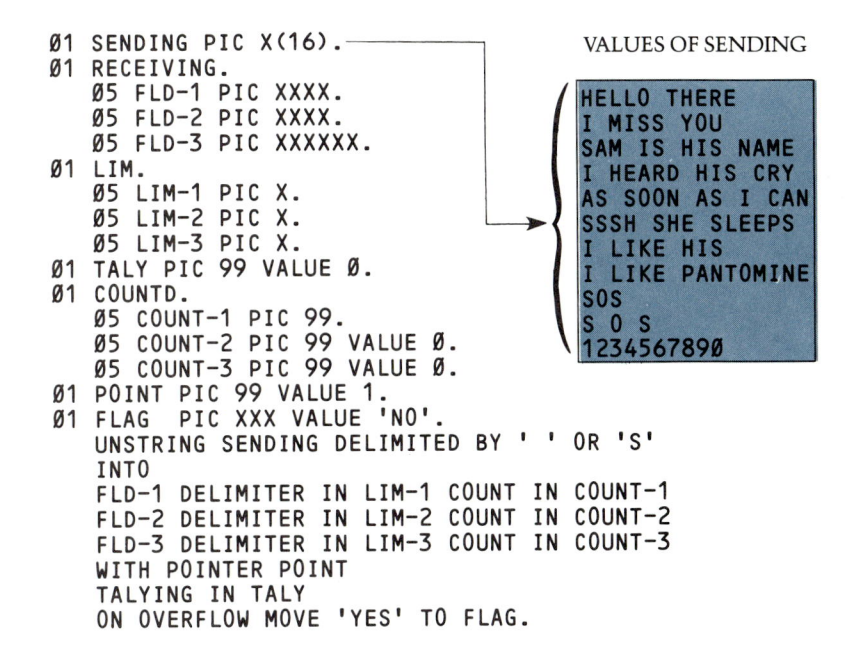

```
01 SENDING PIC X(16).
01 RECEIVING.
   05 FLD-1 PIC XXXX.
   05 FLD-2 PIC XXXX.
   05 FLD-3 PIC XXXXX.
01 LIM.
   05 LIM-1 PIC X.
   05 LIM-2 PIC X.
   05 LIM-3 PIC X.
01 TALY PIC 99 VALUE 0.
01 COUNTD.
   05 COUNT-1 PIC 99.
   05 COUNT-2 PIC 99 VALUE 0.
   05 COUNT-3 PIC 99 VALUE 0.
01 POINT PIC 99 VALUE 1.
01 FLAG  PIC XXX VALUE 'NO'.
   UNSTRING SENDING DELIMITED BY ' ' OR 'S'
   INTO
   FLD-1 DELIMITER IN LIM-1 COUNT IN COUNT-1
   FLD-2 DELIMITER IN LIM-2 COUNT IN COUNT-2
   FLD-3 DELIMITER IN LIM-3 COUNT IN COUNT-3
   WITH POINTER POINT
   TALYING IN TALY
   ON OVERFLOW MOVE 'YES' TO FLAG.
```

VALUES OF SENDING

```
HELLO THERE
I MISS YOU
SAM IS HIS NAME
I HEARD HIS CRY
AS SOON AS I CAN
SSSH SHE SLEEPS
I LIKE HIS
I LIKE PANTOMINE
SOS
S O S
1234567890
```

ANSWERS

1. a. IHAVESEEN THE LIGHT.*******
   b. I CAME,I CAME,I CAME,I CAME,I CAME,Ib
   c. I CAME, I SAW, I CONQUERED, I SIGHED,

2.

SENDING											
HELLO THER E	HELL	THER	bbbbb	05	05	00	b	b	b	03	14	YES
I MISS YOU	Ibbb	MI	bbbbb	01	02	00	b	S	S	03	07	YES
SAM IS HIS NAME	bbbb	AM	Ibbbb	00	02	01	S	b	S	03	07	YES
I HEARD HIS CRY	Ibbb	HEAR	HIbbb	01	05	02	b	b	S	03	12	YES
AS SOON AS I CAN	Abbb	bbbb	bbbbb	01	00	00	S	b	S	03	05	YES
SSSH SHE SLEEPS	bbbb	bbbb	bbbbb	00	00	00	S	S	S	03	04	YES
I LIKE HIS	Ibbb	LIKE	HIbbb	01	04	02	b	b	S	03	11	YES
I LIKE PANTOMINE	Ibbb	LIKE	PANTOM	01	04	09	b	b	b	03	17	NO
SOS	bbbb	Obbb	bbbbb	00	01	00	S	S	b	03	05	YES
S O S	bbbb	bbbb	Obbb	00	00	01	S	b	b	03	05	YES
1234567890	1234	bbbb	bbbbb	10	00	00	b	b	b	03	14	YES

7-3-4 THE EXAMINE STATEMENT

The EXAMINE verb is available in 1968 ANSI COBOL compilers. In the 1974 ANSI COBOL the EXAMINE verb has been replaced by the INSPECT verb, which is significantly more powerful than the EXAMINE verb. Some 1974 compilers feature both verbs and some feature only the INSPECT verb! The reader should consult his/her installation's manual to identify the particular verb that is supported.

The EXAMINE statement is used to count the number of times a particular character appears in a string of characters. It can also be used to replace a particular character in the character string by another user-designated character.

The EXAMINE statement has two formats:

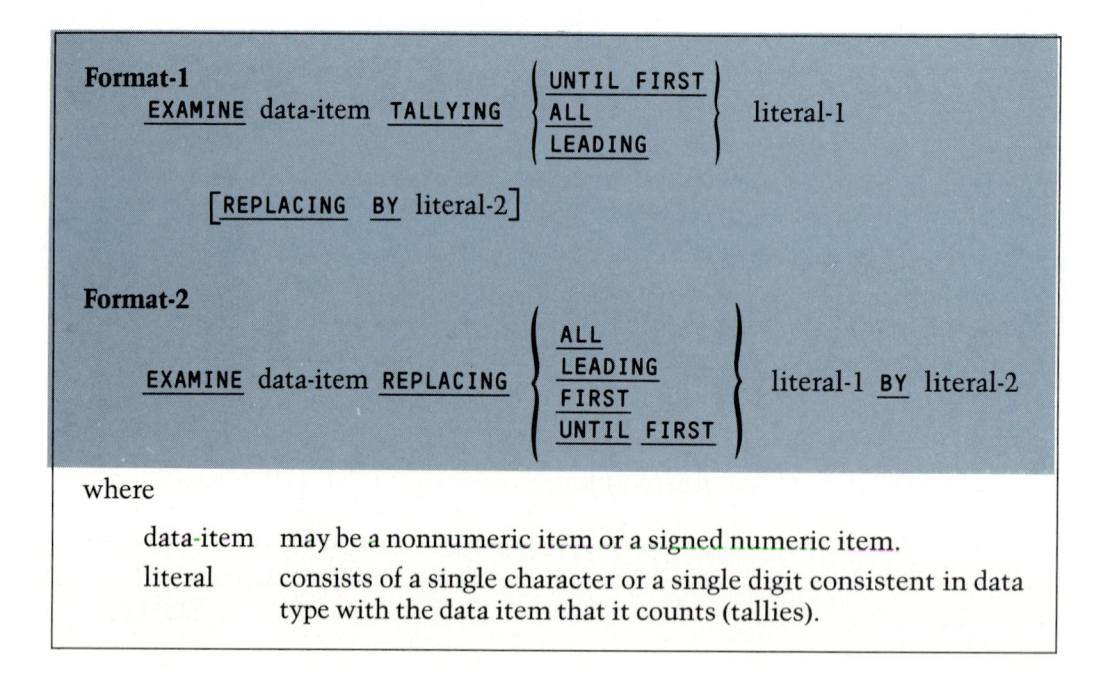

Format-1

$$\underline{\text{EXAMINE}} \text{ data-item } \underline{\text{TALLYING}} \left\{ \begin{array}{l} \text{UNTIL FIRST} \\ \underline{\text{ALL}} \\ \underline{\text{LEADING}} \end{array} \right\} \text{ literal-1}$$

$$[\underline{\text{REPLACING}} \ \underline{\text{BY}} \ \text{literal-2}]$$

Format-2

$$\underline{\text{EXAMINE}} \text{ data-item } \underline{\text{REPLACING}} \left\{ \begin{array}{l} \underline{\text{ALL}} \\ \underline{\text{LEADING}} \\ \underline{\text{FIRST}} \\ \underline{\text{UNTIL FIRST}} \end{array} \right\} \text{ literal-1 } \underline{\text{BY}} \text{ literal-2}$$

where

    data-item   may be a nonnumeric item or a signed numeric item.

    literal   consists of a single character or a single digit consistent in data type with the data item that it counts (tallies).

These two formats and their options are discussed in the following paragraphs. Examples of the various forms of EXAMINE statements are shown in Figure 7-7.

EXAMINE Format-1.

The EXAMINE process automatically creates a data item called TALLY, which stores a count of characters whose value depends on the ALL, UNTIL FIRST, and LEADING options. No record description entry should be provided by the user to describe TALLY. The reserved word TALLY, whose internal picture is numeric, can be used in arithmetic, relational, and MOVE operations. TALLY is reset to 0 at the start of each EXAMINE statement.

Option TALLYING ALL

    `EXAMINE data-item TALLYING ALL literal-1`

The EXAMINE statement counts the number of times literal-1 occurs in the string of characters specified by the EXAMINE verb and stores that number in TALLY. If the REPLACING option is used, literal-2 is substituted for each occurrence of literal-1. Literal-1 consists of just one character.

ADDITIONAL FEATURES AND REPORTS

Option TALLYING UNTIL FIRST

`EXAMINE data-item TALLYING UNTIL FIRST literal-1`

The EXAMINE statement stores in TALLY the count of all characters encountered before the first occurrence of literal-1. The EXAMINE process starts at the left-most character of the string and proceeds to the right, one character at a time. If the REPLACING option is used, all characters are replaced by literal-2 until literal-1 or the right-hand boundary of the string is encountered. Literal-1 consists of just one character.

FLD BEFORE	EXAMINE INSTRUCTION	FLD AFTER	TALLY
AARDVARK	EXAMINE FLD TALLYING UNTIL FIRST 'V'. Count number of characters up to but not including the first V.	AARDVARK	4
AARDVARK	EXAMINE FLD TALLYING ALL 'A'. Count occurrence of letter A in FLD.	AARDVARK	3
AARDVARK	EXAMINE FLD TALLYING LEADING 'A'. Count number of leading A's.	AARDVARK	2
1234 3122	EXAMINE FLD TALLYING ALL 3. Count occurrence of digit 3.	1234 3122	2
WE AM US	EXAMINE FLD TALLYING UNTIL FIRST SPACE. MOVE TALLY TO FIRST-WORD-OUT. EXAMINE FLD TALLYING ALL SPACES. COMPUTE NO-WORDS = TALLY + 1.	WE AM US	2 3
1.000.789,0	EXAMINE FLD TALLYING ALL '.' REPLACING BY ','.	1,000,789,0	2
NEW YORK	EXAMINE FLD TALLYING UNTIL FIRST 'Y' REPLACING BY SPACES.	␣␣␣␣YORK	4
NEW YORK	EXAMINE FLD TALLYING UNTIL FIRST 'A' REPLACING BY ' '. (All positions are replaced by spaces since character A did not occur.)	␣␣␣␣␣␣␣␣	8
0003.45	EXAMINE FLD TALLYING LEADING ZEROS REPLACING BY SPACES.	␣␣␣3.45	3
9091	EXAMINE FLD TALLYING LEADING ZEROS.	9091	0
0030000	EXAMINE FLD TALLYING LEADING ZEROS REPLACING BY SPACES.	␣␣30000	
0003.45	EXAMINE FLD REPLACING LEADING '0' BY '*'.	***3.45	
1234567	EXAMINE FLD REPLACING FIRST 5 BY 0. Replace first occurrence of 5 by a 0.	1234067	
1234567	EXAMINE FLD REPLACING UNTIL FIRST 5 BY 0. Replace all digits up to but not including 5 by 0's.	0000567	

FIGURE 7-7
EXAMPLE OF EXAMINE STATEMENTS

Option TALLYING LEADING

> `EXAMINE` data-item `TALLYING LEADING` literal-1

The EXAMINE statement stores in TALLY the count of occurrences of literal-1 prior to encountering a character other than literal-1, in other words it counts all leading characters specified by literal-1. If the REPLACING option is used, the substitution of literal-2 for literal-1 terminates as soon as a character other than literal-1 or the right-hand boundary of the string is encountered. Literal-1 consists of just one character.

EXAMINE Format-2.

This form of the EXAMINE statement is identical to the format-1 statement, except that no TALLY is used. Format-2 allows the REPLACING FIRST option, which is not available in format-1. When the REPLACING FIRST option is used, the first occurrence of literal-1 is replaced by literal-2.

The EXAMINE statement can be very useful during input validation where it can be used in conjunction with the various class condition statements. For example, suppose a course number consists of three alphabetic characters (course title) followed by three numeric digits. The registrar wants to find the current enrollment for a particular course and types in the course number followed by a query code. To ensure that the course title is valid, the program needs to check that the first three characters are letters of the alphabet (not blanks or other nonalphabetic characters). This requires two types of tests:

```
05 COURSE-ID.
   05 COURSE-TITLE PIC XXX.
   05 COURSE-NO    PIC 999.
         .
         .
   IF COURSE-TITLE IS NOT ALPHABETIC            If title contained a blank space, it would be invalid but
      DISPLAY 'INVALID COURSE TITLE - RETYPE'   would not be caught by the test for NOT
   ELSE                                         ALPHABETIC.
      EXAMINE COURSE-TITLE TALLYING ALL ' '     If title contains one or more blanks, then display an
      IF TALLY > 0                              error message.
         DISPLAY 'BLANKS IN COURSE TITLE - RETYPE'.
   PERFORM CHECK-COURSE-DIGITS.                 Go and screen the digit field.
```

We also need to replace any leading blanks in COURSE–NO by zeros, but we cannot use the EXAMINE verb since blanks are not numeric digits. However, we can achieve that objective by redefining COURSE–NO:

```
05 COURSE-NO PIC 999.
05 COURSE REDEFINES COURSE-NO PIC XXX.
      .
      .
EXAMINE COURSE REPLACING ALL SPACES BY ZEROS.
```

The EXAMINE statement can also be used on group items. Suppose, for example, that TEXT1 is a table whose entries contain a passage of prose and we want to determine whether the passage contains more than 50 sentences. The following code could be used:

ADDITIONAL FEATURES AND REPORTS   325

```
01 PROSE.
    05 TEXT1 OCCURS 100 PIC X(256).           PROSE contains 25600
        .                                     characters.
        .
    EXAMINE PROSE TALLYING ALL '.'.           Assume periods are used only as
    IF TALLY > 50 PERFORM ...                 end-of-sentence indicators (no
                                              abbreviations or decimal points
                                              expected).
```

For another example using the EXAMINE statement on a group item, assume all FILLER fields in a heading line need to be set to asterisks for a special visual effect. The following code could be used:

```
01 HEADER-1.
    05 FILLER     PIC X(5) VALUE SPACES.
    05 LAST-NAME  PIC X(20).
    05 FILLER     PIC X(5) VALUE SPACES.
    05 SS-NO      PIC 9(9).
    05 FILLER     PIC X(5) VALUE SPACES.
        .
    EXAMINE HEADER-1 REPLACING ALL SPACES BY '*'.
```

7-3-5 THE INSPECT STATEMENT

The INSPECT statement essentially allows one to examine a string of characters to perform the following types of functions:

1. Count the number of occurrences of a specified character in the string (TALLYING option).

2. Replace a specified character within the string by another character (REPLACING option).

In many INSPECT versions it is possible to count the occurrence of consecutive characters (instead of just one character), for example, to count how many times salesman name HARRIS occurs in a field of names. The two forms of the INSPECT verb are shown in Figure 7–8.

The following examples should help you understand the mechanics of the INSPECT statement.

EXAMPLE 1 The INSPECT TALLYING form

The TALLY automatically counts the occurrence of a character within a string. The counter should be initialized to 0.

TEXT-LINE PIC X(30) | S | S | H | , | | T | H | E | | M | I | S | S | U | S | ' | | I | S | | S | L | E | E | P | I | N | G | . | |

```
INSPECT TEXT-LINE TALLYING
    COUNT-1 FOR ALL '.'.              COUNT-1 = 1    There is only one period in the examined field.

INSPECT TEXT-LINE TALLYING
    COUNT-2 FOR LEADING 'S'.          COUNT-2 = 2    Since the left-most character in the examined field is
                                                     an S and there are two of them, the count is 2.
```

TEXT-LINE PIC X(30) `SSH, THE MISSUS' IS SLEEPING.`

INSPECT TEXT-LINE TALLYING COUNT-3 FOR CHARACTERS.	COUNT-3 = 29	There are altogether 29 characters in the examined field.
INSPECT TEXT-LINE TALLYING COUNT-4 FOR ALL 'I' AFTER INITIAL 'S'.	COUNT-4 = 3	There are 3 occurrences of the letter I after the first letter S in the examined field.
INSPECT TEXT-LINE TALLYING COUNT-5 FOR LEADING 'S' AFTER INITIAL 'S'.	COUNT-5 = 1	The leading character in the examined field is an S. Since there is only one S after that, the count is equal to 1.
INSPECT TEXT-LINE TALLYING COUNT-6 FOR CHARACTERS AFTER INITIAL ' '.	COUNT-6 = 24	Following the first blank space encountered, there are an additional 24 characters in the examined field.
INSPECT TEXT-LINE TALLYING COUNT-7 FOR CHARACTERS BEFORE INITIAL '.'.	COUNT-7 = 28	There are 28 characters before the occurrence of the first period in the examined field.
INSPECT TEXT-LINE TALLYING COUNT-8 FOR LEADING 'S' BEFORE INITIAL "'".	COUNT-8 = 2	There are two leading S's in the examined field. These are the very first two S's in the field.
INSPECT TEXT-LINE TALLYING COUNT-9 FOR LEADING 'S' AFTER INITIAL 'U'.	COUNT-9 = 1	The leading character after the first U is S.
INSPECT TEXT-LINE TALLYING COUNT-10 FOR LEADING 'S' AFTER INITIAL 'M'.	COUNT-10 = 0	The leading character after the first M is the letter I and not S; hence there are no leading S's in the examined field.

EXAMPLE 2: The INSPECT REPLACING form

TEXT-LINE PIC X(30) `SSH, THE MISSUS' IS SLEEPING.`

INSPECT TEXT-LINE REPLACING
    ALL ',' BY '.'.
TEXT-LINE: SSH, THE MISSUS' IS SLEEPING.
             SSH. THE MISSUS' IS SLEEPING.
Replace all occurrences of a comma by a period.

INSPECT TEXT-LINE REPLACING
    LEADING 'S' BY 'A'.
TEXT-LINE: SSH. THE MISSUS' IS SLEEPING.
             AAH. THE MISSUS' IS SLEEPING.
Replace the leading S's, if any, by the letter A.

INSPECT TEXT-LINE REPLACING
    FIRST 'P' BY 'B'.
TEXT-LINE: AAH. THE MISSUS' IS SLEEPING.
             AAH. THE MISSUS' IS SLEEBING.
Replace first occurrence of P by the letter B.

INSPECT TEXT-LINE REPLACING
    CHARACTERS BY SPACE
        AFTER INITIAL 'L'.
TEXT-LINE: AAH. THE MISSUS' IS SLEEBING.
             AAH. THE MISSUS' IS SL
Replace all characters after the first L with spaces.

INSPECT TEXT-LINE REPLACING
    CHARACTERS BY '/'
        BEFORE INITIAL '.'.
TEXT-LINE: AAH. THE MISSUS' IS SL
             ///. THE MISSUS' IS SL
Replace all characters preceding the first period by slashes.

ADDITIONAL FEATURES AND REPORTS 327

```
INSPECT TEXT-LINE REPLACING        TEXT-LINE:   ///. THE MISSUS' IS SL
    ALL ' ' BY '*'                              ///. THE MISSUS' *************
        AFTER INITIAL "'".         Replace all characters following the first " ' " by asterisks.

INSPECT TEXT-FILE REPLACING        TEXT-LINE:   ///. THE MISSUS' *************
    CHARACTERS BY '%'                           ///. THE MISSUS' *************
        AFTER 'X'.                 No character X is found and hence no replacement.
```

EXAMPLE 3: The INSPECT TALLYING/REPLACING

```
MOVE 0 TO COUNT-1.
INSPECT TEXT-LINE TALLYING         before   S S H , | T H E | M I S S U S ' | I S | S L U U P I N G .
    COUNT-1 FOR ALL ' '
        AFTER INITIAL '.'          TEXT-LINE
    REPLACING
    FIRST 'U' BY '!'               after    S S H , | T H E | M I S S ! S ' | I S | S L U U P I N G .
        AFTER INITIAL SPACE.
```
COUNT-1 = 1 (only 1 blank after the 1st period).

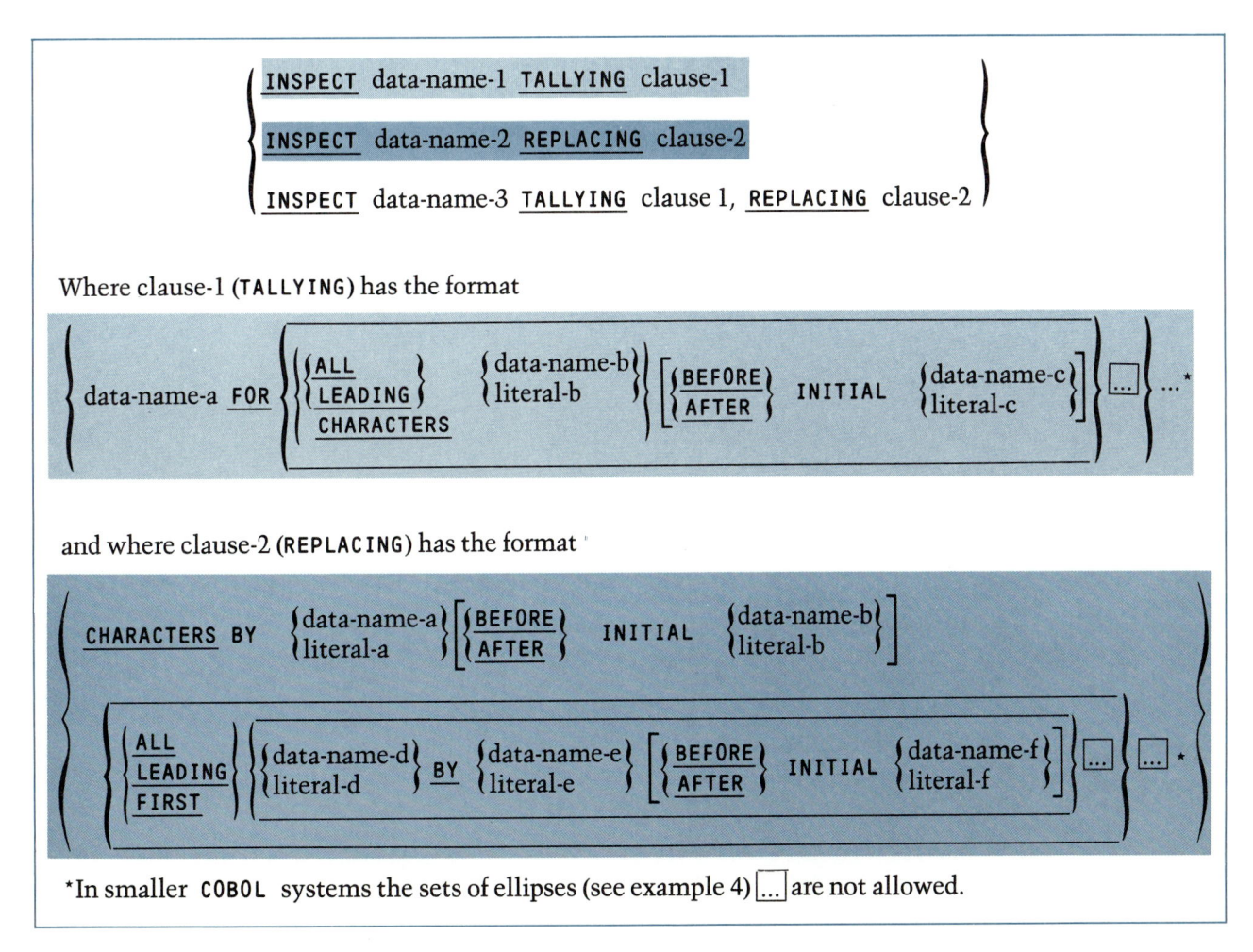

$$\left\{\begin{array}{l}\underline{\text{INSPECT}}\ \text{data-name-1}\ \underline{\text{TALLYING}}\ \text{clause-1}\\ \underline{\text{INSPECT}}\ \text{data-name-2}\ \underline{\text{REPLACING}}\ \text{clause-2}\\ \underline{\text{INSPECT}}\ \text{data-name-3}\ \underline{\text{TALLYING}}\ \text{clause 1, }\underline{\text{REPLACING}}\ \text{clause-2}\end{array}\right\}$$

Where clause-1 (TALLYING) has the format

$$\left\{\text{data-name-a}\ \underline{\text{FOR}}\ \left\{\left\{\begin{array}{l}\underline{\text{ALL}}\\ \underline{\text{LEADING}}\end{array}\right\}\left\{\begin{array}{l}\text{data-name-b}\\ \text{literal-b}\end{array}\right\}\left[\left\{\begin{array}{l}\underline{\text{BEFORE}}\\ \underline{\text{AFTER}}\end{array}\right\}\ \text{INITIAL}\ \left\{\begin{array}{l}\text{data-name-c}\\ \text{literal-c}\end{array}\right\}\right]\right\}\dots\right\}\dots*$$

and where clause-2 (REPLACING) has the format

$$\left\{\begin{array}{l}\underline{\text{CHARACTERS}}\ \text{BY}\ \left\{\begin{array}{l}\text{data-name-a}\\ \text{literal-a}\end{array}\right\}\left[\left\{\begin{array}{l}\underline{\text{BEFORE}}\\ \underline{\text{AFTER}}\end{array}\right\}\ \text{INITIAL}\ \left\{\begin{array}{l}\text{data-name-b}\\ \text{literal-b}\end{array}\right\}\right]\\ \left\{\begin{array}{l}\underline{\text{ALL}}\\ \underline{\text{LEADING}}\\ \underline{\text{FIRST}}\end{array}\right\}\left\{\left\{\begin{array}{l}\text{data-name-d}\\ \text{literal-d}\end{array}\right\}\ \underline{\text{BY}}\ \left\{\begin{array}{l}\text{data-name-e}\\ \text{literal-e}\end{array}\right\}\left[\left\{\begin{array}{l}\underline{\text{BEFORE}}\\ \underline{\text{AFTER}}\end{array}\right\}\ \text{INITIAL}\ \left\{\begin{array}{l}\text{data-name-f}\\ \text{literal-f}\end{array}\right\}\right]\right\}\dots\end{array}\right\}*$$

*In smaller COBOL systems the sets of ellipses (see example 4) [...] are not allowed.

FIGURE 7–8
THE GENERAL FORM OF THE INSPECT VERB

EXAMPLE 4: In COBOL systems that allow the sets of ellipses (see Figure 7–8) the following sequences of clauses can be part of the INSPECT statement:

```
INSPECT TEXT-LINE TALLYING
        COUNT-1 FOR ALL '.' CHARACTERS 'IS' AFTER INITIAL ','
        COUNT-2 FOR LEADING ZERO AFTER INITIAL '$'
                REPLACING
        CHARACTERS BY '/' AFTER INITIAL WS-COUNT.
INSPECT TEXT-LINE TALLYING
        COUNT-1 FOR LEADING ZERO
        COUNT-2 FOR ALL SPACES AFTER INITIAL '.'
                REPLACING
        ALL '/' BY '-', LEADING '0' BY ' ' AFTER INITIAL '0'
        LEADING 'Z' BY ZERO BEFORE INITIAL '9'.
```

7-3-6 DO IT NOW

Specify the contents of FLD (if FLD is changed), and determine the value of the various counters:

1. ```
   MOVE 0 TO K.
   INSPECT FLD TALLYING K FOR ALL 'IS'.
   ```
   `HIS SIS IS ISIS`

2. ```
   MOVE 0 TO K1, K2.
   INSPECT FLD TALLYING
       K1 FOR CHARACTERS BEFORE '3'
       K2 FOR CHARACTERS AFTER '3'.
   ```
   `1112 3 449`

3. ```
   INSPECT FLD
       REPLACING ALL 1 BY 0
       AFTER INITIAL 1.
   ```
   `123151`
   `021011`

4. ```
   INSPECT FLD REPLACING ALL 'A' BY 'Z'
                          'B' BY 'Y'
                          'C' BY 'X'
       AFTER INITIAL 'A'.
   ```
   `MAAXBYC`

5. ```
   MOVE 0 TO K.
   INSPECT FLD TALLYING K FOR CHARACTERS
       REPLACING ALL 'DAD' BY 'SON'.
   ```
   `MOM LOVES DAD`

6. ```
   INSPECT FLD TALLYING K FOR
       LEADING 'E' BEFORE INITIAL 'I'.
   ```
   `TEEPEI`
   `EERIE`
   `TIER`

7. INSPECT FLD TALLYING K
   FOR ALL 'L' REPLACING LEADING
   'A' BY 'E' AFTER INITIAL 'L'.

T	I	L	L	E	A	T
T	A	L	L	A		
T	A	L	A			
L	A	M	A			

8. INSPECT FLD REPLACING CHARACTERS
   BY ' ' BEFORE INITIAL '1'.

   | 0 | 0 | 0 | 1 |
   | 2 | 3 | 1 | 4 |

ANSWERS

1. K = 5
3. 123050 and 021000
4. MAZXYYX
7. TILLEAT   TALLE   TALE   LEMA
   K = 2   K = 2   K = 1 K = 1

7–4 REPORTS

7–4–1 CHARACTERISTICS OF A REPORT

The observation that computer-produced reports should be easy to read, easy to understand, and attractively and efficiently designed appears so evident that one might feel this subject warrants no further comments. Yet the physical appearance of a report is of dramatic importance. Every day, decisions by people in all walks of life are based on computer-produced reports—detailed reports, summarized reports, et cetera.

A good report is self-explanatory (and obviously accurate), self-contained, and organized in such a way as to allow the reader to capture the essence of the report as well as the detail. These characteristics should be reflected in a design that is neat, clear, and pleasant to the eye. It would be difficult to list all the ingredients that make up an ideal report, but a partial list of the most common attributes follows.

Figure 7–9 displays many of the usual headings, subheadings, detailed lines, and various summary lines that form the underpinning of a report.

1. Major or documentary headings:
   a. Identification of the purpose of the report (what is the report about?), for example, class rosters, income statement, payroll, bank statement, ledger balance, financial statement, or inventory analysis.
   b. Date of the report or transaction.
   c. Identification of the company, agency, school, department, et cetera.

2. Subheadings: Titles or labels should be centered over each column of data listed, for example, name, addresses, beginning inventory, ending inventory. Two lines may be needed for certain titles to avoid crowded or abbreviated headings. In certain cases the appearance of the report can be improved by underlining certain headings.

3. The transaction or detail lines should be formatted so that information is not crowded. Sufficient blank spaces should separate each detail line field. Numeric fields should be edited to avoid leading 0's, to provide currency symbols, et cetera.

4. Summary results (subtotals) should be provided within the body of the detail lines to sum up the characteristics of particular classes of items, for example, total sales for one particular salesperson, or subtotal stock on hand for given part numbers.

5. Overall summary results. In many instances the report should include or conclude with a total of subtotals, for example, total inventory versus summarized inventories by category or departments.

In addition to these general considerations, there are physical considerations that affect the appearance or display of the report on the output form or visual screen. The report should be centered, fields should be properly aligned under their respective headings, double or triple spacing should be used between various headings and their associated detail lines, and between summary results, et cetera.

In many instances a report consists of several pages. In such cases additional information should be specified on each page of the report to help the reader digest the information. Each page should be numbered at the top or at the bottom of the page or both. Because a limited number of lines (16 to 64 lines, depending on the hardware) is available on the printer form or CRT screen, only a certain number of transaction lines (in addition to the various headers) can be

```
                    G. SIMS APPAREL COMPANY
                      INVENTORY EVALUATION
                           05/06/86

                         UNIT COST              EXTENDED
            QUANTITY   COST    MARKET      COST        MARKET      LOWER COST
MENS DEPT
  SUITS       300    $100.00  $ 92.00   $ 30,000.00  $ 27,600.00
  COATS       200      60.00    65.00     12,000.00    13,000.00
  SHOES        50      40.00    60.00      2,000.00     3,000.00
  SHIRTS     1000      12.00    73.00     12,000.00    13,000.00
  TOTAL                                   56,000.00  $ 56,600.00   $ 56,000.00

LADIES DEPT
  DRESSES     400    $ 60.00  $ 65.00   $ 24,000.00  $ 26,000.00
  COATS       185     184.00   200.00     34,040.00    37,000.00
  SHOES       600      40.00    30.00     24,000.00    18,000.00
  LINGERIE    500      36.00    30.00     18,000.00    15,000.00
  TOTAL                                  $100,040.00  $ 96,000.00   $ 96,000.00

INVENTORY AT LOWER COST/MARKET                                     $152,000.00
```

FIGURE 7-9

AN INVENTORY EVALUATION

ADDITIONAL FEATURES AND REPORTS   331

displayed on a particular page. Line count considerations must thus be included in the logic of the program. Finally, footing information should be provided on the bottom of the page to reflect current totals or counts of items up to that particular page. The last page of the report, of course, should provide overall totals and descriptive explanations for any other numerical results listed.

7-4-2 PROBLEM EXAMPLE: A MULTIPAGE REPORT

Let us try to write a program to produce a report with the features discussed in section 7-4-1.

Each record of an input file consists of a student name, a social security number, and a grade, as shown below. Write a program to produce a multipage roster of grades, similar to the following:

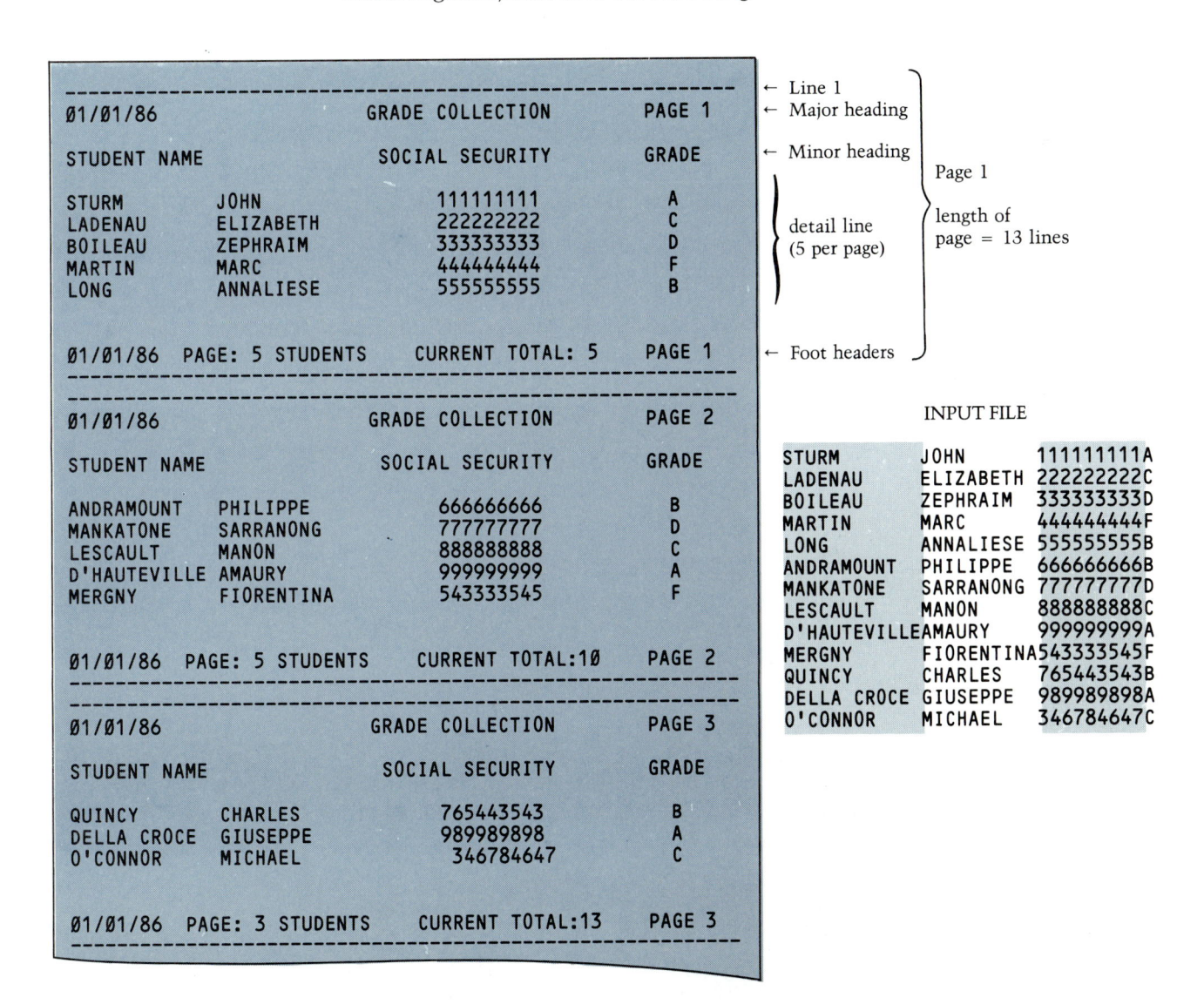

```
-----------------------------------------------------------      ← Line 1
01/01/86              GRADE COLLECTION            PAGE 1         ← Major heading

STUDENT NAME          SOCIAL SECURITY             GRADE          ← Minor heading

STURM       JOHN           111111111               A
LADENAU     ELIZABETH      222222222               C                  detail line
BOILEAU     ZEPHRAIM       333333333               D                  (5 per page)
MARTIN      MARC           444444444               F
LONG        ANNALIESE      555555555               B


01/01/86  PAGE: 5 STUDENTS    CURRENT TOTAL: 5    PAGE 1         ← Foot headers
-----------------------------------------------------------
01/01/86              GRADE COLLECTION            PAGE 2

STUDENT NAME          SOCIAL SECURITY             GRADE

ANDRAMOUNT  PHILIPPE       666666666               B
MANKATONE   SARRANONG      777777777               D
LESCAULT    MANON          888888888               C
D'HAUTEVILLE AMAURY        999999999               A
MERGNY      FIORENTINA     543333545               F


01/01/86  PAGE: 5 STUDENTS    CURRENT TOTAL:10    PAGE 2
-----------------------------------------------------------
-----------------------------------------------------------
01/01/86              GRADE COLLECTION            PAGE 3

STUDENT NAME          SOCIAL SECURITY             GRADE

QUINCY      CHARLES        765443543               B
DELLA CROCE GIUSEPPE       989989898               A
O'CONNOR    MICHAEL        346784647               C



01/01/86  PAGE: 3 STUDENTS    CURRENT TOTAL:13    PAGE 3
-----------------------------------------------------------
```

Page 1 length of page = 13 lines

INPUT FILE

```
STURM        JOHN        111111111A
LADENAU      ELIZABETH   222222222C
BOILEAU      ZEPHRAIM    333333333D
MARTIN       MARC        444444444F
LONG         ANNALIESE   555555555B
ANDRAMOUNT   PHILIPPE    666666666B
MANKATONE    SARRANONG   777777777D
LESCAULT     MANON       888888888C
D'HAUTEVILLE AMAURY      999999999A
MERGNY       FIORENTINA  543333545F
QUINCY       CHARLES     765443543B
DELLA CROCE  GIUSEPPE    989989898A
O'CONNOR     MICHAEL     346784647C
```

The two dashed lines simulate the beginning and end of a page. In this particular example each page consists of 13 lines, 5 of which are used to list the student records and 8 for top and foot headings. Many COBOL systems allow you to skip to the top of a new page (fan-fold forms or paper roll) by means of the statement

WRITE ... AFTER ADVANCING PAGE or some mnemonic other than PAGE. The length of the page is set in the SPECIAL–NAMES paragraph or in the printer file FD entry, depending on the system used (see section 7–5 question 1 for details).

The major heading at the top of the page displays the date and the particular page number. The foot header also gives the date, the page number, the number of students listed per page and the running total of students listed so far (current up-to-the-page student subtotals). The last page of the report generally lists fewer student records then the preceding page(s), although it may be a full page (for example, 10 student records would fit exactly on two full pages).

Program Analysis

The pseudo code to solve this problem is shown in Figure 7–10, and the COBOL program in Figure 7–11. The central idea in this type of problem is to keep track of the number of lines written so that the program can skip to a new page whenever a certain number of records have been written on the current page. Skipping to a new page requires writing out the foot headers on the current page and writing top headings on the next page. In the example considered here, a page consists of 5 top header lines, 3 foot headers, and 5 student record lines.

Just prior to processing a new page, a line counter is set to 0 (lines 48 and 149). After the top-of-page headers are written, the line counter is incremented by 8 to reflect the number of lines committed to top and bottom headers (line 130). At this point there are only 5 more lines available on the page for student records. Student records are then read and written and the line counter is incremented by 1 for each record (line 146). When the value of the line counter is 13, 5 student records have been processed and the final 3 lines for the foot headers are written. The line counter is then reset to 0 (line 149). Then the next record is read; if it is the end-of-file record, the report is complete, since line count is 0 (line 161); otherwise, the top headers are printed and the record just read is processed.

If the end of file occurs before the end of the page is reached (student line count is between 1 and 5), the foot headers are printed (lines 107 and 161.)

Test Your Understanding of the Program

1. Change the code so that the foot headings on the last page appear in the same physical location as on all preceding pages, i.e., at the usual "bottom" position.

2. Change the logic of the problem so that when the end of page is detected, you simply perform WRITE-FOOT-HEADINGS and WRITE-TOP-HEADINGS in succession. With this approach the IF statement at line 134 is not needed. (Be careful, though! You do not want top headings on the last page if there are no student entries to list.)

7-4-3 CONTROL BREAKS

In the preceding section, we discussed the physical aspects of reports, and in chapters 4 and 6 we discussed certain coding techniques to produce such summary statistics as counts, averages, and grand totals. In real-life business applications, more refined summaries are generally needed. For example, in a supermarket an item file might be arranged into categories of goods such as perishables, dairy products, and meats. The manager may need an inventory re-

```
* a multipage grade roster
    Initialize date fields in the top and bottom heading lines
    set page-count to 0
    set students-per-page to 0
    set total-number-students to 0
    set line-count to 0
    set page-length to desired number of lines
* page length should include number of lines needed for top and bottom headings
read student record
perform process-record until end of file
perform last-page-decision
stop

process-record.
    if line-count = 0
    then
        perform write-top-headings
    endif
    write student record
    add 1 to line-count
    add 1 to students-per-page
    if line-count = page-length
    then
        perform write-foot-headings
        set line-count to 0
    endif
    read student record

write-top-headings
    add 1 to page-count
    set students-per-page to 0
    write headings at top of page
    add to line-count number of lines taken by top and bottom headings

write-foot-headings
    add students-per-page to total-number-students
    write foot headings

last-page-decision
    if line-count ≠ 0
    then
        perform write-foot-headings
    endif
```

FIGURE 7-10
A MULTIPAGE REPORT

port by category showing market and cost figures. In a school, a personnel file might be arranged by department number—an administrator may wish to obtain a list and a count of teachers within each department. In a similar situation, a department head may wish to obtain a report at the start of a semester displaying a list of courses broken down into course sections with the name of the teacher for each entry and total enrollment for each course. Or a publishing company may need a financial sales report broken down by author publications.

```
 1:     IDENTIFICATION DIVISION.
 2:     PROGRAM-ID. MULTIPAGE REPORT.
 3:     AUTHOR. JONES.
 4: ****************************************************************
 5: * OBJECTIVE: PRODUCE MULTIPAGE GRADE ROSTER REPORT WITH PAGE    *
 6: *            & FOOT HEADINGS. PAGE HEADINGS IDENTIFY DATE AND   *
 7: *            PAGE NUMBER; FOOT CAPTIONS DISPLAY NO. OF STUDENTS *
 8: *            PER PAGE & RUNNING STUDENT COUNT FOR EACH PAGE     *
 9: *                                                               *
10: * DISK INPUT: DATE, STUDENT NAME, SS. NUMBER AND GRADE          *
11: *                                                               *
12: * OUTPUT: DATE, PAGE NO., STUDENT NAME, SS. NO., GRADE,         *
13: *         NO. OF STUDENTS PER PAGE & RUNNING PAGE TOTALS        *
14: ****************************************************************
15:     ENVIRONMENT DIVISION.
16:     CONFIGURATION SECTION.
17:     SOURCE-COMPUTER. IBM.
18:     OBJECT-COMPUTER. IBM.
19:     INPUT-OUTPUT SECTION.
20:     FILE-CONTROL.
21:         SELECT REPORT-FILE ASSIGN TO PRINTER.
22:         SELECT ROSTER-FILE ASSIGN TO DISK
23:         ORGANIZATION IS LINE SEQUENTIAL.
24:     DATA DIVISION.
25:     FILE SECTION.
26:     FD  ROSTER-FILE
27:         LABEL RECORDS ARE STANDARD
28:         VALUE OF FILE-ID IS 'MULTIPAG'
29:         DATA RECORD IS INPUT-RECORD.
30:     01  INPUT-RECORD PIC X(32).
31:     FD  REPORT-FILE
32:         LABEL RECORDS ARE OMITTED
33:         DATA RECORD IS PRINT-LINE.
34:     01  PRINT-LINE PIC X(62).
35: *
36:     WORKING-STORAGE SECTION.
37: *
38: *       INDEPENDENT ITEMS
39: *
40:     01  DATE-N-FLAGS.
41:         05 WS-EOF  PIC X(03) VALUE 'NO'.
42:         05 WS-DATE PIC Z9/99/99.
43: *
44: *   WS-PAGE-SIZE IS TOTAL NO LINES PER PAGE
45: *
46:         05 WS-PAGE-SIZE        PIC 99 VALUE 13.
47:     01  COMPUTATIONAL-ITEMS.
48:         05 WS-LINE-COUNT          PIC 99   VALUE 0.
49:         05 WS-PAGE-COUNT          PIC 99   VALUE 0.
50:         05 WS-STUDENT-SUBTOTAL    PIC 9999 VALUE 0.
51:         05 WS-STUDENT-TOTAL       PIC 999  VALUE 0.
52: *
53: *       FILE INPUT RECORD DESCRIPTION
54: *
55:     01  ROSTER-RECORD.
56:         05 IR-NAME        PIC X(12).
57:         05 IR-FIRST       PIC X(10).
58:         05 IR-SOCSEC      PIC X(09).
59:         05 IR-SCORE       PIC X.
60: *
61: *       OUTPUT FILE RECORD DESCRIPTION
62: *
63:     01  MAJOR-HEADING.
64:         05 MH-DATE PIC BBX(08).
65:         05 FILLER  PIC X(21) VALUE SPACES.
66:         05 FILLER  PIC X(18) VALUE 'GRADE COLLECTION'.
67:         05 FILLER  PIC X(05) VALUE SPACES.
68:         05 FILLER  PIC X(04) VALUE 'PAGE'.
69:         05 MH-PAGE PIC Z9.
70:     01  SUB-HEADING.
71:         05 FILLER  PIC X(03) VALUE SPACES.
72:         05 FILLER  PIC X(12) VALUE 'STUDENT NAME'.
73:         05 FILLER  PIC X(16) VALUE SPACES.
74:         05 FILLER  PIC X(15) VALUE 'SOCIAL SECURITY'.
75:         05 FILLER  PIC X(08) VALUE SPACES.
76:         05 FILLER  PIC X(38) VALUE 'GRADE'.
77:     01  FOOT-HEADING.
78:         05 FH-DATE              PIC BBX(08).
79:         05 FILLER                PIC X(03) VALUE SPACES.
80:         05 FILLER                PIC X(05) VALUE 'PAGE:'.
81:         05 FH-STUDENT-PER-PAGE PIC Z9.
```

FIGURE 7-11
A MULTIPAGE REPORT

```
 82:          05  FILLER        PIC X(01) VALUE SPACES.
 83:          05  FILLER        PIC X(08) VALUE 'STUDENTS'.
 84:          05  FILLER        PIC X(06) VALUE SPACES.
 85:          05  FILLER        PIC X(14) VALUE 'CURRENT TOTAL:'.
 86:          05  FH-SUBTOTAL   PIC Z9.
 87:          05  FILLER        PIC X(03) VALUE SPACES.
 88:          05  FILLER        PIC X(04) VALUE 'PAGE'.
 89:          05  FH-PAGE       PIC Z9.
 90:      01  DETAIL-LINE.
 91:          05  FILLER        PIC X(03) VALUE SPACES.
 92:          05  DL-NAME       PIC X(12).
 93:          05  FILLER        PIC X(01) VALUE SPACES.
 94:          05  DL-FIRST      PIC X(11).
 95:          05  FILLER        PIC X(09) VALUE SPACES.
 96:          05  DL-SOCSEC     PIC X(09).
 97:          05  FILLER        PIC X(11) VALUE SPACES.
 98:          05  DL-SCORE      PIC X(01).
 99:     *
100:      PROCEDURE DIVISION.
101:      100-COORDINATING-MODULE.
102:          OPEN INPUT ROSTER-FILE.
103:          OPEN OUTPUT REPORT-FILE.
104:          PERFORM 200-DATE-INITIALIZATION.
105:          PERFORM 300-READ-RECORD.
106:          PERFORM 500-PROCESS-RECORD UNTIL WS-EOF = 'YES'.
107:          PERFORM 800-LAST-PAGE-TASK.
108:          CLOSE ROSTER-FILE, REPORT-FILE.
109:          STOP RUN.
110:     *
111:      200-DATE-INITIALIZATION.
112:          ACCEPT WS-DATE FROM DATE.
113:     *    IF FEATURE NOT AVAILABLE READ DATE FROM SEPARATE FILE
114:          MOVE WS-DATE TO FH-DATE, MH-DATE.
115:     *
116:      300-READ-RECORD.
117:          READ ROSTER-FILE INTO ROSTER-RECORD
118:              AT END MOVE 'YES' TO WS-EOF.
119:     *
120:      400-WRITE-TOP-HEADINGS.
121:          MOVE 0 TO WS-STUDENT-SUBTOTAL.
122:          ADD  1 TO WS-PAGE-COUNT.
123:          MOVE WS-PAGE-COUNT TO MH-PAGE.
124:          MOVE ALL '-' TO PRINT-LINE.
125:          WRITE PRINT-LINE AFTER 1 LINE.
126:          WRITE PRINT-LINE FROM MAJOR-HEADING AFTER 1 LINE.
127:          WRITE PRINT-LINE FROM SUB-HEADING   AFTER 3 LINES.
128:          MOVE SPACES TO PRINT-LINE.
129:          WRITE PRINT-LINE AFTER 1 LINE.
130:          ADD 8 TO WS-LINE-COUNT.
131:     *    THIS COUNT REPRESENTS TOP & BOTTOM HEADINGS
132:     *
133:      500-PROCESS-RECORD.
134:          IF WS-LINE-COUNT = 0
135:              PERFORM 400-WRITE-TOP-HEADINGS.
136:          PERFORM 600-PROCESS-ITEM-READ.
137:          PERFORM 300-READ-RECORD.
138:     *
139:      600-PROCESS-ITEM-READ.
140:          MOVE IR-NAME    TO DL-NAME.
141:          MOVE IR-FIRST   TO DL-FIRST.
142:          MOVE IR-SOCSEC  TO DL-SOCSEC.
143:          MOVE IR-SCORE   TO DL-SCORE.
144:          WRITE PRINT-LINE FROM DETAIL-LINE AFTER 1 LINE.
145:          ADD 1 TO WS-STUDENT-SUBTOTAL.
146:          ADD 1 TO WS-LINE-COUNT.
147:          IF WS-LINE-COUNT = WS-PAGE-SIZE
148:              PERFORM 700-WRITE-FOOT-HEADINGS
149:              MOVE 0 TO WS-LINE-COUNT.
150:     *
151:      700-WRITE-FOOT-HEADINGS.
152:          ADD WS-STUDENT-SUBTOTAL   TO WS-STUDENT-TOTAL.
153:          MOVE WS-STUDENT-SUBTOTAL TO FH-STUDENT-PER-PAGE.
154:          MOVE WS-STUDENT-TOTAL     TO FH-SUBTOTAL.
155:          MOVE WS-PAGE-COUNT        TO FH-PAGE.
156:          WRITE PRINT-LINE FROM FOOT-HEADING AFTER 3 LINES.
157:          MOVE ALL '-' TO PRINT-LINE.
158:          WRITE PRINT-LINE AFTER 1 LINE.
159:     *
160:      800-LAST-PAGE-TASK.
161:          IF WS-LINE-COUNT NOT = 0
162:              PERFORM 700-WRITE-FOOT-HEADINGS.
```

FIGURE 7–11
(continued)

The common theme in all of these examples is that input data is frequently arranged into groups of items. These groups must then be processed and summarized into a final output product that also preserves group characteristics. Processing this type of data structure requires that we know when a group starts and ends so that we can count the number of group entries, accumulate related entry fields within each group, et cetera. To illustrate such a process, consider the following input file, where each record consists of a salesperson number, a date of sales, and a sales amount. Let us assume that all records for a given salesperson occur in a group; parenthetically, this does not imply that the records are sorted in sequence by salesperson number.

```
                          Salesperson              Item
                          number    Date of        code     Sales
                                    sale                    amount

Records for               ⎡1002    010786    A1    22256
salesperson 1002          ⎢1002    011086    B3    07895
                          ⎣1002    012386    X2    09500
Records for               ⎡2103    010886    BB    00995
salesperson 2103          ⎣2103    010986    B3    01905
                          ⎡3250    011586    A1    33378
Records for               ⎢3250    011886    X3    06795
salesperson 3250          ⎣3250    012586    S2    56000
```

Given this type of data, a report could be produced to show total sales as well as summary sales for each salesperson. Such a summary report is shown in Figure 7–12. Totals for each salesperson are called *intermediate* or *minor* totals.

Notice that in this example the input file is intentionally organized into groups of salesperson numbers to produce a summary report arranged in a similar fashion. In this application the salesperson number plays a leading role—it determines the grouping of the data on the output report. All other fields play secondary roles. Had management wanted a report summarized by item code or

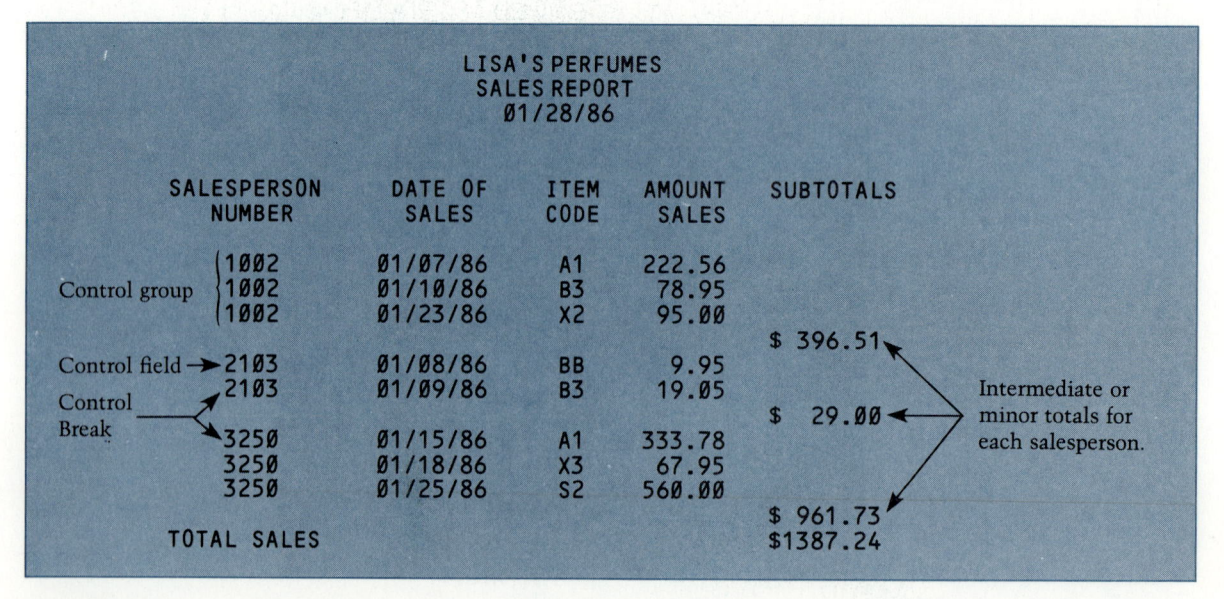

```
                        LISA'S PERFUMES
                         SALES REPORT
                           01/28/86

              SALESPERSON   DATE OF    ITEM    AMOUNT     SUBTOTALS
              NUMBER        SALES      CODE    SALES

             ⎧1002         01/07/86    A1       222.56
Control group⎨1002         01/10/86    B3        78.95
             ⎩1002         01/23/86    X2        95.00
                                                         $ 396.51
Control field→2103         01/08/86    BB         9.95                  Intermediate or
              2103         01/09/86    B3        19.05                  minor totals for
Control                                                  $  29.00       each salesperson.
Break         3250         01/15/86    A1       333.78
              3250         01/18/86    X3        67.95
              3250         01/25/86    S2       560.00
                                                         $ 961.73
              TOTAL SALES                                $1387.24
```

FIGURE 7–12
A SAMPLE CONTROL BREAK REPORT

ADDITIONAL FEATURES AND REPORTS 337

by date, then the item code or date would become the lead or control field, requiring the input file to be arranged by item code or date.

Depending on the type of summary report needed, one particular input field must be designated as a lead field to control the layout of the output report. This, of course, requires that the input data be arranged in appropriate groups. Later on we will see how we can sort an input file by key (control) fields to allow us to produce various types of summary reports based on particular control fields.

Processing an input file organized into control groups requires that we recognize breaks between successive control groups. For that reason, this type of problem is referred to as a *control break problem*. To illustrate the control break programming technique, let us consider a very simple case dealing with a salesperson summary report.

Problem Specification

Each record of an input file contains a salesperson number and a sales amount. Write a program to read an input file (shown below) and produce a summary sales report similar to the following one:

```
                OUTPUT                                    INPUT FILE

    SALESPERSON    SALES      TOTALS
        111       100.00                          Salesperson
        111        50.00     $ 150.00              number
                                                     ↓      sales
        222        30.00     $  30.00
                                                  111010000
        333       150.00                          111005000
        333       250.00     $ 400.00             222003000
                                                  333015000
    TOTAL SALES              $ 580.00             333025000
```

Discussion

Let us assign the following names to the various items that are to be processed:

    salesperson: refers to the salesperson number read from each record

    sales: sales value read from each record

    total-sales: accumulates all sales

    subtotal: accumulates each salesperson's subtotals

    previous-salesperson: Given any two consecutive salesperson groups, previous-salesperson refers to the salesperson number of the first of these two groups.

The basic idea in producing this type of report is to keep accumulating a minor total until a change occurs in the salesperson number. If the record read pertains to the same salesperson as the preceding record, the sales amount read is added to the current salesperson total (minor total). If the record read pertains to a new salesperson a *control break* has been found. At this point the minor total for the previous salesperson is printed, and the accumulator for the new minor total is reset to 0.

The decision as to whether the salesperson just read belongs to the current group or to a new group is made by storing the current salesperson number in previous-salesperson before the next number is read into salesperson. These two values are then compared. If they contain the same number, the record belongs to the current group. Otherwise, a different salesperson number has been read and a control break has occurred.

To start the comparison process between previous-salesperson and salesperson, the first salesperson number is assigned to previous-salesperson.

The logic of the program is described in flowchart form in Figure 7–13 and in pseudo code as follows:

control break logic
    initialize total and subtotal to 0
    read salesperson number and sales
    set previous-salesperson to salesperson number
    perform process-record until end of file
    write subtotal and total sales
    stop
process-record.
    if previous-salesperson is different from salesperson (control break occurs)
    then
        write subtotal
        reset subtotal to 0 (to prepare for subtotal of salesperson just read)
        reset previous-salesperson number to salesperson number (so that we are sure to compare the next salesperson number with the most current (recent) salesperson number)
    endif
    add sales to total and to subtotal
    write salesperson number and sales
    read salesperson number and sales

One way to really understand the control break logic is to trace through the pseudo code using a dummy input file and to record along the way the various values taken on by all data items. Such a tabulation process is carried out in Figure 7–14; the reader can walk through the code and see what is happening at each step. Take the time to analyze this visual walk-through to see that the logic indeed works! The actual COBOL code and structured chart to solve this problem are shown in Figure 7–15.

Test Your Understanding of the Program

1. Change the pseudo code of the control break problem so that total sales is the result of accumulating the various subtotals.

2. Does the following flowchart solve the control break problem outlined in the above pseudo code?
   How would you write the pseudo code for this flowchart? What changes would you make to make it a "structured" flowchart?

ADDITIONAL FEATURES AND REPORTS 339

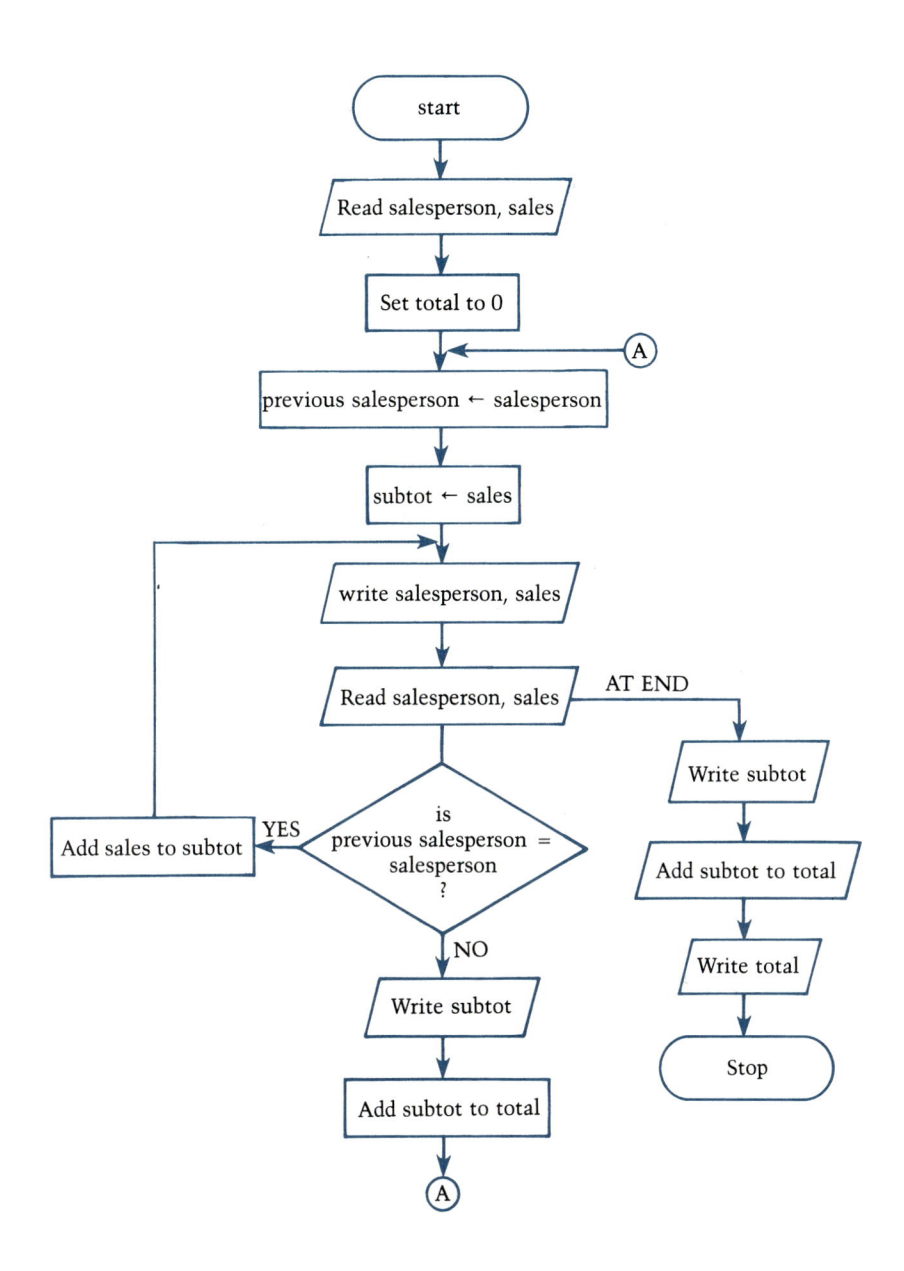

7-4-4 MULTILEVEL CONTROL BREAKS

Section 7-4-3 discussed a simple summary report (sales-by-salesperson report) where various groups of input records gave rise to corresponding summary lines. When a summary report contains summary lines from more than one type of group, it becomes a *multilevel* report. In the program of Figure 7-15 total sales were summarized for each salesperson, while grand totals were listed for the entire sales group. Perhaps this sales group was one of many groups within a particular sales division of a large company. The division's sales manager may wish to obtain a summary report for each sales group, while the company's chief sales executive may need a summary sales report listing division, region (group), and salesperson sales. Figure 7-16 displays an unsophisticated summary sales report by division, region, and salesperson number.

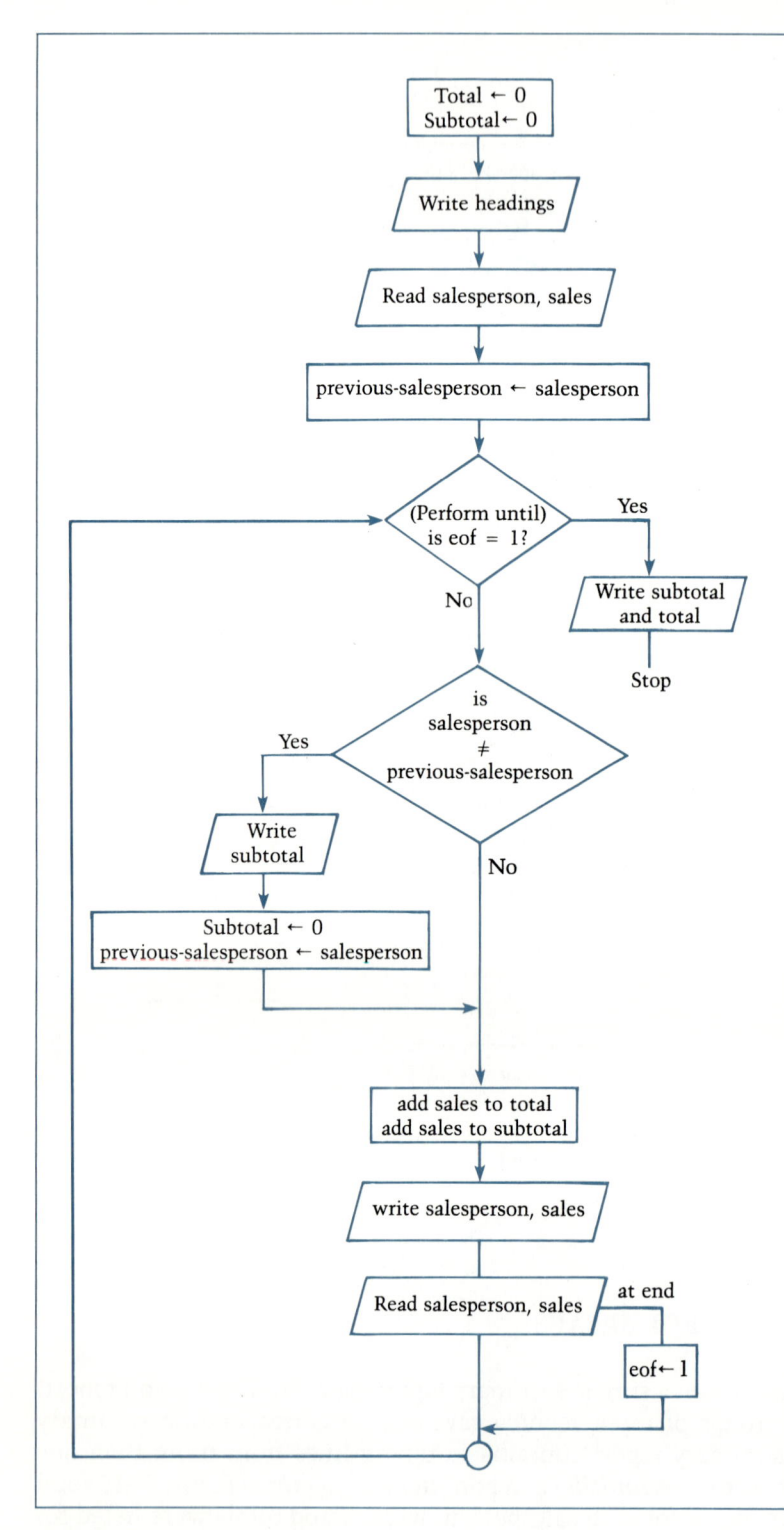

Total accumulates the sum of all sales. *Subtotal* accumulates the totals for each salesperson. Read a salesperson number and call it *salesperson*. Since the procedure involves comparing two succeeding salespersons' numbers, we need two different names for the salespersons' numbers: in general, one for the previous (old) salesperson, *previous-salesperson*, and the other for the new salesperson number, *salesperson*. To start the comparison procedure, we initialize previous-salesperson to salesperson. The first time, of course, these two numbers will be equal.

The end-of-file test here represents the COBOL PERFORM statement at line 95. Keep reading records until the end of file has been detected by the READ statement at the end of paragraph (lines 110–111). If it is the end of file, print the last salesperson's totals and the grand total and stop.

The first time through the procedure, the two salesperson numbers are equal so we add *sales* to both *total* and *subtotal* and print the record just read—actually we want to do this whenever the old salesperson number equals new salesperson number. If the new number is different from the previous number, this means we have encountered a new salesperson and it is time to print the subtotals of the previous salesperson. We must also reset *subtotal* to 0 in order to start accumulating new subtotals for the salesperson whose number has just been read. We also reset the previous salesperson number *previous-salesperson* to the new number just read, since we will need to compare that number with the next number to be read. If this step were omitted, we would always be comparing the new number with the salesperson number from the very first record. This is clearly incorrect, as we always want to compare two consecutive salesperson numbers.

Whether or not the salesperson numbers are the same, we compute a new *total* and *subtotal* and print a complete line with salesperson number and amount of sales.

Finally we read another record. If the end of file is encountered, the paragraph at line 130 will cause the last salesperson subtotals to be printed as well as the overall totals; if the end of file has not been reached, paragraph 300–PROCESS–RECORD will process the information on the record just read.

FIGURE 7–13
A CONTROL BREAK PROBLEM

	Salesperson	Previous salesperson	Sales	Subtotal	Total-Sales

```
total = 0 .........................
subtotal = 0 ......................                    0    0
write headings
read salesperson, sales ............  111         100
previous-salesperson = salesperson..       111
perform process-record until end file
perform write-totals
stop

process-record
  if salesperson ≠ previous-salesperson  111  111
  then write subtotal
    subtotal = 0
    previous-salesperson = salesperson
  endif
  add sales to total ..............                    100
  add sales to subtotal ...........              100
  write salesperson, sales
  read salesperson, sales .........  111         050

process-record
  if salesperson ≠ previous-salesperson  111  111
  then write subtotal
    subtotal = 0
    previous-salesperson = salesperson
  endif
  add sales to total ..............                    150
  add sales to subtotal ...........              150
  write salesperson, sales
  read salesperson, sales .........  222         300

process-record
  if salesperson ≠ previous-salesperson  222  111
  then write subtotal
    subtotal = 0 ...................             0
    previous-salesperson = salesperson..     222
  endif
  add sales to total ..............                    450
  add sales to subtotal ...........              300
  write salesperson, sales
  read salesperson, sales .........  333         150

process-record
  if salesperson ≠ previous-salesperson  333  222
  then write subtotal
    subtotal = 0 ...................             0
    previous-salesperson = salesperson      333  333
  endif
  add sales to total ..............                    600
  add sales to subtotal ...........              150
  write salesperson, sales
  read salesperson, sales .........  333         200

process-record
  if salesperson ≠ previous-salesperson  333  333
  then write subtotal
    subtotal = 0
    previous-salesperson = salesperson
  endif
  add sales to total ..............                    800
  add sales to subtotal ...........              350
  write salesperson, sales
  read salesperson, sales .........  end
                                     file

write-totals
  write subtotal
  write total
```

OUTPUT FILE

NUMBER SALES TOTALS

111   100

111   050

                150

222   300

                300

333   150

333   200

                350
                800

INPUT FILE

111 100
111 050
222 300
333 150
333 200

Salesperson | Sales

FIGURE 7-14
CONTROL BREAK TABULATION

```
1:     IDENTIFICATION DIVISION.
2:     PROGRAM-ID. BREAK-CONTROL.
3:     AUTHOR. JONES.
4:  ****************************************************************
5:  * OBJECTIVE: PRODUCE A SALES SUMMARY REPORT LISTING EACH SALES- *
6:  *            PERSON'S VARIOUS SALES TRANSACTIONS, EACH SALES-   *
7:  *            PERSON'S SUBTOTAL AND THE GRAND TOTAL SALES.       *
8:  *                                                               *
9:  * INPUT:     EACH RECORD CONTAINS A SALESPERSON'S NUMBER AND A  *
10: *            SALES AMOUNT. ALL RECORDS FOR A GIVEN SALESPERSON  *
11: *            OCCUR IN A GROUP.                                  *
12: *                                                               *
13: * OUTPUT:    SALESPERSON'S NUMBER, SALESPERSON'S SALES TRANS-   *
14: *            ACTIONS, SALESPERSON'S SALES SUBTOTAL AND GRAND    *
15: *            SALES TOTAL                                        *
16: ****************************************************************
17:     ENVIRONMENT DIVISION.
18:     CONFIGURATION SECTION.
19:     SOURCE-COMPUTER. IBM.
20:     OBJECT-COMPUTER. IBM.
21:     INPUT-OUTPUT SECTION.
22:     FILE-CONTROL.
23:         SELECT REPORT-FILE ASSIGN TO PRINTER.
24:         SELECT SALES-FILE  ASSIGN TO DISK
25:         ORGANIZATION IS LINE SEQUENTIAL.
26: *
27:     DATA DIVISION.
28:     FILE SECTION.
29: *
30:     FD  SALES-FILE
31:         LABEL RECORDS ARE STANDARD
32:         VALUE OF FILE-ID IS 'SALESMAN'
33:         DATA RECORD IS INPUT-RECORD.
34:     01  INPUT-RECORD PIC X(09).
35:     FD  REPORT-FILE
36:         LABEL RECORDS ARE OMITTED
37:         DATA RECORD IS PRINT-LINE.
38:     01  PRINT-LINE PIC X(132).
39: *
40:     WORKING-STORAGE SECTION.
41: *
42: *       INDEPENDENT ITEMS
43: *
44:     01  FLAGS.
45:         05  WS-EOF PIC 9    VALUE 0.
46:             88 END-OF-FILE VALUE IS 1.
47: *
48:     01  COMPUTATIONAL-ITEMS.
49:         05 WS-PREVIOUS-SALESPERSON PIC 999.
50:         05 WS-SUBTOTAL             PIC 9999V99    VALUE 0.
51:         05 WS-TOTAL-SALES          PIC 99999V99   VALUE 0.
52: *
53: *       INPUT RECORD DESCRIPTION
54: *
55:     01  SALES-RECORD.
56:         05 SR-SALESPERSON-NUMBER PIC 999.
57:         05 SR-SALES              PIC 9999V99.
58: *
59: *       OUTPUT LINE DESCRIPTIONS
60: *
61:     01  MAJOR-HEADING.
62:         05 FILLER              PIC X(05) VALUE SPACES.
63:         05 FILLER              PIC X(11) VALUE 'SALESPERSON'.
64:         05 FILLER              PIC X(05) VALUE SPACES.
65:         05 FILLER              PIC X(05) VALUE 'SALES'.
66:         05 FILLER              PIC X(09) VALUE SPACES.
67:         05 FILLER              PIC X(47) VALUE 'TOTALS'.
```

OUTPUT

SALESPERSON	SALES	TOTALS
111	23.65	
111	345.60	$ 369.25
222	1,000.00	$1,000.00
333	98.00	
333	788.99	$ 886.99
444	1,024.00	
444	2,090.50	
444	987.00	$4,101.50
555	890.00	
555	1,000.00	
555	1,234.50	
555	789.56	$3,914.06
TOTAL SALES		$10,271.80

INPUT FILE

SR-SALESPERSON-NUMBER

```
111002365
111034560
222100000
333009800
333078899
444102400
444209050
444098700
555089000
555100000
555123450
555078956
```

SR-SALES

FIGURE 7–15
A CONTROL BREAK PROGRAM

```cobol
69: 01  DETAIL-LINE.
70:     05  FILLER         PIC X(07) VALUE SPACES.
71:     05  DL-SALESPERSON-NUMBER PIC ZZZ9.
72:     05  FILLER         PIC X(07) VALUE SPACES.
73:     05  DL-SALES       PIC ZZ,ZZZ.99.
74:*
75: 01  SALESPERSON-SUBTOTAL-LINE.
76:     05  FILLER         PIC X(34) VALUE SPACES.
77:     05  SS-SUBTOTAL    PIC $Z,ZZZ.99.
78:*
79: 01  TOTAL-SUMMARY-SALES.
80:     05  FILLER         PIC X(05) VALUE SPACES.
81:     05  FILLER         PIC X(11) VALUE 'TOTAL SALES'.
82:     05  FILLER         PIC X(17) VALUE SPACES.
83:     05  TS-TOTAL-SALES PIC $$$,$$$.99.
84:*
85: 01  BLANK-LINE         PIC X(132) VALUE SPACES.
86:*
87: PROCEDURE DIVISION.
88: 100-COORDINATING-MODULE.
89:     OPEN INPUT  SALES-FILE
90:          OUTPUT REPORT-FILE.
91:     PERFORM 200-WRITE-HEADINGS.
92:     READ SALES-FILE INTO SALES-RECORD
93:         AT END MOVE 1 TO WS-EOF.
94:     MOVE SR-SALESPERSON-NUMBER TO WS-PREVIOUS-SALESPERSON.
95:     PERFORM 300-PROCESS-RECORD UNTIL END-OF-FILE.
96:     PERFORM 700-WRITE-LAST-TOTALS.
97:     CLOSE SALES-FILE, REPORT-FILE.
98:     STOP RUN.
99:*
100: 200-WRITE-HEADINGS.
101:    WRITE PRINT-LINE FROM MAJOR-HEADING AFTER 1 LINE.
102:    MOVE SPACES TO PRINT-LINE.
103:    WRITE PRINT-LINE FROM BLANK-LINE AFTER 1 LINE.
104:*
105: 300-PROCESS-RECORD.
106:    IF SR-SALESPERSON-NUMBER NOT = WS-PREVIOUS-SALESPERSON
107:        PERFORM 400-CONTROL-BREAK.
108:    PERFORM 500-UPDATE-TOTALS.
109:    PERFORM 600-WRITE-DETAIL-LINE.
110:    READ SALES-FILE INTO SALES-RECORD
111:        AT END MOVE 1 TO WS-EOF.
112:*
113: 400-CONTROL-BREAK.
114:    MOVE WS-SUBTOTAL TO SS-SUBTOTAL.
115:    WRITE PRINT-LINE FROM SALESPERSON-SUBTOTAL-LINE
116:        AFTER ADVANCING 0 LINE.
117:    WRITE PRINT-LINE FROM BLANK-LINE AFTER 1 LINE.
118:    MOVE SR-SALESPERSON-NUMBER TO WS-PREVIOUS-SALESPERSON.
119:    MOVE ZERO                  TO WS-SUBTOTAL.
120:*
121: 500-UPDATE-TOTALS.
122:    ADD SR-SALES TO WS-SUBTOTAL.
123:    ADD SR-SALES TO WS-TOTAL-SALES.
124:*
125: 600-WRITE-DETAIL-LINE.
126:    MOVE SR-SALESPERSON-NUMBER TO DL-SALESPERSON-NUMBER.
127:    MOVE SR-SALES              TO DL-SALES.
128:    WRITE PRINT-LINE FROM DETAIL-LINE AFTER 1 LINE.
129:*
130: 700-WRITE-LAST-TOTALS.
131:    MOVE WS-SUBTOTAL    TO SS-SUBTOTAL.
132:    MOVE WS-TOTAL-SALES TO TS-TOTAL-SALES.
133:    WRITE PRINT-LINE FROM SALESPERSON-SUBTOTAL-LINE
134:        AFTER ADVANCING 0 LINE.
135:    WRITE PRINT-LINE FROM TOTAL-SUMMARY-SALES
136:        AFTER ADVANCING 2 LINES.
```

FIGURE 7–15

(continued)

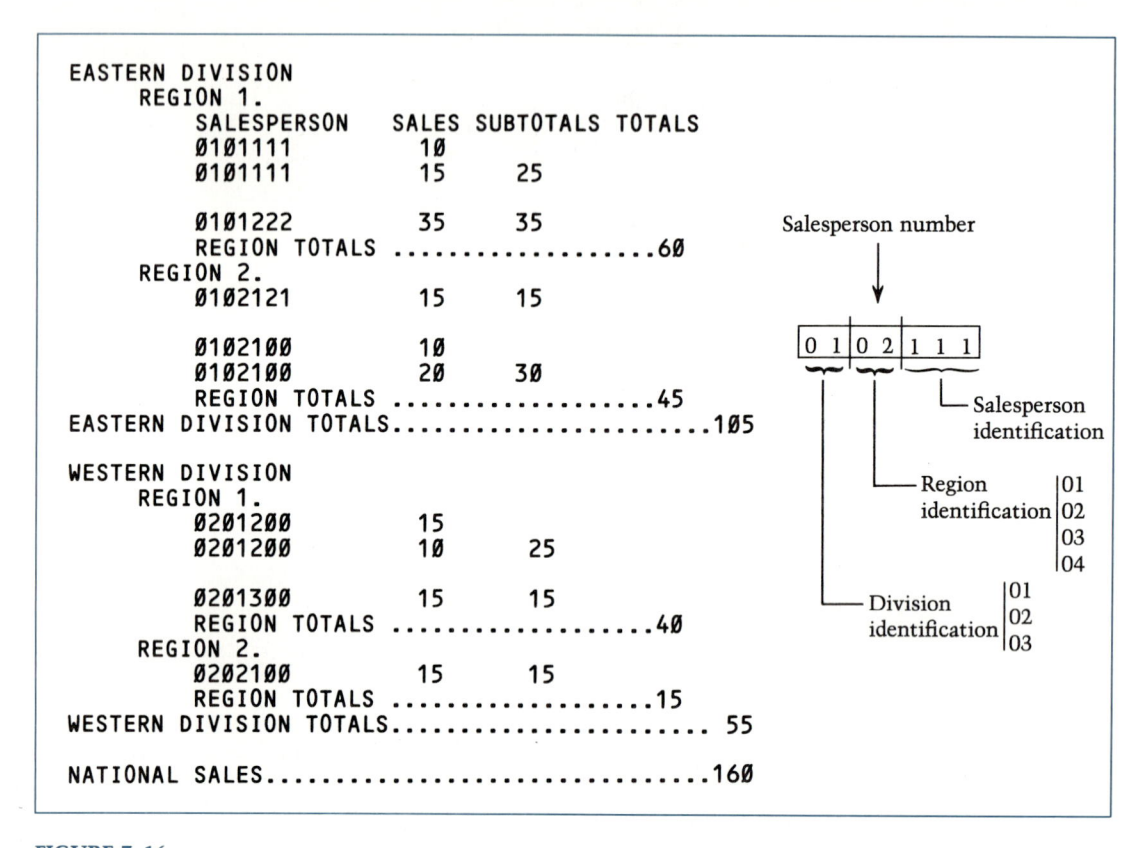

```
EASTERN DIVISION
    REGION 1.
        SALESPERSON   SALES  SUBTOTALS  TOTALS
        0101111         10
        0101111         15       25

        0101222         35       35
        REGION TOTALS ...................60
    REGION 2.
        0102121         15       15

        0102100         10
        0102100         20       30
        REGION TOTALS ...................45
EASTERN DIVISION TOTALS.......................105

WESTERN DIVISION
    REGION 1.
        0201200         15
        0201200         10       25

        0201300         15       15
        REGION TOTALS ...................40
    REGION 2.
        0202100         15       15
        REGION TOTALS ...................15
WESTERN DIVISION TOTALS....................... 55

NATIONAL SALES................................160
```

FIGURE 7-16

A THREE-LEVEL CONTROL BREAK PROBLEM

In Figure 7-16 note that the salesperson number consists of a division code prefix, a region code, and the employee number.

Assuming that the input file consists of a list of all salesperson numbers sorted by division, region, and employee number, the logic to produce the summary report shown in Figure 7-16 is based on recognizing three levels of control breaks: division, region, and employee number.

As an example of a specific two-level control break problem, consider the following programming problem:

Problem Specification

Each record of an input file consists of two entries: a salesperson number and a sales amount. Each salesperson number has seven digits. The first two digits identify the salesperson by region, and the remaining five digits are the salesperson's employee number. All salespersons records are grouped by region, and within each region records are grouped by employee numbers (see the following sample input file).

Write a program to produce a summary report of sales by salesperson and by region. The salesperson's subtotal should appear on the same line as the last sales entry. The printout should indicate the total sales amount for all regions and should skip to the top of a new page whenever a page consists of more than 23 lines (a page includes top-of-page headings). Major and minor headings should appear at the top of each numbered page. Sample input and output files are shown on the next page.

OUTPUT

```
    SALES REPORT                          PAGE 1
    SALESPERSON   SALES    SUBTOTALS    TOTALS
REGION  9
        0988888    9.00      $9.00

        REGION TOTALS ................   $9.00

REGION 10
        1011111   54.78
        1011111   60.00
        1011111   70.00    $184.78

        1022222   67.00
        1022222   78.90    $145.90

        1033333   34.00
        1033333   66.00    $100.00

        REGION TOTALS ................  $430.68


    SALES REPORT                          PAGE 2
    SALESPERSON   SALES    SUBTOTALS    TOTALS
REGION 11
        1144444   78.90     $78.90

        1155555   67.00
        1155555   78.00    $145.00

        REGION TOTALS ................  $223.90
TOTALS                                   $663.58
```

page consists of 23 lines

INPUT FILE

Salesperson number
Region number | Sales amount

```
0988888  0900
1011111  5478
1011111  6000
1011111  7000
1022222  6700
1022222  7890
1033333  3400
1033333  6600
1144444  7890
1155555  6700
1155555  7800
```

Program Analysis

The logic to solve this problem is captured in flowchart form in Figure 7–17; it is essentially the same as the logic of the one-level control break problem of section 7–4–3. The COBOL code itself is shown in Figure 7–18. Note the two control breaks in the code at line 127 and line 141. Every time a record is read, the region is first tested to determine whether a region break has occurred. If it is the same region, the employee number just read is tested with the previous employee number to determine whether a salesperson break has occurred. In the event of a salesperson break, the previous salesperson's subtotals are printed. If a division break occurs, the last salesperson's subtotals are printed first, followed by the region's total sales.

The subject of page size and page breaks merits further consideration. Let us agree that each page consists of exactly 23 lines (an arbitrary decision). This means that when the statement WRITE PRINT-LINE ... AFTER ADVANCING PAGE is carried out, the printer will skip an appropriate number of lines on the current page to advance the carriage (print-bar-element) to the top of a new page. For example, if the printer is at line 10 and the AFTER ADVANCING PAGE clause is invoked, the page interval made up of lines 11, 12, 13, ..., and 23 will be left blank. Likewise if the printer is at line 20, three blank lines will separate the current page from the top of the next page. The implementation of the PAGE feature may vary from one system to another—on some systems the length of a page can be specified in the LINAGE clause in the file description FD entry (line 34 in Figure 7–18), and on other systems the word PAGE may be equated to a particular channel number corresponding to punched holes in a paper carriage tape that guides the line printer's vertical movement. The correspondence between a mnemonic name, such as PAGE, and an actual channel number is specified in the SPECIAL NAMES paragraph of the CONFIGURATION section.

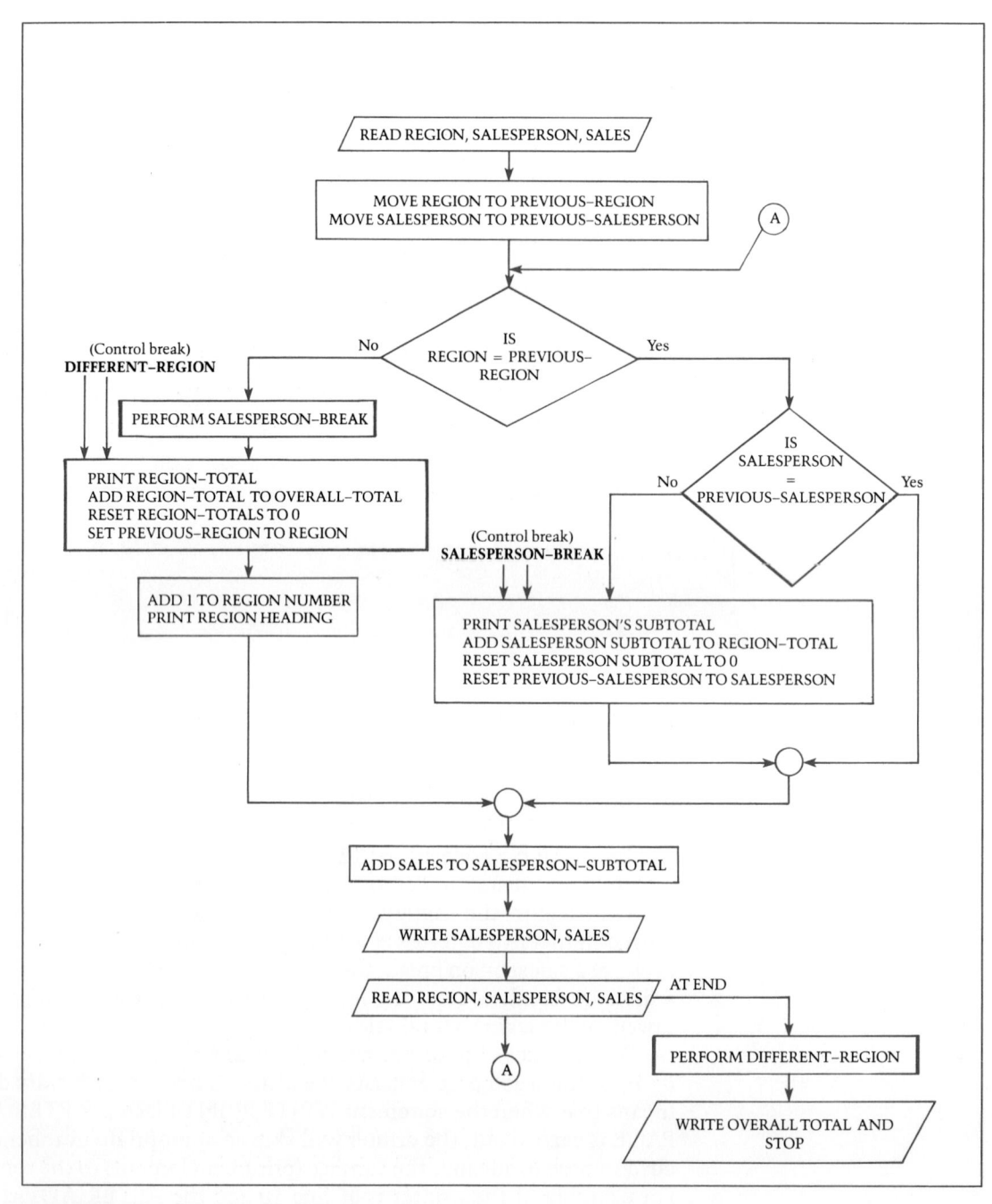

FIGURE 7–17
A TWO–LEVEL CONTROL BREAK PROBLEM.

Let us also agree that all pages will start with identical headings (caption, page number, and minor headings) at the very top of the page (beginning on line 1) and, furthermore, that a minimum of two blank lines will be provided at the bottom (foot) of each page.

Because of the variety of line breaks that can occur from one page to the next, care must be exercised when deciding when to skip to the top of a new page. Such a decision rests primarily on the value of the line counter, but it also depends on the type of line that comes up for printing as the end of the page is approached. Page-to-page breaks may occur at various points in the report, and each type of page break requires special treatment:

1. A salesperson's break: requires an accompanying REGION number on the next page to improve comprehension.

2. A salesperson's summary break: two WRITE operations that are not consecutive in the COBOL code (lines 171 and 160) must be performed together either before or after the page break, since the summary entry must be written on the same line as the last sales entry.

3. A region break: a caption, such as REGION 11, should not occur by itself on the last line of a page since it would be meaningless—it should await the next page.

4. A region summary line (region totals): requires double spacing after it.

5. The overall total for all regions: may have to be specified by itself on the last page if there is no more room at the foot of the current page.

6. Special page-formatting considerations, spelled out by managerial staff, may proscribe one or more of the page breaks discussed in items 1–5.

Thus, many different end-of-page tests are included in the COBOL code of Figure 7–18: at lines 131 (to take care of item 3 above), 145 (for items 2 and 4) and 169 (for item 1).

Test Your Understanding of the Program

1. Add the code to take care of item 5 in the page-to-page break discussed above. The COBOL code in Figure 7–18 does not address this problem.

2. To better understand the page break process, simulate a 10-line page and use the data file shown in the problem specification to see what "happens" to page breaks. Use the constant 5 instead of 18 at lines 131 and 161, and use 6 instead of 19 at line 145.

7-5 YOU MIGHT WANT TO KNOW

1. Since reports are so common, does COBOL support a report type feature where the programmer can, for example, specify the physical format of a report and the system takes care of the necessary code to accumulate various sums, produce totals, increment and reset accumulators and counters, print the detail lines and page numbers, and check for control breaks?

```
 1: IDENTIFICATION DIVISION.
 2: PROGRAM-ID. MULTI LEVEL-CONTROL-BREAK.
 3: AUTHOR. JONES.
 4: ******************************************************************
 5: * OBJECTIVE: PRODUCE A MULTILEVEL AND MULTIPAGE SUMMARY SALES    *
 6: *            REPORT BASED ON SALESPERSON AND REGION.             *
 7: *                                                                *
 8: * INPUT:     REGION NUMBER, SALESPERSON NUMBER AND SALES AMOUNT. *
 9: *                                                                *
10: * OUTPUT:    REGION NUMBER, SALESPERSON NUMBER, SALES AMOUNT,    *
11: *            SUBTOTALS, REGION TOTALS AND TOTAL SALES FIGURE.    *
12: ******************************************************************
13: ENVIRONMENT DIVISION.
14: CONFIGURATION SECTION.
15: SOURCE-COMPUTER. IBM.
16: OBJECT-COMPUTER. IBM.
17: INPUT-OUTPUT SECTION.
18: FILE-CONTROL.
19:     SELECT REPORT-FILE ASSIGN TO PRINTER.
20:     SELECT SALES-FILE  ASSIGN TO DISK
21:     ORGANIZATION IS LINE SEQUENTIAL.
22: *
23: DATA DIVISION.
24: FILE SECTION.
25: *
26: FD  SALES-FILE
27:     LABEL RECORDS ARE STANDARD
28:     VALUE OF FILE-ID IS 'MLTIBRK'
29:     DATA RECORD IS INPUT-RECORD.
30: 01  INPUT-RECORD PIC X(12).
31: FD  REPORT-FILE
32:     LABEL RECORDS ARE OMITTED
33:     DATA RECORD IS PRINT-LINE
34:     LINAGE IS 23 LINES.
35: 01  PRINT-LINE PIC X(132).
36: *
37: WORKING-STORAGE SECTION.
38: *
39: *   INDEPENDENT ITEMS
40: *
41: 01  FLAGS.
42:     05 WS-EOF PIC 9    VALUE 0.
43:        88 END-OF-FILE VALUE IS 1.
44: *
45: 01  COMPUTATIONAL-ITEMS.
46:     05 WS-PREVIOUS-REGION      PIC 99.
47:     05 WS-PREVIOUS-SALESPERSON PIC 9(05).
48:        88 FIRST-RECORD VALUE IS 1.
49:     05 WS-SALESPERSON-SUBTOT PIC 9999V99 VALUE 0.
50:     05 WS-REGION-TOTALS      PIC 9999V99 VALUE 0.
51:     05 WS-OVERALL-TOTALS     PIC 9999V99 VALUE 0.
52:     05 WS-LINE-COUNT         PIC 99      VALUE 0.
53:     05 WS-PAGE-COUNT         PIC 99      VALUE 0.
54: *
55: *   INPUT RECORD DESCRIPTION
56: *
57: 01  SALES-RECORD.
58:     05 SR-SALESPERSON-FIELD.
59:        10 SR-REGION      PIC 99.
60:        10 SR-SALESPERSON PIC 9(05).
61:     05 FILLER            PIC X.
62:     05 SR-SALES          PIC 99V99.
63: *
64: *   OUTPUT LINE DESCRIPTIONS
65: *
66: 01  MAJOR-HEADING.
67:     05 FILLER PIC X(10) VALUE SPACES.
68:     05 FILLER PIC X(12) VALUE 'SALES REPORT'.
69:     05 FILLER PIC X(19) VALUE SPACES.
70:     05 FILLER PIC X(05) VALUE 'PAGE'.
71:     05 MH-PAGE-NUMBER PIC 9.
72: 01  MINOR-HEADING.
73:     05 FILLER     PIC X(07) VALUE SPACES.
74:     05 FILLER     PIC X(14) VALUE 'SALESPERSON'.
75:     05 FILLER     PIC X(08) VALUE 'SALES'.
76:     05 FILLER     PIC X(12) VALUE 'SUBTOTALS'.
77:     05 FILLER     PIC X(06) VALUE 'TOTALS'.
78: 01  REGION-LINE.
79:     05 FILLER     PIC X(01) VALUE SPACES.
80:     05 FILLER     PIC X(07) VALUE 'REGION'.
81:     05 RL-REGION PIC Z9.
82: 01  DETAIL-LINE.
83:     05 FILLER         PIC X(09) VALUE SPACES.
84:     05 DL-SALESPERSON PIC 9(07).
85:     05 FILLER         PIC X(05) VALUE SPACES.
86:     05 DL-SALES       PIC ZZ.99.
87: 01  SALESPERSON-SUMMARY.
88:     05 FILLER    PIC X(30) VALUE SPACES.
89:     05 SS-TOTALS PIC $$$$.99.
90: 01  REGION-SUMMARY.
91:     05 FILLER    PIC X(09) VALUE SPACES.
92:     05 FILLER    PIC X(14) VALUE 'REGION TOTALS'.
93:     05 FILLER    PIC X(17) VALUE ALL '.'.
94:     05 RS-TOTALS PIC $$$$.99.
95: 01  SUMMARY-LINE.
96:     05 FILLER    PIC X(01) VALUE SPACES.
97:     05 FILLER    PIC X(38) VALUE 'TOTALS'.
98:     05 SL-TOTALS PIC $$$$$.99.
99: 01  BLANK-LINE   PIC X(132) VALUE SPACES.
```

INPUT FILE

Salesperson number
region | Sales

Salesperson/region	Sales
0910888	0900
1011111	5478
1011111	6000
1011111	7000
1022222	6700
1022222	7890
1033333	3400
1033333	5678
1144444	7890
1155555	6700
1155555	7800
1266666	8975
1377777	8769
1377777	7800
1377777	0980
1377777	8900
1377777	4500
1488888	0560
1488888	0980
1488888	7000
1488888	3000
1488888	2000
1488888	3400
1488888	5400
1488888	2000
1488888	5000

FIGURE 7-18

A MULTILEVEL CONTROL BREAK PROBLEM

```
101:   PROCEDURE DIVISION.
102:   100-COORDINATING-MODULE.
103:       OPEN INPUT SALES-FILE
104:            OUTPUT REPORT-FILE.
105:       PERFORM 150-READ-INITIALIZE.
106:       PERFORM 200-WRITE-HEADINGS.
107:       PERFORM 300-PROCESS-RECORD UNTIL END-OF-FILE.
108:       PERFORM 800-FINAL-WRITES.
109:       CLOSE REPORT-FILE, SALES-FILE.
110:       STOP RUN.
111: *
112:   150-READ-INITIALIZE.
113:       READ SALES-FILE INTO SALES-RECORD
114:            AT END MOVE 1 TO WS-EOF.
115:       MOVE SR-REGION TO WS-PREVIOUS-REGION, RL-REGION.
116:       MOVE SR-SALESPERSON TO WS-PREVIOUS-SALESPERSON.
117: *
118:   200-WRITE-HEADINGS.
119:       ADD 1 TO WS-PAGE-COUNT.
120:       MOVE WS-PAGE-COUNT TO MH-PAGE-NUMBER.
121:       WRITE PRINT-LINE FROM MAJOR-HEADING AFTER PAGE.
122:       WRITE PRINT-LINE FROM MINOR-HEADING AFTER 2 LINES.
123:       WRITE PRINT-LINE FROM REGION-LINE   AFTER 2 LINES.
124:       MOVE 4 TO WS-LINE-COUNT.
125: *
126:   300-PROCESS-RECORD.
127:       IF SR-REGION = WS-PREVIOUS-REGION
128:           PERFORM 400-SAME-REGION
129:       ELSE
130:           PERFORM 500-DIFFERENT-REGION
131:           IF WS-LINE-COUNT IS GREATER THAN 18
132:               PERFORM 200-WRITE-HEADINGS
133:           ELSE
134:               WRITE PRINT-LINE FROM REGION-LINE AFTER 2
135:               ADD 2 TO WS-LINE-COUNT.
136:       PERFORM 700-PRINT-RECORD-JUST-READ.
137:       READ SALES-FILE INTO SALES-RECORD
138:            AT END MOVE 1 TO WS-EOF.
139: *
140:   400-SAME-REGION.
141:       IF SR-SALESPERSON NOT = TO WS-PREVIOUS-SALESPERSON
142:           PERFORM 600-DIFFERENT-SALESPERSON.
143: *
144:   500-DIFFERENT-REGION.
145:       IF WS-LINE-COUNT IS GREATER THAN 19
146:           PERFORM 200-WRITE-HEADINGS.
147:       PERFORM 600-DIFFERENT-SALESPERSON.
148:       MOVE SR-REGION        TO WS-PREVIOUS-REGION.
149:       MOVE SR-REGION        TO RL-REGION.
150:       MOVE WS-REGION-TOTALS TO RS-TOTALS.
151:       ADD  WS-REGION-TOTALS TO WS-OVERALL-TOTALS.
152:       WRITE PRINT-LINE FROM REGION-SUMMARY AFTER 1 LINE.
153:       ADD  1 TO WS-LINE-COUNT.
154:       MOVE 0 TO WS-REGION-TOTALS.
155: *
156:   600-DIFFERENT-SALESPERSON.
157:       ADD WS-SALESPERSON-SUBTOT  TO WS-REGION-TOTALS.
158:       MOVE SR-SALESPERSON TO WS-PREVIOUS-SALESPERSON.
159:       MOVE WS-SALESPERSON-SUBTOT TO SS-TOTALS.
160:       WRITE PRINT-LINE FROM SALESPERSON-SUMMARY AFTER 0.
161:       WRITE PRINT-LINE FROM BLANK-LINE AFTER 1 LINE.
162:       ADD  1 TO WS-LINE-COUNT.
163:       MOVE 0 TO WS-SALESPERSON-SUBTOT.
164: *
165:   700-PRINT-RECORD-JUST-READ.
166:       ADD SR-SALES TO WS-SALESPERSON-SUBTOT.
167:       MOVE SR-SALESPERSON-FIELD TO DL-SALESPERSON.
168:       MOVE SR-SALES             TO DL-SALES.
169:       IF WS-LINE-COUNT IS GREATER THAN 18
170:           PERFORM 200-WRITE-HEADINGS.
171:       WRITE PRINT-LINE FROM DETAIL-LINE AFTER 1 LINE.
172:       ADD 1 TO WS-LINE-COUNT.
173: *
174:   800-FINAL-WRITES.
175:       PERFORM 500-DIFFERENT-REGION.
176:       MOVE WS-OVERALL-TOTALS TO SL-TOTALS.
177:       WRITE PRINT-LINE FROM SUMMARY-LINE AFTER 2.
```

OUTPUT →

```
     SALES REPORT                      PAGE 1
     SALESPERSON   SALES   SUBTOTALS   TOTALS
REGION  9
        0910888     9.00    $9.00
        REGION TOTALS .................    $9.00
REGION 10
        1011111    54.78
        1011111    60.00
        1011111    70.00   $184.78

        1022222    67.00
        1022222    78.90   $145.90

        1033333    34.00
        1033333    56.78    $90.78
        REGION TOTALS .................$421.46

     SALES REPORT                      PAGE 2
     SALESPERSON   SALES   SUBTOTALS   TOTALS
REGION 11
        1144444    78.90    $78.90

        1155555    67.00
        1155555    78.00   $145.00
        REGION TOTALS .................$223.90
REGION 12
        1266666    89.75    $89.75
        REGION TOTALS .................  $89.75
REGION 13
        1377777    87.69
        1377777    78.00

     SALES REPORT                      PAGE 3
     SALESPERSON   SALES   SUBTOTALS   TOTALS
REGION 13
        1377777     9.80
        1377777    89.00
        1377777    45.00   $309.49
        REGION TOTALS .................$309.49
REGION 14
        1488888     5.60
        1488888     9.80
        1488888    70.00
        1488888    30.00
        1488888    20.00
        1488888    34.00
        1488888    54.00
        1488888    20.00

     SALES REPORT                      PAGE 4
     SALESPERSON   SALES   SUBTOTALS   TOTALS
REGION 14
        1488888    50.00   $293.40
        REGION TOTALS .................$293.40
TOTALS                                 $1347.00
```

FIGURE 7–18
(continued)

Answer: Yes. REPORT WRITER is a special-purpose language subset of COBOL available in many COBOL compilers. It permits a flexible and convenient method of producing reports. Report characteristics are declared in report description entries in the DATA division. The programmer then initiates, generates, and terminates the report in the PROCEDURE division by actually using such report-writer commands as INITIATE, GENERATE, and TERMINATE. The compiler then automatically generates the code in the PROCEDURE division to move the data, construct detail lines, count line and page numbers, produce headings and footing lines, sum various totals, and check for control breaks. For further information, the reader is advised to check his/her installation's technical reference manual.

2. How do I tell the printer to skip to the top or bottom of a page, or for that matter to any particular line on the output form?

    Answer: Printer control can be effected through the ADVANCING feature of the WRITE statement. In many installations using very fast line printers (different than the ones used with microcomputers) a carriage control tape is physically mounted on the printing device (see Figure 7–19). Through the SPECIAL–NAMES paragraph in the CONFIGURATION SECTION, the user can specify in his/her own words 12 distinct types of printer action for line positioning, for example:

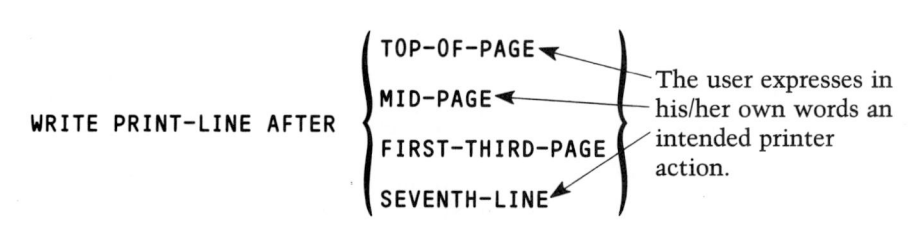

```
                        ┌ TOP-OF-PAGE      ┐
                        │ MID-PAGE         │    The user expresses in
WRITE PRINT-LINE AFTER  │                  │    his/her own words an
                        │ FIRST-THIRD-PAGE │    intended printer
                        │ SEVENTH-LINE     │    action.
                        └                  ┘
```

where TOP–OF–PAGE, MID–PAGE, FIRST–THIRD–PAGE, and SEVENTH–LINE are user-chosen expressions (called *mnemonic names*) to control vertical printer movement. To convey the meaning of these expressions to the compiler, the user equates or assigns the chosen mnemonic names (user-chosen expressions) to predefined hardware functions in the SPECIAL–NAMES paragraph of the CONFIGURATION SECTION. The 12 hardware functions (called *channels*) that are recognized by the COBOL compiler may vary from one manufacturer to the other. For IBM compilers the 12 hardware functions are identified by the reserved words C01, C02, ..., C012 and are defined as follows:

C01   Channel 1 Generally used for skipping to the top of a new page.

C12   Channel 12 Generally used for skipping to the bottom of a page.

C02

C03 ⎫
 . ⎬ Channels 2–11: User choice for printer action.
 . ⎪
C11 ⎭

These functions are made known to the printer by perforating its carriage control tape in the desired channels (see Figure 7–19) to obtain 12 distinct printer vertical line positions. Most carriage control tapes are already prepunched for certain standard actions, such as ejection to the top of a new page (generally associated with the function C01), so if the user who wishes to define his/her own printing parameters, such as MID-PAGE skip or SUMMARY-RESULTS skip, he/she must prepare (punch) the carriage control tape accordingly. The tape is then inserted into a drive wheel in the printer device.

For example, to cause the printer to skip to the 33rd line of the output form using the statement AFTER ADVANCING TO MID-PAGE, the user would punch a hole in the carriage control tape at line 33 (see Figure 7–19) in any of the 12 channels, for example, Channel 3. In the SPECIAL-NAMES paragraph he/she would equate MID-PAGE to C03 or CHANNEL 3 (Burroughs) as follows:

```
        CONFIGURATION SECTION.
        SPECIAL-NAMES.
            C03 IS MID-PAGE.         ⎫
            C07 IS SUMMARY-RESULTS.  ⎬ IBM Compilers
            CHANNEL 3 IS MID-PAGE.      ⎫ BURROUGHS
            CHANNEL 1 IS TOP-OF-PAGE.   ⎬ Compilers
```

Figure 7–19 illustrates the carriage control tape and the printer form (output page).

The SPECIAL-NAMES feature is very useful for professional COBOL programmers who may want to use the various hardware functions C01, C02, ... to skip to predetermined line positions on the output form for such purposes as major headings, subheadings, summary lines, and footing lines. This feature is also extremely convenient for writing on business forms already containing preprinted information (letterheads, invoices, checks, et cetera) at a predefined page depth; the hardware functions can then be adjusted to pinpoint the exact line on the form where entries or results are to be printed. Thus in many COBOL shops, there are programs that require the operator to mount particular carriage control tapes.

In any event, the beginning programmer can always find out what punches already exist on the printer's carriage control tape and use these punches by assigning them mnemonic names through the SPECIAL-NAMES paragraph. In many non-IBM compilers the ADVANCING clause may specify a mnemonic name (such as MID-PAGE), the channel number itself (AFTER CHANNEL 3), or the reserved word PAGE (to skip to the top of a new page—AFTER ADVANCING PAGE). In many instances the WRITE statement may also specify what action is to be taken when the end of the page is reached; one form of such a WRITE statment is:

```
WRITE record-name FROM area-name

    ⎡ ⎧BEFORE⎫                   ⎧CHANNEL integer-1⎫ ⎤
    ⎢ ⎨      ⎬ ADVANCING TO      ⎨Integer-2   LINES⎬ ⎥
    ⎢ ⎩AFTER ⎭                   ⎪Mnemonic-name    ⎪ ⎥
    ⎣                            ⎩PAGE             ⎭ ⎦

    ⎡    ⎧END-OF-PAGE⎫                              ⎤
    ⎢ AT ⎨           ⎬ statement  [ELSE statement]  ⎥
    ⎣    ⎩EOP        ⎭                              ⎦
```

TOP-OF-PAGE

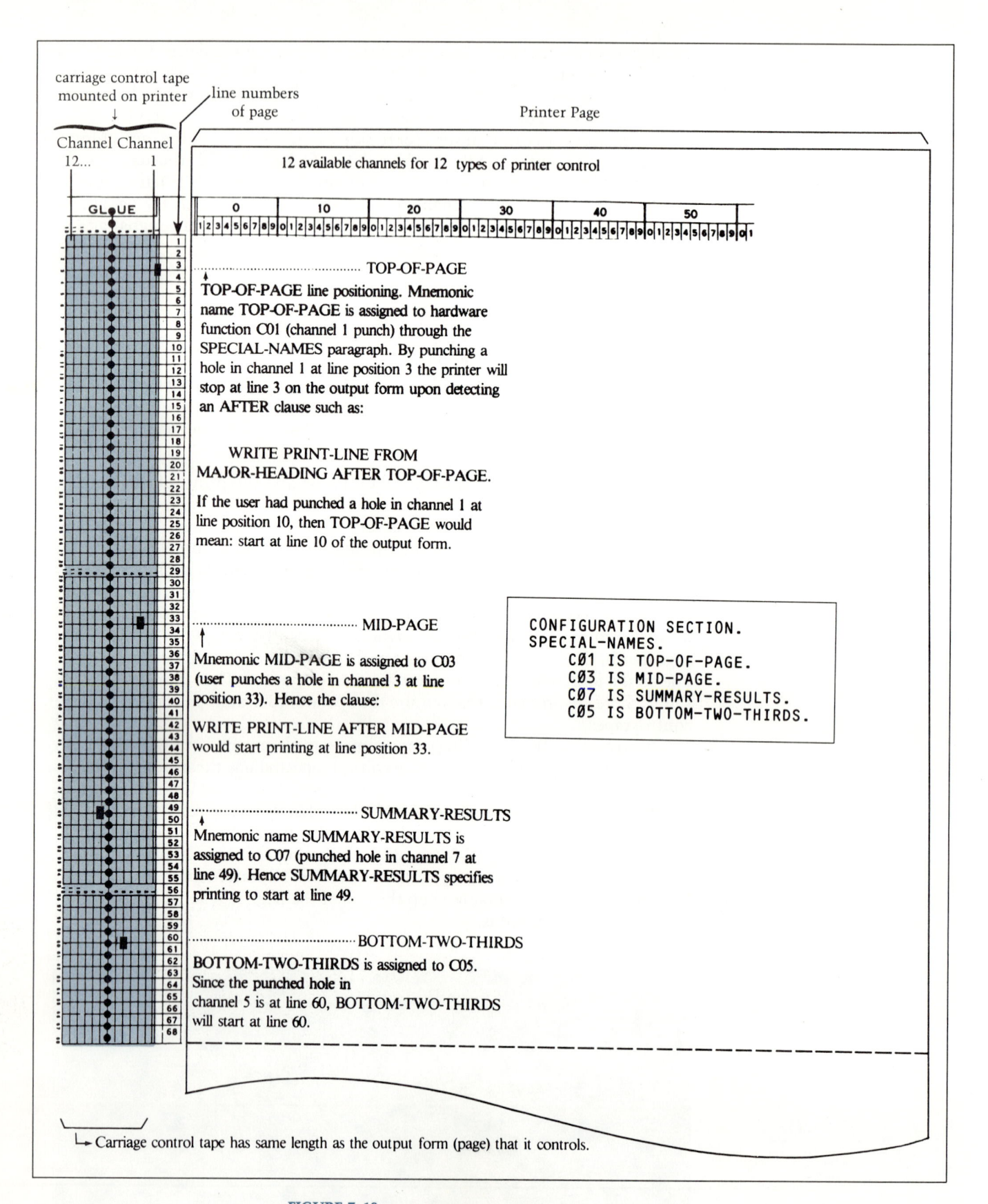

TOP-OF-PAGE line positioning. Mnemonic name TOP-OF-PAGE is assigned to hardware function C01 (channel 1 punch) through the SPECIAL-NAMES paragraph. By punching a hole in channel 1 at line position 3 the printer will stop at line 3 on the output form upon detecting an AFTER clause such as:

WRITE PRINT-LINE FROM
MAJOR-HEADING AFTER TOP-OF-PAGE.

If the user had punched a hole in channel 1 at line position 10, then TOP-OF-PAGE would mean: start at line 10 of the output form.

MID-PAGE

Mnemonic MID-PAGE is assigned to C03 (user punches a hole in channel 3 at line position 33). Hence the clause:

WRITE PRINT-LINE AFTER MID-PAGE
would start printing at line position 33.

```
CONFIGURATION SECTION.
SPECIAL-NAMES.
    C01 IS TOP-OF-PAGE.
    C03 IS MID-PAGE.
    C07 IS SUMMARY-RESULTS.
    C05 IS BOTTOM-TWO-THIRDS.
```

SUMMARY-RESULTS

Mnemonic name SUMMARY-RESULTS is assigned to C07 (punched hole in channel 7 at line 49). Hence SUMMARY-RESULTS specifies printing to start at line 49.

BOTTOM-TWO-THIRDS

BOTTOM-TWO-THIRDS is assigned to C05. Since the punched hole in channel 5 is at line 60, BOTTOM-TWO-THIRDS will start at line 60.

↳ Carriage control tape has same length as the output form (page) that it controls.

FIGURE 7-19
SPECIAL-NAMES AND CARRIAGE CONTROL TAPE

The reader should consult his/her technical reference manual for such useful features.

These hardware functions should not be used on a printer with no carriage control tape, as a runaway paper situation could occur when the printer searches for a nonexistent punch on a nonexistent tape.

3. Can the SPECIAL-NAMES paragraph be used for purposes other than defining carriage control functions?

    Answer: Yes. One clause allows a currency symbol other than the dollar sign to be recognized in PICTURE clauses. The currency symbol chosen must be a nonnumeric, single character literal and may not be any of the following:

    a. Digits 0 through 9.
    b. Alphabetic characters A, B, C, D, J, L, P, R, S, V, X, Z or the space.
    c. Special characters * − , . ; ( ) + " '.

    If the CURRENCY SIGN clause is not present, the currency symbol ($) is used in the PICTURE clause. The sterling pound sign £ is often used.

    Another option allows one to exchange the commas for periods in an edited field. (In Europe $1,000,000.56 is written as $1.000.000,56.) With the DECIMAL POINT IS COMMA option, the computer aligns the "decimal" point on the comma in the report field. The forms of these two clauses are:

    ```
    SPECIAL-NAMES.
         CURRENCY SIGN IS literal.   Literal could be 'F', for example (francs).
         DECIMAL POINT IS COMMA.
    ```

4. **Multiple Redefinition of an Input Record.** In many cases, an input file contains several types of records—records with different lengths that are interspersed in the data file. Since there is only one input area into which input records are read, how can I define that area to capture two or more different types of record layouts? (Remember the REDEFINES statement cannot be used at the 01 level in the FILE section.)

    Answer: The record descriptions for each of the various types of input records are typed following the FD entry describing the particular file, i.e., if the file consists of six different types of records, then six of the level record description entries must be specified following the FD entry for that file. Remember that these six record entries share the same area of storage. For example:

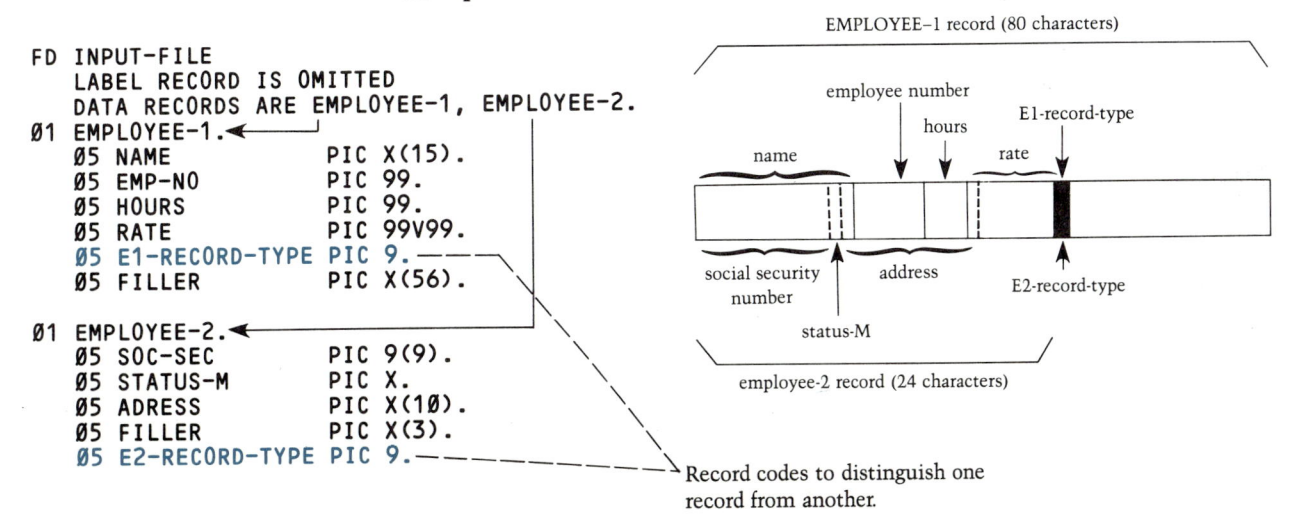

```
FD INPUT-FILE
   LABEL RECORD IS OMITTED
   DATA RECORDS ARE EMPLOYEE-1, EMPLOYEE-2.
01 EMPLOYEE-1.
   05 NAME            PIC X(15).
   05 EMP-NO          PIC 99.
   05 HOURS           PIC 99.
   05 RATE            PIC 99V99.
   05 E1-RECORD-TYPE  PIC 9.
   05 FILLER          PIC X(56).
01 EMPLOYEE-2.
   05 SOC-SEC         PIC 9(9).
   05 STATUS-M        PIC X.
   05 ADRESS          PIC X(10).
   05 FILLER          PIC X(3).
   05 E2-RECORD-TYPE  PIC 9.
```

Record codes to distinguish one record from another.

In the PROCEDURE DIVISION either E1–RECORD–TYPE or E2–RECORD–TYPE could be tested to determine whether the input record should be referred to as EMPLOYEE–1 or EMPLOYEE–2.

The multiple definition of an input/output record produces the same results as the REDEFINES clause. The system does not reserve separate memory areas for the multiple records. Only one area is used, i.e., all input records are successively stored in the same memory area. It is the user's responsibility to determine which form of the record is to be processed; this is done through the data item names referenced in the PROCEDURE division.

7-6 EXERCISES

7-6-1 TEST YOURSELF

1. True or False:

   a. In the PROCEDURE DIVISION, SOC–SEC and SEC can be used interchangeably.

   ```
   05 SOC-SEC PIC 9(9).
   05 SEC REDEFINES SOC-SEC.
      10 FILLER PIC 9(4).
      10 FILLER PIC 9(5).
   ```

   b. If you expect to read different types of records, you can use the REDEFINES clause at the 01 level to capture different record descriptions in the input record in the FILE section.

   c. The VALUE clause may be used in the same entry as the REDEFINES clause.

   d. The PICTURE clause may not be used in the same entry as the REDEFINES clause.

   e. A subordinate entry in the input/output record may not contain the REDEFINES clause.

2. For each of the following coding segments, answer the following:
   (1) Is the code valid or invalid?
   (2) How many memory positions does the lowest level number record description entry reserve?
   (3) Identify in diagram form the areas defined and redefined.
   For example, given the following coding segment, the answers would be as follows:

   ```
   01 X.
      05 A PIC XX.
      05 B PIC 9V9.
   01 Z REDEFINES X.
      05 C PIC 9.
      05 D PIC XXX.
   ```

   Answers:
   1. Valid
   2. Level 01 reserves 4 positions.
   3.

   ```
          A      B
       ┌────┬───┬────┐
       │    │   │    │
       └────┴───┴────┘
          C      D
   ```

a. 01 INPUT-REC.
       10 A   PIC 999.
       10 FILLER PIC X(5).
       10 C   PIC 9V9.
       10 FILLER PIC X(70).
   01 DUMMY REDEFINES INPUT-REC.
       10 TEMP-1 PIC X(60).
       10 TEMP-2 PIC 9(18).

b. 05 FAMILY.
       10 CHILD-1 PIC A(10).
       10 CHILD-2 PIC A(15).
       10 TOM REDEFINES CHILD-1 PIC A(10).
       10 CHILD-3 PIC A(10).

c. 01 RESOURCE.
       10 DEPT   PIC X(8).
       10 FILLER PIC XX.
       10 TASK   PIC 9(10).
       10 KODE REDEFINES TASK PIC XX.

d. FD INPUT-FILE
       DATA RECORD IS CAR.
   01 CAR.
       05 MODEL PIC A(5).
       05 FILLER PIC X(75).
   01 NEW-CAR REDEFINES CAR.
       05 NEW MODEL PIC A(5).
       05 FILLER PIC X(75).

e. 01 XYZ.
       05 A PIC X(10).
       05 B PIC 9.9.
       05 C REDEFINES B PIC AAA.

f. 01 X.
       05 B PIC X(10).
       05 C REDEFINES B PIC 9(10).
       05 D REDEFINES B.
           10 E PIC X(5).
           10 F PIC 9(5).

g. 01 A PIC X(80).
   01 B REDEFINES A.
       15 C PIC X(60).
       15 D PIC X.

h. 01 X.
       05 A PIC 9(10).
       05 B REDEFINES A PIC X(10).
       05 C REDEFINES B PIC 9(5)V9(5).

i. 01 X.
       05 A PIC 9.9.
       05 B PIC XXX.
       06 C REDEFINES B PIC XXX.

j. 01 INPUT-REC.
       05 NAME PIC A(10).
   01 NEW-REC REDEFINES INPUT-REC PIC X(80).

k. 01 INPUT-RECORD.
       05 NAME PIC A(10).
       05 COST REDEFINES NAME.
           10 EMP-NO PIC 999.
           10 FILLER PIC XX.
           10 AMT   PIC 999V99.
       05 FILLER PIC X(70).
   01 IN-OPTION REDEFINES INPUT-RECORD.
       05 A PIC 9(9).
       05 B PIC X(71).

l. 01 A PIC X(80).
   01 B REDEFINES A PIC 9(9).

m. 01 A PIC X(80) VALUE ALL '*'.
   01 B REDEFINES A.
       05 C PIC X(20).
       05 D REDEFINES C.
           10 E PIC 9(10).
           10 F PIC A(10).
       05 G PIC X(60).

3. Display the contents of AMT as a result of the various MOVEs starting at 255 and ending at 290.

```
210 WORKING-STORAGE SECTION.        245 PROCEDURE DIVISION.
215 01 X.                            250 MAIN-L.
220     05 AMT PIC 999V99 VALUE 23.47. 255     MOVE AMT TO Z.
225     05 B REDEFINES AMT.          260     MOVE 38 TO Z.
230         10 Y PIC A.              265     MOVE Z TO T.
235         10 Z PIC 9.              270     MOVE REC TO T.
240         10 T PIC XXX.            275     MOVE Z TO AMT.
242     05 REC REDEFINES AMT PIC 99999. 280     MOVE 'HOUSE' TO Y.
                                     285     MOVE T TO B.
                                     290     STOP RUN.
```

4. Without using class tests, write the code to test whether FLDA PIC 999 is a numeric item. Print an appropriate message in either case.

5. Specify the value of FLDA, TALLY, I, and J.

		FLDA
a.	EXAMINE FLDA TALLYING LEADING ZEROES REPLACING BY SPACES.	000304
b.	EXAMINE FLDA TALLYING ALL ',' REPLACING BY '.'.	1,325,051.3
c.	EXAMINE FLDA TALLYING UNTIL FIRST '.' REPLACING BY ' '.	I AM. .
d.	EXAMINE FLDA REPLACING ALL '/' BY SPACES.	08/16/82
e.	EXAMINE FLDA REPLACING FIRST SPACE BY '$'.	ƀƀƀ34
f.	EXAMINE FLDA REPLACING UNTIL FIRST '1' BY ZERO.	$ƀ**1.56
g.	EXAMINE FLDA REPLACING LEADING ZEROS BY SPACES.	00100
h.	EXAMINE FLDA TALLYING LEADING '0'.	001003

In each of the following assume the counters I and J are set to 0 initially.

i.	INSPECT FLDA REPLACING SPACES BY '*'.	WE AM US
j.	INSPECT FLDA TALLYING I FOR ALL '1'.	1,213.14
k.	INSPECT FLDA TALLYING I FOR LEADING SPACES REPLACING ALL ZEROS BY SPACES.	ƀƀƀ2100

l.	INSPECT FLDA TALLYING
	  I FOR CHARACTERS BEFORE '.'
	  J FOR CHARACTERS AFTER '.'.
		1324.56

m.	INSPECT FLDA TALLYING I FOR CHARACTERS BEFORE INITIAL '$'.	+$$$.99
n.	INSPECT FLDA TALLYING I FOR LEADING 'MY'.	MYOMY
o.	INSPECT FLDA REPLACING ALL '*' BY ZEROS.	$***5.03
p.	INSPECT FLDA REPLACING CHARACTERS BY SPACES.	ABCD.L
q.	INSPECT FLDA TALLYING I FOR ALL 'AM' REPLACING ALL '.ƀ' BY ';*'.	MAAM.ƀDAM.ƀA

r.	INSPECT FLDA REPLACING LEADING '*' BY ZEROES
	    REPLACING FIRST SPACE BY '$'
	    REPLACING ALL 'CR' BY 'DB'.
		ƀƀ***3.24CR*
		00131012
		000.05

s.	INSPECT FLDA REPLACING ALL '1' BY '2' AFTER INITIAL '3'.	HILL
t.	INSPECT FLDA REPLACING ALL ZEROS BY '*' BEFORE INITIAL '.'.	256010
u.	INSPECT FLDA REPLACING FIRST 'I' BY 'E'.	
v.	INSPECT FLDA TALLYING I FOR CHARACTERS BEFORE INITIAL '0'.	

w.	INSPECT FLDA REPLACING ALL '1' BY '2'
	                          '3' BY '4'
	                          '5' BY '6' AFTER INITIAL 7.
		13573

7-6-2 PROGRAMMING EXERCISES

1. A data file consists of records, each containing the following information concerning items produced at the XYZ manufacturing plant: a department number, an item number, a quantity, and a cost per item. Assume the file has been sorted into order by ascending department number. Write a program to produce a summary report as follows:

```
       DEPARTMENT      ITEM     QUANTITY    COST/ITEM    VALUE     TOTALS

           15          1389         4          3.20      12.80
           15          3821         2          7.00      14.00
                                                                   26.80
           16          0122         8          2.50      20.00
                                                                   20.00
           19          1244        100         0.03       3.00
           19          1245         20         4.00      80.00
           19          2469         4         16.00      64.00
                                                                  147.00

                                                     GRAND TOTAL  193.80
```

Could you alter the program to write each subtotal on the same line as the last entry for each department? Make your own data file.

2. An input file consists of several packets of records, each containing grades obtained by different classes. Each packet is identified by a header record specifying the course title and the section number. One student grade (0–100) is typed per record. Write a complete program to determine the percentage of passing grades for each section (passing grades are grades over 60). List the grades starting at the top of a new numbered page for each new section. The pages for each section should be numbered 1, 2, 3, et cetera. Provide appropriate headers.

To simplify testing of your program, assume each output page will contain only 4 student grades; i.e., assume a page is no more than 10 lines including the various headers. The input and output have the following forms: (draw hyphenated lines to indicate end of page)

INPUT FILE

Course title   Section number
     ↓   ↓
```
ALGEBRA        102  ⎫
090                 ⎪
080                 ⎬ Packet 1
073                 ⎪
 .                  ⎭
 .
 .
ECONOMICS 103       ⎫
022                 ⎪
032                 ⎬ Packet 2
010                 ⎪
 .                  ⎭
 .
 .
```

OUTPUT

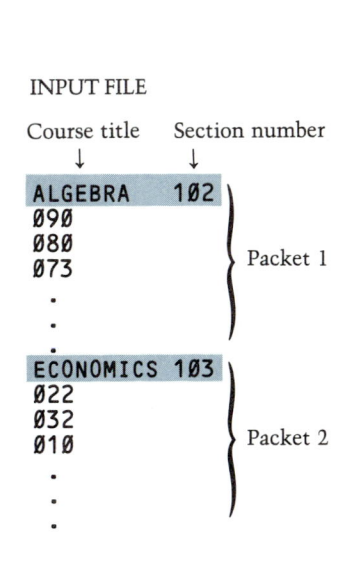

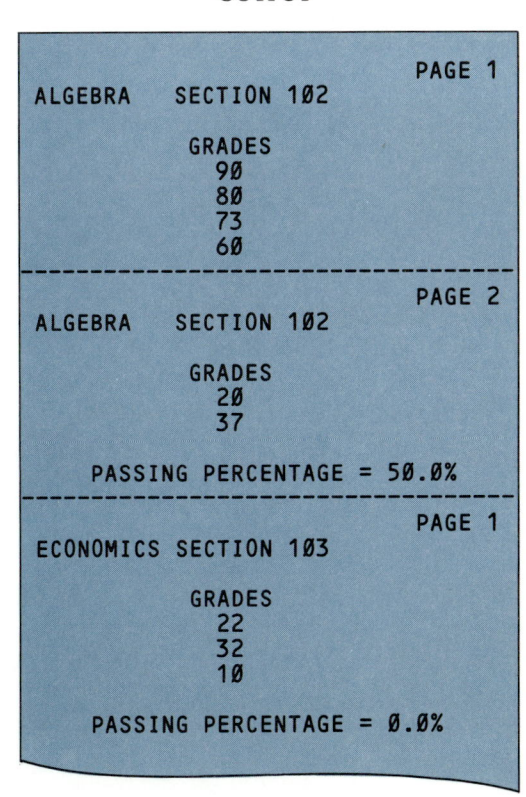

```
                                          PAGE 1
ALGEBRA      SECTION 102

                GRADES
                  90
                  80
                  73
                  60
------------------------------------------
                                          PAGE 2
ALGEBRA      SECTION 102

                GRADES
                  20
                  37

      PASSING PERCENTAGE = 50.0%
------------------------------------------
                                          PAGE 1
ECONOMICS SECTION 103

                GRADES
                  22
                  32
                  10

      PASSING PERCENTAGE = 0.0%
```

3. The following string contains a sentence without spaces between words, where the first word is 1 character long, the second word is 2 characters long, the third word is 3 characters long, ..., up to the ninth word which is 9 characters long.

SENTENCE = 'IAMTOOMUCHTIREDEATINGSAUSAGEAMERICANJALAPINOS'

Using the various character manipulation statements, write a program to:

a. Print each word on a separate line.
b. Separate each word by a blank space and print the entire sentence on one line.

4. Charlie's Eatery has now computerized their operations. Each record of the daily transaction file contains two items: a meal code (B = breakfast, L = lunch, D = dinner) and the cost of the order. All records occur in groups, first the breakfasts, then the lunches, and then the dinners. The management of Charlie's would like to obtain a summarized report displaying total breakfast costs, total lunch costs, et cetera. In addition, the following information is needed:

The day's total sales.
The average breakfast cost.
The lowest cost dinner order.
No meal order should exceed $800.00.

Invalid input records should be listed on output with the message "Invalid meal codes" to identify any unrecognized meal code or "Invalid meal cost" to identify any invalid cost.

Write a program to produce a report similar to the one shown below. Note that the invalid input records are printed on the report with explanatory comments; some invalid records require two error messages.

```
                CHARLIE'S EATERY REPORT

MEAL         COST        TOTALS

BREAKFAST    5.25
BREAKFAST    2.75
                                     C00575    INVALID MEAL CODE
BREAKFAST    3.50        $ 11.50

LUNCH       11.50
LUNCH        5.50
                                     400900    INVALID MEAL CODE
                                     I01000    INVALID MEAL CODE
LUNCH       23.00
                                     L01.0A    INVALID MEAL COST
                                     A0190L    INVALID MEAL CODE
                                               INVALID MEAL COST
LUNCH       17.00        $ 57.00

DINNER     100.00
DINNER      55.00
DINNER      45.50
                                     D90000    MEAL COST OVER 800
                                     A90000    MEAL COST OVER 800
                                               INVALID MEAL CODE
DINNER      10.50
DINNER      10.00        $221.00
                                               Invalid records are printed

TOTAL RECEIPTS           $289.50

AVERAGE BREAKFAST COST =   3.83
MINIMUM DINNER COST    =  10.00
```

5. An input file consists of packets of sales transaction records; the first record in any packet identifies a parts number, a parts quantity, and a reorder level. Succeeding records in the packet represent sale transactions (number of parts sold) for the given part. Write a program to produce a sales summary similar to the report shown below and identify any part that needs to be reordered (quantity on hand less than or equal to reorder level).

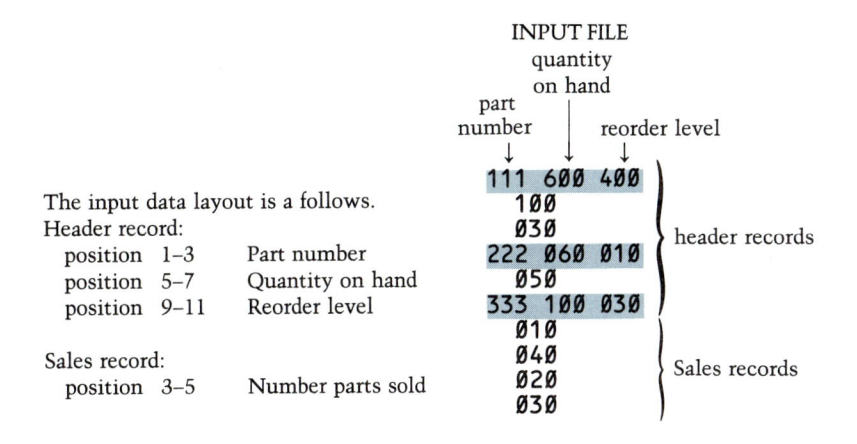

The input data layout is a follows.
Header record:
   position 1–3   Part number
   position 5–7   Quantity on hand
   position 9–11 Reorder level

Sales record:
   position 3–5   Number parts sold

INPUT FILE

```
          part    quantity
         number   on hand   reorder level
            ↓        ↓          ↓
          111      600        400   ⎫
          100                       ⎬ header records
          030                       ⎭
          222      060        010
          050
          333      100        030
          010
          040                       ⎫
          020                       ⎬ Sales records
          030                       ⎭
```

REPORT

```
              STOCK LEVEL ANALYSIS

PARTS NUMBER       SOLD           ON HAND

    111            100
                    30
                                    470
    222             50
                                     10     REORDER
    333             10
                    40
                    20
                    30
                                      0     REORDER
```

6. A large supermarket is organized into departments such as meats, perishables, and dairy products. The supermarket's management would like to follow the monthly sales trends in the various departments. They have instructed their data processing staff to produce monthly reports that will identify departments showing unusually sluggish or unusually active sales: If the current month's sales are more than 15% greater than the average of the previously recorded monthly sales for that department, an appropriate message such as HIGH should be printed. If the current month's sales are less than 90% of the average of the previously recorded monthly sales, then a different message such as LOW should be printed.

    All departments have sales records for at least the last three months, and some have records going back beyond three months. The input file consists of records that are arranged in sequence by department number. Within each department the monthly sales are arranged in ascending date order. Write a program to produce a report similar to the one on the following page (the most recent month is *not* reflected in the average):

OUTPUT

NO.	DATE	SALES	AVERAGES	ALERT
11	02/01	15,000.40		
	03/01	14,000.55		
	04/01	14,500.20		
	05/01	13,800.48	14,500.38	
22	01/01	23,400.64		
	02/01	30,500.88		
	03/01	32,600.46		
	04/01	29,400.00		
	05/01	25,000.00	28,975.56	LOW
33	02/01	40,000.80		
	03/01	45,876.20		
	04/01	44,784.88		
	05/01	51,080.40	43,553.96	HIGH

INPUT

Dept. No. ↓ Date ↓ Amount ↓

1102011500040 ⎫
1103011400055 ⎬ Last 3 months' sales records for dept. 11.
1104011450020 ⎭
1105011380048 ← Current monthly sales for dept. 11.
2201012340064
2202013050088
2203013260046
2204012940000
2205012500000
3302014000080
3303014587620
3304014478488
3305015108040 ← Current monthly sales for dept. 33

7. Write a program to read a principal, an interest rate, and a mortgage duration to produce an amortization schedule similar to the one shown below (see chapter 6, exercise 13, section 6–6–2). Note that in the example shown below the entire report consists of 8 pages, of which only the first and last are shown. Be sure to number each page and print the last payment.

First page (1)

AMORTIZATION TABLE   PAGE 1
PRINCIPAL $40000.00   INTEREST 7.75   DURATION 25 YEARS
REGULAR PAYMENT $302.10

NO.	INTEREST	AMORTIZED	BALANCE	INTEREST TO DATE
1	258.33	43.77	39956.20	258.33
2	258.05	44.05	39912.20	516.38
3	257.77	44.33	39867.90	774.15
4	257.48	44.62	39823.20	1031.63
5	257.19	44.91	39778.30	1288.82
6	256.90	45.20	39733.10	1545.72
7	256.61	45.49	39687.60	1802.33
8	256.32	45.78	39641.90	2058.65
9	256.02	46.08	39595.80	2314.67
10	255.72	46.38	39549.40	2570.39
11	255.42	46.68	39502.70	2825.81
12	255.12	46.98	39455.70	3080.93
YR. 1	3080.93	544.27		
1	254.82	47.28	39408.50	3335.75
2	254.51	47.59	39360.90	3590.26
3	254.21	47.89	39313.00	3844.47
4	253.90	48.20	39264.80	4098.37
5	253.58	48.52	39216.30	4351.95
6	253.27	48.83	39167.40	4605.22
7	252.96	49.14	39118.30	4858.18
8	252.64	49.46	39068.80	5110.82
9	252.32	49.78	39019.00	5363.14
10	252.00	50.10	38968.90	5615.14
11	251.67	50.43	38918.50	5866.81
12	251.35	50.75	38867.80	6118.16
YR. 2	3037.23	587.97		
1	251.02	51.08	38816.70	6369.18
2	250.69	51.41	38765.30	6619.87
3	250.36	51.74	38713.50	6870.23
4	250.02	52.08	38661.50	7120.25
5	249.69	52.41	38609.00	7369.94
6	249.35	52.75	38556.30	7619.29
7	249.01	53.09	38503.20	7868.30
8	248.67	53.43	38449.80	8116.97
9	248.32	53.78	38396.00	8365.29
10	247.97	54.13	38341.90	8613.26
11	247.62	54.48	38287.40	8860.88
12	247.27	54.83	38232.60	9108.15
YR. 3	2989.99	635.21		

Last page (8)

AMORTIZATION TABLE   PAGE 8
PRINCIPAL $40000.00   INTEREST 7.75   DURATION 25 YEARS
REGULAR PAYMENT $302.10

NO.	INTEREST	AMORTIZED	BALANCE	INTEREST TO DATE
1	62.64	239.46	9459.37	49515.90
2	61.09	241.01	9218.36	49577.00
3	59.54	242.56	8975.80	49636.60
4	57.97	244.13	8731.67	49694.50
5	56.39	245.71	8485.96	49750.90
6	54.81	247.29	8238.67	49805.70
7	53.21	248.89	7989.78	49858.90
8	51.60	250.50	7739.28	49910.50
9	49.98	252.12	7487.16	49960.50
10	48.35	253.75	7233.41	50008.90
11	46.72	255.38	6978.03	50055.60
12	45.07	257.03	6721.00	50100.70
YR. 23	647.37	2977.83		
1	43.41	258.69	6462.31	50144.10
2	41.74	260.36	6201.95	50185.80
3	40.05	262.05	5939.89	50225.90
4	38.36	263.74	5676.16	50264.20
5	36.66	265.44	5410.72	50300.90
6	34.94	267.16	5143.55	50335.80
7	33.22	268.88	4874.68	50369.00
8	31.48	270.62	4604.05	50400.50
9	29.73	272.37	4331.68	50430.30
10	27.98	274.12	4057.56	50458.20
11	26.21	275.89	3781.67	50484.40
12	24.42	277.68	3503.99	50508.90
YR. 24	408.20	3217.00		
1	22.63	279.47	3224.52	50531.50
2	20.83	281.27	2943.25	50552.30
3	19.01	283.09	2660.16	50571.30
4	17.18	284.92	2375.24	50588.50
5	15.34	286.76	2088.48	50603.90
6	13.49	288.61	1799.87	50617.30
7	11.62	290.48	1509.39	50629.00
8	9.75	292.35	1217.04	50638.70
9	7.86	294.24	922.80	50646.60
10	5.96	296.14	626.66	50652.50
11	4.05	298.05	328.61	50656.60
12	2.12	328.61	0.00	50658.70

LAST PAYMENT = $330.73

YR. 25   149.84   3503.99

8. An input file consists of an unknown number of records each containing seven fields, as follows:

Positions 1–10:	Author name	PIC X(10).
Positions 11–20:	Book title	PIC X(10).
Positions 21–25:	Number of copies sold	PIC 99999.
Positions 26–30:	Number of copies returned	PIC 99999.
Positions 31–34:	Cost of book	PIC 99V99.
Positions 35–36:	Contract percentage, for example, 15% of net sales PIC V99.	
Positions 37–39:	Percentage of royalties if book is coauthored PIC 9V99. (For example if there are three authors, each gets 33.3% of royalties.)	

An example of an input file is shown below (All records for the same author occur in a group):

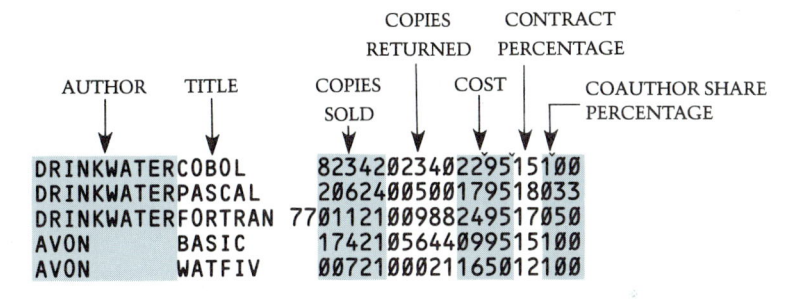

```
                         COPIES   CONTRACT
                         RETURNED PERCENTAGE
AUTHOR     TITLE    COPIES    COST   COAUTHOR SHARE
                    SOLD                PERCENTAGE

DRINKWATERCOBOL     8234202340229515100
DRINKWATERPASCAL    2062400500179518033
DRINKWATERFORTRAN   7701121009882495170500
AVON      BASIC     1742105644099515100
AVON      WATFIV    0072100021165012100
```

Write a program to compute net sales, total royalty amount, and author royalty due. The report should specify the author's name, the book title, the number of copies sold, the number of copies returned, the author percentage expressed in a nonfractional form, as well as the contract royalty rate. For each author, compute the subtotals given on the following output, and compute the grand totals for all authors.

```
                                 PUBLICATION REPORT

                   COPIES                    NET        ROYALTY    COAUTHOR     ROYALTY   ROYALTY
AUTHOR     TITLE    SOLD    RETURNS   COST   SALES      AMOUNT     PERCENTAGE   RATE      DUE

DRINKWATER COBOL    82,342  2,340    $22.95  $1,836,045.90  275,406.88  100.00%   15%   $ 75,406.88
DRINKWATER PASCAL   20,624  500      $17.95     361,225.80   65,020.64   33.00%   18%   $ 21,456.81
DRINKWATER FORTRAN 77 1,121 988      $24.95       3,318.35      564.11   50.00%   17%   $    282.05

           SUBTOTALS 104,087 3,828           2,200,590.05  340,991.63                    $ 97,145.74

AVON       BASIC    17,421  5,644    $9.95     117,181.15   17,577.17  100.00%   15%   $ 17,577.17
AVON       WATFIV      721     21    $16.50     11,550.00    1,386.00  100.00%   12%   $  1,386.00

           SUBTOTALS  18,142  5,655           128,731.15   18,963.17                      18,963.17

                    -------  -----          ------------  ----------                    -----------
           TOTALS:  122,229  9,493          2,329,321.20  359,954.80                    $116,108.91
```

9. A large clothing store keeps track of its inventory by department (1 = men's wear, 2 = ladies' wear, 3 = girls' wear, and 4 = boys' wear). The store's inventory file consists of four packets of data, each packet represent-

ing a particular department. A typical input file is shown below; each record consists of a department number, an item description, an item quantity, a cost figure, and a market figure (cost to the customer).

```
                    Cost to
           Item     Store
    Dept.           │    Cost to
    No.  Quantity   │    Customer
    │    │          │    │
    1SUITS   0300100092
    1COATS   0200060065
    1SHIRTS  1000012013
    1DRESSES 0400060065
    2COATS   0185184200
    2SHOES   0600040030
    3JEANS   0200040035
    3SHOES   0200030034
    4JEANS   0300042043
```

a. Write a program to process the input file to compute the store's inventory at lower cost (the lesser of cost or market value for each whole department). The output should be similar to the following:

```
                PAN AMERICAN APPAREL COMPANY
                     INVENTORY EVALUATION
                          05/06/86

                       UNIT COST           EXTENDED
           QUANTITY   COST    MARKET     COST        MARKET      LOWER COST

MENS DEPT
  SUITS      300     100.00    92.00   $ 30,000.00   27,600.00
  COATS      200      60.00    65.00     12,000.00   13,000.00
  SHIRTS    1000      12.00    13.00     12,000.00   13,000.00
  TOTAL                                $ 54,000.00 $ 53,600.00   $ 53,600.00
LADIES DEPT
  DRESSES    400      60.00    65.00     24,000.00   26,000.00
  COATS      185     184.00   200.00     34,040.00   37,000.00
  SHOES      600      40.00    30.00     24,000.00   18,000.00
  TOTAL                                $ 82,040.00 $ 81,000.00   $ 81,000.00
GIRLS DEPT
  JEANS      200      40.00    35.00      8,000.00    7,000.00
  SHOES      200      30.00    34.00      6,000.00    6,800.00
  TOTAL                                $ 14,000.00 $ 13,800.00   $ 13,800.00
BOYS DEPT
  JEANS      300      42.00    43.00     12,600.00   12,900.00
  TOTAL                                $ 12,600.00 $ 12,900.00   $ 12,600.00

INVENTORY AT LOWER COST                                          $161,000.00
```

The program should compute the subtotals for each of the four departments as well as the grand total.

b. Compute the lower cost inventory line by line instead of for the whole department. For example, for the men's department the lower cost inventory is 27,600 + 12,000 + 12,000 = 51,600.00

10. All academic departments at Franzia College are charged for the use of the college's computer system. The amount charged is based on the utilization of six specific resources:

ADDITIONAL FEATURES AND REPORTS 363

RESOURCES	INPUT CODE	COST IN CENTS
Cards read	10	.0012/card
Cards punched	11	.0012/card
Lines printed	20	.0003/line
CPU time (seconds)	30	.0600/second
Memory (words)	40	.0012/word
I/O operations	50	.0013/operation

Utilization of any of the above resources is recorded on data records like those shown in the sample input file below:

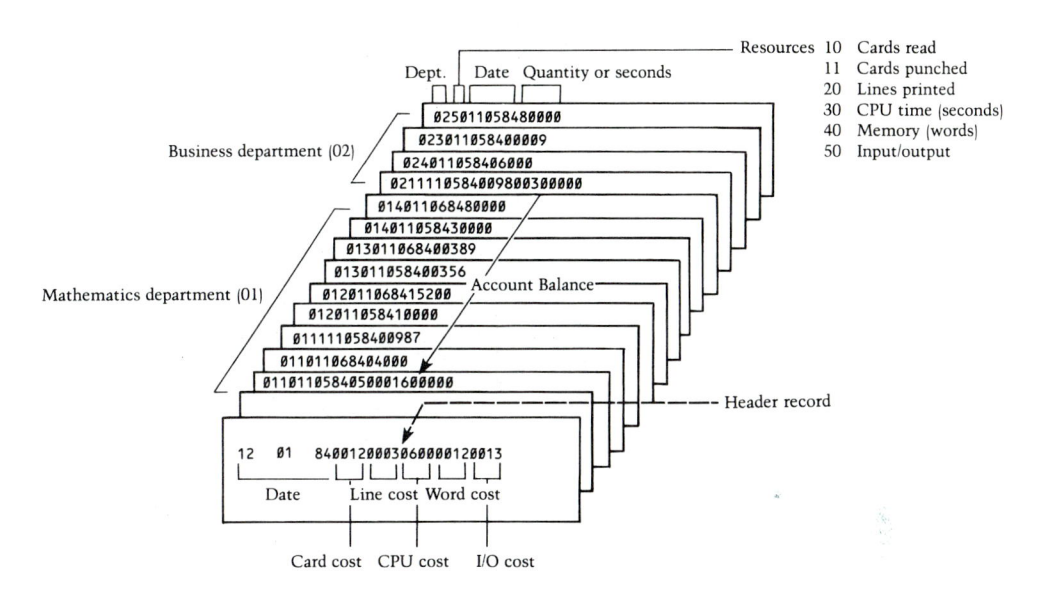

```
                                                    Resources  10 Cards read
                                                               11 Cards punched
                    Dept.  Date  Quantity or seconds           20 Lines printed
                                                               30 CPU time (seconds)
                         0250110584800000                      40 Memory (words)
                        0230110584000009                       50 Input/output
Business department (02) 0240110584060000
                        02111105840098003000000
                       0140110684800000
                      0140110584300000
                     0130110684000389
                    0130110584000356   Account Balance
Mathematics department (01) 01201106841520000
                   0120110584100000
                  0111110584000987
                 0110110684040000
                0110110584050001600000
                                                  ── Header record
         12  01  84001200030600000120013
             └┘ └┘└┘└┘└┘└┘
             Date Line cost Word cost

             Card cost  CPU cost  I/O cost
```

Item Positions

1–2	Department code	01 Math 02 Business 03 Chemistry	PIC 99
3–4	Resources code		PIC 99
5–10	Date of computer transaction		PIC X(6)
11–15	Amount used (no. of cards, seconds, etc.)		PIC 99999
16–22	For header records: department balance		PIC 99999V99

The first record of the input file is a header record that identifies the date of the report and the five costs associated with the six resources. All remaining transaction records are grouped by department; within each department, transaction records are grouped by resources.

In addition to the department code, resource code, date of computer transaction, and amount of resource used, the very first transaction record for each department (department header record) contains an account balance for the department, i.e., how much money is left to spend (position 16–22).

Write a program to produce a billing statement similar to the output shown on next page. Note that the numeric codes for the various departments have been converted to words (MATHEMATICS, BUSINESS, and so forth). Codes for resources have also been expressed in words. New account balances should be computed for each department.

```
                    COMPUTER RESOURCES BILLING STATEMENT

12 01 84 DEPT: MATHEMATICS
PREVIOUS BALANCE                                                    $16,000.00
    110584 CARDS READ              05000 @ .0012      6.00
    110684 CARDS READ              04000 @ .0012      4.80
                                                             10.80
    110584 CARDS PUNCHED           00987 @ .0012      1.18
                                                              1.18
    110584 LINES PRINTED           10000 @ .0003      3.00
    110684 LINES PRINTED           15200 @ .0003      4.56
                                                              7.56
    110584 CPU TIME (SECS)         00356 @ .0600     21.36
    110684 CPU TIME (SECS)         00389 @ .0600     23.34
                                                             44.70
    110584 MEMORY (WORDS)          30000 @ .0012     36.00
    110684 MEMORY (WORDS)          80000 @ .0012     96.00
                                                            132.00
    TOTAL COMPUTER CHARGE                                   196.24

NEW ACCOUNT BALANCE                                                 $15,803.76


12 01 84 DEPT: BUSINESS
PREVIOUS BALANCE                                                    $3,000.00
    110584 CARDS PUNCHED           00980 @ .0012      1.17
                                                              1.17
    110584 MEMORY (WORDS)          06000 @ .0012      7.20
                                                              7.20
    110584 CPU TIME (SECS)         00009 @ .0600       .54
                                                               .54
    110584 INPUT/OUTPUT (SECS) 80000 @ .0013        104.00
                                                            104.00
    TOTAL COMPUTER CHARGE                                   112.91

NEW ACCOUNT BALANCE                                                 $2,887.09
```

Publication 5055 is one of many textbooks published by the North Publishing Company. Publication 5055's author is Witter, and the text is sold in many educational institutions in numerous states. The company's sales department keeps track of the books' sales, by state, as shown in the sample input file below.

INPUT FILE

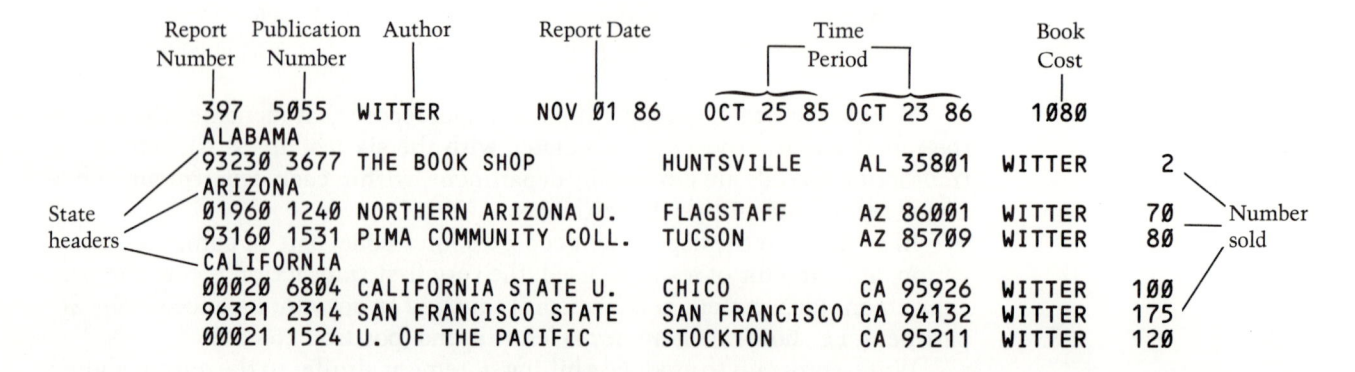

```
Report   Publication   Author            Report Date          Time             Book
Number   Number                                               Period           Cost

 397      5055    WITTER              NOV 01 86    OCT 25 85  OCT 23 86       1080
ALABAMA
 93230    3677    THE BOOK SHOP                    HUNTSVILLE      AL 35801   WITTER    2
ARIZONA
 01960    1240    NORTHERN ARIZONA U.              FLAGSTAFF       AZ 86001   WITTER   70
 93160    1531    PIMA COMMUNITY COLL.             TUCSON          AZ 85709   WITTER   80
CALIFORNIA
 00020    6804    CALIFORNIA STATE U.              CHICO           CA 95926   WITTER  100
 96321    2314    SAN FRANCISCO STATE              SAN FRANCISCO   CA 94132   WITTER  175
 00021    1524    U. OF THE PACIFIC                STOCKTON        CA 95211   WITTER  120
```

State headers — ALABAMA, ARIZONA, CALIFORNIA

Number sold

The report number, the publication number, the author name, the date of the report, the time span that the report covers, and the cost per book are typed on the first record of the input file. The rest of the input file contains groups of state header records followed by sales records for each state. Each sales record contains an order and an invoice number, an institution, an address, the author's name and a number of books sold.

Write a program to produce a yearly summary report similar to the one shown below; every page of the report is numbered, and each page starts with the same headings as the one on the first page.

To avoid typing many input data records, assume a page is 20 lines long (including 5 header lines and 2 blank lines at the bottom of the page). If a list of sales for a particular state is to be carried over to the next page, the resumption of the list of sales on that new page should be preceded by the name of the state (see printout below).

```
REPORT # 397       NEW SALES FOR OCT 25 85 THRU OCT 23 86              PAGE 1
PUB 5055 WITTER                                                        NOV 01 86

ORDER INV#  NAME                  LOCATION                PUBLICATION VOLS AMOUNT
ALABAMA
93230 3677  THE BOOK SHOP         HUNTSVILLE   AL 35801   WITTER         2   21.60

TOTAL ALABAMA                                                            2   21.60

ARIZONA
01960 1240  NORTHERN ARIZONA U.   FLAGSTAFF    AZ 86001   WITTER        70  756.00
93160 1531  PIMA COMMUNITY COLL.  TUCSON       AZ 85709   WITTER        80  864.00

TOTAL ARIZONA                                                          150 1620.00

CALIFORNIA
00020 6804  CALIFORNIA STATE U.   CHICO        CA 95926   WITTER       100 1080.00

. . . . . . . . . . . . . . . . . . . . . . . . . . . . . . . . . . . . . . . .

REPORT # 397       NEW SALES FOR OCT 25 85 THRU OCT 23 86              PAGE 2
PUB 5055 WITTER                                                        NOV 01 86

ORDER INV#  NAME                  LOCATION                PUBLICATION VOLS AMOUNT
CALIFORNIA
96321 2314  SAN FRANCISCO STATE   SAN FRANCISCO CA 94132  WITTER       175 1890.00
00021 1524  U. OF THE PACIFIC     STOCKTON     CA 95211   WITTER       120 1296.00

TOTAL CALIFORNIA                                                       395 4266.00

TOTAL PUB 5055                                                         547 5907.60
```

Sam the Baker finds himself spending more time doing bookkeeping than baking cakes and loaves of bread. He and his part-time work force bake three types of cakes and two types of bread. Sam pays his part-time employees (they don't work every day) by the number of cakes/loaves that they produce: for each cake Sam pays the equivalent of 20 minutes of time, and for each loaf he pays the equivalent of 10 minutes of time. He then figures out the amount of time corresponding to the number of cakes/loaves produced by each employee and pays them at the rate of $4.00 per resulting hour.

Sam doesn't know much about bookkeeping and accounting procedures; through trial and error he has finally settled on producing the three types of reports shown in Figure 7–20 to reflect the data in the input file shown below.

Report 1 is essentially a payroll report that identifies the number of cakes/loaves produced by each employee, the employee's corresponding time on the job in hours and minutes, and the employee's pay.

Report 2 displays the detailed production costs for the various goods produced by each employee as well as the detailed sales receipts and the profit margin for each item.

Report 3 illustrates summary entries relating to receipts, production costs, and net profit.

The input file is organized by worker records, where each record represents a day's contribution of cakes/loaves. Workers may work anywhere from one to six days. A sample input file is shown below:

```
                    Cakes         Loaves
                   / | \          / \
Name              1  2  3        1   2     3 types of cakes; 2 types of loaves
PARTRIDGE L      00 03 03       02  06
PARTRIDGE L      01 02 02       03  01     Partridge baked 6 cakes
PARTRIDGE L      01 00 00       06  00     and 8 loaves the first day
THOMPSON M       10 10 10       00  00
THOMPSON M       05 05 00       05  10     Robison came to work only 1 day and
ROBISON M        20 10 00       10  40     baked 30 cakes and 50 loaves.
```

Write a program to produce the three weekly reports for Sam, as shown in Figure 7–20. Note that each report starts at the top of a new page.

The table of production costs (cost of ingredients) is as follows:

	Cakes			Loaves	
	1	2	3	1	2
Cost ingredients	$2.00	$3.00	$1.50	$0.50	$0.75
Selling price	$5.00	$6.50	$4.00	$1.50	$2.50

The formula to compute the gross profit margin is:

$$\text{Profit margin} = (\text{Selling price} - \text{Cost}) / \text{Cost} \times 100$$

14. Assume an input file consists of records as shown below. All records are sorted in division, region, and salesperson order. Write a program to produce the following report:

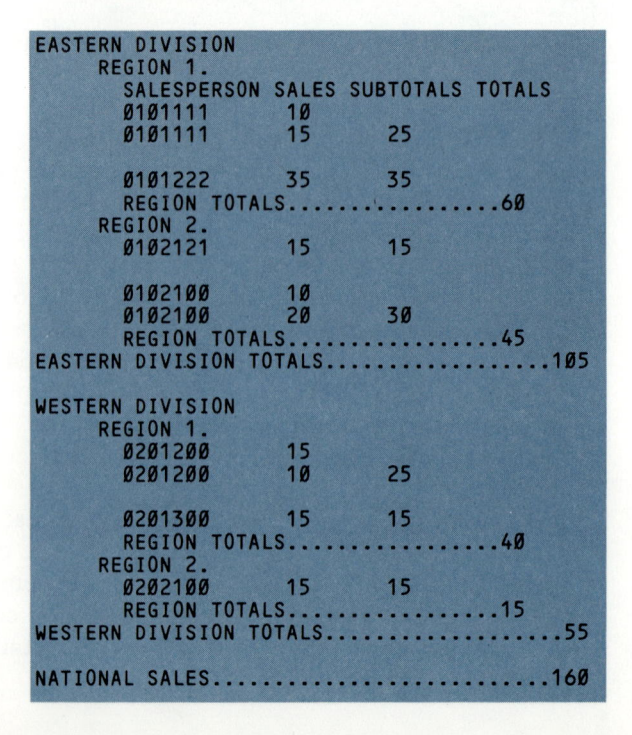

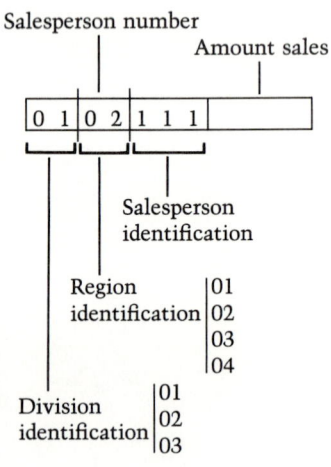

```
EASTERN DIVISION
    REGION 1.
        SALESPERSON  SALES  SUBTOTALS  TOTALS
        0101111       10
        0101111       15      25

        0101222       35      35
        REGION TOTALS.................60
    REGION 2.
        0102121       15      15

        0102100       10
        0102100       20      30
        REGION TOTALS.................45
EASTERN DIVISION TOTALS...................105
WESTERN DIVISION
    REGION 1.
        0201200       15
        0201200       10      25

        0201300       15      15
        REGION TOTALS.................40
    REGION 2.
        0202100       15      15
        REGION TOTALS.................15
WESTERN DIVISION TOTALS...................55

NATIONAL SALES.........................160
```

Salesperson number — Amount sales

`0 1 | 0 2 | 1 1 1 | `

Salesperson identification

Region identification: 01, 02, 03, 04

Division identification: 01, 02, 03

```
                SAM'S PAYROLL DATA SHEET
                    CAKES           LOAVES
    EMPLOYEE     1    2    3      1    2      HRS MNS      PAY

    PARTRIDGE L  0    3    3      2    6       3  20      13.33
    PARTRIDGE L  1    2    2      3    1       2  20       9.33
    PARTRIDGE L  1    0    0      6    0       1  20       5.33
                --   --   --     --   --      -- --      -----
        TOTALS   2    5    5     11    7       7  00      27.99

    THOMPSON M  10   10   10      0    0      10  00      40.00
    THOMPSON M   5    5    0      5   10       5  50      23.33
                --   --   --     --   --      -- --      -----
        TOTALS  15   15   10      5   10      15  50      63.33

    ROBISON M   20   10    0     10   40      18  20      73.33
                --   --   --     --   --      -- --      -----
        TOTALS  20   10    0     10   40      18  20      73.33

  ------------------------------------------------------------

            SAM'S DETAILED PRODUCTION COSTS
                         CAKES                LOAVES
                   1       2       3       1       2

  UNITS PROCESSED 37      30      15      26      57

  INGREDIENT COST 74.00   90.00   22.50   13.00   42.75
  PERSONNEL  COST 49.33   40.00   20.00   17.33   38.00
                  -----   -----   -----   -----   -----
          TOTALS 123.33  130.00   42.50   30.33   80.75

  SALES RECEIPTS 185.00  195.00   60.00   39.00  142.50

  PROFIT MARGIN   50.00   50.00   41.17   28.58   76.47

  ------------------------------------------------------------

            SAM'S SUMMARY COSTS AND PROFITS

        TOTAL SALES RECEIPTS              621.50

        TOTAL INGREDIENT COSTS    242.25
        TOTAL LABOR COSTS         164.66

        TOTAL PRODUCTION COSTS            406.91
                                          ------
                     NET PROFIT           214.59
                     PROFIT MARGIN  52.73
```

FIGURE 7–20
SAM'S REPORTS

7-6-3 Answers to Self Test

1. a. False; SOC-SEC is a numeric field whereas SEC is alphanumeric (group item).
   b. False; cannot redefine 01 level
   c. False
   d. False
   e. False

2. a. Valid; 80 positions

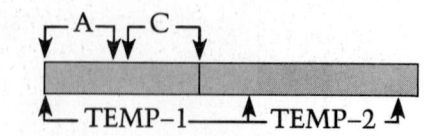

   b. Invalid; TOM may redefine only the immediately preceding entry, i.e., CHILD-2.
   c. Invalid; Length of KODE should equal length of TASK.
   d. Invalid; No REDEFINES is allowed in the FILE section for 01 levels.
   e. Valid; 13 positions 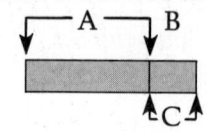
   f. Valid; 10 positions 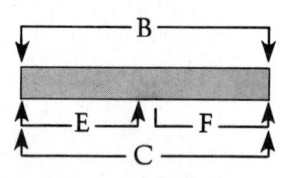
   g. Valid; 80 positions 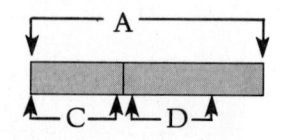
   h. Avoid redefining a record that is itself REDEFINEd.
   i. Invalid; an 06 level should not redefine an 05 level.
   j. Valid; 80 positions 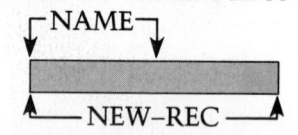
   k. Valid; 80 positions 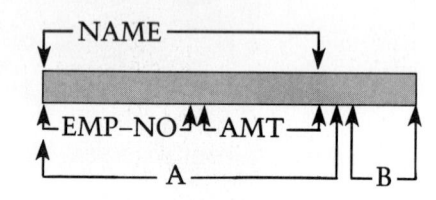
   l. Valid
   m. Valid if not input or output record in FILE section.
   n. Valid; 80 positions

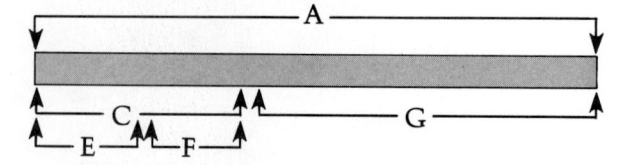

3.
```
000245 PROCEDURE DIVISION.
000250 MAIN-L.
000255     MOVE AMT TO Z.
000260     MOVE 38 TO Z.
000265     MOVE Z TO T.
000270     MOVE REC TO T.
000275     MOVE Z TO AMT.
000280     MOVE 'HOUSE' TO Y.
000285     MOVE T TO B.
000290     STOP RUN.
```

	Y	Z		T	
	0	3	3	4	7
	0	8	3	4	7
	0	8	8		
	0	8	0	8	8
	0	0	8	0	0
H	0	8	0	0	
8	0	0			

REC

4.
```
    WORKING-STORAGE.
    01 FLDA PIC 999.
    01 NUM REDEFINES FLDA.
       05 D1 PIC 9.
          88 NUM1 VALUE 0 THRU 9.
       05 D2 PIC 9.
          88 NUM2 VALUE 0 THRU 9.
       05 D3 PIC 9.
          88 NUM3 VALUE 0 THRU 9.
             .
             .
       MOVE 'NUMERIC' TO MSSG-LINE.
       IF NOT NUM1 MOVE 'NOT NUMERIC' TO MSSG-LINE.
       IF NOT NUM2 MOVE 'NOT NUMERIC' TO MSSG-LINE.
       IF NOT NUM3 MOVE 'NOT NUMERIC' TO MSSG-LINE.
       WRITE PRINT-LINE FROM MSSG-LINE.
```

5.
a. TALLY = 3; ᵇᵇᵇ304
b. TALLY = 2; 1.325.051.3
c. TALLY = 4; ᵇᵇᵇᵇ.
d. 08 16 82
e. $ᵇᵇ34
f. 00001.56
g. ᵇᵇ100
h. TALLY = 2
i. WE*AM*US
j. I = 3
k. I = 0; ᵇᵇᵇ21ᵇᵇ
l. I = 4; J = 2
m. I = 1
n. I = 1
o. $0005.03
p. All spaces
q. I = 2;   MAAM;*DAM;*A
r. $ᵇ0003.24DB*
s. 00132022
t. ***.05
u. HELL
v. I = 3
w. 13574

CHAPTER 8

ONE- AND TWO-DIMENSIONAL TABLES

8–1 ONE-DIMENSIONAL TABLES

8–2 ELEMENTS OF THE COBOL LANGUAGE

8–3 TABLE MANIPULATION

8–4 TWO-DIMENSIONAL TABLES

8–5 WRITING PROGRAMS

8–6 THREE-DIMENSIONAL TABLES

8–7 YOU MIGHT WANT TO KNOW

8–8 EXERCISES

INTRODUCTION Tables are necessary for the solution of many problems. This chapter shows how tables are declared, subscripted, manipulated, used, and input and output in COBOL. The OCCURS clause and the PERFORM VARYING/AFTER statement are introduced, and the internal structure of tables is also described. Examples show the use of one-, two-, and three-dimensional tables.

8-1 ONE-DIMENSIONAL TABLES

8-1-1 BACKGROUND AND JUSTIFICATION

Some problems can only be solved with the use of tables; consider the following examples.

EXAMPLE 1: Suppose an input file consists of five records, where each record contains a score. We want to print the difference between each score and the average score. Computing the average of the scores poses no problem: each time a score is read, it can be accumulated into SUM through the statement ADD SCORE TO SUM. But a problem arises when the average has been computed and it is time to determine the difference between each score and the average: the scores that have been read are no longer in memory, since only one data item was used to store each score successively.

Determining the difference between each score and the average requires the computer to remember (store) the scores as they are read, so that after the average is computed, the computer can remember (retrieve) each score one at a time and compute the difference between it and the average. The computer can remember these scores only if it stores them in different memory locations, i.e., if each score is provided with a separate name, as shown in Figure 8-1. But the code in Figure 8-1 is laborious and impractical because each score is individually processed. What would happen if the input file consisted of 100 scores or, even worse, an unknown number of scores? Another major problem with the approach in Figure 8-1 is that we can no longer use the READ technique that we have been using in all our COBOL programs. We cannot use the same READ INTO statement over and over to read the input records, since each READ INTO statement must specify a different data name!

Obviously all the scores have to be stored in memory if we want to be able to refer to them at any given time in our program. The score storage structure in Figure 8-1 certainly does that, but it does not allow us to refer to a score by its

```
01  INPUT-RECORD PIC 999.      PROCEDURE DIVISION.
WORKING-STORAGE SECTION.       100-MAIN-LOGIC.
01  SCORE-RECORD.                  OPEN INPUT INPUT-FILE.
    05  SCORE-1 PIC 999.           READ INPUT-RECORD INTO SCORE-1 AT END...
    05  SCORE-2 PIC 999.           READ INPUT-RECORD INTO SCORE-2 AT END...
    05  SCORE-3 PIC 999.           READ INPUT-RECORD INTO SCORE-3 AT END...
    05  SCORE-4 PIC 999.           READ INPUT-RECORD INTO SCORE-4 AT END...
    05  SCORE-5 PIC 999.           READ INPUT-RECORD INTO SCORE-5 AT END...
01  SCORE-DIFFERENCE.              COMPUTE AVERAGE = (SCORE-1 + SCORE-2
    05  DIF-1   PIC S999.               + SCORE-3 + SCORE-4 + SCORE-5) / 5.
    05  DIF-2   PIC S999.          COMPUTE DIF-1 = SCORE-1 - AVERAGE.
     .                             COMPUTE DIF-2 = SCORE-2 - AVERAGE.
     .                                  .
                                        .
                                        .
```

FIGURE 8-1
AVERAGE AND GRADE DEVIATION

position in the list of scores, i.e., it does not allow us to ask or answer the following types of questions:

- How far down the list is score 98? Is it the 9th, 10th, or 20th score?
- Which is the largest score? Is it the 2nd, the 3rd, or the 4th, . . . ?
- What is the value of the 11th score?
- Can we read a value for POSITION (a number between 1 and the number of scores) and start printing all scores starting from POSITION on? In other words, if POSITION is 7, then print the 7th, 8th, 9th, . . . score; or if POSITION is 11, then start printing with the 11th score?

The conventional data structure in Figure 8–1 does *not* provide us with such capability.

What we need is an indexing data structure (a high-sounding name for a list or a table) that enables us to refer to an element within a table by its position. Thus, if SCORE is the name of the entire list of scores, then SCORE (3) would refer to the 3rd score in that list (the number 3 enclosed in parentheses is called a *subscript*). Likewise if POSITION has value 4, then SCORE (POSITION) refers to SCORE (4) or the 4th score of the list. With this subscripting capability we can then index a table and access successive table entries simply by manipulating the subscript (adding 1 to the subscript to get us to the next table entry). Thus a problem such as "given a table of 100 scores, determine how many exceed the value 90" can be restated as "determine the number of times SCORE (POSITION) is greater than 90 for values of POSITION ranging from 1 to 100 in increments of 1." Similarly, the problem of the numerous READ statements in Figure 8–1 can now be resolved by carrying out the following instruction as POSITION varies from 1 to 5:

```
READ INPUT-FILE INTO SCORE (POSITION)
    AT END MOVE 1 TO WS-EOF.
```

The first time this instruction is carried out, POSITION is 1 and we read the first score into memory location SCORE (1); POSITION is then 2 and we read the next score into SCORE(2), et cetera.

SCORE (1) is called a *subscripted data name.* Subscripted data names can be processed in exactly the same way as ordinary data names. For example, if AMOUNT and SCORE (1) have both pictures 999 then we can MOVE 48 TO SCORE (2) just as we can MOVE 48 TO AMOUNT. The main difference between the two is that we know what data item precedes SCORE (2) (i.e., SCORE (1)) and what data item follows it (i.e., SCORE (3)), whereas we do *not* know, nor do we really care to know, what data name comes before or after AMOUNT. This concept of order makes it possible to process tables of information. So far we have been able to process only one data item at a time. **Now, with tables, we can process lists of items—a very powerful capability indeed!**

EXAMPLE 2: Another problem that would be difficult to solve without tables is this: Given the tax table shown in Figure 8-2, write a program to compute the amount of tax owed on an adjusted gross income read from an input record.

The problem is, how can the computer compute the tax if it doesn't have the tax tables in its memory? This type of problem obviously requires a data structure different from any we have encountered so far. One approach might be to create an income table INCOME, a tax table TAX, and a percent-over table PERCENTAGE as shown in Figure 8-3 and store these in memory. Then, for example, we could compute the tax due on an adjusted income of $9,800 by successively comparing $9,800 with the first, second, third, ... entries of table INCOME until an entry is found that is larger than 9800, in this case, the sixth entry of table INCOME or INCOME(6). The tax due on $9,800 would then be:

DUE = $1,380 + 22% over $8,000

DUE = 5th entry of TAX + 5th entry of PERCENTAGE * (9800 − 5th entry of INCOME)

DUE =   TAX(5)   +   PERCENTAGE(5)   * (9800 −   INCOME(5))

The last statement is actually the correct COBOL expression to compute the tax due.

8-1-2 Definition of a Table

In terms of structure, a table is nothing more than a "chunk" of memory that is divided into a number of equal contiguous parts. For example, the following diagram represents a table:

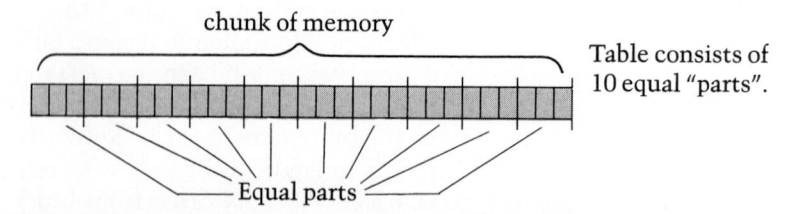

chunk of memory

Table consists of 10 equal "parts".

Equal parts

In terms of syntax, this chunk of memory is a group item that is further subdivided into a number of data items, each with an identical picture field. All these data items bear the same name, which must be followed by a subscript enclosed in parentheses. Just as in the case of record description entries, the name of the group item is different from that of its subordinate items. For example:

ONE- AND TWO-DIMENSIONAL TABLES

SCORE–RECORD:

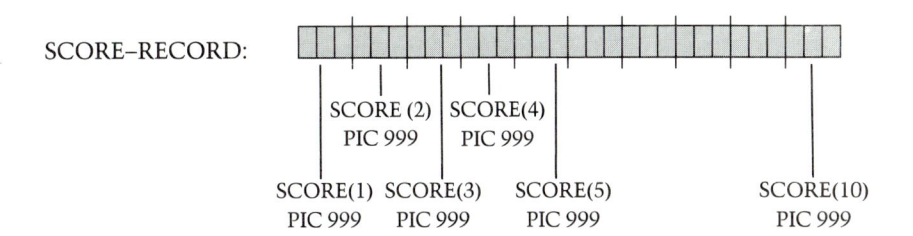

SCORE(1) PIC 999
SCORE(2) PIC 999
SCORE(3) PIC 999
SCORE(4) PIC 999
SCORE(5) PIC 999
SCORE(10) PIC 999

Technically speaking, SCORE–RECORD is not itself a table, but simply a group item. The table in this case is SCORE, whose elements occur 10 times.

In terms of data, a table is a collection of data values with identical characteristics whose use in a program warrants their being organized under one common name as multiple occurrences of related values. For example:

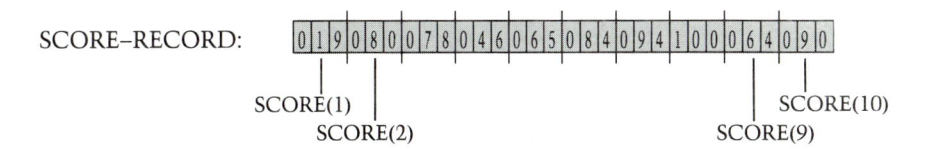

SCORE–RECORD: 019 080 078 046 065 084 094 100 064 090

SCORE(1)
SCORE(2)
SCORE(9)
SCORE(10)

All 10 related values are captured under one name to facilitate processing.

ADJUSTED INCOME	BUT NOT OVER—	TAX	OF THE AMOUNT OVER—
$ 1,000	$ 2,000	$ 140 + 15%	$ 1,000
$ 2,000	$ 3,000	$ 290 + 16%	$ 2,000
$ 3,000	$ 4,000	$ 450 + 17%	$ 3,000
$ 4,000	$ 8,000	$ 620 + 19%	$ 4,000
$ 8,000	$ 12,000	$ 1,380 + 22%	$ 8,000
$ 12,000	$ 16,000	$ 2,260 + 25%	$ 12,000
$ 16,000	$ 20,000	$ 3,260 + 28%	$ 16,000
$ 20,000	$ 24,000	$ 4,380 + 32%	$ 20,000
$ 24,000	$ 28,000	$ 5,660 + 36%	$ 24,000
$ 28,000	$ 32,000	$ 7,100 + 39%	$ 28,000
$ 32,000	$ 36,000	$ 8,660 + 42%	$ 32,000
$ 36,000	$ 40,000	$ 10,340 + 45%	$ 36,000
$ 40,000	$ 44,000	$ 12,140 + 48%	$ 40,000
$ 44,000	$ 52,000	$ 14,060 + 50%	$ 44,000
$ 52,000	$ 64,000	$ 18,060 + 53%	$ 52,000
$ 64,000	$ 76,000	$ 24,420 + 55%	$ 64,000
$ 76,000	$ 88,000	$ 31,020 + 58%	$ 76,000
$ 88,000	$100,000	$ 37,980 + 60%	$ 88,000
$100,000	$120,000	$ 45,180 + 62%	$100,000
$120,000	$140,000	$ 57,580 + 64%	$120,000
$140,000	$160,000	$ 70,380 + 66%	$140,000
$160,000	$180,000	$ 83,580 + 68%	$160,000
$180,000	$200,000	$ 97,180 + 69%	$180,000
$200,000	.....	$110,980 + 70%	$200,000

FIGURE 8–2
A TAX TABLE

ADJUSTED INCOME	BUT NOT OVER—	TAX	OF THE AMOUNT OVER—
$ 1,000	$ 2,000	$ 140 + 15%	$ 1,000
$ 2,000	$ 3,000	$ 290 + 16%	$ 2,000
$ 3,000	$ 4,000	$ 450 + 17%	$ 3,000
$ 4,000	$ 8,000	$ 620 + 19%	$ 4,000
$ 8,000	$ 12,000	$ 1,380 + 22%	$ 8,000
$ 12,000	$ 16,000	$ 2,260 + 25%	$ 12,000
$ 16,000	$ 20,000	$ 3,260 + 28%	$ 16,000
$ 20,000	$ 24,000	$ 4,380 + 32%	$ 20,000
$ 24,000	$ 28,000	$ 5,660 + 36%	$ 24,000
$ 28,000	$ 32,000	$ 7,100 + 39%	$ 28,000
$ 32,000	$ 36,000	$ 8,660 + 42%	$ 32,000

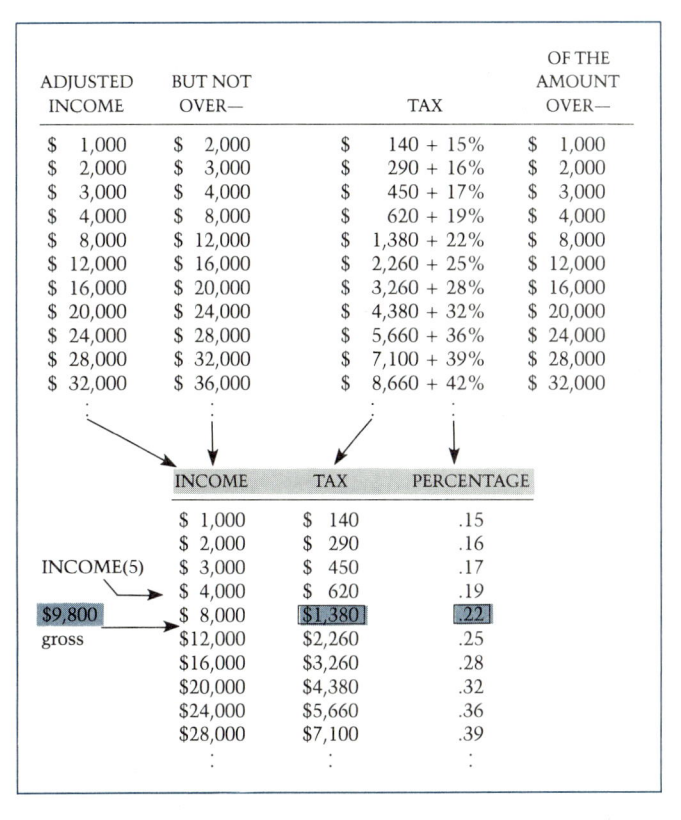

INCOME	TAX	PERCENTAGE
$ 1,000	$ 140	.15
$ 2,000	$ 290	.16
INCOME(5) $ 3,000	$ 450	.17
$ 4,000	$ 620	.19
$9,800 gross → $ 8,000	$1,380	.22
$12,000	$2,260	.25
$16,000	$3,260	.28
$20,000	$4,380	.32
$24,000	$5,660	.36
$28,000	$7,100	.39

FIGURE 8–3
STRUCTURING A TAX TABLE

EXAMPLE 1: A sales table may contain each day's sales for one week

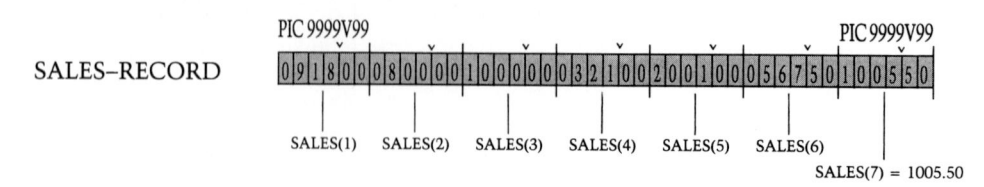

SALES–RECORD

```
PIC 9999V99                                                    PIC 9999V99
091800 080000 100000 032100 200100 056750 100550
SALES(1) SALES(2) SALES(3) SALES(4) SALES(5) SALES(6)
                                                    SALES(7) = 1005.50
```

Each entry has the same picture field PIC 9999V99.

EXAMPLE 2: A table may consist of numeric edited fields

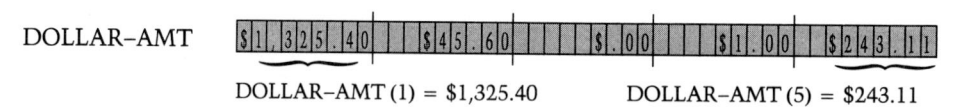

DOLLAR–AMT

```
$1,325.40   $45.60   $.00   $1.00   $243.11
DOLLAR–AMT (1) = $1,325.40      DOLLAR–AMT (5) = $243.11
```

Each entry has the same picture field PIC $$,$$$.99.

EXAMPLE 3: A class roster table may consist of a name and corresponding score

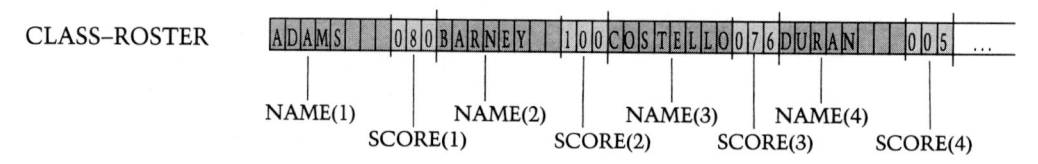

CLASS–ROSTER

```
ADAMS   080 BARNEY   100 COSTELLO 076 DURAN   005 ...
NAME(1)     NAME(2)      NAME(3)      NAME(4)
    SCORE(1)    SCORE(2)      SCORE(3)     SCORE(4)
```

Each name entry has picture PIC X(8)
Each score entry has picture PIC 999.

Another way to visualize a table is to use a tree-like representation:

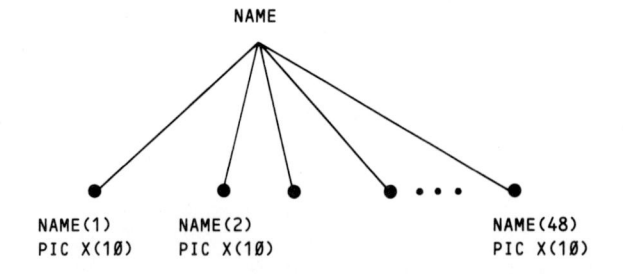

NAME

NAME(1)   NAME(2)   ...   NAME(48)
PIC X(10) PIC X(10)   PIC X(10)

NAME is the name given to the tree/branch (table), and all terminal leaves are the elements of the table; each leaf is numbered and identified by an identical PICTURE clause.

All end points (leaves) must be numbered (subscripted) and must have the same PICTURE clause.

Declaring a Table

Before a table can be used in the PROCEDURE division, it must be defined or declared in the DATA division. Declaring a table requires that we

1. give a name to the group item that is to be subdivided into equal parts, and
2. specify the name and picture of the table entries through the OCCURS verb.

Declaring a table simply means allocating memory space; the OCCURS statement does *not* initialize tables to blanks or zeroes. To declare SCORE as a table consisting of 100 scores each 3 digits long, we write:

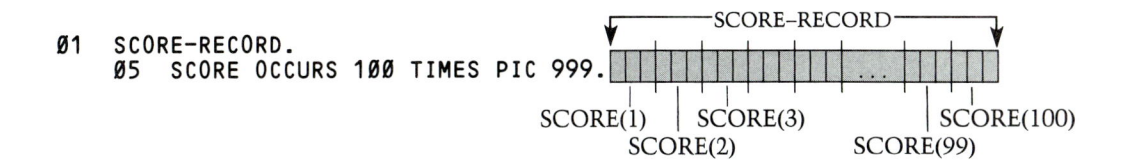

```
01  SCORE-RECORD.
    05   SCORE OCCURS 100 TIMES PIC 999.
```

```
                                          ┌──────SCORE-RECORD──────┐
                                          ┌─┬─┬─┬─┬─┬─┬─┬─┬─┬─┐...┌─┬─┬─┐
                                          └─┴─┴─┴─┴─┴─┴─┴─┴─┴─┘   └─┴─┴─┘
                                          SCORE(1)  SCORE(3)        SCORE(100)
                                                SCORE(2)        SCORE(99)
```

The 05 level declaration states that PIC 999 occurs 100 times in succession. It does not initialize table elements (SCORE(1), SCORE(2) ...) to any value. SCORE-RECORD is a group data item that refers to a block of memory 300 memory positions (characters) long, since the PICTURE 999 is repeated 100 times. In turn, this block SCORE-RECORD is logically divided into 100 data items each 3 numeric positions long. The names of these data items are SCORE(1), SCORE(2), SCORE(3), ..., SCORE(99), SCORE(100). The name of the table is the name given to what OCCURS, i.e., SCORE, and the integers 1, 2, ... 99, 100 in parentheses are the subscripts.

It is very important to understand the difference between SCORE-RECORD, SCORE, and SCORE(3) and how each is used:

SCORE-RECORD is the name given to an alphanumeric string of 300 consecutive digits. Since it does not OCCUR more than once, it is invalid to subscript it; i.e.,
SCORE-RECORD (1) is invalid.

SCORE(3) is the data name of the third item in the table and its value might be 100. The subscript is enclosed in parentheses; it identifies the position of the element within the table.

SCORE is the name of the table and may be used only with a subscript since it OCCURS 100 times. A reference to SCORE without a subscript is invalid.

Examples:

MOVE SCORE-RECORD TO WS-TEMP.	Move 300 characters (digits) in SCORE-RECORD to WS-TEMP.
MOVE SCORE-RECORD (1) TO LINE-OUT.	Invalid. SCORE-RECORD is not a table name and cannot be used with subscripts.
ADD SCORE (2) TO SCORE (3).	Add the 3d grade to the 2d grade and store the result in SCORE(3).
MOVE SCORE TO SCORE-TEMP.	Invalid reference to SCORE. SCORE must be used with a subscript since it occurs more than once.

To give the reader a feeling for the elegance and power of tables, let us write the code to solve example 1 in section 8-1-1.

Problem specification: An input file consists of a maximum of 100 records, each consisting of one score. Write a program to compute the average score and print the scores along with the difference between each score and the average. For example, the following input file would give rise to the output shown below:

OUTPUT

GRADES	DEVIATION
56	-13.6
78	8.4
89	19.4
45	-24.6
80	10.4

INPUT FILE

056
078
089
045
080

378   UNDERSTANDING STRUCTURED COBOL

This problem can be broken down into the following two tasks:

1. Reading the scores into table SCORE and accumulating them at the same time.
2. Printing the scores and the difference between each score and the average.

Let us illustrate these two tasks independently.

Task 1: Reading the scores into table SCORE

```
                                          WORKING-STORAGE SECTION.
                                          01  COUNTER PIC 999 VALUE 1.
                                          01  SCORE-RECORD.
                                              05  SCORE OCCURS 100 TIMES PIC 999.
63:    READ SCORE-FILE INTO SCORE (COUNTER)
64:        AT END MOVE 1 TO WS-EOF.
65:    PERFORM 200-ADD-SCORES UNTIL END-OF-FILE.
66:    COMPUTE WS-NO-SCORES = COUNTER - 1.
67:    COMPUTE WS-AVERAGE =
68:        WS-SUM-SCORES / WS-NO-SCORES.
69:
70:
71:
72:
73:
74: *
75:    200-ADD-SCORES.
76:        ADD SCORE (COUNTER) TO WS-SUM-SCORES.
77:        ADD 1 TO COUNTER.
78:        READ SCORE-FILE INTO SCORE (COUNTER)
79:            AT END MOVE 1 TO WS-EOF.
```

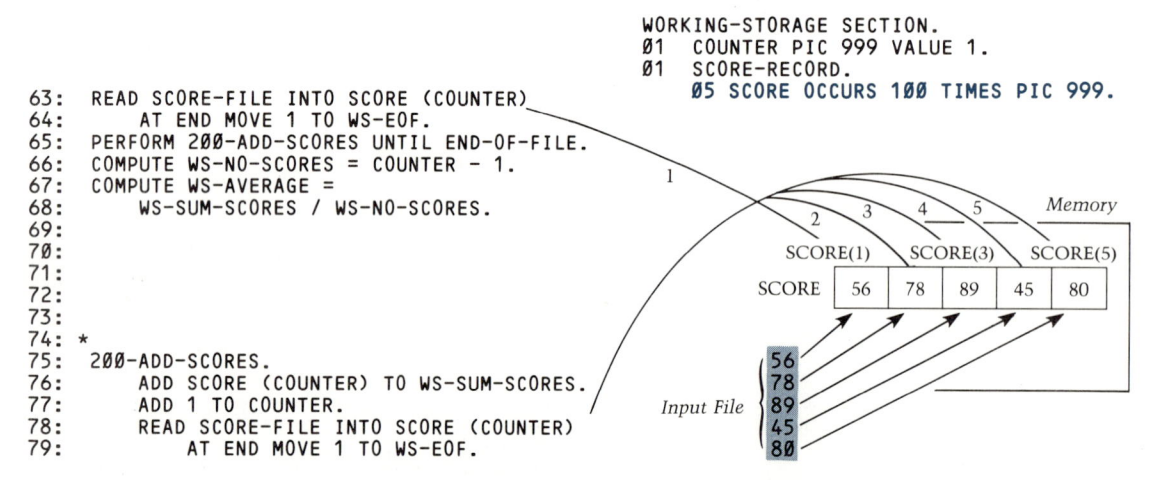

In this code, COUNTER is used as a subscript for the SCORE table. It is initially set to 1 in WORKING-STORAGE so that when the READ statement at line 63 is carried out, the first score in the input file is stored into SCORE (COUNTER), which is SCORE (1) since COUNTER is 1. The remaining scores are read in paragraph 200–ADD–SCORES at line 78. The first time through that paragraph, COUNTER becomes 2 at line 77. The READ statement at line 78 reads the second score from the input file and places it into SCORE (COUNTER) or SCORE (2) since COUNTER = 2. This process of reading a score and placing it in the next available slot in the table goes on until the end of file is detected. The value of COUNTER at that point includes the count of the end-of-file record, hence 1 is subtracted from COUNTER at line 66 to make it equal to the total number of scores read. Line 67 computes the average. Note that the accumulation of the scores takes place at line 76.

Task 2: Printing the elements of table SCORE and the difference between each score and the average

```
68: MOVE 1 TO COUNTER.
69: PERFORM 300-WRITE-DIFFERENCE UNTIL
70:     COUNTER IS GREATER THAN WS-NO-SCORES.
71:
72:
73:
74:
75:
76:
77:
78:
79:
80: 300-WRITE-DIFFERENCE.
81:     COMPUTE DL-DIFFERENCE =
82:         SCORE (COUNTER) - WS-AVERAGE.
83:     MOVE SCORE (COUNTER) TO DL-SCORE.
84:     WRITE PRINT-LINE FROM DETAIL-LINE.
85:     ADD 1 TO COUNTER.
```

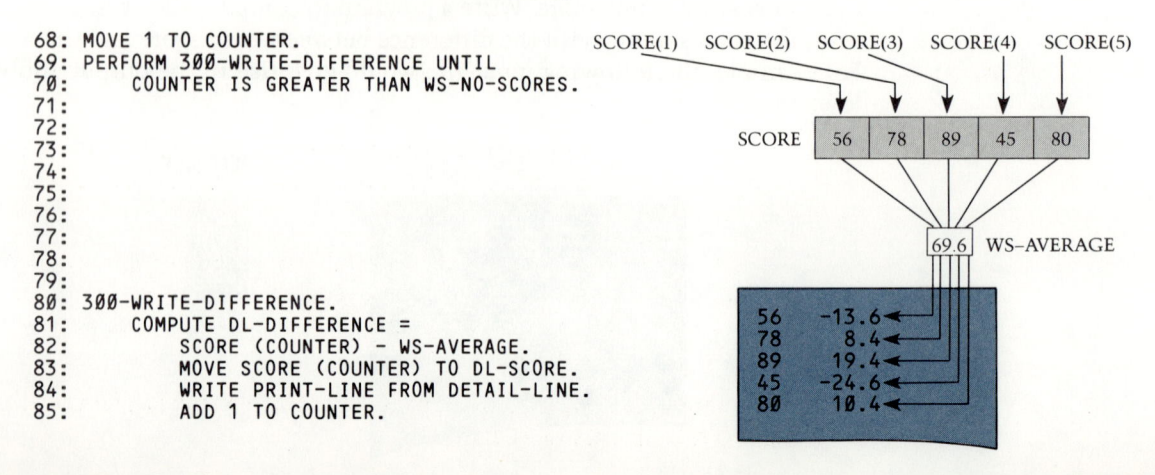

The first time through paragraph 300-WRITE-DIFFERENCE, the subscript is equal to 1; hence DL-DIFFERENCE = SCORE (1) − WS-AVERAGE = 56 − 69.6 = −13.6. The detail line is then printed and COUNTER becomes 2 at line 85. The same process is repeated until all scores and their differences from the average have been printed. (Question: What is the final value of COUNTER?)

The complete problem is shown in Figure 8–4.

8-2 ELEMENTS OF THE COBOL LANGUAGE

8-2-1 THE OCCURS CLAUSE

Tables are declared through the OCCURS clause, which reserves a specific number of entries for a particular table. The general form of the OCCURS clause is shown in Figure 8–5.

After you have declared a table to be a particular size, say TAX OCCURS 100, you must make sure that any subscripts used with table TAX do not exceed 100. This is easier said than done! If your program uses TAX (LEVEL), then LEVEL must be less than or equal to 100. If for some reason LEVEL exceeds 100, many systems will give an execution-time error, such as "invalid index." However, other systems may not, and then the table values become unpredictable. The fact that TAX OCCURS 100 times, however, does not mean that all 100 entries of TAX must be used or referred to when processing the table.

Beginning programmers often ask what the size of a table should be. The answer varies with the particular application, of course! Many times the problem gives a maximum number of entries or records to be processed; then that maximum figure can be used for the size. If no clue is given, choose a reasonable limit for the particular application and stay within it. Since the OCCURS allocates memory storage, you must be careful not to exceed your computer's memory!

8-2-2 SUBSCRIPTS

Subscripts are used with table names to locate specific elements within the table. Rules concerning subscripts are:

1. Subscripts can be either numeric literals or data names. Some compilers allow arithmetic expressions.

2. A subscript must evaluate to a positive integer value (no fractional part). It may vary from 1 to the integer limit stated in the OCCURS clause and may not exceed that integer limit.

3. Subscripts may be used only in conjunction with data names that have been defined in the OCCURS clause. If a group item is a table name, then subscripts must be used not only with the group item name but also with any of the subordinate data items of the group item.

4. If the subscript is a data name, it must be defined in the DATA division just like any regular data item name.

```
13:  *
14:      DATA DIVISION.
15:      FILE SECTION.
16:  *
17:      FD  SCORE-FILE
18:          LABEL RECORDS ARE STANDARD
19:          VALUE OF FILE-ID IS 'SCOREFILE'
20:          DATA RECORD IS INPUT-AREA.
21:      01  INPUT-AREA PIC 999.
22:      FD  REPORT-FILE
23:          LABEL RECORDS ARE OMITTED
24:          DATA RECORD IS PRINT-LINE.
25:      01  PRINT-LINE PIC X(80).
26:  *
27:      WORKING-STORAGE SECTION.
28:  *
29:  *       INDEPENDENT ITEMS
30:  *
31:      01  FLAGS.
32:          05  WS-EOF  PIC 9   VALUE 0.
33:              88 END-OF-FILE VALUE IS 1.
34:  *
35:      01  SUBSCRIPTS.
36:          05  COUNTER     PIC 99 VALUE 1.
37:  *
38:      01  ACCUMULATORS-N-COUNTERS.
39:          05  WS-AVERAGE    PIC 999V99.
40:          05  WS-SUM-SCORES PIC 9999 VALUE 0.
41:          05  WS-NO-SCORES  PIC 999.
42:  *
43:  *       OUTPUT LINE DESCRIPTIONS
44:  *
45:      01  MAJOR-HEADING.
46:          05  FILLER      PIC X(11) VALUE '  SCORES'.
47:          05  FILLER      PIC X(13) VALUE 'DIFFERENCE'.
48:      01  DETAIL-LINE.
49:          05  FILLER      PIC X(03) VALUE SPACES.
50:          05  DL-SCORE    PIC ZZ9.
51:          05  FILLER      PIC X(05) VALUE SPACES.
52:          05  DL-DIFFERENCE PIC ---9.99.
53:  *
54:  *       TABLE DEFINITION
55:  *
56:      01  SCORE-RECORD.
57:          05 SCORE OCCURS 100 TIMES PIC 999.
58:  *
59:      PROCEDURE DIVISION.
60:      100-MAIN-LOGIC.
61:          OPEN OUTPUT REPORT-FILE, INPUT SCORE-FILE.
62:          WRITE PRINT-LINE FROM MAJOR-HEADING AFTER 1 LINE.
63:          READ SCORE-FILE INTO SCORE (COUNTER)
64:              AT END MOVE 1 TO WS-EOF.
65:          PERFORM 200-ADD-SCORES UNTIL END-OF-FILE.
66:          COMPUTE WS-NO-SCORES = COUNTER - 1.
67:          COMPUTE WS-AVERAGE   = WS-SUM-SCORES / WS-NO-SCORES.
68:          MOVE 1 TO COUNTER.
69:          PERFORM 300-WRITE-DIFFERENCE UNTIL
70:              COUNTER IS GREATER THAN WS-NO-SCORES.
71:          CLOSE REPORT-FILE, SCORE-FILE.
72:          STOP RUN.
73:  *
74:      200-ADD-SCORES.
75:          ADD SCORE (COUNTER) TO WS-SUM-SCORES.
76:          ADD 1 TO COUNTER.
77:          READ SCORE-FILE INTO SCORE (COUNTER)
78:              AT END MOVE 1 TO WS-EOF.
79:  *
80:      300-WRITE-DIFFERENCE.
81:          COMPUTE DL-DIFFERENCE = SCORE (COUNTER) - WS-AVERAGE.
82:          MOVE SCORE (COUNTER) TO DL-SCORE.
83:          WRITE PRINT-LINE FROM DETAIL-LINE.
84:          ADD 1 TO COUNTER.
```

INPUT FILE

056
078
089
045
080

Subscript COUNTER is used to flip through the elements of table SCORE

SCORES	DIFFERENCE
56	-13.60
78	8.40
89	19.40
45	-24.60
80	10.40

SCORE table

| 0 5 6 | 0 7 8 | 0 8 9 | 0 4 5 | 0 8 0 | ... | | |

SCORE(1)   SCORE(3)   SCORE(5)   SCORE(100)

FIGURE 8–4

A SIMPLE TABLE EXAMPLE

5. The following coding rules must be observed:

```
                                    at least one blank space (not required by 1974 ANSI COBOL)
                                    ↓
MOVE 1986 TO YEAR (COUNTER).
          ‾‾‾‾  ↑         ↑
       table name   No spaces between the
                   subscript and the parentheses
```

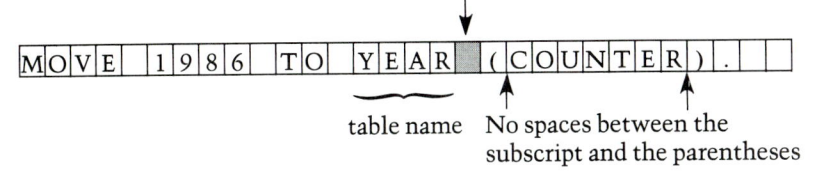

Examples: Valid subscripted data names

```
SALES (3)
TIM   (KOUNT)
RUNNING-TIME (RACE-NO-2)
```

$$\begin{Bmatrix} \text{level-number data-name } \underline{\text{OCCURS}} \text{ integer [TIMES] [picture]} \\ \text{level-number data-name [picture] } \underline{\text{OCCURS}} \text{ integer [TIMES]} \end{Bmatrix}$$

where:

- Level number can be any level number except 01, 77, 88, or 66.
- Data-name can be any group item or elementary data item name in the FILE or WORKING–STORAGE section.
- Integer specifies the maximum number of entries for the table, i.e., the number of times the common picture field occurs. It must be an integer greater than 0. Data-names may not be used to specify the size of the table.
- The VALUE clause may not be used to initialize a data item that OCCURS or any subordinate item of a data-name that OCCURS.
- Data-name must be subscripted when used in the PROCEDURE division. If data-name is a group item, then *any* subordinate items of data-name must also be subscripted.
- In the REDEFINES clause, the REDEFINES may not specify either of the following:
  1. a data item that OCCURS.
  2. a subordinate item of an item that OCCURS.
  3. an OCCURS clause within the REDEFINES clause.
- The OCCURS clause does *not* initialize table entries to any value.

Examples:

```
01  NAME-RECORD.                       01  NAME-RECORD.
    05  NR-NAME OCCURS 100 TIMES PIC X(15).   05  NR-NAME OCCURS 100 TIMES.
                                               10  NR-FIRST PIC X(08).
                                               10  NR-LAST  PIC X(07).
```

FIGURE 8-5
THE OCCURS CLAUSE

INVALID SUBSCRIPTED DATA NAMES	EXPLANATION
ITEM (1.5)	Subscript must be an integer value.
SALES (3)	Blank space before closing parenthesis.
SALES (YEAR + 1)	YEAR + 1 is neither an integer nor a data name (may be valid on some compilers).
SALES (YEAR(3))	Subscript may not be a subscripted data name.
TABLE-TAX (3.)	Illegal period in the subscript.
AMOUNT (0)	Subscript may not be 0.
TIME-DAY (SECONDS)	Space following the open parenthesis.
MONTH-RECORD (-3)	Negative subscript.

It is important to differentiate between the subscript value and the corresponding table element value. The value of WEEK (3) has nothing to do with the number 3; for example, WEEK (3) might be equal to −31.8. Also, note that the same subscript can be used to refer to elements from different tables, for example, MONTH(INDX) and YEAR(INDX).

Let us now consider a few examples of tables in terms of their declaration, structure, interpretation, and possible use.

EXAMPLE 1:

TABLE DECLARATION

```
05 SALES-LIST OCCURS 4 TIMES.
   10 SL-NO PIC 999.
   10 SL-SALES PIC 999V99.
```

MEMORY ARRANGEMENT

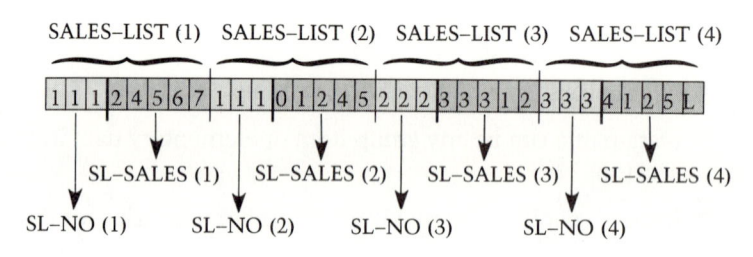

SALES-LIST (1) SALES-LIST (2) SALES-LIST (3) SALES-LIST (4)

`1 1 1 2 4 5 6 7 | 1 1 1 0 1 2 4 5 | 2 2 2 3 3 3 1 2 | 3 3 3 4 1 2 5 L`

SL-NO (1), SL-SALES (1), SL-NO (2), SL-SALES (2), SL-NO (3), SL-SALES (3), SL-NO (4), SL-SALES (4)

POSSIBLE OUTPUT

SALESPERSON NUMBER	AMOUNT SALES
1 1 1	2 4 5 6 7
1 1 1	0 1 2 4 5
2 2 2	3 3 3 1 2
3 3 3 4 1 2 5 L	CHECK RECORD

SL-NO(1) → 1 1 1
SL-SALES(2) → 0 1 2 4 5
SALES-LIST(4) — 8 alphanumeric characters

TREELIKE INTERPRETATION

SALES-LIST (1) ... SALES-LIST (4)
SL-NO (1) SL-SALES (1) SL-NO (2) SL-SALES (2) ... SL-NO (4) SL-SALES (4)

Note that each SALES-LIST entry is a group data item consisting of two elementary items, SL-NO (three positions) and SL-SALES (5 positions). Since SALES-LIST occurs four times, this means that SL-NO and SL-SALES also occur 4 times, hence both SL-NO and SL-SALES must be subscripted. Because SALES-LIST "OCCURS", SALES-LIST itself must be subscripted, and hence the following statements would be illegal:

ONE- AND TWO- DIMENSIONAL TABLES 383

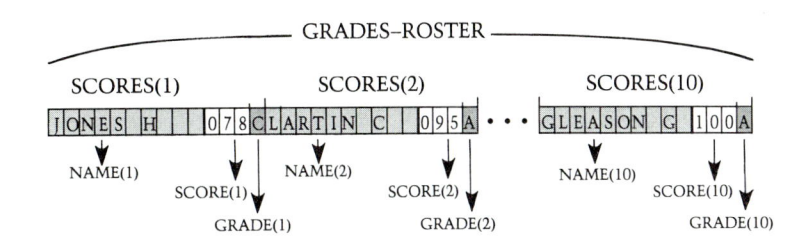

```
MOVE SALES-LIST TO LINE-OUT.     Illegal; no subscript.
ADD SL-SALES TO TOTAL-SALES.     Illegal; no subscript.
```

Note that SALES–LIST (3) is an alphanumeric string consisting of eight characters (digits), thus it cannot be processed numerically.

Also remember that no table subscript should ever exceed the size declared in the OCCURS clause. In this example it would be invalid to refer to SALES–LIST (5), SL–NO (6), or SL–SALES (ITEM) where ITEM is **not** an integer in the range 1–4.

EXAMPLE 2:

TABLE DECLARATION

```
01 GRADES-ROSTER.
   05 SCORES OCCURS 10 TIMES.
      10 NAME  PIC X(10).
      10 SCORE PIC 999.
      10 GRADE PIC A
```

MEMORY ARRANGEMENT

─── GRADES-ROSTER ───

SCORES(1)   SCORES(2)   ...   SCORES(10)

| J | O | N | E | S | | H | | | | 0 | 7 | 8 | C | L | A | R | T | I | N | | C | | | | 0 | 9 | 5 | A | ... | G | L | E | A | S | O | N | | G | | 1 | 0 | 0 | A |

NAME(1)   SCORE(1)   NAME(2)   SCORE(2)   NAME(10)   SCORE(10)
          GRADE(1)   GRADE(2)   GRADE(10)

POSSIBLE OUTPUT

```
      NAME       SCORE    GRADE
NAME(1)→ JONES H    78       C
         LARTIN C   95       A    ←GRADE(2)
         SMITH K   48T   INVALID GRADE
            .        .        .
            .        .        .
         GLEASON G 100       A
           ↑       ↑
       SCORE(3)  SCORE(10)
```

TREELIKE INTERPRETATION
GRADES-ROSTER

SCORES(1)   SCORES(2) ...   SCORES(10)

NAME(1) GRADE(1)   NAME(10) GRADE(10)
    SCORE(1)   SCORE(2)

In this example, GRADES–ROSTER is a group item data name. It identifies a collection of 10 records, each 14 characters long. To create a copy of the entire table in memory, the following instruction could be used:

MOVE GRADES–ROSTER TO DUPLICATE–ROSTER.

and 140 characters would be moved. GRADES–ROSTER is the name given to the overall ten entries of the table. Since it does not OCCUR more than once, the group data name GRADES–ROSTER is not subscripted. SCORES, on the other hand, OCCURS 10 times and hence must be subscripted. Its subitems NAME, SCORE, and GRADE also occur 10 times each (subordinate entries of SCORES) and hence each of these entries must be subscripted in the PROCEDURE division.

EXAMPLE 3:

TABLE DECLARATION

```
01 DIRECTORY.
   03 SALESPERSON-REC OCCURS 100 TIMES.
      05 NAME     PIC X(20).
      05 SALES-ID.
         10 DEPT  PIC 99.
         10 NUMBR PIC 9(4).
      05 SALES    PIC 9(4)V99.
```

TREELIKE STRUCTURE

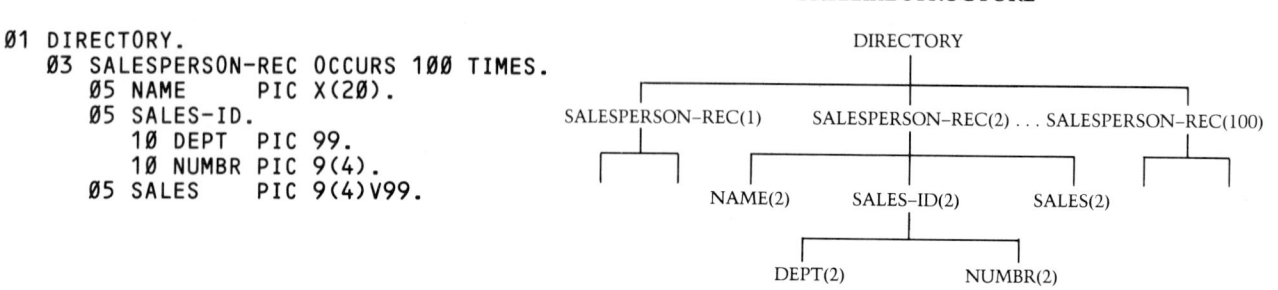

```
                          DIRECTORY
         ┌───────────────────┼───────────────────┐
SALESPERSON-REC(1)   SALESPERSON-REC(2) ... SALESPERSON-REC(100)
                  ┌──────────┼──────────┐
               NAME(2)   SALES-ID(2)  SALES(2)
                          ┌────┴────┐
                       DEPT(2)   NUMBR(2)
```

The physical sequence of data names in memory would be as follows:

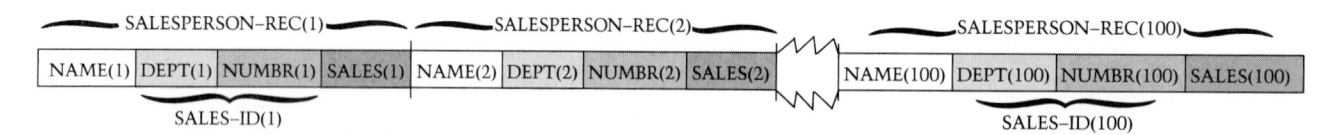

```
──SALESPERSON-REC(1)──  ──SALESPERSON-REC(2)──     ──SALESPERSON-REC(100)──
|NAME(1)|DEPT(1)|NUMBR(1)|SALES(1)|NAME(2)|DEPT(2)|NUMBR(2)|SALES(2)| ... |NAME(100)|DEPT(100)|NUMBR(100)|SALES(100)|
         ──SALES-ID(1)──                                                      ──SALES-ID(100)──
```

In this example DIRECTORY represents a block of $100 \times (20 + 2 + 4 + 6) = 3,200$ storage positions. Logically that record is divided into 100 entries: SALESPERSON-REC (1), SALESPERSON-REC (2), ..., SALESPERSON-REC (100). Each of these 100 entries consists of three subfields. One of these subfields, SALES-ID, is further subdivided into two subfields.

Any reference to SALESPERSON-REC, NAME, SALES-ID, DEPT, NUMBR, or SALES in the PROCEDURE division must be accompanied by subscripts.

EXAMPLE 4: Tables can always be represented by different data structures. Consider the following table

Company Name	Earnings	Dividends	Recent Price	Yield	P/E Ratio
Airborne Ltd.	$2.46	$1.20	21	5.7%	8.5
Fisher Bros.	2.95	0.52	23	2.3	7.8
K mart Corp.	2.96	0.84	22	3.8	7.4
McDonald's	4.53	0.56	42	1.3	9.3
Reynolds Ltd.	5.21	2.10	36	5.8	6.9
Tektronix	4.66	0.84	60	1.4	12.9
Texas Oil	2.28	0.24	42	0.6	18.4
Viacom Int'l	2.35	0.32	44	0.7	18.7

which can be declared in either of the following ways:

CASE 1
```
04 GROWTH-STOCK.
   05 DESCRIPTION OCCURS 8 TIMES PIC X(30).
   05 EARNINGS    OCCURS 8 TIMES PIC 9V99.
   05 DIVIDENDS   OCCURS 8 TIMES PIC 9V99.
   05 PRICE       OCCURS 8 TIMES PIC 99.
   05 YIELD       OCCURS 8 TIMES PIC 9V9.
   05 P-E-RATIO   OCCURS 8 TIMES PIC 99V9.
```

CASE 2
```
04 GROWTH-STOCK OCCURS 8 TIMES.
   05 DESCRIPTION PIC X(30). ⎫
   05 EARNINGS    PIC 9V99.  ⎪
   05 DIVIDENDS   PIC 9V99.  ⎬ all within
   05 PRICE       PIC 99.    ⎪  OCCURS
   05 YIELD       PIC 9V9.   ⎪
   05 P-E-RATIO   PIC 99V9.  ⎭
```

In any event, regardless of the data structure used, EARNINGS (2) will still refer to 2.95 after the tables have been loaded into memory. The only difference between the two data structures is in their memory arrangement.

CASE 1

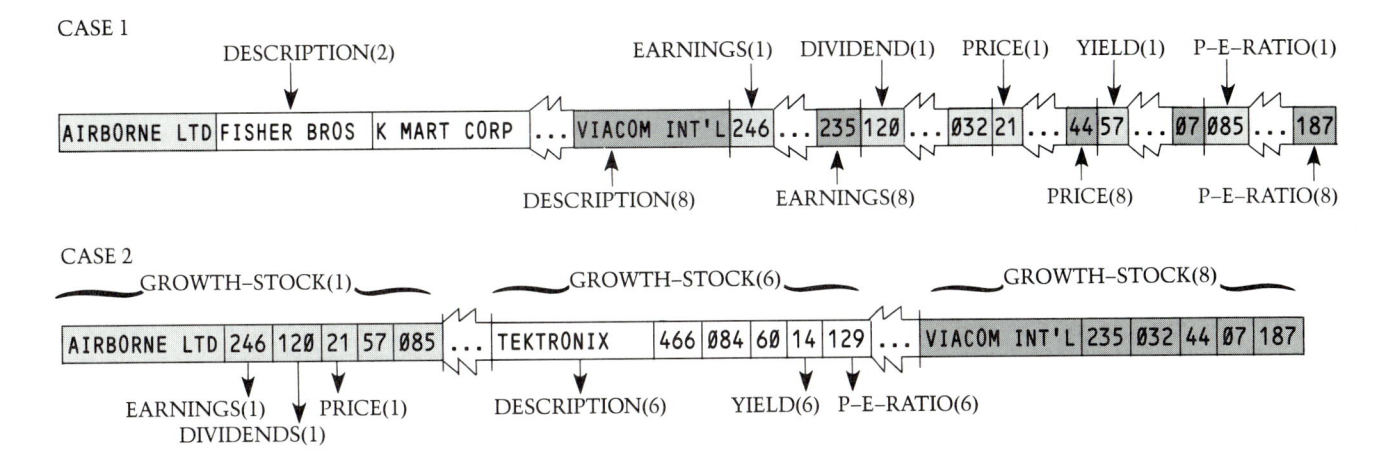

```
                DESCRIPTION(2)              EARNINGS(1)  DIVIDEND(1)  PRICE(1)  YIELD(1)  P-E-RATIO(1)
                      ↓                          ↓           ↓           ↓         ↓          ↓
┌─────────────┬────────────┬─────────────┬┄┄┄┬─────────────┬───┬┄┄┄┬───┬───┬┄┄┄┬───┬───┬┄┄┄┬───┬───┬┄┄┄┬───┐
│AIRBORNE LTD │FISHER BROS │K MART CORP  │...│VIACOM INT'L │246│...│235│120│...│032│ 21│...│ 44│ 57│...│ 07│085│...│187│
└─────────────┴────────────┴─────────────┴┄┄┄┴─────────────┴───┴┄┄┄┴───┴───┴┄┄┄┴───┴───┴┄┄┄┴───┴───┴┄┄┄┴───┘
                                                ↑                ↑                           ↑              ↑
                                         DESCRIPTION(8)     EARNINGS(8)                   PRICE(8)     P-E-RATIO(8)
```

CASE 2

```
  ⎴⎴⎴GROWTH-STOCK(1)⎴⎴⎴          ⎴⎴⎴GROWTH-STOCK(6)⎴⎴⎴           ⎴⎴⎴GROWTH-STOCK(8)⎴⎴⎴
┌─────────────┬───┬───┬──┬──┬───┬┄┄┄┬──────────┬───┬───┬──┬──┬───┬┄┄┄┬─────────────┬───┬───┬──┬──┬───┐
│AIRBORNE LTD │246│120│21│57│085│...│ TEKTRONIX│466│084│60│14│129│...│VIACOM INT'L │235│032│44│07│187│
└─────────────┴───┴───┴──┴──┴───┴┄┄┄┴──────────┴───┴───┴──┴──┴───┴┄┄┄┴─────────────┴───┴───┴──┴──┴───┘
         ↓    ↓   ↓    ↓               ↓                    ↓    ↓
     EARNINGS(1) PRICE(1)          DESCRIPTION(6)        YIELD(6) P-E-RATIO(6)
         DIVIDENDS(1)
```

In each case the same number of memory positions is reserved: 344 positions.

In case 1 GROWTH-STOCK refers to an alphanumeric string of 344 characters. No subscripts can be used on GROWTH-STOCK.

In Case 2 any reference to GROWTH-STOCK must include subscripts. Each GROWTH-STOCK entry identifies 43 alphanumeric characters.

EXAMPLE 5:

```
01  ITEM-INV.
    10  ITEM-A OCCURS 2 TIMES PIC 9.
    10  ITEM-B OCCURS 3 TIMES PIC 9.
    10  ITEM-C OCCURS 4 TIMES.
        15  PART-NO  PIC XX.
        15  PART-QTY PIC 999.
```

ITEM-INV refers to a block of $2 + 3 + 4(2 + 3) = 25$ characters.

All data names subordinate to ITEM-C must be subscripted.

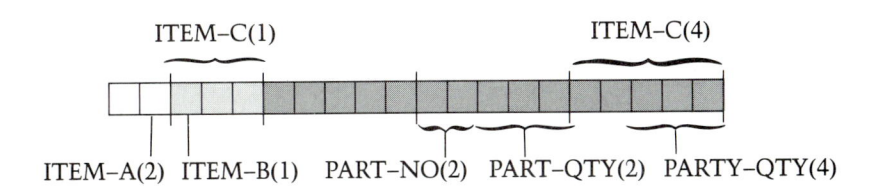

```
                  ITEM-C(1)                          ITEM-C(4)
                ⎴⎴⎴⎴⎴⎴⎴                          ⎴⎴⎴⎴⎴⎴⎴
┌─┬─┬─┬─┬─┬─┬─┬─┬─┬─┬─┬─┬─┬─┬─┬─┬─┬─┬─┬─┬─┬─┬─┬─┬─┐
└─┴─┴─┴─┴─┴─┴─┴─┴─┴─┴─┴─┴─┴─┴─┴─┴─┴─┴─┴─┴─┴─┴─┴─┴─┘
   ↑    ↑     ⎵⎵⎵     ⎵⎵⎵       ⎵⎵⎵
ITEM-A(2) ITEM-B(1) PART-NO(2) PART-QTY(2) PARTY-QTY(4)
```

8-2-3 DO IT NOW

1. Each record of an input file (no more than 100 records) contains a grade. Write a program to compute the grade average and determine the number of grades above the average. Sample input and output are shown on the following page. Grades above the average should be identified with an asterisk on output.

```
           OUTPUT                              INPUT

    ┌─────────────────────────┐              065
    │                         │              071
    │        GRADES           │              089
    │                         │              100
    │         65              │              078
    │         71              │
    │         89  *           │
    │        100  *           │
    │         78              │
    │                         │
    │ AVERAGE = 80.60         │
    │ NO. GRADES ABOVE AVERAGE = 2
    └─────────────────────────┘
```

2. Specify the table structure(s) needed to determine a tax amount from the following columns. How many tables would you need? Discuss your approach to solving this problem.

If the amount on Form 1040, line 37 is: Over—	But not over—	Enter on Form 1040, line 38	of the amount over—
$0	$3,400	—0—	
3,400	5,500	...... 11%	$3,400
5,500	7,600	$231 + 12%	5,500
7,600	11,900	483 + 14%	7,600
11,900	16,000	1,085 + 16%	11,900
16,000	20,200	1,741 + 18%	16,000
20,200	24,600	2,497 + 22%	20,200
24,600	29,900	3,465 + 25%	24,600
29,900	35,200	4,790 + 28%	29,900
35,200	45,800	6,274 + 33%	35,200
45,800	60,000	9,772 + 38%	45,800
60,000	85,600	15,168 + 42%	60,000
85,600	109,400	25,920 + 45%	85,600
109,400	162,400	36,630 + 49%	109,400
162,400	....	62,600 + 50%	162,400

3. True or false:

   a. Subscripts used in conjunction with tables must be declared in the DATA division.
   b. A subscript that evaluates to a negative value will cause a compilation error.
   c. A subscripted data name can itself be the subscript of a table element.
   d. The same subscript may be used by different tables.
   e. A table name without subscripts can be MOVEd as a group item.
   f. If A OCCURS 10 TIMES PIC 99, a reference to A in the PROCEDURE division implies a reference to 20 alphanumeric characters.
   g. A subscript outside the range of its table will cause a compiler error.

4. Determine whether the following table declarations are valid or invalid; if valid, specify the number of storage positions allocated to each table. Also

graphically illustrate the arrangement of table elements by name and position in the internal representation of the table.

a. ```
01 FIRST1.
    02 TAB OCCURS 30 TIMES PIC 99V99.
```

b. ```
01  CLASS.
    05 TABL OCCURS 10 PIC X(10).
        10  DEPT OCCURS 4 TIMES.
            15 A PIC X.
            15 B PIC 9.
```

c. ```
01 SECOND.
    02 EL OCCURS 6.
        04 1-EL PIC 9(5).
        04 2-EL PIC XXX.
        04 3-EL PIC X(20).
```

d. ```
01  TABL OCCURS 7 TIMES PIC 9.
```

e. ```
05 GRADE OCCURS 10 TIMES.
    10 NAME PIC X(20).
    10 SCORE PIC 999 VALUE 0.
  05 TEST OCCURS 3 TIMES PIC 9 VALUE 0.
```

f. ```
05 NAME OCCURS 5 TIMES PIC X(20).
        .
        .
        .
IF NAME (6) > NAME (5) ...
```

SELECTED ANSWERS

1. See Figure 8-6 on page 388.
3. a. T   c. F   e. F   g. F (The compiler can't know.)
4. b. Invalid; a picture clause is not allowed for TABL (it is a group item).
   c. Valid: 168 positions.

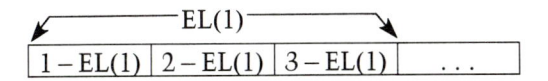

```
       ┌──────EL(1)──────┐
       │1–EL(1)│2–EL(1)│3–EL(1)│ ... │
```

d. Invalid, OCCURS may not be specified at the 01 level.

8-3 TABLE MANIPULATION

When working with tables it is often necessary to initialize table entries to certain values, to create or duplicate tables, to interchange elements within tables, to merge two or more tables into one, to search or accumulate table entries, to

```
130   DATA DIVISION.                              540       05 AVERAGE         PIC 999V99.
140   FILE SECTION.                               560   PROCEDURE DIVISION.
150   FD PRINT-FILE                               570   MAIN-LOGIC.
160      LABEL RECORDS ARE OMITTED                580       PERFORM 10-INITIALIZATION.
170      DATA RECORD IS PRINT-LINE.               590       PERFORM 15-READ-GRADES UNTIL EOF = 1.
180   01 PRINT-LINE         PIC X(133).           600       MOVE 1 TO NO-GRADES.
190   FD INPUT-FILE                               610       COMPUTE AVERAGE = TOTAL / NO-GRADES.
200      LABEL RECORDS ARE OMITTED                620       MOVE 0 TO I.
210      DATA RECORD IS INPUT-RECORD.             630       PERFORM 20-PROCESS-WRITE NO-GRADES TIMES.
220   01 INPUT-RECORD.                            640       PERFORM 30-PRINT-RESULTS-AND-CLOSE.
230      05 IR-GRADE        PIC 999.              650       STOP RUN.
250   WORKING-STORAGE SECTION.                    660   *
260   01 HEADER-1.                                670   10-INITIALIZATION.
270      05 FILLER          PIC X(16) VALUE SPACES. 680       OPEN INPUT INPUT-FILE.
280      05 FILLER          PIC X(06) VALUE 'GRADES'. 690     OPEN OUTPUT PRINT-FILE.
290   01 DETAIL-LINE.                             700       WRITE PRINT-LINE FROM HEADER-1 AFTER 1.
300      05 FILLER          PIC X(18) VALUE SPACES. 710      MOVE SPACES TO PRINT-LINE.
310      05 DL-GRADE        PIC ZZ9.              720       WRITE PRINT-LINE AFTER 1.
320      05 FILLER          PIC XX VALUE SPACES.  730       READ INPUT-FILE AT END MOVE 1 TO EOF.
330      05 DL-FLAG         PIC X.                740   *
340   *                                           750   15-READ-GRADES.
350   01 GRADE-RECORD.                            760       ADD 1      TO I.
360      05 GRADE OCCURS 5 TIMES PIC 999.         770       MOVE IR-GRADE TO GRADE (I)
370   *                                           780       ADD IR-GRADE  TO TOTAL.
380   01 AVERAGE-LINE.                            790       READ INPUT-FILE AT END MOVE 1 TO EOF.
390      05 FILLER          PIC X(08) VALUE SPACES. 800    *
400      05 FILLER          PIC X(09) VALUE 'AVERAGE='. 810 20-PROCESS-WRITE.
410      05 AL-AVERAGE      PIC ZZZ.99.           820       MOVE SPACES TO DL-FLAG.
415   *                                           830       ADD 1 TO I.
420   01 SUMMARY-LINE.                            840       IF GRADE (I) GREATER THAN AVERAGE
430      05 FILLER          PIC X(08) VALUE SPACES. 850         MOVE "*" TO DL-FLAG
440      05 FILLER          PIC X(26) VALUE       860         ADD 1 TO COUNT-ABOVE-AV.
445                         'NO. GRADES ABOVE AVERAGE='. 870  MOVE GRADE (I) TO DL-GRADE.
450      05 SL-ABOVE-AV     PIC Z9.               880       WRITE PRINT-LINE FROM DETAIL-LINE AFTER 1.
460   *                                           890   *
470   01 COUNTERS.                                900   30-PRINT-RESULTS-AND-CLOSE.
480      05 I               PIC 999   VALUE 0.   910       MOVE AVERAGE       TO AL-AVERAGE.
490      05 COUNT-ABOVE-AV  PIC 999   VALUE 0.   920       MOVE COUNT-ABOVE-AV TO SL-ABOVE-AV.
500      05 NO-GRADES       PIC 999.              930       WRITE PRINT-LINE FROM AVERAGE-LINE AFTER 2.
510   01 FLAGS-N-ACCUMULATORS.                    940       WRITE PRINT-LINE FROM SUMMARY-LINE AFTER 1.
520      05 EOF             PIC 9     VALUE 0.   950       CLOSE INPUT-FILE.
530      05 TOTAL           PIC 999   VALUE 0.   960       CLOSE PRINT-FILE.
```

FIGURE 8-6
FINDING GRADES ABOVE THE AVERAGE

sort tables, and so on. This section illustrates certain commonly used table manipulation techniques to help the reader get a better grasp of the table subscript mechanism. In the following discussions it is assumed that the tables have been properly declared and in some cases that values have been read into them.

8-3-1 TABLE INITIALIZATION

One technique for initializing table elements to particular values is presented here. Other methods for initializing tables will be discussed in section 8-3-9.

Suppose that table AMOUNT is of size 100 and we wish to set all entries to 0's, i.e., set AMOUNT (1), AMOUNT (2), ..., AMOUNT (100) equal to 0. The following methods could be used.

Method 1

```
MOVE 1 TO COUNTER.
PERFORM 300-ZERO-OUT UNTIL COUNTER > 100.

300-ZERO-OUT.
    MOVE 0 TO AMOUNT (COUNTER).
    ADD 1 TO COUNTER.
```

ONE- AND TWO- DIMENSIONAL TABLES   389

Method 2 An easier method:

```
01  AMOUNT-RECORD.
    05 AMOUNT OCCURS 100 TIMES PIC 9.

    MOVE ZEROS TO AMOUNT-RECORD.
```

This MOVE instruction will propagate 0's throughout the 100 positions of AMOUNT–RECORD.

8-3-2 THE PERFORM VARYING STATEMENT.

In Method 1 for table initialization, the subscript COUNTER must first be initialized to 1 before the PERFORM . . . UNTIL COUNTER > 100 statement is executed. Then the subscript must be incremented by 1 in the 300 paragraph.

A very convenient extension of the PERFORM statement allows the programmer to specify these two functions (initialization and incrementation of the subscript) in the PERFORM statement itself. This extension, the PERFORM VARYING statement, has a built-in mechanism that initializes a counter and increments that counter automatically each time the procedure specified in the PERFORM statement is carried out.

The general form of the PERFORM VARYING is:

> PERFORM paragraph-name VARYING data-name-1
> FROM initial-value BY increment-value UNTIL condition

where data-name-1 is any data item name and initial-value and increment-value can be a numeric literal or a data item name representing a numeric value.

The function performed by the PERFORM VARYING can be visualized in flowchart form as follows:

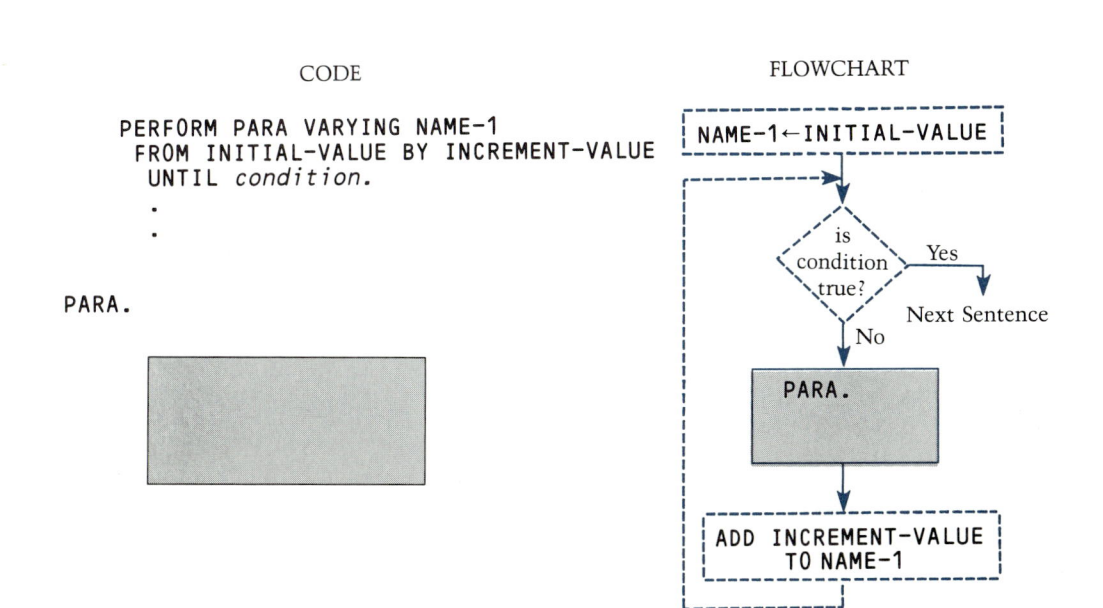

CODE

```
PERFORM PARA VARYING NAME-1
    FROM INITIAL-VALUE BY INCREMENT-VALUE
    UNTIL condition.
    .
    .

PARA.
```

FLOWCHART

NAME-1 ← INITIAL-VALUE

is condition true? — Yes → Next Sentence

No ↓

PARA.

ADD INCREMENT-VALUE TO NAME-1

For example, to initialize the 100 elements of AMOUNT to zeros, the following code could be used:

```
PERFORM ZERO-OUT VARYING COUNTER FROM 1 BY 1 UNTIL COUNTER > 100.
    .
    .
ZERO-OUT.
    MOVE 0 TO AMOUNT (COUNTER).
```

The VARYING feature is naturally very convenient for handling table elements (subscripts), but it can also be used for many other purposes that do not involve tables. Consider the problem of computing the sum of the first 50 even numbers: SUM = 2 + 4 + 6 + 8 + . . . + 98 + 100. The following code could be used:

```
    MOVE 0 TO SUM1.
    PERFORM EVEN-SUM VARYING EVEN FROM 2 BY 2 UNTIL EVEN > 100.
    .
    .
EVEN-SUM.
    ADD EVEN TO SUM1.
```

The values taken on by EVEN will be 2, 4, 6, . . ., 100, and SUM1 will accumulate the sum of these numbers.

Examples:

VALID PERFORM VARYING SENTENCES

1. PERFORM TABLE-LOOK-UP VARYING ENTRY-1 FROM 1 BY 1 UNTIL
      ENTRY-1 > MAX-ENTRY.

2. PERFORM SUMMATION VARYING X FROM -1 BY .05
      UNTIL SUM1 GREATER THAN SUM-1 OR SUM-2.

3. PERFORM EXPERIMENT VARYING TEMPERATURE FROM FREEZING BY
      X-CENTIGRADES UNTIL TEMPERATURE GREATER THAN BOILING.

4. PERFORM TABLE-PRINT VARYING EMP-NO FROM 10 BY -1 UNTIL
      LIST (EMP-NO) = 'ADAMSON' OR EMP-NO = 1.

Following are some invalid or incorrect **PERFORM VARYING** sentences. (Some COBOL compilers may accept example 3.)

1. PERFORM PARA VARYING COUNTER FROM 1 TO 5. The TO word is invalid.

2. PERFORM PARA VARYING X BY 1 FROM 5
      UNTIL X > 0. Should be FROM 5 BY 1.

3. PERFORM PARA VARYING X FROM Y + 1 BY
      2 * INC UNTIL I = 10.5. Expression Y + 1 or 2 * INC may not be allowed.

4. PERFORM SUM-IT VARYING DAYS FROM 2 BY 2
      UNTIL DAYS = 7. Example 4 is syntactically correct, but an infinite loop would result from the code, since DAYS will never take on the value 7 (unless DAYS is changed in SUM-IT).

8-3-3 TABLE INITIALIZATION AND DUPLICATION

Assume tables AMOUNT, TAX and TEMP are of size 100 and that we want to:

1. Copy the first N (N ≤ 100) elements of AMOUNT into table TEMP, and
2. Set the first N entries of table TAX equal to the value X–INIT.

The following code could be used:

```
PERFORM SET-DUP VARING COUNTER FROM 1 BY 1 UNTIL COUNTER > N.
       .
       .
SET-DUP.
    MOVE AMOUNT (COUNTER) TO TEMP (COUNTER).
    MOVE X-INIT            TO TAX (COUNTER).
```

Copy the first N entries of AMOUNT into table TEMP.
Move the constant value X-INIT into the first N elements of table TAX.

Sum of Two Tables

Sometimes it may be necessary to set a table C equal to the sum of two other tables A and B in such a way that C(1) = A(1) + B(1), C(2) = A(2) + B(2), ..., C(100) = A(100) + B(100), for example

```
A →  3. | -1. | 2. | 5. | ... | 8. | 10.
                                              +
B → -1  | 2.  | 3. | 17.| ... | 6. | 9.
    ─────────────────────────────────────
C →  2. | 1.  | 5. | 22.| ... | 14.| 19.
```

The following code could be used:

```
PERFORM TABLE-ADD VARYING SUBSCRIPT FROM 1 BY 1
    UNTIL SUBSCRIPT > 100.
      .
      .
TABLE-ADD.
    COMPUTE C (SUBSCRIPT) = A (SUBSCRIPT) + B (SUBSCRIPT).
```

8-3-4 TABLE ACCUMULATION

Assume table SALES contains

| 10050 | 20050 | 30050 | 25000 | 30000 | 20000 | 40000 |

and we wish to compute the total sales (the sum of the seven entries). The following code could be used:

```
MOVE 0 TO TOTAL-SALES.
PERFORM 200-ACCUMULATE-SALES VARYING DAYS
    FROM 1 BY 1 UNTIL DAYS GREATER THAN 7.

200-ACCUMULATE-SALES.
    ADD SALES (DAYS) TO TOTAL-SALES.
```

When paragraph 200-ACCUMULATE-SALES is carried out,

The 1st time DAYS=1; we add SALES (1) TO TOTAL-SALES or 100.50 to 0 to get 100.50

The 2nd time DAYS=2; we add SALES (2) TO TOTAL-SALES or 200.50 to 100.50 to get 301.00

The 3rd time DAYS=3; we add SALES (3) TO TOTAL-SALES or 300.50 to 301.00 to get 601.50

The 4th time DAYS=4; we add SALES (4) TO TOTAL-SALES or 250.00 to 601.50 to get 851.50

The 5th time DAYS=5; we add SALES (5) TO TOTAL-SALES or 300.00 to 851.50 to get 1151.50

The 6th time DAYS=6; we add SALES (6) TO TOTAL-SALES or 200.00 to 1151.50 to get 1351.50

The 7th time DAYS=7; we add SALES (7) TO TOTAL-SALES or 400.00 to 1351.50 to get 1751.50

8-3-5 TABLE MERGE

Suppose A and B are tables of size 5 and we want to create a third table C whose entries are to be set equal to A(1), B(1), A(2), B(2), . . ., A(5), B(5),

Method 1

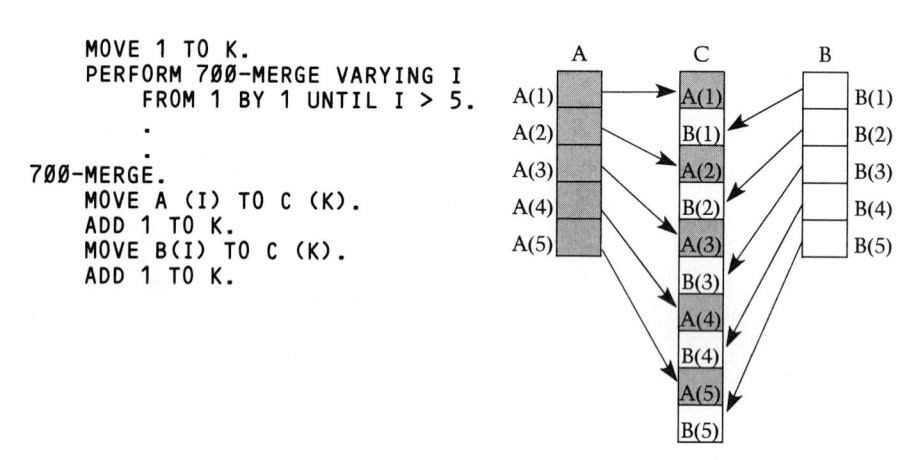

```
    MOVE 1 TO K.
    PERFORM 700-MERGE VARYING I
        FROM 1 BY 1 UNTIL I > 5.
        .
        .
700-MERGE.
    MOVE A (I) TO C (K).
    ADD 1 TO K.
    MOVE B(I) TO C (K).
    ADD 1 TO K.
```

Method 2

```
    MOVE 1 TO K.
    PERFORM 700-MERGE VARYING
        I FROM 1 BY 2 UNTIL I > 10.
        .
        .
700-MERGE.
    MOVE A (K) TO C (I).
    COMPUTE L = I + 1.
    MOVE B (K) TO C (L).
    ADD 1 TO K.
```

Method 3

```
    PERFORM 700-MERGE VARING
        I FROM 1 BY 1 UNTIL I > 5.
        .
        .
700-MERGE.
    COMPUTE ODD  = 2 * I - 1.
    COMPUTE EVEN = 2 * I.
    MOVE A (I) TO C (ODD).
    MOVE B (I) TO C (EVEN).
```

8-3-6 REVERSING ELEMENTS IN A TABLE

Suppose A is a table of size N, where N has been defined previously, and we want to interchange the elements of A as follows:

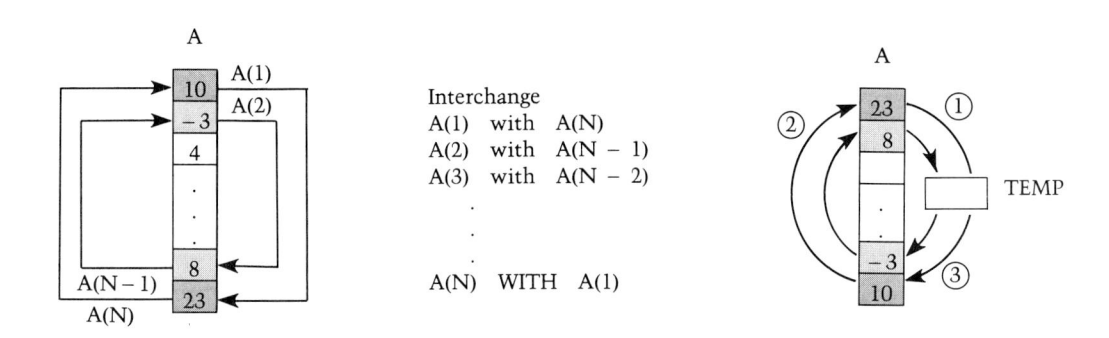

To interchange two memory locations, A(1) and A(N) for example, we must use a temporary storage area TEMP and take the following steps:

1. MOVE A (1) TO TEMP   Save A(1) before we replace
2. MOVE A (N) TO A (1)   A(1) with A(N), and then move
3. MOVE TEMP TO A (N)   TEMP into A(N).

Note that one interchange moves two values. The general procedure can be coded as follows:

```
COMPUTE L = N / 2.                    Since each interchange involves two
PERFORM INTERCHANGE VARYING I         table entries, there will need to be
    FROM 1 BY 1 UNTIL I > L.          only N/2 interchanges.
    .                                 If N is odd, the median element
    .                                 stays the same and the interchange
    .                                 procedure does not affect it.
INTERCHANGE.
    COMPUTE K = N - I + 1.            K generates the numbers N, N - 1 ...,
    MOVE A (I) TO TEMP.               TEMP is a temporary storage area needed to
    MOVE A (K) TO A (I).              preserve A(1) before the statement A(1) =
    MOVE TEMP TO A (K).               A(N) is executed; otherwise the value in A(1)
                                      would be destroyed.
```

8-3-7 TABLE SEARCH

EXAMPLE 1 Suppose GRADE-RECORD is a table of size 100, containing names and test scores as follows:

```
05 GRADE-RECORD OCCURS 100 TIMES.
    10 NAME  PIC X(15).        Name of student.
    10 GRADE PIC 999.          Student score.
```

Let us write the code segment that will print the names of the students whose test scores fall in the open interval 75 to 80. Note that GRADE(WS-SUB) is the grade obtained by the student whose name is NAME(WS-SUB).

```
        PERFORM 10-SEARCH VARYING WS-SUB
            FROM 1 BY 1 UNTIL WS-SUB > 100.
              .
              .
    10-SEARCH.
        IF GRADE (WS-SUB) > 75 AND < 80
            MOVE NAME (WS-SUB) TO DL-NAME
            WRITE PRINT-LINE FROM DETAIL-LINE.
```

Search through table GRADE for grades in the interval 75–80.

If WS–SUB = 3 and GRADE(3) is in the interval 75 to 80, then we want to print NAME(WS–SUB), which is NAME(3).

EXAMPLE 2: A directory of 100 names and corresponding account numbers is stored in tables as follows:

```
01 DIRECTORY OCCURS 100 TIMES.
    05 NAME    PIC X(20).
    05 ACCOUNT PIC 9999.
```

Let us write the code to look up Mr. Beauregard's account number. An error message should be printed if no such name exists in the directory.

Two methods for solving this problem are presented. The first method makes use of a flag or switch that is set to 0 (turned off) before the search process starts, indicating that no such name (Beauregard) has yet been found (obviously). Within the search process itself, the switch is turned on (set to 1) if a match is found. At the conclusion of the search routine, the switch is queried to determine whether to print an error message (no name) or whether to print the account number.

Method 1: Use of a Switch.

```
    MOVE 'BEAUREGARD' TO DL-NAME, EL-NAME.
    MOVE 0 TO SWITCH.
    PERFORM NAME-SEARCH VARYING ACCT-NO
        FROM 1 BY 1 UNTIL SWITCH = 1
            OR ACCT-NO GREATER THAN 100.
    IF SWITCH = 0
        MOVE 'NO SUCH NAME' TO EL-MESSG
        WRITE PRINT-LINE FROM ERROR-LINE
    ELSE
        WRITE PRINT-LINE FROM DETAIL-LINE.
          .
          .
NAME-SEARCH.
    IF NAME (ACCT-NO) = 'BEAUREGARD'
        MOVE ACCOUNT (ACCT-NO) TO DL-ACCOUNT
        MOVE 1 TO SWITCH.
```

Set the switch to 0 to indicate that the name Beauregard has not yet been found. If a match for Beauregard is found, then the switch is turned to 1, and the PERFORM statement is no longer executed since the condition SWITCH = 1 is satisfied. If no match is found, this implies that the subscript ACCT-NO has exceeded 100 and the PERFORM statement is no longer executed since ACCT-NO > 100.

If the condition ACCT-NO > 100 had been omitted from the PERFORM statement, there would be an execution error (invalid index) at the sentence IF NAME(ACCT-NO) = BEAUREGARD, since ACCT-NO would be 101. Note that after the PERFORM statement the switch is tested to determine whether to write an error message or to write the account number.

Method 2: The Name Test is Part of the PERFORM Statement.

```
MOVE 'BEAUREGARD' TO DL-NAME, EL-NAME.
PERFORM NAME-SEARCH VARYING ACCT-NO
    FROM 1 BY 1 UNTIL ACCT-NO > 100
    OR NAME (ACCT-NO) = 'BEAUREGARD'.
IF ACCT-NO > 100
    MOVE 'NAME NOT FOUND' TO EL-MESSG
ELSE
    MOVE ACCOUNT (ACCT-NO) TO DL-ACCOUNT
    WRITE PRINT-LINE FROM DETAIL-LINE.
      .
      .
      .
NAME-SEARCH.
    EXIT.
```

In this case the PERFORM statement does everything. In fact, there really isn't any need for a paragraph NAME–SEARCH to be processed since the PERFORM itself goes through the names in the directory and stops when it encounters a name equal to BEAUREGARD. If it doesn't find a match, then the value of ACCT–NO will exceed 100 at the end of the PERFORM.

Since, grammatically speaking, the PERFORM needs the name of a paragraph to be executed, we specify the name of a paragraph which has as its sole instruction the COBOL key word EXIT. EXIT is a null operation and must be the only word specified in the paragraph in which it appears.

If no name match exists, an "invalid index" execution-time error may occur on some systems as a result of evaluating NAME (ACCT–NO) when ACCT–NO is 101 (NAME occurs only 100 times and 101 is out of the range of the table size).

8-3-8 DO IT NOW

In problems 1 through 4, simply write the appropriate PROCEDURE division statements.

1. Write the code to fill successive elements of a table with the values 5, 7, 9, 11, . . ., 225. Do not use a READ statement.

2. The Miles Furniture Store is going out of business. All different store items have been labeled 1, 2, 3, . . ., 100 (100 different items in all). The cost per item and the number of items in stock have been recorded as follows: COST(1) is the cost of item 1 and QUAN(I) is the number of items I. Assume the COST and QUAN tables have already been read in. Write a program segment to compute the Miles furniture inventory in dollars.

3. A table A supposedly contains 20 elements already sorted in ascending order. Write the code to perform a sequence check. Print YES if the table is in sequence; otherwise print NO.

4. Read in a group of savings account numbers and amounts on deposit (ranging from 0.00 to 99999.99). There will be a maximum of 15 accounts and deposits. Write the code to:

    1. Print the account numbers of all accounts containing deposits of 50,000.00 or more.

    2. *Then* print all the account numbers of accounts containing deposits between 10,000.00 and 50,000.00

5. State whether the following statements are valid or invalid. If valid, state the number of times paragraph A will be executed, assuming the VARYING counter is not changed in paragraph A.

   a. PERFORM A VARYING X FROM 1 BY 1 UNTIL X > 70.
   b. PERFORM A ONE-HUNDRED TIMES.
   c. PERFORM A VARYING I FROM 1 BY -1 UNTIL I > 8.
   d. PERFORM A 100.
   e. PERFORM A UNTIL I = 3.

6. Will both of the following coding segments compute the average of 10 scores stored in table SCORE?

   a.   MOVE 0 TO WS-TOTAL.
          MOVE 1 TO COUNTER.
          PERFORM 100-ADD-SCORES
              UNTIL COUNTER > 10.
          COMPUTE WS-AVERAGE =
              WS-TOTAL / COUNTER.

      100-ADD-SCORES.
          ADD SCORES (COUNTER) TO WS-TOTAL.
          ADD 1 TO COUNTER.

   b.   MOVE 0 TO WS-TOTAL.
          PERFORM 100-ADD-SCORES VARYING COUNTER
              FROM 1 BY 1 UNTIL COUNTER > 10.

      100-ADD-SCORES.
          ADD SCORES (COUNTER) TO WS-TOTAL.
          COMPUTE WS-AVERAGE = WS-TOTAL / COUNTER.

SELECTED ANSWERS

2.   MOVE 0 TO WS-INVENTORY.
       PERFORM 100-CALCULATE-INVENTORY VARYING
           ITEM FROM 1 BY 1 UNTIL ITEM > 100.

   100-CALCULATE-INVENTORY.
       COMPUTE WS-PART = COST (ITEM) * QUAN (ITEM).
       ADD WS-PART TO WS-INVENTORY.

5. a. Valid; paragraph A will be performed 70 times.
   b. Valid; depends on the value of ONE-HUNDRED.
   c. Invalid; logic error as I becomes negative.
   d. Valid; A will be performed 100 times.

6. Part a does not compute the average correctly since COUNTER is 11 when the average is computed. Part b does, but the code is inefficient (why?).

8-3-9 TABLE INITIALIZATION THROUGH THE REDEFINES CLAUSE

So far we have always been able to initialize data names in the DATA division through the VALUE clause. The VALUE clause, however, cannot be used to initialize tables. Consider the following invalid examples:

Example:

1. To initialize an array of KOUNT to zeros, we may *not* write the following code:

   INVALID
   ```
   05 KOUNT OCCURS 10 TIMES PIC 999 VALUE 0.
   ```

   The VALUE clause cannot be used to initialize any data name that OCCURS. This rule makes sense—to which element of KOUNT would the value 0 apply?

2. To initialize the table NAME to blanks and the table KOUNT to 1's, we may *not* write the following code:

   INVALID
   ```
   05 NAME-COUNT OCCURS 10 TIMES.
      10 NAME  PIC X(10) VALUE SPACES
      10 KOUNT PIC 999   VALUE 1
   ```
   The VALUE clause may not be used with a table element description entry.

   The VALUE clause may *not* be specified in a record description entry that contains an OCCURS clause or in an entry that is subordinate to a group data item that OCCURS. In other words, the VALUE clause cannot be used directly to initialize tables.

   Two approaches can be taken to initialize tables. One approach involves moving values into tables during the PROCEDURE division, and the other involves using the REDEFINES clause discussed in section 7-1-1. With the first approach, the following code could be used to initialize the tables in the second example above.

```
       MOVE 0 TO COUNTER.                  Initialize subscript.
       PERFORM 100-INITIALIZE 10 TIMES.
           .
           .
   100-INITIALIZE.
       ADD 1 TO COUNTER.
       MOVE SPACES TO NAME (COUNTER).      Insert blanks in each entry of the NAME table.
       MOVE 1 TO KOUNT (COUNTER).          Initialize all elements of KOUNT to 1.
```

   The REDEFINES clause offers a convenient method for initializing tables of small size as shown in the following examples:

EXAMPLE 1 Suppose we wanted to initialize the table DAYS to the days of the week, i.e.:

```
DAYS (1) = 'MONDAY'
DAYS (2) = 'TUESDAY'
    .
    .
DAYS (7) = 'SUNDAY'
```

We cannot define the table DAYS as:

```
05 DAYS OCCURS 7 TIMES.
    10 DAYS (1) PIC X(8) VALUE 'MONDAY'.
    10 DAYS (2) PIC X(8) VALUE 'TUESDAY'.
        .
        .
```

for two reasons:

1. This structure implies that DAYS(1) would occur 7 times, since DAYS(1) is subordinate to DAYS.

2. Record description entries may not be subscripted nor can they have a VALUE clause!

What we can do is create a group data structure with seven subordinate items initialized to the seven days of the week through the VALUE clause. We then superimpose the table DAYS over that structure in such a way that DAYS(1) corresponds to the first subordinate item of the group data structure. This can be done with the following code:

```
05 DAYS-OF-WEEK.

    10 FILLER PIC X(9) VALUE 'MONDAY'.
    10 FILLER PIC X(9) VALUE 'TUESDAY'.
    10 FILLER PIC X(9) VALUE 'WEDNESDAY'.
    10 FILLER PIC X(9) VALUE 'THURSDAY'.
    10 FILLER PIC X(9) VALUE 'FRIDAY'.
    10 FILLER PIC X(9) VALUE 'SATURDAY'.
    10 FILLER PIC X(9) VALUE 'SUNDAY'.

05 WEEK-NAME REDEFINES DAYS-OF-WEEK.
   10 DAYS OCCURS 7 TIMES PIC X(9).
```

DAYS-OF-WEEK can, of course, be written more compactly, as follows:

```
05 DAYS-OF-WEEK PIC X(63) VALUE
    'MONDAY   TUESDAY  WEDNESDAYTHURSDAY FRIDAY   SATURDAY SUNDAY'.
```

It should be noted that we could have defined WEEK-NAME as:

```
05 WEEK-NAME.
   10 DAYS OCCURS 7 TIMES PIC X(9).
```

and then MOVEd DAYS-OF-WEEK to WEEK-NAME to obtain the same result. However, it is important to note that the REDEFINES preserves memory storage and does not reallocate another area of memory 63 characters long, as this latter code does.

EXAMPLE 2: In the state of Florida the names of all college courses are described with a 3-alphabetic character prefix and a 4-digit code. For example, an American history course label might have the following prefix and code:

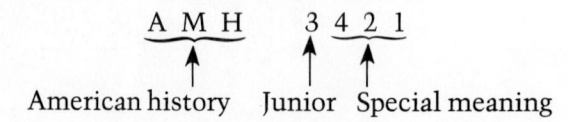

$$\underbrace{A\ M\ H}_{\text{American history}}\ \underbrace{3}_{\text{Junior}}\ \underbrace{4\ 2\ 1}_{\text{Special meaning}}$$

ONE- AND TWO- DIMENSIONAL TABLES

Let us create a table of course titles in such a way that we can index this table by complete course title (AMH3421), by course prefix (AMH), or by the course's 4-digit code (3421):

```
05 COURSE-DIRECTORY.

    07 FILLER PIC X(7) VALUE "FRE1100".
    07 FILLER PIC X(7) VALUE "GER2201".
    07 FILLER PIC X(7) VALUE "SPN1010".
    07 FILLER PIC X(7) VALUE "RUS2200".
          .
          .
          .
05 COURSE-LISTING REDEFINES COURSE-DIRECTORY.
    10 COURSE OCCURS 6 TIMES.
        05 PREFIX PIC X(3).
        05 KODE   PIC 9(4).
```

In memory we get the following linear arrangement

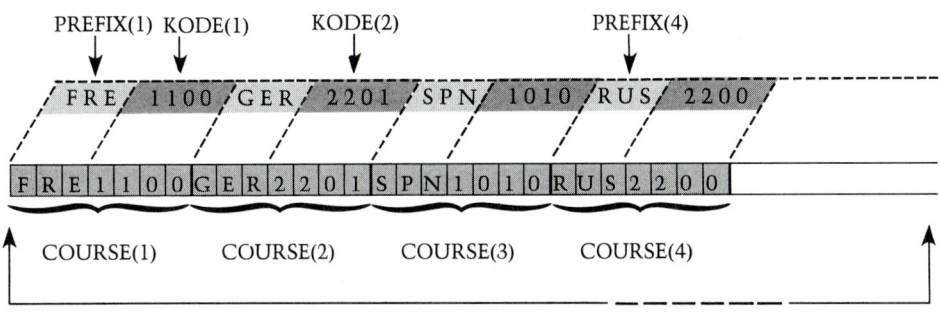

Note again that COURSE-LISTING or COURSE DIRECTORY refers to a string of at least 28 characters, and that neither COURSE-LISTING nor COURSE-DIRECTORY may be subscripted.

COURSE (1) refers to a string of 7 characters.
PREFIX (1) refers to a string of 3 characters.
KODE (1) refers to a 4-digit numeric field.

EXAMPLE 3: Assume GRADE-ROSTER is a table containing 100 entries, each of which consists of a name, a score, and a sex code. We want to determine the number of names starting with the letter F. We need to write the proper data structure to redefine the grade roster so that we can process the first character of each name. The following structure could be used:

```
01 CLASS-RECORD.
    05 GRADE-ROSTER OCCURS 100 TIMES.
        10 NAME  PIC X(10).
        10 SCORE PIC 999.
        10 SEX   PIC A.
01 DUP-RECORD REDEFINES CLASS-RECORD.
    05 DUP-ROSTER OCCURS 100 TIMES.
        10 FIRST-LETTER  PIC X.          Identifies the first letter of each
        10 FILLER        PIC X(13).      name, i.e., the 1st, 15th, 29th, ...
                                         characters of CLASS-RECORD.
```

Allocation of memory for this data structure can be visualized as follows:

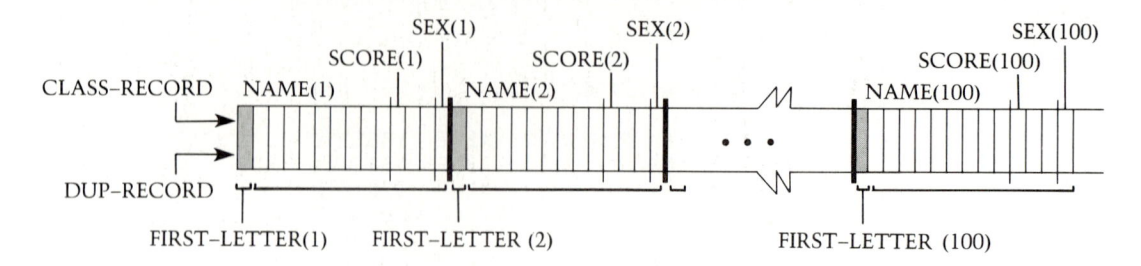

[Diagram showing memory layout of CLASS-RECORD / DUP-RECORD with NAME(1), SCORE(1), SEX(1), NAME(2), SCORE(2), SEX(2), ..., NAME(100), SCORE(100), SEX(100), and FIRST-LETTER(1), FIRST-LETTER(2), ..., FIRST-LETTER(100).]

Note that we *cannot* redefine NAME within GRADE-ROSTER as follows:

```
01  CLASS-RECORD.
    05  GRADE-ROSTER OCCURS 100 TIMES.
        10  NAME PIC X(10).
        10  DUP-NAME REDEFINES NAME.        INVALID (since NAME OCCURS!)
            15  FIRST-LETTER   PIC X.
            15  FILLER         PIC X(09).
        10  SCORE PIC 999.
        10  SEX   PIC X.
```

The REDEFINES clause may not specify a data item name that OCCURS directly or indirectly.

8-3-10   SEARCHING FOR A MAXIMUM OR A MINIMUM VALUE

Suppose the table SCORES contains 10 scores and we want to determine the value of the highest score and its location. Finding the location of the highest score means determining its position in the table, i.e., is it the 1st, 2nd, 3rd, ..., score. The following partial code determines the largest score as well as its position in the table.

```
MOVE SCORES (1) TO WS-MAX-SCORE.
MOVE 1          TO WS-MAX-LOCATION.
PERFORM 300-TABLE-SEARCH VARYING INDX
   FROM 2 BY 1 UNTIL INDX > 10.

300-TABLE-SEARCH.
   IF WS-MAX-SCORE < SCORES (INDX)
      MOVE SCORES (INDX) TO WS-MAX-SCORE
      MOVE INDX          TO WS-MAX-LOCATION.
```

Before the search process is started, assume that the largest score is SCORES (1).

If the highest score so far is less than the score just referenced, replace WS-MAX-SCORE by SCORES (INDX) and remember its location in WS-MAX-LOCATION.

To start comparing successive grades, WS-MAX-SCORE is initially set to the first grade of the table. It is then compared to SCORES (2). If WS-MAX-SCORE is greater than SCORES (2), then WS-MAX-SCORE is compared to SCORES (3), ..., until a grade is found that is larger than WS-MAX-SCORE. Then the larger grade (SCORES (INDX)) is stored into WS-MAX-SCORE. In general, any grade that is larger than the current largest grade is moved into WS-MAX-SCORE.

A similar procedure can be used to search for a minimum value.

8-3-11   TABLE INPUT/OUTPUT

Values can be loaded into a table by means of the REDEFINES clause, as shown in example 1 in Section 8-3-9. Most of the time, though, data will be read from an input file and moved directly into a table structure.

ONE- AND TWO- DIMENSIONAL TABLES

The subscripting of the table can be done by using the PERFORM VARYING, through an independent subscript or with the READ INTO option. Consider the following problem:

Each record of an input file contains a student name and a test score. Write the code to read the student names and scores into a table structure. No more than 100 records are expected. The following two data structures can be used to define tables NAME and SCORE.

STRUCTURE 1

```
01 INPUT-RECORD.
    05 IR-NAME   PIC X(20).
    05 IR-SCORE  PIC 999.

01 TABLES.
    05 ROSTER OCCURS 100 TIMES.
        10 NAME  PIC X(20).
        10 SCORE PIC 999.
```

INPUT DATA

```
NIXON T  048
JONES S  078
    .
    .
CUNE  A  100
```
No more than 100 records.

STRUCTURE 2

```
01 INPUT-RECORD.
    05 IR-NAME   PIC X(20).
    05 IR-SCORE  PIC 999.

01 TABLES.
    05 NAME  OCCURS 100 TIMES PIC X(20).
    05 SCORE OCCURS 100 TIMES PIC 999.
```

Three methods for loading the names and scores are presented; each method can load the names and scores into either data structure.

Method 1: Independent Subscript.

```
    READ INPUT-FILE
        AT END MOVE 1 TO EOF.
    MOVE 0 TO INDX.
    PERFORM LOAD-TABLES UNTIL EOF = 1.
        .
        .
LOAD-TABLES.
    ADD 1 TO INDX.
    MOVE IR-NAME  TO NAME  (INDX).
    MOVE IR-SCORE TO SCORE (INDX).
    READ INPUT-FILE AT END
        MOVE 1 TO EOF.
```

Read the first input record.

The subscript INDX is used to identify the table entries into which successive names and scores are to be moved.

The first time, INDX is 1 and the input data will be moved into the first entry of tables NAME and SCORE.

Note that INDX will reflect the number of elements read into both tables when the end of file is encountered; i.e., there will be INDX names in table NAME.

The process of reading and loading the input data into the two tables can be visualized in Figure 8–7.

Method 2: Using the PERFORM/VARYING statement.

```
10      READ INPUT-FILE
15          AT END MOVE 1 TO EOF.
20      PERFORM LOAD-TABLES VARYING INDX
25          FROM 1 BY 1 UNTIL EOF = 1.
28      COMPUTE WS-RECORDS = INDX - 1.
    .
30  LOAD-TABLES.
40      MOVE IR-NAME TO NAME (INDX).
50      MOVE IR-SCORE TO SCORE (INDX).
60      READ INPUT-FILE
65          AT END MOVE 1 TO EOF.
```

Note that with this method, the final value of INDX will reflect the count of the end-of-file record, since INDX is automatically incremented by 1 each time paragraph LOAD-TABLES is carried out.
For example, if the input file contains only 1 record, the value for INDX will be 2. Hence 1 is subtracted from INDX at line 28.

402 UNDERSTANDING STRUCTURED COBOL

```
Structure 1:  05   ROSTER OCCURS 100 TIMES.
              10     NAME   PIC X(20).
              10     SCORE  PIC 999.
```

```
Structure 2:  05   NAME  OCCURS 100 TIMES PIC X(20).
              05   SCORE OCCURS 100 TIMES PIC 999.
```

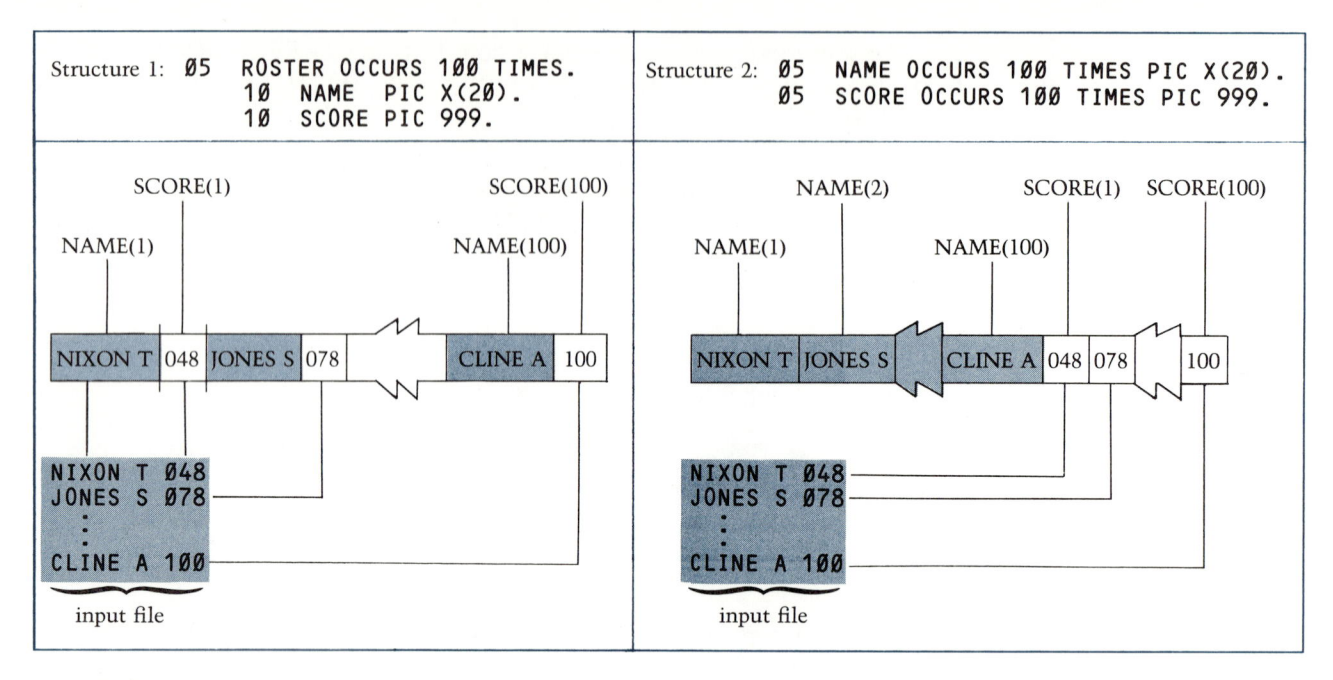

FIGURE 8-7
LOADING TABLES WITH TWO TABLE STRUCTURES

Method 3: The READ INTO Option.

```
01 TABLES.                              01 INPUT-RECORD.
   03 ROSTER OCCURS 100 TIMES.             05 IR-NAME  PIC X(20).
      05 NAME  PIC X(20).                  05 IR-SCORE PIC 999.
      05 SCORE PIC 999.
   .
   .
      PERFORM LOAD-TABLES VARYING INDX
         FROM 1 BY 1 UNTIL EOF = 1.
   LOAD-TABLES.
      READ INPUT-FILE INTO ROSTER (INDX)
         AT END MOVE 1 TO EOF.
```

Since ROSTER(INDX) is 23 positions long, each execution of the READ INTO statement moves the 23 positions of the input record to the next 23 positions of ROSTER. This means that the 20 characters IR-NAME are moved into NAME(INDX) and the next 3 digits IR-SCORE are moved into SCORE(INDX).

This method is very convenient when no filler fields separate the data items in the input record. If FILLER fields do separate the data items in the input record, these FILLER fields can be included in the table structures. However, they do waste memory positions.

As in Method 2, the final value of INDX will be one more than there are records in the input file.

Note that with this approach the prime READ method is not used, i.e., there is only one READ statement. The prime READ method would have to be used, of course, if the records were to be processed as they are read. In such a case the first READ statement would be:

```
READ INPUT-FILE INTO ROSTER (1) AT END MOVE 1 TO EOF.
PERFORM LOAD-TABLES VARYING INDX FROM 1 BY 1 UNTIL EOF = 1.
```

ONE- AND TWO- DIMENSIONAL TABLES

Tables as Input Records

Sometimes a table can be carved out of the input record itself. Consider the following case: An input record consists of a student's name followed by the student's 10 scores. The objective is to load the SCORES into a table. The following data structure could be used to reserve a table for the 10 SCORES—note that the table is part of the input record itself and is declared in the FILE section and not in WORKING-STORAGE.

```
FILE SECTION.
FD  INPUT-FILE
    LABEL RECORDS ARE OMITTED
    DATA RECORD IS STUDENT-REC.
01  STUDENT-REC.
    05 NAME PIC X(10).
    05 SCORE OCCURS 10 TIMES PIC 999.
```

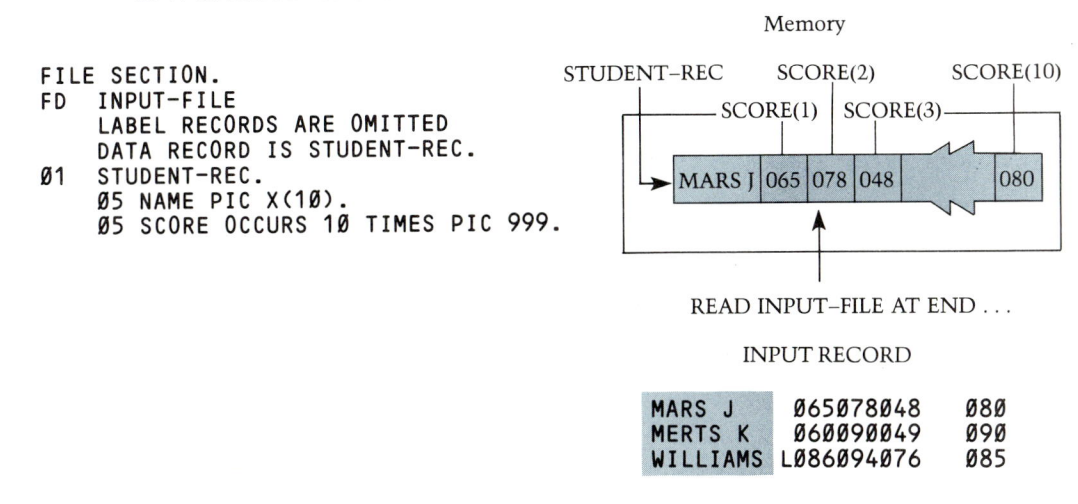

Memory

STUDENT-REC   SCORE(2)   SCORE(10)
        SCORE(1) | SCORE(3)
MARS J | 065 | 078 | 048 | ... | 080

READ INPUT-FILE AT END ...

INPUT RECORD

```
MARS J     065078048    080
MERTS K    060090049    090
WILLIAMS L 086094076    085
```

Table Output

The design of the output line obviously dictates the way in which table elements are to be printed. For example, if table GRADE contains N grades (N < 20), the programmer may wish to print all N grades on one line, or 4 grades per line, or one grade per line.

Case 1: One grade is to be printed per line.

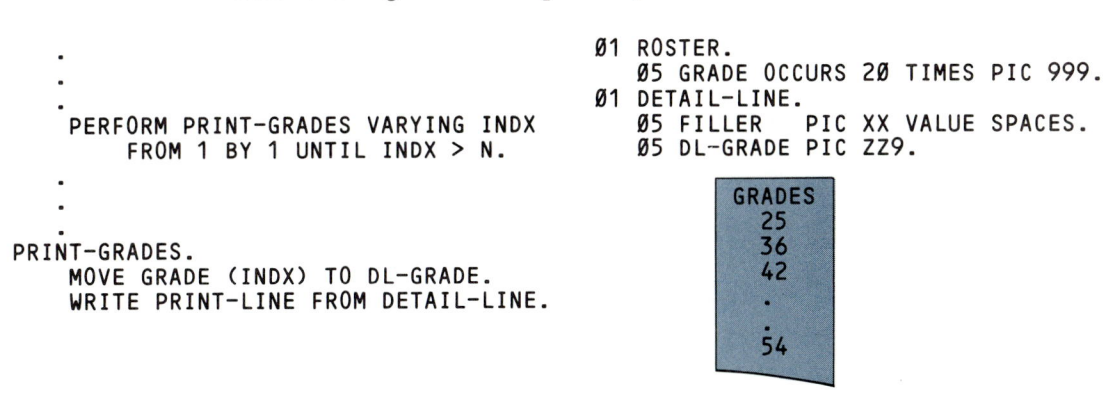

```
        .
        .
        .
    PERFORM PRINT-GRADES VARYING INDX
        FROM 1 BY 1 UNTIL INDX > N.
        .
        .
        .
PRINT-GRADES.
    MOVE GRADE (INDX) TO DL-GRADE.
    WRITE PRINT-LINE FROM DETAIL-LINE.
```

```
01 ROSTER.
   05 GRADE OCCURS 20 TIMES PIC 999.
01 DETAIL-LINE.
   05 FILLER  PIC XX VALUE SPACES.
   05 DL-GRADE PIC ZZ9.
```

```
GRADES
  25
  36
  42
   .
   .
  54
```

Case 2: All N grades are to be printed on one line.

```
    MOVE SPACES TO DETAIL-LINE.
    PERFORM PRINT-GRADES VARYING INDX
        FROM 1 BY 1 UNTIL INDX > N.
    WRITE PRINT-LINE FROM DETAIL-LINE.
        .
        .
        .
PRINT-GRADES.
    MOVE GRADES (INDX) TO DL-GRADE (INDX)..
```

```
01 ROSTER.
   05 GRADE OCCURS 20 TIMES PIC 999.
01 DETAIL-LINE.
   05 FILLER PIC X(2) VALUE SPACES.
   05 DL-GRADE OCCURS 20 TIMES PIC BBBZZ9.
```

3 blank spaces

```
        GRADES
25   36   42 ... 54
```

Note the three blank spaces separating the grades on the output (BBBZZ9). The same result could have been obtained using the following table structure:

```
05 DETAIL-LINE OCCURS 20 TIMES.    or    01 DETAIL-LINE.
   10 FILLER   PIC X(3).                    05 DL-GRADE PIC ZZZZZ9 OCCURS 20.
   10 DL-GRADE PIC ZZ9.
```

Case 3: Four entries are to be printed per line.

```
    MOVE 0 TO COUNTER.                     01 DETAIL-LINE.
    MOVE SPACES TO DETAIL-LINE.               05 GRADE-DETAIL OCCURS 4 TIMES.
    PERFORM PRINT-GRADES VARYING INDX            08 FILLER PIC XX.
       FROM 1 BY 1 UNTIL INDX > NO-GRADES.       08 ITEM   PIC ZZ9.
       .
       .
PRINT-GRADES.
    ADD 1 TO COUNTER.
    MOVE GRADE (INDX) TO ITEM (COUNTER).
    IF COUNTER = 4 OR INDX = NO-GRADES
       WRITE PRINT-LINE FROM DETAIL-LINE
       MOVE 0 TO COUNTER
       MOVE SPACES TO DETAIL-LINE.
```

COUNTER counts up to 4 for the 4 entries per line.
Each successive grade is moved in its position on the line. If 4 grades have been moved into the detail line or there are no more grades in the GRADE table, it is time to print the line. COUNTER is then reset to 0 to prepare for a new output line, which is blanked out in case the next line contains fewer than 4 grades.

The diagram below illustrates the way in which grades are moved into the detail line.

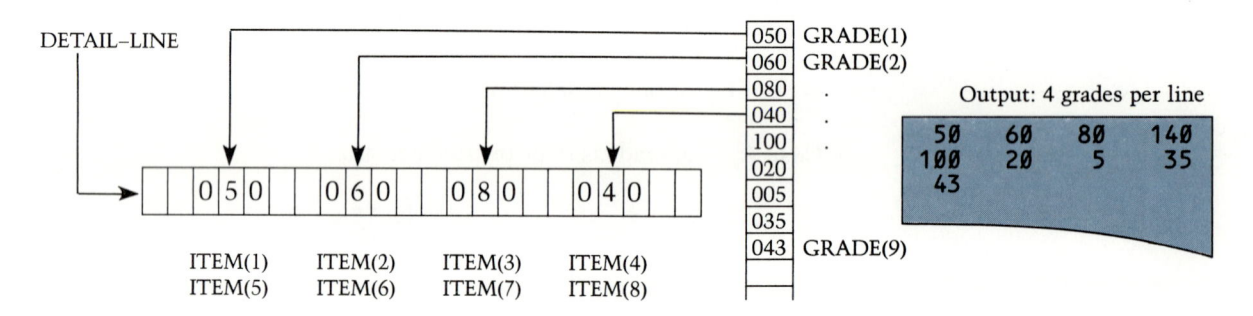

```
DETAIL-LINE                                   050  GRADE(1)
                                              060  GRADE(2)
                                              080
                                              040           Output: 4 grades per line
                                              100            50   60   80   140
     | 050 | 060 | 080 | 040 |                020           100   20    5    35
                                              005            43
                                              035
      ITEM(1) ITEM(2) ITEM(3) ITEM(4)         043  GRADE(9)
      ITEM(5) ITEM(6) ITEM(7) ITEM(8)
```

8-3-12 DO IT NOW

1. Write the COBOL code to add a bonus of 10 points to the 32nd score of a table of 100 scores, if that score is the highest score.

2. Assume SCORE is a table containing 100 scores. What will be the value of TEMP as a result of carrying out the following code?

```
        MOVE 1 TO K.
        PERFORM 100-PROCESS VARYING I FROM 2 BY 1 UNTIL I > 100.
        MOVE SCORE (K) TO TEMP.

    100-PROCESS.
        IF SCORE (I) > SCORE (K)
           MOVE I TO K.
```

3. In method 3 of section 8-3-11 (the READ INTO option), what happens if there are exactly 100 scores? Could an invalid index occur when processing ROSTER(101)?

4. Assume table SALES contains sales figures for seven consecutive days. Write the partial code to print the following:

```
DAYS        SALES

  1         100.50
  2         300.50
  3         400.00
  .
  .
  7         256.50
```

5. Table SOC-SEC contains 100 different social security numbers. Write the partial code to determine whether ITEM (which also contains a social security number) matches any number in the table. Print one of the following messages: MATCH or NO MATCH.

6. A table SCORE contains 100 scores, supposedly arranged in ascending order.

   a. Write the partial code to print *all* scores, then after *all* scores have been printed, write either the message IN SEQUENCE or the message OUT OF SEQUENCE, whichever is appropriate.
   b. Stop printing the scores as soon as a score is found to be out of sequence, but still print the appropriate message, IN SEQUENCE or OUT OF SEQUENCE.

7. Write the code to produce the following tables (generating the numbers in the PROCEDURE division).

```
a. 1 2 3 4 5 6 7 8 9 10      b. 1 2 3 4 5 6 7 8 9 10
   1 2 3 4 5 6 7 8 9            2 3 4 5 6 7 8 9 10
   1 2 3 4 5 6 7 8                3 4 5 6 7 8 9 10
   1 2 3 4 5 6 7                    4 5 6 7 8 9 10
   1 2 3 4 5 6                        5 6 7 8 9 10
   1 2 3 4 5                            6 7 8 9 10
   1 2 3 4                                7 8 9 10
   1 2 3                                    8 9 10
   1 2                                        9 10
   1                                           10
```

8. A table contains 27 numbers that can be either positive or negative. Write a program to print the positive numbers and the negative numbers 4 per line as follows:

```
-14  -12  -34  -56
 -2   -6  -45  -67
          .
          .
-34  -23

+12  +56  +90  +21
+56  +89   +6   +4
          .
          .
+78
```

SELECTED ANSWERS

2. TEMP contains the largest score and K is the position of the largest score.

6. b.
```
        MOVE 1 TO I.
        MOVE 'IN SEQUENCE' TO MESSG.
        PERFORM TASK UNTIL MESSG = 'OUT OF SEQUENCE' OR I > 99.
        DISPLAY MESSG.
    TASK.
        IF SCORE (I) > SCORE (I + 1)
            MOVE 'OUT OF SEQUENCE' TO MESSG.
        ADD 1 TO I.
```

7. a.
```
        PERFORM LOAD-1 VARYING I FROM 1 BY 1 UNTIL I > 10.
        PERFORM XYZ    VARYING I FROM 10 BY -1 UNTIL I < 1.
        STOP RUN.
    LOAD-1.
        MOVE I TO NUMB (I).
    XYZ.
        WRITE PRINT-LINE FROM DETAIL-LINE.
        MOVE ZEROS TO NUMB (I).
```

8.
```
        PERFORM PROC VARYING I              WORKING-STORAGE SECTION.
            FROM 1 BY 1 UNTIL I > 27.       77 M PIC 9  VALUE 0.
        PERFORM POS-WRITE VARYING I         77 K PIC 99 VALUE 0.
            FROM 1 BY 1 UNTIL I > K.        77 L PIC 99 VALUE 0.
        MOVE SPACES TO PRINT-LINE.          77 I PIC 99.
        WRITE PRINT-LINE.                   01 TABS.
        MOVE L TO K.                            05 A OCCURS 27 TIMES PIC 99.
        MOVE NEG-TAB TO PLUS-TAB.           01 DETAIL-LINE.
        MOVE 0 TO M.                            05 FILLER PIC X(5) VALUE SPACES.
        PERFORM POS-WRITE VARYING I             05 NUMB OCCURS 4 PIC -(4)9.
            FROM 1 BY 1 UNTIL I > K.        01 PLUS-TAB.
                                                05 POS OCCURS 16 PIC S99.
    PROC.                                   01 NEG-TAB.
        IF A(I) > 0                             05 NEG OCCURS 16 PIC S99.
            ADD 1 TO K
            MOVE A (I) TO POS (K)
        ELSE
            ADD 1 TO L
            MOVE A (I) TO NEG (L).
    POS-WRITE.
        ADD 1 TO M.
        MOVE POS (I) TO NUMB (M).
        IF M = 4 OR I = K
            MOVE 0 TO M
            WRITE PRINT-LINE FROM DETAIL-LINE
            MOVE SPACES TO DETAIL-LINE.
```

8-4 TWO-DIMENSIONAL TABLES

8-4-1 GENERAL BACKGROUND

Much of the information that we deal with in our everyday lives is arranged in rows and columns. In a movie house, in an airplane, or in a typical classroom, seats are identified by their row and column (aisle) positions. For some of us, looking up our taxes means reading a number at the intersection of an income level row and a number of dependents column. Chess boards and teachers' grade notebooks are also examples of two-dimensional tables.

The power of a two-dimensional table lies in its "lookup" procedure, which allows us to access any entry in the table directly, without searching through all the table entries. We access the table entries by specifying the row and column. For example, in the sales tax deduction table shown below, the deduction allowed a family with four children and an income of $8,000 to $8,999 is $117.

	INCOME TABLE	\multicolumn{6}{c}{NUMBER OF CHILDREN}
		1	2	3	4	5	6
	$ 0,000.	35.	48.	49.	59.	59.	60.
	$ 3,000.	44.	58.	61.	71.	73.	75.
	$ 4,000.	51.	68.	72.	82.	85.	88.
	$ 5,000.	58.	76.	82.	91.	97.	100.
	$ 6,000.	64.	84.	91.	100.	107.	112.
	$ 7,000.	70.	92.	100.	109.	117.	123.
7th entry →	$ 8,000. →	76.	99.	108.	(117.)	127.	133.
	$ 9,000.	81.	106.	116.	124.	136.	143.
	$10,000.	86.	112.	124.	131.	145.	153.
	$11,000.	91.	118.	132.	138.	154.	163.
	$12,000.	96.	124.	139.	145.	162.	172.
	$13,000.	101.	130.	146.	151.	170.	181.
	$14,000.	106.	136.	153.	157.	178.	190.
	$15,000.	110.	141.	160.	163.	186.	198.
	$16,000.	114.	146.	167.	169.	194.	206.
	$17,000.	118.	151.	173.	175.	201.	214.
	$18,000.	122.	156.	179.	181.	208.	222.
	$19,000.	126.	161.	185.	186.	215.	230.

Once the correct income entry has been located in the INCOME table (position 7 for $8,000), we simply look up the figure at the 7th row and 4th column of the table, i.e., we use the number of children to identify the proper column directly (with no IF statements). This table is an example of a two-dimensional table consisting of 18 rows and 6 columns; entries in the table can be successively accessed by varying the row and/or column subscript.

8-4-2 INTERNAL REPRESENTATION

Consider the following class roster where each horizontal line consists of a student name and three test scores.

	TEST 1	TEST 2	TEST 3
ADAMS	78	44	94
BORING	58	66	84
CATTIX	49	58	64
STOUT	59	68	91

Here the data is physically arranged in rows and columns. This is another example of a two-dimensional table from which it is easy to retrieve information. For example, to determine STOUT's score on the second test, we simply look up the entry found at the intersection of the 4th row and the 2nd column. If we name the score table SCORE, then each table entry can be identified by the name of the table and its row and column. For example:

SCORE (4, 1) = 59 and SCORE (2, 3) = 84

Note that the first subscript always refers to the row, while the second subscript refers to the column.

In the computer's memory, however, two-dimensional tables are arranged in linear fashion so that we cannot really talk about rows and columns. We can still think about the concept of rows and columns, but they are not really necessary to our understanding of two-dimensional tables. It is just as easy to visualize the class roster as the following arrangement of information:

```
ADAMS         BORING         CATTIX         STOUT
78  44  94    58  66  84    49  58  64    59  68  91
```

With this linear arrangement, we can still retrieve STOUT's second score easily—we simply look up the 4th name entry and its 2nd score, and in the process we never think about rows or columns! In the linear arrangement, each name occurs four times, and for each name a score occurs three times. This leads, in a very natural way, to the following table declaration: (leading 0's are left out)

```
01 ROSTER-RECORD.
   05 STUDENT-RECORD OCCURS 4 TIMES
      10 NAME PIC X(06).
      10 SCORE OCCURS 3 TIMES PIC 999
```

ADAMS	BORING	CATTIX	STOUT
78 44 94	58 66 84	49 58 64	59 68 91

This structure can be interpreted as follows:

- There are four student records: STUDENT–RECORD (1), STUDENT–RECORD (2), ...

- Each student record consists of two items:

  1. a name, and
  2. three test scores.

With such a table structure, we can talk about NAME (1), NAME (2), ..., but we cannot talk about SCORE (3), since there are many score 3's—one for ADAMS, one for BORING, et cetera. We need to pinpoint more accurately which score 3 we are talking about (is it the first student's score, the second student's score, ..., ?)—and the only way we can do that is to use another subscript, as in:

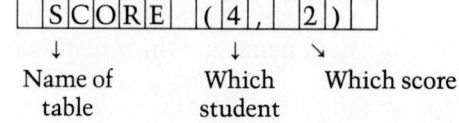

SCORE (4, 2)

↓ Name of table   ↓ Which student   ↘ Which score

Note that the first subscript always corresponds to the first OCCURS clause (it can vary from 1 to 4) and the second subscript to the second OCCURS clause (it varies from 1 to 3).

The reader probably expected two subscripts for SCORE anyway (at least from a syntax point of view)! After all, SCORE is a subordinate item of STUDENT-RECORD, which OCCURS, so it qualifies for at least one subscript; but in addition SCORE itself OCCURS, hence another subscript. The memory arrangement corresponding to this table structure is shown in Figure 8-8. Note that only SCORE is a two-dimensional table.

Just as in the case of one-dimensional tables, it is very important that the subscripts of a two-dimensional table stay within the size limits declared in the various OCCURS statements.

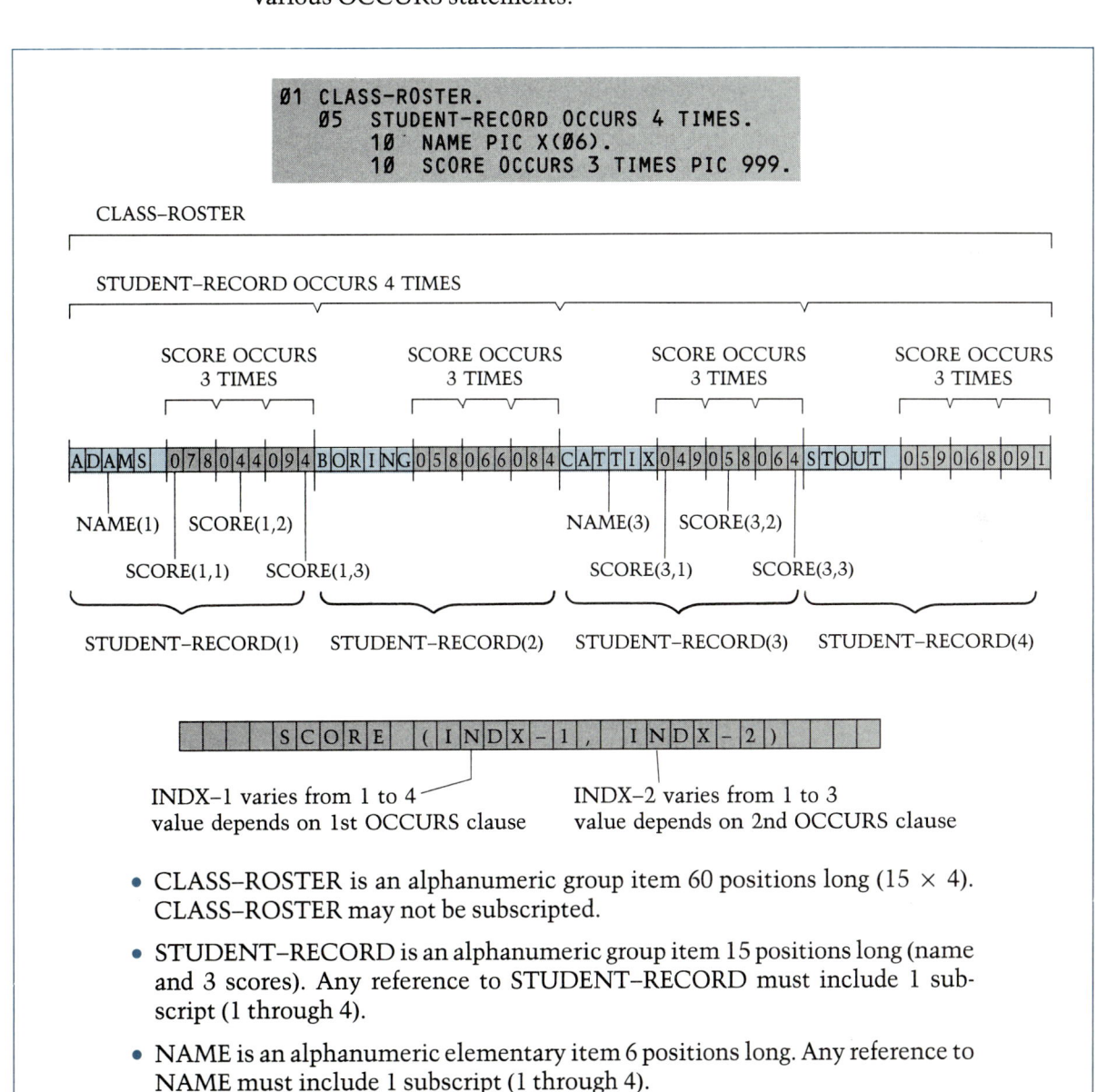

```
01 CLASS-ROSTER.
    05  STUDENT-RECORD OCCURS 4 TIMES.
        10  NAME PIC X(06).
        10  SCORE OCCURS 3 TIMES PIC 999.
```

CLASS-ROSTER

STUDENT-RECORD OCCURS 4 TIMES

SCORE OCCURS 3 TIMES | SCORE OCCURS 3 TIMES | SCORE OCCURS 3 TIMES | SCORE OCCURS 3 TIMES

ADAMS 078044094 BORING 058066084 CATTIX 049058064 STOUT 059068091

NAME(1) | SCORE(1,2) | NAME(3) | SCORE(3,2)
SCORE(1,1) SCORE(1,3) | SCORE(3,1) SCORE(3,3)

STUDENT-RECORD(1) STUDENT-RECORD(2) STUDENT-RECORD(3) STUDENT-RECORD(4)

SCORE (INDX-1, INDX-2)

INDX-1 varies from 1 to 4 — value depends on 1st OCCURS clause

INDX-2 varies from 1 to 3 — value depends on 2nd OCCURS clause

- CLASS-ROSTER is an alphanumeric group item 60 positions long (15 × 4). CLASS-ROSTER may not be subscripted.

- STUDENT-RECORD is an alphanumeric group item 15 positions long (name and 3 scores). Any reference to STUDENT-RECORD must include 1 subscript (1 through 4).

- NAME is an alphanumeric elementary item 6 positions long. Any reference to NAME must include 1 subscript (1 through 4).

- SCORE is a numeric picture field 3 positions long. Any reference to SCORE must include 2 subscripts.

FIGURE 8-8
A TWO-DIMENSIONAL TABLE STRUCTURE

Alternate Table Structure

Another way to declare the table structure shown in Figure 8–8 is:

```
01 CLASS-ROSTER.
   05 NAME OCCURS 4 TIMES PIC X(06).
   05 STUDENT-SCORES OCCURS 4 TIMES.
      10 SCORE OCCURS 3 TIMES PIC 999.
```

In this structure the names occur first, followed by all scores. The memory arrangement would be as follows:

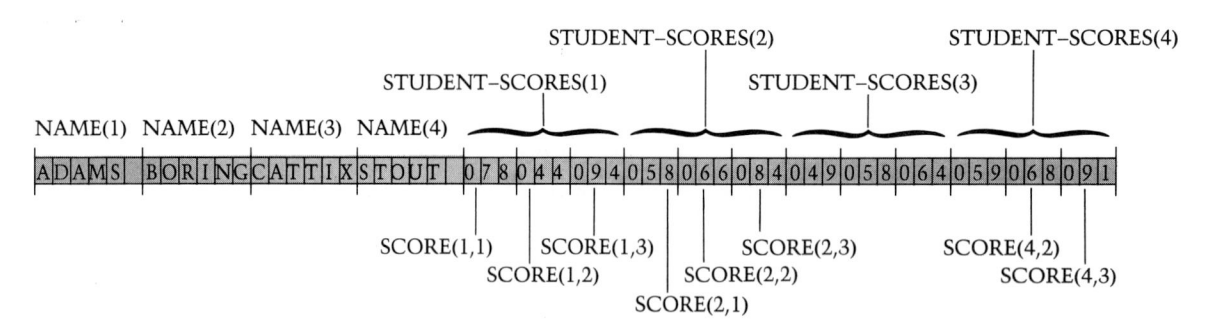

```
                                          STUDENT-SCORES(2)              STUDENT-SCORES(4)
                      STUDENT-SCORES(1)              STUDENT-SCORES(3)
NAME(1) NAME(2) NAME(3) NAME(4)
|ADAMS|BORING|CATTIX|STOUT|078044094058066084049058064059068091|
                        SCORE(1,1)   SCORE(1,3)   SCORE(2,3)   SCORE(4,2)
                             SCORE(1,2)   SCORE(2,2)        SCORE(4,3)
                                     SCORE(2,1)
```

Note that STUDENT–SCORES (1) is an *alphanumeric* field 9 characters long (078044094).

8-4-3 SUBSCRIPTS

The rules on subscripts for two-dimensional tables are the same as the rules for one-dimensional tables (see section 8-2-2). The following coding considerations must be observed:

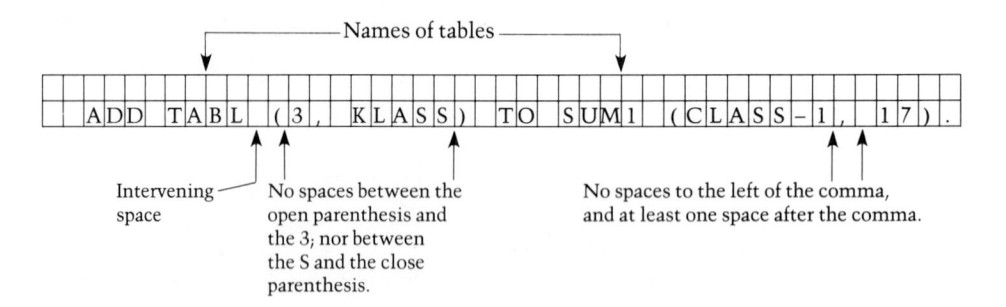

```
                        ──── Names of tables ────
                        ↓                       ↓
        |ADD|TABL|(3,|KLASS)|TO|SUM1|(CLASS-1,|17)|.
                ↑    ↑                        ↑  ↑
         Intervening  No spaces between the   No spaces to the left of the comma,
         space        open parenthesis and    and at least one space after the comma.
                      the 3; nor between
                      the S and the close
                      parenthesis.
```

Note: In 1974 ANSI COBOL, spaces to the left and to the right of the parenthesis are not required, and subscripts may be simple arithmetic expressions. Refer to your technical COBOL manual for special features.

8-4-4 MORE TABLE STRUCTURES

EXAMPLE 1 A two-dimensional table is used by a very small company (10 employees) to store personnel data, as follows:

ONE- AND TWO- DIMENSIONAL TABLES

NAME	MONTHLY BASE PAY	MEDICAL DEDUCTIONS	INCOME TAX PERCENTAGE	PENSION PLAN PERCENTAGE
ADAMS	1000.75	128.00	.243	.045
BILLS	978.00	98.00	.165	.010
.	.	.	.	.
.	.	.	.	.
↓	↓	↓	↓	↓
NAME(2)	EMPLOYEE–DATA(2,1)	EMPLOYEE–DATA(2,2)	EMPLOYEE–DATA(2,3)	EMPLOYEE–DATA(2,4)

Let us design a COBOL table structure to capture this information:

```
01 PERSONNEL-DATA.
   05 NAME OCCURS 10 TIMES PIC X(15).
   05 EMPLOYEE-RECORDS OCCURS 10 TIMES.
      10 EMPLOYEE-DATA OCCURS 4 TIMES PIC 9999V9999.
```

With this table we can then compute the net pay of employee number 6, as follows (our computation includes 7.05% social security withholding):

```
COMPUTE TAX-PERCENTAGE = .0705 + EMPLOYEE-DATA (6, 3) + EMPLOYEE-DATA (6, 4).
COMPUTE NET-PAY = EMPLOYEE-DATA (6, 1) * (1 - TAX-PERCENTAGE) - EMPLOYEE-DATA (6, 2).
```

EXAMPLE 2 Substantially more complex arrangements can be declared as follows:

NAME	MATH		AVG	ENGLISH			AVG	TOT-AVG
MARTIN	20	40	30.0	50	60	70	60.0	45.0
SHEET	10	50	30.0	40	50	60	50.0	40.0
LONG	70	80	75.0	70	80	90	80.0	77.5
SMITH	10	20	15.0	90	90	90	90.0	52.5

This table can be declared as follows:

```
01 GRADE-RECORD.
   05 STUDENT-RECORD OCCURS 4 TIMES.
      10 NAME           PIC X(20).
      10 MATH-GRADES    PIC 999 OCCURS 2 TIMES.
      10 MATH-AVG       PIC 999V9.
      10 ENGLISH-GRADES PIC 999 OCCURS 3 TIMES.
      10 ENGLISH-AV     PIC 999V9.
      10 TOT-AVG        PIC 999V9.
```

GRADE-RECORD refers to a string of 188 characters.
Total length = 4(20 + 2(3) + 4 + 3(3) + 4 + 4) = 4 × 47.
STUDENT-RECORD(2) refers to 47 characters.
NAME(3) has value LONG.
MATH-GRADES(3,2) has numerical value 80.
MATH-AV(4) has numerical value 15.
ENGLISH-GRADES(2,3) has value 60.
ENGLISH-AVG(3) has value 80.
TOT-AVG(2) has value 40.

EXAMPLE 3 Assume the following table represents the volume of shares transacted on the New York Stock Exchange and on the American Stock Exchange for a given 4-week period.

	DAYS									
	1		2		3		4		5	
	NYSE	AMEX	NYSE	AMEX	NYSE	AMEX	NYSE	AMEX	NYSE	AMEX
Week 1	31	15	28	17	33	9	22	14	28	16
Week 2	28	17	14	15	31	11	23	15	30	14
Week 3	25	14	20	18	30	12	25	16	29	11
Week 4	28	17	21	17	31	14	28	12	21	13

Such a table can be declared as a two-dimensional table, as follows:

```
01 MONTH-VOLUME.               MONTH-VOLUME refers to a string of 80 characters.
   02 WEEK OCCURS 4 TIMES.     WEEK(3) refers to 20 characters (3rd row).
      05 DAYS OCCURS 5 TIMES.  DAYS(1,1) refers to the character string 3115.
         10 NYSE PIC 99.       NYSE(2,3) refers to the numerical value 31.
         10 AMEX PIC 99.
```

8-4-5 DO IT NOW

1. Determine whether the following table declarations are valid or invalid; if valid, specify the number of storage positions allocated to each table. Also illustrate the sequence of table elements by name and position in the internal representation of the table.

   a. ```
      01 CLASS-ROSTER.
          05 NAME OCCURS 4 TIMES PIC X(10).
              10 SCORE OCCURS 3 TIMES PIC 999.
      ```

   b. ```
      05  A OCCURS 2 TIMES.
          10  B OCCURS 3 TIMES PIC 9.
          10  C OCCURS 2 TIMES PIC X.
          10  X PIC Z.
      ```

   c. ```
      01 TAB.
          05 A OCCURS 3.
              06 B OCCURS 9 PIC $$,$$$.99.
      ```

   d. ```
      01  4-TAB.
          05  1-EL OCCURS 3.
              07  2-EL OCCURS 5.
                  10  A PIC 9.
                  10  B PIC X(5).
                  10  C PIC ----.
      ```

2. Given the code:
   ```
   01 TAB1.
      10 X OCCURS 10.
         15 Y OCCURS 5 PIC XXX.
         15 Z OCCURS 6 PIC AA.
         15 FILLER     PIC XX.
         15 W OCCURS 4.
            20 A PIC XX.
            20 B PIC 9V9.
   ```

a. Are references to W(3), B(2), Y(1), X(11), W(4,9), Z(9,4), Y(5,10) legal?
b. Identify the number of storage positions reserved for each of the following: TAB1, X(1), Y(5,3), B(5,4).

3. Consider the following record definition:

```
01 TABL.
    05 SCORE OCCURS 4 TIMES.
        10 GRADE PIC 99.
```

Do GRADE(1) and SCORE(1) refer to the same memory positions? Can they be used interchangeably?

4. Do the following pairs of record description entries define similar table structures? Identify differences within each pair.

a.
```
01 TABL.
    05 REGION OCCURS 20 PIC 9(4).
    05 DEPT   OCCURS 5  PIC 99.
    05 EMP    OCCURS 99 PIC X(10).
```
```
01 TABL.
    05 REGION OCCURS 20 PIC 9(4).
    06 DEPT   OCCURS 5  PIC 99.
    07 EMP    OCCURS 99 PIC X(10).
```

b.
```
01 TABL.
    05 CLASS OCCURS 20 TIMES.
        10 A PIC A.
        10 B PIC A.
        10 C PIC A.
```
```
01 TABL.
    10 A OCCURS 20 PIC A.
    10 B OCCURS 20 PIC A.
    10 C OCCURS 20 PIC A.
```

c.
```
01 GRADE-ROSTER.
    05 STUDENT OCCURS 8.
        10 NAME  PIC A(10).
        10 SCORE PIC 999.
```
```
01 STUDENT-NAMES.
    05 NAME OCCURS 8 PIC A(10).
01 STUDENT-SCORES.
    05 SCORE OCCURS 8 PIC 999.
```

d.
```
01 A.
    05 B OCCURS 5.
        10 C OCCURS 5 PIC 99.
```
```
01 X.
    05 B OCCURS 5 PIC 99.
01 Z.
    05 C OCCURS 5 PIC 99.
```
```
01 A.
    05 B OCCURS 5.
        10 D OCCURS 5.
            15 C PIC 99.
```

5. Find any errors in the following codes:

a.
```
77 ITEM PIC 9(9).
77 TEM REDEFINES ITEM PIC A(9).
```

b.
```
77 TAB OCCURS 5 TIMES PIC A(4).
```

c.
```
01 DETAIL-LINE.
    05 FILLER PIC X(17) VALUE SPACES.
    05 DL-IT OCCURS 5 TIMES.
        10 DL-TYPE PIC A(6).
        10 FILLER  PIC XXX VALUE SPACES.
        10 DL-NO   PIC 99.
```

d.
```
01 LIST.
    05 SUB-LIST OCCURS THREE TIMES PIC 9.
    05 EMP-NO   OCCURS 10 TIMES PIC 9(4).
    05 DEP-NO   OCCURS 18 TIMES PIC 9(7).
```

e.
```
01 PLANT OCCURS 4 TIMES PIC 999.
```

f. 05 SCHOOL OCCURS 3 TIMES PIC X(10).
       10 DEPT OCCURS 8 TIMES.
          15 HEAD   PIC A(10).
          15 TEACHER PIC X(8).

g. 01 PART.
       05 N OCCURS 2 TIMES.
          10 N (1)   PIC 99.
          10 FILLER   PIC XXX.
          10 N (2)   PIC 9.

h. 01 ROSTER.
       05 FILLER PIC 99.
       05 TAB OCCURS 4 TIMES.
       05 R-PAY PIC ZZ.99.

i. 01 TAB.
       05 A (1) PIC XX VALUE "I".
       05 A (2) PIC XX VALUE "B".
       05 A (3) PIC XX VALUE "C".

SELECTED ANSWERS

1. a. Invalid; NAME is a group item and cannot have a picture field.
   c. Valid; 243 positions.

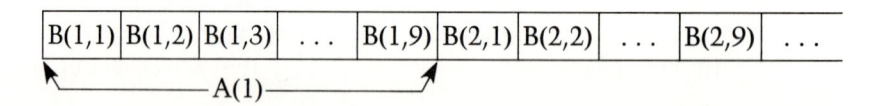

   | B(1,1) | B(1,2) | B(1,3) | ... | B(1,9) | B(2,1) | B(2,2) | ... | B(2,9) | ... |

   ←————— A(1) —————→

   d. Valid; 150 positions.

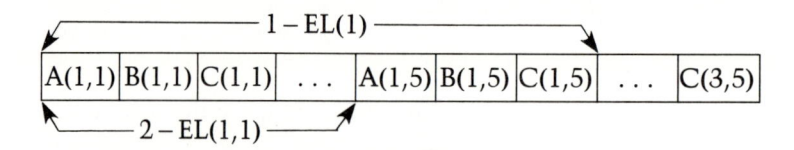

   ←————— 1–EL(1) —————→

   | A(1,1) | B(1,1) | C(1,1) | ... | A(1,5) | B(1,5) | C(1,5) | ... | C(3,5) |

   ←—— 2–EL(1,1) ——→

2. a. Invalid; W is a two-dimensional table.
      Invalid; B is a two-dimensional table.
      Invalid; Y is a two-dimensional table.
      X(11) is invalid; size of table X is 10.
      W(4,9) is invalid. However, W(9,4) is valid.
      Z(9,4) is valid.
      Y(5,10) is invalid. However, Y(10,5) is valid.
   b. Length of TAB1 = 450.
      Length of X(1)   = 45.
      Length of Y(5,3) = 3.
      Length of B(5,4) = 2.

3. GRADE(1) and SCORE(1) refer to the same memory positions. However, SCORE is alphanumeric, whereas GRADE is numeric.

4. a. The second structure is invalid; both REGION and DEPT should have no PICTURE clauses.

b. In both cases A, B, and C are tables of size 20. TABL in either case refers to 60 positions. In the first structure CLASS is also a table.
c. Similar structures for NAME and SCORE.

5. a. Valid.
   b. No OCCURS in 77 levels.
   c. No VALUE clause allowed in a table entry.
   d. THREE is not allowed.
   e. No OCCURS verb at the 01 level.
   f. Invalid PICTURE clause for SCHOOL since SCHOOL is a group item.

8-4-6 PROCESSING TWO-DIMENSIONAL TABLES

Two-dimensional tables can be processed in essentially the same way as one-dimensional tables. Since two subscripts are needed to identify a particular table entry, we will generally need two PERFORM VARYING statements to process a two-dimensional table: one PERFORM will control the row subscript while the other PERFORM will control the column subscript.

EXAMPLE 1: Row Sum Computations. Assume, for example, that we have a table SCORE with 3 rows and 4 columns and that we want to store the sum of each row into STUDENT(1), STUDENT(2) and STUDENT(3):

	TEST1	TEST2	TEST3	TEST4
SCORE:	80	70	60	20
	40	20	60	50
	90	20	50	80

STUDENT(1) = 80 + 70 + 60 + 20 = 230
STUDENT(2) = 40 + 20 + 60 + 50 = 170
STUDENT(3) = 90 + 20 + 50 + 80 = 240

One method is to process the table by rows; i.e., we compute the sum of the first row, then the sum of the second row, and so on. First we fix the row index to 1 and let the column index vary from 1 to 4 to capture the elements of the first row. We then repeat the procedure for row index = 2, and again for row index = 3.

```
        PERFORM 200-STUDENT-ROW-SUM VARYING STUDENT-NO
            FROM 1 BY 1 UNTIL STUDENT-NO IS GREATER THAN 3.

    200-STUDENT-ROW-SUM.
        MOVE 0 TO ROW-SUM.
        PERFORM 300-COLUMN-TESTS VARYING TEST
            FROM 1 BY 1 UNTIL TEST IS GREATER THAN 4.
        MOVE ROW-SUM TO STUDENT (STUDENT-NO).

    300-COLUMN-TESTS.
        ADD SCORE (STUDENT-NO, TEST) TO ROW-SUM.
```

EXAMPLE 2: Column Interchange. Another illustration will help clarify the subscript mechanism of a two-dimensional table. Suppose we want to interchange column 3 and column 17 of a table TABL (17 rows and 23 columns). This interchange procedure can be accomplished by moving the first element of column 3 into a temporary area TEMP, then moving the first element of column 17 into the vacated column 3 position and, finally, moving the saved value in TEMP into position 1 of column 17. This process is then repeated with the 2nd, 3rd, . . . elements of both columns. The code to perform the interchange procedure is as follows:

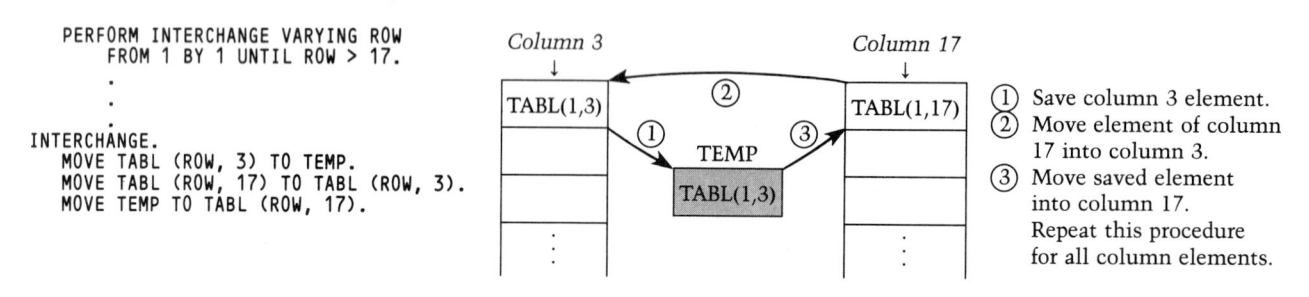

```
PERFORM INTERCHANGE VARYING ROW
    FROM 1 BY 1 UNTIL ROW > 17.
     .
     .
     .
INTERCHANGE.
    MOVE TABL (ROW, 3) TO TEMP.
    MOVE TABL (ROW, 17) TO TABL (ROW, 3).
    MOVE TEMP TO TABL (ROW, 17).
```

① Save column 3 element.
② Move element of column 17 into column 3.
③ Move saved element into column 17.
Repeat this procedure for all column elements.

EXAMPLE 3: Suppose that we want to use the table shown below to determine:

1. Total AMEX sales for the 4-week period.
2. The number of days in which the NYSE volume fell below 31 million shares.
3. Total volume of shares during the third week.
4. The total Friday volume of shares for both boards combined for the four-week period.

	NYSE	AMEX	NYSE	AMEX	NYSE	AMEX	NYSE	AMEX	NYSE	AMEX
Week 1	31	15	28	17	33	9	22	14	28	16
Week 2	28	17	14	15	31	11	23	15	30	14
Week 3	25	14	20	18	30	12	25	16	29	11
Week 4	28	17	21	17	31	14	28	13	21	13

Table declaration

```
01 MONTH-VOLUME.
   05 WEEK OCCURS 4 TIMES.
      10 DAYS OCCURS 5 TIMES.
         15 NYSE PIC 999.
         15 AMEX PIC 999.
```

To compute the AMEX sales for the 4-week period, we need to compute:
AMEX(WEEK,1) + AMEX(WEEK,2) + AMEX(WEEK,3) + AMEX(WEEK,4) + AMEX(WEEK,5)
for values of WEEK initially equal to 1, then 2, then 3, then 4. Hence we need one PERFORM statement to control the row (WEEK) subscript, as follows:

```
1       MOVE 0 TO TOT-AMEX-SHARES.
2       PERFORM ROW-SEARCH VARYING WEEK FROM 1 BY 1 UNTIL WEEK > 4.

3  ROW-SEARCH.
4       COMPUTE ROW-SUM = AMEX (WEEK, 1) + AMEX (WEEK, 2) +
                 AMEX (WEEK, 3) + AMEX (WEEK, 4) + AMEX (WEEK, 5).
5       ADD ROW-SUM TO TOT-AMEX-SHARES.
```

Note that line 4 is the sum of the entries AMEX(WEEK,DAY) as DAY varies from 1 to 5, so that lines 4 and 5 can be rewritten with a PERFORM structure:

ONE- AND TWO- DIMENSIONAL TABLES

```
1    MOVE 0 TO TOT-AMEX-SHARES.
2    PERFORM ROW-SEARCH VARYING WEEK FROM 1 BY 1 UNTIL WEEK > 4.
3 ROW-SEARCH.
4    COMPUTE ROW-SUM = AMEX (WEEK, 1) + AMEX (WEEK, 2) +
              AMEX (WEEK, 3) + AMEX (WEEK, 4) + AMEX (WEEK, 5).
5    ADD ROW-SUM TO TOT-AMEX-SHARES.
```

can be written as

```
PERFORM DAY-SEARCH VARYING DAY
    FROM 1 BY 1 UNTIL DAY > 5.
DAY-SEARCH.
    ADD AMEX (WEEK, DAY) TO TOT-AMEX-SHARES.
```

The remaining parts of the problem follow essentially the same approach as used for the first part of the problem. We will now expand the code just written to include the last three parts of the problem. Two methods are possible. The first involves processing the table by rows as we did in part 1, i.e., for a fixed row (WEEK = 1, for instance) the column subscript DAY is varied from 1 to 5. This approach suggests two PERFORM statements; the outer PERFORM statement varies the WEEK from 1 to 4 while the inner PERFORM varies the DAY from 1 to 5 for each value of the WEEK. The reader should keep in mind that a row actually consists of column elements, i.e., to move along a row means to fix the row subscript and vary the column index from 1 to N (N being the number of elements in each row, i.e., the number of columns).

Row processing approach:

```
MOVE 0 TO TOT-AMEX-SHARES.
MOVE 0 TO NYSE-BELOW-31.
MOVE 0 TO FRIDAY-SALES.
MOVE 0 TO 3RD-WEEK-SALES.
PERFORM ROW-SEARCH VARYING WEEK
    FROM 1 BY 1 UNTIL WEEK > 4.

ROW-SEARCH.
    ADD NYSE (WEEK, 5), AMEX (WEEK, 5)
        TO FRIDAY-SALES.
    PERFORM DAY-SEARCH VARYING DAY
        FROM 1 BY 1 UNTIL DAY > 5.
DAY-SEARCH.
    ADD AMEX (WEEK, DAY) TO TOT-AMEX-SHARES.
    IF NYSE (WEEK, DAY) LESS THAN 31
        ADD 1 TO NYSE-BELOW-31.
    IF WEEK = 3
        ADD NYSE (3, DAY), AMEX (3, DAY)
            TO 3RD-WEEK-SALES.
```

Total AMEX sales for 4-week period.
Number of days for which NYSE shares < 31 million.
4 consecutive Fridays' total sales (both boards).
Total volume during 3rd week.

Compute total Friday sales over a 4-week period. Column subscript is set to 5 to indicate Friday (5th day).

Compute total AMEX shares during 4-week period.
Count NYSE sales below 31 million.

Compute 3rd week's total sales.

Column processing approach

When the table is processed by columns, the outer PERFORM statement varies the columns from 1 to 5, and the inner PERFORM varies the rows from 1 to 4.

```
PERFORM COLUMN-SEARCH VARYING DAY
    FROM 1 BY 1 UNTIL DAY > 5.
         .
         .
COLUMN-SEARCH.
    ADD NYSE (3, DAY), AMEX (3, DAY) TO 3RD-WEEK-SALES.
    PERFORM VERTICAL-SEARCH VARYING WEEK
        FROM 1 BY 1 UNTIL WEEK > 4.
VERTICAL-SEARCH.
    ADD AMEX (WEEK, DAY) TO TOT-AMEX-SHARES.
    IF NYSE (WEEK, DAY) LESS THAN 31
        ADD 1 TO NYSE-BELOW-31.
    IF DAY = 5
        ADD NYSE (WEEK, 5), AMEX (WEEK, 5) TO FRIDAY-SALES.
```

8-4-7 INPUT/OUTPUT AND INITIALIZATION OF TWO-DIMENSIONAL TABLES

In the ensuing discussion, the following two-dimensional table SCORE will be used for illustration:

```
01 ROSTER-TABLE.
   05 STUDENT-RECORD OCCURS 3 TIMES.
      10 SCORE OCCURS 5 TIMES PIC 99.
```

```
          SCORE
11  12  13  14  15
21  22  23  24  25
31  32  33  34  35
```

Initialization through the REDEFINES

Suppose we want to load SCORE with the data shown above. If the data in SCORE is a table of constants that never changes from one program application to the next, the user may be tempted to define these values in the WORKING-STORAGE area and use the REDEFINES clause to provide a name to each entry as follows:

```
01 CONSTANT-VALUES.
   05 FILLER PIC 9(10) VALUE 1112131415.
   05 FILLER PIC 9(10) VALUE 2122232425.
   05 FILLER PIC 9(10) VALUE 3132333435.

01 TABLE-OF-CONSTANTS REDEFINES CONSTANT-VALUES.
   05 STUDENT-RECORD OCCURS 3 TIMES.
      10 SCORE OCCURS 5 TIMES.
```

A PICTURE of X(10) could have been used just as well as 9(10).

SCORE is now a 2-dimensional table containing the values specified in the group data structure CONSTANT-VALUES.

STUDENT-RECORD(1) refers to the alphanumeric string 1112131415. Note that CONSTANT-VALUES could have been defined as a 30-character string:

```
01 CONSTANT-VALUES PIC X(30) VALUE '111213141521222324253132333435'.
```

Initialization through the READ Statement

A two-dimensional table can be loaded in memory by reading data into successive rows, one after the other, or in column fashion, one column after the other. The key factor in loading a two-dimensional table is knowing or deciding the order in which the data entries are arranged in the input file. There are many possible input data layouts for the SCORE table, for example

1. 11 12 13 14 15
   21 22 23 24 25   Each input record represents one row of the table.
   31 32 33 34 35   There are three records in all.

2. 11 21 31
   12 22 32
   13 23 33   Each input record represents one column of the table.
   14 24 34   There are five records in all.
   15 25 35

3. 111213141521222324253132333435   All rows are typed on one record.

4. 112131122232132333142434152535   All columns are typed on one record.

ONE- AND TWO- DIMENSIONAL TABLES

The physical arrangement of the input data obviously dictates the way in which the table is to be loaded. The following coding segments will load the SCORE table with data layouts 1 and 2 above.

Case 1
Table SCORE

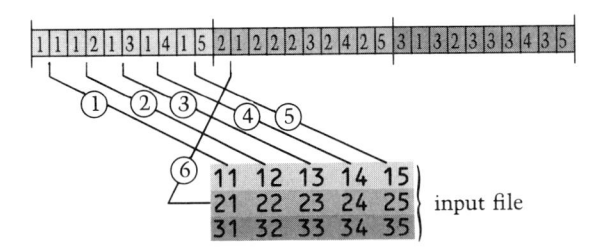

```
01  GRADE-RECORD.
    05 GRADE OCCURS 5 TIMES PIC 99.

    READ SCORE-FILE INTO GRADE-RECORD
        AT END MOVE 1 TO WS-EOF.
    PERFORM LOAD-TABLE VARYING STUDENT
        FROM 1 BY 1 UNTIL WS-EOF = 1.
        .
        .
LOAD-TABLE.
    PERFORM STUDENT-ROW VARYING TEST
        FROM 1 BY 1 UNTIL TEST > 5.
    READ SCORE-FILE INTO GRADE-RECORD
        AT END MOVE 1 TO WS-EOF.
STUDENT-ROW.
    MOVE GRADE (TEST) TO SCORE (STUDENT, TEST).
```

The grades are recorded in row fashion on each data record. Altogether there are three input records. When STUDENT is 1, GRADE(TEST) will be moved in SCORE(1,TEST) as TEST varies from 1 to 5. This means the first five test scores on the first record will be transferred into the first row of SCORE.

Case 2
Table SCORE

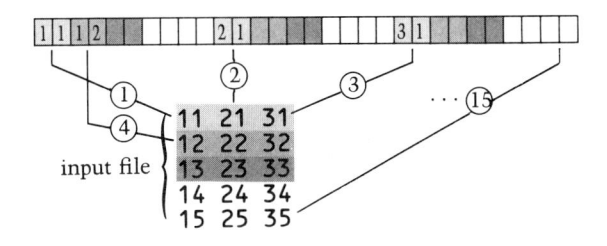

```
01  GRADE-RECORD.
    05 GRADE OCCURS 3 TIMES PIC 99.

    READ SCORE-FILE INTO GRADE-RECORD
        AT END MOVE 1 TO WS-EOF.
    PERFORM LOAD-TABLE VARYING TEST
        FROM 1 BY 1 UNTIL WS-EOF = 1.
        .
        .
LOAD-TABLE.
    PERFORM TEST-ROW VARYING STUDENT
        FROM 1 BY 1 UNTIL STUDENT > 3.
    READ SCORE-FILE INTO GRADE-RECORD
        AT END MOVE 1 TO WS-EOF.
TEST-ROW.
    MOVE GRADE (STUDENT) TO SCORE (STUDENT, TEST).
```

The grades are recorded in column fashion on each data record. Altogether there are five data records. When TEST is 1, GRADE (STUDENT) will be moved into table entries SCORE(STUDENT, 1) as STUDENT varies from 1 to 3. This means the first three test scores on the first record will be transferred into the first column of SCORE.

A fast method of loading a two-dimensional table when the input file is arranged in row order (as in case 1 above) is to read the first record (row) into the first row of the table, then the second record into the second row of the table, et cetera, for example:

```
01  GRADE-RECORD.
    05  GRADE OCCURS 5 TIMES PIC 99.
01  ROSTER-TABLE.
    05  STUDENT-RECORD OCCURS 3 TIMES.
        10  TESTS OCCURS 5 TIMES PIC 99.

    READ SCORE-FILE INTO STUDENT-RECORD (1)
        AT END MOVE 1 TO WS-EOF.
    PERFORM LOAD-TABLE VARYING STUDENT
        FROM 2 BY 1 UNTIL WS-EOF = 1.
LOAD-TABLE.
    READ SCORE-FILE INTO STUDENT-RECORD (STUDENT)
        AT END MOVE 1 TO WS-EOF.
```

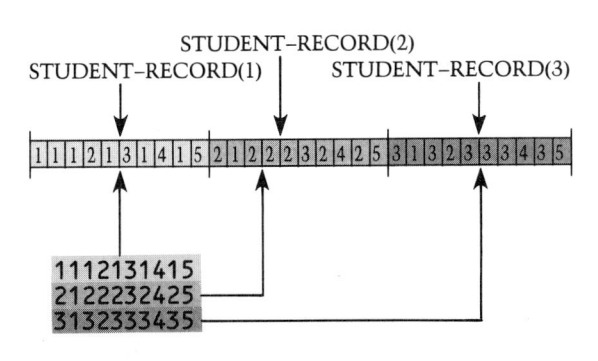

input file

Note that the first READ statement would not be needed if the sole objective were to load the table directly in memory (without processing the records as they are read). In that case, the FROM clause should specify 1 instead of 2.

Output of Two-Dimensional Tables.

To edit and print the elements of TABL in the format shown below, the following code could be used:

```
         TABL                                          TABL
      in memory                           edited and printed on the output form

   1000  0586  0786  1014  0055            $100.0     $ 58.6     $ 78.6     $101.4     $  5.5
   0084  2156  0080  2011  0658 — WRITE→   $  8.4     $215.6     $  8.0     $201.1     $ 65.8
   0880  0250  0860  2000  7051            $ 88.0     $ 25.0     $ 86.0     $200.0     $705.1
```

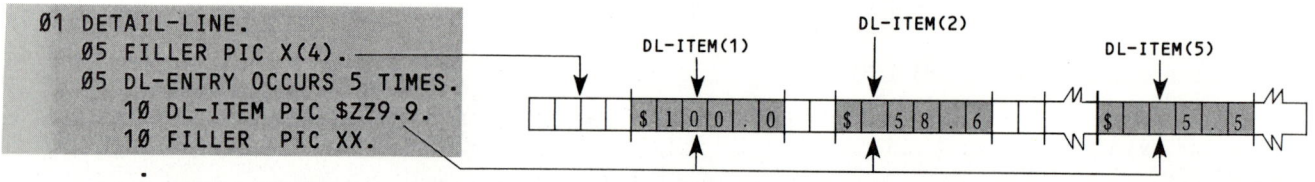

```
01 DETAIL-LINE.
   05 FILLER PIC X(4).
   05 DL-ENTRY OCCURS 5 TIMES.
      10 DL-ITEM PIC $ZZ9.9.
      10 FILLER  PIC XX.
```

```
   MOVE SPACES TO DETAIL-LINE.             Blank out the DETAIL-LINE to make sure the FILLER gets
   PERFORM ROW-CONTROL VARYING R-INDX      blanked out. Print three rows; initially R-INDX is 1 (1st row).
      FROM 1 BY 1 UNTIL R-INDX > 3.
      .
      .
      .
ROW-CONTROL.
   PERFORM COLUMN-CONTROL VARYING C-INDX   When R-INDX = 1 move the five elements of the first row of
      FROM 1 BY 1 UNTIL C-INDX > 5.        TABL into the five fields of DETAIL-LINE (i.e., DL-ITEMs).
   WRITE PRINT-LINE FROM DETAIL-LINE.      The line is then printed. The same procedure is repeated for
                                           R-INDX = 2 and R-INDX = 3.
COLUMN-CONTROL.
   MOVE TABL (R-INDX, C-INDX) TO DL-ITEM (C-INDX).   Initialize the output line with 5 edited items.
```

8-4-8 THE PERFORM VARYING . . . AFTER VARYING . . . STATEMENT.

The user may find it convenient at times to use an extension of the PERFORM statement to handle the subscripts of two-dimensional tables. This option allows the user to initialize and increment two subscripts in one PERFORM statement in the sequence shown in Figure 8-9.

To illustrate the use of the PERFORM VARYING shown in Figure 8-9, assume that TABL consists of 10 rows and 5 columns, and that we want to add all the elements of TABL and also determine the row and column position of the largest element in TABL, for example, the largest element of TABL might be located at ROW = 3 and COLUMN = 5. The following code could be used:

```
01 TABLE-DEFINITION.
    05 ROW OCCURS 10 TIMES.
        10 COLUM OCCURS 5 TIMES.
            15 TABL PIC 99.
    .
    MOVE 1 TO R-MAX, C-MAX.
    MOVE TABL (1, 1) TO LARGEST.
    MOVE 0 TO TOTAL-SUM.
    PERFORM PARA VARYING R-INDX
        FROM 1 BY 1 UNTIL R-INDX > 10
        AFTER C-INDX
        FROM 1 BY 1 UNTIL C-INDX > 5.
    MOVE R-MAX TO DL-ROW.
    MOVE C-MAX TO DL-COLUMN.
    MOVE LARGEST TO DL-LARGEST.
    MOVE TOTAL-SUM TO DL-TOTAL.
    .
PARA.
    ADD TABL (R-INDX, C-INDX) TO TOTAL-SUM.
    IF LARGEST < TABL (R-INDX, C-INDX)
        MOVE R-INDX TO R-MAX
        MOVE C-INDX TO C-MAX
        MOVE TABL (R-INDX, C-INDX) TO LARGEST.
```

Table consists of 10 rows and 5 columns.

To start the search, assume the largest number is at row 1 column 1; i.e., we assume TABL(1,1) is initially the largest value—this will change of course.

Process all 50 elements of TABL in row fashion. R–INDX initially is 1 and C–INDX cycles through 1 to 5; then R–INDX is 2 and C–INDX runs the gamut 1 thru 5, et cetera.

At any given time R–MAX and C–MAX indicate the row and column position of the largest table element found so far i.e., that element is TABL (R–MAX, C–MAX).

Accumulate the sum of the elements of TABL. If the current maximum is less than the next entry, reset the coordinates of the maximum to the newest coordinates R–INDX and C–INDX.

8-4-9 DO IT NOW

1. A two-dimensional table A of size 5 by 5 is typed one row per input record. Write the COBOL code to:

    a. Read in the table and write out each column on one line, that is, write out the columns in row fashion.
    b. Calculate the sum of the elements of the third row.
    c. Find the largest value in the first column.
    d. Create a one-dimensional table B consisting of five elements initialized to zero. Calculate the sum of each column of A, storing the result in the corresponding column position of B.
    e. Compute the sum of the entries of the first diagonal.
    f. Compute the sum of the entries of the second diagonal.
    g. Write the code to determine the smallest element of A and its position in the table, i.e., the row and column at which it is located.
    h. Add corresponding elements of rows 2 and 3 of A, storing results in row 3, i.e., A(3,1) = A(3,1) + A(2,1), et cetera.
    i. Interchange column 3 and row 3.
    j. Accept values for I and J such that both I and J are in the interval 1 through 5 and interchange row I with row J.

2. Write the code to compute the payroll for the problem in example 1, section 8-4-4.

3. Look up the paragraph entitled "Initialization through the READ Statement" in section 8-4-7. Write the code to load the SCORE table from the input files shown in parts 3 and 4.

422 UNDERSTANDING STRUCTURED COBOL

```
PERFORM paragraph-name VARYING data-name-1
    FROM initial-value-1 BY increment-value-1 UNTIL condition-1
    AFTER data-name-2
    FROM initial-value-2 BY increment-value-2 UNTIL condition-2.
```

FLOWCHART INTERPRETATION

- MOVE initial-value-1 TO data-name-1
- ADD increment-value-2 TO data-name-2
- condition-1 true? → Yes → Exit
- No ↓
- condition-2 true? → Yes
- No ↓
- carry out paragraph-name
- MOVE initial-value-2 TO data-name-2
- MOVE initial-value-2 TO data-name-2
  ADD increment-value-1 TO data-name-1

EXAMPLE

```
PERFORM PARA VARYING INDX-1
    FROM 1 BY 1 UNTIL INDX-1 > 2
    AFTER INDX-2
    FROM 1 BY 1 UNTIL INDX-2 > 3.
PARA.
    DISPLAY INDX-1, ' ', INDX-2.
```

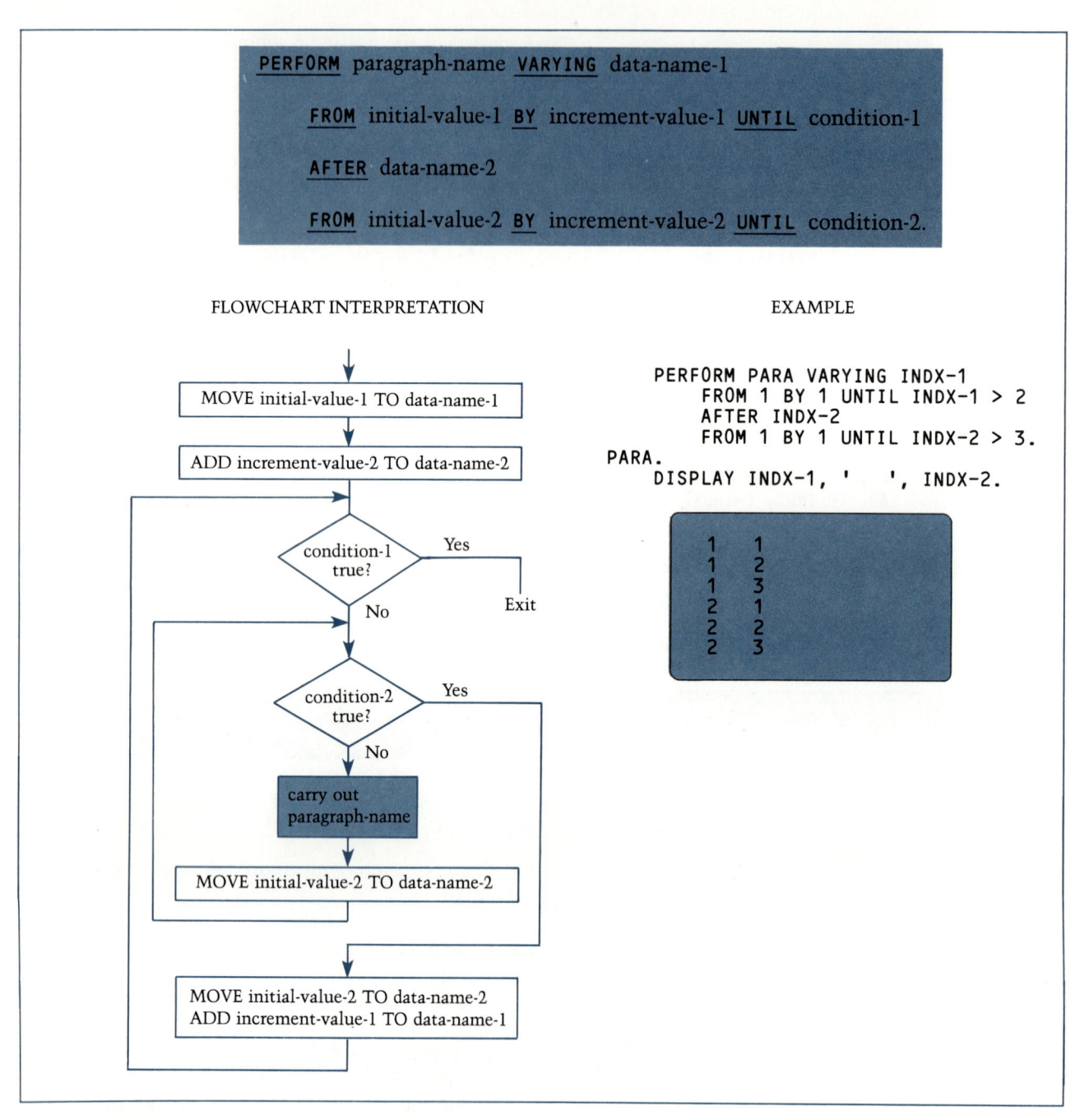

```
1  1
1  2
1  3
2  1
2  2
2  3
```

FIGURE 8–9
THE PERFORM VARYING/AFTER STATEMENT

4. Is the following structure equivalent to the PERFORM VARYING/AFTER shown in Figure 8–9?

```
         PERFORM para-temp VARYING data-name-1
             FROM initial-value-1 BY increment-value-1 UNTIL condition-1.
Para-temp.
         PERFORM paragraph-name VARYING data-name-2
             FROM initial-value-2 BY increment-value-2 UNTIL condition-2.
```

ONE- AND TWO- DIMENSIONAL TABLES

SELECTED ANSWERS

1.
```
        FD  INPUT-FILE
            LABEL RECORDS ARE STANDARD
            DATA RECORD IS INPUT-REC.
        01 INPUT-REC.
            05 LINE1 OCCURS 5 PIC 99.
        WORKING-STORAGE SECTION.
        01 SUBSCRIPTS.
            05 ROW PIC 99.
            05 I   PIC 9.
            05 J   PIC 9.
            05 COL PIC 9.
        01 COMPUTATIONAL-ITEMS.
            05 SUN   PIC 99.
            05 ROW-3 PIC 999.
            05 LARG  PIC 99.
            05 TEMP  PIC 99.
        01 TAB1.
            05 R OCCURS 5.
                06 C OCCURS 5.
                    07 A PIC 99.
        01 TAB2.
            05 B OCCURS 5 PIC 99.
```

```
        PROCEDURE DIVISION.
        MAIN-LOGIC.
```

a.   OPEN INPUT INPUT-FILE, OUTPUT PRINT-FILE.
      PERFORM XYZ VARYING ROW FROM 1 BY 1 UNTIL ROW > 5.
      PERFORM WRITE-TAB VARYING COL FROM 1 BY 1 UNTIL COL > 5.

b.   MOVE 0 TO ROW-3.
      PERFORM ROW-3-ADD VARYING COL FROM 1 BY 1 UNTIL COL > 5.

c.   MOVE A (1, 1) TO LARG.
      PERFORM LARG-FIND VARYING ROW FROM 2 BY 1 UNTIL ROW > 5.

d.   MOVE ZEROS TO TAB2.
      PERFORM SUM-COLUMN VARYING COL FROM 1 BY 1 UNTIL COL > 5.

e.   MOVE 0 TO SUN.
      PERFORM DIAG-1-SUM VARYING ROW FROM 1 BY 1 UNTIL ROW > 5.

f.   MOVE 0 TO SUN.
      PERFORM DIAG-2-SUM VARYING ROW FROM 1 BY 1 UNTIL ROW > 5.

g.   MOVE 1 TO I, J.
      MOVE A (1, 1) TO TEMP.
      PERFORM POSITION-SMALL VARYING ROW FROM 1 BY 1 UNTIL ROW > 5
                                    AFTER   COL FROM 1 BY 1 UNTIL COL > 5.

h.   PERFORM ROW-3-ACC VARYING COL FROM 1 BY 1 UNTIL COL > 5.

i.   PERFORM INTERCHANGE VARYING ROW FROM 1 BY 1 UNTIL ROW > 5.

```
     j.    ACCEPT I, J.
           PERFORM SWAP VARYING COL FROM 1 BY 1 UNTIL COL > 5.
           .
     XZY.
           READ INPUT-FILE INTO R (ROW).
     WRITE-TAB.
           PERFORM LOAD-COL VARYING ROW FROM 1 BY 1 UNTIL ROW > 5.
           WRITE PRINT-LINE FROM INPUT-REC.
     LOAD-COL.
           MOVE A (ROW, COL) TO LINE1 (ROW).
     ROW-3-ADD.
           ADD A (3, COL) TO ROW-3.
     LARG-FIND.
           IF LARG IS LESS THAN A (ROW, 1)
               MOVE A (ROW, 1) TO LARG.
     SUM-COLUMN.
           MOVE 0 TO SUN.
           PERFORM ROW-PROCESS VARYING ROW FROM 1 BY 1 UNTIL ROW > 5.
           MOVE SUN TO B (COL).
     ROW-PROCESS.
           ADD A (ROW, COL) TO SUN.
     DIAG-1-SUM.
           ADD A (ROW, ROW) TO SUN.
     DIAG-2-SUM.
           COMPUTE COL = 6 - ROW.
           ADD A (ROW, COL) TO SUN.
     POSITION-SMALL.
           IF TEMP GREATER THAN A (ROW, COL)
               MOVE A (ROW, COL) TO TEMP
               MOVE ROW TO I
               MOVE COL TO J.
     ROW-3-ACC.
           ADD A (2, COL) TO A (3, COL).
     INTERCHANGE.
           MOVE A (ROW, 3) TO TEMP.
           MOVE A (3, ROW) TO A (ROW, 3).
           MOVE TEMP       TO A (3, ROW).
     SWAP.
           MOVE A (I, COL) TO TEMP.
           MOVE A (J, COL) TO A (I, COL).
           MOVE TEMP       TO A (J, COL).
```

8-5 WRITING PROGRAMS

8-5-1 TABLE LOOKUP

Table look-up is a fast and efficient method to access data in a table directly, without searching the table elements, something like looking up your taxes in the tax table (fast and painful!). Consider the following example:

Problem Specification

United Package Service uses a cost delivery system based on article weight and destination zone. The rate per pound is given in the following table (page 425).

Let us write a program that will read an input file where each record contains two entries: a destination zone and a shipment weight. The program should print the destination zone, the weight, and the corresponding shipping cost. The rate table should be initialized in the DATA division.

ONE- AND TWO- DIMENSIONAL TABLES

ZONE CODE	COST PER POUND	MEANING
1	$ .55	The cost to ship 1 pound to zone 1 is $ .55.
2	$ .80	.
3	$1.03	The cost to ship 1 pound to zone 3 is $1.03.
4	$1.30	.
5	$1.75	.
6	$2.01	.

Program Analysis

The program to solve this problem is shown in Figure 8–10.

To understand the problem, let us look at the following example. Suppose we wanted to send a two-pound parcel to zone 6. We would look up zone 6 and identify the corresponding cost per pound entry, which is $2.01. Since the parcel weighs two pounds, the total cost would be 2 * 2.01 = 4.02. An attractive output design might be:

```
ZONE    WEIGHT    COST

 6       2.0      4.02
 2       3.5      2.80
```

A convenient way to look up the cost associated with a particular zone is to create a table RATE such that RATE(1) = $.55, RATE(2) = $.80, . . ., RATE(6) = $2.01. In this way, if the zone is 6, for example, we can immediately look up the sixth entry of RATE ($2.01). In general, the cost associated with zone ZONE is simply RATE(ZONE). Hence if we read a zone ZONE and a weight WEIGHT, the corresponding shipment cost is simply WEIGHT * RATE(ZONE) (see line 85).

The program in Figure 8–10 reads a zone ZONE and a weight WEIGHT and prints the zone ZONE, the weight WEIGHT, and the resulting cost RATE(ZONE)*WEIGHT.

Note how the rate table is created at line 67 through the REDEFINES statement. Line 65 identifies the six costs per pound.

8-5-2 A FREQUENCY DISTRIBUTION

Problem Specification: Each record of an input file contains a score (1–100). Write a program to determine the number of times each score occurs. The input and output will have the following form:

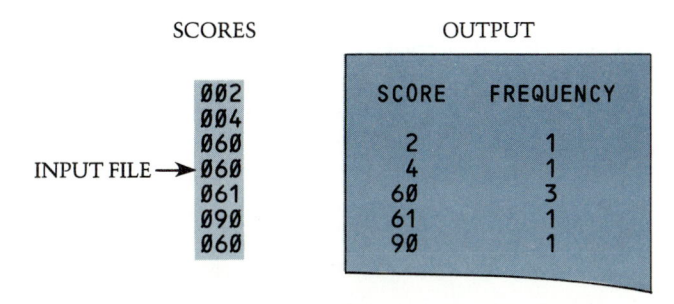

```
          SCORES              OUTPUT

           002           SCORE    FREQUENCY
           004
           060             2          1
INPUT FILE→060             4          1
           061            60          3
           090            61          1
           060            90          1
```

426 UNDERSTANDING STRUCTURED COBOL

```
 1:    IDENTIFICATION DIVISION.
 2:    PROGRAM-ID. TABLE-LOOKUP.
 3:    AUTHOR. JONES.
 4:   **************************************************************
 5:   * OBJECTIVE: GIVEN A PACKAGE WEIGHT AND A DESTINATION ZONE    *
 6:   *            COMPUTE CORRESPONDING COST                       *
 7:   *                                                             *
 8:   * INPUT:     DESTINATION ZONE AND WEIGHT                      *
 9:   *                                                             *
10:   * OUTPUT:    ZONE NUMBER, WEIGHT AND SHIPMENT COST            *
11:   **************************************************************
12:    ENVIRONMENT DIVISION.
13:    CONFIGURATION SECTION.
14:    SOURCE-COMPUTER. IBM.
15:    OBJECT-COMPUTER. IBM.
16:    INPUT-OUTPUT SECTION.
17:    FILE-CONTROL.
18:        SELECT REPORT-FILE ASSIGN TO PRINTER.
19:        SELECT MAILING-FILE ASSIGN TO DISK
20:        ORGANIZATION IS LINE SEQUENTIAL.
35:    WORKING-STORAGE SECTION.
36:   ********************************
37:   *    INDEPENDENT ITEMS          *
38:   ********************************
39:    01 FLAGS.
40:        05 WS-EOF PIC 9  VALUE 0.
41:           88 END-OF-FILE IS 1.
42:   *
43:   *    INPUT RECORD DESCRIPTION
44:   *
45:    01 PACKAGE-RECORD.
46:        05 PR-ZONE   PIC 9.
47:        05 PR-WEIGHT PIC 999V9.
48:   ********************************
49:   *    OUTPUT LINE DESCRIPTIONS  *
50:   ********************************
51:    01 MAJOR-HEADING.
52:        05 FILLER PIC X(08) VALUE ' ZONE'.
53:        05 FILLER PIC X(10) VALUE ' WEIGHT'.
54:        05 FILLER PIC X(64) VALUE ' COST'.
55:    01 DETAIL-LINE.
56:        05 FILLER   PIC X(03) VALUE SPACES.
57:        05 DL-ZONE  PIC 9.
58:        05 FILLER   PIC X(04) VALUE SPACES.
59:        05 DL-WEIGHT PIC ZZZ9.9.
60:        05 FILLER   PIC X(03) VALUE SPACES.
61:        05 DL-COST  PIC ZZZ.99.
62:   ********************************
63:   *    TABLE DEFINITION           *
64:   ********************************
65:    01 RATE-TABLE PIC X(18) VALUE '055080103130175201'.
66:    01 DUPLICATE-TABLE REDEFINES RATE-TABLE.
67:        05 RATE PIC 9V99 OCCURS 6 TIMES.
68:   *
69:    PROCEDURE DIVISION.
70:    100-MAIN-LOGIC.
71:        OPEN OUTPUT REPORT-FILE, INPUT MAILING-FILE.
72:        PERFORM 200-INITIALIZATION.
73:        READ MAILING-FILE INTO PACKAGE-RECORD
74:            AT END MOVE 1 TO WS-EOF.
75:        PERFORM 300-COMPUTE-POSTAGE UNTIL END-OF-FILE.
76:        CLOSE REPORT-FILE, MAILING-FILE.
77:        STOP RUN.
78:   *
79:    200-INITIALIZATION.
80:        WRITE PRINT-LINE FROM MAJOR-HEADING AFTER 1 LINE.
81:        MOVE SPACES TO PRINT-LINE.
82:        WRITE PRINT-LINE AFTER ADVANCING 1 LINE.
83:   *
84:    300-COMPUTE-POSTAGE.
85:        COMPUTE DL-COST ROUNDED = RATE (PR-ZONE) * PR-WEIGHT.
86:        MOVE PR-ZONE   TO DL-ZONE.
87:        MOVE PR-WEIGHT TO DL-WEIGHT.
88:        WRITE PRINT-LINE FROM DETAIL-LINE AFTER 1 LINE.
89:        READ MAILING-FILE INTO PACKAGE-RECORD
90:            AT END MOVE 1 TO WS-EOF.

21:   *
22:    DATA DIVISION.
23:    FILE SECTION.
24:   *
25:    FD MAILING-FILE
26:       LABEL RECORDS ARE STANDARD
27:       VALUE OF FILE-ID IS 'TBLOOKUP'
28:       DATA RECORD IS INPUT-AREA.
29:    01 INPUT-AREA PIC X(05).
30:    FD REPORT-FILE
31:       LABEL RECORDS ARE OMITTED
32:       DATA RECORD IS PRINT-LINE.
33:    01 PRINT-LINE PIC X(80).
34:   *
```

INPUT FILE

60020
20035
30125
10050
28750
60458

PR-ZONE PR-WEIGHT

ZONE	WEIGHT	COST
6	2.0	4.02
2	3.5	2.80
3	12.3	12.67
1	5.0	2.75
2	875.0	700.00
6	45.8	92.06

RATE TABLE

RATE(1) = .55
RATE(2) = .80
RATE(3) = 1.03
RATE(4) = 1.30
RATE(5) = 1.75
RATE(6) = 2.01

Read a destination zone PR-ZONE and a package weight PR-WEIGHT.

TABLE LOOKUP

The cost will equal the weight times the rate for that particular zone, i.e., RATE(PR-ZONE). Print out the zone, weight and cost for each input record.

FIGURE 8-10

A TABLE LOOKUP PROBLEM

ONE- AND TWO- DIMENSIONAL TABLES 427

Program Analysis

The solution to the problem is shown in Figure 8–11.

Given a list of scores in the range 1 to 100, we must determine how many times score 1 appears, how many times score 2 appears, and so forth. It is possible that many of these scores will not appear at all in the input list.

Since we do not know what scores will occur, we need 100 different counters to count all possible score occurrences. Since it would be quite impractical to have 100 different data names to count the occurrence of each of the 100 scores, we will use 100 table elements as counters to count all possible score occurrences. We need to choose which of the table elements will count which score. We decide on the following scheme:

FREQUENCY-COUNT(1) will count the occurrence of score 1.

FREQUENCY-COUNT(2) will count the occurrence of score 2.

.
.
.

FREQUENCY-COUNT(36) will count the occurrence of score 36, and

.
.
.

FREQUENCY-COUNT(SCORE) will count how many times score appears in the input list.

Initially all these counters are set to zeros (line 82). Then every time we read a score, we use that score as the subscript of FREQUENCY-COUNT to designate which counter to increment, i.e., the key instruction in the program is:

```
ADD 1 TO FREQUENCY-COUNT (SR-SCORE)    (line 85)
```

For example, if SCORE = 61, then we add 1 to the counter that keeps track of scores 61: ADD 1 TO FREQUENCY-COUNT(61). After all the scores have been read, the set of counters will appear as follows:

INPUT SCORES   SET OF 100 COUNTERS

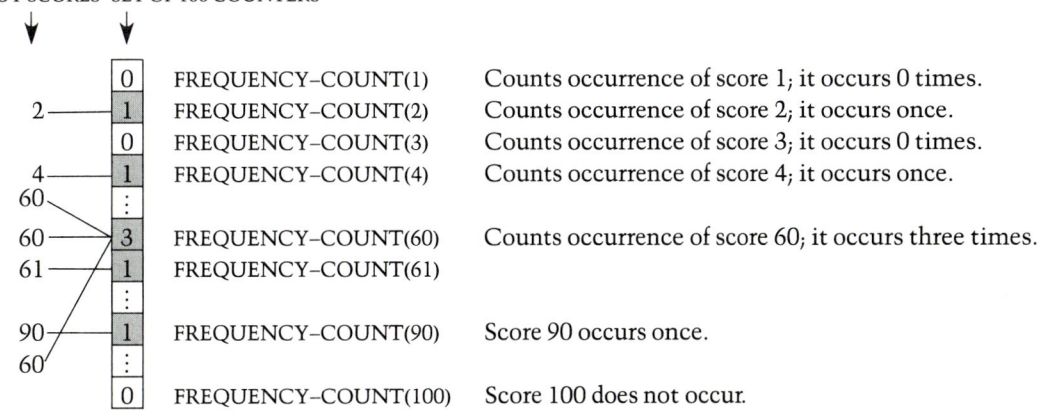

Input	Counter	Name	Description
	0	FREQUENCY-COUNT(1)	Counts occurrence of score 1; it occurs 0 times.
2	1	FREQUENCY-COUNT(2)	Counts occurrence of score 2; it occurs once.
	0	FREQUENCY-COUNT(3)	Counts occurrence of score 3; it occurs 0 times.
4	1	FREQUENCY-COUNT(4)	Counts occurrence of score 4; it occurs once.
60	⋮		
60	3	FREQUENCY-COUNT(60)	Counts occurrence of score 60; it occurs three times.
61	1	FREQUENCY-COUNT(61)	
	⋮		
90	1	FREQUENCY-COUNT(90)	Score 90 occurs once.
60	⋮		
	0	FREQUENCY-COUNT(100)	Score 100 does not occur.

When all the scores have been read, we must print all those scores whose frequency counts are nonzero. This means going through the table of counters, starting with FREQUENCY-COUNT(1), and asking the question: Is FREQUENCY-COUNT(1) = 0? If FREQUENCY-COUNT(1) = 0 there were

```
 1:     IDENTIFICATION DIVISION.
 2:     PROGRAM-ID. FREQUENCY DISTRIBUTION.
 3:     AUTHOR. JONES.
 4: ****************************************************************
 5: * OBJECTIVE: GIVEN A SET OF SCORES, PRODUCE A LISTING OF THE   *
 6: *            SCORES AND THEIR CORRESPONDING FREQUENCY. THE     *
 7: *            SCORES SHOULD BE IN ASCENDING NUMERIC SEQUENCE.   *
 8: *                                                              *
 9: * INPUT:     ONE SCORE PER RECORD.                             *
10: *                                                              *
11: * OUTPUT:    A SCORE AND CORRESPONDING FREQUENCY COUNT.        *
12: ****************************************************************
13:     ENVIRONMENT DIVISION.                46: *******************************
14:     CONFIGURATION SECTION.               47: *   INPUT RECORD DESCRIPTION  *
15:     SOURCE-COMPUTER. IBM.                48: *******************************
16:     OBJECT-COMPUTER. IBM.                49: 01 SCORE-RECORD.
17:     INPUT-OUTPUT SECTION.                50:    05 SR-SCORE    PIC 999.
18:     FILE-CONTROL.                        51: *******************************
19:         SELECT REPORT-FILE ASSIGN TO PRINTER. 52: *   OUTPUT LINE DESCRIPTIONS  *
20:         SELECT SCORE-FILE ASSIGN TO DISK      53: *******************************
21:         ORGANIZATION IS LINE SEQUENTIAL.     54: 01 MAJOR-HEADING.
22: *                                            55:    05 FILLER PIC X(08) VALUE ' SCORE '.
23:     DATA DIVISION.                           56:    05 FILLER PIC X(12) VALUE '  FREQUENCY'.
24:     FILE SECTION.                            57: 01 DETAIL-LINE.
25: *                                            58:    05 FILLER    PIC X(03) VALUE SPACES.
26:     FD SCORE-FILE                            59:    05 DL-SCORE  PIC ZZ9.
27:        LABEL RECORDS ARE STANDARD            60:    05 FILLER    PIC X(07) VALUE SPACES.
28:        VALUE OF FILE-ID IS 'FREQENCY'        61:    05 DL-FREQUENCY PIC Z9.
29:        DATA RECORD IS INPUT-AREA.            62: *******************************
30:     01 INPUT-AREA PIC X(10).                 63: *      TABLE DEFINITIONS      *
31:     FD REPORT-FILE                           64: *******************************
32:        LABEL RECORDS ARE OMITTED             65: 01 FREQUENCY-COUNT-TABLE.
33:        DATA RECORD IS PRINT-LINE.            66:    05 FREQUENCY-COUNT OCCURS 100 TIMES PIC 999.
34:     01 PRINT-LINE PIC X(80).
35: *
36:     WORKING-STORAGE SECTION.
37: *******************************
38: *       INDEPENDENT ITEMS     *
39: *******************************
40:     01 FLAGS.
41:        05 WS-EOF PIC 9    VALUE 0.
42:           88 END-OF-FILE VALUE IS 1.
43:     01 SUBSCRIPTS.
44:        05 SCORE   PIC 999.
45: *    SR-SCORE IS ALSO USED AS A SUBSCRIPT
67: *
68:     PROCEDURE DIVISION.
69:     100-MAIN-LOGIC.
70:         OPEN OUTPUT REPORT-FILE, INPUT SCORE-FILE.
71:         PERFORM 200-INITIALIZATION.
72:         READ SCORE-FILE INTO SCORE-RECORD
73:             AT END MOVE 1 TO WS-EOF.
74:         PERFORM 300-SCORE-FREQUENCY-COUNT UNTIL END-OF-FILE.
75:         PERFORM 400-WRITE-FREQUENCY-COUNTS VARYING
76:             SCORE FROM 1 BY 1 UNTIL SCORE GREATER THAN 100.
77:         CLOSE REPORT-FILE, SCORE-FILE.
78:         STOP RUN.
79: *
80:     200-INITIALIZATION.
81:         WRITE PRINT-LINE FROM MAJOR-HEADING AFTER 1 LINE.
82:         MOVE ZEROS TO FREQUENCY-COUNT-TABLE.
83: *
84:     300-SCORE-FREQUENCY-COUNT.
85:         ADD 1 TO FREQUENCY-COUNT (SR-SCORE).
86:         READ SCORE-FILE INTO SCORE-RECORD
87:             AT END MOVE 1 TO WS-EOF.
88: *
89:     400-WRITE-FREQUENCY-COUNTS.
90:         IF FREQUENCY-COUNT (SCORE) IS NOT EQUAL TO ZERO
91:             MOVE SCORE                  TO DL-SCORE
92:             MOVE FREQUENCY-COUNT (SCORE) TO DL-FREQUENCY
93:             WRITE PRINT-LINE FROM DETAIL-LINE AFTER 1 LINE.
```

INPUT FILE
002
004
060
060
061
090
060

SCORE	FREQUENCY
2	1
4	1
60	3
61	1
90	1

FREQUENCY-COUNT-TABLE

occurrence of score 60

FREQUENCY-COUNT(90)

FIGURE 8–11

A FREQUENCY DISTRIBUTION PROBLEM

no scores equal to 1, so we do not print score 1. If FREQUENCY–COUNT(1) = 3, this means that score 1 occurred three times in the list, so we write score 1 and its corresponding frequency, 3. In general, if the answer to the question, Is FREQUENCY–COUNT(SCORE) = 0?, is yes, then SCORE is *not* printed, otherwise SCORE and its corresponding frequency count FREQUENCY–COUNT(SCORE) are printed.

Test Your Understanding of the Program

1. Modify the program to process an input file consisting of *one* input record containing all scores. The first entry in the record specifies the number of scores in the record, for example

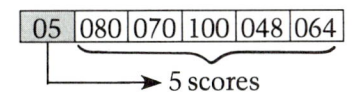

   | 05 | 080 | 070 | 100 | 048 | 064 |

   → 5 scores

2. Modify the program to produce a sorted list of scores, i.e., if score 64 occurs 3 times, print 64, 64, 64. Scores should be written one per line with no frequency count entry.

8–5–3 BAR GRAPHS

One picture is worth a thousand words. It is often desirable to produce graphic output from a computer. A scientific problem may require the graph of a function. A business problem might require a bar graph; for example, trends in sales volumes might be detected more easily in picture form than in table form. Consider the following problem.

Problem Specification

Weekly sales data for a company is shown below. To visualize the sales trend graphically, we can represent the daily sales by a corresponding number of asterisks * on one line to obtain the following bar graph:

DAY	SALES
1	10
2	30
3	24
4	6
5	5
6	8
7	1

```
DAYS
  1  **********
  2  ******************************
  3  ************************
  4  ******
  5  ****
  6  ********
  7  *
     0000000000111111111122222222223
     1234567890123456789012345678990

     AMOUNT IN THOUSANDS
```

1st–gradation–line
2nd–gradation–line

Maximum sales volume for week

Note the two gradation lines where $\overset{0}{1}$ is read as 1, $\overset{0}{2}$ is read as 2 and $\overset{3}{0}$ is read as 30. The last gradation on the gradation lines indicates the largest volume for the entire week. The gradations run from 1 to the maximum sales volume for the week.

Program Analysis

The program to solve this problem is shown in Figure 8–12. Note how a sales amount is read and a corresponding number of asterisks equal to the sales is stored in table DL–STAR (line 92). Also note how the table is printed (line 87).

The two gradation lines are stored in two tables (lines 63 and 66). The upper gradation table is filled with the numbers 000000000111111111222222..., and the lower gradation table contains 1234567890123456.... To generate the upper gradation table, the counter WS–INCREMENT is set to 0 and incremented successively by 0.1. Theoretically, WS–INCREMENT takes on values 0.1, 0.2, 0.3, ..., 0.9, 1.0, 1.1, 1.2, ..., 1.9, 2.0. ... However, by moving WS–INCREMENT to a PICTURE 9 field (1ST–GRADATION–LINE at lines 63–65 and 104), the fractional digits are truncated, thereby generating a sequence of nine 0's, ten 1's, ten 2's, et cetera. Similarly, at line 105, if INDX varies from 1 to maximum sales in increments of 1, and if INDX (PIC 99) is moved to a PICTURE 9 field (2ND–GRADATION–LINE at lines 66–68 and 105), then the value of INDX is truncated to the left of the units position (PICTURE 9 instead of 99) to yield the repeating pattern 1234567890123.... For example 12 becomes 2, 13 becomes 3 et cetera.

Test Your Understanding of the Program

1. Display the output if line 29 is changed to 01 INPUT–AREA PIC X(01).

2. Change the logic of the program so that only one gradation line is used in the DATA division, i.e., delete lines 66–68.

3. Modify the logic of the program to process an input file where the seven daily sales volume are recorded on just one input record.

8-5-4 INVENTORY UPDATE PROGRAM

Problem Specification: An input file consists of two sets of records:

1. The first set of records is the master file, which contains an item inventory at the start of the business day. Each master file record contains a part number and a corresponding item stock quantity. The end of the master file is identified by a record containing the characters EOF in the first three positions of the record. Let us assume that the master file contains no more than 100 records.

2. The second set of records, which follows the master file, shows the transactions for each of the various items during that day. Transaction records have the same format as the master file records: they contain the item number and the corresponding total number of items sold that day.

Write a program to update the master file against the transaction file and produce a new master file at the end of the day. A reorder notice should accompany any item number for which fewer than 10 items remain in stock. A list of invalid item numbers, if any, should be printed before the final master file is

ONE- AND TWO- DIMENSIONAL TABLES

```cobol
 1:   IDENTIFICATION DIVISION.
 2:   PROGRAM-ID. GRAPH-TABLE.
 3:   AUTHOR. JONES.
 4:   ***************************************************************
 5:   * OBJECTIVE: PRODUCE A SALES BAR GRAPH SHOWING DAILY SALES    *
 6:   *                                                             *
 7:   * INPUT:     SALES AMOUNT                                     *
 8:   *                                                             *
 9:   * OUTPUT:    DAYS, NUMBER OF CONTIGUOUS ASTERISKS EQUAL TO    *
10:   *            SALES AMOUNT                                     *
11:   ***************************************************************

12:   ENVIRONMENT DIVISION.
13:   CONFIGURATION SECTION.
14:   SOURCE-COMPUTER. IBM.
15:   OBJECT-COMPUTER. IBM.
16:   INPUT-OUTPUT SECTION.
17:   FILE-CONTROL.
18:       SELECT REPORT-FILE ASSIGN TO PRINTER.
19:       SELECT SALES-FILE  ASSIGN TO DISK
20:       ORGANIZATION IS LINE SEQUENTIAL.
21:   *
22:   DATA DIVISION.
23:   FILE SECTION.
24:   *
25:   FD  SALES-FILE
26:       LABEL RECORDS ARE STANDARD
27:       VALUE OF FILE-ID IS 'GRAPH'
28:       DATA RECORD IS INPUT-AREA.
29:   01  INPUT-AREA PIC X(02).
30:   FD  REPORT-FILE
31:       LABEL RECORDS ARE OMITTED
32:       DATA RECORD IS PRINT-LINE.
33:   01  PRINT-LINE PIC X(80).
34:   *
35:   WORKING-STORAGE SECTION.
36:   ********************************
37:   *     INDEPENDENT ITEMS        *
38:   ********************************
39:   01  COMPUTATIONAL-ITEMS.
40:       05  WS-DAYS      PIC 9   VALUE 0.
41:       05  WS-MAX-SALES PIC 99  VALUE 0.
42:       05  WS-INCREMENT PIC 9V9 VALUE 0.
43:   01  SUBSCRIPTS.
44:       05  INDX         PIC 99.
45:   ********************************
46:   *    INPUT RECORD DESCRIPTION  *
47:   ********************************
48:   01  SALES-AMOUNT     PIC 99.
49:   ********************************
50:   *    OUTPUT LINE DESCRIPTIONS  *
51:   ********************************
52:   01  MAJOR-HEADING    PIC X(80) VALUE ' DAYS'.
53:   01  DETAIL-LINE.
54:       05  FILLER       PIC X(04).
55:       05  DL-DAY       PIC 9.
56:       05  FILLER       PIC X(02).
57:       05  DL-STAR      PIC X OCCURS 72 TIMES.
58:   01  GRADATION-CAPTION PIC X(80) VALUE
59:       '           AMOUNT IN THOUSANDS'.
60:   ********************************
61:   *      TABLE DEFINITIONS       *
62:   ********************************
63:   01  1ST-GRADATION-LINE.
64:       05  FILLER PIC X(07) VALUE SPACES.
65:       05  AL-GRADATION-1 PIC 9 OCCURS 72 TIMES.
66:   01  2ND-GRADATION-LINE.
67:       05  FILLER PIC X(07) VALUE SPACES.
68:       05  AL-GRADATION-2 PIC 9 OCCURS 72 TIMES.
69:   *
70:   PROCEDURE DIVISION.
71:   100-MAIN-LOGIC.
72:       OPEN OUTPUT REPORT-FILE, INPUT SALES-FILE.
73:       WRITE PRINT-LINE FROM MAJOR-HEADING AFTER 1 LINE.
74:       PERFORM 200-GRAPH-PROCESS 7 TIMES.
75:       PERFORM 400-PRINT-GRADATION-LINES.
76:       CLOSE REPORT-FILE, SALES-FILE.
77:       STOP RUN.
78:   *
79:   200-GRAPH-PROCESS.
80:       READ SALES-FILE INTO SALES-AMOUNT
81:           AT END DISPLAY 'CHECK INPUT FILE' STOP RUN.
82:       MOVE SPACES TO DETAIL-LINE.
83:       PERFORM 300-INSERT-STARS VARYING INDX
84:           FROM 1 BY 1 UNTIL INDX GREATER THAN SALES-AMOUNT.
85:       ADD 1 TO WS-DAYS.
86:       MOVE WS-DAYS TO DL-DAY.
87:       WRITE PRINT-LINE FROM DETAIL-LINE AFTER 1 LINE.
88:       IF SALES-AMOUNT IS GREATER THAN WS-MAX-SALES
89:           MOVE SALES-AMOUNT TO WS-MAX-SALES.
90:   *
91:   300-INSERT-STARS.
92:       MOVE '*' TO DL-STAR (INDX).
93:   *
94:   400-PRINT-GRADATION-LINES.
95:       MOVE SPACES TO 1ST-GRADATION-LINE, 2ND-GRADATION-LINE.
96:       PERFORM 500-PREPARE-GRADATION-LINES VARYING INDX
97:           FROM 1 BY 1 UNTIL INDX GREATER THAN WS-MAX-SALES.
98:       WRITE PRINT-LINE FROM 1ST-GRADATION-LINE AFTER 1 LINE.
99:       WRITE PRINT-LINE FROM 2ND-GRADATION-LINE AFTER 1 LINE.
100:      WRITE PRINT-LINE FROM GRADATION-CAPTION  AFTER 2 LINE.
101:  *
102:  500-PREPARE-GRADATION-LINES.
103:      ADD 0.1 TO WS-INCREMENT.
104:      MOVE WS-INCREMENT TO AL-GRADATION-1 (INDX).
105:      MOVE INDX         TO AL-GRADATION-2 (INDX).
```

INPUT FILE
↓
10
30
24
06
05
08
01

```
DAYS
 1  **********
 2  ******************************
 3  ************************
 4  ******
 5  *****
 6  ********
 7  *
    0000000000111111111122222222223
    1234567890123456789012345678901

    AMOUNT IN THOUSANDS
```

FIGURE 8-12

A BAR GRAPH

printed. Invalid items are incorrectly recorded items in the transaction file for which there are no corresponding items in the master file. The input and output should be similar to:

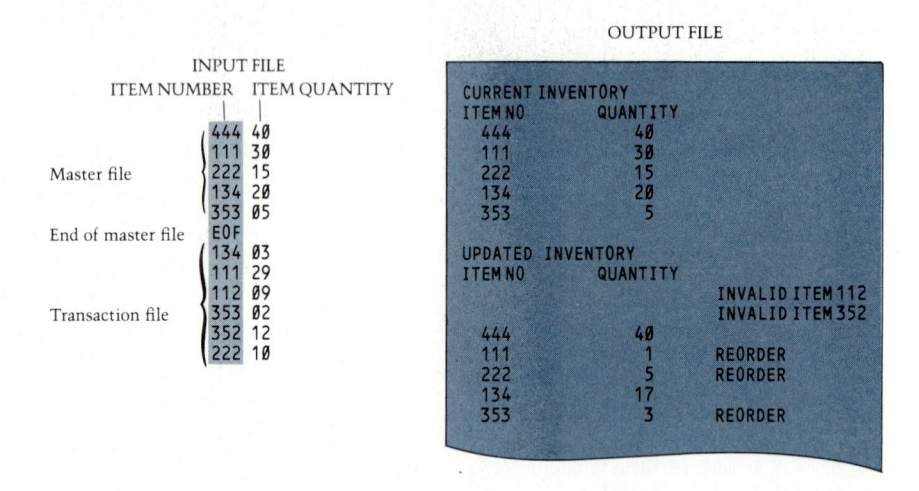

```
                    INPUT FILE                         OUTPUT FILE
              ITEM NUMBER   ITEM QUANTITY
                    |           |              CURRENT INVENTORY
                   444         40              ITEM NO      QUANTITY
                   111         30                444           40
   Master file     222         15                111           30
                   134         20                222           15
                   353         05                134           20
                                                 353            5
   End of master file  EOF
                   134         03              UPDATED INVENTORY
                   111         29              ITEM NO      QUANTITY
                   112         09                                       INVALID ITEM 112
   Transaction file 353        02                                       INVALID ITEM 352
                   352         12
                   222         10                444           40
                                                 111            1       REORDER
                                                 222            5       REORDER
                                                 134           17
                                                 353            3       REORDER
```

Program Analysis

In the input file shown above, the master file consists of five items that represent the inventory at the beginning of the business day. Sales are reflected in the updated master file by subtracting the number of units sold for each item from the corresponding master item quantity. For example, originally there are 20 of item 134; 3 of these are sold during the day, hence the updated master file quantity for item 134 should be 17 (20 − 3).

The master file should be read into two tables: one containing the master item numbers (in this case there are five) and the other containing the corresponding item quantities.

We then read the transaction file one record at a time; every time an item is read (sold), the master file is updated to reflect the current number of items in stock. This requires a search of the master table to identify which master file item number is to be updated. In the transaction for item 134, we look for an entry equal to 134 in the master item table; in this case it is the fourth entry of the table. We then subtract the item quantity (3) from the fourth element of the master file quantity table.

If there is an invalid item number in the transaction file, there will be no matching item in the master item table. If this should happen, we print the invalid item and read the next record. When all transaction records have been read, the updated master file is printed, two entries at a time. If the quantity entry is less than 10, a reorder message is printed.

The program to solve this problem is shown in Figure 8–13.

Step by Step Analysis. The headings for the current inventory are printed by paragraph 200 (from line 98).

Paragraph 400 creates the master file by reading all item numbers and their corresponding stock levels into the table INVENTORY–TABLE. The item number and the quantity are read into two subordinate tables, MASTER–ITEM–NO and MASTER–QUANTITY. The process of reading the master file terminates when the characters EOF are encountered in the input file (line 119). Note the REDEFINES clause at line 62, which allows the first three characters of the input record to be tested for alphanumeric content. The number of items in the master file (WS–NO–MASTER–RECORDS) is one less than the value of MASTER–COUNT, which includes the end-of-file record (see line 120). The inventory is printed on the output form as it is read into memory (line 128).

The headings for the updated inventory are also printed by paragraph 200 (this time from line 100). Note that line 121 has changed the heading to UPDATED INVENTORY.

Now that the current inventory is in memory, paragraph 500 reads and processes the transaction file one record at a time until the end of file is encountered. Paragraph 600 is executed until the transaction record matches an item number in the master file or until TRANSACTION–COUNT is greater than the number of items in the master file (i.e., all the items in the master file have been checked for a match). If there is a match between an item in the transaction file and an item in the master file, lines 146 and 147 update the item quantity and store it back into the quantity array MASTER–QUANTITY. The flag WS–SWITCH is also set to FOUND to indicate that a match was found (line 145). If no match was found, WS–SWITCH remains equal to NOT FOUND (as set in line 133) and an error message is printed by paragraph 700. In either case, another transaction record is then read and processed (line 140).

When the end of file is encountered, control is passed to the PERFORM UNTIL at line 103; since WS–EOF = 1, line 104 is executed. Paragraph 800 prints the updated file. Any item number with stock quantity less than 10 is flagged on the output with the message REORDER. That entry in the detail line (line 159) is then blanked out in case there is no need to reorder the next item.

Test Your Understanding of the Program

1. Give at least two good reasons why transaction records are not stored in a table. Project coding consequences if a table was used.

2. Change the code so that the master file and transaction files are read from two separate input files.

3. At line 133, WS–SWITCH is initialized to the value NOT FOUND. This initialization is carried out for every record—when in fact most transaction records *do* have matches in the master file. Is this an efficient practice? Could you make changes to the code to increase efficiency?

4. Make the necessary changes to the code so that the list of invalid items physically follows the updated inventory. In the present case this list precedes the updated inventory.

8-5-5 A FREQUENCY DISTRIBUTION

Problem Specification:

Data have been gathered on the smoking habits of students at a university. Each student's class (1 = freshman, 2 = sophomore, 3 = junior, 4 = senior, 5 = graduate) and a code representing the student's smoking habits (1 = don't smoke, 2 = one pack or less a day, 3 = more than one pack a day) have been recorded, with each record containing data for one student. Let us write a program to gen-

434 UNDERSTANDING STRUCTURED COBOL

```
 1: IDENTIFICATION DIVISION.
 2: PROGRAM-ID. INVENTORY-PROBLEM.
 3: AUTHOR. JONES.
 4: ****************************************************************
 5: * OBJECTIVE: A MASTER FILE CONSISTING OF ITEM NUMBERS & CORRES- *
 6: *            PONDING STOCK QUANTITIES IS READ FROM AN INPUT FILE*
 7: *            INTO A MASTER TABLE. TRANSACTION RECORDS ARE THEN  *
 8: *            READ AND UPDATED AGAINST THE MASTER FILE. A REORDER*
 9: *            NOTICE ACCOMPANIES ANY ITEM FOR WHICH FEWER THAN 10*
10: *            ITEMS REMAIN IN STOCK. UNRECOGNIZED ITEM NUMBERS   *
11: *            ARE LISTED ON THE OUTPUT.                          *
12: *                                                               *
13: * INPUT:  ITEM NUMBER AND CORRESPONDING ITEM STOCK QUANTITY     *
14: *                                                               *
15: * OUTPUT: MASTER TABLE BEFORE AND AFTER THE UPDATE              *
16: *         REORDER MESSAGES IF ITEM STOCK LEVEL IS LESS THAN 10  *
17: *         LIST OF UNRECOGNIZED ITEM NUMBERS                     *
18: ****************************************************************
19: ENVIRONMENT DIVISION.
20: CONFIGURATION SECTION.
21: SOURCE-COMPUTER. IBM.
22: OBJECT-COMPUTER. IBM.
23: INPUT-OUTPUT SECTION.
24: FILE-CONTROL.
25:     SELECT REPORT-FILE ASSIGN TO PRINTER.
26:     SELECT INVENTORY-FILE ASSIGN TO DISK
27:         ORGANIZATION IS LINE SEQUENTIAL.
28: *
29: DATA DIVISION.
30: FILE SECTION.
31: *
32: FD  INVENTORY-FILE
33:     LABEL RECORDS ARE STANDARD
34:     VALUE OF FILE-ID IS 'INVENTRY'
35:     DATA RECORD IS INPUT-AREA.
36: 01  INPUT-AREA PIC X(10).
37: FD  REPORT-FILE
38:     LABEL RECORDS ARE OMITTED
39:     DATA RECORD IS PRINT-LINE.
40: 01  PRINT-LINE PIC X(80).
41: *
42: WORKING-STORAGE SECTION.
43: ********************************
44: *     INDEPENDENT ITEMS         *
45: ********************************
46: 01  FLAGS.
47:     05  WS-EOF PIC 9     VALUE 0.
48:         88 END-OF-FILE VALUE IS 1.
49:     05  WS-SWITCH      PIC X(09).
50: *
51: 01  SUBSCRIPTS.
52:     05 MASTER-COUNT      PIC 99.
53:     05 TRANSACTION-COUNT PIC 99.
54: *
55: 01  COMPUTATIONAL-ITEMS.
56:     05 WS-NO-MASTER-RECORDS PIC 99.
57: ********************************
58: *     INPUT RECORD DESCRIPTION  *
59: ********************************
60: 01  INPUT-RECORD.
61:     05 IR-ITEM-NO                  PIC 999.
62:     05 IR-FLAG REDEFINES IR-ITEM-NO PIC XXX.
63:     05 FILLER                      PIC X(04).
64:     05 IR-QUANTITY                 PIC 999.
65: ********************************
66: *     OUTPUT LINE DESCRIPTIONS  *
67: ********************************
68: 01  MAJOR-HEADING.
69:     05 FILLER              PIC X(06) VALUE SPACES.
70:     05 MH-INVENTORY-STATUS PIC X(73) VALUE
71:                                  'CURRENT INVENTORY'.
72: 01  MINOR-HEADING.
73:     05 FILLER      PIC X(06) VALUE SPACES.
74:     05 FILLER      PIC X(11) VALUE 'ITEM NO'.
75:     05 FILLER      PIC X(63) VALUE 'QUANTITY'.
76: 01  DETAIL-LINE.
77:     05 FILLER       PIC X(08) VALUE SPACES.
78:     05 DL-ITEM-NO   PIC ZZ9.
79:     05 FILLER       PIC X(08) VALUE SPACES.
80:     05 DL-QUANTITY  PIC ZZ9.
81:     05 FILLER       PIC X(05) VALUE SPACES.
82:     05 DL-ORDER-MSG PIC X(12) VALUE SPACES.
83: 01  INVALID-PART-LINE.
84:     05 FILLER       PIC X(27) VALUE SPACES.
85:     05 FILLER       PIC X(13) VALUE 'INVALID ITEM'.
86:     05 IP-INVALID-NO PIC ZZ9.
87: *
88: *   TABLE DEFINITIONS
89: *
90: 01  INVENTORY.
91:     05 INVENTORY-TABLE OCCURS 100 TIMES.
92:         10 MASTER-ITEM-NO   PIC 999.
93:         10 MASTER-QUANTITY  PIC 999.
```

```
Item    Stock
number  level
  ↓       ↓
 444    040  ⎫
 111    030  ⎪
 222    015  ⎬ Master
 134    020  ⎪ file
 353    005  ⎭
 EOF
 134    003  ⎫
 111    029  ⎪
 112    009  ⎪
 353    002  ⎬ Transaction
 352    012  ⎪ file
 222    010  ⎭
```

```
CURRENT INVENTORY
ITEM NO.   QUANTITY
  444        40
  111        30
  222        15
  134        20
  353         5

UPDATED INVENTORY
ITEM NO    QUANTITY
                              INVALID ITEM 112
                              INVALID ITEM 352
  444        40
  111         1    REORDER
  222         5    REORDER
  134        17
  353         3    REORDER
```

FIGURE 8–13
AN INVENTORY PROBLEM

ONE- AND TWO- DIMENSIONAL TABLES

```
 94:   *
 95:   PROCEDURE DIVISION.
 96:   100-MAIN-LOGIC.
 97:       OPEN OUTPUT REPORT-FILE, INPUT INVENTORY-FILE.
 98:       PERFORM 200-WRITE-HEADINGS.
 99:       PERFORM 300-LOAD-N-WRITE-MASTER-FILE.
100:       PERFORM 200-WRITE-HEADINGS.
101:       READ INVENTORY-FILE INTO INPUT-RECORD
102:           AT END MOVE 1 TO WS-EOF.
103:       PERFORM 500-PROCESS-TRANSACTIONS UNTIL END-OF-FILE.
104:       PERFORM 800-WRITE-UPDATED-INVENTORY VARYING
105:           MASTER-COUNT FROM 1 BY 1 UNTIL
106:               MASTER-COUNT > WS-NO-MASTER-RECORDS.
107:       CLOSE REPORT-FILE, INVENTORY-FILE.
108:       STOP RUN.
109:   *
110:   200-WRITE-HEADINGS.
111:       WRITE PRINT-LINE FROM MAJOR-HEADING AFTER 2 LINES.
112:       WRITE PRINT-LINE FROM MINOR-HEADING AFTER 1 LINE.
113:   *
114:   300-LOAD-N-WRITE-MASTER-FILE.
115:       READ INVENTORY-FILE INTO INPUT-RECORD
116:           AT END DISPLAY 'NO MASTER FILE'
117:               STOP RUN.
118:       PERFORM 400-READ-INVENTORY VARYING
119:           MASTER-COUNT FROM 1 BY 1 UNTIL IR-FLAG = 'EOF'.
120:       COMPUTE WS-NO-MASTER-RECORDS = MASTER-COUNT - 1.
121:       MOVE 'UPDATED INVENTORY' TO MH-INVENTORY-STATUS.
122:   *
123:   400-READ-INVENTORY.
124:       MOVE IR-ITEM-NO   TO MASTER-ITEM-NO  (MASTER-COUNT).
125:       MOVE IR-QUANTITY TO MASTER-QUANTITY (MASTER-COUNT).
126:       MOVE IR-ITEM-NO   TO DL-ITEM-NO.
127:       MOVE IR-QUANTITY TO DL-QUANTITY.
128:       WRITE PRINT-LINE FROM DETAIL-LINE AFTER 1 LINE.
129:       READ INVENTORY-FILE INTO INPUT-RECORD
130:           AT END MOVE 1 TO WS-EOF.
131:   *
132:   500-PROCESS-TRANSACTIONS.
133:       MOVE 'NOT FOUND' TO WS-SWITCH.
134:       PERFORM 600-UPDATE-MASTER
135:           VARYING TRANSACTION-COUNT FROM 1 BY 1
136:           UNTIL TRANSACTION-COUNT > WS-NO-MASTER-RECORDS
137:               OR WS-SWITCH IS EQUAL TO 'FOUND'.
138:       IF WS-SWITCH IS EQUAL TO 'NOT FOUND'
139:           PERFORM 700-UNRECOGNIZED-ITEM-NO.
140:       READ INVENTORY-FILE INTO INPUT-RECORD
141:           AT END MOVE 1 TO WS-EOF.
142:   *
143:   600-UPDATE-MASTER.
144:       IF IR-ITEM-NO = MASTER-ITEM-NO (TRANSACTION-COUNT)
145:           MOVE 'FOUND' TO WS-SWITCH
146:           SUBTRACT IR-QUANTITY
147:               FROM MASTER-QUANTITY (TRANSACTION-COUNT).
148:   *
149:   700-UNRECOGNIZED-ITEM-NO.
150:       MOVE IR-ITEM-NO TO IP-INVALID-NO.
151:       WRITE PRINT-LINE FROM INVALID-PART-LINE AFTER 1 LINE.
152:   *
153:   800-WRITE-UPDATED-INVENTORY.
154:       MOVE MASTER-ITEM-NO  (MASTER-COUNT) TO DL-ITEM-NO.
155:       MOVE MASTER-QUANTITY (MASTER-COUNT) TO DL-QUANTITY.
156:       IF MASTER-QUANTITY (MASTER-COUNT) IS LESS THAN 10
157:           MOVE 'REORDER' TO DL-ORDER-MSG.
158:       WRITE PRINT-LINE FROM DETAIL-LINE AFTER 1 LINE.
159:       MOVE SPACES TO DL-ORDER-MSG.
```

Go read the master records and store the data into MASTER–ITEM–NO and MASTER–QUANTITY tables. Read the first transaction record and keep reading the transaction records until the end of file is reached.

Write the updated master file.

This paragraph is carried out from lines 98 and 100. The major heading is different in each case.

Read the first master record. If none exists stop the program with an error message.

Read the master record and store the data into two tables (item-number and quantity). The end of the master file is reached when EOF is read.

Read the item number and the corresponding stock level and store these two values into the two subordinate tables of INVENTORY–TABLE.

Set WS–SWITCH to NOT FOUND. If a match is found, then the switch is set to FOUND.

If the transaction number was not found in the master table, print an error message.

This paragraph updates the master file with a transaction record. If the transaction item number matches a number in the master file, set switch to FOUND.

Print error message if a transaction item number has no match in the item number table.

Write out the entries of the updated inventory (item number and stock quantity). Determine if item number < 10; if so, print a reorder message.

FIGURE 8–13
(continued)

erate a frequency table showing students' smoking habits by class. The input and output should be similar to the following:

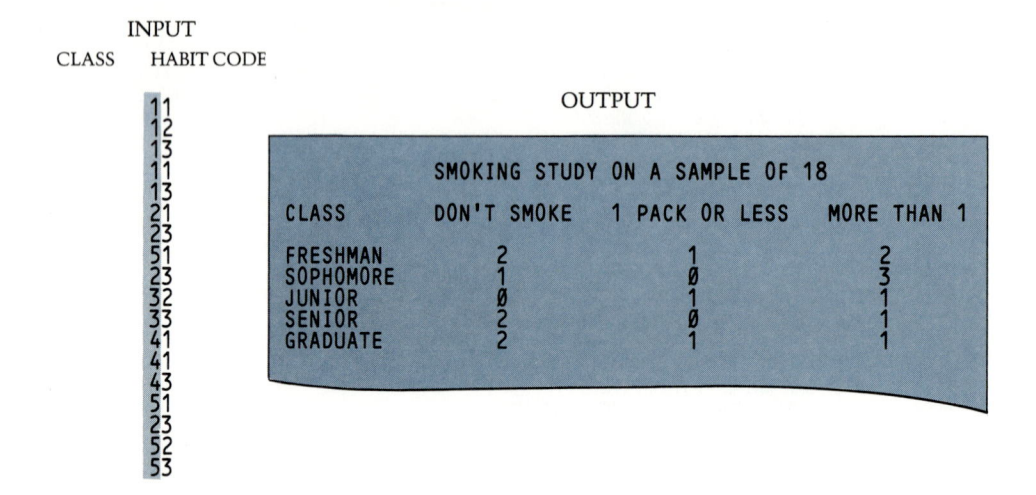

```
        INPUT
CLASS   HABIT CODE
  1 1
  1 2
  1 3
  1 1
  1 3                         OUTPUT
  2 1
  2 3         SMOKING STUDY ON A SAMPLE OF 18
  5 1
  2 3     CLASS      DON'T SMOKE   1 PACK OR LESS   MORE THAN 1
  3 2
  3 3     FRESHMAN        2              1               2
  4 1     SOPHOMORE       1              0               3
  4 1     JUNIOR          0              1               1
  4 3     SENIOR          2              0               1
  5 1     GRADUATE        2              1               1
  2 3
  5 2
  5 3
```

Program Analysis

The code to solve this problem is shown in Figure 8–14.

This problem essentially deals with counting, i.e., we need to count how many freshmen do not smoke, how many freshmen smoke one pack or less a day, how many freshmen smoke in excess of one pack, and so forth. Altogether we need 15 counters (5 student classifications and 3 habits). One simple way to solve the problem manually is to draw a table with 5 rows and 3 columns, and proceed as follows:

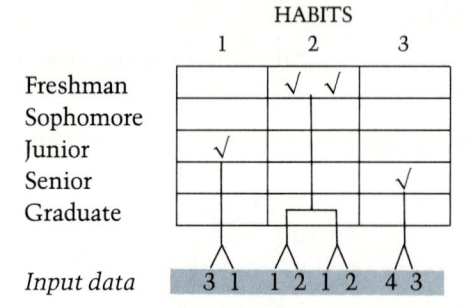

```
              HABITS
           1    2    3
Freshman  |   | √ √ |   |
Sophomore |   |     |   |
Junior    | √ |     |   |
Senior    |   |     | √ |
Graduate  |   |     |   |

Input data  3 1  1 2 1 2  4 3
```

If the first record is 3,1 (3 = junior, 1 = no smoke), we place a check mark in the box at row 3 and column 1. We read the next record (1,2) and check the corresponding box. We repeat the process until we run out of records, then we add up the checks in each box.

This table shows the counts (frequencies) obtained by processing the four data records shown.

To simulate this process in our program, we create a two-dimensional table KOUNT (line 81) with 5 rows and 3 columns, where each entry serves as a counter. Initially, these counters are set to 0 (line 92). Then every time we read a class and a habit code, we add 1 to the corresponding table entry, e.g., if class = 1 and habit = 2, we add 1 to KOUNT(class,habit), which is KOUNT(1,2), see line 101. When all data have been read, table KOUNT will contain the 15 summary counts.

Test Your Understanding of the Program

1. What is the purpose of line 116? Is it necessary? Should it be carried out more than once? Could the DETAIL-LINE be blanked out in the DATA division?

ONE- AND TWO- DIMENSIONAL TABLES 437

2. Change the logic of the program to allow for an input file consisting of only one record containing all pairs of response code, i.e., 111213112351 ... 5253.

3. Add an error check for out-of-range values on input.

8-5-6 A WAREHOUSE PROBLEM

Problem Specification:

You own six warehouses across the country; each warehouse stocks five particular items. The stock quantities for each of the five items are recorded in a data file, with one record for each warehouse. Write a program to read the data into a two-dimensional table and produce the output shown below. Make the program general enough to handle up to 15 warehouses.

Identify on the output any item that is out of stock in three or more warehouses. Also print those warehouses and item numbers where the stock is below 10. When listing those item numbers with stock levels less than 10, note that commas separate each item, i.e., the list should terminate with an item number, not a comma.

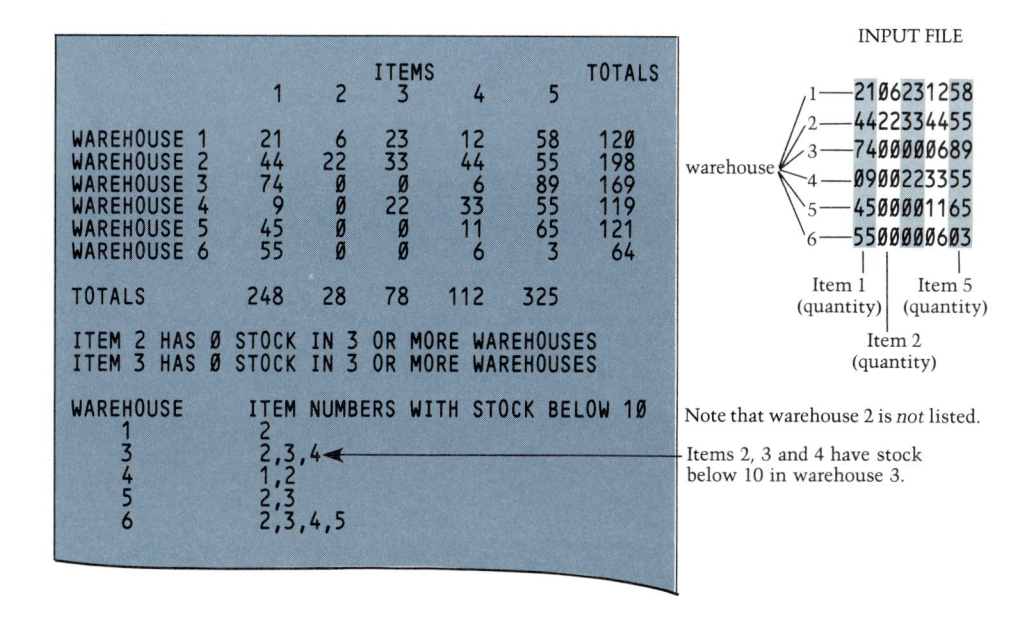

```
                        ITEMS                TOTALS
                1    2    3    4    5
WAREHOUSE 1    21    6   23   12   58    120
WAREHOUSE 2    44   22   33   44   55    198
WAREHOUSE 3    74    0    0    6   89    169
WAREHOUSE 4     9    0   22   33   55    119
WAREHOUSE 5    45    0    0   11   65    121
WAREHOUSE 6    55    0    0    6    3     64

TOTALS        248   28   78  112  325

ITEM 2 HAS 0 STOCK IN 3 OR MORE WAREHOUSES
ITEM 3 HAS 0 STOCK IN 3 OR MORE WAREHOUSES

WAREHOUSE       ITEM NUMBERS WITH STOCK BELOW 10
    1           2
    3           2,3,4
    4           1,2
    5           2,3
    6           2,3,4,5
```

INPUT FILE

1—2106231258
2—4422334455
3—7400000689
warehouse
4—0900223355
5—4500001165
6—5500000603

Item 1 | Item 5
(quantity) | (quantity)
Item 2
(quantity)

Note that warehouse 2 is *not* listed.

Items 2, 3 and 4 have stock below 10 in warehouse 3.

Program Analysis

The problem consists of five parts:

1. Reading the input records into a two-dimensional table
2. Computing the sum of each row of the table.
3. Computing the sum of each column of the table.
4. Searching each column to determine whether three or more entries are 0.
5. Searching each row to find entries that are less than 10.

The last part is probably the most interesting part of the problem. It requires us to look at a row and identify in that row the column number whose

```
 1:     IDENTIFICATION DIVISION.
 2:     PROGRAM-ID. SMOKING-SURVEY.
 3:     AUTHOR. JONES.
 4: ****************************************************************
 5: * OBJECTIVE: PRODUCE A TWO-DIMENSIONAL TABLE SHOWING SMOKING   *
 6: *            HABITS BY STUDENT CLASSIFICATION AND NUMBER OF    *
 7: *            CIGARETTE PACKS SMOKED.                           *
 8: *                                                              *
 9: * INPUT: STUDENT CLASSIFICATION CODE AND SMOKING HABIT CODE    *
10: *            1   DON'T SMOKE                                   *
11: *            2   1 PACK OR LESS                                *
12: *            3   MORE THAN 1 PACK                              *
13: *                                                              *
14: * OUTPUT: SEE OUTPUT TABLE BELOW                               *
15: ****************************************************************
16:     ENVIRONMENT DIVISION.
17:     CONFIGURATION SECTION.
18:     SOURCE-COMPUTER. IBM.
19:     OBJECT-COMPUTER. IBM.
20:     INPUT-OUTPUT SECTION.
21:     FILE-CONTROL.
22:         SELECT REPORT-FILE ASSIGN TO PRINTER.
23:         SELECT SURVEY-FILE ASSIGN TO DISK
24:         ORGANIZATION IS LINE SEQUENTIAL.
25:     DATA DIVISION.
26:     FILE SECTION.
27:     FD  SURVEY-FILE
28:         LABEL RECORDS ARE STANDARD
29:         VALUE OF FILE-ID IS 'SMOKE'
30:         DATA RECORD IS INPUT-AREA.
31:     01  INPUT-AREA PIC X(02).
32:     FD  REPORT-FILE
33:         LABEL RECORDS ARE OMITTED
34:         DATA RECORD IS PRINT-LINE.
35:     01  PRINT-LINE PIC X(80).
36: *
37:     WORKING-STORAGE SECTION.
38: ********************************
39: *       INDEPENDENT ITEMS      *
40: ********************************
41:     01  FLAGS-AND-COUNTERS.
42:         05 WS-EOF    PIC 9  VALUE 0.
43:         05 WS-COUNT PIC 99 VALUE 0.
44: *
45:     01  SUBSCRIPTS.
46:         05 R-INDX    PIC 9.
47:         05 C-INDX    PIC 9.
48: ********************************
49: *     INPUT RECORD DESCRIPTION *
50: ********************************
51:     01  SURVEY-RECORD.
52:         05 SR-CLASS  PIC 9.
53:         05 SR-HABIT  PIC 9.
54: ********************************
55: *     OUTPUT LINE DESCRIPTIONS *
56: ********************************
57:     01  MAJOR-HEADING.
58:         05 FILLER PIC X(12) VALUE SPACES.
59:         05 FILLER PIC X(16) VALUE 'SMOKING STUDY ON'.
60:         05 FILLER PIC X(13) VALUE ' A SAMPLE OF'.
61:         05 MH-SAMPLE-COUNT PIC Z9.
```

INPUT FILE

```
11
12
13
13
21
22
22
32
33
51
51
52
53
53
53
41
41
41
43
```

Student classification — Student habit

```
              SMOKING STUDY ON A SAMPLE OF 19
   CLASS    DON'T SMOKE   1 PACK OR LESS   MORE THAN 1

 FRESHMAN        1               1              2
 SOPHOMORE       1               2              0
 JUNIOR          0               1              1
 SENIOR          3               0              1
 GRADUATE        2               1              3
```

FIGURE 8–14
A TWO-DIMENSIONAL FREQUENCY COUNT

ONE- AND TWO- DIMENSIONAL TABLES

```
 63:   01  MINOR-HEADING.
 64:       05  FILLER  PIC X(01) VALUE SPACES.
 65:       05  FILLER  PIC X(09) VALUE 'CLASS'.
 66:       05  FILLER  PIC X(14) VALUE 'DON''T SMOKE'.
 67:       05  FILLER  PIC X(17) VALUE '1 PACK OR LESS'.
 68:       05  FILLER  PIC X(89) VALUE 'MORE THAN 1'.
 69:  ******************************
 70:  *     TABLE DEFINITIONS       *
 71:  ******************************
 72:   01  DETAIL-LINE.
 73:       05  FILLER      PIC X(01) VALUE SPACES.
 74:       05  DL-CLASS    PIC X(16).
 75:       05  DL-HABIT OCCURS 3 TIMES.
 76:           10  DL-COUNT PIC Z9.
 77:           10  FILLER   PIC X(13).
 78:  *
 79:   01  SMOKE-HABIT-TABLE.
 80:       05  CLASSIFICATION OCCURS 5 TIMES.
 81:           10  KOUNT OCCURS 3 TIMES PIC 99.
 82:  *
 83:   01  CLASS-LIST PIC X(45) VALUE
 84:       'FRESHMAN SOPHOMOREJUNIOR   SENIOR    GRADUATE'.
 85:  *
 86:   01  DUPLICATE-LIST REDEFINES CLASS-LIST.
 87:       05  KLASS OCCURS 5 TIMES PIC X(09).
 88:  *
 89:   PROCEDURE DIVISION.
 90:   100-MAIN-LOGIC.
 91:       OPEN OUTPUT REPORT-FILE, INPUT SURVEY-FILE.
 92:       MOVE ZEROS TO SMOKE-HABIT-TABLE.-------------------- Zero out all counters.
 93:       READ SURVEY-FILE INTO SURVEY-RECORD
 94:           AT END MOVE 1 TO WS-EOF.
 95:       PERFORM 200-UPDATE-TABLE UNTIL WS-EOF = 1.
 96:       PERFORM 300-PRINT-TABLE.
 97:       CLOSE SURVEY-FILE, REPORT-FILE.
 98:       STOP RUN.
 99:  *
100:   200-UPDATE-TABLE.
101:       ADD 1 TO KOUNT (SR-CLASS, SR-HABIT).
102:       ADD 1 TO WS-COUNT.
103:       READ SURVEY-FILE INTO SURVEY-RECORD
104:           AT END MOVE 1 TO WS-EOF.
105:  *
106:   300-PRINT-TABLE.
107:       MOVE WS-COUNT TO MH-SAMPLE-COUNT.
108:       WRITE PRINT-LINE FROM MAJOR-HEADING AFTER 1 LINE.
109:       WRITE PRINT-LINE FROM MINOR-HEADING AFTER 1 LINE.
110:       MOVE SPACES TO PRINT-LINE.
111:       WRITE PRINT-LINE AFTER ADVANCING 1 LINE.
112:       PERFORM 400-PRINT-REPORT-LINE VARYING R-INDX
113:           FROM 1 BY 1 UNTIL R-INDX IS GREATER THAN 5.
114:  *
115:   400-PRINT-REPORT-LINE.
116:       MOVE SPACES        TO DETAIL-LINE.
117:       MOVE KLASS (R-INDX) TO DL-CLASS.
118:       PERFORM 500-PREPARE-LINE VARYING C-INDX
119:           FROM 1 BY 1 UNTIL C-INDX GREATER THAN 3.
120:       WRITE PRINT-LINE FROM DETAIL-LINE AFTER 1 LINE.
121:  *
122:   500-PREPARE-LINE.
123:       MOVE KOUNT (R-INDX, C-INDX) TO DL-COUNT (C-INDX).
```

UPDATE THE FREQUENCY COUNT

A class code and a smoking habit code have been read; update the corresponding counter, i.e., if KOUNT (3,2) is presently 3, and a class code of 3 and a smoking code of 2 have been read, then KOUNT (3,2) is incremented by 1 to become 4.

KLASS(1) = FRESHMAN
KLASS (2) = SOPHOMORE
.
.
KLASS(5) = GRADUATE

FIGURE 8–14
(continued)

corresponding table element is less than 10. It is that column number (item number) that we need to print, not the entry (stock). The program to solve this problem is shown in Figure 8–15.

In the code for parts 1, 2, and 3, the table is read and processed one row (input record) at a time. Line 114 reads the first record and stores the five item quantities into ROW–INVENTORY(1), meaning that the first quantity, 21, is automatically stored into WI–INVENTORY(1, 1), 06 is stored into WI–INVENTORY(1, 2), . . ., and 58 into WI–INVENTORY(1, 5). As each warehouse record is read, the corresponding row sum is computed (line 131), while partial column totals are accumulated into the five slots of table CT–COL–TOTALS at line 144. The detail line is then printed (line 135) before a new record is read. When the entire table has been printed, the column totals are printed (line 117).

For the fourth part of the problem, we check each column (line 165) for entries that have value 0. If there are three or more zero entries in a particular column, we print the column number (item number) and the message (line 160). WS–ZERO–ITEM–COUNT is used as a counter to count each occurrence of a zero entry—if that counter is less than 3, no message is printed.

For the fifth part of the problem, we analyze each row and record in the table SL–ITEMS the item numbers whose stock level is below 10. The counter COUNT–BELOW–10 counts these items (line 185); this count is always less than or equal to 5. When each row has been examined, we print the elements of tables SL–ITEMS and SL–COMMA; there are COUNT–BELOW–10 of each of them (line 181), but note how we replace the right-most comma by a blank space at line 180.

8–6 THREE-DIMENSIONAL TABLES

8–6–1 DEFINITION

A three-dimensional table is a data structure whose elements can be accessed using three subscripts. In some simple problems, one might view a three-dimensional table as a cube that can be sliced into several two-dimensional tables; but like two-dimensional tables, three-dimensional tables are stored linearly in memory, so in most cases, conjuring the geometry of a cube may not prove to be too helpful. Three OCCURS clauses are needed to identify such a table.

Example: To declare TABL as a table with 3 rows, 5 columns, and a depth of 3, the following code could be used:

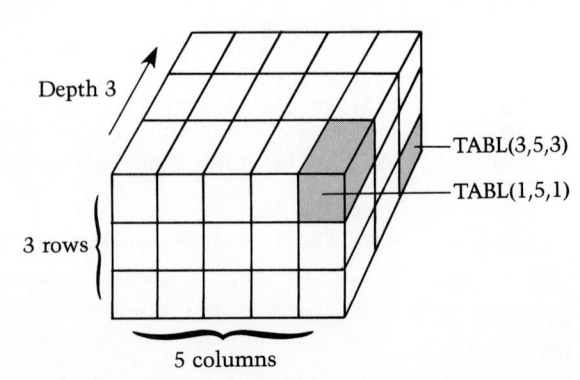

```
01 3D-TABLE.
   05 ROW OCCURS 3 TIMES.
      06 COLUMN OCCURS 5 TIMES.
         07 DEPTH OCCURS 3 TIMES.
            08 TABL PIC 99V99.
```

ONE- AND TWO- DIMENSIONAL TABLES

Each of the 45 table elements can be identified by three subscripts. For example,

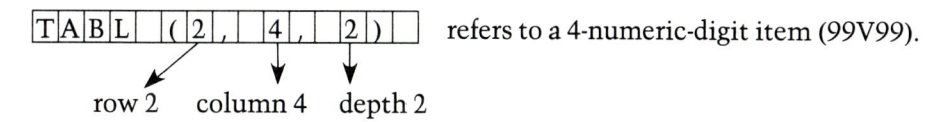

TABL (2, 4, 2)   refers to a 4-numeric-digit item (99V99).
row 2 column 4 depth 2

A three dimensional structure could be used to handle the following type of problem: A company has two factories, each factory containing three shops, each shop having four machines. A study of the repair records of machines (machine down-time expressed in hours) is to be made. The log of repairs is recorded in a table called LOG. For example, the technical manager may want to compile the number of hours lost for each machine in shop 1, factory 2, or he/she may need to know which shops in both factories exceeded 100 hours in down-time for machine 4, et cetera. Using a three-dimensional table to identify the various factories, shops, and machines can greatly facilitate the logic of the program. Such a table could be declared as follows:

```
01 COMPANY-XYZ.
   05 FACTORY OCCURS 2 TIMES.
      10 SHOP OCCURS 3 TIMES.
         20 TOOL OCCURS 4 TIMES.
            25 LOG PIC 999V99.
```

LOG (2,1,3)
Factory Shop Machine tool

The number of storage positions reserved for such a table is $2 \times 3 \times 4 \times 5 = 120$.

An example of the internal representation of this table is shown in Figure 8–16.

COMPANY-XYZ														
FACTORY(1)												FACTORY(2)	
SHOP(1,1)				SHOP(1,2)				SHOP(1,3)				SHOP(2,1)	
LOG(1,1,1)	LOG(1,1,2)	LOG(1,1,3)	LOG(1,1,4)	LOG(1,2,1)	LOG(1,2,2)	LOG(1,2,3)	LOG(1,2,4)	LOG(1,3,1)	LOG(1,3,2)	LOG(1,3,3)	LOG(1,3,4)	LOG(2,1,1)	LOG(2,1,2)	...
01010	02020	01015	00900	00800	00550	01000	01400	01800	00030	02010	02030	04000	02600	...

References to items in the above table are as follows:

- LOG(1,3,2) refers to the number of hours lost on machine tool 2, shop 3, factory 1 (0030).
- TOOL(1,2,3) is identical to LOG(1,2,3), except it is an alphanumeric item.
- SHOP(1,1) refers to all hours lost in shop 1, factory 1. In terms of data, SHOP(1,1) refers to an alphanumeric item equal to 10102020010150900.
- FACTORY(1) refers to an alphanumeric string of 60 characters ($3 \times 4 \times 5$). It encompasses all shops in factory 1.
- COMPANY-XYZ covers the two factories. COMPANY-XYZ consists of a string of 120 characters (digits). A reference to COMPANY-XYZ may not include subscripts.
- LOG(2,4,1) is an invalid data name since the second subscript, 4, does not OCCUR that many times in the declaration of the table.

FIGURE 8–16
INTERNAL REPRESENTATION OF A THREE-DIMENSIONAL TABLE

```cobol
 1:    IDENTIFICATION DIVISION.
 2:    PROGRAM-ID. WAREHOUSE-PROBLEM.
 3:    AUTHOR. JONES.
 4:   ****************************************************************
 5:   * OBJECTIVE: PRODUCE AN INVENTORY REPORT LISTING VARIOUS WARE-  *
 6:   *            HOUSES AND THE ITEM STOCK QUANTITIES AT EACH OF THE*
 7:   *            WAREHOUSES. THE REPORT SHOULD LIST THOSE ITEMS THAT*
 8:   *            HAVE ZERO STOCK IN 3 OR MORE WAREHOUSES AND IDEN-  *
 9:   *            TIFY THE WAREHOUSE(S) AND PART NUMBERS WHERE THE   *
10:   *            STOCK IS BELOW 10.                                 *
11:   *                                                               *
12:   * INPUT:     5 ITEM QUANTITIES PER RECORD (WAREHOUSE).          *
13:   *                                                               *
14:   * OUTPUT:    1. A TWO-DIMENSIONAL TABLE OF WAREHOUSES AND ITEM  *
15:   *               NUMBERS AND STOCK LEVELS.                       *
16:   *            2. LIST OF ITEMS WITH ZERO STOCK LEVEL IN THREE    *
17:   *               OR MORE WAREHOUSES.                             *
18:   *            3. A LIST OF WAREHOUSE NUMBERS AND LIST OF ITEMS   *
19:   *               NUMBERS WITH STOCK LEVEL BELOW 10.              *
20:   ****************************************************************
21:    ENVIRONMENT DIVISION.
22:    CONFIGURATION SECTION.
23:    SOURCE-COMPUTER. IBM.
24:    OBJECT-COMPUTER. IBM.
25:    INPUT-OUTPUT SECTION.
26:    FILE-CONTROL.
27:        SELECT REPORT-FILE ASSIGN TO PRINTER.
28:        SELECT WAREHOUSE-FILE ASSIGN TO DISK
29:            ORGANIZATION IS LINE SEQUENTIAL.
30:   *
31:    DATA DIVISION.
32:    FILE SECTION.
33:   *
34:    FD  WAREHOUSE-FILE
35:        LABEL RECORDS ARE STANDARD
36:        VALUE OF FILE-ID IS 'WRHOUSE'
37:        DATA RECORD IS INPUT-RECORD.
38:    01  INPUT-RECORD PIC X(10).
39:    FD  REPORT-FILE
40:        LABEL RECORDS ARE OMITTED
41:        DATA RECORD IS PRINT-LINE.
42:    01  PRINT-LINE PIC X(80).
43:   *
44:    WORKING-STORAGE SECTION.
45:   ******************************
46:   *     INDEPENDENT ITEMS       *
47:   ******************************
48:    01  FLAGS.
49:        05  WS-EOF PIC 9   VALUE 0.
50:            88 END-OF-FILE VALUE IS 1.
51:   *
52:    01  SUBSCRIPTS.
53:        05  COUNT-BELOW-10 PIC 9.
54:        05  WAREHOUSE      PIC 9 VALUE 1.
55:        05  ITEM           PIC 9.
56:   *
57:    01  COMPUTATIONAL-ITEMS.
58:        05  WS-ZERO-ITEM-COUNT PIC 99.
59:        05  WS-NO-HOUSES       PIC 99.
60:        05  WS-ROW-TOTAL       PIC 999 VALUE 0.
61:   ******************************
62:   *    OUTPUT LINE DESCRIPTIONS *
63:   ******************************
64:    01  BLANK-LINE PIC X(80) VALUE SPACES.
65:    01  HEADER-1.
66:        05  FILLER PIC X(21) VALUE SPACES.
67:        05  FILLER PIC X(14) VALUE 'ITEMS'.
68:        05  FILLER PIC X(06) VALUE 'TOTALS'.
69:    01  HEADER-2.
70:        05  FILLER PIC X(14) VALUE SPACES.
71:        05  FILLER PIC X(17) VALUE
72:                '1   2   3   4   5'.
73:    01  HEADER-3.
74:        05  FILLER     PIC X(13) VALUE ' WAREHOUSE'.
75:        05  FILLER     PIC X(66) VALUE 'ITEM NUMBER'.
76:    01  ZERO-STOCK-LINE.
77:        05  FILLER     PIC X(06) VALUE ' ITEM'.
78:        05  SL-ITEM-NO PIC 9.
79:        05  FILLER     PIC X(46) VALUE
80:               ' HAS 0 STOCK ITEM IN 3 OR MORE WAREHOUSES'.
81:   ******************************
82:   *     TABLE RECORDS           *
83:   ******************************
84:    01  DETAIL-LINE.
85:        05  FILLER       PIC X(10) VALUE 'WAREHOUSE'.
86:        05  DL-WAREHOUSE PIC Z9.
87:        05  DL-QTY       PIC BB99 OCCURS 5 TIMES.
88:        05  FILLER       PIC X(04) VALUE SPACES.
89:        05  DL-ROW-TOTAL PIC ZZ9.
90:   *
91:    01  TOTALS-LINE.
92:        05  FILLER       PIC X(12) VALUE ' TOTALS'.
93:        05  TL-COL-TOTALS PIC BZZ9 OCCURS 5 TIMES.
94:   *
95:    01  WAREHOUSE-INVEN.
96:        05  ROW-INVENTORY           OCCURS 15 TIMES.
97:            10  ITEM-LIST           OCCURS  5 TIMES.
98:                15 WI-INVENTORY PIC 99.
99:   *
100:   01  COLUMN-TOTALS.
101:       05  CT-COL-TOTALS PIC 999 OCCURS 5 TIMES.
102:  *
103:   01  SUMMARY-LINE.
104:       05  FILLER       PIC X(03) VALUE SPACES.
105:       05  SL-WAREHOUSE PIC Z9.
106:       05  FILLER       PIC X(10) VALUE SPACES.
107:       05  LIST-ITEMS OCCURS 5 TIMES.
108:           10  SL-ITEMS PIC 9.
109:           10  SL-COMMA PIC X.
```

INPUT FILE

```
2106231258
4422334455
7400000689
0900223355
4500001165
5500000603
```

```
                              ITEMS           TOTALS

                      1    2    3    4    5

        WAREHOUSE  1  21   06   23   12   58    120
        WAREHOUSE  2  44   22   33   44   55    198
        WAREHOUSE  3  74   00   00   06   89    169
        WAREHOUSE  4  09   00   22   33   55    119
        WAREHOUSE  5  45   00   00   11   65    121
        WAREHOUSE  6  55   00   00   06   03     64

        TOTALS       248   28   78  112  325

        ITEM 2 HAS 0 STOCK ITEM IN 3 OR MORE WAREHOUSES
        ITEM 3 HAS 0 STOCK ITEM IN 3 OR MORE WAREHOUSES

        WAREHOUSE    ITEM NUMBER
        1            2
        3            2,3,4
        4            1,2
        5            2,3
        6            2,3,4,5
```

FIGURE 8-15

A WAREHOUSE PROBLEM

```
110:    PROCEDURE DIVISION.
111:    100-MAIN-LOGIC.
112:        OPEN OUTPUT REPORT-FILE, INPUT WAREHOUSE-FILE.
113:        PERFORM 200-WRITE-HEADINGS.
114:        READ WAREHOUSE-FILE INTO ROW-INVENTORY (1)
115:            AT END MOVE 1 TO WS-EOF.
116:        PERFORM 300-READ-PROCESS UNTIL END-OF-FILE.
117:        PERFORM 500-PREPARE-COLUMN-TOTALS VARYING
118:            ITEM FROM 1 BY 1 UNTIL ITEM GREATER THAN 5.
119:        PERFORM 600-ZERO-STOCK-LEVEL-SEARCH.
120:        PERFORM 900-BELOW-10-INVENTORY-PROCESS.
121:        CLOSE REPORT-FILE, WAREHOUSE-FILE.
122:        STOP RUN.
123:    *
124:    200-WRITE-HEADINGS.
125:        WRITE PRINT-LINE FROM HEADER-1   AFTER 1 LINE.
126:        WRITE PRINT-LINE FROM HEADER-2   AFTER 2 LINE.
127:        WRITE PRINT-LINE FROM BLANK-LINE AFTER 1 LINE.
128:        MOVE ZEROS TO COLUMN-TOTALS.
129:    *
130:    300-READ-PROCESS.
131:        PERFORM 400-ROW-COLUMN-SUMMATION
132:            VARYING ITEM FROM 1 BY 1 UNTIL ITEM GREATER THAN 5.
133:        MOVE WAREHOUSE    TO DL-WAREHOUSE.
134:        MOVE WS-ROW-TOTAL TO DL-ROW-TOTAL.
135:        WRITE PRINT-LINE FROM DETAIL-LINE AFTER 1 LINE.
136:        MOVE 0 TO WS-ROW-TOTAL.
137:        ADD  1 TO WAREHOUSE.
138:        READ WAREHOUSE-FILE INTO ROW-INVENTORY (WAREHOUSE)
139:            AT END MOVE 1 TO WS-EOF.
140:    *
141:    400-ROW-COLUMN-SUMMATION.
142:        MOVE WI-INVENTORY (WAREHOUSE, ITEM) TO DL-QTY (ITEM).
143:        ADD  WI-INVENTORY (WAREHOUSE, ITEM) TO WS-ROW-TOTAL.
144:        ADD  WI-INVENTORY (WAREHOUSE, ITEM) TO CT-COL-TOTALS (ITEM).
145:    *
146:    500-PREPARE-COLUMN-TOTALS.
147:        MOVE CT-COL-TOTALS (ITEM) TO TL-COL-TOTALS (ITEM).
148:    *
149:    600-ZERO-STOCK-LEVEL-SEARCH.
150:        WRITE PRINT-LINE FROM TOTALS-LINE AFTER 2 LINES.
151:        WRITE PRINT-LINE FROM BLANK-LINE  AFTER 1 LINE.
152:        COMPUTE WS-NO-HOUSES = WAREHOUSE - 1.
153:        PERFORM 700-ZERO-SEARCH VARYING
154:            ITEM FROM 1 BY 1 UNTIL ITEM GREATER THAN 5.
155:    *
156:    700-ZERO-SEARCH.
157:        MOVE 0 TO WS-ZERO-ITEM-COUNT.
158:        PERFORM 800-ZERO-COLUMN VARYING WAREHOUSE
159:            FROM 1 BY 1 UNTIL WAREHOUSE > WS-NO-HOUSES.
160:        IF WS-ZERO-ITEM-COUNT IS EQUAL TO 3 OR IS GREATER THAN 3
161:            MOVE ITEM TO SL-ITEM-NO
162:            WRITE PRINT-LINE FROM ZERO-STOCK-LINE AFTER 1 LINE.
163:    *
164:    800-ZERO-COLUMN.
165:        IF WI-INVENTORY (WAREHOUSE, ITEM) IS EQUAL TO 0
166:            ADD 1 TO WS-ZERO-ITEM-COUNT.
167:    *
168:    900-BELOW-10-INVENTORY-PROCESS.
169:        WRITE PRINT-LINE FROM HEADER-3 AFTER 2 LINES.
170:        PERFORM 1000-SEARCH-BELOW-10 VARYING WAREHOUSE
171:            FROM 1 BY 1 UNTIL WAREHOUSE GREATER THAN WS-NO-HOUSES.
172:    *
173:    1000-SEARCH-BELOW-10.
174:        MOVE SPACES TO SUMMARY-LINE.
175:        MOVE ZERO   TO COUNT-BELOW-10.
176:        PERFORM 1100-ROW-SEARCH VARYING ITEM
177:            FROM 1 BY 1 UNTIL ITEM IS GREATER THAN 5.
178:        IF COUNT-BELOW-10 IS GREATER THAN ZERO
179:            MOVE WAREHOUSE TO SL-WAREHOUSE
180:            MOVE SPACES    TO SL-COMMA (COUNT-BELOW-10)
181:            WRITE PRINT-LINE FROM SUMMARY-LINE AFTER 1 LINE.
182:    *
183:    1100-ROW-SEARCH.
184:        IF WI-INVENTORY (WAREHOUSE, ITEM) IS LESS THAN 10
185:            ADD 1 TO COUNT-BELOW-10
186:            MOVE ITEM TO SL-ITEMS (COUNT-BELOW-10)
187:            MOVE ',' TO SL-COMMA (COUNT-BELOW-10).
```

Read inventory stock consisting of five different items per record for each warehouse. Each row represents the inventory for one warehouse.

Print the sum of each column entries and print the item numbers whose corresponding stock levels are zero in three or more warehouses.

Initialize the five-element table COLUMN-TOTALS to 0's. This table is used to store the sum of the entries for each of the five columns.

Position the sum of each of the five columns on the output line.

Determine the number of warehouses.

Find the number of zero entries in each column. If there are more than three 0's in a column, print that column, i.e., the item number.

Is an inventory item at zero stock level? If affirmative, count it in item-count.

Identify the warehouse number in which any stock item is below 10. List such items and the corresponding warehouse number. Note the commas separating the items.

Identify in each warehouse (row) inventory items that number fewer than 10.
If there are items with stock below 10 in a particular row, list the item numbers on the output line and separate them with a comma. Note that the last comma is blanked out (line 180).

Search each row for an inventory item whose stock is below 10. Any such item found (ITEM) is placed on the output line with a comma to the right of the item.

FIGURE 8–15
(*continued*)

8-6-2 THE PERFORM VARYING AFTER STATEMENT

The user may sometimes find it convenient to use an extension of the PERFORM statement to manipulate subscripts for three-dimensional tables. This option allows the user to initialize and increment three subscripts in one PERFORM statement in the sequence shown in the general form in Figure 8–17.

8-6-3 A THREE-DIMENSIONAL TABLE PROBLEM

Problem Specification

Each record of an input file (maximum of 100 records) consists of a student name followed by eight scores. The first four scores were obtained on mathematics tests, and the last four scores were obtained on computer science tests. Write a program to compute the class average (over all tests in both disciplines) and "pass" those students whose averages on both mathematics and computer tests are above the overall class average (place two asterisks by their grades). Sample input and output files are as follows:

```
                TEST 1         TEST 2         TEST 3         TEST 4
              MATH  COMP    MATH  COMP    MATH  COMP    MATH  COMP
STEVENSON L    10    40      20    50      30    60      40    70
GLEASON G      20    60      30    70      40    80      50    90
ANDREAS L      65    70      45    70      90    80      64    90   **
MICKAEL P      60    50      50    60      80    80      30    90

CLASS AVERAGE = 57.31
```

```
INPUT FILE

STEVENSON L 010020030040040050060070
GLEASON G   020030040050060070080090
ANDREAS L   065045090064070070080090
MICKAEL P   060050080030050060080090
            ‾‾‾‾‾‾‾‾‾‾‾‾ ‾‾‾‾‾‾‾‾‾‾‾‾
            Math scores  Computer scores
```

Program Analysis

The program to solve this problem is shown in Figure 8–18.

First the scores are read into the three-dimensional table GRADE (lines 127–128). For the first record, the first four math grades in SR–MATH–SCORES (line 55) are stored as one block of digits into SUBJECT(1,1) while the first four computer grades in SR–COMPUTER–SCORES (line 56) are stored as one block into SUBJECT(1,2). Note that SUBJECT(1,1) is a group item name for GRADE(1,1,1), GRADE(1,1,2), GRADE(1,1,3) and GRADE(1,1,4); likewise SUBJECT(1,2) is a group item name for GRADE(1,2,1), GRADE(1,2,2), GRADE(1,2,3) and GRADE(1,2,4). When the second record is read the four math scores are stored into SUBJECT(2,1) or GRADE(2,1,1), ..., GRADE(2,1,4), and so forth.

The PERFORM VARYING/AFTER/AFTER statement (lines 103–106) is used to compute the sum of all entries of table GRADE and the class average is calculated at line 136.

A flag (or a counter) WS–ABOVE–CLASS–AVERAGE–FLAG is used at line 159 to determine whether or not a student's math average or computer average exceeds the class average. If the flag is equal to 2 at line 149, then the student's average on both tests exceeded the class average and the student record is flagged on the output.

ONE- AND TWO- DIMENSIONAL TABLES   445

> PERFORM paragraph-name VARYING data-name-1
>
> FROM initial-value-1 BY increment-value-1 UNTIL condition-1
>
> AFTER data-name-2
>
> FROM initial-value-2 BY increment-value-2 UNTIL condition-2
>
> AFTER data-name-3
>
> FROM initial-value-3 BY increment-value-3 UNTIL condition-3.

FLOWCHART INTERPRETATION

- MOVE initial-value-1 TO data-name-1
- MOVE initial-value-2 TO data-name-2
- MOVE initial-value-3 TO data-name-3

condition 1 true? — Yes → next statement
No ↓
condition 2 true? — Yes
No ↓
condition 3 true? — Yes
No ↓
Carry out paragraph-name
Add increment-value-3 TO data-name-3

MOVE initial-value-3 TO data-name-3
ADD increment-value-2 TO data-name-2

MOVE initial-value-2 TO data-name-2
ADD increment-value-1 TO data-name-1

EXAMPLE

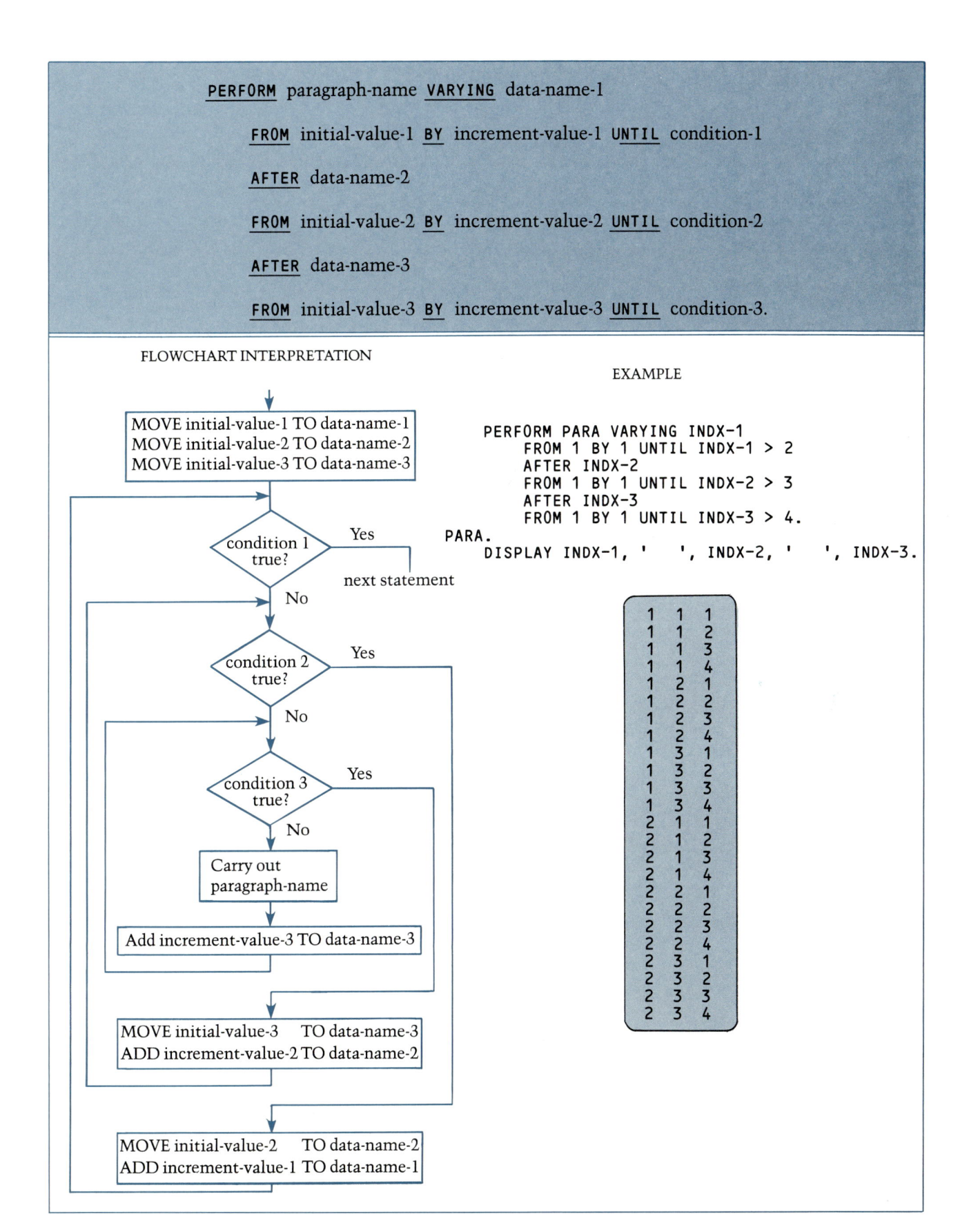

```
PERFORM PARA VARYING INDX-1
    FROM 1 BY 1 UNTIL INDX-1 > 2
    AFTER INDX-2
    FROM 1 BY 1 UNTIL INDX-2 > 3
    AFTER INDX-3
    FROM 1 BY 1 UNTIL INDX-3 > 4.
PARA.
    DISPLAY INDX-1, ' ', INDX-2, ' ', INDX-3.
```

```
1 1 1
1 1 2
1 1 3
1 1 4
1 2 1
1 2 2
1 2 3
1 2 4
1 3 1
1 3 2
1 3 3
1 3 4
2 1 1
2 1 2
2 1 3
2 1 4
2 2 1
2 2 2
2 2 3
2 2 4
2 3 1
2 3 2
2 3 3
2 3 4
```

FIGURE 8–17
THE PERFORM VARYING/AFTER/AFTER STATEMENT

446 UNDERSTANDING STRUCTURED COBOL

```
 1:      IDENTIFICATION DIVISION.
 2:      PROGRAM-ID. 3-DIMENSIONAL-PROBLEM.
 3:      AUTHOR. JONES.
 4:     ****************************************************
 5:     * OBJECTIVE: USE A 3 DIMENSIONAL TABLE TO RECORD & PROCESS  *
 6:     *            STUDENT SCORES. COMPUTE AN OVERALL CLASS AVERAGE*
 7:     *            AND FLAG THOSE STUDENT ENTRIES WHOSE AVERAGES  *
 8:     *            EXCEED BOTH THE MATH & COMPUTER CLASS AVERAGE. *
 9:     *                                                            *
10:     * INPUT: STUDENT NAME, 4 MATH SCORES AND 4 COMPUTER SCORES  *
11:     *                                                            *
12:     * OUTPUT: SEE OUTPUT TABLE BELOW                             *
13:     ****************************************************

14:      ENVIRONMENT DIVISION.
15:      CONFIGURATION SECTION.
16:      SOURCE-COMPUTER. IBM.
17:      OBJECT-COMPUTER. IBM.
18:      INPUT-OUTPUT SECTION.
19:      FILE-CONTROL.
20:          SELECT REPORT-FILE ASSIGN TO PRINTER.
21:          SELECT STUDENT-FILE ASSIGN TO DISK
22:          ORGANIZATION IS LINE SEQUENTIAL.
23:      DATA DIVISION.
24:      FILE SECTION.
25:      FD  STUDENT-FILE
26:          LABEL RECORDS ARE STANDARD
27:          VALUE OF FILE-ID IS 'THREEDIM'
28:          DATA RECORD IS INPUT-AREA.
29:      01  INPUT-AREA PIC X(35).
30:      FD  REPORT-FILE
31:          LABEL RECORDS ARE OMITTED
32:          DATA RECORD IS PRINT-LINE.
33:      01  PRINT-LINE PIC X(80).

34:      WORKING-STORAGE SECTION.
35:     *******************************
36:     *   INDEPENDENT ITEMS          *
37:     *******************************
38:      01  FLAGS-AND-COUNTERS.
39:          05  WS-EOF             PIC 9  VALUE 0.
40:          05  WS-NO-STUDENTS     PIC 99 VALUE 0.
41:          05  WS-ABOVE-CLASS-AVERAGE-FLAG PIC 9 VALUE 0.
42:      01  COMPUTATIONAL-N-ACCUMULATORS.
43:          05  WS-AVERAGE    PIC 999V99.
44:          05  WS-SUM-GRADES PIC 9999 VALUE 0.
45:          05  WS-SCORE      PIC 999.
46:      01  SUBSCRIPTS.
47:          05  R-INDX       PIC 999.
48:          05  C-INDX       PIC 9.
49:          05  D-INDX       PIC 9.
50:     *******************************
51:     *   INPUT RECORD DESCRIPTION  *
52:     *******************************
53:      01  STUDENT-RECORD.
54:          05  SR-NAME           PIC X(11).
55:          05  SR-MATH-SCORES    PIC 9(12).
56:          05  SR-COMPUTER-SCORES PIC 9(12).
57:     *******************************
58:     *   OUTPUT LINE DESCRIPTIONS  *
59:     *******************************
60:      01  CLASS-AVERAGE-LINE.
61:          05  FILLER     PIC X(14).
62:          05  FILLER     PIC X(15) VALUE 'CLASS AVERAGE='.
63:          05  CA-AVERAGE PIC ZZ9.99.
64:      01  BLANK-LINE PIC X(80) VALUE SPACES.
65:     *******************************
66:     *   TABLE DEFINITIONS         *
67:     *******************************
68:      01  MAJOR-HEADING.
69:          05  FILLER      PIC X(14) VALUE SPACES.
70:          05  CAPTION OCCURS 4 TIMES.
71:              10  MH-CAPTION PIC X(05).
72:              10  MH-TEST-NO PIC 9.
73:              10  FILLER     PIC X(05).
74:     *
75:      01  MINOR-HEADING.
76:          05  FILLER   PIC X(13).
77:          05  MH-TITLE PIC X(11) OCCURS 4 TIMES.
78:     *
79:      01  DETAIL-LINE.
80:          05  DL-NAME     PIC X(13).
81:          05  GRADES OCCURS 4 TIMES.
82:              10  DL-MATH     PIC ZZ9.
83:              10  FILLER      PIC X(02).
84:              10  DL-COMPUTER PIC ZZ9.
85:              10  FILLER      PIC X(03).
86:          05  DL-ASTERISKS PIC X(02).
87:     *
88:      01  ROSTER.
89:          05  STUDENT              OCCURS 100 TIMES.
90:              10  STUDENT-NAME PIC X(11).
91:              10  SUBJECT          OCCURS 2 TIMES.
92:                  15  NO-TESTS     OCCURS 4 TIMES.
93:                      20  GRADE PIC 999.
```

input file

GRADE(1,1,2) GRADE(4,2,4)

```
STEVENSON L010020030040040050060070
GLEASON G  020030040050060070080090
ANDREAS L  065045090064070080090
MICKAEL P  060050080030050060080090
```

GRADE(4,1,1)   Math scores   Computer scores

	TEST 1 MATH COMP	TEST 2 MATH COMP	TEST 3 MATH COMP	TEST 4 MATH COMP	
STEVENSON L	10 40	20 50	30 60	40 70	
GLEASON G	20 60	30 70	40 80	50 90	
ANDREAS L	65 70	45 70	90 80	64 90	**
MICKAEL P	60 50	50 60	80 80	30 90	

CLASS AVERAGE = 57.31

varies from 1 to 100   varies from 1 to 4
varies from 1 to 2

GRADE(R-INDX, C-INDX, D-INDX)

Student   Subject   Test number
           1 = Math
           2 = Computers

FIGURE 8–18

A THREE-DIMENSIONAL TABLE PROBLEM

ONE- AND TWO-DIMENSIONAL TABLES

```
 95:     PROCEDURE DIVISION.
 96:     050-MAIN-LOGIC.
 97:         OPEN OUTPUT REPORT-FILE, INPUT STUDENT-FILE.
 98:         PERFORM 100-INITIALIZATION.
 99:         READ STUDENT-FILE INTO STUDENT-RECORD
100:             AT END MOVE 1 TO WS-EOF.
101:         PERFORM 300-LOAD-TABLE VARYING R-INDX
102:             FROM 1 BY 1 UNTIL WS-EOF = 1.
103:         PERFORM 400-COMPUTE-AVERAGE VARYING R-INDX
104:             FROM 1 BY 1 UNTIL R-INDX > WS-NO-STUDENTS
105:             AFTER C-INDX FROM 1 BY 1 UNTIL C-INDX > 2
106:             AFTER D-INDX FROM 1 BY 1 UNTIL D-INDX > 4.
107:         PERFORM 500-PROCESS-STUDENTS.
108:         CLOSE STUDENT-FILE, REPORT-FILE.
109:         STOP RUN.
110:     *
111:     100-INITIALIZATION.
112:         MOVE SPACES TO MAJOR-HEADING, MINOR-HEADING.
113:         PERFORM 200-INSERT-TEST-CAPTIONS VARYING D-INDX
114:             FROM 1 BY 1 UNTIL D-INDX GREATER THAN 4.
115:         WRITE PRINT-LINE FROM MAJOR-HEADING AFTER 1 LINE.
116:         WRITE PRINT-LINE FROM MINOR-HEADING AFTER 1 LINE.
117:         WRITE PRINT-LINE FROM BLANK-LINE    AFTER 1 LINE.
118:     *
119:     200-INSERT-TEST-CAPTIONS.
120:         MOVE 'TEST'      TO MH-CAPTION (D-INDX).
121:         MOVE D-INDX      TO MH-TEST-NO (D-INDX).
122:         MOVE 'MATH COMP' TO MH-TITLE (D-INDX).
123:     *
124:     300-LOAD-TABLE.
125:         ADD 1 TO WS-NO-STUDENTS.
126:         MOVE SR-NAME             TO STUDENT-NAME (R-INDX).
127:         MOVE SR-MATH-SCORES      TO SUBJECT (R-INDX, 1).
128:         MOVE SR-COMPUTER-SCORES  TO SUBJECT (R-INDX, 2).
129:         READ STUDENT-FILE INTO STUDENT-RECORD
130:             AT END MOVE 1 TO WS-EOF.
131:     *
132:     400-COMPUTE-AVERAGE.
133:         ADD GRADE (R-INDX, C-INDX, D-INDX) TO WS-SUM-GRADES.
134:     *
135:     500-PROCESS-STUDENTS.
136:         COMPUTE WS-AVERAGE = WS-SUM-GRADES / ( WS-NO-STUDENTS * 8).
137:         PERFORM 600-COMPUTE-STUDENT-AVERAGES VARYING R-INDX
138:             FROM 1 BY 1 UNTIL R-INDX GREATER THAN WS-NO-STUDENTS.
139:         WRITE PRINT-LINE FROM BLANK-LINE AFTER 1 LINE.
140:         MOVE WS-AVERAGE TO CA-AVERAGE.
141:         WRITE PRINT-LINE FROM CLASS-AVERAGE-LINE AFTER 1 LINE.
142:     *
143:     600-COMPUTE-STUDENT-AVERAGES.
144:         MOVE SPACES TO DETAIL-LINE.
145:         MOVE STUDENT-NAME (R-INDX) TO DL-NAME.
146:         MOVE 0 TO WS-ABOVE-CLASS-AVERAGE-FLAG.
147:         PERFORM 700-TWO-AVERAGE-TESTS VARYING C-INDX
148:             FROM 1 BY 1 UNTIL C-INDX GREATER THAN 2.
149:         IF WS-ABOVE-CLASS-AVERAGE-FLAG = 2
150:             MOVE '**' TO DL-ASTERISKS.
151:         WRITE PRINT-LINE FROM DETAIL-LINE AFTER 1 LINE.
152:     *
153:     700-TWO-AVERAGE-TESTS.
154:         MOVE 0 TO WS-SUM-GRADES.
155:         PERFORM 800-SUBJECT VARYING D-INDX
156:             FROM 1 BY 1 UNTIL D-INDX GREATER THAN 4.
157:         COMPUTE WS-SUM-GRADES = WS-SUM-GRADES / 4.
158:         IF WS-SUM-GRADES GREATER THAN WS-AVERAGE
159:             ADD 1 TO WS-ABOVE-CLASS-AVERAGE-FLAG.
160:     *
161:     800-SUBJECT.
162:         MOVE GRADE (R-INDX, C-INDX, D-INDX) TO WS-SCORE.
163:         ADD WS-SCORE TO WS-SUM-GRADES.
164:         IF C-INDX = 1
165:             MOVE WS-SCORE TO DL-MATH (D-INDX)
166:         ELSE
167:             MOVE WS-SCORE TO DL-COMPUTER (D-INDX).
```

Read at most 100 student records.
Go and compute the sum of all grades.

Identify the test number captions 1, 2, 3, and 4.

Prepare both major and minor headings:
 TEST 1   TEST 2   TEST 3   TEST 4
MATH COMP ...   MATH COMP

Keep track of total number of students.

Store the first four math test scores in GRADE(1,1,1), GRADE(1,1,2), GRADE(1,1,3), and GRADE(1,1,4) and the first four computer test scores in GRADE(1,2,1), GRADE(1,2,2), GRADE(1,2,3), and GRADE(1,2,4).

Compute the class average of all scores.
Go and compute each student's average in both the math tests and the computer tests.

Assume the math and computer averages for each student are below the class average (FLAG = 0). The value of FLAG will be changed when student averages above the class average occur.

If FLAG = 2, this means that the student's two averages were above the class average, in which case asterisks are printed on the line. Print the student's scores on one line.

Compute the two averages for each student. If a student average exceeds the class average, the value 1 is added to FLAG; i.e., if FLAG = 2, this means that both the student's averages are above the class average.

FIGURE 8–18
(*continued*)

Testing Your Understanding of the Program

1. What is the reason for line 144?

2. Could you reduce the number of levels in the definition of the GRADE table (line 88–93)? What do you lose if you do?

3. Modify the program to include English in the report (in addition to math and computers) with four English test scores.

8-7 YOU MIGHT WANT TO KNOW

1. Does COBOL allow tables of more than three dimensions?

   Answer: Yes, some systems such as the Burroughs 68 and 6900 allow for 49 dimensions!

2. Is there any limit to the size of a multidimensional table?

   Answer: Theoretically, no. Practically, yes. Restrictions on table sizes are dictated by the size of the memory of the particular system. For example, on a system with memory size of 124,000 memory positions, the following table will exceed the memory size:

   ```
   01 NAME-TABLE.
       03 ROWS OCCURS 130 TIMES.
           04 COLUMN OCCURS 50 TIMES.
               10 NAME PIC X(20).
   ```

   The programmer requiring large tables should check on memory availability at his/her particular installation.

3. Can I index condition names?

   Answer:
   Yes. For example:

   ```
   05 COLORS OCCURS 10 TIMES.
       10 COLOR1 PIC X(7).
           88 BLUE VALUE 'BLUE'.
       10 COLOR2 PIC X(7).
           88 RED VALUE 'RED'.
   ```

   In the PROCEDURE division we can write:

   ```
   IF BLUE (I) AND RED (I)...
   ```
   to mean
   ```
   IF COLOR1 (I) = 'BLUE' AND
   COLOR2 (I) = 'RED'...
   ```

4. The other day I saw the following in one of my friend's programs:

   ```
   IF YEARS OF CENSUS-TABLE (I, K)
   ```

   Is this a valid reference to an element of CENSUS-TABLE? Shouldn't YEARS be the subscripted data name?

   Answer: The above is valid. Suppose CENSUS-TABLE is defined as follows:

   ```
   02 CENSUS OCCURS 5 TIMES.
       05 CENSUS-TABLE OCCURS 10 TIMES.
           10 YEARS  PIC 9999.
           10 MONTHS PIC 99.
           10 DAYS   PIC 99.
   ```

The YEARS OF CENSUS–TABLE (3,4) is equivalent to YEARS (3,4). This is the way "qualified" data names are subscripted.

5. Searching a table for a particular value or entry must surely be such a common task. I wonder why COBOL doesn't provide the user with a COBOL verb that will perform just that task. Is there such a verb?

   Answer: Yes. A convenient way to perform a linear or binary search is provided through the COBOL verb SEARCH. This feature is described in full in chapter 9.

6. Sorting tables must also be a very common activity in processing tables. Does COBOL offer a built-in procedure that allows the user to sort without having to write the code?

   Answer: Yes, a SORT verb exists; it is discussed in chapter 9, along with the bubble and mini/max sort procedures for systems not supporting the SORT feature.

8-8 EXERCISES

8-8-1 TEST YOURSELF

1. True or false:

   a. In the statement PERFORM PARA VARYING X FROM 1 BY 1 UNTIL X > 10, it is illegal to change the value of X in PARA.
   b. To initialize the table KOUNT to 0's, the following statement is valid (answer true or false for each statement):

   ```
   01 COUNTING.                        (i)   MOVE ZEROS TO KOUNT.
       05 KOUNT OCCURS 10 PIC 99.      (ii)  MOVE 0 TO COUNTING.
                                       (iii) MOVE ALL '0' TO COUNTING.
                                       (iv)  MOVE ZEROS TO COUNTING.
                                       (v)   MOVE '0' TO COUNTING.
   ```

   c. The OCCURS clause may be used at the 01 level if that particular level is redefined.
   d. The REDEFINES clause may not be used in the same entry as the OCCURS clause.
   e. The VALUE clause may not be used in the same entry as the OCCURS clause.
   f. The VALUE clause may be used in the same entry as the REDEFINES clause.
   g. The PICTURE clause may not be used in the same entry as the REDEFINES clause.
   h. The REDEFINES clause may not be used in the description of an input/output record.

2. Are the following statements valid or invalid? If valid, state the number of times paragraph A will be executed, assuming the VARYING counter is not changed by the user in paragraph A.

   ```
   a. PERFORM A VARYING K BY 1 UNTIL K = 1 OR K = 10.
   b. PERFORM A VARYING A FROM 1 BY 1 UNTIL A > 5.
   c. PERFORM A VARYING L FROM -1 BY -1 UNTIL K = 3.
   d. PERFORM A 10 TIMES VARYING K FROM 1 BY 1.
   ```

3. For each of the following coding segments, answer the following questions:

   (i) Is the code valid or invalid?
   (ii) How many memory positions are used by the group item (lowest level number)?
   (iii) Identify in diagram form the areas defined and redefined.

   For example, given the following record description entries, the answers would be as follows:

   ```
   01  X.
       05  A PIC 9999V99.
       05  B PIC XXXX.
   01  Z REDEFINES X.
       05  C OCCURS 3 PIC 99V9.
       05  FILLER PIC X.
   ```

   Answers:
   (i) Valid.
   (ii) 01 level reserves 10 positions.
   (iii) Diagram showing areas A and B on top, C spanning below.

   a. ```
      05 TABL OCCURS 20.
          10 A PIC XXX.
          10 B OCCURS 5 TIMES.
          10 C REDEFINES B.
          10 D PIC 9.
      ```

   b. ```
      05  A OCCURS 10 PIC 999.
      05  B REDEFINES A PIC 9(30).
      ```

   c. ```
      01 X.
          05 A PIC 99V9.
          05 B PIC XXX.
      01 Y REDEFINES X.
          05 C OCCURS 6 PIC 9.
      ```

   d. ```
      01  X PIC 9(+).
      01  B REDEFINES X.
          05  B OCCURS 9 PIC 9.
      ```

   e. ```
      05 X PIC X(30).
      05 B REDEFINES X.
      05 C OCCURS 30 TIMES.
          10 A PIC X.
      ```

   f. ```
      05  X PIC X(20).
      05  B REDEFINES X.
          10  C OCCURS 10 PIC X.
          10  D OCCURS 10 PIC 9.
      ```

   g. ```
      01 X.
          05 A OCCURS 10 PIC 99.
      01 B REDEFINES X PIC 9.
      ```

   h. ```
      01  X.
          05  GRADE PIC 99 OCCURS 5.
      01  SCORE REDEFINES X.
      01  NAME PIC A(10).
      ```

   i. ```
      04 ROST.
          05 ROSTER OCCURS 10 PIC X(10).
      04 CLAS OCCURS 5 REDEFINES ROST.
          10 NAME PIC A(10).
          10 ADRS PIC X(10).
      ```

   j. ```
      01  TAB.
          05  TABL OCCURS 10 TIMES PIC X(8).
      01  CLAS REDEFINES TAB.
          10  A OCCURS 5 TIMES.
              15  B OCCURS 4 TIMES.
                  20  C PIC 9999.
      ```

   k. ```
      01 X.
          04 GRADE PIC 99 OCCURS 5.
      01 SCORE REDEFINES X.
          05 NAME PIC A(10).
      ```

   l. ```
      02  TAB.
          05  TABL OCCURS 5 TIMES PIC 99.
      02  ARRAY REDEFINES TAB PIC X(20).
      ```

   m. ```
      03 ROST.
          05 ROSTER OCCURS 100.
              15 STUDENT PIC A(8).
              15 FILLER PIC XX.
      03 CLAS REDEFINES ROST.
          10 SIZ OCCURS 50 TIMES.
              15 GRADE   PIC 999.
              15 FILLER PIC X(7)
              15 LAS   PIC A(10).
      ```
      ```

n.
```
04 TAB.
    05 TABL OCCURS 20.
        10 A PIC XXX.
        10 B.
            11 X PIC 9(10) OCCURS 5.
        10 C REDEFINES B PIC X(50).
        10 D PIC X.
    04 CLAS REDEFINES TAB.
        10 E OCCURS 10 TIMES PIC X(58).
        10 F OCCURS 10 TIMES PIC X(50).
```

o.
```
01 KODE PIC X(80).
01 KAST REDEFINES KODE.
    05 A PIC X(40).
    05 B PIC X(40).
01 KOT REDEFINES KODE.
    05 C OCCURS 5 PIC X(20).
01 KAT REDEFINES KODE.
    05 D OCCURS 10.
        10 E PIC 99.
        10 F PIC XX.
```

p.
```
01 TAB.
    05 RATE OCCURS 3 PIC 999V99.
01 CLAS REDEFINES TAB.
    05 FILLER PIC 999V99 VALUE .75.
    05 FILLER PIC 999V99 VALUE .65.
    05 FILLER PIC 999V99 VALUE .35.
```

4. Given the code:

```
01 TAB1.
    05 X OCCURS 4 TIMES.
        10 A PIC 99.
        10 B PIC A(8).
        10 C OCCURS 20 PIC S99V9.
```

   a. Are references to A(5), B(2), and C(1) legal?
   b. Identify the number of storage positions for TAB1, X(4), and table C.

5. What type of error would result from executing the following code?

```
77 I PIC 9.
        .
        .
        PERFORM PARA VARYING I FROM 1 BY 1 UNTIL I > 12.
        .
        .
    PARA.
        MOVE CR-RECORD TO A (I).
```

6. Will both of the following coding segments compute the average of 10 grades? (Table G contains the grades.)

a.
```
    MOVE 0 TO WS-SUM.
    MOVE 1 TO I.
    PERFORM ADD-GRADES UNTIL I > 10.
    COMPUTE AVE = WS-SUM / I.
        .
        .
ADD-GRADES.
    ADD G (I) TO WS-SUM.
    ADD 1 TO I.
```

b.
```
    MOVE 0 TO WS-SUM.
    PERFORM ADD-GRADES VARYING I
        FROM 1 BY 1 UNTIL I > 10.
    MOVE AVE TO AVE-OUT.

ADD-GRADES.
    ADD G (I) TO WS-SUM.
    COMPUTE AVE = WS-SUM / I.
```

7. Determine the value of ITEM(1), ITEM(2), and ITEM(3) given the following:

```
05 RECOR.
   10 FILLER PIC X(5) VALUE "AIRPLANE".
   10 FILLER PIC X(3) VALUE "CAR".
   10 FILLER PIC X(7) VALUE "BICYCLE".
05 PART REDEFINES RECOR.
   10 ITEM OCCURS 3 TIMES PIC X(5).
```

8. Given a table A of size 100, write the code to generate the following output:

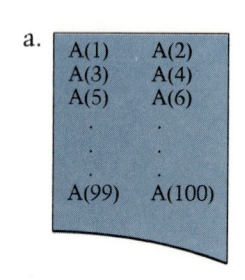

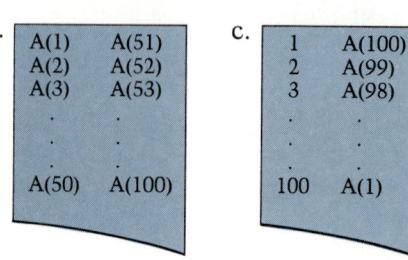

a.
```
A(1)    A(2)
A(3)    A(4)
A(5)    A(6)
 .       .
 .       .
 .       .
A(99)   A(100)
```

b.
```
A(1)    A(51)
A(2)    A(52)
A(3)    A(53)
 .       .
 .       .
 .       .
A(50)   A(100)
```

c.
```
1      A(100)
2      A(99)
3      A(98)
.       .
.       .
.       .
100    A(1)
```

d.
```
              A(2)
              A(4)
              A(6)
               .
               .
               .
              A(100)
A(1)   A(2)   A(3) ...A(9)   A(10)
A(11)  A(12)  A(13)...A(19)  A(20)
                .
                .
                .
A(91)  A(92)  A(93)...A(99)  A(100)
```

9. A and B are tables of size 100 and 50, respectively. Write the code to store the numbers 1, 2, 3, ..., 100 into table A, and the first 50 positive odd integers starting at 101 into table B. Do not read data from input records, and use only one PERFORM statement to load both tables.

10. An input file consists of at least 2 records; each record contains 7 numbers. Write the code to read the first 20 numbers (or 14 if there are only 2 records) into table A. Disregard all other remaining input by flushing it out, i.e., by reading but not storing the remaining records until the end of file is encountered.

11. Write the code to produce the following tables:

a.
```
10
10 9
10 9 8
10 9 8 7
10 9 8 7 6
10 9 8 7 6 5
10 9 8 7 6 5 4
10 9 8 7 6 5 4 3
10 9 8 7 6 5 4 3 2
10 9 8 7 6 5 4 3 2 1
```

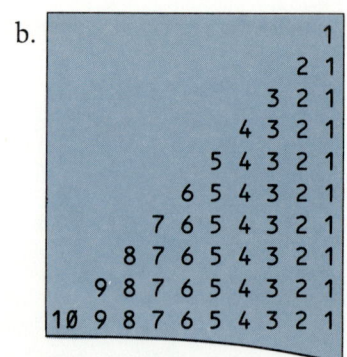

b.
```
                    1
                  2 1
                3 2 1
              4 3 2 1
            5 4 3 2 1
          6 5 4 3 2 1
        7 6 5 4 3 2 1
      8 7 6 5 4 3 2 1
    9 8 7 6 5 4 3 2 1
10  9 8 7 6 5 4 3 2 1
```

12. Write the code to produce the following multiplication tables:

```
1 x 1 = 1    2 x 1 = 2    3 x 1 = 3    4 x 1 = 4    5 x 1 = 5    6 x 1 = 6    7 x 1 = 7    8 x 1 = 8
1 x 2 = 2    2 x 2 = 4    3 x 2 = 6    4 x 2 = 8    5 x 2 = 10   6 x 2 = 12   7 x 2 = 14   8 x 2 = 16
1 x 3 = 3    2 x 3 = 6    3 x 3 = 9    4 x 3 = 12   5 x 3 = 15   6 x 3 = 18   7 x 3 = 21   8 x 3 = 24
1 x 4 = 4    2 x 4 = 8    3 x 4 = 12   4 x 4 = 16   5 x 4 = 20   6 x 4 = 24   7 x 4 = 28   8 x 4 = 32
1 x 5 = 5    2 x 5 = 10   3 x 5 = 15   4 x 5 = 20   5 x 5 = 25   6 x 5 = 30   7 x 5 = 35   8 x 5 = 40
1 x 6 = 6    2 x 6 = 12   3 x 6 = 18   4 x 6 = 24   5 x 6 = 30   6 x 6 = 36   7 x 6 = 42   8 x 6 = 48
```

ONE- AND TWO- DIMENSIONAL TABLES   453

13. Assume table A consists of 11 entries, the first 10 of which contain numbers arranged in ascending sequence. Read a number X and insert it in its proper position in table A. For example, if X = 23 and table A is:

    |10|20|30|40|50|60|70|80|90|95| | New table: |10|20|23|30|40|50|60|70|80|90|95|

14. If A is a table of size 10 by 6, initialize the first column of A with 1's, the second column with 2's, the third column with 3's, . . ., up to column 6 with 6's.

15. Read in two tables C and D of size 3 by 3 given the following 80-position input record: (Each table element has PIC 9.).

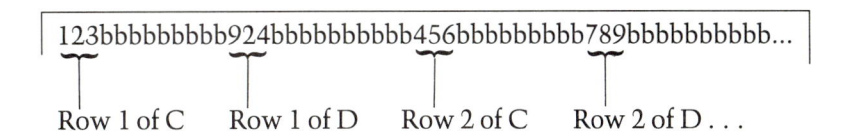

    123bbbbbbbbb924bbbbbbbbbb456bbbbbbbbb789bbbbbbbbbb...
    ⎵   ⎵   ⎵   ⎵
    Row 1 of C   Row 1 of D   Row 2 of C   Row 2 of D . . .

16. Assume a two dimensional table F of size 40 × 17 that already contains data. Write the code to store the rows of the table F sequentially into a one-dimensional table G of size 680 (40 × 17), as follows:

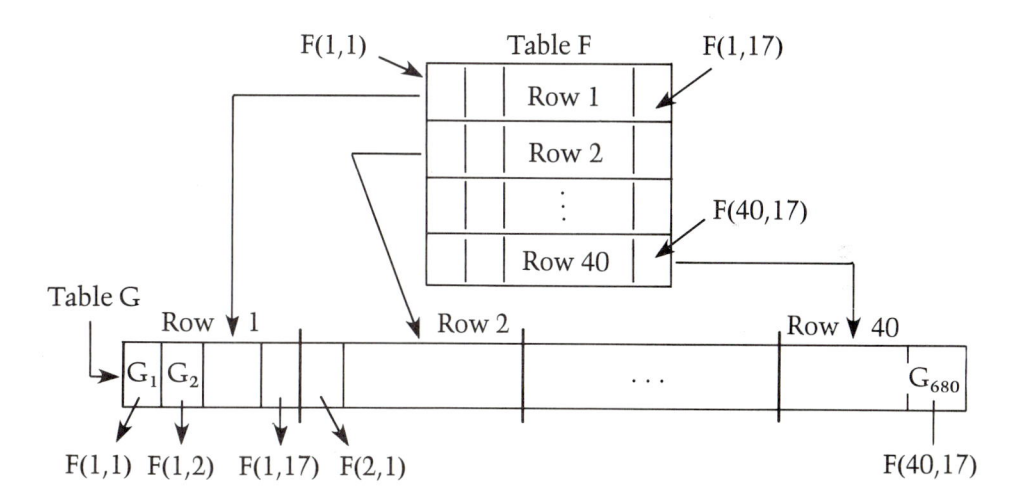

    [diagram showing Table F with rows 1 through 40, F(1,1) to F(40,17), mapped into Table G with elements G₁ G₂ ... G₆₈₀, where F(1,1), F(1,2), F(1,17), F(2,1) ... F(40,17) correspond to positions in G]

17. Assume table A (3 rows, ten columns) has been read in; write the code to compute the sum of the column elements of A and produce a printout similar to the following, including the headers, table elements, and sums.

```
                        FINAL

        COLUMN 1    COLUMN 2    COLUMN 3    . . .    COLUMN 10

        A(1,1)      A(1,2)      A(1,3)      . . .    A(1,10)
        A(2,1)      A(2,2)      A(2,3)      . . .    A(2,10)
        A(3,1)      A(3,2)      A(3,3)      . . .    A(3,10)
        ------      ------      ------               -------

        XXX         XXX         XXX                  XXX
```

18. Assume table A has size 3 by 4 and we want to store the sum of each row in ROW(1), ROW(2), and ROW(3) and the sum of each column in COL(1), COL(2), ..., COL(4) as shown in the illustration below.

```
      A              Row sums
                        ↓
  | 1| 2| 3| 4|       10
  | 5| 6| 7| 8|       26
  | 9|10|11|12|       42
   15 18 21 24  ←——————— Column sums
```

Will the following code "work"?

```
01 TAB.
   05 ROW OCCURS 3 PIC 99.
   05 COL OCCURS 4 PIC 99.
       .
       .
       .
   MOVE ZEROS TO TAB.
   PERFORM SUM-UP VARYING I FROM 1 BY 1 UNTIL I > 3
                     AFTER J FROM 1 BY 1 UNTIL J > 4.
SUM-UP.
   ADD A (I, J) TO ROW (I).
   ADD A (I, J) TO COL (J).
```

19. Assume the following tables A, B, and D contain the following data:

```
       A                    B              D
  | 1| 2| 3| 4|    |10| 20| 30| 40|     |500|
  | 5| 6| 7| 8|    |50| 60| 70| 80|
  | 9|10|11|12|    |90|100|110|120|
```

Write the code to produce the following output lines:

a. 1   2   3   4 ... 12   10 20 30 40 ... 120   500

b. 1   2   3   4   10   20   30   40   500
    5   6   7   8   50   60   70   80   500
    9 10 11 12   90 100 110 120   500

c. 1   5   9   500   10 50   90
    2   6 10   500   20 60 100
    3   7 11   500   30 70 110
    4   8 12   500   40 80 120

d. 1 10   2   20   3   30   4   40
    5 50   6   60   7   70   8   80
    9 90 10 100 11 110 12 120

20. Generate the input statements to read the following input records into WORKING–STORAGE into the specified tables A and B. The size of the tables and the number of entries for tables A and B should reflect the exact number of entries shown in each case.

a. A(1,1) A(2,1) A(3,1) A(4,1)   record #1
    A(1,2) A(2,2) A(3,2) A(4,2)   record #2
    A(1,3) A(2,3) A(3,3) A(4,3)   record #3

ONE- AND TWO- DIMENSIONAL TABLES   455

    b. A(1,1) A(1,2) A(1,3)   record #1
        A(1,4) A(1,5) A(1,5)   record #2
        B(1)   B(2)   B(3)   record #3
        B(4)   B(5)   B(6)   record #4

    c. A(1,1) B(1,1) A(2,1) B(2,1)   record #1
        A(3,1) B(3,1) A(4,1) B(4,1)   record #2
        A(5,1) B(5,1) A(6,1) B(6,1)   record #3

    d. A(,11) B(1,1) A(2,1) B(1,2)   record #1
        A(3,1) B(1,3) B(4,1) B(1,4)   record #2
        A(5,1) B(1,5) A(6,1) B(1,6)   record #3

    e. A(1,1) A(1,2) A(1,3) B(1,1) B(1,2)   record #1
        A(2,1) A(2,2) A(2,3) B(2,1) B(2,2)   record #2
            .
        A(9,1) A(9,2) A(9,3) B(9,1) B(9,2)   record #9

21. Tables A and B contain integers between 1 and 100. Table A has 10 elements, and table B has 16. Write the code to print the numbers that are common to both tables and the number of equal elements.

Example   *Output*

A: | 3 | 5 | 3 | 7 | 9 |

B: | 5 | 3 | 7 | 3 | 8 |

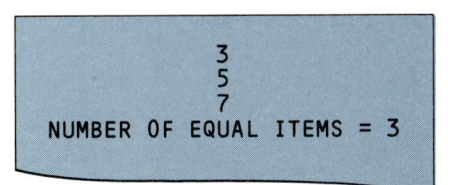

```
3
5
7
NUMBER OF EQUAL ITEMS = 3
```

22. First load table A with any 20 integers between 1 and 20. Then write the code to perform a frequency distribution on the numbers in table A. The output should list the numbers in ascending order and their corresponding frequency, as follows:

```
NUMBERS    1  3  4  5  10  12  13  14  15  17  18  19
FREQUENCY  1  4  2  1   1   1   2   2   1   2   2   1
```

23. Determine whether a table that has 10 numbers (not necessarily integers) has any two equal entries.

8-8-2 PROGRAMMING EXERCISES

General One-Dimensional Problems

1. Each record in a file consists of six data items (a student name followed by five test scores), for example:

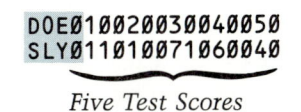

```
DOE0100200300400500
SLY0110100710600400
```

    Five Test Scores

There are at most 100 records. Write a program to read the data into a two-dimensional table. For example, A(3,I), with I ranging from 1 to 5, represents the third student's test scores. Compute the average score for each student and the average score on each test. The output should have the following format:

```
NAME         TEST1   TEST2   TEST3   TEST4   TEST5   AVERAGE
DOE           10      20      30      40      50      30.0
SLY           11      10      71      60      40      38.4

AVERAGE/TEST  10.5    15.0    50.5    50.0    45.0
```

2. At the beginning and at the end of each month, members of the U-WATCH-UR-WEIGHT club are weighed in. Each member's name and initial and terminal weights are typed on a record. Write a program to read such records and print out each member's name, initial and final weight, and weight loss. Also print the average weight loss for the group and the number of members whose weight loss was greater than the average weight loss. For example:

```
    GREEN    200   180   20   *
    FARAH    130   120   10
    TODINI   161   154    7

AVERAGE WEIGHT LOSS IS 12.3 POUNDS
1 MEMBER WITH WEIGHT LOSS OVER 12.3 POUNDS
```

Note that a * is printed beside the name of each member whose weight loss is above the average.

3. For each student in a class, there is one record with his/her name and 10 test scores. The student's average is based on his/her nine best scores. Write a program to read the input records and produce an output similar to the following:

```
              GRADE REPORT

NAME: WOODRUFF      AVERAGE = 60.0
TESTS:   10  20  30  40  50  60  70  80  90  100

NAME: ZIEGLER       AVERAGE = 58.9
TESTS:  100  50  60  40  35  65  80  20  30  70
```

4. The correct answers (1,2,3, or 4) to a multiple choice test of 10 questions are recorded on the first record of an input file. Succeeding records contain the name of a student and the student's 10 answers. Write the code to compute each student's final score (each question is worth 10 points). The input and output have the following form:

```
         Input file              NAME          SCORES            GRADE
    1123142433
    JONES  1123142433            JONES   1 1 2 3 1 4 2 4 3 3     100
    HILL   1123111324            HILL    1 1 2 3 1 1 1 3 2 4      50
    CLAM   4123142432            CLAM    4 1 2 3 1 4 2 4 3 2      80
```

5. A data file contains the following information (maximum of 100 records):

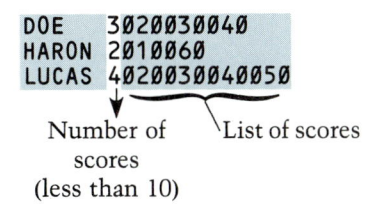

```
    DOE   3020030040
    HARON 2010060
    LUCAS 4020030040050
          ↓         _____
       Number of    List of scores
        scores
      (less than 10)
```

If the average of all the scores in the input file is less than 80, five points are added to the average of each student; otherwise 5 points are subtracted from the average of each student. Write a program to produce the following output:

```
   NAME    TEST1   TEST2   TEST3   TEST4 ... TEST10   AVERAGE   UPDATED AVERAGE

   DOE      20      30      40                         30.00        35.00
   HARON    10      60                                 35.00        40.00
   LUCAS    20      30      40      50                 35.00        40.00
             .       .       .       .                   .            .
             .       .       .       .                   .            .
             .       .       .       .                   .            .
```

6. Klinkon Headquarters has received personnel secrets for the spaceship Renderprize from two of its spies.

The First Spy Reports		The Second Spy Reports	
NUMBER	NAME	NUMBER	TITLE
455-30-1980	Kiik	465-29-9136	Engineer
465-29-9136	Skolly	432-98-2316	Navigator
408-32-6166	Spark	446-66-2366	Navigator
432-98-2316	Thekov	433-27-8107	Doctor
492-38-7213	Uhula	455-30-1980	Captain
433-27-8107	Mc Joy	408-32-6166	First Officer
446-66-2366	Lusu	492-38-7213	Communications

As a Klinkon programmer, your job is to program the computer to match up crew member names with their titles. (Star Fleet Command has evidence that when Klinkon programmers make syntax errors, they mysteriously disappear!) Write the code to produce a list of numbers and the corresponding names and titles, i.e.

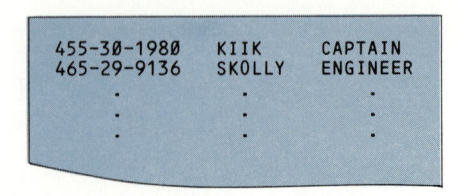

```
455-30-1980    KIIK      CAPTAIN
465-29-9136    SKOLLY    ENGINEER
     .           .          .
     .           .          .
     .           .          .
```

7. Repeat the inventory problem of section 8-5-4 and print a reorder notice whenever the stock falls below ten percent of the original stock. Identify any item that has not been sold that day with two asterisks on the output. List all invalid items after the updated inventory has been printed. The output should be similar to:

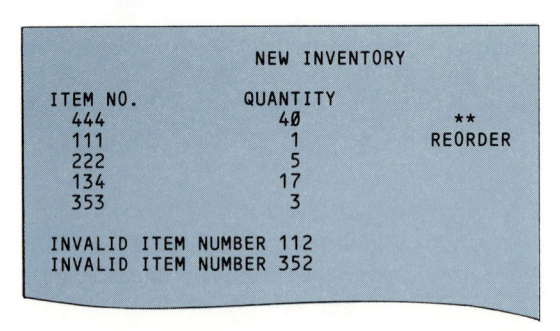

```
                 NEW INVENTORY

    ITEM NO.       QUANTITY
       444            40           **
       111             1                  REORDER
       222             5
       134            17
       353             3

    INVALID ITEM NUMBER 112
    INVALID ITEM NUMBER 352
```

8. Given a list of names with the table structure shown below, write a program to count the number of identical family names and list them on the output along with the number of times they occur.

```
01 TABL.
   05 LIST OCCURS 20 TIMES.
      10 FAMILY PIC A(10).
      10 FIRS1  PIC A(8).
```

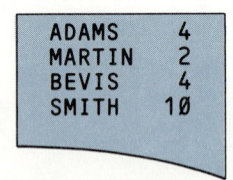

```
ADAMS     4
MARTIN    2
BEVIS     4
SMITH    10
```

9. At the Kilpatrick Community College, General Mathematics MS101 has always been offered in the traditional teacher/lecture format. This year, for the first time, students may take MS101 using a self-paced approach to instruction through a computer-assisted instructional method (CAI). Because of the novelty of the CAI approach, the mathematics faculty has formulated the following policies concerning grades and tests for those taking MS101 in the CAI mode:

   1. Students may take one, two, or three tests during the semester.

   2. The final score is based on the student's average score, scaled as follows: If the CAI class average AV is less than 80 (the standardized average for the traditional teacher/lecture form), then the difference 80 − AV should be added to each student's average score; otherwise, the difference, AV − 80, is subtracted from each student's average. The input data is formatted as follows:

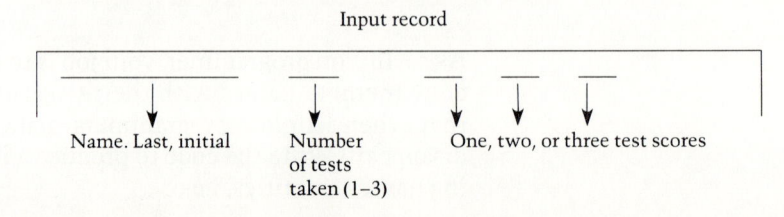

Input record

Name. Last, initial | Number of tests taken (1-3) | One, two, or three test scores

ONE- AND TWO- DIMENSIONAL TABLES 459

Write a program to produce the following score information. For example, the following input data would produce the output shown:

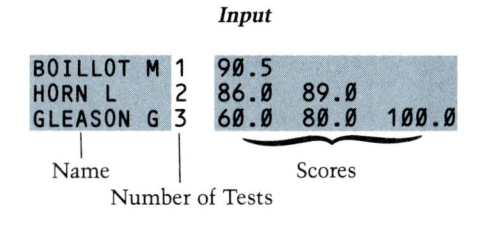

Input

```
BOILLOT M  1  90.5
HORN L     2  86.0  89.0
GLEASON G  3  60.0  80.0  100.0
```
Name | Number of Tests | Scores

Output

STUDENT NAME	AVERAGE	SCALED AVERAGE
BOILLOT M.	90.5	84.5
HORN L.	87.5	81.5
GLEASON G.	80.0	74.0

AVERAGE 86.0

Can you rewrite the code for this exercise in such a way that each student's scores are printed after the student name but before the average?

10. The department of psychology offers a maximum of ten sections of introduction to psychology. Each section contains no more than 25 students. At the end of the semester final grades for each section are recorded as follows:

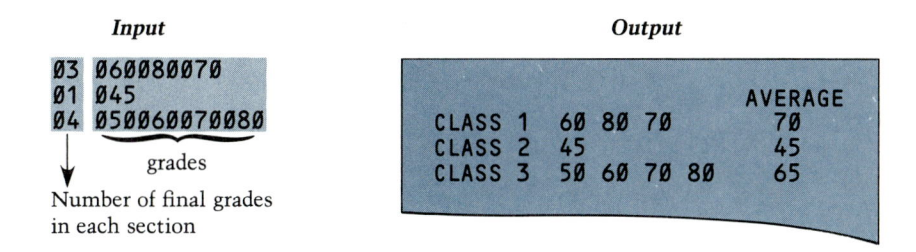

Input

```
03  060080070
01  045
04  050060070080
```
↓ grades
Number of final grades in each section

Output

		AVERAGE
CLASS 1	60 80 70	70
CLASS 2	45	45
CLASS 3	50 60 70 80	65

a. Write a program to produce the output shown above.
b. Write a program to produce the following output showing the class averages:

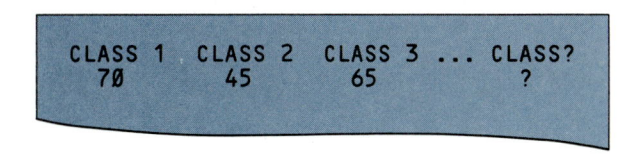

```
CLASS 1  CLASS 2  CLASS 3  ...  CLASS?
   70       45       65            ?
```

Note that there might be fewer than ten classes.

11. The personnel department of a small insurance company maintains a payroll file for its insurance representatives, who work in different states. Each employee's record contains (among other information) the following data:

EMPLOYEE NAME	HOURS WORKED	RATE OF PAY	STATE TAX
Anton D.	45	10.00	.05

Read an unknown number of input records (maximum 100). Load one table with the employee names and load a two-dimensional table with the corresponding set of three entries per record. Then

a. Compute and print each employee's pay before and after tax.
b. Compute the total payroll for the firm (not including state tax withholding).
c. Give a $1,000 bonus to the employee with lowest hourly rate if he/she has worked more hours than any other employee. This condition may or may not be satisfied.

Overtime is paid at 1.5 times the regular rate. The output should be similar to:

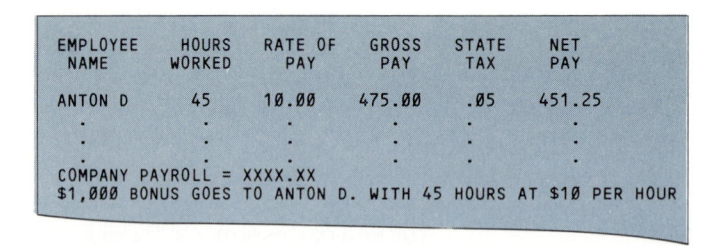

```
EMPLOYEE    HOURS    RATE OF    GROSS    STATE    NET
NAME        WORKED   PAY        PAY      TAX      PAY

ANTON D     45       10.00      475.00   .05      451.25
   .         .          .          .       .         .
   .         .          .          .       .         .
   .         .          .          .       .         .
COMPANY PAYROLL = XXXX.XX
$1,000 BONUS GOES TO ANTON D. WITH 45 HOURS AT $10 PER HOUR
```

12. At the end of every semester, Dr. Landrum, head of the business data systems department, likes to check grade reports of the department's freshman class (100 students at most). Each student's final grades in three subject areas are entered on records, one record per student, for example:

SMITH	58	78	44
Student Name	Accounting I	Business Law	Principles of Management

Enter all student names in an array NAME, and enter each student's grades into a corresponding two-dimensional table G. For example, G(3,2) represents the third student's score in Business Law.

Using the array G, write a program for Dr. Landrum to

a. Compute the average score of each student across all disciplines.
b. Compute the freshman average score for Accounting I, the average score for Business Law, and average score for Principles of Management.
c. List all students whose three final scores are all above the freshman average scores for each of the three subject areas.
d. Award a prize to student(s) with highest score in principles of management. Print the name(s) of the recipient(s).
e. Award a scholarship to any student who obtains the three highest scores in the three subject areas (if there is such a student).

The output should be similar to the following report:

```
                  SEMESTER END REPORT
                       BUSINESS
                ACCT. I    LAW    MANAGEMENT    AVERAGE
    HORNET        40        50        60          50.0
    BOIL          50        90        40          60.0
    SMITHEN       20        60        10          30.0

    CLASS AVERAGE 36.7      66.7      36.7

    STUDENT NAMES WHOSE 3 TESTS EXCEED THE 3 CLASS AVERAGES
                         BOIL
    AWARD GOES TO HORNET
    SCHOLARSHIP IS AWARDED TO NO ONE
```

Interactive Problems.

1. Dr. X is an information-science teacher. He keeps track of his students' names and their respective grades as follows:

STUDENT	GRADE 1	GRADE 2	TOTAL
MARGULIES	91	56	147
GLEASON	40	50	90
HORN	50	65	115
MONISH	70	70	140
⋮	⋮	⋮	⋮

   a. Write a program to read input records and create such a two dimensional table for about ten students.

   b. Add the necessary code (using the ACCEPT statement) to allow Dr. X to correct his file in the event grades are recorded incorrectly. Grade changes are read according to the following format:

   STUDENT NAME   GRADE 1   GRADE 2

   For grades that need not be changed, enter a negative number. For example, HORN −1 98 means change HORN's second grade to 98 and compute the new total. When all changes have been made, print or display the updated roster.

2. You have been asked to write an on-line reservation system for a small commuter airline company. Each plane has 5 rows of seats, with 4 seats per row, and can carry up to 20 passengers. The ticket agent is to ask each passenger's name and his or her row and seat preference; the name and seat request are then entered on a computer terminal. If the seat requested is available, the system should reserve that seat. If that seat is already taken, the system is to assign the first available seat, starting with row 1, row 2, . . ., up to row 5. A message should appear on the screen as soon as the seating capacity has been reached. When all passenger requests have been taken care of, the program should print the seating arrangement, by passenger name, as shown:

```
ENTER ROW THEN SEAT AND NAME
11BOILLOT
ENTER ROW THEN SEAT AND NAME
11ADKINS
ENTER ROW THEN SEAT AND NAME
44FORD
ENTER ROW THEN SEAT AND NAME
44CABERAS
ENTER ROW THEN SEAT AND NAME
0000000000
```

System displays the cue on the terminal.
The agent enters the passenger's request and name.

11 means row 1 and seat 1.

When the agent enters the special code 00, the system prints the seating arrangement.

```
             FINAL SEATING ARRANGEMENT

ROW 1    BOILLOT   ADKINS    CABERAS   _____
ROW 2    _____   _____   _____   _____
ROW 3    _____   _____   _____   _____
ROW 4    _____   _____   _____   FORD
ROW 5    _____   _____   _____   _____
```

Note that ADKINS is assigned 1,2 and that CABERAS is assigned 1,3!

Note that the program instructs the printer to underline each seat.

3. The Language Department at Johns College offers five courses and is now registering students. Each student completes a form with his/her name and one course number. More than one course can be taken by the same student, in which case the student fills out different forms. The list of courses, the maximum enrollment per class, and the room number in which each class meets are described as follows:

COURSE	SIZE	ROOM NO
FRE 110	5	204
FRE 120	10	200
GER 100	6	100
SPN 100	10	212
SPN 105	15	220

a. Each record of the input file consists of a student name and a course number. Write a program to read this file and provide the following enrollment information:

INPUT

```
ADAMS  FRE 110
BEVIS  GER 100
ADAMS  FRE 120
ADAMS  SPN 100
KERR   SPN 105
```

OUTPUT

COURSE	ROOM NO	ENROLLMENT	MAX ENROLLMENT
FRE 110	204	5	5
FRE 120	200	6	10
.			
.			
.			
SPN 105	220	4	15

If a course is filled, either identify that course by placing a * next to the maximum enrollment figure or list the students who could not enroll.

b. At the conclusion of the enrollment procedure, the department head would like to be able to inquire directly in this data base to obtain any of the following:

INFORMATION REQUIRED	QUERY CODE	ITEM
A list of student names in any particular course	1	Course number
A list of courses taken by a particular student	2	Student name
An actual class size for a particular room	3	Room number
(Query code 4 stops the inquiry process.)		

ONE- AND TWO- DIMENSIONAL TABLES 463

For example, the following set of queries would produce the output below:

```
Query Code

1 FRE 120  ──►   COURSE; FRE 120
2 ADAMS    ──►   ADAMS
3 413            SPRING
3 200             .
4                 .
                 LOVE
                 ─────────────────────────────────
                 LIST OF COURSES TAKEN BY ADAMS
                          FRE 110
                          FRE 120
                          SPN 100
                 ─────────────────────────────────
                 ** INCORRECT ROOM NUMBER 413 **
                 ─────────────────────────────────
                 NUMBER STUDENTS IN 200 IS 8
                 ─────────────────────────────────
```

Write a program to accept the query information and produce the requested information (perform input validation on all fields). Another option for inquiries (instead of numerical codes) is for the computer to display a menu of inquiries.

4. The Furnishmatic Warehouse Company is a national distribution center for five types of furniture items: chairs, tables, desks, beds, and sofas. Each item comes in two styles, referred to henceforth as style A and style B. The company keeps track of outgoing shipments as follows: The first five records of the daily transaction file identify the particular furniture items by numeric code and specify the stock on hand for each item at the start of the business day. These five records are not updated during the day. Subsequent records identify transaction shipments as they occured during the day; these records specify the numeric code for the item, the quantity shipped, and the particular style. For example, a sample input file could be visualized as follows:

Item code	In stock Style A	In stock Style B		Item code
1	2000	1000		1 = Chairs
2	1000	0500		2 = Tables
3	0500	0200	Header records	3 = Desks
4	1000	1000		4 = Beds
5	0500	0200		5 = Sofas
1	100	A		
1	050	B		
2	400	A	Shipments	
1	100	B		
5	100	B		

a. Write the program to produce the following end-of-day transaction summary:

```
            SHIPMENTS             ENDING STOCK LEVEL
         STYLE A    STYLE B       STYLE A      STYLE B

CHAIRS     100        150          1900          850
TABLES     400          0           600          500
DESKS        0          0           500          200
BEDS         0          0          1000         1000
SOFAS        0        100           500          100
```

b. This part requires interactive communication with the computing system through the ACCEPT verb or the READ statement through the terminal. Write the code to carry out the inquiries described in the following paragraphs.

The warehouse agent would like to make the inventory processing system more flexible; he would like to ask the computer questions in addition to entering the regular item transactions shown in part a on the terminal. The agent settles on two forms of inquiry. One informs him of the current stock level of all items when he types the query code INVEN on the screen (terminal). The computer's response should appear on the screen as follows:

```
           STYLE A     STYLE B
CHAIRS      1900         850
TABLES       600         500
DESKS        500         200
BEDS        1000        1000
SOFAS        500         100
```

The other form of inquiry allows the agent to enter a numeric item code and a corresponding style; the computer responds with the number of such items that have already been shipped out. Both the query and the response should appear on the screen as follows:

```
1    B
CHAIRS    STYLE B    SHIPMENT: 150
```

In order for the agent to enter regular transactions in addition to the two forms of inquiry discussed above, the program must be written in such a way that the terminal constantly polls the agent by leaving the following messages on the terminal when idle:

```
TO ENTER REGULAR TRANSACTIONS:          ENTER 1
TO DISPLAY CURRENT INVENTORY:           ENTER INVEN
TO DETERMINE NUMBER OF ITEMS SHIPPED:   ENTER 2
TO TERMINATE:                           ENTER 3
```

For example, a typical dialogue between agent and terminal might be as follows: The characters in blue identify the agent's inquiries.

```
TO ENTER REGULAR TRANSACTIONS         ENTER 1
TO DISPLAY CURRENT INVENTORY          ENTER INVEN
TO DETERMINE NUMBER OF ITEMS SHIPPED  ENTER 2
TO TERMINATE                          ENTER 3
1
ENTER TRANSACTION
1  100  A
TO ENTER REGULAR TRANSACTIONS ENTER 1
TO DISPLAY CURRENT INVENTORY ENTER INVEN
TO DETERMINE NUMBER OF ITEMS SHIPPED ENTER 2
TO TERMINATE ENTER 3
INVEN
             STYLE A     STYLE B
CHAIRS       1900        1000
TABLES       1000         500
DESKS         500         200
BEDS         1000        1000
SOFAS         500         100
TO ENTER REGULAR TRANSACTIONS ENTER 1
TO DISPLAY CURRENT INVENTORY ENTER INVEN
TO DETERMINE NUMBER OF ITEMS SHIPPED ENTER 2
TO TERMINATE ENTER 3
2
ENTER SELECTION
1  B
CHAIRS   STYLE B   SHIPMENT: 80
```

    c. The agent still feels that the process in part b is awkward. He would rather have the computer display a menu of possible inquiries to which he could give a simple response. For example, a menu to take care of part b of this exercise would appear on the screen as:

```
STOCK LEVEL MENU
WHAT TYPE OF ITEM?
1
WHAT STYLE?
B
WHAT DETAIL CODE?
2
```

Write the code to allow this type of interaction.

5. The Medical Center Clinic maintains a patient file where the patient's medical history is recorded on one or more records. Multiple records are used for patients having undergone some form of surgery. The first record identifies the patient's name, address, insurance company, vital statistics, et cetera. Subsequent records for a multirecord patient identify the surgical intervention (transplants, fractures, excisions, et cetera), the name of the physician in charge, the date of the operation, and a list of drugs used in connection with the operation. A separate record is created for each surgical intervention. A special record identification code is typed in position 1 of any record: a code of 1 indicates the first of possibly many records for a given patient; a code of 2 identifies a surgery record (not all patients have such records). Code 2 records follow a code 1 record (only one code 1 record per patient). An example of an input file is as follows.

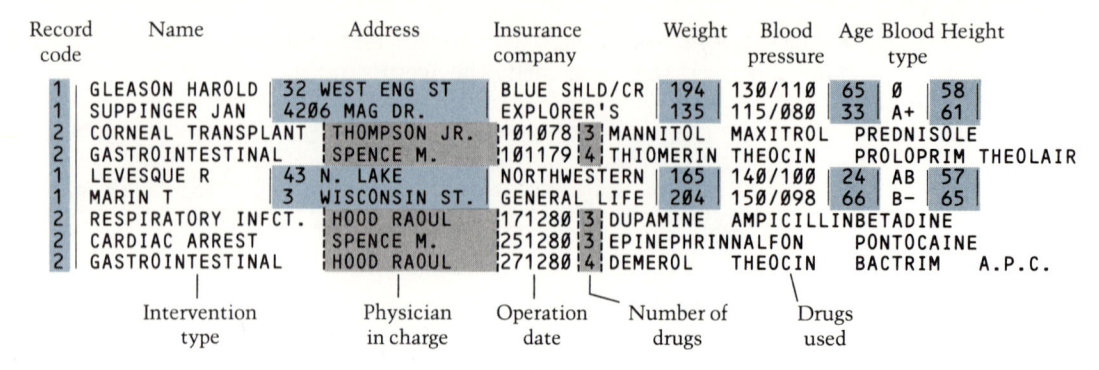

```
Record    Name            Address           Insurance         Weight  Blood    Age Blood Height
code                                        company                   pressure     type
  1  GLEASON HAROLD   32 WEST ENG ST    BLUE SHLD/CR  194  130/110  65  Ø    58
  1  SUPPINGER JAN    4206 MAG DR.      EXPLORER'S    135  115/080  33  A+   61
  2  CORNEAL TRANSPLANT  THOMPSON JR.   101078  3  MANNITOL  MAXITROL   PREDNISOLE
  2  GASTROINTESTINAL    SPENCE M.      101179  4  THIOMERIN THEOCIN    PROLOPRIM  THEOLAIR
  1  LEVESQUE R       43 N. LAKE        NORTHWESTERN  165  140/100  24  AB   57
  1  MARIN T          3 WISCONSIN ST.   GENERAL LIFE  204  150/098  66  B-   65
  2  RESPIRATORY INFCT.  HOOD RAOUL     171280  3  DUPAMINE  AMPICILLIN BETADINE
  2  CARDIAC ARREST      SPENCE M.      251280  3  EPINEPHRIN NALFON    PONTOCAINE
  2  GASTROINTESTINAL    HOOD RAOUL     271280  4  DEMEROL   THEOCIN    BACTRIM    A.P.C.
        │                    │             │    │                         │
   Intervention         Physician     Operation  Number of            Drugs
     type                in charge       date     drugs                used
```

Write a program to compile a list of the names and addresses of all patients. For example:

```
GLEASON HAROLD        32 WEST ENG ST
SUPPINGER JAN         4206 MAG DR.
LEVESQUE R            43 N. LAKE
MARIN T               3 WISCONSIN ST
```

The center's director wishes to obtain a list of the drugs that have been used in connection with any gastrointestinal operation carried out at the center. Write the code to oblige the director (see sample output below). How would you generalize this procedure to cover any type of intervention and not just a gastrointestinal intervention?

```
PATIENT NAME          INTERVENTION: GASTROINTESTINAL

SUPPINGER JAN         THIOMERIN   THEOCIN    PROLOPRIN   THEOLAIR
MARIN T               DEMEROL     THEOCIN    BACTRIM     A.P.C.
```

6. Write a program to accept an income figure and compute itemized sales tax deductions using the following instructions and table:

Your itemized deduction for general sales tax paid can be estimated from these tables. To use the tables:

Step 1—Figure your total available income.

Step 2—Count the number of exemptions for you and your family. Do not count exemptions claimed for being 65 or over or blind as part of your family size.

Step 3 A—If your total available income is not over $40,000, find the income line on the table and read across to find the amount of sales tax for your family size.

Step 3 B—If your income is over $40,000, but not over $100,000, find the deduction listed on the income line "$38,001–$40,000" for your family size. For each $5,000 (or part of $5,000) of income over $40,000, increase the deduction by the amount listed on the line "$40,000–$100,000."

Step 3 C—If your income is over $100,000, your sales tax deduction is limited to the deduction for income of $100,000. To figure your sales tax deduction, use Step 3 B but don't go over $100,000

ALABAMA

INCOME	FAMILY SIZE					OVER
	1	2	3	4	5	5
$1–$8,000	93	115	122	131	142	160
$8,001–$10,000	109	132	142	153	165	185
$10,001–$12,000	124	147	161	173	187	208
$12,001–$14,000	138	161	178	191	206	228
$14,001–$16,000	152	174	194	209	225	248
$16,001–$18,000	164	186	210	226	242	266
$18,001–$20,000	176	197	225	242	259	284
$20,001–$22,000	188	208	239	257	275	301
$22,001–$24,000	199	218	253	271	290	317
$24,001–$26,000	210	228	266	285	305	332
$26,001–$28,000	221	238	279	299	320	347
$28,001–$30,000	231	247	291	313	334	362
$30,001–$32,000	241	256	303	326	347	376
$32,001–$34,000	251	265	315	338	360	390
$34,001–$36,000	261	274	327	350	373	403
$36,001–$38,000	271	282	338	362	386	416
$38,001–$40,000	280	290	349	374	399	429
$40,001–$100,000 (See Step 3B)	14	15	17	19	20	21

Computational Problems

1. The following integers have been recorded on a record.

    36, 27, 43, 18, 5, 6, 9, 33, 45, 34, 22, 42

   Write a program to read these numbers into a table and accomplish the following:

   a. Compute the average (mean) of these 12 numbers, rounded to the nearest whole number.
   b. Compute the difference between each of these 12 numbers and the mean (subtract the mean from each number) and store each of these deviations in a table.
   c. Determine which of the 12 numbers in the table deviates the most from the mean (this corresponds to the deviation having the largest absolute value) and print that number (not its deviation).

   The output should be as follows:

   ```
   ARRAY     DEVIATION

   36            9
   27            Ø
   43           16
    .            .
    .            .
    .            .
   42           15

   NUMBER DEVIATING MOST FROM MEAN IS 5
   ```

2. Using the schedule shown below, write a program to read an adjusted gross income and compute and print the amount of tax owed.

Not over $3,400	No tax.
Over $3,400 but not over $5,500	14% of excess over $3,400
Over $5,500 but not over $7,600	$294, plus 16% of excess over $5,500
Over $7,600 but not over $11,900	$630, plus 18% of excess over $7,600
Over $11,900 but not over $16,000	$1,404, plus 21% of excess over $11,900
Over $16,000 but not over $20,200	$2,265, plus 24% of excess over $16,000
Over $20,200 but not over $24,600	$3,273, plus 28% of excess over $20,200
Over $24,600 but not over $29,900	$4,505, plus 32% of excess over $24,600
Over $29,900 but not over $35,200	$6,201, plus 37% of excess over $29,900
Over $35,200 but not over $45,800	$8,162, plus 43% of excess over $35,200
Over $45,800 but not over $60,000	$12,720, plus 49% of excess over $45,800
Over $60,000 but not over $85,600	$19,678, plus 54% of excess over $60,000
Over $85,600 but not over $109,400	$33,502, plus 59% of excess over $85,600
Over $109,400 but not over $162,400	$47,544, plus 64% of excess over $109,400
Over $162,400 but not over $215,400	$81,464, plus 68% of excess over $162,400
Over $215,400	$117,504, plus 70% of excess over $215,400

3. The Triple Star Corporation maintains a file in which each record contains a date (year) and the yearly sales in millions of dollars. These figures lie be-

tween 0 and 70 million. Write a program to produce a graph of this data, similar to the following one:

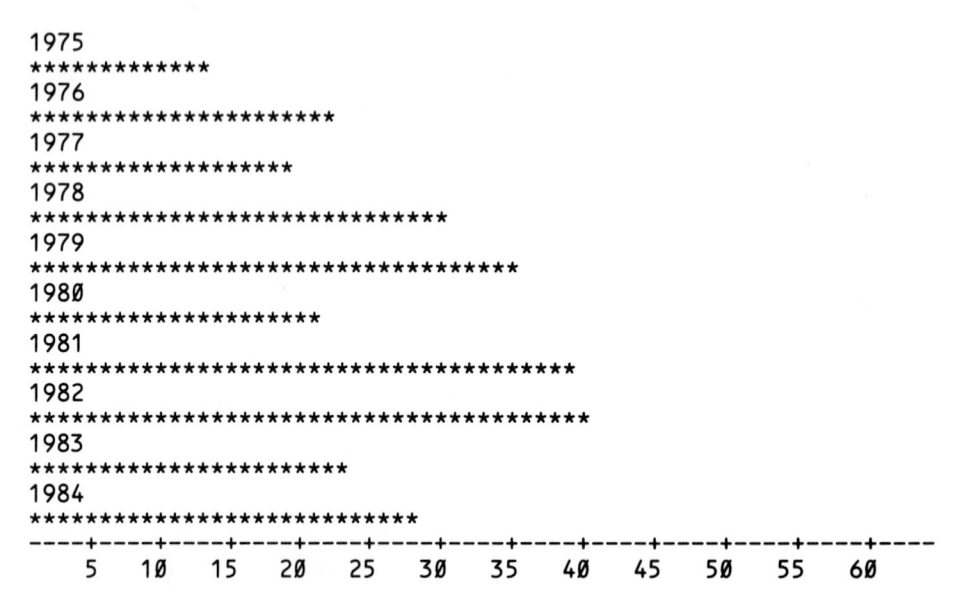

```
1975
*************
1976
***********************
1977
*******************
1978
*******************************
1979
**************************************
1980
*********************
1981
*******************************************
1982
*****************************************
1983
************************
1984
****************************
----+----+----+----+----+----+----+----+----+----+----+----+----
    5   10   15   20   25   30   35   40   45   50   55   60
```

Make sure your program prints the last unit line, i.e., ----+----+----, and the graduations 0,5,10,15,...

4. Write a program to read an unknown number of grades and calculate the standard deviation of those grades using the following formula:

$$SD = \sqrt{\frac{(x_1 - \bar{x})^2 + (x_2 - \bar{x})^2 + (x_3 \times \bar{x})^2 + \ldots + (x_n - \bar{x})^2}{n(n - 1)}}$$

where n = number of grades;
$\bar{x}$ = average of grades;
$x_1, x_2, x_3, \ldots, x_n$ are the grades.

5. An encyclopedia company has hired part-time salespeople. The name of each salesperson and the number of encyclopedia sets he/she has sold are recorded on separate data records (one record per salesperson). Each salesperson is paid $90.00 for each set sold, as well as $15.00 extra for each set (or fraction) sold over the average number of sets sold by all the salespeople. Write a program to print the name, the number of sets sold, and the amount earned by each employee. For example, if the average number of sets sold is 5.8 and a salesperson has sold 8 sets, the difference is 2.2, which counts as 3 sets over the average (the fractional part counts as an entire set). Do not forget to print the average number of sets sold.

6. The Meals on Wheels Company operates a fleet of vans used for the delivery of cold foods at various local plants and construction sites. The management is thinking of purchasing a specially built $18,000 van equipped to deliver hot foods. This new addition to the fleet is expected to generate after-tax earnings $E_1, E_2, \ldots, E_6$ (as displayed below) over the next six years, at which time the van's resale value will be zero. Projected repair and maintenance costs $C_0, C_1, C_2, \ldots, C_6$ over the six years are also shown below.

PROJECTED EARNINGS		PROJECTED COSTS		
E_1	$2,500	C_0	$18,000	(purchase cost of the van)
E_2	2,500	C_1	1,000	
E_3	3,000	C_2	1,500	
E_4	4,500	C_3	2,000	
E_5	6,000	C_4	2,000	
E_6	6,000	C_5	2,100	
		C_6	2,400	

The decision to purchase the van depends on the benefit/cost ratio (BCR) (grossly speaking, earnings/expenditures) given by the formula

$$\text{BCR} = \frac{E_1(1+i)^6 + E_2(1+i)^5 + \ldots + E_6(1+i)^1}{C_0 + C_1(1+i)^6 + C_2(1+i)^5 + \ldots + C_6(1+i)^1}$$

where i is the rate of investment of earnings by the company. If BCR > 1, then the company should acquire the van. Write a program to determine how high the investment rate (i) would have to be raised to permit the purchase of the vehicle. The program should compute the BCR for investment rates starting at 6% and increasing by amounts of 0.1%. The output should be as follows:

```
BENEFIT/COST RATIO      INVESTMENT RATE
        .                      6.0
        .                      6.1
        .                       .
        .                       .
        .                       .
```

Stop when the BCR is greater than 1 and print the following message:

`PURCHASE OF VAN REQUIRES INVESTMENT RATE OF XX.XX.`

7. Wrap-around sales averaging. The management of Food Stores, Inc., likes to compare their monthly sales with a running average of their sales for the preceding 11 months. Write a program to read sales data for the preceding 11 months (Jan. to Nov. '85) and read "dummy" sales projections for the next 12 months (Dec. '85 through Nov. '86). Then compute the preceding 11-month's running average for Dec. '85 through Nov. '86. The process can be visualized as follows:

```
Jan.-Nov. 1985                      Dec. '85-Nov.'86
                                                            11-months
J F M A M J J A S O N       D J F M A M ...N           running average
10 11 12 10 11 14 10 11 12 11 12    13                         11.27
   11 12 10 11 14 10 11 12 11 12    13 16                      11.54
      12 10 11 14 10 11 12 11 12    13 16 11                   12.00
         10 11 14 10 11 12 11 12    13 16 11 13                11.90
                  .                       .                       .
                  .                       .                       .
                  .                       .                       .
```

For the month of December, for example, management will compare the December volume (13) with the running average of the 11 previous months, 11.27

$$[(10 + 11 + 12 + 10 + 11 + 14 + 10 + 11 + 12 + 11 + 12)/11]$$

The output should be similar to:

```
MONTHS      11-MONTH RUNNING AVERAGE    MONTH SALES

DECEMBER            11.27                   13
JANUARY             11.54                   16
FEBRUARY            12.00                   11
MARCH               11.90                   13
   .                   .                     .
   .                   .                     .
```

8. Systems planning involves estimating development time and projecting costs associated with the completion of a particular task. An example might be planning for the construction of a house. A list of tasks and time schedule might be as follows:

SEQUENCE OF EVENTS	TASK DESCRIPTION	TIME IN DAYS
1	Laying of foundation	15
2	Plumbing installment	12
3	Frame and roof	20
4	Electrical work	7
5	Plastering	4
6	Carpentry	7
7	Landscaping	3

Write a program to produce a bar graph to represent the duration of each task as follows:

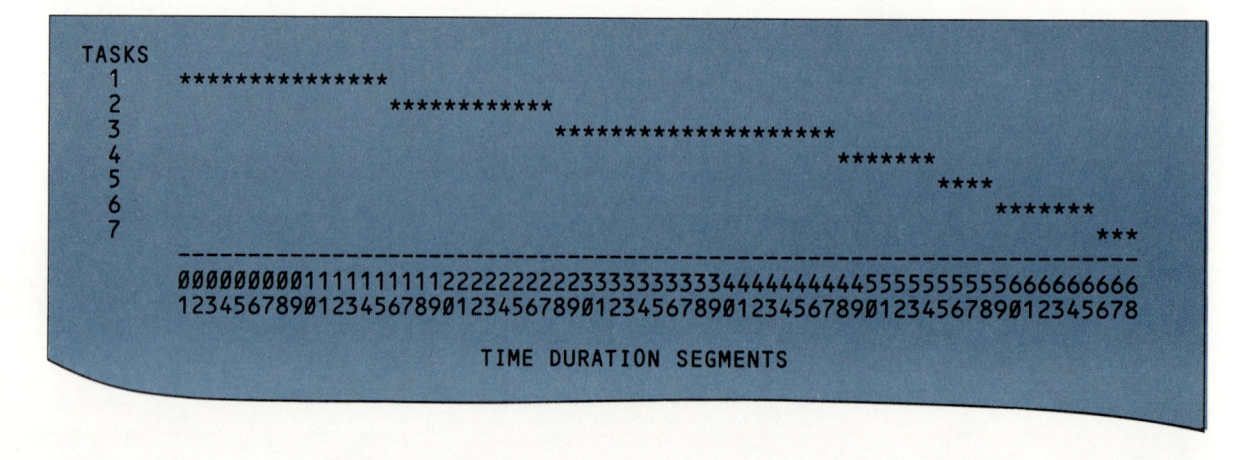

```
TASKS
  1   ***************
  2                  ************
  3                              ********************
  4                                                  *******
  5                                                         ****
  6                                                             *******
  7                                                                    ***
      ----------------------------------------------------------------------
      0000000000111111111122222222223333333333444444444455555555556666666666
      1234567890123456789012345678901234567890123456789012345678901234567890

                          TIME DURATION SEGMENTS
```

9. The XYZ Company manufactures four products, P1, P2, P3, and P4. Each of these products must undergo some type of operation on five different machines, A, B, C, D, and E. The time (in units of hours) required for each of these products on each of the five machines is shown below:

ONE- AND TWO- DIMENSIONAL TABLES 471

	A	B	C	D	E
P1	.2	.2	.1	.58	.15
P2	.26	.1	.13	.61	.3
P3	.5	.21	.56	.45	.27
P4	.6	.17	1.3	.25	.31

For example, product P1 requires .2 hour on machine A, .2 hour on machine B, .1 hour on machine C, and so on.

a. The XYZ Company has been requested to fill an order of 356 products P1, 257 products P2, 1,058 products P3, and 756 products P4. Write a program to determine the total number of hours that *each* machine will be used.

b. The XYZ Company is renting the five machines A, B, C, D, and E from a tooling company. The hourly rental cost for each machine is as follows:

Machines	A	B	C	D	E
Rental cost/hour	$10.00	$5.75	$3.50	$10.00	$5.76

Write a program to compute the total rental expense for all the machines to fill the order in part a.

One- and Two-Dimensional Business Problems

1. The Swivel Cast Company sells casters nationwide. Its present stock level of casters, their designations, and their list prices are reflected in the following table:

COMMODITY NUMBER	DESCRIPTION	LIST PRICE	STOCK LEVEL
112	Sq. shank swivel	1.10	500
131	Flat top rigid	1.12	500
172	Ext. shank with brk.	2.00	200
321	Bolt and nut shank	3.15	150
441	Rnd. spr. ring stem	4.21	300
621	Bolt and nut shank	9.95	600

Customer orders are transcribed on a record as follows:

INPUT FILE

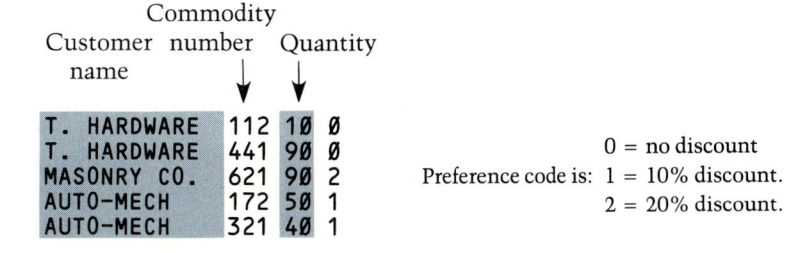

```
                  Commodity
Customer   number   Quantity
  name       ↓         ↓

T. HARDWARE   112  10  0
T. HARDWARE   441  90  0
MASONRY CO.   621  90  2
AUTO-MECH     172  50  1
AUTO-MECH     321  40  1
```

Preference code is:
0 = no discount
1 = 10% discount.
2 = 20% discount.

All transactions records are arranged in customer order groups.

a. Write a program to read a file of customer orders and to print customer invoices, while simultaneously updating the inventory. (Assume that no order will deplete any stock in this part of the problem.) Any preference code 0 with an order exceeding $100 gets a 10% discount rate. The invoices should be similar in format to the following:

```
INVOICE DATE: 17/06/86             SWIVEL CAST COMPANY
SOLD TO     : T. HARDWARE

QUANTITY    COMMODITY   DESCRIPTION            PRICE    AMOUNT

   10          112      SQ. SHANK SWIVEL        1.10     11.00
   90          441      RND. SPR. RING STEM     4.21    378.90

                                                        389.90
                                             DISCOUNT     0.00
                                                       $389.90
----------------------------------------------------------------
INVOICE DATE: 17/06/86             SWIVEL CAST COMPANY
SOLD TO     : MASONRY CO.

QUANTITY    COMMODITY   DESCRIPTION            PRICE    AMOUNT

   90          621      BOLT AND NUT SHANK      9.95    895.50

                                                        895.50
                                             DISCOUNT   179.10
                                                       $716.40
----------------------------------------------------------------
```

b. Write the code to print the original inventory, and when all invoices have been printed, print the end-of-day updated inventory. A reorder message should accompany any commodity item whose stock is less than 20% of the original inventory level. A typical inventory listing is as follows:

```
COMMODITY NO       DESCRIPTION            STOCK

    112         SQ. SHANK SWIVEL           400
    131         FLAT TOP RIGID             500
    172         EXT. SHANK WITH BRK.        39     RE-ORDER
    321         BOLT AND NUT SHANK         100
    441         RND. SPR. RING STEM         15     RE-ORDER
    621         BOLT AND NUT SHANK         500
```

c. In part a it was assumed that no order would deplete any stock. Modify your program to assume that this is no longer the case, i.e., that there are two possible cases: (1) Certain orders may be partially filled, in which case the invoice should specify the number of items sold (items still available) and the number of items placed on order (currently unavailable items). (2) The order cannot even be filled partially, in which case the invoice should specify that the particular item is out of stock.

ONE- AND TWO- DIMENSIONAL TABLES

2. The Personnel Director at Manpower Co. wants certain information about its employees according to the region and the department in which they work. Its directory file consists of 8-digit employee numbers with the following format:

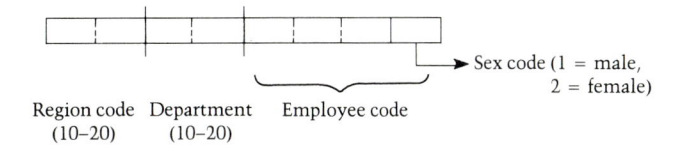

```
┌──────┬──────┬────────┬──┐
│      │      │        │  │───► Sex code (1 = male,
└──────┴──────┴────────┴──┘           2 = female)
Region code  Department  Employee code
  (10-20)     (10-20)
```

Certain departments may not exist in some regions, for example, departments 11 and 12 may not exist in region 10. All regions, however, have at least one department. The directory file is not arranged in any particular order and should not be sorted for this problem.

   a. The Director wants the DP personnel to write a program to allow direct inquiry in the personnel file to capture such information as:
      (i) Number of males/females per region or per department.
      (ii) Number of males/females in a given region and department.
      (iii) Number of males/females in the entire company.

   Design a system to oblige the director's wishes.

   b. Write the code to produce the following:
      (i) The list of employees by region.
      (ii) The list of employees by department across all regions.

   Use Format 1 and then Format 2 below for your output.

Format 1:

```
REGION 10
    10101111
    10131112
       .
REGION 11
    11101211
       .
REGION 20
    20151012
       .
DEPARTMENT 10
    10101111
    10104444
    13101012
       .
DEPARTMENT 20
    10201081
    11201072
```

Format 2:

```
REGION 10        10101111  10131112  10131021
                 10151002
REGION 11        11101211  11131521  11131532
                 11141341  11161721
    .
    .
REGION 20        20151012
DEPARTMENT 10    10101111  10104441  13101012
                 15101012
    .
DEPARTMENT 20    10201081  11201072
```

Note that in Format 2 there are 3 employee numbers per line.

3. Trans-X-Motor Co. sells automobiles, trucks, campers and accessories. Salespeople's commissions vary according to the type of vehicle sold. The commission rate code (1–7) is the last digit of the 5-digit vehicle identification number (unit number) and it indicates a percentage of sales, as follows:

VEHICLE	CODE	COMMISSION (PERCENTAGE OF RETAIL PRICE)		
New car	1	.06		Bonus of $200 for each sale exceeding $12,000
Used car	2	.03	For	
New truck	3	.065	cars	or
Used truck	4	.025	only	Bonus of $100 for each sale in the interval $6,000 to $12,000
New camper	5	.07		
Used camper	6	.02		
Accessories	7	.04		

Input records consist of the following entries: salesperson name, date of transaction, unit number, retail price, and wholesale price. Assume the records are sorted by salesperson and date. A typical input file might be as follows:

```
                                    Commission code
     Name         Date    Id-number / Retail   Wholesale
QUICK JOHNNY     111286    A1111     06426     05200
QUICK JOHNNY     111286    A1212     14254     11000
SALES SAMMY      111286    T1006     08200     07100
SALES SAMMY      121286    X1017     00700     00580
COMBO JOAN       111286    A2001     18500     15000
```

a. Write a program to produce a commission report, organized by salesperson, using a table look-up procedure based on the commission code to identify the various commission rates. The output should be similar to:

```
NAME       DATE        ITEM    COMMISSION     TOTALS

QUICK J    11/12/86    A1111     485.56
QUICK J    11/12/86    A1212     627.62
                                              1113.18
SALES S
   .
   .
   .
```

b. Generate a report to summarize:
   (i) Each salesperson's commission.
   (ii) The profit made on each of the salesperson's total sales.
   (iii) The gross margin associated with each salesperson.

Definitions: Profit = markup − commission

Markup = retail price − wholesale price

Gross margin = profit/retail

The output should be similar to the following (you may want to include a retail column/entry).

```
        SALESMAN    COMMISSION    PROFIT     GROSS MARGIN

        QUICK J      1113.18      3,366.82      .163
        SALES S       192.00      1,028.00      .116
        COMBO J      1310.00      2,190.00      .118

TOTAL COMMISSION     2615.18
TOTAL PROFIT                      6,584.82
AVERAGE PROFIT MARGIN                           .137
```

ONE- AND TWO- DIMENSIONAL TABLES

c. Management would also like a daily sales report showing each salesperson's commissions, as well as individual and total retail sales. The output should be similar to:

```
DATE        SALESMAN    COMMISSION      RETAIL      TOTALS

11/12/86    QUICK J       1113.18    20,680.00
            SALES S        164.00     8,200.00
            COMBO J       1310.00    18,500.00
                                                  47,380.00
12/12/86    SALES S         28.00       700.00
                                                     700.00
                                       TOTAL RETAIL   $48,080.00
```

4. Professor X's grade roster (100 records maximum) contains the following information:

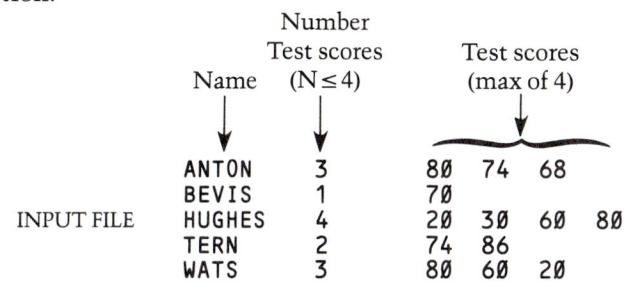

```
                        Number
                      Test scores       Test scores
              Name     (N ≤ 4)          (max of 4)
                ↓        ↓                  ↓
              ANTON      3          80  74  68
              BEVIS      1          70
INPUT FILE    HUGHES     4          20  30  60  80
              TERN       2          74  86
              WATS       3          80  60  20
```

Write the code to read the name and number of tests into one-dimensional tables, NAME and NO and read the grades into a two-dimensional table GRADES. **Then** print the following report:

TABLES

NAME	NO	GRADES			
ANTON	3	80	74	68	
BEVIS	1	70			
HUGHES	4	20	30	60	80
TERN	2	74	86		
WATS	3	80	60	20	
⋮	⋮	⋮	⋮	⋮	⋮

OUTPUT

```
NAME      TESTS    TEST 1   TEST 2   TEST 3   TEST 4
ANTON       3        80       74       68
BEVIS       1        70
HUGHES      4        20       30       60       80
TERN        2        74       86
WATS        3 b.     80       60       20
```

5. An input file contains at most 100 records. Each record contains a student name, the number of tests the student took that semester, and the test scores themselves (see sample input below). Students may take only the final if they want to, or both the 12 weeks test and the final, or the 6 and 12 weeks tests and the final. The tests are recorded on the input record in the following order: final, 12 weeks test (test 2), 6 weeks test (test 1).

Write the code to first read the input data into tables NAME, GRADES, and N (number of tests), but do *not* accumulate or compute anything during this initial reading phase. After the scores have been read into the two-dimensional table GRADES, process the data as follows: List the names, the scores, and the test averages of all students who took three tests. Provide similar lists of the students who took two tests and those who took one test. Finally, print the class averages for the three tests. A sample output is shown below.

No grades other than the scores read from the input record should be stored in the GRADES table, i.e., unused elements of GRADES should not be initialized to 0's or to any other values.

The input and output have the following form:

SAMPLE INPUT

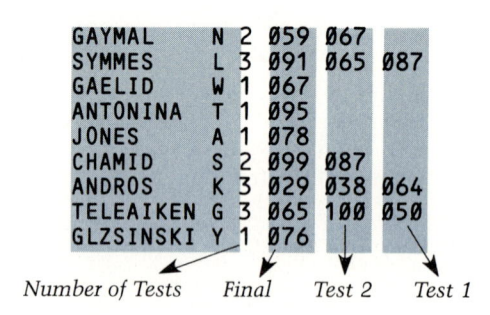

```
GAYMAL     N 2 059 067
SYMMES     L 3 091 065 087
GAELID     W 1 067
ANTONINA   T 1 095
JONES      A 1 078
CHAMID     S 2 099 087
ANDROS     K 3 029 038 064
TELEAIKEN  G 3 065 100 050
GLZSINSKI  Y 1 076
```

Number of Tests   Final   Test 2   Test 1

SAMPLE OUTPUT

```
NAME            TEST 1    TEST 2    FINAL    AVERAGE

SYMMES     L      87        65        91       81.0
ANDROS     K      64        38        29       43.7
TELEAIKEN  G      50       100        65       71.7

GAYMAL     N                67        59       63.0
CHAMID     S                87        99       93.0

GAELID     W                          67       67.0
ANTONINA   T                          95       95.0
JONES      A                          78       78.0
GLZSINSKI  Y                          76       76.0

AVERAGE           67.0      71.4      73.2
```

TABLES

GRADES

59	67	
91	65	87
67		
95		
78		
99	87	
29	38	64
65	100	50
76		

N

2
3
1
1
1
2
3
3
1

6. The East Publishing Company needs sales estimates for five of its textbooks. Each of the company's three regional offices submit their sales estimates three times during the year, in January, March, and May. Projections are recorded on records in chronological time order; i.e., the first three records reflect the three regional offices' estimates for the month of January (in units of a thousand).

Textbooks

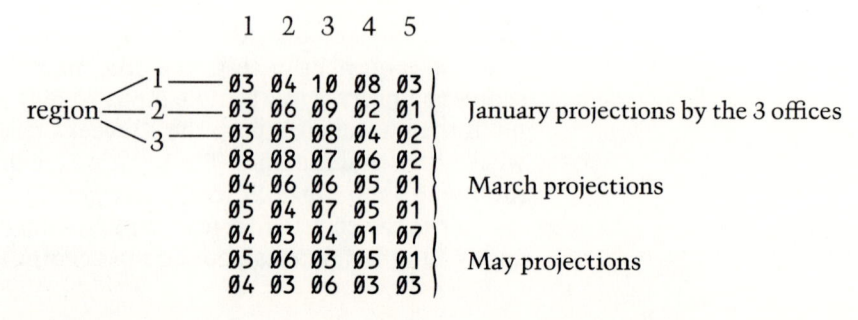

          1   2   3   4   5

```
          ╱1── 03 04 10 08 03 ⎫
region ──2── 03 06 09 02 01 ⎬ January projections by the 3 offices
          ╲3── 03 05 08 04 02 ⎭
              08 08 07 06 02 ⎫
              04 06 06 05 01 ⎬ March projections
              05 04 07 05 01 ⎭
              04 03 04 01 07 ⎫
              05 06 03 05 01 ⎬ May projections
              04 03 06 03 03 ⎭
```

ONE- AND TWO- DIMENSIONAL TABLES 477

Write a program to read an input file similar to the one shown and produce three different kinds of reports identified as a, b, and c. For report a, be sure to store the names of the months in a table to simplify the output operation.

a.

```
                        TEXTBOOKS
JANUARY PROJECTION     3   4  10   8   3
                       3   6   9   2   1
                       3   5   8   4   2
JANUARY AVERAGES      3.0 5.0 9.0 4.7 2.0
-----------------------------------------
MARCH   PROJECTION    8   8   7   6   2
                      4   6   6   5   1
                      5   4   7   5   1
MARCH   AVERAGES     5.7 6.0 6.7 5.3 1.3
-----------------------------------------
MAY     PROJECTIONS   4   3   4   1   7
                      5   6   3   5   1
                      4   3   6   3   3
MAY     AVERAGES     4.3 4.0 4.3 3.0 3.7
-----------------------------------------
AVERAGE PROJECTIONS  4.3 5.0 6.7 4.3 2.3
```

b.

```
                         TEXTBOOKS
                       1   2   3   4   5
REGION 1               3   4  10   8   3
                       8   8   7   6   2
                       4   3   4   1   7
REGION PROJECTIONS     5   5   7   5   4
-----------------------------------------
REGION 2               3   6   9   2   1
                       4   6   6   5   1
                       5   6   3   5   1
REGION PROJECTIONS     4   6   6   4   1
-----------------------------------------
REGION 3               3   5   8   4   2
                       5   4   7   5   1
                       4   3   6   3   3
REGION PROJECTIONS     4   4   7   4   2
-----------------------------------------
PROJECTION AVERAGES   4.3 5.0 6.7 4.3 2.3
```

c.

```
      JANUARY            MARCH              MAY
  3   4  10   8   3    8   8   7   6   2    4   3   4   1   7
  3   6   9   2   1    4   6   6   5   1    5   6   3   5   1
  3   5   8   4   2    5   4   7   5   1    4   3   6   3   3

           BOOK        PROJECTION (AVERAGE)
            1                 4.3
            2                 5.0
            3                 6.7
            4                 4.3
            5                 2.3
```

7. A discount store buys products from different manufacturers. A manufacturer's suggested retail price (MSRP) is given with every item purchased. The discount store records in an input file each item number, the manufacturer's suggested retail price, and the discount price the store plans to charge the consumer. Let us assume there are a maximum of 15 items. Write a program to produce three paragraphs listing items selling below, at, and above the MSRP. Item numbers should be printed four per line. The input and output should be similar to the following:

```
              INPUT
   Item                Customer
  number    MSRP         cost                    OUTPUT

   2222     2000         1000
   3333     2000         2000       BELOW MSRP
   1111     2000         1000         2222    1111    8888    1100
   8888     3000         2000
   4444     5600         5600       AT    MSRP
   5555     6000         9000         3333    4444    6666    1000
   1100     4500         4200         1200    1300
   6666     7800         7800
   7777     2300         2400       ABOVE MSRP
   1000     5600         5600         5555    7777    9999
   9999     6500         6800
   1200     4500         4500
   1300     2000         2000
```

Hint: Since the item numbers must be printed by groups (at, above, or below the MSRP), three tables are needed to store the three groups of item numbers. A two-dimensional table TABS (see below) is created where TABS(1,I), as I goes from 1 to K, is used to store the item numbers that sell for less than the MSRP. K counts the number of items below the MSRP.

Likewise, TABS(2,I), with I varying from 1 to J, is used to store the item numbers selling at the MSRP. J counts the number of items at the MSRP. Finally, TABS(3,I), as I varies from 1 to L, stores the L items selling above the MSRP.

```
01 AT-ABOVE-BELOW.
    05 LEVELS OCCURS 3 TIMES.
        10 TABS OCCURS 15 TIMES PIC 9999.
```

```
                    TABS(1,2)
         TABS(1,1)  |  TABS(1,3)            Below MSRP
            ↓       ↓      ↓                    ↓
         |2222|1111|8888|1100|    |    |    LEVELS(1)
         |3333|4444|6666|1000|1200|1300| ... LEVELS(2) → At MSRP
         |5555|7777|9999|    |    |    |    LEVELS(3)
            ↑       ↑                           ↑
        TABS(3,1)  TABS(3,2)                Above MSRP
```

8. You are tabulating returns from a primary election in which five candidates were running for office: Aiken, Andover, Hilary, Martin, and Watson. Each vote is recorded on one record with two entries per record. The first entry is a number identifying the party of the voter (1 = Democrat, 2 = Republican, 3 = Independent). The second entry identifies the name of the candidate.

   a. Write a program to determine the total number of votes obtained by each candidate. If a candidate obtains six or more votes from any party, print the number of votes from that party and the party. For example:

CANDIDATE	TOTAL VOTES	PARTY	NUMBER OF VOTES
AIKEN	4		
WATSON		DEMOCRAT	6
WATSON	21	INDEPENDENT	10
ANDOVER	8		
HILARY	14	INDEPENDENT	10
MARTIN		DEMOCRAT	6
MARTIN		REPUBLICAN	6
MARTIN	20	INDEPENDENT	8

   Note for example that Mr. Watson must have gotten five votes from the Republican party; the name of the party is not printed, however, since he did not obtain at least six votes from that party.

   b. List the candidates who obtained votes from each of the three parties. For the example given above, the output might be:

   ```
   WATSON
   MARTIN
   ```

   c. Identify candidates who received votes from one or more Democrats, from one or more Republicans, et cetera. Given the above input, the output could be as follows:

```
BY AT LEAST 1 DEMOCRAT:    AIKEN   ANDOVER MARTIN WATSON
BY AT LEAST 1 REPUBLICAN:  MARTIN  HILARY  WATSON
BY AT LEAST 1 INDEPENDENT: ANDOVER HILARY  MARTIN WATSON
```

9. LUXURMART is an exclusive clothing store where Luxurmart members are required to maintain $1,000 in their accounts at all times. Members charge all purchases on Luxur credit cards. Write a main program to create a master member file (table) consisting of member names with an initial $1,500 credit for all members.

   There are several types of transactions that require members' accounts to be updated. Some members return merchandise that must be credited to their accounts. Other members purchase items; if a purchase causes a member's credit to fall below $1,000, a message should be printed requesting the member to write a check for an amount to bring his/her credit back to $1,000. If the name listed on a transaction is not on the master file, an appropriate message should be printed. Transaction records contain member names and dollar amounts for credit or debit.

   Write a program to produce an updated member file after all transaction records have been processed. Sample input and output data are shown below.

   INPUT

   Master File

   ```
   PELLON   106.00
   MOCKER   500.00
   NIARCO   -10.00
   HOWARD  -600.00
   NIARCO    -5.00
   ```

   OUTPUT

   ```
   **NO MATCHING NAME FOR MOCKER**
   --HOWARD MUST PAY 100.00 NOW-

        UPDATED MATER FILE
        HOWARD    900.00
        NIARCO   1485.00
        PELLON   1606.00
        ROCKER   1500.00
   ```

10. Repeat the preceding exercise with the following variation:

    To simplify and minimize transcription errors, the transaction records contain tag numbers, instead of dollar amounts, for items purchased or returned. D or C signifies debit or credit, respectively. For example:

    HOWARD   9 D   means debit Howard's account by whatever item 9 costs.
    NIARCO 10 C   means credit Niarco's account by the value of item 10.

    To allow for the above create a table of costs for the different items as in:

ITEM TAG	COST
1	44.50
2	100.75
3	94.50
.	.
.	.
.	.
10	46.00

11. The following is the daily schedule of a small Pennsylvania airline.

FLIGHT NUMBER	ORIGIN	STOPS	PLANE CAPACITY	DEPARTURE TIME
700	State College	Harrisburg Baltimore Washington	5	7:05 A.M.
701	Washington	Harrisburg State College	5	9:00 A.M.
430	State College	Harrisburg Baltimore Washington	5	4:15 P.M.
431	Washington	Baltimore Harrisburg State College	5	8:15 P.M.

A program is needed to process reservation requests. The planes are very small; there is a maximum of five passengers per flight. If a plane is full, assume the passenger will accept the next available flight. After all transactions have been processed, print a listing by flight and stops of the passengers scheduled. Use a three-dimensional table to store reservations.

The output should have the following form:

```
DATE    FLIGHT                          PASSENGER
2/25    700     STATE COLLEGE TO        B. BALDRIGE
                HARRISBURG              H. DAVIS
                                        .
                                        .
                                        .
                HARRISBURG      TO      B. BALDRIGE
                BALTIMORE               H. DAVIS
                                        .
                                        .
                                        .
                BALTIMORE       TO      H. DAVIS    (Baldridge gets off at Baltimore)
                WASHINGTON
        701     WASHINGTON      TO      A. CHARLES
                HARRISBURG
                                        .
                                        .
                                        .
                HARRISBURG      TO      (Charles gets off in Harrisburg)
                STATE COLLEGE
                                TO      .
                                        .
                                        .
        430     STATE COLLEGE TO        .
                HARRISBURG
                .                       .
                .                       .
                .                       .
        431     .                       .
                .                       .
                .                       .
2/26    700     .                       .
                .                       .
                .                       .
```

Write a program for maintaining passenger reservations for three days, using the following list of reservation requests:

Transactions (Requests for Seats)

NAME	DATE DESIRED	FROM	TO	FLIGHT NUMBER
B. Baldrige	2/25	State College	Baltimore	700
W. Bartlett	2/26	Harrisburg	State College	431
W. Broderick	2/25	Harrisburg	Washington	430
R. Cheek	2/26	Baltimore	State College	431
E. Cooley	2/27	State College	Washington	700
H. Davis	2/25	State College	Washington	700
S. Dalles	2/26	Harrisburg	State College	431
L. Donald	2/25	Baltimore	Washington	700
F. John	2/26	Baltimore	Harrisburg	431
L. Line	2/26	Washington	State College	431
M. Dohert	2/25	State College	Baltimore	700
W. Howard	2/26	Washington	Harrisburg	431
J. Jacks	2/25	Washington	State College	431
J. Jacks	2/26	State College	Washington	430
G. Holland	2/26	Harrisburg	Washington	700
G. Holland	2/27	Washington	Harrisburg	431
C. Italia	2/26	State College	Washington	700
C. Italia	2/26	Washington	Harrisburg	431
H. Kent	2/25	Baltimore	Harrisburg	431
H. Kent	2/27	Harrisburg	Baltimore	430
C. Murray	2/25	State College	Washington	700
C. Murray	2/26	Washington	State College	431
R. Steel	2/25	State College	Washington	700
R. Steel	2/25	Washington	State College	431
A. Charles	2/25	Washington	Harrisburg	701
A. Charles	2/26	Harrisburg	Washington	430
A. Jabbari	2/25	State College	Washington	700
B. Jolly	2/27	Baltimore	Harrisburg	431
J. Hay	2/26	State College	Harrisburg	430
D. Day	2/27	Washington	State College	431
C. Mead	2/25	State College	Baltimore	700
Z. Mattern	2/26	Washington	Harrisburg	431
D. Davidson	2/25	Harrisburg	State College	431
M. West	2/26	State College	Washington	700
L. Mudd	2/27	Baltimore	Harrisburg	431
R. Frat	2/25	Washington	Harrisburg	701

12. Project: Given the Rent-a-Car cost table shown below, write a program to compute a customer's invoice based on the following input parameters:

- Odometer-out and odometer-in readings.
- Vehicle type.
- Rental period (time-out and time-in readings).
- Location of receiving station (a destination fee is charged if the receiving station is not the renting station; see explanations below).
- State sales tax.
- Optional insurance.
- Amount owed if gas tank is not returned full.

TYPE	SCHEDULE 1 FREE MILES 150 DAILY	SCHEDULE 1 FREE MILES 1050 WEEKLY	SCHEDULE 2 TIME & MILEAGE DAILY	SCHEDULE 2 TIME & MILEAGE WEEKLY	SCHEDULES 1 & 2 MILEAGE CHARGE	EXTRA HOURS
Chevette Corolla Omni	24.95	140.00	18.00	100.80	.18	3.60
2-dr. Fairmont 2-dr. Citation	26.95	151.20	19.00	106.40	.20	4.00
4-dr. Fairmont 4-dr. Citation	28.95	162.40	20.00	112.00	.22	4.40
2-dr. Cutlass Monte Carlo Thunderbird Pickup truck	30.95	173.60	22.00	123.20	.22	4.60
4-dr. Caprice 4-dr. Cutlass	32.95	184.80	25.00	140.00	.24	4.80
Impala wagon Cadillac Ville	44.95	256.95	32.00	166.50	.25	5.20
Van 12 passengers	44.95	256.95	25.00	152.00	.26	7.00

Explanations:

The schedule 1 daily rate includes a mileage allowance of 150 miles, and the weekly rate includes a mileage allowance of 1050 miles. The mileage charge column indicates the additional cost for each mile above the mileage allowance for the different car types.

Schedule 2 does not include a mileage allowance. The cost per mile is specified in the mileage charge column.

Before the client takes possession of the car he or she must specify in advance the particular rental plan (Schedule 1 daily, Schedule 1 weekly, Schedule 2 daily, or Schedule 2 weekly). The invoice is then computed based on the agreed plan when the vehicle is returned.

The extra hours column specifies the additional hourly charge for each hour that the vehicle is used in excess of one day or in excess of one week. (Actually, the company's unwritten policy is not to charge the renter for up to two hours beyond the daily/weekly deadline.)

Passenger collision insurance is optional, and costs $3.75 per day.

Destination fee: There is no extra fee if the vehicle is returned to the renting station; however, if the receiving station is not the renting station, an additional cost of 14 cents per mile is charged to the customer for the total number of miles driven, including the mileage allowance.

The final invoice should include a state tax (4% of final invoice).

Time-in and time-out are recorded using the Julian date system; i.e., if time-out is at DAY = 230 and HOURS = 13, this means the 230th day of the year at 1 PM.

Following are some invoice examples for Chevettes with no destination fee (local use).

Example 1. DAYS = 3, MILEAGE = 1050

- Schedule 1: DAILY cost = 3 * 24.95 + 600 mi. @ .18 = 74.85 + 108 = $182.85
- Schedule 1: WEEKLY cost = $140.00
- Schedule 2: DAILY cost = 3 * 18 + 1050 mi. @ .18 = 54 + 189 = $243.00.

Example 2. DAYS = 6, MILEAGE = 210

- Schedule 1: WEEKLY cost = $140.00
- Schedule 2: WEEKLY cost = 100.80 + 210 * .18 = $138.60

Example 3. DAYS = 5, MILEAGE = 50

- Schedule 2: DAILY cost = 5 * 18 + .18 * 50 = $99.00
- Schedule 2: WEEKLY cost = 100.80 + .18 * 50 = $109.80

Example 4. DAYS = 1, MILEAGE = 40, 2 extra hours

- Schedule 1: DAILY cost = 24.95 + 2 hours @ 3.60 = $32.15
- Schedule 2: DAILY cost = 18.00 + 2 hours @ 3.60 + 40 * .18 = $32.40

The following examples show complete printed outputs:

```
UNIT NUMBER        234
MAKE               FORD.         MODEL      THUNDERBIRD
LICENSE PLATE      KP9007        STATE      AL.

MILES OUT          5500          TIME OUT   DAY  2 HOURS 12
MILES IN           6730          TIME IN    DAY 18 HOURS 16
MILES DRIVEN       1230          TIME USED  DAYS 16 HOURS  4
LESS MILES ALLOWED    0
CHARGEABLE MILES   1230          @  .22          270.60
SCHEDULE 2
PER WEEK           3    WEEKS    @ 123.20        369.60
                                 SUBTOTAL        640.20

INSURANCE         16    DAYS     @ 3.75           60.00
DESTINATION FEE 1230    MILES    @  .14          172.20

                                 TAXABLE CHARGE  872.40
                                 STATE TAX        34.90
TOP TANK                                          10.66
                                 NET AMOUNT      917.96
```

```
UNIT NUMBER        102
MAKE               CHEV.         MODEL      CHEVETTE
LICENSE PLATE      BL6420        STATE      FL.

MILES OUT          8520          TIME OUT   DAY 21 HOURS 14
MILES IN           9600          TIME IN    DAY 26 HOURS 14
MILES DRIVEN       1080          TIME USED  DAYS  5 HOURS  0
LESS MILES ALLOWED  750
CHARGEABLE MILES    330          @  .18           59.40
SCHEDULE 1
PER DAY   150 MI. 5     DAYS     @ 24.95         124.75

INSURANCE          5    DAYS     @ 3.75           18.75
DESTINATION FEE 1080    MILES    @  .14          151.20

                                 TAXABLE CHARGE  354.10
                                 STATE TAX        14.16
TOP TANK                                          10.00
                                 NET AMOUNT      378.26
```

8-8-3 SELECTED ANSWERS TO TEST YOURSELF

1. e. T f. F g. F h. F

2. b. Invalid; A is used both as a paragraph name and as a counter.
   c. Valid; depends on paragraph A.

3. a. Invalid; B has no PICTURE clause.
   b. Cannot REDEFINES a data item that occurs (A). Also, PIC 9(30) is invalid.
   c. Valid; 6 positions.

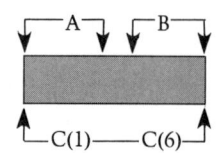

   d. Invalid; multiple use of B.
   e. Invalid; no PICTURE for B.
   i. Invalid; cannot have OCCURS and REDEFINES at the same time.
   j. Valid; The B's represent alphanumeric strings of 4 characters each. The C's represent numeric items, each 4 digits long. 80 positions in all.

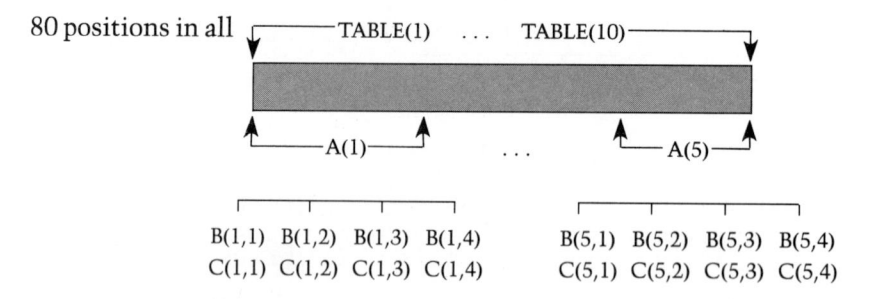

   k. Valid; 10 positions.

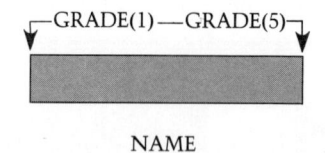

   m. Valid; 1000 positions.

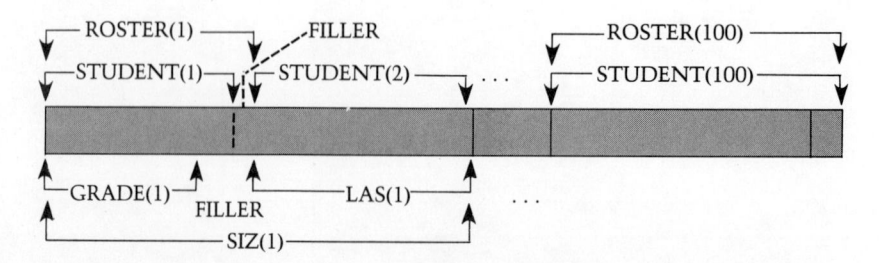

5. Execution error; invalid subscript when I becomes 0; i.e., I will never be 10 since the picture for I is 9.

6. Part a does not compute the average of 10 scores; the last value of I is 11. Part b will compute the average of 10 grades.

8. d.
```
        MOVE SPACES TO DETAIL-LINE.
        PERFORM PARA-1 VARYING I
            FROM 2 BY 2 UNTIL I > 100.
        MOVE 0 TO K.
        MOVE SPACES TO ENTRIES-LINE.
        PERFORM PARA-2 VARYING I
            FROM 1 BY 1 UNTIL I > 100.
            .
            .
    PARA-1.
        MOVE A (I) TO DL-2.
        WRITE PRINT-LINE FROM DETAIL-LINE.
    PARA-2.
        ADD 1 TO K.
        MOVE A (I) TO ITEM (K).
        IF K > 9
            WRITE PRINT-LINE FROM ENTRIES-LINE
            MOVE 0 TO K.
```

```
01 DETAIL-LINE.
   05 FILLER PIC X(20).
   05 DL-2 PIC 99.
01 ENTRIES-LINE.
   05 FILLER PIC X(5).
   05 ENTRY OCCURS 10 TIMES.
      10 ITEM PIC 99.
      10 FILLER PIC XX.
```

10.
```
        MOVE 0 TO I.
        PERFORM PROCESS-PARA UNTIL EOF = 1.
            .
            .
    PROCESS-PARA.
        READ INPUT-FILE AT END MOVE 1 TO EOF.
        IF EOF NOT = 1
        IF I = 20 NEXT SENTENCE
        ELSE
            PERFORM LOAD-7 VARYING K FROM 1 BY 1
                UNTIL K > 7 OR I = 20.
    LOAD-7.
        ADD 1 TO I.
        MOVE NUMB (K) TO A (I).
```

```
01 INPUT-REC.
   05 NUMB OCCURS 7 PIC 99.
```

12.
```
    PROCEDURE DIVISION.
    MAIN-LOGIC.
        OPEN OUTPUT PRINT-FILE.
        PERFORM P-1 VARYING J
            FROM 1 BY 1 UNTIL J > 6.
            .
            .
    P-1.
        PERFORM P-2 VARYING I
            FROM 1 BY 1 UNTIL I > 8.
        WRITE PRINT-LINE FROM DETAIL-LINE.
    P-2.
        COMPUTE PROD = I * J.
        MOVE I TO K (I).
        MOVE J TO L (I).
        MOVE PROD TO M (I).
        MOVE "*" TO AST (I).
        MOVE "=" TO EQAL (I).
```

```
WORKING-STORAGE SECTION.
77  I    PIC 99.
77  J    PIC 99.
77  PROD PIC 999.
01  DETAIL-LINE.
    05 FILLER PIC X VALUE " ".
    05 ENTRY OCCURS 8 TIMES.
       10 K    PIC 9B.
       10 AST  PIC XX.
       10 L    PIC 9B.
       10 EQAL PIC XX.
       10 M    PIC Z9BBB.
```

13.
```
     PERFORM LOAD-1 VARYING I FROM 1 BY 1        WORKING-STORAGE SECTION.
         UNTIL X < A (I) OR I > 10.              77 I PIC 99.
     PERFORM ARR.                                77 K PIC 99.
     MOVE X TO A (I).                            77 L PIC 99.
         .                                       77 S PIC 99.
 LOAD-1.                                         77 X PIC 99.
     EXIT.                                       01 TAB.
 ARR.                                                05 A OCCURS 11 PIC 99.
     COMPUTE S = I + 1.
     PERFORM IT VARYING K FROM 11 BY -1
         UNTIL K < S.
 IT.
     COMPUTE L = K - 1.
     MOVE A (L) TO A (K).
```

18. Yes

19. The following WORKING-STORAGE is used for parts a, b, c, and d.
```
         WORKING-STORAGE SECTION.
         77  D  PIC 999 VALUE 500.
         77  I  PIC 9.
         77  J  PIC 9.
         77  L  PIC 99.
         01  T1 PIC X(24) VALUE "010203040506070809101112".
         01  TAB-A REDEFINES T1.
             05 A-1 OCCURS 3 TIMES.
                10 A OCCURS 4 TIMES PIC 99.
         01  T2 PIC X(36) VALUE "010020030040050060070080090100110120".
         01  TAB-B REDEFINES T2.
             05 B-1 OCCURS 3 TIMES.
                10 B OCCURS 4 TIMES PIC 999.
```

a.
```
     PROCEDURE DIVISION.
     MAIN-LOGIC.
         OPEN OUTPUT PRINT-FILE.
         PERFORM WRITE-1 VARYING I FROM 1 BY 1 UNTIL I > 3
                 AFTER           J FROM 1 BY 1 UNTIL J > 4.
         MOVE D TO C3.
         WRITE PRINT-LINE FROM                          01 DETAIL-LINE.
             DETAIL-LINE AFTER 1.                           05 C1 OCCURS 12 PIC ZZ9.
         STOP RUN.                                          05 FILLER PIC X(5) VALUE " ".
     WRITE-1.                                              05 C2 OCCURS 12 PIC ZZ99.
         COMPUTE L = (I - 1) * 4 + J.                      05 FILLER PIC XXX VALUE " ".
         MOVE A (I, J) TO C1 (L).                           05 C3 PIC 999.
         MOVE B (I, J) TO C2 (L).
```

b.
```
     PROCEDURE DIVISION.
     MAIN-LOGIC.
         OPEN OUTPUT PRINT-FILE.
         MOVE SPACES TO DETAIL-LINE.
         PERFORM WRITE-1 VARYING I FROM 1
             BY 1 UNTIL I > 3.
             .
     WRITE-1.
         PERFORM W-2 VARYING J FROM 1 BY 1             01 DETAIL-LINE.
             UNTIL J > 4.                                  05 C1 OCCURS 4 PIC ZZ9.
         MOVE D TO C3.                                     05 FILLER PIC X(5) VALUE " ".
         WRITE PRINT-LINE FROM DETAIL-LINE.                05 C2 OCCURS 4 PIC ZZ9.
     W-2.                                                  05 FILLER PIC X(4) VALUE " ".
         MOVE A (I, J) TO C1 (J).                          05 C3 PIC 999.
         MOVE B (I, J) TO C2 (J).
```

c. PROCEDURE DIVISION.
   MAIN-LOGIC.
       OPEN OUTPUT PRINT-FILE.
       PERFORM WRITE-1 VARYING I FROM 1
           BY 1 UNTIL I > 4.
       .
   WRITE-1.
       MOVE SPACES TO DETAIL-LINE.
       PERFORM W-2 VARYING J FROM 1 BY 1   01 DETAIL-LINE.
           UNTIL J > 3.   05 C1 OCCURS 3 PIC ZZ9.
       MOVE D TO C3.   05 FILLER PIC X(5) VALUE " ".
       WRITE PRINT-LINE FROM DETAIL-LINE.   05 C3 PIC 999.
   W-2.   05 FILLER PIC XXX VALUE " ".
       MOVE A (J, I) TO C1 (J).   05 C2 OCCURS 3 PIC ZZ99.
       MOVE B (J, I) TO C2 (J).

CHAPTER 9

SEARCHING AND SORTING

9-1 INDEXING

9-2 THE SEARCH FEATURE

9-3 SORTING

9-4 SORTING WITHOUT THE SORT STATEMENT

9-5 PROGRAMMING EXERCISES

INTRODUCTION This chapter covers two important data processing activities: searching and sorting. Searching a table for a particular value requires that the table be indexed instead of being subscripted, so the INDEXED BY and SET clauses are first introduced, then the SEARCH and SEARCH ALL verbs are explained and illustrated. Sorting the elements of a list into a particular order can be accomplished using a built-in SORT feature or with a user-written sorting routine. The built-in SORT statement and the extended SORT input and output procedures with RETURN and RELEASE statements are explained, and two examples of user-written sorting routines are also presented. The use of sections in the PROCEDURE division is also discussed.

9–1 INDEXING

9–1–1 INDEXING VERSUS SUBSCRIPTING

Chapter 8 showed how subscripts could be used to identify table entries by name—the name of the table is specified first, followed by a subscript in parentheses to indicate the position or location of the entry within the table. For example, KLASS (3) refers to the third entry of the table KLASS.

Indexing is an alternative to subscripting. Indexing requires the use of the INDEXED BY clause, which must be specified in the OCCURS clause of the table to be indexed. As far as the programmer is concerned, there is no visual difference between a subscripted table entry and an indexed table entry—they look exactly alike, i.e., KLASS (ID) is a valid reference to a subscripted table entry as well as a valid reference to an indexed table entry. In terms of code execution, indexing is more efficient and results in a faster run time than subscripting. Equally important, indexing allows the programmer use the SEARCH feature, an extremely convenient and flexible option that enables the user to search a table for a particular entry or value. Such a search can be accomplished only if the table to be searched is indexed. The SEARCH feature is discussed in section 9–2.

In terms of syntax, the differences between subscripting and indexing are shown in Figure 9–1.

In the example in Figure 9–1, if INDX is a subscript, the value of INDX is 04. If INDX is an index, the statement SET INDX TO 4 causes the internal value of INDX to be 9, i.e., TAB (INDX) is 9 positions away from the origin of the table; however, as far as the programmer is concerned, the value 4 specified by the SET statement indicates the fourth entry in the table.

SEARCHING AND SORTING

SUBSCRIPTING	INDEXING
1. The subscript must be identified in the DATA division by a PICTURE clause.	1. A reference to an indexed table entry must consist solely of the table name and the name of the index, i.e., TABL (3) is invalid since 3 is not an index name.
2. The subscript can be manipulated just like any other data item name: it can be MOVEd, processed arithmetically, compared, et cetera.	2. The index specified by the INDEXED BY clause must not be defined in the DATA DIVISION, i.e., the system furnishes the index with an internal PICTURE that is not made available to the user.
	3. The INDEXED BY clause must be specified in the OCCURS clause of the table(s) to be indexed.
3. The value of the subscript INDX in TAB(INDX) is an integer value that reflects the position or location of the table entry, i.e., it indicates whether the entry is first, second, third, et cetera.	4. The index specified by the INDEXED BY clause may not be MOVED or processed arithmetically (added, multiplied, et cetera). The index can be set to values through the SET and PERFORM statements, and it can be used in IF statements.
	5. The internal value of the index INDX in TAB (INDX) is equal to the total number of memory positions separating the indexed entry from the beginning of the table, i.e., if INDX is SET TO 4 (made to point to the 4th element) and each table entry has PICTURE 999, the internal value of INDX is 9, since 9 memory positions separate the 4th entry (the occurence position) from the start of the table. Note that the programmer works only with the occurence value of the index (4) and not with its internal value (9).

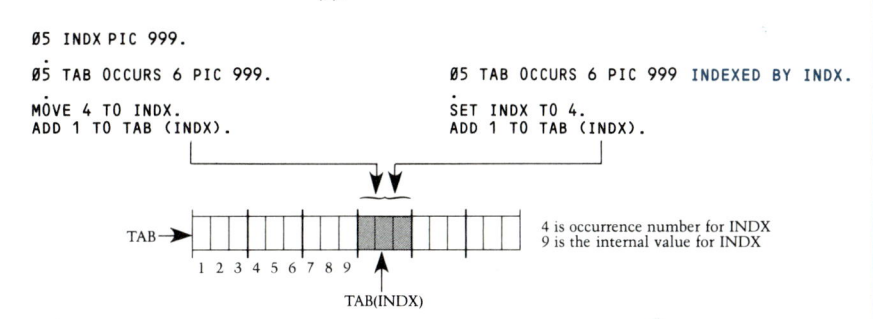

```
05 INDX PIC 999.
.
05 TAB OCCURS 6 PIC 999.              05 TAB OCCURS 6 PIC 999 INDEXED BY INDX.

MOVE 4 TO INDX.                       SET INDX TO 4.
ADD 1 TO TAB (INDX).                  ADD 1 TO TAB (INDX).
```

TAB → [| | | | | | | | | | | |]   4 is occurrence number for INDX
       1 2 3 4 5 6 7 8 9   9 is the internal value for INDX
              TAB(INDX)

FIGURE 9–1
SUBSCRIPTING VERSUS INDEXING

The general form of the INDEXED BY clause is:

INDEXED BY index-name-1 [index-name-2 . . .]

where
The INDEXED BY clause must be specified in the OCCURS clause and index-name-1 and 2 are user chosen names that must *not* have corresponding picture clauses.

Examples:

(1) 05 GRADES OCCURS 10 TIMES   (2) 05 GRADES OCCURS 10 TIMES
       PIC 99 INDEXED BY K.   INDEXED BY K PIC 99.

(3) 05 EMP-ID OCCURS 100 TIMES   (4) 05 KLASS OCCURS 10 TIMES
       INDEXED BY IND1, IND2.   INDEXED BY ROW.
    10 DEPT-NO PIC 999.   10 NAME PIC X(20).
    10 EMP-NO PIC 99.   10 HABIT OCCURS 5 TIMES
                                              INDEXED BY COL.
                                           15 SMOKE PIC 999.

In the fourth example, KLASS(ROW), NAME(ROW), HABIT(ROW,COL), and SMOKE(ROW,COL) are all valid references to table entries. KLASS(3) is incorrect since the index must be a data name and not an integer. HABIT(ROW) is also incorrect since HABIT requires two indexes.

The INDEXED BY option is specified in the OCCURS clause, and index-name-1, index-name-2 are user-chosen names that represent various index names with which to index the table.

Index-name-1 and index-name-2 must *not* be declared as record entries in the DATA DIVISION and, as is the case with subscripts, the value of the index name must not exceed the size of the table specified in the OCCURS clause.

ANSI 74 COBOL permits relative indexing, which means that the index may be followed by the + or − symbol and an unsigned numeric literal as in:

table-entry (index-name [{±} literal-1])

For example, TAB (INDX + 3) refers to the INDX + 3rd element of TAB: that is, if INDX is 2, TAB (INDX + 3) refers to the fifth element of TAB.

An index name must be unique, meaning that two INDEXED BY clauses may not specify the same index. An index name can only be used for the table which specified that particular index name through the INDEXED BY clause.

Note that a table with a declared index can also be subscripted, i.e., we can use both index names or subscripts for the same table.

9-1-3 THE SET CLAUSE

As we have noted, the index is declared only in the OCCURS clause. The user must not define the index in the DATA division. To the programmer, the index is a special data item that has no visible PICTURE clause. Because of that peculiarity, the index cannot be manipulated in the same way as other data items. For example, an index cannot be DISPLAYED or processed with the MOVE, COMPUTE, ADD, SUBTRACT, MULTIPLY, or DIVIDE instructions. There are a limited number of instructions that can process an index. These instructions are:

1. The SET UP BY, the SET DOWN BY, and the PERFORM VARYING statements, which modify (vary) the index by incrementing or decrementing it.

2. The PERFORM VARYING and the SET TO statement, which initialize the index to particular values.

3. The IF statement.

4. The PERFORM . . . UNTIL condition, where the index is a component of the condition.

The general forms of the SET clause are:

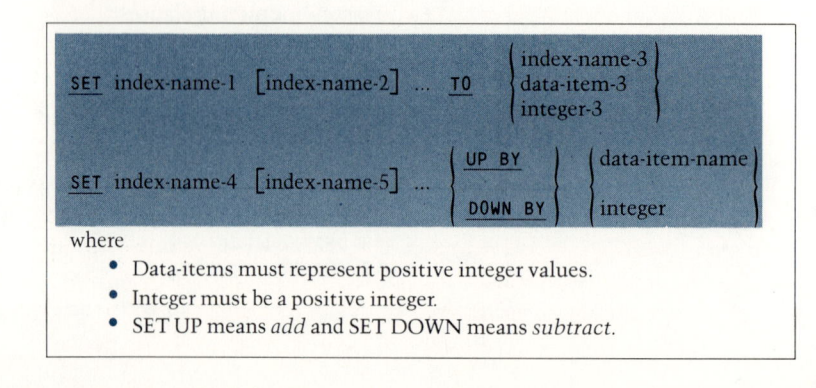

```
SET index-name-1 [index-name-2] ... TO   { index-name-3  }
                                         { data-item-3   }
                                         { integer-3     }

SET index-name-4 [index-name-5] ... { UP BY   }  { data-item-name }
                                    { DOWN BY }  { integer        }
```
where
- Data-items must represent positive integer values.
- Integer must be a positive integer.
- SET UP means *add* and SET DOWN means *subtract*.

Examples:

1. SET IND TO 5.
   MOVE 1 TO TAB (IND).

   The SET verb uses the position number (occurrence) 5 to calculate the internal value of IND. If TAB entries have PIC 999, then the internal value of IND corresponding to 5 is $4 \times 3 = 12$.

2. SET INDEX-1 TO IND.

   The value of index IND (as defined in the preceding example) is "moved" into INDEX-1.

3. SET INDEX-2 TO KLASS.

   If KLASS is not an index, it must have a positive integer value.

4.   PERFORM TRANS VARYING K
      FROM 1 BY 1 UNTIL K > 10.
         .
         .
   TRANS.
      ADD 1 TO TAB (K).

   If K is an index that has been specified in the INDEXED BY clause, K is initialized to 1 by the PERFORM verb. K is then successively incremented by 1.

   Add 1 to each of the 10 entries in TAB.

5. SET EMP-FLAG UP BY 10.

   If EMP-FLAG initially pointed to the first element of TAB, then TAB (EMP-FLAG) now refers to the 11th element of TAB. (Add 10 to EMP-FLAG.)

6. SET EMP-FLAG DOWN BY AMT.

   If EMP-FLAG pointed initially to the 15th element of TAB and AMT = 10, then TAB (EMP-FLAG) now refers to the 5th element of TAB. (Subtract 10 from EMP-FLAG.)

Figure 9-2 illustrates the coding difference between subscripting and indexing.

9-2 THE SEARCH FEATURE

Searching is a data processing activity frequently associated with tables. It is often necessary to determine whether a particular item exists in a table, or it may be necessary, for example, to look up a particular account number to determine the balance in that account. The COBOL verbs SEARCH and SEARCH ALL provide the user with a convenient means to search one-, two- or three-dimensional tables. Both SEARCH verbs require that the tables to be searched be indexed; i.e., the SEARCH verbs cannot be used with subscripted tables.

The main difference between SEARCH and SEARCH ALL is efficiency and speed. SEARCH ALL is much faster than SEARCH, but SEARCH ALL requires that the table entries be in either ascending or descending sequence, and that certain entries be declared through the KEY phrase as key fields in the OCCURS clause. Furthermore, some compilers restrict the types of conditions that can be used to look up table entries when the SEARCH ALL option is used. For example, we might want to search the table TAB for a particular entry equal to or less than ITEM, but the SEARCH ALL verb may specify only conditions involving equality; i.e., it is valid to say something like "search table until TAB (INDX) = ITEM," but it may not be valid to say "search table until TAB (INDX) < ITEM" depending on the particular compiler. Such restrictions do not exist with the SEARCH verb.

> The President of XYZ College wants to obtain a list of students whose grade point averages exceed 3.8. GRADE-ROSTER consists of 5,000 records each containing a student name and the student's grade point average. Write the code to print such a list.

SUBSCRIPTING	INDEXING

``
77 INDX PIC 9999.
01 GRADE-ROSTER.
   05 GPA-TABLE OCCURS 5000 TIMES.
      10 NAME PIC X(20).
      10 GPA PIC 9V99.
``
	``
	01 GRADE-ROSTER.
	   05 GPA-TABLE OCCURS 5000 TIMES
	            INDEXED BY INDX.
	      10 NAME PIC X(20).
	      10 GPA PIC 9V99.
	``

Option 1:
``
    MOVE 1 TO INDX.
    PERFORM PRINT-LIST UNTIL INDX > 5000.
      .
      .
PRINT-LIST.
    IF GPA (INDX) > 3.8
       MOVE NAME (INDX) TO DL-NAME
       WRITE PRINT-LINE FROM D-LINE.
    ADD 1 TO INDX.
``
	``
	    SET INDX TO 1.
	    PERFORM PRINT-LIST UNTIL INDX > 5000.
	      .
	      .
	PRINT-LIST.
	    IF GPA (INDX) > 3.8
	       MOVE NAME (INDX) TO DL-NAME
	       WRITE PRINT-LINE FROM D-LINE.
	    SET INDX UP BY 1.
	``

Option 2:
``
    PERFORM PRINT-LIST VARYING INDX
       FROM 1 BY 1 UNTIL INDX > 5000.
      .
      .
PRINT-LIST.
    IF GPA (INDX) > 3.8
       MOVE NAME (INDX) TO DL-NAME
       WRITE PRINT-LINE FROM D-LINE.
``
	``
	    PERFORM PRINT-LIST VARYING INDX
	       FROM 1 BY 1 UNTIL INDX > 5000.
	      .
	      .
	PRINT-LIST.
	    IF GPA (INDX) > 3.8
	       MOVE NAME (INDX) TO DL-NAME
	       WRITE PRINT-LINE FROM D-LINE.
	``

FIGURE 9-2
SUBSCRIPTING VERSUS INDEXING

9-2-1 THE SEARCH VERB

The general form of the SEARCH verb is shown in Figure 9-3. The WHEN clauses specify the condition(s) under which the SEARCH terminates. These clauses are evaluated in the order in which they appear in the SEARCH sentence. When any condition specified by the WHEN is satisfied, the corresponding imperative statements (there can be any number of them) are carried out. These imperative statements may not be conditional statements or PERFORM UNTIL statements. After execution of these imperative statements, control is passed to the next sentence and the search is terminated. The SEARCH also terminates when the end of the table is reached.

The conditions specified in the WHEN clauses can be relation conditions, class conditions, condition names, or sign conditions. Compound conditions may be used, for example, WHEN (SEX = 1 OR AGE > 65) is permissible.

SEARCHING AND SORTING

```
                PROCEDURE DIVISION                                      DATA DIVISION

  SEARCH table-name  [ VARYING { index-name-1 } ]       05 table-name OCCURS integer TIMES
                               { data-item-1  }              [picture-clause]
  [AT END imperative-statement-1...]                          INDEXED BY index-name-2

  WHEN condition-1 { imperative-statement-2... }
                   { NEXT SENTENCE              }

  [ WHEN condition-2 { imperative-statement-3... } ] ...
                     { NEXT SENTENCE              }
```

where

- Imperative-statements can be MOVE, DISPLAY, ADD, PERFORM statements but *not* conditional statements such as IF, PERFORM...UNTIL, et cetera.
- The WHEN clause specifies the condition under which a table-name entry is to be looked up.
- Condition can be a relation, a class, or a sign condition or a condition name.
- The AT END specifies what to do if the search is unsuccessful.
- Index-name-2 (**not index-name-1**) is the index used to search table-name entries.
- The VARYING option is discussed in item 4 below.

Example: Display the employee number corresponding to "HALL" in EMPLOYEE table.

```
05 EMPLOYEE OCCURS 10 TIMES         SET IND TO 1.
    INDEXED BY IND.                 SEARCH EMPLOYEE
   10 EMP-NAME PIC X(10).                AT END DISPLAY 'NOT FOUND'
   10 EMP-NUMB PIC 9999.                 WHEN EMP-NAME (IND) = 'HALL'
                                             DISPLAY EMP-NUMB (IND).
```

FIGURE 9–3
THE GENERAL FORM OF THE SEARCH STATEMENT

The VARYING option is discussed on page 496.

If at the start of the SEARCH instruction the value of the index is less than or equal to the number of entries in the table, the following actions take place:

1. The conditions in the WHEN clause(s) are evaluated in the order in which these are written.

2. If none of the conditions is satisfied, the index for table-name is incremented to reference the next table element, and step (1) is repeated.

3. If, upon evaluation, one of the WHEN conditions is satisfied, the search terminates immediately and the imperative statement(s) associated with that condition is/are executed; control is then passed to the next sentence. The value of the index-name is equal to the position number of the table entry that was "found."

4. If the end of the table is reached without any WHEN condition being satisfied, or if the initial value for index-name exceeds the number of table entries (as declared in the OCCURS clause), the SEARCH terminates and control is passed to the next sentence.

5. The imperative statements of the AT END option are carried out only if none of the WHEN clauses is satisfied or if the initial value of index-name exceeds the number of entries in the table.

Several points with regard to the use of the SEARCH verb should be noted.

1. Table entries in the table to be searched need not be arranged in any particular sequence.

2. The table-name specified by the SEARCH must be the table-name that is declared in the OCCURS clause where the INDEXED BY option is specified. The index used to search table-name is the one specified by the INDEXED BY option. For example, in Figure 9–3 we cannot write SEARCH EMP–NAME because EMP–NAME is *not* the table-name declared in the OCCURS clause. Note, however, that it is perfectly valid to index any subordinate items of table-name.

It is also possible to search two- or three-dimensional tables as follows:

```
05 PLANT OCCURS 5 TIMES INDEXED BY ROW.
   10 MACHINE-ID PIC X(8).
   10 MACHINE OCCURS 10 TIMES INDEXED BY COL.
      15 HOURS-LOST PIC 999V99.
```

With this data structure, the following SEARCHes can be specified:

```
SEARCH PLANT                            or    SEARCH MACHINE
    WHEN MACHINE-ID (ROW) = "LATHE" ...         WHEN HOURS-LOST (ROW, COL) = 48...
```

3. A SET or a PERFORM VARYING statement must establish the initial value of the index before the SEARCH process is carried out. This means that the search can start in the middle of the table! The user may set the index to 1 or to any other positive integer value. The index will then be incremented automatically by 1 as the search proceeds from one table element to the next.

4. The VARYING option of the SEARCH verb can be used to vary the index of a table other than the table being searched. In that case, the value of the VARYING index takes on the same values as the SEARCH index. Consider the following example:

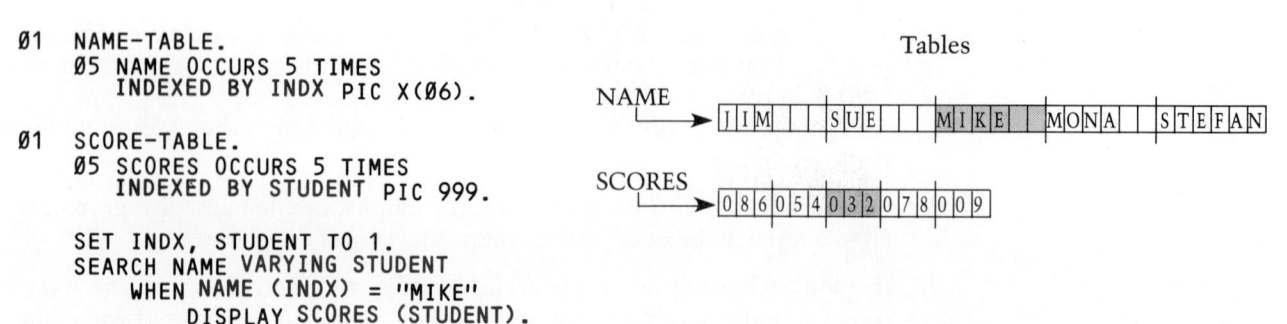

```
01  NAME-TABLE.
    05 NAME OCCURS 5 TIMES
        INDEXED BY INDX PIC X(06).

01  SCORE-TABLE.
    05 SCORES OCCURS 5 TIMES
        INDEXED BY STUDENT PIC 999.

    SET INDX, STUDENT TO 1.
    SEARCH NAME VARYING STUDENT
        WHEN NAME (INDX) = "MIKE"
            DISPLAY SCORES (STUDENT).
```

Tables

NAME → | JIM | SUE | MIKE | MONA | STEFAN |

SCORES → | 086 | 054 | 032 | 078 | 009 |

The WHEN condition is satisfied when INDX is 3. Since STUDENT is an index for table SCORES and since it is also specified in the VARYING option of the

SEARCHING AND SORTING   497

SEARCH statement, STUDENT takes on the same values as INDX and hence SCORES (STUDENT) = SCORES (3) = 032. It would have been incorrect to write SCORES(INDX) since INDX can only be used to index NAME.

To better understand the mechanics of the SEARCH verb and its various phrases, consider the following two examples:

EXAMPLE 1: Each entry of a grade roster table consists of a student's name and score. These GRADE-ROSTER entries are sorted in alphabetical name sequence. Write the code to accept a student's name and print the student's score. If the name of the student is not present in the table, print an appropriate error message.

```
26:   01 GRADE-ROSTER.
27:      05 GRADE-TABLE OCCURS 100 TIMES
28:            INDEXED BY INDX.
39:         10 NAME  PIC X(08).
30:         10 TEST  PIC 999.
31: *
32:   PROCEDURE DIVISION.
33:   100-COORDINATING-MODULE.
34:      OPEN INPUT STUDENT-FILE.
35:      PERFORM 200-LOAD-TABLE VARYING INDX
36:         FROM 1 BY 1 UNTIL WS-EOF = 1.
37:      ACCEPT WS-NAME.
38:      PERFORM 300-PROCESS-RECORDS
39:         UNTIL WS-NAME = 'XXX'.
40:      CLOSE STUDENT-FILE.
41:      STOP RUN.
42: *
43:   300-PROCESS-RECORDS.
44:      SET INDX TO 1.
45:      SEARCH GRADE-TABLE
46:         AT END MOVE 'END' TO WS-FLAG

47:         WHEN WS-NAME < NAME (INDX)
48:            MOVE 'END' TO WS-FLAG


49:         WHEN WS-NAME = NAME (INDX)
50:            NEXT SENTENCE.
51:      IF WS-FLAG = 'END'
52:         DISPLAY 'NO NAME FOUND'
53:      ELSE
54:         DISPLAY TEST (INDX).
55:      ACCEPT WS-NAME.
56: *
57:   200-LOAD-TABLE.
58:      READ STUDENT-FILE
59:         INTO GRADE-TABLE (INDX)
60:         AT END MOVE 1 TO WS-EOF.
```

GRADE-TABLE:
```
ADAMS  T  087
BUNDY  L  085
DINGEL M  100
FALLS  S  078
HIRT   J  060
LOOMIS P  078
```

Load GRADE-TABLE with names and scores. Accept a student name and determine if it is in the table. If it is, display the student's corresponding score.

Initialize index to start of NAME table.
If the AT END clause is taken, then the name is beyond the last name in the table. For example, if WS-NAME = "POTTER" then control is passed to line 51.
If WS-NAME is less than the very next name, then WS-NAME is not in the table, i.e., if WS-NAME = "CANTY", the search is stopped after comparing the first three entries (since CANTY is less than DINGEL). Control is passed to line 51.
If there is a match, go to line 51 and print the test score.
If no match was found as a result of either line 46 or line 48, print an error message
otherwise
display the student's score.
Accept another student name.

EXAMPLE 2: Consider the table of caloric requirements, shown below, for females desiring to sustain their weight. To keep one's weight (WEIGHT-IN) at the same level, one must search through the weight column and read the corresponding number of calories; intake of that number of calories will result in no weight gain or loss. For example,

If WEIGHT–IN is equal to 146, the sustaining calories = 2550.

If WEIGHT–IN is equal to 149, the sustaining calories = 2600.

If WEIGHT–IN is below 109, the caloric requirement = 1900.

Let us write the code to look up one's sustaining caloric requirement for a given weight WEIGHT–IN.

```
01 TAB-CONSTANT.
    05 FILLER PIC X(18) VALUE "109114120124130134".
    05 FILLER PIC X(18) VALUE "139145149156159164".
    05 FILLER PIC X(16) VALUE "1920200021202190".
    05 FILLER PIC X(16) VALUE "2240230024002550".
    05 FILLER PIC X(16) VALUE "2600272028002900".

01 TAB-SEARCH REDEFINES TAB-CONSTANT.
    05 WEIGHT OCCURS 12 PIC 999   INDEXED BY K.
    05 CALORY OCCURS 12 PIC 9999  INDEXED BY L.
```

Weight	Calories
below 109	1900
109	1920
114	2000
120	2120
124	2190
130	2240
134	2300
139	2400
145	2550
149	2600
156	2720
159	2800
164	2900
over 164	3000

```
05: SET K, L TO 1.
10: SEARCH WEIGHT VARYING L
15:     AT END MOVE 3000 TO CAL-OUT
```
Detecting the end of the weight table indicates that WEIGHT–IN exceeds the last weight value in the table; i.e., the number of sustaining calories is 3000. Control is passed to line 65.

```
20:     WHEN WEIGHT-IN < 109
25:         MOVE 1900 TO CAL-OUT
```
Any weight less than 109 requires 1900 calories.

```
30:     WHEN WEIGHT-IN < WEIGHT (K)
35:         SET L DOWN BY 1
40:         MOVE CALORY (L) TO CAL-OUT
```
Decrement the index by 1 and record the correct number of calories. Then go to line 65.

```
45:     WHEN WEIGHT-IN = WEIGHT (K)
50:         MOVE CALORY (L) TO CAL-OUT
```
Record the number of calories and go to line 65.

```
55:     WHEN WEIGHT-IN > 164
60:         MOVE 3000 TO CAL-OUT.
```
Record number of calories and go to line 65.

```
65: WRITE PRINT-LINE FROM CALORY-LINE.
```
Print the number of calories required.

Statement 55 might seem redundant in view of statement 15. However, statement 15 is executed only after the entire table has been searched; the presence of statement 55 makes the search more efficient, since a weight above 164 causes the search to terminate for the first value of the index K. In the absence of statement 55, all 12 table elements would have to be searched before the AT END option would become activated.

9-2-2 THE SEARCH ALL STATEMENT

The general form of the SEARCH ALL statement is shown in Figure 9–4.

Several points with regard to the use of the SEARCH ALL verb should be noted:

1. The SEARCH ALL is faster than the SEARCH statement. It uses a binary search process discussed in example 8 section 9.5.1.

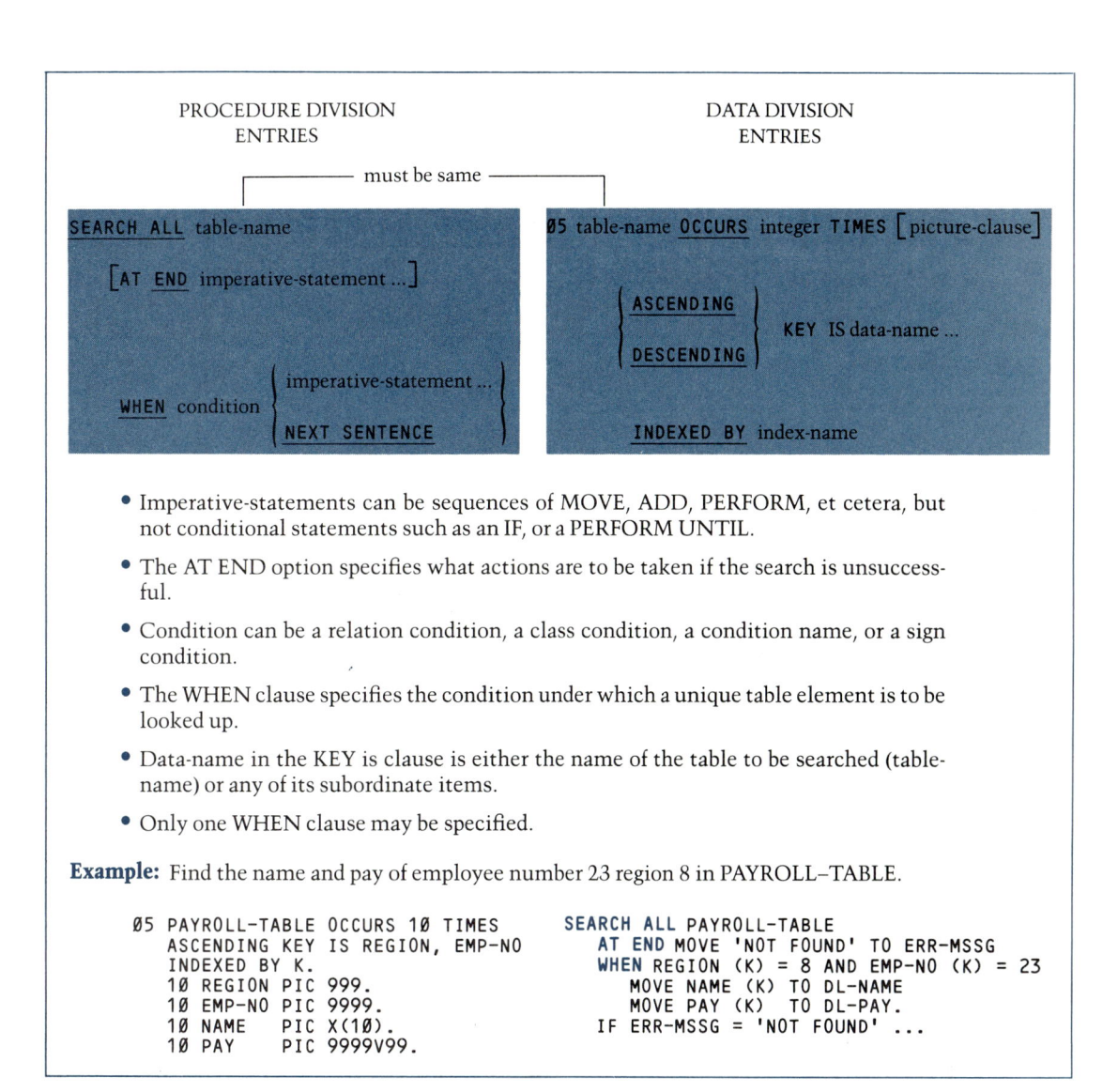

```
                PROCEDURE DIVISION              DATA DIVISION
                    ENTRIES                       ENTRIES
                          ┌─── must be same ───┐
    SEARCH ALL table-name                  05 table-name OCCURS integer TIMES [picture-clause]

        [AT END imperative-statement ...]
                                                  ⎧ ASCENDING  ⎫
                                                  ⎨            ⎬  KEY IS data-name ...
                                                  ⎩ DESCENDING ⎭
                      ⎧ imperative-statement ... ⎫
        WHEN condition ⎨                          ⎬
                      ⎩ NEXT SENTENCE             ⎭  INDEXED BY index-name
```

- Imperative-statements can be sequences of MOVE, ADD, PERFORM, et cetera, but not conditional statements such as an IF, or a PERFORM UNTIL.
- The AT END option specifies what actions are to be taken if the search is unsuccessful.
- Condition can be a relation condition, a class condition, a condition name, or a sign condition.
- The WHEN clause specifies the condition under which a unique table element is to be looked up.
- Data-name in the KEY is clause is either the name of the table to be searched (table-name) or any of its subordinate items.
- Only one WHEN clause may be specified.

Example: Find the name and pay of employee number 23 region 8 in PAYROLL–TABLE.

```
05 PAYROLL-TABLE OCCURS 10 TIMES        SEARCH ALL PAYROLL-TABLE
   ASCENDING KEY IS REGION, EMP-NO         AT END MOVE 'NOT FOUND' TO ERR-MSSG
   INDEXED BY K.                           WHEN REGION (K) = 8 AND EMP-NO (K) = 23
   10 REGION PIC 999.                         MOVE NAME (K) TO DL-NAME
   10 EMP-NO PIC 9999.                        MOVE PAY (K)  TO DL-PAY.
   10 NAME   PIC X(10).                    IF ERR-MSSG = 'NOT FOUND' ...
   10 PAY    PIC 9999V99.
```

FIGURE 9–4
THE SEARCH ALL STATEMENT

2. The index that is used to search table-name must be the index specified in the OCCURS clause that declares table-name. This index is *automatically* initialized by the SEARCH ALL process, i.e., no SET statement should be used to initialize the index when using SEARCH ALL.

3. Table items that are to be searched *must* be declared in the ASCENDING or DESCENDING KEY clauses. These item names, referred to as data-name in Figure 9–4, are either subordinate items of table-name or table-name itself. In any event, the ASCENDING/DESCENDING data names *must* already be sorted in the declared sequence order. Note that in the example in Figure 9–4, NAME and PAY are *not* key fields and hence neither of these items need be in any type of sequence. Within the SEARCH ALL statement, both DESCENDING and ASCENDING key data names can be specified.

4. The WHEN phrase can be specified only *once* in the SEARCH ALL sentence. Furthermore, many compilers require that the condition specified in the WHEN clause test only for equality of key fields to some value; i.e., no relational operator other than the equal sign can be used in the condition. The condition may be a compound condition, but only the AND connector can be used. After execution of the imperative statement(s), execution resumes at the next sentence.

5. The optional AT END clause specifies what action is to be taken if the end of the table has been reached before the WHEN condition has been satisfied or if the index is greater than the highest possible occurrence number for table-name. After the AT END action is taken, control resumes at the next sentence.

Example:

Each entry of table ACCOUNTS consists of a year (2-digit number), a month, a day (any number between 1 and 31), and a sales amount. Write the code to print the sales amount corresponding to a particular year, month, and day. The table consists of sales entries for the last 10 years, except for certain holidays and weekends. Let us find the sales for May 7, 1981:

```
01 SALES-RECORDS.
   05 ACCOUNTS OCCURS 3653 TIMES
       DESCENDING KEY YEAR
       ASCENDING KEY MONTH, DAY
       INDEXED BY INDX.
       10 YEAR  PIC 99.
       10 MONTH PIC 99.
       10 DAY   PIC 99.
       10 SALES PIC 999V99.
```

A maximum of 3653 entries for the last 10 years. Years are in descending order starting with the most recent year. For each given year the monthly entries will be in ascending sequence, and for each month the days will be in ascending order.

Two options are shown:

```
SEARCH ALL ACCOUNTS
    AT END MOVE 'NOT FOUND' TO FLAG
    WHEN YEAR (INDX)    = 81
      AND MONTH (INDX) = 5
      AND DAY (INDX)   = 7
        NEXT SENTENCE.
IF FLAG = 'NOT FOUND'
    DISPLAY 'NO SALES THAT DAY'
ELSE
    DISPLAY SALES (INDX).
```

```
SEARCH ALL ACCOUNTS
    AT END DISPLAY 'NO SALES THAT DAY'
    WHEN YEAR (INDX)  = 81 AND
         MONTH (INDX) = 5  AND
         DAY (INDX)   = 7
        DISPLAY SALES (INDX).
```

9-2-3 A TWO-DIMENSIONAL TABLE SEARCH

The following example illustrates the use of indexing, the SEARCH with the VARYING option, and the SEARCH ALL statements.

Example: Let us read two one-dimensional tables DETAILED–CENSUS and SUMMARIZED–CENSUS stored on a disk into memory. The first table DETAIL–CENSUS contains the number of births and deaths that have occurred in each of five states for each of the last five years in units of 10,000. Each table entry contains a year, a number of births and a number of deaths. The second table SUMMARIZED–TABLE contains the total number of births and deaths that have occurred in each of the states over the entire five-year period. For example:

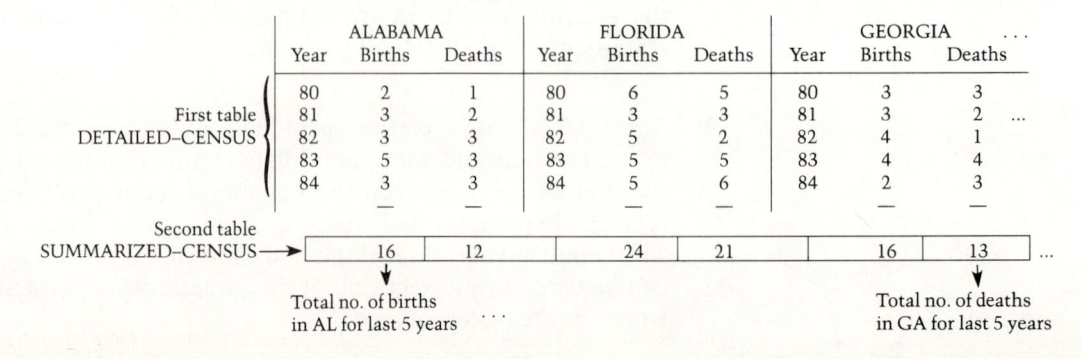

		ALABAMA			FLORIDA			GEORGIA	
	Year	Births	Deaths	Year	Births	Deaths	Year	Births	Deaths
First table DETAILED–CENSUS	80	2	1	80	6	5	80	3	3
	81	3	2	81	3	3	81	3	2
	82	3	3	82	5	2	82	4	1
	83	5	3	83	5	5	83	4	4
	84	3	3	84	5	6	84	2	3
Second table SUMMARIZED–CENSUS →		16	12		24	21		16	13

Total no. of births in AL for last 5 years

Total no. of deaths in GA for last 5 years

SEARCHING AND SORTING

Let us write a program to read these two tables into memory and produce an output similar to the one shown below. The program will accept a given year and a given state and print the corresponding number of births and deaths that occurred that year as well as the total number of births and deaths for that state for the last 5 years.

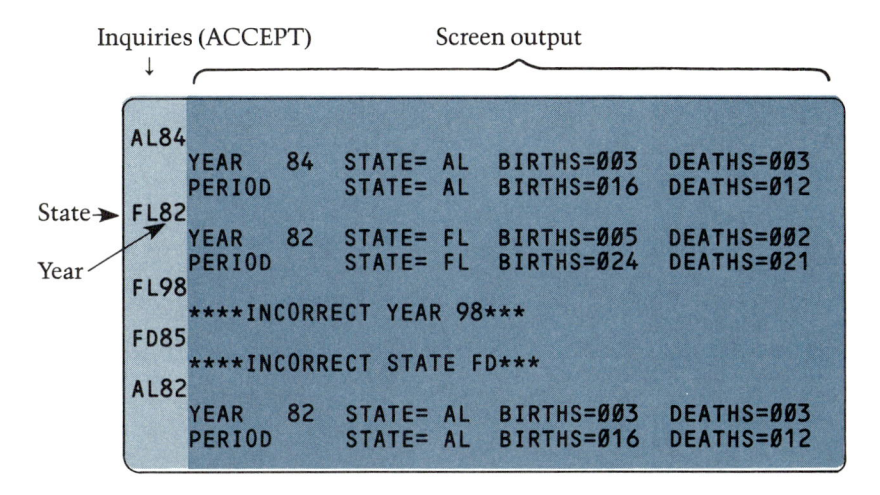

```
                 Inquiries (ACCEPT)         Screen output
                         ↓
         AL84
              YEAR    84   STATE= AL   BIRTHS=003   DEATHS=003
              PERIOD       STATE= AL   BIRTHS=016   DEATHS=012
State→   FL82
              YEAR    82   STATE= FL   BIRTHS=005   DEATHS=002
Year          PERIOD       STATE= FL   BIRTHS=024   DEATHS=021
         FL98
              ****INCORRECT YEAR 98***
         FD85
              ****INCORRECT STATE FD***
         AL82
              YEAR    82   STATE= AL   BIRTHS=003   DEATHS=003
              PERIOD       STATE= AL   BIRTHS=016   DEATHS=012
```

The program to solve this problem is shown in Figure 9–5. Note that the first SEARCH (line 88) uses the index ST to locate the position of the desired state in the table. The second SEARCH ALL (line 99) uses index YR to search the years within that state to match the input year. The desired entries are then DETAIL–BIRTH (ST, YR) and DETAIL–DEATH (ST, YR) at lines 110–111.

9–3 SORTING

9–3–1 AN OVERVIEW

Given a list of any type of unprocessed or raw information, such as a list of names or employee numbers, one's first impulse is generally to sort out these items into some particular order (descending or ascending) so that looking them up will be a great deal easier. Hence it should come as no surprise that sorting is one of the most practiced forms of data processing (for directories, tax tables, book retrieval, identifications, and so forth).

Most main-frame COBOL compilers have built-in SORT features that the programmer can conveniently use without having to write the actual COBOL code. However, most microcomputer COBOL compilers do not have such a SORT feature. For those who do not have the SORT feature, two sorting procedures are discussed in section 9–4.

9–3–2 THE SORT FEATURE

Built-in SORT features can be conveniently used by specifying

1. The name of a disk/tape file to be sorted.
2. The various record keys to be used for sequencing purposes.
3. The name of a user-designated file into which the sorted file will be stored.

```
 1:    IDENTIFICATION DIVISION.
 2:    *******************************
 3:    *   CENSUS PROGRAM            *
 4:    *******************************
 5:    PROGRAM-ID. CENSUS-SEARCH.
 6:    AUTHOR. JONES.
 7:    ENVIRONMENT DIVISION.
 8:    CONFIGURATION SECTION.
 9:    SOURCE-COMPUTER. IBM.
10:    OBJECT-COMPUTER. IBM.
11:    INPUT-OUTPUT SECTION.
12:    FILE-CONTROL.
13:    *
14:        SELECT CENSUS-FILE ASSIGN TO DISK
15:        ORGANIZATION IS LINE SEQUENTIAL.
16:    *
17:    DATA DIVISION.
18:    FILE SECTION.
19:    *
20:    FD  CENSUS-FILE
21:        LABEL RECORDS ARE STANDARD
22:        VALUE OF FILE-ID IS 'CENSUS'
23:        DATA RECORD ARE DETAILED-CENSUS
24:            SUMMARIZED-CENSUS.
25:    01  DETAILED-CENSUS PIC X(110).
26:    01  SUMMARIZED-CENSUS PIC X(20).
27:    WORKING-STORAGE SECTION.
28:    01  INDEPENDENT-ITEMS.
29:        05 STATE-FLAG PIC X(09).
30:        05 YEAR-FLAG  PIC X(09).
31:    *
32:    *   SCREEN INQUIRY (STATE, YEAR)
33:    *
34:    01  INQUIRY.
35:        05 STATE PIC XX.
36:        05 YEAR  PIC 99.
37:    *
38:    *   SCREEN OUTPUT
39:    *
40:    01  SUMMARY-LINE.
41:        05 FILLER-1 PIC X(13) VALUE '     YEAR'.
42:        05 SL-YEAR  PIC Z(02).
43:        05 FILLER   PIC X(10) VALUE ' STATE='.
44:        05 SL-STATE PIC X(02).
45:        05 FILLER   PIC X(09) VALUE ' BIRTHS='.
46:        05 SL-BIRTH PIC 9(03).
47:        05 FILLER   PIC X(09) VALUE ' DEATHS='.
48:        05 SL-DEATH PIC 9(03).
49:    *
50:    *   TABLES
51:    *
52:    01  DETAIL-CENSUS-TABLE.
53:        05 DETAIL-STATE-TABLE OCCURS 5 INDEXED BY ST.
54:           10 STATE-ABBREV PIC XX.
55:           10 DETAIL-CENSUS OCCURS 5 TIMES
56:                 ASCENDING KEY IS YEAR
57:                 INDEXED BY YR.
58:              15 DETAIL-YEAR  PIC 99.
59:              15 DETAIL-BIRTH PIC 9.
60:              15 DETAIL-DEATH PIC 9.
61:    *
62:    01  SUMMARY-CENSUS-TABLE.
63:        05 SUMMARY-STATE OCCURS 5 TIMES
64:              INDEXED BY ST-05.
65:           10 SUMMARY-BIRTHS PIC 99.
66:           10 SUMMARY-DEATHS PIC 99.
```

ALABAMA			FLORIDA			GEORGIA		
Year	Births	Deaths	Year	Births	Deaths	Year	Births	Deaths
80	2	1	80	6	5	80	3	3
81	3	2	81	3	3	81	3	2
82	3	3	82	5	2	82	4	1
83	5	3	83	5	5	83	4	4
84	3	3	84	5	6	84	2	3
Totals	16	12		24	21		16	13

AL8021813282338353843FL806581338252835584 56GA8033813282418344 8423 ...
161224211613 ...

Total number of births for Alabama in past five years
Total number of deaths for Georgia in past five years

Screen input: State, Year — Screen output:

```
AL84
     YEAR    84  STATE= AL  BIRTHS=003  DEATHS=003
     PERIOD      STATE= AL  BIRTHS=016  DEATHS=012
FL82
     YEAR    82  STATE= FL  BIRTHS=005  DEATHS=002
     PERIOD      STATE= FL  BIRTHS=024  DEATHS=021
FL98
     ****INCORRECT YEAR 98***
FD85
     ****INCORRECT STATE FD***
AL82
     YEAR    82  STATE= AL  BIRTHS=003  DEATHS=003
     PERIOD      STATE= AL  BIRTHS=016  DEATHS=012
```

FIGURE 9–5

A SEARCH AND SEARCH ALL EXAMPLE

```
67:  *
68:  PROCEDURE DIVISION.
69:  *
70:  100-COORDINATING-MODULE.
71:      OPEN INPUT CENSUS-FILE.
72:      PERFORM 200-LOAD-TWO-CENSUS-TABLES.
73:      ACCEPT INQUIRY.
74:      PERFORM 300-CENSUS-INQUIRY
75:          UNTIL INQUIRY = '9999'.
76:      CLOSE CENSUS-FILE.
77:      STOP RUN.
78:  *
79:  200-LOAD-TWO-CENSUS-TABLES.
80:      READ CENSUS-FILE INTO DETAIL-CENSUS-TABLE
81:          AT END STOP RUN.
82:      READ CENSUS-FILE INTO SUMMARY-CENSUS-TABLE
83:          AT END STOP RUN.
84:  *
85:  300-CENSUS-INQUIRY.
86:      SET ST, ST-05 TO 1.
87:      MOVE 'FOUND' TO STATE-FLAG, YEAR-FLAG.
88:      SEARCH DETAIL-STATE-TABLE VARYING ST-05
89:          AT END MOVE 'NOT FOUND' TO STATE-FLAG
90:          WHEN STATE = STATE-ABBREV (ST)
91:              NEXT SENTENCE.
92:      IF STATE-FLAG = 'NOT FOUND'
93:          DISPLAY '    ****INCORRECT STATE ', STATE, '***'
94:      ELSE
95:          PERFORM 400-DETERMINE-YEAR.
96:      ACCEPT INQUIRY.
97:  *
98:  400-DETERMINE-YEAR.
99:      SEARCH ALL DETAIL-CENSUS
100:         AT END MOVE 'NOT FOUND' TO YEAR-FLAG
101:         DISPLAY '    ****INCORRECT YEAR ', YEAR, '***'
102:         WHEN DETAIL-YEAR (ST, YR) = YEAR
103:             NEXT SENTENCE.
104:     IF YEAR-FLAG = 'FOUND'
105: *
106: *   DISPLAY CENSUS FOR THE ONE YEAR PERIOD
107: *
108:         MOVE YEAR               TO SL-YEAR
109:         MOVE STATE              TO SL-STATE
110:         MOVE DETAIL-BIRTH (ST, YR) TO SL-BIRTH
111:         MOVE DETAIL-DEATH (ST, YR) TO SL-DEATH
112:         DISPLAY SUMMARY-LINE
113: *
114: *   DISPLAY CENSUS FOR THE FIVE YEAR PERIOD
115: *
116:         MOVE 0 TO SL-YEAR
117:         MOVE '   PERIOD'         TO FILLER-1
118:         MOVE SUMMARY-BIRTHS (ST-05) TO SL-BIRTH
119:         MOVE SUMMARY-DEATHS (ST-05) TO SL-DEATH
120:         DISPLAY SUMMARY-LINE
121:         MOVE '     YEAR' TO FILLER-1.
```

FIGURE 9–5

(continued)

Examples of sorts using the SORT feature are shown in Figure 9–6 and explained in the following paragraphs.

Case 1: The disk/tape input file GRADE-FILE is sorted in four different ways: in ascending name order, in descending name order, in ascending score order, and in descending score order. In the PROCEDURE code,
SORT is a key word telling COBOL to start the sorting process.
SORT-FILE is a work file that is used by COBOL to sort.
USING identifies the name of the user disk/tape file to be sorted.
GIVING specifies the name of the user file into which the sorted file is to be stored.

Case 2: This is a variation of case 1 where more than one key field is used to specify the order in which the records are to be sorted. Note the combination, within one sort, of the ASCENDING and DESCENDING options.

Case 3: This sort option allows the user to read an input file and choose records from that input file for sorting. This option is made possible through the INPUT procedure, which allows the user to select records for the sorting process. Once COBOL has sorted the file into its own work file, another option, the OUTPUT procedure, allows the user to selectively retrieve records from the sorted work file to create various output files, print reports from the sorted work file, et cetera.

9–3–3 THE BASIC AND EXTENDED SORTS

In discussing the SORT feature, we will differentiate between the basic SORT, which sorts all records of a given disk/tape file, and the extended SORT, which allows the user to send the sort-file selected records from one or more input files and to selectively retrieve records from the COBOL sort-file as in case 3 in Figure 9–6. For a better understanding of the mechanics and the components of the sort process, we will discuss three sort programs: a basic sort, an extended sort with the INPUT PROCEDURE (section 9–2–4), and an extended sort with the OUTPUT PROCEDURE (section 9–2–6). Consider the following example of a basic sort:

A disk data file GRADE-ROSTER contains student names and scores. We want to:

1. Sort the roster in ascending name sequence.

2. Store the resulting file in a user disk file named SORTED-NAMES.

3. Print the sorted file SORTED-NAMES.

The process can be visualized as follows:

```
   GRADE-ROSTER                SORTED-NAMES              PRINTOUT

  YOUNG   ARNIE   79    SORT   KING    DEBBIE   81     KING    DEBBIE   81
  KING    DEBBIE  81    ──►    LORD    JIM      66     LORD    JIM      66
  LORD    JIM     66           YOUNG   ARNIE    79     YOUNG   ARNIE    79
```

The program to solve this problem is shown in Figure 9–7. All records of the disk-file specified by the USING verb (GRADE-ROSTER in this instance) are moved into the COBOL sort work-file. This work-file (SORT-FILE) is specified

SEARCHING AND SORTING

Case 1: Single-Key Sort

GRADE-FILE (disk file)

NAME	SCORE
YOUNG ARNIE	84
KING DEBBIE	81
LORD JIM	66

Sequence:
1. ASCENDING KEY NAME
2. ASCENDING KEY SCORE
3. DESCENDING KEY SCORE
4. DESCENDING KEY NAME

Sorted files:

1. KING DEBBIE 81 / LORD JIM 66 / YOUNG ARNIE 84
2. LORD JIM 66 / KING DEBBIE 81 / YOUNG ARNIE 84
3. YOUNG ARNIE 84 / KING DEBBIE 81 / LORD JIM 66
4. YOUNG ARNIE 84 / LORD JIM 66 / KING DEBBIE 81

PROCEDURE code (for #2):
```
SORT SORT-FILE
    ON ASCENDING KEY SCORE
    USING GRADE-FILE
    GIVING SORTED-FILE-2.
```

PROCEDURE code (for #4):
```
SORT SORT-FILE
    ON DESCENDING NAME
    USING GRADE-FILE
    GIVING SORTED-FILE-4.
```

Case 2: Multiple Keys

GRADE-FILE

CLASS	LAST	FIRST	SCORE
2	JONES	ABE	84
1	JONES	SAM	92
2	JONES	ABE	78

DESCENDING KEY IR-SCORE, IR-CLASS:
1 JONES SAM 92
2 JONES ABE 84
2 JONES ABE 78

ASCENDING KEY IR-CLASS, IR-LAST, IR-FIRST, IR-SCORE:
1 JONES SAM 92
2 JONES ABE 78
2 JONES ABE 84

ASCENDING KEY IR-LAST, IR-FIRST DESCENDING KEY IR-CLASS, IR-SCORE:
2 JONES ABE 84
2 JONES ABE 78
1 JONES SAM 92

```
SORT SORT-FILE
    ASCENDING IR-LAST, IR-FIRST
    DESCENDING IR-CLASS, IR-SCORE
    USING GRADE-FILE
    GIVING SORTED-FILE-7.
```

Case 3: Selective Sort

The user controls what goes into and out of the SORT-FILE. In the following example, the user does not wish to have class 1 records participate in the sort. Once the sort is completed, the user prints records only from the sorted file in which the scores are above 80.

INPUT FILE

2	JONES ABE	84
1	JONES SAM	92
2	JONES ABE	78

Class   Name   Score

```
SORT SORT-FILE
    ON ASCENDING KEY SCORE
    INPUT  PROCEDURE OMIT-CLASS-1
    OUTPUT PROCEDURE PRINT-ABOVE-80.
    .
    :
OMIT-CLASS-1.
    Read input-file and transmit to SORT-FILE
    all records except class-1 records.
PRINT-ABOVE-80.
    Print those records from SORT-FILE
    where SCORE > 80.
```

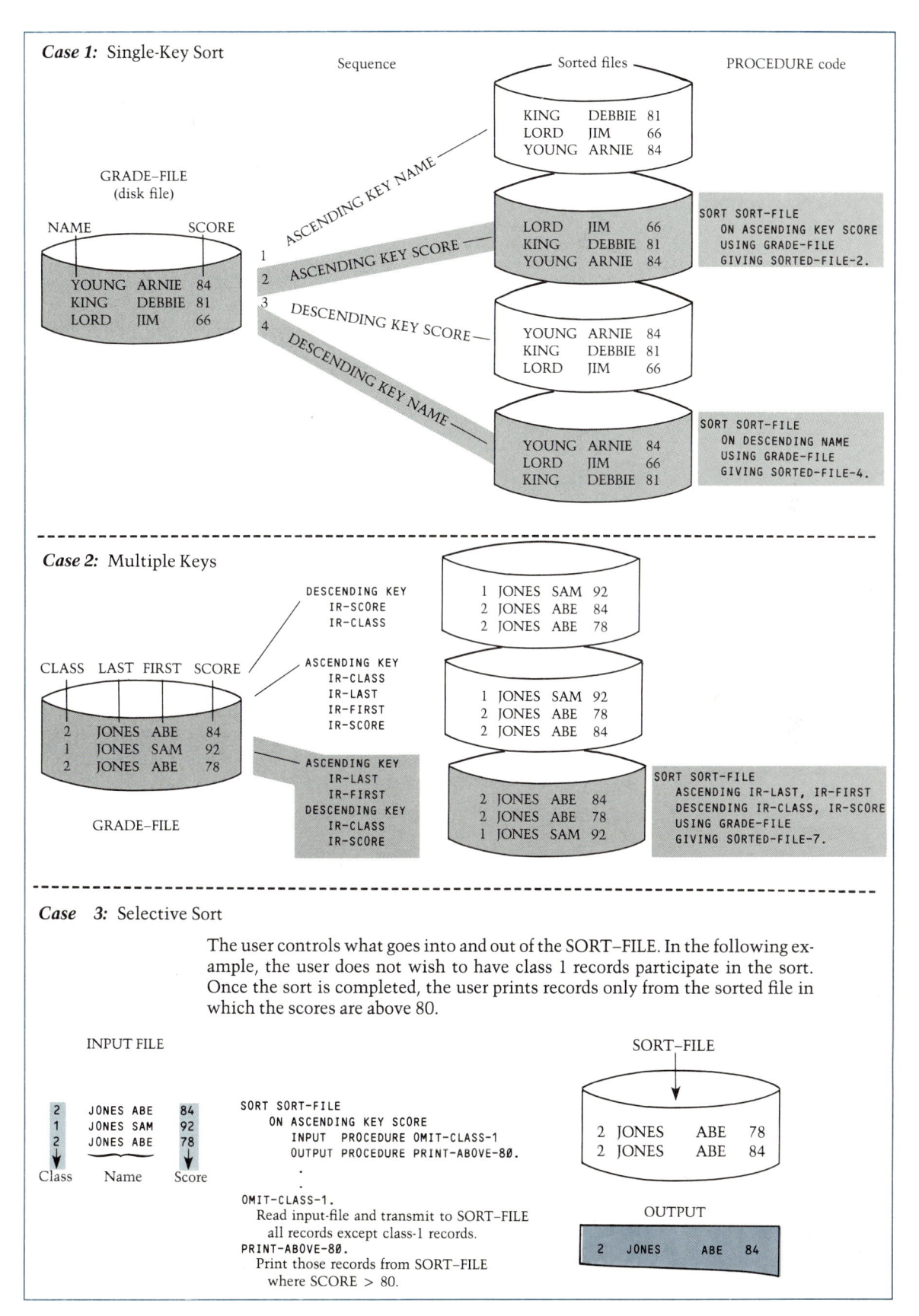

SORT-FILE:
2 JONES ABE 78
2 JONES ABE 84

OUTPUT:
2 JONES ABE 84

FIGURE 9–6
DIFFERENT TYPES OF SORTS

506   UNDERSTANDING STRUCTURED COBOL

```
050 FILE-CONTROL.
060     SELECT GRADE-ROSTER ASSIGN TO DISKPACK.
070     SELECT SORTED-NAMES ASSIGN TO DISKPACK.
080*
090     SELECT SORT-FILE    ASSIGN TO DISKPACK.
100*
110     SELECT PRINT-FILE   ASSIGN TO PRINTER.
115*
120 DATA DIVISION.
130 FILE SECTION.
140 FD  GRADE-ROSTER
150     RECORD CONTAINS 15 CHARACTERS
160     LABEL RECORDS ARE STANDARD.
170 01  ROSTER-REC.
180     05 RR-NAME  PIC X(12).
190     05 RR-SCORE PIC 999.
200 FD  SORTED-NAMES
210     RECORD CONTAINS 15 CHARACTERS
220     LABEL RECORDS ARE STANDARD.
230 01  NAMES-REC PIC X(15).
240*
250 SD  SORT-FILE
260     RECORD CONTAINS 15 CHARACTERS.
270 01  SORT-REC.
280     05 SR-NAME PIC X(12).
290     05 FILLER  PIC 999.
300*
310 FD  PRINT-FILE
320     LABEL RECORDS ARE OMITTED.
330 01  PRINT-LINE.
340     05 FILLER    PIC X(05).
350     05 PRINT-REC PIC X(75).
360 WORKING-STORAGE SECTION.
380 77  EOF-NAME PIC 9 VALUE 0.
390*
400 PROCEDURE DIVISION.
410 10-MAIN-LOGIC SECTION.
420     SORT SORT-FILE
430        ON ASCENDING KEY SR-NAME
440        USING GRADE-ROSTER
450        GIVING SORTED-NAMES.
460*
470     OPEN INPUT SORTED-NAMES
480          OUTPUT PRINT-FILE.
490     MOVE "SORTED NAMES" TO PRINT-REC.
500     WRITE PRINT-LINE AFTER 1.
510     READ SORTED-NAMES INTO PRINT-REC
515        AT END MOVE 1 TO EOF-NAME.
520     PERFORM 20-PRINT-NAMES UNTIL EOF-NAME = 1.
530     CLOSE SORTED-NAMES, PRINT-FILE.
540     STOP RUN.
550*
560 20-PRINT-NAMES.
570     WRITE PRINT-LINE AFTER 1.
580     READ SORTED-NAMES INTO PRINT-REC
585        AT END MOVE 1 TO EOF-NAME.
```

GRADE-ROSTER contains the names to be sorted (see line 440). COBOL will store the sorted file in SORTED-NAMES (line 450). SORT-FILE is a work file that must be reserved by the user for the SORT. COBOL uses it to sort GRADE-ROSTER file. PRINT-FILE is the output file, a terminal in this case. It could have been assigned to the printer.

GRADE-ROSTER

YOUNG	ARNIE	79
KING	DEBBIE	81
LORD	JIM	66

In this case the input records have been typed as a data file on disk.

SORTED-NAMES

KING	DEBBIE	81
LORD	JIM	66
YOUNG	ARNIE	79

Result of the instruction at line 420.

Note that the COBOL work-file description is specified by the SD entry, <u>not</u> the typical FD entry. Since SR-NAME is the only key used to sequence the file, no other item in the record need be specified by name; i.e., all other entries may be grouped into filler fields.

Note that neither SORT-FILE, GRADE-ROSTER, or SORTED-NAMES is opened by the user before the SORT process. SORT-FILE is the user name given to the COBOL work file. GRADE-ROSTER is the name of the file to be sorted. All records without exception will be sorted. The sorted file is stored in the user file SORTED-NAMES.

Once the sort is completed, the SORTED-NAMES file is opened by the user (it was closed by the SORT feature), and the contents of the file are printed.

FIGURE 9-7
SORTING GRADES

by the SORT verb in the PROCEDURE division (line 420). When all the GRADE-ROSTER records have been moved into the SORT-FILE, COBOL sorts these records in the order specified by the ASCENDING or DESCENDING key(s) in the SORT sentence (line 430). This key or keys must be defined in the record description of the SORT-FILE record (line 280). At the conclusion of the SORT process, the sorted file is stored in the file designated by the GIVING clause (line 450).

9-3-4 THE SORT STATEMENT

The various files needed by the SORT are specified in the ENVIRONMENT and DATA divisions, while the COBOL instruction to initiate the SORT is found in the PROCEDURE division.

ENVIRONMENT DIVISION Sort Entries

The SELECT/ASSIGN clauses for the files to be used by the SORT are standard SELECT/ASSIGN clauses. The name given to the SORT work-file is user-chosen. This work-file is no longer available to the user after the SORT is over.
Thru the ASSIGN/SELECT clauses the user:

1. Specifies the various input files needed by the SORT statement.
2. Designates a disk/tape file into which the sorted file is to be stored.
3. Reserves a work file to be used by the sort system.

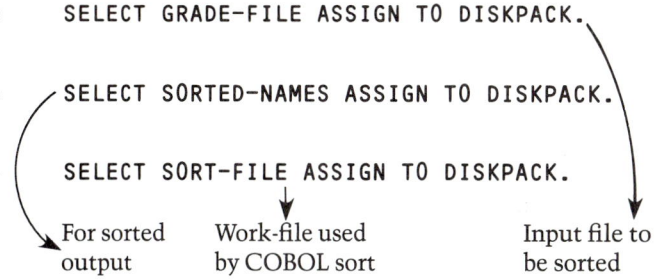

```
SELECT GRADE-FILE ASSIGN TO DISKPACK.
SELECT SORTED-NAMES ASSIGN TO DISKPACK.
SELECT SORT-FILE ASSIGN TO DISKPACK.
```

For sorted output / Work-file used by COBOL sort / Input file to be sorted

DATA DIVISION Sort Entries

All files declared through the SELECT/ASSIGN clauses must have corresponding file description entries (FD) in the DATA division, **except for the COBOL sort-file, which must be declared with an SD (sort description)** entry, not with the FD entry. In the SD entry, the options BLOCK CONTAINS and LABEL RECORDS must *not* be specified. Multiple record definitions may be specified in the SD entry; i.e., a sort file may define multiple 01 level record descriptions.

Any entries (group items or elementary data items) specified in the COBOL sort-file can be used as sequence keys by the SORT system (they will be designated by the SORT verb in the PROCEDURE division). Any signed numeric key causes the SORT process to sequence the file algebraically, i.e., negative values are lower in sequence than positive values. Any group item will be treated as an alphanumeric field.

Only those entries that are to be used as sequence keys need to be specified in the sort-file record. All other entries may be combined into FILLER fields. However, for documentation and readability, the programmer may wish to itemize all entries by name in the sort-file record.

In the DATA division the programmer should:

1. Specify SD and not FD for the sort-file definition.
2. Not use BLOCK CONTAINS or LABEL RECORDS in the SD entry.
3. Specify all key fields in the sort file record that are to be used for sequencing by the SORT. Other fields not used for sequencing can be grouped together into FILLER fields.

```
SD  SORT-FILE
    DATA RECORD IS SORT-REC.
01  SORT-REC.
    05 FILLER     PIC X.
    05 AGE        PIC 999.
    05 SS-NO      PIC X(9).
    05 GROUP-ITEM.
       10 AMT     PIC S999V99.
       10 KLASS   PIC 9.
```

Any record description in SORT–REC can be used to sequence the file. For example, AGE, SS–NO, GROUP-ITEM (6-alphanumeric-position item), AMT, and KLASS could be keys specified in ASCENDING or DESCENDING sequence in the SORT instruction.

PROCEDURE DIVISION SORT Statements

The SORT-related statements that can be used in the PROCEDURE division are:

1. The SORT statement.
2. The RELEASE statement.
3. The RETURN statement.

The general forms of these statements are shown in Figure 9–10 (see section 9-3-6). Discussion of the RELEASE and the RETURN statements is deferred to the discussion of extended sorts.

In the basic SORT problem in Figure 9–7, where we sorted a disk file GRADE-ROSTER in ascending name order and stored the sorted file on a disk file named SORTED-NAMES, the only statement required in the PROCEDURE division is the SORT statement, whose basic form is shown as follows:

```
SORT sort-file-name ON  { ASCENDING  }  KEY  name-1  [ name-2 ] ...
                        { DESCENDING }

                  [ ON  { ASCENDING  }  KEY  name-4  [ name-5 ] ... ] ...
                        { DESCENDING }

                    USING  file-name-1  [ file-name-2 ] ...

                    GIVING  file-name-3
```

The SORT feature automatically OPENs and CLOSEs the sort-file and all files associated with the USING and GIVING clauses. Hence, at the time the SORT statement is executed, none of the aforementioned files must be opened by the user, nor should these files be closed right after the completion of the sort.

The sort-file-name is a user chosen name which must be defined in the SD entry of the DATA division.

Keys cannot be described with an OCCURS clause, nor can they be subordinate to entries that contain an OCCURS clause.

The maximum number of keys that can be used in a sort application may vary from one compiler to another (12 keys are not uncommon). Also, the maximum number of memory positions that can be allocated for a key may vary from one system to another (IBM—270 positions; Burroughs—35,535).

The USING clause specifies the name of the user file that is to be sorted. All records from the user file are moved to the COBOL work-file, where the records are then sorted according to the set of keys specified in the SORT statement. When the entire sort is completed, the sorted file is stored in the file specified by the GIVING clause.

Many SORTs can be executed in a single COBOL program.

As shown in the general form of the SORT statement, numerous keys can be used in one sort application. When more than one key is used, the first key listed in the SORT statement becomes the *major* key, while all remaining keys (*minor* keys) are listed in order of decreasing significance.

The terms ASCENDING or DESCENDING are optional for minor keys. If not specified, the order of the minor keys is that specified by the major key. A combination of ascending and descending minor keys can also be specified.

Examples:

1. ```
   SORT SORT-FILE
       ON ASCENDING  SS-NUM      Major key
                     EMP-NO      Minor key-1  } ASCENDING
                     DEPT-NO     Minor key-2  } order assumed
                     .
                     .
                     .
   ```

2. ```
   SORT SORT-FILE
       ON DESCENDING IR-LAST     Major key
                     IR-FIRST    Descending
       ON ASCENDING  IR-TEST1 } → Ascending      } Minor keys
                     IR-TEST2 }
       ON DESCENDING IR-CLASS } → Descending
                     IR-YEAR  }
                     .
                     .
   ```

To better understand the significance of multiple keys, examples of key and sequence combinations are shown below. Assume the file to be sorted contains the following records:

LAST	FIRST	MIDDLE	CLASS	SCORE
JONES	JIM	A	1	050
JONES	JIM	A	2	060
JONES	JIM	H	1	060
JONES	JIM	A	2	080
MARY	SUE	L	1	040

The following coding segments will result in the following sorted files:

		LAST	FIRST	MIDDLE	CLASS	SCORE
SORT SORT-FILE		JONES	JIM	H	1	060
ON ASCENDING	IR-KLASS	JONES	JIM	A	1	050
	IR-LAST	MARY	SUE	L	1	040
ON DESCENDING	IR-SCORE	JONES	JIM	A	2	080
		JONES	JIM	A	2	060

		LAST	FIRST	MIDDLE	CLASS	SCORE
SORT SORT-FILE		MARY	SUE	L	1	040
ON DESCENDING	IR-LAST	JONES	JIM	H	1	060
	IR-FIRST	JONES	JIM	A	2	080
	IR-MIDDLE	JONES	JIM	A	2	060
	IR-SCORE	JONES	JIM	A	1	050

		LAST	FIRST	MIDDLE	CLASS	SCORE
SORT SORT-FILE		JONES	JIM	A	2	080
ON DESCENDING	IR-SCORE	JONES	JIM	H	1	060
ON ASCENDING	IR-CLASS	JONES	JIM	A	2	060
	IR-LAST	JONES	JIM	A	1	050
ON DESCENDING	IR-MIDDLE	MARY	SUE	L	1	040

9-3-5 THE EXTENDED SORT: THE INPUT PROCEDURE

When the basic SORT and the USING option are used, all records in the file designated by the USING clause are sorted. The user cannot select certain records from the USING file to release (make available) to the sort-file; all records are automatically released to the sort-file. With the INPUT PROCEDURE, the user can designate one or more files and selectively release any record from any of these files to the SORT process, i.e., the SORT can feed from different files and from selected records within each file.

Consider the following input file GRADE–ROSTER, where each record consists of a name, a student classification code (1 = freshman, 2 = sophomore, 3 = junior, 4 = senior), and a test score. Let us write a program to release to the COBOL sort-file all sophomore records found in GRADE–ROSTER and create a sophomore disk file arranged in descending test score order, and by ascending alphabetical name sequence (minor key). Let us also print the sorted sophomore disk file. The problem can be visualized as follows:

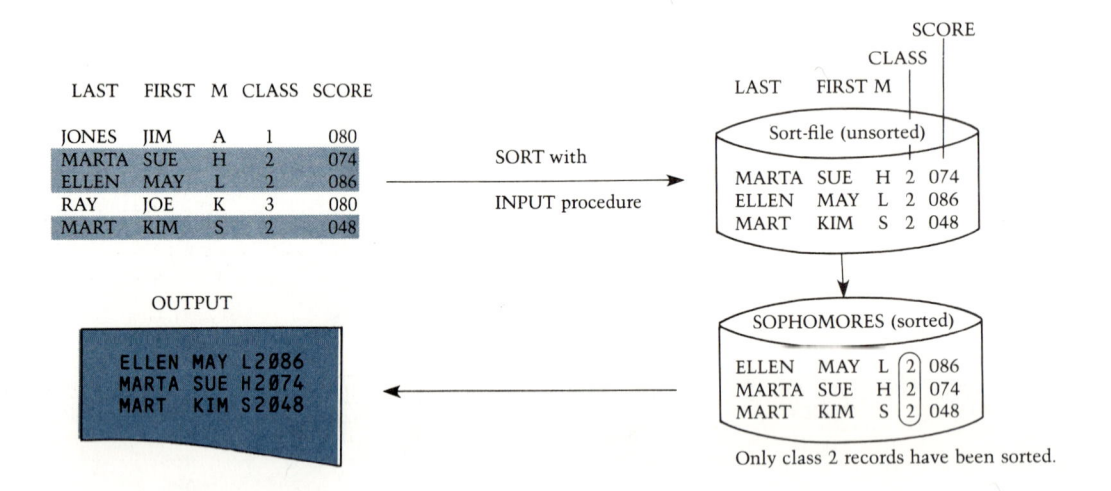

```
        LAST   FIRST  M  CLASS  SCORE                                       SCORE
                                                                       CLASS
        JONES  JIM    A    1     080                           LAST    FIRST  M
        MARTA  SUE    H    2     074      SORT with               Sort-file (unsorted)
        ELLEN  MAY    L    2     086   ────────────────►        MARTA  SUE    H  2  074
        RAY    JOE    K    3     080      INPUT procedure       ELLEN  MAY    L  2  086
        MART   KIM    S    2     048                            MART   KIM    S  2  048

                OUTPUT                                             SOPHOMORES (sorted)
          ┌──────────────────┐                                   ELLEN  MAY    L  2  086
          │ ELLEN  MAY L2086 │   ◄────────────────────────      MARTA  SUE    H  2  074
          │ MARTA  SUE H2074 │                                   MART   KIM    S  2  048
          │ MART   KIM S2048 │
          └──────────────────┘                              Only class 2 records have been sorted.
```

The program to solve this problem is shown in Figure 9–8.

The format of the extended sort in the context of the INPUT PROCEDURE is shown in Figure 9–9.

The INPUT PROCEDURE must consist of one or more consecutive sections. (Sections will be discussed on pages 512–514). These sections may make use of any COBOL statements (except the SORT statement) to select, create, or modify records that the user would like to submit or release to the sort-file.

Records prepared by the user are transferred to the COBOL sort-file by means of the RELEASE verb. The RELEASE option can be used *only* for this particular operation. It has essentially the same meaning as the WRITE statement.

Many COBOL compilers require that the INPUT PROCEDURE section(s) be activated only by the INPUT PROCEDURE statement in the SORT sentence. Other compilers are less restrictive and may allow the INPUT PROCEDURE section(s) to be carried out by various PERFORM statements in the COBOL program.

The THRU option in the INPUT PROCEDURE of the SORT statement must be used if the INPUT PROCEDURE terminates in a section other than the ones in which it started. This is to ensure proper return from the INPUT PROCEDURE to the SORT sentence when the INPUT PROCEDURE is completed. The compiler inserts a return mechanism at the end of the last section of the INPUT PROCEDURE (the one specified by the THRU statement). When

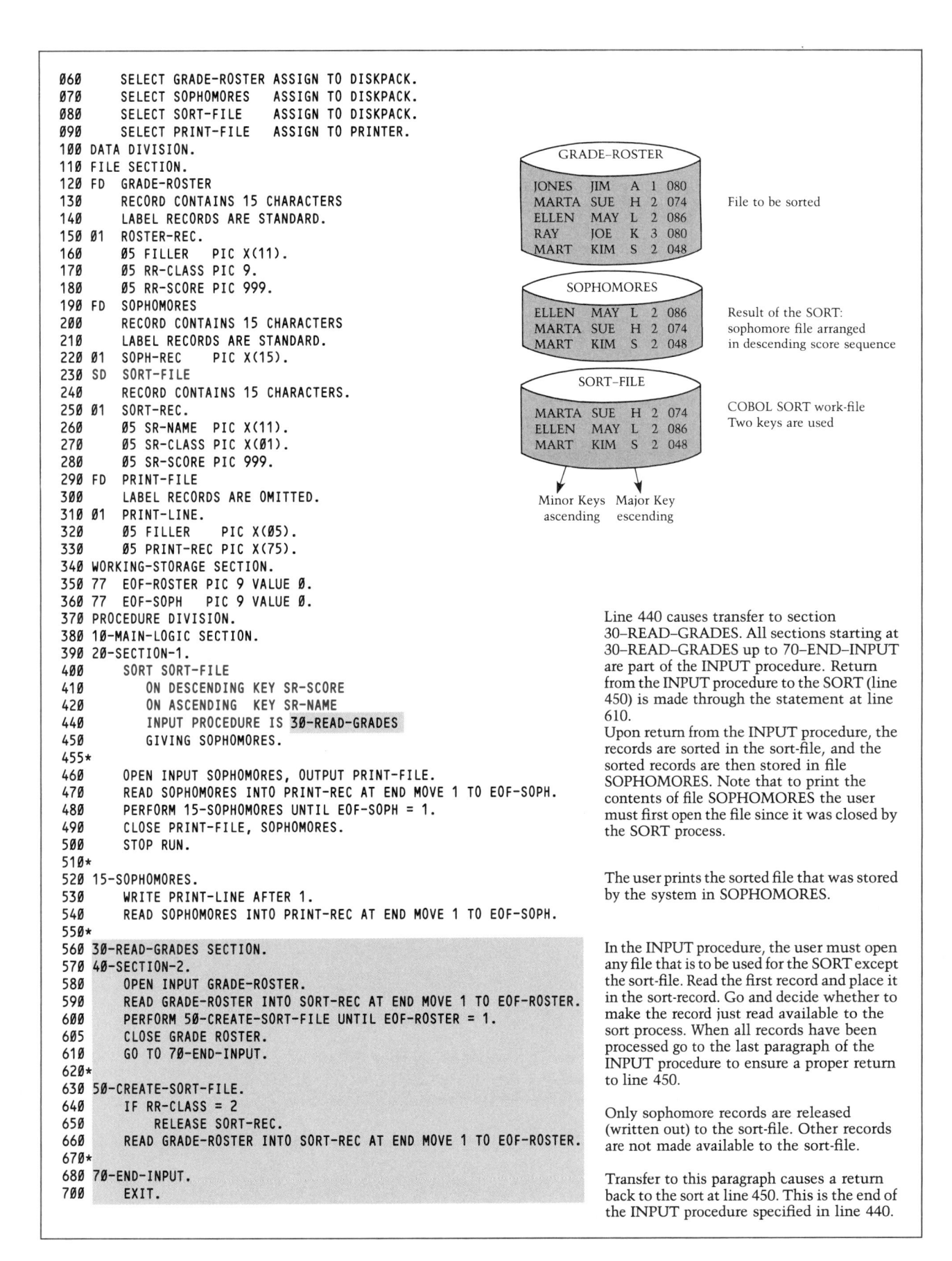

```
060     SELECT GRADE-ROSTER ASSIGN TO DISKPACK.
070     SELECT SOPHOMORES   ASSIGN TO DISKPACK.
080     SELECT SORT-FILE    ASSIGN TO DISKPACK.
090     SELECT PRINT-FILE   ASSIGN TO PRINTER.
100 DATA DIVISION.
110 FILE SECTION.
120 FD  GRADE-ROSTER
130     RECORD CONTAINS 15 CHARACTERS
140     LABEL RECORDS ARE STANDARD.
150 01  ROSTER-REC.
160     05 FILLER    PIC X(11).
170     05 RR-CLASS  PIC 9.
180     05 RR-SCORE  PIC 999.
190 FD  SOPHOMORES
200     RECORD CONTAINS 15 CHARACTERS
210     LABEL RECORDS ARE STANDARD.
220 01  SOPH-REC     PIC X(15).
230 SD  SORT-FILE
240     RECORD CONTAINS 15 CHARACTERS.
250 01  SORT-REC.
260     05 SR-NAME   PIC X(11).
270     05 SR-CLASS  PIC X(01).
280     05 SR-SCORE  PIC 999.
290 FD  PRINT-FILE
300     LABEL RECORDS ARE OMITTED.
310 01  PRINT-LINE.
320     05 FILLER    PIC X(05).
330     05 PRINT-REC PIC X(75).
340 WORKING-STORAGE SECTION.
350 77  EOF-ROSTER PIC 9 VALUE 0.
360 77  EOF-SOPH   PIC 9 VALUE 0.
370 PROCEDURE DIVISION.
380 10-MAIN-LOGIC SECTION.
390 20-SECTION-1.
400     SORT SORT-FILE
410         ON DESCENDING KEY SR-SCORE
420         ON ASCENDING  KEY SR-NAME
440         INPUT PROCEDURE IS 30-READ-GRADES
450         GIVING SOPHOMORES.
455*
460     OPEN INPUT SOPHOMORES, OUTPUT PRINT-FILE.
470     READ SOPHOMORES INTO PRINT-REC AT END MOVE 1 TO EOF-SOPH.
480     PERFORM 15-SOPHOMORES UNTIL EOF-SOPH = 1.
490     CLOSE PRINT-FILE, SOPHOMORES.
500     STOP RUN.
510*
520 15-SOPHOMORES.
530     WRITE PRINT-LINE AFTER 1.
540     READ SOPHOMORES INTO PRINT-REC AT END MOVE 1 TO EOF-SOPH.
550*
560 30-READ-GRADES SECTION.
570 40-SECTION-2.
580     OPEN INPUT GRADE-ROSTER.
590     READ GRADE-ROSTER INTO SORT-REC AT END MOVE 1 TO EOF-ROSTER.
600     PERFORM 50-CREATE-SORT-FILE UNTIL EOF-ROSTER = 1.
605     CLOSE GRADE ROSTER.
610     GO TO 70-END-INPUT.
620*
630 50-CREATE-SORT-FILE.
640     IF RR-CLASS = 2
650         RELEASE SORT-REC.
660     READ GRADE-ROSTER INTO SORT-REC AT END MOVE 1 TO EOF-ROSTER.
670*
680 70-END-INPUT.
700     EXIT.
```

GRADE-ROSTER

JONES	JIM	A	1	080
MARTA	SUE	H	2	074
ELLEN	MAY	L	2	086
RAY	JOE	K	3	080
MART	KIM	S	2	048

File to be sorted

SOPHOMORES

ELLEN	MAY	L	2	086
MARTA	SUE	H	2	074
MART	KIM	S	2	048

Result of the SORT: sophomore file arranged in descending score sequence

SORT-FILE

MARTA	SUE	H	2	074
ELLEN	MAY	L	2	086
MART	KIM	S	2	048

COBOL SORT work-file
Two keys are used

Minor Keys ascending   Major Key descending

Line 440 causes transfer to section 30-READ-GRADES. All sections starting at 30-READ-GRADES up to 70-END-INPUT are part of the INPUT procedure. Return from the INPUT procedure to the SORT (line 450) is made through the statement at line 610.

Upon return from the INPUT procedure, the records are sorted in the sort-file, and the sorted records are then stored in file SOPHOMORES. Note that to print the contents of file SOPHOMORES the user must first open the file since it was closed by the SORT process.

The user prints the sorted file that was stored by the system in SOPHOMORES.

In the INPUT procedure, the user must open any file that is to be used for the SORT except the sort-file. Read the first record and place it in the sort-record. Go and decide whether to make the record just read available to the sort process. When all records have been processed go to the last paragraph of the INPUT procedure to ensure a proper return to line 450.

Only sophomore records are released (written out) to the sort-file. Other records are not made available to the sort-file.

Transfer to this paragraph causes a return back to the sort at line 450. This is the end of the INPUT procedure specified in line 440.

FIGURE 9-8
THE INPUT PROCEDURE

control passes from the last section of the INPUT PROCEDURE to the SORT, all records released into the sort-file are then sorted.

In the program in Figure 9–8 observe the following:

1. It is the programmer's responsibility to open and close any of the files needed in the INPUT PROCEDURE for release of records to the sort-file.

2. The INPUT PROCEDURE in this program consists of one section. The last section 70–END–INPUT is necessary to return from the INPUT PROCEDURE to the SORT sentence. Control is passed to this section by means of the GO TO statement at line 610. Without the GO TO statement, paragraph 50–CREATE–SORT–FILE would be executed one more time (one too many times) before the return to the SORT sentence.

SECTIONS

Since the extended SORT feature makes use of sections, a brief discussion on sections is presented here.

Just as the ENVIRONMENT and the DATA DIVISIONS have sections, so can the PROCEDURE DIVISION. A section in the PROCEDURE DIVISION consists of one or more successive paragraphs that are logically related. A section must be identified by a section name (section name rules are identical to paragraph name rules), followed by the word SECTION. The section name applies to all paragraphs following the section name until a new section name is encountered, or until the end of the PROCEDURE DIVISION has been encountered.

Since a section is a procedure, control can be passed to a section through the PERFORM/UNTIL statement, in the same way as control is passed to a paragraph through the PERFORM/UNTIL. When the section has been PERFORMed, return is automatically made to the PERFORM/UNTIL statement to determine whether to PERFORM the section again or to pass control to the statement following the PERFORM statement.

The general structure of the PROCEDURE DIVISION with sections is:

```
PROCEDURE DIVISION
[Section-name-1 SECTION.]
Paragraph-name-1.
     Sentences . . .
          .
[Paragraph-name-3.
     sentences . . . ]  . . .

[Section-name-2 SECTION.]
[Paragraph-name-4.
     sentences . . . ]

[Paragraph-name-6.
     sentences . . . ]  . . .
```

Some COBOL compilers require that a section header should immediately follow the PROCEDURE DIVISION entry if sections are to be used in a program. Some compilers may also require that each section be followed immediately by a paragraph name. The example on the opposite page shows a PROCEDURE DIVISION with sections.

SEARCHING AND SORTING 513

$$\underline{\text{SORT}} \text{ sort-file ON} \begin{Bmatrix} \underline{\text{ASCENDING}} \\ \underline{\text{DESCENDING}} \end{Bmatrix} \text{KEY name-1} \ldots$$

$$\begin{Bmatrix} \underline{\text{USING}} \text{ file-name-1} \\ \underline{\text{INPUT PROCEDURE}} \text{ is section-name-1 } [\underline{\text{THRU}} \text{ section-name-3}] \end{Bmatrix}$$

$$\underline{\text{GIVING}} \text{ file-name-3}$$

	Domain of the INPUT PROCEDURE
Section-name-1. Section-name-2. ⋮ Section-name-3.	Identify those records from the various input files that are to be submitted (released) to the sort process. These records are made available one by one to the sort file through the verb <u>RELEASE</u> sort-record-name <u>FROM</u> name-2

The INPUT PROCEDURE specifies one or more section names (THRU option) within which the records to be passed along to the sort process are selected.

The INPUT PROCEDURE, coded by the user, is executed when the INPUT PROCEDURE statement is encountered in the SORT statement. When the INPUT procedure is completed, i.e., all records have been selected and released to the sort, the user must transfer to the last section of the INPUT procedure so that proper return to the SORT sentence is made.

The RELEASE sort-record-name FROM name-2 option allows transfer of record name-2 (defined in the DATA division) to the COBOL sort file. This is equivalent to moving name-2 to sort-record-name and then releasing sort-record-name.

FIGURE 9-9
THE INPUT PROCEDURE FORMAT

Example:

```
010     PROCEDURE DIVISION.
020     100-MAIN SECTION.
030     100-LOGIC-1.
040         PERFORM 200-INITIALIZE.
050         PERFORM 350-READ-TRANS.
060         PERFORM 300-WRITE-PROCESS UNTIL EOF = 1.
                .
070     200-INITIALIZE SECTION.
080     200-LOGIC-2.
090         MOVE AMT TO DL-AMT.
100         MOVE TAX TO DL-TAX.

110     300-WRITE-PROCESS SECTION.
120     300-LOGIC-3.
130         PERFORM 400-HEADER.
                .
                .
140         ADD 1 TO KOUNT.
150     350-READ-TRANS.
160         READ INPUT-FILE
170             AT END MOVE 1 TO EOF.

180     400-HEADER SECTION.
190     400-LOGIC-4.
200         WRITE PRINT-LINE FROM HEADER AFTER 1.
```

Many compilers do not require the user to specify a paragraph name after a section header; i.e., the paragraph names at lines 30, 80, 120, and 190 could be omitted.

Note that a PERFORM statement in one section may PERFORM a paragraph within another section (see line 50).

A PERFORM statement may also PERFORM a section, in which case control is returned to the PERFORM statement after the complete section has been carried out. In line 60, for example, performing section 300–WRITE–PROCESS means that paragraph 300–LOGIC–3 is first executed, followed by paragraph 350–READ–TRANS.

Sections can also be executed by means of the PERFORM . . . THRU . . . UNTIL, as shown in the following example.

Example:

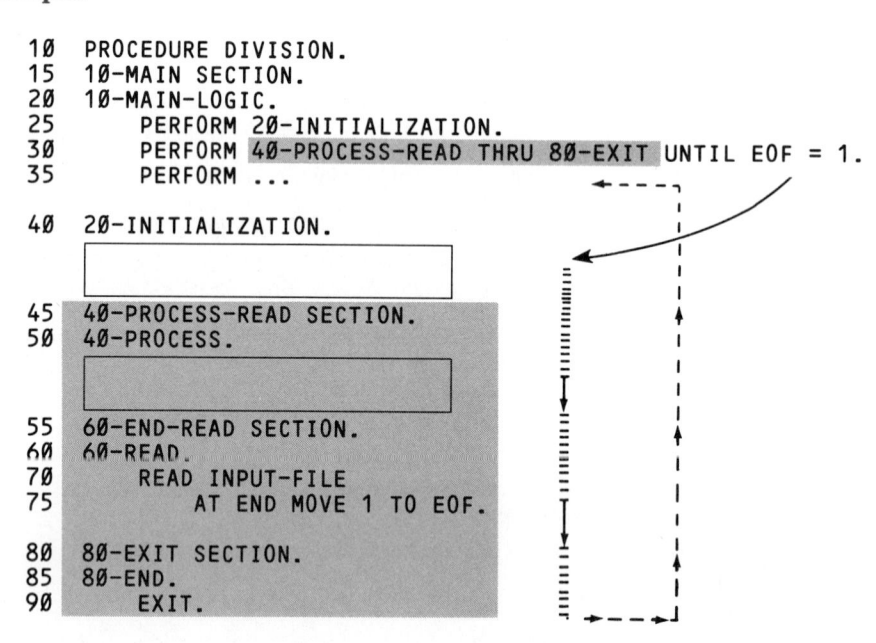

```
10   PROCEDURE DIVISION.
15   10-MAIN SECTION.
20   10-MAIN-LOGIC.
25       PERFORM 20-INITIALIZATION.
30       PERFORM 40-PROCESS-READ THRU 80-EXIT UNTIL EOF = 1.
35       PERFORM ...

40   20-INITIALIZATION.


45   40-PROCESS-READ SECTION.
50   40-PROCESS.


55   60-END-READ SECTION.
60   60-READ.
70       READ INPUT-FILE
75           AT END MOVE 1 TO EOF.

80   80-EXIT SECTION.
85   80-END.
90       EXIT.
```

All sections from 40–PROCESS–READ through 80–EXIT are carried out until the end of file EOF is set to 1, at which time control is passed to line 35.

9-3-6 THE EXTENDED SORT: THE OUTPUT PROCEDURE

The general form of the procedural (INPUT or OUTPUT) SORT statement is shown in Figure 9–10.

If the GIVING option is specified in the SORT sentence, all sorted records in the sort-file are automatically transferred to the file specified by the GIVING clause; i.e., the user has no control over what goes into the GIVING file. Many times, though, the programmer may want to selectively process the records that are in the sort-file, as shown in the following example:

Suppose a COBOL sort-file contains a grade roster that has been sorted by student classification, and we want to create separate disk files for each of the four classes, i.e., freshman, sophomore, et cetera, where each file is sorted in descending score order (major key) and by ascending name (minor key). Furthermore, we want to list the names of all honors students (grade > 95) regardless of class. The problem can be visualized as follows in terms of input and output (only freshman and sophomore classes are shown here and in the following illustrations):

SEARCHING AND SORTING 515

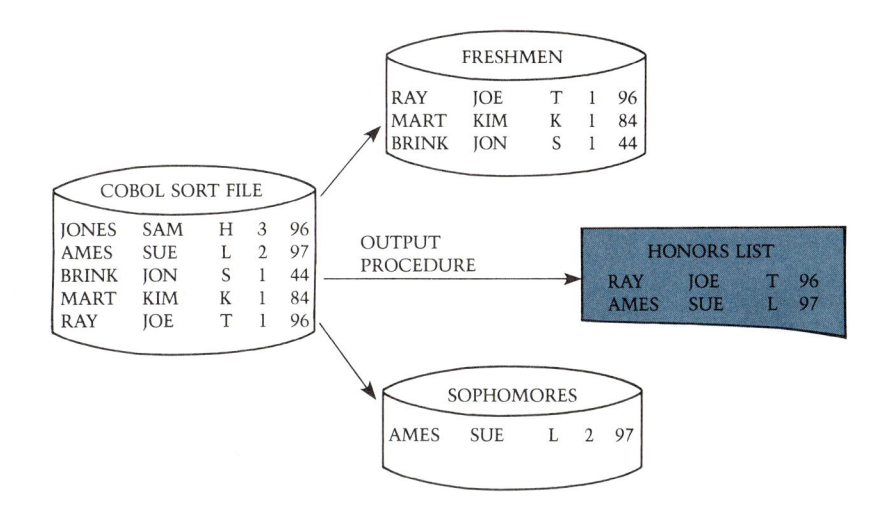

```
                    ┌─────────────────────┐
                    │      FRESHMEN       │
                    │ RAY    JOE   T 1 96 │
                    │ MART   KIM   K 1 84 │
                    │ BRINK  JON   S 1 44 │
                    └─────────────────────┘
┌─────────────────────┐
│   COBOL SORT FILE   │
│ JONES  SAM   H 3 96 │         ┌──────────────────────┐
│ AMES   SUE   L 2 97 │ OUTPUT  │     HONORS LIST      │
│ BRINK  JON   S 1 44 │─────────│ RAY    JOE   T   96  │
│ MART   KIM   K 1 84 │PROCEDURE│ AMES   SUE   L   97  │
│ RAY    JOE   T 1 96 │         └──────────────────────┘
└─────────────────────┘
                    ┌─────────────────────┐
                    │     SOPHOMORES      │
                    │ AMES   SUE  L 2 97  │
                    └─────────────────────┘
```

The program to solve this problem is shown in Figure 9–11. Note the RETURN verb at lines 530 and 660. The RETURN verb is used exclusively to read records from the COBOL sort-file. Also note the AT END clause in those lines to specify what action is to be taken when the end of the sort-file has been encountered. Just as in the case of the INPUT PROCEDURE, a GO TO statement is generally needed in the OUTPUT PROCEDURE (line 560) to transfer to the last section of the OUTPUT PROCEDURE and return control to the SORT sentence. If no GO TO statement has been specified, paragraph 40–READ–SORTED–FILE would have been carried out one too many times. If the OUTPUT procedure consisted of only one paragraph, then no GO TO statement would be needed.

Finally, it should be pointed out that both the INPUT and the OUTPUT procedures can be used concurrently in the SORT feature. In such a case neither the GIVING nor the USING clause can be used.

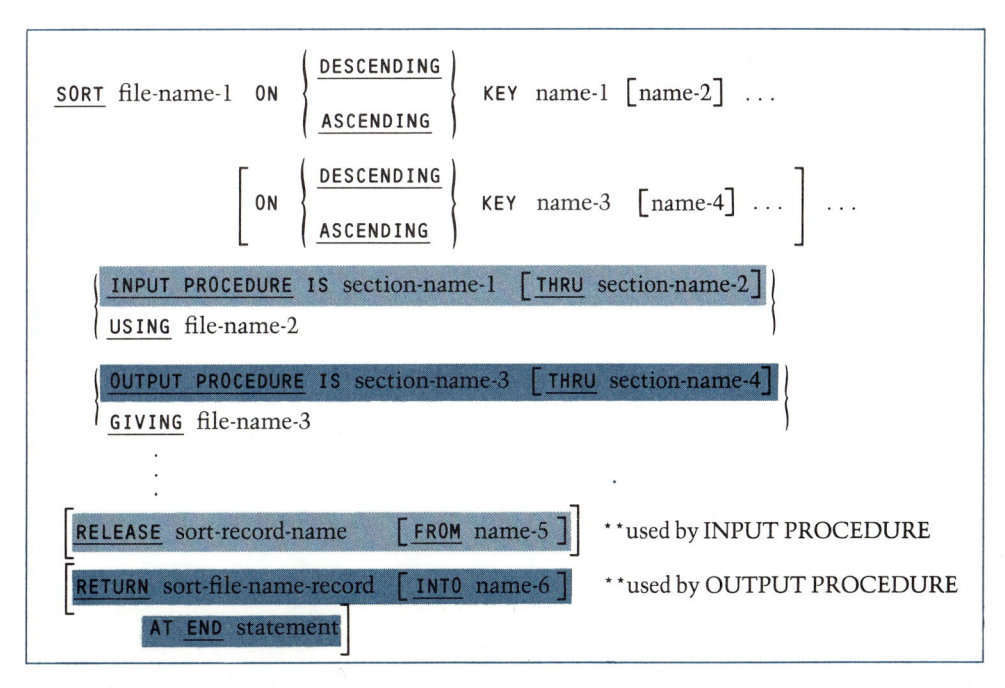

```
SORT file-name-1 ON  { DESCENDING }  KEY name-1 [name-2] ...
                     { ASCENDING  }

              [ ON   { DESCENDING }  KEY name-3 [name-4] ... ] ...
                     { ASCENDING  }

     { INPUT PROCEDURE IS section-name-1 [THRU section-name-2] }
     { USING file-name-2                                        }

     { OUTPUT PROCEDURE IS section-name-3 [THRU section-name-4] }
     { GIVING file-name-3                                        }
                              .
                              .
                              .
     [ RELEASE sort-record-name       [FROM name-5] ]    **used by INPUT PROCEDURE
     [ RETURN sort-file-name-record   [INTO name-6] ]    **used by OUTPUT PROCEDURE
              [ AT END statement ]
```

FIGURE 9–10
THE GENERAL FORM OF THE SORT STATEMENTS

516   UNDERSTANDING STRUCTURED COBOL

```
060     SELECT GRADE-ROSTER ASSIGN TO DISKPACK.
070     SELECT FRESHMEN     ASSIGN TO DISKPACK.
080     SELECT SOPHOMORES   ASSIGN TO DISKPACK.
090     SELECT SORT-FILE    ASSIGN TO DISKPACK.
100     SELECT PRINT-FILE   ASSIGN TO PRINTER.
110 DATA DIVISION.
120 FILE SECTION.
130 FD  GRADE-ROSTER
140     RECORD CONTAINS 15 CHARACTERS
150     LABEL RECORDS ARE STANDARD.
160 01  ROSTER-REC PIC X(15).
170 FD  FRESHMEN
180     RECORD CONTAINS 15 CHARACTERS
190     LABEL RECORDS ARE STANDARD.
200 01  FRESH-REC PIC X(15).
210 FD  SOPHOMORES
220     RECORD CONTAINS 15 CHARACTERS
230     LABEL RECORDS ARE STANDARD.
240 01  SOPH-REC PIC X(15).
250 SD  SORT-FILE
260     RECORD CONTAINS 15 CHARACTERS.
270 01  SORT-REC.
280     05 SR-NAME  PIC X(11).
285     05 SR-CLASS PIC 9.
290     05 SR-SCORE PIC 999.
300 FD  PRINT-FILE
310     LABEL RECORDS ARE OMITTED.
320 01  PRINT-LINE.
330     05 FILLER   PIC X(05).
340     05 PL-NAME  PIC X(11).
350     05 PL-SCORE PIC ZZ9.
360 WORKING-STORAGE SECTION.
370 77 EOF-SORT-FILE PIC 9 VALUE 0.
380 PROCEDURE DIVISION.
390 10-MAIN-LOGIC SECTION.
400 20-SECTION1.
410     SORT SORT-FILE
420         ON ASCENDING  KEY SR-CLASS
430         ON DESCENDING KEY SR-SCORE
440         USING GRADE-ROSTER
450         OUTPUT PROCEDURE IS 30-PROCESS.
460     CLOSE PRINT-FILE.
470     STOP RUN.
480*
490 30-PROCESS SECTION.
500 31-SECTION2.
510     OPEN OUTPUT FRESHMEN SOPHOMORES PRINT-FILE.
520     MOVE SPACES TO PRINT-LINE.
530     RETURN SORT-FILE AT END MOVE 1 TO EOF-SORT-FILE.
550     PERFORM 40-READ-SORTED-FILE UNTIL EOF-SORT-FILE = 1.
555     CLOSE FRESHMEN, SOPHOMORES.
560     GO TO 50-END-OUTPUT-PROCEDURE.
570*
580 40-READ-SORTED-FILE.
600     IF SR-SCORE > 95
610         MOVE SR-NAME  TO PL-NAME
620         MOVE SR-SCORE TO PL-SCORE
630         WRITE PRINT-LINE AFTER 1.
640     IF SR-CLASS = 1 WRITE FRESH-REC FROM SORT-REC.
650     IF SR-CLASS = 2 WRITE SOPH-REC  FROM SORT-REC.
660     RETURN SORT-FILE AT END MOVE 1 TO EOF-SORT-FILE.
670*
680 50-END-OUTPUT-PROCEDURE.
700     EXIT.
```

GRADE-ROSTER

JONES	SAM	H	3	96
AMES	SUE	L	2	97
BRINK	JON	S	1	44
MART	KIM	K	1	84
RAY	JOE	T	1	96

FRESHMEN

RAY	JOE	T	1	96
MART	KIM	S	1	84
BRINK	JON	S	1	44

SOPHOMORES

| AMES | SUE | L | 2 | 97 |

OUTPUT

```
RAY  JOE T 96
AMES SUE L 97
```

Line 410 says:
Sort the file GRADE-ROSTER and leave sorted file in SORT-FILE.
Line 450 says:
Go and separate the freshmen class from the sophomore class. When control is transferred to 50-END-OUTPUT-PROCEDURE, the output procedure will be complete; return will be made to line 460.

The output procedure is responsible for opening all files except the SORT-FILE. The RETURN verb is synonymous to the READ verb except that it is used exclusively to read records from the COBOL sort-file. When all sort-file records have been processed, transfer is made to the last paragraph of the OUTPUT PROCEDURE, which causes a return to the SORT sentence.

Print the list of honor students.

Separate the classes. Read the next record from the sort file. When the end of file is reached, line 680 is executed, causing an automatic return to line 470.

FIGURE 9-11

THE OUTPUT PROCEDURE

9-4 SORTING WITHOUT THE SORT STATEMENT

Two methods for sorting, the bubble sort and the mini/max sort are discussed in this section. Both methods are easy to understand, and they will give the reader some insight in the sorting process. In the "real world" of sorting, however, these two methods may not be suited to sort very long lists; other very excellent sorts are available (see exercise 8 in section 9-5-2).

9-4-1 THE BUBBLE SORT

Let us illustrate the bubble sort with an example.
Assume the following list of numbers is to be sorted in *ascending* sequence:

| 4 | 5 | 3 | 2 |

The bubble sort begins by comparing the first and second numbers and interchanging the first number with the second number if the first number is greater than the second number. Then we move on to the second and third numbers and perform an interchange if the second is greater than the third (this time we interchange 5 and 3). Then we move on to the third and fourth numbers (5 and 2) and perform an interchange if necessary (in this case we interchange 2 and 5). In this way we ensure that the largest number is continuously moved to the right. At the end of this first pass through the list, the order is:

| 4 | 3 | 2 | 5 |

We now repeat the procedure on a second pass:
Compare the first pair 4, 3 and interchange to obtain 3, 4.

Compare the second pair 4, 2 and interchange to obtain 2, 4.

Compare the third pair 4, 5; no interchange.

Actually we did not need to process the third pair, since we already know that the largest number is in the last position. At the end of the second pass, the second largest number is in the second-to-last position and the order is:

| 3 | 2 | 4 | 5 |

We now carry out the same procedure for the third time.

Compare the first pair 3, 2 and interchange to obtain 2, 3.

Compare the second pair 3, 4; no interchange.

Compare the third pair 4, 5; no interchange.

Actually, we only needed to compare the first pair of numbers, since we know the last two numbers are already in order.
Thus at the end of the third pass the numbers are sorted.

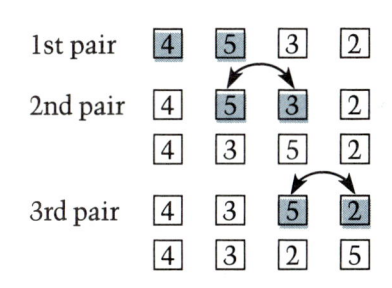

1st pair | 4 | 5 | 3 | 2 |

2nd pair | 4 | 5 | 3 | 2 |
         | 4 | 3 | 5 | 2 |

3rd pair | 4 | 3 | 5 | 2 |
         | 4 | 3 | 2 | 5 |

The largest number is now in the right-most position

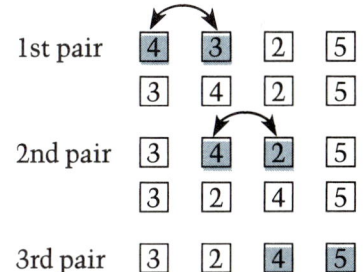

1st pair | 4 | 3 | 2 | 5 |
         | 3 | 4 | 2 | 5 |

2nd pair | 3 | 4 | 2 | 5 |
         | 3 | 2 | 4 | 5 |

3rd pair | 3 | 2 | 4 | 5 |

The second-largest number is now in the next-to-last position.

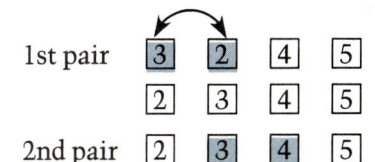

1st pair | 3 | 2 | 4 | 5 |
         | 2 | 3 | 4 | 5 |

2nd pair | 2 | 3 | 4 | 5 |

3rd pair | 2 | 3 | 4 | 5 |

| 2 | 3 | 4 | 5 |

Bubble Sort Program

Write a program using the bubble sort to sort a group of grades into ascending sequence. A maximum of 10 records, each containing a grade, will be read. The program to perform this sort is shown in Figure 9–12. A sample input and output are shown as follows:

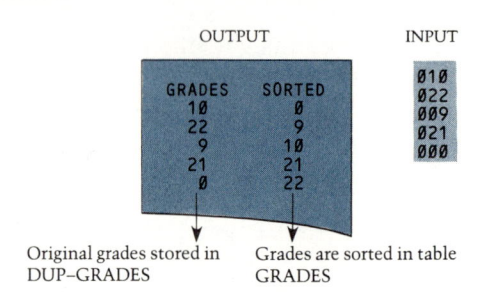

```
                    OUTPUT           INPUT
              GRADES    SORTED       010
                10        0          022
                22        9          009
                 9       10          021
                21       21          000
                 0       22
```

Original grades stored in DUP–GRADES   Grades are sorted in table GRADES

The sorting algorithm requires two loops. An outer loop (statement 510) controls the positioning of the largest element in the right-most position of the ever-shrinking table (positions 5, 4, 3, . . .), and an inner loop (statement 660) shifts the largest element to the right-most position of the shrinking table through the interchange procedure (statements 690–740). The outer loop controls the number of passes; if a table has N elements, then N − 1 passes are required.

9-4-2 THE MINI/MAX SORT

Another method that can be used to sort a table of numbers into ascending (or descending) order is to determine the location (position) of the smallest element in the table and interchange that element with the first element of the table. At the end of the first search pass, the smallest element is in the first position. The table is then searched for the next smallest element, with the search starting at position 2 of the table; the smallest element is then swapped with the number in position 2 of the table. At the end of the second search pass, the first two elements of the table are in ascending sequence order. The search for the next smallest number starts in position 3, and the same search-and-interchange process is repeated until the last two (right-most) table elements are processed. Using this sorting procedure, a table of N elements will require N − 1 passes for the search-and-interchange procedure. During the first pass, N elements will be compared, while in the last pass only two elements will be compared. Let's see how this sort process works, using the same example we used with the bubble sort:

	Array G		
Begin 1st pass	4 5 3 2	Find location of smallest score and switch places with first score (GRADES(1)).	Search for smallest value starts at position 1.
End 1st pass	2 5 3 4		
Begin 2nd pass	2 5 3 4	Find location of smallest score and switch places with first score of remaining array, i.e., GRADES(2).	Search for smallest value starts at position 2.
End 2nd pass	2 3 5 4		
Begin 3rd pass	2 3 5 4	Find location of smallest score and switch places with first score of remaining array (GRADES(3)).	Search for smallest value starts at position 3.
End 3rd pass	2 3 4 5		

SEARCHING AND SORTING

```
240 WORKING-STORAGE SECTION.
250 01  SUBSCRIPTS-N-COUNTERS.
260     05 I           PIC 99.
270     05 J           PIC 99.
280     05 L           PIC 99.
290     05 NO-GRADES   PIC 99 VALUE 0.
300     05 NO-PASSES   PIC 99.
310 01  FLAGS-N-TEMP-LOCATIONS.
320     05 EOF         PIC 9 VALUE 0.
330     05 TEMP        PIC 999.
340 01  GRADE-COLLECTION.
350     05 GRADES      PIC 999 OCCURS 10 TIMES.
360     05 DUP-GRADES  PIC 999 OCCURS 10 TIMES.
370 01  HEADER.
380     05 FILLER      PIC X(10) VALUE " GRADES".
390     05 FILLER      PIC X(20) VALUE "SORTED".
400 01  DETAIL-LINE.
410     05 FILLER      PIC X(04) VALUE SPACES.
420     05 DL-GRADE    PIC ZZ9.
430     05 FILLER      PIC X(06) VALUE SPACES.
440     05 DL-SORTED   PIC ZZ9.
450 PROCEDURE DIVISION.
460 05-MAIN-LOGIC.
470     OPEN INPUT INPUT-FILE, OUTPUT PRINT-FILE.
480     READ INPUT-FILE AT END MOVE 1 TO EOF.
490     PERFORM 10-READ-GRADES VARYING I FROM 1
495         BY 1 UNTIL EOF = 1.
500     COMPUTE NO-PASSES = NO-GRADES - 1.
510     PERFORM 20-PROCESS-PASSES VARYING L FROM
520         NO-PASSES BY -1 UNTIL L LESS THAN 1.
530     WRITE PRINT-LINE FROM HEADER AFTER 1.
540     PERFORM 40-WRITE-RESULTS VARYING I FROM 1
550         BY 1 UNTIL I GREATER THAN NO-GRADES.
560     CLOSE PRINT-FILE, INPUT-FILE.
570     STOP RUN.
580*
590 10-READ-GRADES.
600     MOVE IR-GRADE TO DUP-GRADES (I).
610     MOVE IR-GRADE TO GRADES (I).
620     ADD 1 TO NO-GRADES.
630     READ INPUT-FILE AT END MOVE 1 TO EOF.
640*
650 20-PROCESS-PASSES.
660     PERFORM 30-INTERCHANGE-PROCESS VARYING
670         I FROM 1 BY 1 UNTIL I GREATER L.
680*
690 30-INTERCHANGE-PROCESS.
700     COMPUTE J = I + 1.
710     IF GRADES (I) > GRADES (J)
720         MOVE GRADES (I) TO TEMP
730         MOVE GRADES (J) TO GRADES (I)
740         MOVE TEMP       TO GRADES (J).
750*
760 40-WRITE-RESULTS.
770     MOVE DUP-GRADES (I) TO DL-GRADE.
780     MOVE GRADES (I)     TO DL-SORTED.
790     WRITE PRINT-LINE FROM DETAIL-LINE AFTER 1.
```

```
130 DATA DIVISION.
140 FILE SECTION.
150 FD  PRINT-FILE
160     LABEL RECORDS ARE STANDARD
170     DATA RECORD IS PRINT-LINE.
180 01  PRINT-LINE PIC X(133).
190 FD  INPUT-FILE
200     LABEL RECORDS ARE STANDARD
205     DATA RECORD IS INPUT-RECORD.
210 01  INPUT-RECORD.
220     05 IR-GRADE PIC 999.
```

GRADES	SORTED	Input
45	5	045
26	26	026
78	45	078
45	45	045
5	78	005

Original grades stored in DUP-GRADES

Grades are sorted in table GRADES

Read the grades into two tables. The number of passes is one less than the number of grades. Perform the interchange process a number of times equal to NO–PASSES. Since the largest number is moved to the right-most position by pass 1, the second pass needs only move the next-to-largest element to the next-to-last position. On the third pass, the third largest element will be moved into the third-from-last position, et cetera. In general, L controls the size of the shrinking table; thus L is decremented by 1 for each pass.

Read the grades and store them in two tables, GRADES and DUP–GRADES. The latter table allows the program to print both the original list of grades and the sorted list of grades.

Go and perform the interchange process. The first time L will be one less than the number of grades. The second time L will be two less than the number of grades. The final value for L will be 1.

Compare two consecutive grades. If the first is greater than the second, interchange them so that the larger of the two is continuously pushed to the right.

FIGURE 9–12
THE BUBBLE SORT

To better understand the complete sort program, let's start by writing the code for the first pass, which determines the position of the smallest element of the table and performs the interchange of the smallest number with the number in the first position of the table. Assume table GRADES contains a number of grades equal to NO-GRADES.

In the following code, K keeps track of the position of the current smallest number as the code analyses each successive element of table GRADES. Referring to the example above, in the first pass, K is initially 1 and then takes on the value 4, since the smallest number (2) is in position 4.

```
MOVE 1 TO K.
MOVE GRADES (1) TO WS-MIN.

PERFORM SERCH VARYING I FROM 2
    BY 1 UNTIL I > NO-GRADES.
```

Initially the pointer K points to the first element of the table; Assume GRADES(1) is the smallest element. K will then be changed whenever a smaller number is encountered.
The first time through SERCH, I is set to 2 since there is no reason to compare GRADES(1) with GRADES(1). Compare however many elements there are in the table (NO-GRADES).

```
MOVE GRADES (1) TO WS-TEMP.
MOVE WS-MIN   TO GRADES (1).
MOVE WS-TEMP TO GRADES (K).
    .
    .
SERCH.
    IF WS-MIN > GRADES (I)
        MOVE I TO K
        MOVE GRADES (I) TO WS-MIN.
```

At the completion of the search procedure, K identifies the location of the smallest number, and WS-MIN is the smallest number in the table. Interchange WS-MIN with the grade at position K.

If WS-MIN is greater than GRADES(I), then the smallest element so far is at position I, so we reset K to I to keep track of the current location of the smallest element. If WS-MIN is less than or equal to GRADES(I), then K still points to the smallest number in the table, hence K remains unchanged.

To generalize the above code to the complete sort program, K must take on the value 1 for the first pass, then the value 2 for the second pass, et cetera, up to NO-GRADES − 1 for the last pass (the number of passes is one less than the number of grades). The interchange process will require that we move GRADES(2) to WS-TEMP on the second pass, GRADES(3) to WS-TEMP on the third pass, et cetera. Hence an additional (outer) loop is required to control K and to position the succeeding smallest values into locations GRADES(1), GRADES(2), GRADES(3), . . ., GRADES(NO-GRADES). The complete code is shown in Figure 9–13.

9–5 PROGRAMMING EXERCISES

9–5–1 EXERCISES USING SEARCH

Write a program to store the weight charts in Figure 9–14 into two tables and write the code to accept an individual's height, his/her current weight, frame size, and sex code in order to look up the individual's corresponding ideal weight. One's ideal weight, in the context of this problem, is defined to be the average of the two extreme weights displayed in Figure 9–14 for

```
250 WORKING-STORAGE SECTION.
260 01  SUBSCRIPTS-N-COUNTERS.
270     05 I          PIC 99.
280     05 J          PIC 99.
290     05 K          PIC 99.
300     05 NO-GRADES  PIC 99 VALUE 0.
310     05 NO-PASSES  PIC 99.
320 01  FLAGS-N-TEMP-LOCATIONS.
330     05 EOF        PIC 9 VALUE 0.
340     05 TEMP       PIC 999.
345     05 MIN        PIC 999.
350 01  GRADE-COLLECTION.
360     05 GRADES     PIC 999 OCCURS 10 TIMES.
370     05 DUP-GRADES PIC 999 OCCURS 10 TIMES.
380 01  HEADER.
390     05 FILLER     PIC X(10) VALUE "   GRADES".
400     05 FILLER     PIC X(20) VALUE "SORTED".
410 01  DETAIL-LINE.
420     05 FILLER     PIC X(04) VALUE SPACES.
430     05 DL-GRADE   PIC ZZ9.
440     05 FILLER     PIC X(06) VALUE SPACES.
450     05 DL-SORTED  PIC ZZ9.
455*
460 PROCEDURE DIVISION.
470 05-MAIN-LOGIC.
480     OPEN INPUT INPUT-FILE, OUTPUT PRINT-FILE.
490     READ INPUT-FILE AT END MOVE 1 TO EOF.
500     PERFORM 10-READ-GRADES VARYING I FROM 1
510         BY 1 UNTIL EOF = 1.
520     COMPUTE NO-PASSES = NO-GRADES - 1.
530     PERFORM 20-PROCESS-PASSES VARYING J FROM
540         1 BY 1 UNTIL J > NO-PASSES.
550     WRITE PRINT-LINE FROM HEADER AFTER 1.
560     PERFORM 40-WRITE-RESULTS VARYING I FROM 1
570         BY 1 UNTIL I GREATER THAN NO-GRADES.
580     CLOSE PRINT-FILE, INPUT-FILE.
590     STOP RUN.
600*
610 10-READ-GRADES.
620     MOVE IR-GRADE TO DUP-GRADES (I).
630     MOVE IR-GRADE TO GRADES (I).
640     ADD 1 TO NO-GRADES.
650     READ INPUT-FILE AT END MOVE 1 TO EOF.
660*
670 20-PROCESS-PASSES.
680     MOVE J TO K.
685     MOVE GRADES (J) TO MIN.
690     PERFORM 30-SEARCH-LARGEST VARYING
700         I FROM J BY 1 UNTIL I > NO-GRADES.
710     MOVE GRADES (J) TO TEMP.
720     MOVE MIN        TO GRADES (J).
730     MOVE TEMP       TO GRADES (K).
735*
740 30-SEARCH-LARGEST.
750     IF MIN > GRADES (I)
760         MOVE I TO K
765         MOVE GRADES (I) TO MIN.
770*
780 40-WRITE-RESULTS.
790     MOVE DUP-GRADES (I) TO DL-GRADE.
800     MOVE GRADES (I)     TO DL-SORTED.
810     WRITE PRINT-LINE FROM DETAIL-LINE AFTER 1.
```

```
130 DATA DIVISION.
140 FILE SECTION.
150 FD  PRINT-FILE
160     LABEL RECORDS ARE OMITTED
170     DATA RECORD IS PRINT-LINE.
180 01  PRINT-LINE PIC X(133).
190 FD  INPUT-FILE
200     LABEL RECORDS ARE STANDARD
210     DATA RECORD IS INPUT-RECORD.
220 01  INPUT-RECORD.
230     05 IR-GRADE PIC 999.
```

OUTPUT

GRADES	SORTED
45	5
26	26
78	45
45	45
5	78

INPUT

045
026
078
045
005

The number of passes is one fewer than the number of grades. The first pass will interchange the smallest element in the table with the first number in the table (then the smallest grade will be the first element of the table). The second pass will interchange the smallest of the remaining elements of the table with the second number in the table, i.e., the second smallest element will now be in the second position of the table.

Print the original as well as the sorted grades.

Read the grades into tables GRADES and DUP–GRADES.

J takes on the values 1, 2, 3, ..., NO–PASSES. K is the pointer used to keep track of the position of the smallest grade in each search. At the conclusion of the first interchange procedure, the smallest grade is stored in GRADES(1). At the conclusion of the second interchange, the second smallest grade is moved to GRADES(2). The numbers thus are in ascending sequence.

Find the position of the smallest element and record its position in K and its value in MIN.

Write out contents of both tables—the original as well as the sorted table.

FIGURE 9–13
THE MINI/MAX SORT

	FEMALES				MALES		
HEIGHT	SMALL FRAME	MEDIUM FRAME	LARGE FRAME	HEIGHT	SMALL FRAME	MEDIUM FRAME	LARGE FRAME
4 ft. 10 in.	92–98	96–107	104–119	5 ft. 2 in.	112–120	118–129	126–141
4 ft. 11 in.	94–101	98–110	106–122	5 ft. 3 in.	115–123	121–133	129–144
5 ft. 0 in.	96–104	101–113	109–125	5 ft. 4 in.	118–126	124–136	132–148
5 ft. 1 in.	99–107	104–116	112–128	5 ft. 5 in.	121–129	127–139	135–152
5 ft. 2 in.	102–110	107–119	115–131	5 ft. 6 in.	124–133	130–143	138–156
5 ft. 3 in.	105–113	110–122	118–134	5 ft. 7 in.	128–137	134–147	142–161
5 ft. 4 in.	108–116	113–126	121–138	5 ft. 8 in.	132–141	138–152	147–166
5 ft. 5 in.	111–119	116–130	125–142	5 ft. 9 in.	136–145	142–156	151–170
5 ft. 6 in.	114–123	120–135	129–146	5 ft. 10 in.	140–150	146–160	155–174
5 ft. 7 in.	118–127	124–139	133–150	5 ft. 11 in.	144–154	150–165	159–179
5 ft. 8 in.	122–131	128–143	137–154	6 ft. 0 in.	148–158	154–170	164–184
5 ft. 9 in.	126–135	132–147	141–158	6 ft. 1 in.	152–162	158–175	168–189
5 ft. 10 in.	130–140	136–151	145–163	6 ft. 2 in.	156–167	162–180	173–194
5 ft. 11 in.	134–144	140–155	149–168	6 ft. 3 in.	160–171	167–185	178–199
6 ft. 0 in.	138–148	144–159	153–173	6 ft. 4 in.	164–175	172–190	182–204

FIGURE 9–14
MALE/FEMALE WEIGHT CHARTS

one's given height and frame size. For example, the ideal weight for a medium-frame, 6-foot man is 162 lb. [(170 + 154)/2]. For females between ages 18–25, one pound should be subtracted for each year under age 25. Solve the problem by using indexes (not subscripts) without the SEARCH verb, and then solve the problem with the SEARCH feature. The printout should also indicate by how many pounds the individual in question is overweight or underweight.

2. Repeat exercise 1, but store both tables in a two-dimensional table.

3. The results of the program in exercise 1 tell whether an individual is overweight, underweight, or just right! The tables in Figure 9–15 display caloric requirements for those who wish to maintain their ideal weight or those who wish to alter their weight. Write a program to accept an individual's height, sex code, and frame size to determine the individual's ideal weight, using the height/frame size tables in Figure 9–14.

    The program should also read an individual's current weight (in addition to the physical characteristics described above) and prescribe a weight control plan. Three plans may be offered:

    a. Diet Plan: The individual's weight exceeds the weight interval corresponding to his/her ideal weight as shown in Figure 9–14. In this case, print a diet plan specifying the number of daily "reducing calories" for the individual. For example, if the medium-frame man described in exercise 1 weighs 176 lb., he is considered overweight and his daily caloric intake should be limited to 2460 calories.

    b. On Target Plan: The individual's weight falls within the interval corresponding to his/her ideal weight as shown in Figure 9–14. In this case the corresponding number of "sustaining calories" should be prescribed. For

SEARCHING AND SORTING

	FEMALES			MALES	
IDEAL WEIGHT	SUSTAINING CALORIES	REDUCING CALORIES	IDEAL WEIGHT	SUSTAINING CALORIES	REDUCING CALORIES
105 to 109	1920	1200	125 to 129	2640	1940
110 to 114	2000	1300	130 to 134	2700	2000
115 to 119	2100	1400	135 to 139	2780	2080
120 to 124	2190	1450	140 to 144	2840	2140
125 to 129	2250	1500	145 to 149	2920	2220
130 to 134	2300	1550	150 to 154	3000	2300
135 to 139	2400	1600	155 to 159	3080	2380
140 to 144	2500	1650	160 to 164	3160	2460
145 to 149	2600	1700	165 to 169	3240	2540
150 to 154	2700	1750	170 to 174	3320	2620
155 to 159	2800	1800	175 to 179	3420	2720
160 to 164	2900	1900	180 and over	3550	2830
165 and over	3000	2000			

FIGURE 9–15
CALORIC REQUIREMENTS FOR IDEAL WEIGHTS

example, if the man in exercise 1 weighed 164 lb., his daily caloric requirement would be 3160.

c. Gain Plan: The individual's weight falls below the interval corresponding to his/her ideal weight as shown in Figure 9–14, in which case the Gain Plan should prescribe 5% more calories than the number of indicated "sustaining calories" for that interval.

The following considerations also apply to these plans:

(1) If the individual is a nervous type of person, the daily caloric figure should be increased by 10%.
(2) If the individual performs heavy physical labor, the daily caloric figure should be increased by 15%.
(3) If the individual is a sedentary, rather inactive type, then the daily caloric requirement should be decreased by 8%.

4. Assume you have recorded your daily caloric intake for the last six weeks in tables similar to the ones shown here. Write a program to compute the "totals" column for each week and print the tables shown in Figure 9–16 with all the captions. Furthermore, write the program in such a way that you can enter a week number (1–6), a day, and a particular meal and have the computer recall and print your caloric intake for that meal. Use the SEARCH verb.

5. You have a home computer and you have stored your four favorite breakfast recipes, including the total calories for each, in tables in memory. Write a program to accept a maximum number of calories that you allow yourself for a particular breakfast, and have the computer provide you with a choice of menus whose caloric content must be below the maximum specified.

WEEK 1

	Breakfast	Lunch	Dinner	Total
1st Day				
2nd Day				
3rd Day				
4th Day				
5th Day				
6th Day				
7th Day				

WEEK 2

	Breakfast	Lunch	Dinner	Total
1st Day				
2nd Day				
3rd Day				
4th Day				
5th Day				
6th Day				
7th Day				

WEEK 3

	Breakfast	Lunch	Dinner	Total
1st Day				
2nd Day				
3rd Day				
4th Day				
5th Day				
6th Day				
7th Day				

FIGURE 9–16
CALORIC DIARIES

For example, given the various breakfasts shown below, if you specified 205 calories, only Breakfast No. 3 would be listed. If, on the other hand, you specified 230 calories, then all four breakfasts would be printed. Note that the list of breakfasts should be printed vertically, not horizontally (as shown):

Breakfast No. 1 (Calories....226)	Breakfast No. 2 (Calories....224)	Breakfast No. 3 (Calories....201)	Breakfast No. 4 (Calories....217)
½ Medium Grapefruit Soft Boiled Egg Slice Protein Bread (may be toasted) ½ pat of Butter Black Coffee	8 oz. Glass Tomato Juice Fried Egg Slice Protein Bread (may be toasted) ½ pat of Butter Black Coffee	8 oz. Glass Tomato Juice Poached Egg Slice Protein Bread (may be toasted) ½ pat of Butter Black Coffee	½ Cantaloupe One-egg Omelet Slice Protein Bread (may be toasted) ½ pat of Butter Black Coffee

6. The two tables shown on top of page 525 show life expectancy figures and the number of years a savings amount will last if it is invested at a fixed interest rate and if a fixed percentage of the amount is withdrawn consistently every year. For example, if one's savings earns 10% interest and one with-

SEARCHING AND SORTING 525

draws 10% of the amount every year, the withdrawal process can go on indefinitely; however, if 11% of the amount is withdrawn every year, then the withdrawal process will last only 25 years.

LIFE EXPECTANCY

AGES	MALE	FEMALE
65	13.4	17.5
66	12.8	16.7
67	12.2	16.0
68	11.7	15.3
69	11.2	14.6
70	10.7	13.9
71	10.2	13.2
72	9.7	12.6
73	9.2	12.0
74	8.8	11.4
75	8.4	10.8

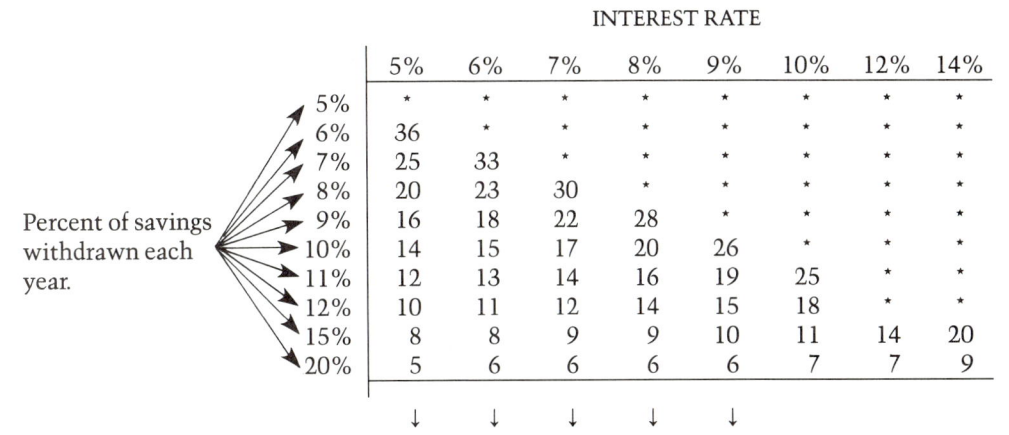

INTEREST RATE

Percent of savings withdrawn each year.

	5%	6%	7%	8%	9%	10%	12%	14%
5%	*	*	*	*	*	*	*	*
6%	36	*	*	*	*	*	*	*
7%	25	33	*	*	*	*	*	*
8%	20	23	30	*	*	*	*	*
9%	16	18	22	28	*	*	*	*
10%	14	15	17	20	26	*	*	*
11%	12	13	14	16	19	25	*	*
12%	10	11	12	14	15	18	*	*
15%	8	8	9	9	10	11	14	20
20%	5	6	6	6	6	7	7	9

Number of years savings will last.
*Money will last indefinitely.

    a. Write a program to store both tables in memory, and write the code to accept an interest rate and a withdrawal percentage and determine the number of years the withdrawal process can continue. For example, savings earning 8% interest with an 11% withdrawal rate will last for 16 years.

    b. Given an individual's age (65 or over), a sex code, a savings amount, and an interest rate, determine the largest possible yearly savings withdrawal that will leave the individual as close to broke as possible (as allowed by the table) at the time of death!

        For example, a male, age 75, with $10,000 in savings at 10% interest rate, has a life expectancy of 8.4 years. His maximum percentage of withdrawal is then 15%. Twenty percent would be too high (the withdrawal process could last only 7 years). Hence his maximum yearly withdrawal would be $1500. (This would still leave a little extra for funeral expenses!)

        Another example: A male, age 65, with $10,000 savings invested at 7% interest rate, has a life expectancy of 13.4 years. His maximum withdrawal would be 11%, for a yearly withdrawal of $1,100.

7. The tables shown in Figure 9–17 are sales tax tables for four states. Write a program to accept an income and a family size and have the computer print out the lowest state tax deduction of the four states. Identify the state and the tax on the output. Be sure to read the instructions for steps A, B, and C.

8. The SEARCH verb uses a sequential approach to searching; i.e., the search starts at the first element of the table and proceeds with the next sequential table element until the desired search condition is met (there is a match in the table). The entries in the table need not be in any particular type of order. Thus, if a table contains 1000 elements and the entry to be located is the 1000th entry, the search will examine the first 999 elements before the search is successful.

    The SEARCH ALL uses a different approach, which requires that all table elements to be searched be sorted into either ascending or descending order. The technique used in this case is the halving process, which is essentially a guessing game. The table is split into two sections at the mid-

	Alabama						Arizona					Arkansas						California			
Income	Family size					Over	Family size				Over	Family size					Over	Family size		Over
	1	2	3	4	5	5	1&2	3	4	5	5	1	2	3	4	5	5	1&2	3&4	5	5
$1–$8,000	93	115	122	131	142	160	99	116	120	129	141	78	97	102	100	116	132	135	147	155	164
$8,001–$10,000	109	132	142	153	165	185	116	136	141	150	163	91	111	118	127	135	152	147	173	183	193
$10,000–$12,000	124	147	161	173	187	203	131	154	160	170	184	103	123	134	143	153	170	167	198	208	219
$12,001–$14,000	133	161	178	191	206	228	145	171	178	189	203	115	134	148	158	169	187	185	220	232	243
$14,001–$16,000	152	174	194	209	225	248	158	187	195	206	221	125	145	161	173	184	202	204	242	255	266
$16,001–$18,000	164	186	210	226	242	266	171	202	212	223	238	135	154	174	186	198	217	222	263	276	288
$18,001–$20,000	176	197	225	242	259	287	183	216	227	239	254	145	163	185	199	212	231	233	282	297	300
$20,001–$22,000	188	208	239	257	275	301	194	230	242	254	270	154	172	198	212	225	245	254	301	317	330
$22,001–$24,000	199	218	253	271	290	317	205	244	257	268	285	163	181	209	224	238	258	270	320	336	349
$24,001–$26,000	210	228	266	285	305	332	216	257	271	282	299	172	189	220	235	250	270	285	338	355	368
$26,001–$28,000	221	238	279	299	320	347	226	269	285	296	313	180	197	230	246	262	282	299	355	373	386
$28,001–$30,000	231	247	291	313	334	362	236	281	298	310	327	188	204	240	257	273	294	313	372	391	404
$30,001–$32,000	241	256	303	326	347	376	246	293	311	323	340	196	211	250	268	284	305	327	389	408	422
$32,001–$34,000	251	265	315	338	360	390	256	305	324	336	353	204	218	260	278	295	316	341	405	425	439
$34,001–$36,000	261	274	327	350	373	403	265	317	337	348	365	211	225	270	288	306	326	354	421	441	455
$36,001–$38,000	271	282	338	362	386	416	274	328	349	360	377	218	232	279	298	316	336	367	436	457	471
$38,001–$40,000	280	290	349	374	399	429	283	338	361	372	389	225	239	283	308	326	346	380	451	473	487
$40,001–$100,000 (See Step B)	14	15	17	19	20	21	14	17	18	19	19	11	12	14	15	16	17	19	23	24	24

Step A—If your total available income is not over $40,000, find the income line for your state on the tables and read across to find the amount of sales tax for your family size.

Step B—If your income is over $40,000 but not over $100,000, find the deduction listed on the income line "$38,001–$40,000" for your family size and State. For each $5,000 (or part of $5,000) of income over $40,000, increase the deduction by the amount listed for the line "$40,001–$100,000."

Step C—If your income is over $100,000, your sales tax deduction is limited to the deduction for income of $100,000. To figure your sales tax deduction, use Step B but don't go over $100,000.

FIGURE 9–17
STATE TAXES

point. The desired entry is either in the right section or in the left section. If it is in the right section, that section is again split into two subsections, and the desired number is in one or the other subsection. This splitting-in-half procedure is carried out until the desired entry has been found. This search process is sometimes called the *binary search*. The table is divided in half, then in quarters, then in eighths, then in sixteenths, and so on.

A table with 4 entries (2^2) requires at most 2 comparisons.
A table with anywhere from 5 to 8 entries (2^3) requires at most 3 comparisons.
A table with anywhere from 9 to 16 entries (2^4) requires at most 4 comparisons.
A table with anywhere from 17 to 32 entries (2^5) requires at most 5 comparisons.

.
.
.

A table with up to 1024 entries (2^{10}) requires at most 10 comparisons.

Hence, to search for a specific value in a table with 1024 entries (2^{10}) requires only 10 comparisons!

When the table is split into sections, the end points of a section are identified by two pointers, L (left) and R (right). Initially L = 0 and R = number of entries + 1. The method can be visualized by studying the following example, where we want to determine whether 51 is in table A, which has 11 elements.

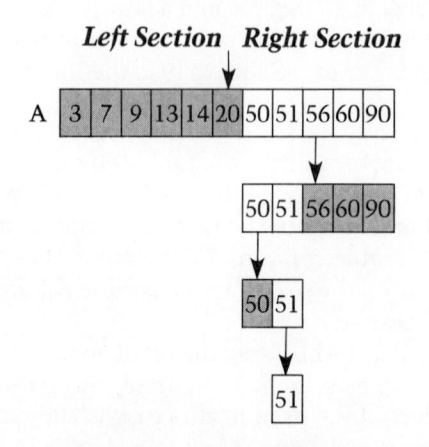

Left Section *Right Section*

A | 3 | 7 | 9 | 13 | 14 | 20 | 50 | 51 | 56 | 60 | 90 |

$L = 0, R = 12, \text{Midpt} = \frac{0 + 12}{2} = 6$

51 > A(6). Throw out the left section.

$L = 6, R = 12, \text{Midpt} = \frac{6 + 12}{2} = 9$

| 50 | 51 | 56 | 60 | 90 |

51 < A(9). Throw out the right section.

$L = 6, R = 9, \text{Midpt} = \frac{6 + 9}{2} = 7$

| 50 | 51 |

51 > A(7). Throw out the left section.

$L = 7, R = 9, \text{Midpt} = \frac{7 + 9}{2} = 8$

| 51 |

51 = A(8)   FOUND IT!

SEARCHING AND SORTING

Note that the number 51 was found in four moves as opposed to the eight moves that would have been required if a sequential search had been performed.

Write a program to perform a binary search on an array containing no more than 50 elements.

9-5-2 EXERCISES DEALING WITH SORTING

1. For each student in a class, you have one record with his/her account number in columns 1–4 and ten test scores **in no specific order** in columns 5–34. The student's average is based on his/her nine best scores. Write a program to produce the following output at the top of a new page:

   ```
                    GRADING REPORT
   ACCOUNT NUMBER:   3214 AVERAGE = 71.4
   TESTS              27  44  48  51  60  80  84  86  94  96
   ACCOUNT NUMBER:   2134 AVERAGE = 65.2
   TESTS              24  47  66  68  72  74  79  80  82  86
   ```

   All ten test scores should be printed in ascending order.

2. An input file consists of an unknown number of grades in random order (one per record). Write a program to compute and print the median. The median is the score that divides a distribution of scores into two equal parts. For example,

   10, 30, 87, 12   The median is (12 + 30)/2 = 21
                    (Half are above 21, half are below 21.)

   53, 16, 99   The median is 53 (Half are above 53, half below 53.)

3. A radio station has hired you to write a program to help them plan their air time. You are given twenty input records at most, with the following entries on each record:

   1st entry: Record identification
   2nd entry: Record type (1 = Punk rock, 2 = Acid rock, 3 = Classical)
   3rd entry: Playing time (3.6 means 3 minutes and 6/10 of a minute)

   Write a program to

   a. Read the input file and store the record identification, the record type, and the playing time into three separate tables.
   b. Sort the three tables in ascending order by playing time.
   c. Print the sorted tables with each record identification, record type, and corresponding playing time on one output line (3 data items/line).
   d. Determine total playing time for each type of record and print the result as:

   ```
   PUNK ROCK    14.6
   ACID ROCK    21.0
   CLASSICAL     9.2
   ```

   e. Determine the classical record with the playing time closest to 2.4 minutes and print the located record's identification and playing time.

4. The BOISUPP company employs a variable number of salespersons. The input file consists of records of sales by each salesperson. The records are not arranged in any particular sequence. For example, a typical data file might be:

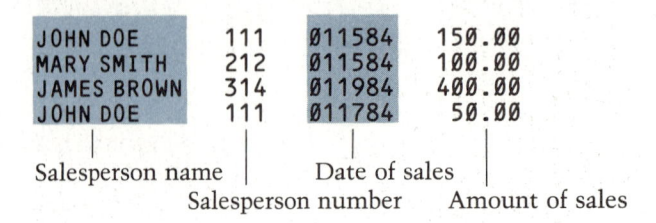

```
JOHN DOE      111    011584    150.00
MARY SMITH    212    011584    100.00
JAMES BROWN   314    011984    400.00
JOHN DOE      111    011784     50.00
    |          |        |         |
Salesperson    |     Date of sales|
   name   Salesperson number   Amount of sales
```

The management wants to print out a monthly sales report to summarize the total sales for each salesperson and the total amount of all sales. Also, a salesperson-of-the-month award will go to the salesperson with highest sales for the month. Entries are to be listed in ascending order by salesperson number and date of sales. Arrange the output in the following form:

```
SALESPERSON              DATE OF     AMOUNT OF      TOTAL SALES/
NAME            NUMBER    SALES        SALES        SALESPERSON

JOHN DOE          111    01 15 84     150.00
                         01 17 84      50.00          200.00

MARY SMITH        212    01 15 84     100.00          100.00

JAMES BROWN       314    01 19 84     400.00          400.00

                                    TOTAL SALES       700.00
**AWARD GOES TO JAMES BROWN**
```

a. Write a program to read a transaction file and produce a summary report like the one shown. Be sure to include more than one transaction for some of the salespersons and note that in such a case you print the name and number of the salesperson only once.
b. Produce an alternative report by ascending date of sales.
c. Produce an alternative report by descending sales totals and ascending salesperson number (if two or more total sale entries are equal).

5. Write a program to record in a table P the relative ascending order position of each element of table A. For example, if

table A = | 51 | 20 | 90 | 80 | 100 | then   table P = | 2 | 1 | 4 | 3 | 5 |

1 is stored in P(2), to indicate that the 2nd element of A is the smallest (20).

2 is stored in P(1), to indicate that the 1st element of A is the next-to-smallest (51).

.
.
.

5 is stored in P(5), to indicate that the 5th element of A is the largest (100).

The following elements of A would then be in ascending numerical sequence:

A(P(1)), A(P(2)), A(P(3)), . . . A(P(50))

In what programming situation would this sort algorithm be preferable to the bubble or mini/max sorts? Write the code to print out the table A with the subscripts shown above to make sure table P is correct.

6. You work for the National Weather Service. They are going to measure changes in wind direction by sending up 3 balloons on each of 5 different days. Each of the 15 balloons is assigned a unique integer identification number (ID) between 100 and 999 (in no particular order). One balloon is released in the morning, one is released at noon, and one is released in the evening on each of the five days. When the balloons are returned, the ID number, the day each balloon was sent up (1, 2, 3, 4, or 5), and the distance traveled will be recorded, with one record for each balloon (see the following table of test data). Write a program to:

   a. Read the test data records shown below into three tables (identification, day and distance).
   b. Sort the tables into ascending order by ID number.
   c. Print the sorted table with three entries per line (ID, day, and distance).
   d. Find the maximum distance traveled for each day (5 maximums). Print the ID, day, and maximum distance for each of the 5 days (print the results for the first day, then the second, third, et cetera).
   e. Find the average distance traveled by balloons released on the first and fifth days combined and print this average distance (one result).

   Input: 15 records with 3 data items/record: ID, day and distance.

   Output: 15 printed lines of sorted ID's and corresponding days and distances (ID, day, distance).
   5 printed lines of maximum distances for each day (1 through 5) (ID, day, distance).
   1 printed line of the average distance traveled on the first and fifth days (average).

   Use the following test data.

Identification	Day	Distance
123	2	143.7
269	3	976.4
120	1	370.2
460	5	980.8
111	1	111.3
986	4	1320.6
629	3	787.0
531	2	429.2
729	2	726.1
833	4	433.1
621	3	962.4
143	4	714.3
972	5	320.1
410	5	820.4
511	1	1240.0

7. You are the organizer for the National Swimming Finals. You want to have a program that will seed the swimmers in the correct preliminary heat (race). You have 36 swimmers, each with an identification number and a submitted time. The swimming pool has only six lanes, so only six swim-

mers can swim at a time. The procedure for seeding is to (1) sort the swimmers according to submitted times, and (2) assign to the first heat the swimmers with the first, seventh, thirteenth, . . ., and thirty-first fastest times. (Note that a person whose time is 52.1 is *faster* than someone whose time is 55.8.) The swimmers in the second heat should be those with the second, eighth, fourteenth, . . ., and thirty-second fastest times. Swimmers should be assigned to the other four heats in a similar manner.
Write a program to:

a. Read a file in which each record contains an integer ID and a submitted time, and store these data into two tables.
b. Sort both tables in ascending order *by time*.
c. Starting with the first heat, print the heat number, then print the ID number and time of each swimmer in that heat in ascending order by time. Repeat for each heat.
d. Print on a separate line (1) the number of swimmers who swam faster than the average submitted time and (2) the average submitted time.

8. Two sort methods have been presented in this chapter, the bubble and the mini/max sort. These two sorting techniques are not the most efficient methods, however. An extremely efficient sorting method is the Shell-Metzner sort displayed here in flowchart form. In an article entitled "A Comparison of Sorts" in *Creative Computing*, Volume 2, John Grillo compared the three methods and determined that to sort 100,000 numbers would take 7.1 days, 3.8 days, and 15 minutes for the bubble, mini/max, and Shell-Metzner sort, respectively. To sort 10,000,000 numbers would take 93 years, 50 years, and 2.5 days respectively! Write a program to sort N numbers using the following flowchart.

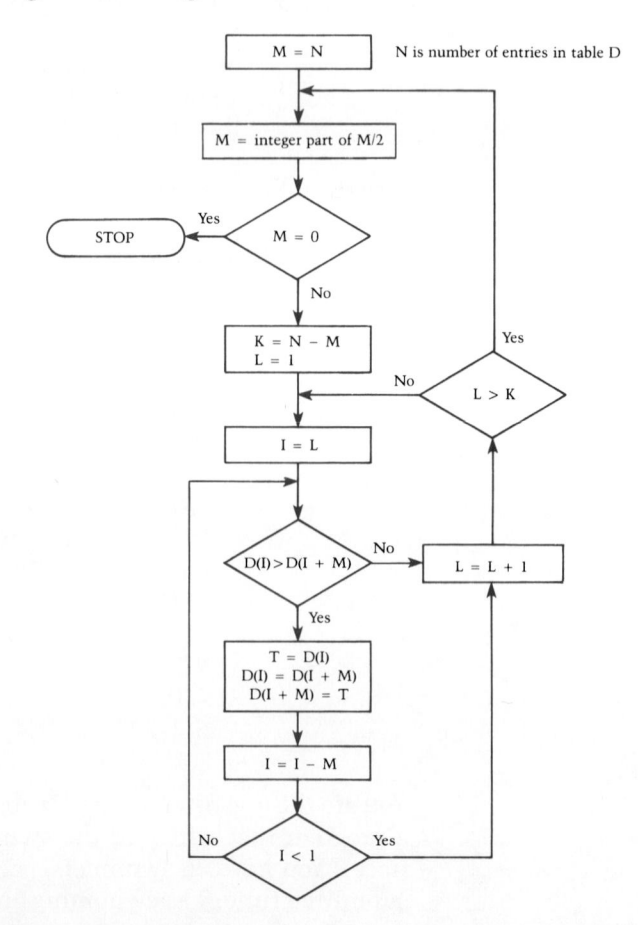

CHAPTER 10

SEQUENTIAL FILE PROCESSING

10–1   PROBLEM EXAMPLE: CREATION OF A TAPE/DISK DATA FILE THROUGH COBOL

10–2   FILES AND PHYSICAL DEVICES

10–3   SEQUENTIAL FILE PROCESSING

10–4   COMMON FILE-PROCESSING TASKS

10–5   A MULTIPLE-FILE PROGRAMMING PROBLEM: GRADE REPORT

10–6   YOU MIGHT WANT TO KNOW

10–7   PROGRAMMING EXERCISES

532   UNDERSTANDING STRUCTURED COBOL

INTRODUCTION Files are necessary for storing large quantities of data: the need for files and the physical characteristics of various file-storage mediums are described in this chapter, which then concentrates on the use of sequential files in COBOL. This chapter shows how to create files in COBOL, how sequential files are organized, and what COBOL statements are used to process such files. Programs for merging and updating files are discussed; examples are given of both a full sequential update and a partial in-place update using the REWRITE statement and the OPEN EXTEND option.

10-1 PROBLEM EXAMPLE: CREATION OF A TAPE/DISK DATA FILE THROUGH COBOL

Each record of an input file created through a text editor, consists of an item number, an item description, an item quantity, and a corresponding item cost. Write a COBOL program to read this file and then write it on disk or tape; then write a separate COBOL program to print the contents of the COBOL created disk/tape file. The input to the first program (and the output produced by the second program) is as follows:

```
Item    Item         Item      Item
number  description  quantity  cost

0900LOVE SEAT       20  09800
0950HUTCH TOP       20  08400
1500SOFA            14  08500
1700LOVE SEAT       17  08400
1800DOUBLE SOFA     24  18600
3000ARMCHAIR        24  16699
4000LOUNGE CHAIR    08  06700
```

The two programs to solve this problem are shown in Figures 10–1 and 10–2.

Each computer manufacturer's COBOL differs in the way in which a physical device (tape or magnetic disk) is associated with a particular file in the SELECT/ASSIGN clause. Lines 13 through 30 of Figure 10–1 display the five most common SELECT/ASSIGN specifications.

The simplest SELECT/ASSIGN clause for assigning files to tape or disk is offered by microcomputer systems such as IBM COBOL:

```
SELECT MASTER-FILE ASSIGN TO DISK
    ORGANIZATION IS SEQUENTIAL.
      .
      .
      .
FD  MASTER-FILE
    LABEL RECORDS ARE STANDARD
    VALUE OF FILE-ID IS 'OLDMASTR'.
```

where

> MASTER–FILE is the disk file name used in the PROCEDURE division to refer to the output file.
>
> ORGANIZATION IS SEQUENTIAL should be specified instead of LINE SEQUENTIAL. The LINE SEQUENTIAL clause should be specified only if the disk file is created through a text editor.
>
> 'OLDMASTR' is the name under which the output disk file is catalogued.

Burroughs' COBOL also has a simple device assignment specification:

```
SELECT MASTER-FILE ASSIGN TO 5 * 10 DISKPACK.
```

DISKPACK is a system name recognized as a particular disk unit; 5 * 10 specifies the area of the disk needed and MASTER–FILE becomes the name under which the file is catalogued on the tape or disk.

A third more complicated device assignment specification (for the novice programmer) is that used by IBM for main frame computers:

```
SELECT MASTER-FILE ASSIGN DA-S-DISKFILE.
```

where DA and S have special meaning to the compiler and where DISKFILE is a user-chosen name to identify the disk file, which must be further defined/described through additional *job control language* parameters outside the COBOL program. These parameters identify the particular device, the area of the disk to be used, et cetera. Such job control statements generally follow the source program. The user should check with his/her installation for the specific details.

The new disk file created in Figure 10–1 and catalogued under the name OLDMASTR becomes the input file to the listing program of Figure 10–2. As each OLDMASTR record is read, it is listed on the printer. Note the name INPUT–FILE given to the input file in Figure 10–2. The name MASTER–FILE could have been used just as well.

10–2 FILES AND PHYSICAL DEVICES

10–2–1 FILE CONCEPTS

Mr. X wants to use a computer to keep track of the inventory at his store. The part numbers and corresponding quantities are recorded on a disk file. Later, as parts are sold or as parts are added to the inventory, the parts file can be updated. Then, on either a daily or a weekly basis, reports can be produced to list the number of parts on hand, and to identify those parts that need to be ordered, et cetera.

Such an information-processing system inevitably leads to the following file-processing considerations: Once the initial file is created, certain procedures must be defined to maintain the file, i.e., to keep the file current. Inventory files must be updated when parts are sold or added to the inventory. In the case of personnel or payroll files, new employees are hired, others retire and

```
 1:  IDENTIFICATION DIVISION.
 2:  PROGRAM-ID. CREATE-FILE.
 3:  *****************************************
 4:  * C R E A T I N G   A   D I S K - F I L E *
 5:  *****************************************
 6:  AUTHOR. JONES.
 7:  ENVIRONMENT DIVISION.
 8:  CONFIGURATION SECTION.
 9:  SOURCE-COMPUTER. IBM.
10:  OBJECT-COMPUTER. IBM.
11:  INPUT-OUTPUT SECTION.
12:  FILE-CONTROL.
13:      SELECT INPUT-FILE ASSIGN TO DISK
14:          ORGANIZATION IS LINE SEQUENTIAL.
15:      SELECT MASTER-FILE ASSIGN TO DISK
16:          ORGANIZATION IS SEQUENTIAL.
17:  ******************************************************
18:  *     SELECT MASTER-FILE ASSIGN DA-S-DISKFILE.        *
19:  *                                                    *
20:  *                                                    *
21:  *                                                    *
22:  *     SELECT MASTER-FILE ASSIGN TO OUTPUT 'DISK'.    *
23:  *                                                    *
24:  *                                                    *
25:  *                                                    *
26:  *     SELECT MASTER-FILE ASSIGN 5 * 10 DISKPACK.     *
27:  *                                                    *
28:  *                                                    *
29:  *                                                    *
30:  *     SELECT MASTER-FILE ASSIGN TO UT-S-SYSTAPE.     *
31:  ******************************************************
32:  DATA DIVISION.
33:  FILE SECTION.
34:  *
35:  FD  INPUT-FILE
36:      LABEL RECORDS ARE STANDARD
37:      VALUE OF FILE-ID IS 'TRANSACT'.
38:  01  INPUT-AREA.
39:      05 IR-ITEM   PIC 9999.
40:      05 IR-DESCR  PIC X(13).
41:      05 IR-QTY    PIC 99.
42:      05 FILLER    PIC X.
43:      05 IR-COST   PIC 999V99.
44:  *                                    MOVE
45:  FD  MASTER-FILE
46:      LABEL RECORDS ARE STANDARD
47:      VALUE OF FILE-ID IS 'OLDMASTR'.
48:  01  MASTER-AREA PIC X(25).
49:  *
50:  WORKING-STORAGE SECTION.
51:  01  FLAGS.
52:      05 WS-EOF PIC 9 VALUE 0.
53:  *
54:  PROCEDURE DIVISION.
55:  100-MAIN-LOGIC.
56:      OPEN INPUT INPUT-FILE
57:           OUTPUT MASTER-FILE.
58:      READ INPUT-FILE INTO MASTER-AREA
59:          AT END MOVE 1 TO WS-EOF.
60:      PERFORM 200-READ-WRITE UNTIL WS-EOF = 1.
61:      CLOSE INPUT-FILE, MASTER-FILE.
62:      STOP RUN.
63:  *
64:  200-READ-WRITE.
65:      WRITE MASTER-AREA.
66:      READ INPUT-FILE INTO MASTER-AREA
67:          AT END MOVE 1 TO WS-EOF.
```

IBM microcomputer COBOL. If the input file is created by a text editor then LINE SEQUENTIAL must be specified (line 14). Writing a file on disk by means of the COBOL WRITE statement requires the SEQUENTIAL attribute (line 16).

IBM: (line 18) The user-chosen name DISKFILE is also specified in the job control statements to identify the disk and the disk area onto which the master file is to be written.

Tandy Microcomputer: (line 22) No job control statements needed. User-chosen name DISK specifies area onto which file is to be written.

Burroughs: (line 26) The file is written on disk and the external name (catalogued name) of the file is MASTER-FILE.

IBM: (line 30) The output file would be written on magnetic tape. Job control statements are needed to link tape and SYSTAPE.

INPUT-FILE

IR-ITEM	IR-DESCR	IR-QTY	IR-COST
0900	LOVE SEAT	20	09800
0950	HUTCH TOP	20	08400
1500	SOFA	14	08500
1700	LOVE SEAT	17	08400
1800	DOUBLE SOFA	24	18600
3000	ARMCHAIR	24	16699
4000	LOUNGE CHAIR	08	06700

The catalogued name of the COBOL-written disk file is OLDMASTR (line 47); it cannot be edited by a text editor.

Read the first record from input file into the output record area for the disk output file.

Write the output record area onto disk. Note that there is no ADVANCING clause since the output device is not a printer.

FIGURE 10–1
CREATING A DISK FILE THROUGH COBOL

```
 1:     IDENTIFICATION DIVISION.
 2:     PROGRAM-ID.  CREATE-FILE.
 3:     ************************************************************
 4:     * R E A D I N G   A   C O B O L   C R E A T E D   D I S K   F I L E *
 5:     ************************************************************
 6:     AUTHOR. JONES.
 7:     ENVIRONMENT DIVISION.
 8:     CONFIGURATION SECTION.
 9:     SOURCE-COMPUTER. IBM.
10:     OBJECT-COMPUTER. IBM.
11:     INPUT-OUTPUT SECTION.
12:     FILE-CONTROL.
13:         SELECT REPORT-FILE ASSIGN TO PRINTER.
14:         SELECT INPUT-FILE ASSIGN TO DISK                IBM microcomputer
15:         ORGANIZATION IS SEQUENTIAL.
16:     ****************************************************
17:     *   SELECT INPUT-FILE   ASSIGN DA-S-DISKFILE.    *   IBM
18:     *                                                *
19:     *                                                *
20:     *   SELECT INPUT-FILE   ASSIGN 20 * 40 DISKPACK. *   BURROUGHS
21:     *                                                *
22:     *                                                *
23:     *   SELECT INPUT-FILE   ASSIGN TO INPUT 'DISK'.  *   Tandy
24:     *                                                *
25:     *                                                *
26:     *   SELECT INPUT-FILE   ASSIGN TO UT-S-SYSTAPE.  *   IBM tape file
27:     ****************************************************
28:     DATA DIVISION.                                      Catalogued name is OLDMASTR
29:     FILE SECTION.
30:     *
31:     FD  INPUT-FILE
32:         LABEL RECORDS ARE STANDARD
33:         VALUE OF FILE-ID IS 'OLDMASTR'.
34:     01  INPUT-AREA.
35:         05  IR-ITEM   PIC 9999.
36:         05  IR-DESCR  PIC X(13).
37:         05  IR-QTY    PIC 99.
38:         05  FILLER    PIC X.
39:         05  IR-COST   PIC 999V99.
40:     *
41:     FD  REPORT-FILE
42:         LABEL RECORDS ARE OMITTED.
43:     01  PRINT-LINE PIC X(80).
44:     *
45:     WORKING-STORAGE SECTION.
46:     01  FLAGS.
47:         05  WS-EOF PIC 9 VALUE 0.
48:     *
49:     PROCEDURE DIVISION.
50:     100-MAIN-LOGIC.
51:         OPEN INPUT INPUT-FILE
52:              OUTPUT REPORT-FILE.
53:         READ INPUT-FILE INTO PRINT-LINE
54:             AT END MOVE 1 TO WS-EOF.
55:         PERFORM 200-READ-WRITE UNTIL WS-EOF = 1.
56:         CLOSE INPUT-FILE, REPORT-FILE.
57:         STOP RUN.
58:     *
59:     200-READ-WRITE.
60:         WRITE PRINT-LINE AFTER 1 LINE.
61:         READ INPUT-FILE INTO PRINT-LINE
62:             AT END MOVE 1 TO WS-EOF.
```

INPUT-FILE

```
0900LOVE SEAT      20 09800
0950HUTCH TOP      20 08400
1500SOFA           14 08500
1700LOVE SEAT      17 08400
1800DOUBLE SOFA    24 18600
3000ARMCHAIR       24 16699
4000LOUNGE CHAIR   08 06700
```

WRITE

REPORT-FILE

```
0900LOVE SEAT      20 09800
0950HUTCH TOP      20 08400
1500SOFA           14 08500
1700LOVE SEAT      17 08400
1800DOUBLE SOFA    24 18600
3000ARMCHAIR       24 16699
4000LOUNGE CHAIR   08 06700
```

FIGURE 10–2
READING A DISK FILE

some may be fired, the marital status and the number of exemptions may change, certain employees may be promoted thereby causing a change in their pay/salary formula, et cetera. Clearly the files must be updated to reflect such changes before paychecks can be written. In any type of information-processing system, one or more of the following tasks will generally need to be performed:

1. Creating files.
2. Merging files, i.e., combining the records of two or more files into one new file.
3. Adding records.
4. Deleting records.
5. Changing individual items within file records.
6. Generating detailed or summary reports.

Such processes are illustrated in Figure 10-3, where a master file is created and then run against a transaction file to produce a newly updated master file. In real-life applications, of course, the updated master file becomes the current master file, which then evolves into new updated master files as a result of new transactions.

10-2-2 THE NEED FOR EXTERNAL STORAGE MEDIA

Most business applications of computers require the processing of masses of data (mailing lists, directories, catalogues, et cetera) that cannot be wholly contained in memory at one time because of the sheer volume of data. Other applications, such as payrolls and inventories, require that an existing body of data be changed or updated frequently. Both types of data are generally stored temporarily on some external storage medium. Typical external storage media are magnetic tape, magnetic disk, flexible magnetic disks (diskettes) and hard disks, which are now commonly used on microcomputer systems. COBOL allows the user to select and work with all these storage media.

In selecting a particular storage medium, the user should consider carefully the following storage characteristics: portability, storage capacity, processing speeds, cost, and convenience.

10-2-3 MASS STORAGE DEVICES

Magnetic Tape

With the rapidly changing technology of mass storage devices, magnetic tapes, like punched cards, are becoming less and less common in most typical computing installations. However, their distinct advantages over most other types of external storage devices, particularly magnetic disks, lie in the following:

1. Their portability and size, i.e., the ease with which they can be carried and sent through the mails.
2. Their relative low cost. For example, a typical 2400-foot tape may sell for $20.00 or so and may hold approximately 40 million characters (the equivalent of roughly 40 copies of this book).
3. Their ease of storage. Tapes can be stored on shelves like books on library racks. The Social Security and Internal Revenue Service main offices serve as repositories for literally hundreds of thousands of magnetic tapes (see Figure 10-4).

SEQUENTIAL FILE PROCESSING

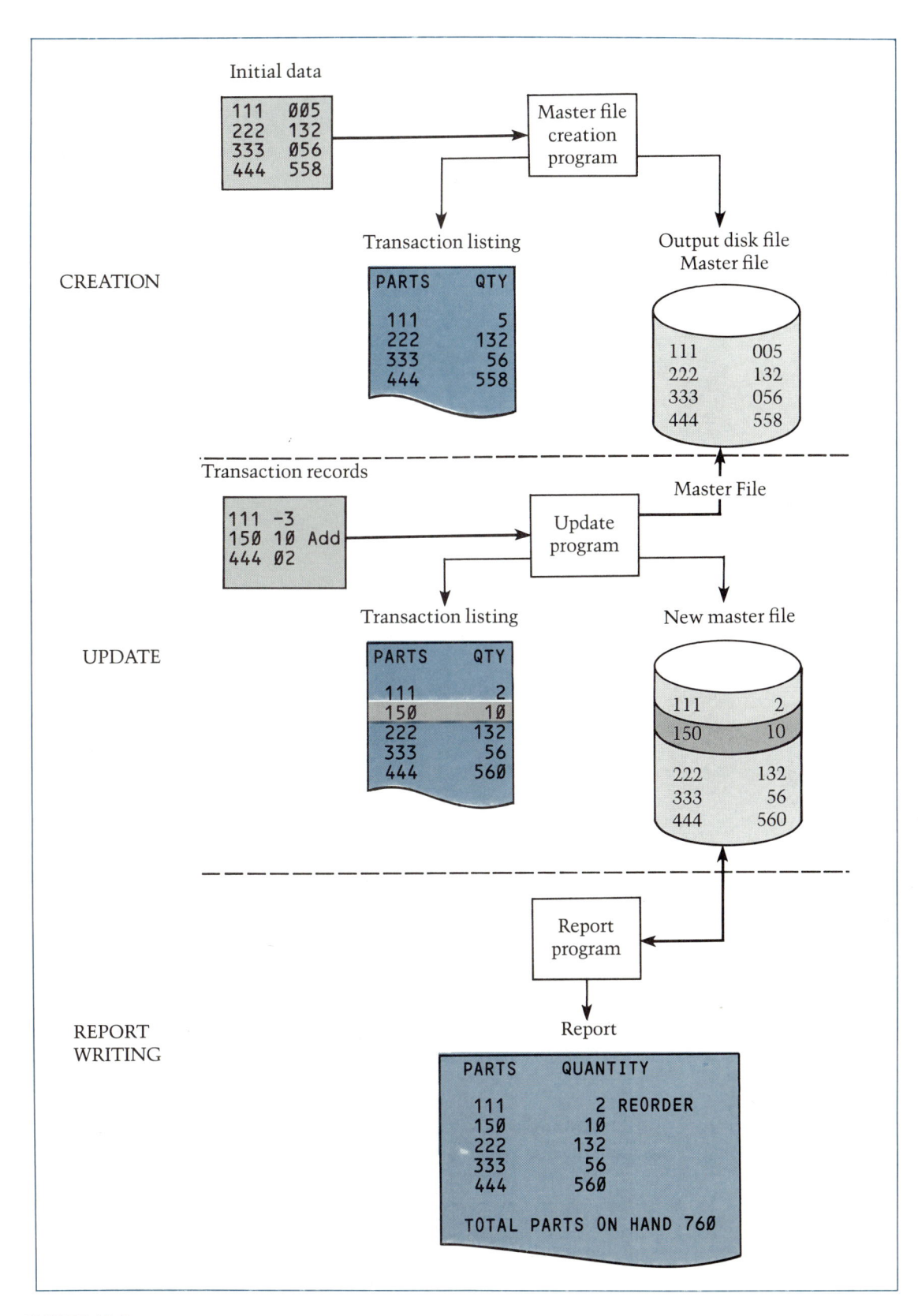

FIGURE 10–3
FILE-PROCESSING TASKS

FIGURE 10–4
MAGNETIC TAPE LIBRARY

Physical Characteristics

Data can be recorded on tapes using different densities. Typical recording densities are 800, 1600, and 6,250 characters per inch of tape (two or three pages of this text could be compressed into one inch of tape with a recording density of 6,250 characters per inch). Each character is represented by a vertical combination of magnetic spots, as shown in Figure 10–5.

Typical tape drives (physical devices on which magnetic tapes are mounted for reading and writing purposes; see Figure 10–5) can read up to 200 inches of tape per second. Thus at a density of 1600 characters per inch, approximately 300,000 characters can be read per second (the average human eye can read anywhere from 50 to 150 characters per second). All magnetic tapes are externally and internally labeled for identification and security reasons. Such internal labels can be processed by the operating system, through COBOL, if the user so desires.

Blocking

Records on magnetic tape are usually *blocked* to optimize transmission of data between tape and memory and to economize on the use of tape. To better grasp the meaning of blocking, consider a record that is 80 columns long; i.e., every

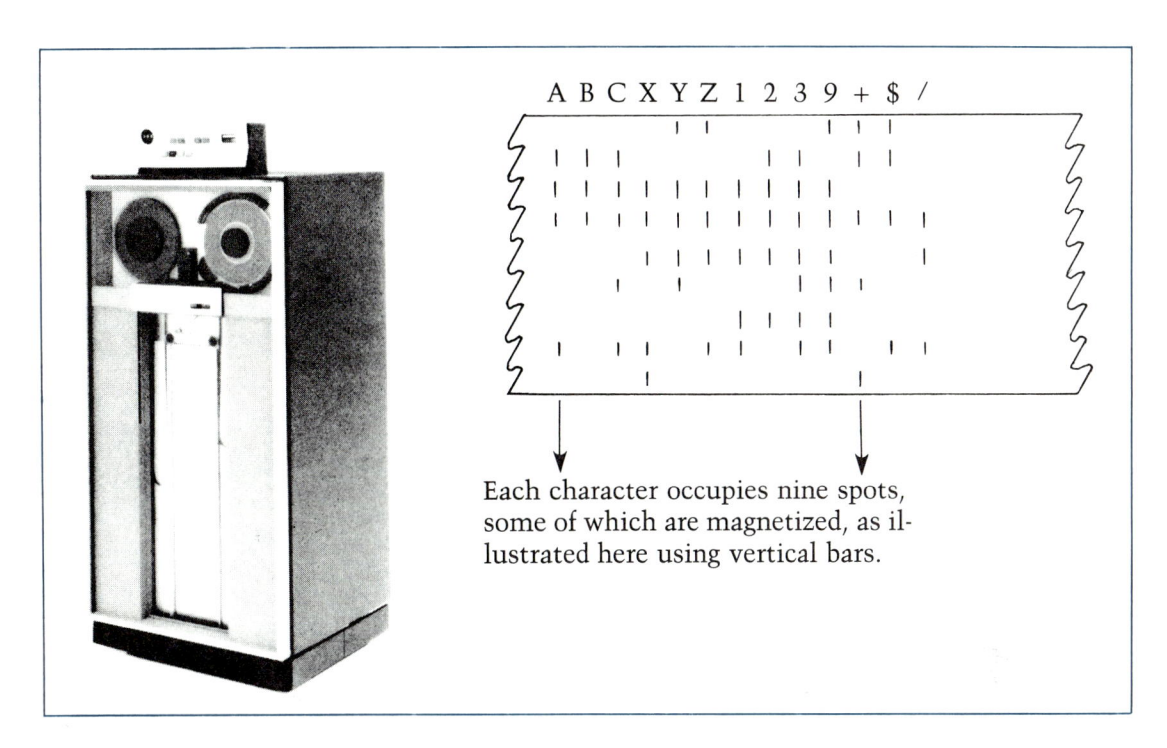

FIGURE 10–5
A MAGNETIC TAPE DRIVE AND SAMPLE NINE-CHANNEL TAPE CHARACTERS.
(Courtesy of IBM Corporation)

time the computer reads a record, it physically reads 80 columns of information. To the programmer, such a record generally represents one logical record, i.e., a record that is further subdivided into many logically related fields or subfields, which add up to 80 positions and whose descriptions are provided in the FILE or WORKING–STORAGE section of the DATA division.

Since magnetic tape is a continuous unbroken strip of tape, neither a physical nor a logical record is limited to 80 characters. A physical tape record can be arbitrarily large or small. The programmer, for instance, may decide that all his/her physical records are going to be 80 characters (positions) long or that they are all going to be 1600 positions long. At this point there is no distinction between physical and logical records. On the tape itself, however, all such blocks of data (whether 80 or 1600 characters long) would be separated from one another by interrecord gaps (called IRG or IBG, interblock gaps). Tape drives require that each physical record (block of data) be separated from one another by 0.6 inch of tape. Such gaps allow the tape drive to stop and start and allow tape positioning ahead of or after a particular record. The following diagram shows how physical records of different size are arranged on tape (one record is 80 characters long, while the other is 16,000 characters long):

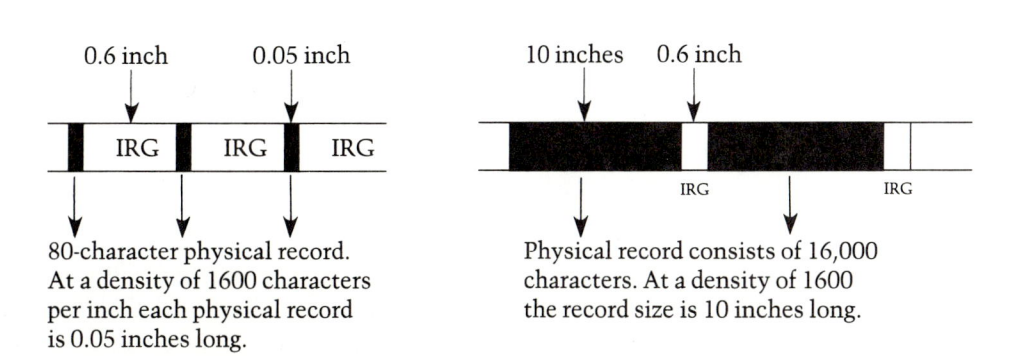

80-character physical record. At a density of 1600 characters per inch each physical record is 0.05 inches long.

Physical record consists of 16,000 characters. At a density of 1600 the record size is 10 inches long.

The important point to keep in mind is that when data is read from a tape, a complete physical record (block of data) between two interrecord gaps is read, not just one item of the record, then another item of the same record, et cetera. In our examples, either 0.05 inch (80 characters) or 10 inches (16,000 characters) is read at one time from tape (disk) to memory.

The programmer often works with small records—for example, records that are 40 or 80 positions long. Writing such records on tape means that each physical record is minuscule (0.025 or 0.05 inch for a 40- or 80-character record) in comparison to the interrecord gaps that separate each physical record. With such small record lengths, 90% of the tape is consumed by interrecord gaps; this is not only wasteful in terms of tape, but also inefficient in terms of the many READ or WRITE statements needed to capture all the minuscule physical records.

To make tape processing more efficient, logical records are grouped together to form a block of data (physical record) of more reasonable size. The programmer, for example, might specify that 10 logical records of 80 positions each will make up one physical record. Such a block of data (physical record) will then be $10 \times 80 = 800$ characters long and will occupy 0.5 inch of tape if a recording density of 1600 is used, as opposed to 5.9 inches of tape if ten separate physical records had been used (9 interrecord gaps + 10 times 0.05 = 5.9 inches). Logical records have thus been blocked. The following diagram illustrates a physical record consisting of 10 logical records, each 80 characters long.

10 logical records make up one physical record.
A block of 10 logical records, each 80 positions, occupies half an inch of tape at 1600 density.

When there are 10 records per physical tape record and a blocking factor of 10 is specified for an input file in a COBOL program, 10 logical records are actually read into memory at one time every time data is transmitted from tape to memory. As far as the programmer is concerned, however, each READ statement actually processes only one logical record, i.e., the system automatically makes available one logical record at a time for each READ statement. This process is known as *deblocking* and is performed automatically by the COBOL program/system whenever the BLOCK clause is specified in the file description paragraph. For an output file the BLOCK clause will specify the number of records to be written in a block on the disk/tape file. The system will automatically accumulate 10 logical records in its output *buffer* (memory area) before it writes them on tape as one block of data.

The reader may wonder why all the data that is to be stored on tape cannot be blocked into one gigantic physical record, to save on tape space and to cause only one physical transmission of data between tape and memory. The reason against such a practice is threefold:

1. Most tape drives limit a physical record to no more than approximately 32,000 characters.

2. If a READ or WRITE error occurs during an input/out operation on tape (bad tape area), the entire physical record may be lost.

3. Transmission of a 32,000-character record from tape to memory (or vice versa) would require a memory area of 32,000 positions into which the rec-

ord is to be received (or from which the record is to be written to tape). This is a very large chunk of memory, and many systems cannot afford to use such large areas of memory for input/output purposes.

Magnetic Disk

Data is recorded in the form of magnetic spots along a series of concentric circles or tracks on each surface of a magnetic disk plate. The number of tracks and the number of disk plates vary from one device to another. In any event, each track holds the same number of characters whether it is the innermost or the outermost track. Figure 10–6 shows a magnetic disk drive, a diskette, and a hard disk (microcomputer).

Magnetic tape is a sequential storage medium; i.e., if a record positioned near the end of the tape is to be retrieved, the entire tape must be read before the desired record is processed. The amount of time required for accessing any record on tape precludes using magnetic tape in situations where instantaneous retrieval of data is required. The main advantages of magnetic disk over magnetic tape are:

1. Records can be accessed directly without searching through preceding records. Access time is measured in fractions of a second.

2. Storage capabilities. Many magnetic disks can literally store hundreds of millions of characters.

3. For disk files whose records are not organized sequentially, individual records can be modified right where the physical records actually lie. This cannot be done with tapes.

4. Similarity to tape. Data can be organized on disk the same way as data can be organized on magnetic tape.

Just as with magnetic tape, disk records can also be blocked to optimize disk-processing efficiency. Because of the many hardware differences between magnetic disks, the reader is advised to consult his/her installation's technical reference manual to determine the best procedure for blocking records. As in the case of magnetic tapes, internal file labels on magnetic disks can be processed through COBOL.

FIGURE 10–6
MAGNETIC DISK DRIVES, DISKETTES, AND HARD DISK

10-3 SEQUENTIAL FILE PROCESSING

Due to the sequential nature of magnetic tape, records are generally stored on tape in sequential fashion according to some particular identification field within the record itself; i.e., associated with each record is some identifying field, sometimes referred to as the *key* field. For example, a personnel file might use the employee's social security or employee number as a key field or record key, as shown in the diagram below:

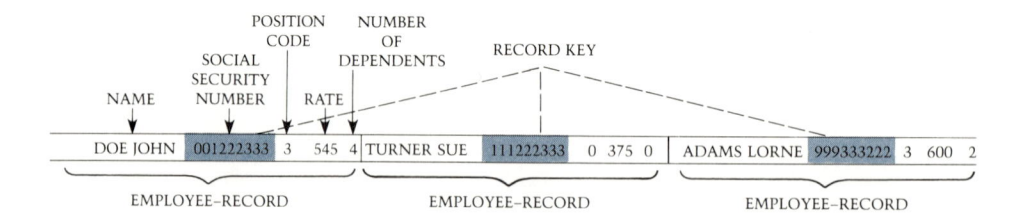

```
                  POSITION    NUMBER
                    CODE        OF
           SOCIAL            DEPENDENTS    RECORD KEY
           SECURITY
   NAME    NUMBER    RATE
    ↓         ↓       ↓  ↓        ↓              |
  DOE JOHN 001222333 3 545 4 | TURNER SUE 111222333 0 375 0 | ADAMS LORNE 999333222 3 600 2
  _____/   _____/       _____/
       EMPLOYEE-RECORD           EMPLOYEE-RECORD               EMPLOYEE-RECORD
```

An accounts receivable file might use the customer's account number as a key field. A name field for a key may not be a judicious selection since identical names may occur. In any event, key fields are used for record identification during a file update or an inquiry process.

A common way to organize a file is to prepare the records in such a way that key fields are arranged in sequential order (either ascending or descending). Such files can then be recorded on either magnetic tape or on disk. If ascending sequence is used, each succeeding record has a key field value larger than the key field of the preceding record. It should be noted that disk files need not be organized sequentially; other types of file organization, such as indexed sequential, are discussed in chapter 11.

Files in which records are organized sequentially are most often accessed in sequential fashion; i.e., the original records are processed by the program one after the other, in the order the records were recorded when the file was created. The logic to process sequentially organized files is essentially independent of the particular device on which the file is stored; i.e., the logic is the same whether the sequential file is stored on tape or on disk.

10-3-2 CREATION OF A SEQUENTIAL FILE

Records must first be sorted in sequence by key order. Data files can be created by means of text editors. Such files can then be read and processed by COBOL. **A COBOL program however, cannot update such data files directly;** i.e., it cannot insert or delete an item in the original data file in the same way the user can edit his/her file through the text editor. COBOL is not capable of such a function when a data file is not created through COBOL itself (the text editor's data file format is different from COBOL's file format). COBOL can save and reuse an updated file only if that file has been written by a COBOL program and stored on some external storage medium.

SEQUENTIAL FILE PROCESSING

It should be noted that when sequential files on tape are updated, the new updated file is always produced on another reel of tape. Changes cannot be made directly on the existing tape since, for example, all existing records to the right of an insert record would have to be propagated to the right! In the case of a disk file, the situation is somewhat different. If a full sequential update is to be performed (physical deletion, insertion of records, and changes to existing record fields) then a new updated file is always produced in another disk area, just as in the case of magnetic tape. Some COBOL systems, however, permit in-place updates, meaning that a particular field within an existing disk record can be changed and written over the same track area that it formerly occupied. The file is thus updated in place and no new file is created in the process. Such systems also make it possible to add records to the file by placing the added records after the last original record of the file. In these cases, those added records are not merged or sorted with the original records, and the file must be sorted before it can be processed sequentially. The features that deal with in-place sequential updates using the REWRITE and EXTEND statements, are discussed in detail in section 10-4-4.

Note that updating a sequential file **in place** does not generate a backup file. Indeed, should logical or hardware errors occur during the update process or should the file be inadvertently destroyed or lost (e.g., by fire or theft), all the original information would be lost. In most computer information-processing systems, at least two (and generally more) generations of backup files and associated transaction files are preserved.

10-3-3 COBOL INSTRUCTIONS FOR SEQUENTIAL FILES

ENVIRONMENT DIVISION Features

The general form for the SELECT and ASSIGN statement is:

```
SELECT file-name ASSIGN TO system-name-1
[ ORGANIZATION IS SEQUENTIAL ]
[ ACCESS MODE IS SEQUENTIAL  ]
```

where system-name-1 is a system name describing the particular hardware device.

The ORGANIZATION clause specifies the logical structure of the file. This clause is optional; it is used mainly for documentation purposes and to differentiate sequential organization from other types of organization such as indexed organization (discussed in chapter 11).

The ACCESS mode specifies the order in which records are read and written. The absence of this clause implies ACCESS MODE IS SEQUENTIAL.

DATA DIVISION Features.

Each SELECT/ASSIGN entry must have a corresponding file description entry in the FD entry of the FILE section. Additional clauses that can be specified in the FD entry when working with sequential files are shown on the next page:

```
FD file-name

[BLOCK CONTAINS [integer-1 TO] integer-2 {RECORDS / CHARACTERS}]

[RECORD CONTAINS [integer-3 TO] integer-4 CHARACTERS]

LABEL {RECORD IS / RECORDS ARE} {STANDARD / OMITTED}
```

If logical records are blocked (see section 10-2-3), the BLOCK CONTAINS clause must be used. If each logical record constitutes one physical block, the BLOCK clause may be omitted. Integer-1 and integer-2 refer to the minimum and maximum size of the physical record, respectively. If both integer-1 and integer-2 are specified, the physical record is a variable length record. If only integer-2 is specified, the physical record is a fixed length record.

Fixed length records

Example:

```
FD STUDENT-GRADES
    BLOCK CONTAINS 10 RECORDS
    LABEL RECORDS ARE STANDARD
    DATA RECORD IS STUDENT-REC.
01 STUDENT-REC
    SR-TEST1 PIC 999V99.
    SR-TEST2 PIC 999V99.
    SR-FINAL PIC 999.
```

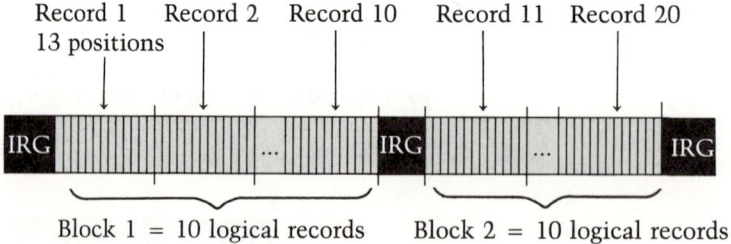

Record 1, Record 2, Record 10, Record 11, Record 20
13 positions

Block 1 = 10 logical records   Block 2 = 10 logical records

1 physical record = 1 block = 10 × 13 = 130 positions
Each block of data contains exactly 10 records.

The first READ STUDENT–GRADES statement in the PROCEDURE division will cause a block of 10 logical records to be read from the particular tape/disk device into a special area of memory called an *input buffer*; at the same time, the first logical record is moved into the FD input record area. The second time the READ statement is carried out, the second logical record, already in the input buffer, is moved to the FD input record area. This process continues until, finally, the tenth time the READ statement is carried out, the tenth logical record in the input buffer is moved into the FD record area. This procedure of making logical records available for each execution of the READ statement is called *deblocking*; deblocking is performed automatically by the system without the user ever becoming aware of it. The eleventh time the READ statement is carried out, a new block of data (10 logical records) is read and the dispersion of these 10 logical records proceeds in the manner described above. Writing with blocked records implies that the physical transfer of the block of logical records to the tape/disk is delayed until a sufficient number of logical records have been collected in the buffer to constitute a block.

SEQUENTIAL FILE PROCESSING 545

Variable length records Records can be made variable in length in either of two ways:

1. By specifying multiple record definitions and records of different sizes in the FILE section.
2. By using the DEPENDING ON clause in table description entries in the FILE SECTION.

EXAMPLE 1:

```
FD PAYROLL
   LABEL RECORDS ARE STANDARD
   RECORD CONTAINS 50 TO 80 CHARACTERS
   BLOCK CONTAINS 1 RECORDS
   DATA RECORDS ARE TYPE1, TYPE2.
01 TYPE1.
   05 FILLER PIC X(50).
01 TYPE2.
   05 FILLER PIC X(80).
```

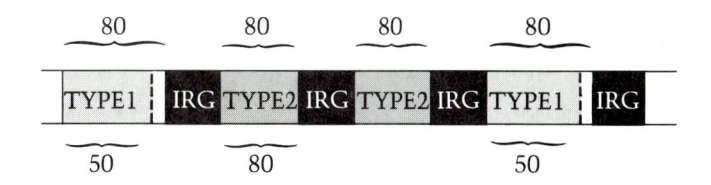

$$\underbrace{}_{80}\ \underbrace{}_{80}\ \underbrace{}_{80}\ \underbrace{}_{80}$$

| TYPE1 | IRG | TYPE2 | IRG | TYPE2 | IRG | TYPE1 | IRG |

$$\underbrace{}_{50}\ \underbrace{}_{80}\ \underbrace{}_{50}$$

It is assumed these records are moved into record description entries in WORKING–STORAGE.

EXAMPLE 2:

```
FD STUDENT-GRADES
   BLOCK CONTAINS 1 RECORDS
   LABEL RECORDS ARE STANDARD
   RECORD CONTAINS 15 TO 30 CHARACTERS
   DATA RECORD IS STUDENT-REC.
01 STUDENT-REC.
   05 SR-NAME PIC X(14).
   05 SR-NO-QUIZZES PIC 9.  ◄────┐
   05 SCORES OCCURS 0 TO 5 TIMES PIC 999
      DEPENDING ON  SR-NO-QUIZZES. ────┘
```

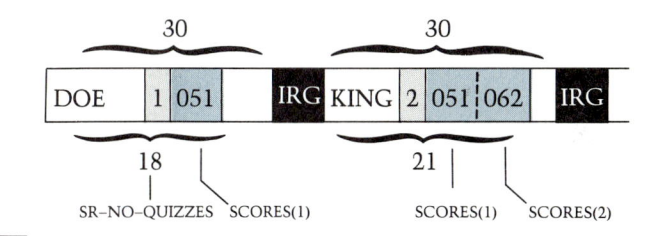

$$\underbrace{}_{30}\ \underbrace{}_{30}$$

| DOE | 1 | 051 | IRG | KING | 2 | 051 | 062 | IRG |

  18   21
SR-NO-QUIZZES SCORES(1)   SCORES(1) SCORES(2)

STUDENT-REC can occupy anywhere from 15 characters (14 positions for NAME and 1 position for NO-QUIZZES) to 30 characters (15 for NAME and NO-QUIZZES and 15 for 5 possible test scores). Hence the block size is 30 characters.

The LABEL RECORDS clause is required for all files. If the LABEL RECORD IS STANDARD option is specified for a given file, the operating system (or COBOL itself) will automatically write internal label records on any device that is designated as an output file. These labels will then be processed or inspected before the file is processed. Header and trailer labels are written at the beginning and at the end of the data file and will generally deal with identification, dates, number of records, et cetera. In an installation with literally thousands of tapes/ disk packs, it is critical that the program process the intended tape/disk pack.

If LABEL RECORDS ARE OMITTED, no label processing is performed by the system, i.e., labels are not written by the system on the data file. In such a case, the user may or may not want to write his/her own labels (as a special first record, for example).

PROCEDURE Division Statements

For tape or disk processing, the OPEN and CLOSE statements must appear in the PROCEDURE division. The general forms of the OPEN and CLOSE verbs are as follows:

```
OPEN  { INPUT  }  file-name ...
      { OUTPUT }
      { I-O    }

CLOSE  file-name  [ { REEL } WITH { NO REWIND } ] ...
                  [ { UNIT }      { LOCK      } ]
```

The OPEN statement initiates the processing of mass storage files. If STANDARD labels are used, the opening of an input file causes the internal labels to be checked in accordance with the system conventions for input label checking. If an error condition arises, the operating system will terminate the program. When an output file is opened with the standard label option, the appropriate header label is written.

The I–O option can be used only for disk files. It allows the program to process a file both as an input and an output file; i.e., a record can be read from one file and then rewritten (changed) on the same file.

Any file may be opened with the INPUT, OUTPUT and I–O attribute in the same program. Each subsequent OPEN for a given file must be preceded by the execution of a CLOSE statement. However, a file that has been locked (LOCK option) may not be reopened during the execution of the program that locked the file (protection of file).

The CLOSE verb can be carried out only on files that have been previously OPENed. When an output file is closed, a new trailer label is written on the file if the STANDARD LABEL option is specified, and an end-of-file mark is written on the file. If a STOP RUN is executed before a particular output file is closed, the end-of-file marker may not be written on that file, leading to potential problems. A file that has been CLOSEd cannot be processed without an intervening OPEN.

When a tape file is closed, the tape is rewound automatically. The NO REWIND option prevents the tape from being rewound. This option can be used, for example, to write different files on one particular tape. Some applications may require processing of multireel tapes or multidisk units. In such a case, when an intermediary tape/unit has been processed, the option REEL will close the physical unit while leaving the particular file still logically opened.

10-4 COMMON FILE-PROCESSING TASKS

10-4-1 INTRODUCTION

As discussed in section 10–1, file-processing applications generally involve processing distinct master and transaction files that are usually stored on various external storage media. The records in sequential files are sorted in a particular

SEQUENTIAL FILE PROCESSING   **547**

order; typically, a particular item or a group item that is present in all the records of the files is selected as a key to order the various records. This key is then used by the program to process the records sequentially. The key also identifies each record uniquely. Names are not generally "good" keys, since names may be identical. In a personnel file, social security numbers insure uniqueness. When updating sequentially organized files, both master and transaction files must be sequenced on the same key.

Updating a file generally involves one or more of the following activities:

1. Adding new records (merging a transaction file with a master file).
2. Deleting existing records from a file.
3. Changing record items within a file.

10-4-2 MERGING

Many file-processing activities deal with the merging of files. Suppose that two files are sorted into ascending (or descending) order by a key field common to both file records and that we want to combine the two files into a single file that is also sorted into ascending (or descending) key order. For example, one of the files could be a transaction file and the other a master file. A straightforward approach for solving this problem is illustrated in Figure 10-7. The letter T refers to the transaction key record and the letter M to the master key record. Initially, both T and M are read. If T is less than M, the transaction record is written on the new file (the one producing the merged file). If T is greater than M, the master file record is written on the new file. Eventually one of the files will run out of records and all remaining records of the last active file will be copied on the new file.

The COBOL code to capture the logic of Figure 10-7 is shown in Figure 10-8. TRANSACTION-FILE consists of records that contain a furniture item number, an item description, an item quantity, and an item cost. A master file

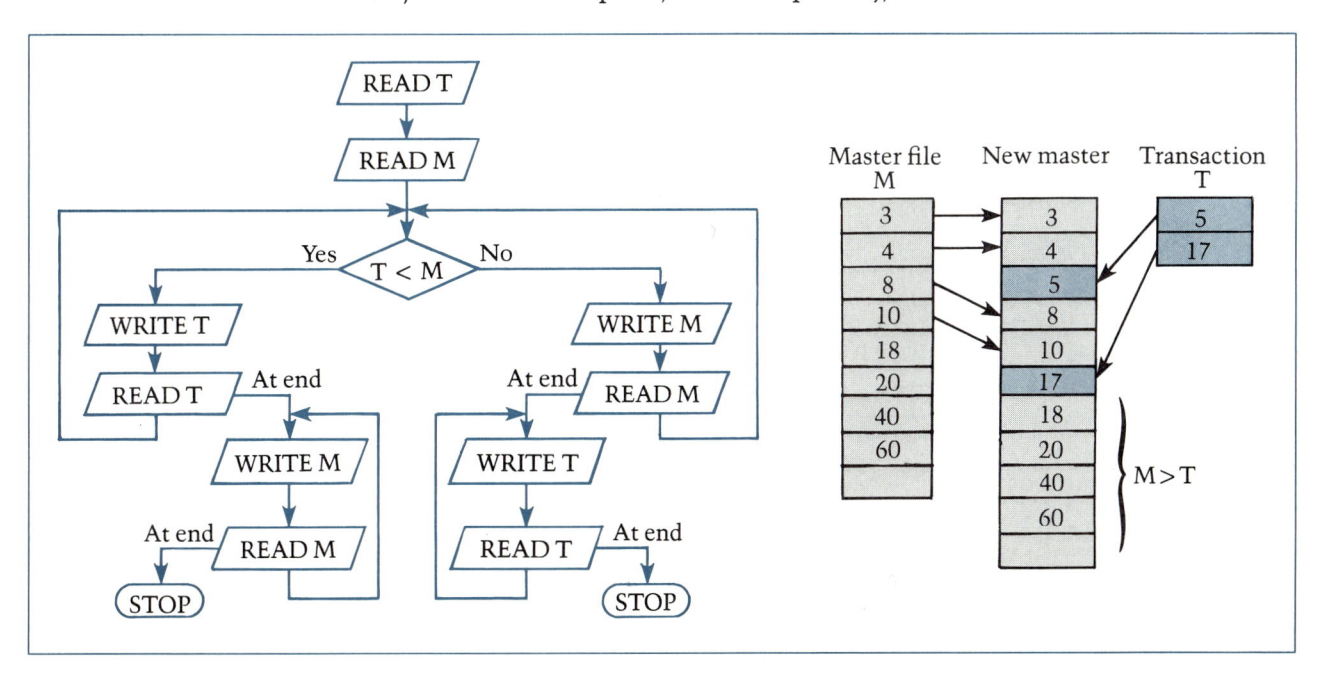

FIGURE 10-7
A FIRST TRY AT MERGING

548   UNDERSTANDING STRUCTURED COBOL

```
005    IDENTIFICATION DIVISION.
010    PROGRAM-ID. MERGE.
015    *******************************
020    * A  M E R G E   P R O B L E M *
025    *******************************
030    AUTHOR. JONES.
035    ENVIRONMENT DIVISION.
040    CONFIGURATION SECTION.
050    SOURCE-COMPUTER. IBM.
060    OBJECT-COMPUTER. IBM.
070    INPUT-OUTPUT SECTION.
080    FILE-CONTROL.
090    *
100    SELECT TRANSACTION-FILE ASSIGN TO DISKPACK.
110    SELECT MASTER-FILE      ASSIGN TO DISKPACK.
120    SELECT NEW-MASTER-FILE  ASSIGN TO DISKPACK.
130    SELECT PRINT-FILE       ASSIGN TO PRINTER.
140    *
150    DATA DIVISION.
160    FILE SECTION.
170    *
180    FD  TRANSACTION-FILE
190        LABEL RECORDS ARE STANDARD
200        DATA RECORD IS TRANSACTION-RECORD.
210    01  TRANSACTION-RECORD.
220        05 TRANSACTION-KEY PIC 9(06).
230        05 TR-DESCR        PIC X(15).
240        05 TR-PART-QTY     PIC 99.
250        05 TR-PART-COST    PIC 999V99.
260    *
270    FD  MASTER-FILE
280        LABEL RECORDS ARE STANDARD
290        DATA RECORD IS MASTER-RECORD.
300    01  MASTER-RECORD.
310        05 MASTER-KEY      PIC 9(06).
320        05 MR-DESCR        PIC X(15).
330        05 MR-PART-QTY     PIC 99.
340        05 MR-PART-COST    PIC 999V99.
350    *
360    FD  NEW-MASTER-FILE
370        LABEL RECORDS ARE STANDARD
380        DATA RECORD IS NEW-MASTER-RECORD.
390    01  NEW-MASTER-RECORD PIC X(28).
400    *
410    FD  PRINT-FILE
420        LABEL RECORDS ARE OMITTED
430        DATA RECORD IS PRINT-LINE.
440    01  PRINT-LINE PIC X(132).
450    *
460    WORKING-STORAGE SECTION.
470    77  EOF-MASTER-FILE     PIC 9 VALUE 0.
480        88 END-OF-MASTER-FILE      VALUE IS 1.
490    77  EOF-TRANSACTION-FILE PIC 9 VALUE 0.
500        88 END-OF-TRANSACTION-FILE VALUE IS 1.
510    *
```

TRANSACTION-FILE
```
192400BUFFET CHAIR    2009500
192705SEATING PIECE   1504450
193810LAZY JOE        2611999
```

MASTER-FILE
```
192598CAPTAINS CHAIR  3090000
192695CATKIN CHAIR    1014599
192700MATES CHAIR     0910000
193656TRESTLE BENCH   1516000
193800HUTCH TOP       1319999
```

NEW-MASTER-FILE
```
192400BUFFET CHAIR    2009500
192598CAPTAINS CHAIR  3090000
192695CATKIN CHAIR    1014599
192700MATES CHAIR     0910000
192705SEATING PIECE   1504450
193656TRESTLE BENCH   1516000
193800HUTCH TOP       1319999
193810LAZY JOE        2611999
```

MASTER-FILE resides on disk. Each MASTER-FILE record on disk occupies 28 positions.

NEW-MASTER-FILE also resides on disk. Each NEW-MASTER-FILE record on disk will occupy 28 positions.

FIGURE 10-8
MERGING FILES: VERSION 1

```
520    PROCEDURE DIVISION.
530    MAIN-LOGIC.
540        OPEN INPUT   TRANSACTION-FILE
550                     MASTER-FILE
560            OUTPUT   NEW-MASTER-FILE
570                     PRINT-FILE.
580  *
590        READ TRANSACTION-FILE
600            AT END DISPLAY "NO TRANSACTION DATA" STOP RUN.
610        READ MASTER-FILE
620            AT END DISPLAY "CHECK MASTER FILE " STOP RUN.
630  *
640        PERFORM MERGE-TRANSACTION-MASTER UNTIL
650            END-OF-TRANSACTION-FILE AND END-OF-MASTER-FILE.
660
670        CLOSE TRANSACTION-FILE
680              MASTER-FILE
690              NEW-MASTER-FILE
700              PRINT-FILE.
710        STOP RUN.
720  *
730    MERGE-TRANSACTION-MASTER.
740        IF TRANSACTION-KEY < MASTER-KEY
750            WRITE NEW-MASTER-RECORD FROM TRANSACTION-RECORD
760            WRITE PRINT-LINE        FROM TRANSACTION-RECORD
770            READ TRANSACTION-FILE
780                AT END MOVE 1 TO EOF-TRANSACTION-FILE
790                       PERFORM COPY-REST-OF-MASTER-FILE
800                       UNTIL END-OF-MASTER-FILE
804  *
808  *
809  *
810        ELSE
820            WRITE NEW-MASTER-RECORD FROM MASTER-RECORD
830            WRITE PRINT-LINE        FROM MASTER-RECORD
840            READ MASTER-FILE
850                AT END MOVE 1 TO EOF-MASTER-FILE
860                       PERFORM  COPY-REST-OF-TRANSACTION-FILE
870                       UNTIL END-OF-TRANSACTION-FILE.
880  *
885  *
887  *
890    COPY-REST-OF-MASTER-FILE.
900        WRITE NEW-MASTER-RECORD FROM MASTER-RECORD.
910        WRITE PRINT-LINE        FROM MASTER-RECORD.
920        READ MASTER-FILE
930            AT END MOVE 1 TO EOF-MASTER-FILE.
940  *
950    COPY-REST-OF-TRANSACTION-FILE.
960        WRITE NEW-MASTER-RECORD FROM TRANSACTION-RECORD.
970        WRITE PRINT-LINE        FROM TRANSACTION-RECORD.
980        READ TRANSACTION-FILE
990            AT END MOVE 1 TO EOF-TRANSACTION-FILE.
```

Read a transaction record on the input file.

Read a record from the master file stored on disk or tape.

Go and merge both files until the end of file has been encountered on both files.

If the transaction key < master key, write out the transaction record on the new master file, then read the next transaction record and carry out the process again. If there are no more transaction records, go and copy all remaining master file records onto the new master file. When the end of file is encountered in the master file, control returns to line 650.

If the transaction key > master key, go and write the master record on the new master file and read the next master record. If there are no master records, go and copy all remaining transaction file records onto the new file. When the end of file is encountered on the transaction file, return is made to line 650.

Copy all remaining records of the master file onto the new master file.

Copy all remaining records of the transaction file onto the new master file.

FIGURE 10–8
(continued)

(MASTER–FILE) on disk contains similarly formatted records. The program in Figure 10–8 merges both files to produce NEW–MASTER–FILE, which is stored on disk (or tape). For example

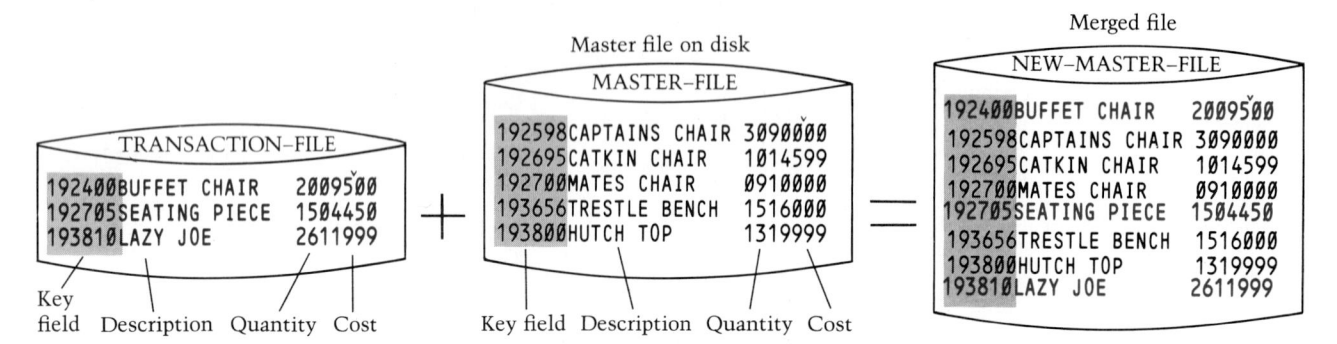

```
                                   Master file on disk           Merged file
                                      MASTER-FILE             NEW-MASTER-FILE

       TRANSACTION-FILE         192598CAPTAINS CHAIR 3090000  192400BUFFET CHAIR    2009500
                                192695CATKIN CHAIR   1014599  192598CAPTAINS CHAIR 3090000
  192400BUFFET CHAIR  2009500   192700MATES CHAIR    0910000  192695CATKIN CHAIR   1014599
  192705SEATING PIECE 1504450 + 193656TRESTLE BENCH  1516000 = 192700MATES CHAIR   0910000
  193810LAZY JOE      2611999   193800HUTCH TOP      1319999  192705SEATING PIECE  1504450
                                                              193656TRESTLE BENCH  1516000
  Key                                                         193800HUTCH TOP      1319999
  field Description Quantity Cost  Key field Description Quantity Cost  193810LAZY JOE      2611999
```

The key record used in the merging process is the six-digit furniture item number field.

An Improved Merging Technique with Sequence Check

A closer look at the flowchart of Figure 10–7 or at the program of Figure 10–8 reveals that the program could be improved in terms of structure. The two paragraphs COPY-REST-OF-MASTER-FILE and COPY-REST-OF-TRANSACTION-FILE (lines 890–990) in Figure 10–8 that copy the remaining records of the last active file when the end of the other file has been encountered are actually not necessary. Instead, when the end of file is encountered on one file, the record key for that file is set to its highest possible value (all 9's in this example) so that on subsequent key comparisons, the record keys of the remaining file will all be less than 999999 and hence all corresponding records of the last active file will automatically be written on the new file.

The improved flowchart and its corresponding COBOL code are shown in Figures 10–9 and 10–10, respectively. When the end of the remaining active file is reached, the corresponding record key for that file is also set to 999999, at which point the statement at line 670, PERFORM...UNTIL TRANSACTION-KEY = 999999 AND MASTER-KEY = 999999, is satisfied and the merging process stops. Note that instead of moving 999999 to TRANSACTION-KEY, we could have moved HIGH-VALUES to TRANSACTION-KEY. HIGH-VALUES is a figurative constant that sets a particular data item to its highest collating value. Since HIGH-VALUES is an alphanumeric literal, both keys should be declared with an X PICTURE.

Figure 10–10 also performs a sequence check on the transaction file (input file). Such a check should always be performed before creating a master file. Note that, to start the comparison (for the sequence check) between the first and second transaction keys, at line 770, the PREVIOUS-TRANSACTION-KEY is initialized to 0 at line 470. The figurative constant LOW-VALUE could also have been used to initialize PREVIOUS-TRANSACTION-KEY.

Note that the output listing identifies the records that are out of sequence, while those that are in sequence are merged.

10-4-3 CHANGING, INSERTING, AND DELETING RECORDS

As we have seen in section 10-4-2, the merging process combines two files into one, allowing the user to add new records to an existing file. Many times, though, we may want to selectively change one or more items within a particu-

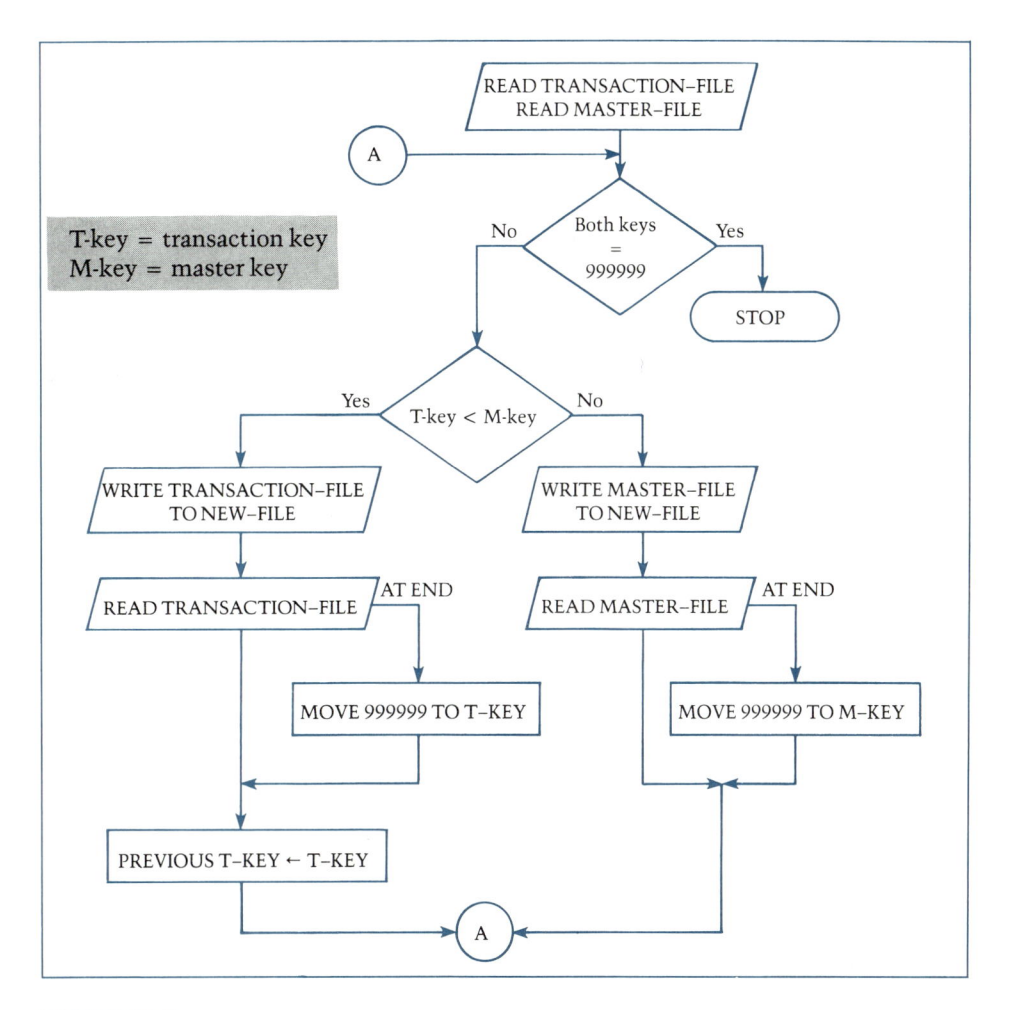

FIGURE 10-9
AN IMPROVED MERGE

lar record(s) or delete any number of records from the file. Because of hardware considerations, we cannot change one or more items in a record without rewriting the entire record onto a new file if sequential access methods are used to process the file (adding just one record implies rewriting an entire new master file!).

Let's consider, for example, how the inventory file maintenance system of a furniture retailer might work. New furniture models are added to the current line of furniture (new unit entries are inserted into the current inventory file), discontinued models are taken out of stock (units are deleted from the inventory), and supplier cost increases may force the retailer to reprice some or all furniture items in stock (cost changes in the existing inventory records). In addition, incoming shipments (receipts) of current models, and outgoing shipments (sales) of units also affect the current inventory. Master stock level entries need to be updated to reflect new stock levels.

Deleting or changing a particular record in a master file implies that a transaction record must identify which record in the master file is to be changed or deleted; i.e., for such an operation to take place, the transaction key must match a master file key. In addition, a transaction code is needed to indicate whether the particular transaction is a deletion or a change. Also, since more than one item in a record might be changed, other change codes or transaction codes may be needed to specify the particular operation and the particular item within the record.

552   UNDERSTANDING STRUCTURED COBOL

```
001    IDENTIFICATION DIVISION.
005    ***************************************
010    * M E R G I N G   T W O   F I L E S *
015    ***************************************
020    PROGRAM-ID. MERGE-FILES.
030    ENVIRONMENT DIVISION.
040    CONFIGURATION SECTION.
050    SOURCE-COMPUTER. BURROUGHS.
060    OBJECT-COMPUTER. BURROUGHS.
070    INPUT-OUTPUT SECTION.
080    FILE-CONTROL.
090    *
100    SELECT TRANSACTION-FILE ASSIGN TO DISKPACK.
110    SELECT MASTER-FILE      ASSIGN TO DISKPACK.
120    SELECT NEW-MASTER-FILE  ASSIGN TO DISKPACK.
130    SELECT PRINT-FILE       ASSIGN TO PRINTER.
140    *
150    DATA DIVISION.
160    FILE SECTION.
170    *
180    FD  TRANSACTION-FILE
190        LABEL RECORDS ARE STANDARD
200        DATA RECORD   IS TRANSACTION-RECORD.
210    01  TRANSACTION-RECORD.
220        05 TRANSACTION-KEY PIC 9(06).
230        05 TR-DESCR        PIC X(15).
240        05 TR-PART-QTY     PIC 99.
250        05 TR-PART-COST    PIC 999V99.
260    *
270    FD  MASTER-FILE
280        LABEL RECORDS ARE STANDARD
290        DATA RECORD   IS MASTER-RECORD.
300    01  MASTER-RECORD.
310        05 MASTER-KEY      PIC 9(06).
320        05 MR-DESCR        PIC X(15).
330        05 MR-PART-QTY     PIC 99.
340        05 MR-PART-COST    PIC 999V99.
350    *
360    FD  NEW-MASTER-FILE
370        LABEL RECORDS ARE STANDARD
380        DATA RECORD IS NEW-MASTER-RECORD.
390    01  NEW-MASTER-RECORD PIC X(28).
400    *
410    FD  PRINT-FILE
420        LABEL RECORDS ARE OMITTED
430        DATA RECORD IS PRINT-LINE.
440    01  PRINT-LINE PIC X(132).
450    *
460    WORKING-STORAGE SECTION.
470    77  PREVIOUS-TRANSACTION-KEY PIC 9(6) VALUE 0.
480    *
490    01  ERROR-LINE.
500        05 FILLER   PIC XXX    VALUE " **".
510        05 EL-ERROR PIC 9(6).
520        05 FILLER   PIC X(71)  VALUE " OUT OF SEQUENCE**".
```

Disk file to be updated

TRANSACTION FILE

192400BUFFET CHAIR   2009500
192200SEATING CHAIR   1508000
192300SEATING CHAIR   1509000
192705SEATING CHAIR   1407800
192605LAZY JOE   2014500

MASTER-FILE

192598CAPTAINS CHAIR 3090000
192695CATKIN CHAIR   1014599
192700MATES CHAIR   0910000
193656TRESTLE BENCH   1516000
193800HUTCH TOP   1319999

Transaction key

UPDATE PROGRAM

Updated file

NEW-MASTER-FILE

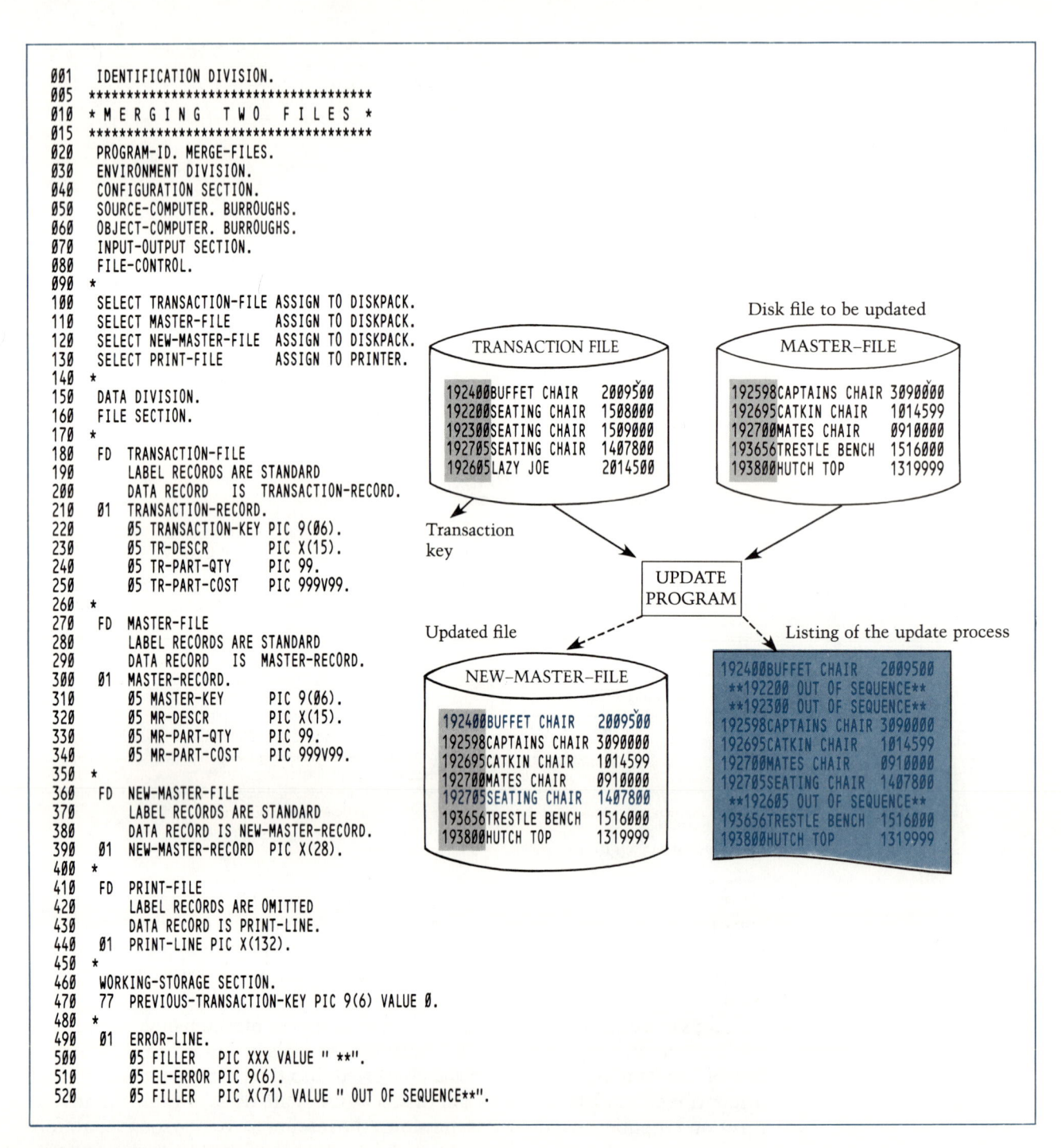

192400BUFFET CHAIR   2009500
192598CAPTAINS CHAIR 3090000
192695CATKIN CHAIR   1014599
192700MATES CHAIR   0910000
192705SEATING CHAIR   1407800
193656TRESTLE BENCH   1516000
193800HUTCH TOP   1319999

Listing of the update process

192400BUFFET CHAIR   2009500
192200 OUT OF SEQUENCE
192300 OUT OF SEQUENCE
192598CAPTAINS CHAIR 3090000
192695CATKIN CHAIR   1014599
192700MATES CHAIR   0910000
192705SEATING CHAIR   1407800
192605 OUT OF SEQUENCE
193656TRESTLE BENCH   1516000
193800HUTCH TOP   1319999

FIGURE 10–10

MERGING FILES: IMPROVED VERSION

```
550    PROCEDURE DIVISION.
560    MAIN-LOGIC.
570        OPEN INPUT   TRANSACTION-FILE
580                     MASTER-FILE
590             OUTPUT  NEW-MASTER-FILE
600                     PRINT-FILE.
620        PERFORM READ-TRANSACTION-FILE.
630        PERFORM READ-MASTER-FILE.
670        PERFORM SEQUENCE-CHECK-AND-MERGE UNTIL
680            TRANSACTION-KEY = 999999 AND MASTER-KEY = 999999.
700        CLOSE TRANSACTION-FILE
710              MASTER-FILE
720              NEW-MASTER-FILE
730              PRINT-FILE.
740        STOP RUN.
750    *
760    SEQUENCE-CHECK-AND-MERGE.
770        IF TRANSACTION-KEY < PREVIOUS-TRANSACTION-KEY
810            MOVE TRANSACTION-KEY TO EL-ERROR
820            WRITE PRINT-LINE FROM ERROR-LINE AFTER 1
821            PERFORM READ-TRANSACTION-FILE
822        ELSE
823            MOVE TRANSACTION-KEY TO PREVIOUS-TRANSACTION-KEY
824            PERFORM MERGE-TRANSACTION-MASTER.
830    *
840    MERGE-TRANSACTION-MASTER.
850        IF TRANSACTION-KEY < MASTER-KEY
860            WRITE NEW-MASTER-RECORD FROM TRANSACTION-RECORD
870            WRITE PRINT-LINE       FROM TRANSACTION-RECORD
880            PERFORM READ-TRANSACTION-FILE
900        ELSE
910            WRITE NEW-MASTER-RECORD FROM MASTER-RECORD
920            WRITE PRINT-LINE       FROM MASTER-RECORD
930            PERFORM READ-MASTER-FILE.
940    *
941    READ-TRANSACTION-FILE.
942        READ TRANSACTION-FILE
943            AT END MOVE 999999 TO TRANSACTION-KEY.
944    *
945    READ-MASTER-FILE.
946        READ MASTER-FILE
947            AT END MOVE 999999 TO MASTER-KEY.
```

Read the first transaction file record.
Read the first master file record.
Verify ascending sequence of transaction records and merge if appropriate.

If the next transaction record is less than the previous transaction record, the transaction record just read is out of sequence. Write an error message. Go and read the next transaction record.

If record is in sequence, go and merge.

If transaction key is less than the master key, go and write the transaction record on new file and read a new transaction record.

If master key is less than the transaction key, go and write the master record; then go and read a new master record.

If this is the end of the transaction file, move highest value into the transaction key. All master keys from then on will be less than the transaction key; hence all master records will be transferred to the new file.

The process in the preceding paragraph is carried out for the master file.

FIGURE 10–10
(continued)

Program Update Example

Consider the transaction file and the old master file in Figure 10–11. The master file consists of records containing an item number (master key), an item description, a quantity on hand, and a corresponding item cost. The transaction file consists of a transaction key, an item description, an item quantity, a corresponding item cost, and a one-digit transaction code defined as follows:

TRANSACTION CODE	OPERATION
1	Delete record.
2	Insert record.
3	Replace cost entry in master file by cost entry in transaction file.
4	Add transaction item quantity to item quantity in master file.

554   UNDERSTANDING STRUCTURED COBOL

TRANSACTION FILE RECORDS.

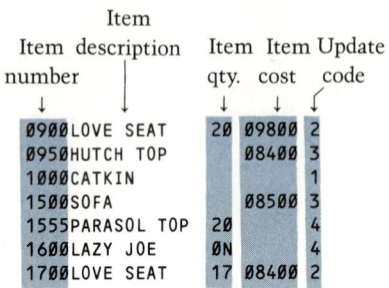

```
        Item
Item description  Item  Item  Update
number            qty.  cost  code
   ↓       ↓       ↓     ↓     ↓
0900LOVE SEAT     20   09800  2
0950HUTCH TOP          08400  3
1000CATKIN                    1
1500SOFA               08500  3
1555PARASOL TOP   20          4
1600LAZY JOE      0N          4
1700LOVE SEAT     17   08400  2
```

Meaning of Update Code

Insert new item no. 0900 in its appropriate place in the master file.
Replace the cost of item 950 by $84.00 in the master file.
Delete item 1000 from the master file.

Subtract 5 (0N = −5) from current stock of item 1600 in master file.

MASTER FILE RECORDS

```
Item     Item         Item  Item
Number   Description  Qty.  Cost
  ↓         ↓          ↓     ↓
1000CATKIN         30  09000
1500SOFA           34  09800
1600LAZY JOE       21  14500
3000ARMCHAIR       17  16699
```

THE UPDATE PROCESS

OLD-MASTER-FILE
```
1000CATKIN      30 09000
1500SOFA        34 09800
1600LAZY JOE    21 14500
3000ARMCHAIR    17 16699
```

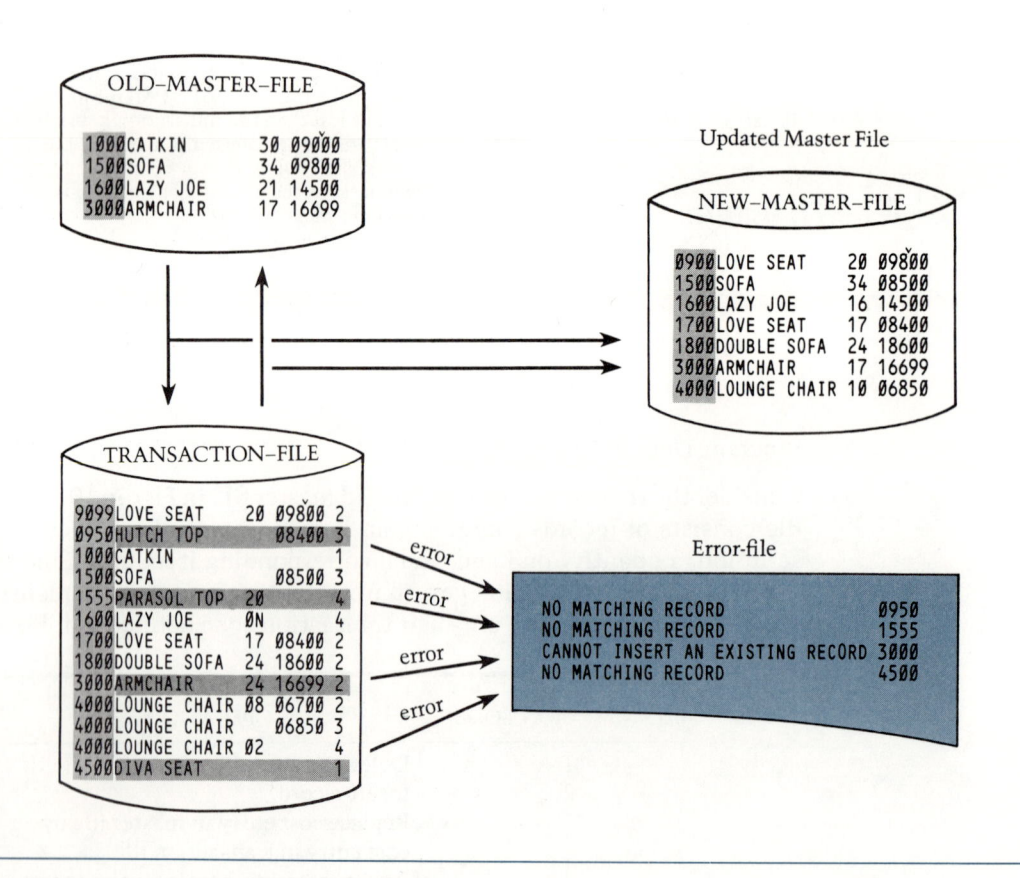

Updated Master File

NEW-MASTER-FILE
```
0900LOVE SEAT      20 09800
1500SOFA           34 08500
1600LAZY JOE       16 14500
1700LOVE SEAT      17 08400
1800DOUBLE SOFA    24 18600
3000ARMCHAIR       17 16699
4000LOUNGE CHAIR   10 06850
```

TRANSACTION-FILE
```
9099LOVE SEAT       20 09800 2
0950HUTCH TOP          08400 3
1000CATKIN                   1
1500SOFA               08500 3
1555PARASOL TOP     20       4
1600LAZY JOE        0N       4
1700LOVE SEAT       17 08400 2
1800DOUBLE SOFA     24 18600 2
3000ARMCHAIR        24 16699 2
4000LOUNGE CHAIR    08 06700 2
4000LOUNGE CHAIR       06850 3
4000LOUNGE CHAIR    02       4
4500DIVA SEAT                1
```

Error-file
```
NO MATCHING RECORD              0950
NO MATCHING RECORD              1555
CANNOT INSERT AN EXISTING RECORD 3000
NO MATCHING RECORD              4500
```

FIGURE 10-11
FILES IN A COMPLETE UPDATE SYSTEM

Both the master file and the transaction file *must* be arranged in ascending item number sequence if a sequential update is to be successful. It is, of course, possible to introduce errors (other than sequence errors in master and transaction file) in the update process through the transaction records. Errors can occur when an attempt is made to:

1. Delete a record that does not exist in the master file (transaction code = 1 and no match for transaction key in master file).

2. Insert a record that already exists in the master file (transaction code = 2 and transaction key already exists in master file).

3. Make a change to a record not present in the master file (transaction code = 3 or 4 and transaction key is not present in master file).

Step-by-Step Analysis

The complete logic to solve the inventory update problem is illustrated in flowchart form in Figure 10–12 and in Figure 10–13 for the COBOL program.

It is easy to get lost in the maze of activity in the flowchart or in the program code. Yet the logic of the problem revolves around one very simple but crucial observation: when a record is MOVEd to the new-master-record for output purposes, it is not actually written on disk at that time. The signal for the actual WRITE operation depends on what the next record is! For example, suppose we have just moved an insert record (e.g., item number 900) to new-master-record. It is "too early" to WRITE new-master-record, since the next transaction record could specify a change for item 900 (e.g., a change in its cost or quantity field). If this is the case, the change can easily be made while the record for item 900 is still in new-master-record. If, however, the next transaction record involves a different item number, *then* it is time to write the contents of new-master-record (item 900) onto disk.

In the flowchart of Figure 10–12, first a master (M–KEY) and a transaction (T–KEY) record are read. The master record is automatically moved to the new master record (N–KEY) but not yet written onto disk. This move initializes N–KEY to the value of M–KEY. The following table summarizes the various actions that need to be taken, depending on the transaction key and the new key.

COMPARISON OF KEYS	POSSIBLE ACTION
T–KEY = N–KEY	1. Could be a delete record. 2. Could be a change record. 3. Could be an error if the transaction code indicates an insert operation.
T–KEY < N–KEY	1. Transaction record is probably an insertion record. 2. Error if transaction code specifies anything but an insertion operation.
T–KEY > N–KEY	The master record needs to be written on the new master file since the current transaction record does not affect the master record.

If T-KEY is less than N-KEY (the new master-file record not yet written) and the transaction code calls for an insertion, the transaction record is moved into the new master record, thus resetting N-KEY to T-KEY. Then a new transaction record is read with key T-KEY. Since the transaction records are assumed to be in sequence, T-KEY > N-KEY and the first transaction record is written onto disk. The old master record, which has not yet been processed, is then moved into the NEW-MASTER-RECORD, which causes N-KEY to be reset to M-KEY (master key). T-KEY and N-KEY are compared, and if T-KEY is less than N-KEY, the same sequence of activities is repeated (i.e., insert records).

At this juncture, however, two other possibilities can occur: T-KEY = N-KEY or T-KEY > N-KEY.

> If T-KEY = N-KEY and the transaction code is a deletion (neither an insert nor a change), the new master file record, which contains the item to be deleted, is simply not written onto disk; then a new transaction record and a new master record are read. If the transaction code is a change code, the designated items in the new master record are changed and a new transaction code is read. Since the new T-KEY will be greater than N-KEY (the transaction records are assumed to be in sequence), the changed master file record will be written onto disk.
> If T-KEY = N-KEY and the transaction code specifies an insert operation, the transaction record should be checked, since this is clearly an error.
> If T-KEY is greater than N-KEY, this implies that either all appropriate changes to the master record have been made, or that no changes are contemplated. In either case, the master record or the changed master record is written onto the new disk file. A new master record is then read, and a sequence of steps similar to those described above is repeated.

Ultimately, both T-KEY and M-KEY will be set to their highest value (end-of-file conditions) and the update process will be terminated. If the very last record read is a valid insert transaction, or a record that was in the process of being changed, then that last record is written onto disk (line 78).

It is, of course, possible that more than one transaction will affect one particular master record. Conceivably a record could be deleted, immediately recreated, and then immediately changed, as in the following example:

```
0100    CHAIR                  1    Delete record 100.
0100    CHAIR    20   5000     2    Recreate a new record 100 by insertion.
0100    CHAIR    20   6000     3    Correct the previous insert, i.e., change
                                    quantity to 60.
```

The reader is urged to go through the flowchart step by step, using a variety of transaction files, in order to understand the update process. Some "trace through" examples of the flowchart are shown below. The master and transaction files are shown in the first two columns (the item description has been omitted since it does not play a key role in the update process). The updated records stored on disk are shown in the right-most column. T-KEY refers to the transaction record key, M-KEY refers to the master file record key, and N-KEY refers to the key of the new master record, i.e., the one which will ultimately be written on the disk/tape (NEW-MASTER-FILE). Hence N-KEY is either T-KEY or M-KEY, depending on which record is moved into the new master record.

SEQUENTIAL FILE PROCESSING

OLD-MASTER-RECORD		TRANSACTION-RECORD				NEW-MASTER-RECORD			M-KEY	T-KEY	N-KEY	FILE-JUST-READ	Records stored on disk
Key	Qty Cost	Key	Qty	Cost	Code	Key	Qty	Cost					
90	20 98.00	80	20	54.00	2	90	20	98.00	—	80	90	MASTER	80 20 54.00
/*		/*				80	20	54.00	90	9999	80	TRANSACTION	90 20 98.00
						90	20	98.00			90	MASTER	End of run
90	20 98.00	95	20	64.00	2	90	20	98.00	90	95	90	MASTER	90 20 98.00
/*		/*				90	20	98.00	9999	9999	90	MASTER	95 20 64.00
						95	20	64.00			95	TRANSACTION	End of run
80	20 90.00	80	20	95.00	3	80	20	90.00	80	80	80	MASTER	80 20 95.00
/*						80	20	95.00	9999	9999	80		End of run
						80	20	95.00			80		
80	20 40.00	80	20	40.00	1	80	20	40.00	80	80	80	MASTER	End of run
/*		/*				80	20	40.00	9999	9999	80	MASTER	
80	20 40.00	70	30	45.00	4	80	20	40.00	80	70	80	MASTER	Error message
/*		75	40	80.00	2	75	40	80.00	75		75	TRANSACTION	75 40 80.00
		78	50	40.00	2	78	50	40.00	78		78	TRANSACTION	78 50 40.00
		/*				80	20	40.00	9999	9999	80	MASTER	80 20 40.00

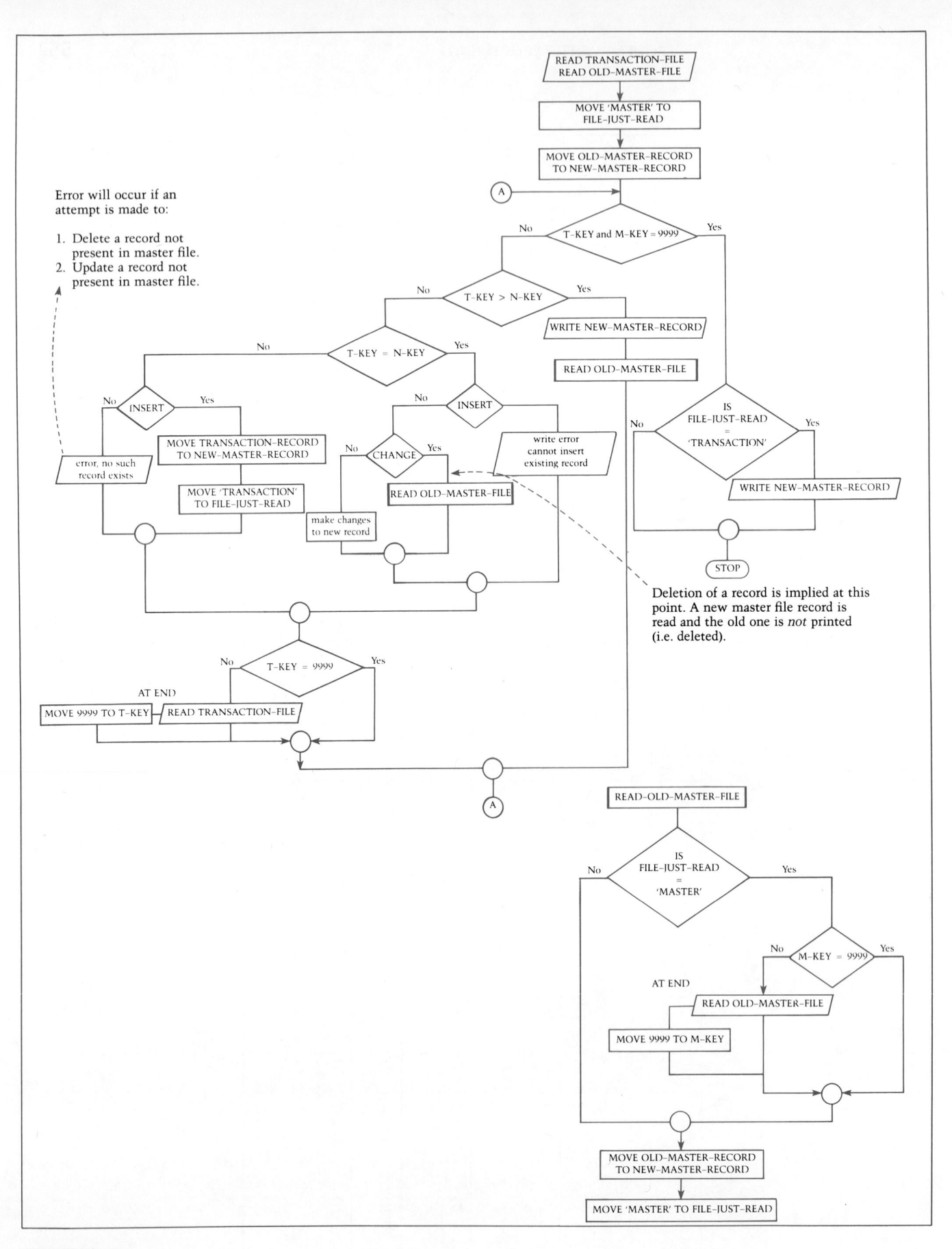

FIGURE 10–12
FLOWCHART FOR A SEQUENTIAL UPDATE

10-4-4 A PARTIAL IN-PLACE UPDATE—THE REWRITE FEATURE

Section 10-4-3 discussed a full sequential update resulting in the creation of a new file. This full update allowed the user to insert and delete records and change fields within records. A more limited update that involves only deletions and changes to records and does not result in the creation of a new file is possible in COBOL compilers that support the REWRITE feature. (See your COBOL technical reference manual for the availability of the REWRITE statement; look under sequential ORGANIZATION.) This update is performed in place. Changed records are rewritten on the same track area that they formerly occupied. Records to be deleted are simply flagged by the program, i.e., a particular item within the record is used to reflect the status of the record. If the record is to be deleted, the status flag is set to 1 to reflect inactive status. A 0 status flag indicates an active record. Thus a deleted record is not physically removed from the disk; instead it is logically removed from consideration. In the logic of the program, you simply test the status flag to determine the active/inactive status of the record.

There are both advantages and disadvantages to in-place updates. The advantages are:

1. The updated file never changes its catalogued name. Thus there is no need to swap the catalogued names of the new and old master files at the conclusion of the update, since the old master file and the new master file are one and the same!
2. There is an economy of disk storage space, since the file is updated in place.
3. Deleted records are still present in the file and can be analyzed, listed, or reactivated at any time.
4. In a multiuser/sharing environment, the file is available to users during the update process.
5. The logic of the update process is fairly straightforward and easy to understand compared to the logic of the update section 10-4-3.

The disadvantages are:

1. Records cannot be inserted sequentially in the file. (The OPEN EXTEND feature can be used to add records to the file, but they will not be in sequence. Such records physically follow the last original record in the file.)
2. No back-up file is available. Of course a copy can be made after the update, but if there is a disk crash in the course of the update process, the file will be lost or damaged.
3. The deleted records may soon start to accumulate and stagnate in the file as more and more records are deleted. This could result in inefficiency or performance degradation. (In addition, each record must be checked for active or inactive status!) To be sure, a new, compressed file can be recreated every so often to discard all inactive records and yield a new file on a separate disk area.

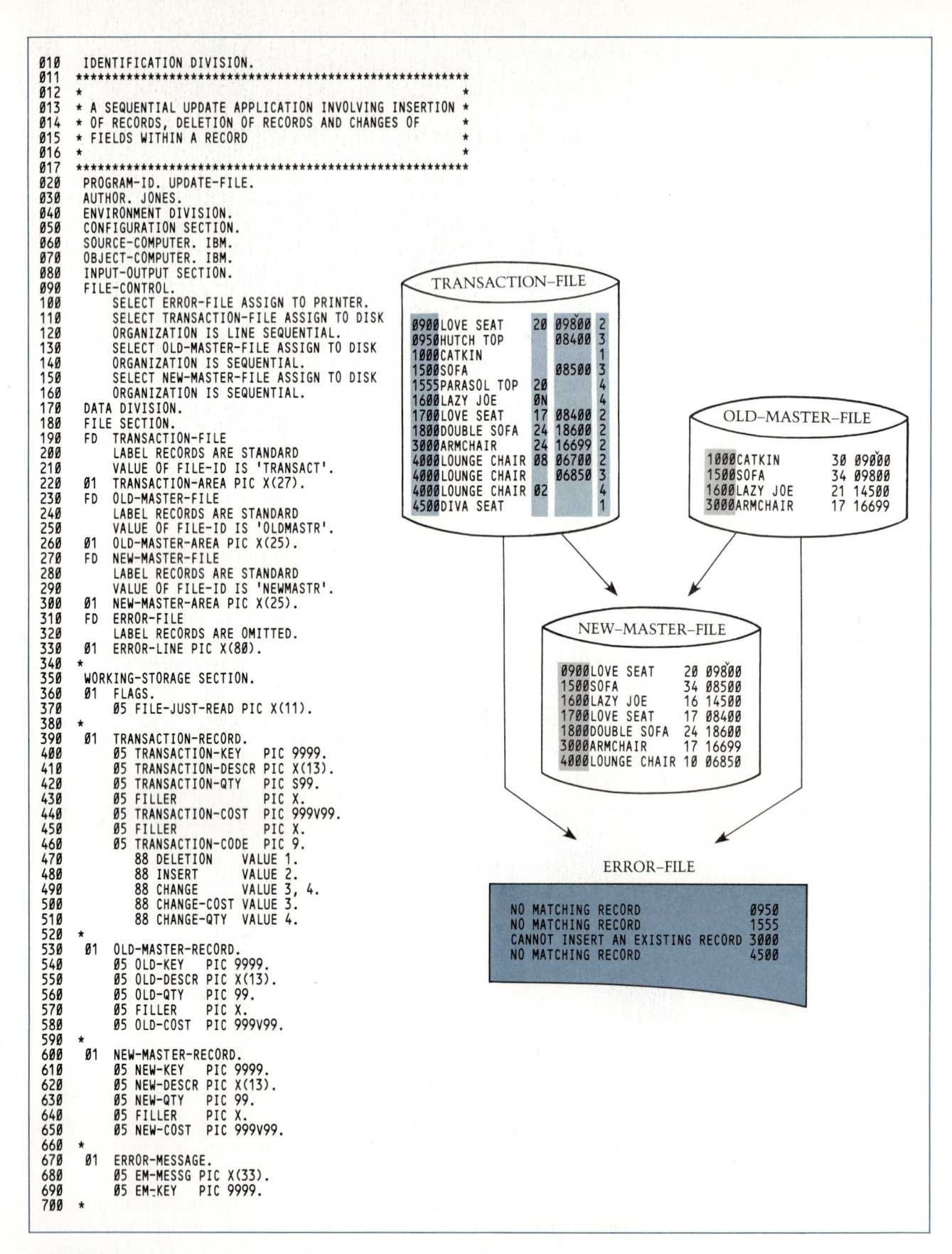

```
010    IDENTIFICATION DIVISION.
011    ********************************************************
012    *                                                      *
013    * A SEQUENTIAL UPDATE APPLICATION INVOLVING INSERTION  *
014    * OF RECORDS, DELETION OF RECORDS AND CHANGES OF       *
015    * FIELDS WITHIN A RECORD                               *
016    *                                                      *
017    ********************************************************
020    PROGRAM-ID. UPDATE-FILE.
030    AUTHOR. JONES.
040    ENVIRONMENT DIVISION.
050    CONFIGURATION SECTION.
060    SOURCE-COMPUTER. IBM.
070    OBJECT-COMPUTER. IBM.
080    INPUT-OUTPUT SECTION.
090    FILE-CONTROL.
100        SELECT ERROR-FILE ASSIGN TO PRINTER.
110        SELECT TRANSACTION-FILE ASSIGN TO DISK
120        ORGANIZATION IS LINE SEQUENTIAL.
130        SELECT OLD-MASTER-FILE ASSIGN TO DISK
140        ORGANIZATION IS SEQUENTIAL.
150        SELECT NEW-MASTER-FILE ASSIGN TO DISK
160        ORGANIZATION IS SEQUENTIAL.
170    DATA DIVISION.
180    FILE SECTION.
190    FD  TRANSACTION-FILE
200        LABEL RECORDS ARE STANDARD
210        VALUE OF FILE-ID IS 'TRANSACT'.
220    01  TRANSACTION-AREA PIC X(27).
230    FD  OLD-MASTER-FILE
240        LABEL RECORDS ARE STANDARD
250        VALUE OF FILE-ID IS 'OLDMASTR'.
260    01  OLD-MASTER-AREA PIC X(25).
270    FD  NEW-MASTER-FILE
280        LABEL RECORDS ARE STANDARD
290        VALUE OF FILE-ID IS 'NEWMASTR'.
300    01  NEW-MASTER-AREA PIC X(25).
310    FD  ERROR-FILE
320        LABEL RECORDS ARE OMITTED.
330    01  ERROR-LINE PIC X(80).
340    *
350    WORKING-STORAGE SECTION.
360    01  FLAGS.
370        05 FILE-JUST-READ PIC X(11).
380    *
390    01  TRANSACTION-RECORD.
400        05 TRANSACTION-KEY   PIC 9999.
410        05 TRANSACTION-DESCR PIC X(13).
420        05 TRANSACTION-QTY   PIC S99.
430        05 FILLER            PIC X.
440        05 TRANSACTION-COST  PIC 999V99.
450        05 FILLER            PIC X.
460        05 TRANSACTION-CODE  PIC 9.
470           88 DELETION    VALUE 1.
480           88 INSERT      VALUE 2.
490           88 CHANGE      VALUE 3, 4.
500           88 CHANGE-COST VALUE 3.
510           88 CHANGE-QTY  VALUE 4.
520    *
530    01  OLD-MASTER-RECORD.
540        05 OLD-KEY   PIC 9999.
550        05 OLD-DESCR PIC X(13).
560        05 OLD-QTY   PIC 99.
570        05 FILLER    PIC X.
580        05 OLD-COST  PIC 999V99.
590    *
600    01  NEW-MASTER-RECORD.
610        05 NEW-KEY   PIC 9999.
620        05 NEW-DESCR PIC X(13).
630        05 NEW-QTY   PIC 99.
640        05 FILLER    PIC X.
650        05 NEW-COST  PIC 999V99.
660    *
670    01  ERROR-MESSAGE.
680        05 EM-MESSG PIC X(33).
690        05 EM-KEY   PIC 9999.
700    *
```

TRANSACTION-FILE

```
0900LOVE SEAT     20 09800 2
0950HUTCH TOP        08400 3
1000CATKIN                 1
1500SOFA             08500 3
1555PARASOL TOP   20       4
1600LAZY JOE      0N       4
1700LOVE SEAT     17 08400 2
1800DOUBLE SOFA   24 18600 2
3000ARMCHAIR      24 16699 2
4000LOUNGE CHAIR 08 06700 2
4000LOUNGE CHAIR    06850 3
4000LOUNGE CHAIR 02       4
4500DIVA SEAT              1
```

OLD-MASTER-FILE

```
1000CATKIN       30 09800
1500SOFA         34 09800
1600LAZY JOE     21 14500
3000ARMCHAIR     17 16699
```

NEW-MASTER-FILE

```
0900LOVE SEAT    20 09800
1500SOFA         34 08500
1600LAZY JOE     16 14500
1700LOVE SEAT    17 08400
1800DOUBLE SOFA  24 18600
3000ARMCHAIR     17 16699
4000LOUNGE CHAIR 10 06850
```

ERROR-FILE

```
NO MATCHING RECORD                0950
NO MATCHING RECORD                1555
CANNOT INSERT AN EXISTING RECORD  3000
NO MATCHING RECORD                4500
```

FIGURE 10–13
A COMPLETE SPEQUENTIAL UPDATE

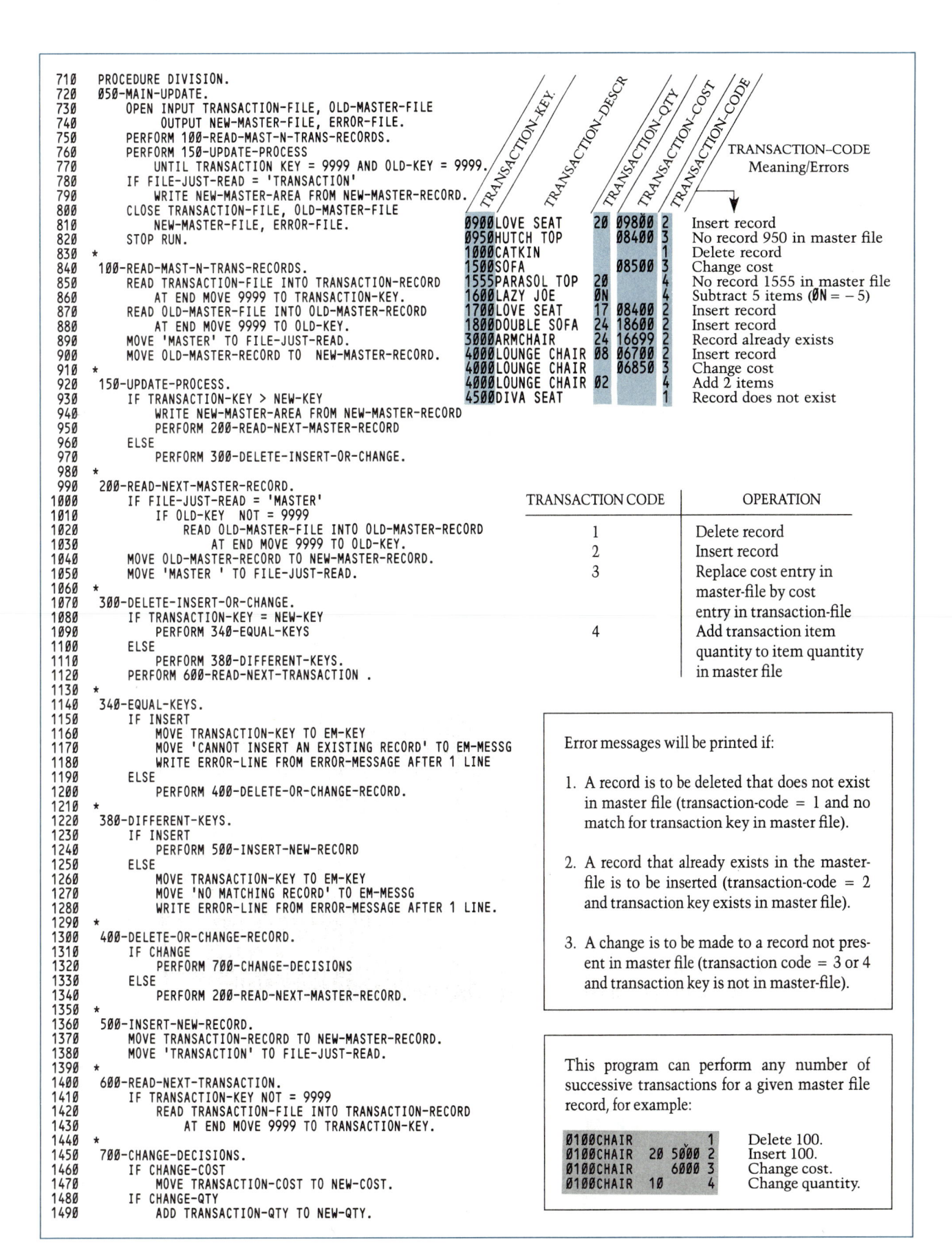

```
710     PROCEDURE DIVISION.
720     050-MAIN-UPDATE.
730         OPEN INPUT TRANSACTION-FILE, OLD-MASTER-FILE
740              OUTPUT NEW-MASTER-FILE, ERROR-FILE.
750         PERFORM 100-READ-MAST-N-TRANS-RECORDS.
760         PERFORM 150-UPDATE-PROCESS
770             UNTIL TRANSACTION KEY = 9999 AND OLD-KEY = 9999.
780         IF FILE-JUST-READ = 'TRANSACTION'
790             WRITE NEW-MASTER-AREA FROM NEW-MASTER-RECORD.
800         CLOSE TRANSACTION-FILE, OLD-MASTER-FILE
810              NEW-MASTER-FILE, ERROR-FILE.
820         STOP RUN.
830     *
840     100-READ-MAST-N-TRANS-RECORDS.
850         READ TRANSACTION-FILE INTO TRANSACTION-RECORD
860             AT END MOVE 9999 TO TRANSACTION-KEY.
870         READ OLD-MASTER-FILE INTO OLD-MASTER-RECORD
880             AT END MOVE 9999 TO OLD-KEY.
890         MOVE 'MASTER' TO FILE-JUST-READ.
900         MOVE OLD-MASTER-RECORD TO  NEW-MASTER-RECORD.
910     *
920     150-UPDATE-PROCESS.
930         IF TRANSACTION-KEY > NEW-KEY
940             WRITE NEW-MASTER-AREA FROM NEW-MASTER-RECORD
950             PERFORM 200-READ-NEXT-MASTER-RECORD
960         ELSE
970             PERFORM 300-DELETE-INSERT-OR-CHANGE.
980     *
990     200-READ-NEXT-MASTER-RECORD.
1000        IF FILE-JUST-READ = 'MASTER'
1010            IF OLD-KEY  NOT = 9999
1020                READ OLD-MASTER-FILE INTO OLD-MASTER-RECORD
1030                    AT END MOVE 9999 TO OLD-KEY.
1040        MOVE OLD-MASTER-RECORD TO NEW-MASTER-RECORD.
1050        MOVE 'MASTER ' TO FILE-JUST-READ.
1060    *
1070    300-DELETE-INSERT-OR-CHANGE.
1080        IF TRANSACTION-KEY = NEW-KEY
1090            PERFORM 340-EQUAL-KEYS
1100        ELSE
1110            PERFORM 380-DIFFERENT-KEYS.
1120        PERFORM 600-READ-NEXT-TRANSACTION .
1130    *
1140    340-EQUAL-KEYS.
1150        IF INSERT
1160            MOVE TRANSACTION-KEY TO EM-KEY
1170            MOVE 'CANNOT INSERT AN EXISTING RECORD' TO EM-MESSG
1180            WRITE ERROR-LINE FROM ERROR-MESSAGE AFTER 1 LINE
1190        ELSE
1200            PERFORM 400-DELETE-OR-CHANGE-RECORD.
1210    *
1220    380-DIFFERENT-KEYS.
1230        IF INSERT
1240            PERFORM 500-INSERT-NEW-RECORD
1250        ELSE
1260            MOVE TRANSACTION-KEY TO EM-KEY
1270            MOVE 'NO MATCHING RECORD' TO EM-MESSG
1280            WRITE ERROR-LINE FROM ERROR-MESSAGE AFTER 1 LINE.
1290    *
1300    400-DELETE-OR-CHANGE-RECORD.
1310        IF CHANGE
1320            PERFORM 700-CHANGE-DECISIONS
1330        ELSE
1340            PERFORM 200-READ-NEXT-MASTER-RECORD.
1350    *
1360    500-INSERT-NEW-RECORD.
1370        MOVE TRANSACTION-RECORD TO NEW-MASTER-RECORD.
1380        MOVE 'TRANSACTION' TO FILE-JUST-READ.
1390    *
1400    600-READ-NEXT-TRANSACTION.
1410        IF TRANSACTION-KEY NOT = 9999
1420            READ TRANSACTION-FILE INTO TRANSACTION-RECORD
1430                AT END MOVE 9999 TO TRANSACTION-KEY.
1440    *
1450    700-CHANGE-DECISIONS.
1460        IF CHANGE-COST
1470            MOVE TRANSACTION-COST TO NEW-COST.
1480        IF CHANGE-QTY
1490            ADD TRANSACTION-QTY TO NEW-QTY.
```

TRANSACTION-KEY	TRANSACTION-DESCR	TRANSACTION-QTY	TRANSACTION-COST	TRANSACTION-CODE	TRANSACTION-CODE Meaning/Errors
0900	LOVE SEAT	20	09800	2	Insert record
0950	HUTCH TOP		08400	3	No record 950 in master file
1000	CATKIN			1	Delete record
1500	SOFA		08500	3	Change cost
1555	PARASOL TOP	20		4	No record 1555 in master file
1600	LAZY JOE	0N		4	Subtract 5 items (0N = −5)
1700	LOVE SEAT	17	08400	2	Insert record
1800	DOUBLE SOFA	24	18600	2	Insert record
3000	ARMCHAIR	24	16699	2	Record already exists
4000	LOUNGE CHAIR	08	06700	2	Insert record
4000	LOUNGE CHAIR		06850	3	Change cost
4000	LOUNGE CHAIR	02		4	Add 2 items
4500	DIVA SEAT			1	Record does not exist

TRANSACTION CODE	OPERATION
1	Delete record
2	Insert record
3	Replace cost entry in master-file by cost entry in transaction-file
4	Add transaction item quantity to item quantity in master file

Error messages will be printed if:

1. A record is to be deleted that does not exist in master file (transaction-code = 1 and no match for transaction key in master file).

2. A record that already exists in the master-file is to be inserted (transaction-code = 2 and transaction key exists in master file).

3. A change is to be made to a record not present in master file (transaction code = 3 or 4 and transaction key is not in master-file).

This program can perform any number of successive transactions for a given master file record, for example:

0100CHAIR			1	Delete 100.
0100CHAIR	20	5000	2	Insert 100.
0100CHAIR		6000	3	Change cost.
0100CHAIR	10		4	Change quantity.

FIGURE 10-13

(continued)

The REWRITE Statement

The REWRITE statement replaces a logical record on a sequential disk file. The general form of the REWRITE statement is:

> REWRITE record-name   FROM data-name

Before a record can be rewritten, the corresponding file in which changes are to be made must be opened in I–O mode, that is, the program must be able to read the file (I for input) and at the same time write on the file (O for output).

The file must be in existence before the REWRITE statement can be used.

The REWRITE statement replaces the disk record that was accessed by the most recent successfully completed READ statement. The record to be rewritten (the replacement record) should be the same length as the record it is to replace; otherwise, truncation of the replacement record will occur if the replacement record is too long, or unpredictable data will fill in the record if the replacement record is too short.

The REWRITE statement can be executed repeatedly for just one READ operation. This can be very advantageous when transaction files contain successive changes for just one record. (See the first two records of the transaction file in Figure 10–14.)

The WRITE statement cannot be used for files opened in I–O mode.

An In-Place Delete-and-Change Sequential Update

Problem Specification. A sequential file called MASTER–FILE consists of records whose layout is shown below. Let us assume that MASTER–FILE is a file created by a COBOL program (not by a text editor) using ORGANIZATION IS SEQUENTIAL. The first item in the master record is a code/flag specifying the status of the record (0 = active, 1 = inactive), followed by the item number serving as the key for the update.

Let us write a program to update MASTER–FILE with a TRANSACTION–FILE whose record format is also shown below. Note that the last item in the transaction record, TRANSACTION–CODE, specifies the update action:
(1) If the transaction code is 0, the corresponding master record is to be deleted.
(2) If the transaction code is 3, the specified cost field in the transaction record replaces the cost field in the master record.
(3) If the transaction code is 4, the specified quantity field in the transaction record is added to the quantity field in the master record.

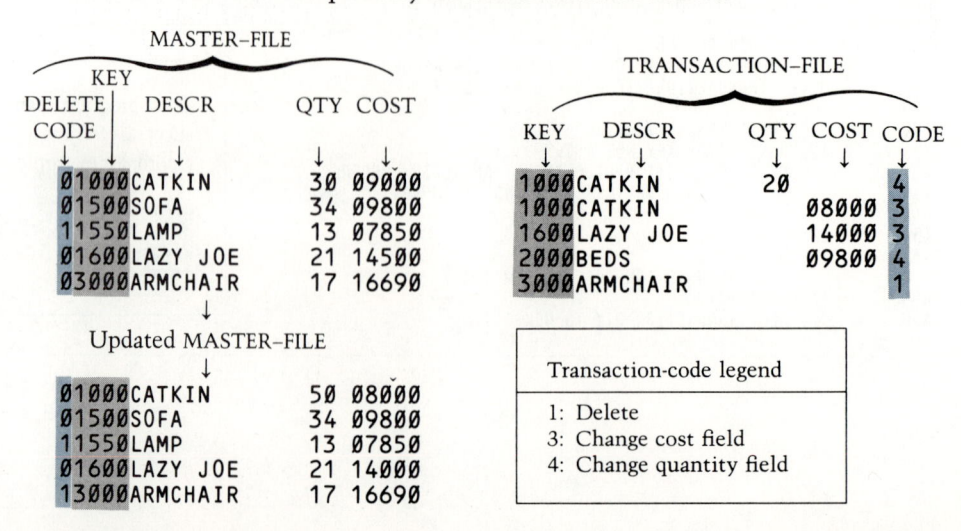

```
              MASTER-FILE
        ⎧―――――――――――――――――⎫                    TRANSACTION-FILE
        KEY                                ⎧――――――――――――――――――――――⎫
DELETE|   DESCR      QTY   COST         KEY    DESCR      QTY  COST  CODE
CODE
  ↓   ↓              ↓     ↓              ↓      ↓         ↓    ↓     ↓
 01000CATKIN         30    09000         1000CATKIN       20          4
 01500SOFA           34    09800         1000CATKIN            08000  3
 11550LAMP           13    07850         1600LAZY JOE          14000  3
 01600LAZY JOE       21    14500         2000BEDS              09800  4
 03000ARMCHAIR       17    16690         3000ARMCHAIR                 1
                     ↓
         Updated MASTER-FILE
                     ↓                        Transaction-code legend
 01000CATKIN         50    08000             1: Delete
 01500SOFA           34    09800             3: Change cost field
 11550LAMP           13    07850             4: Change quantity field
 01600LAZY JOE       21    14000
 13000ARMCHAIR       17    16690
```

Problem Analysis A program to solve this problem is shown in Figure 10–14. Records are rewritten on disk at line 90 to reflect changes to either the cost or quantity fields. Records are also rewritten at line 96 to delete a record, i.e., to change the status (delete) code of the master record from 0 to 1.

If a transaction record has no match in the master file, an error-message is displayed at line 81.

Note that the first two transaction records in the transaction file identify the same record. Each transaction record indicates a different change for the same master record, and the REWRITE statement at line 90 takes care of the two changes.

The statement PERFORM 200–READ–MASTER–FILE UNTIL DELETE–CODE = 0 OR MASTER–KEY = 9999 at line 62 and 63 searches for active records and skips over inactive records in the master file. Records with a DELETE–CODE equal to 1 (inactive) are read but not processed.

The EXTEND Option

Some COBOL systems allow records to be added to a sequential file through the use of the EXTEND option in the OPEN statement. When the OPEN EXTEND statement is carried out, the disk (or tape) file is positioned immediately after the last logical record of the file so that any records written are added to the "tail end" of the file. These records are not merged with the original records; thus the entire file now needs to be sorted. The form of the OPEN EXTEND statement is:

> **OPEN EXTEND** file-name...

The file must already exist on disk before the OPEN EXTEND statement is executed.

10-4-5 DO IT NOW

1. Write a program to:
   a. Create a sequential file where each record consists of a student name and a test score. Then close the file.
   b. Create a transaction file where each record consists of a name and a transaction code (1 or 2) with the following code meanings:

      code = 1: add 10% of class average to score if score exceeds 95
      code = 2: delete any record with a score entry less than 50

      Then, using the logic of Figure 10–13 or Figure 10–14, write the code to update the file. No resulting scores should exceed 100. Make sure that your transaction file contains at least one name that does not appear in the master file. (This warrants an error message on output.) Print the updated file. Produce a listing of student names in descending score order.

564   UNDERSTANDING STRUCTURED COBOL

```
01:     IDENTIFICATION DIVISION.
02:     PROGRAM-ID. REWRITE-FILE.
03:     ****************************************************************
04:     * S E Q U E N T I A L   U P D A T E   W I T H   R E W R I T E *
05:     ****************************************************************
06:     AUTHOR. JONES.
07:     ENVIRONMENT DIVISION.
08:     CONFIGURATION SECTION.
09:     SOURCE-COMPUTER. IBM.
10:     OBJECT-COMPUTER. IBM.
11:     INPUT-OUTPUT SECTION.
12:     FILE-CONTROL.
13:         SELECT TRANSACTION-FILE ASSIGN TO DISK
14:             ORGANIZATION IS LINE SEQUENTIAL.
15:         SELECT MASTER-FILE ASSIGN TO DISK
16:             ORGANIZATION IS SEQUENTIAL.
17:     DATA DIVISION.
18:     FILE SECTION.
19:     FD  TRANSACTION-FILE
20:         LABEL RECORDS ARE STANDARD
21:         VALUE OF FILE-ID IS 'TRANSACT'.
22:     01  TRANSACTION-RECORD.
23:         05 TRANSACTION-KEY    PIC 9999.
24:         05 TRANSACTION-DESCR  PIC X(13).
25:         05 TRANSACTION-QTY    PIC S99.
26:         05 FILLER             PIC X.
27:         05 TRANSACTION-COST   PIC 999V99.
28:         05 FILLER             PIC X.
29:         05 TRANSACTION-CODE   PIC 9.
30:             88 DELETION       VALUE 1.
32:             88 CHANGE         VALUE 3, 4.
33:             88 CHANGE-COST    VALUE 3.
34:             88 CHANGE-QTY     VALUE 4.
35:     *
36:     FD  MASTER-FILE
37:         LABEL RECORDS ARE STANDARD
38:         VALUE OF FILE-ID IS 'MASTER'.
39:     01  MASTER-RECORD.
40:         05 DELETE-CODE   PIC 9.
41:         05 MASTER-KEY    PIC 9999.
42:         05 MASTER-DESCR  PIC X(13).
43:         05 MASTER-QTY    PIC 99.
44:         05 FILLER        PIC X.
45:         05 MASTER-COST   PIC 999V99.
47:     *
48:     PROCEDURE DIVISION.
49:     050-MAIN-UPDATE.
50:         OPEN INPUT TRANSACTION-FILE
51:              I-O   MASTER-FILE.
52:         PERFORM 100-READ-MAST-N-TRANS-RECORDS.
53:         PERFORM 300-UPDATE-PROCESS
54:             UNTIL TRANSACTION-KEY = 9999 AND MASTER-KEY = 9999.
55:         CLOSE TRANSACTION-FILE, MASTER-FILE.
56:         STOP RUN.
57:     *
58:     100-READ-MAST-N-TRANS-RECORDS.
59:         READ TRANSACTION-FILE
60:             AT END MOVE 9999 TO TRANSACTION-KEY.
61:         MOVE 1 TO MASTER-KEY, DELETE-CODE.
62:         PERFORM 200-READ-MASTER-FILE
63:             UNTIL DELETE-CODE = 0 OR MASTER-KEY = 9999.
64:     *
65:     200-READ-MASTER-FILE.
66:         READ MASTER-FILE.
67:             AT END MOVE 9999 TO MASTER-KEY.
```

TRANSACTION-FILE

			CODE	
KEY	DESCR	QTY COST		
1000	CATKIN	20	4	change cost
1000	CATKIN	08000	3	change quantity
1600	LAZY JOE	14000	3	
2000	BEDS	09800	4	
3000	ARMCHAIR		1	delete record

MASTER-FILE

DELETE CODE

KEY	DESCR	QTY	COST
0 1000	CATKIN	30	09000
0 1500	SOFA	34	09800
1 1550	LAMP	13	07850
0 1600	LAZY JOE	21	14500
0 3000	ARMCHAIR	17	16690

After the update

KEY	DESCR	QTY	COST
0 1000	CATKIN	20	08000
0 1500	SOFA	34	09800
1 1550	LAMP	13	07850
0 1600	LAZY JOE	21	14000
1 3000	ARMCHAIR	17	16690

Read the first record from the master file and the first record from the transaction file.

Initialize DELETE-CODE to 1 so that 200-READ-MASTER-FILE is carried out the first time. Keep reading the master file until an active record is found (one not flagged by a 1).

FIGURE 10-14
A SEQUENTIAL UPDATE WITH THE REWRITE STATEMENT

```
68:  *
69:  300-UPDATE PROCESS.
70:      IF TRANSACTION-KEY = MASTER-KEY AND CHANGE
71:          PERFORM 400-CHANGE-DECISIONS
72:      ELSE
73:          IF TRANSACTION-KEY = MASTER-KEY AND DELETION
74:              PERFORM 500-DELETE-RECORD
75:          ELSE
76:              IF TRANSACTION-KEY > MASTER-KEY
77:                  MOVE 1 TO DELETE-CODE
78:                  PERFORM 200-READ-MASTER-FILE
79:                      UNTIL DELETE-CODE = 0 OR MASTER-KEY = 9999
80:              ELSE
81:                  DISPLAY 'NO MATCH IN MASTER FILE'
82:                  READ TRANSACTION-FILE
83:                      AT END MOVE 9999 TO TRANSACTION-KEY.
84:  *
85:  400-CHANGE-DECISIONS.
86:      IF CHANGE-COST
87:          MOVE TRANSACTION-COST TO MASTER-COST.
88:      IF CHANGE-QTY
89:          ADD TRANSACTION-QTY TO MASTER-QTY.
90:      REWRITE MASTER-RECORD.
91:      READ TRANSACTION-FILE
92:          AT END MOVE 9999 TO TRANSACTION-KEY.
93:  *
94:  500-DELETE-RECORD.
95:      MOVE 1 TO DELETE-CODE.
96:      REWRITE MASTER-RECORD.
97:      READ TRANSACTION-FILE
98:          AT END MOVE 9999 TO TRANSACTION-KEY.
99:      PERFORM 200-READ-MASTER-FILE
100:         UNTIL DELETE-CODE = 0 OR MASTER-KEY = 9999.
```

Comments (right column):
- Lines 70–71: If both keys match and the transaction code specifies a change, go to line 85.
- Lines 73–75: If both keys match and the transaction code specifies a deletion, go and delete record (line 94).
- Lines 76–79: If transaction key > master key, there is a possible match for the transaction in the next coming master records.
- Lines 80–83: If transaction key < master key, then there is no match for the transaction record, for if there were it would have been picked up earlier.
- Line 87: Make the necessary cost changes.
- Lines 89–90: Make the necessary quantity adjustments and write these changes on the disk.
- Lines 95–96: Flag the master record to be deleted with a 1 in DELETE code and write the entire record on disk.

FIGURE 10–14
(*continued*)

2. Trace through the program of Figure 10–14 using the master and transaction files shown below, and determine the final contents of the master file.

MASTER FILE

	Delete code	Key	Quantity	Cost
a.	0	100	20	40
	0	200	5	17
b.	1	100	20	40
c.	1	100	20	40
	0	200	5	17
d.	0	100	20	40
	0	200	5	17
	0	300	15	20

TRANSACTION FILE

	Key	Quantity	Cost	Code
a.	120	5	10	3
b.	100	2	40	1
c.	200	−5	17	4
	200	15	17	4
d.	100	20	38	3
	200			1
	300	10	10	4

3. This exercise deals with the REWRITE and EXTEND feature discussed in section 10-4-4. Complete problem 1.b. with the following additions:

   a. Use the EXTEND option to add records to your master file.
   b. Update the master file.
   c. Sort the entire master file.
   d. Produce a listing of student names in descending score order.

10–5 A MULTIPLE-FILE PROGRAMMING PROBLEM: GRADE REPORT

At the end of the semester, students' final grades are recorded in a file called GRADE–ROSTER–FILE. The file is organized sequentially using each student's social security number as a key. Identical social security numbers occur in groups, i.e., a group contains a particular student's grades in every course taken by the student, for example

GRADE–ROSTER–FILE

```
           ⎧ 111222333GLEASON JIM NG 100A061286
           ⎪ 111222333GLEASON JIM HES102B061286
Student 1  ⎨ 111222333GLEASON JIM BY1104C061286
           ⎪ 111222333GLEASON JIM BY2106D061286
           ⎩ 111222333GLEASON JIM PSY108F061286
Student 2  { 212356553WOLFE MONA  PSY108B061286
             212356553WOLFE MONA  BY2106A061286
```

Fields: Social Security | Name | Course Number | Grade | Date

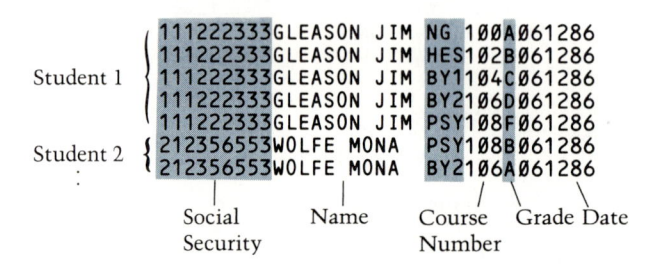

The Registrar's office also has a list of student names organized sequentially by social security key on a disk file called STUDENT–ADMISSION–FILE. In addition to the student's name and social security number, each disk record contains the student's current cumulative hours, cumulative grade point, major field of study, and classification. An example of STUDENT–ADMISSION–FILE is:

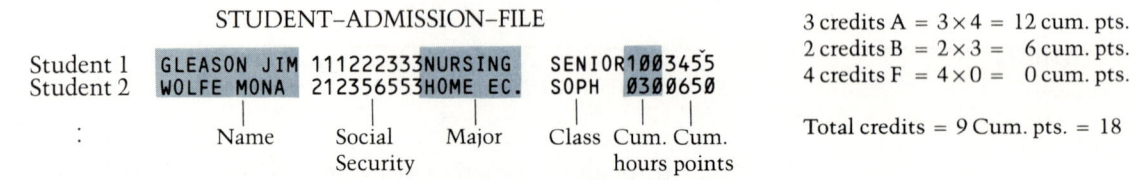

STUDENT–ADMISSION–FILE

```
Student 1   GLEASON JIM 111222333NURSING   SENIOR1003455
Student 2   WOLFE MONA  212356553HOME EC.  SOPH  0300650
```

Fields: Name | Social Security | Major | Class | Cum. hours | Cum. points

3 credits A = 3 × 4 = 12 cum. pts.
2 credits B = 2 × 3 = 6 cum. pts.
4 credits F = 4 × 0 = 0 cum. pts.

Total credits = 9 Cum. pts. = 18

Since the records of the GRADE–ROSTER–FILE indicate neither the number of credits nor the verbal descriptions of the courses, a file called COURSE–CATALOG–FILE is used as a course identification directory for looking up the number of credits for each course and the corresponding verbal description. Courses are identified by their three-digit course numbers. An example of such a file is shown below:

COURSE–CATALOG–FILE

```
100NURSING II         4     → Course number 100 is Nursing II,
102EL. NUTRITION      3        a four-credit course.
104MICROBIOLOGY       3
106MICROBIOLOGY LAB   1
108GEN. PSYCHOLOGY    3
```

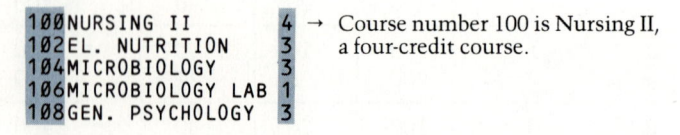

Let us write a program that will:

1. Read the GRADE–ROSTER–FILE and print each student's end-of-semester grade report.

2. Compute the student's grade point average for the semester, as well as his/her cumulative grade point average.

3. Print the total hours for the semester, as well as the total cumulative hours.

4. Update the cumulative points and cumulative hours in the student admission file.

The student's end-of-semester grade report should have the following form:

```
FIELD STUDY     CLASS     STUDENT NAME              DATE          SS. NUMBER
NURSING         SENIOR    GLEASON JIM               06 12 86      111222333
*****************************************************************************
      COURSE    NUMBER    DESCRIPTION       HOURS    GRADE    POINTS    GPA
***************CUMULATIVE TOTALS            100               345.5
      NG        100       NURSING II        4        A        16.0
      HES       102       EL. NUTRITION     3        B        9.0
      BY1       104       MICROBIOLOGY      3        C        6.0
      BY2       106       MICROBIOLOGY LA   1        D        1.0
      PSY       108       GEN. PSYCHOLOGY   3        F        0.0
*****************************************************************************
                          SEMESTER TOTALS   14                32.0      2.285
                          CUM.    TOTALS    114               377.5     3.311
```

The relationships between the various transaction files and the master file is shown in Figure 10–15. This figure illustrates the way in which data is captured from the various files to produce a complete end-of-semester grade report. The COBOL program to solve this problem is shown in Figure 10–16.

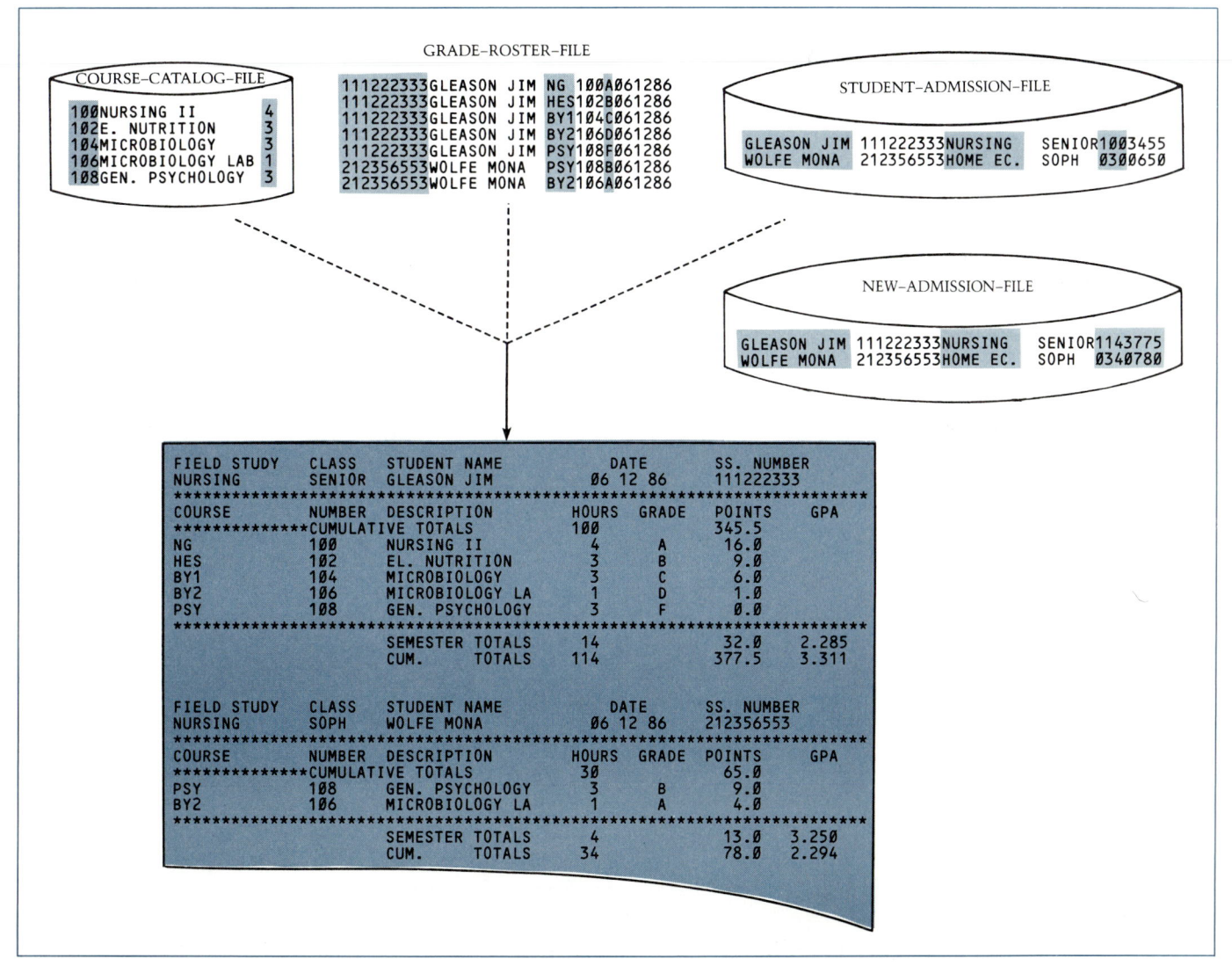

FIGURE 10–15

THE CREATION OF AN END-OF-SEMESTER GRADE REPORT

```
0100     SELECT GRADE-ROSTER-FILE    ASSIGN TO DISKPACK.
0110     SELECT COURSE-CATALOG-FILE  ASSIGN TO DISKPACK.
0120     SELECT STUDENT-ADMISSION-FILE ASSIGN TO DISKPACK.
0130     SELECT NEW-ADMISSION-FILE   ASSIGN TO DISKPACK.
0140     SELECT PRINT-FILE           ASSIGN TO PRINTER.
0160 DATA DIVISION.
0170 FILE SECTION.
0190 FD  GRADE-ROSTER-FILE
0200     LABEL RECORDS ARE STANDARD
0210     DATA RECORD IS STUDENT-GRADE-ROSTER.
0230 01  STUDENT-GRADE-ROSTER.
0240     05  SS-NO       PIC 9(9).
0250     05  NAME        PIC X(12).
0260     05  COURSE      PIC XXX.
0270     05  COURSE-NO   PIC 999.
0280     05  GRADE       PIC X.
0290     05  DATE-ENTRY  PIC 9(6).
0310 FD  COURSE-CATALOG-FILE
0320     LABEL RECORDS ARE STANDARD
0330     DATA RECORD IS COURSE-INFORMATION-RECORD.
0340 01  COURSE-INFORMATION-RECORD.
0350     05  COURSE-ID   PIC 999.
0360     05  COURSE-NAME PIC X(17).
0370     05  NO-CREDIT   PIC 9.
0390 FD  STUDENT-ADMISSION-FILE
0400     LABEL RECORDS ARE STANDARD
0410     DATA RECORD IS STUDENT-ADMISSION-RECORD.
0420 01  STUDENT-ADMISSION-RECORD.
0430     05  CONSTANT-INFO.
0440         10  FILE-NAME      PIC X(12).
0450         10  FILE-SS-NO     PIC 9(9).
0460         10  MAJOR          PIC X(10).
0470         10  CLASSIFICATION PIC X(6).
0480     05  CUM-HOURS     PIC 999.
0490     05  CUM-POINTS    PIC 999V9.
0510 FD  NEW-ADMISSION-FILE
0520     LABEL RECORDS ARE STANDARD
0530     DATA RECORD IS NEW-ADMISSION-RECORD.
0540 01  NEW-ADMISSION-RECORD.
0550     05  NEW-CONSTANT-INFO.
0560         10  NEW-FILE-NAME      PIC X(12).
0570         10  NEW-FILE-SS-NO     PIC 9(9).
0580         10  NEW-MAJOR          PIC X(10).
0590         10  NEW-CLASSIFICATION PIC X(06).
0600     05  NEW-CUM-HOURS   PIC 999.
0610     05  NEW-CUM-POINTS  PIC 999V9.
0630 FD  PRINT-FILE
0640     LABEL RECORDS ARE STANDARD
0650     DATA RECORD IS PRINT-LINE.
0660 01  PRINT-LINE  PIC X(80).
0680 WORKING-STORAGE SECTION.
0690 01  VARIOUS-END-FILE-FLAGS.
0700     05  EOF-COURSE-CATALOG  PIC 9 VALUE 0.
0710         88  END-CATALOG            VALUE 1.
0720     05  EOF-GRADE-ROSTER    PIC 9 VALUE 0.
0730         88  END-ROSTER             VALUE 1.
0750 01  ACCUMULATORS-N-SUBSCRIPTS.
0760     05  I               PIC 9.
0770     05  OLD-SS-NO       PIC 9(9).
0780     05  WS-SEM-HRS      PIC 999   VALUE 0.
0790     05  WS-SEM-QUAL-PTS PIC 999   VALUE 0.
0800     05  WS-QUAL-PTS     PIC 999V99.
0810     05  STARS           PIC X(71) VALUE ALL "*".
0820 01  HEADER1.
0830     05  FILLER PIC X(12) VALUE "FIELD STUDY".
0840     05  FILLER PIC XX    VALUE SPACES.
0850     05  FILLER PIC X(5)  VALUE "CLASS".
0860     05  FILLER PIC XXX   VALUE SPACES.
0870     05  FILLER PIC X(12) VALUE "STUDENT NAME".
0880     05  FILLER PIC X(11) VALUE SPACES.
0890     05  FILLER PIC XXXX  VALUE "DATE".
0900     05  FILLER PIC X(8)  VALUE SPACES.
0910     05  FILLER PIC X(10) VALUE "SS. NUMBER".
0930 01  ENTRY-HEADER1.
0940     05  EH-MAJOR   PIC X(11).
0950     05  FILLER     PIC XXX    VALUE SPACES.
0960     05  EH-CLASS   PIC X(6).
0970     05  FILLER     PIC XX     VALUE SPACES.
0980     05  EH-NAME    PIC X(12).
0990     05  FILLER     PIC X(9)   VALUE SPACES.
1000     05  EH-DATE    PIC 99B99B99.
1010     05  FILLER     PIC X(6)   VALUE SPACES.
1020     05  EH-SS-NO   PIC 9(9).
1040 01  HEADER2.
1050     05  FILLER  PIC X(12) VALUE "COURSE".
1060     05  FILLER  PIC XX    VALUE SPACES.
1070     05  FILLER  PIC X(6)  VALUE "NUMBER".
1080     05  FILLER  PIC XX    VALUE SPACES.
1090     05  FILLER  PIC X(12) VALUE "DESCRIPTION".
1100     05  FILLER  PIC X(7)  VALUE SPACES.
1110     05  FILLER  PIC X(5)  VALUE "HOURS".
1120     05  FILLER  PIC XX    VALUE SPACES.
1130     05  FILLER  PIC X(5)  VALUE "GRADE".
1140     05  FILLER  PIC XXXX  VALUE SPACES.
1150     05  FILLER  PIC X(6)  VALUE "POINTS".
1160     05  FILLER  PIC XXXX  VALUE SPACES.
1170     05  FILLER  PIC XXX   VALUE "GPA".
1190 01  DETAIL-LINE.
1200     05  DL-COURSE  PIC XXX.
1210     05  FILLER     PIC X(11) VALUE SPACES.
1220     05  DL-NUMBER  PIC 999.
1230     05  FILLER     PIC X(5)  VALUE SPACES.
1240     05  DL-DESCR   PIC X(16).
1250     05  FILLER     PIC X(5)  VALUE SPACES.
1260     05  DL-HOURS   PIC 9.
1270     05  FILLER     PIC X(6)  VALUE SPACES.
1280     05  DL-GRADE   PIC X.
1290     05  FILLER     PIC X(6)  VALUE SPACES.
1300     05  DL-POINTS  PIC ZZ9.9.
1320 01  CUMULATION-LINE.
1330     05  FILLER    PIC X(14) VALUE ALL "*".
1340     05  FILLER    PIC X(17) VALUE "CUMULATIVE TOTALS".
1350     05  FILLER    PIC X(10) VALUE SPACES.
1360     05  CL-HOURS  PIC ZZ9.
1370     05  FILLER    PIC X(13) VALUE SPACES.
1380     05  CL-POINTS PIC ZZ9.9.
1400 01  SUMMARY-LINE-1.
1410     05  FILLER     PIC X(22) VALUE SPACES.
1420     05  FILLER     PIC X(20) VALUE "SEMESTER TOTALS".
1430     05  SL1-HOURS  PIC ZZ9.
1440     05  FILLER     PIC X(12) VALUE SPACES.
1450     05  SL1-POINTS PIC ZZ9.9.
1460     05  FILLER     PIC X(4)  VALUE SPACES.
1470     05  SL1-GPA    PIC 9.999.
1490 01  SUMMARY-LINE-2.
1500     05  FILLER     PIC X(22) VALUE SPACES.
1510     05  FILLER     PIC X(20) VALUE "CUM.     TOTALS".
1520     05  SL2-HOURS  PIC ZZ9.
1530     05  FILLER     PIC X(12) VALUE SPACES.
1540     05  SL2-POINTS PIC ZZ9.9.
1550     05  FILLER     PIC X(4)  VALUE SPACES.
1560     05  SL2-GPA    PIC 9.999.
```

FIGURE 10-16

AN END-OF-SEMESTER TRANSCRIPT REPORT

SEQUENTIAL FILE PROCESSING 569

```
1580    01  COURSE-INFORMATION.
1590        05  COURSE-TABLE OCCURS 110 TIMES.
1600            10  COURSE-DESCR    PIC X(15).
1610            10  COURSE-CREDIT   PIC 9.
1620    *
1630    01  GRADE-VALUES PIC X(32) VALUE
1640            "A 40B+35B 30C+25C 20D+15D 10F 00".
1650    01  GRADE-TABLE REDEFINES GRADE-VALUES.
1660        05  GRADE-TAB OCCURS 8 TIMES.
1670            10  LETTER-GRADE  PIC XX.
1680            10  GRADE-POINT   PIC 9V9.
1690    *
1694    *
1696    *
1700    PROCEDURE DIVISION.
1710    MAIN-LOGIC.
1720        OPEN INPUT GRADE-ROSTER-FILE
1730                   COURSE-CATALOG-FILE
1740                   STUDENT-ADMISSION-FILE
1750             OUTPUT NEW-ADMISSION-FILE
1760                    PRINT-FILE.
1770        PERFORM LOAD-COURSE-CATALOG UNTIL END-CATALOG.
1780        PERFORM CONTROL-BREAK-INITIALIZATION.
1790        PERFORM READ-PROCESS-WRITE UNTIL END-ROSTER.
1800        PERFORM SUMMARY-TRANSCRIPT.
1810        CLOSE GRADE-ROSTER-FILE, COURSE-CATALOG-FILE
1820              STUDENT-ADMISSION-FILE, PRINT-FILE
1830              NEW-ADMISSION-FILE.
1840        STOP RUN.
1850    *
1854    *
1856    *
1860.   LOAD-COURSE-CATALOG.
1870        READ COURSE-CATALOG-FILE
1880            AT END MOVE 1 TO EOF-COURSE-CATALOG.
1890        IF NOT END-CATALOG
1900            MOVE COURSE-NAME TO COURSE-DESCR (COURSE-ID)
1910            MOVE NO-CREDIT   TO COURSE-CREDIT (COURSE-ID).
1920    ***** RETURN TO LINE 1780
1921    *
1930    CONTROL-BREAK-INITIALIZATION.
1940        READ GRADE-ROSTER-FILE
1950            AT END MOVE 1 TO EOF-GRADE-ROSTER.
1960        MOVE SS-NO TO OLD-SS-NO.
1970        PERFORM TRANSCRIPT-HEADERS.
1980        PERFORM WRITE-RECORD.
1990    ***** RETURN TO LINE 1780
1991    *
2000    TRANSCRIPT-HEADERS.
2010        WRITE PRINT-LINE FROM HEADER1 AFTER 3.
2020        PERFORM SEARCH-STUDENT-ADMISSION-FILE UNTIL
2030            SS-NO = FILE-SS-NO.
2040        MOVE MAJOR TO EH-MAJOR.
2050        MOVE CLASSIFICATION TO EH-CLASS.
2060        MOVE FILE-NAME      TO EH-NAME.
2070        MOVE FILE-SS-NO     TO EH-SS-NO
2080        MOVE DATA-ENTRY     TO EH-DATE.
2090        WRITE PRINT-LINE FROM ENTRY-HEADER1 AFTER 1.
2100        MOVE STARS TO PRINT-LINE, WRITE PRINT-LINE.
2110        WRITE PRINT-LINE FROM HEADER2 AFTER 1.
2120        MOVE CUM-HOURS   TO CL-HOURS.
2130        MOVE CUM-POINTS  TO CL-POINTS.
2140        WRITE PRINT-LINE FROM CUMULATION-LINE AFTER 1.
2150    ***** RETURN 1ST TIME TO LINE 1970 AND THEN TO 2520
```

```
FIELD STUDY   CLASS    STUDENT NAME          DATE       SS. NUMBER
NURSING       SENIOR   GLEASON JIM          06 12 86    111222333
****************************************************************
COURSE        NUMBER   DESCRIPTION    HOURS  GRADE   POINTS   GPA
**************CUMULATIVE TOTALS         100            345.5
NG            100      NURSING II      4       A       16.0
HES           102      EL. NUTRITION   3       B        9.0
BY1           104      MICROBIOLOGY    3       C        6.0
BY2           106      MICROBIOLOGY LA 1       D        1.0
PSY           108      GEN. PSYCHOLOGY 3       F        0.0
****************************************************************
                       SEMESTER TOTALS 14             32.0  2.285
                       CUM.    TOTALS 114            377.5  3.311
```

```
111222333GLEASON JIM  NG 100A061286
111222333GLEASON JIM  HES102B061286
111222333GLEASON JIM  BY1104C061286      100 NURSING II         4
111222333GLEASON JIM  BY2106D061286      102 EL. NUTRITION      3
111222333GLEASON JIM  PSY108F061286      104 MICROBIOLOGY       3
212356553WOLFE MONA   PSY108B061286      106 MICROBIOLOGY LAB   1
212356553WOLFE MONA   BY2106A061286      108 GEN. PSYCHOLOGY    3
```

↑ GRADE-ROSTER-FILE   ↑ COURSE-CATALOG-FILE

NEW-ADMISSION-FILE
↓

```
GLEASON JIM 111222333NURSING   SENIOR1143775
WOLFE MONA  212356553HOME EC   SOPH  0340780
```

Load the list of courses into a directory so that by looking up a particular course number, the number of credits for that course can be determined. COURSE–TABLE allows up to 110 course entries. For example, the number of credits for course 102 is simply COURSE-CREDIT (102) = 3.

Read the first student record in GRADE–ROSTER–FILE.

Write out the header (first five lines) of the end-of-semester grade report as shown in paragraph TRANSCRIPT-HEADERS. Print the first record of the first student in GRADE–ROSTER–FILE, i.e. print the results of the first student's first course.

Paragraph TRANSCRIPT–HEADERS produces the following five lines of information:

```
FIELD STUDY   CLASS    STUDENT NAME          DATE       SS. NUMBER
HOME EC.      SOPH     WOLFE MONA           06 12 86    212356553
****************************************************************
COURSE        NUMBER   DESCRIPTION    HOURS  GRADE   POINTS   GPA
**************CUMULATIVE TOTALS          30             65.0
```

Print the number of credits/hours previously earned by the student. If freshman, hours = 0.

FIGURE 10–16
(continued)

```
2160 SEARCH-STUDENT-ADMISSION-FILE.
2170     READ STUDENT-ADMISSION-FILE
2180         AT END DISPLAY "NO SUCH RECORD IN ADMISSIONS"
2190             STOP RUN.
2200**** RETURN TO LINE 2020
2201*
2210 WRITE-RECORD.
2220     ADD  COURSE-CREDIT (COURSE-NO) TO CUM-HOURS.
2230     ADD  COURSE-CREDIT (COURSE-NO) TO WS-SEM-HRS.
2240     MOVE COURSE-CREDIT (COURSE-NO) TO DL-HOURS.
2250     MOVE GRADE            TO DL-GRADE.
2260     PERFORM COMPUTE-QUALITY-POINTS VARYING I FROM
2270         1 BY 1 UNTIL GRADE = LETTER-GRADE (I).
2280     COMPUTE WS-QUAL-PTS =
2290         COURSE-CREDIT (COURSE-NO) * GRADE-POINT (I).
2300     ADD WS-QUAL-PTS  TO WS-SEM-QUAL-PTS.
2310     ADD WS-QUAL-PTS  TO CUM-POINTS.
2320     MOVE WS-QUAL-PTS TO DL-POINTS.
2330     MOVE COURSE      TO DL-COURSE.
2340     MOVE COURSE-NO   TO DL-NUMBER.
2350     MOVE COURSE-DESCR (COURSE-NO) TO DL-DESCR.
2360     WRITE PRINT-LINE FROM DETAIL-LINE AFTER 1.
2370**** RETURN 1ST TIME TO LINE 1980 AND THEN TO 2530
2371*
2380 COMPUTE-QUALITY-POINTS.
2390     EXIT.
2400
2410 READ-PROCESS-WRITE.
0420     READ GRADE-ROSTER-FILE
2430         AT END MOVE 1 TO EOF-GRADE-ROSTER.
2440     IF NOT END-ROSTER
2450         PERFORM PROCESS-WRITE.
2460**** RETURN TO LINE 1790
2461*
2470 PROCESS-WRITE.
2480     IF SS-NO NOT = OLD-SS-NO
2490         PERFORM SUMMARY-TRANSCRIPT
2500         MOVE ZERO  TO WS-SEM-QUAL-PTS, WS-SEM-HRS
2510         MOVE SS-NO TO OLD-SS-NO
2520         PERFORM TRANSCRIPT-HEADERS.
2530         PERFORM WRITE-RECORD.
2540**** RETURN TO LINE 2450
2541*
2550 SUMMARY-TRANSCRIPT.
2555     MOVE STARS TO PRINT-LINE. WRITE PRINT-LINE.
2560     COMPUTE SL1-GPA = WS-SEM-QUAL-PTS / WS-SEM-HRS.
2570     COMPUTE SL2-GPA = CUM-POINTS / CUM-HOURS.
2580     MOVE WS-SEM-QUAL-PTS TO SL1-POINTS.
2590     MOVE WS-SEM-HRS     TO SL1-HOURS.
2600     MOVE CUM-HOURS      TO SL2-HOURS.
2610     MOVE CUM-POINTS     TO SL2-POINTS.
2620     WRITE PRINT-LINE FROM SUMMARY-LINE-1 AFTER 1.
2630     WRITE PRINT-LINE FROM SUMMARY-LINE-2 AFTER 1.
2635     MOVE CONSTANT-INFO TO NEW-CONSTANT-INFO.
2640     MOVE CUM-POINTS    TO NEW-CUM-POINTS.
2650     MOVE CUM-HOURS     TO NEW-CUM-HOURS.
2660     WRITE NEW-ADMISSION-RECORD.
2670**** RETURN TO LINE 2490 AND LAST TIME TO 1800
```

The admission file is searched for a social security number that matches the student's social security number in GRADE-ROSTER-FILE.

Typical output lines produced by paragraph WRITE-RECORD are shown as follows:

```
PSY 108 GEN. PSYCHOLOGY 3 B 9.0
BY2 106 MICROBIOLOGY LA 1 A 4.0
```

Note that, for example:

COURSE-CREDIT (100) = 4 credits and
COURSE-DESCR (100) = Nursing II.

Line 2260 determines the quality points associated with each particular letter grade; i.e., if GRADE = LETTER-GRADE (I) = C+, then the corresponding number of points for LETTER-GRADE (I) is GRADE-POINT (I) = 2.5.

Read a student record from GRADE-ROSTER-FILE.

If the student record just read does not belong to the previous student group, complete the end-of-semester report for the previous student; i.e., compute total semester hours, quality points, and GPA, and also compute the cumulative hours, quality points, and GPA.

Print the headers for the next end-of-semester grade report for the student record just read.

SUMMARY-TRANSCRIPT produces the following three lines of information:

```
*****************************************************************
         SEMESTER TOTALS      4         13.0  3.250
         CUM.    TOTALS      34         78.0  2.294
```

Update STUDENT-ADMISSION-FILE by creating a NEW-ADMISSION-FILE. Cumulative totals are updated.

FIGURE 10-16
(concluded)

10-6 YOU MIGHT WANT TO KNOW

1. When a sequential master file is updated using sequential access, a new master file is created either on a new tape or on a new area of disk. How does one tell the system that this updated file is to serve as the master file for the next update run without changing the SELECT/ASSIGN statement to identify the new file?

    Answer: If both files are tape files, the operator simply relabels the newly updated tapes as the current master tape and keeps the original master tape as a backup tape. The adhesive label is replaced. The internal labels, if any, can also be renamed.

    If a magnetic disk is used, special system commands/instructions (utility programs) allow the user to rename the updated file as the current file. This simply results in a name change in the disk directory.

2. What happens if I forget to close a disk file or a tape file?

    Answer: It depends on the system and on the file organization. Such an omission could lead to potential problems. Many systems will issue a warning during the compilation process.

3. What are some major advantages and disadvantages of magnetic tape?

    Answer: Advantages: Low cost storage is a major one. Magnetic tape is probably the least expensive form of storage for data that is seldom used. Portability, size, and weight are other advantages. Disadvantages: Any transactions to be stored on tape must first be batched and sorted into sequence before they can be processed. Tape records cannot be changed nor can records be inserted without rewriting the entire tape. If one record needs to be changed and the tape contains 200,000 records, all 200,000 records have to be rewritten!

4. What are the major advantages and disadvantages of magnetic disks?

    Answer: Advantages: If you need to read the 100,001st record on a magnetic tape, you must first read the 100,000 records that precede it. On magnetic disk, depending on the organization method used to store the records, the 100,001st record can be retrieved just as quickly as the first record! Hence, for any application that requires near instantaneous retrieval of records, magnetic disk is vastly superior to magnetic tape. For that reason, disks are used for on-line file updating when frequent inquiries into data files are required (on-line registrations, airline reservation systems, et cetera). Also, records can be changed without rewriting all the remaining records of the file.

    Disadvantages: Not as light nor as portable as magnetic tapes. Diskpacks are 20 to 50 times more expensive than magnetic tapes, and disk drives are significantly more expensive than tape drives.

5. What are the physical factors that affect speed in retrieving records on disk?

    Answer: a. *Access motion time.* This is the time it generally takes for the access arm of the disk drive to position itself over the desired disk track (groove). It is frequently measured in fractions of a second, typically 100 to 200 milliseconds.

b. *Rotational delay.* Disks spin anywhere from 100 to 2500 revolutions per second, depending on the model. Rotational delay is the average time it takes a record on a disk track to become positioned under the read/write heads. This delay is measured in milliseconds, typically 15 milliseconds.

c. *Data transfer.* This is the time that it takes the system to capture data on a track and transfer it to memory, typically 100 thousand to one million characters per second.

6. What different types of file organizations can be used on direct access storage devices?

   Answer: Files can be organized essentially in three different ways:

   a. *Sequential organization.* Records are stored in a sequence based on a unique identifier called a key. Each record (except the first and last) has a predecessor and a successor. This relationship between records is established when the file is written and does not change unless records are added or deleted. Both magnetic tapes and disks support this type of organization.

   Sequential file organization is most desirable in situations where the volume of transactions is high and where it is not necessary to update records as transactions occur. For example, in a billing application, customer statements would be prepared at scheduled intervals and then collected or batched together for one daily or weekly update run.

   b. *Direct access organization.* The record addressing scheme is based on a relationship between the record key and the record's physical location on the track. A new master file is not created when a direct access file is updated. A record that is deleted is actually only flagged and is not physically deleted; an updated record is changed and then rewritten on the same file.

   Direct access organization is used in applications where the time it takes to locate and process a particular record must be minimized.

   c. *Indexed sequential organization.* Initially, the records are stored sequentially by key order just as they would be in sequential organization. In addition, an index is created to identify certain record keys and their corresponding record disk addresses. A record can then be located by matching the desired record key against the index table to obtain the approximate disk area where the record lies. The search for the record then starts at that approximate area and proceeds in sequential fashion until the particular record is found. This process is a little like looking for someone's house in an unfamiliar neighborhood or city. One heads directly to the area identified by the street and then proceeds sequentially by visual inspection of numbers (keys) until the particular number is located.

   Indexed sequential organization is a compromise between sequential and direct access organizations. It is not as fast as sequential processing when nearly every record in the file must be processed, nor is it as fast as direct processing when instantaneous responses to inquiries are needed. An indexed sequential file organization is ideally suited to an inventory-type application where just a few weekly updates are required and where on-line queries to the file do not mandate instantaneous responses.

   Note that when a file is updated using either direct or indexed sequential file access, a change in one particular record does not cause other records to be displaced and rewritten as in the case of sequential access.

7. What considerations determine the selection of a particular file organization?

   Answer:

   a. File size.
   b. File activity. *Activity* refers to the proportion of records processed during an update run. A 100% activity file refers to a file in which all records are processed during a typical update run, while a 5% activity file refers to a file where only 5% of the records are typically processed. Generally speaking, high activity files benefit from sequential organization.
   c. Volatility. *Volatility* refers to the frequency of changes made to a file during a certain time period. Direct access processing is suited to low activity and high volatility files.

10–7 PROGRAMMING EXERCISES

1. The Grand Order of Beavers bills its members for dues on a monthly basis. The Vice-Exalted Flat Tail has been performing this task by hand, but since a computer system has become available, he feels that the billing could be made more efficient using a computerized system. Design and implement a system to maintain membership rolls and produce bills and associated reports. Payments should be processed in small batches as they are received. Include a feature for dropping a member if his dues are in arrears by three months or more.

2. In the program of Figure 10–16, which produced the end-of-semester grade report, include the code to change a student name in STUDENT–ADMISSION–FILE whenever matching social security numbers in GRADE–ROSTER–FILE and STUDENT–ADMISSION–FILE do not identify the same student name. This could happen, for instance, if a name change due to marriage occurs during the semester.

3. A personnel file consists of records identifying an employee's social security number, employee number, year-to-date gross pay, and year-to-date net pay. The file is organized sequentially by social security number key and is already stored on disk. Write a program to read the personnel file on disk and from that file create a similar personnel file organized by ascending employee number key rather than by social security number. List the contents of the new file.

4. Modify the update program of Figure 10–13, where transaction records can be inserted, changed, or deleted, to include the code to perform a sequence check on the transaction file.

5. Figure 10–16 did not include data validation. Rewrite the program to take care of the following situations:

   a. A social security number in GRADE–ROSTER–FILE has no corresponding match in STUDENT–ADMISSION–FILE. In such a case, print an appropriate error message identifying the name of the student not listed in the STUDENT–ADMISSION–FILE.
   b. A course number in the GRADE–ROSTER–FILE has been incorrectly typed and is not found in the course directory. Type an appropriate mes-

sage and abort the report for that student. Note that in such a case successive social security numbers may still belong to that student. Such records should be flushed out before continuing with the next record(s) for a different student.

c. The grade specified in the GRADE–ROSTER–FILE is incorrectly recorded; i.e., the grade is neither F, D, C, B, or A. Abort the current report and continue with the next report.

6. Dr. Teach keeps her students' grades on diskettes on her own microcomputer system. She has already entered the following information on each student into her master file: name, two test scores, and two blank entries for the final average and the corresponding letter grade. Dr. Teach's input data might be similar to:

Name	Test 1	Test 2	Average	Grade
DOE J	80	90	?	?
HILL K	60	62	?	?
⋮				

A = 90 or above
B+ = 85–89
B = 80–84
C+ = 75–79
C = 60–74
D = 50–59
F = below 50

Dr. Teach is now ready to write a program to compute each student's final score and corresponding letter grade. She realizes that in some cases, either or both test scores may have to be changed. Some students have withdrawn from the class and need their names deleted from the master file. Write a program to:

a. Create a class file arranged alphabetically by student name. Each record should contain a name, two test scores, and two initially blank fields for the final average and the letter grade.
b. Create a transaction file consisting of change records. Such records can cause deletion of certain records or changes in either one or both test scores. Use change codes of your choice.
c. Print an updated grade roster file listing the names of the students and their scores and letter grades. Identify transaction names that do not have matches in the master file.

The master file, transaction file, and output have the following form:

```
MASTER FILE              TRANSACTION FILE                          OUTPUT

DOE JOE     050070      DOE JOE     DELETE
LIKE SALLY  080090      LIKE SALLY  CHANGE1070    NAME          T1   T2   AVG   GRADE
TASS MIKE   065070      TASS MIKE   CHANGE1080
TURAN LEO   080070      TURAN LEO   CHANGE2080    LIKE SALLY    70   90   80    B
                        TURAN LEO   CHANGE1060    TASS MIKE     80   70   75    C+
                        AMIGO LUIS  CHANGE1060    TURAN LEO     60   80   70    C
                                                  NO MATCH FOR AMIGO
```

7. The Furniture Company has stock in three different warehouses. The controller/dispatcher needs to know at any given time the number of particular furniture items at each of the three warehouses. He may also need to know the number of each particular item in one warehouse. Initially, the stock of items in all warehouses is as follows:

	WAREHOUSE 1	WAREHOUSE 2	WAREHOUSE 3
TABLES	100	100	50
DESKS	123	44	76
CHAIRS	789	234	12
BEDS	67	456	90
SOFAS	10	50	20
LAMPS	100	200	100

The controller has at his fingertips a terminal where he can inquire about a particular item. For example, when he types "BEDS," the system furnishes him with the number of beds at the three warehouses.

   a. Write a program to allow the following communications between the dispatcher and the data base:

```
ENTER REQUEST
BEDS
          WAREHOUSE1    WAREHOUSE2    WAREHOUSE3
              67            456           90        TOTAL 613

ENTER REQUEST
WAREHOUSE3
          TABLES   DESKS   CHAIRS   BEDS   SOFAS   LAMPS
            50      76       12      90      20     100     TOTAL 348

ENTER REQUEST
CHAIRS
          WAREHOUSE1    WAREHOUSE2    WAREHOUSE3
             789           234           12        TOTAL 1035

ENTER REQUEST
```

Note that the message ENTER REQUEST is printed after each request has been satisfied. If the dispatcher enters an invalid request, the system should print an appropriate error message to force him to his request.

   b. How would you design a program to update the master file? Do so.

8. WKNE station's meteorologist has access to a master file containing weather data on most of the cities that lie within a 50-mile radius of the WKNE broadcasting station. Each record contains the name of the city and its record high and low temperatures for each of the past 20 years. The master file records have the following layout:

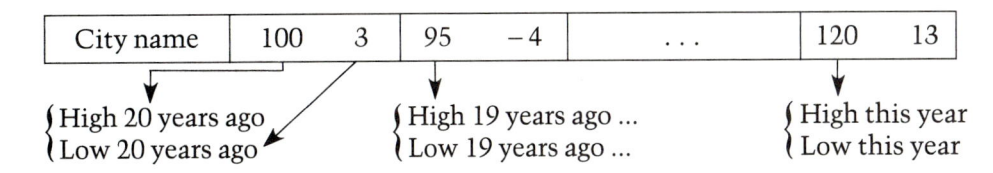

| City name | 100 | 3 | 95 | −4 | ... | 120 | 13 |

{ High 20 years ago / Low 20 years ago }   { High 19 years ago ... / Low 19 years ago ... }   { High this year / Low this year }

   a. Write a program to read a data file where each record contains the name of a city and the corresponding high and low temperatures for the day. These records have the following form:

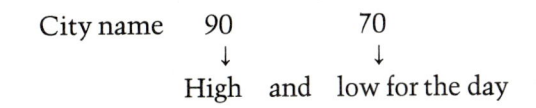

   City name   90   70
               ↓   ↓
              High and low for the day

The program should list the high and low temperatures of the day for the name of the city read and indicate whether any temperature records were broken during the day. A typical listing might be:

```
CITY           HIGH     LOW

ATMORE          98       70
BEULAH          95       68    PREVIOUS RECORD HI WAS 94 IN 1971
CHUMUCKLA       92       65    PREVIOUS RECORD LO WAS 66 IN 1979
MILTON          98       62
MARYESTHER     100       58    PREVIOUS RECORD HI WAS 98 IN 1974
                               PREVIOUS RECORD LO WAS 60 IN 1981
PACE            94       71    PREVIOUS RECORD LO WAS 72 IN 1984
```

Make sure to update the master file when record temperatures are broken; i.e., change the records in the master file to identify new highs or lows.

b. Design an on-line inquiry system to allow the meteorologist to perform the following functions:
   i. Key in a city name and a year and list the high and low for that city and year.
   ii. Key in a city name and identify the year(s) of its record high and low for the last 20 years. Print the city, year(s), and record high and low.
   iii. Key in a year and identify the city (cities) with the record high and low for that year.
   iv. Produce a listing arranged by year, identifying the record high and low for each city during the year. Over the 20-year period the output might be as follows:

```
YEAR     CITIES          HI      LO

1966     ATMORE          94      15
         BEULAH          91      21
         CHUMUCKLA       96      16
         MILTON          89      23
         MARYESTHER      90      20
         PACE            94       9

1967     ATMORE          98      10
         BEULAH          94      16
         CHUMUCKLA       89      14
                 .
                 .
                 .
1985     ATMORE          91      10
         BEULAH          90      12
                 .
         PACE            99      20
```

9. The Chique Boutique is an exclusive ladies' fashion store where members are required to maintain at least $1,000 in their accounts at all times. Members charge purchases on Chique Boutique credit cards. Members may return merchandise, in which case their account is credited appropriately.

Purchases may cause a member's credit to fall below $1,000, in which case a notice is sent to the member requesting that a check be written to bring back the member's credit to at least $1,000.

A transaction file for the month consists of various purchase records sorted by ascending customer numbers. Such records include a customer number, an item number and description, and a date of purchase. Multiple transactions (if there are more than one) for an individual customer occur in groups.

a. Write a program to create a master file consisting of customer numbers, customer names, and an initial balance of over $1,500 for each member.
b. Write a program to update the master file and produce a monthly customer invoice similar to the following:

```
CHIQUE BOUTIQUE
ACCT NO: 1215
DATE 02/05/86

                              DATE        BALANCE      PURCHASES
                                          10000.00
***JOVANT BOOTS               01/20/86     360.00
   ENSEMBLE LINGERIE          01/25/86                    550.75
   FLEURETTE FOUNDATION       01/25/86                    145.25
   PENDANT 20 KT.             01/27/86                   2600.00
                                          7064.00       3296.00
```

Note that *** is a credit entry (return).

```
CHIQUE BOUTIQUE
ACCT NO: 1315
DATE 02/05/86

                              DATE        BALANCE      PURCHASES
                                           2000.00
   NEGLIGEE EXQUIS            01/15/86                    600.00
   PEIGNOIR BROCADE           01/20/86                    400.00
   ILUNA ESSENCE 6 OZ. FL     01/23/86                    300.00
                                           700.00       1300.00

PLEASE REMIT MINIMUM OF $300.00
```

c. The Chique Boutique sales department would like to produce the following monthly sales activity report by ascending customer account number:

```
MONTHLY SALES REPORT: APRIL 1986

ACCOUNT NO.    TOTAL SALES    CUSTOMER BALANCE

   1215           3296.00          7064.00
   1315           1300.00           700.00
   1446          10432.00          5600.00
   1502          15028.00         13364.00
```

Write the code to generate such a report.

d. Write the code to produce a sales summary report for the internal auditor; this report shows the sales for each day of the month as follows:

```
        SUMMARY DAILY SALES

    DATE                SALES

   01/02/86           23452.00
   01/03/86           13452.00
   01/04/86           33400.70
      :                  :
```

e. Write another code for the auditor to produce a summary of daily sales by items, as follows:

```
DETAILED DAILY SALES
   DATE      ITEMS       SALES        TOTALS

  01/02/86
               112        344.00
               209        246.00
               321        410.00
               400      22452.00
                                      23,452.00
  01/03/86
               112        344.00
               216      10000.00
               312       3108.00
                                      13,452.00
     :          :           :            :
```

10. The Tricity College library staff is thinking about using computers to assist them in dealing with the high volume of book transactions. Four types of transactions must be considered:

   (1) Books checked in.   (3) New books put into circulation.
   (2) Books checked out.   (4) Old books withdrawn from circulation.

   Books have an 8-digit numeric code identification, the last two digits of which indicate a multicopy identification number:

   ```
            1 1 1 1 2 0 0 1
            1 1 1 1 2 0 0 3
   ```
   Book number ⎯⎦   ⎣⎯ Copy identification number (1–20)
             Number of copies in library

   The library clerks deal manually with four types of files:

   (1) The CHECK–IN–OUT–FILE.
       This file consists of a daily list of books that have been checked in or checked out. The record layout for each file is as follows:

Item	Nature
1	Book number identification
2	Disposition code (1 = check in, 2 = check out)
3	Julian date (025 means Jan. 25, 365 is Dec. 31)
4	Patron's identity (1 = faculty, 2 = student)
5	Patron's telephone number

```
            Book id.          Patron
              ↓                 ↓
           11112002      1 034 1 4345410
           11112017      2 034 1 4762500
           22220201      2 034 2 4785660
               |              |   |    |
           copies           Date    Telephone
           Book no.      Disposition code
              Copy number     Patron
                              identity
```

(2) **The NEW–BOOK–FILE.**
This file consists of books that have been either purchased or donated and do not exist in the master file. The record layout for such file records is:

Item	Nature
1	Book number identification
2	Year of edition
3	Disposition status (1 = available, 2 = reserve)
4	Author
5	Acquisition code (1 = purchased, 2 = donation)

(3) **The DELETE–FILE.**
Transaction records in this file allow the librarian to delete books from the master file or to change the status field of a particular book. The record layout for such file records is:

Item	Nature
1	Book number identification
2	Change code $\begin{cases} 1 = \text{delete} \\ 2 = \text{make status available} \\ 3 = \text{make status reserve} \end{cases}$

```
   ┌─ All 1130 books are deleted from the inventory.
   ▼
  1 1 3 0 | 1
  1 4 0 0 | 2   ← change code
          ▲
          └─ All 1400 books are now changed to available
             status (however many there were).
```

(4) **The MASTER–FILE.**
All records in the master file have the following layout:

Item	Nature
1	Book identification number
2	Author
3	Edition Year
4	Status disposition (1 = on loan, 2 = on shelf)
5	Date loaned (0 if book is not loaned)
6	Patron's identity (1 = faculty, 2 = student, 3 = on the shelf)
7	Acquisition code (1 = purchased, 2 = donation)
8	Reserve status (1 = available, 2 = reserve)
9	Patron's telephone number

Write a program to perform the following tasks:

a. Create the above four files and store them on disk. Assume the records are arranged sequentially according to the 8-digit book identification number.

b. Print the four disk files.
c. i. Assume that all disk file records are in sequence and that all transaction records are valid; i.e., transaction keys all have corresponding keys in the master file. Update MASTER–FILE with CHECK–IN–OUT–FILE.
   ii. Print a listing of the updated file.
   iii. Print a list of telephone numbers of patrons who possess overdue books. A book is overdue if it has been kept 30 days or more. A fine of 10 cents a day is charged for each day over 30 days. This report should indicate the telephone number, the number of days overdue, the original checkout day, and the corresponding fine in dollars and cents. No fines are listed for faculty members. Books that have not been returned after a 100-day overdue period are considered stolen. Flag such books on the output to allow the librarian to charge the patron for the cost of the book plus the 100-day fine. (These books will be deleted in part f. of this exercise by their inclusion in the DELETE–FILE.)
   iv. List each book identification number of MASTER–FILE and summarize for each volume the number of copies in (on the shelf) or out (on loan). The report should be similar to:

```
BOOK IDENTIFICATION    IN    OUT
     1111 20 03
     1111 20 08
     1111 20 17
                        3     17
     2000 18 02
     2000 18 12
                        2     16
          :
```

   v. Determine the percentage of books currently held by faculty and the percentage of books currently held by the students.
d. i. Update the current MASTER–FILE with NEW–BOOK–FILE; i.e., merge the two files. It is understood that no book in NEW–BOOK–FILE exists in the current MASTER–FILE. (See part g. for additions of books that currently exist in the master file.) Print an updated inventory listing.
   ii. During the update pass (i.e., do not reprocess the master file), keep track of all the book identification numbers that have been donated, and print a list of such titles at the conclusion of the update process.
e. i. Identify any author who has written two or more different books. Specify the author and corresponding list of books.
   ii. Produce a list of books arranged by ascending author order.
f. i. Update MASTER–FILE with DELETE–FILE.
   ii. Print the list of books that have been deleted (all such books are assumed to be currently on the shelf). Remember, there may be more than one of the same title.
   iii. Any book that has not been returned 100 days after the checkout date is considered stolen and hence should be deleted and brought to the attention of the librarian by means of an appropriate message.
   iv. Print the updated file.

g. On many occasions, the library purchases additional copies of existing books. Design a system to allow the librarian to add these books to the master file. Such purchases of new books can give rise to the following situations: Either the new books purchased need to be added to similar copies already on the shelf, in which case the quantity of existing books on hand needs to be changed; or the books to be added are newer editions, in which case all books with edition years less than that of the new edition must be taken out of circulation, i.e., deleted. If this is the case, the librarian would like to obtain a list of all books that are to be deleted, so that these entries can be added to the DELETE file of part f. of this problem. Write the code to take care of these possibilities.

CHAPTER 11

INDEXED SEQUENTIAL FILES

11–1 INDEXED FILES

11–2 PROCESSING AN INDEXED FILE SEQUENTIALLY (ACCESS MODE IS SEQUENTIAL)

11–3 PROCESSING RECORDS RANDOMLY

11–4 PROCESSING AN INDEXED FILE DYNAMICALLY

11–5 EXERCISES

INTRODUCTION In contrast to sequential file processing, an indexed file-processing system permits random inquiries or random updates to be made in the file; records in an indexed file are retrieved through specified primary or alternate keys. This chapter explains how to create indexed files and how to process them sequentially, randomly, and dynamically. The FILE STATUS entry and the START option are also introduced.

11-1 INDEXED FILES

11-1-1 SEQUENTIAL VERSUS INDEXED FILES

Recall from chapter 10 the characteristics of sequential file processing:

1. The records in a sequential file are organized in sequence based on a unique record key.

2. Updating a sequential file requires that all transaction records already be sorted in record key sequence (ascending or descending).

3. A new master file, physically distinct from the old master file, is always created as a result of a sequential update; this is true regardless of the number of transaction records, be it one or one thousand!

This type of file organization can be ideal in many information-processing environments where transactions can be accumulated, sorted in batches, and periodically run against a master sequential file. In other types of situations this approach may be less than ideal, especially in cases where random inquiries or random updates are to be processed on the spot or within a short time interval. In such a case, different file-processing methods must be used: one suitable method involves indexed files. An indexed file-processing system can be characterized as follows:

1. The user can access and process a particular record sequentially or directly (randomly) by identifying the particular record key called the *primary key*. When processing records randomly, no search of prior records is necessary. Internally, retrieving a record randomly is somewhat like using a table look-up procedure to retrieve a particular entry from a table. Thus an indexed file system can enable a bank employee to look up a customer's credit balance almost instantaneously, regardless of whether the record is the first or the last in the file, quite unlike a sequential search.

2. Only direct access files can be indexed. Such files must be stored on direct access storage devices such as magnetic disks, drums, and diskettes, but not on magnetic tapes.

3. Unlike sequential file updates, which create a new physical master file, no new master file is created as a result of updating an indexed file. Records can be added to the file, but this does not cause adjacent records to be physically relocated. Changes can be made to a particular record on the same track area that the record occupies. similarly, records can be deleted without altering the physical sequence of records in the file. Such records are simply flagged by the system as unavailable to the user.

4. In certain COBOL indexed files there are alternate keys, in addition to the primary record key, that can be used to randomly access records. For example, in a file organized by employee number (primary key), the employee name can be designated as an alternate key. This would allow the programmer to obtain a list of employee names in alphabetical order simply by reading the file and specifying the name as a key. Such alternate keys, of course, must be predesignated and specified at the time the indexed file is created. Direct record inquiries can then be made by specifying the alternate key. The reader should check with his/her system's COBOL technical manual to determine whether alternate keys are available.

5. Because of such flexibility, processing indexed files is more expensive than processing sequential files in terms of system overhead (hidden bookkeeping chores performed by the system). Also, more disk storage space is utilized than with sequential files. Deleted records are still physically present in the file. When numerous records have been added or deleted, the user can reorganize the indexed file by reading it sequentially and recopying it as an indexed file under a new name, or the user can use a system program (called a utility program) to reduce or compact the file. The issue of backup files is obviously central, since no old master file is available when updating an indexed sequential file. Careful consideration must be given to this subject, which is outside the scope of this text.

The implementation of indexed files at the ENVIRONMENT, DATA, and PROCEDURE DIVISION levels may vary slightly from one COBOL compiler to another. The following discussion of indexed files applies to the COBOL 74 implementation of indexed files.

11-1-2 OVERVIEW OF INDEXED FILES

Records within an indexed file may be accessed or retrieved through one or more keys (depending on the system) that are defined at the time the indexed file is created. **The number of such keys, their PICTURE descriptions, and their physical positions in the record cannot be changed later when the file is processed.**

There are two types of keys: a primary key (only one is allowed) and alternate keys (up to 256,) although many systems do not support alternate keys. A primary key is a particular data item in a record whose PICTURE and physical location in the record are the same for all the records in the file. The value of its primary key distinguishes a particular record from all other records in the file, i.e., it gives the record a unique identification. Indexed files are sorted on the basis of the primary key (in a personnel file, a social security number is a good primary key since no two employees can have the same social security number). It should be noted that **once the indexed file is created, it is no longer possible to**

change the value of a record's primary key, unless, of course, the record is deleted and a new record with a different key value is added to the file.

Other data items in a record can be selected as alternate keys to provide an alternate path to records in an indexed file. When an alternate key is specified in an indexed file, the system expects no two alternate key values in the file to be identical, otherwise identification of a record by its alternate key would no longer be unique (there is a provision, however, to allow duplicate values in a file for an alternate key). Alternate keys are generally used to look up records and *cannot* be used to add records to a file. They can be used to change or delete records by retrieving an appropriate record, although such a practice is discouraged unless the primary key is first verified. Since an indexed file is organized sequentially by primary key, records are added to a file through the primary key, and records should be changed or deleted through the primary key.

11–1–3 ENVIRONMENT DIVISION ENTRIES

Indexed files must be created sequentially, i.e., records must be organized by ascending primary key value. Once the indexed file has been created, it can then be processed sequentially, randomly, or dynamically (a combination of sequential and random access); the user specifies the desired mode through the ACCESS MODE clause in the SELECT clause, as shown in Figure 11–1.

The clauses listed in Figure 11–1 can appear in any order following the SELECT verb.

The ORGANIZATION IS INDEXED entry specifies the logical structure of the file. This organization cannot be changed subsequently; i.e., it is not possible to change later on to ORGANIZATION IS SEQUENTIAL and hope to process the file sequentially as described in chapter 10.

Once the indexed file has been created, the ACCESS MODE can be used to specify the way in which the records are to be accessed. If SEQUENTIAL ACCESS mode is specified, then all records for that particular application must be processed sequentially, i.e., they are read, stored, or changed in sequential fashion by ascending primary key. The alternate key(s) can also be used to retrieve records; the records are automatically retrieved, based on their ascending alternate key values (the system figures out their ascending key values).

```
SELECT file-name ASSIGN TO direct-access-device-name

    ORGANIZATION IS INDEXED

   ⎡                  ⎧ SEQUENTIAL ⎫ ⎤
   ⎢ ACCESS MODE IS   ⎨ RANDOM     ⎬ ⎥
   ⎣                  ⎩ DYNAMIC    ⎭ ⎦

    RECORD KEY IS data-name-1

   [ ALTERNATE RECORD KEY IS data-name-2  [WITH DUPLICATES] ] ...

    FILE STATUS IS data-name-3
```

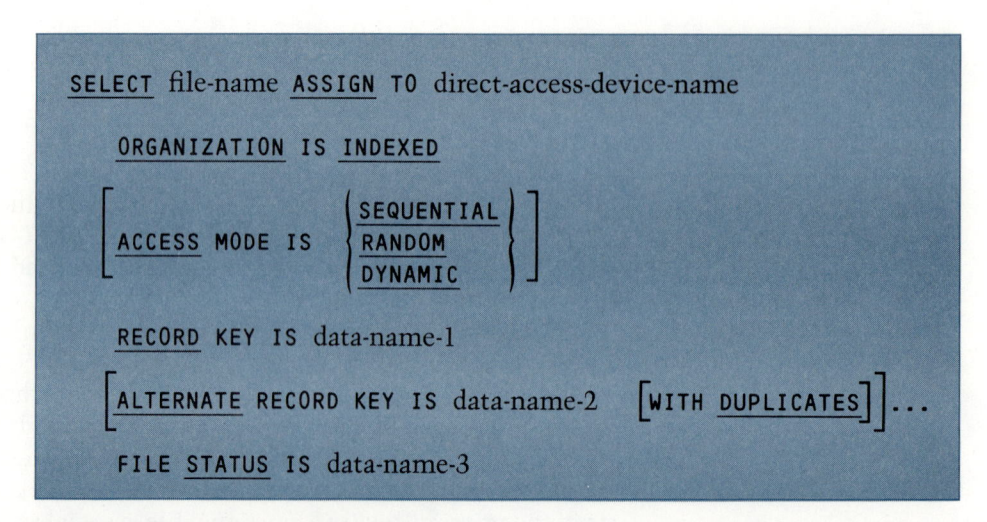

FIGURE 11–1

THE SELECT ENTRY FOR INDEXED FILES

If the RANDOM ACCESS mode is specified, records are retrieved randomly by specifying the primary key or an alternate key (if any exist).

When the DYNAMIC ACCESS mode is specified, records in the file can be accessed either sequentially or randomly in the same program.

If the ACCESS MODE clause is omitted, SEQUENTIAL access is implied.

The RECORD KEY specifies the data item to be used as the primary key. The data name specified by the RECORD KEY clause *must* be described in the record associated with the FD entry for the indexed file. In the case of multiple records, any field from any of the record descriptions can be used as long as it occupies the same position in all of the records, and as long as its PICTURE field is the same in all the records.

Many COBOL compilers require that the primary and alternate keys be alphanumeric and not greater than 256 characters in length.

The ALTERNATE RECORD KEY entry specifies other fields in the FD record area that can be used as alternate keys. The number of such keys, their PICTUREs, and their physical locations within the record are set at file creation time and may not be changed subsequently. Records may be retrieved through these alternate keys. An error will occur if a record that is to be added to the file contains an alternate key value that already exists in the indexed file—in such a case the record will not be added. Such an error will not occur, however, if the option WITH DUPLICATES is specified, i.e., it is then permissible to have records in the file contain the same value for a given alternate key; if such a record is to be accessed, the system will retrieve the first such record, i.e., the one with the lowest primary key value.

The FILE STATUS entry specifies a two-character alphanumeric item that must be described by the programmer in WORKING–STORAGE. This data item is updated by the system any time an input/output operation (OPEN, CLOSE, START, READ, WRITE, REWRITE, or DELETE instruction) is carried out on the indexed file. The FILE–STATUS entry reflects the outcome of any input/output operation in terms of its success or failure (can't find a record for a particular key, for example), and the status item can be tested by the user. A table of values for this file status word is shown in Figure 11–2.

1ST CHARACTER	2D CHARACTER	MEANING
0	0	Successful completion.
0	2	Duplicate keys exist (with DUPLICATES option).
1	0	AT END (end-of-file condition).
2	1	Sequence error for sequential READ.
2	2	Attempt to write duplicate keys.
2	3	No record found with that key.
2	4	Boundary violation. Insufficient disk space.
3	0	Hardware input/output error.
9	0	Incorrect OPEN mode or unsuccessful READ statement for a sequential DELETE or REWRITE.
9	1	File not opened.
9	2	Cannot open—file closed!
9	3	Cannot open—file is locked!
9	4	Invalid OPEN—no DD statement (job control).
9	5	Invalid device specification.
9	6	Undefined pointer status.
9	7	Invalid record length.

(Rows 9,1 through 9,7: May vary depending on system)

FIGURE 11–2
STATUS KEY MEANING

11-1-4 CREATING AN INDEXED FILE

An indexed file **must** be created sequentially. The COBOL entries for creating an indexed sequential file are shown in Figure 11-3.

When creating an indexed file, the input records must already be in ascending primary key value order (i.e., each key value must be greater than the preceding key value). The clause ORGANIZATION IS INDEXED is required; this specifies an indexed organization as opposed to a sequential file organization (ORGANIZATION IS SEQUENTIAL). The internal record arrangement on disk is different for the two types of file organization. Indexed organization cannot be changed to sequential organization later, but this does not mean that the indexed file cannot be accessed sequentially—it can, if the user specifies ACCESS MODE IS SEQUENTIAL. The point is that an indexed file is processed internal-

---

ENVIRONMENT DIVISION entries:

```
SELECT file-name ASSIGN TO direct-access-device-name
    ORGANIZATION IS INDEXED
    [ACCESS MODE IS SEQUENTIAL]
    RECORD KEY IS data-name-1
    [ALTERNATE RECORD IS data-name-2 [WITH DUPLICATES]]...
    [FILE STATUS IS data-name-3]
```

DATA DIVISION entries:

```
FD file-name
    [BLOCK CONTAINS  integer-1 TO  integer-2  { RECORDS   } ]
                                              { CHARACTERS }
    [RECORD CONTAINS [integer-3 TO] integer-4 CHARACTERS]
    LABEL RECORDS ARE STANDARD
    [DATA RECORDS ARE record-name-1 [record-name-2] ...]
```

PROCEDURE DIVISION entries:

```
OPEN OUTPUT file-name
    WRITE record-name [FROM data-name-4]  INVALID KEY imperative-statement ...
```

INVALID KEY error conditions:	
WRITE:	Key values are not in ascending order from one WRITE to the next WRITE. The allocated disk space is exceeded.

FIGURE 11-3
COBOL ENTRIES TO CREATE AN INDEXED FILE

ly with keys, whereas no keys are used internally with sequential files. When an indexed file is processed sequentially, keys are still used internally to access the records, even though this may not be apparent to the user.

The entry ACCESS MODE IS SEQUENTIAL can be omitted; it specifies that the records are arranged in ascending primary key value sequence. The absence of such a clause implies sequential access.

The RECORD KEY entry is mandatory; it specifies the name of the user-designated field in the input record that is to be used by the system to sequence the file. The actual record key name must be present in the FD record description entry associated with the indexed file. This key, called the primary key, can be used subsequently to access records in the file either sequentially or randomly. Each record key must have a value that is unique in the file, i.e., no two record key values can be the same, since the system would not be able to differentiate one record from the other.

The user can optionally designate alternate keys (system permitting). These keys allow the system and the user to retrieve a record by a key other than its primary key. The values of alternate keys, just like the values of the primary key, must be unique within the file; otherwise identification of the record is not unique. However, if the option WITH DUPLICATES is used, then an alternate key may have the same value in more than one record; in other words, an alternate key value may be present in two or more records.

Once the file has been created, it is no longer possible to change the primary key to a different field in the record, nor is it possible to change the key's length or its PICTURE. The name of the key itself may be changed, of course, from one program to the next, for example, in the creation program the primary key might be called ISAM-KEY, and in subsequent programs processing the indexed file the primary key might be called EMP-NUMBER;—**the important point is that the primary key's PICTURE, its position in the record, and its length must not be changed.**

The FILE STATUS clause, if used, must designate a user-specified data item consisting of two alphanumeric characters into which a value will be moved by the system. This two-character code reflects possible error outcomes as a result of OPEN, WRITE, and CLOSE instructions relating to the indexed file. The user can then test these values and take appropriate action. The first character of the FILE STATUS word is referred to as status key 1, and the second character is referred to as status key 2 (see Figure 11-2).

The FD entries are identical to the entries we have specified for the files we have discussed so far. If multiple records are present, each record must describe the primary and secondary keys (if any). These keys should have the same position and PICTURE in each record. The key names themselves will be different, and one of these names must be specified in the RECORD KEY entry. Even though records may vary in length, the primary or alternate keys should be fixed in length.

In the PROCEDURE DIVISION, the OPEN clause *must* specify OUTPUT and the file name. **Once the indexed file has been created, it should *never* be opened as an OUTPUT file, since the contents of the file would be automatically destroyed by the system to prepare for the creation of a new file!**

The WRITE statement releases one logical record to the disk file (output file), then this logical record is no longer available in the FD record area for that file.

The WRITE statement should specify the INVALID KEY clause. This clause will be activated during the creation of an indexed file if the primary key of the record to be written is not in sequence or if the record contains a key whose value has already been written onto disk as part of another record. In either event the record is not written and the imperative statements are executed. The imperative statements must be nonconditional statements; if particular conditions are to be tested, an imperative statement such as PERFORM ERROR-TEST can be used—within that paragraph IF sentences can then test the FILE STATUS or test for other conditions.

11-1-5 PROGRAM EXAMPLE

An input file, shown in Figure 11-4, consists of records containing an item number (primary key), an item description (alternate key), an item quantity, and an item cost. Let us write a program to create an indexed sequential file from such an input file. Figure 11-4 shows the program and the resulting indexed file INVENTORY-FILE stored on disk; an error printout is also provided to identify errors that occurred while trying to write certain records onto disk. Note that out-of-sequence input records are not written onto the file; the same is true for records whose key values are already present in the file.

If alternate keys are used in the program, as shown at lines 17, 82, and 83, the resulting indexed file and error output file would appear as:

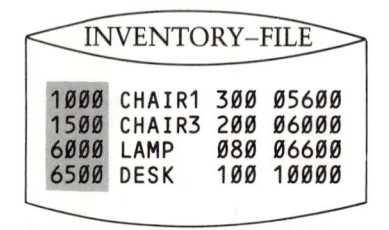

```
   INVENTORY-FILE                    ERROR-FILE
  1000 CHAIR1 300 05600      KEY SEQUENCE ERROR: 1400
  1500 CHAIR3 200 06000      KEY SEQUENCE ERROR: 1480
  6000 LAMP   080 06600      DUPLICATE KEY     : 2000
  6500 DESK   100 10000
```

The record with key value 2000 is not written onto the indexed file since the alternate key CHAIR3 occurs more than once in the input file. Remember that key values must be unique in the file—otherwise they are useless for retrieval purposes!

11-2 PROCESSING AN INDEXED FILE SEQUENTIALLY (ACCESS MODE IS SEQUENTIAL)

11-2-1 AN OVERVIEW

The following types of tasks can be carried out on an indexed file when ACCESS MODE IS SEQUENTIAL:

1. Creating an indexed file (using the WRITE instruction).
2. Reading the contents (or part of the contents) of an indexed file based on the primary or alternate keys (using the READ instruction).
3. Changing fields within records (using the READ and then the REWRITE instructions).
4. Deleting records from the file (using the READ and then the DELETE instructions).

Note that operations 3 and 4 above do not result in the creation of a new master file (distinct from the original master file) on disk, as would happen if the file organization were sequential (chapter 10).

New records *cannot* be added to an indexed file when accessing the file sequentially (ACCESS MODE IS SEQUENTIAL). This can be accomplished only when the ACCESS MODE IS RANDOM.

The WRITE instruction should be used at only one time—when creating the indexed file.

A special instruction START (discussed in the next section) allows the user to skip records and start processing records anywhere in the file. The START instruction can be used in tasks 2, 3, and 4.

Indexed files can be opened in INPUT, OUTPUT, or I–O mode. INPUT allows READ operations, OUTPUT is only for creating the file for the first time, and I–O is for changing and deleting records.

The various input/output statements that can be used to manipulate indexed files sequentially are shown in Figure 11–5. Many of these input/output instructions can be used only in conjunction with certain options of the OPEN verb (see table in Figure 11–5).

Opening an indexed file as OUTPUT when ACCESS MODE IS SEQUENTIAL is **fatal**—the contents of the file will be destroyed. (The system thinks you are about to create an indexed file!)

Indexed files must be opened before they can be processed. If LOCK is specified in the CLOSE statement, then the LOCKed file cannot be reopened during the program run.

11-2-2 THE START VERB

Just as in the case of files that were processed sequentially (discussed in chapter 10), the READ statement for indexed files with ACCESS IS SEQUENTIAL also reads records one after the other in key order sequence starting with the very first record of the file. This means that if you want to start processing the file at a particular key entry, you must read each record and test the primary key to determine if you have reached your starting point. This is tedious and requires that you write the code to skip the unwanted records. With the START feature, access to the desired record is immediate!

In essence the START option allows the user to start processing an indexed file at any particular record in the file by specifying the desired record's key. This key can be either the primary key or an alternate key. The START feature makes sequential processing of records more efficient as it allows the program to skip over many records and start right in the middle of (or anywhere else in) a file.

The general form of the START statement is shown in Figure 11–5. Filename is the name of the indexed file, and the KEY option specifies the key that is to be used to identify the "start" record.

The KEY phrase can specify the primary key, the alternate key(s), or the first subitem of any of the keys if the keys themselves are group items. The three conditions specified in the START clause allow the user to start not only right at the specified record key value (KEY EQUAL TO data-name), but also at the first record that satisfies a particular condition such as KEY GREATER THAN data-name or KEY NOT LESS THAN data-name. For example, if the file consisted of a list of names, BURNS, DAVON, STEVENS, STEWARD, ..., the user might want to start in the file at the first name greater than STEVENS. Processing would then start at STEWARD and continue in sequence based on as-

```
01: IDENTIFICATION DIVISION.
02: PROGRAM-ID. CREATE-FILE.
03: ****************************************
04: * C R E A T I N G   A N   I N D E X E D   F I L E *
05: ****************************************
06: AUTHOR. JONES.
07: ENVIRONMENT DIVISION.
08: CONFIGURATION SECTION.
09: SOURCE-COMPUTER. IBM.
10: OBJECT-COMPUTER. IBM.
11: INPUT-OUTPUT SECTION.
12: FILE-CONTROL.
13: *
14:     SELECT INVENTORY-FILE ASSIGN TO DISK
15:     ORGANIZATION IS INDEXED
16:     RECORD KEY   IS IR-ITEM-NO
17: *****ALTERNATE RECORD KEY IS IR-ITEM-DESCR
18:     FILE STATUS IS SEQUENCE-FLAG.
19: *
20:     SELECT INPUT-FILE ASSIGN TO DISK
21:     ORGANIZATION IS LINE SEQUENTIAL.
22: *
23:     SELECT ERROR-FILE ASSIGN TO PRINTER.
24: *
25: DATA DIVISION.
26: FILE SECTION.
27: *
28: FD  INPUT-FILE
29:     LABEL RECORDS ARE STANDARD
30:     VALUE OF FILE-ID IS 'INVENTRY'
31:     DATA RECORD IS INPUT-RECORD.
32: 01  INPUT-RECORD PIC X(21).
33: *
34: FD  INVENTORY-FILE
35:     LABEL RECORDS ARE STANDARD
36:     BLOCK CONTAINS 10 RECORDS
37:     RECORD CONTAINS 21 CHARACTERS
38:     VALUE OF FILE-ID IS 'INVEN'
39:     DATA RECORD IS INVENTORY-RECORD.
40: 01  INVENTORY-RECORD.
41:     05 IR-ITEM-NO    PIC X(04).
42:     05 FILLER        PIC X.
43:     05 IR-ITEM-DESCR PIC X(06).
44:     05 FILLER        PIC X.
45:     05 IR-ITEM-QTY   PIC 999.
46:     05 FILLER        PIC X.
47:     05 IR-ITEM-COST  PIC 999V99.
48: *
49: FD  ERROR-FILE
50:     LABEL RECORDS ARE OMITTED.
51: 01  ERROR-LINE PIC X(80).
52: *
53: WORKING-STORAGE SECTION.
54: 01  FLAGS.
55:     05 WS-EOF PIC 9 VALUE 0.
56:     05 SEQUENCE-FLAG PIC X(02).
57: 01  ERROR-MESSG.
58:     05 FILLER    PIC X VALUE SPACES.
59:     05 EM-MESSG PIC X(20).
60:     05 EM-KEY    PIC X(04).
```

INVENTORY-FILE is an indexed file and thus has a different logical structure than a sequential file (see line 15). Records are written onto the file in sequential key record order. The primary and alternate keys are specified in the SELECT clause; they must also be defined in the DATA division. Either key may be used to access a particular record. FILE STATUS allows the user to test whether input records are in primary key order or if two or more records have the same key value. In the first case, out-of-sequence records are not written onto the indexed file, and in the second case only the first record is written.

```
        ITEM         ITEM
     DESCRIPTION    COST
ITEM           ITEM
NUMBER       QUANTITY            ─INPUT-FILE

1000  CHAIR1  300  05600
1500  CHAIR3  200  06000
1400  CHAIR2  100  08000 }  These two input records are
1480  TABLE1  400  10000 }  out of sequence and will not be
2000  CHAIR3  500  05000    written onto the indexed file.
6000  LAMP    080  06600
6500  DESK    100  10000
```

INDEXED FILE
↓

```
INVENTORY-FILE
1000  CHAIR1  300  05600
1500  CHAIR3  200  06000
2000  CHAIR3  500  05000
6000  LAMP    080  06600
6500  DESK    100  10000
```

This file is catalogued on disk under name 'INVENTRY' (see line 30).

```
KEY SEQUENCE ERROR: 1400
KEY SEQUENCE ERROR: 1480
```

Error messages are printed by line 84 as a result of testing the status flag (line 80). Two input records were out of sequence.

FIGURE 11-4
CREATION OF AN INDEXED FILE

INDEXED SEQUENTIAL FILES

INPUT-FILE

ITEM NUMBER	ITEM DESCRIPTION	ITEM QUANTITY	ITEM COST
1000	CHAIR1	300	05600
1500	CHAIR3	200	06000
1400	CHAIR2	100	08000
1480	TABLE1	400	10000
2000	CHAIR3	500	05000
6000	LAMP	080	06600
6500	DESK	100	10000

Primary → (Item Number column)   Alternate key → (Item Description column)

Creation of the indexed sequential file ← **File creation program** → Reject out of sequence records

INVENTORY-FILE

1000	CHAIR1	300	05600
1500	CHAIR3	200	06000
2000	CHAIR3	500	05000
6000	LAMP	080	06600
6500	DESK	100	10000

ERROR-FILE

```
KEY SEQUENCE ERROR: 1400
KEY SEQUENCE ERROR: 1480
```

```
61: *
62: PROCEDURE DIVISION.
63: 100-MAIN-LOGIC.
64:     OPEN INPUT INPUT-FILE.
65:     OPEN OUTPUT INVENTORY-FILE, ERROR-FILE.
66:     READ INPUT-FILE INTO INVENTORY-RECORD
67:         AT END MOVE 1 TO WS-EOF.
68:     PERFORM 200-CREATE-INDEXED-FILE
69:         UNTIL WS-EOF = 1.
70:     CLOSE ERROR-FILE, INVENTORY-FILE, INPUT-FILE.
71:     STOP RUN.
72: *
73: 200-CREATE-INDEXED-FILE.
74:     WRITE INVENTORY-RECORD
75:         INVALID KEY PERFORM 300-ERROR-TEST.
76:     READ INPUT-FILE INTO INVENTORY-RECORD
77:         AT END MOVE 1 TO WS-EOF.
78: *
79: 300-ERROR-TEST.
80:     IF SEQUENCE-FLAG = '21'
81:         MOVE 'KEY SEQUENCE ERROR:' TO EM-MESSG.
82: *****IF SEQUENCE-FLAG = '22'
83: *****    MOVE 'DUPLICATE KEY      :' TO EM-MESSG.
84:     WRITE ERROR-LINE FROM ERROR-MESSG AFTER 1.
```

OPEN OUTPUT is required when creating an indexed file.
Read the first input record and copy that record into the indexed file INVENTORY-FILE, then keep reading and transferring the next input records to the indexed file.

Move the input record to the indexed file record and write the record onto disk. If an error occurs as a result of the WRITE, go find out why at ERROR-TEST. Read the next transaction record.

If the error code is 21, the record just read is out of sequence. The record in error is not written, and an error message is printed. If the error code is 22, the alternate key of the transaction record just read has a value that is identical to one that has already been written onto disk. This is an error, and the record is not written.

FIGURE 11–4
(continued)

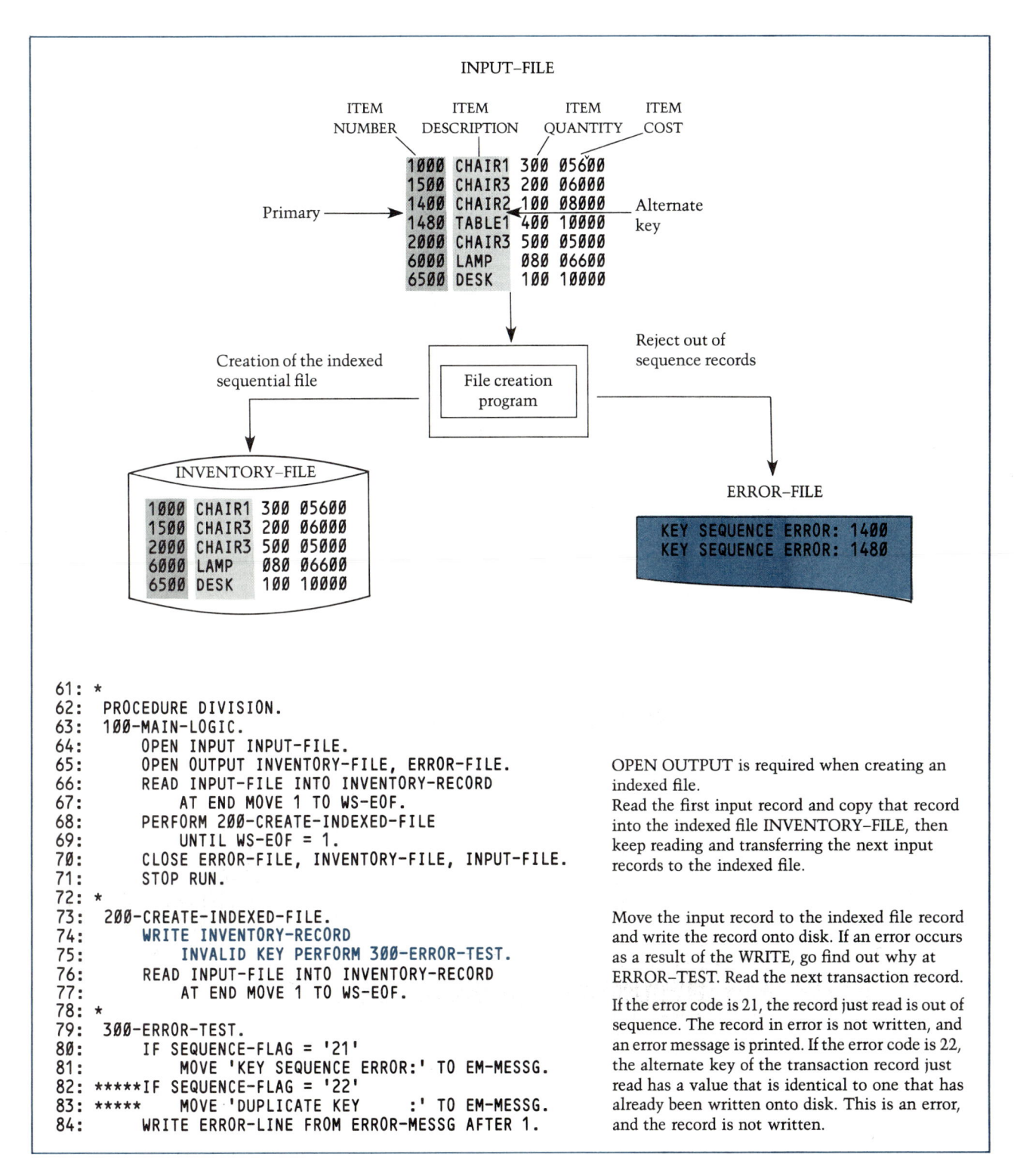

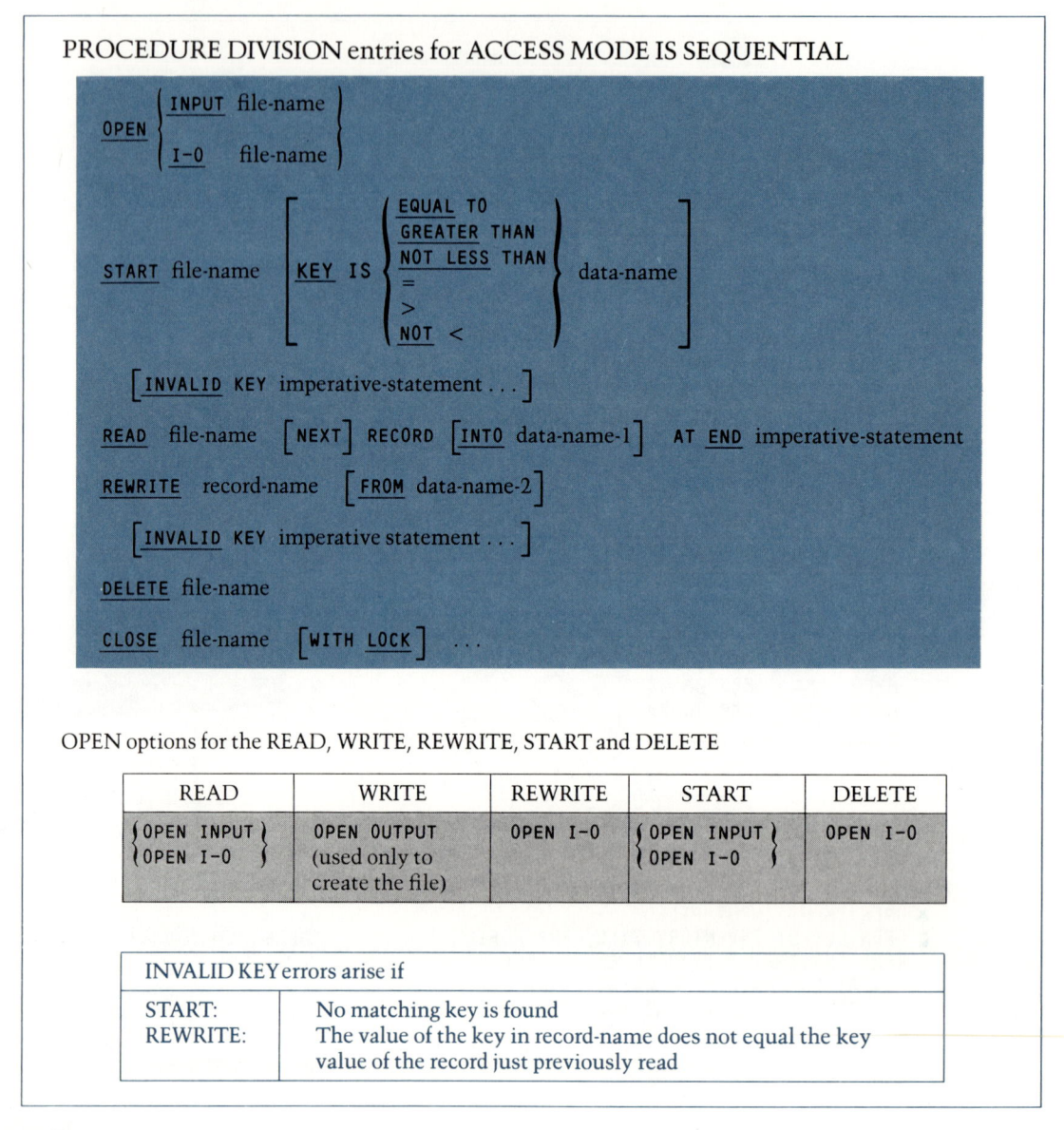

PROCEDURE DIVISION entries for ACCESS MODE IS SEQUENTIAL

```
OPEN  { INPUT file-name }
      { I-O   file-name }

START file-name [ KEY IS { EQUAL TO        } data-name ]
                         { GREATER THAN    }
                         { NOT LESS THAN   }
                         { =               }
                         { >               }
                         { NOT <           }

    [ INVALID KEY imperative-statement ... ]

READ file-name [NEXT] RECORD [INTO data-name-1]  AT END imperative-statement

REWRITE record-name [FROM data-name-2]

    [ INVALID KEY imperative statement ... ]

DELETE file-name

CLOSE file-name [WITH LOCK] ...
```

OPEN options for the READ, WRITE, REWRITE, START and DELETE

READ	WRITE	REWRITE	START	DELETE
{ OPEN INPUT } { OPEN I-O }	OPEN OUTPUT (used only to create the file)	OPEN I-O	{ OPEN INPUT } { OPEN I-O }	OPEN I-O

INVALID KEY errors arise if	
START: REWRITE:	No matching key is found The value of the key in record-name does not equal the key value of the record just previously read

FIGURE 11–5

COBOL ENTRIES TO PROCESS AN EXISTING INDEXED FILE SEQUENTIALLY

cending name order. Note that the name could have been specified as a primary key or as an alternate key.

If the KEY phrase is not specified, the starting record is identified by the value of the primary key, and the condition EQUAL TO is assumed; i.e., the START points to the record specified by the primary key.

The INVALID KEY option is activated if the condition specified is not satisfied by any record in the file; i.e., no key can be found that is EQUAL to (or GREATER THAN or NOT LESS THAN) the value specified in the RECORD KEY or in the ALTERNATE RECORD KEY field.

Note that the START does not actually read a record—it merely locates or points to a desired record in the file, causing the next READ statement associated with the file to capture a record at the position indicated by the START. To understand the START mechanism, consider the following coding segments:

INDEXED SEQUENTIAL FILES

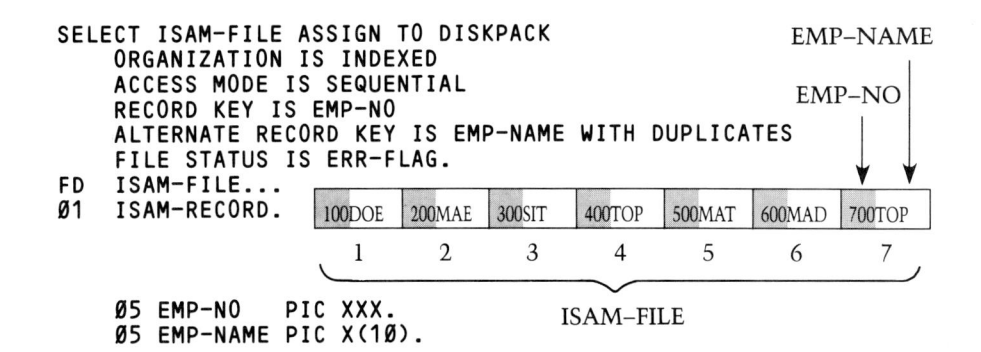

```
    SELECT ISAM-FILE ASSIGN TO DISKPACK              EMP-NAME
        ORGANIZATION IS INDEXED
        ACCESS MODE IS SEQUENTIAL                    EMP-NO
        RECORD KEY IS EMP-NO
        ALTERNATE RECORD KEY IS EMP-NAME WITH DUPLICATES
        FILE STATUS IS ERR-FLAG.
 FD ISAM-FILE...
 01 ISAM-RECORD.    100DOE 200MAE 300SIT 400TOP 500MAT 600MAD 700TOP
                      1      2      3      4      5      6      7
                                     ISAM-FILE
    05 EMP-NO   PIC XXX.
    05 EMP-NAME PIC X(10).
```

To start reading the file at employee number 400, the following code could be used:

```
    MOVE '400' TO EMP-NO.
    START ISAM-FILE
    INVALID KEY DISPLAY ERR-FLAG.
    READ ISAM-FILE ...
```

If the KEY clause is omitted from the START instruction, the START will point to the record with primary key 400. If key 400 is not in the file, the INVALID KEY will be activated.

Alternate keys can be used as follows:

```
    MOVE 'MAD' TO EMP-NAME.
    START ISAM-FILE
        KEY GREATER EMP-NAME
        INVALID KEY DISPLAY ERR-FLAG.
    READ ISAM-FILE ...

    MOVE 'TOP' TO EMP-NAME.
    START ISAM-FILE
        KEY = EMP-NAME
        INVALID KEY
            DISPLAY ERR-FLAG.
    READ ISAM-FILE ...
```

START will point to the first record whose alternate key is greater than MAD, which is MAE (record 2). If MAE had been specified, then MAT would be the next record.

START will point to record 4, which is the first occurrence of duplicate key TOP (since the primary key 400 occurs before the primary key 700). A subsequent START with alternate key value TOP will still point to record 4 and not to record 7.

The START feature has many useful applications. For example, to print all employee names of ISAM-FILE from the letter M to the letter Z in alphabetical sequence, the following code can be used:

```
    MOVE 'M' TO EMP-NAME.
    START ISAM-FILE
        KEY NOT < EMP-NAME
        INVALID KEY DISPLAY ERR-FLAG.
    PERFORM LIST-NAMES
        UNTIL WS-EOF = 1.
        .
LIST-NAMES.
    READ ISAM-FILE AT END
        MOVE 1 TO WS-EOF.
    IF WS-EOF NOT = 1 DISPLAY ISAM-REC.
```

The alternate key EMP-NAME is now used for the READ operation starting with the first name that is not less than M. Using the sample file shown above, the list of names displayed would be in alphabetical order as follows:

```
600 MAD
200 MAE
500 MAT
300 SIT
400 TOP
700 TOP
```

To determine whether name MOP is present in the file, the following code could be used:

```
MOVE 'MOP' TO EMP-NAME.
START ISAM-FILE INVALID KEY DISPLAY 'NO MOP'.
```

EQUAL TO is the implied condition for the START, since the KEY IS clause is not present in the START instruction.

11-2-3 A PROGRAM TO LIST PART OF AN INDEXED FILE

Problem Specification:

An indexed sequential inventory file consists of a part number designated as the primary key, an item description designated as an alternate key, an item quantity, and an item cost. Write a program to allow a user to list the inventory records starting at an item description specified by the user through the ACCEPT statement. (The list of items should be in alphabetical sequence, of course.)

Program Analysis

The program to solve this problem is shown in Figure 11-6. Through the alternate key, the program is made to list the item descriptions in alphabetical order starting with the ACCEPTed item description CHAIR3 (line 910). The START verb (line 920) is used to home in immediately on CHAIR3. This sets up the alternate key for the READ operation at line 830. From then on, the system weaves its way alphabetically through the remaining item descriptions (line 980).

If CHAIR3 is not in the file, the program will list all other item descriptions that would follow CHAIR3, since the condition NOT LESS THAN is specified at line 930.

11-2-4 DELETING RECORDS

Records can be deleted only if the file has been opened as an I–O file. Any record that is to be deleted must first be successfully read from the indexed file. The DELETE instruction deletes the most recent record that was successfully read from the file. Other input/output operations on other files may take place, however, between the associated READ and the DELETE instruction.

Deletion of a record causes the record to be logically removed from the file, but this does not necessarily result in the physical removal of the record from the disk area. The record is flagged by the system as a deleted record and ignored on subsequent input operations for that file.

The user should realize that deleting a record is permanent—the record is gone forever as far as the programmer is concerned. Therefore, before deleting a record, the user should verify that the particular record read is indeed the one to be deleted! A listing or a copy of deletion records should be made for backup or documentation purposes in case something goes wrong!

Executing a DELETE instruction does not affect the contents of the record area associated with the indexed file, i.e., the copy of the record to be deleted is still in the record area.

Note that there is no INVALID KEY clause associated with the DELETE instruction (nowhere to go if something "wrong" happens); the last record read is simply removed!

INDEXED SEQUENTIAL FILES

```
000390 IDENTIFICATION DIVISION.
000400 PROGRAM-ID. INDEXED-FILES.
000410************************************************
000420*  P R I N T I N G   A N   I N D E X E D   F I L E *
000430************************************************
000440 ENVIRONMENT DIVISION.
000450 CONFIGURATION SECTION.
000460 SOURCE-COMPUTER. BURROUGHS.
000470 OBJECT-COMPUTER. BURROUGHS.
000480 INPUT-OUTPUT SECTION.
000490 FILE-CONTROL.
000500 SELECT ISAM-FILE ASSIGN TO  DISKPACK
000510          ORGANIZATION       IS INDEXED
000520          ACCESS MODE        IS SEQUENTIAL
000530          RECORD KEY         IS IR-ITEM-NO
000540          ALTERNATE RECORD KEY IS IR-ITEM-DESCR
000550          FILE STATUS        IS WRITE-ERROR.
000560 SELECT PRINT-FILE ASSIGN TO PRINTER.
000570 DATA DIVISION.
000580 FILE SECTION.
000590 FD  PRINT-FILE
000600     LABEL RECORDS ARE OMITTED
000610     DATA RECORD IS PRINT-LINE.
000620 01  PRINT-LINE PIC X(132).
000630*
000640 FD  ISAM-INVENTORY
000650     BLOCK CONTAINS 10 RECORDS
000660     LABEL RECORDS ARE STANDARD
000670     DATA RECORD IS ISAM-RECORD
000680     RECORD CONTAINS 18 CHARACTERS.
000690 01  ISAM-RECORD.
000700     05  IR-ITEM-NO    PIC XXXX.
000710     05  IR-ITEM-DESCR PIC X(6).
000720     05  IR-ITEM-QTY   PIC 999.
000730     05  IR-ITEM-COST  PIC 999V99.
000740*
000750 WORKING-STORAGE SECTION.
000760 01  FLAGS.
000770     05  WRITE-ERROR   PIC XX.
000780     05  ISAM-EOF      PIC 9 VALUE 0.
000790*
000800 PROCEDURE DIVISION.
000810 MAIN-LOGIC.
000820     PERFORM 10-INITIALIZATION.
000830     READ ISAM-INVENTORY INTO PRINT-LINE
000840          AT END MOVE 1 TO ISAM-EOF.
000850     PERFORM 20-LIST-ISAM-FILE UNTIL ISAM-EOF = 1.
000860     CLOSE ISAM-INVENTORY, PRINT-FILE.
000870     STOP RUN.
000880*
000890 10-INITIALIZATION.
000900     OPEN INPUT ISAM-INVENTORY, OUTPUT PRINT-FILE.
000910     ACCEPT IR-ITEM-DESCR.   (Assume chair3)
000920     START ISAM-INVENTORY
000930          KEY IS NOT LESS THAN IR-ITEM-DESCR
000940              INVALID KEY DISPLAY WRITE-ERROR.
000950*
000960 20-LIST-ISAM-FILE.
000970     WRITE PRINT-LINE AFTER 1.
000980     READ ISAM-INVENTORY INTO PRINT-LINE
000990          AT END MOVE 1 TO ISAM-EOF.
```

The file is to be processed as a sequential file.

The records will be accessed by the alternate key. (Records could also be accessed by specifying the primary key.)

The program prints a list of records starting with an item description provided by the user (see line 910), e.g. CHAIR3.

ISAM-INVENTORY

```
1000CHAIR130005600
1500CHAIR320006000
6000LAMP  08006600
6500DESK  10010000
```
} Inventory-file

This inventory will produce the following list of records when CHAIR3 is specified as the starting record:

```
1500CHAIR320006000
6500DESK  10010000
6000LAMP  08006600
```
} Item descriptions in order

Note that the records are in alphabetical order by item description.

Go and open the various files and determine the item description that will start the list. The user tells the system which item description should begin the list of records to be printed (CHAIR3 in this example). If the particular item description is not present in the file, the list will start with the record whose item description is greater than the item description entered.

The records are then read and written sequentially as they appear in the file.

FIGURE 11–6

PRINTING A PARTIAL INDEXED FILE

For example, to delete a record whose primary key value is 600 in the indexed file ISAM–FILE, the following code can be used:

Approach 1:

```
READ ISAM-FILE AT END MOVE 1 TO WS-EOF.
PERFORM DELETE-PARA UNTIL WS-EOF = 1
    OR WS-FLAG = "FOUND".
    .
    .
    .
DELETE-PARA.
    IF PRIMARY-KEY = "600"
        DELETE ISAM-FILE
        MOVE "FOUND" TO WS-FLAG.
    READ ISAM-FILE AT END MOVE 1 TO WS-EOF.
```

Search the file sequentially until the record with primary key value 600 is found. Then delete it and stop the search process.

Make sure you have the right record!

Approach 2:

```
MOVE "600" TO PRIMARY-KEY.
START ISAM-FILE
    INVALID KEY PERFORM TEST-ERROR.
READ ISAM-FILE AT END MOVE 1 TO WS-EOF.
IF PRIMARY-KEY = "600"
    DELETE ISAM-FILE
ELSE ...
```

Skip directly to record 600 if it exists and then delete it.

Make sure it is record 600 that is about to be deleted!

11-2-5 CHANGING RECORDS

Records are changed by means of the REWRITE instruction (see Figure 11–5). Records can be changed only when the file has been opened as an I–O file. The record length of the new record must be the same as the length of the record it replaces, and the primary key value should not be changed!

The transaction file of the records to be changed must be in ascending primary key order. Master file records are read until a match between a master and a transaction key occurs. The programmer then makes the necessary changes to the record, and the newly changed record is logically released (BLOCKSIZE may have been specified) to the file by means of the REWRITE statement. Intervening master file records must be read (unless START is used) but need not be rewritten. The START instruction can be used to skip over master file records if desired.

The changes can be made directly in the FD record area associated with the indexed file or in WORKING–STORAGE if the READ INTO option is used; similarly, the changed record can be rewritten (REWRITE) from the FD record area or from WORKING–STORAGE if the REWRITE FROM option is used.

If the primary key of a record needs to be changed, the user should first delete the record and then add it to the file using the WRITE statement with ACCESS MODE IS RANDOM (see section 11-4). Alternate keys may be changed as long as their new value does not duplicate existing alternate key values in the file. This restriction does not apply if the option WITH DUPLICATES defined the keys at the time the file was created.

The REWRITE instruction activates the INVALID KEY clause if the primary key of the new record does not match the primary key of the last successfully read record of the indexed file or if the file record was successfully read but also deleted just before the REWRITE operation.

INDEXED SEQUENTIAL FILES

11-2-6 A SEQUENTIAL UPDATE PROGRAM

Problem Specification

An input transaction file (TRANSACTION-FILE) consists of records similar to those shown below, where each record consists of an invoice number, an item number, and a number of items sold. The transaction records are arranged in ascending order by item number (primary key). Note that identical item numbers may occur in a group in the transaction file (different sales for the same item).

An indexed file MASTER-FILE also consists of records arranged in ascending item number sequence. Each master file record consists of an item number, a current item stock level, and a corresponding cost figure for the item in question.

Write a program to update the master file by changing the stock levels for the various items sold that day. The program should also produce an end-of-day sales report containing the invoice numbers, the item numbers, the quantity sold, the sales amount for each transaction, and a total daily sales figure. Invalid transactions should be flagged on output. Examples of the input and output files are in the following sketch of the update process.

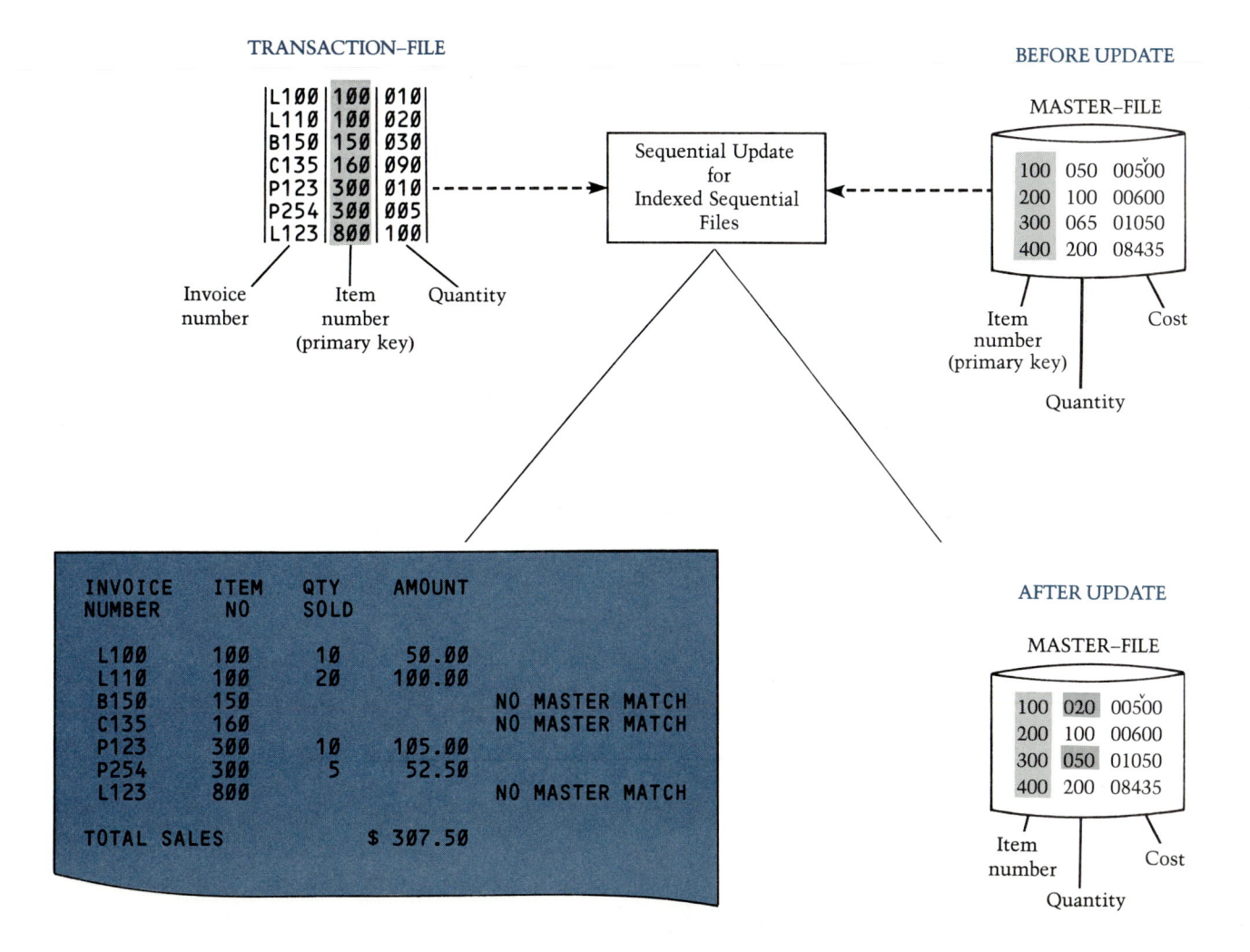

```
TRANSACTION-FILE                                              BEFORE UPDATE

 L100 100 010                                                  MASTER-FILE
 L110 100 020
 B150 150 030                                                  100  050  00500
 C135 160 090         Sequential Update                        200  100  00600
 P123 300 010     ←      for              ←                    300  065  01050
 P254 300 005         Indexed Sequential                       400  200  08435
 L123 800 100             Files

   Invoice   Item    Quantity                                Item            Cost
   number   number                                          number
           (primary key)                                  (primary key)
                                                                Quantity


 INVOICE    ITEM   QTY    AMOUNT                              AFTER UPDATE
 NUMBER     NO     SOLD
                                                               MASTER-FILE
  L100      100    10     50.00
  L110      100    20    100.00                                100  020  00500
  B150      150              NO MASTER MATCH                   200  100  00600
  C135      160              NO MASTER MATCH                   300  050  01050
  P123      300    10    105.00                                400  200  08435
  P254      300     5     52.50
  L123      800              NO MASTER MATCH                 Item            Cost
                                                           number
 TOTAL SALES            $ 307.50                                Quantity
```

The logic outlining the solution to the problem is shown in flowchart form in Figure 11-7, and the COBOL code is shown in Figure 11-8.

```
                              Set REC–CHANGE to "NO"
                              Read TRANSACTION–FILE
                              Read MASTER–FILE
                              Set TR–FLAG to "NO"
                              Set MAST–FLAG to "NO"
```

```
        (A) ─────────────────►◇ end of        ──Yes──► Write the last changed record
                                transaction file        onto disk, if any, and print
                                                        summary results and stop.
                                    │No
                                    ▼
```

Legend
T = Transaction key
M = Master key

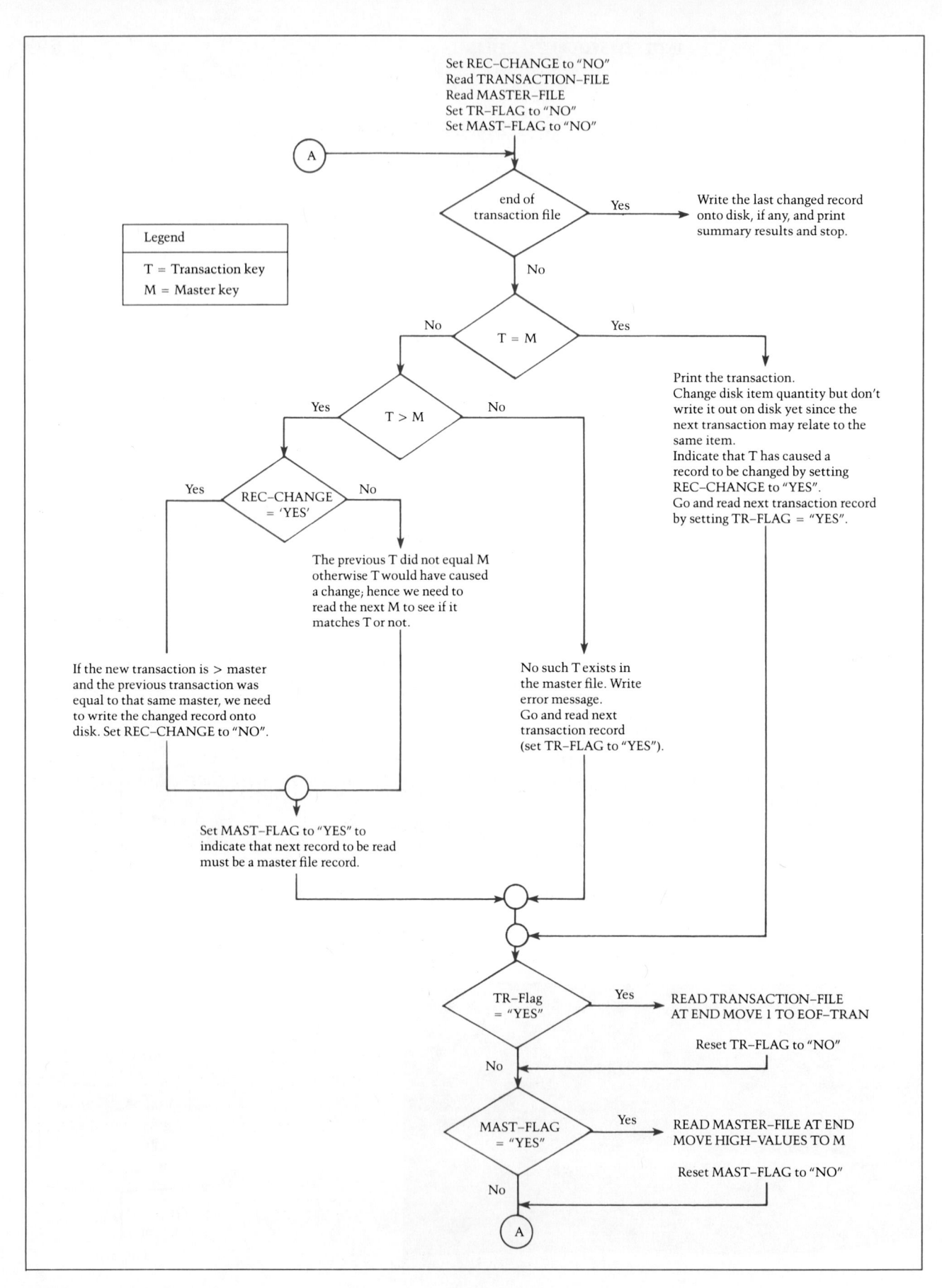

```
                       ──No──◇ T = M ──Yes──┐
                              │             │
                              ▼             │
                   ──Yes──◇ T > M ──No──┐   │
                          │             │   │
                          ▼             │   │
               ──Yes──◇ REC–CHANGE ──No─┤   │
                       = 'YES'          │   │
```

Print the transaction.
Change disk item quantity but don't
write it out on disk yet since the
next transaction may relate to the
same item.
Indicate that T has caused a
record to be changed by setting
REC–CHANGE to "YES".
Go and read next transaction record
by setting TR–FLAG = "YES".

The previous T did not equal M
otherwise T would have caused
a change; hence we need to
read the next M to see if it
matches T or not.

If the new transaction is > master
and the previous transaction was
equal to that same master, we need
to write the changed record onto
disk. Set REC–CHANGE to "NO".

No such T exists in
the master file. Write
error message.
Go and read next
transaction record
(set TR–FLAG to "YES").

Set MAST–FLAG to "YES" to
indicate that next record to be read
must be a master file record.

```
                    ◇ TR–Flag    ──Yes──► READ TRANSACTION–FILE
                      = "YES"              AT END MOVE 1 TO EOF–TRAN
                        │                  Reset TR–FLAG to "NO"
                        │No
                        ▼
                    ◇ MAST–FLAG  ──Yes──► READ MASTER–FILE AT END
                      = "YES"              MOVE HIGH–VALUES TO M
                        │                  Reset MAST–FLAG to "NO"
                        │No
                        ▼
                       (A)
```

FIGURE 11–7
LOGIC TO SEQUENTIALLY UPDATE AN INDEXED SEQUENTIAL FILE

11-2-7 DO IT NOW

1. Suppose INVENTORY-FILE is an indexed file that has already been created. You now want to process that file sequentially (ACCESS MODE IS SEQUENTIAL). Specify the particular types of operations that you could carry out on INVENTORY-FILE if you opened the file as follows:

   a. OPEN INPUT
   b. OPEN OUTPUT
   c. OPEN I-O

2. How could you reread an indexed file sequentially (ACCESS MODE IS SEQUENTIAL) in the same program? Assume you do not know what the first record is.

3. All of the following statements refer to an indexed file where ACCESS MODE IS SEQUENTIAL. State whether each statement is true or false.

   a. An indexed file can be processed sequentially if ORGANIZATION IS SEQUENTIAL is specified.
   b. The WRITE statement can be used to write records to an existing indexed file.
   c. As a result of creating an indexed file, it is possible that some of the records in the file are not in ascending key order.
   d. It is possible to create an indexed file in descending key order.
   e. If the ACCESS clause is not specified, the indexed file can only be processed sequentially.
   f. The FILE STATUS word must be defined in the FILE section.
   g. The primary key must always be the very first data item in the record.
   h. An indexed file may consist of records where each record consists of only the primary key.
   i. It is not possible to add or insert records in the indexed file.
   j. The FILE STATUS word can be tested by an IF statement in the same sentence as the INVALID KEY phrase.
   k. The following entry is syntactically correct:

   ```
   SELECT MASTER-FILE ASSIGN TO DISK
   ORGANIZATION IS INDEXED
   RECORD-KEY IS MR-ITEM
   FILE-STATUS IS ERR-FLAG.
   ```

   l. This statement is valid: `READ INVENTORY-FILE`
       `INVALID KEY DISPLAY INVEN-REC.`
   m. The START option causes the system to place the targeted record in the input record area.
   n. The REWRITE instruction can be used to change the value of a primary key directly.
   o. The statement

   `DELETE INVEN-FILE INVALID KEY DISPLAY ST-FLAG` is valid.

   p. This statement is grammatically valid:

   ```
   START INVEN-FILE KEY EQUAL TO "P"
       INVALID KEY DISPLAY "NOT FOUND".
   ```

602 UNDERSTANDING STRUCTURED COBOL

```
000005 IDENTIFICATION DIVISION.
000010 PROGRAM-ID. UPDATE.
000011****************************************************
000012* A  S E Q U E N T I A L  I N D E X E D  U P D A T E *
000013****************************************************
000015 ENVIRONMENT DIVISION.
000020 CONFIGURATION SECTION.
000025 SOURCE-COMPUTER. IBM.
000030 OBJECT-COMPUTER. IBM.
000035 INPUT-OUTPUT SECTION.
000040 FILE-CONTROL.
000045*
000050     SELECT TRANSACTION-FILE ASSIGN TO DISK.
000055     SELECT PRINT-FILE ASSIGN  TO PRINTER.
000060     SELECT MASTER-FILE ASSIGN TO DISK
000065         ORGANIZATION IS INDEXED
000070         ACCESS MODE  IS SEQUENTIAL
000075         RECORD KEY   IS MR-ITEM
000080         FILE STATUS  IS REWRITE-ERROR.
000085 DATA DIVISION.
000090 FILE SECTION.
000095 FD  TRANSACTION-FILE
000097     VALUE OF FILE-ID IS "TRANSACT"
000100     LABEL RECORDS ARE STANDARD.
000105 01  TRAN-REC.
000110     05  TR-INVOICE  PIC X(04).
000115     05  FILLER      PIC X.
000120     05  TR-ITEM     PIC 999.
000125     05  FILLER      PIC X.
000130     05  TR-QTY      PIC 999.
000135 FD  MASTER-FILE
000140     LABEL RECORDS ARE STANDARD
000142     VALUE OF FILE-ID IS "MASTER"
000145     RECORD CONTAINS 13 CHARACTERS.
000150 01  MASTER-REC.
000155     05  MR-ITEM     PIC XXX.
000160     05  FILLER      PIC X.
000165     05  MR-QTY      PIC 999.
000170     05  FILLER      PIC X.
000175     05  MR-COST     PIC 999V99.
000180 FD  PRINT-FILE
000185     LABEL RECORDS ARE STANDARD.
000190 01  PRINT-LINE PIC X(132).
000195 WORKING-STORAGE SECTION.
000200 01  FLAGS-N-ACCUMULATORS.
000205     05  EOF-TRAN      PIC 9 VALUE 0.
000210     05  WS-FLAG       PIC XXX VALUE "YES".
000215     05  MAST-FLAG     PIC XXX VALUE "YES".
000220     05  REC-CHANGE    PIC XXX VALUE "NO".
000225     05  REWRITE-ERROR PIC XX.
000230     05  TOTAL-SALES   PIC 9999V99 VALUE 0.
000235     05  WS-COST       PIC 9999V99.
000240 01  HEADER-1.
000245     05  FILLER PIC X(11) VALUE " INVOICE".
000250     05  FILLER PIC X(07) VALUE "ITEM".
000255     05  FILLER PIC X(07) VALUE "QTY".
000260     05  FILLER PIC X(06) VALUE "AMOUNT".
000265 01  HEADER-2.
000270     05  FILLER PIC X(12) VALUE " NUMBER".
000275     05  FILLER PIC X(06) VALUE "NO".
000280     05  FILLER PIC X(04) VALUE "SOLD".
000285 01  DETAIL-LINE.
000290     05  FILLER     PIC X(02) VALUE SPACES.
000295     05  DL-INVOICE PIC X(04).
000300     05  FILLER     PIC X(05) VALUE SPACES.
000305     05  DL-ITEM    PIC 999.
000310     05  FILLER     PIC X(04) VALUE SPACES.
000315     05  DL-QTY     PIC ZZ9.
000320     05  FILLER     PIC X(03) VALUE SPACES.
000325     05  DL-AMOUNT  PIC ZZZ9.99.
000330     05  DL-ERROR   PIC X(23).
000335 01  SUMMARY-LINE.
000337     05  FILLER   PIC X(20) VALUE " TOTAL SALES".
000338     05  SL-SALES PIC $ZZZZ.99.
```

TRANSACTION-FILE

TR-INVOICE	TR-ITEM	TR-QTY
L100	100	010
L110	100	020
B150	150	030
C135	160	090
P123	300	010
P254	300	005
L123	800	100

MASTER-FILE before update

MR-ITEM	MR-QTY	MR-COST
100	050	00500
200	100	00600
300	065	01050
400	200	08435

MASTER-FILE after update

MR-ITEM	MR-QTY	MR-COST
100	020	00500
200	100	00600
300	050	01050
400	200	08435

Indicates end of TRANSACTION-FILE.
Used as flags to indicate whether next record to be read is a transaction or a master file record.

Used by FILE-STATUS.
Computes cost associated with a particular transaction.

OUTPUT

INVOICE NUMBER	ITEM NO	QTY SOLD	AMOUNT	
L100	100	10	50.00	
L110	100	20	100.00	
B150	150			NO MASTER MATCH
C135	160			NO MASTER MATCH
P123	300	10	105.00	
P254	300	5	52.50	
L123	800			NO MASTER MATCH
TOTAL SALES			$ 307.50	

FIGURE 11–8

A SEQUENTIAL UPDATE FOR AN INDEXED FILE

INDEXED SEQUENTIAL FILES

```
340 PROCEDURE DIVISION.
345 10-MAIN-LOGIC.
350     OPEN INPUT   TRANSACTION-FILE
355          OUTPUT  PRINT-FILE
360          I-O     MASTER-FILE.
365     WRITE PRINT-LINE FROM HEADER-1 AFTER 1.
370     WRITE PRINT-LINE FROM HEADER-2 AFTER 1.
372     MOVE SPACES TO PRINT-LINE.
374     WRITE PRINT-LINE AFTER 1
375     PERFORM 60-READ-FILES.
380     PERFORM 20-UPDATE-MASTER UNTIL EOF-TRAN = 1.
385     IF REC-CHANGE = "YES"
390         REWRITE MASTER-REC INVALID KEY
395             DISPLAY TR-ITEM, REWRITE-ERROR.
400     MOVE TOTAL-SALES TO SL-SALES.
405     WRITE PRINT-LINE FROM SUMMARY-LINE AFTER 2.
410     CLOSE PRINT-FILE, TRANSACTION-FILE, MASTER-FILE.
415     STOP RUN.
420*
425 20-UPDATE-MASTER.
430     IF TR-ITEM = MR-ITEM
435         SUBTRACT TR-QTY FROM MR-QTY
440         MOVE "YES" TO REC-CHANGE, WS-FLAG
445         COMPUTE WS-COST = TR-QTY * MR-COST
450         ADD  WS-COST     TO TOTAL-SALES
455         MOVE WS-COST     TO DL-AMOUNT
460         MOVE TR-INVOICE  TO DL-INVOICE
465         MOVE TR-ITEM     TO DL-ITEM
470         MOVE TR-QTY      TO DL-QTY
475         WRITE PRINT-LINE FROM DETAIL-LINE AFTER 1
480     ELSE
485         IF TR-ITEM > MR-ITEM
490             PERFORM 30-WRITE-RECORD-OR-READ-MASTER
495         ELSE
500             MOVE SPACES      TO DETAIL-LINE
505             MOVE TR-INVOICE  TO DL-INVOICE
510             MOVE TR-ITEM     TO DL-ITEM
515             MOVE "  NO MASTER MATCH" TO DL-ERROR
520             WRITE PRINT-LINE FROM DETAIL-LINE AFTER 1.
525             MOVE SPACES TO DETAIL-LINE
530             MOVE "YES" TO WS-FLAG.
535     PERFORM 60-READ-FILES.
540*
545 30-WRITE-RECORD-OR-READ-MASTER.
550     IF REC-CHANGE = "YES"
555         MOVE "NO" TO REC-CHANGE
560         REWRITE MASTER-REC INVALID KEY
565             DISPLAY TR-ITEM, REWRITE-ERROR.
570     MOVE "YES" TO MAST-FLAG.
575*
580 60-READ-FILES.
585     IF WS-FLAG = "YES"
590         MOVE "NO" TO WS-FLAG
595         READ TRANSACTION-FILE AT END MOVE 1 TO EOF-TRAN.
600     IF MAST-FLAG = "YES"
605         MOVE "NO" TO MAST-FLAG
610         READ MASTER-FILE
615             AT END MOVE HIGH-VALUES TO MR-ITEM.
```

Transaction records must already be sorted in ascending key sequence order. The item number is the record key. MASTER-FILE must be opened as an input/output file since records will be changed in all probability.

Go and read the first transaction record and the first master file record to get the process underway. If the last changed record has not yet been written onto the master disk file, now is the time.

Print the summary results.

If the transaction key is equal to the master key, change the quantity field in the master record but do not write the record yet; the next transaction key could be identical to the current transaction key. The only time the changed record is physically written onto disk is when the next transaction key is different from the current transaction key. We indicate that a record has been changed by setting the flag REC-CHANGE to "YES".

If T–Key ≠ M–Key, there are three possible outcomes: If T–Key < M–Key, the only possible outcome is that no match corresponds to T–Key in the master file. For example, if the first transaction key is 20 and the first master key is 30, then T–Key = 20 has no match in the masterfile.
If T–Key > M–Key, then two possible cases arise:
• The previous record was changed and needs to be written out onto disk (if REC–CHANGE = "YES"),
• or if the previous record was not changed (REC–CHANGE = "NO"), a match for the transaction record has not yet been found in the master file. For example, assume the first transaction key is 80 and the first three master keys are 20, 30, and 80. T–Key is larger than the first two master keys, so no record has been changed yet—more master records need to be read until T–Key = M–Key, at which time item 80 will be updated. Of course, it is possible that there will be no match for T–Key = 80; if, for example, the first three records of the master file are 20, 30, and 90, then 80 has no match (T–Key < M–Key).
In paragraph 60-READ-FILES the next record to be read depends on the state of either TR-FLAG or MAST-FLAG.

FIGURE 11–8
(continued)

4. Write the code to perform the following operations using ACCESS MODE IS SEQUENTIAL.
   a. Create an indexed file where each record contains a name and a score.
   b. Print the honor roll, i.e., the names of students with scores exceeding 90.
   c. List students whose last names start with M through Z. Do this without using the START verb, then with the START verb.
   d. If your system permits, use the score as an alternate key and provide a list of students by name in ascending score order. Assume that there are no two equal scores.
   e. Suppose you cannot use the ALTERNATE KEY feature; how would you solve part d?
   f. Add a bonus of five points added to the scores of all students whose scores exeed the average. No scores should exceed 100.
   g. Delete from the file all records whose corresponding name fields start with the letter M.
   h. Delete all student records whose score fields fall below 50.

SELECTED ANSWERS

1. a. You can READ records and use the START verb. You may not DELETE or REWRITE records.
   b. You have destroyed the file, simply by opening it as an OUTPUT file!

2. Close the file and reOPEN it or use the START verb with a key ≥ LOW-VALUES.

3. a. False. An indexed file cannot be processed sequentially under a sequential organization.
   c. False. The system does not write the records that are out of order.
   e. True.
   g. False. It can be any field in the record, but it must be specified through the RECORD KEY at when the file is created.
   i. True.
   k. False. The hyphen in FILE–STATUS is invalid.
   m. False. The READ instruction must be carried out first.
   p. False. The EQUAL TO must specify a data item name that is a key.

11-3 PROCESSING RECORDS RANDOMLY

11-3-1 AN OVERVIEW

To process records randomly, the clause ACCESS MODE IS RANDOM must be specified in the SELECT/ASSIGN statement. In this mode records are not processed in any particular sequence. Transaction files and on-line inquiries need not be arranged in any order. Records are accessed by their primary or alternate keys, i.e., a value is moved into the RECORD KEY or the ALTERNATE RECORD KEY field prior to executing an input/output instruction.

The COBOL entries that can be used to process an indexed file randomly are shown in Figure 11–9.

INDEXED SEQUENTIAL FILES 605

ENVIRONMENT DIVISION entries for ACCESS MODE IS RANDOM

SELECT file-name ASSIGN to device-name
    ORGANIZATION IS INDEXED
    ACCESS MODE IS RANDOM
    RECORD KEY IS data-name-1
    [ALTERNATE RECORD KEY IS data-name-2 [WITH DUPLICATES]] ...
    [FILE STATUS IS data-name-3]

PROCEDURE DIVISION entries for ACCESS MODE IS RANDOM

OPEN { INPUT / OUTPUT / I-O } file-name ...

READ file-name RECORD [INTO data-name-4]
    [KEY IS data-name-5]
    [INVALID KEY imperative-statement ...]

WRITE record-name [FROM data-name-6] [INVALID KEY imperative-statement ...]

REWRITE record-name [FROM data-name-7] [INVALID KEY imperative-statement ...]

DELETE file-name [INVALID KEY imperative-statement ...]

CLOSE file-name [WITH LOCK] ...

OPEN options for the READ, WRITE, REWRITE, and DELETE

READ	WRITE	REWRITE	DELETE
{OPEN INPUT} / {OPEN I-O}	{OPEN OUTPUT} / {OPEN I-O}	OPEN I-O	OPEN I-O

INVALID KEY errors if:	
READ:	Key does not refer to an existing key in the file.
WRITE:	The file already contains a record with the same key value.
	The allocated disk space is exceeded.
REWRITE	The new record's key value does not equal to that of any record in the file.
DELETE	No matching record (with the same primary key) can be found.

FIGURE 11-9
COBOL ENTRIES TO PROCESS AN INDEXED FILE RANDOMLY

The following types of file-processing activities can take place in random mode:

1. Locate and retrieve a record by its primary or its alternate key (READ operation).
2. Change a field in a particular record (REWRITE operation).
3. Add a record to the indexed file (WRITE operation).
4. Delete a particular record (DELETE operation).

Note that the START clause cannot be used when processing records randomly. The OUTPUT mode should not be selected for the OPEN statement since this will result in erasing the indexed file. Keep in mind also that the keys used for random access must be identical to the keys that were defined when the file was created in terms of number of keys, PICTURE, length, and key position within the record; the names themselves may differ, of course.

Permissible input/output operations that can be used in conjunction with the various OPEN options are illustrated in Figure 11-9.

11-3-2 READING RECORDS: THE READ STATEMENT

Records can be retrieved by the record's primary key or by any of its alternate keys (see READ instruction in Figure 11-9). The KEY clause in the READ statement can specify the primary key (RECORD KEY) or any of the alternate keys specified in the ALTERNATE RECORD KEY clause. If the KEY clause is omitted, the primary key is assumed; i.e., record retrieval will be based on whatever value is present in the READ record description entry corresponding to the primary key field. Before the READ statement is executed, the programmer should move the appropriate key value of the record to be read into the primary key field.

Records can be retrieved in any order; for example, an airline employee might check on passenger reservations based on random inquiry.

Note that the READ statement differs from the READ statement used in ACCESS MODE IS SEQUENTIAL. The INVALID KEY clause is activated if no record in the file has a key that matches the key specified by the primary or alternate key of the READ record area.

As an example, suppose the indexed file ISAM-FILE has primary key ISAM-KEY and alternate key ALT-KEY. We want to display the record whose primary key value is in SS-NO and the record whose alternate key value is to be entered on-line on the screen (for example, HASTINGS). The following code segments could be used:

```
MOVE SS-NO TO ISAM-KEY.          DISPLAY "ENTER EMPLOYEE NAME".
READ ISAM-FILE                   ACCEPT ALT-KEY.  → (HASTINGS)
    INVALID KEY MOVE 1 TO WS-FLAG. READ ISAM-FILE
IF WS-FLAG = 1                       KEY IS ALT-KEY
    DISPLAY "NO KEY MATCH"           INVALID KEY MOVE 1 TO WS-FLAG.
ELSE                             IF WS-FLAG-1
    DISPLAY ISAM-RECORD.             DISPLAY "NO MATCHING KEY"
                                 ELSE
                                     DISPLAY ISAM-RECORD.
```

11-3-3 CHANGING RECORDS: THE REWRITE STATEMENT

The REWRITE instruction is used to change records; the procedure is identical to changing records when ACCESS MODE IS SEQUENTIAL. The primary key of the record to be changed must not be modified, and the length of the substitute record must be the same as the original record. The file whose records are to be changed should be opened in I-O mode.

It is recommended, though not mandatory (unlike sequential access mode), that a record be read and verified before it is changed. The user may, however, change a record directly by specifying the record key in the REWRITE statement without first reading the record. Either primary or alternate keys may be specified in the READ statement to identify the record to be changed. Changes are then made to the FD record area or in WORKING–STORAGE if the READ INTO statement is used. The changed record is then released for output from the FD record area or from WORKING–STORAGE through the REWRITE or the REWRITE FROM instruction, respectively. The logical record released is no longer available in the record area if the REWRITE instruction is successful.

Alternate keys may be changed, but the new keys cannot duplicate values that already exist for that key in the indexed file (unless such keys were defined with the DUPLICATES option in the file creation program).

The INVALID KEY is activated if the primary key of the substitute record has no match in the indexed file or if an attempt is made to change a record to an alternate key value that duplicates an existing value for that key in the file (if, of course, the alternate key was not declared with the DUPLICATES option).

11-3-4 ADDING RECORDS: THE WRITE STATEMENT

Records may be added to the file in any particular order by using the WRITE instruction (see Figure 11–9). The indexed file must be opened as I–O. The primary key determines the position that the record will occupy in the file. The primary key and other alternate keys, if any, must be present in the FD record area associated with the WRITE and must conform to the original key descriptions as defined in the file creation program.

Variable size records can be added to the file as long as the clause RECORD CONTAINS integer-1 TO integer-2 CHARACTERS was present in the FD description of the indexed file at the time of its creation (variable size records occur with tables of varying lengths (DEPENDING ON option) or with multiple defined records).

As many records can be added to the file as disk space will permit (the user may have to explicitly reserve the disk area through job control or workflow statements).

The record to be added is moved into the FD record area associated with the WRITE statement and is then written on disk; it can be written directly from WORKING–STORAGE if the WRITE FROM option is used.

The WRITE statement will activate the INVALID KEY if:

1. A file record with the same key (either the primary key or the alternate key if the DUPLICATES option was not specified) already exists in the file.

2. There is insufficient space on the disk to write the record.

11-3-5 DELETING RECORDS: THE DELETE STATEMENT

Deleting records is accomplished through the DELETE instruction (see Figure 11–9). The indexed file must be opened as an I–O file. For verification purposes it is recommended that records be read first before they are actually deleted. The record identified by the primary key in the FD record area associated with file-name is logically removed from the file by the DELETE file-name instruction, i.e., no READ operation is necessary to delete a record.

Execution of the DELETE statement does not affect the contents of the record area associated with the file-name.

The DELETE instruction activates the INVALID KEY if no file record matches the primary key specified by the DELETE statement.

11-3-6 A RANDOM UPDATE PROGRAM

An indexed file MASTER-FILE consists of records shown in Figure 11-10. Each master file record consists of an item number (primary key), an item description (alternate key), an item quantity, and an item cost. Each record of a transaction file, TRANSACTION-FILE, contains an item number (primary key), an item description (alternate key), an item quantity, an item cost, and a transaction code defined as follows:

CODE	MEANING
1	Delete record from file.
2	Add record to file.
3	Change the cost-data-field in the designated record.
4	Change the quantity-field in the designated record.

The transaction records are not arranged in any particular key sequence order.

Write a program to update the MASTER-FILE with the TRANSACTION-FILE. Appropriate error messages should be printed if an attempt is made to:

1. Add to the MASTER-FILE a record that already exists.
2. Delete or change a record that does not exist in the file.
3. Add or change a record to duplicate a key already in the file.

The update process and the input and output parameters are illustrated in Figure 11-10. The program to solve this problem is shown in Figure 11-11.

Many types of error conditions may occur as a result of conflicts in transaction codes or duplicate key values. For example:

1. To successfully add a record, the following three conditions must be satisfied:

   a. The primary key of the record to be added must not exist in the master file (line 345).
   b. The transaction code must be a 2 (line 380).
   c. The record added must not contain an alternate key value that already exists as an alternate key value in the file (lines 400 and 535).

2. To successfully change or delete a record, the following three conditions be satisfied:

   a. The primary key of the record to be changed must exist in the master file (line 355).
   b. The transaction code must be either a 3 or a 4 for a change or a 1 for a deletion (lines 435, 470, and 505).
   c. The alternate key value, realistically, should not be changed; but if it is changed, it should not equal the value of an existing alternate key (lines 525 and 550).

Note that adding records to the master file is carried out through the WRITE statement at line 400, while changing records is carried out through the REWRITE statements at lines 445 and 480. When changing a record, care must be exercised to make sure that neither the primary key nor the alternate key values are changed. In that perspective, note the importance of line 430, which moves the transaction alternate key field to the master record to allow the system to check for duplicate alternate keys in the event a record is to be changed.

INDEXED SEQUENTIAL FILES

```
                TRANSACTION-FILE                                          BEFORE UPDATE

        ITEM-DESCR   ITEM-COST                                              MASTER-FILE

ITEM-NO      ITEM-QTY      CODE                                        NO  DESCR  QTY   COST

2300  FILE   0980  06600   2 | Add                                    1111 CHAIR  1000  02600
1000  CHAIR  0300  08900   2 | Add                                    1222 FAN    2000  01300
5555  BENCH                1 | Delete              ┌─────────┐        2222 DESK   1000  20000
4444  LAMP         08800   3 | Change cost   ----→ │ Update  │ ←----  4444 LAMP   0100  08500
1111  CHAIR  0300  02600   2 | Add                 │ Program │        5555 BENCH  0010  06500
2222  DESK   2000          4 | Change quantity     └─────────┘
6000  COUCH                1 | Delete
2222  DESK         08900   3 | Change cost              1: Delete
4444  DESK   0200          4 | Change quantity          2: Add
3000  FILE   0800  05000   2 | Add                      3: Change cost
                                                        4: Change quantity

                                                                          AFTER UPDATE

                                                                           MASTER-FILE

                                                                       1111 CHAIR  1000 02600
                                                                       1222 FAN    2000 01300
                                                                       2222 DESK   2000 08900
                                                                       2300 FILE   0980 06600
                                                                       4444 LAMP   0100 08800
```

Error messages during the update process

```
ITEM 1000: CANNOT ADD. CONTAINS EXISTING ALTERNATE KEY
ITEM 1111: CANNOT ADD RECORD THAT EXISTS IN FILE
ITEM 6000: CANNOT DELETE/CHANGE NONEXISTENT RECORD IN MASTER
ITEM 4444: CANNOT CHANGE. CONTAINS EXISTING ALTERNATE KEY
ITEM 3000: CANNOT ADD. CONTAINS EXISTING ALTERNATE KEY
```

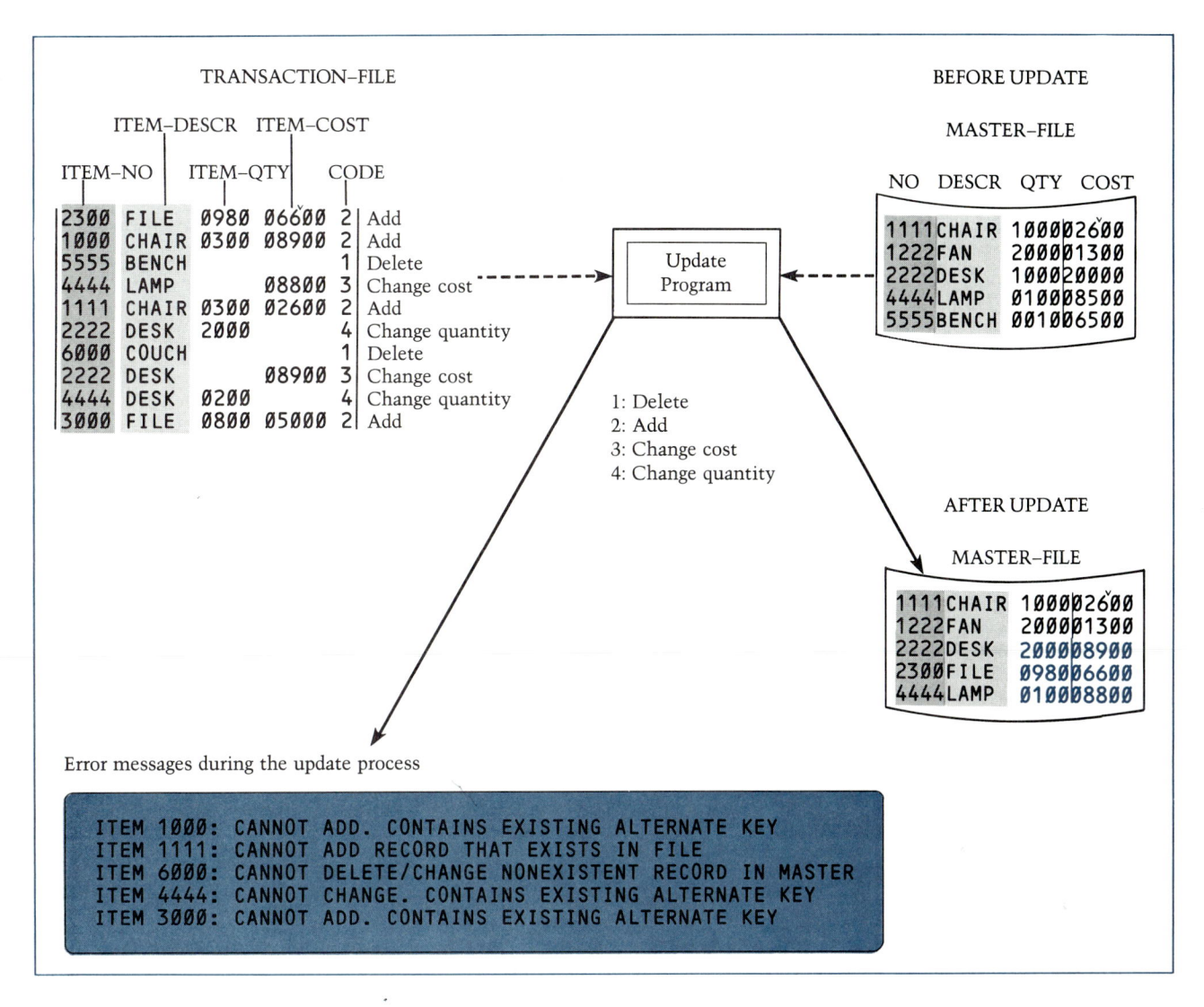

FIGURE 11-10
AN INDEXED SEQUENTIAL FILE UPDATE (RANDOM)

Consider, for example, what would have happened if line 430 had been omitted when processing the next-to-last transaction file item, 4444 DESK 0200, with the transaction code of 4 (change quantity). As a result of line 325, MOVE TR-ITEM-NO TO MR-ITEM-NO, MASTER-RECORD contains:

MASTER-RECORD | 4444 | old information |

As a result of the READ MASTER-FILE at line 330, MASTER-RECORD contains:

MASTER RECORD | 4444 | LAMP | 0100 | 08500 |

As a result of the change instruction at line 440, MASTER-RECORD now contains:

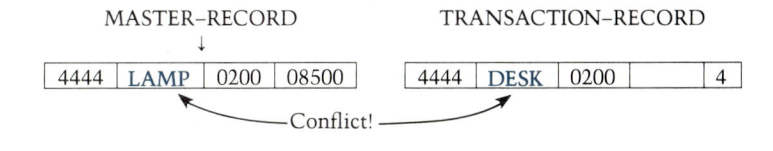

MASTER-RECORD   TRANSACTION-RECORD

| 4444 | LAMP | 0200 | 08500 | | 4444 | DESK | 0200 | 4 |
            ←———— Conflict! ————→

```
005 IDENTIFICATION DIVISION.
010 PROGRAM-ID. RANDOM-FILE.
012***********************************************
013* U P D A T I N G   A   R A N D O M   F I L E *
014***********************************************
015 ENVIRONMENT DIVISION.
020 CONFIGURATION SECTION.
025 SOURCE-COMPUTER. BURROUGHS.
030 OBJECT-COMPUTER. BURROUGHS.
035 INPUT-OUTPUT SECTION.
040 FILE-CONTROL.
045 SELECT TRANSACTION-FILE ASSIGN TO DISK.
050*
055 SELECT MASTER-FILE ASSIGN TO DISK
060         ORGANIZATION    IS INDEXED
065         ACCESS MODE     IS RANDOM
070         RECORD KEY      IS MR-ITEM-NO
075         ALTERNATE RECORD IS MR-ITEM-DESCR
080         FILE STATUS     IS ERROR-FLAG.
085*
090 DATA DIVISION.
095 FILE SECTION.
100*
105 FD  TRANSACTION-FILE
110     LABEL RECORDS ARE STANDARD
112     VALUE OF FILE-ID IS "TRANSACT"
115     DATA RECORD IS TRANSACTION-RECORD.
120 01  TRANSACTION-RECORD.
125     05  TR-ITEM-NO      PIC XXXX.
130     05  FILLER          PIC X.
135     05  TR-ITEM-DESCR   PIC X(5).
140     05  FILLER          PIC X.
145     05  TR-ITEM-QTY     PIC 9999.
150     05  FILLER          PIC X.
155     05  TR-ITEM-COST    PIC 999V99.
160     05  FILLER          PIC X.
165     05  TR-CODE         PIC 9.
170         88  DELETION       VALUE 1.
175         88  INSERT         VALUE 2.
108         88  CHANGE-COST    VALUE 3.
105         88  CHANGE-QTY     VALUE 4.
105*
200 FD  MASTER-FILE
205     LABEL RECORDS ARE STANDARD
208     VALUE OF FILE-ID IS "MASTER"
210     DATA RECORD IS MASTER-RECORD
215     RECORD CONTAINS 18 CHARACTERS.
220 01  MASTER-RECORD.
225     05  MR-ITEM-NO      PIC XXXX.
230     05  MR-ITEM-DESCR   PIC X(5).
235     05  MR-ITEM-QTY     PIC 9999.
240     05  MR-ITEM-COST    PIC 999V99.
245*
250 WORKING-STORAGE SECTION.
252 01  FLAGS.
255     05  ERROR-FLAG      PIC XX.
260     05  TRANS-EOF       PIC XXX     VALUE "NO".
265     05  ISAM-READ-KEY   PIC X(07)   VALUE "MATCH".
270*
```

Errors listed on the screen

```
ITEM 1000: CANNOT ADD. CONTAINS EXISTING ALTERNATE KEY
ITEM 1111: CANNOT ADD RECORD THAT EXISTS IN FILE
ITEM 6000: CANNOT DELETE/CHANGE NONEXISTENT RECORD IN MASTER
ITEM 4444: CANNOT CHANGE. CONTAINS EXISTING ALTERNATE KEY
ITEM 3000: CANNOT ADD. CONTAINS EXISTING ALTERNATE KEY
```

TRANSACTION-FILE

```
                    TR-ITEM-QTY
   TR-ITEM-DESCR          TR-ITEM-COST
TR-ITEM-NO                      TR-CODE

2300 FILE  0980 06600 2  Add
1000 CHAIR 0300 08900 2  Add
5555 BENCH            1  Delete
4444 LAMP       08800 3  Change cost
1111 CHAIR 0300 02600 2  Add
2222 DESK  2000       4  Change quantity
6000 COUCH            1  Delete
2222 DESK       08900 3  Change cost
4444 DESK  0200       4  Change quantity
3000 FILE  0800 05000 2  Add
```

MASTER-FILE before update

```
1111CHAIR 100002600
1222FAN   200001300
2222DESK  100020000
4444LAMP  010008500
5555BENCH 001006500
```

IR-ITEM-NO   IR-ITEM-COST
IR-ITEM-DESCR IR-ITEM-QTY

MASTER-FILE after update

```
1111CHAIR 100002600
1222FAN   200001300
2222DESK  200008900
2300FILE  098006600
4444LAMP  010008800
```

FIGURE 11-11
A RANDOM UPDATE

```
275 PROCEDURE DIVISION.
280 MAIN-LOGIC.
285     OPEN INPUT TRANSACTION-FILE.
290     OPEN I-O MASTER-FILE.
295     READ TRANSACTION-FILE AT END MOVE 1 TO TRANS-EOF.
300     PERFORM UPDATE-MASTER-FILE UNTIL TRANS-EOF = 1.
305     CLOSE TRANSACTION-FILE, MASTER-FILE.
310     STOP RUN.
315*
320 UPDATE-MASTER-FILE.
325     MOVE TR-ITEM-NO TO MR-ITEM-NO.
330     READ MASTER-FILE INVALID KEY
335         MOVE "NOMATCH" TO ISAM-READ-KEY.
340     IF ISAM-READ-KEY = "NOMATCH"
345         PERFORM INSERT-OR-ERROR
350     ELSE
355         PERFORM DELETE-CHANGE-OR-ERROR.
360     MOVE "MATCH" TO ISAM-READ-KEY.
365     READ TRANSACTION-FILE AT END MOVE 1 TO TRANS-EOF.
370*
375 INSERT-OR-ERROR.
380     IF INSERT
385         MOVE TR-ITEM-DESCR TO MR-ITEM-DESCR
390         MOVE TR-ITEM-QTY   TO MR-ITEM-QTY
395         MOVE TR-ITEM-COST  TO MR-ITEM-COST
400         WRITE MASTER-RECORD INVALID KEY PERFORM ERROR-TEST
405     ELSE
410         DISPLAY "ITEM", TR-ITEM-NO
410         ": CANNOT DELETE/CHANGE NONEXISTENT RECORD IN MASTER".
420*
425 DELETE-CHANGE-OR-ERROR.
430     MOVE TR-ITEM-DESCR TO MR-ITEM-DESCR.
435     IF CHANGE-COST
440         MOVE TR-ITEM-COST TO MR-ITEM-COST
445         REWRITE MASTER-RECORD
450             INVALID KEY DISPLAY "ITEM", TR-ITEM-NO
455             ": CANNOT CHANGE. CONTAINS EXISTING ALTERNATE KEY "
460     ELSE
465*
470         IF CHANGE-QTY
475             MOVE TR-ITEM-QTY TO MR-ITEM-QTY
480             REWRITE MASTER-RECORD
485                 INVALID KEY DISPLAY "ITEM", TR-ITEM-NO
490                 ": CANNOT CHANGE. CONTAINS EXISTING ALTERNATE KEY"
495         ELSE
500*
505             IF DELETION
510                 DELETE MASTER-FILE
515             ELSE
520                 DISPLAY "ITEM", TR-ITEM-NO
525                 ": CANNOT ADD RECORD THAT EXISTS IN FILE".
530*
535 ERROR-TEST.
540     IF ERROR-FLAG= "22"
545         DISPLAY "ITEM", TR-ITEM-NO
550         ": CANNOT ADD. CONTAINS EXISTING ALTERNATE KEY "
555     ELSE
560         DISPLAY "INSUFFICIENT DISK STORAGE SPACE FOR RECORD".
```

I-O is required since the master file is to be updated. Read the first transaction record, and go and update the record as well as all other transaction records.

Move the transaction primary key to the RECORD KEY to retrieve the record in the master file that matches the transaction record. If there is no such corresponding record (primary key) in the file, set up a flag.
If there is no match, this means that the record is to be added (transaction code = 2), or it is an error if the transaction code specifies a change or a deletion. If there is a match, this means that the record is to be deleted or changed, or it means an error if the transaction code specifies an insert (addition). Line 360 resets the error flag to "MATCH" for the next MASTER-FILE READ operation at line 330.

If it is an insert (line 380), copy all the transaction data items into the master file record. If the transaction record specifies an alternate key value that already exists in the master file or if there is no space left on disk for the record, print error message (535). If the record is to be added (primary key does not exist in master file) but the transaction code does not specify an addition operation, print an error message at line 415.

The statement at line 430 forces the system to check for duplicate key values at statements 445 and 480.
In the case of a change operation (435 and 470), the only error condition that can be encountered in the REWRITE process is if the transaction record specifies an alternate key value that already exists in the master file. Obviously the transaction item description should match the corresponding item description in the master file record—unless the item description is to be changed; caution must be exercised in that event. Line 510 does not require an INVALID KEY clause in this particular case since the record was read at line 330 and is known to exist in the file.

Line 545 is activated if an addition to the file is indicated but the transaction record specifies an alternate key value already present in the master file.

FIGURE 11-11
(continued)

and as a result of the REWRITE statement at line 445, the above record would be stored in the indexed file! But something is not right! The transaction record specifies a 200 desk change, but the actual record written on disk reflects 200 lamps! The program did not verify that the alternate keys were equal before it made the change and rewrote the record on the disk. Such a situation can be avoided by testing for equality of the transaction and master record alternate keys or letting the system take care of it by moving the alternate key value DESK into the master record alternate key area MR-ITEM-DESCR; then when the REWRITE instruction is carried out, the system will realize that the alternate key value DESK already exists in the file, and it will not change the record in question—instead an error message will be printed as a result of the INVALID KEY clause (line 450).

11-4 PROCESSING AN INDEXED FILE DYNAMICALLY

11-4-1 A DYNAMIC ACCESS PROBLEM EXAMPLE: AN AIRLINE ON-LINE RESERVATION SYSTEM

Problem Specification:

An indexed file, PASSENGER-FILE, is stored on disk and contains the names of passengers and their corresponding seat numbers. The RECORD KEY for the file is the passenger name. Write a program to allow a counter agent to interact with the file and perform the following functions in any order at any given time from his/her terminal:

1. Assign a seat number to a passenger whose name is accepted from the terminal. Both the name and seat number are then added to the file.

2. Obtain at any given time a passenger list showing each passenger name in alphabetical order and his/her seat number.

3. Cancel passenger reservations: a passenger name is accepted from the terminal and then deleted from the file.

4. Look up the seat number of any given passenger.

5. Change a passenger's seat number to another seat number.

6. Bring the on-line session to a close at any given time.

The initial passenger file might be similar to the following:

```
ARMONK  K    050
SIMMONS S    100     Assume this indexed file
SIMS    L    033     is already stored on the disk
SIMS    P    077
          .    .
          .    .
```

The program should react to possible error situations as follows:

1. Ask the agent to retype the code for a desired function if that code is mistyped.

2. Since the file is organized by name key and since each name must be unique in the file, the program should tell the agent to extend names with a numeric digit if a duplicate name is encountered while the agent is trying to assign a seat number. For example, if JONES M is already present in the file and another JONES M is to be assigned a seat, the agent will enter JONES M 1 for the new name and then assign a seat number; that transaction will then be recorded on disk.

3. In any of the tasks 3, 4, and 5 specified above, the agent will be asked to retype any names that have been spelled incorrectly on the terminal. The system will know that such names are incorrect because they will not be present in the file.

A typical session between the agent and the terminal is shown in Figure 11–12. The following inquiry codes are used by the agent to carry out the six functions discussed earlier:

- LI: List the passengers in alphabetical order (and seats)
- RE: Assign seat numbers to passengers (reservation)
- CH: Change a passenger seat to another seat
- SE: Look up a passenger's seat (search)
- CA: Cancel a reservation (delete name of passenger)
- TE: Terminate session

Study Figure 11–12 carefully to appreciate the scope of the task.

Conceptual Overview of Task

In a problem of this type we need to (1) read an indexed file sequentially (obtain a list of passengers in alphabetical sequence) and (2) access records randomly (look up, cancel, reserve, et cetera). Recall that ACCESS MODE IS RANDOM does not allow us to read records sequentially; in RANDOM mode the value of the key (or the name, in this problem) must first be moved to the record key before a record can be read. On the other hand, ACCESS MODE IS SEQUENTIAL does not allow us to retrieve a record directly without first searching all records that precede it. To satisfy this dual need for sequential and random access, COBOL provides us with ACCESS MODE IS DYNAMIC.

Step-by-Step Program Analysis

The program to solve the problem is shown in Figure 11–13. Note that PASSENGER–FILE is an input and output file opened in I–O mode (line 49).

The agent selects the particular function (RE, LI, CA, et cetera) at lines 55–58.

One characteristic of all of the functions selected by the agent is that either the function is carried out immediately without any problem, or else it is not carried out right away because of certain errors—in this case we keep trying to carry out the function until the errors are resolved. This explains the PERFORM UNTIL statements at lines 64, 69, 74, 84, and 89.

In the case of the reservation function (paragraph 400-RESERVATION at line 94), it is possible that a duplicate name will be encountered while trying to assign a seat to a passenger. The START verb at line 97 essentially checks for duplicate names. RR–KEY, the name of the passenger, is the starting point for the

```
LI
***LIST PASSENGERS
NAMES           SEAT

ARMONK S        050
SIMMONS K       100     Initial indexed file
SIMS L          033     stored on disk.
SIMS P          077
...............................
ENTER SELECTION
RT
INVALID INQUIRY CODE
...............................
ENTER SELECTION
RE
***RESERVATION
ENTER NAME
DOBERMAN J
ENTER SEAT
22
SEAT 022 CONFIRMED FOR DOBERMAN J
...............................
ENTER SELECTION
SIMS L
INVALID INQUIRY CODE
...............................
ENTER SELECTION
RE
***RESERVATION
ENTER NAME
SIMS L
DUPLICATE NAME; USE NAME EXTENSION
ENTER NAME
SIMS L 1
ENTER SEAT
55
SEAT 055 CONFIRMED FOR SIMS L 1
...............................
ENTER SELECTION
LI
***LIST PASSENGERS
NAMES           SEAT

ARMONK S        050
DOBERMAN J      022
SIMMONS K       100
SIMS L          033
SIMS L 1        055
SIMS P          077
...............................
ENTER SELECTION
CH
***CHANGE SEATS
SIMS L
ENTER NEW SEAT NUMBER
76
SEAT 076 CONFIRMED FOR SIMS L
...............................
ENTER SELECTION
CH
***CHANGE SEATS
ENTER NAME
SIMS L1
NO SUCH NAME: RETYPE
ENTER NAME
SIMS L 1
ENTER NEW SEAT NUMBER
74
SEAT 074 CONFIRMED FOR SIMS L 1
...............................
ENTER SELECTION
CA
***CANCELLATION
ENTER NAME
DOBERMAN J                                to next column
```

Legend

LI: List
RE: Reserve seat
CH: Change seat
SE: Search seat
CA: Cancel
TE: Terminate

```
DOBERMAN J      SEAT 022 CANCELLED
...............................
ENTER SELECTION
CA
***CANCELLATION
ENTER NAME
ARMONK K
NO SUCH PASSENGER EXISTS
ENTER NAME
ARMONK S
ARMONK S        SEAT 050 CANCELLED
...............................
ENTER SELECTION
LI
***LIST PASSENGERS
NAMES           SEAT

SIMMONS K       100
SIMS L          076
SIMS L 1        074
SIMS P          077
...............................
ENTER SELECTION
SE
***SEAT LOOK-UP
ENTER NAME
SIMMONS K
SIMMONS K       SEAT NUMBER: 100
...............................
ENTER SELECTION
SE
***SEAT LOOK-UP
ENTER NAME
SIMS B
NO SUCH PASSENGER EXISTS
ENTER NAME
SIMS P
SIMS P          SEAT NUMBER:077
...............................
ENTER SELECTION
RE
***RESERVATION
ENTER NAME
YOUNG F
ENTER SEAT
106
SEAT 106 CONFIRMED FOR YOUNG F
...............................
ENTER SELECTION
RE
***RESERVATION
ENTER NAME
MARRIOTT E
ENTER SEAT
063
SEAT 063 CONFIRMED FOR MARRIOTT E
...............................
ENTER SELECTION
LI
***LIST PASSENGERS
NAMES           SEAT

MARRIOTT E      063
SIMMONS K       100
SIMS L          076
SIMS L 1        074
SIMS P          077
YOUNG F         106
...............................
ENTER SELECTION
TE
```

FIGURE 11-12
ON-LINE INQUIRY SYSTEM

START verb. If that name is not in the file, the INVALID KEY option is activated and PASSENGER-MATCH is set to the value NO. If the name is in the file, then PASSENGER-MATCH is equal to YES as a result of line 95. The test at line 99 causes the name and seat number to be recorded in the file at line 101 if the name is not present (PASSENGER-MATCH = 'NO'); if the name is present it asks the agent to submit an extended name so that on the next reservation try, the extended name will *not* be found in the file in which case a reservation will be made.

The reader may wonder why we could not have used WRITE PASSENGER-RECORD INVALID KEY instead of using the START verb at line 97 to reserve a seat. A WRITE statement with the INVALID KEY clause would also tell us whether or not a duplicate name existed on the file, and just like the START statement, the WRITE statement would not write the record on disk if the name was a duplicate name. But the WRITE statement must also write a record specifying the assigned seat number, and such a seat number has not yet been assigned (line 100). If the seat were assigned prior to the WRITE statement and the name was duplicate then assigning a seat number would be useless since the record would never be written. Thus, we first check for name validity with the START statement; if it is a valid name, *then* we assign a number and write it out at line 101. Otherwise, we make up an extended name (line 104) and assign a seat number on the next execution of paragraph 400-RESERVATION.

In the look-up function at paragraph 500-SEAT-LOOKUP (line 106), we move the name that is to be retrieved (line 109) into the record key. The READ statement at line 110 determines whether or not there is a match in the file. If the INVALID KEY is activated, the key must have been misspelled by the agent. The PERFORM UNTIL at line 69 forces the agent to retype the name until it is correct. The name and corresponding seat number is then displayed (line 113).

When using the LIST function, we need to start reading at the "top" of the list. The form of the sequential READ statement using dynamic access mode is:

READ PASSENGER **NEXT RECORD** AT END ... (line 129; NEXT required)

The OPEN verb always causes the READ ... NEXT RECORD to start at the very first record of the file. From then on, the READ ... NEXT RECORD reads the next logical record until the end of file is encountered (AT END). The only way to reread the file (in our case this must be done every time the LIST function is involved) is to use the START verb (line 80-81) to point the READ statement back to the first record of the file. The condition NOT LESS THAN RR-KEY at line 81, where RR-KEY contains LOW-VALUES, ensures that the READ operation starts at the very first record in the file.

In the case of the cancellation function at paragraph 600-CANCELLATION (line 115), the record to be cancelled is first read at line 118. The seat associated with the record to be deleted (RR-SEAT) is then displayed on the screen at line 122. The DELETE INVALID KEY could, of course, have been used without the READ statement; in that case however, the cancelled seat number could not have been displayed on the screen since the DELETE instruction does not make RR-SEAT available to the program.

If an invalid inquiry code is typed (line 91), an error message is printed and the operator retypes the function code at line 92.

11-4-2 PERMISSIBLE OPERATIONS IN DYNAMIC MODE

The COBOL entries that can be used to process an indexed file in DYNAMIC mode are shown in Figure 11-14. DYNAMIC mode must be specified in the ACCESS entry.

```
 1:  IDENTIFICATION DIVISION.
 2:  PROGRAM-ID. RANDOM-UPDATE.
 3:  ********************************************************
 4:  * P R O C E S S I N G   A   D Y N A M I C   F I L E *
 5:  ********************************************************
 6:  AUTHOR. JONES.
 7:  ENVIRONMENT DIVISION.
 8:  CONFIGURATION SECTION.
 9:  SOURCE-COMPUTER. IBM.
10:  OBJECT-COMPUTER. IBM.
11:  INPUT-OUTPUT SECTION.
12:  FILE-CONTROL.
13: *
14:      SELECT PASSENGER-FILE ASSIGN TO DISK
15:          ORGANIZATION IS INDEXED
16:          ACCESS       IS DYNAMIC
17:          RECORD KEY   IS RR-KEY.
18: *
19:  DATA DIVISION.
20:  FILE SECTION.
21: *
22:  FD  PASSENGER-FILE
23:      LABEL RECORDS ARE STANDARD
24:      VALUE OF FILE-ID IS 'AIRLINE'.
25:  01  PASSENGER-RECORD.
26:      05  RR-KEY.
27:          10 RR-NAME PIC X(10).
28:          10 RR-EXT  PIC X(02).
29:      05  RR-SEAT   PIC 999.
30: *
31:  WORKING-STORAGE SECTION.
32:  01  FLAGS.
33:      05 END-FILE      PIC 9.
34:      05 PASSENGER-MATCH PIC XXX.
35:          88 NO-MATCH      VALUE IS 'NO'.
36:          88 MATCH         VALUE IS 'YES'.
37:  01  SCREEN-INQUIRY-FIELD.
38:      05 INQUIRY PIC XX.
39:          88 RESERVATION   VALUE IS 'RE'.
40:          88 SEAT-LOOK-UP  VALUE IS 'SE'.
41:          88 CANCELLATION  VALUE IS 'CA'.
42:          88 LIST          VALUE IS 'LI'.
43:          88 CHANGE-SEATS  VALUE IS 'CH'.
44:          88 SESSION-END   VALUE IS 'TE'.
45:  01  FIRST-NAME PIC X(10) VALUE LOW-VALUE.
46: *
47:  PROCEDURE DIVISION.
48:  100-MAIN-LOGIC.
49:      OPEN I-O PASSENGER-FILE.
50:      PERFORM 200-ACCEPT-INQUIRY.
51:      PERFORM 300-ON-LINE-PROCESS UNTIL SESSION-END.
52:      CLOSE PASSENGER-FILE.
53:      STOP RUN.
54: *
55:  200-ACCEPT-INQUIRY.
56:      DISPLAY '.................................'.
57:      DISPLAY 'ENTER SELECTION'.
58:      ACCEPT INQUIRY.
59: *
60:  300-ON-LINE-PROCESS.
61:      IF RESERVATION
62:          DISPLAY '***RESERVATION'
63:          MOVE 'YES' TO PASSENGER-MATCH
64:          PERFORM 400-RESERVATION UNTIL NO-MATCH
65:      ELSE
66:          IF SEAT-LOOK-UP
67:              DISPLAY '***SEAT LOOK-UP'
68:              MOVE 'NO' TO PASSENGER-MATCH
69:              PERFORM 500-SEAT-LOOKUP UNTIL MATCH
```

PASSENGER-FILE is an existing indexed file that was created using ACCESS MODE IS SEQUENTIAL.

The PASSENGER-MATCH flag is used to determine whether or not a name typed on the screen has a corresponding match in the file.

Airline employee types a selection code.
RE: Reserve seat for passenger
SE: Look up seat number for a given passenger
CA: Cancel seat for a given passenger
LI: List current passenger names and seats
CH: Change seat for a given passenger
TE: Terminate session

FIRST-NAME is used to point to the start of the file.

Accept inquiry from screen.
Process inquiries until user types in TErminate.

Employee types either RE, SE, CA, LI, CH or TE.

If this is a reservation request, line 63 forces the PERFORM statement at line 64 to be carried out. If there is a passenger with the same name, use a name extension, e.g., if JONES M is already in the file, type in JONES M 1.

FIGURE 11-13
AIRLINE RESERVATION PROGRAM USING DYNAMIC ACCESS

INDEXED SEQUENTIAL FILES

```
 70:            ELSE
 71:              IF CANCELLATION
 72:                  DISPLAY '***CANCELLATION'
 73:                  MOVE 'NO' TO PASSENGER-MATCH
 74:                  PERFORM 600-CANCELLATION UNTIL MATCH
 75:              ELSE
 76:                  IF LIST
 77:                      DISPLAY '***LIST PASSENGERS'
 78:                      DISPLAY 'NAMES            SEAT'
 79:                      DISPLAY ' '
 80:                      MOVE LOW-VALUES TO RR-KEY
 81:                      START PASSENGER-FILE KEY NOT LESS THAN RR-KEY
 82:                      PERFORM 750-READ-PASSENGER-FILE
 83:                      MOVE 0 TO END-FILE
 84:                      PERFORM 700-LIST-PASSENGERS UNTIL END-FILE = 1
 85:                  ELSE
 86:                      IF CHANGE-SEATS
 87:                          DISPLAY '***CHANGE SEATS'
 88:                          MOVE 'NO' TO PASSENGER-MATCH
 89:                          PERFORM 800-CHANGE-SEATS UNTIL MATCH
 90:                      ELSE
 91:                          DISPLAY 'INVALID INQUIRY CODE'.
 92:         PERFORM 200-ACCEPT-INQUIRY.
 93: *
 94:   400-RESERVATION.
 95:       MOVE 'YES' TO PASSENGER-MATCH.
 96:       DISPLAY 'ENTER NAME', ACCEPT RR-KEY.
 97:       START PASSENGER-FILE KEY IS EQUAL TO RR-KEY
 98:           INVALID KEY MOVE 'NO' TO PASSENGER-MATCH.
 99:       IF NO-MATCH
100:           DISPLAY 'ENTER SEAT', ACCEPT RR-SEAT
101:           WRITE PASSENGER-RECORD
102:           DISPLAY 'SEAT', RR-SEAT, ' CONFIRMED FOR ', RR-KEY
103:       ELSE
104:           DISPLAY 'DUPLICATE NAME; USE NAME EXTENSION'.
105: *
106:   500-SEAT-LOOKUP.
107:       MOVE 'YES' TO PASSENGER-MATCH.
108:       DISPLAY 'ENTER NAME'.
109:       ACCEPT RR-KEY.
110:       READ PASSENGER-FILE RECORD
111:           INVALID KEY MOVE 'NO' TO PASSENGER-MATCH
112:                       DISPLAY 'NO SUCH PASSENGER EXISTS'.
113:       IF MATCH DISPLAY RR-KEY, ' SEAT NUMBER: ', RR-SEAT.
114: *
115:   600-CANCELLATION.
116:       MOVE 'YES' TO PASSENGER-MATCH.
117:       DISPLAY 'ENTER NAME'. ACCEPT RR-KEY.
118:       READ PASSENGER-FILE RECORD
119:           INVALID KEY MOVE 'NO' TO PASSENGER-MATCH
120:                       DISPLAY 'NO SUCH PASSENGER EXISTS'.
121:       IF MATCH DISPLAY RR-KEY, ' SEAT ', RR-SEAT, ' CANCELLED'
122:           DELETE PASSENGER-FILE.
123: *
124:   700-LIST-PASSENGERS.
125:       DISPLAY RR-KEY, ' ', RR-SEAT.
126:       PERFORM 750-READ-PASSENGER-FILE.
127: *
128:   750-READ-PASSENGER-FILE.
129:       READ PASSENGER-FILE NEXT RECORD AT END MOVE 1 TO END-FILE.
130: *
131:   800-CHANGE-SEATS.
132:       MOVE 'YES' TO PASSENGER-MATCH.
133:       DISPLAY 'ENTER NAME'.
134:       ACCEPT RR-KEY.
135:       REWRITE PASSENGER-RECORD
136:           INVALID KEY MOVE 'NO' TO PASSENGER-MATCH
137:                       DISPLAY 'NO SUCH NAME: RETYPE'.
138:       IF MATCH
139:           DISPLAY 'ENTER NEW SEAT NUMBER', ACCEPT RR-SEAT
140:           DISPLAY 'SEAT ', RR-SEAT, ' CONFIRMED FOR ', RR-KEY.
```

Cancel seat for particular passenger. If the name is mistyped, type it again as many times as necessary.

To list the passengers, we read the file sequentially starting with the very first name in the file. The START verb is used to point to the "lowest" alphabetical name in the list. Keep reading the names until the end of the file is reached.

Change seats for a given passenger. If the name is mistyped, retype it as many times as necessary.

Accept the name for a reservation. START checks whether the name is already present in the file. If it is present, add an extension to the name and reserve a seat. If it is not present, enter a seat number and assign it to passenger name.

Accept name of passenger and place it in the RECORD KEY so that the READ can capture it. Note the word RECORD in the READ statement.

Cancel seat for a given passenger.

Accept name and read corresponding record to identify seat number. If name is not found print error message, otherwise delete record.

List the names of all passengers. Display each name and seat.

The very first record of the indexed file is identified by lines 80 and 81.

Change the seat for a given passenger.

Accept passenger name and store the name in the RECORD KEY so that the REWRITE knows which seat to change. If there is no such name, print an error message.

FIGURE 11–13
(*continued*)

Just as in RANDOM mode, transaction files and on-line inquiries need not be arranged in any particular order if an indexed file is to be updated.

The types of file processing activities that can be carried out in dynamic mode are:

1. Locate and retrieve a record by its primary or alternate key (READ format-2 in Figure 11-14).

2. Read records sequentially (READ format-1 in Figure 11-14). The START verb can be used to position the READ at a certain record in the file—from that point on, the file can be processed sequentially.

3. Change any number of fields in a particular record (REWRITE operation).

4. Insert or add a record to the file (WRITE operation).

5. Delete a particular record (DELETE operation).

The input/output operations that are permitted in conjunction with the various OPEN options are shown in the table in Figure 11-14.

Reading Records Sequentially: The READ . . . NEXT RECORD . . .

Dynamic mode allows the programmer to read an indexed file sequentially, in conceptually the same way as sequential files are read under ORGANIZATION IS SEQUENTIAL (chapter 10).

The READ statement must specify NEXT, and the AT END tells the program what to do when the end of file has been reached. The INTO option is also available. The OPEN statement causes the READ . . . NEXT to start at the very first record in the file. In some applications, though, it may be necessary to re-read the file (in sequential fashion) from the beginning. Since random insert transactions are likely to affect the value of the first record, the simplest way to point back to the beginning of the file is as follows:

```
MOVE LOW-VALUES TO MR-KEY.
START MASTER-FILE KEY IS NOT LESS THAN MR-KEY.
READ MASTER-FILE NEXT RECORD . . .
```

where MR-KEY is the primary key associated with MASTER-FILE. In this case the lowest characters in the character-collating sequence are moved to MR-KEY. The START verb will then point to the first key value in the file that is greater than or equal to LOW-VALUES and that will be the first record in the file.

Reading Records Randomly: The READ Statement

The use of the READ statement (format 2) for random retrieval of records through the READ file-name RECORD is identical to that of the READ statement using ACCESS MODE IS RANDOM (section 11-3-2).

Changing Records: The REWRITE Statement

There are no differences in syntax or use between the random and dynamic REWRITE statements (see section 11-3-3). Records can of course be changed in sequential order through the use of the sequential READ; as each record is read sequentially, the REWRITE statement can be used to change it.

ENVIRONMENT DIVISION entries for ACCESS MODE IS DYNAMIC

```
SELECT file-name ASSIGN to device-name
    ORGANIZATION IS INDEXED
    ACCESS MODE  IS DYNAMIC
    RECORD KEY   IS data-name-1
    [ALTERNATE RECORD KEY IS data-name-2  [WITH DUPLICATES]] ...
    [FILE STATUS IS data-name-3]
```

PROCEDURE DIVISION entries for ACCESS MODE IS DYNAMIC

```
OPEN  { INPUT  }  file-name ...
      { OUTPUT }
      { I-O    }
```

format-1
sequential access
READ file-name NEXT RECORD [INTO data-name-1]
    [AT END imperative-statement ...]

format-2
direct retrieval
READ file-name RECORD [INTO data-name-1]
    [KEY   data-name-2]
    [INVALID KEY imperative-statement ...]

WRITE record-name FROM data-name-1][INVALID KEY imperative-statement ...]

START file-name KEY IS { GREATER THAN } data-name
                        { NOT LESS THAN }
                        { EQUAL TO   }
    [INVALID KEY imperative-statement ...]

DELETE file-name RECORD [INVALID KEY imperative-statement ...]
REWRITE record-name [FROM data-name] [INVALID KEY imperative-statement ...]

OPEN options for the READ, WRITE, START, DELETE, and REWRITE

READ	WRITE	START	DELETE	REWRITE
{OPEN INPUT} {OPEN I-O}	{OPEN OUTPUT} {OPEN I-O}	{OPEN INPUT} {OPEN I-O}	OPEN I-O	OPEN OUTPUT

INVALID KEY errors and AT END conditions	
READ	End of file (AT END) for format-1 type READ.
	Key does not refer to an existing key in the file.
WRITE	The file already contains a record with the same key value.
	The allocated disk space is exceeded.
START	No matching record is found.
DELETE	No matching record is found.
REWRITE	No matching record is found.

FIGURE 11–14
COBOL ENTRIES TO PROCESS AN INDEXED FILE IN DYNAMIC MODE

Adding Records: The WRITE Statement

There are no differences in syntax or use between the random and dynamic WRITE statements (see section 11-3-4).

Deleting Records: The DELETE Statement

There are no differences in syntax or use between the random and dynamic DELETE statements (see section 11-3-5). Records can be deleted in sequential fashion through the use of the sequential READ; the DELETE statement can be used to delete each record as it is read sequentially.

11-5 EXERCISES

1. Are the following statements true or false? If false, explain why.
   a. To start a sequential READ operation at the record with key value JONES, you can MOVE 'JONES' to the record key and immediately use the READ file-name NEXT RECORD ... instruction.
   b. All input/output operations that can be carried out in ACCESS IS RANDOM can also be carried out in ACCESS IS DYNAMIC.
   c. The FILE STATUS word can reflect an end-of-file condition as a result of an INVALID KEY clause being activated when dynamic mode is used.
   d. When the DELETE statement is used, the record to be deleted is moved into the input area of the corresponding file.

2. Print the records of an indexed file using ACCESS MODE IS DYNAMIC, starting at a key value that is ACCEPTed. Printout should be in order by ascending key value.

3. Print the records of an indexed file in ascending key value using ACCESS MODE IS RANDOM.

4. Print the contents of an indexed file in descending key value. Assume no more than 100 records. Use the DYNAMIC mode.

5. An indexed file contains a list of names (the name is the RECORD KEY). Write the code to delete all records in the name interval M through T (for example, delete MASON, SIMS, and TORO, but not LAMBERT or ULAN).

6. Each record of an indexed file contains a name (key value) and a score. Write the code to do the following:

   a. Add 10% of the class average to each score. No resulting score should exceed 100.
   b. Delete all records with scores below 50.
   c. Print the names of all students whose scores exceed 90, *then* print the names of all students whose scores are between 50 and 70.

7. For what operations would you use the START verb in DYNAMIC mode, other than in conjunction with the READ NEXT RECORD?

8. The last record key value of indexed file ROSTER is the name JOHNSON. Write the code to read an ORGANIZATION IS SEQUENTIAL transaction file consisting of names in alphabetical sequence starting with the letter M, and add the names of the transaction file to the indexed file. The records in the two files have identical formats. Be as efficient as possible.

INDEXED SEQUENTIAL FILES   **621**

9. Two indexed files have identical record formats. Write the code to merge the two files into one file or the other.

10. Two indexed files have identical record formats with the same keys. Write the code to delete all records that are common to both files.

11. Modify the airline reservation program of Figure 11–13, so that

   a. The agent can print out the number of seats that have been assigned so far.
   b. The agent can enter a seat number and determine the name of its occupant.
   c. The system will print an error message if the agent assigns a seat number that has already been given to another passenger.
   d. The agent can print out a list of all unreserved seats.
   e. The agent can print out the seating arrangement of the airplane starting with row 1. Each row contains four seats, and there are 40 rows. Place the name of each passenger in his/her seating position. For example:

   ```
   Row 1    ADAMS J      SKULLS K    DENNIS M    *****
   Row 2    *****        SIMS L      *****       LONG G
   Row 3    WONG K       *****       BELL P      BELL M
   Row 4    ARTEMIS L    GORDON K    SUWAMI L    JENKINS L
   ```

12. Each record of an indexed file contains the bank account number of a customer, the name of the customer, and a balance amount.

   a. Write a program to create such an indexed file.

   For the following transactions it would be preferable to use ACCEPT/DISPLAY statements for input/output. If you cannot use your terminal in the interactive mode, create a regular data file that will be read by the program. Then write the code to carry out the following functions on the indexed file you have created:

   b. Subtract from each account a monthly service charge fee of $6.50.
   c. List all records at any given time during the program.
   d. Change the name of a customer.
   e. Delete specified records.
   f. Compute and print the total amount deposited by all customers.
   g. Accept an account number and a deposit (positive number) or a debit (negative number), and update the balance of that account.
   h. Print the account number and customer name for any account in debit. Print the debit, to which is added a $10.00 penalty charge.
   i. Add new account numbers whenever needed.
   j. Provide the bank with a current list of accounts with balances exceeding $100,000.

13. A hospital maintains a patient file where each record contains the following information:

   a. Patient identification number (record key).
   b. Patient name.
   c. Date of admission and date of discharge (latter field is initially blank). Express the dates in Julian form and omit the year. For example 033 is February 2nd and 364 is December 30th.

d. Weight in and weight out (the latter is left blank until the patient's discharge).
e. Name of patient's doctor.
f. A maximum of 10 drugs to which the patient is allergic. This particular entry is comprised of one data item specifying the number of allergies, followed by a table containing a maximum of ten drugs, for example

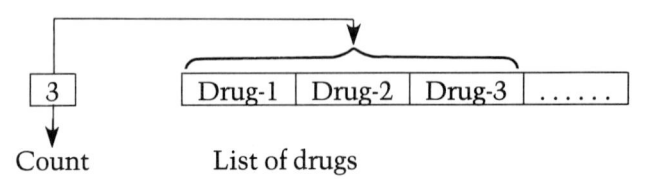

```
   3        | Drug-1 | Drug-2 | Drug-3 | ......
   ↓
 Count          List of drugs
```

g. A table, initially consisting of 10 blank entries, to be used to record drugs administered to the patient and corresponding dosage (expressed in units). The format is as follows:

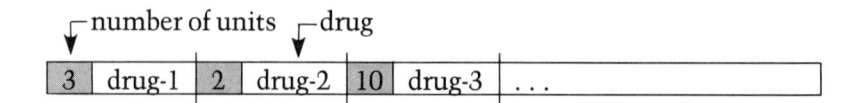

```
 ┌number of units  ┌drug
 ↓                 ↓
| 3 | drug-1 | 2 | drug-2 | 10 | drug-3 | ...
```

Write a program to create an indexed file containing the information in items 1–7.

Then write another program to allow the medical staff to ask questions about and to update a particular patient record. For each of the following actions, the patient's I.D. number and a special query code should be entered:

aa. Enter a patient I.D. number and print the name of the patient's doctor.
bb. Print the list of drugs to which the patient is allergic.
cc. Record any drug administered to the patient and the number of units.
dd. Print the list of drugs administered to the patient.
ee. Delete a particular drug from the patient's list of drug allergies.
ff. Add a drug to the patient's list of drug allergies (limited to a maximum of 10).
gg. ACCEPT a particular drug and determine if the patient is allergic to it.
hh. When a patient is discharged from the hospital, fill in his/her discharge date.
ii. Compute the number of days the patient spent at the hospital.
jj. Record the patient's weight on his/her discharge day.
kk. Print the patient's total room cost ($200 per day). Print the patient's total weight gain or loss. Print the total number of days he/she spent at the hospital.
ll. Compute each patient's drug bill. To produce this bill you will need to read a sequential file DRUG where all drugs and corresponding unit costs have been recorded. Print each of the patient's drugs and its corresponding cost, as well as the total cost.

APPENDIX A:

USAGE Clause and RENAMES

A-1 THE USAGE CLAUSE

DATA TYPES

The USAGE clause specifies the form in which a data item is to be represented in the computer's memory. The programmer never *needs* to use this clause. However, in many instances, the USAGE clause can significantly affect the efficiency of a COBOL program. Not only can it affect the physical size of the program by reducing the number of memory/storage positions needed to represent numeric data, but it can also speed up the execution of the program by optimizing arithmetic operations. Such savings of memory storage and time are important considerations for large production programs that are run frequently.

The user can specify any of three data USAGES for numeric data items: COMPUTATIONAL, DISPLAY, and COMPUTATIONAL-3 (on some compilers). This implies three distinct internal number representations for numeric data. Alphanumeric data has a unique internal representation called DISPLAY mode, and all alphanumeric characters essentially occupy one memory position. Thus USAGE for alphanumeric data is limited to DISPLAY. The general form of the USAGE clause is:

```
              ⎧ COMPUTATIONAL or COMP      ⎫
              ⎪ DISPLAY                    ⎪
USAGE IS      ⎨ COMPUTATIONAL-3 or COMP-3* ⎬
              ⎪ INDEX                      ⎪
              ⎩                            ⎭

*COMP-3 is non-standard (used by IBM)
```

The USAGE clause can be used at any level of data description. It can be specified at the group level, in which case it applies to each elementary item in the group, or it can be specified at the elementary item level. The clause itself should be placed after the PICTURE clause but before the VALUE clause (if present).

The following paragraphs provide a brief discussion of the four types of USAGE clauses.

Usage Is Display.

(This is sometimes referred to as ZONED, EBCDIC, or character format.) This is the usage that has been used unknowingly to declare all data items up to this point in this text. The absence of the USAGE clause in a record description entry implies that the USAGE is DISPLAY for the item described.

Alphanumeric fields (PIC X), alphabetic fields (PIC A), and numerically edited fields (PIC $$,$$$.99) are all examples of DISPLAY usage fields.

Numeric fields (PIC S99V99) in DISPLAY mode occupy as many memory positions as there are digits in the PICTURE field (in some compilers the S occupies a position by itself).

Examples:

```
                                                    MEMORY POSITIONS
77 A PIC S9V99 USAGE IS DISPLAY VALUE .45.          | 0 | 4 | 5 |

01 TAB USAGE IS DISPLAY.
   05 B PIC XXXX.                                   |   |   |   |   |
   05 C PIC $$,$$$.99.                              |   |   |   |   |   |   | . |   |   |
   05 D PIC S999 VALUE -23.                         | 0 | 2 | 3̄ |
   05 E PIC AAA VALUE "CAT".                        | C | A | T |
```

Since group item TAB is DISPLAY usage, all subitems of TAB are DISPLAY. Of course, only D could be of different usage since it is the sole numeric item.

The USAGE IS DISPLAY option should be used in the following cases:

1. When describing numeric input fields where the input data will be read from terminals or ACCEPTed by a CRT or by some other character-set-sensitive input device (keyboards, et cetera).

2. When describing output fields for printers, videos, terminals, and other character-set-sensitive output devices.

3. When describing any alphabetic, alphanumeric, and numerically edited fields.

Usage Is Computational.

COMPUTATIONAL (or COMP) usage can be used only on numeric data items. Most computers perform arithmetic operations on numeric values that are expressed internally in binary form (1's and 0's). Similarly, subscripting is ultimately carried out with binary subscript values. This means that if DISPLAY-type data items are to be processed arithmetically or logically (compared) or used as subscripts, the computer must first convert these items from DISPLAY format to binary format, which naturally takes more time. Hence, any data items that are to be used as counters, accumulators, numeric independent data items, or subscripts should be specified as COMP USAGE (binary) to make the program more efficient.

Keep in mind, however, that numeric record description entries that are to be processed by input/output devices such as printers, and monitors must be declared as DISPLAY usage and not COMPUTATIONAL.

The difference between a COMP item and a DISPLAY item is in the length of the internal field allocated for that item. For example, on an IBM 370 system an 18-digit DISPLAY numeric item is reduced to 8 memory positions when it is in COMP form. The following table illustrates memory position differences between DISPLAY and COMP usages (for IBM 370 systems).

DIGITS IN PICTURE CLAUSE	STORAGE POSITIONS DISPLAY	COMP
1–4	1–4	2
5–9	5–9	4
10–18	10–18	8

These numbers will vary, of course, from one computer system to another.

Examples:

```
77 AMT PIC IS S9(3) DISPLAY VALUE -1.  |0|0|I|
77 AMT PIC IS S9(3) COMP    VALUE -1.  |F|F|    hexadecimal notation
                                        ↑ ↑
                                       Binary no. (2 positions)
```

When a DISPLAY item is MOVEd into a COMP field, the item is converted to the USAGE form of the receiving field.

Usage Is Computational-3 (Packed decimal).

Some compilers (IBM, for example) allow the user to specify USAGE IS COMP-3 (COMPUTATIONAL-3). Numeric data is then converted to packed decimal format, which in essence reduces the size of the DISPLAY field by a factor of 2. The reader should consult an IBM (or other) reference manual to determine the optimal conditions under which COMP-3 can be used.

Other compilers, in addition to IBM, allow the user to specify COMP-1 and COMP-2 usage (on some compilers these might be called COMP-4 and COMP-5). Data items specified as such are then converted to single- and double-precision numbers. These numbers are expressed internally in terms of a fractional part and an exponent and are used to express numbers with very large magnitudes. The user is advised to consult his/her technical reference manual to determine the optimal conditions under which COMP-1 and COMP-2 can be used. Once again, neither COMP, COMP-1, nor COMP-2 should be used to describe input/output records that are to be processed by character-sensitive devices (monitors, printers).

Usage Is Index.

This is another option for the USAGE clause, for example:

```
77  I  PIC 99 USAGE IS INDEX.
```

The index described must be an elementary item. In this case the data item I can be used to store the value of another index for future reference. The SET clause can be used to initialize I.

THE SYNCHRONIZED CLAUSE

The SYNCHRONIZED or SYNC clause may appear only at the elementary data item level. Since this clause affects the proper alignment of data items with regard to internal word boundaries, the reader is advised to check his/her reference manual for the technical details. It should be noted that this clause should be used only with COMP, COMP-1, COMP-2, and COMP-3 entries. For example, an entry using the SYNCHRONIZED clause might be as follows:

```
77 AMT PIC S999V99 SYNC USAGE IS COMP VALUE -31.27.
```

MASS STORAGE CONSIDERATIONS AND THE USAGE CLAUSE

Numeric data read from a text edited file accepted by a CRT must generally be converted from DISPLAY to COMPUTATIONAL before it can be processed by the arithmetic unit. Similarly, printers and CRTs require that numerically computed results be converted to DISPLAY form before being printed. Numeric data, however, can be stored on mass storage devices such as magnetic tape or disk in either DISPLAY, COMPUTATIONAL, COMP-1, COMP-2, OR COMP-3 form. Data items that have been written onto disk/tape in COMP form or in a form other than DISPLAY do not need to be converted back to COMP when read back from disk/tape to memory. This can save storage space on the external storage device and speed up arithmetic processing, since the data is already in a form that can be handled directly by the CPU arithmetic unit. For example, the following record could be written out on disk as:

```
                                                     Positions
01 DISK-RECORD
   05 NAME PIC X(20).                                20 characters
   05 FLD-1 PIC S99999      USAGE IS COMP.           4 binary
   05 FLD-2 PIC S9(5)V999   USAGE IS COMP-3.         5 packed
   05 FLD-3 PIC S99V999     USAGE IS COMP-2.         8 floating point
```

A-2 66 LEVEL DATA ITEMS: THE RENAMES CLAUSE

The RENAMES clause can be useful occasionally when the programmer needs to give an alternate name to a data item name, or when he/she needs to refer to a group of consecutive record description entries using just one name, i.e., this clause allows the user to group a set of successive record entries under one umbrella name.

To a certain extent, the RENAMES clause is similar to the REDEFINES clause, except that it cannot change the PICTURE fields of the items that it renames (the PICTURES remain the same).

The general format for the RENAMES clause is

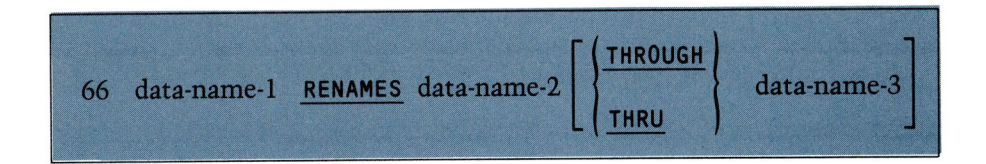

$$66 \text{ data-name-1 } \underline{\text{RENAMES}} \text{ data-name-2 } \left[\begin{Bmatrix} \text{THROUGH} \\ \text{THRU} \end{Bmatrix} \text{ data-name-3} \right]$$

where

66 is a level number (margin A) exclusively reserved for the RENAMES clause.

A 66-level entry cannot rename another 66-level entry, nor can it rename an 01-, 77-, or 88-level entry.

All 66-level entries associated with a logical record must immediately follow the record's last record description entry.

If data-name-3 is specified, then data-name-1 becomes a group item and represents all entries up to and including data-name-3 and all subordinate items of data-name-3 if data-name-3 is a group item.

Neither data-name-2 nor data-name-3 may have an OCCURS clause in its record description entry or be subordinate to an item that has an OCCURS clause in its record description entry.

Some examples of RENAMES clauses are as follows:

EXAMPLE 1:

```
01 FLDA.
    05 A.
        10 A1 PIC X.
        10 A2 PIC XXX.
        10 A3 PIC XX.
        10 A4 PIC XX.
    05 X.
        10 X1 PIC XX.
        10 X2 PIC X(6).
        10 X3 PIC X(8).
66 B RENAMES A.                  B is an alphanumeric item comprising A1 thru A4.
66 C RENAMES A.                  C is an alphanumeric item comprising A1 thru A4.
66 D RENAMES A1 THRU A3.         D consists of 6 characters.
66 E RENAMES A4 THRU X2.         E consists of a string of 10 characters.
66 F RENAMES A2 THRU X.          F consists of A2 thru X3 (23 characters).
66 G RENAMES A  THRU X.          G consists of A1 thru X3 (24 characters).
01 FLDB.
    03 AMT PIC 999V99 VALUE 112.3.
66 Z RENAMES AMT.                Another name for AMT is Z.
```

EXAMPLE 2:

```
01 STUDENT-RECORD.
   05 LAST-NAME   PIC X(20). ⎫
   05 MIDDLE-NAME PIC X(10). ⎬ FULL-NAME
   05 FIRST-NAME  PIC X(10). ⎭
   05 BIRTH-DATE.
      10 DAYS  PIC 99.           ⎫
      10 MONTH PIC 99. ⎫         ⎬ ANNIVERSARY
      10 YEAR  PIC 99. ⎭ MONTH-YEAR ⎭

66 FULL-NAME   RENAMES LAST-NAME THRU FIRST-NAME.
66 MONTH-YEAR  RENAMES MONTH THRU YEAR.
66 ANNIVERSARY RENAMES BIRTH-DATE.
   .
   .
   .
IF MONTH-YEAR < "1181"
   MOVE FULL-NAME TO DL-NAME.    Move last, middle, and first name.
```

APPENDIX B

American National Standard COBOL Format Summary and Reserved Words

No word in the following list should appear as a programmer-defined name. The keys that appear before some of the words have the following meanings:

- (xa) the word is an IBM extension to American National Standard COBOL.
- (xac) the word is an IBM extension to both American National Standard COBOL and CODASYL COBOL.
- (ca) the word is a CODASYL COBOL reserved word not incorporated in American National Standard COBOL or in IBM American National Standard COBOL.
- (sp) the word is an IBM function-name established in support of the SPECIAL-NAMES function.
- (spn) the word is used by an IBM American National Standard COBOL compiler.
- (asn) before a word means that the word is defined by American National Standard COBOL.

	ACCEPT		CALL
	ACCESS	(xa)	CANCEL
	ACTUAL	(xac)	CBL
	ADD	(xa)	CD
(asn)	ADDRESS		CF
	ADVANCING		CH
	AFTER	(xac)	CHANGED
	ALL	(xa)	CHARACTER
	ALPHABETIC		CHARACTERS
(ca)	ALPHANUMERIC	(asn)	CLOCK-UNITS
	ALPHANUMERIC-EDITED		CLOSE
	ALTER	(asn)	COBOL
	ALTERNATE		CODE
	AND		COLUMN
(xa)	APPLY	(spn)	COM-REG
	ARE		COMMA
	AREA	(xa)	COMMUNICATION
	AREAS		COMP
	ASCENDING	(xa)	COMP-1
	ASSIGN	(xa)	COMP-2
	AT	(xa)	COMP-3
	AUTHOR	(xa)	COMP-4
			COMPUTATIONAL
(xac)	BASIS	(xa)	COMPUTATIONAL-1
	BEFORE	(xa)	COMPUTATIONAL-2
	BEGINNING	(xa)	COMPUTATIONAL-3
	BLANK	(xa)	COMPUTATIONAL-4
	BLOCK		COMPUTE
(ca)	BOTTOM		CONFIGURATION
	BY	(sp)	CONSOLE

	CONTAINS		
	CONTROL		
	CONTROLS		
	COPY		
(xac)	CORE-INDEX		
	CORR		
	CORRESPONDING		
(xa)	COUNT		
(sp)	CSP		
	CURRENCY		
(xac)	CURRENT-DATE		
(spn)	CYL-INDEX		
(spn)	CYL-OVERFLOW		
(sp)	C01		
(sp)	C02		
(sp)	C03		
(sp)	C04		
(sp)	C05		
(sp)	C06		
(sp)	C07		
(sp)	C08		
(sp)	C09		
(sp)	C10		
(sp)	C11		
(sp)	C12 DATA		
(xa)	DATE		
	DATE-COMPILED		
	DATE-WRITTEN		
(xa)	DAY		
(ca)	DAY-OF-WEEK		
	DE		
(xac)	DEBUG		
(ca)	DEBUG-CONTENTS		
(ca)	DEBUG-ITEM		
(ca)	DEBUG-LINE		
(ca)	DEBUG-NAME		
(ca)	DEBUG-SUB-1		
(ca)	DEBUG-SUB-2		
(ca)	DEBUG-SUB-3		
(ca)	DEBUGGING		
	DECIMAL-POINT		
	DECLARATIVES		
(xa)	DELETE		
(xa)	DELIMITED		
(xa)	DELIMITER		
	DEPENDING		
(xa)	DEPTH		
	DESCENDING		

(xa)	DESTINATION
	DETAIL
(ca)	DISABLE
(xac)	DISP
	DISPLAY
(xac)	DISPLAY-ST
(ca)	DISPLAY-n
	DIVIDE
	DIVISION
	DOWN
(ca)	DUPLICATES
(xa)	DYNAMIC
(xa)	ECI
(xac)	EJECT
	ELSE
(xa)	EMI
(ca)	ENABLE
	END
	END-OF-PAGE
(xa)	ENDING
	ENTER
(xac)	ENTRY
	ENVIRONMENT
(xa)	EOP
	EQUAL
(ca)	EQUALS
	ERROR
(xa)	ESI
	EVERY
	EXAMINE
(ca)	EXCEEDS
(xa)	EXCEPTION
(xac)	EXHIBIT
	EXIT
(xa)	EXTEND
(spn)	EXTENDED-SEARCH
	FD
	FILE
	FILE-CONTROL
	FILE-LIMIT
	FILE-LIMITS
	FILLER
	FINAL
	FIRST
	FOOTING
	FOR
	FROM

	GENERATE		MULTIPLE	(ca)	REFERENCES	(xa)	SUB-QUEUE-2
	GIVING		MULTIPLY	(ca)	RELATIVE	(xa)	SUB-QUEUE-3
	GO				RELEASE		SUBTRACT
(xac)	GOBACK	(xac)	NAMED	(xac)	RELOAD		SUM
	GREATER		NEGATIVE		REMAINDER	(ca)	SUPERVISOR
	GROUP		NEXT		REMARKS	(xa)	SUPPRESS
			NO	(ca)	REMOVAL	(ca)	SUSPEND
	HEADING	(xac)	NOMINAL		RENAMES	(xa)	SYMBOLIC
	HIGH-VALUE		NOT	(xac)	REORG-CRITERIA		SYNC
	HIGH-VALUES		NOTE		REPLACING		SYNCHRONIZED
(ca)	HOLD	(spn)	NSTD-REELS		REPORT	(sp)	SYSIN
			NUMBER		REPORTING	(spn)	SYSIPT
	I-O		NUMERIC		REPORTS	(spn)	SYSLST
	I-O-CONTROL	(ca)	NUMERIC-EDITED	(xac)	REREAD	(sp)	SYSOUT
(xac)	ID				RERUN	(spn)	SYSPCH
	IDENTIFICATION		OBJECT-COMPUTER		RESERVE	(sp)	SYSPUNCH
	IF	(ca)	OBJECT-PROGRAM		RESET	(sp)	SO1
	IN		OCCURS		RETURN	(sp)	SO2
	INDEX		OF	(xac)	RETURN-CODE		
(ca)	INDEX-n		OFF		REVERSED	(ca)	TABLE
	INDEXED		OMITTED		REWIND		TALLY
	INDICATE		ON	(xa)	REWRITE		TALLYING
(ca)	INITIAL		OPEN		RF		TAPE
(ca)	INITIALIZE		OPTIONAL		RH	(ca)	TERMINAL
	INITIATE		OR		RIGHT		TERMINATE
	INPUT	(xa)	ORGANIZATION		ROUNDED	(xa)	TEXT
	INPUT-OUTPUT	(xac)	OTHERWISE		RUN		THAN
(xac)	INSERT		OUTPUT			(xac)	THEN
(ca)	INSPECT	(xa)	OVERFLOW	(ca)	SA		THROUGH
	INSTALLATION				SAME		THRU
	INTO		PAGE		SD	(xa)	TIME
	INVALID		PAGE-COUNTER		SEARCH	(xac)	TIME-OF-DAY
	IS	(xac)	PASSWORD		SECTION		TIMES
			PERFORM		SECURITY		TO
	JUST		PF		SEEK	(ca)	TOP
	JUSTIFIED		PH	(xa)	SEGMENT	(xac)	TOTALED
			PIC		SEGMENT-LIMIT	(xac)	TOTALING
	KEY		PICTURE		SELECT	(xac)	TRACE
			PLUS	(xa)	SEND	(xac)	TRACK
	LABEL	(xa)	POINTER		SENTENCE	(xac)	TRACK-AREA
(xac)	LABEL-RETURN		POSITION	(xa)	SEPARATE	(xac)	TRACK-LIMIT
	LAST	(xac)	POSITIONING		SEQUENTIAL	(xac)	TRACKS
	LEADING		POSITIVE	(xac)	SERVICE	(xa)	TRAILING
(xac)	LEAVE	(xac)	PRINT-SWITCH		SET	(xac)	TRANSFORM
	LEFT	(ca)	PRINTING		SIGN		TYPE
(xa)	LENGTH		PROCEDURE		SIZE		
	LESS	(ca)	PROCEDURES	(xac)	SKIP1	(ca)	UNEQUAL
(ca)	LIBRARY		PROCEED	(xac)	SKIP2		UNIT
	LIMIT	(ca)	PROCESS	(xac)	SKIP3	(xa)	UNSTRING
	LIMITS		PROCESSING		SORT		UNTIL
(ca)	LINAGE	(xa)	PROGRAM	(xac)	SORT-CORE-SIZE		UP
(ca)	LINAGE-COUNTER		PROGRAM-ID	(xac)	SORT-FILE-SIZE		UPON
	LINE			(ca)	SORT-MERGE	(spn)	UPSI-0
	LINE-COUNTER	(xa)	QUEUE	(xac)	SORT-MESSAGE	(spn)	UPSI-1
	LINES		QUOTE	(xac)	SORT-MODE-SIZE	(spn)	UPSI-2
(xa)	LINKAGE		QUOTES	(spn)	SORT-OPTION	(spn)	UPSI-3
	LOCK			(xac)	SORT-RETURN	(spn)	UPSI-4
	LOW-VALUE		RANDOM		SOURCE	(spn)	UPSI-5
	LOW-VALUES		RD		SOURCE-COMPUTER	(spn)	UPSI-6
			READ		SPACE	(spn)	UPSI-7
(spn)	MASTER-INDEX	(xac)	READY		SPACES		USAGE
	MEMORY	(xa)	RECEIVE		SPECIAL-NAMES		USE
(xa)	MERGE		RECORD		STANDARD		USING
(xa)	MESSAGE	(xac)	RECORD-OVERFLOW	(xa)	START		
	MODE	(xa)	RECORDING		STATUS		
	MODULES		RECORDS		STOP		VALUE
(xac)	MORE-LABELS		REDEFINES	(xa)	STRING		VALUES
	MOVE		REEL	(xa)	SUB-QUEUE-1		VARYING

APPENDIX C

General Form of COBOL Statements

Format notation:

NOTATION*	MEANING
UPPER CASE WORDS	Reserved words.
UPPER CASE UNDERLINED WORDS	Required reserved words.
lowercase	Programmer-supplied items.
[optional]	Optimal entry.
{Either one / or the other}	Select one entry of the list.
...	Item may be optimally repeated.

*In many compilers characters may be typed in uppercase, lowercase, or a combination of both.

General Format for IDENTIFICATION DIVISION

IDENTIFICATION DIVISION.

PROGRAM-ID. program-name.

[AUTHOR. [comment-entry] ...]

[INSTALLATION. [comment-entry] ...]

[DATE-WRITTEN. [comment-entry] ...]

[DATE-COMPILED. [comment-entry] ...]

[SECURITY. [comment-entry] ...]

General Format for ENVIRONMENT DIVISION

ENVIRONMENT DIVISION.

CONFIGURATION SECTION.

SOURCE-COMPUTER. computer-name [WITH DEBUGGING MODE].

OBJECT-COMPUTER. computer-name

$\left[\text{, MEMORY SIZE integer} \begin{Bmatrix} \text{WORDS} \\ \text{CHARACTERS} \\ \text{MODULES} \end{Bmatrix} \right]$

[, PROGRAM COLLATING SEQUENCE IS alphabet-name]

[, SEGMENT-LIMIT IS segment-number] .

$\Big[$ SPECIAL-NAMES . , implementor-name

$\begin{Bmatrix} \underline{\text{IS}} \text{ mnemonic-name } [\text{, } \underline{\text{ON}} \text{ STATUS } \underline{\text{IS}} \text{ condition-name-1 } [\text{, } \underline{\text{OFF}} \text{ STATUS } \underline{\text{IS}} \text{ condition-name-2}]] \\ \underline{\text{IS}} \text{ mnemonic-name } [\text{, } \underline{\text{OFF}} \text{ STATUS } \underline{\text{IS}} \text{ condition-name-2 } [\text{, } \underline{\text{ON}} \text{ STATUS } \underline{\text{IS}} \text{ condition-name-1}]] \\ \underline{\text{ON}} \text{ STATUS } \underline{\text{IS}} \text{ condition-name-1 } [\text{, } \underline{\text{OFF}} \text{ STATUS } \underline{\text{IS}} \text{ condition-name-2}] \\ \underline{\text{OFF}} \text{ STATUS } \underline{\text{IS}} \text{ condition-name-2 } [\text{, } \underline{\text{ON}} \text{ STATUS } \underline{\text{IS}} \text{ condition-name-1}] \end{Bmatrix}$

$\left[\text{, alphabet-name IS} \begin{Bmatrix} \text{STANDARD-1} \\ \text{NATIVE} \\ \text{implementor-name} \\ \text{literal-1} \left[\begin{Bmatrix} \text{THROUGH} \\ \text{THRU} \end{Bmatrix} \text{literal-2} \atop \text{ALSO literal-3 [, ALSO literal-4] ...} \right] \\ \quad \left[\text{literal-5} \left[\begin{Bmatrix} \text{THROUGH} \\ \text{THRU} \end{Bmatrix} \text{literal-6} \atop \text{ALSO literal-7 [, ALSO literal-8] ...} \right] \right] ... \end{Bmatrix} \right]$

[, CURRENCY SIGN IS literal-9]

[, DECIMAL-POINT IS COMMA] .

APPENDIX C: General Form of COBOL Statements

continued from page C2

[INPUT-OUTPUT SECTION.

FILE-CONTROL.

    {file-control-entry} ...

[I-O-CONTROL.

    [; RERUN [ON $\begin{Bmatrix} \text{file-name-1} \\ \text{implementor-name} \end{Bmatrix}$]

        EVERY $\begin{Bmatrix} [\text{END OF}] \begin{Bmatrix} \underline{\text{REEL}} \\ \underline{\text{UNIT}} \end{Bmatrix} \text{OF file-name-2} \\ \text{integer-1 } \underline{\text{RECORDS}} \\ \text{integer-2 } \underline{\text{CLOCK-UNITS}} \\ \text{condition-name} \end{Bmatrix}$] ...

    [; SAME $\begin{bmatrix} \underline{\text{RECORD}} \\ \underline{\text{SORT}} \\ \underline{\text{SORT-MERGE}} \end{bmatrix}$ AREA FOR file-name-3 {, file-name-4} ...] ...

    [; MULTIPLE FILE TAPE CONTAINS file-name-5 [POSITION integer-3]

        [, file-name-6 [POSITION integer-4]] ...]] .

General Format for FILE-CONTROL Entry (ENVIRONMENT DIVISION)

FORMAT 1:

SELECT [OPTIONAL file-name]

    ASSIGN TO implementor-name-1 [, implementor-name-2] ...

    [; RESERVE integer-1 $\begin{bmatrix} \underline{\text{AREA}} \\ \underline{\text{AREAS}} \end{bmatrix}$]

    [; ORGANIZATION IS SEQUENTIAL]

    [; ACCESS MODE IS SEQUENTIAL]

    [; FILE STATUS IS data-name-1].

FORMAT 2:

<u>SELECT</u> file-name

    <u>ASSIGN</u> TO implementor-name-1 [, implementor-name-2] ...

    [; <u>RESERVE</u> integer-1 [<u>AREA</u> / <u>AREAS</u>]]

    ; <u>ORGANIZATION</u> IS <u>RELATIVE</u>

    [; <u>ACCESS</u> MODE IS { <u>SEQUENTIAL</u> [, <u>RELATIVE</u> KEY IS data-name-1] / { <u>RANDOM</u> / <u>DYNAMIC</u> } , <u>RELATIVE</u> KEY IS data-name-1 }]

    [; <u>FILE</u> <u>STATUS</u> IS data-name-2] .

FORMAT 3:

<u>SELECT</u> file-name

    <u>ASSIGN</u> TO implementor-name-1 [, implementor-name-2] ...

    [; <u>RESERVE</u> integer-1 [<u>AREA</u> / <u>AREAS</u>]]

    ; <u>ORGANIZATION</u> IS <u>INDEXED</u>

    [; <u>ACCESS</u> MODE IS { <u>SEQUENTIAL</u> / <u>RANDOM</u> / <u>DYNAMIC</u> }]

    ; <u>RECORD</u> KEY IS data-name-1

    [; <u>ALTERNATE</u> <u>RECORD</u> KEY IS data-name-2 [WITH <u>DUPLICATES</u> ...]]

    [; <u>FILE</u> <u>STATUS</u> IS data-name-3] .

FORMAT 4:

<u>SELECT</u> file-name <u>ASSIGN</u> TO implementor-name-1 [, implementor-name]

General Format for DATA DIVISION

<u>DATA</u> <u>DIVISION</u>.

<u>FILE</u> <u>SECTION</u>.

FD file-name

APPENDIX C: General Form of COBOL Statements

$$\left[\text{; } \underline{\text{BLOCK}} \text{ CONTAINS } \left[\text{integer-1 } \underline{\text{TO}} \right] \text{ integer-2 } \left\{ \begin{array}{l} \underline{\text{RECORDS}} \\ \underline{\text{CHARACTERS}} \end{array} \right\} \right]$$

$$\left[\text{; } \underline{\text{RECORD}} \text{ CONTAINS } \left[\text{integer-3 } \underline{\text{TO}} \right] \text{ integer-4 CHARACTERS} \right]$$

$$\text{; } \underline{\text{LABEL}} \left\{ \begin{array}{l} \underline{\text{RECORD}} \text{ IS} \\ \underline{\text{RECORDS}} \text{ ARE} \end{array} \right\} \left\{ \begin{array}{l} \underline{\text{STANDARD}} \\ \underline{\text{OMITTED}} \end{array} \right\}$$

$$\left[\text{; } \underline{\text{VALUE}} \text{ OF implementor-name-1 IS } \left\{ \begin{array}{l} \text{data-name-1} \\ \text{literal-1} \end{array} \right\} \right.$$

$$\left. \left[\text{; implementor-name-2 IS } \left\{ \begin{array}{l} \text{data-name-2} \\ \text{literal-2} \end{array} \right\} \right] \ldots \right]$$

$$\left[\text{; } \underline{\text{DATA}} \left\{ \begin{array}{l} \underline{\text{RECORD}} \text{ IS} \\ \underline{\text{RECORDS}} \text{ ARE} \end{array} \right\} \text{ data-name-3 } \left[\text{, data-name-4} \right] \ldots \right]$$

$$\left[\text{; } \underline{\text{LINAGE}} \text{ IS } \left\{ \begin{array}{l} \text{data-name-5} \\ \text{integer-5} \end{array} \right\} \text{ LINES } \left[\text{, WITH } \underline{\text{FOOTING}} \text{ AT } \left\{ \begin{array}{l} \text{data-name-6} \\ \text{integer-6} \end{array} \right\} \right] \right.$$

$$\left. \left[\text{, LINES AT } \underline{\text{TOP}} \left\{ \begin{array}{l} \text{data-name-7} \\ \text{integer-7} \end{array} \right\} \right] \left[\text{, LINES AT } \underline{\text{BOTTOM}} \left\{ \begin{array}{l} \text{data-name-8} \\ \text{integer-8} \end{array} \right\} \right] \right]$$

$$\left[\text{; } \underline{\text{CODE-SET}} \text{ IS alphabet-name} \right]$$

$$\left[\text{; } \left\{ \begin{array}{l} \underline{\text{REPORT}} \text{ IS} \\ \underline{\text{REPORTS}} \text{ ARE} \end{array} \right\} \text{ report-name-1 } \left[\text{, report-name-2} \right] \ldots \right] .$$

$$\left[\text{record-description-entry} \right] \ldots \right] \ldots$$

$$\left[\underline{\text{SD}} \text{ file-name} \right.$$

$$\left[\text{; } \underline{\text{RECORD}} \text{ CONTAINS } \left[\text{integer-1 } \underline{\text{TO}} \right] \text{integer-2 CHARACTERS} \right]$$

$$\left[\text{; } \underline{\text{DATA}} \left\{ \begin{array}{l} \underline{\text{RECORD}} \text{ IS} \\ \underline{\text{RECORDS}} \text{ ARE} \end{array} \right\} \text{ data-name-1 } \left[\text{, data-name-2} \right] \ldots \right] .$$

$$\left. \left\{ \text{record-description-entry} \right\} \ldots \right] \ldots \right]$$

$$\left[\underline{\text{WORKING-STORAGE SECTION}}. \right.$$

$$\left. \left[\begin{array}{l} \text{77-level-description-entry} \\ \text{record-description-entry} \end{array} \right] \ldots \right]$$

$$\left[\underline{\text{LINKAGE SECTION}}. \right.$$

$$\left. \left[\begin{array}{l} \text{77-level-description-entry} \\ \text{record-description-entry} \end{array} \right] \ldots \right]$$

$$\left[\underline{\text{COMMUNICATION SECTION}}. \right.$$

$$\left[\text{communication-description-entry} \right.$$

$$\left. \left. \left[\text{record-description-entry} \right] \ldots \right] \ldots \right]$$

[REPORT SECTION.

[RD report-name

  [; CODE literal-1]

  [; {CONTROL IS / CONTROLS ARE} {data-name-1 [, data-name-2] ... / FINAL [, data-name-1 [, data-name-2] ...]}]

  [; PAGE [LIMIT IS / LIMITS ARE] integer-1 [LINE / LINES] [, HEADING integer-2]

  [, FIRST DETAIL integer-3] [, LAST DETAIL integer-4]

  [, FOOTING integer-5]] .

{report-group-description-entry} ...] ...]

General Format for DATA DIVISION Description Entries

FORMAT 1:

level-number {data-name-1 / FILLER}

  [; REDEFINES data-name-2]

  [; {PICTURE / PIC} IS character-string]

  [; [USAGE IS] {COMPUTATIONAL / COMP / DISPLAY / INDEX}]

  [; [SIGN IS] {LEADING / TRAILING} [SEPARATE CHARACTER]]

  [; OCCURS {integer-1 TO integer-2 TIMES DEPENDING ON data-name-3 / integer-2 TIMES}

  [{ASCENDING / DESCENDING} KEY IS data-name-4 [, data-name-5] ...] ...

    [INDEXED BY index-name-1 [, index-name-2] ...]]

  [; {SYNCHRONIZED / SYNC} [LEFT / RIGHT]]

  [; {JUSTIFIED / JUST} RIGHT]

  [; BLANK WHEN ZERO]

  [; VALUE IS literal] .

APPENDIX C: General Form of COBOL Statements   C7

FORMAT 2:

66 data-name-1; <u>RENAMES</u> data-name-2 $\left[\left\{\dfrac{\underline{THROUGH}}{\underline{THRU}}\right\} \text{data-name-3}\right]$.

FORMAT 3:

88 condition-name; $\left\{\dfrac{\underline{VALUE}\ IS}{\underline{VALUES}\ ARE}\right\}$ literal-1 $\left[\left\{\dfrac{\underline{THROUGH}}{\underline{THRU}}\right\} \text{literal-2}\right]$

$\left[, \text{literal-3} \left[\left\{\dfrac{\underline{THROUGH}}{\underline{THRU}}\right\} \text{literal-4}\right]\right]$ ... .

General Format for PROCEDURE DIVISION

FORMAT 1:

<u>PROCEDURE DIVISION</u> [<u>USING</u> data-name-1 [, data-name-2] ...] .

[<u>DECLARATIVES</u>.

{section-name <u>SECTION</u> [segment-number] . declarative-sentence

[paragraph-name. [sentence] ...] ... } ...

<u>END DECLARATIVES</u>.]

{section-name <u>SECTION</u> [segment-number] .

[paragraph-name. [sentence] ...] ... } ...

FORMAT 2:

<u>PROCEDURE DIVISION</u> [<u>USING</u> data-name-1 [, data-name-2] ...] .

{paragraph-name. [sentence] ... } ...

General Format for Verbs

<u>ACCEPT</u> identifier [<u>FROM</u> mnemonic-name]

<u>ACCEPT</u> identifier <u>FROM</u> $\left\{\begin{array}{l}\underline{DATE}\\ \underline{DAY}\\ \underline{TIME}\end{array}\right\}$

<u>ACCEPT</u> cd-name <u>MESSAGE COUNT</u>

<u>ADD</u> $\left\{\begin{array}{l}\text{identifier-1}\\ \text{literal-1}\end{array}\right\}$ $\left\{\begin{array}{l}\text{, identifier-2}\\ \text{, literal-2}\end{array}\right\}$ ... <u>TO</u> identifier-m [<u>ROUNDED</u>]

[, identifier-n [<u>ROUNDED</u>]] ... [; <u>ON SIZE ERROR</u> imperative-statement]

$\underline{\text{ADD}} \begin{Bmatrix} \text{identifier-1} \\ \text{literal-1} \end{Bmatrix} , \begin{Bmatrix} \text{identifier-2} \\ \text{literal-2} \end{Bmatrix} \begin{bmatrix} , \text{identifier-3} \\ , \text{literal-3} \end{bmatrix} \ldots$

$\underline{\text{GIVING}}$ identifier-m [$\underline{\text{ROUNDED}}$] [, identifier-n [$\underline{\text{ROUNDED}}$]] ...

[; $\underline{\text{ON}}$ $\underline{\text{SIZE}}$ $\underline{\text{ERROR}}$ imperative-statement]

$\underline{\text{ADD}} \begin{Bmatrix} \underline{\text{CORRESPONDING}} \\ \underline{\text{CORR}} \end{Bmatrix}$ identifier-1 $\underline{\text{TO}}$ identifier-2 [$\underline{\text{ROUNDED}}$]

[; $\underline{\text{ON}}$ $\underline{\text{SIZE}}$ $\underline{\text{ERROR}}$ imperative-statement]

$\underline{\text{ALTER}}$ procedure-name-1 $\underline{\text{TO}}$ [$\underline{\text{PROCEED}}$ $\underline{\text{TO}}$] procedure-name-2

[, procedure-name-3 $\underline{\text{TO}}$ [$\underline{\text{PROCEED}}$ $\underline{\text{TO}}$] procedure-name-4] ...

$\underline{\text{CALL}} \begin{Bmatrix} \text{identifier-1} \\ \text{literal-1} \end{Bmatrix}$ [$\underline{\text{USING}}$ data-name-1 [, data-name-2] ...]

[; $\underline{\text{ON}}$ $\underline{\text{OVERFLOW}}$ imperative-statement]

$\underline{\text{CANCEL}} \begin{Bmatrix} \text{identifier-1} \\ \text{literal-1} \end{Bmatrix} \begin{bmatrix} , \text{identifier-2} \\ , \text{literal-2} \end{bmatrix} \ldots$

$\underline{\text{CLOSE}}$ file-name-1 $\begin{bmatrix} \begin{Bmatrix} \underline{\text{REEL}} \\ \underline{\text{UNIT}} \end{Bmatrix} \begin{bmatrix} \underline{\text{WITH}} \underline{\text{NO}} \underline{\text{REWIND}} \\ \underline{\text{FOR}} \underline{\text{REMOVAL}} \end{bmatrix} \\ \underline{\text{WITH}} \begin{Bmatrix} \underline{\text{NO}} \underline{\text{REWIND}} \\ \underline{\text{LOCK}} \end{Bmatrix} \end{bmatrix}$

$\begin{bmatrix} , \text{file-name-2} \begin{bmatrix} \begin{Bmatrix} \underline{\text{REEL}} \\ \underline{\text{UNIT}} \end{Bmatrix} \begin{bmatrix} \underline{\text{WITH}} \underline{\text{NO}} \underline{\text{REWIND}} \\ \underline{\text{FOR}} \underline{\text{REMOVAL}} \end{bmatrix} \\ \underline{\text{WITH}} \begin{Bmatrix} \underline{\text{NO}} \underline{\text{REWIND}} \\ \underline{\text{LOCK}} \end{Bmatrix} \end{bmatrix} \end{bmatrix}$

$\underline{\text{CLOSE}}$ file-name-1 [$\underline{\text{WITH}}$ $\underline{\text{LOCK}}$] [, file-name-2 [$\underline{\text{WITH}}$ $\underline{\text{LOCK}}$]] ...

$\underline{\text{COMPUTE}}$ identifier-1 [$\underline{\text{ROUNDED}}$] [, identifier-2 [$\underline{\text{ROUNDED}}$]] ...

= arithmetic-expression [; $\underline{\text{ON}}$ $\underline{\text{SIZE}}$ $\underline{\text{ERROR}}$ imperative-statement]

$\underline{\text{DELETE}}$ file-name $\underline{\text{RECORD}}$ [; $\underline{\text{INVALID}}$ $\underline{\text{KEY}}$ imperative-statement]

$\underline{\text{DISABLE}} \begin{Bmatrix} \underline{\text{INPUT}} [\underline{\text{TERMINAL}}] \\ \underline{\text{OUTPUT}} \end{Bmatrix}$ cd-name $\underline{\text{WITH}}$ $\underline{\text{KEY}} \begin{Bmatrix} \text{identifier-1} \\ \text{literal-1} \end{Bmatrix}$

$\underline{\text{DISPLAY}} \begin{Bmatrix} \text{identifier-1} \\ \text{literal-1} \end{Bmatrix} \begin{bmatrix} , \text{identifier-2} \\ , \text{literal-2} \end{bmatrix} \ldots$ [$\underline{\text{UPON}}$ mnemonic-name]

$\underline{\text{DIVIDE}} \begin{Bmatrix} \text{identifier-1} \\ \text{literal-1} \end{Bmatrix}$ $\underline{\text{INTO}}$ identifier-2 [$\underline{\text{ROUNDED}}$]

[, identifier-3 [$\underline{\text{ROUNDED}}$]] ... [; $\underline{\text{ON}}$ $\underline{\text{SIZE}}$ $\underline{\text{ERROR}}$ imperative-statement]

APPENDIX C: General Form of COBOL Statements

$\underline{\text{DIVIDE}} \begin{Bmatrix} \text{identifier-1} \\ \text{literal-1} \end{Bmatrix} \underline{\text{INTO}} \begin{Bmatrix} \text{identifier-2} \\ \text{literal-2} \end{Bmatrix} \underline{\text{GIVING}} \text{ identifier-3 } [\underline{\text{ROUNDED}}]$

$[, \text{identifier-4 } [\underline{\text{ROUNDED}}]] \ldots [; \underline{\text{ON}} \underline{\text{SIZE}} \underline{\text{ERROR}} \text{ imperative-statement}]$

$\underline{\text{DIVIDE}} \begin{Bmatrix} \text{identifier-1} \\ \text{literal-2} \end{Bmatrix} \underline{\text{BY}} \begin{Bmatrix} \text{identifier-2} \\ \text{literal-2} \end{Bmatrix} \underline{\text{GIVING}} \text{ identifier-3 } [\underline{\text{ROUNDED}}]$

$[, \text{identifier-4 } [\underline{\text{ROUNDED}}]] \ldots [; \underline{\text{ON}} \underline{\text{SIZE}} \underline{\text{ERROR}} \text{ imperative-statement}]$

$\underline{\text{DIVIDE}} \begin{Bmatrix} \text{identifier-1} \\ \text{literal-1} \end{Bmatrix} \underline{\text{INTO}} \begin{Bmatrix} \text{identifier-2} \\ \text{literal-2} \end{Bmatrix} \underline{\text{GIVING}} \text{ identifier-3 } [\underline{\text{ROUNDED}}]$

$\underline{\text{REMAINDER}} \text{ identifier-4 } [; \underline{\text{ON}} \underline{\text{SIZE}} \underline{\text{ERROR}} \text{ imperative-statement}]$

$\underline{\text{DIVIDE}} \begin{Bmatrix} \text{identifier-1} \\ \text{literal-1} \end{Bmatrix} \underline{\text{BY}} \begin{Bmatrix} \text{identifier-2} \\ \text{literal-2} \end{Bmatrix} \underline{\text{GIVING}} \text{ identifier-3 } [\underline{\text{ROUNDED}}]$

$\underline{\text{REMAINDER}} \text{ identifier-4 } [; \underline{\text{ON}} \underline{\text{SIZE}} \underline{\text{ERROR}} \text{ imperative-statement}]$

$\underline{\text{ENABLE}} \begin{Bmatrix} \underline{\text{INPUT}} \ [\underline{\text{TERMINAL}}] \\ \underline{\text{OUTPUT}} \end{Bmatrix} \text{cd-name } \underline{\text{WITH}} \underline{\text{KEY}} \begin{Bmatrix} \text{identifier-1} \\ \text{literal-1} \end{Bmatrix}$

$\underline{\text{ENTER}} \text{ language-name } [\text{routine-name}] \ .$

$\underline{\text{EXIT}} \ [\underline{\text{PROGRAM}}] \ .$

$\underline{\text{GENERATE}} \begin{Bmatrix} \text{data-name} \\ \text{report-name} \end{Bmatrix}$

$\underline{\text{GO}} \ \underline{\text{TO}} \ [\text{procedure-name-1}]$

$\underline{\text{GO}} \ \underline{\text{TO}} \text{ procedure-name-1 } [, \text{procedure-name-2}] \ldots , \text{procedure-name-n}$

$\quad \underline{\text{DEPENDING}} \ \underline{\text{ON}} \text{ identifier}$

$\underline{\text{IF}} \text{ condition;} \begin{Bmatrix} \text{statement-1} \\ \underline{\text{NEXT}} \ \underline{\text{SENTENCE}} \end{Bmatrix} \begin{Bmatrix} ; \underline{\text{ELSE}} \text{ statement-2} \\ ; \underline{\text{ELSE}} \ \underline{\text{NEXT}} \ \underline{\text{SENTENCE}} \end{Bmatrix}$

$\underline{\text{INITIATE}} \text{ report-name-1 } [, \text{report-name-2}] \ldots$

$\underline{\text{INSPECT}} \text{ identifier-1 } \underline{\text{TALLYING}}$

$\quad , \text{identifier-2 } \underline{\text{FOR}} \left\{ \left\{, \begin{Bmatrix} \underline{\text{ALL}} \\ \underline{\text{LEADING}} \\ \underline{\text{CHARACTERS}} \end{Bmatrix} \begin{Bmatrix} \text{identifier-3} \\ \text{literal-1} \end{Bmatrix} \left[\begin{Bmatrix} \underline{\text{BEFORE}} \\ \underline{\text{AFTER}} \end{Bmatrix} \underline{\text{INITIAL}} \begin{Bmatrix} \text{identifier-4} \\ \text{literal-2} \end{Bmatrix} \right] \right\} \ldots \right\} \ldots$

$\underline{\text{INSPECT}} \text{ identifier-1 } \underline{\text{REPLACING}}$

$\left\{ \begin{matrix} \underline{\text{CHARACTERS}} \ \underline{\text{BY}} \begin{Bmatrix} \text{identifier-6} \\ \text{literal-4} \end{Bmatrix} \left[\begin{Bmatrix} \underline{\text{BEFORE}} \\ \underline{\text{AFTER}} \end{Bmatrix} \underline{\text{INITIAL}} \begin{Bmatrix} \text{identifier-7} \\ \text{literal-5} \end{Bmatrix} \right] \\ \left\{, \begin{Bmatrix} \underline{\text{ALL}} \\ \underline{\text{LEADING}} \\ \underline{\text{FIRST}} \end{Bmatrix} \right\} \left\{, \begin{Bmatrix} \text{identifier-5} \\ \text{literal-3} \end{Bmatrix} \underline{\text{BY}} \begin{Bmatrix} \text{identifier-6} \\ \text{literal-4} \end{Bmatrix} \left[\begin{Bmatrix} \underline{\text{BEFORE}} \\ \underline{\text{AFTER}} \end{Bmatrix} \underline{\text{INITIAL}} \begin{Bmatrix} \text{identifier-7} \\ \text{literal-5} \end{Bmatrix} \right] \right\} \ldots \end{matrix} \right\} \ldots$

INSPECT identifier-1 TALLYING

$$\left\{, \text{identifier-2 } \underline{\text{FOR}} \left\{\left\{, \left\{\begin{matrix}\underline{\text{ALL}}\\ \underline{\text{LEADING}}\\ \underline{\text{CHARACTERS}}\end{matrix}\right\} \left\{\begin{matrix}\text{identifier-3}\\ \text{literal-1}\end{matrix}\right\} \left[\left\{\begin{matrix}\underline{\text{BEFORE}}\\ \underline{\text{AFTER}}\end{matrix}\right\} \text{INITIAL} \left\{\begin{matrix}\text{identifier-4}\\ \text{literal-2}\end{matrix}\right\}\right]\right\} \ldots \right\} \ldots$$

REPLACING

$$\left\{\left\{\underline{\text{CHARACTERS}} \underline{\text{BY}} \left\{\begin{matrix}\text{identifier-6}\\ \text{literal-4}\end{matrix}\right\} \left[\left\{\begin{matrix}\underline{\text{BEFORE}}\\ \underline{\text{AFTER}}\end{matrix}\right\} \text{INITIAL} \left\{\begin{matrix}\text{identifier-7}\\ \text{literal-5}\end{matrix}\right\}\right]\right.\right.$$

$$\left.\left\{, \left\{\begin{matrix}\underline{\text{ALL}}\\ \underline{\text{LEADING}}\\ \underline{\text{FIRST}}\end{matrix}\right\}\right\} \left\{, \left\{\begin{matrix}\text{identifier-5}\\ \text{literal-3}\end{matrix}\right\} \underline{\text{BY}} \left\{\begin{matrix}\text{identifier-6}\\ \text{literal-4}\end{matrix}\right\} \left[\left\{\begin{matrix}\underline{\text{BEFORE}}\\ \underline{\text{AFTER}}\end{matrix}\right\} \text{INITIAL} \left\{\begin{matrix}\text{identifier-7}\\ \text{literal-5}\end{matrix}\right\}\right]\right\} \ldots \right\} \ldots$$

MERGE file-name-1 ON $\left\{\begin{matrix}\underline{\text{ASCENDING}}\\ \underline{\text{DESCENDING}}\end{matrix}\right\}$ KEY data-name-1 [, data-name-2] ...

[ON $\left\{\begin{matrix}\underline{\text{ASCENDING}}\\ \underline{\text{DESCENDING}}\end{matrix}\right\}$ KEY data-name-3 [, data-name-4] ...] ...

[COLLATING SEQUENCE IS alphabet-name]

USING file-name-2, file-name-3 [, file-name-4] ...

$$\left\{\begin{matrix}\underline{\text{OUTPUT}} \underline{\text{PROCEDURE}} \text{ IS section-name-1} \left[\left\{\begin{matrix}\underline{\text{THROUGH}}\\ \underline{\text{THRU}}\end{matrix}\right\} \text{section-name-2}\right]\\ \underline{\text{GIVING}} \text{ file-name-5}\end{matrix}\right\}$$

MOVE $\left\{\begin{matrix}\text{identifier-1}\\ \text{literal}\end{matrix}\right\}$ TO identifier-2 [, identifier-3] ...

MOVE $\left\{\begin{matrix}\underline{\text{CORRESPONDING}}\\ \underline{\text{CORR}}\end{matrix}\right\}$ identifier-1 TO identifier-2

MULTIPLY $\left\{\begin{matrix}\text{identifier-1}\\ \text{literal-1}\end{matrix}\right\}$ BY identifier-2 [ROUNDED]

[, identifier-3 [ROUNDED]] ... [; ON SIZE ERROR imperative-statement]

MULTIPLY $\left\{\begin{matrix}\text{identifier-1}\\ \text{literal-1}\end{matrix}\right\}$ BY $\left\{\begin{matrix}\text{identifier-2}\\ \text{literal-2}\end{matrix}\right\}$ GIVING identifier-3 [ROUNDED]

[, identifier-4 [ROUNDED]] ... [; ON SIZE ERROR imperative-statement]

OPEN $\left\{\begin{matrix}\underline{\text{INPUT}} \text{ file-name-1} \left[\begin{matrix}\underline{\text{REVERSED}}\\ \underline{\text{WITH NO REWIND}}\end{matrix}\right] \left[, \text{file-name-2} \left[\begin{matrix}\underline{\text{REVERSED}}\\ \underline{\text{WITH NO REWIND}}\end{matrix}\right]\right] \ldots\\ \underline{\text{OUTPUT}} \text{ file-name-3} [\text{WITH } \underline{\text{NO}} \text{ REWIND}] [, \text{file-name-4} [\text{WITH } \underline{\text{NO}} \text{ REWIND}]] \ldots\\ \underline{\text{I-O}} \text{ file-name-5} [, \text{file-name-6}] \ldots\\ \underline{\text{EXTEND}} \text{ file-name-7} [, \text{file-name-8}] \ldots\end{matrix}\right\} \ldots$

APPENDIX C: General Form of COBOL Statements

$$\underline{\text{OPEN}} \begin{Bmatrix} \underline{\text{INPUT}} \text{ file-name-1 } [\text{, file-name-2}] \ldots \\ \underline{\text{OUTPUT}} \text{ file-name-3 } [\text{, file-name-4}] \ldots \\ \underline{\text{I-O}} \text{ file-name-5 } [\text{, file-name-6}] \ldots \end{Bmatrix} \ldots$$

$$\underline{\text{PERFORM}} \text{ procedure-name-1} \left[\begin{Bmatrix} \underline{\text{THROUGH}} \\ \underline{\text{THRU}} \end{Bmatrix} \text{ procedure-name-2} \right]$$

$$\underline{\text{PERFORM}} \text{ procedure-name-1} \left[\begin{Bmatrix} \underline{\text{THROUGH}} \\ \underline{\text{THRU}} \end{Bmatrix} \text{ procedure-name-2} \right] \begin{Bmatrix} \text{identifier-1} \\ \text{integer-1} \end{Bmatrix} \underline{\text{TIMES}}$$

$$\underline{\text{PERFORM}} \text{ procedure-name-1} \left[\begin{Bmatrix} \underline{\text{THROUGH}} \\ \underline{\text{THRU}} \end{Bmatrix} \text{ procedure-name-2} \right] \underline{\text{UNTIL}} \text{ condition-1}$$

$$\underline{\text{PERFORM}} \text{ procedure-name-1} \left[\begin{Bmatrix} \underline{\text{THROUGH}} \\ \underline{\text{THRU}} \end{Bmatrix} \text{ procedure-name-2} \right]$$

$$\underline{\text{VARYING}} \begin{Bmatrix} \text{identifier-2} \\ \text{index-name-1} \end{Bmatrix} \underline{\text{FROM}} \begin{Bmatrix} \text{identifier-3} \\ \text{index-name-2} \\ \text{literal-1} \end{Bmatrix}$$

$$\underline{\text{BY}} \begin{Bmatrix} \text{identifier-4} \\ \text{literal-3} \end{Bmatrix} \underline{\text{UNTIL}} \text{ condition-1}$$

$$\left[\underline{\text{AFTER}} \begin{Bmatrix} \text{identifier-5} \\ \text{index-name-3} \end{Bmatrix} \underline{\text{FROM}} \begin{Bmatrix} \text{identifier-6} \\ \text{index-name-4} \\ \text{literal-3} \end{Bmatrix} \right.$$

$$\underline{\text{BY}} \begin{Bmatrix} \text{identifier-7} \\ \text{literal-4} \end{Bmatrix} \underline{\text{UNTIL}} \text{ condition-2}$$

$$\left[\underline{\text{AFTER}} \begin{Bmatrix} \text{identifier-8} \\ \text{index-name-5} \end{Bmatrix} \underline{\text{FROM}} \begin{Bmatrix} \text{identifier-9} \\ \text{index-name-6} \\ \text{literal-5} \end{Bmatrix} \right.$$

$$\left. \underline{\text{BY}} \begin{Bmatrix} \text{identifier-10} \\ \text{literal-6} \end{Bmatrix} \underline{\text{UNTIL}} \text{ condition-3} \right] \right]$$

$\underline{\text{READ}}$ file-name RECORD $[\underline{\text{INTO}}$ identifier$]$ $[; \underline{\text{AT}} \underline{\text{END}}$ imperative-statement$]$

$\underline{\text{READ}}$ file-name $[\underline{\text{NEXT}}]$ RECORD $[\underline{\text{INTO}}$ identifier$]$

$[; \underline{\text{AT}} \underline{\text{END}}$ imperative-statement$]$

$\underline{\text{READ}}$ file-name RECORD $[\underline{\text{INTO}}$ identifier$]$ $[; \underline{\text{INVALID}}$ KEY imperative-statement$]$

$\underline{\text{READ}}$ file-name RECORD $[\underline{\text{INTO}}$ identifier$]$

$[; \underline{\text{KEY}}$ IS data-name$]$

$[; \underline{\text{INVALID}}$ KEY imperative-statement$]$

$\underline{\text{RECEIVE}}$ cd-name $\begin{Bmatrix} \underline{\text{MESSAGE}} \\ \underline{\text{SEGMENT}} \end{Bmatrix}$ $\underline{\text{INTO}}$ identifier-1 $[; \underline{\text{NO}} \underline{\text{DATA}}$ imperative-statement$]$

$\underline{\text{RELEASE}}$ record-name $[\underline{\text{FROM}}$ identifier$]$

RETURN file-name RECORD [INTO identifier] ; AT END imperative-statement

REWRITE record-name [FROM identifier]

REWRITE record-name [FROM identifier] [; INVALID KEY imperative-statement]

SEARCH identifier-1 [VARYING { identifier-2 / index-name-1 }] [; AT END imperative-statement-1]

; WHEN condition-1 { imperative-statement-2 / NEXT SENTENCE }

[; WHEN condition-2 { imperative-statement-3 / NEXT SENTENCE }] ...

SEARCH ALL identifier-1 [; AT END imperative-statement-1]

; WHEN { data-name-1 { IS EQUAL TO / IS = } { identifier-3 / literal-1 / arithmetic-expression-1 } / condition-name-1 }

[AND { data-name-2 { IS EQUAL TO / IS = } { identifier-4 / literal-2 / arithmetic-expression-2 } / condition-name-2 }] ...

{ imperative-statement-2 / NEXT SENTENCE }

SEND cd-name FROM identifier-1

SEND cd-name [FROM identifier-1] { WITH identifier-2 / WITH ESI / WITH EMI / WITH EGI }

[{ BEFORE / AFTER } ADVANCING { { { identifier-3 / integer } [LINE / LINES] } / mnemonic-name / PAGE }]

SET { identifier-1 [, identifier-2] ... / index-name-1 [, index-name-2] ... } TO { identifier-3 / index-name-3 / integer-1 }

SET index-name-4 [, index-name-5] ... { UP BY / DOWN BY } { identifier-4 / integer-2 }

SORT file-name-1 ON { ASCENDING / DESCENDING } KEY data-name-1 [, data-name-2] ...

[ON { ASCENDING / DESCENDING } KEY data-name-3 [, data-name-4] ...] ...

$$\left[\text{COLLATING } \underline{\text{SEQUENCE}} \text{ IS alphabet-name} \right]$$

$$\left\{ \begin{array}{l} \underline{\text{INPUT}} \underline{\text{ PROCEDURE}} \text{ IS section-name-1} \left[\left\{ \begin{array}{l} \underline{\text{THROUGH}} \\ \underline{\text{THRU}} \end{array} \right\} \text{section-name-2} \right] \\ \underline{\text{USING}} \text{ file-name-2 } \left[\text{ , file-name-3} \right] \ldots \end{array} \right\}$$

$$\left\{ \begin{array}{l} \underline{\text{OUTPUT}} \underline{\text{ PROCEDURE}} \text{ IS section-name-3} \left[\left\{ \begin{array}{l} \underline{\text{THROUGH}} \\ \underline{\text{THRU}} \end{array} \right\} \text{section-name-4} \right] \\ \underline{\text{GIVING}} \text{ file-name-4} \end{array} \right\}$$

$$\underline{\text{START}} \text{ file-name} \left[\underline{\text{KEY}} \left\{ \begin{array}{l} \text{IS } \underline{\text{EQUAL}} \text{ TO} \\ \text{IS } = \\ \text{IS } \underline{\text{GREATER}} \text{ THAN} \\ \text{IS } > \\ \text{IS } \underline{\text{NOT}} \underline{\text{ LESS}} \text{ THAN} \\ \text{IS } \underline{\text{NOT}} < \end{array} \right\} \text{data-name} \right]$$

$$\left[\text{; } \underline{\text{INVALID}} \text{ KEY imperative-statement} \right]$$

$$\underline{\text{STOP}} \left\{ \begin{array}{l} \underline{\text{RUN}} \\ \text{literal} \end{array} \right\}$$

$$\underline{\text{STRING}} \left\{ \begin{array}{l} \text{identifier-1} \\ \text{literal-1} \end{array} \right\} \left[\begin{array}{l} \text{, identifier-2} \\ \text{, literal-2} \end{array} \right] \ldots \underline{\text{DELIMITED}} \text{ BY} \left\{ \begin{array}{l} \text{identifier-3} \\ \text{literal-3} \\ \underline{\text{SIZE}} \end{array} \right\}$$

$$\left[\text{, } \left\{ \begin{array}{l} \text{identifier-4} \\ \text{literal-4} \end{array} \right\} \left[\begin{array}{l} \text{, identifier-5} \\ \text{, literal-5} \end{array} \right] \ldots \underline{\text{DELIMITED}} \text{ BY} \left\{ \begin{array}{l} \text{identifier-6} \\ \text{literal-6} \\ \underline{\text{SIZE}} \end{array} \right\} \right] \ldots$$

$$\underline{\text{INTO}} \text{ identifier-7} \left[\text{WITH } \underline{\text{POINTER}} \text{ identifier-8} \right]$$

$$\left[\text{; ON } \underline{\text{OVERFLOW}} \text{ imperative-statement} \right]$$

$$\underline{\text{SUBTRACT}} \left\{ \begin{array}{l} \text{identifier-1} \\ \text{literal-1} \end{array} \right\} \left[\begin{array}{l} \text{, identifier-2} \\ \text{, literal-2} \end{array} \right] \ldots \underline{\text{FROM}} \text{ identifier-m } \left[\underline{\text{ROUNDED}} \right]$$

$$\left[\text{, identifier-n } \left[\underline{\text{ROUNDED}} \right] \right] \ldots \left[\text{; ON } \underline{\text{SIZE}} \underline{\text{ ERROR}} \text{ imperative-statement} \right]$$

$$\underline{\text{SUBTRACT}} \left\{ \begin{array}{l} \text{identifier-1} \\ \text{literal-1} \end{array} \right\} \left[\begin{array}{l} \text{, identifier-2} \\ \text{, literal-2} \end{array} \right] \ldots \underline{\text{FROM}} \left\{ \begin{array}{l} \text{identifier-m} \\ \text{literal-m} \end{array} \right\}$$

$$\underline{\text{GIVING}} \text{ identifier-n } \left[\underline{\text{ROUNDED}} \right] \left[\text{, identifier-o } \left[\underline{\text{ROUNDED}} \right] \right] \ldots$$

$$\left[\text{; ON } \underline{\text{SIZE}} \underline{\text{ ERROR}} \text{ imperative-statement} \right]$$

$$\underline{\text{SUBTRACT}} \left\{ \begin{array}{l} \underline{\text{CORRESPONDING}} \\ \underline{\text{CORR}} \end{array} \right\} \text{ identifier-1 } \underline{\text{FROM}} \text{ identifier-2 } \left[\underline{\text{ROUNDED}} \right]$$

$$\left[\text{; ON } \underline{\text{SIZE}} \underline{\text{ ERROR}} \text{ imperative-statement} \right]$$

$$\underline{\text{SUPPRESS}} \text{ PRINTING}$$

TERMINATE report-name-1 [, report-name-2] ...

UNSTRING identifier-1

$$\left[\underline{\text{DELIMITED}} \text{ BY } [\underline{\text{ALL}}] \begin{Bmatrix} \text{identifier-2} \\ \text{literal-1} \end{Bmatrix} \left[, \underline{\text{OR}} \; [\underline{\text{ALL}}] \begin{Bmatrix} \text{identifier-3} \\ \text{literal-2} \end{Bmatrix} \right] \ldots \right]$$

INTO identifier-4 [, DELIMITER IN identifier-5] [, COUNT IN identifier-6]

[, identifier-7 [, DELIMITER IN identifier-8] [, COUNT IN identifier-9]] ...

[WITH POINTER identifier-10] [TALLYING IN identifier-11]

[; ON OVERFLOW imperative-statement]

$$\underline{\text{USE}} \; \underline{\text{AFTER}} \; \text{STANDARD} \begin{Bmatrix} \underline{\text{EXCEPTION}} \\ \underline{\text{ERROR}} \end{Bmatrix} \text{PROCEDURE ON} \begin{Bmatrix} \text{file-name-1 } [, \text{file-name-2}] \ldots \\ \underline{\text{INPUT}} \\ \underline{\text{OUTPUT}} \\ \underline{\text{I-O}} \\ \underline{\text{EXTEND}} \end{Bmatrix}$$

$$\underline{\text{USE}} \; \underline{\text{AFTER}} \; \text{STANDARD} \begin{Bmatrix} \underline{\text{EXCEPTION}} \\ \underline{\text{ERROR}} \end{Bmatrix} \text{PROCEDURE ON} \begin{Bmatrix} \text{file-name-1 } [, \text{file-name-2}] \ldots \\ \underline{\text{INPUT}} \\ \underline{\text{OUTPUT}} \\ \underline{\text{I-O}} \end{Bmatrix}$$

USE BEFORE REPORTING identifier.

$$\underline{\text{USE FOR DEBUGGING}} \text{ ON} \left[\begin{Bmatrix} \text{cd-name-1} \\ [\underline{\text{ALL REFERENCES OF}}] \text{ identifier-1} \\ \text{file-name-1} \\ \text{procedure-name-1} \\ \underline{\text{ALL PROCEDURES}} \end{Bmatrix} \right.$$

$$\left. \begin{bmatrix} \text{cd-name-2} \\ , [\underline{\text{ALL REFERENCES OF}}] \text{ identifier-2} \\ \text{file-name-2} \\ \text{procedure-name-2} \\ \underline{\text{ALL PROCEDURES}} \end{bmatrix} \ldots \right] .$$

WRITE record-name [FROM identifier-1]

$$\left[\begin{Bmatrix} \underline{\text{BEFORE}} \\ \underline{\text{AFTER}} \end{Bmatrix} \text{ADVANCING} \begin{Bmatrix} \begin{Bmatrix} \text{identifier-2} \\ \text{integer} \end{Bmatrix} \begin{bmatrix} \text{LINE} \\ \text{LINES} \end{bmatrix} \\ \begin{Bmatrix} \text{mnemonic-name} \\ \underline{\text{PAGE}} \end{Bmatrix} \end{Bmatrix} \right]$$

$$\left[; \text{AT} \begin{Bmatrix} \underline{\text{END-OF-PAGE}} \\ \underline{\text{EOP}} \end{Bmatrix} \text{imperative-statement} \right]$$

WRITE record-name [FROM identifier] [; INVALID KEY imperative-statement]

APPENDIX C: General Form of COBOL Statements

General Format for Conditions

Relation Condition:

$$\begin{Bmatrix} \text{identifier-1} \\ \text{literal-1} \\ \text{arithmetic-expression-1} \\ \text{index-name-1} \end{Bmatrix} \begin{Bmatrix} \text{IS [NOT] } \underline{\text{GREATER}} \text{ THAN} \\ \text{IS [NOT] } \underline{\text{LESS}} \text{ THAN} \\ \text{IS [NOT] } \underline{\text{EQUAL}} \text{ TO} \\ \text{IS [NOT] } \underline{>} \\ \text{IS [NOT] } \underline{<} \\ \text{IS [NOT] } \underline{=} \end{Bmatrix} \begin{Bmatrix} \text{identifier-2} \\ \text{literal-2} \\ \text{arithmetic-expression-2} \\ \text{index-name-2} \end{Bmatrix}$$

Class Condition:

$$\text{identifier IS [\underline{NOT}]} \begin{Bmatrix} \underline{\text{NUMERIC}} \\ \underline{\text{ALPHABETIC}} \end{Bmatrix}$$

Sign Condition:

$$\text{arithmetic-expression IS [\underline{NOT}]} \begin{Bmatrix} \underline{\text{POSITIVE}} \\ \underline{\text{NEGATIVE}} \\ \underline{\text{ZERO}} \end{Bmatrix}$$

Condition-Name Condition:

condition-name

Switch-Status Condition:

condition-name

Negated Simple Condition:

<u>NOT</u> simple-condition

Combined Condition:

$$\text{condition} \left\{ \begin{Bmatrix} \underline{\text{AND}} \\ \underline{\text{OR}} \end{Bmatrix} \text{condition} \right\} \ldots$$

Abbreviated Combined Relation Condition:

$$\text{relation-condition} \left\{ \begin{Bmatrix} \underline{\text{AND}} \\ \underline{\text{OR}} \end{Bmatrix} [\underline{\text{NOT}}] \left[\text{relational-operator} \right] \text{object} \right\} \ldots$$

Miscellaneous Formats

Qualification:

$$\begin{Bmatrix} \text{data-name-1} \\ \text{condition-name} \end{Bmatrix} \left[\begin{Bmatrix} \underline{\text{OF}} \\ \underline{\text{IN}} \end{Bmatrix} \text{data-name-2} \right] \dots$$

$$\text{paragraph-name} \left[\begin{Bmatrix} \underline{\text{OF}} \\ \underline{\text{IN}} \end{Bmatrix} \text{section-name} \right]$$

$$\text{text-name} \left[\begin{Bmatrix} \underline{\text{OF}} \\ \underline{\text{IN}} \end{Bmatrix} \text{library-name} \right]$$

Subscripting:

$$\begin{Bmatrix} \text{data-name} \\ \text{condition-name} \end{Bmatrix} \left(\text{subscript-1} \; [, \text{subscript-2} \; [, \text{subscript-3}]] \right)$$

Indexing:

$$\begin{Bmatrix} \text{data-name} \\ \text{condition-name} \end{Bmatrix} \left(\begin{Bmatrix} \text{index-name-1} \; [\{\pm\} \; \text{literal-2}] \\ \text{literal-1} \end{Bmatrix} \right.$$

$$\left[, \begin{Bmatrix} \text{index-name-2} \; [\{\pm\} \; \text{literal-4}] \\ \text{literal-3} \end{Bmatrix} \left[, \begin{Bmatrix} \text{index-name-3} \; [\{\pm\} \; \text{literal-6}] \\ \text{literal-5} \end{Bmatrix} \right] \right] \bigg)$$

Identifier: Format 1

$$\text{data-name-1} \left[\begin{Bmatrix} \underline{\text{OF}} \\ \underline{\text{IN}} \end{Bmatrix} \text{data-name-2} \right] \dots \left[\text{subscript-1} \; [, \text{subscript-2} \; [, \text{subscript-3}]] \right]$$

Identifier: Format 2

$$\text{data-name-1} \left[\begin{Bmatrix} \underline{\text{OF}} \\ \underline{\text{IN}} \end{Bmatrix} \text{data-name-2} \right] \dots \left[\left(\begin{Bmatrix} \text{index-name-1} \; [\{\pm\} \; \text{literal-2}] \\ \text{literal-1} \end{Bmatrix} \right. \right.$$

$$\left[, \begin{Bmatrix} \text{index-name-2} \; [\{\pm\} \; \text{literal-4}] \\ \text{literal-3} \end{Bmatrix} \left[, \begin{Bmatrix} \text{index-name-3} \; [\{\pm\} \; \text{literal-6}] \\ \text{literal-5} \end{Bmatrix} \right] \bigg) \right]$$

General Format for Copy Statement

$$\underline{\text{COPY}} \text{ text-name } \left[\left\{ \begin{matrix} \underline{\text{OF}} \\ \underline{\text{IN}} \end{matrix} \right\} \text{ library-name} \right]$$

$$\left[\text{REPLACING} \left\{ , \begin{Bmatrix} ==\text{pseudo-text-1}== \\ \text{identifier-1} \\ \text{literal-1} \\ \text{word-1} \end{Bmatrix} \underline{\text{BY}} \begin{Bmatrix} ==\text{pseudo-text-2}== \\ \text{identifier-2} \\ \text{literal-2} \\ \text{word-2} \end{Bmatrix} \right\} \ldots \right]$$

Index

$ symbol 128
* editing symbol 128
+ editing symbol 135
+ symbol 128
+ symbol, screen 181
, instead of . SPECIAL–NAMES 353
– editing symbol 135
– symbol 128
– symbol, screen 181
. in the IF ELSE 210
/ symbol 128
2-dim tables, column interchange 415
2-dim tables, raw sum computations 415
3-dimensional table problem 444
3-dimensional tables 440
77 level items 86
9 numeric data description, a 1st look 47
9, numeric picture 78
< in condition 214
= in condition 214
> in condition 214

ACCEPT, formatted screens 198
ACCEPT, numeric data entry 180
ACCEPT, an overview 178, 179
ACCEPT DATE 186
ACCEPT DAY 186
ACCEPT format 1 180
ACCEPT format 2, 3 184, 186
ACCEPT FROM TIME example 191
ACCEPT TIME 186
ACCEPT, alphanumeric data entry 180
ACCESS MODE IS DYNAMIC 586, 619
ACCESS MODE IS RANDOM 586
  general form 605
  overview 604
ACCESS MODE IS SEQUENTIAL 543, 586, 590
access motion time 571
accumulating positive integers 234
accumulation examples 233–234
accumulation process 227, 232–236
accumulation of table elements 391
accumulation of 2-dim table elements 416

accumulator 233
ADD 95, 150
  instruction 141
adding records, random access 607
adding table elements 391
addition/subtraction 97
ADVANCING option 90
AFTER 90
  with INSPECT 327
AFTER/BEFORE ADVANCING clause 92
airline reservation problem 461
  2-dim 480
    algebraic expression 96
ALL
  figurative constant 65
  with INSPECT 327
  with string 317
  with unstring 317
ALPHABETIC in class test 225
ALPHABETIC, testing in IF ELSE 213
alphanumeric characters, collating sequence 267
alphanumeric data entry, ACCEPT 180
alphanumeric data items 78
alphanumeric fields, screen entry 189
alphanumeric processing of data items 46, 47
alternate keys with indexed files 585
ALTERNATE RECORD KEY 586
  dynamic access 619
  random access 605
American National Standard COBOL B1
amortization schedule 280, 360
AND 268
  logical operator 214
  with SEARCH ALL 499
ANS, ANSI COBOL standards 25
apostrophes 65
Applications program 7
area A & B, 67–70
Arithmetic and logic unit 4
arithmetic operations 93–98
  general format 150
  precedence 215
  rule of precedence 97
ASCENDING with SORT 508

ASCENDING KEY with SEARCH ALL 499
ASCII code, collating sequence 266
ASCII code in comparisons 224
ASSIGN 75
  clause 44
asterisk, column 7, 67
asterisk editing symbol 134
asterisks, comments 42
AT END 93
AUTHOR entry 74
AUTO
  screen 195
  screen entry 196
AUTO–SKIP
  ACCEPT 186
  screen 188
average of grades, computation of 235

B symbol 128
BACKGROUND–COLOR, screen entry 196
backspace key, screen processing 198
backtrack, screen processing 198
bar graphs, 2-dim table 429
BEEP, ACCEPT 186
BEFORE 90
  with INSPECT 327
BELL
  problem example 199
  screen entry 196
benefit cost ratio 287
binary format in USAGE clause a2
binary search, SEARCH ALL 525–526
BLANK LINE, screen entry 196
blank lines 155
BLANK SCREEN, screen entry 196
BLANK WHEN ZERO 155
  screen entry 196
BLINK, screen entry 196
BLOCK CONTAINS 544
  with SD entry 507
blocking 538–540
braces, use of
brackets, use of 62
break even point formula 292
bubble sort 517–518
bugs 103
business forms 178

caloric diaries 524
caloric table for weights 523
capitalized words 62
carriage control 350
carriage tape 352
cataloging data files 35, 36
catalogued data file 192
Central processing unit 4
Changing records
  in indexed files 598
  in-place update 562
  random access 606
  in sequential file 550
CHANNEL, page control 351
channels, printer line control 350
character manipulating statements 312–313
character manipulation
  EXAMINE 322
  INSPECT 325–329
character set 63
CHARACTERS with INSPECT 327
characters, internal representation 266
charts, structured 260–261
check protection character 134
class condition 213
  general form C15
class tests 225
  example in program 258–259, 265
  student billing problem 255–257
clause, structure 61
clock, picture of 204
CLOSE 90
  indexed files 594
  random access 605
  sequential 546
COBOL 8
  a file processing language 24, 42
  a first COBOL program 36, 39
  history 24
  microcomputers 26
COBOL character set 63
COBOL coding sheet 66
COBOL elements
  a hierarchy diagram 59
  general conventional notation 62
COBOL language, structure 58
COBOL program, structure of elements 61
COBOL statements, general form C1
CODASYL 24
coding form 67
coding sheet 66
COL, screen location 182
collating sequence 224–225
collation of characters 224–225
collation sequence, alphanumeric data 266
colors 196
column 7 42, 66, 67
COLUMN NUMBER, screen entry 196
columns 1–6, 66, 67
columns 73–80, 71–72
columns 8–72, 68, 69
comma, the editing symbol 133

commas 71
comments lines 42
Comments pseudo code 16
comparisons
  nonnumeric 224
  numeric 223–224
  type of 223
  valid & invalid 267
compile time errors 102, 103
Compilers 7, 8
compiling and executing a program 42, 43
compound arithmetic 93
compound conditions 213
  evaluation of 216
  examples 214, 215
  implied subject operator 268
  logical operators 214
  omission of subject 267
  with SEARCH ALL 499
compound interest 172
COMPUTE 90, 95, 150
COMPUTE statements
  examples 96
  invalid examples 96
Computer system 4
concatenation 313
condition name, VALUE clause
condition names 309–311
  THRU option 311
condition
  class testing 213
  general form 214
  in PERFORM 228–229
  relational 213
  with SEARCH ALL 499
  sign 213
  subject and object 213
conditions
  compound 213–216
  general form C15
  in the IF ELSE 213
  precedence 215
  short form compound 267–269
  with WHEN in SEARCH 494–495
CONFIGURATION SECTION 74, 75
  with SPECIAL-NAMES 352
constants
  definition & composition 64
  literal & figurative 64
continuation, hyphen, 68
control break, multilevel 339–347
control breaks 332–339
control structures 242
Control unit 4
Coordinating module 11
COPY, general form C17
CORRESPONDING option 154
COUNT with UNSTRING 317
counter
  lines in report 332
  pages in report 332
  with PERFORM VARYING 389
  use of 232–233
counting 232
CPU 4

CR editing symbol 137, 138
CR symbol 128
creating indexed files 586, 590, 592–593
creation of a sequential file 542
credit symbol 137, 138
cue, screen 187
currency symbol 131
CURRENT-DATE 155
cursor, screen cue 187

Data description: chapter 1, 14
Data dictionary 16
DATA DIVISION 75
  entries for indexed files 588
  a 1st look 42
  general form C5
  a 2nd look 44, 49
data file
  catalogue 192
  creation of 36
data item description, general form 62
data item description entry 79
data item names, rules on composition 60
data item type 78
data items 75, 77–80, chapter 1, 10
  hierarchy 44, 47
  illustrative examples
  independent 86
  invalid 80
  length, type 46, 47
  subordinate with OCCURS 381
data movement 85
data names
  invalidity subscripted 382
  qualified 154
DATA RECORD IS 83
DATA RECORDS ARE, multiple redefinition 353
data transfer 125
  arithmetic operations 141–152
data transfer rate 572
data validation 247
  car rental problem 251
  in program example 265
  student billing problem 255
data validation model 261
data-item, declaring 48
DATE 155
DATE, ACCEPT 186
DATE-COMPILED entry 74
DATE-WRITTEN entry 74
DAY, ACCEPT 186
DB editing symbol 137, 138
DB symbol 128
debit symbol 137, 138
debug 103
debugging, ACCEPT, DISPLAY 179
debugging, DISPLAY 184
decimal point
  implied 117
  screen 181
  screen cue 187
  with SPECIAL-NAMES 353
decimal points, an overview 116, 117

INDEX

decision structure 11, 14, 208
declaration of tables, examples 382–385
DELETE
  dynamic access 619
  random access 605
  random delete 607
  with indexed files 594
deleting random records 607
deleting records
  indexed file 596
  in-place update 562
  in sequential files 550
DELIMITED, unstring 317
DELIMITED BY, string option 313–315
DELIMITER with UNSTRING 317
density tape 539
DEPENDING ON 545
depreciation calculations 281
DESCENDING KEY with SEARCH ALL 499
DESCENDING with SORT 508
design, top down 244
design testing 247
detail lines 48, 84–85
diagram, structured 260
Dijkstra 26
direct access organization of files 572
directory on disk 37
disk containing program & data file, diagram 40
disk directory, files on disk
disk file, printing a 193
DISPLAY
  debugging 184
  erase 191
  examples 183
  formatted screens 198
  statement, general form 182
  type A1
  an overview 178, 179
DIVIDE 150
  instruction 146, 147
dividend 148
DIVISION, IDENTIFICATION 73
Divisions 16, 42, 58
divisor 148
Documentation 16
  column 7, 67
  of data items 86
  paragraph names 60
  of program 42
DOWN bY with SET clause 492
DYNAMIC access mode indexed files 618

Easter Sunday 172
EBCDIC code 224
  collating sequence 266
editing 35
  characters 128
  process 122–152
  with the + and − sign 135, 136
  with the / symbol 138
  with the B symbol 138

with the check protection character * 134
with the comma 133
with the CR and DB symbols 137, 138
with the currency symbol 131
with the decimal point 129, 130
with the Z symbol 130, 131
elementary data item 78, 81
elementary item, screen 196
ellipsis, use of 62
ELSE sentence 209
ELSE with WRITE statement 351
EMPTY-CHECK, ACCEPT 186
END with SEARCH 495
END with SEARCH ALL 499
end-of-file flags, a 1st look 48, 49
END-OF-PAGE with WRITE 351
ENVIRONMENT DIVISION 73–75
  entries for indexed files 588
  a 1st look 42
  general form C2, 63
  a 2nd look 44
EOP 351
EQUAL in condition 214
ERASE 182
error flags, data validation 255–257
errors 102–104
EXAMINE examples 355–356
EXAMINE statement 322
Execution of a program 8, 43
execution time errors 102–104
exponentiation 97
EXTEND, for sequential files 563
extended SORT 510
extended SORT, OUTPUT PROCEDURE 514
extending a sequential file 563

false statement 213
FD 82–83
FD entry, a 1st look 44
Fields: chapter 1, 10
figurative constants 64, 79
file activity 573
file concepts 533
file description, general discussion 42, 43
file organization
  an overview 572
  general discussion 542
file processing tasks, diagram 537, 546
FILE section & REDEFINES 305
FILE SECTION skeletal form 82
FILE section, a 1st look 44, 47
file size 573
FILE STATUS
  dynamic access 619
  for indexed files 586
  random access 605
file chapter 1 10
  checking for end of file 48, 49
  merging 547
  saving 35
  volatility 573

FILE–CONTROL
  general form of entries C3
  paragraph 75
files 533
  illustrative example 24
  saving 35
FILLER fields, a 1st look 48
fixed length records 544
flags, data validation 255
Flexible diskettes 3
Floppy disks 3
Flowchart 26, 27
  break control problem 340
  complete sequential update 558
  an improved sequential file merge 551
  indexed sequential update 600
  merging of files 547
  multilevel break control 346
  PERFORM VARYING AFTER AFTER AFTER 445
  representation of PERFORM VARYING 389
  Shell Metzner sort 530
  student billing problem 256
foot headers 332
FOREGROUND–COLOR, screen entry 196
form of COBOL elements 62, 63, appendix C
form of COBOL statements C1
format notation of COBOL statements C1
formatted screens 194–201
  ACCEPT 198
  DISPLAY 198
  problem example 198–201
formula to compute interest on principal 235
frequency distribution
  1-dim table 425
  2-dim table 433
FULL
  screen 195
  screen entry 196

gaps, tape 539
gas-pumping machine 204
GIVING
  with SORT 508
  with the OUTPUT PROCEDURE 514
GO TO with the extended SORT procedure 515
Grillo, John 530
group item 78, 81
  ACCEPT entry 180
  screen entry 181
grouping 97
  via parentheses 215

Hardware 3
hierarchy charts 21
hierarchy of operations 215
high level languages 7, 8

HIGH–VALUE (S) figurative constants 65
HIGHLIGHT
  problem example 199
  screen entry 196
hyphen: continuation, 68
hyphens 16, 60

I–O, open sequential files 546
I–O, opening indexed files 594
IBG 539
IDENTIFICATION DIVISION 73, 74
  a 1st look 42
  general format C1
  a 2nd look 43, 44
identification field 71
IF 90
IF class tests 225
IF ELSE IF ELSE . . . 217
IF ELSE structure 217
IF ELSE, discussion of multilevel structures 218
IF IF . . . ELSE ELSE 217
IF statement, the simple IF 211
IF statements, multilevel structure 216–223
If then else: chapter 1, 14
IF with index 492
IF, sign tests 227
implied decimal point 117
independent data items 86
index expression 492
INDEXED BY
  general form 491
  with SEARCH ALL 499
indexed file
  activities in random access 605
  adding random records 607
  adding records dynamically 620
  changing random records 606
  changing records (REWRITE) 598
  creation 592
  deleting random records 607
  deleting records 596
  dynamic access type activities 618
  dynamic change of records 618
  dynamic delete 620
  dynamic processing 612
  example of deleting records 598
  listing 596
  processing sequentially 590
  random process 604–612
  random update 608
indexed files
  creation of 586
  an overview 585
  reading random records 606
  a sequential update problem 599
  START 591
indexed sequential organization, overview 572
indexing 490–491
  general form C16
  relative 492
  versus subscripting 491

initialization of tables 391
  thru REDEFINES 396–397
  of 2-dim tables 418
input and output areas, diagram 46
input area 44, 45, 84
input of numbers with decimal points 119–121
INPUT PROCEDURE 510
  domain of 513
  program example 511
input processing, a diagram 52
input record, multiple redefinition 353
input records, 44, 45
input records as tables 403
INPUT, sequential files 546
INPUT–OUTPUT SECTION 75
input/output 85
  record description entry 83
  of tables 400–404
  of 2-dim tables 418–421
insert of records, sequential file 550
insertion characters 128
INSPECT
  examples of 355, 356
  general form 327
INSTALLATION entry 74
inter record gaps 539
interactive communication 178
interchange procedure in sorting 520
interest on daily average balance 285
interest rates, using nested PERFORMS 236
interest table on amount saved 525
internal representation
  of numbers 118
  of 3-dim table 441
  of 2-dimensional table 407
INTO
  string option 313–315
  with UNSTRING 317
INVALID KEY
  indexed file creation 588
  indexed files 594
  random access 605
INVALID KEY errors
  dynamic access 619
  for index file creation 588
  random access 605
  with indexed files 594
invalid subscripted data names 382
INVALID with REWRITE, indexed files 594
inventory update problem, 1-dim 430
IRG 539
iteration structure 243

JUSTIFIED, screen entry 196

key
  major with SORT 508–509
  minor with SORT 509
  primary & secondary with START 591
key fields with SEARCH ALL 499
KEY IS, random access 605

KEY phrase with START 591
KEY with indexed files, general form 594
Keyboard 3
keys for indexed files 587
klinkon headquarters 457

LABEL RECORD with SORT 507
LABEL RECORDS ARE OMITTED clause 44
LABEL RECORDS ARE STANDARD 83
LABEL RECORDS for disks 544–545
labels 44
languages 26
layout design 99, 102
layout of records 44, 47
LEADING 120
  with INSPECT 327
LESS in condition 214
level 01 46
level numbers & REDEFINES 305
level numbers with tables 381
levels of data items in record structure 45, 47
levels, subordinate levels 46
library program assignment 578
life expectancy tables 525
LIN, screen location 182
LINAGE clause, page control 346
line counters 332
LINE entry, screen 196
line numbers 35
listing an indexed file 596
literal constants definition
literals
  in condition names 310
  non-numeric 65
  numereic 64
loading a 2-dim table row-wise 419
LOCK 591
  open sequential files 546
logic 8
logical errors 103, 104
logical operators OR AND OR 214
logical operators, precedence 215
logical records 540
  blocking 544
looping structure 11, 13, 243
LOW–VALUE(S) figurative constant 65
lower-case words 62

machine language code 8
magnetic disks 4, 541, 571
magnetic tape 4, 536
  advantages 571
  physical characteristics 538
major key with SORT 509
margin A & B, 68, 69
mass storage devices 3, 536
maximum/minimum value in table 400
meals on wheels 287
median 527

memory 4
  allocation of records 48
  arrangement of tables 382–385
menus 178
merge of tables 392
merging of files 547
merging sequential files 548
  with sequence check 550, 552
mini-max sort 518
minor key with SORT 509
minutes 189
mnemonic names for printer control 352
modules chapter 1, 10, 20
month 155
monthly mortgage formula 173
mortgage payment formula 285
MOVE 90
  general form 63, 125
  between alphanumeric fields 126
  between numeric fields 125, 126
  from numeric to numeric edited fields 127
MOVE CORRESPONDING 154
multilevel break control problem 339
multilevel IF structures 216–223
multipage report 331, 333
multiple file programming problem 566
multiple key sort 505
multiple record definition 545
multiple record definition for SD entry 507
multiple redefinition of input record 353
multiple redefinition of output record 354
multiplication/division 97
MULTIPLY 150
MULTIPLY instruction 144, 145

names, condition names 309–311
names, paragraphs 59
NEGATIVE in sign tests 227
negative number, internal representation 120
negative numbers 118, 119
negative numbers, screen entry 188
negative sign 118
nested IF statements 216
nesting of paragraphs 235–236
NEXT SENTENCE 209
  examples of 212, 213
  with SEARCH 495
  with SEARCH ALL 499
NO REWIND, open sequential files 546
NO–ECHO, ACCEPT 186
nonnumeric comparisons 224
nonnumeric literal 65, 79
NOT 268
  =, <, > 214
  EQUAL in condition 214
  greater in condition 214

less in condition 214
  logical operators 214
numbers with decimal points, input of 119–121
numeric comparisons 223
numeric data entry, ACCEPT 180
numeric data items 78
numeric edited field, screen 181
numeric edited fields 122, 123
  screen prompt 186, 187
numeric expression 96
numeric fields
  example of invalid fields 122
  screen prompt 186, 187
  valid examples 122
numeric items 116
numeric literals, definition 64
numeric processing of data items 46, 47
NUMERIC
  class tests 225
  testing in IF ELSE 213

object code 8
object of condition 213
OBJECT–COMPUTER 75–76
OCCURS & VALUE clause 397
OCCURS clause, overview 379
OCCURS
  general form 381
  with the INDEXED BY 491
  with REDEFINES 381
  with SEARCH ALL 499
  with 2-dimensional tables 409
ON SIZE ERROR option 150, 151
on-line reservation problem 461
one-dimensional tables, background 372
OPEN 90
  dynamic access 619
  indexed files 594
  random access 605
  sequential files 546
OPEN EXTEND, sequential files 563
OPEN options with indexed files 594
OPEN OUTPUT for indexed file creation 589, 591
operations, hierarchy of 215
operators, relational 214
OR 268
OR logical operator 214–215
OR with UNSTRING 317
ORGANIZATION IS INDEXED 586
  random process 605
ORGANIZATION IS LINE SEQUENTIAL 75
ORGANIZATION IS SEQUENTIAL 543
output
  area 44, 45
  lines 83
  processing, a diagram 52
  record 84–85
  sequential files 546

of tables 403
of 2-dim tables 420
OUTPUT PROCEDURE 514
  a diagram 515
  a program example 516
OVERFLOW
  string option 313–315
  with UNSTRING 317

PAGE 90
  after advancing 345
  considerations 332
  control 350
  counter 332
  ejection 345
paper form, line control 352
paragraph name readability 16
paragraph names 59
paragraphs 11, 58, 73
  nesting of 235
parentheses, precedence of operations 215
parenthesis, placement of 95–96
passes for sorting 516–519
payroll program, screen processing 198–201
PERFORM 90
  with SECTIONS 513–514
  the simple PERFORM 227–228
PERFORM statement 11, 13, 27
PERFORM THRU 513–514
PERFORM UNTIL chapter 1, 12
  with condition names 310–311
  discussion and form 228–230
PERFORM VARYING
  examples 390
  with index 492
  loading tables 400–404
PERFORM VARYING .. AFTER VARYING 40, 389, 421, 444
period in the IF ELSE 210
periods 71
physical record 539
PICTURE 79
  a 1st look 47
  screen entry 196
picture clause 78
PICTURE clause, implied decimal point 117
picture field for screen entry 180, 181
PICTURE fields in class tests 226
POINTER
  string option 313–315
  with UNSTRING 317
POSITIVE, sign test 227
POSITIVE in condition 213
precedence, rule of 97
prefix 86
prefix in data item names 46, 47
primary key with indexed files 585, 606
Primary storage 4
printer control tape 352
problem specification 241

PROCEDURE DIVISION 89–99
   a closer look 49, 51
   entries for indexed files 588
   with extended SORT 512
   a 1st look 42
   general form 90, C1
processing records randomly, indexed file 604
processing 2-dimensional tables 415–417
Program development: a 1st example
program development process 238–239
program
   compiling and running 42
   structure layout 61
programming activities 238
programming example
   bubble sort 519
   a multi page report 331
   SEARCH and SEARCH ALL 502–503
   sorting grades with SORT 506
programming problem
   inventory update 430
   billing program 249–257
   break control 337–339
   car rental 249–251
   checkbook analysis 160, 161
   computing student bills 245
   creating a disk file 534
   creating an indexed file 590, 592
   deviation of scores 380
   dynamic indexed file 612–625
   frequency distribution 425
   improved merging files 552
   in place update program 564
   indexed sequential update 602
   merging sequential 548
   mini-max sort 521
   multilevel break level 345
   printing an indexed file 597
   a random file update 610
   reading a disk file 535
   receptionist 189–191
   sequence check & highest 263
   sequential update 560
   3-dim problem example 444
   transcript problem 568
   2-dim bar graph 429
   2-dim frequency 433
   2-dim table lookup 424
   2-dim warehouse 437
programming program, student billing 251–257
Programs 7
PROGRAM-ID 73, 74
PROMPT option, alphanumeric fields 189
PROMPT, ACCEPT 186
Pseudo code 8, 9, 17
   of PERFORM 228–229
   practical considerations 231–232
   sequence structure 242–243
   solution to 1st program: chapter 1, 11

punctuation 71
   valid & invalid 71
puzzles with IF ELSE 221

qualification formats C16
qualified data names 154
quotation marks 65
QUOTE figurative constant 65
quotient 148

random access, reading records 606
random file update 608
random files, types of activities 605
random process of indexed files 604
READ 90
   a 1st look 47
READ dynamic in random fashion 618
READ INTO 93
   feature 94
   for reading tables 402
READ NEXT RECORD, dynamic access 619–620
READ NEXT RECORD INTO, indexed files 594
READ RECORD INTO, random access 605
READ RECORD KEY INVALID, dynamic access 619
Readability 16
reading records, random access 606
record, declaring 48
record description 80–81, 83
record description entries, a 1st look 46, 47
record description examples 84
RECORD KEY
   dynamic access 619
   for indexed files 586
   random files 605
records chapter 1 10
   changing in indexed file 598
   changing, inserting, deleting 550
   and data items 77
   deleting in indexed file 596
   fixed length 544
   illustrative examples 24
   input/output & processing diagram 52
   memory allocation 48
   variable length 545
REDEFINES
   general form 305
   to initialize table elements 396–397
   justification 300–303
   with OCCURS clause 381
   program examples 306
   with tables 397–399
   and 2-dim tables 418
REEL, sequential files 546
refinement process, diagram 244
relational operator omitted in compound 268
relational operators, symbol or verbal 214
relative indexing, 492

RELEASE
   with extended SORT 510
   with INPUT PROCEDURE 513
REMAINDER clause 148
REMAINDER option used in program example 184, 185
RENAMES clause, general form A4–5
rent a car project 482
replacement characters 128
REPLACING with INSPECT 327
report items 122
REPORT WRITER 350
reports 329
   miltipage 331
REQUIRED
   screen 195
   screen entry 196
reserved words 42, 182, B1
RETURN with SORT 508
   a program example 516
RETURN with the OUTPUT PROCEDURE 515
REVERSE VIDEO
   problem example 199
   screen entry 196
reversing table elements 392
REWRITE
   dynamic access 619
   random access changing records 606
   sequential in place update 559, 562
REWRITE.. FROM
   indexed files 594
   random access 605
rotational delay 572
ROUNDED OPTION 149
running a COBOL program on your system 40, 41
running a program 42

S symbol 118, 119
screen cue 187
screen editing, ACCEPT examples 183
screen elementary item 196
screen entry, negative numbers 188
screen fields, skip over 198
screen formatted output examples 197
screen formatting, problem example 198, 199
screen group item, general form 195
screen
   input character validation 181
screen items 195
screen location coordinates 182
screen location problem example 191
screen-name 196
screen processing problem example 200, 201
SCREEN SECTION 194, 195
screen tools 178
screens
   formatted 194–201
   predesigned 178
scrolling 195
SD for SORT 507
SEARCH ALL 498
   binary search 526

INDEX

program examples 500–503
versus SEARCH 498–499
SEARCH
  discussion of 525
  general form 495
  important points 496
  program example 497–498
  of 2-dim tables 417
searching for a maximum/minimum value 400
secondary storage devices 4
SECTION examples of use 513–514
sections 58, 512
SECURE
  screen 195
  screen entry 196
SECURITY entry 74
SELECT clause 44
SELECT/ASSIGN 75
  dynamic mode 619
  for indexed files 586
  for sequential files 532, 543
  random files 605
selection structure 208, 243
selective key sort 505
semicolons 71
sentences 60
SEPARATE CHARACTER clause 120, 121
sequence check 550
Sequence structure 11, 14, 208, 242
sequence, collation of characters 224–225
sequential file
  a basic overview 572
  creation of 542
  COBOL instructions 543
  extending the file 563
  in-place change 562
  in-place deletion 562
  in-place update 559
  multiple files 566
  processing characteristics 584
  program update 553
sequential update problem 599
sequential update with REWRITE 564
sequential versus indexed files 584
SET clause 492–493
Shell Metzner sort 530
shopping basket 292
SIGN clause 120, 121
sign condition 213
SIGN conditions, general form C15
SIGN IS 120, 121
sign representation 120
sign tests, general form 227
signed numbers 78
  input of 119, 121
simple arithmetic 93
simple conditions
  general form 213
  subject and object 213
simple PERFORM 227–228
single key sort 505
Software 3, 6

SORT
  BASIC SORT 504
  DATA DIVISION entries 507
  ENVIRONMENT SORT entries 507
  examples with keys 509
  extended 510, 514
  feature 501–516
  general form 508
  general form with extended procedures 515
  OUTPUT PROCEDURE 514
  with PROCEDURE DIVISION statements 508
  Shell Metzner procedure 530
sort-file with SORT 507
sorting
  an overview 501
  bubble and mini-max sort 517–521
  a disk file 504
Source code 8
SOURCE–COMPUTER 75–76
SPACES, definition 65
SPECIAL–NAMES
  with CURRENCY clause 353
  with DECIMAL POINT 353
  page control 350
standard deviation 286
  1-dim table problem 469
START
  dynamic access 619
  examples of 595–596
  general form, indexed files 594
  with indexed files 591
state tax tables 526
statements
  COBOL general form C1
  structure 61
status key meaning 587
stepwise refinement 244
STOP RUN 155
STRING 313–315
Structure 11
  diagrams 20
  of COBOL language 58
  of COBOL program 61
  the IF ELSE general form 209
  of record 44, 47
structured charts 260–261
structured diagrams 20, 260–261
Structured programming, historical development, 26
structures, multilevel IFs 216–221
Subitems 24, 47, 77
subject of condition 213
subject, omitted in compound condition 267
subordinate data items and the OCCURS 381
subordinate items 81
subordinate levels 46
subscripted data items, examples 376–377
subscripting versus indexing 490
subscripting, general form C16
subscripts
  rule & definition 379

3-dim table 441
  for 2-dimensional tables 409, 410
Subtasks 10
SUBTRACT 95, 144, 150
symbols, used in conditions 214
syntax 58
syntax errors 103
system considerations, your system 40, 41
systems planning problem 470

table accumulation 391
table declaration 376–377
  examples of 382–385
  for 2-dimensional tables 408
table definition 374
table initialization 388
  and duplication 391
  thru REDEFINES 396–397
table input/output 400–404
table lookup, 2-dim table 424
table merge 392
table output 403
table processing, a 1st example 378
table search examples 393–395
table size 381, 383
table structures 383–385
  2-dim table examples 410–412
table
  a 1st program, deviation of scores 377
  OCCURS clause 381
  reversing elements 392
  sum of tables 391
  2-dim accumulation of elements 416
tables
  background & justification 372
  copying 383
  indexing, general form C16
  as input records 403
  memory arrangement 382–385
  OCCURS for 2-dimensional tables 409
  processing 2-dimensional tables 415–417
  searching for a maximum/minimum value 400
  subscripting, general form C16
  subscripts 3-dimensional 441
  3-dimensional 440
  3-dimensional internal representation 441
  2-dimensional 407–421
  2-dimensional column interchange 415
  2-dimensional input/output 418–421
  2-dimensional internal representation 407
  2-dimensional loading row-wise 419
  2-dimensional output 420
  2-dimensional row sum computation 415
  2-dimensional search of elements 417

2-dimensional table initialization REDEFINES 418
TALLYING
  with INSPECT 327
  with UNSTRING 317
tasks 10
tax tables, earning 467
terminals 3
testing a design 247
testing, DISPLAY, ACCEPT 179
tests
  class 225
  sign tests 226
text editor commands 40, 41
text editor
  creating a data file 36
  typing a COBOL program 35, 36, 41
  screen display 36, 37
THRU with condition names 311–312
THRU with the extended SORT procedure 510
TIME 155
time interval computation 189
TIME, ACCEPT 186
time, picture of clock 204, 205
TIMES in simple PERFORM 227
TIMES, with the OCCURS 381
top down design 10, 244
top down process example 245
TRAILING 120
transaction code 553
translation programs 7
true statement 213
two-dimensional tables 407
type 78

UNDERLINE, screen entry 196
UNIT, open sequential files 546
UNSTRING 316–319
  examples of 320
UNTIL condition, in PERFORM 228–230
UP BY with SET clause 492
update program, sequential files 553
update, a random file 608
UPON, DISPLAY instruction 182
USAGE clause, storage considerations A4
USAGE IS COMPUTATIONAL 3, A1
USAGE IS DISPLAY A1
USAGE IS INDEX A1
USING with SORT 508
utility program to print disk file 192

V symbol 117
V symbol in screen picture 180, 181
validation
  car rental problem 251
  input characters on screen 181
  of input data 247–249
  student billing problem 255–257
  use of flags 253–257
VALUE 79
  general form for condition names 312
VALUE clause & REDEFINES 305
VALUE clause in condition names 310
VALUE in the OCCURS clause 381, 397
VALUE IS, screen entry 196
VALUE OF FILE–ID 83
variable length records 545

VARYING with PERFORM 389–390
VARYING with SEARCH 495
volatility 573

walk through of break control problem 341
warehouse problem, 2-dim table 437
warnings 103
weight charts 522
WHEN with SEARCH 495
WHEN with SEARCH ALL 499
windows 204
WITH DUPLICATES 586
WORKING–STORAGE SECTION 83–86
WORKING–STORAGE
  a 1st look 48, 49
  general form C5
wrap around sales average problem 469
WRITE 90–91
  adding random records 607
  dynamic access 619
  for indexed files 588
  with SPECIAL–NAMES 351
WRITE.. FROM, random access 605

X picture 47, 78

year 155

Z symbol 128
ZERO in sign test 227
zero suppression character 130
ZERO, ZEROES, ZERO 64